Bay of Biscay

Cedeira

Castro Urdiales
San Sebastián
Zarautz
Bermeo
Laredo
Santander
Oviedo
Sotres

GALICIA
ASTURIAS
CANTABRIA
Bilbao
BASQUE
COUNTRY
Pamplona

Santiago
de Compostela
León
NAVARRA
Haro
La Guardia
Ezcaray
LA RIOJA
Tudela
Huesca
Arties

ANDORRA

Cambados
El Grove
Compludo
Burgos
ARAGON
Seo
de Urgel
La Escala

Bayona
CASTILLA
Y LEÓN
Aranda
de Duero
Zaragoza
CATALUNYA

Toro
Almonacid
de la Sierra
Barcelona

Sepúlveda
Tarragona

S P A I N

Salamanca
Segovia
MADRID
Alcalá
de Henares
Albarracín
VALENCIA

Madrid
Chinchón
Cuenca
Castellón
de la Plana

Lagartera
Toledo
CASTILLA-LA MANCHA
Valencia
El Palmar
Mallorca
Menorca
Maho

PORTUGAL
Cáceres
Trujillo
Guadalupe
Las Pedroñeras
Cullera
Dénia
Ibiza
San Antonio
Palma

EXTREMADURA
Mérida
Almagro
Albacete
BALEARIC ISLAND

Elche

Jabugo
Cazalla
de la
Sierra
Córdoba
Baeza
Úbeda
Murcia
MURCIA

Baena
ANDALUCIA
Sevilla
Antequera
Mediterranean Sea

Sanlúcar de Barrameda
Málaga

Cádiz

ATLANTIC
OCEAN

ALGERIA

MOROCCO

E

Praise for
1,000 SPANISH RECIPES
by Penelope Casas

From the moment *The Foods and Wines of Spain* came out in the early 1980s, I became a great fan of Penelope Casas. Penny gives us the true cuisine of Spain. The legacy of an extraordinary cook, *1,000 Spanish Recipes* will now become my reference source when I try any Spanish dishes at home. These are the dishes I could enjoy every day—from tortilla to gazpacho, from fried cod sticks, hake, or piquillo peppers to flan de manzana and peaches in red wine.

—Jacques Pépin, Chef, cookbook author, and host of numerous PBS-TV cooking series

What a triumph! Penelope Casas has poured her vast talents into her last book, which, with its 1,000 recipes, is a compendium and the only Spanish cookbook you will need on your shelf. Whether you wish to entertain with tapas or cook chickpeas, or sardines or quail, the recipes are all here, with little accompanying stories or bits of history to entertain and enlighten.

—Madhur Jaffrey, Cookbook author, TV presenter, and actress

Without the enthusiasm and passion of my good friend Penelope Casas, it is impossible to understand the popularity of Spanish cooking in the United States. With her great knowledge, successful books, and now the legacy of her admirable work *1,000 Spanish Recipes*, Penelope has revealed, like nobody else, the popular, genuine, and homey cuisine of her beloved adoptive country.

—Juan Mari Arzak, Chef, restaurateur

Through her sensitivity and passion, Penelope Casas offers this memorable sample of the richness of Spanish cuisine. *—Ferran Adrià, Chef of elBulli*

I have had a love affair with Spain and Spanish cuisine for nearly 25 years and I owe a great deal of that to Penelope Casas. Unknowingly, Ms. Casas was directly responsible for my decision to become a chef and, more importantly, to focus on Spanish food. I was a teenager, about to embark on a year abroad in Burgos, Spain and as a part of my preparation, I had a research project I needed to present to my Spanish class. I decided to do my project on Tapas and my teacher gave me a stack of Penelope Casas' books. They were the first cookbooks I ever owned and still sit proudly on their own shelf, in my office. In *1,000 Spanish Recipes*, an incredible collection of Ms. Casas' diverse repertoire of recipes, there are countless wonderful gems that show how profound an impact this tireless student of Spanish cuisine continues to have on the subject.

—Seamus Mullen, Chef, cookbook author, restaurateur

Spanish cooking couldn't be understood without someone like Penelope and her amazing books, like *1,000 Spanish Recipes*. She shows us how to love a country by its cuisine, its ingredients, and the people who tell its stories through their cooking.

—José Andrés, Chef/Owner of ThinkFoodGroup and Dean of Spanish Studies, International Culinary Center

1,000
SPANISH
Recipes

Penelope Casas

Houghton Mifflin Harcourt
Boston New York

For information about permission to reproduce selections from this book, write to trade.permissions@hmhco.com or to Permissions, Houghton Mifflin Harcourt Publishing Company, 3 Park Avenue, 19th Floor, New York, New York 10016.

www.hmhco.com

Library of Congress Cataloging-in-Publication Data

Casas, Penelope.
1,000 Spanish recipes / Penelope Casas.
pages   cm
ISBN 978-0-470-16499-0 (hardback);
ISBN 978-0-544-30908-1 (ebk)
1. Cooking, Spanish. I. Title. II. Title: One thousand
Spanish recipes.
TX723.5.S7C3572 2014
641.5946 — dc23
2014016739

PUBLISHER: Natalie Chapman

EXECUTIVE EDITOR: Linda Ingroia

JACKET DESIGNER: Jeff Faust,
    Chrissy Kurpeski

INTERIOR DESIGNER: Greta D. Sibley

MANUFACTURING MANAGER: Kevin Watt

JACKET ILLUSTRATOR: Gina Triplett

Printed in the United States of America

DOC 10 9 8 7 6 5 4 3 2

4500692150

To my husband, Luis, my daughter, Elisa,
and my granddaughter, Ruby

Contents

In Celebration of Penelope Casas

A Tribute to My Wife by Luis Casas

In the summer of 1962, Penelope came to Spain to study at Madrid University. She had just finished her sophomore year at Vassar, where she was majoring in Spanish studies. She had registered at the School of *Filosofía y Letras* in Madrid to attend summer courses intended for foreign students. At that time, Penelope was quite knowledgeable in Spanish culture, and her Spanish, although not perfect, was good enough to partake in conversation. She was nineteen and it was the first time that she was traveling by herself, and to Europe. I went to the airport to pick her up and bring her to my home, where she would be living for two months that summer with my mother, me, and another American student. I arrived at the airport not knowing what she looked like and somewhat concerned about not finding her, but when I saw this very pretty, elegant girl stylishly dressed in an attractive green summer dress, with short dark hair and beautiful eyes, I approached her and said, "You are Penelope!" She said, "Yes," and at that moment we started a relationship that lasted fifty years.

Penelope had learned a lot in school about Spanish culture, but coming from a Greek family with a mother who was mostly limited to Greek or French cuisine, she didn't know much about Spanish cooking. As soon as she arrived in Spain, she integrated herself very easily and took a lot of pleasure in her new environment, immersing herself in a different lifestyle and totally new way of eating. From the first day, she was enamored of Spanish cuisine and sampled many ingredients for the first time. Her mother disliked olive oil and garlic because of their strong flavor, but they became two of Penny's favorite ingredients. She adapted herself perfectly to Spanish hours and did not mind at all to have lunch at two in the afternoon or dinner after ten in the evening. As a matter of fact, years later while living in New York, she still liked to keep that schedule.

My mother, Clara, Basque by birth but raised mostly in Madrid, did not cook every day, but she always supervised the cooking of Pilar, my childhood nanny who continued working and living in our home for over thirty years. Under my mother's tutelage, she became a great cook. Penelope assisted on multiple occasions in the kitchen helping Pilar with whatever she was preparing for lunch. On these occasions, my mother liked to be present and give Penny further, more specific instructions about Spanish gastronomy. Penny always had a little notebook with her that eventually became an inseparable part of her during her life, taking notes on anything new that she learned (my family still has her close to 350 "little notebooks!"). The influence of my mother and Pilar was fundamental in Penelope's later career as a successful writer of Spanish cookbooks. Pilar taught Penny to cook the best tortilla (Spanish omelet), not surprising as Pilar was a native of Galicia, a region well known for the quality of the potatoes and where the best tortilla is made. She also told her how to make the best white sauce, referred to by its French name, béchamel, by Spaniards. She also taught her the best way to cook fish (*a la Romana*—dipped in flour and egg, then deep fried), as well as many other techniques that Penny would document in her little notebooks, which years later remained a never-ending source of information.

The summer that Penelope came to Madrid, I was a medical student, and in the morning, I used to go to the University Hospital while Penny went to the School of Philosophy. Most days we would meet at around one before going home for lunch. But on the way home, we'd meet friends and we'd do something that for Penny became one of her most cherished pastimes—*ir de tapeo* (to go for tapas). Without making a telephone call or making a date, you could, on the spur of the moment, go to a bar and always find friends available to talk and share a drink and some appetizers (tapas). This aspect of Spanish culture fascinated her, and tapas became a key reason that Penny was attracted to Spanish cuisine.

I still remember many of Penny's favorite bars and taverns: Gayango for *Flamenquines* (Fried Pork and Ham Rolls, page 81) and mussels fried with béchamel (Stuffed Fried Mussels, page 36), Fiesta Alegre for piquillo peppers stuffed with hake, Los Caracoles for delicious snails (Snails, Madrid Style, page 45), El Abra for its croquettes and *Soldaditos de Pavía* (Fried Cod Sticks, page 44), small sticks of cod fish fried *a la Romana*, and El Abuelo for their marvelous grilled shrimp (Grilled Shrimp over Coarse Sea Salt, page 27). I could continue without end, for in the two months that Penny spent in Madrid that summer, we went all over trying to locate the best food and tapas. Penny continued her quest

for the best tapas all throughout her life, not only in Madrid but all over Spain. We looked for them in the most out-of-the-way villages, and with our friends, we created many unforgettable memories.

Penny had a wide-eyed curiosity for all things Spanish, and her enthusiasm for her adopted country pushed her to learn as much as she could. She loved its people, history, philosophy of life, cuisine, art, and even its bullfighting. Penny particularly appreciated Romanesque art, sculpture, frescos, and architecture, and she'd go out of her way to locate an ancient stone carving or a forgotten chapel in a remote village the same way that she would seek out an unusual and delicious recipe. She used to equate Romanesque art and cooking, saying "Two very simple and pleasant ways of satisfying yourself: one fulfills your soul and the other your body." At the end of that summer, she went back to the United States and to her studies at Vassar.

Penny came back to Spain the following summer, this time speaking almost perfect Spanish and with a clear idea of what she wanted to do and learn. Obviously cooking was one of her primary interests, and that summer she did not limit herself to Madrid. We traveled to Segovia, Salamanca, Burgos, and Toledo. She was always interested in local culinary specialties and filled up quite a few of her little notebooks that summer. She became addicted to roast baby lamb, *chorizo*, Serrano ham, freshwater crayfish, and black sausage, and while traveling through the Mediterranean coast in Valencia, Penny discovered one of her favorite dishes in Spain, *Arroz Negro* or Black Rice (page 318). She spent quite a few mornings in Valencia at La Pepica, in Dénia at El Pegoli, and in Castellón at La Tasca del Puerto working in the kitchen of these restaurants and learning the proper technique for preparing the perfect paella.

Penny and I got married the following year. We lived in Madrid for three years while I was finishing my studies in medical school, and Penny continued to increase her knowledge of Spain and particularly of Spanish cuisine by observing my mother and many friends. It was around the mid-1970s that *La Nueva Cocina Vasca* (nouvelle Basque cuisine) appeared in Spain, with the revolutionary Juan Mari Arzak as its main representative. This new gastronomic movement was at that time considered the ultimate in cooking in Spain and in a way competed with the similar trend in France. Obviously Penny was quite interested, so we went to San Sebastián and Bilbao in the northern Basque Country to find out what the new techniques were. She became very friendly with Juan Mari Arzak and Pedro Subijana, the better known nouvelle chefs. She worked with them in their kitchens and even went with them to the markets to get to know the produce and the ingredients that they were using. Juan Mari and Pedro have continued to be good friends for many years, and Penny was very fond of visiting them in their beautiful restaurants to try their latest dishes.

But in spite of all the innovations and amazing new techniques, such as the ones later used by Ferran Adrià of El Bulli (also a good friend), Penny stayed loyal to traditional Spanish cooking, which was apparent in her seven previous books on Spanish cuisine. I think that she considered all these radical new techniques, such as "molecular cuisine," cooking with foams, or the deconstruction of traditional recipes of Ferran Adrià, more of a curiosity. We were once invited by one of the best-known chefs in Spain for a dinner of avant garde cuisine at his restaurant. The dinner lasted from 10 pm to 3 am. We were served 28 dishes followed by 8 desserts. At the end of dinner, we sat with the chef for a drink and a talk. Penny found the meal very interesting, but when the chef invited her to come back the following day, she uncharacteristically "invented" an excuse. She could not handle that type of meal two days in a row. The following day, we went to a restaurant not too far away where we had a simple, traditional dinner, a relief after the five-hour, 36-course meal of the night before.

It was around 1979 that Penelope met and became a close friend of Craig Claiborne, the food editor at the *New York Times*. Craig had written an article in the *Times* about Spanish food, but the spelling of the dish and the recipe were wrong. Penny wrote to him with a correction which led to more correspondence, a dinner prepared by Penny for Craig, and then a lasting friendship for many years. Craig was instrumental in getting Penny her first book deal with Judith Jones at Knopf (Julia Child's editor). Her first book, *The Foods and Wines of Spain*, was published in 1981 to public and critical acclaim and was awarded the National Prize of Gastronomy in Spain. Her second book, *Tapas: The Little Dishes of Spain*, initiated the trend for tapas bars in the United States, until then totally unknown to the American public. The first tapas bar to hit the dining scene was The Ballroom with chef Felipe Rojas Lombardi (collaborator and disciple of James Beard). Both of Penny's books are still in print and have become classics of gastronomic literature.

Other books followed, including *Delicioso, Paella,* and *La Cocina de Mama.* She wrote multiple articles for the *New York Times, Saveur, Food and Wine*, and many other publications. The Spanish government awarded her the Cross of the Order of Civil Merit, and posthumously, the King of Spain awarded her the title of Dame of the Order of Isabel La Católica, the highest civil decoration in Spain in 2013.

This book that I am introducing is her last. For a few years she had been fighting a chronic and debilitating condition, but thankfully, her mind was not affected, and she took on this job with the same enthusiasm and purpose that she manifested in everything that she did in life. She finished the last chapter of the book on a Tuesday and she was radiant, happy, and proud of herself for having completed the most extensive book project of her career. She died five days later. It is a great book, and I hope that all of you realize who Penny was and what she has represented in the gastronomic history of this country. I am sure that her legacy will last for many years.

A Tribute to My Mother by Elisa Casas

My mom's recipe box tells the story of her life. The early, faded recipe cards ("From the recipe file of Penny Fexas") display the writing of a 1950s teenager who loved to cook and was eager to start a recipe collection of her own. She had a talent for baking (though all her life she said she didn't) and would think nothing of baking a pie, from scratch, as an after-school snack. She learned techniques from my grandmother, whose expertise was Greek cuisine. Many of the early cards reflect her love of Greek food, with recipes of my great-grandmother's, such as *Kourambiedes, Spanakopita,* and *Keftedes.* Some of the cards also reflect the times, with all-American recipes such as Roquefort Sour Cream Dip (still a staple in my family), Roast Beef, Aunt Libby's Rainbow Cake, and one that simply says "Hamburgers."

During her college years, she visited Madrid and fell in love with Spain: its cuisine, its culture, and my father, a medical student at the time. *Tascas* (tapas bars) were her favorite, and she eagerly frequented them and absorbed all the knowledge she could about Spanish food. Her college roommate said she never forgot the very first time my mom made a paella, upon her return from Spain in 1962. She miscalculated the time it would take to prepare such an elaborate dish, and my grandfather, who liked to eat at 6 pm, became impatient. My grandmother had to prepare a sandwich for him, but the rest of the family ate the paella, which apparently was delicious, at 10 pm, like real Spaniards.

When she moved to Spain in 1965, her recipe cards multiplied quickly, as she was settling in

with a new husband and a new baby (me), and she cooked frequently. She acquired many techniques from my Spanish grandmother, Clara, who was an excellent cook, and she became proficient quickly. While my dad was in school, my mom prepared elaborate meals: usually Spanish, as she was honing her skills, but often also things she missed from home such as Stuffed Cabbage, Baked Chicken, and Lentil Soup (the cards now read, "From the recipe file of Penny Casas.")

In the early 1970s, my handwriting starts to appear in the recipe box. I was a teenager when my mom took a temporary full-time job and asked me to cook dinner one night a week. I was eager to help, because *Seventeen* magazine had just started a recipe column! I made dishes such as Oriental Stir Fry and Stuffed Shells with Ricotta and Spinach, and those recipes became family staples. At this time, international cuisine became very trendy in New York, and my parents and their friend Marsha started an international food club (they were the only members). They frequented obscure restaurants in Manhattan, trying new things like sushi, chicken mole, and fondue. Her recipe cards from this period reflect this new experimentation, including dishes such as Indonesian Rice, Armenian Meat Pies, Cold Sesame Noodles, Kielbasa, and Pesto.

But during the 1970s, we were also visiting Spain frequently, and she was making more and more culinary discoveries as we traveled across the country. Many recipe cards of this period document her resourcefulness, with everything from a simple Club Sandwich from the Alfonso XIII, a hotel she loved in Sevilla, to *Gambas en Salsa Verde* (Shrimp with Green Sauce) from a restaurant in Galicia.

This was also the time that she really became an expert in Spanish cuisine, at a time when no one in the United States understood what it was. She religiously carried a small notebook with her and jotted down recipes and historical notes for future articles and, later, for her books. Whenever she asked a Spanish chef for a recipe, even before she became "La Penelope" (what they called her in Spain when she became well known), they were honored that an American was taking an interest in their culinary heritage. Years later, she and my dad went back to many of these restaurants and awarded them the *Garbanzo de Plata* (The Silver Chickpea), an honor that they bestowed on the best chefs in Spain.

After my mom got her first book deal, my dad and I were her guinea pigs, eating "experiments" every night until I left for college. At the time, I took her cooking for granted, and although I knew that the other moms didn't make their kids *Arroz Negro* (Black Rice Paella) or gourmet cakes for their birthday, or *angulas* (baby eels) on New Year's Eve, each dinner was just an everyday meal to us. On my dad's birthday, he would always want the simplest fare: fried eggs, Spanish style. Regardless of her expertise, my mom always worried that she would accidentally break the yolks. She was very modest; she always said, "If you can read, you can cook," and followed even her own recipes meticulously. In the 1980s, she would have huge, elaborate tapas parties, and everyone was impressed that she did it all on her own.

As I got older, I would help my mom with big family meals like Thanksgiving. The recipe cards for all the fixings were bundled together in her recipe box, easy to find when we needed them. She insisted on preserving our traditional meal dish-for-dish and refused to remove the Pineapple Jello Mold, a relic from the 1950s, from the menu, even though we all found it ghastly. She wasn't a food snob; she occasionally loved to eat things like raw ground beef, McDonald's Filet-O-Fish, Milky Way bars, cookie dough, cold sesame noodles, and, believe it or not, airplane food. On those rare nights when both my

dad and I went out, she would always make herself *Avgolemono*, a Greek egg and lemon soup that my dad and I abhorred. But despite her traditional inclinations, my mom was also intrigued by nouvelle cuisine. She reveled in the attention Spain received for its inventive "new Basque cuisine" in the 1980s and was fascinated with it, trying the odd food combinations, scientific procedures, and "deconstructed" dishes that friends Juan Mari Arzak and Ferran Adrià were experimenting with.

One Christmas, I was appalled to realize that her apple pie recipe, something that she had been perfecting all her life, only existed on one torn, grease-stained index card. Thousands of Spanish recipes were saved on her computer, of course, and preserved in her books, but she never thought to digitize our most beloved family recipes. Perhaps I was thinking about preserving our family traditions more than usual because this was around the time that my daughter Ruby was born. Soon Ruby started pulling recipe cards out of the box for things like Butter Cookies and Biscuits, but for her favorite dish, Penchie's Pasta, there was no recipe card—it was something my mom threw together especially for her. When I tried to recreate it at home, Ruby would say, "It's not as good as Penchie's."

After my mom passed away, I received many letters and emails from fans who said they felt that they knew her through her books. Some said that they read her books like autobiographies, the way I read her recipe box. She was passionate about Spain, and her love of Spanish cuisine was profound, which was apparent in her books. This, her last book, is a testament to the knowledge she acquired over her lifetime and for me is like a journey through my own life as well.

Penelope's author photo taken at home for *The Foods and Wines of Spain*, 1979. *Luis Casas*

Penelope with Jacques Pépin and Craig Claiborne at a reception for *The Foods and Wines of Spain* at Cafe San Martin, Manhattan, New York, 1983. *Luis Casas*

Penelope with the owner of El Faro restaurant in Cádiz, Spain, 1999. *Luis Casas*

Penelope with Ferran Adrià, at the Madrid Fusion event, Madrid, Spain, 2003. *Luis Casas*

Acknowledgments

Although it has been thirty-two years since the publication of my first book, *The Foods and Wines of Spain*, I am pleased to say that many of the friends and professionals whom I acknowledged in that book are still a part of my life and continue to offer incomparable support and advice.

For fifty years, I have traveled to Spain with my husband Luis, and we have dined in beautiful restaurants and discovered down-to-earth *mesones y tavernas*. Many of those chefs and owners enthusiastically shared old family recipes with me, and many have become dear friends that we visit year after year.

Candida Acebo, who runs a small five-table restaurant along The Way of Saint James in the quaint village of Compludo and serves simple, though extraordinary, fare. Cinta Gutierrez, of Els Pescadors de L'Escala, who taught me about Catalan cuisine. Digna Prieto, of Crisol in O Grove, a small Galician fishing village. Pedro Narro, in the magnificent village of Albarracín, where he runs El Chorro, a delightful tavern. The always-smiling brothers Hermoso, Fernando and Paco, from Sanlúcar de Barrameda, who own Casa Bigote and serve the best fish dishes in southern Spain. Fray Juan Barrera, master of monacal cuisine, who runs the kitchen at the Guadalupe Monastery. Salvador Lucero of Bar Bahia in Cádiz, probably the most authentic chef I have ever met. Ruperto Blanco, quintessential Andalusian and a master at cooking Moorish-influenced cuisine at Casa Ruperto in Sevilla. And lastly, my dear friend Tomás Herranz, from the great Cenador del Prado in Madrid, who recently passed away. He was a remarkable chef and a wonderful man.

I want to extend my thanks to some chefs who were responsible for bringing Spain to the forefront of international cuisine. My friends Juan Mari Arzak of Arzak and Pedro Subijana of Akelarre, both from San Sebastian. Ferran Adrià of El Bulli in Catalunya. Gonzalo Córdoba of El Faro in Cádiz. My dear friend Irene España of Casa Irene, in the beautiful Valley of Aran high up in the Pyrenees. Paco Patón, a longtime friend in charge of the kitchen at the Hotel Urban in Madrid. I've known Lucio Blázquez of the famed Casa Lucio in Madrid since I first visited Spain in 1962 and have spent many afternoons in his kitchen, laughing and learning his techniques. In New York, I need to thank our old friend Ramón San Martín of Cafe San Martín, who for 35 years has always extended a helping hand, Rufino López of Solera, and Jesús Manso (Lolo) of Socarrat and La Nacional.

My dear friend Marsha Stanton has always given me support and encouragement, tasting new dishes and offering her opinions since the time of my

first book. Pilar Vico's advice was always wise and on point, and she has been an invaluable resource and friend for many years. My mother-in-law, Clara Orozco, introduced me to Spanish cooking over fifty years ago. Like many Basques, she was an excellent cook, and many of her recipes are still among my favorites.

My husband's cousin Rafael Salgado and some of Luis's friends, Chalo Pelaez, Pepe Sanz, Pepe and Carmen González, and Pepe and Paqui Delfin, have explored the gastronomic panorama of Spain with me and have directed me to unusual locations where we have experienced incredibly inventive dishes and exceptional tapas. Their good taste and knowledge were an invaluable resource to me for over fifty years.

I want to dedicate a few words to Craig Claiborne from the *New York Times*. In 1979, he encouraged me to write my first book and helped me get my first publishing deal. I was honored by his confidence in me, and I have missed him over the years. I feel his legacy in this book.

I want to thank my editor, Linda Ingroia, for her patience, encouragement, and guidance, her dedication to this project, and her attention to detail. Also Kristi Hart, the copy editor, deserves thanks for her incredibly finessed work on consistency and clarity. I also want to thank others on the Houghton Mifflin Harcourt team who supported the book in so many ways—Natalie Chapman, publisher; Marina Padakis, managing editor; Jackie Beach, production editor, Greta Sibley, designer, and Melissa Lotfy and Jeff Faust, cover designers.

My husband Luis, my daughter Elisa, and my granddaughter Ruby were very supportive during the long process of writing this book and seeing it through to publication. As always, Luis's encyclopedic knowledge of Spain, his excellent memory, and his astute suggestions were essential. And a big thanks to my cousin, Stephanie Phillips, who assisted in researching and organizing the manuscript.

Introduction to 1,000 Spanish Recipes

Penelope Casas

My first visit to Spain was fifty years ago when I lived in Madrid as a foreign exchange student. I was immediately enchanted by their culture and lifestyle, and I quickly learned that Spaniards are as passionate about their cuisine as they are about their country. They take immense pride in the freshness of their ingredients, and they will spare no expense to acquire them. As they say in Spain, they live to eat (*vivir para comer*) as opposed to eat to live (*comer para vivir*).

Every meal in Spain is an occasion unto itself, which often entails socializing with old friends as well as making new ones. Eating in this leisurely fashion often takes up a good part of each day, starting with breakfast, followed by a midmorning snack and early afternoon tapas. These delicious and incredibly varied appetizers (known as "the little dishes of Spain") can be as filling as a main meal. It is not uncommon for Spaniards to saunter from restaurant to restaurant, seeking whatever unique *tapa* that particular chef is famous for. The night usually involves multiple glasses of wine, sangria, or sherry and always seems to include lively conversation. Tapas are not just a way of eating in Spain—they are a way of life. But these delicious bite-size morsels do not deter the average Spaniard from also indulging in heavier meals. Dinner, *la cena*, and especially lunch, *la comida*, are consumed heartily despite all the in-between snacking. In fact, the Spanish workday grinds to a halt for the traditional long lunch, which consists of three different courses that are savored for several hours.

Spaniards have an expression, *"Viva Yo!"* which translates in English to "Long Live Me!" This somewhat epicurean attitude towards life is reflected by their love of delicious food, fine wine, and good companionship. Nobody in Spain waits until the weekend to enjoy life, as this is considered a priority on a daily basis. Spaniards eat as they live—with unabashed gusto.

When I fell in love with Spanish culture and cuisine, I wanted to learn everything possible about it. In the 1970s and 1980s, there were almost no Spanish cookbooks on American bookshelves, and my friend, the famed *New York Times* food critic Craig Claiborne, suggested that I write one. He had been to my house on numerous occasions and had sampled many of my Spanish dishes. With his support and encouragement, my first book, *The Foods and Wines of Spain*, was born.

Long before then, I had married my husband, Dr. Luis Casas, a *Madrileño* (native of Madrid) who just happened to be the son of the family that hosted me as a foreign exchange student. His father had died long ago in the Spanish Civil War, but it was his mother who first taught me how to cook. Luis and I spent many years living in Spain before moving back to New York. As I researched this book, and then my six subsequent others, it became readily apparent that in order to capture the varying culinary styles of the different regions of Spain, I would have to visit them myself.

Year after year, Luis and I traveled extensively throughout the different provinces of Spain, acquiring recipes from restaurants, friends, and especially friends' *mamas y yayas* (mothers and grandmothers). I studied the cookbook of Rupert Nola, chef to King Ferdinand, the first known Spanish cookbook dating back to 1525. I pored over handwritten old family recipes from anyone who was kind enough to share them. I visited monasteries and convents, which proved to be some of the only places where some unusual recipes were kept alive. More importantly, I had the opportunity to watch as many of these dishes were actually being prepared. I stood next to elderly women in the small kitchens of their modest homes, and I stood next to world-renowned chefs in magnificent three-star restaurants. I learned that even though the style of cooking in Spain has changed dramatically throughout the years, everyone maintains a soft spot in his or her heart for the dishes of childhood.

With Luis as my eager tour guide and my daughter Elisa in tow, we scoured the coast of Spain for the seafood, the mountains of Castilla for the succulent pig and roast baby lamb, and the rice fields of Valencia for the traditional dishes, the most famous, of course, being their unparalleled paella. To my surprise, some of my favorite recipes were procured from the tiny, remote villages we drove through along the way.

After each trip, I went back to my home in New York and experimented with every dish myself, refining some recipes and recreating others. I frequently held dinner parties—some small and intimate, some large and boisterous—where my recipes were put to the test. I sought the opinions of my tireless friends and family, and I soon figured out that the easiest way to judge the most popular dish was that, invariably, it was the one to disappear from the table first.

I initially found that many Americans shared some major misconceptions about Spanish food. Many people automatically associated it with Mexican or Latin American food, when in fact these cuisines have little in common. One of the most distinctive differences is that Spanish food in general is not hot or spicy. The Spanish cooking style is subtle and refined as well as simple and down to earth.

Because of the vast diversity of eating habits and cooking styles found in the different regions and provinces, Spain does not really have a national cuisine. There are of course a handful of dishes that are popular nationwide, such as gazpacho, *tortilla de patata* (potato omelets), *gambas al ajillo* (shrimp in garlic sauce) and of course paella. But because Spaniards insist upon only the finest and freshest ingredients, much of what they eat is dictated by the climate and geography of where they live.

Spain has the longest coastline in Europe and some of the richest fishing grounds in the world, so seafood features prominently wherever it is accessible. In Spain's northernmost area, the region of Galicia, where recipes reflect their ancient Celtic heritage, has extraordinary seafood and shellfish, especially their famed scallops. Inland, there are lush green mountainous areas for animals to graze, and I believe that Galicians also have the finest veal in Spain.

Asturias, slightly east along the coast, is famed for its legendary bean dish, *fabada*. This robust and hearty stew was born from economic necessity and was originally used to warm the bellies of the local shepherds. These days *fabadas* are often enhanced with meat, seafood, and *chorizo*, and they are as popular today as they were back then.

The Basque region is well-known for its famous fish soup *marmitako*, which some say comes from the French word for "metal soup kettle." There are many different versions of this recipe, but they all invariably include either pimientos or dried sweet red chile peppers called *ñoras*.

Catalunya, an area of diverse landscapes, is in my opinion the most gastronomically exciting region of Spain. The chefs there tend to be especially creative and imaginative with their recipes. The Pyrenees Mountains, the port city of Barcelona, and the jagged Costa Brava shoreline are all located here. Catalan-style cooking reflects the incredible surplus of fine and easily obtained ingredients.

Valencia, often called Levante (land of the sunrise), could also be called the land of rice as endless rice recipes are prepared and eaten on a daily basis. Valencians have created numerous incarnations of rice dishes, but of course the most popular is their famed paella.

Andalucía, the southern-most region, has a warmer climate and access to freshly caught seafood, vine-ripened vegetables, and a variety of delectable meats. Gazpacho of the bright red variety is said to have originated there, and the chilled, refreshing thirst-quencher is often still enjoyed on a daily basis.

Castilla, an historic region, recently split into Castilla Y León and Castilla-La Mancha, with the Madrid region nestled in between. They are home to *cocido*, an enticing meal-in-a-pot, made with chickpeas, meat, and sausages. These hearty dishes can be found simmering for hours in restaurants and homes everywhere. *Chorizo*, now commonly found in most areas, is undoubtedly at its best in the region, as are suckling pigs and baby lambs. Madrid, being a metropolitan Mecca as well as the country's capital, is lucky enough to have access to restaurants specializing in recipes from every region.

Extremadura, a dry region that is home to some of Spain's most breathtaking villages, has a cuisine similar to that of Castilla. Stews with poultry and meat are more commonly served than other preparations, and simple pastry dishes can also be found.

Aragon and Navarra, with its varied terrain of mountains, valleys, and rivers are known for its game and its most delicious trout. *Chilindrón* dishes, meat and poultry made with the region's famed mild red pepper, are always a staple. Recipes featuring *chilindrón* have gained in popularity and have now made their way through almost all the regions of Spain.

The Canary Islands, until recently, did not play a major role in the cuisine of Spain. But times have changed, and now many of their locally found ingredients, such as bananas, fish, and tiny tender potatoes have become key ingredients in more than a few Spanish recipes.

This book is an accumulation of my favorite recipes that I have acquired from different regions over many years. Some are simple and some require several hours of preparation, but none of them are especially difficult to make at home. When a dish calls for an ingredient that is only found in Spain, I try to suggest its alternative American counterpart, as well as provide a list of specialty stores where you will be sure to find them. Some of the more old-fashioned recipes demand hand mashing with a mortar, but an electric mini-processor often works just as well. Every dish can be adapted to today's busy lifestyle, and almost all of them are perfectly suited for the health conscious. Because Spain produces more olive oil than any other country in the world, it permeates their cuisine, providing enormous nutritional benefits. *1,000 Spanish Recipes* is a comprehensive guide for seasoned cooks and beginners alike. I hope you have as much fun eating and preparing these recipes as I did collecting and creating them. *¡Salud!*

Homemade Ingredients

There are a number of ingredients or recipe components that can be storebought but when made from scratch almost always provide better taste and texture to Spanish dishes, or really any cooking. I prefer to make my own bread crumbs and croutons, mayonnaise, and garlic sauce (alioli), which don't take very much time at all. Whenever possible I also prefer to prepare broths or cooking liquids (fish, vegetable, chicken, meat), pate, pimientos (roasted, peeled, and seeded peppers), puff pastry, sausage, and tomato sauce—not all at once but when I know I want to make special dishes.

For the recipes in this book, I sometimes call for either homemade or storebought versions of these ingredients. The dishes will still be excellent with high-quality storebought ingredients but as you cook through this book continue adding more of these ingredients to your "homemade" repertoire. Just remember to consider the time required to prepare these components as you plan for the main recipes.

Glossary of Spanish Ingredients

AGUARDIENTE, also called *orujo*, is a powerful Spanish liquor, popular as a drink in Galicia, and used very sparingly in cooking. Its Italian equivalent, grappa, is widely available here in the United States, and although it has a higher alcohol volume than the Spanish liquor, it is an adequate substitute.

ALIOLI, or garlic sauce, is a combination of olive oil (preferably extra-virgin) and garlic, sometimes with a touch of egg. You can make your own or buy it bottled.

ANCHOVIES (*boquerones*) that are vertically packed in olive oil and in bottles are usually superior to those packed in tins. Spain's best anchovies come from the Mediterranean in Catalunya and the Cantabrian Sea in the Basque Country. When anchovies are fresh, they are known as *boquerones*, and if the filets are marinated in vinegar, they become a popular tapa called *Boquerones en Vinagre* (Marinated Fresh Anchovies, page 15).

ASPARAGUS (white) originated in the region of Navarra, where they are painstakingly grown by covering young shoots with earth to prevent them from turning green. Spaniards insist that canned or bottled white asparagus are far superior to fresh—which is often the case since fresh white asparagus rapidly loses quality, and factory-processed asparagus are cooked at their peak of freshness and flavor. White asparagus are most often served with a vinaigrette or mayonnaise as a salad course and are also used as a salad ingredient.

BACON, SLAB, is simply bacon in a single piece, rather than in thin slices. It is often used in Spanish cooking, cut into small cubes or cut into chunks. Although thin-sliced bacon will give the desired flavor, it burns too easily and cannot take the heat that the cubes of bacon can. It also does not provide texture. Slab bacon is often found in supermarkets.

BEANS, dried in Spain, are of the highest quality and are grown in several varieties, some of which have become easier to find, others are still specialty items. Chickpeas (*garbanzos*) are amongst Spain's favorite beans and are a key ingredient in Spain's *cocidos* (stews); they can now be found in supermarkets. Oversized kidney-shaped beans (*judiones*) and other large white beans like *fabas asturianas* are favored in Spanish bean stews. Beans the size of a pea are popular in Catalunya and sometimes served as a vegetable side course, and red beans (*caparrones*) are preferred in the Basque Country. Other beans that are common and featured in this book include deep-red beans (*alubias rojas*), butter beans (*habas grandes*), and black beans (*frijoles negros*). Spanish lentils are not processed for fast cooking but are superior in taste and texture to lentils found in U.S. supermarkets. They will need an overnight soaking, like any other dried bean.

CANELONES are dried pasta squares, which in Spanish cooking are boiled, then filled, typically with meat, and rolled.

CAPERBERRIES are formed from the fruit of the caper bush once the flowers have faded. They make great tapas.

CAPERS are the flowers of the caper bush that proliferate in warm, Mediterranean climates. When the buds are at their smallest, they are known as nonpareil capers and are very attractive in salads and marinades. But the quality is no different from larger, less expensive capers.

CHEESES, SPANISH, are finally available in this country in more than a dozen varieties. They are an exciting addition, bearing little resemblance to the hundreds of other cheeses already sold here. Some of the best-known and most popular kinds are the following:

- *queso manchego,* a sheep milk cheese from La Mancha in central Spain, can be semi-soft when lightly cured or as hard as Parmesan (but not as strong tasting) when left to age. It is the most popular cheese in Spain and a great favorite of mine.
- *queso de Cabrales* and *queso de Valdeón* are pungent yet smooth blue cheeses, sometimes wrapped in leaves, from the mountainous northern area of Spain. Made from a mixture of cow, goat, and sheep milk, they are strictly artisan cheeses, produced in mountain caves and rural kitchens in very small quantities.
- *queso del roncal* comes from the Spanish Pyrenees and is made from sheep and cow milk. It is usually well-cured and a bit similar in taste to *queso manchego.*
- *queso de Idiazabal* is made in the Basque Country in northern Spain. It is a semi-soft sheep milk cheese with a smoky taste.
- *queso tetilla,* shaped like a large chocolate kiss, comes from Galicia. It is mild and creamy but, at the same time, slightly pungent and works well in recipes calling for a cheese that melts easily.
- *queso torta del casar,* is a unique and runny sheep milk cheese from Extremadura that is mild but with a bite. It has become popular in *vanguardista* cooking.

- *torta de la serena* is a similar soft sheep's milk cheese. Brie or Camembert can be substituted for either.

CIDER (*sidra*) is a hard, very dry cider that is the typical drink of Asturians in northern Spain, often replacing wine as a lunch or dinner accompaniment. It is also used to make sauces for meat and fish. Use only hard cider available here in liquor stores. It is a bit sweeter than the Asturian cider (and therefore not as appropriate as a dinner drink), but it works very well in cooking. A sparkling cider imported from Spain is often found in Spanish markets. This product is quite sweet and meant to be used as champagne, not a cooking liquid.

CLAMS AND MUSSELS, CANNED, are among the other wonderful Spanish fish products prepared in brine, raw cockles (*berberechos al natural*), and pickled mussels (*mejillones en escabeche*), both of which make tasty tapas.

CODFISH, DRIED, SALTED (*bacalao*) is a favorite in Spain in interior areas with no access to the sea as well as in the north, where fresh fish are plentiful. Its strong flavor is not to everyone's liking, but when well prepared in an interesting sauce, it can be outstanding. Look for cod that is well-dried and white—avoid pieces that have a yellow cast to them. Cod that has been boned and skinned before drying is much easier to handle and eat. Each cod recipe gives instructions for preparation of cod suitable to that recipe, but all call for a soaking period of 24 to 36 hours to remove the salt.

HAM, CURED (*jamón serrano*) is used in a surprising variety of Spanish recipes. Italian prosciutto is the closest cured ham available here. Try to find prosciutto that is not too salty or dry. Italian capicolla is also an acceptable substitute. Never substitute Spanish cooking ham—it will give an entirely different flavor that is not appropriate for Spanish cooking. Many recipes call for cured ham cut into small cubes (¼ inch) or into chunks. Buy the ham, therefore, in slices at least ¼ inch thick. When larger pieces are required—for example in soups—it is best to cut the narrow end of the ham in a piece at least 1 inch thick.

LARD, or solidified rendered pork fat, is used in baking as well as frying, sautéing, and basting meat and fowl. Although used sparingly in this book, when it is called for, it lends a special flavor to foods, and I recommend its use. However, for main courses, olive oil may be substituted; in baking, vegetable shortening may be substituted. When buying lard, look for packages that say "100% pure lard" (such as the Tobin brand), and skip those that contain chemical preservatives. Better yet, render your own lard from "leaf lard" available in butcher shops.

MEMBRILLO is a quince preserve that is well loved in Spain as a dessert, typically accompanied by manchego cheese.

MORCILLA is a Spanish blood sausage often used in stews as well as sliced and fried as an accompaniment to eggs or as an appetizer. When it is of excellent quality, it is one of my favorite sausages. The *morcilla* found vacuum-packed is usually not very good. Look for the unpackaged kinds found in Spanish markets. The type labeled "Argentinian" is quite good, but I most enjoy the *morcilla* that contains rice, sometimes called "Columbian style." If top-quality *morcilla* cannot be found, it can usually be omitted from recipes without drastically changing the flavor.

OLIVE OIL is the oil used almost exclusively in Spanish cooking—except in dessert making, when salad oil is used. Butter rarely enters into a Spanish recipe. Olive oil is an unsaturated fat and therefore excellent for those watching their cholesterol. It may be strongly flavored (the "virgin" oils) with grassy or fruity notes or mild tasting. Which one you use is a matter of personal preference (I often call for fruity extra-virgin olive oil when it makes a positive difference.) Excellent Spanish olive oils are available in Spanish markets (Carbonell brand is my favorite). They are also found disguised under Italian names in supermarkets. You may use olive oil from any country in Spanish cooking—the important thing to decide is whether you want your oil strong tasting or mild. (See also "Olive Oil," page 148.)

PAPRIKA, ground sweet red peppers, can be made from many different varieties of red peppers. For authentic flavor, use paprika (*pimentón*) imported from Spain. There are many varieties on the shelf, but I specified in my recipes whether to use sweet, bittersweet, or hot *pimentón* in the recipes. I usually prefer Spanish smoked paprika for richer flavor.

PEPPERS

- **dried hot red chile peppers** are a common ingredient in many Spanish dishes, used to give a slight hotness to a sauce. They are often added in a single piece or are broken into large pieces, and the seeds are not used. They are not meant to be eaten. You may substitute crushed red pepper, available in supermarkets, but this will contain the pepper seeds, which will give extra spiciness. Using crushed pepper will also mean that the pepper pieces will be distributed throughout a sauce, which is not always desirable.

- **dried sweet red peppers** (*ñoras, pimientos, romescos, or pimientos choriceros*) lend a wonderfully earthy taste to foods and are used in several rice dishes, and are essential to two of the most outstanding dishes of Spain, *Bacalao a la Vizcaína* (Salt Cod, Basque Style, page 406) and *Gran Romesco de Pescado* (fish with romesco sauce). Although hot red peppers of numerous varieties can be found here in Mexican and South American markets, the dried sweet peppers are harder to get. The closest I have found to the sweet red pepper used in Spain is an elongated pepper called "New Mexico" (Anaheim), which has just a slight piquantness that it loses in cooking. (New Mexico peppers need to be cored with kitchen shears, because the skin is tougher than on other peppers.) It is well worth the effort to find Spanish dried sweet peppers for the special character they give to several dishes in the book. I have tried a combination of paprika and pimientos as a substitute (about 3 teaspoons paprika and 1 pimiento to each dried red pepper), but I really do not find this mixture an adequate substitute.

- **frying peppers** (*padrón*) are named after the Spanish town where they originated. Most are mild although occasionally you'll get a hot one.
- **piquillo peppers** are heart-shaped and thick-fleshed shiny chiles that ripen from green to red and grow to about 4 inches long. Often found jarred.

PIMIENTOS is the Spanish word for peppers, but in English it has come to mean red peppers that are prepared by cooking, peeling, and seeding. Pimientos are used extensively in Spanish cooking. If using canned pimientos, purchase only those imported from Spain—domestic pimientos are mushy and fall apart in cooking. It is of course preferable to make your own, especially since red peppers seem to be available now year-round. Simply place the red peppers in a roasting pan and bake at 350°F for 30 minutes, turning occasionally. Peel off the skin and remove the seeds and the core. They may be refrigerated for several days, either wrapped in foil or in a covered container.

RICE, SHORT-GRAIN, sometimes called pearl rice, is the only kind of rice used in Spanish cooking. It has a nutty taste and a chewy texture that are especially important for paella and for the cold rice tapas in this book. You can find it imported from Spain and Italy, but it is also grown in California. Short-grain rice turns mushy when overcooked, so the recipe cooking times should be carefully observed. If you can't find Spanish rice, Italian Arborio is a fine substitute.

SAFFRON (*azafrán*), an Arab word for "yellow," consists of the stigmas of a purple crocus flower. Saffron adds color and a distinct flavor, somewhat akin to tea, to Spanish rice dishes as well as other main courses. Most of the world's saffron comes from Spain, and because of the arduous process of collection, it is the most expensive spice in the world. Its strong flavor means that it is always used in small quantities. Substitutes, such as turmeric and Mexican marigold petals, will lack the flavor and aroma of saffron and should not be used in Spanish cooking. (See also "Saffron," page 295.)

SALT, COARSE, sometimes called Kosher or sea salt, is recommended for use in all recipes calling for salt, although in some it is more important than others. Meat and poultry that are sprinkled with salt before sautéing fry better when coarse salt is used. It is also much better for sprinkling on foods already cooked, for it does not penetrate the food as much as fine salt does. Coarse salt is essential for the fish dish *Urta a la Sal* (Porgy Baked in Salt, page 374). If, however, the salt is going to dissolve in cooking, fine salt will do just as well. I have indicated coarse salt in recipes where that type of salt is most important.

SAUSAGES, SPANISH

- *butifarra* **sausage** is a white sausage that comes from Catalunya. It is spiced with cinnamon, nutmeg, and cloves and used extensively in Catalan cooking. If *butifarra* cannot be found, Italian-style sweet sausage or breakfast sausage are passable substitutes.
- *chorizo* **sausage** is the most typical Spanish sausage, heavily scented with paprika and garlic. It is eaten cold and sliced or fried as an appetizer. You can make your own *chorizo*, or buy it in any Spanish specialty food store, as well as some supermarkets. Spanish-style *chorizo*, as opposed to South American style, is mild. *Chorizo* that is less cured is most often used in cooking while the harder and drier *chorizo* are eaten as cold cuts. Most *chorizo* is prepared in links; you can also find soft *chorizo* sold in bulk, which is used for sautéed dishes and for fillings.
- *sobrasada* **sausage** is a soft, spreadable *chorizo* from the Balearic Islands that also makes a terrific tapa. It can be found in specialty food stores in the United States and is also available through mail order.

SHERRY/WINES, SPANISH

Sherry is the quintessential Spanish wine, the perfect *aperitivo* with tapas and a popular accompaniment with shellfish and fish. Sherry is also an essential element in Spanish cooking, lending a distinctive flavor, and sherry vinegar is used all over Spain. There are three basic types of sherry: fino and manzanilla (dry), medium-sweet (Oloroso), and sweet (cream).

Jerez, as it is known in Spain, has been produced since the 8th century in the Andalucian towns between Jerez de la Frontera, Puerto de Santa Maria and Sanlucar de Barrameda. The three most important elements in its production are the Palomino grape, the "Albariza" soil, and the very special microclimate that provides its slightly salty flavor.

SQUID, in all its many varieties, is a favorite seafood in Spain. It is delicious when quickly fried as well as slowly stewed. Many fish markets sell squid already cleaned (at a higher price) or will clean it for you. To clean it yourself, hold the body of the squid in one hand and pull out the tentacles with the other. Reserve the tentacles if they are called for in a recipe, cutting off all waste material but leaving the tentacles in one piece. Remove the skin from the body of the squid and pull off the fins. Turn the squid inside out, remove the cartilage, and wash the body well under running water. Turn the squid to the outside again and dry well on paper towels.

TURRÓN is a Spanish almond and honey candy of Arab origin that comes in a crackling hard bar (*Alicante* style) and in a soft marzipan-like form (*Jijona* style). Both are available imported from Spain, especially during the Christmas season, in Spanish markets. *Turrón* is excellent eaten as a candy and is used besides in desserts, such as Turrón Ice Cream, page 648. Despite a visit to a *turrón* factory in Jijona, Spain, and innumerable attempts to produce a recipe for this candy, I have not been able to create a *turrón* that measures up to the imported candy.

Glossary of Spanish Cooking Equipment

CAZUELAS are earthenware casserole dishes that are ubiquitous to Spain, used both for cooking—in the oven or on top of the stove—and for serving. They come in many sizes, from individual tapa size to large casserole dishes. Before using it for the first time, soak it in water for several hours. You might also want to use a flame tamer when placing it directly on a gas stovetop.

Foods undoubtedly cook more evenly in *cazuelas*, and liquids do not evaporate as easily as in metal cookware. Some say *cazuelas* impart a distinctive taste to the food. In any case, their rustic look is charming for serving tapas as well as roasted and simmering dishes, and they retain heat much better than other cookware. Do not subject earthenware to sudden changes of temperature—heat gradually and cool slowly.

CHURRO PRESS is a traditionally metal device (although now available in plastic), like a pastry tube but larger and wider, to make Spanish wand-shaped breakfast fritters (*churros*).

MORTARS hold a place of honor in every Spanish kitchen—be it a rustic village kitchen or a high-tech city kitchen. Nothing beats the mortar and its companion, the pestle, to unlock flavor, especially from herbs, spices, and garlic. Its purpose is not just to mince and mix but to commingle ingredients in a way that a food processor can never do. If there is any one item that you should have in order to cook Spanish style, it is without question the mortar. The one most commonly used in Spain is charming—bright yellow ceramic dabbed with green.

PAELLA PANS are the typically wide flat pans with handles that are specifically designed to make authentic paellas. Use the inexpensive steel pans (rather than stainless steel) that are used in Valencia, homeland of paella. True, these pans will discolor with use, but because they heat so rapidly, they give the best results.

A NOTE ABOUT THE RECIPE SYMBOLS IN THIS BOOK

Ⓥ indicates the recipe is vegetarian; **Ⓥ*** indicates that the recipe can be made vegetarian with one ingredient change, such as using vegetable broth instead of chicken broth or omitting bacon in the recipe. You can make your own adaptations based on your diet or preferences.

Menu Suggestions

Most Spanish meals consist of at least three courses. This is a sample of some of my favorite menu selections, some easy to make and some slightly more difficult, but all of them combining tastes and textures that are well suited for each other.

The list is divided into four categories. The first part consists of menus that can be served every day, such as lunches, brunches, and family dinners. The second part emphasizes regional cooking and provides recipes for popular menus created in the style for which that particular region is best known. The third part contains meals with some elaborate recipes that are best suited for dinner parties. The fourth part suggests menus for meals that are made up entirely of tapas alone. In Spain, it is common to sometimes have a supper that is comprised only of tapas. Bear in mind that, of course, all these menus can be mixed and matched to suit your particular preferences.

Everyday Menus

COLD SUMMER MENU

White Gazpacho, Málaga Style (page 186)

Braised Marinated Quail (page 476)

Green Bean Salad (page 158)

Cinnamon-Flavored Ice Milk (page 670)

Powdered Sugar Cookies, Seville Style (page 582)

HEARTY WINTER MENU

Asturian Bean Stew (page 213)

Mixed Salad, San Isidro Style (page 155)

Rice Pudding, Asturian Style (page 636)

SEAFOOD DELIGHT

Mussels in Green Sauce (page 37)

Basque Tuna Soup (page 202)

Garlic Green Beans (page 247)

assorted fruit and cheese

LIGHT DINNER

Eggplant with Shrimp and Ham (page 244)

Watercress and Carrot Salad with
Anchovy Dressing (page 160)

Orange Ice Cream Cake (page 588)

LUNCHEON MENU

Tomato and Green Pepper Pies (page 136)

Gently Scrambled Eggs with Shrimp
and Spinach (page 108)

Fig and Candied Squash Pastries (page 620)

BRUNCH MENU

Spanish Potato Omelet (page 118)

Asturian sausage or Catalan sausage

Basic Long Loaf (Baguette) Bread (page 126)

Almond and Marmalade Puff
Pastry Strips (page 617)

TRADITIONAL CHRISTMAS EVE DINNER

Onion and Almond Soup (page 192)

Baked Porgy, Madrid Style (page 376)

Roast turkey

Baked Red Cabbage and Apples (page 240)

Assorted fruit and cheese

Turrón candy

Marzipan Candies (page 668)

Regional Menus

GALICIAN DINNER

Galician Meat, Potato, Greens,
and Bean Soup (page 211)

Pork Pie (page 139)

Galician Almond Cake (page 585)

ASTURIAN DINNER

Onion, Tuna, and Tomato Omelet (page 125)

Pork Chops with Apples in
Cider Sauce (page 531)

Walnut-Filled Turnovers (page 619)

BASQUE DINNER

Crabmeat with Brandy and Wine (page 420)

Butterflied Porgy, Bilbao Style (page 374)

Green Beans and Cured Ham (page 248)

Fried Custard (page 635)

CASTILIAN DINNER

Tripe Stew, Madrid Style (page 228)

Partridges in Escabeche (page 472)

Peas with Cured Ham (page 257)

Breakfast Fritters (page 599)

CATALAN DINNER

Baked Sausage and Mushrooms (page 550)

Mixed Shellfish in Brandy and
Tomato Sauce (page 425)

Vegetable Salad in Romesco Sauce (page 156)

Sugar-Crusted Custard (page 632)

ANDALUCIAN DINNER

Baked Eggs with Ham,
Sausage, and Asparagus (page 113)

Porgy Baked in Salt (page 374)

Custard-Filled Cake Roll (page 591)

VALENCIAN DINNER

Marinated Frog Legs (page 431)

Valencia's Traditional Paella (page 325)

Potato and Orange Salad (page 153)

Orange-Almond Cake (page 587)

RIOJA DINNER

Mixed Vegetables, Rioja Style (page 276)

Chicken with Red Peppers (page 454)

Spicy Potatoes (page 51)

Pears in Wine Sauce (page 661)

Dinner Party Menus

Gazpacho, Andalusian Style (page 185)

Mixed Chicken and Seafood Paella (page 326)

Escarole Salad with Tomato and
Cumin Dressing (page 159)

Caramel Custard (Flan) (page 627)

~~~~~~

Shrimp Cocktail, Spanish Style (page 25)

Duck with Sherry and Green
Olives, Sevilla Style (page 481)

Roasted Potatoes with Bell Pepper (page 269)

Escarole-Tomato Salad, Murcia Style (page 165)

Prune Ice Cream with Orange
Liqueur Sauce (page 650)

"Cat's Tongue" Cookies (page 576)

~~~~~~

Garlic Soup, Castilian Style (page 191)

Turbot in Romesco Sauce (page 383)

Cucumber, Tomato, and Pepper Salad (page 147)

Sugar-Crusted Custard (page 632)

~~~~~~

Shellfish and Fish Vinaigrette (page 22)

Seafood-Flavored Rice, Alicante Style (page 299)

Eggplant, Artichoke, Pepper, and
Tomato Salad (page 163)

assorted fruit and cheese

~~~~~~

Veal Chops with Ham,
Mushrooms, and Pimiento (page 556)

Poor Man's Potatoes (page 264)

Frozen Orange Custard with
Blackberry Sauce (page 647)

~~~~~~

Tripe Stew, Madrid Style (page 228)

Boiled Beef and Chickpea
Dinner (page 227)

Cream-Filled Fritters (page 601)

~~~~~~

Garlic Soup, Castilian Style (page 191)

Pickled Trout (page 366)

Roast Lamb, Castilian Style (page 527)

Eggplant with Cheese (page 243)

Custard-Filled Dessert Crepes (page 625)

Tapas Menus

TAPAS AS A MEAL

Chicken Liver Pâté with Sherry Glaze (page 99)

Spicy Pimientos (page 48)

Clam Pie (page 137)

Chicken in Garlic Sauce (page 62)

~~~~~~

Sautéed Artichokes and Cured Ham (page 234)
Smoked Salmon Toast (page 98)
Duck and Serrano Ham Pâté (page 100)

Clams in Almond Sauce (page 34)
Fish and Vegetable Salad (page 181)
Grilled Shrimp over Coarse Sea Salt (page 27)
Monkfish Marinera (page 401)

Olive "Paste" and Blue Cheese Canapé (page 89)
Tuna Escabeche (page 17)
Andalusian Rice Salad (page 169)
Vegetable Salad in Romesco Sauce (page 156)

Vegetarian Tapas

Fried Cheese Canapé (page 94)
Tomato and Green Pepper Pies (page 136)
Vegetable Medley, Andalusian Style
(page 279) with fried quail egg (optional)
Cumin-Flavored Mushroom Salad (page 151)
Broiled Asparagus with Brie (page 53)

Tapas Extravaganza

Marinated Mussels (page 20)
Clams in Green Sauce (page 33)
Cumin-Flavored Mushroom Salad (page 151)
Pâté with Turkey Breast (page 103)
Fresh Sardine Pie (page 136)
Shrimp in Piparrada Sauce (page 26)
Spanish Potato Omelet (page 118)
Manchego Cheese with Quince Paste (page 92)
Sausages with Sweet-and-Sour Figs (page 551)
Mushrooms Stuffed with Lemon (page 49)
Fresh Fish Spread (page 97)
Baked Stuffed Squid in Almond Sauce (page 429)
Pork Ribs in Garlic Sauce (page 55)
Black Sausage in Puff Pastry (page 77)
Shrimp Tartlets (page 83)
Chicken and Cured Ham Croquettes (page 70)
Chorizo "Lollipops" (page 56)

The Recipes

Tapas

SKEWERED BITES (BANDERILLAS)

Sample Banderillas

Banderilla Dressing ⓥ

Black Olives Marinated in Paprika ⓥ

Olives with Garlic and Paprika ⓥ

Marinated Green Olives ⓥ

Potato and Seafood Banderilla

Chorizo and Bread Banderilla

Egg Tapa

Fried Pork Skins with Anchovies

MARINATED AND PICKLED DISHES

Pickled Eggplant, Almagro Style ⓥ

"Russian" Potato and Vegetable Salad

Butter Beans in Caper Vinaigrette

Tuna-Filled Pickle

Pickled Fresh Sardines

Marinated Fresh Anchovies

Fresh Anchovies with Pickled Beets and Onions

Marinated Fresh Anchovy Layered with Eggplant

Marinated and Fried Fresh Anchovies

Stuffed Pickles

Tuna Escabeche

Pickled Fresh Tuna with Grilled Vegetables

Pickled Mackerel with Lemon and Orange

Marinated and Fried Small Fish

ⓥ = Vegetarian ⓥ* = Vegetarian with one change

Marinated Mussels

Marinated Octopus

Marinated Fried Shark

Tuna Tartare with Avocado, Pickle, and Capers

Shellfish and Fish Vinaigrette

Escabeche of Asparagus with Fresh Anchovies

Prawns in Clove-Scented Marinade

Lobster in Vinaigrette with Saffron,
Brandy, and Hard-Boiled Egg

Headcheese Vinaigrette

COOKED SHELLFISH

Shrimp in Garlic Sauce

Shrimp Cocktail, Spanish Style

Batter-Fried Shrimp

Shrimp in Piparrada Sauce

Shrimp with Sherry and Ham

Grilled Shrimp over Coarse Sea Salt

Shrimp with Bacon

Béchamel-Coated Fried Shrimp

Clams Fisherman Style

Clams, Andalusian Style

Clams in White Wine Sauce

Clams in Romesco Sauce

Clams in Spicy Tomato Sauce

Grilled Clams with Thin-Sliced Shrimp

Clams, Botín Style

Clams in Green Sauce

Clams with Green Pepper and Tomato

Clams in Almond Sauce

Baked Stuffed Clams

Mussels "My Way"

Mussels, Galician Style

Stuffed Fried Mussels

Mussels in White Wine Sauce

Mussels in Green Sauce

Baked Mussels and Mushrooms

Mussels in Spicy Tomato Sauce

Scallops Wrapped in Bacon
with Pomegranate Sauce

Crab Crepes

COOKED FISH, SQUID, AND OCTOPUS

Swordfish in Saffron Sauce

Fried Squid "a la Romana"

Batter-Fried Squid Tentacles

Fried Stuffed Baby Squid

Small Squid in Beer Sauce

Dried Cod in Garlic Mayonnaise

Fried Cod Sticks

Baby Eels in Garlic Sauce

Snails, Madrid Style

Marinated Octopus

Fish Roll with Pine Nuts and Cheese

COOKED VEGETABLES

Stewed Zucchini, Peppers, and Tomatoes **V**

Almond-Stuffed Dates Wrapped in Bacon

Chickpeas in Onion Sauce **V**

Spicy Pimientos **V***

Fried Salted Almonds **V**

Mushrooms Stuffed with Lemon **V**

Pork-Stuffed Mushrooms

Mushrooms Segovia Style

Mushrooms in Garlic Sauce

Grilled Oyster Mushrooms
with Oil and Garlic **V**

Spicy Potatoes **V**

Potato Chips with Octopus and Garlic Sauce

Figs Wrapped in Ham with Soft Cheese

Batter-Fried Onion Rings **V**

Broiled Asparagus with Brie **V**

Deep-Fried Leeks **V**

COOKED MEAT DISHES

Spicy Pork Skewers

Marinated Pork Loin

Chorizo Simmered in White Wine

Pork Ribs in Garlic Sauce

Chorizo "Lollipops"

Chorizo and Apples in Hard Cider Sauce

Fresh Ham with Orange and Walnut Sauce

Beef Tenderloin Tips in Garlic Sauce

Sausage Rolled in Cabbage Leaves

Pork Meatballs

Tiny Meatballs in Saffron Sauce

Meatballs in Semisweet Sherry

Meatballs Filled with Cheese in
Green and Red Pepper Sauce

Partridge Meatballs

Lamb Meatballs in Brandy Sauce

Pork Tenderloin with Tomato and Onion Salad

Chicken in Garlic Sauce

Quail with Pearl Onions and Pine Nuts

CROQUETTES AND
FRIED PASTRIES

Fried Ham and Cheese Sandwiches

Fried Cheese Balls

Soft Cheese Croquettes Ⓥ

Zucchini Croquettes Ⓥ

Swiss Chard Croquettes Ⓥ

Eggplant Fritters Filled with
Anchovies and Cheese

Potato and Cheese Puffs Ⓥ

Mushroom Croquettes with Apple Cider

Zucchini and Shrimp Puffs

Fried Anchovies Filled with Spinach

Paella Croquettes

Spinach, Pine Nut, and Raisin Croquettes Ⓥ

Chicken and Cured Ham Croquettes

Partridge and Cheese Croquettes

Ham and Fresh Pork Croquettes

Fried Zucchini and Cheese Rolls

Salt Cod and Potato Puffs

Chorizo Puffs

Red Bell Peppers in Puff Pastry Ⓥ

Spinach and Pear in Puff Pastry

Mushrooms and Piquillo
Peppers in Puff Pastry Ⓥ

Anchovies and Piquillo Peppers in Puff Pastry

Puff Pastry with Mushrooms and
Shrimp in Sparkling Wine Sauce

Potatoes and Vegetables in Puff Pastry

Black Sausage in Puff Pastry

Frog Legs and Shrimp in Puff Pastry

Shrimp in Puff Pastry

Blue and Cream Cheese Pastries with
Raisins and Cream Sherry Ⓥ

Cheese, Olive, and Caper Phyllo

Shrimp Pancakes

Codfish Pancakes

Fried Pork and Ham Rolls

Crunchy Potato Nests Filled
with Ham and Tomato

Puff Pastry Tartlet Shells **Ⓥ**

Mushroom Tartlets **Ⓥ**

Shrimp Tartlets

Crab Tartlets

MINI TURNOVERS
(*EMPANADILLAS*)

Tuna Turnovers with Tomato

Fried Tuna, Peas, and Peppers Turnovers

Veal and Chorizo Turnovers

Baked Turnovers with Tomatoes,
Peppers, Onion, Egg, Tuna, and Peas

Spicy Meat Turnovers

CANAPÉS AND PÂTÉS

Garlic and Tomato Bread **Ⓥ**

Egg and Mushroom Canapé **Ⓥ**

Roasted Vegetable and Strawberry Toasts

Black Olive Paste

Olives, Capers, and Anchovies Paste

Olive "Paste" and Blue Cheese Canapé **Ⓥ**

Green Olive "Paste" Canapé

Anchovy and Pimiento Spread

Avocado Dip **Ⓥ**

Avocado, Egg, and Anchovy Canapé

Pâté with Pine Nut and Orange Zest Syrup

Mushroom and Quince Toast with
Garlic Sauce and Cured Ham

Manchego Cheese with Quince Paste **Ⓥ**

Goat Cheese in Cherry Tomatoes
with Orange Marmalade **Ⓥ**

Goat Cheese, Piquillo Peppers,
and Honey Canapé **Ⓥ**

Creamed Blue Cheese with Brandy **Ⓥ**

Blue Cheese and Pine Nut Canapé **Ⓥ**

Cabrales Blue Cheese Toast with
Liqueur, Honey, and Almonds **Ⓥ**

Marinated Lettuce Canapés **V**

Fried Cheese Canapé **V**

Canapé of Mackerel and Serrano Ham

Clam Toast

Canapé of Eggs, Hake, and Zucchini

Marinated Tuna and Tomato on Bread Triangles

Fresh Fish Spread

Fish, Mayonnaise, and Lettuce Spread

Smoked Salmon Toast

Anchovy, Chicken, and Tomato Canapé

Pâté with Fresh Figs

Chicken Liver Pâté with Sherry Glaze

Duck and Serrano Ham Pâté

Partridge and Chicken Liver Pâté

Potato, Liver Pâté, Mushroom,
and Caramelized Apple

Parmesan Wafers with Liver Pâté

Pâté with Turkey Breast

*T*apas, the little dishes of Spain, are the most representative foods in Spanish cuisine. Any food can be a tapa, but the main characteristics are that tapas should be served in small portions, served promptly in a pleasant, friendly environment, and be affordable. In Spain, tapas bars are plentiful and offer both traditional dishes and regional cuisine. Tapas from the Mediterranean shoreline are quite different from those from Castile or those from Galicia, in the north. The variations are infinite, and traveling is the best way to get acquainted with all that tapas have to offer.

But going out for tapas (or as Spaniards say, *ir de tapeo*) is not just a way of eating. It's a way of life. Spaniards love tapas bars because they can mingle in convivial surroundings and converse about politics, gossip, sports, and bullfighting. They do this while drinking wine or beer and sharing tapas with each other. Tapas bars allow people to communicate, socialize, and relax after work with family, friends, and co-workers. Having a drink and something delicious to eat just makes it a more enjoyable environment.

For many years tapas have been a staple of Spanish gastronomy, and much has been written about their origin. Even though tapas can be found in every region of Spain, its beginnings can be traced to Andalucía and principally to Sevilla, known for its warm climate, friendly people, and slow-paced atmosphere. Literally translated, *tapa* means "lid" or "cover." Traditionally, when a glass of sherry or wine was served, a small tapa, such as a slice of chorizo or cheese or a small dish with olives, was placed on top of the glass. The tapa was usually complimentary and served as an incentive for the client to purchase another drink.

Tapas are varied, usually based in the cooking of the regions where the bars are located. They can be very simple, such as slices of ham, chorizo, or cheese, or a small plate of almonds or olives, or they can be more elaborate, involving sophisticated sauces such as mayonnaise, vinaigrette, or *romesco*, a pepper-based sauce. In different regions, tapas have their own character and even a unique name, such as in the Basque provinces where tapas are known as *pinchos* and consist frequently of a toothpick skewering different ingredients or a simple slice of bread with something on top of it.

In the past few years, modern tapas bars have opened all over Spain, and tapas have become quite sophisticated due to the influence of several inventive chefs such as Juan Mari Arzak and Ferran Adrià. Innovative and creative techniques have taken tapas to a new level: *La Nueva Cocina*, or Spain's new cuisine, has taken the gourmet world by storm.

Throughout the years, I have served tapas in my house to family and friends instead of a formal dinner. At my tapas parties, friends can serve themselves from the many dishes available, sit where they please, and mingle with one another freely. I strongly recommend serving tapas when entertaining.

Skewered Bites

(Banderillas)

Banderillas are a separate class of tapas, consisting of marinated fish, meat, olives, vegetables, and other ingredients skewered together with a toothpick. They are very easy to prepare, and you can mix and match any ingredients you want to create different taste sensations. It is important that you put everything on the toothpick in your mouth at once so the flavors will blend. *Banderillas* derived their name from their resemblance to the colorful, ornamental darts used in bullfighting.

Sample Banderillas

MAKES 1 TAPA

Here are four examples of typical Spanish bande-rillas—simple bite-size ingredient stacks to serve with drinks or at parties, usually skewered on tooth-picks. Ingredients can be added or omitted according to personal preference. Each combination creates a different taste. Experiment to see which you like best.

1 pitted green olive (with or without pimiento), preferably Spanish

One (¼-inch) crosswise slice dill or cornichon pickle

One (¾-inch) piece (jarred) piquillo pepper or pimiento

One (¾-inch) chunk canned or jarred white or light meat tuna, drained

1 cooked shrimp, shelled and deveined

One (2-inch) cooked asparagus tip

Mayonnaise (mayonesa, page 359), to taste

1 wedge small hard-boiled egg

1 rolled anchovy fillet, with or without capers

1 pitted black olive, preferably Spanish

Mayonnaise (mayonesa, page 359), to taste

½ small hard-boiled egg, cut crosswise and trimmed at the bottom to sit flat

1 small cooked shrimp, shelled and deveined

One (¾-inch) square piece Serrano (Spanish cured mountain) ham or prosciutto, cut from a slice ⅛ inch thick

Mayonnaise (mayonesa, page 359), to taste

Parsley, for garnish

For each of these tapas, add the ingredients to a skewer in the order they are listed and garnish as directed. Increase the ingredient amounts for the number of tapas you want to serve. They are usually served at room temperature.

Banderilla Dressing Ⓥ

Picada

MAKES ENOUGH TO DRESS 20 BANDERILLAS

The recipe for this picada sauce comes from Tito of the Bar Cascabel in Madrid, which specializes in banderillas. Picada—a finely chopped mixture of garlic, parsley, pickle, and oil—adds an interesting flavor to just about any banderilla you can think of. Picada sauce should be made in a food processor and processed until as smooth as possible.

3 tablespoons finely chopped fresh flat-leaf parsley

3 garlic cloves, finely chopped

2 tablespoons dill or cornichon pickle, finely chopped

3 tablespoons olive oil

Place the parsley, garlic, and pickle in a food processor and process until smooth. With the motor running, gradually add the oil. Process until as smooth as possible. Serve at room temperature, or store up to 5 days in a covered container in the refrigerator and bring to room temperature to serve.

Black Olives Marinated in Paprika Ⓥ

Aceitunas Negras con Mojo

MAKES 6 TO 8 SERVINGS

Though most Spanish olives that find their way to the United States are green, black olives are more frequently used for tapas in Spain. This well-seasoned marinade enhances their flavor with a recipe that calls for cumin, reflecting a Moorish influence.

PREPARE AT LEAST 10 DAYS IN ADVANCE

One (7-ounce) jar black olives, preferably Spanish, drained

5 garlic cloves, lightly smashed

½ teaspoon ground hot paprika, such as Spanish smoked

1 tablespoon ground bittersweet paprika, such as Spanish smoked

1 teaspoon dried oregano

2 sprigs thyme

¼ teaspoon ground cumin

One (2-inch) strip orange peel (orange part only)

2 sprigs parsley

2 tablespoons extra-virgin olive oil

⅓ cup vinegar

Combine all the ingredients in a glass jar with a tight-fitting lid, add water to cover, and shake well. Let marinate in the refrigerator at least 10 days, stirring occasionally. Serve cold or at room temperature.

Olives with Garlic and Paprika Ⓥ

Aceitunas con Pimentón

MAKES 4 SERVINGS

Two of the most common ingredients in Spanish cuisine, olives and pimentón (paprika) are used in an infinite number of dishes. Here they take center stage in the company of several spices and herbs also quite prevalent in Spanish cooking. You can keep them in the refrigerator for weeks — they just keep getting better.

PREPARE AT LEAST 3 DAYS IN ADVANCE

½ cup black olives, preferably Spanish

2 garlic cloves, lightly smashed

⅛ teaspoon ground hot paprika, such as Spanish smoked, or ground cayenne pepper

¼ teaspoon ground bittersweet paprika, such as Spanish smoked

½ teaspoon dried oregano

½ teaspoon dried thyme

¼ teaspoon ground cumin

2 teaspoons finely chopped fresh flat-leaf parsley

½ teaspoon vinegar

3 tablespoons extra-virgin olive oil

Combine all the ingredients in a glass jar with a tight-fitting lid and shake well. Let marinate in the refrigerator at least 3 days. Serve cold or at room temperature.

Marinated Green Olives Ⓥ
Aceitunas Verdes Aliñadas

MAKES 6 TO 8 SERVINGS

Spaniards love olives and they are often served complimentary with drinks at tapas bars. In this recipe, the flavor of green olives is enhanced by garlic, thyme, rosemary, and oregano.

PREPARE AT LEAST 3 DAYS IN ADVANCE

One (7-ounce) jar green olives (with pits), preferably
    Spanish, lightly crushed
6 garlic cloves, lightly smashed
One (2-inch) strip orange peel (orange part only)
2 sprigs thyme
2 sprigs rosemary
3 bay leaves
½ teaspoon fennel seeds
½ teaspoon dried oregano
¼ cup vinegar

Combine all the ingredients in a glass jar with a tight-fitting lid, add water to cover, and shake well. Let marinate in the refrigerator at least 3 days. Discard the bay leaves. Serve cold or at room temperature.

Potato and Seafood Banderilla
Pincho de Patata, Huevo, Atún y Gamba

MAKES 8 TAPAS (4 SERVINGS)

Some banderillas *such as this one gain in flavor when left refrigerated overnight, giving the separate ingredients the time to fully blend together. This* banderilla *of potato, egg, tuna, and shrimp is sometimes served with an additional onion-and-oil dressing.*

2 small potatoes
Kosher or sea salt
8 small shrimp
3 tablespoons extra-virgin olive oil
1 slice onion, separated into rings
1 large hard-boiled egg, cut into 8 slices
One (7-ounce) can white or light meat tuna, drained
    and separated into ½-inch chunks
8 (½-inch) pieces onion, such as Vidalia or other
    sweet onion
Mayonnaise (mayonesa, page 359), to taste
Finely chopped fresh flat-leaf parsley, for garnish

1. Place the potatoes in a small saucepan with cold water to cover and add salt. Cover and bring to a simmer over low heat. Cook about 20 minutes or until tender when pierced with a knife. Drain and let cool slightly. Peel and cut each potato into 4 (¼-inch) slices. Reserve.

2. Meanwhile, sprinkle the shrimp with salt. Bring a small saucepan of water to a boil over high heat. Add the shrimp, reduce the heat to low, and simmer until pink, 2 to 3 minutes. Drain and let cool. Remove the shell and the vein.

3. In a serving dish just large enough to hold the 8 potato slices, add the oil and spread to coat the bottom. Add salt and arrange the onion rings in the dish and arrange the potato slices over the onions. Top each potato with a slice of egg and a chunk of tuna. On each toothpick, add 2 pieces of onion and top with 1 shrimp. Attach to the potato-egg-tuna layer. Dab with the mayonnaise and sprinkle with the parsley. Serve at room temperature or refrigerate up to 24 hours and bring to room temperature to serve.

Chorizo and Bread Banderilla
Pincho de Chorizo

MAKES 8 TAPAS (4 SERVINGS)

Chorizo, *Spain's famous well-seasoned sausage, adds tremendous flavor to every dish it is a part of. This combination of* chorizo *and a bread cube is simple but delicious and is a typical part of any tapas selection.*

1 teaspoon olive oil

¼ pound (2 links) chorizo, each cut into 4 pieces

1 tablespoon dry red or white wine

1 (½-inch) slice long-loaf (baguette) bread, cut into quarters

1. Heat the oil in a medium skillet over medium heat. Add the chorizo and cook, stirring, until browned on all sides. Add the wine and cook, stirring gently, until the wine is absorbed.

2. On each toothpick, add 1 piece of sausage and top with 1 piece of bread. Serve hot.

Egg Tapa
Pincho de Huevo

MAKES 2 TAPAS (1 SERVING)

In Spain, small appetizers meant to be eaten with toothpicks are called pinchos. *There are innumerable varieties of them that combine different tastes and textures. This* pincho *consists of hard-boiled egg, shrimp, pimiento-stuffed olives, and anchovies — an interesting and unusual blend of flavors.*

Kosher or sea salt

2 small shrimp

2 teaspoons mayonnaise (mayonesa, page 359)

1 large hard-boiled egg, halved lengthwise

2 pimiento-stuffed olives, preferably Spanish

2 rolled anchovy fillets

1. Sprinkle the shrimp with salt. Bring a small saucepan of water to a boil over high heat. Add the shrimp, reduce the heat to low, and simmer until pink, 2 to 3 minutes. Drain, let cool, and remove the shell and the vein.

2. Spoon 1 teaspoon of the mayonnaise on the yolk of each egg. Insert a toothpick in the center of the egg (the egg white should be on the bottom), then add 1 shrimp on top of the egg, 1 olive, and 1 anchovy. Serve at room temperature.

Fried Pork Skins with Anchovies
Corteza de Cerdo con Anchoa

MAKES 4 TO 6 SERVINGS

This tapa doesn't really require recipe directions, but the basic ingredients and steps are provided below. Fried pork rinds can usually be found in the potato chip section of your supermarket. Make at least two per person.

PREPARE SEVERAL HOURS IN ADVANCE

¼ pound Marinated Fresh Anchovies (page 15; partial recipe)

1 small bag fried pork rinds

Prepare the anchovies. On each toothpick, add 1 small pork rind and top with 1 anchovy. Serve at room temperature.

Pickled Eggplant, Almagro Style ⓥ

Berenjena de Almagro en Escabeche

MAKES 4 SERVINGS

La Mancha, land of Don Quixote, was for centuries considered a gastronomic wasteland, but in the last few years its cuisine has been rediscovered. Now many of its products have reached new highs, such as Manchego cheese, which is number one in popularity all over the Spain and fast becoming a staple in the United States. Almagro, in the middle of La Mancha, is proud of the eggplants grown there and the restaurant Mesón del Corregidor is a good place to savor the local fare.

2 small eggplants (about 3 ounces each)

1 tablespoon olive oil

3 tablespoons finely chopped onion

3 tablespoons finely chopped green bell pepper

3 tablespoons finely chopped tomato

¼ teaspoon ground cumin

¼ teaspoon dried oregano

1 (½-inch) piece red chile pepper, seeded

Kosher or sea salt

Freshly ground black pepper

2 tablespoons wine vinegar

2 tablespoons water

Parsley, for garnish

1. Place the eggplants in a medium saucepan, add water to cover and salt, and bring to a boil over high heat. Reduce the heat to low, cover, and simmer 5 minutes or until tender. Drain and let cool. Cut off the stems and cut each in half lengthwise.

2. Heat the oil in a medium skillet over medium heat. Add the eggplant and cook 1 minute per side. Transfer the eggplant to a platter. Add the onion, bell pepper, tomato, cumin, oregano, chile pepper, salt, and black pepper and cook, stirring, until the vegetables are softened, about 5 minutes. Transfer to the platter.

3. Reduce the heat to low and return the eggplant to the skillet, cut side up. Add the vinegar and water and simmer until only a small amount of liquid remains, 10 to 15 minutes. Remove from the heat and let cool. Sprinkle with parsley. Serve at room temperature or refrigerate to chill and serve cold.

"Russian" Potato and Vegetable Salad

Ensaladilla Rusa

MAKES 6 SERVINGS

Cerveceria Alemana in Santa Ana Square in the center of Madrid is considered by many to be the Mecca of Ensaladilla Rusa. *We do not know where the name "Russian" comes from, but after the Civil War, since anything Russian was anathema, this salad was renamed* Ensaladilla Nacional. *The new name did not catch on.*

PREPARE SEVERAL HOURS IN ADVANCE

½ pound red waxy potatoes

¼ pound carrots, peeled, such as ready-to-eat baby carrots

¼ cup frozen peas, thawed

3 ounces canned or jarred white or light meat tuna, drained and flaked

10 small pitted green olives, preferably Spanish

continues...

½ cup mayonnaise (mayonesa, page 359), thinned
 with 1 teaspoon water

Kosher or sea salt

2 ounces cooked very small shrimp, shelled and
 deveined (optional)

1 large hard-boiled egg, cut into eighths, for garnish

Pimiento strips, for garnish

1. Place the potatoes in a small saucepan and add cold water to cover and salt. Cover and bring to a simmer over low heat. Cook about 15 minutes or until tender when pierced with a knife. Do not overcook. Drain and let cool slightly. Peel.

2. Meanwhile, place the carrots in another small saucepan and add cold water to cover and salt. Cover and bring to a simmer over low heat. Cook about 5 minutes or until tender. Do not overcook.

3. Cut the potatoes and carrots into ⅜-inch cubes. Place in a large bowl and fold in the peas, tuna, olives, and shrimp, if using. Fold in the mayonnaise and shape into a mound. Garnish with the egg and pimiento. Refrigerate overnight to chill and serve cold.

Butter Beans in Caper Vinaigrette
Judiones en Vinagreta de Alcaparras

MAKES 4 SERVINGS

This refreshing summer salad includes smoked salmon and trout, a good amount of capers, and canned beans. Judiones *are the large broad beans found in Castilla and the neighboring province of La Rioja, where they are called* pochas. *Use those if you can find them; otherwise, butter beans are fine.*

3 tablespoons extra-virgin olive oil

1 teaspoon white wine vinegar

Kosher or sea salt

Freshly ground black pepper

⅛ teaspoon sugar

One (15-ounce) can butter beans, drained

One (1-inch) wedge sweet onion, such as Vidalia,
 slivered

2 teaspoons capers (nonpareil preferred), rinsed and
 drained

1 tablespoon finely chopped fresh flat-leaf parsley

1 teaspoon finely chopped fresh dill

8 (½-inch) squares thinly sliced smoked salmon

8 (½-inch) squares thinly sliced smoked trout fillet,
 skinned

Whisk together the oil, vinegar, salt, pepper, and sugar in a medium bowl. Gently stir in the beans with a flexible rubber spatula, then fold in the onion, capers, parsley, dill, salmon, and trout. Let sit at least 1 hour to meld flavors. Serve at room temperature or refrigerate at least 2 hours and serve cold.

Tuna-Filled Pickle
Pepinillo Relleno

MAKES 2 TAPAS (1 SERVING)

Baby dill pickles stuffed with tuna are a bit of an acquired taste for many Americans but a very popular tapa in Spain. Increase all the ingredients for as many servings as needed.

2 teaspoons canned or jarred white or light meat
 tuna, drained and flaked

Salt

Freshly ground black pepper

2 baby dill pickles

2 teaspoons finely chopped onion

2 pimiento-stuffed green olives, preferably Spanish

Combine the tuna, salt, and pepper in a small bowl. Cut a slit lengthwise in each pickle without cutting all the way through. Fill with the tuna, sprinkle with the onion, top with an olive, and secure with a toothpick. Serve at room temperature.

Pickled Fresh Sardines
Sardinas en Escabeche

MAKES 6 SERVINGS

Sardines, plentiful along all the coasts of Spain, are common in tapas prepared many different ways. Spaniards have a special affection for sardines as they are found in summer at small chiringuitos, beach-side eateries, where they are the most popular dish. Escabeche is not only an ancient way to preserve food, mainly game and fish, but also a popular way to intensify the flavor of the dish.

1 pound small fresh sardines

All-purpose flour, for dusting

2 tablespoons olive oil

½ medium onion, thinly sliced and separated into rings

5 garlic cloves

Peel of 1 lemon (yellow part only)

6 peppercorns

3 bay leaves

¼ cup vinegar

Kosher or sea salt

Water

1. Remove the heads and bones from the sardines, rinse well, pat dry, and dust with flour. Heat the oil in a small skillet over medium heat. Add the sardines and cook, turning occasionally, until golden on all sides. Transfer with a slotted spoon to paper towels and let dry, reserving the oil. Then transfer to an earthenware casserole dish or Dutch oven.

2. Heat the reserved oil over medium heat. Add the onion and garlic and cook, stirring, until the garlic is golden. Add the lemon, peppercorns and bay leaves and remove from the heat. Transfer to a small saucepan and stir in the vinegar, salt, and water. Bring to a boil over high heat, reduce the heat to low, and simmer about 5 minutes. Pour over the sardines and let cool. Refrigerate until 30 minutes before serving. Discard the bay leaves. If using earthenware, serve at room temperature in the dish, or transfer to a platter.

Marinated Fresh Anchovies
Boquerones en Vinagre

MAKES 4 TO 6 SERVINGS

This is one of the most popular tapas in Spain. You can find it in the north, in the south, by the sea, or in the middle of Castile—refreshing and delicious! I always remember the ones I ate in Córdoba across from the Arab Mosque in a very simple bar that for years had the reputation of having the best boquerones in the country. If anchovies are unavailable, you may substitute smelts.

PREPARE AT LEAST 6 HOURS IN ADVANCE

½ pound fresh very small anchovies, cleaned and heads and tails removed

¼ cup white wine vinegar

Kosher or sea salt

2 garlic cloves, finely chopped

1 tablespoon finely chopped fresh flat-leaf parsley

Extra-virgin olive oil

1. Place the anchovies in a strainer and run cold water over them until the water runs clear. Remove the spines and divide into fillets. Let dry on paper towels.

2. Combine the vinegar and salt in a flat-bottom bowl. Add the anchovies and fold to coat. Cover and let marinate in the refrigerator at least 6 hours up to overnight.

3. Drain and place the anchovies on a platter in layers. Sprinkle with the garlic and parsley and season with salt. Pour oil over the anchovies to cover, ensuring that the oil penetrates to the bottom layer. Serve cold or at room temperature.

Fresh Anchovies with Pickled Beets and Onions
Anchoas Frescas con Remolacha en Escabeche

MAKES 4 SERVINGS

Fresh anchovies are fished locally in small boats along the coast of Spain. They are prepared many different ways, but here they are combined with beets and onions.

PREPARE AT LEAST 6 HOURS IN ADVANCE

½ pound Marinated Fresh Anchovies (page 15)

¼ cup finely chopped pickled beets

4 teaspoons finely chopped onion

Prepare the anchovies. Arrange on individual plates or a platter. Sprinkle with the beets and onions. Serve cold or at room temperature.

Marinated Fresh Anchovy Layered with Eggplant
Boquerones en Vinagre con Berenjena Asada

MAKES 4 SERVINGS

Roasted eggplant adds an interesting twist to these marinated anchovies.

PREPARE AT LEAST 6 HOURS IN ADVANCE

¼ pound Marinated Fresh Anchovies (page 15; partial recipe)

4 baby eggplants (¼ pound each), ends trimmed

Kosher or sea salt

Freshly ground black pepper

1 tablespoon extra-virgin olive oil, plus oil for brushing

1 medium tomato, coarsely chopped (about ⅔ cup)

2 tablespoons extra-virgin olive oil

2 tablespoon finely chopped fresh flat-leaf parsley

1 garlic clove, finely chopped

1. Prepare the anchovies. Preheat the oven to 400°F. Using a vegetable peeler, peel the eggplants in thin, alternating strips to create a stripe effect. Cut into ¼-inch lengthwise slices. Arrange in a roasting pan and season with salt and pepper. Brush with oil. Roast 15 minutes or until tender.

2. Meanwhile, drain the marinade from the anchovies. On a serving platter, arrange half of the eggplant in a single layer, cover with half of the anchovies in a single layer. Repeat with the remaining eggplant and anchovies and cut the layers in half crosswise.

3. Place the tomato, oil, salt, and pepper in a food processor and process until smooth. Divide among 4 small individual plates, about 2 teaspoons each.

4. In a small bowl, combine the parsley, I tablespoon oil, the garlic, and salt. Drizzle over the eggplant. Arrange the eggplant and anchovies on top of the tomato sauce on each plate and serve.

Marinated and Fried Fresh Anchovies
Boquerones en Vinagre Fritos

MAKES 4 TO 6 SERVINGS

Because anchovies are so popular in Spain, there are numerous ways to prepare them. In this tapa, the anchovies are first marinated, then fried.

½ pound fresh anchovies, cleaned and filleted

2 garlic cloves

⅛ teaspoon salt

1 tablespoon finely chopped fresh flat-leaf parsley

1 tablespoon fresh lemon juice

All-purpose flour, for dredging

2 large eggs, lightly beaten

Olive oil, for frying

1. Place the anchovies in a small bowl. In a mortar or mini-processor, mash the garlic, salt, and parsley. Stir in the lemon juice. Spread the garlic mixture over the anchovies. Cover and let marinate in the refrigerator 2 hours.

2. Heat at least ½ inch of oil in a medium skillet over medium-high heat (or better still, use a deep fryer set at 360°F) until it turns a cube of bread light brown in 60 seconds. Place the flour and eggs in separate shallow bowls. Dredge the anchovies in the flour, dip in the egg, and place in the oil. Cook, turning once, until golden, about 5 minutes. (Cook in batches if needed to avoid overcrowding.) Let drain on paper towels. Serve hot.

Stuffed Pickles
Pepinillos Rellenos

MAKES 1 TAPA (1 SERVING)

Los Pepinillos ("The Pickles") was a bar in Madrid that had been around for centuries. They had barrels of pickles categorized into a numbering system in which #1 was the mildest and #5 was the spiciest. This recipe for a pickle stuffed with anchovies is of the mild variety—and the most popular pickle they sold.

2 anchovy fillets, one (¼-inch-thick) strip of pickled
    herring, or 2 Marinated Fresh Anchovies (page
    15; partial recipe)
1 very small dill gherkin, halved lengthwise

Place 1 anchovy on top of 1 pickle half. Cover with the other pickle half and secure with a toothpick. Serve cold or at room temperature.

Tuna Escabeche
Escabechado de Bonito

MAKES 4 SERVINGS

Fried and then marinated, this tuna tapa is a classic escabeche.

2 tablespoons olive oil
¾ pound tuna steaks, about 1 inch thick
2 medium onions, thinly sliced and separated
    into rings
2 medium carrots, cut into very thin 2-inch strips
1 medium zucchini, cut into very thin 2-inch strips
1 tablespoon cider vinegar
Kosher or sea salt

1. Heat the oil in a medium skillet over medium heat. Increase the heat to high, add the tuna and cook briefly, turning once and seasoning each side with salt, until seared. Transfer to a platter, reserving the oil.

2. Reduce the heat to medium low, add the onion, carrot, and zucchini to the skillet, and cook, stirring, until softened, about 8 minutes. Sprinkle with the vinegar and cook, stirring, until just absorbed. Return the tuna to the skillet and cook, turning once, until just cooked through (just barely pink inside), about 5 minutes. Remove from the heat and let cool.

3. Cut the tuna into thin slices. Arrange on a serving platter with the vegetables. Serve at room temperature or refrigerate at least 2 hours and serve cold.

Pickled Fresh Tuna with Grilled Vegetables

Atún Fresco con Verduras Asadas

MAKES 4 TO 6 SERVINGS

In this very refreshing tapa, pickled fresh tuna is mixed with grilled red pepper, eggplant, white onion, and garlic. The tuna should be cut into chunks and served over the grilled vegetables. This is usually served after refrigerating the marinated fish for a day.

PREPARE 24 HOURS IN ADVANCE

One (2-inch) wedge red onion, slivered

1 medium red bell pepper, thinly sliced

1 small eggplant, thinly sliced crosswise

1 medium tomato, thinly sliced

Kosher or sea salt

6 tablespoons extra-virgin olive oil, plus oil for drizzling

One (2-inch) wedge white onion

2 garlic cloves

1 bay leaf

2 tablespoons sherry vinegar or red wine vinegar

2 tablespoons dry white wine

¼ teaspoon dried thyme

¼ teaspoon dried basil

2 sprigs parsley

2 whole cloves

4 peppercorns

¾ pound tuna steak, about 1 inch thick

I. Place a broiler rack about 4 inches from the heat source and preheat the broiler. (cover the broiler pan with foil for easier cleanup, if you like.) Arrange the red onion, bell pepper, eggplant, and tomato in a broiler pan and broil until softened. Remove from the broiler, season with salt, and drizzle with the oil. Let cool slightly, then coarsely chop the tomato and eggplant. Reserve.

2. Heat the 6 tablespoons oil in a medium skillet over low heat. Add the white onion, garlic, and bay leaf and cook, stirring and pressing the garlic with a wooden spoon to release its flavor, until the onion softens. Stir in all the remaining ingredients except the tuna and bring to a boil, then lower heat and simmer about 30 minutes. Let cool. Add the tuna and spoon some sauce over the top. Cover and simmer over low heat about 10 minutes, turning once, until cooked through. Let cool. Let marinate in the refrigerator 24 hours.

3. Place the vegetables on a serving platter. Discard the bay leaf, cut the tuna into chunks, and arrange over the vegetables. Serve hot.

Pickled Mackerel with Lemon and Orange

Escabeche de Caballa con Cítricos

MAKES 4 TO 6 SERVINGS

Mackerel works very well in the vinegar marinade escabeche due to the firmness of its flesh—it doesn't fall apart in the tart brine. This recipe adds the brightness of citrus juices.

PREPARE 8 TO 12 HOURS IN ADVANCE

1 tablespoon sugar

2 tablespoons vinegar

2 cups water

Peel of 1 lemon (yellow part only), cut into very thin strips

Peel of 1 orange (orange part only), cut into very thin strips

3 tablespoons fresh lemon juice

3 tablespoons fresh orange juice

2 bay leaves

2 sprigs thyme

7 whole cardamom pods

4 whole cloves

1 tablespoon freshly grated ginger

Kosher or sea salt

Freshly ground black pepper

2 tablespoons olive oil

½ pound onions, slivered

5 garlic cloves, finely chopped

1½ pounds mackerel

1. In a medium saucepan over medium heat, stir together the sugar, vinegar, and 2 cups water; stir until the sugar syrup caramelizes (turns golden). Stir in the juices, bay leaves, thyme, cardamom, cloves, ginger, salt, and pepper. Reduce the heat to low and simmer until blended and slightly thickened.

2. Heat the oil in a medium skillet over medium heat. Add the onion and garlic and cook, stirring, until the onion is wilted and transparent and the garlic golden, about 5 minutes. Stir into the sugar mixture.

3. Cut the mackerel into bite-size pieces and add to the marinade. Bring the marinade to a simmer over low heat and cook until the mackerel is heated through. Let cool. Discard the bay leaves. Cover and let marinate in the refrigerator overnight. Serve cold.

Marinated and Fried Small Fish
Boquerones Don Pedro

MAKES 4 TO 6 SERVINGS

These tiny fish are a specialty at Meson de Don Pedro, a hundred year old tavern on the very lively Don Pedro Street in Old Madrid. Rumor has it that this was the location where famous painter Francisco de Goya was stabbed by a jealous husband.

PREPARE AT LEAST 4 HOURS IN ADVANCE

2 garlic cloves, finely chopped

1 bay leaf, crumbled

4 peppercorns

Pinch of dried oregano

¼ teaspoon ground cumin

¼ cup red wine vinegar

Freshly ground white pepper

Salt

2 tablespoons water

1 pound very small fish, such as smelts (about 20 to a pound), cleaned and heads left on

Flour, such as semolina, for dredging

Olive oil, for frying

Kosher or sea salt

1. In a shallow bowl, mix the garlic, bay leaf, peppercorns, oregano, cumin, vinegar, white pepper, salt, and water. Add the fish and turn to coat. Cover and let marinate in the refrigerator at least 4 hours, turning occasionally. Drain and discard the bay leaf.

2. Heat at least ½ inch of oil in a medium skillet over medium-high heat (or better still, use a deep fryer set at 360°F) until it turns a cube of bread light brown in 60 seconds. Place the flour in a shallow bowl. Season both sides of each fish with salt, dredge in the flour, and place in the oil. Cook, turning once, until well browned and crisp, about 5 minutes. Transfer with a slotted spoon to paper towels and let drain. Sprinkle with coarse salt and serve.

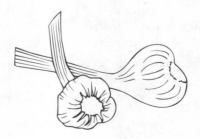

Marinated Mussels

Mejillones a la Vinagreta

MAKES 4 TO 6 SERVINGS

This is one of my favorite recipes and one that I have prepared many, many times at home for friends and family, who always react with enthusiastic approval. In Spain, you can find these mussels in a lot of bars and restaurants served as tapas.

PREPARE 8 TO 12 HOURS IN ADVANCE

½ cup extra-virgin olive oil

3 tablespoons red wine vinegar

1 teaspoon capers (nonpareil preferred), rinsed and drained

1 tablespoon finely chopped onion

1 tablespoon finely chopped pimiento, such as (jarred) piquillo pepper

1 tablespoon finely chopped fresh flat-leaf parsley

Kosher or sea salt

Freshly ground black pepper

2 dozen medium mussels

1. In a medium bowl, whisk together the oil and vinegar, then stir in the capers, onion, pimiento, parsley, salt, and pepper.

2. Rinse the mussels well. Cut or pull off the beards. Discard any with cracked shells or that do not close tightly when touched. Place I cup water in a large skillet, add the mussels, and bring to a boil over high heat. Transfer the mussels as they open to another medium bowl and let cool.

3. Remove the mussels from the shells, reserving half of the shells. Add the mussels to the bowl with the marinade and stir to coat. Cover and let marinate in the refrigerator overnight.

4. Meanwhile, clean the reserved shells well, cover, and reserve in the refrigerator until ready to serve. Place I mussel in each shell half and spoon marinade over the top. Serve cold.

Marinated Octopus

Pulpo a la Vinagreta

MAKES 4 SERVINGS

A wonderful and refreshing octopus salad prepared Andalusian style, this recipe comes from Bar Miami in Sevilla, one of my favorite cities in Spain. Preparing the octopus is labor-intensive but produces the freshest, most tender dish.

PREPARE 9 TO 13 HOURS IN ADVANCE

2 (¾-pound) octopus, cleaned

12 cups water

1 bay leaf

½ medium onion

4 peppercorns

2 sprigs parsley

Salt

½ cup extra-virgin olive oil

3 tablespoons red wine vinegar

1 tablespoon finely chopped onion

1 garlic clove, finely chopped

1 tablespoon finely chopped fresh flat-leaf parsley

Salt

Freshly ground black pepper

1. Before cooking the octopus, tenderize it by throwing it with force into the cleaned kitchen sink. Repeat at least 10 times.

2. In a large pot, bring the water to a boil over high heat. Dunk the octopus in the boiling water for a few seconds, remove and repeat 2 more times, leaving the octopus out of the water a minute between dunkings. Transfer to a platter. Add the bay leaf, onion, peppercorns, parsley, and salt to the pot and bring to a boil again over high heat, if necessary.

3. Return the octopus to the pot, reduce the heat to low, cover, and simmer until tender, about I hour, depending on the size of the octopus. Drain,

discard the bay leaf, and let cool. Scrape off any loose skin. Cut the body and tentacles into bite-size pieces with scissors.

4. In a small bowl, whisk together the oil, vinegar, onion, garlic, parsley, salt, and pepper. Add the octopus and mix to coat. Cover and let marinate in the refrigerator overnight. Serve cold or at room temperature.

Marinated Fried Shark
Palometas Adobadas

MAKES 4 SERVINGS

This recipe comes from Cádiz, a beautiful city in Andalucía by the Atlantic Ocean where there is a great tradition of cooking fish. Locally this dish is called bienmesabe, *literally "it tastes good to me," and I cannot imagine a better way to describe it.*

PREPARE 8 TO 12 HOURS IN ADVANCE

1 tablespoon vinegar

½ teaspoon ground bittersweet paprika, such as Spanish smoked

½ teaspoon dried oregano

2 garlic cloves, mashed in a garlic press or mortar

¼ teaspoon crushed red pepper

Kosher or sea salt

¾ pound shark or other mild fish, cut into 1-inch chunks

All-purpose flour, for dredging

Olive oil, for frying

1. In a medium bowl, mix the vinegar, paprika, oregano, garlic, chile flakes, and salt. Add the shark and mix to coat. Cover and let marinate in the refrigerator overnight. Drain and pat dry with paper towels.

2. Heat at least 1½ inches of oil in a large skillet over medium-high heat (or better still, use a deep fryer set at 360°F) until it turns a cube of bread light brown in 60 seconds. Place the flour in a shallow bowl. Dredge all sides of the shark in the flour, and place in the oil. Cook, turning occasionally, until golden on all sides. Let drain on paper towels. Serve.

Tuna Tartare with Avocado, Pickle, and Capers
Tartar de Atún con Aguacate y Alcaparras

MAKES 2 SERVINGS

A wonderful version of tuna tartare, this recipe combines different tastes and textures. It is imperative that the tuna be of sushi quality. The hot sauce gives this tapa an extra kick.

2 tablespoons extra-virgin olive oil

¼ pound sushi-grade tuna steak, cut into chunks

1 medium avocado, chopped

1 cornichon pickle, finely chopped

1 teaspoon capers (nonpareil preferred), rinsed and drained

1 teaspoon Worcestershire sauce

Several drops hot sauce, such as Tabasco

Kosher or sea salt

Freshly ground black pepper

1 tablespoon balsamic vinegar

1 tablespoon fresh lemon juice

Lettuce leaves, for serving (optional)

Combine all the ingredients in a medium bowl and let sit at least 1 hour in the refrigerator to meld flavors. Bring to room temperature for serving. Line a platter with lettuce leaves, if using, and place the tuna in the center.

Shellfish and Fish Vinaigrette
Salpicón de Mariscos y Pescados

MAKES 4 SERVINGS

Salpicón, from the Spanish salpicar, *means to cut into small pieces. This dish can be found in many bars and restaurants either as a tapa or as a first course.*

PREPARE 8 TO 12 HOURS IN ADVANCE

1 small (1- to 1½-pound) live lobster

1 pound large shrimp

1 pound monkfish

Vinaigrette

½ cup extra-virgin olive oil

¼ cup vinegar

Kosher or sea salt

Freshly ground black pepper

1 tablespoon Dijon mustard

2 medium scallions, finely chopped

6 small cornichon pickles, finely chopped

1 pimiento, such as (jarred) piquillo pepper, finely chopped

1 large hard-boiled egg, finely chopped

2 tablespoons finely chopped fresh flat-leaf parsley

I. Bring a large pot of salted water to a boil over high heat. Add the lobster upside-down and head first, cover, and cook until the shell is red, 12 to 15 minutes. Drain and let cool. In a separate pot, boil the shellfish and fish briefly in salted water to cover until the shrimp has just turned pink and the fish is just cooked through. Remove the shells from the shellfish and cut the shellfish and fish into ¾-inch pieces.

2. Prepare the vinaigrette: In a large bowl, whisk together the oil, vinegar, mustard, salt, and pepper. Stir in the scallions, pickles, pimiento, hard-boiled egg, and parsley.

3. Add the shellfish and fish to the vinaigrette and stir to coat evenly. Cover and let marinate in the refrigerator overnight. Serve cold

Escabeche of Asparagus with Fresh Anchovies
Escabeche de Espárrago con Boquerones

MAKES 4 TO 6 SERVINGS

Fresh anchovies paired with fresh asparagus make a delicious combination.

½ pound asparagus spears

¾ pound fresh anchovies, cleaned and heads removed

Kosher or sea salt

All-purpose flour, for dredging

2 tablespoons olive oil

⅛ teaspoon saffron threads, crumbled

Kosher or sea salt

⅓ cup wine vinegar

2 tablespoons olive oil

10 garlic cloves, thinly sliced

10 peppercorns

Peel of ½ orange (orange part only), cut into several pieces

1 bay leaf

I. Place the asparagus in a medium skillet with water to cover, add salt, and bring to a boil over high heat. Reduce the heat to low, cover, and simmer 5 to 10 minutes or until crisp-tender. Reserve.

2. Meanwhile, heat at least ½ inch of oil in a medium skillet over medium-high heat (or better still, use a deep fryer set at 360°F) until it turns a cube of bread light brown in 60 seconds. Place the flour in a shallow bowl. Season both sides of each anchovy with salt, dredge in the flour, and place in the oil. Cook, turning once, until golden, about 5 minutes. Let drain on paper towels. Reserve.

3. In a mortar or mini-processor, mash the saffron, then whisk in the salt, vinegar, and oil. Pour into a small saucepan and stir in the garlic, peppercorns, orange peel, bay leaf, and asparagus. Bring to a simmer over medium heat and cook just until blended. Remove from the heat, cover, and let sit 15 to 30 minutes. Discard the bay leaf. Place the fish on a serving platter, pour the sauce around the fish, and serve. Or refrigerate the fish and sauce separately at least 2 hours and serve cold, pouring the sauce around the fish before serving.

Prawns in Clove-Scented Marinade

Langostinos con Clavo

MAKES 4 SERVINGS

Dried red chile pepper add spiciness to this delicious preparation of shrimp marinated with cloves, thyme, and peppercorns. It is best with medium to large shrimp.

PREPARE AT LEAST 24 HOURS IN ADVANCE

3 tablespoons olive oil

4 whole cloves

3 cups water

1 cup dry white wine

2 thin slices medium onion

½ carrot, peeled and thinly sliced

1 thin slice lemon

2 sprigs parsley

½ teaspoon dried thyme

1 bay leaf

½ dried red chile pepper, seeded

6 peppercorns

Salt

1 pound medium or large shrimp, in their shells

1. Place all the ingredients except the shrimp in a medium saucepan and bring to a boil over high

Marinades, escabeche, and adobos have been used for centuries to preserve food, but even after the advent of refrigeration, they continue to be popular for their varied capacity to provide intense flavor. They are especially appreciated in the summer months since adobos and escabeche are served refrigerated or at room temperature. They are mostly used to prepare fish, such as sardines, mackerel, tuna and shark, and game including quail, partridge, rabbit, and hare.

Escabeche is simple to make and includes ingredients such as olive oil, vinegar, garlic, onion, bay leaves, white wine, black pepper, thyme and lemon juice. Here is a traditional recipe for escabeche:

~~~~~~~

In a medium skillet, heat about ½ cup of oil over medium heat. Add 4 or 5 garlic cloves and cook, stirring, until golden. Add ¾ cup red wine vinegar and ¾ cup dry white wine. Add also 2 or 3 bay leaves, ¼ teaspoon thyme, and 6 to 7 peppercorns. Boil a few minutes, then let cool. Pour the liquid over the fish or meat that you have already cooked separately, making sure you cover it completely. Arrange a few slices of lemon on top and then refrigerate a couple of days to meld flavors. Serve at room temperature.

heat. Reduce the heat to low and simmer about 10 minutes. Add the shrimp, return to a boil, and cook until the shrimp are pink, 2 to 3 minutes.

2. Remove the shrimp, reserving the cooking liquid. Remove their shells, and place in a medium bowl. Bring the reserved liquid to a boil again over high heat and cook until reduced by half. Let cool. Discard the bay leaf, pour over the shrimp, and stir to coat. Cover and refrigerate at least 24 hours. Serve cold.

Lobster in Vinaigrette with Saffron, Brandy, and Hard-Boiled Egg
Langosta en Vinagreta con Azafrán, Coñác y Huevo

MAKES 4 SERVINGS

An elegant and deluxe tapa or first course, this lobster is best when made with Spanish brandy, such as Lepanto, which is made from a sherry base.

PREPARE SEVERAL HOURS IN ADVANCE

4 (1¼- to 1½-pound) live lobsters

3 tablespoons extra-virgin olive oil

¼ cup white wine vinegar

2 tablespoons brandy

1 medium onion, finely chopped (about ⅔ cup)

1 large hard-boiled egg, finely chopped

Kosher or sea salt

Freshly ground black pepper

¼ teaspoon ground hot paprika, such as Spanish smoked

⅛ teaspoon saffron threads, crumbled

1. Bring a large pot of salted water to a boil over high heat. Add the lobster upside-down and head first, cover, and cook about 15 minutes. Drain and let cool. Remove the shell, cut the meat into ¾-inch pieces and place in a medium bowl.

2. In a small bowl, whisk together the oil, vinegar, and brandy. Stir in the onion and egg. Season with salt, pepper, paprika, and saffron. Fold into the lobster. Cover and let marinate in the refrigerator overnight. Serve cold.

Headcheese Vinaigrette
Cabeza de Jabalí a la Vinagreta

MAKES 4 SERVINGS

A perfect tapa for a hot summer day, this is not a cheese at all, but rather an interesting tapa made from calf heads. In Spanish, the word "headcheese" translates to "wild boar's head." When it is mixed with this wonderful vinaigrette, it is light and refreshing. It is much easier to buy the calf's head headcheese already prepared than to make it at home.

PREPARE 8 TO 12 HOURS IN ADVANCE

¼ cup extra-virgin olive oil

2 tablespoons red wine vinegar

2 tablespoons finely chopped fresh flat-leaf parsley

2 tablespoons very thin 2-inch strips dill or cornichon pickle

2 tablespoons very thin 2-inch strips red bell pepper

2 tablespoons finely chopped carrot

8 to 12 small pitted black olives

Kosher or sea salt

Freshly ground black pepper

½ pound headcheese, cut into very thin 2-inch strips

In a small bowl, whisk together the oil and vinegar. Stir in all the remaining ingredients except the headcheese. Place the headcheese in a shallow serving bowl and fold in the dressing. Let marinate in the refrigerator overnight. Serve cold.

Cooked Shellfish

Shrimp in Garlic Sauce
Gambas al Ajillo

MAKES 4 TO 6 SERVINGS

Perhaps the most popular shellfish tapa in Spain, utterly simple and delicious, this recipe relies on chile pepper and plenty of garlic. Do not forget to serve with nice crusty slices of bread to dunk in the sauce.

1 pound small shrimp, shelled and deveined

Kosher or sea salt

6 tablespoons olive oil

4 garlic cloves, thinly sliced

1 dried red chile pepper, seeded

1 tablespoon finely chopped fresh flat-leaf parsley,
    for garnish

In a medium bowl, season the shrimp with salt and let sit 3 minutes. Heat the oil in a shallow earthenware casserole dish or Dutch oven over medium heat. Add the oil, garlic, and chile pepper and cook, stirring, until the garlic is lightly golden. Add the shrimp and cook, stirring, until pink, 3 to 5 minutes. If using earthenware, sprinkle with the parsley and serve hot in the dish, or transfer to a platter.

Shrimp Cocktail, Spanish Style
Cóctel de Gambas

MAKES 6 SERVINGS

A typical Spanish shrimp cocktail consists of a generous amount of tiny shrimp (camarones) served in a tomato and mayonnaise sauce flavored with brandy.

PREPARE AT LEAST 2 HOURS IN ADVANCE

7 cups Cooking Liquid (page 26)

1½ pounds small shrimp, in their shells

Cocktail Sauce

1 cup mayonnaise

1 teaspoon brandy, such as Spanish brandy or Cognac

1 large hard-boiled egg, finely chopped

¼ teaspoon tarragon

½ teaspoon caper or pickle juice

1 tablespoon finely chopped fresh flat-leaf parsley

Salt

Freshly ground black pepper

Shredded lettuce, for garnish

Parsley, for garnish

1. Prepare the cooking liquid. Add the shrimp and simmer over low heat until pink, 2 to 3 minutes. Drain, let cool, and remove the shells and veins.

2. Mix all the cocktail sauce ingredients in a small bowl. Cover and refrigerate the shrimp and the sauce separately and refrigerate at least 2 hours or until ready to use.

3. Arrange the lettuce leaves on a serving platter, place the shrimp in the center, and drizzle with the sauce. Garnish with the parsley and serve.

There are a number of variations of this basic quick fish "cooking liquid," similar to a stock, that helps add flavor and depth to many recipes. It makes 7 cups.

6 cups water

1 cup storebought or homemade Fish Broth or bottled clam juice

1 bay leaf

1 slice lemon

2 sprigs parsley

5 peppercorns

1 slice medium onion

¼ teaspoon dried thyme

Salt

In a large pot, combine the ingredients and bring to a boil over high heat. Reduce the heat to low and simmer 15 minutes.

Batter-Fried Shrimp
Gambas con Gabardina

MAKES 4 SERVINGS

Literally "shrimp in a raincoat," a much-appreciated tapa in Madrid where two bars about two hundred yards from each other claim the honor of serving the best gambas con gabardina in town. One is La Oficina on Carmen Street and the other is Casa Labra on Tetuan Street. Both deserve a visit.

½ pound large shrimp, in their shells

½ cup all-purpose flour

½ cup seltzer

⅛ teaspoon saffron threads, crumbled

Olive oil, for frying

Kosher or sea salt

1. Peel the shrimp, leaving the last tail segment intact. Season with salt. In a small bowl, mix the flour, seltzer, and saffron until well blended.

2. Heat at least ½ inch of oil in a medium skillet over medium-high heat (or better still, use a deep fryer set at 365°F) until it turns a cube of bread light brown in 60 seconds. Hold each shrimp by the tail, dip in the batter, and place in the oil. Cook, turning once, until golden. Transfer with a slotted spoon or spatula to paper towels and let drain. Serve hot.

Shrimp in Piparrada Sauce
Gambas con Salsa Piparrada

MAKES 4 TO 6 SERVINGS

In this Basque specialty, the ingredients are finely minced and used as a dip for cold seafood. "Piparrada" is a Basque word referring to any recipe where the primary ingredients are tomatoes and green peppers.

7 cups Cooking Liquid (at left)

1½ pounds medium or large shrimp, in their shells

1 medium cucumber, finely chopped

1 medium green bell pepper, finely chopped (about 1 cup)

1 small onion, finely chopped (about ⅓ cup)

2 medium ripe tomatoes, finely chopped (about 1⅓ cups)

6 tablespoons extra-virgin olive oil

3 tablespoons red wine vinegar

Salt

Freshly ground black pepper

1. Prepare the cooking liquid. Add the shrimp and simmer until pink, 2 to 3 minutes. Drain, let cool, and remove the shells.

2. In a small bowl, place the cucumber, bell pepper, onion, and tomatoes. In another small bowl, whisk together the oil and vinegar and season with

salt and pepper. Fold into the cucumber mixture. Transfer to a serving bowl.

3. Arrange the shrimp around the rim of the serving bowl for the sauce or on a plate. Serve at room temperature or cover and refrigerate at least 2 hours and serve cold—do not leave overnight because the tomato and pepper will lose their bright colors.

Shrimp with Sherry and Ham
Gambas al Jerez con Jamón

MAKES 4 SERVINGS

What could be more Spanish than shrimp, sherry, and cured ham? A delicious mixture.

2 tablespoons olive oil

3 garlic cloves, finely chopped

1 pound large shrimp, shelled and deveined

¼ pound Serrano (Spanish cured mountain) ham or prosciutto, finely chopped

⅓ cup dry sherry, such as Fino

Kosher or sea salt

Freshly ground black pepper

Heat the oil in a medium skillet over medium heat. Add the garlic and cook, stirring, until lightly golden. Add the shrimp, ham, sherry, salt, and pepper, reduce the heat to low, and cook, stirring, until the shrimp are pink. Serve hot.

Grilled Shrimp over Coarse Sea Salt
Gambas a la Plancha con Sal Gorda

MAKES 6 SERVINGS

In this simple and special way to prepare shrimp, the flavor of the sea shines through in every bite. If you can, visit the El Abuelo bar on Victoria Street in Madrid where the only fare is shrimp a la plancha

sold in huge amounts. The floor is littered with shells; one person's only job is to sweep the floor clean.

Kosher or sea salt

12 medium or large shrimp, in their shells

Olive oil

Sprinkle a stovetop griddle with a good amount of coarse sea salt and heat over medium heat. Arrange the shrimp on the griddle and drizzle with the oil. Cook until pink, turning once. Serve hot.

Shrimp with Bacon
Pincho de Langostino

MAKES 6 TAPAS

This is a fine mix of shrimp and bacon with the unmistakable aroma of dry sherry.

6 large shrimp, shelled and deveined

6 very thin bacon strips

4 tablespoons olive oil

1 tablespoon sherry vinegar or red wine vinegar

¼ cup dry sherry

2 medium tomatoes, finely chopped (about 1⅓ cups)

2 tablespoons heavy cream

2 medium leeks, white parts only, trimmed, well washed, and finely chopped

2 large eggs, lightly beaten

Bread crumbs, for dredging

Salt

1. Wrap each shrimp in a bacon slice and secure with a toothpick. Set aside. Heat 2 tablespoons of the oil in a medium skillet over medium heat. Stir in the vinegar, sherry, and tomatoes and cook until the tomatoes cook down and a sauce develops. Remove from the heat and press through a strainer into a bowl, discarding the solids. Return the sauce to the skillet over medium heat. Add the cream and

continues…

cook, stirring, until thickened and smooth. Remove from the heat and reserve.

2. Meanwhile, in another medium skillet, heat the remaining 2 tablespoons oil over medium heat. Add the leeks and cook, stirring, until crispy. Transfer with a slotted spoon to paper towels and let drain. Reserve.

3. Heat at least ½ inch of oil in a medium skillet over medium-high heat (or better still, use a deep fryer set at 365°F) until it turns a cube of bread light brown in 60 seconds. Place the eggs and bread crumbs in separate shallow bowls. Dip each shrimp in the egg, dredge in the bread crumbs, and place in the oil. Cook, turning once, until browned, about 5 minutes. Let drain on paper towels. Season with salt and sprinkle with the leeks. Serve hot.

Béchamel-Coated Fried Shrimp
Gambas Villeroy

MAKES 6 TO 8 SERVINGS

Béchamel, often called "white sauce," lends its distinctive rich and creamy flavor to many tapas as well as main courses. Here it is superb as a coating for crispy fried shrimp.

7 cups Cooking Liquid (page 26)

1 pound medium or large shrimp, in their shells

5 tablespoons unsalted butter

6 tablespoons all-purpose flour

¾ cups milk

¼ teaspoon fresh lemon juice

2 large eggs, lightly beaten

Bread crumbs, for dredging

Oive oil, for frying

Salt

Freshly ground black pepper

1. Prepare the cooking liquid as instructed in step 1 of the recipe. Add the shrimp and simmer until pink, 2 to 3 minutes. Transfer the shrimp to a medium bowl, reserving the cooking liquid. Remove the shells, return them to the broth. and continue cooking 15 minutes more. Remove from the heat and pass through a strainer, reserving ¾ cup of the broth and discarding the solids. (Reserve the remaining broth for the next time you boil shellfish — it will immensely improve the flavor.)

2. Melt the butter in a medium saucepan over medium heat. Add the flour and cook, stirring, 1 minute. Stir in the reserved broth, the milk, juice, salt, and pepper and cook, stirring constantly, until the sauce is thickened and smooth (it will be very thick; if you coat the back of a spoon you can swipe a clean line through with your finger). Let cool, stirring occasionally.

3. Dip each shrimp in the sauce, coating well on all sides. Place on a dish, cover, and refrigerate at least 1 hour or until the sauce has hardened.

4. Heat at least ½ inch of oil in a medium skillet over medium-high heat (or better still, use a deep fryer set at 365°F) until it turns a cube of bread light brown in 60 seconds. Place the eggs and bread crumbs in separate shallow bowls. Dip each shrimp in the eggs, dredge in the bread crumbs, and place in the oil. (Cook in batches if needed to avoid overcrowding.) Cook, turning once, until browned, about 5 minutes. Let drain on paper towels. Season with salt and pepper. Serve hot.

Clams Fisherman Style
Almejas Pescador

MAKES 6 TO 8 SERVINGS

This is one of the most common and delicious ways to prepare clams — with a sauce that, due to its bright color, is commonly referred in Spain as salsa verde or "green sauce." The name relates to its origin as a dish prepared by fishermen on the way back to home port.

4 dozen small clams, such as Manila or littleneck

¼ cup olive oil

½ cup finely chopped onion

3 garlic cloves, finely chopped

½ cup dry white wine

2 bay leaves

1 tablespoon fresh lemon juice

Several threads of saffron, crumbled

3 tablespoons finely chopped fresh flat-leaf parsley

1. Rinse the clams. Discard any with cracked shells or that do not close tightly when touched.

2. Heat the oil in a medium skillet over medium heat. Add the onion and garlic and cook, stirring, until the onion is wilted and transparent, about 5 minutes. Add the clams, increase the heat to high, and cook, stirring, 1 minute more. Stir in the wine and cook, stirring, until reduced by half.

3. Reduce the heat to medium, add the bay leaves, juice, saffron, and 2 tablespoons of the parsley. Cook, stirring periodically, until the clams open. Discard any unopened clams and the bay leaves. Sprinkle with the remaining 1 tablespoon parsley and serve hot.

Clams, Andalusian Style

Almejas Estilo Andaluz

MAKES 6 TO 8 SERVINGS

The cooking in Andalucía is simple and always uses ingredients that will greatly enhance the flavor of the dish. In this case, it's all about the paprika. Use a good-quality sweet Spanish paprika.

4 dozen small clams, such as Manila or littleneck

¼ cup dry white wine

1 tablespoon ground sweet paprika, such as Spanish smoked

Kosher or sea salt

BÉCHAMEL OR WHITE SAUCE

Béchamel is one of the most popular sauces in Spanish cuisine and loved by everybody in the country. It appears in a multitude of recipes, most notably in a popular tapa called *croquetas*. The preparation is quite simple, and many cooks, professional and amateur alike, take great pride in their béchamel. It has been said that if you are visiting a town away from home and want a good meal, the first thing you ask for at a bar or restaurant is for one *croqueta*. If it is good, it's likely that the chef is experienced and you will get a good meal. If it is not good, look for another eatery. Here is an excellent recipe for a classic béchamel.

~~~~~

Melt 5 tablespoons butter in a medium saucepan over low heat. Add ¾ cup flour and stir about 1 minute. Slowly add, stirring constantly, ¾ cup chicken broth and ¾ cup milk. Season with salt and freshly ground black pepper. Cook, stirring constantly, until smooth and thick. Remove from the heat, spread the sauce on a plate, and refrigerate 1 hour or until firm.

At that point you can handle the sauce well (it should be quite thick) and use it to coat your meat, fish, or vegetable, or you can make croquettes.

1. Rinse the clams. Discard any with cracked shells or that do not close tightly when touched.

2. Heat a medium skillet over medium-high heat. Add the clams and stir in the wine, paprika, and salt. Cover and shake well. Cook until the clams open. Discard any unopened clams. Serve hot.

Clams in White Wine Sauce
Almejas a la Marinera

MAKES 4 TO 6 SERVINGS

Spaniards are partial to tiny clams, called coqui-nas. *Because they are so small, a typical order is comprised of about 50. This is one of the most popular tapas in Spain, but because* coquinas *are nearly impossible to find in the United States, you should substitute the smallest clams you can find.*

2 dozen small clams, such as Manila or littleneck

7 tablespoons olive oil

2 tablespoons finely chopped onion

4 garlic cloves, finely chopped

1 tablespoon all-purpose flour

1 tablespoon ground paprika

2 tablespoons finely chopped fresh flat-leaf parsley

1 cup semisweet white wine

1 bay leaf

1 dried red chile pepper, seeded and cut into 3 pieces

Freshly ground black pepper

Salt

I. Rinse the clams. Discard any with cracked shells or that do not close tightly when touched.

I. Heat the oil in a large shallow casserole dish or Dutch oven over medium heat. Add the onion and garlic and cook, stirring, until the onion is wilted and transparent, about 5 minutes. Increase the heat to medium-high. Add the clams and cook, removing the clams as they open. Return to the pan when all have opened. Discard any unopened clams.

2. Sprinkle in the flour and stir to blend. Add the paprika, parsley, wine, bay leaf, chile pepper, black pepper, and salt and cook, stirring, about 5 minutes more. Discard the bay leaf. If using earthenware, serve hot in the dish, or transfer to a platter.

Clams in Romesco Sauce
Almejas Romesco

MAKES 4 TO 6 SERVINGS

Romesco pepper sauce originated in the region of Tarragona and has been around for nearly a thousand years. Romesco is typically served as an accompaniment for grilled shellfish or mixed seafood dishes. Aguardiente, a strong Spanish liqueur made from the pressing of grape skins, is an important ingredient as it lends a special flavor to this sauce. It can sometimes be found in specialty stores but if unavailable, you can substitute its Italian equivalent, grappa.

PREPARE 8 TO 12 HOURS IN ADVANCE

2 dozen very small clams, such as Manila or littleneck

2 pimientos, cut into thin strips

½ cup red wine vinegar

1 bay leaf

Fish Broth

1 small whole fish, such as whiting, head on, cleaned

¼ cup dry white wine

1½ cups water

½ bay leaf

¼ teaspoon dried thyme

1 small onion

1 small carrot, peeled and halved

6 peppercorns

Salt

3 tablespoons olive oil

2 (¼-inch) slices thin slices long-loaf (baguette) bread

3 garlic cloves

12 blanched almonds

¼ cup dry white wine

1 dried red chile pepper, seeded and crumbled

Salt

Freshly ground black pepper

1 teaspoon aguardiente or grappa

1 tablespoon finely chopped fresh flat-leaf parsley,
    for garnish

1. Rinse the clams. Discard any with cracked shells or that do not close tightly when touched.

2. Prepare the broth: Place all the broth ingredients in a medium saucepan and bring to a boil over high heat. Cover, reduce the heat to low, and simmer 1 hour. Pass through a strainer, reserving 1 cup broth and discarding the solids.

3. Heat the oil in a large shallow earthenware casserole dish or Dutch oven over medium heat. Add the pimientos and cook, stirring, about 2 minutes. Transfer to a blender or food processor, reserving the oil.

4. In the reserved oil over medium heat, add the bread and garlic and cook, turning the bread once and stirring the garlic, until both are golden. Transfer to the blender. Add the almonds and blend until a paste forms. With the motor running, gradually add ¼ cup of the reserved broth until well blended. Add the remaining ¾ cup broth and the wine and blend until smooth.

5. Heat the casserole dish over medium heat. Pass the contents of the blender through a fine-mesh strainer into the dish, pressing with the back of a wooden spoon to extract as much liquid as possible. Discard the solids. Add the chile pepper and season with salt and pepper. Arrange the clams in the dish, cover, and cook until the clams open, removing each as it opens. Discard any unopened clams.

6. Taste and adjust the seasoning, then remove the casserole dish from the heat. Stir in the aguardiente and return the clams to the dish, making sure the clam meat is covered by the sauce. Cover and let sit 1 to 2 hours, stirring occasionally.

7. Reheat the clams in the casserole dish over medium heat until heated through. Sprinkle with the parsley. If using earthenware, serve hot in the dish, or transfer to a platter.

Clams in Spicy Tomato Sauce
Almejas Diablo

MAKES 4 TO 6 SERVINGS

For those who like their food spicy, this is an excellent preparation of clams. The dried red chile peppers give this tomato sauce an added kick.

2 tablespoons olive oil

1 medium onion, finely chopped (about ⅔ cup)

2 garlic cloves, finely chopped

2 medium tomatoes, peeled and finely chopped
    (about 1⅓ cups)

1 tablespoon tomato paste

1 teaspoon ground paprika

½ cup dry white wine

Salt

Freshly ground black pepper

1 tablespoon finely chopped fresh flat-leaf parsley

½ dried red chile pepper, seeded and crumbled

1½ dozen very small clams, such as Manila or
    littleneck

1. Heat the oil in a shallow earthenware casserole dish or Dutch oven over medium heat. Add the onion and garlic and cook, stirring, until the onion is wilted and transparent, about 5 minutes. Stir in all the remaining ingredients except the clams. Cover and cook 10 minutes more.

2. Increase the heat to medium-high. Add the clams and cook uncovered until they open, removing each as it opens. Return to the pan when all have opened. Discard any unopened clams. Cook, stirring occasionally, 5 minutes more. If using earthenware, serve hot in the dish, or transfer to a platter.

Grilled Clams with Thin-Sliced Shrimp

Almejas a la Sartén con Láminas de Langostinos

MAKES 4 TO 6 SERVINGS

This classic tapa of clams, shrimp, shallots, and garlic should be served immediately after preparation.

¼ pound small shrimp, shelled and cut lengthwise into slices as thin as possible

Kosher or sea salt

3 shallots, finely chopped

6 tablespoons olive oil

2½ dozen small Manila clams

5 garlic cloves, thinly sliced

2 chile peppers, seeded and thinly sliced

1. Place a broiler rack about 4 inches from the heat source and preheat the broiler. (Cover the broiler pan with foil for easier cleanup, if you like.) Place shrimp slices on the broiler pan and broil a few minutes, just until pink. Arrange on a platter, season with salt, sprinkle with the shallots, and drizzle with I tablespoon of the oil.

2. Heat the remaining 5 tablespoons of oil in a large skillet over medium heat. Add the clams, cover, and cook, stirring occasionally. Transfer the clams as they open to the platter with the shrimp. Discard any unopened clams.

3. In the same oil over medium heat, add the garlic and chile pepper and cook, stirring, until the garlic is lightly golden. Pour over the shrimp and clams. Serve hot.

Clams, Botín Style

Almejas Botín

MAKES 4 SERVINGS

Casa Botín, in its original location in the Cava Baja—among the oldest and most evocative streets in Madrid—is, according to the Guinness Book of World Records, the oldest restaurant in the world. It was built over an eighteenth-century inn and is a required visit in Madrid. Their clams are one of my favorite tapas.

4 dozen small Manila clams

2 garlic cloves, finely chopped

2 tablespoons finely chopped fresh flat-leaf parsley

⅛ teaspoon saffron threads, crumbled

1 tablespoon olive oil

½ medium onion, finely chopped (about ¼ cup)

1 bay leaf

½ chile pepper, stemmed and seeded

1 teaspoon ground bittersweet paprika, such as Spanish smoked

2 tablespoons tomato sauce

½ cup dry white wine

Kosher or sea salt

1. Rinse the clams. Discard any with cracked shells or that do not close tightly when touched.

2. In a mortar or mini-processor, mash the garlic, parsley, and saffron. Heat the oil in a large skillet over medium heat. Add the onion, bay leaf, and chile pepper and cook, stirring, until the onion is wilted and transparent, about 5 minutes. Add the paprika and tomato sauce and cook, stirring, until incorporated, about 2 minutes more. Add the clams, wine, and salt and cook until the clams begin to open. Stir in the mortar mixture and cook 3 to 5 minutes more. Discard any unopened clams and the bay leaf. Serve hot.

Clams in Green Sauce
Almejas Las Pocholas

MAKES 3 OR 4 SERVINGS

Whenever Ernest Hemingway visited Pamplona for the annual "running of the bulls," he always ate at Las Pocholas, a very popular restaurant named after the six daughters of the original owner, known as Pocholo. Clams in green sauce is one of their signature dishes. Green sauce is commonly served in Spain over various types of fish, but I like it best with clams.

2 dozen small Manila clams or cockles or 1 dozen very small littlenecks

Green Sauce

2 tablespoons olive oil

2 tablespoons finely chopped onion

4 garlic cloves, finely chopped

4 teaspoons all-purpose flour

¼ cup dry white wine

½ cup plus 2 tablespoons storebought or homemade Fish Broth or bottled clam juice

2 tablespoons milk

½ cup finely chopped fresh flat-leaf parsley

Kosher or sea salt

Freshly ground black pepper

1. Rinse the clams. Discard any with cracked shells or that do not close tightly when touched.

2. Prepare the green sauce: Heat the oil in a shallow earthenware casserole dish or Dutch oven over medium heat. Add the onion and cook, stirring, until wilted and transparent, about 3 minutes. Add the garlic and cook, stirring, about 1 minute more. Stir in the flour and cook about 1 minute more. In stages, gradually stir in the wine, then the broth, and then the milk. Add the parsley, salt, and pepper and cook, stirring constantly, until thickened and

smooth. (May be prepared ahead and then reheated before adding the clams.)

3. Reduce the heat to low, add the clams, cover, and cook, removing the clams as they open. Return to the dish when all have opened, making sure the clam meat is covered by the sauce. Discard any unopened clams. If using earthenware, serve hot in the dish, or transfer to a platter.

Clams with Green Pepper and Tomato
Almejas con Pimientos Verdes y Tomate

MAKES 6 SERVINGS

Clams, encountered frequently in Spanish cooking, are prepared in many ways using the local ingredients in each region. This recipe uses tomatoes and peppers, which together with the onion enhance the flavor of the clams.

4 dozen small Manila clams

¼ cup olive oil

1 small onion, finely chopped (about ⅓ cup)

2 green frying peppers, finely chopped

4 medium tomatoes, finely chopped (about 3 cups)

½ cup storebought or homemade Fish Broth or bottled clam juice

¼ cup dry white wine

1. Rinse the clams. Discard any with cracked shells or that do not close tightly when touched.

2. Heat the oil in a large skillet over medium heat. Add the onion and peppers and cook, stirring, until softened, about 5 minutes. Reduce the heat to low, add the tomato, and cook, stirring, until softened and their juices release, about 5 minutes more. Add the clams, broth, and wine and simmer, removing the clams as they open. Return to the skillet when all have opened. Discard any unopened clams. Serve hot.

Clams in Almond Sauce
Almejas en Salsa de Almendra

MAKES 4 SERVINGS

Almonds are plentiful in Spain and are used frequently in cooking. They have a distinctive flavor and mix perfectly with fish and shellfish. They are also used frequently to thicken sauces. Marcona almonds, imported from Spain, are ideal to use and easily found in the United States.

2 dozen small clams, such as Manila or littleneck

2 tablespoons olive oil

8 blanched almonds

1 small onion, finely chopped (about ⅓ cup)

2 garlic cloves, finely chopped

¼ cup dry white wine

¾ cup bottled clam juice

Kosher or sea salt

Freshly ground black pepper

Few threads of saffron

1 tablespoon finely chopped fresh flat-leaf parsley, for garnish

1. Rinse the clams. Discard any with cracked shells or that do not close tightly when touched.

2. Heat the oil in a large skillet over medium heat. Add the almonds and cook, stirring, until lightly browned. Transfer to a plate. Add the onion and garlic to the skillet and cook, stirring, until the onion is wilted and transparent, about 5 minutes.

3. In a mortar or mini-processor, mash the almonds, then stir in the wine, clam juice, salt, pepper, and saffron. Add to the skillet and cook until the liquids are absorbed and the sauce thickens. Add the clams and cook, removing the clams to a platter as they open. Return to the skillet when all have opened. Discard any unopened clams. Sprinkle with the parsley and serve hot.

Baked Stuffed Clams
Almejas al Horno

MAKES 4 TO 6 SERVINGS

The distinctive accent of dry sherry enhances this delicious preparation of baked clams stuffed with seasoned bread crumbs and ham. It's always a favorite at my tapas parties.

1½ dozen medium clams

1 tablespoon olive oil

2 tablespoons finely chopped onion

1 garlic clove, finely chopped

6 tablespoons bread crumbs

2 tablespoons finely chopped Serrano (Spanish cured mountain) ham or prosciutto

1 teaspoon dry sherry, such as Fino

¼ teaspoon fresh lemon juice

Salt

Freshly ground black pepper

¼ teaspoon ground paprika

1 tablespoon finely chopped fresh flat-leaf parsley

Unsalted butter

1. Preheat the oven to 350°F. Unseal the clams with a knife and place in a roasting pan. Bake, removing the clams as they open. Discard any unopened clams. Chop the meat and reserve half of the shells. Leave the oven on.

2. Heat the oil in a small skillet over medium heat. Add the onion and garlic and cook, stirring, until the onion is wilted and transparent, about 5 minutes. Stir in all the remaining ingredients except the butter. Add the clams and cook until heated through.

3. Clean the reserved shells well. Fill each shell with the clam mixture and dot with butter. Arrange in the roasting pan and bake about 10 minutes or until lightly browned. Serve hot.

Mussels "My Way"

Mejillones a Mi Estilo

MAKES 4 TO 6 SERVINGS

This recipe comes from the northern town of El Grove in Galicia where mussels are farmed everywhere and paprika (pimentón) is used enthusiastically. My friend Digna, owner of El Crisol restaurant, cooks mussels "her way."

2 dozen mussels

½ lemon, thinly sliced

3 tablespoons olive oil

1 medium onion, slivered

1 garlic clove, lightly smashed

1 tablespoon ground bittersweet paprika, such as Spanish smoked

¼ teaspoon ground hot paprika, such as Spanish smoked

¼ cup dry white wine

Kosher or sea salt

Freshly ground black pepper

1. Rinse the mussels well. Cut or pull off the beards. Discard any with cracked shells or that do not close tightly when touched.

2. In a large skillet, place the mussels, lemon, and water to cover. Bring to a boil over high heat and cook, removing the mussels as they open. Discard any unopened mussels. Reserve the cooking liquid and lemon. Wipe out the skillet.

3. Heat the oil in the same skillet over medium heat. Add the onion and garlic and cook, stirring, until the onion is wilted and transparent, about 5 minutes. Add the paprikas and wine and cook, stirring occasionally, until cooked down, about 5 minutes more. Add the mussels and the reserved cooking liquid and lemon, and cook until the mussels are heated through. Season with salt and pepper. Serve hot.

Mussels, Galician Style

Mejillones a la Gallega

MAKES 4 TO 6 SERVINGS

This tapa hails from the region of Galicia in the northwestern corner of Spain, where they farm large amounts of mussels.

2 tablespoons olive oil

2 tablespoons finely chopped onion

2 garlic cloves, finely chopped

2 teaspoons ground bittersweet paprika, such as Spanish smoked

⅛ teaspoon ground cayenne pepper

2 dozen medium mussels

Kosher or sea salt

1 tablespoon fresh lemon juice

1 bay leaf

¼ cup dry white wine

1. Rinse the mussels well. Cut or pull off the beards. Drain. Discard any mussels with cracked shells or that do not close tightly when touched.

2. Heat the oil in a large skillet over medium heat. Add the onion and garlic and cook until the onion is wilted and transparent, about 3 minutes. Sprinkle with the paprika and cayenne pepper and add the mussels, salt, juice, bay leaf, and wine. Cook until the mussels open, removing each as it opens. Return to the skillet after all have opened. Discard any unopened mussels and the bay leaf. Serve hot.

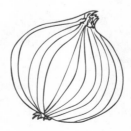

Stuffed Fried Mussels

Tigres

MAKES 6 TO 8 SERVINGS

As far as I know, this tapa originated in a Madrid bar called Gayango, now closed, and was the star attraction. The origin of the name, tigres *(tigers), has been lost and efforts to clarify its meaning have been unsuccessful. Nonetheless, it's a delicious dish.*

2 pounds medium mussels

¾ cup water

1 slice lemon

1 medium onion, finely chopped (about ⅔ cup)

1 medium green bell pepper, finely chopped
    (about ¾ cup)

1 garlic clove, finely chopped

2 tablespoons finely chopped Serrano (Spanish
    cured mountain) ham or prosciutto

2 teaspoons tomato sauce

White Sauce

3 tablespoons unsalted butter

¼ cup all-purpose flour

½ cup milk

Kosher or sea salt

Freshly ground black pepper

Olive oil, for frying

2 large eggs, lightly beaten

Bread crumbs, for dredging

I. Rinse the mussels well. Cut or pull off the beards. Discard any mussels with cracked shells or that do not close tightly when touched.

2. Place the mussels, water, and lemon in a large skillet. Bring to a boil over high heat, removing the mussels as they open. Discard any unopened mussels. Reserve ½ cup of the cooking liquid. Finely chop the meat and reserve half of each shell for filling. Wipe out the skillet.

3. Heat the oil in the same skillet over medium heat. Add the onion and bell pepper and cook, stirring, until softened, about 8 minutes. Add the garlic and ham and cook, stirring, about I minute more. Stir in the tomato sauce, mussels, parsley, salt, and pepper and cook until the sauce and seasonings are absorbed. Divide the mussel mixture among the shell halves and place them in a pan.

4. Prepare the sauce: Melt the butter in a small saucepan over medium heat. Add the flour and, cook, stirring, I to 2 minutes. Gradually pour in the reserved cooking liquid and the milk and cook, stirring constantly, until thickened and smooth. Season with salt and pepper. Let cool, stirring occasionally. Using a teaspoon, cover the filled shells with the sauce, sealing the edges by smoothing with the cupped side of the spoon. Refrigerate at least I hour or until the sauce solidifies.

5. Heat at least I inch of oil in a medium skillet over medium-high heat (or better still, use a deep fryer set at 360°F) until it turns a cube of bread light brown in 60 seconds. Place the eggs and bread crumbs in separate shallow bowls. Dip each mussel in the egg (the whole mussel), dredge in the bread crumbs, and place in the oil. (Cook in batches if needed to avoid overcrowding.) Cook, filled side down, until well browned. Let drain on paper towels. Serve hot.

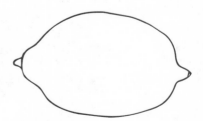

Mussels in White Wine Sauce
Mejillones al Vino Blanco

MAKES 6 TO 8 SERVINGS

This is one of the many ways mussels are prepared in Galicia, the region in northwestern Spain where mussels are so plentiful. Another typical ingredient from this area is the omnipresent paprika.

2 pounds mussels

2 tablespoons olive oil

½ medium onion, finely chopped (about ¼ cup)

1 garlic clove, finely chopped

½ teaspoon all-purpose flour

1 teaspoon ground bittersweet paprika, such as Spanish smoked

¼ teaspoon ground hot paprika, such as Spanish smoked

¼ cup dry white wine

1 slice lemon

2 tablespoons finely chopped fresh flat-leaf parsley

2 bay leaves

1. Rinse the mussels well. Cut or pull off the beards. Discard any mussels with cracked shells or that do not close tightly when touched.

2. Heat the oil in a large skillet over medium heat. Add the onion and garlic and cook, stirring, until the onion is wilted and transparent, about 5 minutes. Stir in the flour and paprika and add the wine, lemon, parsley, bay leaves, and mussels. Reduce the heat to low, cover, and simmer, removing the mussels as they open, about 10 minutes more. Return to the skillet after all have opened. Discard any unopened mussels and the bay leaves. Serve hot.

Mussels in Green Sauce
Mejillones en Salsa Verde

MAKES 4 SERVINGS

Although mussels in green sauce are not commonly found in restaurants in Spain, they are served in almost every Spanish restaurant in the United States. Green sauce (salsa verde) in Spain is typically served with other kinds of seafood, most notably clams, but it is equally delicious with mussels. Be sure to provide plenty of bread for dunking.

2 dozen medium mussels

1 tablespoon olive oil

3 tablespoons finely chopped onion

3 garlic cloves, finely chopped

2 tablespoons all-purpose flour

¾ cup finely chopped fresh flat-leaf parsley

½ cup dry white wine

½ cup bottled clam juice or water

Salt

Freshly ground black pepper

1. Rinse the mussels well. Cut or pull off the beards. Discard any mussels with cracked shells or that do not close tightly when touched.

2. Heat the oil in a large earthenware casserole dish or Dutch oven over medium heat. Add the onion and garlic and cook, stirring, until the onion is wilted and transparent, about 3 minutes. Stir in the flour and cook 1 minute more. Stir in the parsley, wine, clam juice, salt, and pepper. Reduce the heat to low, cover, and simmer 15 minutes more.

3. Increase the heat to medium, add the mussels, cover, and cook 5 minutes. Uncover and cook, removing the mussels as they open. Return to the skillet after all have opened. Discard any unopened mussels. If using earthenware, serve hot in the dish, or transfer to a platter.

Baked Mussels and Mushrooms
Mejillones Gratinados

MAKES 4 SERVINGS

This is a wonderfully rich tapa of mussels and mushrooms baked in a creamy sauce and then covered with grated cheese. For an elegant presentation, serve in scallop shells.

4 dozen medium mussels

1 cup water

1 slice lemon

½ pound mushrooms, thinly sliced

White Sauce

2 large egg yolks

Dash of hot sauce, such as Tabasco

4 tablespoons (½ stick) unsalted butter

¼ cup all-purpose flour

1 cup milk

1 tablespoon fresh lemon juice

Pinch of saffron

Freshly ground black pepper

¼ cup grated aged cheese, such as Manchego

Unsalted butter

1. Rinse the mussels well. Cut or pull off the mussel beards. Discard any mussels with cracked shells or that do not close tightly when touched.

2. In a large skillet, place the mussels, water, and lemon and bring to a boil over high heat. Cook until the mussels open, removing each as it opens. Discard any unopened mussels. Reserve 1 cup of the cooking liquid. Remove the meat from the shells and place in a large bowl. Add the mushrooms and stir to combine. Discard the shells.

3. Prepare the sauce: Beat the egg yolks in a small bowl and stir in the hot sauce. Melt the butter in a small saucepan over medium heat. Stir in the flour and cook 1 minute more. Gradually stir in the reserved cooking liquid, the milk, lemon juice, saffron, and pepper. Cook, stirring constantly, until thickened and smooth. Reduce the heat to low, add the egg mixture, and cook, stirring constantly, until thickened.

4. Preheat the oven to 450°F. Place the mussels and mushrooms in a shallow earthenware casserole dish or Dutch oven or divide among individual casserole dishes or large scallop shells. Pour the sauce over the top, sprinkle with the cheese, and dot with butter. Bake about 10 minutes or until bubbly and lightly browned. If using earthenware, serve hot in the dish, or transfer to a platter.

Mussels in Spicy Tomato Sauce
Mejillones en Tomate con Ajo, Guindilla, Cebolla y Vino

MAKES 4 TO 6 SERVINGS

One of the attractions of this recipe is the delicious sauce it creates. The dish should be served with some slices of bread to allow dunking.

2 dozen small mussels

3 tablespoons olive oil

2 large onions, finely chopped (about 2 cups)

1 cup canned crushed tomato

1 dried red chile pepper, stemmed and seeded

⅛ teaspoon sugar

Kosher or sea salt

Freshly ground black pepper

3 garlic cloves, finely chopped

2 tablespoons finely chopped fresh flat-leaf parsley

¼ cup white wine

1. Rinse the mussels well. Cut or pull off the mussel beards. Discard any mussels with cracked shells or that do not close tightly when touched.

2. Heat the oil in a medium skillet over medium heat. Add the onion and cook, stirring, until wilted

and transparent, about 5 minutes. Reduce the heat to low. Add the tomato, chile pepper, sugar, salt, and black pepper and cook, stirring occasionally, about 10 minutes. In a mortar or mini-processor, mash the garlic and parsley, stir in the wine, then stir into the tomato mixture in the skillet. Add the mussels, and cook, until the mussels open, removing each as it opens. Return to the skillet after all have opened. Discard any unopened mussels. Serve hot.

Scallops Wrapped in Bacon with Pomegranate Sauce
Vieiras Envueltas en Tocino

MAKES 4 SERVINGS

Either as a tapa or a first course, this recipe boasts great flavor as well as a nice presentation. The dish, quite innovative, is a creation of Solera, a fine Spanish restaurant in midtown Manhattan run by its owner Rufino, who was born in Galicia where scallops are plentiful and their shells considered an emblem of this region.

Pomegranate Sauce

1 tablespoon olive oil

1 shallot, finely chopped

3 garlic cloves, finely chopped

3 tablespoons onion, finely chopped

2 tablespoons finely chopped carrot

2 tablespoons finely chopped celery

¼ cup finely chopped mushrooms, such as brown or white

2 tablespoons finely chopped tomato

1 teaspoon tomato paste

⅓ cup red wine

2½ cups chicken broth or vegetable broth

½ bay leaf

¼ teaspoon dried thyme

½ cup pomegranate juice

8 large sea scallops

6 thin slices bacon, halved crosswise

2 tablespoons pomegranate seeds, for garnish (optional)

Kosher or sea salt

1. Prepare the sauce: Heat the oil in a medium skillet over medium heat. Add the shallot, garlic, onion, carrot, celery, and mushrooms and cook, stirring, about 1 minute. Reduce the heat to low, cover, and cook 5 minutes more. Stir in the tomato and tomato paste and cook about 2 minutes more. Stir in the wine, broth, bay leaf, and thyme, bring to a boil, and cook uncovered, stirring occasionally, about 30 minutes more.

2. Let cool slightly, then pass through a fine-mesh strainer into a small saucepan, pressing with a wooden spoon to extract as much liquid as possible (you should have about 1 cup). Discard the solids. Stir in the pomegranate juice, and bring to a boil. Cook, stirring constantly, until thick and syrupy and reduced to about ⅓ cup. Reserve in a small tightly covered jar.

3. Wrap a piece of bacon around each scallop. Brush a stovetop griddle with olive oil and heat to the smoking point over high heat. Add the scallops, seam of the bacon down, reduce the heat to medium-high, and cook until the seam side of the bacon is browned. Turn and cook until scallops are white and opaque on the inside and the bacon is browned on all sides, about 5 minutes more.

4. On individual plates, spoon about 1 tablespoon of the pomegranate sauce onto each plate. Place 2 scallops on the sauce and garnish with pomegranate seeds, if using. Season with salt and serve hot.

Crab Crepes
Crepes de Txangurro

MAKES 6 SERVINGS

Centollos are the large, sweet spider crabs found along Spain's northern coast. To make this dish, the crabmeat is mixed with a well-seasoned sauce. Since centollos *are rarely available in the United States, Alaskan King crab makes an adequate substitute.*

Crepes

1 large egg

½ cup milk

½ cup water

1 cup all-purpose flour

⅛ teaspoon salt

Crab Filling

1 tablespoon olive oil

2 tablespoons finely chopped leeks (white part only)

2 tablespoons very finely chopped onion

2 tablespoons very finely chopped carrot

½ pound fresh crab meat

2 tablespoons brandy

Marinara Sauce

1 tablespoon olive oil

1 small onion, finely chopped

1 small tomato, finely chopped

¼ cup dry white wine

1 teaspoon finely chopped fresh thyme or ⅛ teaspoon dried thyme

1 bay leaf

2 tablespoons all-purpose flour

2 cups storebought or homemade Fish Broth (page 199; partial recipe) or bottled clam juice

Salt

1. Prepare the crepes: Place all the crepe ingredients in a food processor and process until smooth. Lightly grease a small skillet or crepe pan, preferably 4 inches in diameter and heat. Swirl in just enough batter to coat the pan, about 1 tablespoon. When the crepe has set, turn and cook the other side. Do not brown.

2. Prepare the filling: Heat the oil in a medium skillet over medium heat. Add the leeks, onion, and carrots, cover, and cook 15 minutes or until the vegetables are softened. Add the crab meat, then add the brandy. Standing well away from the skillet, ignite the liquid with a match or kitchen lighter and let die out. Cook 1 minute more and reserve.

3. Prepare the sauce: Heat the oil in a medium skillet over medium heat. Add the onion and cook, stirring, until softened, about 5 minutes. Add the tomato and cook, stirring, until the tomato liquid evaporates. Add the wine, thyme, and bay leaf and cook until the sauce is reduced by half. Stir in the flour and cook 1 minute, then add the fish broth. Simmer 30 minutes. Pass the sauce through a fine-mesh strainer, reserving 1 cup. Discard the solids. Taste for salt.

4. Preheat the oven to 400°F. Place 2 tablespoons crab meat in the center of each crepe, roll up, and place seam side down in a greased baking dish. Pour the reserved sauce over the crepes. Bake 10 minutes. Serve hot.

Cooked Fish, Squid, and Octopus

Swordfish in Saffron Sauce
Pescado en Amarillo

MAKES 4 SERVINGS

The firm texture of swordfish is perfect for this sauce that features the distinctive taste of saffron. This is a favorite of mine from the Bar Bahia on the water-front in Cádiz.

1 tablespoon olive oil

2 tablespoons finely chopped onion

1 garlic clove, finely chopped

1 tablespoon finely chopped green frying peppers

2 tablespoons peeled and finely chopped tomato

1 bay leaf

2 tablespoons brandy

¼ cup chicken broth or vegetable broth

Kosher or sea salt

Freshly ground black pepper

⅛ teaspoon grated or ground nutmeg

Several threads of saffron

¾ pound swordfish or shark, cut into 1½-inch chunks

Heat the oil in a medium skillet over medium heat. Add the onion, garlic, and frying pepper and cook, stirring, until softened, about 5 minutes. Stir in the tomato and bay leaf and cook until the tomato is softened and its juices release, 2 to 3 minutes more. Stir in the brandy, broth, salt, pepper, nutmeg, and saffron and cook 5 minutes more. (The sauce may be prepared in advance and reheated before adding the swordfish.) Add the swordfish, cover, and cook 10 minutes more. Remove the bay leaf. Serve hot.

Fried Squid "a la Romana"
Calamares "a la Romana"

MAKES 6 TO 8 SERVINGS

Fried squid, probably one of the most common dishes in the world, is part of Spanish cuisine as well. The traditional way to fry squid—with a light batter—is very nice (see the next recipe), but I highly recommend trying the "Roman" style of frying (anything) —dipping in egg then flour before cooking it in the hot oil (this recipe). It's quite special and easy to do.

¾ pound small squid, cleaned

2 large eggs, lightly beaten

¾ cup all-purpose flour, for dredging

Kosher or sea salt

Olive oil, for frying

1. Dry the squid tentacles and bodies completely —inside and out—to prevent splattering during frying. Cut the bodies into ½-inch rings, and leave the tentacles whole.

2. Prepare "a la romana": Heat at least ½ inch of oil in a medium skillet over medium-high heat (or better still, use a deep fryer set at 365°F) until it turns a cube of bread light brown in 60 seconds. Place the eggs and flour in separate shallow bowls. Dredge the squid bodies and tentacles in the flour, dip in the egg, and place in the oil. (Cook in batches if needed to avoid overcrowding.) Cook, turning occasionally, until golden, 2 to 3 minutes. Do not overcook or the squid will toughen. Transfer with a slotted spoon to paper towels and let drain. Season with salt and serve hot.

Batter-Fried Squid Tentacles
Tentáculos de Calamar en Tempura

MAKES 4 SERVINGS

The tentacles of a squid may look unsightly, but when prepared properly, they are absolutely delicious (the squid bodies can work just as well). In this classic tapa, squid tentacles are dipped in batter and fried until golden brown. This dish makes a nice main course (to serve two, or double the recipe quantities).

¾ pound small squid tentacles

Batter

1 large egg white

1 cup ice water

2 tablespoons dry white wine

¾ cup all-purpose flour

¼ cup cornstarch

1 teaspoon baking powder

¼ teaspoon baking soda

¼ teaspoon salt

1 tablespoon finely chopped fresh flat-leaf parsley

All-purpose flour, for dredging

Olive oil, for frying

1. Clean the tentacles thoroughly and dry completely to prevent splattering during frying.

2. Prepare the batter: In a large bowl, whisk the egg white until light and frothy. Whisk in the ice water, then whisk in all the remaining batter ingredients until well blended. The batter should be fairly thin.

3. Place the flour for dredging in a small shallow bowl. Heat at least ½ inch of oil in a medium skillet over medium-high heat (or better still, use a deep fryer set at 365°F) until it turns a cube of bread light brown in 60 seconds. Dredge the tentacles in the flour, making sure they are well separated. Dip in the batter, remove with a slotted spoon and place in the oil. (Cook in batches if needed to avoid overcrowding.) Cook until very lightly browned, about 2 minutes. Transfer to paper towels and let drain. (May be kept warm in a 200°F oven up to 30 minutes.) Serve hot.

Fried Stuffed Baby Squid
Calamaritos Rellenos

MAKES 4 SERVINGS

Baby squid is called for in this recipe because larger squid become too tough when fried. The frying should only take several minutes and must be done at the very last moment, but the squid may be stuffed in advance. This is a very popular tapa.

1¼ pounds baby squid with tentacles, bodies about 2 inches long, cleaned

1 tablespoon olive oil

¼ cup finely chopped onion

1 garlic clove, finely chopped

¼ pound Serrano (Spanish cured mountain) ham or prosciutto, finely chopped

⅛ teaspoon ground paprika

2 teaspoons finely chopped fresh flat-leaf parsley

Kosher or sea salt

Freshly ground black pepper

1 teaspoon dry white wine

4 teaspoons bread crumbs

Olive oil, for frying

2 large eggs, lightly beaten

All-purpose flour, for dredging

1. Cut off the squid tentacles and leave the bodies in one piece. Dry the tentacles and bodies completely—inside and out—to prevent splattering during frying. Finely chop the tentacles, and leave the bodies whole.

2. Heat the 1 tablespoon oil in a medium skillet over medium heat. Add the onion and garlic and cook, stirring, until the onion is wilted and

transparent, about 5 minutes. Add the tentacles and ham and cook, stirring, about 2 minutes more. Remove from the heat and stir in the paprika, parsley, salt, pepper, wine, and bread crumbs. Fill each squid body with the tentacle mixture.

3. Heat at least ½ inch of oil in a medium skillet over medium-high heat (or better still, use a deep fryer set at 365°F) until it turns a cube of bread light brown in 60 seconds. Place the eggs and flour in separate shallow bowls. Dredge each squid in the flour, dip in the egg, and place in the oil. (Cook in batches if needed to avoid overcrowding.) Reduce the heat to medium and cook, turning occasionally, until the squid are lightly golden, about 2 minutes. Do not overcook or the squid will toughen. Transfer with a slotted spoon to paper towels and let drain. Season with salt and serve hot.

Small Squid in Beer Sauce
Chipirones en Cerveza

MAKES 4 SERVINGS

This unusual squid recipe from Rincon de Pepe, an exceptional restaurant and tapas bar in Murcia, calls for squid of the small variety. If you can't find small squid, cut a larger squid into rings. The beer sauce completes an excellent dish.

1 pound small squid with tentacles, bodies no more
      than 4 inches long, cleaned

4 tablespoons olive oil

3 garlic cloves, lightly smashed

1 medium onion, such as Vidalia or other sweet onion,
      finely chopped (about ⅔ cup)

1 medium tomato, peeled, seeded, and finely
      chopped (about ⅔ cup)

1 bay leaf

¼ teaspoon sugar

Kosher or sea salt

Freshly ground black pepper

⅓ cup beer

1. Dry the squid completely to prevent splattering during frying. Heat 2 tablespoons of the oil in a medium skillet over medium heat. Add the garlic and cook, stirring, until the garlic turns lightly golden. Stir in the onion, reduce the heat to low, cover, and cook 10 to 15 minutes or until the onion is tender but not browned. Stir in the tomato, bay leaf, sugar, salt, and pepper. Increase the heat to medium and cook, uncovered, about 5 minutes. Reserve.

2. Heat the remaining 2 tablespoons oil in a large skillet over high heat. Add the squid bodies and tentacles and cook about 2 minutes. Stir in the beer, reduce the heat to low, cover, and cook 10 minutes. Stir in the tomato mixture and cook, covered, 25 minutes more. Transfer the squid to a platter. Cook the sauce, uncovered and stirring occasionally, until thickened. Return the squid to the skillet and cook until the squid is tender, about 10 minutes more. Discard the bay leaf and serve hot.

Dried Cod in Garlic Mayonnaise
Bacalao Pil Pil

MAKES 4 SERVINGS

In this Basque signature dish, where only the finest dried salt cod is acceptable, the cod should be cooked slowly in oil, which creates a gelatin that thickens the oil into a mayonnaise-like consistency. When preparing cod, it needs to be soaked first in cold water for 2 or 3 days or else it will be too salty.

PREPARE 24 TO 36 HOURS IN ADVANCE

½ pound dried boneless skinless salt cod, cut into
      thin pieces with the skin on and as many of the
      bones removed as possible

½ cup olive oil

4 garlic cloves, thinly sliced lengthwise

continues...

½ medium-hot dried chile pepper, such as Spanish guindilla, seeded, or ¼ teaspoon crushed red pepper

2 tablespoons lightly beaten egg

1. Place the cod in a medium bowl and add cold water to cover. Cover and let sit in the refrigerator 24 to 36 hours, changing the water several times, until the water no longer tastes salty. Drain well.

2. Heat the oil in a shallow earthenware casserole dish or Dutch oven over low heat. Add the garlic and chile pepper and cook, stirring, until the garlic just begins to turn golden. Remove the garlic and reserve. Add the cod skin side down and cook, shaking the pan constantly, about 3 minutes more. Turn the fish and cook about 3 minutes more. Add 1 tablespoon water, cover, and cook 15 minutes more.

3. Transfer the cod and chile pepper to a warm platter. Cut the cod into four tapas-size portions. Place the egg in a food processor and pulse briefly. With the motor running, gradually pour in the oil from the casserole dish and process until the mixture is a mayonnaise-like consistency. Pour over the cod. Decorate with the garlic and chile pepper. Serve hot.

Fried Cod Sticks
Soldaditos de Pavía

MAKES 4 TO 6 SERVINGS

In English, Soldaditos de Pavía *translates to "Little Soldiers of Pavia," a reference to the Spanish troops who occupied the Italian town of Pavia in the eighteenth century. Because the cod is cut into sticks, it is said to resemble the straight backs of the soldiers. Fried cod sticks are enormously popular and can be found in just about every tapas bar and tavern in Madrid. They're a signature tapa at Casa Labra on Tetuan Street.*

PREPARE 24 TO 36 HOURS IN ADVANCE

¼-pound piece dried boneless skinless salt cod, about ½ inch thick

Fresh lemon juice

Mild olive oil, for frying

Batter

¾ cup all-purpose flour

1½ teaspoons baking powder

⅛ teaspoon salt

¼ cup water

¼ cup milk

3 tablespoons mild olive oil

1. Place the cod in a medium bowl and add cold water to cover. Cover and let sit in the refrigerator 24 to 36 hours, changing the water occasionally, until the water no longer tastes salty. Drain well. Remove any membrane. Cut into strips ½ to ¾ inch wide and 2 inches long. Brush the cod on both sides with lemon juice.

2. Prepare the batter: Combine the flour, baking powder, and salt in a small bowl. Stir in the water, milk, and oil and mix until smooth. (The batter may be prepared in advance, refrigerated, and brought to room temperature before frying.)

3. Heat at least ½ inch of oil in a medium skillet over medium-high heat (or better still, use a deep fryer set at 365°F) until it turns a cube of bread light brown in 60 seconds. Dip the cod in the batter and place in the oil. (Cook in batches if needed to avoid overcrowding.) Cook, turning once, until golden on both sides. Transfer with a slotted spoon to paper towels and let drain. Serve hot.

Baby Eels in Garlic Sauce
Angulas a la Bilbaína

MAKES 1 SERVING

Angulas *are tiny baby eels that are considered a delicacy in Spain. For a long time, the only place I* could find them in New York was at the *Café San Martin*, where they were imported directly from Spain. But in recent years, their popularity has grown and they can now be found in specialty stores. *Angulas* are usually served *a la bilbaína*, with olive oil, garlic, and hot red pepper.

3 tablespoons olive oil

1 large garlic clove, thinly sliced

½ dried red chile pepper, seeded and cut into 3 pieces

¼ pound baby eels

Place the oil, garlic, and chile pepper in a 5-inch individual earthenware casserole dish or small saucepan. Heat over medium-high heat until the garlic begins to sizzle and just turn golden. Immediately add the baby eels, all at once—do not stir. Remove the dish from the heat immediately and cover with a plate. Take the covered dish to the table, then uncover and stir the eels lightly. Serve hot.

Snails, Madrid Style
Caracoles a la Madrileña

MAKES 4 TO 6 SERVINGS

The very best snails I have tasted came from chef Amadeo, the vivacious owner of the 15 de Cascorro bar, named after its street address, and located in the middle of Rastro, Madrid's crowded flea market. Amadeo combines his snails with chorizo *that he gets from the village of Villarcayo, and the results are outstanding. Since fresh snails are nearly impossible to find in the United States, you can substitute periwinkles, which have a similar flavor. The snails taste best the following day, reheated.*

1 pound live periwinkles, 1½ pounds (thawed) frozen unseasoned snails, or 2 dozen canned snails, in their shells

3 tablespoons olive oil

1 medium onion, finely chopped (about ⅔ cup)

1 or 2 dried red chile peppers, seeded and each cut into 3 pieces

4 garlic cloves, finely chopped

¼ pound (2 links) chorizo, thinly sliced

¼ pound Serrano (Spanish cured mountain) ham or prosciutto, cut into ¼-inch cubes

2 teaspoons all-purpose flour

4 teaspoons ground paprika

½ cup tomato sauce

2 cups dry white wine

Salt

¼ cup finely chopped fresh flat-leaf parsley

1. Place the periwinkles in a medium bowl, uncovered, and let sit in the refrigerator until ready to use. Rinse under cold running water for 30 minutes. Drain.

2. Heat the oil in a shallow earthenware casserole dish or Dutch oven over medium heat. Add the onion and cook, stirring, until wilted and transparent, about 5 minutes. Add the chile peppers, garlic, chorizo, and ham and cook, stirring, about 5 minutes more. Sprinkle with the flour and paprika and stir to coat. Stir in the tomato sauce, wine, periwinkles, salt, and 2 tablespoons of the parsley and bring to a boil over medium-high heat. Reduce the heat to low and simmer, stirring occasionally, about 30 minutes more.

3. Sprinkle with the remaining 2 tablespoons parsley. If using earthenware, serve hot in the dish, or transfer to a platter. Or, let cool, cover, and refrigerate overnight, then reheat over medium heat and serve hot.

Marinated Octopus

Pulpo Marinado

MAKES 6 TO 8 SERVINGS

Octopus is very popular in Galicia, in northern Spain. It is traditionally made in large quantities in metal cauldrons and is always served at local festivals. Try to find small octopus, as the large ones may be tough.

PREPARE 8 TO 12 HOURS IN ADVANCE

1½ pounds small octopus, cleaned

Cooking Liquid

12 cups water

1 bay leaf

½ medium onion, peeled

4 peppercorns

2 sprigs parsley

Salt

Dressing

½ cup extra-virgin olive oil

3 tablespoons red wine vinegar

1 tablespoon finely chopped onion

1 garlic clove, finely chopped

1 tablespoon finely chopped fresh flat-leaf parsley

Salt

Freshly ground black pepper

I. Before cooking the octopus, tenderize it by throwing it with force into the kitchen sink, repeating at least 10 times.

2. Prepare the cooking liquid: In a large pot, bring the water to a boil over high heat. Submerge the octopus in the water, then remove it immediately. Repeat 2 times and transfer to a platter. Add the bay leaf, onion, peppercorns, parsley, and salt to the pot and bring to a boil again over high heat.

3. Return the octopus to the pot, reduce the heat to low, cover, and simmer until tender, 1¾ to 3 hours, depending on the size of the octopus. Drain, discard the bay leaf, and let cool. Scrape off any loose skin. Cut the body and tentacles into bite-size pieces.

4. Prepare the dressing: Combine all the dressing ingredients in a medium bowl. Add the octopus and let marinate overnight in the refrigerator. Serve cold or at room temperature.

Fish Roll with Pine Nuts and Cheese

Merluza Rellena de Piñones y Queso

MAKES 4 SERVINGS

This tapa of hake or fresh cod with cheese, bread crumbs, and pine nuts should be rolled, then served in slices.

2 (¼-pound) fish fillets, such as hake or fresh cod

2 tablespoons olive oil plus more, for brushing

Kosher or sea salt

2 tablespoons ground pine nuts

2 tablespoons coarsely grated aged Manchego or Parmesan cheese

2 tablespoons bread crumbs

2 tablespoons finely chopped fresh flat-leaf parsley

Lemon juice from 1 lemon

Pinch of Sugar

I. Preheat the oven to 350°F. Brush a shallow earthenware casserole dish or Dutch oven with oil. Brush both sides of each fish with the oil and season with salt. Sprinkle one side with 2 teaspoons each of the pine nuts, cheese, bread crumbs, and parsley. Roll up the fish and place seam side down in the baking dish. (The fish rolls may be prepared in advance and refrigerated until ready to use.) Brush the tops of the fish rolls with a little more oil and sprinkle with the remaining 1 teaspoon each pine nuts, cheese, bread crumbs, and parsley. Bake 15 minutes.

2. Cut the fish rolls into 1-inch slices and lay on their sides in the casserole dish. Stir the sugar into the lemon juice in a cup or small bowl and drizzle over the fish rolls. If using earthenware, serve hot in the dish, or transfer to a platter.

Stewed Zucchini, Peppers, and Tomatoes Ⓥ
Pisto Manchego

MAKES 6 SERVINGS

A classic vegetable dish that originated in La Mancha ("the land of Don Quixote") in the central plains of Spain, this can be served hot or cold, according to preference. The consistency should not be soupy but rather thick like a stew.

3 tablespoons fruity olive oil

1 medium green bell pepper, cut into ¾-inch squares

1 medium onion, coarsely chopped (about ⅔ cup)

1 medium zucchini, cut into ½-inch cubes (about 6 ounces)

5 garlic cloves, finely chopped

¾ pound tomatoes, peeled and cut into ½-inch cubes

1 tablespoon finely chopped fresh flat-leaf parsley

Kosher or sea salt

Freshly ground black pepper

Heat the oil in a large saucepan over medium heat. Add the bell pepper, onion, zucchini, and garlic and cook, stirring, until the onion is wilted and transparent, about 8 minutes. Add the tomatoes, parsley, salt, and pepper and cook, stirring occasionally, about 30 minutes more. Increase the heat to medium-high and cook until the liquid is reduced—the stew should be thick, not soupy. Serve.

Almond-Stuffed Dates Wrapped in Bacon

Dátiles Rellenos de Almendras Envueltos en Tocino

MAKES 4 TO 6 SERVINGS

Dates, almonds, and bacon are an ideal mix of tastes for this simple tapa, covered in egg and fried until golden.

12 pitted dates
12 blanched almonds
3 thin slices bacon, cut crosswise into quarters
All-purpose flour, for dredging
1 large egg, lightly beaten

1. Fill each date with an almond and close the date. Wrap a strip of bacon around each date. Heat a medium skillet over medium heat. Place the dates in the skillet, seam of the bacon down, and cook until the seam side of the bacon is golden. Turn and cook until the bacon is golden on the other side. Let drain on paper towels.

2. Heat at least ½ inch of oil in a medium skillet over medium-high heat (or better still, use a deep fryer set at 365°F) until it turns a cube of bread light brown in 60 seconds. Place the flour and egg in separate shallow bowls. Dredge each date in the flour, dip in the egg, and place in the oil. Cook, turning once, until just browned. Let drain on paper towels. Serve hot.

Chickpeas in Onion Sauce **Ⓥ**

Garbanzos con Cebolla

MAKES 4 SERVINGS

My mother-in-law loved this recipe. The generous amount of stewed onions it calls for adds a delightful sweetness to the chickpeas.

PREPARE SEVERAL HOURS IN ADVANCE

¼ pound dried chickpeas
1 garlic clove
1 slice medium onion
1 bay leaf
Kosher or sea salt
2 tablespoons olive oil
1 medium onion, coarsely chopped
1 tablespoon peeled and finely chopped tomato

1. Place the chickpeas in a medium bowl, add cold water to cover by 1 inch, and let soak in the refrigerator overnight. Drain and place in a deep earthenware casserole dish or Dutch oven. Add the garlic, onion slice, bay leaf, salt, and water to cover. Bring to a boil over high heat, reduce the heat to low, cover, and simmer 1½ to 2 hours or until the chickpeas are tender. Drain and discard the garlic and bay leaf.

2. Heat the oil in a medium skillet over medium heat. Add the chopped onion and cook, stirring, 1 minute. Add the tomato, reduce the heat to low, cover, and cook until the onion is cooked but not colored, about 15 minutes. Fold into the chickpeas. If using earthenware, serve hot in the dish, or transfer to individual plates.

Spicy Pimientos **Ⓥ***

Pimientos Picantes

MAKES 6 SERVINGS

What makes these red bell peppers especially good is that they are slow cooked, which brings out the intensity of their flavor. If you want to avoid roasting and peeling the fresh bell peppers, you can substitute canned or jarred piquillo *peppers, which are red peppers that are cone-shaped and have a sweet, spicy flavor. They work just as well and can be found in specialty stores. The addition of cayenne pepper makes this dish quite spicy. Make this vegetarian with vegetable broth.*

4 medium red bell peppers or 8 to 10 (jarred) piquillo
  peppers, drained

2 to 3 tablespoons chicken, vegetable broth, or water

2 tablespoons olive oil

4 garlic cloves, lightly smashed

¼ teaspoon ground cayenne pepper

Kosher or sea salt

1. Preheat the oven to 500°F. Place the bell peppers in roasting pan and roast 20 minutes, turning once, 20 minutes or until the skin has bubbled and charred. Transfer the bell peppers to a deep bowl, reserving the juices in the pan. Cover tightly with foil and let sit 15 minutes.

2. Meanwhile, deglaze the pan, adding the chicken broth, stirring, and scraping up any bits of flavor. Reserve.

3. Peel the bell peppers, remove the core and seeds, and cut each into 8 strips. Heat the oil in a medium skillet over low heat. Add the bell peppers, garlic, cayenne pepper, and salt and cook, stirring, about 3 minutes. Add the reserved broth, cover, and cook 5 minutes more. Let cool. Serve at room temperature.

Fried Salted Almonds ⓥ
Almendras Fritas

MAKES 4 TO 6 SERVINGS

The best fried almonds I have ever tasted came from Sevilla, where frying takes precedence over any other method of preparation. Almond trees thrive in many parts of Spain, and almonds are a typical part of a tapa assortment. Some bars serve them complimentary, knowing full well that the saltiness will cause the patrons to order more drinks.

Mild olive oil, for frying

4 ounces blanched almonds, such as Spanish
  Marcona (about ⅓ cup)

Kosher or sea salt

Heat at least ½ inch of oil in a small skillet over medium-high heat (or better still, use a deep fryer set at 365°F) until it turns a cube of bread light brown in 60 seconds. Place the almonds in the oil and cook until lightly golden. Transfer with a slotted spoon to paper towels and let drain. Season with salt and serve hot.

Mushrooms Stuffed with Lemon ⓥ
Champiñones Rellenos con Limón

MAKES 6 SERVINGS

The strong lemon flavor in this easy-to-prepare tapa is very popular.

12 stuffing mushrooms, rinsed and trimmed

2 tablespoons olive oil plus more, for brushing

1 lemon

1 medium sweet onion, such as Vidalia, finely
  chopped

Kosher or sea salt

Freshly ground black pepper

6 tablespoons bread crumbs

2 tablespoons grated aged Manchego or Parmesan
  cheese

2 tablespoons finely chopped fresh flat-leaf parsley

1. Remove the stems and chop finely. Brush the caps with oil. Grate the lemon zest, then squeeze the juice (you will need about 3 tablespoons). Reserve.

2. Preheat the oven to 400°F. Heat the oil in a large skillet over medium heat. Add the onion and mushroom stems and cook, stirring, until softened, about 8 minutes. Season with salt and pepper. Continue cooking until no liquid remains and remove from the heat. Stir in the bread crumbs, lemon juice and zest, cheese, and parsley and mix well. Fill each mushroom cap with the stem mixture. Arrange in a baking dish and bake 15 to 20 minutes or until softened. Serve hot.

Pork-Stuffed Mushrooms
Champiñones Rellenos

MAKES 4 SERVINGS

Almost every tapas bar in Spain has some version of stuffed mushrooms on their menu. They are particularly tasty when stuffed with pork, as in this one filled with a mixture of pork and pine nuts.

¾ pound large mushrooms, rinsed and trimmed

Fresh lemon juice

5 tablespoons unsalted butter

3 tablespoons finely chopped onion

1 garlic clove, mashed in a garlic press or mortar

¼ pound lean ground pork

Salt

Freshly ground black pepper

3 tablespoons bread crumbs

½ teaspoon brandy, such as Spanish brandy or Cognac

1 tablespoon finely chopped fresh flat-leaf parsley

1 tablespoon chopped pine nuts

1. Remove the mushroom stems and chop finely, reserving ½ cup for this recipe and the rest for another use. Sprinkle the caps with lemon juice. Reserve.

2. Heat 4 tablespoons of the butter in a medium skillet over low heat. Add the onion and garlic and cook, stirring, until the onion is wilted and transparent, about 5 minutes. Add the pork and cook, breaking it up and sprinkling with salt and pepper, until it loses its color. Add the mushroom stems and cook 3 minutes more. Remove from the heat. Stir in the bread crumbs, brandy, parsley, pine nuts, and more salt and pepper if necessary.

3. Preheat the oven to 350°F. Fill each of the mushroom caps with the stem mixture and dot with butter. Arrange in a baking dish and bake 15 minutes. Serve hot.

Mushrooms Segovia Style
Champiñones a la Segoviana

MAKES 4 SERVINGS

The province of Segovia is famous for its delectable suckling pigs, so it is no wonder that this regional recipe for mushrooms includes bacon.

¼ cup small cubes (¼ inch) slab bacon

1 garlic clove, finely chopped

1 tablespoon finely chopped fresh flat-leaf parsley

½ pound mushrooms, rinsed, trimmed, and halved or quartered

¼ cup dry white wine

Salt

Freshly ground black pepper

Place the bacon in a medium skillet and heat over medium heat. Cook, stirring, until it begins to brown. Add the garlic, parsley, and mushrooms and cook, stirring, about 2 minutes more. Stir in the wine, salt, and pepper. Increase the heat to high and cook, stirring occasionally, until the liquid evaporates. Serve hot.

Mushrooms in Garlic Sauce
Champiñones al Ajillo

MAKES 4 TO 6 SERVINGS

Garlic sauce (alioli) *is beloved by Spaniards and is used for vegetables, seafood, and poultry. It is particularly well suited as a contrast to the subtle flavor of mushrooms, with a spicy accent of dried red chile pepper.*

3 tablespoons olive oil

3 garlic cloves, finely chopped

1½ teaspoons all-purpose flour

1 cup beef broth, chicken broth, or water

½ dried red chile pepper, seeded and cut into 3 pieces

2 tablespoons finely chopped fresh flat-leaf parsley

2 teaspoons fresh lemon juice

½ pound small (whole) or medium (halved) mushrooms, rinsed and trimmed

1. Heat 2 tablespoons of the oil in a medium skillet over medium heat. Add the garlic and cook until lightly golden and fragrant. Lower the heat if needed so the garlic does not brown. Stir the flour into the pan and cook 1 minute until it absorbs the oil. Slowly pour in the beef broth, stirring, then add the chile pepper, 1 tablespoon of the parsley, and the lemon juice. Continue to cook until the sauce is smooth and thickened.

2. In another medium skillet, heat the remaining 1 tablespoon oil over medium-high heat. Add the mushrooms and cook, stirring, until lightly browned. Add the mushrooms to the sauce and simmer 5 minutes. Sprinkle with the remaining 1 tablespoon parsley and serve hot.

Grilled Oyster Mushrooms with Oil and Garlic Ⓥ
Setas a la Parrilla con Aceite y Ajo

MAKES 4 SERVINGS

A very simple tapa that relies on the earthy flavor of oyster mushrooms, this is easy and fast to prepare.

1 pound oyster mushrooms, rinsed, trimmed, and separated into ears

2 tablespoons olive oil

2 garlic cloves, finely chopped

Kosher or sea salt

2 tablespoons finely chopped fresh flat-leaf parsley

Heat a greased stovetop griddle over high heat. Reduce the heat to medium, add the mushrooms, drizzle with the oil and sprinkle with the garlic, pressing the mushrooms with the back of a pancake turner to flatten. Turn, season with salt, and cook until tender. Sprinkle with the parsley and serve hot.

Spicy Potatoes Ⓥ
Patatas a la Brava

MAKES 4 SERVINGS

Bar Las Bravas, on Callejon del Gato, in Madrid has claimed for many years to have invented this classic tapa of fried potatoes with a spicy tomato sauce. When the dish became wildly popular and a signature Spanish dish, they obtained a patent, which is now framed and displayed at the bar. Some people like to serve the potatoes drizzled with the garlic sauce alioli.

3 tablespoons olive oil

3 medium potatoes, peeled and cut into ½-inch cubes

Kosher or sea salt

Freshly ground black pepper

2 tablespoons finely chopped onion

1 garlic clove, finely chopped

1 cup tomato sauce

¼ cup dry white wine

1 tablespoon finely chopped fresh flat-leaf parsley

½ dried red chile pepper, seeded and crushed

Dash of hot sauce, such as Tabasco

Garlic sauce (optional)

1. Heat 2 tablespoons of the oil in a large skillet over medium heat. Add the potatoes and cook until well browned on all sides. Season with salt and pepper. Cover, reduce the heat to low, and cook until tender, about 20 minutes more.

2. Meanwhile, in a medium saucepan, heat the remaining 1 tablespoon oil over medium heat. Add the onion and garlic and cook, stirring, until the onion is wilted and transparent, about 3 minutes. Stir in the tomato sauce, wine, parsley, chile pepper, hot sauce, salt, and pepper. Cook, stirring occasionally, about 20 minutes—the sauce should be thick. Lightly coat the potatoes with the tomato sauce. If using the garlic sauce, drizzle it lightly over the potatoes as well. Serve hot.

Potato Chips with Octopus and Garlic Sauce

Patatas "Chips" con Pulpo y Alioli

Octopus is a most popular staple in Galicia and seen in every bar in the region. I saw this tapa in Santiago de Compostela at a bar frequented by students from the local university.

PREPARE AT LEAST 2 HOURS IN ADVANCE

½ recipe Garlic Sauce (alioli; page 284)

¼ pound octopus, cleaned

1 medium potato, peeled and thinly sliced

Olive oil, for frying

1 garlic clove, thinly sliced

1 tablespoon ground hot paprika, such as Spanish smoked

2 teaspoons ground sweet paprika, such as Spanish smoked

Kosher or sea salt

1. Prepare the sauce. Before cooking the octopus, tenderize it by throwing it with force into the kitchen sink. Repeat at least 10 times. Bring a large saucepan of water to a boil over high heat. Submerge the octopus in the water and remove it immediately. Repeat 2 more times. Return the octopus to the pot, reduce the heat to low, cover, and simmer until tender, 1¾ to 3 hours. Cut the body into slices and the tentacles into thin medallions and reserve.

2. Heat at least ½ inch of oil in a small skillet over medium-high heat (or better still, use a deep fryer set at 375°F) until it quickly browns a cube of bread. Add the potatoes one at a time to prevent sticking. Season with salt. Cook, turning occasionally, until golden. Transfer with a slotted spoon to paper towels and let drain.

3. On each potato chip, place a little garlic sauce, then 1 garlic slice, and 1 octopus slice. Season with the paprikas and salt. Serve hot.

Figs Wrapped in Ham with Soft Cheese

Brevas con Jamón y Torta de la Serena

MAKES 8 SERVINGS

This tapa combines three of the most common ingredients in the region of Extremadura: figs, torta de la Serena—a soft sheep's milk cheese—and ham. A great combination.

8 figs, halved

16 small pieces Torta de la Serena or Brie cheese, softened and rind removed

8 very thin slices Serrano (Spanish cured mountain) ham or prosciutto, cut in half

Balsamic vinegar

Roll each piece of ham and place on top of 1 fig half. Add 1 piece of cheese and secure with a toothpick. Sprinkle with the vinegar and serve at room temperature.

Batter-Fried Onion Rings ⓥ

Anillos de Cebolla

MAKES 4 TO 5 SERVINGS

Yellow Spanish onion works best for this recipe. Children particularly love onion rings.

½ cup milk

2 large eggs

1 large Spanish (yellow) onion, peeled, cut into ½-inch slices, and separated into rings

All-purpose flour, for dredging

Kosher or sea salt

Olive oil, for frying

1. In a medium bowl, whisk together the milk and eggs. Add the onions and let sit 10 minutes. In a small shallow bowl, combine the flour and salt. Remove the onions from the milk-egg mixture and dredge in the flour. Place on a platter and let sit 10 minutes more.

2. Heat at least ½ inch of oil in a medium skillet over medium-high heat (or better still, use a deep fryer set at 365°F) until it turns a cube of bread light brown in 60 seconds. Place the onions in the oil in a single layer. (Cook in batches if needed to avoid overcrowding.) Cook, turning once, until golden. Transfer with a slotted offset spatula to paper towels and let drain. Serve hot.

Broiled Asparagus with Brie Ⓥ
Espárragos con Brie a la Parrilla

MAKES 6 SERVINGS

Here is another elegant tapa that can be assembled within minutes.

30 very thin cooked asparagus, rinsed and trimmed
6 thin slices Brie cheese, rind removed
Grated aged Manchego or Parmesan cheese
¾ teaspoon ground sweet paprika, such as Spanish smoked
Extra-virgin olive oil, for drizzling

Place a broiler rack about 6 inches from the heat source and preheat the broiler. (Cover the broiler pan with foil for easier cleanup, if you like.) Arrange the asparagus on a broiler pan in groups of five with their bottom ends together and the tips spreading out like a fan. Place 1 slice Brie across the center of each asparagus fan. Sprinkle with the grated cheese and paprika and drizzle with oil. Broil until the cheese is melted, about 1 minute. Do not brown. Transfer to individual serving plates, maintaining the fan shape, and serve hot.

Deep-Fried Leeks Ⓥ
Crujiente de Puerros

MAKES 4 SERVINGS

These simple leeks are easy to prepare but very delicious.

2 leeks (white part only), trimmed and well washed
All-purpose flour, for dredging
Olive oil, for frying
Kosher or sea salt

Cut the leeks lengthwise in half and separate into single layers. Heat at least ½ inch of oil in a large skillet over medium-high heat (or better still, use a deep fryer set at 365°F) until it turns a cube of bread light brown in 60 seconds. Place the flour on a large plate. Dredge each leek in the flour and place in the oil. (Cook in batches if needed to avoid overcrowding.) Cook, turning once, until crisp. Transfer with a slotted offset spatula to paper towels and let drain. Season with salt. Serve hot.

Cooked Meat Dishes

Spicy Pork Skewers
Pincho Moruno

MAKES 4 SERVINGS

These Moorish-style miniature pork kabobs heavily seasoned with cumin and paprika are a very popular Spanish tapa. The best version I have ever tasted came from the Bar Espuela on the Plaza Santa Ana in Madrid, prepared by Hamed de Melilla, the self proclaimed "Shish Kabob King."

PREPARE SEVERAL HOURS IN ADVANCE

6 tablespoons olive oil

½ teaspoon dried thyme

¾ teaspoon ground cumin

½ teaspoon ground bittersweet paprika, such as Spanish smoked

1 teaspoon crushed red pepper

1 bay leaf, crumbled

1 tablespoon finely chopped fresh flat-leaf parsley

Kosher or sea salt

Freshly ground black pepper

1 pound lean pork, cut into ¾- to 1-inch pieces

1. Mix all the ingredients in a medium bowl. Cover and let marinate in the refrigerator overnight, stirring occasionally.

2. Place a broiler rack about 6 inches from the heat source and preheat the broiler. (Cover the broiler pan with foil for easier cleanup, if you like.) Thread the pork onto small skewers and place on a broiler pan. Broil until browned but still juicy, basting with the marinade and turning once. Serve hot.

Marinated Pork Loin
Lomo de Orza

MAKES 6 SERVINGS

Whenever my husband Luis and I travel from Madrid to Barcelona, we always stop for tapas in the old Arab town of Catatayud, where the main street is lined with innumerable tapas bars. This recipe for pork, cooked, then preserved in an oil marinade, is one of the local specialties. Each slice of pork should be cut into ¼-inch strips, then drizzled with the marinade.

PREPARE 24 HOURS IN ADVANCE

¼ pound lean boneless pork loin, cut into 1-inch-thick slices

Kosher or sea salt

Freshly ground black pepper

1 cup plus 2 tablespoons extra-virgin olive oil

1 tablespoon fresh lemon juice

1½ teaspoons finely chopped fresh thyme or ¼ teaspoon dried thyme

¾ teaspoon finely chopped fresh rosemary or ⅛ teaspoon dried rosemary

4 garlic cloves, lightly smashed

1. Season the pork with salt and pepper. Heat 2 tablespoons of the oil in a medium skillet over medium-high heat. Add the pork and cook, turning once, until browned on both sides. Reduce the heat to medium and cook until no longer pink in the center but still juicy, 3 to 5 minutes more. Do not let the pork get dry. Transfer to a shallow earthenware casserole dish in which the slices fit snugly.

2. Add the remaining 1 cup oil to the casserole dish. (The oil should just cover the pork. Depending on the size of your dish, you may need a little more or less.) In a small bowl, combine the juice, thyme, rosemary, garlic, salt, and pepper then drizzle it over the pork and shake the dish a couple of

times to distribute. Cover with foil and let marinate in the refrigerator 24 hours.

3. Remove the pork from the marinade. Cut the slices on the bias into ¼-inch strips and drizzle with the remaining marinade. Serve chilled or at room temperature.

Chorizo Simmered in White Wine
Chorizo al Vino Blanco

MAKES 4 SERVINGS

The wine lends a special depth of flavor to the chorizo in this simple and tasty dish.

1 pound (8 links) chorizo
2 cups dry white wine

Place the chorizo and wine in a shallow earthenware casserole dish or Dutch oven. Prick the chorizo links with a fork. Bring the wine to a boil over high heat. Reduce the heat to low and cook, stirring occasionally, until the wine has been absorbed and reduces a bit and the chorizo is cooked through, about 10 minutes. If using earthenware, serve hot in the dish, or transfer to a platter and cut into chunks.

Pork Ribs in Garlic Sauce
Costillas al Ajillo

MAKES 4 SERVINGS

Here pork, such a popular meat in Spain, is cooked with another beloved ingredient, garlic.

1¾ pounds pork spare ribs, smallest available
3 tablespoons olive oil
½ cup chicken broth or vegetable broth
1 bay leaf

1 large garlic clove
1 tablespoon finely chopped fresh flat-leaf parsley
Kosher or sea salt
Freshly ground black pepper

1. Cut the pork into individual ribs, then cut each rib crosswise into 2-inch pieces. Heat the oil in a deep earthenware casserole dish or Dutch oven over medium heat. Add the ribs and cook, turning occasionally, until browned on all sides. Reduce the heat to low, Add the broth and bay leaf, cover, and simmer 45 minutes. Uncover and cook until most of the broth has evaporated. Skim off part of the fat, leaving about 2 tablespoons in the sauce, and discard.

2. In a mortar or mini-processor, mash the garlic, parsley, salt, and pepper. Stir into the ribs, cover, and let sit 2 minutes. (You may prepare the ribs in advance, but do not add the mortar mixture until the last minute.) Remove the bay leaf. If using earthenware, serve hot in the dish, or transfer to a platter.

Chorizo "Lollipops"
"Chupa Chups" de Chorizo

MAKES 16 TAPAS

A fun tapa with an unusual presentation, chorizo pieces are speared on a stick, as if they were lollipops, then coated with caramelized sugar. This recipe comes from master chef Jaume Sole, who owns Els Fogons de Can Llaudes Restaurant set in a centuries-old chapel in Catalunya.

3 ounces (1½ links) chorizo, skin removed and cut into ⅜-inch slices

½ cup sugar

2 tablespoons water

1 long-loaf (baguette) bread

1. On each of 16 (4- to 6-inch) skewers, thread 1 chorizo vertically, as if it were a lollipop.

2. Place the sugar and water in a heavy small saucepan and cook over medium heat, stirring occasionally, until the sugar dissolves. Increase the heat to medium-high and cook, without stirring, until the mixture turns light amber, occasionally brushing down the sides of the pan with a wet pastry brush and swirling the pan, about 6 minutes more. Remove from the heat.

3. Quickly dip each chorizo into the sugar and place the skewer end in the bread at an angle, being careful not to drip the hot sugar onto your hands. Let cool and snap off any sugar drippings. Place the bread on a tray and serve.

Chorizo and Apples in Hard Cider Sauce
Chorizo a la Sidra

MAKES 4 SERVINGS

Sidra—hard, dry apple cider—is the most popular drink in Asturias as well as a common liquid for cooking. Apple orchards abound in this area, and cider has found its way into many Asturian recipes. I suggest you use the hard cider commonly found in U.S. liquor stores. In this tapa, the sweetness of the apple slices is the perfect contrast to the heavily spiced chorizo *sausage.*

½ pound (4 links) chorizo

2 apples, peeled, cored, and cut into ½-inch slices

1 cup hard cider

Place the chorizo, apples, and ½ cup of the cider in a small skillet and bring to a boil over high heat. Reduce the heat to low, cover, and cook 15 minutes, adding the remaining 1½ cups cider a little at a time as the liquid evaporates. Slice the chorizo and serve with the apples and sauce. Serve hot.

Fresh Ham with Orange and Walnut Sauce
Jamón Fresco con Mermelada de Naranja y Nueces

MAKES 6 SERVINGS

My husband and I were in the old Castilian city of Burgo de Osma when we stopped into the Virrey Palafox restaurant and tasted this exceptional tapa. The sweet orange and walnut sauce is the perfect complement to the savory flavor of fresh ham.

¾ cup orange marmalade, such as imported English

1 tablespoon raisins

2 pitted prunes, cut into small pieces

¼ cup broken walnut meats

3 tablespoons fresh orange juice

1 tablespoon water

6 (¼-inch) slices ham

In a small saucepan, combine ¼ cup of the marmalade, the raisins, and prunes and bring to a simmer over low heat, stirring occasionally. Cover and simmer 10 minutes. Uncover and simmer stirring occasionally, about 5 minutes more. Let cool. Stir in the remaining ½ cup marmalade, the walnuts, juice, and water. Arrange the ham attractively on a serving platter and place the sauce in a small serving bowl. Serve at room temperature.

Beef Tenderloin Tips in Garlic Sauce

Puntitas de Solomillo al Ajillo "Sol y Sombra"

MAKES 4 SERVINGS

Sol y Sombra is a lively Andalusian tapas bar in the Triana section of Seville across the Guadalquivir River. The mood is always festive with flamenco music blasting, bullfighting memorabilia adorning the walls, sawdust on the floor, and cured hams and dried peppers hanging from the ceiling. This dish of tenderloin tips in garlic sauce (alioli) is one of their house specialties.

3 tablespoons fruity olive oil

8 garlic cloves, lightly smashed

¾ pound beef tenderloin tips or steak, cut into 1-inch pieces

Kosher or sea salt

1 tablespoon dry sherry, such as Fino

Heat the oil in a medium skillet over medium-high heat. Add the garlic and beef and cook, stirring, until browned and done as desired. Add salt, stir in the sherry, and transfer to an earthenware casserole dish. Deglaze the skillet, adding several tablespoons of water, stirring, and scraping up any bits of flavor. Stir into the mixture into the casserole dish. If using earthenware, serve hot in the dish, or transfer to a platter.

Sausage Rolled in Cabbage Leaves

Repollo Relleno de Salchicha

MAKES 16 TAPAS

A wonderful tapa in which the savory flavor of sausage is contrasted by the sweetness of the cabbage leaves, these are best when served immediately.

8 cabbage leaves

1 pound sausage links (about 8 sausages)

2 large eggs, lightly beaten

All-purpose flour, for dredging

Olive oil, for frying

1. Place the cabbage leaves in a small saucepan with water to cover. Bring to a boil over high heat, reduce the heat to medium, and cook until tender, about 15 minutes. Drain. Cut each leaf in half lengthwise.

2. Meanwhile, place the sausage in a medium skillet over medium heat and cook, turning occasionally, until browned. Do not overcook. Cut each leaf in half crosswise.

3. Heat at least ½ inch of oil in a medium skillet over medium-high heat (or better still, use a deep fryer set at 365°F) until it turns a cube of bread light brown in 60 seconds. Place the eggs and flour in separate shallow bowls. Wrap each cabbage leaf around 1 sausage, folding in the sides, then rolling up. Dip in the egg, dredge in the flour, and place in the oil. Cook, turning occasionally, until golden. Let drain on paper towels. Serve hot.

Pork Meatballs
Albóndigas de Cerdo

MAKES 20 TAPAS

These small, well seasoned pork meatballs are delicious on their own but even better with garlic sauce (alioli).

2 garlic cloves, mashed in a garlic press or mortar (optional)

Mayonnaise (mayonesa, page 359), to taste (optional)

All-purpose flour, for dredging

2 large eggs, lightly beaten

½ pound ground pork loin

7 tablespoons finely chopped fresh flat-leaf parsley

2 garlic cloves, finely chopped

1 tablespoon finely chopped onion

3 tablespoons bread crumbs

Salt

Freshly ground black pepper

Olive oil, for frying

1. In a small bowl, mix the garlic and mayonnaise, if using, until well blended. Let sit to meld flavors until needed.

2. Place the flour in a shallow bowl and beat I of the eggs in another shallow bowl. In a medium bowl, combine the pork, parsley, garlic, onion, bread crumbs, the beaten egg, salt, and pepper. Shape into I-inch balls.

3. Heat at least ½ inch of oil in a medium skillet over medium-high heat (or better still, use a deep fryer set at 365°F) until it turns a cube of bread light brown in 60 seconds. Beat the remaining I egg in the same shallow bowl. Dip each pork meatball into the egg, dredge in the flour, and place in the oil. Reduce the heat to medium and cook, turning occasionally, until well browned on both sides. Let drain on paper towels. Serve the pork hot with the sauce on the side.

Tiny Meatballs in Saffron Sauce
Albondiguitas al Azafrán

MAKES 5 TO 6 SERVINGS

Distinctively flavored saffron sauce make these wonderful tiny meatballs of veal and pork a special treat that is most likely of Moorish origin. You may prepare them several hours in advance and reheat, but I suggest waiting to add the saffron mixture just before serving.

1 thin slice sandwich-style bread

Milk or water, for soaking

½ pound ground veal

½ pound ground pork

2 garlic cloves, finely chopped

2 tablespoons finely chopped fresh flat-leaf parsley

1 large egg, lightly beaten

1½ teaspoons kosher or sea salt

Freshly ground black pepper

All-purpose flour, for dredging

2 tablespoons olive oil

2 tablespoons finely chopped onion

¼ teaspoon ground paprika, such as Spanish smoked

½ cup veal broth, chicken broth, or vegetable broth

2 tablespoons white wine

Several threads of saffron

Finely chopped fresh flat-leaf parsley, for garnish

1. Cut the crust off the bread and discard, then soak the bread in milk or water and squeeze dry. In a medium bowl, combine the veal, pork, half of the garlic, I tablespoon of the parsley, the egg, bread, the I½ teaspoons salt, and pepper. Shape into I-inch balls. Place the flour in a small shallow bowl. Dredge each meatball in the flour.

2. Over medium heat, heat the oil in a shallow earthenware casserole dish or Dutch oven large enough for all the meatballs to fit in one layer. Add the meatballs and cook, turning occasionally, until

browned on all sides. Add the onion and cook, stirring, until wilted and transparent, about 3 minutes more. Sprinkle in the paprika and cook 1 minute more. Stir in the broth and wine and bring to a boil. Reduce the heat to low, cover, and simmer 40 minutes more.

3. Meanwhile, in a mortar or mini-processor, mash the remaining half of the garlic, the remaining 1 tablespoon parsley, the saffron, and a pinch of salt. Stir into the meatballs and sprinkle with parsley. If using earthenware, serve hot in the dish, or transfer to a platter.

Meatballs in Semisweet Sherry
Albóndigas al Oloroso

MAKES 6 TO 8 SERVINGS

The aroma of the Oloroso sherry is unmistakable and lends the meatballs a special flavor.

2 pounds ground pork

3 large eggs, lightly beaten

5 garlic cloves, finely chopped

1 shallot, finely chopped

2 medium onions, finely chopped (about 1⅓ cups)

Bread crumbs

⅛ teaspoon grated or ground nutmeg

Kosher or sea salt

All-purpose flour, for dredging

5 tablespoons olive oil

½ cup medium sweet sherry, such as Oloroso

1. In a large bowl, combine the meat, eggs, garlic, shallot, half of the onions, the bread crumbs, nutmeg, and salt. Shape into 1-inch balls. Place the flour in a small shallow bowl. Dredge each meatball in the flour.

2. Over medium heat, heat 3 tablespoons of the oil in a shallow earthenware casserole dish or Dutch oven large enough for all the meatballs to fit in one layer. Add the meatballs and cook, turning occasionally, until browned on all sides. Reserve.

3. Heat the remaining 2 tablespoons oil in a small skillet over medium heat. Add the remaining half of the onions and cook, stirring, until wilted and transparent, about 5 minutes. Add the sherry, bring to a boil, and cook, stirring occasionally, until reduced, about 10 minutes more. Add to the meatballs, bring to a simmer over low heat, and simmer 5 minutes more. If using earthenware, serve hot in the dish, or transfer to a platter.

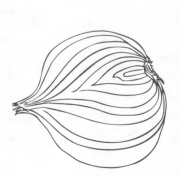
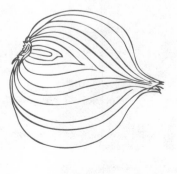

Meatballs Filled with Cheese in Green and Red Pepper Sauce

Albóndigas Rellenas de Queso en Salsa de Pimientos

MAKES 6 TO 8 SERVINGS

Here's a unique spin on albóndigas, *the small meatballs featured at just about every tapas bar in Spain. In this version, the ground pork and veal meatballs are filled with a cube of soft cheese and served over a green and red bell pepper sauce. They are often accompanied by crispy tempura vegetables, which make this a truly exceptional dish.*

1 slice sandwich-style bread, crust removed

Milk, for soaking

3 tablespoons olive oil

¾ cup finely chopped onion

3 tablespoons finely chopped Serrano (Spanish cured mountain) ham or prosciutto

½ pound ground veal

½ pound ground pork

1 large egg, lightly beaten

1½ teaspoons Kosher or sea salt

Generous amount of freshly ground black pepper

2 tablespoons finely chopped fresh flat-leaf parsley

1 medium red bell pepper, finely chopped (about 1 cup)

1 medium green bell pepper, finely chopped (about 1 cup)

1 garlic clove, finely chopped

¼ cup finely chopped onion

¼ pound soft mild cheese, such as mozzarella, cut into ½-inch cubes

All-purpose flour, for dredging

½ teaspoon ground bittersweet paprika, such as Spanish smoked

1½ teaspoons finely chopped fresh thyme or ¼ teaspoon dried thyme

½ cup dry white wine

¼ cup chicken broth or vegetable broth

Tempura Vegetables (optional)

2 cups water

Salt

12 to 16 (⅛-inch) crosswise slices baby eggplant, sprinkled with salt and drained

1 recipe Batter (from Batter-Fried Squid Tentacles, page 42)

12 to 16 (⅛-inch) crosswise slices baby zucchini

1. Soak the bread in the milk and squeeze dry. Over medium heat, heat 1 tablespoon of the oil in a large shallow earthenware casserole dish or Dutch oven large enough for all the meatballs to fit in one layer. Add ½ cup of the onion and the ham and cook, stirring, until the onion is wilted and transparent, about 5 minutes. Transfer to a large bowl and wipe out the casserole dish. Add the veal, pork, egg, salt, pepper, the bread, and 1 tablespoon of the parsley to the bowl with the onion-ham mixture and mix well. Reserve.

2. Heat another 1 tablespoon of the oil in the casserole dish over medium heat. Add the bell peppers, garlic, and the remaining ¼ cup onion and cook, stirring, until the peppers are softened, about 8 minutes. Transfer to a medium bowl, reserve, and wipe out the casserole dish.

3. Shape the meat around each cube of cheese to form a 1¼-inch ball that encloses the cheese. Dredge lightly in the flour. Heat the remaining 1 tablespoon oil in the casserole dish over medium heat. Add the meatballs and cook, turning occasionally, until browned on all sides.

4. Return the pepper mixture to the casserole dish, stir in the paprika and thyme, and pour in the wine and broth. Season with salt and pepper. Bring to a boil over medium-high heat, reduce the heat to low, cover, and simmer 45 minutes. Transfer the meatballs to a warm platter and pass the sauce through a strainer into a small bowl. (May be prepared ahead.) Reserve.

5. Meanwhile, prepare the tempura vegetables, if using: In a medium bowl, mix the water and salt. Add the eggplant and let soak 30 minutes. Drain and let dry on paper towels.

6. Prepare the batter, if using, as instructed in step 1 of Batter-Fried Squid Tentacles. Heat at least ½ inch of oil in a large skillet over medium-high heat (or better still, use a deep fryer set at 365°F) until it turns a cube of bread light brown in 60 seconds. Dip each vegetable in the batter and place in the oil. (Cook in batches if needed to avoid overcrowding.) Cook until golden. Transfer with a slotted spoon to paper towels and let drain.

7. Pour the sauce onto a platter or onto individual dishes, and place the meatballs in the sauce. If garnishing with the tempura vegetables, arrange them over the dish, sprinkle with parsley, and serve hot.

Partridge Meatballs
Albóndigas de Perdiz

MAKES 6 TO 8 SERVINGS

Partridge meatballs with cheese are an interesting twist, bathed in a savory sauce of garlic, onion, bell pepper, and wine.

2 tablespoons olive oil

¼ cup finely chopped onion

¼ cup finely chopped green bell pepper

2 garlic cloves, finely chopped

1 bay leaf

½ cup chicken broth or vegetable broth

2 tablespoons dry white wine

¼ cup bread crumbs

Milk, for soaking

1 partridge or 2 quail, boned and meat finely chopped

2 slices mild cheese, finely chopped

1 large egg

1 tablespoon finely chopped fresh flat-leaf parsley

Kosher or sea salt

Freshly ground black pepper

1 garlic clove, finely chopped

All-purpose flour, for dredging

1. Heat 1 tablespoon of the oil in a medium skillet over medium heat. Add the onion, bell pepper, 2 chopped garlic cloves, and bay leaf and cook, stirring, until the onion is softened, about 5 minutes. Stir in the broth and wine, reduce the heat to low, cover, and simmer 1 hour. Remove the bay leaf.

2. Meanwhile, soak the bread crumbs in the milk until softened and squeeze dry. In a medium bowl, combine the partridge, cheese, egg, parsley, bread crumbs, salt, pepper, and 1 garlic clove. Shape into 1-inch balls. Place the flour in a small shallow bowl. Dredge each meatball in the flour.

3. In a shallow earthenware casserole dish or Dutch oven large enough for all the meatballs to fit in one layer, heat the remaining 1 tablespoon oil over medium heat. Add the meatballs and cook, turning occasionally, until browned on all sides and cooked through. Spoon the sauce over the meatballs. If using earthenware, serve hot in the dish, or transfer to a platter.

Lamb Meatballs in Brandy Sauce
Albóndigas "Sant Climent"

MAKES 8 TO 10 SERVINGS

Many years ago, I found this recipe for these unusual lamb meatballs in brandy sauce in Tahull, a quaint village high up in the Pyrenees Mountains. It is still today one of my favorites. This may be prepared several hours or a day in advance, stored covered in the refrigerator, and then reheated. (The flavor actually improves.)

continues . . .

1 pound ground lamb

1 large egg

2 garlic cloves, mashed in a garlic press or mortar

2 tablespoons finely chopped fresh flat-leaf parsley

Kosher or sea salt

1 tablespoon coarsely ground black pepper

½ cup bread crumbs

2 tablespoons dry red wine

1 tablespoon olive oil

1 small onion, finely chopped (about ⅓ cup)

2 tablespoons brandy

4½ teaspoons tomato sauce

½ cup low-sodium beef or lamb broth

1. In a medium bowl, combine the lamb, egg, garlic, parsley, salt, and pepper. In another medium bowl, soak the bread crumbs in the wine. Add the crumb mixture to the lamb mixture and mix well. Shape into about 30 (1-inch) balls.

2. Over high heat, heat the oil in a shallow earthenware casserole dish or Dutch oven large enough for all the meatballs to fit in one layer. Add the meatballs and cook, turning occasionally, until browned on all sides. Add the onion and cook, stirring, until wilted and transparent. Add the brandy and, standing well away from the casserole dish, ignite the liquid with a match or kitchen lighter, and stir until the flames die out.

3. Stir in the tomato sauce and broth and season with salt. Reduce the heat to low, cover, and simmer 45 minutes. If using earthenware, serve hot in the dish, or transfer to a platter.

Pork Tenderloin with Tomato and Onion Salad
Escarapuches

MAKES 6 TO 8 SERVINGS

While traveling through Extremadura near the frontier with Portugal, in an area of Spain with a

very small population, we could not find a place to have lunch. Finally we arrived in the small village of Barcarrota and found a bar in the main square where we were served these escarapuches, something unknown to us. They were delicious and since then have become a favorite at home.

2 medium ripe tomatoes, cut into ½-inch cubes

1 large onion, slivered (about

1 garlic clove, finely chopped

¼ cup extra-virgin olive oil

1 teaspoon red wine vinegar or sherry vinegar

¼ teaspoon ground cumin

1 tablespoon finely chopped fresh flat-leaf parsley

3 tablespoons dry white wine

¼ teaspoon dried oregano

¼ teaspoon dried thyme

6 peppercorns, smashed

¼ teaspoon red pepper flakes

Kosher or sea salt

1 bay leaf, crumbled

1½ to 2 pounds pork tenderloin

In a medium bowl, combine all the ingredients except the pork and let sit 5 minutes. Cut the pork into ½-inch-thick strips, then cut each strip crosswise into 1-inch pieces. Heat a greased stovetop griddle over high heat. Add the pork and cook, turning once, until no longer pink in the center. Place the pork on a platter and place the tomato salad on top of the pork, removing the bay leaf. Serve hot.

Chicken in Garlic Sauce
Pollo en Salsa de Ajo

MAKES 4 TO 6 SERVINGS

Pollo al ajillo is so popular in Spain that it is featured on just about every menu. For this tapas version of the dish, you can either use chicken wings or a whole chicken cut into bite-size pieces.

8 chicken wings or half of a 3-pound chicken
   cut into tapas-size portions

¼ cup olive oil

8 large garlic cloves

1 tablespoon brandy

½ teaspoon all-purpose flour

2 tablespoons dry white wine

2 tablespoons chicken broth or vegetable broth

Kosher or sea salt

1 tablespoon finely chopped fresh flat-leaf parsley

Few threads of saffron

3 peppercorns

1. Remove and discard the wing tips and split the rest of the wings into two parts. Heat the oil in a large skillet over medium heat. Add the chicken and garlic and cook, stirring the garlic, until the garlic is golden (remove each garlic clove as it turns golden and transfer to a mortar) and the chicken browned on all sides. Add the brandy and, standing well away from the skillet, ignite the brandy with a match or kitchen lighter and let die out. Sprinkle in the flour and stir in the wine, broth, and salt. Reduce the heat to low, cover, and simmer 15 minutes more.

2. In the mortar, mash the reserved garlic, the parsley, saffron, peppercorns, and salt. Stir this mixture into the chicken, cover, and cook 15 minutes more. Serve hot.

Quail with Pearl Onions and Pine Nuts
Codornices con Cebolletas y Piñones

MAKES 4 SERVINGS

This delicious preparation of quail makes an excellent tapa, but it is also substantial enough to be a main course. Because of their small size, I like to serve quail in individual casserole dishes.

2 quail, each butterflied (split in half)

Kosher or sea salt

2 tablespoons olive oil

8 pearl onions, halved lengthwise

2 medium carrots, peeled and thinly sliced

1 garlic clove, finely chopped

2 tablespoons finely chopped (jarred) piquillo
   pepper or pimiento

½ cup dry white wine

¼ cup chicken broth or vegetable broth

2 tablespoons pine nuts

1 tablespoon finely chopped fresh flat-leaf parsley

1 tablespoon finely chopped fresh thyme or
   ½ teaspoon dried thyme

1 bay leaf

Freshly ground black pepper

1. Season the quail with salt. Heat the oil in a shallow earthenware casserole dish or Dutch oven over medium heat. Add the quail and cook, turning once, until browned on both sides. Transfer to a platter. Add the onions, carrots, and garlic to the casserole dish. Reduce the heat to low, cover, and cook until the onions are tender. (May be prepared ahead.) Return the quail and any juices to the casserole dish and add the piquillo peppers, wine, broth, pine nuts, parsley, thyme, bay leaf, salt, and pepper. Cover and cook 15 to 20 minutes more or until the quail are just tender.

2. Transfer the quail to a warm serving platter (or individual casserole dishes). Cook the sauce 1 to 2 minutes more. Remove the bay leaf. Pour over the quail and serve hot.

Fried Ham and Cheese Sandwiches
Emparedados de Jamón y Queso

MAKES 8 TAPAS

My mother-in-law always used to make these delicious fried ham and cheese sandwiches for my husband Luis when he was a child growing up in Madrid. To this day, they remain one of his favorites. They're best when made with a mild cheese, such as Gouda or Jarlsberg.

¼ pound Serrano (Spanish cured mountain) ham or prosciutto, thinly sliced

¼ pound mild cheese, such as Gouda or Jarlsberg, thinly sliced

16 (⅜- to ½-inch) slices long-loaf (baguette) bread, preferably day old and not airy

½ cup milk

2 large eggs, lightly beaten

Olive oil, for frying

1. Fit several layers of ham on each of 8 bread slices, top with layers of cheese, and cover with the remaining bread.

2. Pour the milk into a flat-bottom dish. Briefly dip each sandwich into it, moistening both sides. Place on a dry platter and let sit 20 minutes.

3. Place the eggs in a shallow bowl. Heat at least ½ inch of oil in a large skillet over medium-high heat (or better still, use a deep fryer set at 365°F) until it turns a cube of bread light brown in 60 seconds. Dip both sides of each sandwich in the egg and place in the oil. Cook until golden on both sides, turning once. Transfer with a slotted spatula to paper towels and let drain. Serve hot.

Fried Cheese Balls
Delicias de Queso

MAKES ABOUT 26 TAPAS

Best when made with Swiss, Jarlsberg, or Gouda, these delicate cheese balls are a favorite of my grand-daughter Ruby. The nutmeg adds an earthy flavor.

2 large eggs, separated

½ cup milk

½ cup all-purpose flour

Salt

Freshly ground black pepper

Dash of grated or ground nutmeg

½ pound cheese, such as Swiss, Jarlsberg, or Gouda, coarsely grated

2 tablespoons grated Parmesan cheese

3 tablespoons finely chopped Serrano (Spanish cured mountain) ham or prosciutto

1 teaspoon finely chopped onion

Olive oil, for frying

1. In a small bowl, whisk the egg yolks until lightly colored. Stir in the milk, then gradually add the flour and whisk until smooth.

2. In another small bowl, whisk the egg whites until soft peaks form. Fold half of the yolk mixture into the whites, add the salt, pepper, nutmeg, cheeses, ham, and onion, and fold in the remaining yolk mixture.

3. Heat at least ½ inch of oil in a medium skillet over medium-high heat (or better still, use a deep fryer set at 365°F) until it turns a cube of bread light brown in 60 seconds. Drop the dough by rounded teaspoon into the oil. Cook, turning once, until just golden—do not overcook. Transfer with a slotted spoon to paper towels and let drain. Serve hot.

Soft Cheese Croquettes Ⓥ
Croquetas al Queso de la Serena

MAKES ABOUT 35 TAPAS

Croquetas, *beloved by children and adults alike, are found from the Basque provinces all the way down to Andalucía. They are made with a variety of ingredients, most commonly with chicken, ham, and codfish. These* croquetas, *from the region of Extremadura, use the local cheese, a soft sheep's milk cheese that has a very pleasant, mild flavor.*

5 tablespoons unsalted butter

1 tablespoon olive oil

¾ cup all-purpose flour

1¼ cups milk

Kosher or sea salt

Generous amount of freshly grated black pepper

Generous amount of freshly grated nutmeg

¼ pound La Serena, Brie, or Camembert cheese, rind removed

2 large eggs, lightly beaten

Bread crumbs, for dredging

Olive oil, for frying

I. Melt the butter in a small saucepan over medium heat. Add the flour and cook, stirring constantly, about 3 minutes. Gradually stir in the milk, salt, pepper, and nutmeg. Cook, stirring constantly, until thickened and smooth. Spread the mixture out on a dinner plate and let cool, then refrigerate until firm enough to handle.

2. Shape cheese mixture into 1¼-inch balls. Place the eggs and flour in separate shallow bowls. Heat at least 1 inch of oil in a large skillet over medium-high heat (or better still, use a deep fryer set at 365°F) until it turns a cube of bread light brown in 60 seconds. Dip each croquette in the egg, dredge in the bread crumbs, and place in the oil.

Cook, turning several times, until golden. Transfer with a slotted spoon to paper towels and let drain. Serve hot.

Zucchini Croquettes Ⓥ
Croquetas de Calabacín

MAKES ABOUT 20 TAPAS

Not a very common recipe for croquetas *because of its vegetable base, but these zucchini are very tasty and light.*

2 tablespoons unsalted butter

2 tablespoons olive oil

⅜ cup all-purpose flour

Kosher or sea salt

Freshly ground black pepper

¼ pound zucchini, coarsely grated

2 large eggs, lightly beaten

Bread crumbs, such as regular mixed with Japanese panko, for dredging

Olive oil, for frying

I. Heat the butter and oil in a medium saucepan over medium heat until the butter melts. Add the flour and cook, stirring constantly, until the sauce is thickened and smooth, about 3 minutes. Add the zucchini and cook, stirring occasionally, about 10 minutes more. Spread the mixture out on a dinner plate and let cool, then refrigerate until firm enough to handle.

2. Shape the zucchini mixture into 1-inch balls. Place the eggs and bread crumbs in separate shallow bowls. Heat at least 1 inch of oil in a large skillet over medium-high heat (or better still, use a deep fryer set at 365°F) until it turns a cube of bread light brown in 60 seconds. Dip each croquette in the egg, dredge in the bread crumbs, and place in the oil. Cook, turning several times, until golden. Transfer with a slotted spoon to paper towels and let drain. Serve hot.

Swiss Chard Croquettes Ⓥ
Croquetas de Acelgas

MAKES ABOUT 20 TAPAS

Acelgas, similar to Swiss chard, is a favorite vegetable for Spaniards prepared and eaten in many ways but not usually by itself. In this case, Swiss chard is used to make croquetas, *and the result is excellent.*

½ pound Swiss chard, well washed and thick stems trimmed

3 tablespoons olive oil

2 tablespoons unsalted butter

1 small onion, finely chopped (about ⅓ cup)

½ teaspoon dried oregano

Kosher or sea salt

Freshly ground black pepper

⅛ teaspoon ground nutmeg

2 large eggs, lightly beaten

⅜ cup all-purpose flour

Bread crumbs, such as regular mixed with Japanese panko, for dredging

Olive oil, for frying

1. Place the chard in a large saucepan with water to cover, add salt, and bring to a boil over high heat. Reduce the heat to medium, and cook until tender, about 15 minutes. Drain and chop finely.

2. Heat 1 tablespoon of the oil in a medium skillet over medium heat. Add the onion and cook until wilted, about 5 minutes. Add the chard, salt, pepper, and oregano and cook until the chard wilts and absorbs the seasonings.

3. Meanwhile, heat the butter and the remaining 2 tablespoons oil in a medium saucepan over medium heat until the butter melts. Add the flour and cook, stirring constantly, until the sauce is thickened and smooth, about 3 minutes. Add the chard and cook, stirring occasionally, about 10 minutes more.

Spread the mixture out on a dinner plate and let cool, then refrigerate until firm enough to handle.

4. Shape the chard mixture into 1-inch balls and dip in the beaten egg and coat with the crumbs. Place the eggs and bread crumbs in separate shallow bowls. Heat at least 1 inch of oil in a large skillet over medium-high heat (or better still, use a deep fryer set at 365°F) until it turns a cube of bread light brown in 60 seconds. Dip each croquette in the egg, dredge in the bread crumbs, and place in the oil. Cook, turning several times, until golden. Transfer with a slotted spoon to paper towels and let drain. Serve hot.

Eggplant Fritters Filled with Anchovies and Cheese
Buñuelos de Berenjena Rellenos de Anchoa y Queso

MAKES ABOUT 12 TAPAS

For this tapa a soft, flavorful goat cheese should be used.

3 baby eggplants, about ¼ pound each

1 tablespoon goat cheese (about 1 ounce)

6 small anchovy fillets, finely chopped

All-purpose flour, for dredging

Olive oil, for frying

1. Preheat the oven to 400°F. Lightly oil your hands and rub over the surface of each eggplant. Puncture the skin in a few places with a knife. Place in a roasting pan and bake, turning once, 35 to 40 minutes or until tender. Let cool, peel, and chop finely. Let sit to release any liquid.

2. In a small bowl, combine the cheese and anchovies. Using the eggplant 2 teaspoons at a time, shape into a ball and fill with about ¼ teaspoon of the cheese-anchovy mixture. Heat at least 1 inch of oil in a small skillet over medium-high heat (or

better still, use a deep fryer set at 365°F) until it turns a cube of bread light brown in 60 seconds. Dredge each fritter in the flour and place in the oil. Cook, turning several times, until golden. Transfer with a slotted spoon to paper towels and let drain. Serve hot.

Potato and Cheese Puffs Ⓥ
Buñuelos de Patata y Queso

MAKES ABOUT 18 TAPAS

This crunchy mixture of potatoes and cheese is delightful when served in a pastry puff and is a favorite of children and adults alike. Try to get a good Manchego, the quintessential Spanish cheese. Its characteristic strong flavor gives these buñuelos *a nice Spanish flair.*

1 pound potatoes

2 teaspoons olive oil

⅛ teaspoon lemon zest

3 tablespoons grated aged Manchego or Parmesan cheese

¼ teaspoon grated or ground nutmeg

1 tablespoon all-purpose flour

Kosher or sea salt

Freshly ground black pepper

1 tablespoon milk

1 large egg, lightly beaten

Bread crumbs, for dredging

Olive oil, for frying

1. Place the potatoes in a small saucepan and add cold water to cover and salt. Cover and bring to a simmer over low heat. Cook about 15 minutes or until tender when pierced with a knife. Drain well and let cool slightly. Peel. Pass through a ricer into a medium bowl. Stir in the 2 teaspoons oil, the lemon zest, cheese, nutmeg, flour, salt, and pepper. Stir in the milk and egg.

2. Shape the potato mixture into I-inch balls. Place the bread crumbs in a shallow bowl. Heat at least I inch of oil in a medium skillet over medium-high heat (or better still, use a deep fryer set at 365°F) until it turns a cube of bread light brown in 60 seconds. Dredge each puff in the bread crumbs and place in the oil. Cook, turning once with tongs, until golden. Transfer with a slotted spoon to paper towels and let drain. Serve hot.

Mushroom Croquettes with Apple Cider
Croquetas de Setas con Sidra de Manzana

MAKES ABOUT 35 TAPAS

Apple cider is the preferred drink in Asturias, the mountainous region in northern Spain, and it is also used profusely in cooking. Cider adds an unusual flavor to these mushroom croquettes.

6 tablespoons olive oil

10 medium mushrooms, such as oyster, rinsed, trimmed, and finely chopped

3 tablespoons unsalted butter

¾ cup all-purpose flour

1½ cups milk

¼ cup apple cider

¼ cup chicken broth or vegetable broth

Kosher or sea salt

Freshly ground black pepper

2 large eggs, lightly beaten

Bread crumbs, such as regular mixed with Japanese panko, for dredging

Olive oil, for frying

1. Heat 2 tablespoons of the oil in a medium skillet over medium heat. Add the mushrooms and cook, stirring, until softened.

continues . . .

2. Heat the butter and the remaining 4 tablespoons oil in a medium saucepan over medium heat. Add the flour and cook, stirring constantly, about 3 minutes more, until the sauce is thickened and smooth. Gradually stir in the milk, cider, and broth and cook, stirring occasionally, until blended. Season with salt and pepper, add the mushrooms, and cook, stirring occasionally, until the mushrooms soften, release their juices, and are incorporated into the sauce. Spread the mixture out on a dinner plate and let cool, then refrigerate until firm enough to handle.

3. Shape the mushroom mixture into 1-inch balls. Place the eggs and bread crumbs in separate shallow bowls. Heat at least 1 inch of oil in a large skillet over medium-high heat (or better still, use a deep fryer set at 365°F) until it turns a cube of bread light brown in 60 seconds. Dip each croquette in the egg, dredge in the bread crumbs, and place in the oil. (Cook in batches if needed to avoid overcrowding.) Cook, turning several times, until golden. Transfer with a slotted spoon to paper towels and let drain. Serve hot.

Zucchini and Shrimp Puffs
Buñuelos de Calabacín y Gambas

MAKES ABOUT 12 TAPAS

The dough for these puffs should be made in advance, and allowed to rest to get to the proper consistency. It is also important to fry them right before serving them.

PREPARE SEVERAL HOURS IN ADVANCE

3 ounces shrimp

¼ teaspoon salt

¼ cup all-purpose flour

½ teaspoon baking powder

1 large egg, lightly beaten

½ pound zucchini, coarsely grated

1 large garlic clove, finely chopped

Generous amount of freshly ground black pepper

Olive oil, for frying

1. Bring a small saucepan of water to a boil over high heat. Add the shrimp, reduce the heat to low, and simmer until pink, 2 to 3 minutes. Drain and let cool. Remove the shells and cut into ¼-inch pieces.

2. Combine the salt, flour, and baking powder in a small bowl. Add the egg, zucchini, shrimp, garlic, and pepper and mix well. Cover and refrigerate overnight. Drain off any liquid.

3. Heat at least 1 inch of oil in a small skillet over medium-high heat (or better still, use a deep fryer set at 365°F) until it turns a cube of bread light brown in 60 seconds. Drop the dough by rounded tablespoons into the oil. Cook, turning once, until golden brown. Transfer with a slotted spoon to paper towels and let drain. Serve hot.

Fried Anchovies Filled with Spinach
Boquerones Rellenos de Espinacas

MAKES 6 SERVINGS

The sweetness of the raisins and the mildness of the pine nuts give these anchovies an unusual and appealing flavor. The batter is essential to complete the dish.

1 recipe Batter (from Batter-Fried Squid Tentacles, page 42)

1 tablespoon olive oil

¼ pound fresh spinach

2 dozen fresh anchovies, cleaned, boned, and butterflied

2 tablespoons golden raisins

2 tablespoons pine nuts

All-purpose flour, for dredging

Olive oil, for frying

1. Prepare the batter as instructed in step 1 of the recipe. Heat the 1 tablespoon oil in a small skillet

over medium heat. Add the spinach and cook, stirring, until wilted. Stir in the raisins and pine nuts, and cook, stirring, until incorporated and the pine nuts are fragrant and lightly golden. Fill the cavities of the anchovies and secure closed with toothpicks.

2. Place the flour in a shallow bowl. Heat at least ½ inch of oil in a large skillet over medium-high heat (or better still, use a deep fryer set at 365°F) until it turns a cube of bread light brown in 60 seconds. Reduce the heat to medium. Dip each anchovy into the batter, dredge in the flour, and place in the oil. Cook, turning once, until golden. Transfer with a slotted spoon to paper towels and let drain. Serve hot.

Paella Croquettes
Croquetas de Paella

MAKES 10 TAPAS

Spaniards typically make these croquettes out of paella or other rice dishes left over from the previous day's meal. Whether the paella is made with chicken, fish, or meat (or a combination of all three), the resulting croquettes are delicious.

1 cup leftover paella rice

½ cup chopped cooked chicken, fish, or meat from a paella

2 large eggs, lightly beaten separately

2 tablespoons all-purpose flour

Bread crumbs, for dredging

Olive oil, for frying

1. In a small bowl, mix the rice and the chicken, fish, or meat. Add 1 of the eggs and the 2 teaspoons of flour. With floured hands, shape the rice mixture into 2-inch balls.

2. Place the bread crumbs in a shallow bowl. Heat at least 1 inch of oil in a large skillet over medium-high heat (or better still, use a deep fryer set at 365°F) until it turns a cube of bread light brown in 60 seconds. Dip each croquette in the remaining

1 egg, dredge in the bread crumbs, and place in the oil. Cook, turning several times, until golden. Transfer with a slotted spoon to paper towels and let drain. Serve hot.

Spinach, Pine Nut, and Raisin Croquettes Ⓥ
Croquetas de Espinacas, Piñones y Uvas Pasas

MAKES 12 TAPAS

Most Spanish croquettes contain either meat or fish but this vegetable version, which contains an unusual blend of flavors—spinach, pine nuts, and raisins—is remarkably satisfying. The raisins add sweetness and the pine nuts add a subtle crunch.

4 tablespoons (½ stick) unsalted butter

5 tablespoons olive oil

¾ cup all-purpose flour

1½ cups milk

½ cup vegetable broth or water

2 tablespoons dry sherry, such as Fino

Kosher or sea salt

Freshly ground black pepper

⅛ teaspoon ground nutmeg

2 tablespoons finely chopped pine nuts

2 tablespoons raisins

¼ pound cooked chopped spinach, well drained

1 large egg, lightly beaten

Bread crumbs, for dredging

Olive oil, for frying

1. Heat the butter and oil in a small saucepan over medium heat until the butter melts. Add the flour and cook, stirring constantly, about 2 minutes. Gradually stir in the milk, broth, sherry, salt, pepper, and nutmeg and cook, stirring constantly, until thickened and smooth and it begins to bubble.

continues...

Stir in the pine nuts, raisins, and spinach and cook 1 minute. Let cool slightly, stirring to release the steam. Spread the mixture out on a dinner plate and let cool completely, then refrigerate until firm enough to handle.

2. Place the eggs and bread crumbs in separate shallow bowls. Shape the spinach mixture into 1-inch balls. Dip each croquette in the egg, dredge in the bread crumbs, and place on a plate. Let sit until dry, about 10 minutes.

3. Heat at least 1 inch of oil in a medium skillet over medium-high heat (or better still, use a deep fryer set at 365°F) until it turns a cube of bread light brown in 60 seconds. Place the croquettes in the oil and cook, turning several times, until golden. Transfer with a slotted spoon to paper towels and let drain. Serve hot.

Chicken and Cured Ham Croquettes
Croquetas de Lhardy

MAKES ABOUT 35 TAPAS

The recipe for these unusual chicken and cured ham croquettes comes from Lhardy in Madrid, well known as one of the oldest and most elegant restaurants in Spain. The second floor is a magnificent restaurant, and the first floor is a pastry shop and deli where tapas are served on the honor system. Croquetas de Lhardy are one of their signature tapas.

PREPARE AT LEAST 3 HOURS IN ADVANCE

3 tablespoons unsalted butter

5 tablespoons olive oil

¾ cup all-purpose flour

1½ cups milk

½ cup chicken broth or vegetable broth

Salt

Freshly ground black pepper

Pinch of grated or ground nutmeg

1 cup finely chopped boiled chicken breast

½ cup finely chopped Serrano (Spanish cured mountain) ham or prosciutto

All-purpose flour, for dredging

2 large eggs, lightly beaten

Bread crumbs, for dredging

Olive oil, for frying

1. Heat the butter and 5 tablespoons oil in a medium saucepan over medium heat until the butter melts. Add the flour and cook, stirring constantly, about 3 minutes. Gradually stir in the milk and broth, salt, pepper, and nutmeg and cook, stirring constantly, until the sauce is thickened and smooth. Add the chicken and ham and cook, stirring, until the sauce reaches the boiling point, about 10 minutes more. Let cool, cover, and refrigerate at least 3 hours. (The croquettes may be prepared to this point and refrigerated up to one day ahead.)

2. On a lightly floured work surface, shape the chicken mixture into 1-inch balls (about 1 tablespoon each) with floured hands. Place the eggs and bread crumbs in separate shallow bowls. Heat at least 1 inch of oil in a large skillet over medium-high heat (or better still, use a deep fryer set at 365°F) until it turns a cube of bread light brown in 60 seconds. Dip each croquette in the egg, dredge in the bread crumbs, and place in the oil. (Cook in batches if needed to avoid overcrowding.) Cook, turning several times, until golden. Transfer with a slotted spoon to paper towels and let drain. Serve hot.

Partridge and Cheese Croquettes
Croquetas de Perdiz y Queso

MAKES ABOUT 30 TAPAS

Partridge and quail thrive all over Spain and are popular for hunting and therefore in food preparation as well. Here they are made into croquettes flavored with mild cheese.

3 tablespoons olive oil

1 tablespoon unsalted butter

6 tablespoons all-purpose flour

¾ cup milk

¼ cup chicken broth or vegetable broth

Kosher or sea salt

Freshly ground black pepper

Generous amount of freshly ground nutmeg

1 partridge or 2 quail, boned, skinned, and meat finely chopped

¼ cup finely chopped Serrano (Spanish cured mountain) ham or prosciutto

2 thin slices mild cheese, such as Spanish Tetilla or Fontina, finely chopped

1 tablespoon finely chopped fresh flat-leaf parsley

2 large eggs, lightly beaten

Bread crumbs, for dredging

Olive oil, for frying

1. Heat the 3 tablespoons oil and the butter in a medium saucepan over medium heat until the butter melts. Add the flour and cook, stirring constantly, about 2 minutes until combined. Gradually stir in the milk and broth, salt, pepper, and nutmeg and cook, stirring constantly, until thickened and smooth. Add the partridge, ham, cheese, and parsley and cook, stirring, about 5 minutes more. Let cool slightly, stirring to release the steam. Spread the mixture out on a dinner plate and let cool, then refrigerate until firm enough to handle.

2. With floured hands, shape the partridge mixture into ½-inch balls. Place the eggs and bread crumbs in separate shallow bowls. Heat at least ½ inch of oil in a large skillet over medium-high heat (or better still, use a deep fryer set at 365°F) until it turns a cube of bread light brown in 60 seconds. Dip each croquette in the egg, dredge in the bread crumbs, and place in the oil. Cook, turning several times, until golden. Transfer with a slotted spoon to paper towels and let drain. Serve hot.

Ham and Fresh Pork Croquettes
Croquetas de Jamón y Cerdo

MAKES ABOUT 35 TAPAS

Here, a croquette of ham and fresh pork, with earthy accents of nutmeg and cinnamon.

3 tablespoons unsalted butter

5 tablespoons olive oil

¾ cup all-purpose flour

1½ cups milk

½ cup chicken broth or vegetable broth

Kosher or sea salt

Freshly ground black pepper

Dash of grated or ground nutmeg

Dash of ground cinnamon

½ cup finely chopped Serrano (Spanish cured mountain) ham or prosciutto

1 cup finely chopped cooked fresh lean pork loin

2 large eggs, lightly beaten

Bread crumbs, for dredging

Olive oil, for frying

1. Heat the butter and oil in a medium saucepan over medium heat until the butter melts. Add the flour and cook, stirring constantly, about 3 minutes. Gradually add the milk and broth, then add the salt, pepper, nutmeg, and cinnamon and cook, stirring constantly, until the sauce is thickened and smooth. Reduce the heat to low, add the ham, chicken, and pork, and cook, stirring occasionally, about 10 minutes more. Spread the mixture out on a dinner plate and let cool, then refrigerate until firm enough to handle.

2. With floured hands, shape the pork mixture into 1-inch balls. Place the eggs and bread crumbs in separate shallow bowls. Heat at least 1 inch of oil in a large skillet over medium-high heat (or better still, use a deep fryer set at 365°F) until it turns a cube of bread light brown in 60 seconds. Dip each

continues...

croquette in the egg, dredge in the bread crumbs, and place in the oil. (Cook in batches if needed to avoid overcrowding.) Cook, turning several times, until golden. Transfer with a slotted spoon to paper towels and let drain. Serve hot.

Fried Zucchini and Cheese Rolls
Rollitos de Calabacín y Queso

MAKES 8 TAPAS

A simple fried tapa for anytime. The cheese should be soft and flavorful, such as the Galician tetilla.

1 small zucchini, thinly sliced lengthwise

¼ pound soft cheese, such as tetilla or Fontina, thinly sliced

Kosher or sea salt

1 large egg, lightly beaten

Bread crumbs, for dredging

Olive oil, for frying

1. Bring a medium saucepan of water to boil over high heat. Add the zucchini and cook until softened. Let cool. Place 1 cheese slice on 1 zucchini slice, roll up, and secure with a toothpick.

2. Place the egg and bread crumbs in separate shallow bowls. Heat at least ½ inch of oil in a small skillet over medium-high heat (or better still, use a deep fryer set at 365°F) until it turns a cube of bread light brown in 60 seconds. Dip each roll in the egg, dredge in the bread crumbs, and place in the oil. Cook, turning once, until lightly golden, about 2 minutes. Transfer with a slotted spoon to paper towels and let drain. Serve hot.

Salt Cod and Potato Puffs
Buñuelos de Bacalao

MAKES ABOUT 40 TAPAS

Here the strongly flavored salt cod is contrasted by the mild taste of the potato, enhanced with garlic, and made richer with egg yolks. It is best when served with alioli.

PREPARE 24 TO 36 HOURS IN ADVANCE

½ pound dried boneless skinless salt cod

1 recipe Garlic Sauce (alioli; page 284)

1 medium potato, quartered

2 garlic cloves, mashed in a garlic press or mortar

1 tablespoon finely chopped fresh flat-leaf parsley

Kosher or sea salt

Freshly ground black pepper

2 large egg yolks

Olive oil, for frying

1. Place the cod in a medium bowl and add cold water to cover. Cover and let sit in the refrigerator 24 to 36 hours, changing the water occasionally, until the water no longer tastes salty. Drain well.

2. Prepare the sauce. Place the cod and potatoes in a medium saucepan and add cold water to cover and salt. Cover and bring to a simmer over low heat. Cook about 15 minutes or until the potatoes are tender when pierced with a knife. Drain well and let cool slightly. Peel the potatoes and pass through a ricer into a medium bowl. Crumble the cod and fold into the potatoes. Stir in the garlic, parsley, salt, and pepper, then the egg yolks. Cover and refrigerate 1 hour.

3. Heat at least 1 inch of oil in a large skillet over medium-high heat (or better still, use a deep fryer set at 365°F) until it turns a cube of bread light brown in 60 seconds. Drop the dough by rounded tablespoons into the oil. Cook, turning several times, until golden. Transfer with a slotted spoon to paper towels and let drain. Serve hot with the sauce on the side.

Chorizo Puffs

Hojaldrados de Chorizo

MAKES 16 TAPAS

When making tapas covered in pastry dough, there are a wide variety of ingredients used as fillings. Chorizo, the wonderfully spiced sausage that Spain introduced to the rest of the world, is delicious when served on its own and even better when baked in puff pastry.

½ pound puff pastry dough, homemade (page 135) or storebought

¼ pound (2 links) chorizo, cut into ¼-inch slices

1 large egg yolk, lightly beaten, for brushing

Place an oven rack in the upper position. Preheat the oven to 450°F. Roll the pastry dough out to ⅛-inch thickness and cut into 16 (1½-inch) rounds. Place 1 chorizo in the center of each round, brush the edge of the round with the egg, and cover with a second round. Press the edges with a fork to seal. Place the puffs on a cookie sheet and bake until lightly browned. Serve hot.

Red Bell Peppers in Puff Pastry Ⓥ

Hojaldre de Pimientos Morrones

MAKES 8 TAPAS

This combination of fresh red bell peppers and hollandaise sauce in puff pastry is one of the specialties of Raco d'en Binu, located in the small town on Argentona, which was once considered the premier restaurant in all of Catalunya. Make sure the peppers are sweet and have a deep red color.

½ pound puff pastry dough, homemade (page 135) or storebought

1 large egg yolk, lightly beaten with 1 teaspoon water

4 medium red bell peppers or 8 (jarred) piquillo peppers

Kosher or sea salt

Freshly ground black pepper

Olive oil, for brushing

Hollandaise Sauce

3 egg yolks

1 tablespoon fresh lemon juice

½ cup cold butter, cut into pieces

1. Place an oven rack in the upper position. Preheat the oven to 425°F. Roll the pastry dough to ⅛-inch thickness and cut into 4 (5 x 3-inch) rectangles. Brush the tops with the egg yolk and place on a cookie sheet that has been dampened with water. Bake 10 to 11 minutes or until golden. Let cool.

2. Preheat the oven to 500°F. Place the bell peppers in a roasting pan and roast, turning once, 20 minutes or until the skin has bubbled and charred. Remove from the oven and place the peppers in a deep bowl. Cover tightly with foil and let sit 15 minutes. Peel, core, and seed the peppers.

3. Meanwhile, prepare the peppers: Cut 2 of the bell peppers into 8 (1-inch) strips and reserve. Place the remaining 2 bell peppers in a food processor or blender and process until smooth. Pass through a fine-mesh strainer into a very small saucepan. Stir in a little water until it is the consistency of a thick sauce. Season with salt and pepper. Bring to a simmer over low heat and simmer 1 minute. (May be prepared ahead.)

4. Prepare the hollandaise: In a small saucepan, whisk together the egg yolks and lemon juice. Add half of the butter to the pan. Heat over low heat, whisking constantly, until the butter is melted. Add the remaining butter, whisk until melted and the sauce is thickened. (Be sure that the butter melts and the eggs cook slowly, so the eggs don't curdle; lower the heat if necessary.) If the sauce begins to separate, add a spoon of boiling water and whisk until smooth.

continues...

5. Preheat the oven to 450°F. Split the puff pastry rectangles horizontally in half. Hollow out a depression in the center of each bottom half and fill with the pepper sauce. Arrange 2 reserved bell pepper strips on top, season with salt, then cover with 1 tablespoon hollandaise sauce. Place on a cookie sheet and bake 2 minutes. Cover with the reserved pastry tops and bake 2 minutes more. Serve hot.

Spinach and Pear in Puff Pastry
Hojaldre de Espinaca y Pera

MAKES 4 SERVINGS

I discovered this unusual recipe at La Gabarra restaurant in Madrid, where I was surprised to learn that spinach and pears create a fabulous blend of flavors.

¾ pound puff pastry dough, homemade (page 135) or storebought

½ pound fresh spinach, rinsed, trimmed, and coarsely chopped

1 pear, peeled, cored, and coarsely chopped

Kosher or sea salt

Freshly ground black pepper

Dash of freshly grated or ground nutmeg

Béchamel (White Sauce)

2 tablespoons unsalted butter

2 tablespoons all-purpose flour

½ cup milk

½ cup chicken broth or vegetable broth

1. Place an oven rack in the upper position. Preheat the oven to 450°F. On a floured surface, roll the pastry dough to ⅛-inch thickness and cut into 8 (2½-inch) rounds. With 1½-inch round cookie cutter, score a circle in the center of each round—do not cut all the way through.

2. Bake about 10 minutes or until golden. Remove the scored circle from each round to form a hollow for the filling. Keep the pastry warm until ready to use, or reheat quickly before using.

3. Meanwhile, place the spinach in a large saucepan and sprinkle with a few drops of water. Add the pear and stir to combine. Season lightly with salt and pepper. Cover and cook over low heat until just tender—do not let the spinach or pear get soggy. Drain any remaining liquid.

4. Prepare the sauce: Melt the butter in a small saucepan over medium heat. Add the flour and cook, stirring constantly, 1 to 2 minutes. Gradually stir in the milk and broth and cook, stirring constantly, until thickened and smooth.

5. Stir the sauce into the spinach mixture and season with salt, pepper, and nutmeg. (May be prepared ahead.) Fill the pastry shells with the spinach mixture and serve.

Mushrooms and Piquillo Peppers in Puff Pastry Ⓥ
Hojaldre de Champiñón con Piquillo

MAKES ABOUT 18 TAPAS

Another variation on mushroom-filled puff pastries, this recipe calls for piquillo peppers as well as crushed red pepper, making the mushroom mix more flavorful and spicy.

1 tablespoon olive oil

1 tablespoon finely chopped onion

1 garlic clove, finely chopped

2 tablespoons finely chopped (jarred) piquillo peppers or pimiento

¼ pound mushrooms, rinsed, trimmed, and finely chopped

½ medium-hot dried red chile pepper, such as Spanish guindilla, seeded and crumbled, or ¼ teaspoon crushed red pepper

Kosher or sea salt

Freshly ground black pepper

¼ pound puff pastry dough, homemade (page 135) or storebought

2 teaspoons grated cheese, such as aged Manchego or Parmesan

1. Heat the oil in a medium skillet over medium heat. Add the onion and garlic and cook, stirring, until the onion is wilted and transparent, about 3 minutes. Add the piquillo pepper and cook, stirring, 1 minute, then add the mushrooms, chile pepper, salt, and pepper and cook, stirring, until the mushrooms are softened. Remove from the heat and stir in the cheese.

2. Preheat the oven to 425°F. Roll the pastry dough to ⅛-inch thickness and cut into 18 (1¾-inch) rounds. Place 1 teaspoon of filling in the center of each of 9 rounds. Brush the edge of the round with water, cover with a second round, and press the edge with a fork to seal. (May be prepared ahead and refrigerated.) Place on a cookie sheet that has been dampened with water and bake 7 to 9 minutes or until golden. Serve hot.

Anchovies and Piquillo Peppers in Puff Pastry
Anchoa y Piquillos en Hojaldre

MAKES 6 TO 8 TAPAS

Piquillo peppers are grown in a small area of Navarra in northern Spain. They are of very high quality, sweet and intense in flavor, and are a perfect complement to anchovies.

6 ounces puff pastry dough, homemade (page 135) or storebought

3 (jarred) piquillo peppers, cut into thin strips

3 (jarred) anchovy fillets, cut into several pieces

1. Place an oven rack in the upper position. Preheat the oven to 450°F. Roll the pastry dough to ⅛-inch thickness. With a 2½-inch round scalloped-edge cookie cutter, cut into 6 to 8 rounds and transfer to a cookie sheet. With a 1½-inch round cookie cutter, score a circle in the center of each round about three-quarters of the way through—do not cut all the way.

2. Bake about 8 minutes or until golden brown. Turn off the oven and leave the door slightly ajar 5 minutes more or until thoroughly crisped. Remove the scored circle from each round, discarding any pastry interior, and reserve the circles. Place several piquillo strips in each pastry shell, cover with the anchovies, and top with the pastry circles. Serve.

Puff Pastry with Mushrooms and Shrimp in Sparkling Wine Sauce
Milhojas de Setas y Gambas en Salsa de Cava

MAKES 12 TAPAS

A wonderful tapa, made with cream sauce and puff pastry dough, this is perfectly seasoned with Serrano ham, smoked paprika, and Worcestershire sauce. The recipe comes from Bar Bergara in the bustling Gros district of San Sebastian.

6 ounces puff pastry dough, homemade (page 135) or storebought

1 tablespoon olive oil

2 teaspoons finely chopped shallots

¼ pound shrimp, shelled and finely chopped

3½ ounces mushroom caps, such as shiitake or brown, finely chopped

1 tablespoon finely chopped Serrano (Spanish cured mountain) ham or prosciutto

2 teaspoons finely chopped fresh flat-leaf parsley

1½ teaspoons finely chopped fresh thyme or ¼ teaspoon dried thyme

continues...

¼ teaspoon ground sweet paprika, such as Spanish smoked

2 tablespoons dry sparkling wine, such as Cava or dry white wine

6 tablespoons heavy cream

4 teaspoons grated aged Manchego or Parmesan cheese

Freshly grated or ground nutmeg

4 teaspoons Worcestershire sauce

Kosher or sea salt

Freshly ground black pepper

1. Place an oven rack in the upper position. Preheat the oven to 450°F. Roll the puff pastry to ⅛-inch thickness. With a 2½-inch round scalloped-edge cookie cutter, cut into 12 rounds and transfer to a cookie sheet. With a 1½-inch round cookie cutter, score a circle in the center of each round about ¾ of the way through—do not cut all the way.

2. Bake about 8 minutes or until golden brown. Turn off the oven and leave the door slightly ajar 5 minutes more or until thoroughly crisped. Remove the scored circle from each round, discard any pastry interior, and reserve the circles.

3. Meanwhile, heat the oil in a medium skillet over medium heat. Add the shallots and cook, stirring, about 1 minute. Add the shrimp, mushrooms, ham, parsley, and thyme and cook, stirring, until the mushrooms are slightly softened. Add the paprika and wine and cook, stirring occasionally, until evaporated. Stir in the cream, cheese, nutmeg, Worcestershire sauce, salt, and pepper and cook, stirring, until it is the consistency of a thick sauce. Fill each pastry round with the shrimp mixture and top with the pastry circles. Serve.

Potatoes and Vegetables in Puff Pastry
Pastel de Ensaladilla Rusa

MAKES 6 SERVINGS

Ensaladilla Rusa is a classic and popular tapa on its own, but even better when served in a puff pastry shell. The glaze, made from gelatin and chilled chicken broth, is optional.

1 recipe "Russian" Potato and Vegetable Salad (page 13)

3½ cups Cooking Liquid (page 26; partial recipe)

12 medium to large shrimp, in their shells

1 pound puff pastry dough, homemade (page 135) or storebought

Pickles, thinly sliced lengthwise

Glaze (optional)

1½ teaspoons unflavored gelatin

1 cup cold clarified vegetable or chicken broth

1. Prepare the salad and reserve. Prepare the cooking liquid. Add the shrimp and cook until pink, about 2 minutes. Drain, discard the bay leaf, and let cool. Remove the shells and reserve the shrimp.

2. Preheat the oven to 425°F. Roll the puff pastry into a 6 x 5-inch rectangle. Place on a cookie sheet that has been dampened with water and prick well with a fork all over to within 1 inch of the long edges. Bake 15 minutes, pricking the center of the dough occasionally to keep it from puffing. Reduce the heat to 400°F and bake 5 minutes more or until golden. Let cool.

3. Split the rounds horizontally in half and hollow out the center to make room for the filling. Fill each pastry shell with the salad and arrange the shrimp in rows over the top. Decorate the sides with pickles, pressing them into the salad so they will adhere. Replace the top round. If not using the glaze, serve.

4. Prepare the glaze, if using: In a small saucepan, soften the gelatin in ¼ cup of the broth. Add the remaining ¾ cup broth. Over low heat, cook, stirring, until the gelatin is dissolved. Let cool and refrigerate until the mixture just begins to thicken slightly. Spoon over the pastry top and refrigerate until set but not cold. Serve cool.

Black Sausage in Puff Pastry
Hojaldre de Morcilla

MAKES 10 TAPAS

Second only to chorizo, morcilla *(black sausage) is the most popular sausage in Spain. This recipe for a puff pastry filled with* morcilla *came from our dear friend Tomas Herranz.*

3 tablespoons olive oil

3 tablespoons finely chopped onion

3 ounces black sausage, skin removed and finely chopped

¼ teaspoon dried oregano

¼ teaspoon ground sweet paprika, such as Spanish smoked

Kosher or sea salt

Freshly ground black pepper

¼ pound puff pastry dough, homemade (page 135) or storebought

1. Heat 2 tablespoons of the oil in a small skillet over medium heat. Add the onion and cook, stirring, until wilted and transparent, about 3 minutes. Add the sausage and mash with a wooden spoon. Remove from the heat and stir in the remaining 1 tablespoon oil, the oregano, paprika, salt, and pepper (the mixture should be well seasoned).

2. Preheat the oven to 450°F. Roll the puff pastry into a 9 x 3½-inch rectangle about ⅛ inch thick. Place the sausage mixture in a narrow strip down the center of the pastry. Brush the edge of one long side with water, bring the two sides up, and pinch

to seal. (May be prepared ahead and refrigerated.) Place seam side down on a cookie sheet that has been dampened with water. Bake 7 minutes, reduce the heat to 350°F, and bake 4 minutes more or until well browned. Cut crosswise into 1-inch slices and serve hot.

Frog Legs and Shrimp in Puff Pastry
Hojaldre de Ancas de Rana y Gambas

MAKES 12 TAPAS

I first tasted these pastry puffs at the elegant Príncipe de Viana, a first-class and very beautiful Basque restaurant in Madrid, with waitresses in traditional Basque costumes. Substitute chicken for the frog legs or triple the amount of shrimp.

½ pound puff pastry dough, homemade (page 135) or storebought

4 medium shrimp, shelled

½ pound medium frog legs or ¼ pound boneless skinless chicken breast

4 medium mushrooms, rinsed and trimmed

3 tablespoons unsalted butter

1 scallion (white part only), cut into very thin 2-inch strips

1 teaspoon finely chopped shallots

2 tablespoons dry sherry, such as Fino

6 tablespoons veal or chicken broth

2 teaspoons heavy cream

1. Place an oven rack in the upper position. Preheat the oven to 425°F. Roll the puff pastry to ⅛-inch thickness and cut into 12 (3-inch) rounds. Place on a cookie sheet that has been dampened with water and bake about 7 minutes or until deeply golden. Reserve on the cookie sheet.

continues...

2. Meanwhile, cut the shrimp lengthwise in half, then cut into thin strips. Remove and discard the frog leg bones and cut the meat into long, thin strips. Cut the mushrooms lengthwise into thin slices (with stems), then cut into thin strips.

3. Heat 2 tablespoons of the butter in a medium skillet over medium heat. Add the scallion and shallots and cook, stirring, until just softened. Increase the heat to medium-high, add the frog legs and shrimp and cook, stirring, about 1 minute. Add the mushrooms and cook, stirring, about 1 minute more. Transfer to a plate, reserving the liquid.

4. Melt the remaining 1 tablespoon butter in the skillet over medium heat. Add the sherry, stirring and scraping up any bits of flavor, and cook a few seconds to reduce. Stir in the broth and cream, reduce the heat to low, and simmer, stirring constantly, until the sauce is slightly thickened. Return the frog mixture to the skillet, increase the heat to medium, and cook, stirring constantly, until most of the sauce has been incorporated into the mixture—it should be neither dry nor saucy. (May be prepared ahead.)

5. Preheat the oven to 375°F. Return the puff pastries to the oven and bake 10 to 15 minutes or until heated through. Heat the puff pastry rounds. Split the rounds horizontally in half and hollow out the center to make room for the filling. Fill each bottom round with about 2 teaspoons of the frog mixture and cover with the top round. Serve hot.

Shrimp in Puff Pastry
Milhojas de Langostinos

MAKES 4 TAPAS

A very elegant tapa discovered in a bar in the old quarter of beautiful San Sebastian.

¾ **pound puff pastry dough, homemade (page 135) or storebought**

1 **large egg, lightly beaten**

Sauce

2 **tablespoons olive oil**

2 **medium onions, cut into very thin 2-inch strips**

2 **garlic cloves, finely chopped**

1 **leek (white part only), trimmed, well washed, and cut into very thin 2-inch strips**

1 **tablespoon finely chopped fresh flat-leaf parsley**

1 **medium carrot, peeled, cut into very thin 2-inch strips**

16 **medium shrimp, with shrimp heads and shells removed and shrimp meat separated**

2 **tablespoons brandy**

2 **tablespoons finely chopped tomato**

2 **tablespoons storebought or homemade Fish Broth**

2 **tablespoons olive oil**

1 **teaspoon finely chopped garlic**

8 **clams such as Manila or littleneck**

½ **cup dry white wine**

2 **tablespoons finely chopped fresh flat-leaf parsley**

1. Preheat the oven to 375°F. Roll the pastry dough out into a 16 x 16-inch square that is ⅛ inch thick. Brush the pastry dough with the egg, prick generously with a fork, and place on a cookie sheet. Bake until golden. Let cool. Cut the pastry horizontally in half. Cut both halves into 4 (4-inch) squares (with top and bottom halves). Reserve.

2. Prepare the sauce: Heat the 2 tablespoons oil in a small skillet over low heat. Add the onions, the 2 chopped garlic cloves, the leek, the 1 tablespoon parsley, the carrot, and shrimp heads and shells and cook, stirring, until the vegetables are softened. Press the shrimp heads and shells to extract flavor, then discard. Add the brandy and, standing well away from the skillet, ignite the liquid with a match or kitchen lighter, and stir until the flames die out. Add the tomato and broth and cook, stirring occasionally, until incorporated. Pass through a fine-mesh strainer into a small bowl. Discard the solids.

3. Heat the additional 2 tablespoons oil in a medium skillet over medium heat. Add the 1

teaspoon garlic and cook, stirring, until golden. Stir in the shrimp meat, clams, wine and broth, bring to a boil and cook until the clams open. Discard any unopened clams. Sprinkle with the 2 tablespoons parsley.

4. Place the shrimp over the puff pastry halves, cover with the sauce, and top with the remaining pastry. Bake for several minutes until heated through. Garnish with the clams. Serve hot.

Blue and Cream Cheese Pastries with Raisins and Cream Sherry Ⓥ

Bric de Queso Azúl y Cremoso en Salsa de Uva Pasa y Pedro Ximénez

MAKES 6 TAPAS

If possible, try to get Cabrales blue cheese from Spain. Its strong taste mixes beautifully with the sweetness of the Pedro Ximénez sherry and the raisins.

1 ounce cream cheese

1 ounce blue cheese, such as Cabrales

2 teaspoons trimmed, well washed, and finely chopped leek or scallion (white part only)

4 teaspoons golden raisins

¼ cup very sweet sherry, such as Pedro Ximénez

1 sheet phyllo dough (thawed if frozen)

Olive oil, for frying

1. Combine the cheeses and leek in a small bowl. Combine the raisins and sherry in a small saucepan. Bring to a simmer over low heat and cook, stirring occasionally, until the sherry is syrupy and the raisins are softened.

2. Cut the phyllo dough lengthwise into 16 (3-inch-wide) strips. Cut each strip crosswise into 4 equal

strips. You will end up with 16 (4.5 x 3.5-inch) strips.

3. Place about 1 tablespoon of the cheese mixture in a corner of each strip and fold up like a flag (corner to corner) into a triangle. Seal the ends with water.

4. Heat at least ½ inch of oil in a medium skillet over medium-high heat (or better still, use a deep fryer set at 375°F) until it quickly browns a cube of bread. Place the pastries in the oil and cook, turning once, until lightly golden, about 2 minutes. Transfer with a slotted spoon to paper towels and let drain. Drizzle the pastries with the sauce and serve hot.

Cheese, Olive, and Caper Phyllo

Bric Relleno de Queso, Aceituna y Alcaparra

MAKES 16 TAPAS

A soft tetilla cheese from Galicia is ideal for this filling for phyllo pastry. The cheese mixes very well with the capers and the black olive paste.

1 sheet phyllo dough (thawed if frozen)

3 tablespoons tetilla or Brie cheese, rind removed

2 teaspoons storebought or homemade Black Olive Paste (page 88; partial recipe)

32 capers (nonpareil preferred), rinsed and drained

1. Cut the phyllo dough sheet lengthwise into 4 equal strips. Cut each strip crosswise into 4 equal strips. You will end up with 16 (4.5 x 3.5-inch) strips.

2. Place about 1 teaspoon of the cheese in a corner of each of the dough strips and press some of the olive paste and 2 capers into the cheese. Fold up like a flag (corner to corner) into a triangle. Seal the ends with water.

continues…

3. Heat at least I inch of oil in a medium skillet over medium-high heat (or better still, use a deep fryer set at 375°F) until it quickly browns a cube of bread. Place the pastries in the oil and cook, turning once, until lightly golden, about 2 minutes. Transfer with a slotted spoon to paper towels and let drain. Serve hot.

Shrimp Pancakes
Tortillitas de Camarones

MAKES ABOUT 10 TAPAS

Shrimp pancakes, a specialty of Cádiz, can be found on all local restaurant menus as well as at street stands. They are best when made with camarones (tiny shrimp).

3 tablespoons olive oil

3 tablespoons finely chopped onion

2 tablespoons finely chopped fresh flat-leaf parsley

⅛ teaspoon ground paprika

3 tablespoons all-purpose flour

7 tablespoons water

¾ teaspoon salt

½ teaspoon baking powder

¼ pound small shrimp, shelled and finely chopped

Olive oil, for frying

I. Heat the 3 tablespoons oil in a medium skillet over low heat. Add the onion and parsley and cover, and cook, stirring, until the onion is tender. Stir in the paprika.

2. In a small bowl, mix the flour, water, salt, and baking powder. Stir in the onion mixture and the shrimp. Wipe out the skillet.

3. Heat at least ¼ inch of oil in the skillet over medium-high heat (or better still, use a deep fryer set at 375°F) until it quickly browns a cube of bread. Drop the batter by rounded tablespoons into the oil, spreading it into thin 2½-inch pancakes

with the back of a spoon that has first been dipped in hot oil. Cook, turning once, until golden and crisp on both sides. Transfer with a slotted spatula to paper towels and let drain. Serve hot.

Codfish Pancakes
Tortillitas de Bacalao

MAKES ABOUT 20 TAPAS

These tortillitas, or thin pancakes, are typically from Andalucía, most specifically from the province of Cádiz, where they are masters of frying and have great knowledge of herbs and spices.

PREPARE 26 TO 38 HOURS IN ADVANCE

¼ pound boneless, skinless dried salt cod

1 recipe Garlic Sauce (alioli; page 284)

⅛ teaspoon saffron threads, crumbled

1 cup all-purpose flour

½ teaspoon baking powder

¼ teaspoon baking soda

3 tablespoons finely chopped onion

3 garlic cloves, mashed in a garlic press or mortar

3 tablespoons finely chopped fresh flat-leaf parsley

⅛ teaspoon ground bittersweet paprika, such as Spanish smoked

Kosher or sea salt

Freshly ground black pepper

Olive oil, for frying

I. Place the cod in a medium bowl and add cold water to cover. Cover and let sit in the refrigerator 24 to 36 hours, changing the water occasionally, until the water no longer tastes salty. Drain and flake.

2. Prepare the sauce: In a large bowl, mix the flour, baking powder, baking soda, onion, garlic, parsley, paprika, saffron, salt, and pepper. Stir in the cod and mix well. Cover, and let sit 2 hours.

3. Heat at least ¼ inch of oil in a medium skillet over medium-high heat (or better still, use a deep fryer set at 375°F) until it quickly browns a cube of bread. Drop the batter by rounded tablespoons into the oil, spreading it into thin 2½-inch pancakes with the back of a spoon that has first been dipped in hot oil. Cook, turning once, until golden and crisp on both sides. Transfer with a slotted spatula to paper towels and let drain. Serve hot with the sauce on the side.

Fried Pork and Ham Rolls
Flamenquines

MAKES 6 TO 8 SERVINGS

Just the name of this tapa, "little flamencos," gives a hint of its origin in the city of Sevilla. I first ate flamenquines *at the famous Madrid bar Gayango, sister of the original bar in Sevilla. These were the most popular tapa there.*

1 recipe Béchamel Sauce (page 29)

4 thin slices cooked pork loin, cut into 2½ x 2-inch pieces

4 thin slices Serrano (Spanish cured mountain) ham or prosciutto, cut into 2½ x 2-inch pieces

2 large eggs, lightly beaten

Bread crumbs, for dredging

2 garlic cloves, mashed in a garlic press or mortar

2 tablespoons finely chopped fresh flat-leaf parsley

Olive oil, for frying

1. Prepare the sauce as instructed in step 2 of the recipe. Place 1 ham slice on top of 1 pork slice, roll up, and secure with a toothpick. Dip each roll in the white sauce, coating it completely. Place on a plate and refrigerate at least 1 hour or until the sauce solidifies.

2. Place the eggs in a shallow bowl. Place the bread crumbs in another shallow bowl and mix in the garlic and parsley. Heat at least ½ inch of oil in a medium skillet over medium-high heat (or better still, use a deep fryer set at 365°F) until it turns a cube of bread light brown in 60 seconds. Dip each roll in the egg, dredge in the bread crumbs, and place in the oil. Cook, turning once, until golden. Transfer with a slotted spoon to paper towels and let drain. Serve hot.

Crunchy Potato Nests Filled with Ham and Tomato
Cestillas Crujientes Rellenas

MAKES 8 TAPAS

This is an impressively attractive tapa that can be prepared with many different fillings, in this case, with cockles and ham in a tomato sauce. Making the nest requires a potato nest basket for the deep fryer. It's a specialty item, but you'll want to use it often once you get it.

Potato Nests

6 cups shredded peeled potatoes

Olive oil, for frying

2 tablespoons olive oil

1 medium onion, finely chopped (about ⅔ cup)

4 dozen cockles or very small clams, shelled

1 medium tomato, finely chopped (about ⅔ cup)

2 tablespoons finely chopped Serrano (Spanish cured mountain) ham or prosciutto

1 teaspoon ground bittersweet paprika, such as Spanish smoked

Kosher or sea salt

Freshly ground black pepper

1 tablespoon brandy

1. Prepare the potato nests: Place the potatoes in a medium bowl with cold water to cover and let soak 30 minutes. Drain and let dry on paper towels.

continues . . .

2. Preheat the oven to 200°F. Heat enough oil to cover a potato nest basket in a large skillet over medium-high heat (or better still, use a deep fryer set at 365°F) until it turns a cube of bread light brown in 60 seconds. Dip the potato nest basket into the oil to coat, then line with the potatoes, about ¾ cup per nest. Secure with the smaller nest basket that fits inside. Dip each nest into the oil and cook until lightly browned. Let drain on paper towels then place on a cookie sheet and transfer to a 250°F oven to keep warm until ready to use. Repeat for the remaining 3 nests (for a total of 4).

3. Heat the 2 tablespoons oil in a medium skillet over medium heat. Add the onion and cook, stirring, until wilted and transparent, about 5 minutes. Add the cockles and cook, stirring, transferring each as it opens to a medium bowl. Discard any unopened cockles. When all have been removed, stir in the tomato, ham, paprika, salt, and pepper.

4. Pour the brandy evenly over the ham mixture. Standing well away from the skillet, ignite the liquid with a match or kitchen lighter and shake the pan to distribute the flame evenly. Cover to extinguish. Fill each nest with the sauce and top with about 6 cockles. Serve hot.

Puff Pastry Tartlet Shells Ⓥ
Tartaletas

MAKES ABOUT 65 TAPAS

Puff pastry dough for tartlets can be purchased in many stores, but it is a lackluster substitute for the homemade kind, and it makes a huge difference in the taste of the tartlets. This is a master recipe for puff pastry tartlets that can be made ahead of time and then stored in the refrigerator or freezer.

1 pound puff pastry dough, homemade (page 135) or storebought, chilled

1. Place an oven rack in the upper position. Preheat the oven to 425°F. Use only one-quarter of the pastry dough at a time because the dough must stay chilled. Roll out to less than ⅛ inch thickness and cut into about 16 (1½-inch) rounds.

2. Press the rounds into 1½-inch tartlet molds (I like the ones that are fluted and rounded on the bottom), stretching the dough slightly so it extends a little over the top of the mold.

3. Prick the dough with a fork, cover with another tartlet mold, and weigh it down (you can use dried beans or metal pellets sold for this purpose). If the dough has softened, place in the freezer for a couple of minutes before baking. The dough is ready to use or to store for future use in the refrigerator or freezer.

4. If using immediately, bake about 7 minutes or until golden. Remove the weights and the top mold, prick the tartlets, and bake 1 minute more. Prick again and bake 1 minute more or until golden.

Mushroom Tartlets Ⓥ
Tartaletas de Champiñón

MAKES 20 TAPAS

These delicious mushroom tartlets should be garnished with pieces of pickle and pimiento. It is important that you do not prepare this tapa more than 1 hour in advance or the mushrooms may give off liquid that thins the sauce.

5 tablespoons mayonnaise (mayonesa, page 359), to taste

1 garlic clove, mashed in a garlic press or mortar

1 tablespoon finely chopped fresh flat-leaf parsley

1 teaspoon fresh lemon juice

Salt

Freshly ground black pepper

¼ pound mushrooms, rinsed, trimmed, and finely chopped

20 puff pastry tartlet shells, homemade (page 82) or storebought

Pickles and pimientos, cut into small pieces, for garnish

In a small bowl, mix the mayonnaise, garlic, parsley, lemon juice, salt, and pepper. Fold in the mushrooms and refrigerate 1 hour. Fill each tartlet shell with the mushroom mixture and decorate with the pickle and pimiento and serve.

Shrimp Tartlets
Tartaletas de Gambas

MAKES 24 TAPAS

The shrimp for these tartlets is simmered slowly in onion, garlic, and tomato and then mixed with mayonnaise. The combination of flavors is exceptional.

2 tablespoons fruity olive oil

½ pound small to medium shrimp, in their shells

¼ cup finely chopped onion, such as Vidalia or other sweet onion

2 garlic cloves, finely chopped

1 medium tomato, finely chopped (about ⅔ cup)

¾ cup water

¾ cup storebought or homemade Fish Broth or bottled clam juice

Kosher or sea salt

Freshly ground black pepper

Mayonnaise (mayonesa, page 359), to taste

24 puff pastry tartlet shells, homemade (page 82) or storebought

1. Heat the oil in a medium skillet over medium heat. Add the shrimp, and cook, turning once, until pink. Transfer to a medium bowl. In the remaining oil over medium heat, cook the onion and garlic, stirring, until the onion is wilted and transparent, about 5 minutes. Add the tomato and cook until softened and its juices release, about 5 minutes

more. Return the shrimp to the skillet and stir in the water, broth, salt, and pepper. Bring to a boil, reduce the heat to low, and simmer about 30 minutes. Let the shrimp sit in the liquid until cool. Drain.

2. Remove and discard the shells (or save to make shrimp broth) and chop finely. Combine the shrimp and the mayonnaise in a medium bowl. (May be prepared ahead, covered, and refrigerated.) Fill each tartlet shell with the shrimp mixture. Serve at room temperature.

Crab Tartlets
Tartaletas de Cangrejo

MAKES ABOUT 15 TAPAS

I first tasted these extraordinary tartlets in a restaurant in Bilbao, and this delectable crab mixture soon became one of my favorite tartlet fillings.

5 medium shelled cooked shrimp, finely chopped

5 tablespoons shredded lump crab meat

2 tablespoons finely chopped dill or cornichon pickle

4 tablespoons finely chopped hard-boiled egg

2 tablespoons finely chopped (jarred) piquillo pepper or pimiento

2 tablespoons finely chopped onion, such as Vidalia or other sweet onion

Mayonnaise (mayonesa, page 359), to taste

About 15 puff pastry tartlet shells, homemade (page 82) or storebought

Pimiento or parsley, for garnish

In a medium bowl, combine the shrimp, crab, pickle, egg, piquillo pepper, and onion. Stir in enough mayonnaise to make a smooth, creamy mixture. (May be prepared ahead.) Fill each tartlet shell with the shrimp mixture, garnish with pimiento, and serve.

Mini Turnovers
(*Empanadillas*)

Tuna Turnovers with Tomato
Empanadillas de Atún

MAKES ABOUT 40 TAPAS

Empanadas, savory meat pies, are beloved by Spaniards and can be found prepared with many different fillings. Empanadillas are smaller versions of empanadas that are commonly served as tapas. In Spanish, the suffix "illa" means small, which is how these turnovers differ from pie-size empanadas. Here tuna is complemented by the sweetness of tomatoes.

PREPARE 3 HOURS IN ADVANCE

1 recipe Empanada Dough (page 135)

2 tablespoons olive oil

1 medium onion, finely chopped (about ⅔ cup)

1 garlic clove, finely chopped

One (7-ounce) jarred white or light meat tuna, drained and flaked

¼ cup finely chopped tomato

5 tablespoons tomato sauce

1 pimiento, finely chopped

1 tablespoon finely chopped fresh flat-leaf parsley

Kosher or sea salt

Freshly ground black pepper

1 large hard-boiled egg, finely chopped

Olive oil, for frying

1. Prepare the dough. Roll out to ⅛-inch thickness and cut into 3-inch rounds with an empanadilla or biscuit cutter.

2. Prepare the filling: Heat the 2 tablespoons oil in a medium skillet over medium heat. Add the onion and garlic and cook, stirring, until the onion is wilted and transparent, about 5 minutes. Stir in the tuna, tomato, tomato sauce, pimiento, parsley, salt, and pepper and cook about 10 minutes. Stir in the egg and remove from the heat. Let cool. Place about 1 tablespoon of the filling in the center of each dough round. Fold over and press the edges with a fork to seal.

3. Heat at least 1 inch of oil in a medium skillet over medium-high heat (or better still, use a deep fryer set at 375°F) until it quickly browns a cube of bread. Place the turnovers in the oil and cook, turning once, until lightly golden, about 2 minutes. Transfer with a slotted spoon to paper towels and let drain. Serve hot.

Fried Tuna, Peas, and Peppers Turnovers
Empanadillas de Atún, Guisantes y Pimientos

MAKES ABOUT 40 TAPAS

Turnovers are perfect for parties because they can be filled ahead of time, then kept refrigerated until baking time. This empanadilla *recipe filled with tuna, peas, and green bell pepper is particularly tasty.*

PREPARE 3 HOURS IN ADVANCE

1 recipe Empanada Dough (page 135) or pizza dough

2 tablespoons olive oil

1 medium onion, finely chopped (about ⅔ cup)

3 garlic cloves, finely chopped

1 medium green bell pepper, finely chopped (about 1 cup)

Kosher or sea salt

Freshly ground black pepper

2 medium tomatoes, finely chopped (about 1⅓ cups)

3 tablespoons cooked peas

One (7-ounce) jarred white or light tuna,
    drained and flaked

1 large hard-boiled egg, finely chopped

Olive oil, for frying

1. Prepare the dough. Roll out to ⅛-inch thickness and cut into 3-inch rounds with an empanadilla or biscuit cutter.

2. Heat the 2 tablespoons oil in a medium skillet over medium heat. Add the onion, garlic, and green pepper and cook, stirring, until the vegetables are softened, about 8 minutes. Season with salt and pepper. Stir in the tomatoes, reduce the heat to low, and cook until softened and their juices release, 2 to 3 minutes more. Add the peas, tuna, and egg and cook, stirring, about 2 minutes more. Let cool. Place about 1 tablespoon of the filling in the center of each dough round. Fold over and press the edges with a fork to seal.

3. Heat at least 1 inch of oil in a medium skillet over medium-high heat (or better still, use a deep fryer set at 375°F) until it quickly browns a cube of bread. Place the turnovers in the oil and cook, turning once, until lightly golden, about 2 minutes. Transfer with a slotted spoon to paper towels and let drain. Serve hot.

Veal and Chorizo Turnovers
Empanadillas de Ternera

MAKES ABOUT 40 TAPAS

Some of the finest veal in the world can be found in Spain. These veal turnovers are made even richer and more savory by the addition of heavily spiced chorizo. They are always a hit at my tapas parties.

PREPARE 3 HOURS IN ADVANCE

1 recipe Empanada Dough (page 135)

Veal Filling

1 tablespoon olive oil

1 medium onion, finely chopped (about ⅔ cup)

1 garlic clove, finely chopped

¼ pound (2 links) chorizo, finely chopped

1 pound ground veal

3 tablespoons tomato paste

¼ cup dry white wine

1 pimiento, finely chopped

1 tablespoon finely chopped fresh flat-leaf parsley

1 tablespoon finely chopped green olives, preferably
    Spanish

Kosher or sea salt

Freshly ground black pepper

Olive oil, for frying

1. Prepare the dough. Roll out to ⅛-inch thickness and cut into 3-inch rounds with an empanadilla or biscuit cutter.

2. Heat the 1 tablespoon oil in a large skillet over medium heat. Add the onion and garlic and cook, stirring, until the onion is wilted and transparent, about 5 minutes. Add the chorizo and cook, stirring, about 5 minutes more. Increase the heat to high, add the veal, and cook, stirring, until the veal is lightly browned. Stir in the tomato paste, wine, pimiento, parsley, olives, salt, and pepper. Reduce the heat to low and simmer until the meat is cooked through and the sauce is blended, about 20 minutes.

3. Place about 1 tablespoon of the filling in the center of each dough round. Fold over and press the edges with a fork to seal.

4. Heat at least 1 inch of oil in a medium skillet over medium-high heat (or better still, use a deep fryer set at 375°F) until it quickly browns a cube of bread. Place the turnovers in the oil and cook, turning once, until lightly golden, about 2 minutes. Transfer with a slotted spoon to paper towels and let drain. Serve hot.

Baked Turnovers with Tomatoes, Peppers, Onion, Egg, Tuna, and Peas
Cocotets

MAKES ABOUT 40 TAPAS

These tapas are great to serve at parties. The filling includes tuna and, if possible, it should be Spanish tuna, packed in jars. The quality is exceptional.

1 recipe Empanada Dough (page 135) or pizza dough

2 tablespoons olive oil

1 medium onion, finely chopped (about ⅔ cup)

3 garlic cloves, finely chopped

1 medium green bell pepper, finely chopped (about 1 cup)

2 medium tomatoes, chopped (about 1⅓ cups)

3 tablespoons cooked peas

One (7-ounce) jarred white or light meat tuna in oil or water, drained and flaked

1 large hard-boiled egg, finely chopped

Kosher or sea salt

Freshly ground black pepper

1 large egg, lightly beaten

1. Prepare the dough. Roll out to ⅛-inch thickness and cut into 3-inch rounds with an empanadilla or biscuit cutter.

2. Preheat the oven to 350°F. Heat the oil in a medium skillet over medium heat. Add the onion, garlic, and green pepper and cook, stirring, until the vegetables are softened, about 8 minutes. Stir in the tomatoes, peas, tuna, and hard-boiled egg and cook until the tomatoes are absorbed. Let cool. Place 1 tablespoon of the filling in the center of each dough round, pull up the sides and pinch to seal. Brush with the egg.

3. Bake on a lightly greased cookie sheet about 15 minutes or until a deep golden color. Serve hot or at room temperature.

Spicy Meat Turnovers
Empanadillas de Carne

MAKES ABOUT 40 TAPAS

The recipe for these turnovers filled with ground beef flavored by crushed dried red peppers comes from the Bar Coruña in Santiago de Compostela. They can be served either hot or cold.

1 recipe Empanada Dough (page 135)

2 tablespoons olive oil

1 medium onion, finely chopped (about ⅔ cup)

3 garlic cloves, finely chopped

¼ cup finely chopped green bell pepper

1 pound ground beef

Kosher or sea salt

Freshly ground black pepper

3 tablespoons tomato paste

½ cup water

1½ tablespoons dry white wine

¼ teaspoon crushed red chile pepper

Olive oil, for frying

1. Prepare the dough. Roll out to ⅛-inch thickness and cut into 3-inch rounds with an empanadilla or biscuit cutter.

2. Heat the 2 tablespoons oil in a large skillet over medium heat. Add the onion, garlic, and bell pepper and cook, stirring, until the vegetables are softened, about 8 minutes. Add the beef and cook, stirring, until browned. Season with salt and pepper. Stir in the tomato paste, water, wine, and chile pepper, cover, and cook 10 minutes more. Let cool. Place about 1 tablespoon of the filling in the center of each dough round. Fold over and press the edges with a fork to seal.

3. Heat at least 1 inch of oil in a medium skillet over medium-high heat (or better still, use a deep fryer set at 375°F) until it quickly browns a cube of bread. Place the turnovers in the oil and cook, turning once, until lightly golden, about 2 minutes. Transfer with a slotted spoon to paper towels and let drain. Serve hot.

Canapés and Pâtes

Garlic and Tomato Bread Ⓥ
Pa Amb Tomáquet

MAKES 4 TAPAS

This regional specialty of Barcelona can now be found in many parts of Spain. It is best when served with thick slices of Catalan country bread, which should be toasted and served warm.

5 tablespoons extra-virgin olive oil

4 garlic cloves, mashed in a garlic press or mortar

4 (¾-inch) slices round country bread or long-loaf (baguette) bread

1 very ripe medium tomato

I. Preheat the oven to 350°F. In small bowl, combine the oil and garlic. Place the bread slices on a cookie sheet and toast until lightly crisp. Leave the oven on.

2. Cut the tomato in half crosswise and gently squeeze each half to extract the seeds. Brush the bread with the garlic mixture and rub well with the tomato. Repeat for the other side of the bread. (May be prepared ahead.) Toast again in the oven until crisp. Serve warm.

Egg and Mushroom Canapé Ⓥ
Pincho de Revuelto de Seta

MAKES 8 TO 12 TAPAS

Scrambled eggs on bread as a tapa is common throughout the north of Spain, where they prefer their tapas to be rich and filling. The best version of these garlicky egg and mushroom tapas that I have ever found came from the Basque city of Vitoria.

2 large eggs

4 teaspoons milk

Kosher or sea salt

Freshly ground black pepper

2 tablespoons olive oil

8 medium mushrooms, rinsed, trimmed, and coarsely chopped (about 6 ounces)

2 tablespoons finely chopped fresh flat-leaf parsley

2 garlic cloves, finely chopped

8 to 12 (½-inch) slices long-loaf (baguette) bread

I. Half fill with hot water a skillet that is slightly larger than the one in which the eggs will cook. Bring to a boil over high heat, reduce the heat to low to keep at a simmer. In a small bowl, lightly beat the eggs, milk, salt, and pepper.

2. Heat the oil in a small skillet over high heat. Add the mushrooms and cook about 1 minute. Stir in the parsley, cook a few seconds, then remove from the heat. Add the eggs and place the skillet in the larger skillet of hot water. Stir constantly with a wooden spoon until the eggs are set but still soft. (May be prepared ahead.) Spoon the mixture onto each bread slice. Serve at room temperature.

Roasted Vegetable and Strawberry Toasts
Tostas de Escalivada con Fresón

MAKES ABOUT 12 TAPAS

Chef Sergi Arola of the La Broche restaurant in Madrid always surprises me with his innovative creations. Roasted vegetables are commonly served with tomatoes, but in Sergi's signature version, he omits the tomatoes and instead adds strawberries. A very unique and refreshing tapa that my party guests love.

¼ pound baby eggplant

¼ pound red bell pepper

½ medium onion

2 small strawberries, hulled and thinly sliced lengthwise

4 black olives, finely chopped, preferably Spanish

1 tablespoon finely chopped fresh flat-leaf parsley

1 small garlic clove, mashed in a garlic press or mortar

¼ teaspoon balsamic vinegar

2 teaspoons extra-virgin olive oil

8 (⅜-inch) long-loaf (baguette) bread

Olive oil, for brushing

8 canned or jarred anchovy fillets

16 capers (nonpareil preferred), rinsed and drained

1. Preheat the oven to 500°F. Arrange the eggplant, pepper, and onion in a roasting pan and roast about 20 minutes, turning the eggplant, and pepper once. Let cool, then peel, core, and seed the pepper. Peel the eggplant, cut in half lengthwise, and remove most of the seeds.

2. Coarsely chop the pepper, eggplant, and onion while still warm and transfer to a medium bowl. Fold in the strawberries, olives, parsley, garlic, vinegar and 2 teaspoons oil. Cover and refrigerate 2 hours up to overnight to meld the flavors.

3. Preheat the oven to 350°F. Remove the strawberry mixture from the refrigerator. Place the bread on a cookie sheet and bake until crisp but not browned. Brush with the oil and spread 1 tablespoon of the topping on each bread slice. Place an anchovy diagonally across the top and a caper to either side. Serve at room temperature.

Black Olive Paste
Pâté de Aceituna Negra

MAKES ABOUT 24 TAPAS

Simply spread on bread rounds, this is great over goat cheese or combined with other compatible ingredients of your choice. It's best when made in advance.

PREPARE AT LEAST 2 HOURS IN ADVANCE

40 pitted black olives (about 4 ounces), preferably Spanish

1 small garlic clove, finely chopped

2 teaspoons capers (nonpareil preferred), rinsed, drained, and finely chopped

2 anchovy fillets, finely chopped

2 teaspoons extra-virgin olive oil

24 (¼-inch) slices long-loaf (baguette) bread

Thin pimiento strips, for garnish

Combine all ingredients except the bread in a medium bowl, mashing lightly with a fork. Cover and refrigerate at least 2 hours up to overnight to meld flavors. Spread about ½ teaspoon over each bread slice and top with 1 pimiento strip and serve.

Olives, Capers, and Anchovies Paste
Tapenade

MAKES ABOUT 24 TAPAS

A very simple and tasty spread for toasts (or crackers), this one will disappear quickly.

40 pitted black olives, preferably Spanish

2 garlic cloves

1 tablespoon capers (nonpareil preferred), rinsed and drained

2 or 3 anchovy fillets

6 slices sandwich bread, crust removed, toasted, each cut into 4 triangles

Combine all the ingredients except the toast in a blender and blend until as finely chopped as possible. Spread thinly on each toast triangle and serve at room temperature.

Olive "Paste" and Blue Cheese Canapé ⓥ
Canapé de Pasta de Aceituna Negra y Queso Cabrales

MAKES 12 TAPAS

This canapé originated in Asturias, the region in northern Spain where Cabrales cheese is produced. The paste of black olives, garlic, and crunchy pine nuts is the perfect complement to this strongly flavored cheese. In order for the black olives to give the proper flavor, they must be cured.

¼ pound pitted black olives, preferably Spanish

1 large garlic clove, mashed in a garlic press or mortar

2 tablespoons pine nuts

3 tablespoons extra-virgin olive oil

¼ to ½ pound blue cheese, such as Cabrales, Roquefort, or Gorgonzola, crumbled

12 (¼-inch) slices long-loaf (baguette) bread

Pitted black olives, coarsely chopped, for garnish

Place the ¼ pound olives, the garlic, pine nuts, and olive oil in a food processor and process until as finely chopped as possible. (May be prepared ahead.) Spread thinly on each bread slice. Sprinkle with the blue cheese. Decorate with the chopped olives. Serve at room temperature.

Green Olive "Paste" Canapé
Canapé de Pasta de Aceituna Verde

MAKES ABOUT 12 TAPAS

This paste is terrific when spread on a piece of bread but can also serve as a condiment to enhance other dishes, such as meatballs and salads. The ingredients are quintessentially Spanish—olives, capers, anchovies, almonds, and garlic.

40 pitted green olives, preferably Spanish, coarsely chopped

1 teaspoon capers (nonpareil preferred) rinsed and drained

4 canned or jarred anchovy fillets, coarsely chopped

1 teaspoon finely ground blanched almonds

1 garlic clove, mashed in a garlic press or mortar

¼ cup fruity extra-virgin olive oil

⅛ teaspoon ground cumin

¼ teaspoon ground sweet paprika, such as Spanish smoked

1½ teaspoons finely chopped fresh thyme or ¼ teaspoon dried thyme

Freshly ground black pepper

12 thin slices long-loaf (baguette) bread

Jarred or canned piquillo peppers or pimientos, for garnish

Place all the ingredients except the bread and piquillo peppers in a food processor and process until as finely chopped as possible. Transfer to a mortar and mash. (May be prepared ahead.) Spread thinly on each bread slice and garnish with the piquillo peppers. Serve at room temperature.

Anchovy and Pimiento Spread
Canapé de Anchoa y Pimiento

MAKES 12 TO 16 TAPAS

A highly popular tapa that is very simple to prepare, this anchovy and pimiento spread should be refrigerated, then served on crustless bread triangles.

PREPARE AT LEAST 2 HOURS IN ADVANCE

3 ounces canned anchovy fillets, drained and finely chopped

2 pimientos, finely chopped

½ cup finely chopped Spanish (yellow) onion

1 tablespoon finely chopped fresh flat-leaf parsley

Freshly ground black pepper

1 tablespoon extra-virgin olive oil

1¼ teaspoons red wine vinegar

3 to 4 slices sandwich bread, crust removed

In a small bowl, combine the anchovy, pimientos, onion, parsley, and pepper. Stir in the olive oil and vinegar. Cover and refrigerate at least 2 hours up to overnight. Spread thinly on each bread slice and cut into 4 triangles and serve.

Avocado Dip Ⓥ
Mojo de Aguacate

MAKES 6 SERVINGS

This popular dip is from the semitropical Canary Islands, where avocados and all kinds of fruits and vegetables thrive.

2 avocados, peeled and pitted

2 teaspoons fresh lemon juice

½ teaspoon salt

4 teaspoons extra-virgin olive oil

¼ cup finely chopped fresh cilantro

2 large garlic cloves, mashed in a garlic press or mortar

Bread sticks

Place all the ingredients except the bread sticks in a food processor and process until smooth. Transfer to a small bowl and serve at room temperature with the bread sticks.

Avocado, Egg, and Anchovy Canapé
Canapé de Aguacate, Huevo y Anchoa

MAKES 2 TAPAS

Hard-boiled egg combines perfectly with avocado. The bread should be a loaf of either Italian or French country bread. Increase the ingredients based on the number of pieces you want to serve.

2 thin slices long-loaf (baguette) bread

Olive oil, for brushing

Flat lettuce leaf, torn to fit bread slices

2 crosswise slices large hard-boiled egg

2 crosswise ⅛-inch slices avocado

2 anchovy fillets

2 thin strips (jarred) piquillo peppers, for garnish

1. Preheat the oven to 350°F. Brush the bread with the oil. Place the bread on a cookie sheet and bake until lightly browned, turning once.

2. On each bread slice, place first the lettuce, then 1 egg, 1 avocado, and 1 anchovy. Garnish with the peppers and serve.

Pâté with Pine Nut and Orange Zest Syrup

Pâté con Piñones y Naranja

MAKES 8 TAPAS

Pâté, in spite of its French name, has a long tradition in Spanish gastronomy due to the popularity of hunting and the need to preserve food before refrigeration. I had this tapa at a restaurant in Albarracín, a beautiful village in the mountainous province of Teruel, which is surrounded by forests of pine trees from which pine nuts are foraged. Not far away, in Valencia and Castellón, are plentiful orange groves. To use homemade pâté, make the Chicken Liver Pâté (page 99) without the glaze.

PREPARE AT LEAST 2 HOURS IN ADVANCE

½ cup sugar

½ cup water

Salt

Peel of 1 orange (orange part only), cut into very thin 2-inch strips

¼ cup pine nuts

8 thin slices long-loaf (baguette) bread, toasted if desired

¼ pound liver pâté, storebought or homemade

I. In a small saucepan, combine the sugar, water, salt, orange, and pine nuts. Heat over medium heat and cook, stirring, until the sugar is dissolved. Reduce the heat to low and let simmer 15 minutes more. Let cool completely. Cover and refrigerate at least 2 hours up to overnight to meld flavors.

2. Cut the pâté into thin slices. Place I slice on each bread slice, top with the syrup and serve.

Mushroom and Quince Toast with Garlic Sauce and Cured Ham

Tosta de Setas, Alioli, Membrillo y Jamón

MAKES 16 TAPAS

The key to this recipe is the very special and unusual alioli that has a base of apple and quince, two fruits grown mostly in the north of Spain. With the addition of the mushrooms and the cured ham, the result is a delicious tapa.

1 medium apple, peeled, sliced, and seeded

3 medium quince, peeled, sliced, and seeded or 1 cup quince paste (membrillo)

3 tablespoons olive oil

⅓ pound mushrooms, rinsed, trimmed, and thinly sliced

2 tablespoons honey

1 garlic clove, mashed in a garlic press or mortar

¼ pound Serrano (Spanish cured mountain) ham or prosciutto, thinly sliced

16 thin slices long-loaf (baguette) bread

I. Place the apple, quince, if using the fruit, and honey in a medium saucepan and add water to cover. Cook, stirring, over medium heat until tender. Drain and let cool.

2. Meanwhile, heat the 2 tablespoons oil in a small skillet over medium heat. Add the mushrooms and cook, stirring, until softened and the juices have evaporated.

3. Preheat the oven to 350°F. Transfer the fruit to a food processor and blend until smooth. With the motor running, gradually add the quince paste, if using, the remaining I tablespoon oil and the garlic and blend until smooth.

continues . . .

4. Spread each bread slice generously with the fruit alioli. Top with mushrooms then the ham slices cut to the size of the bread. Place on a cookie sheet and bake until golden. Serve hot or at room temperature.

Manchego Cheese with Quince Paste V

Queso Manchego con Membrillo

MAKES 6 SERVINGS

Quince is a fruit similar to an apple, and it is an excellent complement to a sharp cheese such as Spanish Manchego. This is commonly served as a dessert in Spain but also popular as a tapa. When quince is made into paste form, it is called dulce de membrillo, *which can be found quite easily in specialty food stores in the United States. It is a delicious and memorable blend of flavors that can be served either before or after the main meal.*

2 (¼-pound) wedges aged Manchego cheese or other aged sheep's milk cheese
½ pound quince paste (membrillo) or quince marmalade

Trim the rind from each cheese wedge. Place each wedge on its side and slice into ¼-inch-thick triangles. Slice the quince paste into the same size triangles in the same manner and place on top of the cheese, or if using quince marmalade, spread it over the cheese. (May be prepared ahead.) Serve at room temperature.

Goat Cheese in Cherry Tomatoes with Orange Marmalade V

Queso de Cabra con Tomate Picante y Naranja

MAKES 8 TAPAS

This tapa requires a little work but the results are quite satisfying. The combination of the marmalade, the garlic, and the hot sauce is very intriguing.

8 cherry tomatoes
Kosher or sea salt
Pinch of sugar
2 drops hot sauce, such as Tabasco
1 small garlic clove, finely chopped
¼ pound soft fresh goat cheese, cubed
Peel of 2 oranges (orange part only), cut into very thin 2-inch strips
Storebought or homemade Black Olive Paste (page 88)
Orange marmalade
⅛ teaspoon dried thyme
Extra-virgin olive oil

1. Preheat the oven to 350°F. Cut the top off each tomato. Scoop out the inside. In a cup, mix the salt, sugar, hot sauce, and garlic and sprinkle over the tomatoes. Fill three-quarters full with the cheese.

2. Bake 20 minutes or until the tomatoes have softened and the cheese has melted. Spread each with a little black olive paste then with the marmalade. Sprinkle with the thyme and drizzle with the olive oil. Serve at room temperature.

Goat Cheese, Piquillo Peppers, and Honey Canapé Ⓥ

Canapé de Queso de Cabra con Piquillos y Miel

MAKES 12 TAPAS

A heavenly blend of flavors, this tapa can be prepared in less than 5 minutes. The sweetness of the honey completes the complex flavors of this very memorable canapé.

3 ounces fresh goat cheese
12 plain crackers or Melba toast rounds
4 (jarred) piquillo peppers or pimientos, cut into ½-inch strips
1 tablespoon honey

Spread the goat cheese on the crackers. Top with the pepper strips and drizzle with the honey. Serve at room temperature.

Creamed Blue Cheese with Brandy Ⓥ

Crema de Cabrales al Coñac

MAKES 16 TAPAS

This simple pâté recipe calls for Asturias' famed Cabrales blue cheese, made more flavorful by the distinctive taste of Spanish brandy. The flavor is even better if it is left to sit overnight at room temperature.

16 thin slices long-loaf (baguette) bread
½ pound blue cheese, such as Cabrales, Gorgonzola, or Roquefort, at room temperature
1 teaspoon brandy
Finely chopped fresh flat-leaf parsley, for garnish

1. Preheat the oven to 350°F. Place the bread on a cookie sheet and toast about 5 minutes or until lightly browned and crisp. Let cool.

2. In a small bowl, mash the cheese well with a fork. Mix in the brandy until smooth. (You may serve the cheese mixture right away, or cover and let sit overnight at room temperature or in the refrigerator.)

3. Spread the cheese on each bread slice and garnish with the parsley, or serve the bread and cheese separately and let the guests assemble the toasts themselves.

Blue Cheese and Pine Nut Canapé Ⓥ

Canapé de Cabrales y Piñones

MAKES 20 TAPAS

The recipe for these canapés comes from Asturias, home to Cabrales cheese. If unavailable, you may substitute another blue cheese such as Roquefort or Gorgonzola.

10 tablespoons strong blue cheese, such as Roquefort or Gorgonzola, at room temperature
5 slices sandwich bread, crust removed
5 tablespoons pine nuts
5 pitted black olives, preferably Spanish, sliced

In a small bowl, mash the cheese with a fork until smooth enough to spread. Spread each bread slice with the cheese and cut into 4 triangles. Sprinkle with the pine nuts, pressing down lightly so they adhere to the cheese. Decorate with the olives and serve at room temperature.

Cabrales Blue Cheese Toast with Liqueur, Honey, and Almonds Ⓥ

Tosta de Cabrales con Orujo, Miel y Almendra

MAKES 8 TAPAS

Cabrales blue cheese, a product from the high mountains of Asturias and León, has a characteristic consistency and flavor quite different from other better-known blues. Here it is combined with orujo, a liqueur from northern Spain very similar to grappa, obtained from the stems and skins of the grapes after they are crushed to obtain wine. The resulting flavor is robust and very pleasant.

8 thin slices long-loaf (baguette) bread
Extra-virgin olive oil
¼ pound Cabrales Spanish blue cheese or other blue cheese, softened
2½ tablespoons Spanish orujo or grappa
Honey, for drizzling
Blanched sliced almonds, lightly toasted

1. Preheat the oven to 350°F. Brush the bread with the oil. Bake until lightly browned, turning once.

2. In a small bowl, mash the cheese well with a fork. Mix in the liqueur until smooth. Spread about 1 tablespoon on each bread slice. Drizzle with the honey and sprinkle with the almonds. Serve at room temperature.

Marinated Lettuce Canapés Ⓥ

Canapé de Lechuga a la Vinagreta

MAKES ABOUT 24 TAPAS

These simple miniature lettuce sandwiches are an outstanding creation from the elegant Lhardy restaurant in Madrid. Everything at this restaurant is excellent, and the ambience takes you back to times of old.

PREPARE 8 TO 12 HOURS IN ADVANCE

3 teaspoons mayonnaise (mayonesa, page 359)
6 tablespoons extra-virgin olive oil
3 tablespoons vinegar
Pinch of sugar
Salt
Freshly ground black pepper
1 medium head romaine lettuce (green part only), shredded
12 very thin slices sandwich bread, crust removed

1. Place the mayonnaise in a small bowl. Gradually whisk in the oil, then add the vinegar, sugar, salt, and pepper and whisk until well blended. Place the lettuce in a large bowl, pour in the mayonnaise mixture, and mix well. Cover and refrigerate 8 hours up to overnight.

2. Spread the lettuce mixture on 3 slices of bread and top with the other 3 slices. Press gently, then cut each sandwich on the diagonal twice to make 4 triangles. Serve cold. (If not served right away, wrap loosely in a damp towel until ready to serve.)

Fried Cheese Canapé Ⓥ

Canapé de Queso Frito

MAKES 10 TO 12 TAPAS

In this classic Spanish canapé, the cheese will adhere nicely to the bread after frying.

2 ounces grated aged Manchego or Parmesan cheese
½ cup all-purpose flour
¼ cup plus 1 tablespoon milk
2 tablespoons unsalted butter
⅛ teaspoon salt
Freshly ground black pepper
½ egg, lightly beaten

1 long-loaf (baguette) bread, cut into ¼-inch slices

Olive oil, for frying

1. Combine the cheese and flour in a small bowl. Combine the milk, butter, and salt in a small saucepan and bring to a boil over medium heat. Add the cheese and flour mixture and stir until a semisoft ball forms. Remove from the heat. Add the egg and beat with a whisk until smooth.

2. Heat at least ½ inch of oil in a medium skillet over medium-high heat (or better still, use a deep fryer set at 365°F) until it turns a cube of bread light brown in 60 seconds.

3. With the cup side of a spoon, cover the bread slices with 2 teaspoons of the cheese mixture, pressing to the bread so it adheres well. Place the canapés in the oil, cheese side down, and cook, turning once, until golden. Let drain on paper towels. Serve hot.

Canapé of Mackerel and Serrano Ham

Montadito de Caballa y Jamón

MAKES 8 TAPAS

This simple but very tasty tapa is a specialty of Casa Poli in Madrid and also a favorite of my husband Luis. Mackerel and Serrano ham are a wonderful combination.

PREPARE AT LEAST 2 HOURS IN ADVANCE

¼ pound Serrano (Spanish cured mountain) ham or prosciutto, cut into ¼-inch slices

8 (¼-inch) slices long-loaf (baguette) bread

One (4½-ounce) can mackerel fillets in olive oil, such as imported from Spain

Place the ham on each of the 8 bread slices and top with 1 mackerel fillet. Cover and refrigerate at least 2 hours. Serve cold.

Clam Toast

Tostá de Berberechos

MAKES 8 TAPAS

My mother-in-law Clara Orozco, a Madrileña of Basque descent, always added dried chile pepper to this recipe, which gives the clam toast a spicy accent. It's a very popular tapa in Spain.

6 medium clams, such as Manila or littleneck or 2 (5-ounce) cans Spanish cockles

⅓ cup bottled clam juice or water

2 tablespoons olive oil

1 medium onion, finely chopped (about ⅔ cup)

2 garlic cloves, finely chopped

¼ cup finely chopped fresh flat-leaf parsley

½ medium-hot dried chile pepper, such as Spanish guindilla, seeded and crumbled, or ¼ teaspoon crushed red pepper

4 teaspoons all-purpose flour

4 slices sandwich bread, crust removed and very lightly toasted

1. Rinse the clams. Discard any with cracked shells or that do not close tightly when touched. Remove and finely chop the clam meat.

2. Heat the oil in a medium skillet over low heat. Add the onion, and cook, stirring, until wilted and transparent, about 5 minutes. Cover and cook 20 minutes more or until tender but not colored.

3. Uncover and increase the heat to medium-low. Add the garlic, parsley, and chile pepper and cook 2 to 3 minutes more, then stir in the flour. Increase the heat to medium-high, add the reserved clam juice and the clams, and cook until thick enough to spread. (May be prepared ahead.)

4. Cut each bread slice in half diagonally. Spread with the clam mixture and serve hot.

Canapé of Eggs, Hake, and Zucchini

Canapé de Revuelto de Merluza y Calabacín

MAKES 8 TAPAS

Luis Alberto, who took over Casa Fermín in the city of Oviedo from his father-in-law Luis Gil Lus, is well known for his traditional Asturian dishes such as bean stew (fabada), but he also makes it a point to keep up with the latest trends. This is a sensational egg dish that can be served on its own or as a tapa.

2 large eggs

2 teaspoons milk

Kosher or sea salt

Freshly ground white pepper

1 tablespoon olive oil

2 tablespoons finely chopped onion, such as Vidalia or other sweet onion

½ cup diced zucchini

2 ounces hake or fresh cod, finely chopped

8 thin slices long-loaf (baguette) bread

1. In a small bowl, lightly beat the eggs, milk, salt, and pepper. Heat the oil in a medium skillet over low heat. Add the onion and cook, stirring, until wilted and transparent, about 3 minutes. Add the zucchini, salt, and pepper and cook, stirring, 1 minute more. Cover and cook about 4 minutes more or until the zucchini is tender. Uncover, add the hake, and cook until the fish turns white, about 1 to 2 minutes.

2. Half fill a slightly larger skillet with water and bring to a boil over high heat. Reduce the heat to low and place the skillet with the zucchini mixture in the larger skillet, double boiler fashion. Add the eggs and stir constantly with a wooden spoon until the eggs are set but still quite soft. (May be prepared ahead.)

3. Spoon the mixture onto each bread slice and serve warm or at room temperature.

Marinated Tuna and Tomato on Bread Triangles

Canapé de Atún y Tomate

MAKES 16 TAPAS

This tuna tapa of Basque origin is popular in the fishing town of Bermeo. The recipe calls for canned tuna, but it is important that you use a stronger flavored tuna, not white tuna.

PREPARE 8 TO 12 HOURS IN ADVANCE

One (7-ounce) can or jar white or light meat tuna, drained and flaked

1½ teaspoons red wine vinegar

2 tablespoons finely chopped onion

2 tablespoons finely chopped pimiento

1 tablespoon finely chopped fresh flat-leaf parsley

5 tablespoons tomato sauce or diluted tomato paste

2 tablespoons finely chopped hard-boiled egg

Salt

Freshly ground black pepper

16 thin slices long-loaf (baguette) bread

1 large hard-boiled egg, thinly sliced, for garnish

1. In a small bowl, combine the tuna, vinegar, onion, pimiento, and parsley. Stir in the tomato sauce, chopped egg, salt, and pepper. Cover and let marinate in the refrigerator 8 hours up to overnight.

2. Spread thickly on each of 8 bread slices and top each with another bread slice. Cut each sandwich diagonally to make 4 triangles. Garnish with the egg and serve, 2 pieces per serving.

Fresh Fish Spread
Ensaladilla de Pescado

MAKES 8 TO 10 TAPAS

This recipe comes from Nou Manolín, a popular restaurant and tapas bar in the city of Alicante. It is best when you use a mild fish such as fresh cod, scrod, or tilefish. The addition of potatoes makes this tasty spread thicker and heartier. You can serve it in a bowl with bread on the side or spread on the bread as a canapé.

3½ cups Cooking Liquid (page 26; partial recipe)

8 to 10 thin slices long-loaf (baguette) bread

1 small potato (about 2 ounces)

¼ pound fresh cod, scrod, tilefish, or other mild fish

3 tablespoons mayonnaise (mayonesa, page 359)

½ large hard-boiled egg, finely chopped

2 tablespoons shredded lettuce (white rib portion only)

Kosher or sea salt

Freshly ground black pepper

Finely chopped fresh flat-leaf parsley, for garnish

1. Prepare the cooking liquid. Preheat the oven to 350°F. Place the bread on a cookie sheet and bake about 5 minutes or until lightly golden and crisp. Reserve.

2. Place the potato in a small saucepan and add cold water to cover and salt. Cover and bring to a simmer over low heat. Cook about 10 to 12 minutes or until tender when pierced with a knife. Drain well and let cool slightly. Peel and cut into small cubes. Reserve.

3. Meanwhile, place the fish in a medium saucepan with cooking liquid to cover and bring to a boil over high heat. Reduce the heat to low, cover, and simmer, turning once, 10 minutes. Shred the fish with your fingers into a medium bowl. Fold in the potato, fish, mayonnaise, egg, lettuce, salt, and pepper. (May be prepared ahead.) Spread on each bread slice or serve in a small bowl with the toasted bread. Garnish with the parsley and serve.

Fish, Mayonnaise, and Lettuce Spread
Merluza Bar Parisienne

MAKES ABOUT 6 SERVINGS

This simple fish spread is named after the Bar Parisienne in Cádiz, one of my favorite cities in Spain. I like it best when made with hake or fresh cod steak.

PREPARE 1 HOUR IN ADVANCE

¾ cup dry white wine

2 sprigs parsley

1 scallion, cut into 3 pieces

2 slices medium onion

1 bay leaf

3 peppercorns

Kosher or sea salt

1½ teaspoons finely chopped fresh thyme or ¼ teaspoon dried thyme

1 cup water

½ pound hake or fresh cod steak

¼ cup finely chopped romaine lettuce (white stem portions only)

Mayonnaise (mayonesa, page 359), to taste

Fresh ground black pepper

Thin slices long-loaf (baguette) bread or crackers

1. In a medium skillet, place the wine, parsley, scallion, onion, bay leaf, peppercorns, salt, and thyme and bring to a boil over high heat. Cook, stirring occasionally, until reduced by half. Add the water and fish and return to a boil. Reduce the heat to low, cover, and simmer, turning once, 10 minutes. Drain, remove the bay leaf, and let cool.

continues...

2. Shred the fish with your fingers into a medium bowl. Fold in the lettuce, mayonnaise, salt, and ground pepper. Cover and refrigerate 2 hours up to overnight to meld flavors. Serve cold with the bread.

Smoked Salmon Toast
Tostada de Salmón

MAKES 8 TAPAS

This recipe is from José Ramón Elizondo, owner of Aloña Berri, a bar in San Sebastían. All of his tapas are delicious and always presented in a creative way that is visually pleasing. Most of the items on José's menu are more elaborate, but this simple smoked salmon toast can be made in almost no time at all.

2 ounces smoked salmon, finely chopped
1 tablespoon finely chopped dill pickle
1 tablespoon finely chopped scallions
Mayonnaise (mayonesa, page 359), to taste
Freshly ground black pepper
2 tablespoons finely chopped fresh flat-leaf parsley
8 thin slices long-loaf (baguette) bread

1. Preheat the oven to 450°F. Toast the bread slices on a cookie sheet in the oven for 5 minutes until crisp.

2. In a small bowl, combine the salmon, pickle, scallions, mayonnaise, pepper, and 1 tablespoon of the parsley. (May be prepared ahead.)

3. Spoon onto each bread slice and sprinkle with the remaining 1 tablespoon parsley. Serve at room temperature or refrigerate at least 2 hours and serve cold.

Anchovy, Chicken, and Tomato Canapé
Canapé de Anchoa y Pollo con Tomate

MAKES 10 TAPAS

The flavors in this very unusual combination of ingredients blend beautifully.

10 thin slices long-loaf (baguette) bread
Mayonnaise (mayonesa, page 359), to taste
20 anchovy fillets
2 pimientos, cut into thin strips
¼ cup tomato sauce or diluted tomato paste
Dash of ground cayenne pepper
¼ cup finely chopped boiled chicken
Finely chopped fresh flat-leaf parsley, for garnish

1. Preheat the oven to 450°F. Place the bread on a cookie sheet and toast 5 minutes or until crisp.

2. Spread with the mayonnaise. Cut the anchovies into pieces to fit on the toast and arrange them on top. Spread the anchovies with mayonnaise. Cut the pimientos into 10 strips the length of the toast and place 1 on each canapé.

3. Mix the tomato sauce and cayenne pepper in a small bowl. Spread 1 teaspoon onto each canapé, sprinkle with the chicken, and garnish with the parsley. Serve at room temperature.

Pâté with Fresh Figs
Pâté con Brevas

MAKES 4 SERVINGS

It's easy to prepare this unusual pâté. If you don't have time to make homemade liver pâté, you can purchase a good quality pâté, which should be smooth in texture. The fresh figs add a sweetness that is unexpected and delicious, and the cream lends a pleasant contrast of texture and flavor. To use homemade pâté, follow the Chicken Liver Pâté with Sherry Glaze (below), but omit the glaze.

4 fresh figs, cut into ½-inch crosswise slices

2 ounces pâté, storebought or homemade, cut into ¼-inch slices

¼ cup heavy cream

Parsley sprigs, for garnish

1. Arrange the figs on a serving dish. Cut pieces of pâté about the same size as the figs. Place 1 piece on top of each fig and secure with a toothpick. (May be prepared in advance.)

2. Pour the cream around—not over—the tapas. Garnish with the parsley sprigs and serve at room temperature. If you prepare the figs and pâté in advance, add the cream just before serving.

Chicken Liver Pâté with Sherry Glaze
Pâté de Higaditos al Pedro Ximénez

MAKES 8 SERVINGS

Our dear friend Irene, who owns Casa Irene, a charming restaurant in the majestic Pyrenees Mountains, has given me more recipes than I can count. We visit her every time we go to Spain, and we always know the meal will be spectacular. This is Irene's recipe for chicken liver pâté, glazed in a very sweet sherry, preferably Ximénez sherry.

PREPARE AT LEAST 3 HOURS IN ADVANCE

12 tablespoons (1½ sticks) unsalted butter, softened

½ medium onion, such as Vidalia or other sweet onion, finely chopped (about ¼ cup)

1 garlic clove, finely chopped

½ pound chicken livers

2 teaspoons kosher or sea salt

Generous amount of freshly ground black pepper

1½ teaspoons finely chopped fresh thyme or ½ teaspoon dried thyme

¼ teaspoon freshly ground nutmeg

1½ tablespoons brandy

½ cup heavy cream

¼ cup very sweet (Pedro Ximénez) or cream sherry

¼ tablespoon gelatin powder

Parsley sprigs, for garnish

Thin slices long-loaf (baguette) bread

1. Melt 2 tablespoons of the butter in a medium skillet over low heat. Add the onion and garlic, cover, and cook, stirring occasionally, about 15 minutes or until the onion is softened. Increase the heat to medium, add the chicken livers, salt, pepper, thyme, and nutmeg, and cook, stirring, until the livers are no longer pink in the center.

2. Pour the sherry evenly around the skillet. Standing well away from the skillet, ignite the liquid with a match or kitchen lighter, shaking the pan to prevent burning. Cover to extinguish. Let cool.

3. Transfer the liver mixture to a food processor, add the remaining 10 tablespoons butter, and process until smooth. Add the cream and process until well incorporated. Transfer to custard cups or ramekins, smooth the surface with a spoon, and place in the refrigerator at least 2 hours or until firm.

4. In a small saucepan, combine the sherry and gelatin and let stand 1 minute. Heat over low heat until the gelatin is completely dissolved. Let cool a few minutes, then pour a scant 1 tablespoon over each custard cup. Return to the refrigerator at least 1 hour or until the gelatin has solidified.

5. Bring to room temperature before serving. Garnish with the parsley and serve with the bread.

Duck and Serrano Ham Pâté

Pâté de Pato

This pâté recipe comes from the Ritz Hotel in Madrid, which has been famous since the 1900s. The hotel's restaurant and bar are both exquisite, and this duck pâté with Serrano ham is the best I have ever eaten.

PREPARE AT LEAST 3 DAYS IN ADVANCE

½ pound chicken livers, cut into small pieces

1 duck liver, cut into small pieces

3½ pound duck, skinned, boned, fat removed, and cut into pieces

¾ pound lean boneless pork loin or shoulder

¼ pound pork fat

2 large eggs

2 tablespoons kosher or sea salt

2 tablespoons freshly ground black pepper

1½ teaspoons finely chopped fresh thyme or ¾ teaspoon dried thyme

½ cup dry sherry, such as Fino

¼ cup brandy

2 large garlic cloves, finely chopped

2 tablespoons finely chopped fresh flat-leaf parsley

⅓ cup small cubes (¼ inch) Serrano (Spanish cured mountain) ham or prosciutto (not salty) (about 2 ounces)

Pork fatback or bacon in thin slices

4 bay leaves

1. In a food processor, place the livers, duck, pork, and pork fat and process until a medium (slightly chunky) consistency. With brief pulses, mix in the eggs, salt, pepper, thyme, sherry, brandy, garlic and parsley. Stir in the ham.

2. Bring a medium pot of water to a boil over high heat then remove from the heat. Meanwhile, preheat the oven to 350°F. Line a 9¼ x 5¼-inch loaf pan with strips of fatback and extend over the sides. Pour in the pâté mixture, arrange the bay leaves in a row down the center, then fold over the strips of fatback to cover the pâté. (If they do not cover, add more strips.) Cover the surface and pan rim tightly with foil.

3. Place the loaf pan in a roasting pan. Gently pour about 1 inch of the boiling water into the roasting pan. Bake 2 hours until set. Remove the loaf pan from the water, loosen the foil, and pour off and discard any fat.

4. Place a heavy object (a brick covered with foil is ideal) on top of the foil and let cool. Remove the weight, cover, and refrigerate at least 3 days. Bring to room temperature before serving. Remove the bay leaves and serve.

Partridge and Chicken Liver Pâté

Terrina de Perdiz

MAKES AT LEAST 10 TO 12 SERVINGS

This more elaborate pâté is less coarse than most and has the unique additional flavor of partridge. I always serve it on pumpernickel bread that has been sliced into tapa-size squares.

PREPARE AT LEAST 3 HOURS IN ADVANCE

¼ pound slab bacon, coarsely chopped

Meat from a 1-pound partridge or pheasant or 2 quail, coarsely chopped

1 partridge liver (optional)

1 pound chicken livers, cut into small pieces

¼ cup all-purpose flour

¼ cup dry sherry, such as Fino

2 tablespoons brandy

2 tablespoons heavy cream

2 large eggs

¼ cup kosher or sea salt

¼ teaspoon freshly ground black pepper

½ teaspoon freshly ground nutmeg

1 tablespoon truffles (optional)

Pumpernickel bread, thinly sliced

1. In a food processor, place the bacon, partridge meat, partridge liver, if using, and chicken livers and process until finely chopped. Add the flour and process until smooth. With the motor running, add the sherry, brandy, cream, eggs, salt, pepper, and nutmeg. With brief pulses, mix in the truffles, if using. Transfer to a loaf pan, cover the surface and pan rim tightly with foil. Place a heavy object (a small brick covered with foil is an ideal size and weight) on top of the foil and refrigerate for 2 hours.

2. Remove the weight and refrigerate at least 3 days. Bring to room temperature before serving.

3. Cut bread into small squares. Serve the pâté with the bread.

Potato, Liver Pâté, Mushroom, and Caramelized Apple
Montaditos de Patata, Pâté, Seta y Manzana

MAKES 8 SERVINGS

This innovative tapa is the creation of José Ramón Elizondo, who owns the Aloña Berri bar in San Sebastián. José is very passionate about his tapas, and their presentation rivals that of a 3-star restaurant. This pâté combines potatoes, mushrooms, and caramelized apples, creating a taste sensation that is out of this world. Caramelizing the sugar at the end requires a kitchen torch. If you don't have one, you can place the tapas on a broiler pan and as close to the heat as possible.

2 tiny (1¼-inch) new potatoes

1 Golden Delicious apple, peeled, sliced lengthwise up the core, and cut into 8 (1½-inch) rounds

Apple juice or water

1 tablespoon olive oil

8 oyster mushroom ears, each cut into 1½-inch pieces, or other mushrooms, cut into ¼-inch slices

1 ounce liver pâté, homemade or storebought, cut into ⅛-inch slices

8 tablespoons spiced applesauce

2 teaspoons sugar

1. Place the potatoes in a small saucepan and add cold water to cover and salt. Cover and bring to a simmer over low heat. Cook about 15 minutes or until tender when pierced with a knife. Drain well and let cool slightly. Peel and cut into ¼-inch slices.

2. Place the apples in a small skillet with apple juice to cover. Bring to a boil over high heat, reduce the heat to low, and simmer until the apples are crisp-tender. Drain. Wipe out the skillet.

3. Heat the skillet over medium heat. Add the mushrooms and cook, stirring, 1 minute. Reduce the heat to low, cover, and cook until tender.

4. Place 1 tablespoon of the applesauce on each of 8 small individual plates and cover with a piece of mushroom. Top with 1 slice of pâté, cut to the size of the potatoes, 1 potato, and 1 apple. Sprinkle ¼ teaspoon of the sugar over each apple. Standing well away from the plates, with a home-safe kitchen propane torch, caramelize the sugar. Serve at room temperature.

Parmesan Wafers with Liver Pâté

Corte de Parmesano con Pâté de Higado

MAKES 10 TAPAS

This tapa of liver pâté sandwiched between two cheesy crisp wafers is one of my very favorites. I got the recipe from Chef Paco Roncero at the Casino de Madrid restaurant. Paco has worked for a long time with the famous chef Ferran Adrià of El Bulli ("The Pug"), considered the best restaurant in the world for many years. It is best when served while the pâté is still cold.

Parmesan Wafer

⅓ cup all-purpose flour

½ cup grated Parmesan cheese

4 tablespoons (½ stick) unsalted butter, slightly softened

1 tablespoon beaten egg

¼ pound Chicken Liver Pâté (Page 99; omit the glaze, preferably chilled in a greased mini loaf pan); or chilled purchased duck liver pâté, cut into ¼- to ⅜-inch slices

1. Prepare the wafers: In a food processor, place the flour, cheese, and butter and process until the butter is fully incorporated. Add the egg and process until incorporated into the dough. Cover and refrigerate at least 1 hour (or store in the refrigerator until ready to use, then leave it at room temperature until pliable before using).

2. Preheat the oven to 350°F. Lightly grease a cookie sheet. On a floured surface, roll the dough to ⅛ inch and cut into 10 (2¾ x 1½-inch) rectangles. Place on the cookie sheet and bake about 5 minutes, turning once, until golden brown all over. Let cool. (May be prepared ahead.)

3. Place 1 slice of cold pâté on half of the wafers and top with a second wafer to make sandwiches. Serve while the pâté is still cold.

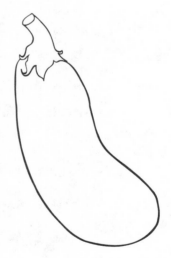

Pâté with Turkey Breast
Pâté Café San Martín

MAKES AT LEAST 10 TO 12 SERVINGS

This tapa is for meat lovers! It features turkey, chicken livers, veal, ham, and two other cuts of pork, which combine deliciously. Here the pâté has a roll of white meat turkey wrapped in ham cooked into the pâté. The recipe came from our dear departed friend Tomás Herranz, who worked for years at the Café San Martín in New York.

When you poach the turkey breast, you can do so in just the broth or, if you wish, add some salt, a few peppercorns, a bay leaf, some thyme, and a sprig of parsley.

PREPARE AT LEAST 3 DAYS IN ADVANCE

½-pound turkey breast, the length of the pâté and 1½ inches wide

Chicken broth or vegetable broth

3 very thin slices boiled deli ham

¾ pound veal, cut into small pieces

¾ pound lean boneless pork loin or shoulder, cut into small pieces

½ pound chicken livers, cut into small pieces

¼ pound pork fat

½ pound liver pâté

2 tablespoons finely chopped fresh thyme or 1 teaspoon dried thyme

½ teaspoon freshly ground nutmeg

¼ cup kosher or sea salt

¼ teaspoon freshly ground black pepper

¼ cup medium-sweet Spanish sherry, such as Oloroso

1 large egg

Pork fatback or bacon, thinly sliced

½ cup whole shelled pistachio nuts, papery outer skin removed

3 bay leaves

1. Tie the turkey breast at intervals with a string. Place in a shallow earthenware casserole dish or Dutch oven with chicken broth to cover. Bring to a boil over high heat, reduce the heat to low, cover, and simmer 10 minutes. Transfer to a plate and let cool. Cut off the string. Wrap the breast in the ham slices.

2. Bring a medium pot of water to a boil over high heat then remove from the heat. Meanwhile, preheat the oven to 350°F. In a food processor, place the veal, pork, chicken livers, pork fat, pâté, thyme, nutmeg, salt, and pepper and process to a medium consistency. With brief pulses, add the sherry and egg until just incorporated.

3. Line a 9¼ x 5¼-inch loaf pan with strips of fatback and extend over the sides. Pour in half of the pâté mixture, sprinkle with half of the pistachio nuts, then place the turkey roll down the center. Add the remaining pâté mixture, then the remaining nuts, pushing them gently into the pâté. Place the bay leaves in a row down the center, then fold over the strips of fatback to cover the pâté. (If they do not cover, add more strips.) Cover tightly with foil.

4. Place the loaf pan in a roasting pan. Gently pour about 1 inch of the boiling water into the roasting pan. Bake 1¾ hours. Remove the pan from the oven and the loaf pan from the larger pan of water, loosen the foil, and pour off any fat.

5. Place a heavy object (a brick covered with foil is ideal) on top of the foil and let cool. Remove the weight, cover, and refrigerate at least 3 days. Remove the bay leaves. Bring to room temperature before serving.

Eggs, Breads, and Empanadas

~~~

FRIED, BAKED, AND BOILED EGGS

Fried Eggs, Spanish Style Ⓥ

Fried Bread

Gently Scrambled Eggs with
Shrimp and Spinach

Baked Eggs with Sliced Tomato and Sausage

Eggs Scrambled with Bacon and Chorizo

Marinated Ground Pork with Fried Eggs

Eggs in a Nest

Sautéed Bread Bits with Peppers,
Grapes, and Fried Eggs

Sautéed Bread Bits with Peppers,
Chorizo, and Fried Eggs

Baked Eggs with Ham, Sausage, and Asparagus

"Crashed" Fried Eggs and Potatoes Ⓥ

Soft-Set Eggs and Scallions Ⓥ

Sliced Eggs with Garlic and Parsley Ⓥ

Shrimp-Stuffed Eggs

Salmon-Stuffed Eggs

~~~

OMELETS

Josefa's Artichoke Omelet Ⓥ

Sausage and Bean Omelet

Marinated Tuna Omelet

Spanish Potato Omelet Ⓥ

Potato Omelet with Garlic and Parsley Ⓥ

Potato and Vegetable Omelet

Old-Fashioned Spanish Potato and Tuna Omelet

Potato Omelet with Ham and Mint

Potato, Chorizo, and Pimiento Omelet

Potato and Banana Omelet Ⓥ

Country-Style Omelet

Ⓥ = Vegetarian Ⓥ* = Vegetarian with one change

Mushroom Omelet

Chickpea Omelet **V**

Lima Bean Omelet

Onion, Tuna, and Tomato Omelet

Cod Omelet

BREADS

Basic Long Loaf **V**

Country-Style Bread **V**

Aranda Bread Tortes **V**

Flat Bread Loaf **V**

Galician Rye Bread **V***

Corn and Barley Bread **V**

Sausage-Stuffed Country Bread

Holiday Bread **V***

Miniature Egg Buns **V**

Sweet Filled Bread Rings **V**

Sugar-Topped Sweet Rolls **V**

Sweet Snail-Shaped Rolls **V**

PIES (EMPANADAS)

Puff Pastry **V**

Empanada Dough **V***

Tomato and Green Pepper Pies **V**

Fresh Sardine Pie

Tuna Pie

Clam Pie

Asturian Chorizo Pie

Pork Pie

Galician Pork and Pepper Pie

Mallorcan Lamb and Sobrasada Pie

Veal Pie of Murcia

Veal Sandwiches

Veal in Puff Pastry

Sausage Buns

This chapter is a bit of a potpourri of different but related food categories, namely eggs, breads, and empanadas. Eggs are an integral part of Spanish cuisine, bread is called for in many egg recipes and used for sandwiches, and empanadas are the savory pies (similar to sealed sandwiches) with various tasty fillings enclosed in empanada dough. You'll also find other doughs here for savory treats.

Spaniards have had a love affair with eggs that goes back hundreds of years. Spanish-Style Fried Eggs (*Huevos Fritos a la Española*) is an enormously popular dish that is usually served for lunch or dinner, often with *migas* (crispy bread bits). Spaniards are very particular about their fried eggs—they must be fried quickly in sizzling hot olive oil, as butter produces an egg that is flat and rubbery. They are usually accompanied by fried potatoes and sometimes with chorizo or a good loaf of country bread.

Because Spaniards are so fond of fried eggs and fried potatoes, it is no wonder that the Spanish Potato Omelet (*Tortilla Española*) is a most beloved dish, served either as a tapa or a main course. Ingredients for omelets (*tortillas*), some served folded but most served as a pie—vary according to region—including dishes such as Potato, Chorizo, and Pimiento Omelet (*Tortilla la Gallega*), Butifarra and White Bean Omelet (*Tortilla Catalana*) featuring a regional white sausage, and Vegetable and Potato Omelet (*Tortilla a la Segoviana*). Some versions are very simple and others more elegant, but the popularity of the omelet in Spain cannot be overstated.

Breads are often eaten in the morning, with tea or coffee, as part of a continental breakfast in an assortment that may include sweet breads such as Sugar-Topped Sweet Rolls (*Suizos*) and Miniature Egg Buns (*Media-Noches*). For lunch and dinner, loaves of crusty bread such as Basic Long Loaf (*Pan de Pueblo*) and Country-Style Bread (*Pan Candeal*) are used for dunking in sauces of the main meal, as well as for sandwiches in the afternoon (and even for thickening dishes like stews). In Spain, table breads and sweet breads are usually sold in different kinds of bakeries. A *panadería* sells regular loaves of bread, while a *pastelería* features sweetbreads and pastries. But the importance of bread dough in Spanish gastronomy goes far and above simple breads served on the side of an entrée.

The use of puff pastry dough in Spanish cooking is enormously popular and has been used for centuries. Many recipes, especially for tapas, rely on Puff Pastry (*Hojaldre*) to turn ordinary dishes into extraordinary ones. Popular tapas such as Puff Pastry with Potatoes and Cheese (*Buñuelos de Patata y Queso*), Puff Pastry with Zucchini and Shrimp (*Buñuelos de Calabacín y Gambas*), and Puff Pastry with Salted Dried Cod (*Buñuelos de Bacalao*) depend on the quality of the puff pastry crust. Puff pastry is very easy to make and can even be stored in the freezer for later use. Empanada Dough for Meat or Fish Pie (*Masa de Empanada*), the unsweetened pizza-like dough that is used for savory meat and fish pies, is equally easy to prepare but requires a different method.

Empanadas (turnovers) and their smaller counterparts, *empanadillas* (hand pies), originated in Galicia. Different versions can be found throughout Spain, mostly along the northern coast. Popular empanadas include Pork Pie (*Empanada de Lomo*), Tuna Pie (*Empanada de Bonito*), and Veal and Chorizo Pie (*Pastel Murciano*, a specialty from the province of Murcia). Empanadas cut into wedges or squares make excellent tapas, and *empanadillas* are often served as tapas. (See Turnovers (Empanadas) in the Tapas chapter, pages 84–86). In larger portions, they make a wonderful main course. I like to serve empanadas freshly baked but at room temperature—they are always a big hit at my parties.

Fried, Baked, and Boiled Eggs

Fried Eggs, Spanish Style Ⓥ
Huevos Fritos a la Española

MAKES 1 SERVING

The only way to make an authentic, traditional Spanish fried egg is to use sizzling-hot olive oil. Butter produces an egg that is rubbery—which is simply not acceptable to a Spaniard. The egg must be cracked into hot oil so the result is light and crunchy. The phrase Spaniards use to describe the golden edges of the fried eggs is vestidos de torero *which translates to "dressed like a bullfighter." This meal is mostly served for lunch or dinner, usually accompanied by fried potatoes, such as Poor Man's Potatoes (page 264).*

Olive oil, or a mixture of olive and salad oils, for frying

2 large eggs, or any number desired, at room temperature

Kosher or sea salt

1. In a medium skillet, heat at least ½ inch of oil over high heat until it reaches the smoking point. Break no more than 2 eggs at a time into the oil. Working quickly with a large spoon, fold the edges of the egg white, which will have spread, up over the yolks, forming a circle. Spread the hot oil over the eggs until they begin to be crunchy around the edges and the yolks have set. The whole process will take about a minute.

2. Transfer the eggs with a slotted spatula to paper towels and let drain slightly. Repeat for as many eggs as desired. Season with salt and serve hot.

EGGS

Eggs are probably the most common, loved, and utilized staple in Spanish cooking. They are used in the preparation of meat, fish, shellfish, and many vegetable recipes, as a principal element in the preparation of desserts, and as a main course. For quite a few years, I lived in Madrid and was always amazed at the love that Spaniards have for their fried eggs (*huevos fritos*) and the frequency that they are ordered at restaurants. In fact, any restaurant in Spain will prepare an egg dish for a customer, even one not on the menu, if requested.

My husband, a native of Madrid, always requests fried eggs for dinner on his birthday. Many years ago, when he was 16 or 17, he spent a couple of days in the countryside near Madrid. He and a friend woke up at five in the morning on a cold, wintry day of November to go hunting. They spent hours walking through the fields and did not shoot their guns even once. After hours of being cold, tired, and uncomfortable, they returned ravenously hungry to the country house where the woman in charge of the kitchen served them a lunch of fried potatoes, fried chorizo sausage, and three or four fried eggs. To this day, my husband swears it was the best meal he ever ate.

A few years ago, I was traveling in Spain while writing one of my books, *La Cocina de Mama*, and had the opportunity to talk to some of Spain's most famous chefs. The question I always asked them was a simple one, "When you were young, what was your favorite dish?" I could not believe that world-renowned chefs such as Juan Mari Arzak, Ferran Adrià, and Lucio Blázques all gave the same answer – "*Huevos fritos!*"

Fried Bread

Migas

Migas, or crispy bread bits, are a popular Spanish accompaniment to fried eggs. Castilla produces a coarse country bread that is perfect for making fried bread. No matter what kind of bread you use, be sure that it is at least 1 or 2 days old because drier bread gets crisp more easily. Fried eggs and bread are delicious on their own but even better when bacon and ham are added. Try chorizo, too.

PREPARE 8 TO 12 HOURS IN ADVANCE

1 day-old loaf bread, not airy, such as Basic Long Loaf (baguette; pan de pueblo; page 126) or Country-Style Loaf (round; pan candeal; page 127) (either of the white breads work perfectly)

2 tablespoons small cubes (¼ inch) slab bacon

3 tablespoons olive oil

3 garlic cloves, 1 whole and 2 finely chopped

Salt

Freshly ground black pepper

¼ teaspoon ground cumin

½ teaspoon ground paprika

2 tablespoons finely chopped onion

2 tablespoons small cubes (¼ inch) Serrano (Spanish cured mountain) ham or prosciutto (about 1 ounce)

1. Remove the crust from the bread, discard the crust, and rip the bread into crouton-size pieces by hand (or cut into cubes if you prefer), and place them on a tray. Dampen by wetting your hand and shaking it over the bread. Repeat several times. Wrap the bread in a towel or foil and let sit overnight. (The bread is moistened so that when they are fried in the skillet, they will remain tender inside.)

2. In a medium skillet over low heat, cook the bacon until it is translucent and the fat is rendered. Transfer with a slotted spoon to paper towels, let drain, and reserve. Add 2 tablespoons of the oil and the whole garlic clove to the skillet. Increase the heat to medium and cook, stirring, until the garlic is well browned, about 4 minutes. Discard the garlic. Add the bread and stir to coat with the oil. Stir in the salt, pepper, cumin, and paprika. Reduce the heat to low and cook, stirring occasionally, until the bread is crisp but not browned, about 30 minutes.

3. Meanwhile, in a small skillet, heat the remaining 1 tablespoon oil over medium heat. Add the onion and the chopped garlic and cook, stirring, until the onion is wilted and transparent, about 3 minutes. Stir in the ham and reserved bacon and cook 1 minute more. Add the bread and stir to combine. At this point, if you wish your bread a little less crisp, sprinkle with 1 tablespoon of oil or a little water. Serve hot.

Gently Scrambled Eggs with Shrimp and Spinach

Revuelto de Langostinos y Espinacas Casa Lucio

This exceptional recipe is from Casa Lucio, an extraordinary restaurant in Old Madrid that has been frequented by the Who's Who of Spanish society for many years. When Lucio brought me into his kitchen and taught me how to make these scrambled eggs with shrimp and spinach, he emphasized that it needs to be completed quickly because the eggs should be very softly set.

4 medium shrimp, shelled, deveined, and each cut into 3 pieces

Kosher or sea salt

2 teaspoons olive oil

¼ cup torn and blanched fresh spinach leaves
    (about 2 cups uncooked), well drained

2 large eggs

1. Place the shrimp in a small bowl, season with salt, and let sit 15 minutes.

2. Heat the oil in a small skillet over medium-high heat. Add the shrimp and cook quickly (less than a minute will do) until they just begin to turn opaque. Stir in the spinach. Break the eggs into the skillet and stir rapidly, removing the skillet from the heat almost immediately. Add salt and continue stirring until the eggs are no longer liquid and just begin to set and the shrimp are pink. Transfer immediately to a plate to prevent further cooking. Serve hot.

Baked Eggs with Sliced Tomato and Sausage
Huevos a la Madrileña

MAKES 1 SERVING

These baked eggs with sliced tomato and rice-filled Spanish black sausage, (morcilla) are out of this world. In Spain, eggs are usually served as a first dinner course or for lunch, but rarely for breakfast. Morcilla, similar to Irish black pudding, can now be found in specialty stores in the United States, but if not available, you may substitute breakfast sausage or sweet Italian sausage.

1 medium tomato, cut into ¼-inch slices

1 tablespoon water

Salt

Freshly ground black pepper

1 large garlic clove, mashed in a garlic press or
    mortar

1 tablespoon finely chopped fresh flat-leaf parsley

1 tablespoon olive oil

4 (¼-inch) slices rice-filled black sausage (morcilla)
    or any breakfast or sweet Italian-style sausage

1 or 2 large eggs

1 tablespoon grated Parmesan cheese

1. Preheat the oven to 450°F. Season the tomatoes with salt, pepper, and garlic and sprinkle with the parsley. Heat the oil in a medium skillet over medium heat. Add the tomatoes and cook, turning once, until softened and their juices release, about 1 minute per side. Transfer to a shallow earthenware casserole dish or Dutch oven and arrange in a single layer.

2. Deglaze the skillet, adding the water, stirring, and scraping up any bits of flavor. Pour over the tomatoes. Wipe out the skillet, grease lightly, and heat over medium heat. Add the sausage and cook, turning once, until lightly browned on each side.

3. Break the egg(s) into the middle of the casserole dish. Place the sausage around the edges and sprinkle everything with the cheese. Transfer to the oven and bake until the egg whites are set but the yolks still soft, about 6 minutes. If using earthenware, serve hot in the dish, or transfer to individual plates.

Eggs Scrambled with Bacon and Chorizo
Duelos y Quebrantos

MAKES 1 SERVING

Eggs and bacon were staples in Castilla in the sixteenth and seventeenth centuries when other more expensive ingredients were not available, but this dish continues to be popular today. Duelos y Quebrantos, *which translates to "sorrow and suffering", was immortalized in the first paragraph of the masterpiece* Don Quijote de la Mancha *as one of the frequent meals of the protagonist.*

1 tablespoon olive oil

¼ cup small cubes (¼ inch) slab bacon (about 2 ounces)

2 tablespoons small pieces (¼ inch) chorizo sausage

2 large eggs

1. Heat the oil in a medium skillet over low heat. Add the bacon and cook, stirring, until browned and crisp. Add the chorizo and cook, stirring, about 1 minute more. Transfer the meat with a slotted spoon to a small bowl, reserving 1 tablespoon of the oil in the skillet.

2. In a medium bowl, beat the eggs lightly with a fork. Stir in the bacon and chorizo. Heat the skillet again over low heat and use a spatula to loosen any particles of meat stuck to the bottom. Increase the heat to high, pour in the egg mixture, and cook, stirring constantly, until the eggs are set but not dry. Serve hot.

Marinated Ground Pork with Fried Eggs
Zorza con Huevos Fritos

MAKES 4 SERVINGS

In typical Galician style, the pork in this recipe is first marinated in paprika-seasoned broth, then sautéed and served with boiled new potatoes. Both paprika and new potatoes are staples in Galicia and are used in many regional dishes. This hearty recipe comes from Mesón Alberto in the historic walled city of Lugo.

PREPARE 8 TO 12 HOURS IN ADVANCE

1 pound lean ground pork

4 teaspoons ground sweet paprika, such as Spanish smoked

½ teaspoon ground hot paprika, such as Spanish smoked

½ teaspoon salt

8 large garlic cloves, finely chopped

¼ cup chicken broth, vegetable broth, or water

4 medium or 8 small (2-inch) new potatoes

1 tablespoon olive oil

4 or 8 large eggs, at room temperature

1. In a medium bowl, mix the pork, paprikas, salt, garlic, and broth. Cover and refrigerate overnight.

2. Place the potatoes in a medium saucepan with cold water to cover and add salt. Cover and bring to a simmer over low heat. Cook about 15 minutes or until tender when pierced with a knife. Drain and let cool slightly. Peel and reserve.

3. Meanwhile, heat the oil in a medium skillet over medium heat. Add the meat mixture and cook, breaking up the meat as it cooks, until lightly browned. Transfer with a slotted spoon to individual plates.

4. Fry the eggs as instructed in Fried Eggs, Spanish Style (page 107). Arrange the potatoes around the

meat on each plate. Arrange the fried eggs over the meat and serve hot.

Eggs in a Nest
Huevos al Nido

MAKES 6 SERVINGS

I owe much of what I have learned about Spanish cooking to my mother-in-law, Clara Orozco, a gifted and highly inventive cook who was always creating new recipes. In order to make these unusual puffed eggs, you first hollow out bread rolls, fill them with tomato sauce and egg yolk, then top them with beaten egg whites that puff during cooking. The presentation, which resembles eggs in a nest, is quite elegant.

2 tablespoons olive oil

1 small onion, finely chopped (about ⅓ cup)

½ cup small cubes (¼ inch) slab bacon

6 tablespoons tomato paste

¾ cup water

Salt

Freshly ground black pepper

6 large rolls, such as hard or challah

6 large eggs

Salad oil, for frying

1. Heat the oil in a small saucepan over medium heat. Add the onion and cook, stirring, until wilted and transparent, about 5 minutes. Add the bacon and cook until the bacon is transparent. Stir in the tomato paste, water, salt, and pepper. Reduce the heat to low and cook 20 minutes, adding more water if necessary. (The sauce should have the consistency of a thick spaghetti sauce.) Let cool.

2. Meanwhile, cut out a circle of bread, about 1½ inches in diameter, from the center top of each roll. Through that opening, hollow out the rolls with a small spoon (espresso size is best) until only ¼ inch thickness remains on the bottom and ½ inch

on the sides. Be careful not to pierce the rolls all the way through. Spoon 3 tablespoons of the sauce into each of the rolls. Separate the eggs, placing the whites in a medium bowl and 1 yolk into each roll. The yolks should remain intact, but if they break, no dire consequences will result.

3. In a medium bowl, beat the egg whites with a hand-held electric beater until stiff peaks form. With a large spoon, cover each roll with egg white forming a smooth dome about 2 inches high in the center. (There may be some egg white left over, depending on the size of the eggs. Refrigerate or discard.)

4. In a medium skillet, heat ½ inch of oil over high heat until it reaches the smoking point, then reduce the heat to medium-high. Place one of the rolls on a slotted pancake turner. Hold it over—not in—the oil. With a large spoon, pour oil over the top of the roll, letting the excess run down into the pan. Continue doing this until the whites are puffed and golden and the roll is crisp, about 1 minute. Slide the roll onto a paper towel and let drain, then place on a warm platter. Repeat for each roll. Serve immediately because the egg whites deflate rapidly. (You can reserve and reuse the oil.)

Sautéed Bread Bits with Peppers, Grapes, and Fried Eggs
Migas Estilo Andaluz

MAKES 4 SERVINGS

Migas, or crispy bread bits, make fried eggs much heartier and are considered comfort food in Spain. They must be prepared with day-old bread and then moistened so that when they are fried in the skillet, they will remain tender inside. In this Andalusian recipe, the migas are combined with fried eggs and frying peppers, with grapes adding a surprising sweetness.

continues ...

8 cups crustless ½-inch pieces day-old country loaf (round) bread

¼ teaspoon kosher or sea salt

½ cup water

3 tablespoons olive oil

¼ cup small cubes (¼ inch) fresh or cured slab bacon or pancetta

6 ounces (3 links) sweet chorizo sausage, thinly sliced or cut into ¼-inch pieces

¼ pound Serrano (Spanish cured mountain) ham or prosciutto, cut into ¼-inch cubes

6 garlic cloves, finely chopped

2 tablespoons finely chopped onion

1½ pounds small green frying peppers (padróns)

2 teaspoons ground sweet paprika, such as Spanish smoked

2 garlic cloves, lightly smashed

Kosher or sea salt

8 large eggs, at room temperature

24 peeled seedless green grapes

1. Place the bread in a large bowl. Dissolve the ¼ teaspoon salt in the water and pour over the bread. With your hands, gradually work the salted water into the bread, dampening it evenly. Reserve.

2. Heat 1 tablespoon of the oil in a large skillet over low heat. Add the bacon and cook, stirring, until it is translucent and the fat is rendered. Add the chorizo, ham, chopped garlic, and onion and cook, stirring, until the onion is wilted and transparent and the meats are slightly crisped. Add the peppers, paprika, and smashed garlic and cook, turning occasionally, until the peppers are softened to taste. Add the bread, stir to combine, and cook until crisp. Season with salt.

3. Fry the eggs as instructed in Fried Eggs, Spanish Style (page 107). Scatter the grapes over the bread. Serve hot with the peppers and the fried eggs on the side.

Sautéed Bread Bits with Peppers, Chorizo, and Fried Eggs
Migas Extremeñas Fray Juan

MAKES 2 SERVINGS

For many years, my husband Luis and I have been friends with Brother Juan Barrera, the very talented cook in charge of the kitchen in the beautiful Guadalupe monastery. His version of the crispy bread bits known as migas *includes peppers and chorizo and are sensational with Spanish fried eggs. As with all* migas, *the bread you use should be a day or two old.*

1 tablespoon olive oil

¼ cup cored, seeded, and finely chopped green frying peppers (padróns)

½ cup small cubes (¼ inch) fresh or cured slab bacon or pancetta

3 tablespoons small pieces (¼ inch) sweet chorizo sausage

2 garlic cloves, lightly smashed

4 cups crustless ½-inch cubes day-old country loaf (round) bread

¼ teaspoon salt

¼ cup water

4 large eggs, at room temperature

1. Heat the oil in a medium skillet over low heat. Add the peppers and cook, stirring, until softened, about 10 minutes. Increase the heat to medium, add the bacon and chorizo, and cook, stirring, until the pork loses its color and the fat from the meats has rendered. Transfer the meat with a slotted spoon to a small bowl and reserve.

2. Add the garlic to the skillet (adding a little more oil if the skillet seems dry), and cook over medium heat, pressing with the back of a wooden spoon, until lightly browned on both sides. Discard the garlic. Add the bread and stir to coat with

the oil. Dissolve the salt in the water and sprinkle over the bread. Reduce the heat to medium-low and cook, stirring frequently, until crispy, about 10 minutes more. Stir in the reserved meat and cook until the bread is crisp and golden. Remove from the heat, cover, and keep warm while preparing the eggs.

3. Heat ¼ inch of oil in a 9-inch skillet over medium-high heat to the smoking point. Break 1 egg into a cup, then slide into the oil. Working very quickly, fold in the edges of the egg white with the aid of a wooden spoon. With a large metal spoon, pour the hot oil over the egg so that it puffs up and becomes crisp around the edges. All this must be done in a matter of seconds so the yolk remains soft.

4. Remove the egg with a metal slotted spatula, rest the egg and spatula briefly on paper towels and let drain, then slide the egg onto one side of a dinner plate. Repeat for the remaining eggs, placing 2 on each plate. Heat the bread and meat mixture and pile in the center of the dish. Serve hot.

Baked Eggs with Ham, Sausage, and Asparagus
Huevos a la Flamenca

MAKES 4 SERVINGS

One of the most popular egg dishes in Spain, Huevos a la Flamenca originated in the city of Seville where the creativity of Andalusian cooking is at its finest. The best version of these baked eggs I ever tasted came from El Burladero, a lively and festive restaurant that is not just filled with bullfighting memorabilia, but often frequented by actual bullfighters. The day I was there, all conversation suddenly came to a halt, and everyone watched in awe as the famous El Litri walked in.

12 asparagus

2 tablespoons olive oil

1 medium onion, finely chopped (about ⅔ cup)

1 garlic clove, finely chopped

6 fresh or canned plum tomatoes, coarsely chopped (about 2 cups)

½ cup chicken broth or vegetable broth

¼ teaspoon ground paprika

Salt

Freshly ground black pepper

¼ pound Serrano (Spanish cured mountain) ham or prosciutto, cut into ¼-inch cubes

¼ pound (2 links) chorizo sausage, cut into ¼-inch slices

8 large eggs

6 tablespoons cooked or thawed frozen peas

2 pimientos, cut into thin strips

2 tablespoons finely chopped fresh flat-leaf parsley

1. Place the asparagus in a medium skillet with water to cover, add salt, and bring to a boil over high heat. Reduce the heat to low, cover, and simmer 5 to 10 minutes or until crisp-tender. Reserve.

2. Preheat the oven to 450°F. Heat the oil in a medium skillet over medium heat. Add the onion and garlic and cook, stirring, until the onion is wilted and transparent, about 5 minutes. Add the tomatoes, broth, paprika, salt, and pepper, cover, and cook 10 minutes or until thickened.

3. Meanwhile, in another medium skillet over medium heat, cook the ham and chorizo, stirring, until cooked through, about 5 minutes.

4. Pour the tomato sauce into 4 individual earthenware ramekins. Break 2 eggs into each dish. Arrange the ham-chorizo mixture, the asparagus, peas, and pimientos attractively around the eggs. Season with salt and pepper and sprinkle the entire dish with the parsley. Bake until the egg whites are set but the yolks still soft, 5 to 6 minutes. Serve hot.

"Crashed" Fried Eggs and Potatoes V

Huevos Estrellados Lucio

MAKES 1 SERVING

Huevos Estrellados is a popular egg dish originated and served at the world-renowned Casa Lucio restaurant in Old Madrid. Owner Lucio Blázquez is a charming and generous man who shared his recipe with me. This is Lucio's creative spin on two dishes dear to most Spaniards' hearts: fried eggs and fried potatoes. He cuts up the egg after it is cooked and blends it with the potatoes, giving this traditional dish a new, exciting spin. Huevos Estrellados is usually the first dish served for dinner since everybody, including the Spanish King, asks for them when dining.

1 medium potato, peeled and cut lengthwise into ½-inch fries

Olive oil, for frying

Salt

2 tablespoons olive oil

2 large eggs, at room temperature

1. Deep-fry the potato in two stages. First, heat at least 1 inch of oil in a small skillet over low heat (or better still, use a deep fryer set at 300°F). Add the potato slices and simmer until softened but not browned. Transfer with a slotted spoon to paper towels and let drain (or let drain in the frying basket).

2. Preheat the oven to 200°F. Heat the oil in the skillet over medium-high heat (or the deep fryer set to 350°F). Return the potatoes to the oil for a few seconds until crisped but not browned. Let drain again. Season with salt, arrange in a shallow individual earthenware casserole dish, and keep warm in the oven.

3. Meanwhile, heat the 2 tablespoons oil in a medium skillet over medium heat until it reaches the smoking point. Break the eggs into the oil and cook very briefly until just set underneath. Rather than flipping, carefully roll them over with the aid of a pancake turner (they should not brown). Season with salt and place over the potatoes. Cut up the eggs and potatoes so that the yolks blend with the potatoes and serve hot.

Soft-Set Eggs and Scallions V

Revuelto de Ajetes

MAKES 1 SERVING

These eggs, made with butter instead of olive oil, are much lighter than most traditional Spanish egg dishes. Their flavor is greatly enhanced by an accent of scallions.

1 tablespoon unsalted butter

5 very thin scallions, cut into 2-inch pieces

3 thin slices long-loaf (baguette) bread, coarsely chopped

2 large eggs

1 tablespoon milk

Salt

1. Melt the butter in a medium skillet over low heat. Add the scallions and cook, stirring, until tender. Transfer with a slotted spoon to paper towels and let drain. Add the bread to the skillet and cook, stirring, until slightly crisp. Reserve.

2. Meanwhile, fill a large skillet halfway with water and bring to a boil over high heat. Reduce the heat to low. In a small bowl, beat the eggs, milk, and salt lightly with a fork. Add the eggs to the medium skillet. Remove the pan immediately from the heat, and place it within the large skillet of water, double-boiler fashion. Stir the eggs gently with a wooden spoon until no longer liquid but still quite soft. Spoon the eggs onto a plate and scatter the cooked scallions and bread over the eggs. Serve hot.

Sliced Eggs with Garlic and Parsley V
Huevos Duros en Alino

MAKES 4 TO 6 SERVINGS

This is simply sliced hard-boiled eggs sauced with a generous amount of garlic and parsley oil and attractively garnished with grated carrot and olives.

PREPARE AT LEAST 2 HOURS IN ADVANCE

2 garlic cloves

¼ cup finely chopped fresh flat-leaf parsley

Kosher or sea salt

Freshly ground pepper (use white pepper if you have it)

⅛ teaspoon ground sweet paprika, such as Spanish smoked

6 tablespoons extra-virgin olive oil

5 large hard-boiled eggs, thinly sliced crosswise

Coarsely grated carrot, for garnish

Black or green olives, preferably Spanish, for garnish

1. In a food processor, combine the garlic, parsley, salt, pepper, and paprika. With the motor running, gradually pour in the oil and process until well blended.

2. Arrange the eggs in a serving dish and season with salt. Pour the sauce over the eggs and garnish with the carrot and olives. Refrigerate at least 2 hours up to overnight and serve cold.

Shrimp-Stuffed Eggs
Huevos Rellenos de Gambas

MAKES 8 STUFFED EGG HALVES

This delicious preparation of hard-boiled eggs filled with a mixture of egg yolk and shrimp is made even better when coated with a light wine sauce.

4 large hard-boiled eggs

¼ cup olive oil

¼ cup finely chopped onion

¼ cup all-purpose flour

2 tablespoons dry white wine

6 tablespoons storebought or homemade Fish Broth or clam juice

½ pound medium shrimp, in their shells

Salt

Freshly ground black pepper

2 teaspoons finely chopped fresh flat-leaf parsley, for garnish

1. Preheat the oven to 350°F and grease a medium baking dish. Cut the eggs in half lengthwise. Remove the yolks, finely chop them, and place yolks in a small bowl. Reserve the whites.

2. Heat the oil in a small skillet over medium heat. Add the onion and cook, stirring, until wilted and transparent, about 3 minutes. Stir in the flour and cook 1 minute. Add the wine and broth and cook, stirring constantly, until thickened and smooth. Remove from the heat.

3. Fill a large saucepan with water, add salt, and bring to a boil over high heat. Add the shrimp and cook until just pink, 2 to 3 minutes. Drain, let cool, and remove and discard the shells. Coarsely chop and place the shrimp in the bowl with the egg yolks. Mix in 2 tablespoons of the sauce and season with salt and pepper.

4. Fill the egg whites with the shrimp mixture and place the stuffed eggs in the baking dish. Pour the remaining sauce over the eggs and bake 10 minutes. Sprinkle with the parsley and serve hot.

Salmon-Stuffed Eggs
Huevos Rellenos de Salmon

MAKES 10 STUFFED EGG HALVES

In this somewhat extravagant tapa, the eggs are hard-boiled, stuffed with a salmon mixture, coated with béchamel, and then fried. The best version I have ever tasted came from the Mallorca shop on Velazquez Street in Madrid. The shop is small but contains a bakery, delicatessen, wine store, cheese shop, and tapas bar—all under one roof. If you are in Madrid, I recommend that you stop by. It is most crowded in the early afternoon.

PREPARE AT LEAST 2 HOURS IN ADVANCE

1 recipe Béchamel Sauce (page 29; omit the nutmeg and add ¾ cup chicken broth)

5 large hard-boiled eggs

Half of a 7¾-ounce can salmon

3 tablespoons tomato sauce

Salt

Freshly ground black pepper

2 teaspoons finely chopped fresh flat-leaf parsley

2 large eggs, for dredging

Bread crumbs, for dredging

Olive oil, for frying

1. Prepare the sauce. Cut the hard-boiled eggs in half lengthwise. Remove the egg yolks and reserve the yolks from 4 halves. (Store the yolks from 6 halves; they will not be used).

2. In a medium bowl, flake the salmon with a fork. Add the egg yolks and crumble them with the fork. Add the tomato sauce, salt, pepper, and parsley and mix well. Fill the egg whites with the mixture and refrigerate at least 1 hour.

3. Cover and coat the stuffed eggs with the sauce and refrigerate 1 hour more or until the sauce hardens.

4. Lightly beat the 2 eggs in a shallow bowl. Add the bread crumbs to a separate shallow bowl. Heat 1 inch of oil in a medium saucepan over medium-high heat (or better still, use a deep fryer set at 365°F) until it turns a cube of bread light brown in 60 seconds. Working in batches, dip each coated, stuffed egg into the beaten eggs to coat it all around, dredge it all over in the bread crumbs, and place it in the oil. Cook, turning gently, until browned all around. Transfer with a slotted spoon to paper towels and let drain. Serve hot or at room temperature.

Omelets

Josefa's Artichoke Omelet ⓥ
Tortilla de Alcachofas de Josefa

MAKES 1 SERVING

This creative yet simple egg dish, a folded omelet, came from Master Chef Ferran Adrià from El Bulli Restaurant, considered one of the finest chefs in the world. Ferran credits his mother, Josefa Acosta, for many of his specialties, including this wonderful artichoke omelet. In order to prepare it properly, the artichoke hearts must be briefly sautéed, then left to sit in the beaten egg before the omelet is made.

1 tablespoon olive oil

2 cooked (steamed or boiled) artichoke hearts, quartered

Kosher or sea salt

2 large eggs, at room temperature

2 teaspoons finely chopped fresh flat-leaf parsley

1. Heat the oil in a 6-inch skillet over medium heat. Add the artichoke hearts and cook, stirring, until lightly browned, 2 to 4 minutes. Season with salt. Transfer with a slotted spoon to a small bowl and let cool, reserving the oil in the skillet.

2. In a small bowl, beat the eggs lightly with a fork and add salt. Stir in the artichokes and let sit 5 minutes.

3. Reheat the oil in the skillet over high heat. Pour in the egg mixture and spread evenly. Cook until the eggs are no longer runny but not completely set, fold the omelet in half, and cook a few seconds more (it should remain juicy within). Sprinkle with the parsley and serve hot.

Sausage and Bean Omelet
Tortilla Catalana

MAKES 1 SERVING

Butifarra, a spicy white sausage made in Catalunya, is called for in many regional recipes. Here it is combined with white beans, creating a French-style folded omelet that is rich and hearty.

1 teaspoon lard or vegetable shortening

1½ tablespoons olive oil

¼ cup slivered onion

5 (½-inch) slices pork sausage (butifarra) or 5 slices sweet Italian-style sausage, cut into pieces

5 tablespoons coarsely chopped tomato

¼ cup cooked dried white beans, drained, or ¼ cup canned white beans, rinsed and drained

Salt

Freshly ground black pepper

2 large eggs

1 tablespoon finely chopped fresh flat-leaf parsley, for garnish

1. Heat the lard and ½ tablespoon of the oil in a medium skillet over low heat. Add the onion and cook, stirring, until wilted and transparent, about 5 minutes. Add the sausage and cook, stirring, until it loses its color. Stir in the tomato, cover, and cook until softened and its juices release, about 3 minutes more.

2. In a small bowl, beat the eggs lightly with a fork. Stir in salt and pepper. In another medium skillet, heat the remaining 1 tablespoon oil over medium heat. Pour in the eggs and cook until the bottom is set. Place the sausage mixture in the center and fold the omelet in half. Continue cooking until done to taste. Sprinkle with the parsley and serve hot.

Marinated Tuna Omelet
Tortilla de Atún Escabechado

MAKES 1 SERVING

Escabeche was an ancient way of preserving fish that is still commonly used today to enhance its natural flavor. This is a very tasty folded omelet in which the tuna is first marinated then sautéed and served with an onion-spiced tomato sauce.

Sauce

1 tablespoon olive oil

1 tablespoon finely chopped onion

½ cup tomato sauce

Salt

Freshly ground black pepper

2 tablespoons olive oil

2 tablespoons finely chopped onion

¾ cup canned or jarred marinated tuna or white or
    light meat tuna in water, drained and flaked

2 large eggs

Salt

Freshly ground black pepper

1. Prepare the sauce: Heat the 1 tablespoon oil in a small skillet over medium heat. Add the onion and cook, stirring, until wilted and transparent, 2 to 3 minutes. Stir in the tomato sauce, salt, and pepper. Reduce the heat to low, cover, and simmer 15 minutes or until slightly thickened.

2. Heat 1 tablespoon of the oil in a medium skillet heat over medium heat. Add the onion and cook, stirring, until wilted, 2 to 3 minutes. Add the tuna and cook, stirring occasionally, about 5 minutes.

3. In a small bowl, beat the eggs lightly with a fork and add pepper. In another medium skillet, heat the remaining 1 tablespoon oil over medium heat. Pour in the eggs and cook until the bottom is set. Place the tuna mixture in the center and fold the omelet in half. Continue cooking until done to taste. Pour the sauce over the omelet and serve hot.

Spanish Potato Omelet ⓥ
Tortilla de Patata a la Española

MAKES 8 SERVINGS

Omelets are a staple in Spanish cuisine and are beloved by children and adults alike. While an omelet is a simple dish to prepare, it is important that you know the proper technique (described below). When serving an omelet as a tapa, you should cut it into 1-inch squares that can be picked up with a toothpick. Omelets in Spain are the quintessential picnic dish.

1 cup olive oil, for frying

4 large potatoes, peeled and cut into ⅛-inch slices

1 large onion, thinly sliced

Kosher or sea salt

4 large eggs

1. Heat the oil in an 8- or 9-inch skillet over medium heat until it sizzles a potato slice. Add the potatoes and onion one slice at a time to prevent sticking, alternating layers of potatoes and onion. Season with salt. Cook, turning occasionally, until the potatoes are tender but not browned, about 20 minutes. Transfer with a slotted spoon or spatula to a colander and let drain. Reserve 4 teaspoons oil and wipe out the skillet.

2. In a large bowl, beat the eggs lightly with a fork and add salt. Add the potatoes and press down until completely covered by the egg mixture. Let sit 15 minutes.

3. Heat 3 teaspoons of the reserved oil in the same skillet over high heat until it reaches the smoking point. Quickly pour in the potato-and-egg mixture and distribute evenly. Reduce the heat to medium-high and cook, shaking the skillet often to prevent

sticking, until the bottom begins to brown. Slide the omelet onto a plate, cover with a second plate, and turn over.

4. Heat the remaining 1 teaspoon reserved oil in the same skillet over high heat to the smoking point. Reduce the heat to medium and slide the omelet back into the skillet. Cook, shaking constantly, until the bottom is browned, using the back of a pancake turner to neatly tuck in the edges. Continue cooking until set in the center but still slightly juicy within. Serve hot or at room temperature.

Potato Omelet with Garlic and Parsley ⓥ
Tortilla de Patata con Ajo y Perejil

MAKES 8 TO 10 SERVINGS

Most omelets are made with a generous amount of onion, but the garlic and parsley take center stage in this very tasty variation on the standard Spanish omelet.

¾ cup olive oil, for frying

4 medium to large baking potatoes, peeled, cut into ⅛-inch slices

½ medium onion, finely chopped (about ⅓ cup)

5 large eggs

Salt

1 garlic clove, finely chopped

2 tablespoons finely chopped fresh flat-leaf parsley

1. Heat the oil in an 8- or 9-inch skillet over medium heat until it sizzles a potato slice. Add the potatoes, one slice at a time to prevent sticking, and the onions, in alternating layers. Season with salt. Cook, turning occasionally, until the potatoes are tender but not browned, about 20 minutes. Transfer with a slotted spoon or spatula to a colander and let drain. Reserve 4 teaspoons oil and wipe out the skillet.

2. In a large bowl, beat the eggs lightly with a fork and add salt. Stir in the garlic and parsley. Add the potatoes and press down until completely covered by the egg mixture. Let sit 10 to 15 minutes.

3. Heat 3 teaspoons of the reserved oil in the same skillet over high heat until it reaches the smoking point. Quickly pour in the potato-and-egg mixture and distribute evenly. Reduce the heat to medium-high and cook, shaking the skillet often to prevent sticking, until the bottom begins to brown. Slide the omelet onto a plate, cover with a second plate, and turn over.

4. Heat the remaining 1 teaspoon reserved oil in the same skillet over high heat to the smoking point. Reduce the heat to medium and slide the omelet back into the skillet. Cook, shaking constantly, until the bottom is browned, using the back of a pancake turner to neatly tuck in the edges. Continue cooking until set in the center but still slightly juicy within. Serve hot or at room temperature.

Potato and Vegetable Omelet
Tortilla a la Segoviana

MAKES 4 TO 6 SERVINGS

Here, carrots, green beans, peas, and asparagus are delicious additions to the typical Spanish potato omelet. Since this dish comes from Segovia, a region well known for its fine meats, it is no surprise this recipe also includes ham and chorizo, making this tortilla that much richer.

½ cup olive oil, for frying

2 medium baking potatoes, peeled and cut into ⅛-inch slices

1 small onion, thinly sliced

Salt

4 large eggs

1 tablespoon finely chopped fresh flat-leaf parsley

continues...

3 tablespoons small cubes (¼ inch) Serrano (Spanish cured mountain) ham or prosciutto

3 tablespoons small pieces (¼ inch) sweet chorizo sausage

1 tablespoon finely chopped pimiento

1 small carrot, cut into ¼-inch cubes

⅓ cup blanched or boiled peas

½ cup blanched or boiled green beans

8 (4-inch) blanched or boiled asparagus tips, cut into 1-inch pieces

1. Heat the oil in an 8- or 9-inch skillet over medium heat until it sizzles a potato slice. Add the potatoes and onion one slice at a time to prevent sticking, alternating layers of potatoes and onion. Season with salt. Cook, turning occasionally, until the potatoes are tender but not browned, about 20 minutes. Transfer with a slotted spoon or spatula to a colander and let drain. Reserve 4 teaspoons oil and wipe out the skillet.

2. In a large bowl, beat the eggs lightly with a fork and add salt. Add the potatoes and onions and the remaining ingredients and stir to combine. Let sit 5 minutes.

3. Heat 3 teaspoons of the reserved oil in the same skillet over high heat until it reaches the smoking point. Quickly pour in the potato-and-egg mixture and distribute evenly. Reduce the heat to medium-high and cook, shaking the skillet often to prevent sticking, until the bottom begins to brown. Slide the omelet onto a plate, cover with a second plate, and turn over.

4. Heat the remaining 1 teaspoon reserved oil in the same skillet over high heat to the smoking point. Reduce the heat to medium and slide the omelet back into the skillet. Cook, shaking constantly, until the bottom is browned, using the back of a pancake turner to neatly tuck in the edges. Continue cooking until set in the center but still slightly juicy within. Serve hot or at room temperature.

Old-Fashioned Spanish Potato and Tuna Omelet
Antigua Tortilla Española

MAKES 4 SERVINGS AS A MAIN COURSE OR 8 TO 10 AS AN APPETIZER

When Christopher Columbus introduced potatoes from the new world to Spain, they quickly became a popular companion for eggs. This version of the typical tortilla Española *includes tuna and is quite delicious. This recipe has always been a favorite of my husband Luis.*

1 cup olive oil, for frying

3 medium potatoes, peeled and cut into ⅛-inch slices

1 medium onion, cut into ⅛-inch slices

Kosher or sea salt

5 large eggs

1 tablespoon finely chopped fresh flat-leaf parsley

1½ teaspoons finely chopped fresh thyme or rosemary or ¼ teaspoon dried thyme or rosemary

4 ounces canned or jarred white or light meat tuna, drained and separated into small chunks

1. Heat the oil in an 8- or 9-inch skillet over medium heat until it sizzles a potato slice. Add the potatoes and onion one slice at a time to prevent sticking, alternating layers of potatoes and onion. Season with salt. Cook, turning occasionally, until the potatoes are tender but not browned, about 20 minutes. Transfer with a slotted spoon or spatula to a colander and let drain. Reserve 4 teaspoons oil and wipe out the skillet.

2. In a large bowl, beat the eggs lightly with a fork and add salt. Add the parsley, thyme, and tuna and stir to combine. Add the potatoes and press down until completely covered by the egg mixture. Let sit 10 to 15 minutes.

3. Heat 3 teaspoons of the reserved oil in the same skillet over high heat until it reaches the smoking point. Quickly pour in the potato-and-egg mixture and distribute evenly. Reduce the heat to medium-high and cook, shaking the skillet often to prevent sticking, until the bottom begins to brown. Slide the omelet onto a plate, cover with a second plate, and turn over.

4. Heat the remaining 1 teaspoon reserved oil in the same skillet over high heat to the smoking point. Reduce the heat to medium and slide the omelet back into the skillet. Cook, shaking constantly, until the bottom is browned, using the back of a pancake turner to neatly tuck in the edges. Continue cooking until set in the center but still slightly juicy within. Serve hot or at room temperature.

Potato Omelet with Ham and Mint
Tortilla a la Navarra

MAKES 4 TO 6 SERVINGS

I discovered this unusual tortilla when my husband and I were traveling through the region of Navarra. It consists of mountain-cured ham flavored with mint, creating a taste quite memorable and unique.

¾ cup olive oil, for frying

4 medium baking potatoes, peeled and cut into ⅛-inch slices

1 small onion, very finely chopped (about ⅓ cup)

5 large eggs

Salt

¼ cup small cubes (¼ inch) Serrano (Spanish cured mountain) ham, or prosciutto or capicolla (about 2 ounces)

2 garlic cloves, finely chopped

2 tablespoons finely chopped fresh flat-leaf parsley

1½ teaspoons finely chopped fresh mint or ¼ teaspoon dried mint

1. Heat the oil in an 8- or 9-inch skillet over medium heat until it sizzles a potato slice. Add the potatoes, one slice at a time to prevent sticking, and the onion, alternating layers of potatoes and onion. Season with salt. Cook, turning occasionally, until the potatoes are tender but not browned, about 20 minutes. Transfer with a slotted spoon or spatula to a colander and let drain. Reserve 4 teaspoons oil.

2. In a large bowl, beat the eggs lightly with a fork and add salt. Stir in the ham, garlic, parsley, and mint. Add the potatoes and press down to completely submerge in the egg mixture. Let sit 10 to 15 minutes.

3. Heat 3 teaspoons of the reserved oil in the same skillet over high heat until it reaches the smoking point. Quickly pour in the potato-and-egg mixture and distribute evenly. Reduce the heat to medium-high and cook, shaking the skillet often to prevent sticking, until the bottom begins to brown. Slide the omelet onto a plate, cover with a second plate, and turn over.

4. Heat the remaining 1 teaspoon reserved oil in the same skillet over high heat to the smoking point. Reduce the heat to medium and slide the omelet back into the skillet. Cook, shaking constantly, until the bottom is browned, using the back of a pancake turner to neatly tuck in the edges. Continue cooking until set in the center but still slightly juicy within. Serve hot or at room temperature.

Potato, Chorizo, and Pimiento Omelet
Tortilla a la Gallega

MAKES 4 TO 6 SERVINGS

This is Galicia's version of the classic Spanish egg and potato omelet. The recipe calls for a generous amount of pimientos, giving this tortilla a rich and interesting flavor.

continues...

1 cup olive oil, for frying

4 medium potatoes, peeled and cut into ⅛-inch slices

1 medium onion, cut into ⅛-inch slices

Salt

5 large eggs

2 ounces (1 link) chorizo sausage, cut into ¼-inch pieces

3 tablespoons finely chopped pimiento

1. Heat the oil in an 8- or 9-inch skillet over medium heat until it sizzles a potato slice. Add the potatoes and onion, one slice at a time to prevent sticking, alternating layers of potatoes and onion. Season with salt. Cook, turning occasionally, until the potatoes are tender but not browned, about 20 minutes. Transfer with a slotted spoon or spatula to a colander and let drain. Reserve 4 teaspoons oil.

2. In a large bowl, beat the eggs lightly with a fork and add salt. In a small skillet over medium heat, cook the chorizo, stirring, about 5 minutes. Add it and the pimiento to the eggs, and stir to combine. Add the potatoes and press down until completely covered by the egg mixture. Let sit 15 minutes.

3. Heat 3 teaspoons of the reserved oil in the same skillet over high heat until it reaches the smoking point. Quickly pour in the potato-and-egg mixture and distribute evenly. Reduce the heat to medium-high and cook, shaking the skillet often to prevent sticking, until the bottom begins to brown. Slide the omelet onto a plate, cover with a second plate, and turn over.

4. Heat the remaining 1 teaspoon reserved oil in the same skillet over high heat to the smoking point. Reduce the heat to medium and slide the omelet back into the skillet. Cook, shaking constantly, until the bottom is browned, using the back of a pancake turner to neatly tuck in the edges. Continue cooking until set in the center but still slightly juicy within. Serve hot or at room temperature.

Potato and Banana Omelet Ⓥ
Tortilla de Patata y Plátano

MAKES 4 TO 6 SERVINGS

Where else but the Canary Islands would you find a tortilla with bananas as one of the ingredients? The warm climate of the Canaries is perfect for bananas to thrive, and they add a lovely sweet accent to this typical egg and potato omelet. The variety of banana grown in the Canaries is smaller and sweeter than the ones found in the United States. I suggest using the smallest ones you can find.

3 tablespoons olive oil

1 medium potato, peeled and cut into ½-inch pieces

Salt

¼ pound semi-ripe bananas, such as baby, peeled and cut into ⅛-inch slices

4 large eggs

1. Heat the oil in an 8-inch skillet over high heat until it reaches the smoking point. Add the potato, stir to coat with the oil, and add salt. Reduce the heat to medium and cook, stirring occasionally, until tender, about 15 minutes. Transfer with a slotted spoon to paper towels and let drain.

2. In the same oil over medium heat, add the bananas and cook, stirring, until lightly browned. Transfer to paper towels, let drain, and reserve. Reserve about 2 teaspoons oil and wipe out the skillet.

3. In a medium bowl, beat the eggs lightly with a fork and add salt. Stir in the potatoes and let sit 5 minutes. Stir in the bananas.

4. Heat the reserved oil in the skillet over high heat until it reaches the smoking point. Quickly pour in the egg mixture and distribute evenly in the skillet. Reduce the heat to medium and cook, shaking the skillet often to prevent sticking, until the edges and bottom begin to brown and the center is less liquid. Slide onto a plate, cover with a second plate, and turn over.

5. If no oil remains in the skillet, add 1 more teaspoon, then slide the omelet back into the hot skillet. Continue cooking until set in the center but still slightly juicy within. Serve hot or at room temperature.

Country-Style Omelet
Tortilla Paisana

MAKES 6 TO 8 SERVINGS

This country-style omelet that includes string beans, peas, and asparagus is one of my very favorite omelets. It should be served cut into wedges, either hot or at room temperature. Tortilla Paisana makes a perfect lunch in the summertime.

3 tablespoons plus 1 teaspoon olive oil

1 medium onion, coarsely chopped

¼ pound (2 links) chorizo sausage, cut into ¼-inch pieces

¼ pound Serrano (Spanish cured mountain) ham or prosciutto, cut into ¼-inch cubes

2 medium potatoes, boiled, peeled, and cut into small pieces

2 pimientos, cut into thin strips

½ cup boiled string beans, halved

½ cup boiled peas

6 cooked asparagus spears, each cut into 4 pieces

8 large eggs

Salt

1. Heat 2 tablespoons of the oil in a 10-inch skillet over medium heat. Add the onion and cook, stirring, until wilted and transparent, about 5 minutes. Add the chorizo, ham, and potatoes and cook, stirring, about 5 minutes. Add the pimientos, beans, peas, and asparagus and cook, stirring, about 5 minutes more. Wipe out the skillet.

2. In a large bowl, beat the eggs lightly with a fork. Add the skillet mixture and salt to the eggs and fold to combine.

3. Heat another 1 tablespoon of the oil in the same skillet over high heat until it reaches the smoking point. Quickly pour in the potato-and-egg mixture and distribute evenly. Reduce the heat to medium-high and cook, shaking the skillet often to prevent sticking, until the edges and bottom begin to brown and the center is less liquid. Slide the omelet onto a plate, cover with a second plate, and turn over.

4. Heat the remaining 1 teaspoon oil in the same skillet over high heat to the smoking point. Reduce the heat to medium and slide the omelet back into the skillet. Cook, shaking constantly, until the bottom is browned, using the back of a pancake turner to neatly tuck in the edges. Continue cooking until set in the center but still slightly juicy within. Serve hot or at room temperature.

Mushroom Omelet
Tortilla de Champiñón

MAKES 1 SERVING

This is a delicious blend of mushrooms, garlic, parsley, and cured ham.

2 tablespoons olive oil

½ pound mushrooms, rinsed, trimmed, and thinly sliced

1 small garlic clove, finely chopped

1 tablespoon finely chopped Serrano (Spanish cured mountain) ham or prosciutto

2 large eggs

Salt

Freshly ground black pepper

1. Heat 1 tablespoon of the oil in a medium skillet over high heat until it reaches the smoking point. Add the mushrooms, garlic, parsley, and ham and cook, stirring, about 2 minutes. Wipe out the skillet.

continues…

2. In a small bowl, beat the eggs lightly with a fork. Add salt, pepper, and the mushroom mixture, and fold to combine.

3. Heat the remaining 1 tablespoon oil over high heat to the smoking point. Quickly pour in the egg mixture and distribute evenly. Reduce the heat to medium-high and cook, shaking the skillet constantly to prevent sticking, until the edges and bottom begin to brown and the center is less liquid, using the back of a pancake turner to neatly tuck in the edges. Use the pancake turner to flip to the other side, adding more oil if necessary, and continue cooking until set in the center but still slightly juicy within. Serve hot.

Chickpea Omelet ⓥ
Tortilla de Garbanzos

MAKES 1 SERVING

The taste and texture of chickpeas combined with the flavors of onion and garlic make a wonderful filling for an omelet — perfect for vegetarians.

2 tablespoons olive oil

2 tablespoons finely chopped onion

1 garlic clove, finely chopped

½ cup drained cooked or drained and rinsed canned chickpeas

2 large eggs

Salt

Freshly ground black pepper

1 tablespoon finely chopped pimiento

1 tablespoon finely chopped fresh flat-leaf parsley

1. Heat 1 tablespoon of the oil in a medium skillet over medium heat. Add the onion and garlic and cook, stirring, until the onion is wilted and transparent, 2 to 3 minutes. Add the chickpeas and cook, stirring, about 5 minutes more. Wipe out the skillet.

2. In a small bowl, beat the eggs lightly with a fork. Stir in salt, pepper, the pimiento, and parsley. Add the chickpea mixture and fold to combine.

3. Heat the remaining 1 tablespoon oil over high heat to the smoking point. Quickly pour in the egg mixture and distribute evenly. Reduce the heat to medium-high and cook, shaking the skillet constantly to prevent sticking, until the edges and bottom begin to brown and the center is less liquid, using a back of the pancake turner to neatly tuck in the edges. Use the pancake turner to flip to the other side, adding more oil if necessary, and continue cooking until set in the center but still slightly juicy within. Serve hot.

Lima Bean Omelet ⓥ*
Tortilla de Habas

MAKES 1 SERVING

In Andalucía, lima beans are commonly fed to fighting bulls to make them stronger for the bullring, besides being a common staple of southern Spanish cooking. Here lima beans are the star attraction in this delicious omelet, made richer by the addition of ham. Leave out the ham and it's a vegetarian dish.

3 tablespoons olive oil

½ medium onion, coarsely chopped

¼ pound lima beans

1 tablespoon finely chopped Serrano (Spanish cured mountain) ham or prosciutto

2 large eggs

Salt

1. Heat 2 tablespoons of the oil in a medium skillet over low heat. Add the onion and cook, stirring, until wilted and transparent, about 5 minutes. Stir in the beans, cover, and cook about 30 minutes or until the beans are tender. Stir in the ham and cook about 5 minutes more. Wipe out the skillet.

2. In a medium bowl, beat the eggs lightly with a fork. Add the bean mixture and salt and mix until well blended. Let sit 5 minutes.

3. Add the remaining 1 tablespoon oil and heat over high heat until it reaches the smoking point. Quickly pour in the egg mixture and distribute evenly. Reduce the heat to medium-high and cook, shaking the skillet constantly to prevent sticking, until the edges and bottom begin to brown and the center is less liquid, using the back of a pancake turner to neatly tuck in the edges. Use the pancake turner to flip to the other side, adding more oil if necessary, and continue cooking until set in the center but still slightly juicy within. Serve hot.

Onion, Tuna, and Tomato Omelet

Tortilla Asturiana

MAKES 1 SERVING

This recipe came from my good friend Sofia Pandiellas, who is a talented cook and a native of Asturias in northern Spain. Her recipe calls for a generous amount of onion, making this omelet especially flavorful.

2 tablespoons olive oil

1 medium onion, thinly sliced

1 small ripe tomato, coarsely chopped (about ½ cup)

2 large eggs

Half of a 7-ounce can white or light meat tuna, drained and flaked

Salt

Freshly ground black pepper

1. Heat 1 tablespoon of the oil in a medium skillet over low heat. Add the onion, cover, and cook, until tender but not browned, about 8 minutes. Stir in the tomato and cook uncovered about 10 minutes more. Let cool slightly. Wipe out the skillet.

2. In a small bowl, beat the eggs lightly with a fork. Add the tuna, salt, pepper, and the onion mixture and fold to combine.

3. Heat the remaining 1 tablespoon oil over high heat until it reaches the smoking point. Quickly pour in the egg mixture and distribute evenly. Reduce the heat to medium-high and cook, shaking the skillet constantly to prevent sticking, until the edges and bottom begin to brown and the center is less liquid, using the back of a pancake turner to neatly tuck in the edges. Use the pancake turner to flip to the other side, adding more oil if necessary, and continue cooking until set in the center but still slightly juicy within. Serve hot.

Cod Omelet

Tortilla de Bacalao

MAKES 1 SERVING

Very popular with Spaniards, dried salted codfish (bacalao) or salt cod is a strong-flavored fish that makes an exceptionally tasty filling for an omelet. Remember that cod needs to be soaked in cold water for at least a day or two in order to reduce its saltiness.

PREPARE 24 TO 36 HOURS IN ADVANCE

¼ pound dried boneless skinless salt cod

2 tablespoons olive oil

1 garlic clove, finely chopped

1 tablespoon finely chopped onion

2 large eggs

Salt

Freshly ground black pepper

1 tablespoon finely chopped fresh flat-leaf parsley

1. Place the cod in a medium bowl with cold water to cover. Cover and let sit in the refrigerator 24 to

continues...

36 hours, changing the water occasionally, until the water no longer tastes salty. Drain. Fill a medium saucepan with water, add the cod, and bring to a boil over high heat. Transfer the cod to a plate and shred with your fingers.

2. Heat 1 tablespoon of the oil in a medium skillet over medium heat. Add the garlic and onion and cook, stirring, until the onion is wilted and transparent, 2 to 3 minutes. Reduce the heat to low, add the cod, and cook about 10 minutes.

3. In a small bowl, beat the eggs lightly with a fork. Add the cod mixture, salt, pepper, and parsley. Let sit 5 minutes.

4. Heat the remaining 1 tablespoon oil over high heat until it reaches the smoking point. Quickly pour in the egg mixture and distribute evenly. Reduce the heat to medium-high and cook, shaking the skillet constantly to prevent sticking, until the edges and bottom begin to brown and the center is less liquid, using the back of a pancake turner to neatly tuck in the edges. Use the pancake turner to flip to the other side, adding more oil if necessary, and continue cooking until set in the center but still slightly juicy within. Serve hot.

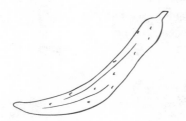

Basic Long Loaf ⓥ
Pan de Pueblo

MAKES 2 LONG LOAVES

This is one of the most popular breads in Spain, and it is very easy to prepare. You can make more dough than you need right away; freeze the rest for later use.

1 package (2½ teaspoons) active dry yeast
1¼ cups warm water (100°F to 110°F)
3¼ cups bread flour or unbleached all-purpose flour
3 teaspoons kosher or sea salt
Cornmeal or bread crumbs, for sprinkling
1 large egg white
1 teaspoon water

1. In a small cup, sprinkle the yeast over ¼ cup of the warm water. Let sit until the yeast is creamy, about 2 minutes. Stir until the yeast dissolves. Mix the flour and salt in a large bowl. Add the softened yeast and the remaining 1 cup warm water and mix with a wooden spoon (the dough will not yet hold together). Turn out onto a lightly floured work surface. Knead until smooth and elastic, adding more flour if necessary, about 5 minutes.

2. Grease a large bowl with oil, place the dough in the bowl, and turn to coat. Cover with a towel and let rise in a warm place (such as an oven turned off) about 3 hours or until double in size.

3. Punch down the dough and knead 5 minutes. Divide into 2 equal parts. Roll out each part into a 20 x 5-inch rectangle. Starting with a long side, roll up tightly jellyroll fashion. Pinch to seal the seam and the ends.

4. Sprinkle a cookie sheet with the cornmeal and place the loaves, seam side down, on the cookie sheet. Cut diagonal slits in the top in several places. Let rise in a warm place 1 hour more or until double in size.

5. Place an oven rack in the upper-middle position. Preheat the oven to 450°F and place a pan of water on the oven floor. Bake the bread 5 minutes. Remove the pan of water and bake 5 minutes more. Lightly beat the egg white and the 1 teaspoon water in a small bowl. Brush this egg wash over the bread and bake 5 to 10 minutes more or until browned and crusty.

Country-Style Bread ⓥ
Pan Candeal

MAKES 1 ROUND LOAF

The preparation of this round loaf of country-style bread was inspired by primitive techniques. It results in a bread that is slightly sour because the dough is aged two days without yeast, then the yeast is added to ensure proper rising. This very hearty bread is perfect for dunking.

PREPARE 48 HOURS IN ADVANCE

3½ cups bread flour or unbleached all-purpose flour
1¼ cups warm water (100°F to 110°F)
1 package (2½ teaspoons) active dry yeast
3 tablespoons kosher or sea salt
Cornmeal or bread crumbs, for sprinkling

1 large egg white
1 tablespoon water

1. In a medium bowl, mix 3 cups of the flour with 1 cup of the warm water until combined. Turn out onto a lightly floured work surface and knead 5 minutes, adding more flour if necessary—the dough should be very firm. Let rest 5 minutes, then knead 5 minutes more. Dust with flour, place in a medium bowl, and cover with foil. Place in a draft-free spot, such as a kitchen cabinet, and let sit 48 hours. The dough should have expanded slightly and have a faint aroma of vinegar.

2. In a small cup, sprinkle the yeast over the remaining ¼ cup warm water. Let sit until the yeast is creamy, about 2 minutes. Stir until the yeast dissolves. Add the remaining ½ cup flour and mix until combined. Place in the bowl with the dough that has been resting and mix until thoroughly combined. Turn out onto a lightly floured work surface and knead about 5 minutes, incorporating in the process salt and as much flour as necessary to form a smooth elastic dough. Grease a large bowl with oil, place the dough in the bowl, and turn to coat. Cover with a towel and let rise in a warm place (such as an oven turned off) 2½ to 3 hours or until double in size.

3. Place an oven rack in the upper-middle position. Preheat the oven to 425°F and place a pan of water on the oven floor. Transfer the dough to an 8-inch round cake pan and bake 5 minutes. Remove the pan of water and bake 10 minutes more. Lightly beat the egg white and the 1 tablespoon water in a small bowl. Brush this egg wash over the bread.

4. Remove the loaf from the pan and place directly on the oven rack. Bake about 2 minutes more, or until the bread sounds hollow when tapped on the bottom.

Due to its climate and soil, Spain has always been fertile ground to grow grains. Even the Romans imported wheat from the Iberian Peninsula to feed the Empire. Castilla, the central region of Spain, is composed of soil that is ideal to grow wheat—so much so that the Castilian provinces of Valladolid, Segovia, Leon, and Palencia are known as *tierra de pan* (the land of bread). The variety of breads available in Spain is very diverse and often based on local recipes and traditions as well as local government regulations. Breads are consistently high quality and usually baked during the night and sold in the early morning in *panaderias*, which sell bread exclusively. Sweet rolls, pastries, pies, and cakes are sold in *pastelerias*.

All Spanish meals are served with bread. At home, of course, bread is a daily staple, bought and eaten fresh daily or sometimes kept for days to use in recipes that call for "stale" bread. The most popular way to use bread in Spain is the tradition of the *bocadillo*, sometimes called a *bocata*. El Bocadillo (literally, the "little bite") is a popular item to snack on at 5 or 6 pm and is served in bars, cafeterias, delicatessens, taverns—everywhere. A *bocadillo* is a small, usually white roll sliced in half and filled with Serrano ham, *chorizo*, Manchego cheese, sausage, canned sardines, tuna, red peppers, or whatever ingredient you like. In fact, a very popular *bocadillo* is made with fried calamari. The *bocadillo* is the basis of the *merienda*, the traditional afternoon snack served prior to tapas and dinner. It is usually accompanied by a glass of beer or wine.

Aranda Bread Tortes Ⓥ
Pan de Aranda

MAKES 1 LARGE OR
2 (9-INCH) ROUND LOAVES

The recipe for this wonderful flat but moist Castilian bread comes from the Mesón de la Villa restaurant in Aranda de Duero. This excellent restaurant is most famous for its delectable roast lamb, but its signature bread is also outstanding.

PREPARE AT LEAST 6 HOURS IN ADVANCE

1½ packages (1 tablespoon) active dry yeast
1½ cups warm water (100°F to 110°F)
3 cups bread flour or unbleached all-purpose flour
1½ teaspoons salt
Cornmeal or all-purpose flour, for sprinkling
Extra-virgin olive oil, for brushing

1. In a small cup, sprinkle the yeast over ¾ cup of the warm water. Let sit until the yeast is creamy, about 2 minutes. Stir until the yeast dissolves. In a food processor, place 2 cups of the flour and the dissolved yeast and process 1 minute. Grease a large bowl with oil, place the dough in the bowl, and turn to coat. Cover with a damp towel and let rise in a warm place (such as an oven turned off) 3 hours.

2. Punch down the dough and return it to the processor. Add the remaining 1 cup flour, the salt, and the remaining ¾ cup warm water. Process 1 minute. Remove with well-floured hands (dough will be quite sticky) and knead briefly on a lightly floured work surface. Return to the oiled bowl, cover with a damp towel, and let rise in a warm place 3 hours more.

3. Place an oven rack in the upper-middle position. Preheat the oven to 400°F and place a pan of water on the floor of the oven. Punch down the dough. For 1 loaf, roll out the dough into an 18-inch round. For 2 loaves, divide the dough in half and roll each into a 9-inch round. Score with a sharp thin knife to within 1 inch of the edge.

4. Sprinkle a cookie sheet with the cornmeal and place the dough on the cookie sheet. Bake 10 minutes. Remove the pan of water and brush the bread with the oil. Bake 5 to 10 minutes more or until lightly browned.

Flat Bread Loaf Ⓥ

Zapatilla

MAKES 2 LONG FLAT LOAVES

Also known as chapata, *this flatbread has become popular in Madrid and can be found in gourmet shops cut into large squares with simple fillings. The dough is made the same way as Aranda Bread Tortes, but the shape and thickness are different.*

1 recipe dough for Aranda Bread Tortes (page 128)
Cornmeal or all-purpose flour, for dusting

1. Prepare the dough and let rise as instructed in steps 1 and 2 of the recipe. Place an oven rack in the upper-middle position. Preheat the oven to 400°F and place a pan of water on the floor of the oven. Punch down the dough. Divide in half and roll each piece into a 16 x 4½-inch rectangle. Cut slits in the top and dust with flour.

2. Sprinkle 2 cookie sheets with the cornmeal and place 1 loaf on each. Bake 10 minutes. Remove the pan of water and bake 5 to 10 minutes more or until lightly browned.

Galician Rye Bread Ⓥ*

Pan Gallego de Centeno

MAKES 1 LARGE ROUND LOAF

Caraway seeds lend their distinctive flavor to this rye bread that originated in Galicia. The loaf is meant to be round with a twisted top characteristic of both breads and cheeses from that region. Make it vegetarian with vegetable shortening.

PREPARE 36 HOURS IN ADVANCE

4½ cups bread flour
2½ cups dark rye flour
½ cup cornmeal
2½ cups warm water (100°F to 110°F)
2 packages (5 teaspoons) active dry yeast
4 teaspoons sugar
2 tablespoons kosher or sea salt
2 tablespoons lard or vegetable shortening, softened
2 teaspoons caraway seeds
Cornmeal or bread crumbs, for sprinkling

1. In a large bowl, mix 3½ cups of the bread flour, the rye flour, cornmeal, and 2 cups of the warm water until combined. Turn out onto a lightly floured work surface and knead 5 minutes, adding more bread flour if necessary—the dough should be very firm. Let rest 5 minutes. Knead until smooth, about 5 minutes more. Dust with flour, place in a large bowl, and cover with foil. Place in a draft-free spot, such as a kitchen cabinet, and let sit 36 hours. The dough should have expanded a bit and have the slight aroma of vinegar.

2. In a small cup, sprinkle the yeast over the remaining ½ cup warm water. Let sit until the yeast is creamy, about 2 minutes. Stir until the yeast dissolves. Add the remaining 1 cup bread flour and mix until combined. Place in the bowl with the

continues . . .

dough that has been resting, add the salt, lard, and caraway seeds, and mix until combined. Turn out onto a lightly floured work surface and knead 5 minutes, adding more flour if necessary.

3. Grease a large bowl with oil, place the dough in the bowl, and turn to coat. Cover with a towel and let rise in a warm place (such as an oven turned off) 2 to 2½ hours or until double in size.

4. Punch down the dough. Knead 5 minutes, adding more flour if necessary. Shape into a ball and twist in the center to make the Galician "cap." Sprinkle a cookie sheet with cornmeal and place the dough on the cookie sheet. Let rise in a warm place 1 hour or until double in size.

5. Place an oven rack in the upper-middle position. Preheat the oven to 425°F and place a pan of water on the oven floor. Bake 5 minutes. Remove the pan of water and bake 5 minutes more. Reduce the heat to 350°F and bake 20 minutes more. Remove the bread from the cookie sheet and place directly on the oven rack. Bake about 2 minutes more or until the bread is well browned and sounds hollow when tapped on the bottom.

Corn and Barley Bread Ⓥ

Pan de Cebada

MAKES 1 LARGE ROUND LOAF

Galicia is the only region where you can find this hearty bread, where it is frequently eaten with sardines, pâté, or marinated cold fish. Corn and barley give this dough a very strong flavor. If you can't find barley flour, purchase whole barley and finely grind it in a coffee grinder.

PREPARE AT LEAST 28 HOURS IN ADVANCE

2 cups cornmeal

3½ cups water

1 cup barley flour

4¾ cups whole wheat flour

2 packages (5 teaspoons) active dry yeast

¼ cup warm water (100°F to 110°F)

5 teaspoons salt

Cornmeal or bread crumbs, for sprinkling

1. In a medium saucepan, mix the cornmeal and the 3½ cups water. Bring to a boil over medium heat, stirring constantly, then continue cooking until quite thick. Let cool.

2. In a large bowl, mix the barley flour, 4½ cups of the whole wheat flour and the softened cornmeal. Turn out onto a lightly floured work surface and knead 5 minutes (it will take a little work before it begins to hold together). Let rest 5 minutes. Knead 5 minutes more, adding more whole wheat flour if necessary. Form into a ball, dust with flour, and place in a large bowl. Cover with foil, place in a warm draft-free spot, such as a kitchen cabinet, and let sit 24 hours.

3. In a small cup, sprinkle the yeast over the ¼ cup warm water. Let sit until the yeast is creamy, about 2 minutes. Stir until the yeast dissolves. Mix in the remaining ¼ cup whole wheat flour. Add the yeast mixture and the salt to the bowl with the dough, and mix until combined. Turn out onto a lightly floured work surface and knead 2 minutes, adding more whole wheat flour if necessary. Let rest 2 minutes. Knead 3 minutes more. Grease a large bowl with oil, place the dough in the bowl, and turn to coat. Cover with a towel and let rise in a warm place (such as an oven turned off) 3 hours—it will not quite double in size.

4. Punch down the dough and knead 5 minutes. Shape into a ball. Sprinkle a cookie sheet with the cornmeal and place the dough on the cookie sheet. Cut two slits in the top. Let rise in a warm place 1 hour more—it will not quite double in size.

5. Place an oven rack in the upper-middle position. Preheat the oven to 425°F and place a pan of water on the oven floor. Bake 5 minutes. Remove the pan

of water and bake 5 minutes more. Reduce the heat to 350°F and bake about 20 minutes more. Remove the bread from the cookie sheet and place directly on the oven rack. Bake about 5 minutes more or until it is well browned and sounds hollow when tapped on the bottom.

Sausage-Stuffed Country Bread
Hornazo

MAKES 1 LARGE LOAF

In Spain, country bread stuffed with chorizo, morcilla, and whole eggs is typically eaten on Easter. This bread, which originated in Castilla, is almost rich and hearty enough to be a meal on its own.

1 recipe Country-Style Bread dough (page 127)
3 tablespoons olive oil
¼ pound slab bacon, cut into ¼-inch cubes
¼ pound black sausage (morcilla), halved crosswise
¼ pound (2 links) chorizo, each halved crosswise
2 hard-boiled eggs, shelled
Cornmeal or bread crumbs, for sprinkling

1. Prepare the dough and let rise as instructed in steps 1 and 2 of the recipe. Heat the oil in a medium skillet over medium heat. Add the bacon, black sausage, and chorizo and cook, stirring, until the bacon is crispy. Transfer with a slotted spoon to paper towels and let drain. Reserve the oil.
2. Punch down the dough and knead in 3 tablespoons of the reserved oil and the bacon, adding more flour if necessary. Shape into a ball. Cut slits in the dough and push in the pieces of black sausage and chorizo and the hard-boiled eggs. Close the dough over the pieces, pinching to seal well. Sprinkle a cookie sheet with cornmeal and place the dough, pinched side down, on the cookie sheet. Flatten the dough slightly. Let rise in a warm place (such as an oven turned off) 1 hour or until double in size.

3. Place an oven rack in the upper-middle position. Preheat the oven to 450°F and place a pan of water on the oven floor. Bake 5 minutes. Remove the pan of water and bake about 15 minutes more or until well browned.

Holiday Bread ⓥ*
Roscón de Reyes

MAKES 1 LARGE BREAD RING

Roscón de Reyes, a wonderful sweetened bread coated with sugar and candied fruit, is only prepared and eaten around January 6th, the Day of the Three Kings. This important Spanish holiday celebrating the Three Wise Men's journey to Spain on camels is beloved by children, because The Wise Men come bearing gifts. If the children have been "good," the Kings leave presents in their shoes. If they have been "bad," the Kings fill their shoes with coal instead of toys. On this special day, even the holiday loaf of bread comes with a surprise—usually either a coin or a ceramic figure is baked into it. According to legend, whoever finds the "surprise" in their piece of bread is brought good luck for the rest of the year.

The orange flower water can be found in specialty shops. Make it vegetarian with vegetable shortening.

1 package (2½ teaspoons) active dry yeast
¾ cup warm water (100°F to 110°F)
1 tablespoon orange flower water or strong tea
½ teaspoon lemon zest
6 whole cloves
¼ pound (1 stick) unsalted butter
1 tablespoon lard or vegetable shortening
½ cup sugar
½ teaspoon salt
3 large eggs

continues...

Eggs, Breads, and Empanadas   131

1 tablespoon brandy, such as Spanish brandy or
   Cognac

½ cup milk, scalded and cooled

5 cups unbleached all-purpose flour

Candied fruit slices, such as orange or lemon

1 teaspoon water

1½ tablespoons sugar, such as coarse, for sprinkling

1. In a small cup, sprinkle the yeast over ¼ cup of the warm water. Let sit until the yeast is creamy, about 2 minutes. Stir until the yeast dissolves. In a small saucepan, add the remaining ½ cup warm water, the orange flower water, zest, and cloves, cover, and cook over low heat 10 minutes. Let cool. Discard the cloves.

2. Meanwhile, in a large bowl using an electric mixer, beat the butter, lard, sugar, and salt until smooth. Beat in 2 of the eggs. Add the brandy, milk, the water-lemon mixture, and the yeast and mix until well blended. Gradually mix in the flour with a wooden spoon until the dough is soft and sticky. Turn out onto a lightly floured work surface and knead until smooth and elastic, adding more flour if necessary, about 5 minutes.

3. Grease a large bowl with oil, place the dough in the bowl, and turn to coat. Cover with a towel and let rise in a warm place (such as an oven turned off) about 2 hours or until double in size. Punch down the dough and knead 5 minutes. Insert a washed and dried good-luck coin or object, such as a silver dollar, half dollar, or a clean miniature ceramic animal.

4. Lightly grease a cookie sheet. Shape the dough into a large ring, pinching the ends to seal well, and place on the cookie sheet. Decorate with the fruit slices, pushing them slightly into the dough. Let rise in a warm place about 1 hour or until double in size.

5. Preheat the oven to 350°F. Lightly beat the remaining 1 egg and the 1 teaspoon water in a small bowl. Brush this egg wash over the dough, sprinkle with the sugar, and bake 35 to 40 minutes or until deep golden brown.

Miniature Egg Buns Ⓥ
Medias-Noches

MAKES 20 BUNS

These small, sweet buns glazed with egg yolks are perfect for tea sandwiches of any kind. Sliced ham and cheese are popular fillings, although these buns are also delicious when simply spread with butter. Medias-Noches (which means "midnight") are mostly used with different fillings for cocktail parties, weddings, and birthdays.

1 package (2½ teaspoons) active dry yeast

¼ cup warm water (100°F to 110°F)

1¾ cups bread flour or unbleached all-purpose flour

½ teaspoon salt

5 teaspoons sugar

3 tablespoons milk

2 large eggs, lightly beaten

2 tablespoons unsalted butter, melted and cooled

1 large egg yolk

1 teaspoon water

1. In a small cup, sprinkle the yeast over the warm water. Let sit until the yeast is creamy, about 2 minutes. Stir until the yeast dissolves. In a medium bowl, combine the flour, salt, and sugar. Add the milk, yeast mixture, the 2 eggs, and the butter and mix until well blended. Turn out onto a lightly floured work surface and knead 5 minutes, adding more flour if necessary and throwing the dough forcefully to the counter several times until smooth and elastic—the dough will be soft but should not be sticky.

2. Divide the dough into 20 equal pieces, each about 1½ inches in diameter. Shape into ovals and place on an ungreased cookie sheet. Flatten slightly. Let rise in a warm place (such as an oven turned off) about 30 minutes or until double in size.

3. Preheat the oven to 350°F. Lightly beat the egg yolk and the 1 teaspoon water in a small bowl. Brush this egg wash over the rolls and bake about 15 minutes or until very well browned. Serve warm, fresh from the oven or reheated.

Sweet Filled Bread Rings ⓥ
Torteles

MAKES 3 (5-INCH) RINGS

Typically enjoyed with mid-morning coffee and for afternoon tea parties, these bread rings are filled with a sweetened mixture of almonds and potato. They are a specialty of Catalunya but are commonly found in cafeterias throughout Spain.

Dough

½ package (1½ teaspoons) active dry yeast

½ cup warm water (100°F to 110°F)

2 cups unbleached all-purpose flour

¼ teaspoon salt

2 large eggs

4 tablespoons sugar

1½ tablespoons salad oil

Melted unsalted butter

1 teaspoon water

Powdered (confectioners) sugar, for dusting

Filling

2 ounces blanched almonds (about ⅓ cup)

¼ cup granulated sugar

3 ounces boiled potato (about ¼ medium potato), peeled

¼ teaspoon lemon zest

Melted unsalted butter

1. Prepare the dough: In a small cup, sprinkle the yeast over ¼ cup of the warm water. Let sit until the yeast is creamy, about 2 minutes. Stir until the yeast dissolves. Add the flour and mix until combined. Turn out onto a lightly floured work surface, and knead lightly, adding more flour if necessary, until a ball forms and the dough is smooth. Cut a slit in the top, wrap in a towel, and let sit in a warm place (such as an oven turned off) while preparing the rest of the dough.

2. In a medium bowl, mix the remaining ¼ cup warm water, the salt, 1 of the eggs, and 2 tablespoons of the granulated sugar. Add the remaining 1½ cups flour and mix until combined. Turn out onto a lightly floured work surface, kneading until all the flour is incorporated. Knead together the 2 balls of dough, gradually incorporating the remaining 2 tablespoons granulated sugar and the oil, adding a little more flour if necessary, until smooth and elastic. Wrap in a towel and let sit in a warm place about 10 minutes.

3. Meanwhile, prepare the filling: In a food processor, place the almonds and process until as finely chopped as possible (but not a paste). With the motor running, gradually add the ¼ cup sugar, then add the potato and zest and process until smooth.

4. Divide the dough into 3 equal pieces. Grease a work surface and a rolling pin, and roll 1 piece of dough into a rectangle about 24 x 5 inches and the thickness of a coin. Brush the dough with some of the melted butter. Place one-third of the filling in a thin cord along one side of the dough, close to the edge. Starting with a long side, roll up, jellyroll fashion. Pinch to seal the seam, then shape into a circle and pinch to seal the ends together. Repeat for the other 2 pieces of dough. Place on a cookie sheet, seam side down, and let rise in a warm place (such as an oven turned off) about 3 hours or until double in size.

5. Place an oven rack in the upper-middle position. Preheat the oven to 400°F. Lightly beat the remaining 1 egg and the 1 teaspoon water in a small bowl. Gently brush this egg wash over the rings and dust with the powdered sugar. Bake about 10 minutes or until lightly browned. Serve warm, fresh from the oven or reheated.

Sugar-Topped Sweet Rolls ⓥ
Suizos

MAKES 12 ROLLS

These sweet rolls are a customary part of any continental breakfast served at a Spanish hotel. Of all the different sweet rolls I have tasted, suizos *are my favorite.*

1 recipe Sweet Filled Bread Rings (page 133)
¼ cup sugar, for topping
1 large egg
1 teaspoon water

1. Prepare and knead the dough as instructed in steps I and 2 of the recipe (do not let rise).

2. Divide the dough into 12 equal pieces. Shape each into an oval and cut a slit in the top lengthwise down the center. Place on a cookie sheet and let rise in a warm place (such as an oven turned off) 3 hours or until double in size. Fill the slit in each roll with I teaspoon sugar.

3. Preheat the oven to 350°F. Lightly beat the egg and water in a small bowl. Brush this egg wash over the roll tops (not the sugared part). Bake 10 to 15 minutes or until well browned. Serve warm, fresh from the oven or reheated.

Sweet Snail-Shaped Rolls ⓥ
Ensaimadas

MAKES 18 ROLLS

Originally from the island of Mallorca, the name ensaimadas *is derived from the shape these sweet rolls take as they are rolled tightly (jellyroll style), resembling snails. They are usually served with breakfast or afternoon tea. The magnificent Mallorca shop on Velazquez Street has been selling* ensaimadas *since the 1940s, and it is still popular today. I highly recommend a visit.*

1 recipe Sweet Filled Bread Rings (page 133)
Melted unsalted butter
Powdered (confectioners) sugar, for dusting

1. Prepare and knead the dough as instructed in steps I and 2 of the recipe (do not let rise).

2. Divide the dough into 9 equal pieces. Take I piece and roll between your palms to form a rope about ½ inch thick. Grease a work surface and a rolling pin and roll out the dough into a 30 x 2-inch rectangle. Brush with melted butter—but not quite to the edges. Starting with a long side, roll up tightly, jellyroll fashion. Pinch to seal well.

3. Cut the roll into 2 equal pieces. Curl each piece loosely into a spiral or "snail" shape. Pinch the end to close the spiral. Repeat for the remaining 8 pieces. Place the snails on a cookie sheet, seam side down, with the ends of the spirals near the edges of the pan to prevent uncurling. Let rise in a warm place (such as an oven turned off) 3 hours or until double in size.

4. Preheat the oven to 350°F. Brush the roll tops with water and dust with the powdered sugar. Bake about 10 minutes or until lightly browned. Let cool slightly and dust again with powdered sugar. Serve warm, fresh from the oven or reheated.

Puff Pastry Ⓥ

Hojaldre

MAKES 2¾ POUNDS

The use of puff pastry in Spanish cooking goes back hundreds of years. It is commonly used for desserts but also very popular with fillings of meats and fish. Any tapa or main course is made more elegant when served in puff pastry, not to mention richer and more delicious. This recipe is simple to make and produces an excellent pastry crust. The dough will keep in your freezer for many weeks.

3 cups unbleached all-purpose flour

1 cup cake flour

1½ teaspoons kosher or sea salt

6½ sticks sweet butter, chilled

1 cup ice cold water

1. In a large bowl, mix the flours and stir in the salt. Cut the sticks of butter lengthwise into quarters then into ½-inch cubes and add to the flour. Rub each of the butter cubes between your fingers to flatten into flakes, combining them at the same time with the flour. Refrigerate 10 minutes (the butter must be kept firm throughout the process). Add the water and stir until the dough holds together loosely.

2. Turn the dough out onto a lightly floured work surface. Pat into an 18 x 8-inch rectangle. Sprinkle the top of the dough with flour. With the aid of a knife, fold lengthwise in thirds, business-letter fashion. Lift the dough, flour the work surface again, flour the top of the dough, then roll out with a rolling pin to the previous size, making the folded sides the width and the open ends the length.

(Remember, all this must be done rapidly—if the butter softens, refrigerate briefly.)

3. Fold up a second time in the same manner, roll out again, then repeat two more times (for a total of four), flouring surfaces as necessary and ending with the dough folded.

4. Cover the dough with plastic wrap and refrigerate 40 minutes. Roll and fold twice more, then the dough is ready to use or to store for future use in the refrigerator or freezer.

Empanada Dough Ⓥ*

Masa de Empanada

DOUGH FOR 11-INCH ROUND PIE OR
10 X 15-INCH RECTANGULAR PIE OR 40
TURNOVERS

Empanadas, savory meat or fish pies, are beloved by Spaniards and can be found prepared with a variety of delicious fillings. Empanadillas are smaller versions of empanadas that are commonly served as tapas or for dinner. This dough, which is not too sweet, is perfect for all types of empanadas and empanadillas. Make it vegetarian with vegetable shortening.

PREPARE AT LEAST 2 HOURS IN ADVANCE

1 package (2½ teaspoons) active dry yeast

¼ cup warm water (100°F to 110°F)

3 tablespoons lard or vegetable shortening

3½ cups unbleached all-purpose flour

1½ teaspoons salt

2 large eggs, lightly beaten

½ cup warm milk (100°F to 110°F)

1. In a small cup, sprinkle the yeast over ¼ cup of the warm water. Let sit until the yeast is creamy, about 2 minutes. Stir until the yeast dissolves. Melt the lard in a small saucepan over low heat. Let cool slightly.

continues . . .

2. Mix the flour and salt in a large bowl. Add the eggs, lard, yeast mixture, and milk and mix until combined. Turn out onto a lightly floured work surface and knead briefly until the dough is smooth and elastic, adding flour as necessary, 2 to 3 minutes.

3. Grease a large bowl with oil, place the dough in the bowl, and turn to coat. Cover with a towel and let rise in a warm place (such as an oven turned off) 1½ hours. Knead the dough 2 to 3 minutes more, then return to the bowl, cover, and let rise 1 hour more. The dough is ready to use or to store for future use in the refrigerator or freezer.

Tomato and Green Pepper Pies **V**
Coca "La Plana"

MAKES 5 SMALL PIES

In the regions of Catalunya and Levante, coca refers to a round, thin bread-like dough which can be sweetened or unsweetened. I got this recipe for delicious tomato and green pepper pies from Merendero La Plana, a charming family-run restaurant in the city of Alicante. A very tasty vegetable empanada.

½ recipe for Empanada Dough (page 135), Basic Long Loaf dough (page 126), or pizza dough

2 tablespoons vegetable oil

½ pound firm ripe tomatoes, cut into very thin slices

2 medium green bell peppers, cut into very thin slices

1 small onion, slivered

2 garlic cloves, finely chopped

Salt

Freshly ground black pepper

15 teaspoons olive oil

1. Prepare the bread dough and let rise as instructed in steps 1 and 2 of the recipe. Punch down the dough and knead in the 1 tablespoon vegetable

oil, adding flour if necessary. Divide into 5 equal pieces. Shape into balls. Roll out each into a 6-inch round about ⅛-inch thick. Curl up the edge to make a rim. Place on a cookie sheet.

3. Preheat the oven to 350°F. Arrange the tomato slices in overlapping circles over each dough round. Cover each pie with 3 bell pepper rings over the tomatoes. Scatter the onion over the pie, sprinkle with the garlic, and season with salt and pepper. Drizzle with the 3 teaspoons olive oil.

4. Bake the pies about 20 minutes or until the vegetables are tender and the crust very lightly golden. Serve hot.

Fresh Sardine Pie
Empanada de Sardinas

MAKES 4 SERVINGS AS A MAIN COURSE OR 8 AS AN APPETIZER

Sardines have a very strong flavor, empanada dough is the perfect complement. This dish is better when you use fresh sardines, but you can substitute dry, salted sardines after proper desalting. They can be served either hot or at room temperature.

PREPARE AT LEAST 2 HOURS IN ADVANCE

1 recipe Empanada Dough (page 135)

4 tablespoons olive oil

½ pound fresh sardines, cleaned (or dry, salted sardines, de-salted)

2 medium onions, thinly sliced

2 pimientos, coarsely chopped

1 medium tomato, coarsely chopped (about ⅔ cup)

Salt

Freshly ground black pepper

Few threads of saffron

1 large egg

1 teaspoon water

1. Prepare the dough. While the dough is rising, heat 2 tablespoons of the oil in a medium skillet over medium heat. Add the sardines and cook, turning once, until golden. Fillet them, leaving the skin on.

2. Wipe out the skillet and heat the remaining 2 tablespoons oil over medium heat. Add the onions and cook, stirring, until wilted and transparent, about 5 minutes. Add the pimientos, tomato, salt, pepper, and saffron, cover, and cook 15 minutes more.

3. Preheat the oven to 350°F. Separate the dough into 2 equal parts. Roll each into a 9-inch round less than ⅛ inch thick. Place 1 round on a greased cookie sheet and arrange the sardines on top of the dough in a pinwheel pattern. Cover with the onion mixture. Cover the pie with the other dough round. Roll up the edges and press to seal well. Cut decorative slits in the top. Lightly beat the egg and water in a small bowl. Brush this egg wash over the dough.

4. Bake about 20 minutes or until golden. Serve hot or at room temperature.

Tuna Pie
Empanada de Bonito

MAKES 4 SERVINGS AS A MAIN COURSE OR 6 AS AN APPETIZER

Another empanada that comes from Galicia, this one is filled with tuna and peppers and seasoned with onion and garlic. If making empanadillas, *the pie should be cut into small square portions.*

PREPARE AT LEAST 3 HOURS IN ADVANCE

1 recipe Empanada Dough (page 135)

2 tablespoons olive oil

2 medium green bell peppers, cut into thin strips

2 medium onions, thinly sliced

3 garlic cloves, finely chopped

One (7-ounce) can white or light meat tuna, drained and flaked

¼ cup tomato sauce

2 tablespoons water

Salt

Freshly ground black pepper

1 large egg, lightly beaten, for brushing

1. Prepare the dough. While the dough is rising, heat the oil in a medium skillet over medium heat. Add the bell peppers, cover, and cook until softened. Add the onion, garlic, tuna, and tomato sauce and cook uncovered, stirring occasionally, until slightly thickened, about 5 minutes more. Stir in the water. Season with salt and pepper.

2. Divide the dough into 2 equal parts. Roll each into a 15 x 10-inch rectangle. Place 1 rectangle on a greased cookie sheet of the same size. Spread the filling over the dough and cover with the second dough rectangle. Roll up the edges and press to seal well. Cut several slits in the top. Let sit 20 minutes in a warm place (such as an oven turned off).

3. Preheat the oven to 350°F. Brush the dough with the egg wash and bake 20 to 30 minutes or until golden. Serve hot or at room temperature.

Clam Pie
Empanada de Berberecho

MAKES 4 SERVINGS AS A MAIN COURSE OR 8 AS AN APPETIZER

In Spanish, cockles (tiny clams) are called berberechos, *which are found in Galicia and make for an exceptional empanada filling.*

PREPARE AT LEAST 3 HOURS IN ADVANCE

1 recipe Empanada Dough (page 135)

2 (6.5 ounce) cans clams, drained, with 3 tablespoons juice reserved

½ cup vegetable oil

2 medium onions, thinly sliced

3 cloves garlic, finely chopped

continues . . .

¾ cup finely chopped pimiento

¼ cup tomato sauce or diluted tomato paste

½ teaspoon ground paprika

Salt

Freshly ground black pepper

1 large egg, lightly beaten, for brushing

1. Prepare the dough. While the dough is rising, coarsely chop the clams. Then heat the oil in a medium skillet over medium heat. Add the onion and garlic and cook, stirring, until the onion is wilted and transparent, about 5 minutes. Drain out all but about 2 tablespoons of the oil and leave the onions and garlic in the skillet.

2. Add the pimiento, clams, tomato sauce, and paprika and cook, stirring occasionally, about 10 minutes. Remove from the heat and stir in the reserved clam juice. Season with salt and pepper.

3. Divide the dough into 2 equal parts. Roll each into a 15 x 10-inch rectangle. Place 1 rectangle on a greased cookie sheet of the same size. Spread the filling over the dough and cover with the second dough rectangle. Roll up the edges and press to seal well. Cut several slits in the top. Let sit 20 minutes in a warm place (such as an oven turned off).

4. Preheat the oven to 350°F. Brush with the egg and bake 20 to 30 minutes or until golden. Serve hot.

Asturian Chorizo Pie
Empanada Asturiana

MAKES 6 SERVINGS AS A MAIN COURSE OR 8 AS AN APPETIZER

This delicious savory meat pie is filled with well-seasoned chorizo and originated in Asturias but is enormously popular all over Spain. It can be served either hot or at room temperature. Definitely one of my favorite empanadas.

PREPARE AT LEAST 3 HOURS IN ADVANCE

1 recipe Empanada Dough (page 135)

2 tablespoons olive oil

2 large onions, coarsely chopped (about 2 cups)

2 garlic cloves, finely chopped

½ pound lean pork loin, cut into thin strips ⅛-inch thick

1 medium ripe tomato, peeled and coarsely chopped (about ⅔ cup)

2 pimientos, cut into thin strips

Pinch of saffron threads

Salt

Freshly ground black pepper

2 hard-boiled eggs, coarsely chopped

¼ cup warm water

1 large egg

1 tablespoon milk

1. Prepare the dough. While the dough is rising, heat the oil in a large skillet over medium heat. Add the onion and garlic and cook, stirring, until the onion is wilted and transparent, about 8 minutes. Add the pork and chorizo and cook, stirring, about 10 minutes. Add the tomato, pimientos, saffron, salt, and pepper, reduce the heat to low, and cook, stirring, until slightly thickened, about 10 minutes more. Scatter the hard-boiled eggs over the top and immediately remove from the heat. Stir in the warm water.

2. Preheat the oven to 350°F. Divide the dough into 2 equal parts. Roll each into a 12-inch round. Place 1 round in an ungreased 11-inch pie plate, extending the edge over the side of the plate. Add the filling and cover with the second dough round. Curl the bottom dough up over the top dough and press to seal well. Cut decorative slits in the top. Lightly beat the egg and milk in a small bowl. Brush this egg wash over the dough.

3. Bake about 30 minutes or until nicely browned. Let sit about 15 minutes. Serve hot or at room temperature.

Pork Pie

Empanada de Lomo

MAKES 4 SERVINGS AS A MAIN COURSE OR
6 AS AN APPETIZER

*Pork, beloved by so many Spaniards, makes a rich
and delicious filling for empanadas. This is the most
popular meat pie served in the region of Galicia. The
pork is heavily spiced with onion, garlic, and paprika,
as well as the distinctive flavor of saffron.*

PREPARE AT LEAST 3 HOURS IN ADVANCE

1 recipe Empanada Dough (page 135)

4 tablespoons vegetable oil

2 medium green bell peppers, cut into very thin strips

¾ pound lean pork loin, cut into very thin ½-inch
    strips

¾ pound veal, cut into very thin ½-inch strips

Salt

Freshly ground black pepper

½ cup dry white wine

1½ teaspoons finely chopped fresh thyme or
    ¼ teaspoon dried thyme

1½ teaspoons finely chopped fresh oregano or
    ¼ teaspoon dried oregano

2 teaspoons ground paprika

Pinch of saffron threads, crumbled

1 large egg, lightly beaten, for brushing

I. Prepare the dough. Heat 2 tablespoons of the
oil in a medium skillet over medium heat. Add the
bell peppers, cover, and cook until tender. Transfer
to a small bowl.

2. Heat the remaining 2 tablespoons oil in the same
skillet over medium-high heat. Add the pork and
veal and cook, stirring, until lightly browned. Season with salt and pepper. Add ¼ cup of the wine
and cook, stirring occasionally, until almost evaporated. Reduce the heat to medium, add the bell
peppers, the reserved onion mixture, the thyme,
oregano, paprika, and saffron. Stir in the remaining
¼ cup wine and cook, stirring occasionally, until
little liquid remains. Season with salt and pepper.

3. Divide the dough into 2 equal parts. Roll each
into a 15 x 10-inch rectangle. Place 1 rectangle on
a greased cookie sheet of the same size. Spread the
filling over the dough and cover with the second
dough rectangle. Roll up the edges and press to seal
well. Cut several slits in the top. Let sit 20 minutes
in a warm place (such as an oven turned off).

3. Preheat the oven to 350°F. Brush the dough with
the egg. Bake 20 to 30 minutes or until golden.
Serve hot or at room temperature.

Galician Pork and Pepper Pie

Empanada Gallega de Raxó

MAKES 4 SERVINGS AS A MAIN COURSE OR
8 TO 10 AS AN APPETIZER

*Galician empanadas are descendants of the Celtic
savory pies still very popular in Ireland and Great
Britain. The word* raxó *translates to "pork."*

PREPARE AT LEAST 5 HOURS IN ADVANCE

1 recipe Empanada Dough (page 135)

3 garlic cloves

2 tablespoons finely chopped fresh flat-leaf parsley

1½ teaspoons finely chopped fresh oregano or
    ¼ teaspoon dried oregano

1½ teaspoons finely chopped fresh thyme or
    ¼ teaspoon dried thyme

Pinch of saffron threads, crumbled

¼ cup olive oil

3 tablespoons dry white wine

¾ pound boneless pork loin, cut into very thin ½-inch
    strips

1 large onion, such as Vidalia or Spanish, slivered

¾ pound green frying peppers (padróns), cored,
    seeded, and cut into very thin strips

continues...

2 teaspoons ground sweet paprika, such as Spanish smoked

¼ pound medium tomatoes, peeled, seeded, and coarsely chopped

¼ cup finely chopped Serrano (Spanish cured mountain) ham or prosciutto (about 2 ounces)

Salt

Freshly ground black pepper

1 large hard-boiled egg, sliced

1 pimiento, cut into very thin strips

1 large egg

1 teaspoon water

1. Prepare the dough. In a mortar or mini-processor, mash the garlic, parsley, oregano, thyme, and saffron. Mix in 1 tablespoon of the oil and the wine. Transfer to a medium bowl, add the pork, and stir to coat well. Cover and let marinate in the refrigerator at least 2 hours. Drain the pork and reserve the marinade.

2. Heat 2 tablespoons of the oil in a medium skillet over medium heat. Add the pork and cook, stirring, until it just loses its color. Add the pork to the reserved marinade.

3. Heat the remaining 1 tablespoon oil in the same skillet over medium heat. Add the onion and peppers and cook, stirring, 1 to 2 minutes. Reduce the heat to low, stir, cover, and cook 15 minutes more. Stir in the paprika and increase the heat to medium. Add the tomato and cook, stirring, until slightly thickened, about 5 minutes more. Stir in the pork with its marinade, the ham, salt, and pepper and continue cooking and stirring until the pork is heated through and the sauce is blended.

4. Preheat the oven to 350°F. Roll the dough into a 28 x 14-inch rectangle. Cut in half crosswise to make two 14-inch squares, then trim the corners to make two 14-inch rounds. Place 1 round on a cookie sheet and spread the pork mixture to within 1 inch of the edge. Arrange the egg slices over the pork and top with the pimiento strips. Cover with the second dough round. Roll up the

edges and press to seal well. Cut several slits in the top. Lightly beat the egg and water in a small bowl. Brush this egg wash over the dough.

5. Bake 30 to 35 minutes or until browned. Let sit a few minutes. Serve hot or at room temperature.

Mallorcan Lamb and Sobrasada Pie
Empanada Mallorquina

MAKES 6 SERVINGS AS A MAIN COURSE OR 8 AS AN APPETIZER

Sobrasada *is the well-seasoned sausage typical of Mallorca, similar in taste to* chorizo *but softer and more spreadable. Here it is combined with lamb, onions, and a touch of saffron, creating an empanada that is sensational. The dough commonly used in Mallorca is different from most—it's made with lard, olive oil, and freshly squeezed orange juice.*

Mallorcan Empanada Dough

2½ cups unbleached all-purpose flour

¼ teaspoon kosher or sea salt

6 tablespoons chilled lard or vegetable shortening, cut into several pieces

3 tablespoons mild olive oil

3 tablespoons fresh orange juice

¼ cup ice water

Filling

2 tablespoons olive oil

1 pound lean lamb, from the leg or shoulder, cut into ½-inch pieces

Kosher or sea salt

Freshly ground black pepper

2 medium onions, such as Vidalia or other sweet onions, slivered

2 garlic cloves, finely chopped

½ cup dry white wine

Scant ⅛ teaspoon saffron threads, crumbled

¼ pound sobrasada or soft cooking chorizo, skinned and finely chopped

1 large egg, lightly beaten, for brushing

1. Prepare the filling: Heat the oil in a large skillet over high heat until it reaches the smoking point. Add the lamb and cook, stirring, until browned on all sides, sprinkling with salt and pepper as it cooks. Transfer to a warm platter. Add the onions and garlic (and a little more oil if necessary) and cook, stirring, until onion is wilted and transparent, about 2 minutes more. Reduce the heat to low, cover, and cook about 20 minutes more.

2. Add the lamb to the skillet and stir in the wine and saffron. Cook uncovered, stirring occasionally, until the liquid is reduced by half. Stir in the sobrasada and cook about 2 minutes more. Let cool.

3. Preheat the oven to 350°F. Divide the dough into 2 equal parts. Roll each between wax paper into a 13-inch round. Place 1 round on an ungreased cookie sheet and spread the meat mixture over the dough to within 1 inch of the edge. Cover with the second dough round. Roll up the edges and press to seal well. With a knife, cut a small hole in the center of the dough. Brush with the egg.

4. Bake about 30 minutes or until nicely browned. Serve hot or at room temperature.

Veal Pie of Murcia
Pastel Murciano

MAKES 6 INDIVIDUAL PIES

The vegetables from Murcia, along the southeastern coast of Spain, are top quality and known for their freshness—especially their sun-ripened tomatoes and peppers. This special empanada made with pie dough and puff pastry combines those vegetables with the delectable veal with outstanding results.

2 ½ pounds puff pastry dough, homemade (page 135) or storebought

Dough

3 cups all-purpose flour

¾ teaspoon salt

½ cup plus 1 tablespoon salad oil

½ cup water

1 medium onion, finely chopped (about ⅔ cup)

1 garlic clove, finely chopped

2 medium green bell peppers, finely chopped (about 2 cups)

2 tablespoons olive oil

¼ pound (2 links) chorizo sausage, cut into ⅛-inch slices

¼ pound Serrano (Spanish cured mountain) ham or prosciutto, cut into ½-inch cubes

½ pound veal, cut into ½-inch pieces

½ pound tomatoes, peeled and coarsely chopped

Salt

Freshly ground black pepper

1 hard-boiled egg, coarsely chopped

1. Prepare the puff pastry if necessary.

2. Prepare the dough: In a medium bowl, mix the flour and salt. Stir in the oil and water. Turn out onto a lightly floured work surface and knead until the dough holds together. Wrap in plastic wrap and let sit 30 minutes.

3. Meanwhile, heat 1 tablespoon of the oil in a medium skillet over medium heat. Add the onions and peppers and cook, stirring, until tender, about 6 to 8 minutes. Transfer the vegetables to a small bowl and reserve. In the same skillet, heat the remaining 1 tablespoon oil over high heat. Add the chorizo, ham, and veal and cook, stirring, until the veal loses its color. Reduce the heat to low, add the pepper and onion mixture, the tomato, salt, and pepper, and simmer until blended, about 10 minutes more. Remove from the heat and stir in the chopped egg.

continues . . .

4. Unwrap the dough and roll out on a lightly floured work surface into a rectangle. Fold lengthwise into thirds, business-letter fashion. Roll again to the previous size, then fold and roll twice more (for a total of four times). Roll out to ⅛-inch thickness. Cut into 6 (6-inch) rounds. Divide and place the filling in the center of each round, spreading until just before the edges.

5. Preheat the oven to 350°F. Roll out the pastry to ⅛-inch thickness. Cut into 1-inch strips and also cut 6 (2-inch) rounds. Arrange a strip (piecing if necessary) in a circle around the edge of the filling and pinch the ends of the puff pastry to seal. Repeat with a second strip in a slightly overlapping concentric circle. Plug the center of each pie with 1 of the pastry rounds, slightly overlapping the edge of the strip. Fold up the sides of the bottom dough and pinch to attach it well to the puff pastry.

6. Bake 25 to 30 minutes or until the puff pastry is golden. Let cool slightly. Serve hot or at room temperature.

Veal Sandwiches
Pepitos de Ternera

MAKES 6 SERVINGS (12 SANDWICHES)

Breaded veal cutlets are adored by Spanish children as well as adults. When made into sandwiches, they are called pepitos *and are commonly served for lunch. The most delicious version of this sandwich I ever tasted was at the bar of the Parador Nacional de Nerja, a magnificent parador with a garden-like atmosphere and a spectacular view of the coastline.*

1 recipe dough from Basic Long Loaf (page 126)

Cornmeal or bread crumbs, for sprinkling

1½ pounds veal cutlet, cut into ¼-inch slices

Kosher or sea salt

At least 5 tablespoons olive oil

Dijon mustard

1. Prepare the bread dough and let rise as instructed in steps 1 and 2 of the recipe.

2. Punch down the dough and knead 5 minutes. Divide the dough into 8 equal pieces. Shape into balls. Roll out each ball into a 6½ x 5½-inch oval. Starting with a long side, roll up tightly, jellyroll fashion. Pinch to seal well. Taper the ends.

3. Sprinkle a baking sheet with the cornmeal and place the rolls seam side down on the sheet. Cut 2 or 3 diagonal slits in the top of each roll. Let rise in a warm place (such as an oven turned off) 1 hour more or until double in size.

4. Bake as instructed in step 4 of the bread recipe. Allow to cool.

5. Meanwhile, when the rolls are almost ready or if you like in advance, season the veal with salt. Heat 5 tablespoons of the oil in a large skillet over medium-high heat. Add the veal and cook, turning once, until lightly browned on each side. Transfer to a warm platter and reserve the oil.

6. Slice open the rolls but do not cut all the way through. Heat the reserved oil in the skillet over medium-high heat. Pierce the crust of one roll with a fork. Place the soft side of the bread on the surface of the hot oil and cook until lightly browned, less than a minute. Repeat for the rest of the rolls, adding more oil to the pan if necessary. Place the meat on the rolls and pour any meat juices remaining on the platter onto the inside of the rolls. Serve hot or at room temperature with the mustard.

Veal in Puff Pastry

Aguja de Ternera

MAKES 10 PASTRIES

If you have a good veal source near you, these crispy puff pastries with a veal filling are simple but delicious. Aguja de Ternera are enormously popular throughout Spain, and many places sell them ready-made.

2¾ pounds puff pastry dough, homemade (page 135) or storebought

1 recipe Veal Filling (from Veal and Chorizo Turnovers [Tapas], page 85)

1. Prepare the pastry if necessary. Prepare the veal filling as directed in step 2 of the recipe.

2. Place an oven rack in the upper-middle position. Preheat the oven to 425°F. Roll out the pastry into 2 (25 x 15-inch) rectangles that are ⅛ inch thick. Cut each into 5 (5 x 3-inch) rectangles.

3. Place 3 tablespoons of the filling along the length of each rectangle. Fold up the sides and ends and press to seal. Place seam side down on a cookie sheet.

4. Bake about 15 minutes or until golden. Serve hot or at room temperature.

Sausage Buns

Bollo Preñado

MAKES 8 BUNS

This version of sausages wrapped in bread is called Bollo Preñado, *which translates in English to "Pregnant Buns." Despite the odd title, these sausage buns are extremely tasty and are best when made with Pan de Pueblo dough (the basic loaf).*

½ recipe dough Basic Long Loaf (page 126)

8 (3-inch) pieces chorizo sausage

8 thick slices bacon, cut into 3-inch pieces

Cornmeal or bread crumbs, for sprinkling

1 large egg, lightly beaten, for brushing

1. Prepare the bread dough and let rise as instructed in steps 1 and 2 of the recipe. Punch down the dough and knead until combined, about 5 minutes. Divide into 8 equal pieces and shape into balls. Roll out each ball into a 5 x 3-inch rectangle.

2. Preheat the oven to 450°F. In the center of each dough rectangle, place 1 piece of chorizo and cover with 1 slice of bacon. Fold up the sides and ends and pinch to seal well. Sprinkle a cookie sheet with the cornmeal. Place the rolls, pinched side down, on the cookie sheet. Let sit in a warm place (such as an oven turned off) 30 minutes.

3. Brush the rolls with the egg. Bake 15 minutes or until golden. Serve hot or at room temperature.

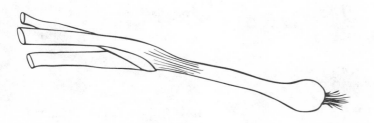

Salads

VEGETABLE SALADS

Cucumber Salad with Honey and Rosemary Ⓥ

Cucumber, Tomato, and Pepper Salad Ⓥ

Tomato and Egg Salad Ⓥ

Pimiento and Tomato Salad

Tomato, Green Pepper, Ham, and Tuna Salad

Tomato and Pepper Salad, Cádiz Style

Tomato, Tuna, and Egg Salad

Tomato and Pepper Salad with Eggs and Ham

Cumin-Flavored Mushroom Salad Ⓥ

Moorish-Style Green Salad with
Cumin and Paprika

Mixed Salad with Pomegranate Seeds Ⓥ

Summer Potato Salad with Sherry Vinaigrette Ⓥ

Potato and Orange Salad Ⓥ

Asparagus Salad with Piquillo
Peppers, Egg, and Anchovies

Cauliflower Salad Ⓥ

Mixed Salad, San Isidro Style

Mixed Salad, Spanish Style

Vegetable Salad in Romesco Sauce Ⓥ

Spinach, Mushroom, and Ham
Salad with Sherry Vinaigrette

Marinated Carrot Salad Ⓥ

Pearl Onions in Sherry Vinegar Ⓥ

Green Bean Salad Ⓥ

Cabbage Salad, San Andrés Style Ⓥ

Swiss Chard with Croutons Ⓥ

Escarole Salad with Tomato
and Cumin Dressing Ⓥ

Watercress and Carrot Salad
with Anchovy Dressing

Cabbage and Watercress Salad Ⓥ

Cabbage and Pomegranate Salad Ⓥ

Endives with Blue Cheese Ⓥ

Fresh Beet Salad Ⓥ

Potato and Beet Salad Ⓥ

Fresh Beets in Romesco Sauce Ⓥ

Andalusian Pepper Salad Ⓥ

Mushroom and Cured Ham Salad

Eggplant, Artichoke, Pepper,
and Tomato Salad Ⓥ

Orange Salad with Onion,
Almonds, and Raisins Ⓥ

Summer Salad Ⓥ

Escarole-Tomato Salad, Murcia Style Ⓥ

Catalan-Style Salad

BEAN AND RICE SALADS

White Bean Salad Ⓥ

Fresh Bean Salad, Catalan Style Ⓥ*

Marinated Chickpeas Ⓥ

Marinated Chickpeas with
Capers and Red Pepper Ⓥ

Lentil Salad Ⓥ

Andalusian Rice Salad

Rice Salad Ring

FISH SALADS

Shrimp and Tomato in Sherry Vinaigrette

Shrimp, Melon, and Apple Salad

Asparagus, Shrimp, and Mushroom Salad

Salad of Tiny Potatoes and Tuna

Pimiento and Tuna Salad, Cazorla Style

Tuna, Egg, and Potato Salad

Red Pepper, Tomato, and Tuna
Salad, Andalusian Style

Cinta's Old-Fashioned Cod and Bean Salad

Codfish Salad with Sweet Onion and Eggs

Orange-Scented Salt Cod, Granada Style

Avocado Salad with Pomegranate
Seeds and Salmon

Escarole, Tomato, Anchovy, and Black
Olive Salad with Xato Dressing

Grilled Mackerel Topped with
Tomato and Pepper Salad

White Bean Salad with Herring

Lobster and Watercress Salad

Lobster Salad, Galician Style

Lobster and Endive Salad

Fish and Lobster Salad

Baby Eel Salad

Fish and Vegetable Salad

 = Vegetarian    = Vegetarian with one change

*M*any Spanish meals are accompanied by an *ensalada*, a refreshing and often colorful salad that complements the richer dishes that are being served. Traditionally salads are presented in one of two ways—either as a course served before the meal or in a big wooden bowl placed in the center of the table. As with *tapas*, which are served in communal bowls or plates for sharing, it is customary for dinner guests to sometimes eat the salad directly from the bowl rather than serving themselves individual portions.

Spaniards are accustomed to only the finest ingredients, and nowhere is this more evident than in their salads. Salads range from the simple mixed salad of lettuce, vine-ripened tomatoes, and onions to more imaginative and creative fare. Romaine is always the lettuce of choice, regarded as far superior to iceberg. In small towns, the freshest of vegetables are purchased from local *huertas*, family plots, while in bigger cities, they are available in markets. Other ingredients commonly found in Spanish salads include olives, tuna, and white asparagus. The white variety of asparagus is more difficult to harvest and therefore priced a bit higher, making it a very popular delicacy in Spain.

And as with the rest of Spanish cuisine, salads vary greatly according to region and geography. In Andalucía, they take advantage of the fish caught daily in the Mediterranean. Salads often feature shrimp, scallops and monkfish, once known as "the poor man's lobster." In Aragon, roasted red bell peppers are the focus of their own small category of popular salads. Catalunya is famed for their *empedrat*, a hearty salad with dried salt cod and white beans. Many of the salads in the southern regions reflect a Moorish influence with the inclusion of spices such as cumin. In the warmer climates of Spain, it is common to include fruits such as raisins and figs. On a hot summer day, there is perhaps nothing more refreshing than an *Ensalada San Andrés*.

All Spanish salads have one thing in common. They are never, ever drowned in dressing because the delicious taste of top-quality vegetables and other ingredients should never be masked. Instead, it should be drizzled with olive oil and a touch of sherry vinegar, which to me is simple perfection. However, not all olive oils are created equal. I use only Spanish olive oil because it is of very high quality and has a wonderfully fruity taste that gives food a characteristic Spanish flavor. Americans now have access to the olive oils of Spain through numerous specialty shops.

Ensaladas refresh the palate and provide a cool, crisp contrast to the texture of the other dishes that are being served. Many of these salad recipes can be prepared hours in advance and left to chill in the refrigerator while your soups or main courses are simmering.

Cucumber Salad with Honey and Rosemary Ⓥ
Pepinos a la Miel de Romero

MAKES 4 SERVINGS

This recipe could not be any simpler and can be prepared in almost no time at all. The honey adds a wonderful sweetness to the cool, crisp cucumbers.

2 pounds medium cucumbers
8 tablespoons honey
Finely chopped fresh rosemary, for garnish

Cut off the ends of the cucumbers and, using a vegetable peeler, partially peel them, leaving strips of dark and light green. Cut each cucumber lengthwise into 4 wedges. Drizzle with the honey, garnish with the rosemary, and serve at room temperature.

Cucumber, Tomato, and Pepper Salad Ⓥ
Ensalada de Piparrada

MAKES 4 TO 6 SERVINGS

This simple salad of Basque origin is delightfully refreshing on a hot summer day. It is also the perfect accompaniment to an outdoor barbecue.

2 medium tomatoes, cut into 1-inch pieces
1 medium cucumber, peeled and cut into 1-inch pieces
1 medium green bell pepper, cut into 1-inch pieces
1 small onion, cut into 1-inch pieces

6 tablespoons extra-virgin olive oil
3 tablespoons red wine vinegar
½ teaspoon sugar
Salt
Freshly ground black pepper

1. In a large bowl, combine the tomatoes, cucumber, bell pepper, and onion.

2. In a small bowl, whisk together the oil, vinegar, sugar, salt, and pepper. Pour over the salad and toss. Refrigerate at least 30 minutes and serve cold.

Tomato and Egg Salad Ⓥ
Ensalada de Tomate y Huevo

MAKES 4 SERVINGS

This recipe is from the personal cookbook of my mother-in-law, who was an inventive cook. Noteworthy about this version of tomato and egg salad is that it doesn't use oil. Instead, the vinegar is tempered by the sugar.

PREPARE AT LEAST 2 HOURS IN ADVANCE

¼ cup red wine vinegar
4 teaspoons sugar
Salt
Freshly ground black pepper
2 large hard-boiled eggs, each cut into 4 wedges
3 medium tomatoes, each cut into 4 wedges
1 small onion, sliced
1 tablespoon finely chopped fresh flat-leaf parsley, for garnish

In a salad bowl, whisk together the vinegar, sugar, salt, and pepper. Fold in the eggs, tomatoes, and onion. Refrigerate at least 2 hours. Sprinkle with the parsley and serve cold.

Spain is the world's leading producer of olive oil and the country where some of the most exquisite olive oils are made. Today, Spain's olive production is concentrated mainly in Catalunya and Andalucía, although other regions such as Castilla, Extremadura, and even Madrid are also cultivating olive oil. Andalucía produces twenty percent of the world's olive oil. It was the Romans who first brought the olive tree and olive press to Spain. Olive trees thrived in the warm climate, and ever since those early times, Spain has been a major exporter, even to countries like France and Italy.

Olive oil is classified as pure, virgin, and extra virgin. Pure is the lowest quality, so it must be refined and processed, then mixed with some virgin oil for flavor. Virgin does not necessarily mean that the oil tastes better, only that it has not been chemically processed. Most Spanish salads are made with extra-virgin olive oil, which has the lowest acidity, generally uses the finest olives, and is most likely to have the best flavor.

In the United States, the use of olive oil has increased as the numerous health benefits are now widely recognized. A selection of Spain's famous olive oils can be found in specialty stores and sometimes even supermarkets. Among the finest extra-virgin olive oils are Núñez de Prado, Rafael Salgado, and Ybarra.

Pimiento and Tomato Salad
Ensalada de Pimiento y Tomate

MAKES 4 TO 6 SERVINGS

So easy to prepare, this light and refreshing salad is perfect to serve with a heavier main course. I recommend making your own pimientos, but they are also readily available in jars.

PREPARE AT LEAST 2 HOURS IN ADVANCE

2 pimientos, cut into thin strips
1 small onion, cut crosswise into 4 slices
4 medium tomatoes, each cut into 8 wedges
Salt
Freshly ground black pepper
2 tablespoons extra-virgin olive oil
2 tablespoons red wine vinegar
½ teaspoon sugar
3 anchovy fillets, finely chopped
1 tablespoon finely chopped fresh flat-leaf parsley, for garnish
12 or more black olives, preferably Spanish, for garnish

1. Place the pimientos in layers in a shallow, flat-bottom bowl. Separate the onions into rings and arrange over the pimientos. Arrange the tomatoes in an attractive design over the onions. Season with salt and pepper.

2. In a small bowl, whisk together the oil, vinegar, sugar, salt, pepper, and anchovies. Pour over the salad. Sprinkle with the parsley and decorate with the olives. Refrigerate at least 2 hours and serve cold.

Tomato, Green Pepper, Ham, and Tuna Salad

Pipirrana Jaenera

MAKES 4 SERVINGS

This salad originated in the province of Jaen, where, Spaniards believe, the best olive oil is produced. Refreshing and colorful, it is as pleasing to the eye as it is to the palate. It makes a perfect light dinner in summertime.

PREPARE AT LEAST 2 HOURS IN ADVANCE

2 large hard-boiled eggs

2 garlic cloves, mashed in a garlic press or mortar

3 tablespoons olive oil

½ slice long-loaf (baguette) bread, soaked and squeezed dry

Salt

Freshly ground black pepper

1½ tablespoons red wine vinegar

1 pound medium tomatoes, cut into ½-inch pieces

¼ pound medium green bell pepper, finely chopped

¾ cup marinated or plain white or light meat tuna, preferably Spanish, drained and flaked

¼ cup very thin strips Serrano (Spanish cured mountain) ham or prosciutto

I. Separate the egg whites and yolks. Finely chop the whites and set aside. In a small bowl, mash the yolks. Place the egg yolks, garlic, oil, and bread in a blender or food processor and blend until smooth. Add the salt, black pepper, and vinegar and blend to incorporate.

2. In a large bowl, combine the tomatoes, bell pepper, egg whites, salt, pepper, tuna, and ham. Fold in the dressing. Refrigerate at least 2 hours and serve cold.

Tomato and Pepper Salad, Cádiz Style

Picadillo a la Gaditana

MAKES 6 SERVINGS

This recipe originated in Cádiz, home to the freshest vine-ripened tomatoes and the sweetest green and red frying peppers. In order to keep the flavor of the vegetables at its very best, the recipe calls for fruity extra-virgin olive oil.

PREPARE AT LEAST 2 HOURS IN ADVANCE

1 pound medium ripe tomatoes, seeded and cut into ½-inch pieces

½ pound green frying (Italian) peppers, cored, seeded, and cut into ½-inch pieces

1 small onion, slivered (about ⅓ cup)

2 ounces canned or jarred white or light meat tuna, drained and separated into chunks

¼ cup fruity extra-virgin olive oil

2 tablespoons sherry vinegar or red wine vinegar

Salt

Freshly ground black pepper

I. In a medium bowl, combine the tomatoes, pepper, onion, and tuna.

2. In a small bowl, whisk together the oil, vinegar, salt, and pepper. Fold into the salad. Refrigerate at least 2 hours and serve cold.

Tomato, Tuna, and Egg Salad
El Mojo

MAKES 6 SERVINGS

This salad is typical of the town of Motilla del Palancar in the province of Cuenca. Since the ingredients are finely chopped, it can also be used as a condiment. A fruity olive oil is best here.

PREPARE AT LEAST 2 HOURS IN ADVANCE

2 medium tomatoes, finely chopped (about 1⅓ cups)

2 tablespoons canned or jarred white or light meat tuna, drained and flaked

2 large hard-boiled eggs, coarsely chopped

4 tablespoons slivered onion

2 tablespoons finely chopped pimiento

4 pitted black olives, preferably Spanish, coarsely chopped

2 garlic cloves, finely chopped

1 tablespoon finely chopped fresh flat-leaf parsley

2 tablespoons extra-virgin olive oil

4 teaspoons wine vinegar, such as white

2 tablespoons water

Salt

Freshly ground black pepper

1. In a medium bowl, combine the tomatoes, tuna, eggs, onion, pimiento, olives, garlic, and parsley.

2. In a small bowl, whisk together the oil, vinegar, water, salt, and pepper. Fold into the salad. Refrigerate at least 2 hours and serve cold.

Tomato and Pepper Salad with Eggs and Ham
Ensalada de El Rocio

MAKES 4 SERVINGS

This recipe originated in the warmer climates of Spain where peppers, tomatoes, and other vegetables are at their very best. The addition of egg and cured Spanish ham make this salad richer and heartier.

¾ pound plum tomatoes

¾ pound red frying peppers (padrónes) or, if available, red bell peppers

¾ pound green frying peppers (padrónes)

2 large hard-boiled eggs

Kosher or sea salt

1 small onion, slivered (about ⅓ cup)

1 large garlic clove, finely chopped

¼ teaspoon ground cumin

2 teaspoons wine vinegar, such as mild white

¼ cup extra-virgin olive oil

¼ pound Serrano (cured mountain ham) or prosciutto, thinly sliced

1. Preheat the oven to 500°F. Place the tomatoes and peppers in a roasting pan and bake 20 minutes. turning once. Let cool slightly, peel, and coarsely chop. Combine and transfer to a platter.

2. Separate the egg whites and yolks. Coarsely chop the whites and finely chop the yolks. Sprinkle both over the tomatoes and peppers. Season with salt and scatter the onion over the salad.

3. In a mortar or mini-processor, mash the garlic, ⅛ teaspoon salt, and the cumin. Stir in the vinegar and oil and pour over the salad. Arrange the ham on top and serve at room temperature.

Cumin-Flavored Mushroom Salad ⓥ

Ensalada de Setas

MAKES 4 TO 6 SERVINGS

This salad combines different types of mushrooms with red bell peppers and a touch of cumin, which lends a distinctive flavor.

PREPARE AT LEAST 2 HOURS IN ADVANCE

½ pound mushrooms, such as a mix of button and puffball or boletus, rinsed and trimmed

½ medium red bell pepper, cut into very thin strips

Dressing

¼ cup extra-virgin olive oil

2 tablespoons fresh lemon juice

1 garlic clove, mashed in a garlic press or mortar

1 tablespoon finely chopped fresh flat-leaf parsley

¼ teaspoon ground cumin

Salt

Freshly ground black pepper

1. Leave the mushrooms whole if they are small; otherwise, cut into halves or quarters. Combine the mushrooms and bell pepper in a medium bowl.

2. Prepare the dressing: In a small bowl, whisk together the dressing ingredients. Pour over the salad and toss. Let marinate at least 1 hour. Serve at room temperature or refrigerate at least 2 hours to chill and serve cold.

Moorish-Style Green Salad with Cumin and Paprika

Ensalada al Estilo Moro

MAKES 4 SERVINGS

Cumin is a wonderful addition to salad dressing, and an idea that comes from the Moors, who controlled southern Spain for many centuries. Paprika came years later, after the discovery of America by Spain. This dressing is excellent on any green or mixed salad.

1 tablespoon finely chopped fresh flat-leaf parsley

2 anchovy fillets, finely chopped

1 large garlic clove, finely chopped

¾ teaspoon ground cumin

½ teaspoon ground sweet paprika, such as Spanish smoked

Kosher or sea salt

Freshly ground black pepper

4 teaspoons wine vinegar

¼ teaspoon Dijon mustard

¼ cup extra-virgin olive oil

4 cups salad greens, such as romaine or mesclun, washed, dried, and torn into pieces

1. In a mortar or mini-processor, mash the parsley, anchovies, garlic, cumin, paprika, and a pinch each of salt and pepper. Add the vinegar and mustard and whisk to combine, then whisk in the oil. Season with salt.

2. Place the greens in a salad bowl. Pour the dressing over the salad and toss. Serve at room temperature or refrigerate at least 2 hours to chill and serve cold.

Mixed Salad with Pomegranate Seeds 🅥

Ensalada de Lechuga con Granadas

MAKES 6 SERVINGS

This wonderful salad was traditionally meant to accompany a stew, but its slightly sweet taste complements many other dishes as well. Pomegranates thrive in the warmer climates of southern Spain, while in the United States their availability is seasonal.

1 pomegranate

Dressing

6 tablespoons extra-virgin olive oil

2 teaspoons sherry vinegar or red wine vinegar

4 teaspoons red wine vinegar

Salt

Freshly ground black pepper

Mixed salad greens, such as romaine, watercress, or mesclun, rinsed and trimmed

½ small onion, slivered (about ⅓ cup)

2 medium scallions, coarsely chopped (about 2 tablespoons)

I. Cut the pomegranate into wedges and separate the seeds. Reserve ¾ cup seeds for the salad. In a mortar or mini-processor, mash enough of the remaining seeds to make 2 tablespoons juice for the dressing.

2. Prepare the dressing: In a small bowl, whisk together the reserved pomegranate juice and the dressing ingredients.

3. In a large bowl, place the greens, onions, and scallions and toss. Pour the dressing over the salad and toss. Scatter the pomegranate seeds over the salad and serve.

Summer Potato Salad with Sherry Vinaigrette 🅥

Ensalada de Patata Veraniega

MAKES 6 SERVINGS

Marinated potatoes are most delicious when combined with cucumber, eggs, peppers, and olives in sherry vinaigrette.

PREPARE AT LEAST 2 HOURS IN ADVANCE

1½ pounds new or red waxy potatoes

¼ cup fresh lemon juice

6 tablespoons extra-virgin olive oil

2 tablespoons sherry vinegar or red wine vinegar

Salt

Freshly ground black pepper

½ pound tomatoes, cut into wedges

2 large hard-boiled eggs, cut into wedges

¼ cup finely chopped small cucumber, peeled or unpeeled

2 medium scallions, finely chopped (about 2 tablespoons)

¼ cup finely chopped green bell pepper

12 black olives, preferably Spanish

I. Place the potatoes and lemon juice in a medium saucepan with cold water to cover and add salt. Cover and bring to a simmer over low heat. Cook about 15 minutes or until tender when pierced with a knife. Drain and let cool slightly. Peel and cut into thin slices. Meanwhile, in a small bowl, whisk together the oil, vinegar, salt, and pepper.

2. In a shallow serving bowl, arrange the potatoes in layers, drizzling each layer lightly with the vinaigrette and seasoning with the salt and pepper.

3. Arrange the tomatoes and eggs over the potatoes. Scatter the cucumber, scallions, bell pepper, and olives over the top. Pour the remaining vinaigrette over the salad and toss. Serve at room temperature or refrigerate at least 2 hours and serve cold.

Potato and Orange Salad V
Ensalada Valenciana

MAKES 4 SERVINGS

Potatoes and oranges might seem like an unusual combination, but they blend together perfectly to create a delightfully refreshing salad. Valencia, well known for its rice paddies, is also home to Spain's finest orange groves.

PREPARE AT LEAST 2 HOURS IN ADVANCE

3 medium red waxy potatoes

½ cup slivered yellow (Spanish) onion

1 orange, peeled and cut into ¼-inch slices, each slice cut into quarters

1 pimiento, cut into thin strips

2 tablespoons red wine vinegar

4 tablespoons extra-virgin olive oil

Salt

Freshly ground black pepper

1. Place the potatoes in a medium saucepan with cold water to cover and add salt. Cover and bring to a simmer over low heat. Cook about 15 minutes or until tender when pierced with a knife. Drain and let cool slightly. Peel and cut into 1-inch pieces.

2. In a large bowl, fold together the potatoes, onion, orange, and pimiento.

3. In a small bowl, whisk together the vinegar and oil. Fold into the salad. Season with salt and pepper. Refrigerate at least 2 hours and serve cold.

SHERRY VINEGAR

There are many different types of vinegars. In Spain, red wine vinegar and white wine vinegar are used mostly for cooking, whereas sherry vinegar is used more frequently for salads. It is called for in recipes when the taste of quality vinegar is important and most especially when cooking Spanish food. Spain is the land of sherry, and obviously this special wine is used to produce magnificent vinegars. Made from the different varieties of sherry such as Fino, Oloroso, and Manzanilla, each one has a distinctive flavor.

Sherry vinegar begins with fine-quality sherry wines made from the indigenous Palomino grape. The vinegar is typically aged for a period of six years before it is ready for bottling. The longer the sherry vinegar is left to age, the better it is and the more the flavor deepens in complexity.

Some Spanish recipes call for a lesser quality vinegar, but when it comes to salads, marinades and sauces, the distinctive taste of sherry vinegar is extremely important. In Spain, the best sherry vinegar comes from Andalucía. There are several excellent brands of imported sherry available in the United States.

Asparagus Salad with Piquillo Peppers, Egg, and Anchovies
Espárragos a la Riojana

MAKES 4 SERVINGS

This recipe gets its name from La Rioja, an area well known for their succulent peppers and sweet young asparagus. When paired with the rather strong taste of anchovies and the added zest of mustard, the result is excellent.

1 pound small asparagus, rinsed and trimmed

2 (jarred) piquillo peppers or 1 pimiento, drained and finely chopped

1 small ripe tomato, peeled and seeded (about ½ cup)

3 anchovy fillets, finely chopped

1 tablespoon red wine vinegar

1 tablespoon extra-virgin olive oil

¼ teaspoon Dijon mustard

Kosher or sea salt

Freshly ground black pepper

1 large hard-boiled egg, finely chopped, for garnish

1 tablespoon finely chopped fresh flat-leaf parsley, for garnish

1. Place the asparagus in a medium skillet with water to cover, add salt, and bring to a boil over high heat. Reduce the heat to low, cover, and simmer 5 to 10 minutes or until crisp-tender. Reserve.

2. In a food processor, place the piquillo peppers, tomato, anchovies, vinegar, oil, mustard, salt, and black pepper and blend until smooth.

3. On individual salad plates, arrange the asparagus in a fan shape. Spoon about 1 tablespoon of the dressing across the asparagus. Sprinkle with the egg and parsley and serve at room temperature.

Cauliflower Salad ⓥ
Ensalada de Coliflor

MAKES 6 SERVINGS

This is a typically Spanish way to prepare cauliflower. It is a very refreshing salad in which the garlic lends a wonderful pungency.

PREPARE AT LEAST 2 HOURS IN ADVANCE

1 small cauliflower (about 1 pound), trimmed and cut into 1-inch florets

2 teaspoons fresh lemon juice

Dressing

¼ cup extra-virgin olive oil

2 tablespoons red wine vinegar

1 garlic clove, mashed in a garlic press or mortar

1 tablespoon capers (nonpareil preferred), rinsed and drained

1 teaspoon ground paprika, preferably Spanish style

Dash of ground cayenne pepper

Salt

3 tablespoons hard-boiled egg, finely chopped, for garnish

1 tablespoon finely chopped fresh flat-leaf parsley, for garnish

1. In a medium saucepan, place 1 inch of water and the lemon juice; add salt. Add the cauliflower and bring to a boil over high heat. Reduce the heat to low, cover, and simmer 8 to 12 minutes or until crisp-tender. Drain and let cool. Cut off the stems close to the florets.

2. Prepare the dressing: In a small bowl, whisk together the dressing ingredients. Pour over the cauliflower and fold until the dressing is absorbed. Taste and adjust seasoning if necessary. Let marinate in the refrigerator at least 2 hours up to overnight. Sprinkle with the egg and parsley and serve cold or at room temperature.

Mixed Salad, San Isidro Style
Ensalada de San Isidro

MAKES 4 SERVINGS

This is a basic, traditional Spanish salad that is popular throughout the various regions of Spain. The essential ingredients are onion, tomato, lettuce, and tuna, while other ingredients such as asparagus and olives (which I like to add), and cucumbers, are optional.

2 tablespoons extra-virgin olive oil

4 tablespoons red wine vinegar

Salt

Freshly ground black pepper

½ head romaine lettuce, rinsed and torn into pieces

2 medium tomatoes, cut into eighths

3 thin slices medium onion

3 to 4 ounces jarred white or light meat tuna , preferably Spanish, drained and flaked

4 (jarred) white asparagus, rinsed, trimmed, and cut in half crosswise (optional)

12 small green olives (with or without pimiento), preferably Spanish

1. In a small bowl, whisk together the oil, vinegar, salt, and pepper.

2. In a salad bowl, combine the lettuce, tomato, onion, tuna, asparagus (if using), and olives (if using). Pour the vinaigrette over the salad, toss, and serve at room temperature.

Mixed Salad, Spanish Style
Ensalada Mixta a la Española

MAKES 4 SERVINGS

This classic Spanish salad is a more embellished and formally plated version of the basic lettuce and tomato salad often served, which is typically brought to the table undressed and then drizzled with olive oil and vinegar. An ensalada mixta is never over seasoned as that would mask the fresh flavor of the fine ingredients.

About 4 cups torn hearts of romaine lettuce

½ medium onion, slivered

1 small carrot, peeled and coarsely grated (about ¼ cup)

10 slices pickled beets, halved

2 small ripe tomatoes, each cut into 8 wedges

2 large hard-boiled eggs, sliced

Kosher or sea salt

Freshly ground black pepper

3 to 4 ounces jarred white or light meat tuna in olive oil, preferably Spanish, separated into chunks

16 small green olives with pits, otherwise rinsed of their brine, preferably Spanish

8 (jarred) large white asparagus, such as Spanish, rinsed and trimmed

Extra-virgin olive oil

Wine vinegar, such as mild white wine vinegar

Place the lettuce on individual salad plates. Scatter the onion over the lettuce and the grated carrot on top. Arrange the beets, tomatoes, and eggs around the edge of the plate. Sprinkle everything with salt and pepper. Place the tuna in the center and scatter the olives over the salad. Arrange the asparagus attractively over the salad. Drizzle with the oil and vinegar and serve at room temperature.

Vegetable Salad in Romesco Sauce ⓥ

Ensalada en Salsa Romesco

MAKES 6 TO 8 SERVINGS

Romesco sauce, made with dried sweet red peppers, garlic, and almonds, originated in Catalunya. It is delicious with fish or shellfish, but here it makes an excellent dressing for a vegetable salad.

PREPARE AT LEAST 2 HOURS IN ADVANCE

Romesco Sauce

1 large ripe tomato

5 garlic cloves

1 dried sweet red pepper (ñora), such as New Mexico (Anaheim)

½ dried red chile pepper, seeded, or ¼ teaspoon crushed red pepper

½ cup water

4½ tablespoons red wine vinegar

½ cup plus 1 tablespoon extra-virgin olive oil

1 thin slice long-loaf (baguette) bread, broken into pieces

5 blanched almonds

Salt

Freshly ground black pepper

1 medium potato, such as red waxy

¼ pound green beans, halved

1 medium zucchini (about 6 ounces), cut into ¼-inch slices, each slice cut in half

½ large hard-boiled egg, sliced

4 thin slices medium onion

½ small cucumber, cut into ¼-inch slices, each slice cut in half

1 small ripe tomato, cut into 8 wedges

10 small pitted green olives (with or without pimiento), preferably Spanish

½ pimiento, cut into thin strips

1 tablespoon finely chopped fresh flat-leaf parsley, for garnish

1. Prepare the sauce: Place the sauce ingredients in a food processor and process until smooth. Let sit 1 hour.

2. Place the potato in a small saucepan with cold water to cover and add salt. Cover and bring to a simmer over low heat. Cook about 15 minutes or until tender when pierced with a knife. Drain and let cool slightly. Peel, cut into thin slices, and season with salt.

3. Place the beans and zucchini in a medium saucepan, add water to cover and salt, and bring to a boil over high heat. Reduce the heat to low, cover, and simmer about 10 minutes or until crisp-tender.

4. In a salad bowl or deep serving dish, arrange the vegetables in layers: first the potato, then the beans, zucchini, egg, onion, cucumber, tomato, olives, and pimiento. Pour the sauce over the vegetables (do not mix). Let sit at least 1 hour. Sprinkle with the parsley. Serve at room temperature or refrigerate at least 2 hours and serve cold.

Spinach, Mushroom, and Ham Salad with Sherry Vinaigrette

Ensalada de Espinaca, Champiñones y Jamón en Vinagreta de Jerez

MAKES 4 TO 6 SERVINGS

The distinctive taste of sherry vinegar is the perfect complement to this spinach salad made with mushrooms and cured ham. The finest sherry vinegar in the world comes from Andalucía and is made from the indigenous Palomino grape.

Dressing

1 tablespoon sherry vinegar or red wine vinegar

¼ teaspoon Dijon mustard

3 tablespoons extra-virgin olive oil

1 tablespoon finely chopped fresh flat-leaf parsley

1 garlic clove, finely chopped

1½ teaspoons finely chopped fresh thyme or ¼ teaspoon dried thyme

Salt

Freshly ground black pepper

About 9 cups fresh baby spinach, well washed

¼ pound mushrooms, rinsed, trimmed, and thinly sliced

½ pound Serrano (Spanish cured mountain) ham or prosciutto, cut into very thin strips

1. Prepare the dressing: In a small bowl, whisk together the vinegar and mustard, then the oil, parsley, garlic, thyme, salt, and pepper.

2. Arrange the spinach on individual salad plates and scatter the mushrooms and ham on top. Spoon the vinaigrette over the salad and serve at room temperature.

Marinated Carrot Salad Ⓥ
Ensalada de Zanahoria O'Merlo

MAKES 4 SERVINGS

I first tasted this salad at O'Merlo, one of the greatest tapas bars in the charming Galician city of Ponte-vedra. The recipe calls for a large amount of vinegar, which lends a tangy flavor to the mayonnaise-coated carrots.

PREPARE 8 TO 12 HOURS IN ADVANCE

½ pound carrots (4 medium), peeled and cut into very thin 2-inch strips

Mayonnaise (mayonesa; page 359)

2 tablespoons white wine vinegar

In a small bowl, mix together the mayonnaise and vinegar. Place the carrots in a shallow bowl and fold in the mayonnaise mixture. Cover and refrigerate overnight to marinate. Serve cold.

Pearl Onions in Sherry Vinegar Ⓥ
Cebolletas al Jerez

MAKES 4 SERVINGS

These delicious pearl onions are enhanced by the distinctive sherry vinegar from Jerez de la Frontera in Andalucía. They can be eaten within 30 minutes or kept for weeks.

¼ pound small pearl onions (no larger than ¾ inch)

1 cup water

4 teaspoons salt

⅔ cup sherry vinegar or red wine vinegar

½ dried red chile pepper, seeded, or ¼ teaspoon crushed red pepper

4 peppercorns

1 bay leaf

2 whole cloves

⅛ teaspoon dried thyme

1. For easy peeling, bring a small pot of water to a boil over high heat, then add the onions and cook 1 minute. Drain, then rinse in cold water. Trim off the stems and slip off the papery skin. If your onions are a little too large, you may remove some extra layers to reduce the size.

2. To remove the onions' sting, in a medium bowl, place the onions, 1 cup water, and the salt and let soak at least 30 minutes. Drain.

3. Place the vinegar in a medium saucepan and bring to a boil over high heat. Add the onions, reduce the heat to low, and simmer until crisp-tender, about 2 minutes. Stir in the chile pepper, peppercorns, bay leaf, cloves, and thyme. Remove from the heat and let sit 30 minutes. Remove the bay leaf and serve at room temperature, or store in a covered container in the refrigerator up to 3 weeks.

Green Bean Salad ⓥ
Judías Verdes a la Vinagreta

MAKES 4 SERVINGS

Green beans are one of the most popular vegetables in Spain. This simple green bean salad garnished with hard-boiled eggs can be prepared in almost no time at all.

PREPARE AT LEAST 2 HOURS IN ADVANCE

¾ pound green beans

4 tablespoons extra-virgin olive oil

2 tablespoons red wine vinegar

Salt

Freshly ground black pepper

⅛ teaspoon sugar

2 tablespoons finely chopped onion

1 tablespoon finely chopped fresh flat-leaf parsley

2 tablespoons finely chopped pimiento

1 large hard-boiled egg, finely chopped, for garnish

1. Place the beans in a medium saucepan, add water to cover and salt, and bring to a boil over high heat. Reduce the heat to low, cover, and simmer 15 minutes or until crisp-tender. Drain, let cool, and transfer to a medium bowl.

2. In a small bowl, whisk together the oil, vinegar, salt, pepper, and sugar. Pour over the beans. Add the onion, parsley, and pimiento and fold to combine. Cover and refrigerate 2 hours up to overnight. Sprinkle with the egg and serve cold.

Cabbage Salad, San Andrés Style ⓥ
Ensalada San Andrés

MAKES 4 SERVINGS

An influence of the Canary Islands on Spanish cuisine is the addition of pineapple to this layered cabbage salad. I first enjoyed this dish on the island of La Palma in the charming village of San Andrés. The quaint restaurant San Andrés sits right in the center of the town's church courtyard and features many exceptional dishes.

Dressing

6 tablespoons extra-virgin olive oil

2 tablespoons fresh lemon juice

Salt

Freshly ground black pepper

1 garlic clove, mashed in a garlic press or mortar

¼ teaspoon ground (or mortar-crushed) cumin

2 tablespoons finely chopped fresh flat-leaf parsley

1 small head (about 1 pound) green cabbage, finely shredded

16 hearts of palm (canned or jarred), drained and cut into ¼-inch slices

2 thin slices pineapple, cut into small wedges

8 thin slices medium tomato

8 thin slices medium green bell pepper

8 thin slices medium onion

¼ cup cooked corn kernels

1 cup coarsely grated carrot (about 2 medium)

Salt

1. Prepare the dressing: In a small bowl, whisk together the dressing ingredients.

2. Arrange a bed of cabbage on a serving platter. Scatter the hearts of palm, pineapple, tomato,

green pepper, and onion over the cabbage. Sprinkle with the corn, carrot, and salt.

3. Pour the dressing over the salad. Serve at room temperature or refrigerate at least 2 hours to chill and serve cold.

Swiss Chard with Croutons ⓥ
Acelgas con Picatostes

MAKES 4 SERVINGS

This preparation of Swiss chard is made that much more delicious with the added crunchiness and flavor of the croutons. I highly recommend that you make the croutons yourself.

1 pound Swiss chard, well washed and thick stems trimmed

Salt

4 tablespoons olive oil

3 dried sweet red chile peppers (ñoras)

5 thin slices long-loaf (baguette) bread, cut into cubes

3 garlic cloves

1 teaspoon ground sweet paprika, such as Spanish smoked

1. Place the chard in a large saucepan, add water to cover and salt, and bring to a boil over high heat. Reduce the heat to medium and cook until just tender, about 15 minutes. Drain, pressing to extract as much liquid as possible.

2. Meanwhile, heat 3 tablespoons of the oil in a medium skillet over medium heat. Add the peppers and cook, stirring, until golden, about 15 minutes. Transfer to a small bowl, reserving the oil. Add the bread and cook, stirring, until golden, about 15 minutes. Transfer to a separate small bowl.

3. In a mortar or mini-processor, mash the garlic, peppers, paprika, and the remaining 1 tablespoon oil. Taste and add salt if needed. Pour the mixture

over the chard and scatter the croutons over the top. Serve at room temperature.

Escarole Salad with Tomato and Cumin Dressing ⓥ
Ensalada Almoraina

MAKES 4 TO 6 SERVINGS

This Andalucian salad has a Moorish influence reflected in the use of cumin and paprika, which lend a wonderfully distinctive flavor.

2 medium ripe tomatoes, peeled, seeded, and coarsely chopped (about 1⅓ cups)

½ teaspoon ground cumin

1 garlic clove, mashed in a garlic press or mortar

1 teaspoon ground paprika

6 tablespoons extra-virgin olive oil

3 tablespoons red wine vinegar

Salt

Freshly ground black pepper

1 head escarole

Black olives, preferably Spanish, for garnish

2 to 3 hard-boiled eggs, sliced or cut into wedges, for garnish

1. In a blender or food processor, place the tomatoes, cumin, garlic, paprika, and 2 tablespoons of the oil and blend until smooth. Add the remaining 4 tablespoons oil, the vinegar, salt, and pepper and blend to incorporate. Wash and dry the escarole and tear into pieces.

2. Arrange the escarole on individual salad plates. Spoon the dressing over the escarole. Garnish with the olives and eggs and serve at room temperature.

Watercress and Carrot Salad with Anchovy Dressing
Ensalada de Berros con Vinagreta de Anchoa

Chef José Barcena of New York's famed San Martín Restaurant was kind enough to provide me with this excellent recipe in which the strong flavor of anchovies is prominently featured.

1 bunch watercress, rinsed and thick stems trimmed

2 medium carrots, cut into very thin strips

Dressing

½ cup extra-virgin olive oil

3 tablespoons red wine vinegar

¼ teaspoon Dijon mustard

3 anchovy fillets, finely chopped

½ teaspoon finely chopped capers

4 teaspoons finely chopped onion

Salt

Freshly ground black pepper

1 tablespoon finely chopped sour pickle

1 tablespoon finely chopped tomato

2 teaspoons finely chopped fresh flat-leaf parsley

1. On individual salad plates, arrange the watercress, covering half the plate, with the stems towards the center. On the other half of the plate, arrange the carrot strips, covering the watercress stems and fanning out from the center.

2. Prepare the dressing: In a small bowl, whisk together the dressing ingredients. Pour over the salad and serve at room temperature.

Cabbage and Watercress Salad ⓥ
Ensalada de Repollo y Berros

The mix of flavors in this salad is typical of the Canary Islands. Not only is the salad tasty, but it also has an unusually colorful presentation.

PREPARE AT LEAST 2 HOURS IN ADVANCE

1½ tablespoons fresh lemon juice

3 tablespoons extra-virgin olive oil

Salt

Freshly ground black pepper

½ cup finely chopped watercress, rinsed and thick stems removed

1 small onion, slivered (about ⅓ cup)

1 small carrot, peeled and coarsely grated (about ¼ cup)

2 cups finely shredded green cabbage

1 cup finely shredded red cabbage

8 or 12 cherry tomatoes

1 tablespoon finely chopped fresh cilantro

In a small bowl, whisk together the lemon juice, olive oil, salt, and pepper. In a salad bowl, toss together the remaining ingredients. Pour the dressing over the salad and toss. Taste and adjust seasoning if necessary. Refrigerate at least 2 hours and serve cold.

Cabbage and Pomegranate Salad ⓥ
Ensalada de Repollo y Granada

The pomegranate is part of the coat of arms in Spain and commemorates the conquest of Granada by the

Spanish Catholic Monarchs Fernando and Isabel in 1492. Pomegranates figure prominently in many Spanish recipes and are quite delicious when combined with cabbage.

4 tablespoons extra-virgin olive oil

2 tablespoons wine vinegar

1 garlic clove, finely chopped

1 teaspoon Dijon mustard

1 tablespoon finely chopped scallion

Kosher or sea salt

Freshly ground black pepper

1 small head green cabbage, finely shredded

4 tablespoons pomegranate seeds

In a small bowl, whisk together the oil, vinegar, garlic, mustard, scallions, salt, and pepper. Add the cabbage and pomegranate seeds and toss. Serve at room temperature.

Endives with Blue Cheese **V**
Endivias con Queso Cabrales

MAKES 4 TO 6 SERVINGS

Endives have cuplike leaves and are especially delicious when filled with a blue cheese mixture. Since they are easy to pick up by hand, they can also be served as tapas.

2 medium endives, separated into leaves, rinsed, and dried (about 24 leaves)

¾ cup blue cheese, such as Roquefort or Gorgonzola, at room temperature

½ cup Mayonnaise (mayonesa; page 359)

2 tablespoons finely chopped fresh flat-leaf parsley, for garnish

I. In a medium bowl, mash the blue cheese with a spoon until smooth. Add the mayonnaise and mix well.

2. Spread 2 teaspoons of the cheese mixture on the green end of each endive leaf. Arrange 4 to 6 leaves on individual salad plates, green tips facing outward. Sprinkle with the parsley and serve at room temperature.

Fresh Beet Salad **V**
Ensalada de Remolacha

MAKES 4 SERVINGS

This fresh beet salad is excellent when prepared with onions and red wine vinegar and served on top of a bed of lettuce.

4 medium beets, trimmed

2 tablespoons extra-virgin olive oil

1 tablespoon red wine vinegar

Salt

Freshly ground black pepper

½ Spanish (yellow) onion, slivered

Lettuce leaves, for presentation

I. Place the beets in a medium saucepan with cold water to cover. Cover and bring to a simmer over low heat. Cook about 1 hour or until tender when pierced with a knife, replenishing the water if necessary. Drain and let cool. Peel and cut into ¼-inch slices.

2. In a small bowl, whisk together the oil, vinegar, salt, and pepper. Place half of the beets in a serving dish. Sprinkle with the salt, pepper, and onions. Pour half of the dressing over the beets. Repeat with a second layer. Refrigerate 30 minutes—the salad should be served cool, not cold. Line a serving platter with the lettuce leaves, spoon the beets over the lettuce, and serve.

Potato and Beet Salad Ⓥ
Ensalada de Patata y Remolacha

MAKES 6 SERVINGS

The potatoes and hard-boiled eggs here make for a heartier version of beet salad that is richer and more filling.

4 medium potatoes, such as red waxy

4 medium fresh beets, trimmed, or 1 (9-ounce) can or jar beets

4 tablespoons vinegar

Salt

Freshly ground black pepper

Mayonnaise (mayonesa; page 359)

2 large hard-boiled eggs, sliced

1. For fresh beets, place in a medium saucepan with cold water to cover. Cover and bring to a simmer over low heat. Cook about 1 hour or until tender when pierced with a knife, replenishing the water if necessary. Drain. (If using canned beets, drain and let dry on paper towels.) Peel and cut into cubes. Place in a medium bowl, add the vinegar and stir to combine. Let sit 1 hour.

2. Meanwhile, place the potatoes in a medium saucepan and add cold water to cover and salt. Cover and bring to a simmer over low heat. Cook about 20 minutes or until tender when pierced with a knife. Drain and let cool slightly. Peel and cut into cubes.

3. Place the beets in a serving dish or in individual dishes. Scatter the potatoes over the beets and season with salt and pepper. Spread the mayonnaise lightly over the potatoes. Sprinkle with the eggs and serve at room temperature.

Fresh Beets in Romesco Sauce Ⓥ
Remolacha en Salsa Romesco

MAKES 6 SERVINGS

This salad is a specialty of chef Jose Maria Llach at the marvelous Quo Vadis restaurant in Barcelona. Also not to be missed at Quo Vadis is their large variety of wild mushrooms that are simply prepared with garlic and parsley. The sauce and beets can be made in advance, but do not combine until serving time.

½ recipe Romesco Sauce (page 156), reducing the oil to 2 tablespoons and thinning with 4 tablespoons water

3 medium beets (about 1½ pounds), trimmed

Finely chopped fresh flat-leaf parsley, for garnish

1. Prepare the sauce. Place the beets in a medium saucepan with cold water to cover. Cover and bring to a simmer over low heat. Cook about 1 hour or until the beets are tender when pierced with a knife, replenishing the water if necessary. Drain and let cool slightly. Peel and cut into 1-inch pieces.

2. Place the beets and sauce in a medium bowl and fold to combine. Transfer to a serving dish. Sprinkle with the parsley and serve at room temperature.

Andalusian Pepper Salad Ⓥ
Ensalada de Pimientos a la Andaluza

MAKES 4 TO 6 SERVINGS

This Andalusian roasted pepper salad is both refreshing and colorful. In Spain, it is common to serve a pepper salad as a side dish for grilled or fried fish.

1½ pounds green bell peppers

1½ pounds red bell peppers

Kosher or sea salt

Freshly ground black pepper

¼ cup finely chopped Spanish (yellow) onion

1 garlic clove, finely chopped

2 tablespoons extra-virgin olive oil

2 teaspoons sherry vinegar or red wine vinegar

1. Preheat the oven to 500°F. Place the bell peppers in a roasting pan and bake, turning once, 20 minutes or until the skin has bubbled and charred. Remove from the oven and place the peppers in a deep bowl. Cover tightly with foil and let sit 15 minutes. Remove the peppers from the bowl, reserving the juices. Peel, core, and seed the peppers. Cut into long strips about ½-inch wide and return to the bowl.

2. Add the salt, pepper, onion, garlic, oil, and vinegar and fold to combine. Cover and refrigerate at least 1 hour and serve cold.

Mushroom and Cured Ham Salad
Ensalada de Champiñón

MAKES 4 TO 6 SERVINGS

Here the savory flavor of the ham is perfectly complemented by the subtle taste of the mushrooms. This salad is best served with El Aliño dressing.

½ cup Mustard Vinaigrette Dressing (El Aliño; page 165)

½ pound mushrooms, rinsed, trimmed, and halved or quartered, or sliced

Fresh lemon juice (from ½ lemon)

¼ cup very thin strips Serrano (Spanish cured mountain) ham or prosciutto

1 tablespoon finely chopped fresh flat-leaf parsley

Prepare the dressing. Place the mushrooms in a medium bowl and sprinkle with lemon juice. Fold in the ham, then the salad dressing and parsley. Refrigerate until ready to serve (but not more than 1 hour or the mushrooms may discolor).

Eggplant, Artichoke, Pepper, and Tomato Salad Ⓥ
Escalibada

MAKES 4 TO 6 SERVINGS

The tastes and textures of this colorful salad are especially nice as they combine a mixture of fresh vegetables with cooked vegetables.

PREPARE AT LEAST 2 HOURS IN ADVANCE

½ pound small Italian eggplants

1 medium green bell pepper

1 medium red bell pepper

2 medium onions

3 artichoke hearts, cooked (if jarred, drained) and sliced

½ pound medium tomatoes, cut into ½-inch pieces

¼ cup extra-virgin olive oil

3 tablespoons fresh lemon juice

1 garlic clove, mashed in a garlic press or mortar

1 tablespoon finely chopped fresh flat-leaf parsley

1 teaspoon capers (nonpareil preferred), rinsed and drained

Salt

Freshly ground white pepper

2 large hard-boiled eggs, cut into wedges, for garnish

1. Preheat the oven to 350°F. Place the eggplant, bell peppers, and onions in a roasting pan and bake about 30 minutes or until wilted, turning occasionally (the onions will still be slightly crunchy). Let cool slightly. Peel the eggplant and peppers and cut into thin strips. Cut the onions into thin slices.

2. Place the eggplant, peppers, onions, artichoke hearts, and tomatoes in a serving bowl.

3. In a small bowl, whisk together the oil, lemon juice, garlic, parsley, capers, salt, and white pepper. Pour over the vegetables and fold to combine. Refrigerate at least 2 hours. Garnish with the eggs and serve cold.

Orange Salad with Onion, Almbonds, and Raisins ⓥ

Ensalada de Naranjas
Tasca del Puerto

MAKES 4 SERVINGS

The Valencia region of Spain has an abundance of orange groves that stretch for miles. This sweet-and-sour mixture of oranges, raisins, onion, and vinegar reflects a Moorish influence. I first tried it at the Tasca del Puerto restaurant in the city of Castellón.

4 teaspoons golden raisins

Dressing

3 tablespoons extra-virgin olive oil

2 teaspoons red wine vinegar, such as raspberry scented

⅛ teaspoon sugar

Salt

Freshly ground black pepper

4 small oranges, peeled, seeded, and cut into ¼-inch slices

20 paper-thin slices red onion

4 teaspoons finely chopped blanched almonds

4 sprigs mint, for garnish

1. Place the raisins in a small bowl with warm water to cover and let soak 15 minutes. Drain.

2. Meanwhile, prepare the dressing: In a small bowl, whisk together the dressing ingredients.

3. Arrange the oranges on individual salad plates or a serving platter. Scatter the onions, almonds, and raisins over the oranges. Pour the dressing over the salad, garnish with the mint, and serve.

Summer Salad ⓥ

Mojete de Verano

MAKES 6 SERVINGS

This delightful salad makes the most of juicy, ripe tomatoes and fresh herbs, plus other ingredients you probably have on hand.

2 large red bell peppers

3 small onions

2 medium ripe tomatoes, finely chopped (about 1⅓ cups)

3 garlic cloves, finely chopped

2 tablespoons vinegar

4 tablespoons extra-virgin olive oil

1 teaspoon ground cumin

Finely chopped fresh oregano

Finely chopped fresh flat-leaf parsley

Salt

1. Preheat the oven to 450°F. Place the peppers and onions in a roasting pan and roast, turning once, 1 hour or until softened and the peppers are charred. Transfer the peppers to a bowl, cover tightly with foil, and let cool, about 15 minutes. Peel the peppers and onions. Cut the peppers into strips and the onions into slivers and arrange on a serving platter.

2. Combine the tomatoes and garlic in a medium bowl. Stir in the vinegar, then the olive oil. Stir in the cumin, oregano, parsley, and salt. Spoon the tomato mixture over the peppers and onions and serve.

Escarole-Tomato Salad, Murcia Style V

Ensalada Murciana

MAKES 4 SERVINGS

Murcia is a region well known for its high quality of vegetables. This salad is attractively arranged in layers, so try to keep them intact when serving.

½ head escarole, washed, dried, and torn into pieces

Kosher or sea salt

½ pound tomatoes, thinly sliced

6 tablespoons extra-virgin olive oil

3 tablespoons red wine vinegar

Freshly ground black pepper

Dash of ground paprika

Dash of sugar

½ bunch watercress, rinsed (leaves only) and dried

1. Place the escarole in a salad bowl and season with salt. Arrange the tomatoes over the escarole and season with a little more salt.

2. In a small bowl, whisk together the oil, vinegar, salt, pepper, paprika, and sugar. Pour carefully over the salad, distributing evenly. Cover with the watercress leaves. Serve, keeping the layers intact.

Catalan-Style Salad

Ensalada Catalana

MAKES 4 TO 6 SERVINGS

Originated in the region of Catalunya, this highly refreshing salad is one of my very favorites. Like so many other salads, this one is perfect when drizzled with El Aliño mustard vinaigrette dressing. When refrigerated overnight, it becomes even more flavorful the next day. Serve this with plenty of good, crusty bread.

PREPARE AT LEAST 2 HOURS IN ADVANCE

*Mustard Vinaigrette Dressing
(El Aliño Dressing)*

1 cup extra-virgin olive oil, or a mixture of extra-virgin olive oil and salad oil

⅓ cup red wine vinegar

1 teaspoon Dijon mustard

1 garlic clove, mashed in a garlic press or mortar

¼ teaspoon sugar

¼ teaspoon finely chopped fresh basil

¼ teaspoon finely chopped fresh thyme

⅛ teaspoon finely chopped fresh marjoram

1 tablespoon freshly grated Parmesan cheese

¼ teaspoon horseradish

1 tablespoon finely chopped fresh flat-leaf parsley

Salt

Freshly ground black pepper

4 large potatoes, such as red waxy

One (3-ounce) jar small pitted green olives (without pimientos), preferably Spanish

1 medium red onion, thinly sliced

1 medium green bell pepper, thinly sliced crosswise

7 ounces white or light meat tuna, preferably Spanish, drained and separated into chunks

continues...

Salt

Freshly ground black pepper

2 large hard-boiled eggs, quartered

2 medium ripe tomatoes, cut into eighths

1. Prepare the dressing: Place the dressing ingredients in a blender or food processor and blend until smooth and creamy.

2. Place the potatoes in a medium saucepan with cold water to cover and add salt. Cover and bring to a simmer over low heat. Cook about 15 minutes or until tender when pierced with a knife. Drain and let cool slightly. Peel and cut into thin slices.

3. Reserve 3 tablespoons of the dressing. Spread 2 tablespoons of the dressing in a large, flat-bottom bowl. Place a thin layer of potatoes in the bowl, and scatter with some of the olives, onion, bell pepper, and tuna. Season with salt and black pepper. Drizzle with some of the dressing. Repeat the layers until all ingredients have been used, except the reserved dressing. Arrange the eggs and tomatoes on top of the salad and drizzle with the reserved 3 tablespoons dressing.

4. Refrigerate at least 2 hours but no more than 4 hours because the potatoes will change texture. Serve cold, cutting through all the layers with a large serving spoon.

White Bean Salad ⓥ
Ensalada de Judías Blancas

MAKES 4 SERVINGS

Spaniards adore their tender white beans, which are primarily found in the region of Asturias. If you can't find white beans, kidney beans may be substituted.

PREPARE AT LEAST 2 HOURS IN ADVANCE

½ **pound dried white or kidney beans, sorted and washed**

1 **medium onion, halved**

1 **bay leaf**

Salt

Freshly ground black pepper

Marinade

2 **tablespoons extra-virgin olive oil**

1 **tablespoon vinegar**

Salt

Freshly ground black pepper

Pinch of sugar

1 **tablespoon finely chopped onion**

1 **tablespoon finely chopped green bell pepper**

1 **tablespoon finely chopped fresh flat-leaf parsley**

Lettuce leaves, for presentation

1. Place the beans in a medium saucepan, add cold water to cover, and let soak overnight. Drain. In the same saucepan, again add cold water to cover and bring to a boil over high heat. Drain and cover again with cold water. Cover and simmer over low heat 1 hour. Add the onion, bay leaf, salt, and pepper, then cover and simmer 1 hour more or until the beans are just tender. Rinse, drain, remove the bay leaf, and let cool.

2. Prepare the marinade: In a small bowl, whisk together the marinade ingredients. Gently fold into the beans. Refrigerate at least 2 hours. Place the lettuce on individual plates and spoon the beans onto the lettuce. Serve cold.

Fresh Bean Salad, Catalan Style **V***
Ensalada de Habas a la Catalana

MAKES 5 TO 6 SERVINGS

Combining the flavor of mint with young fresh beans similar to lima beans reflects a traditional Catalan style of cooking. The lima beans are a fine substitute for this recipe. Leave out the ham and it's vegetarian.

1¼ pounds lima beans, fresh or thawed frozen

2 sprigs mint

½ cup water

Dressing

1 teaspoon Dijon mustard

1 tablespoon sherry vinegar or red wine vinegar

2 tablespoons fruity extra-virgin olive oil

Salt

Freshly ground black pepper

2 teaspoons finely chopped fresh mint

2 ounces Serrano (Spanish cured mountain) ham or prosciutto, cut into very thin strips (about ¼ cup)

½ small head Boston lettuce (about ¼ pound), shredded

Mint sprigs, for garnish

1. Place the beans, the 2 mint sprigs, and the water in a microwave-safe medium bowl. Cover and cook on Medium-High 5 minutes or until the beans are cooked but still firm (or place in a medium saucepan and bring to a boil over high heat. Reduce the heat to low and simmer 10 minutes or until crisp-tender.). Let cool in the cooking liquid. Drain, discard the mint, and transfer to a medium bowl.

2. Prepare the dressing: In a small bowl, whisk together the dressing ingredients.

3. Add the ham and lettuce to the bowl with the beans and fold in the dressing. Garnish with the mint and serve at room temperature.

Marinated Chickpeas **V**
Garbanzos Aliñados

MAKES 4 SERVINGS

Chickpeas, a staple in Spanish cuisine, complement a number of other ingredients but are also wonderful on their own, especially with this simple marinade made more flavorful by the addition of capers.

PREPARE 16 TO 24 HOURS IN ADVANCE

½ pound dried chickpeas or 2 cups canned chickpeas

1 bay leaf

Salt

1 large hard-boiled egg yolk

4 tablespoons extra-virgin olive oil

2 tablespoons red wine vinegar

2 tablespoons finely chopped fresh flat-leaf parsley

1 tablespoon capers (nonpareil preferred), rinsed and drained

1. Place the chickpeas in a medium saucepan, add cold water to cover, and let soak overnight; do not drain. Add the bay leaf, salt, and more water if necessary. Cover and cook 1½ to 2 hours or until tender. Rinse, drain, remove the bay leaf, and let cool. If using canned chickpeas, drain and rinse them.

2. Press the boiled egg yolk through a fine-mesh strainer into a small bowl. Add the oil and vinegar and whisk to combine, then stir in the onion, garlic, 1 tablespoon of the parsley, the capers, and the chickpeas. Refrigerate overnight. Bring to room temperature, sprinkle with the remaining 1 tablespoon parsley, and serve.

Marinated Chickpeas with Capers and Red Pepper ⓥ
Garbanzos Aliñados con Alcaparras

MAKES 4 SERVINGS

Traditionally, Spaniards have always adored chickpeas, adding them to salads as well as soups and stews. Today they are highly esteemed for their nutritional and culinary merits.

¼ cup extra-virgin olive oil

2 tablespoons finely chopped Vidalia onion

2 tablespoons finely chopped red bell pepper

2 tablespoons finely chopped fresh flat-leaf parsley

2 tablespoons red wine vinegar

1 tablespoon capers (nonpareil preferred), rinsed and drained

1 garlic clove, finely chopped

2 cups drained cooked or canned chickpeas (drained and rinsed)

Kosher or sea salt

Freshly ground black pepper

1 large hard-boiled egg yolk, finely chopped, for garnish

In a medium serving bowl, whisk together the oil, onion, red pepper, parsley, vinegar, capers, and garlic. Stir in the chickpeas and season with salt and black pepper. Let sit 1 hour at room temperature. Sprinkle with the egg and serve at room temperature.

Lentil Salad ⓥ
Ensalada de Lentejas

MAKES 4 SERVINGS

Traditionally, lentils were used in soups and stews in order to make them thicker and heartier. This simple lentil salad is quite filling, and the generous amount of onion creates a wonderful pungency.

½ pound dried lentils, picked over, rinsed, and drained

½ medium onion

1 whole clove

1 bay leaf

½ carrot, peeled and cut into small cubes (about ½ cup)

1 garlic clove

Salt

Freshly ground black pepper

¼ cup extra-virgin olive oil

1 tablespoon red wine vinegar

2 tablespoons finely chopped onion

1 garlic clove, mashed in a garlic press or mortar

2 tablespoons finely chopped pimiento

1. Place the lentils in a medium saucepan with water to cover. Add the onion, clove, bay leaf, carrot, whole garlic clove, salt, and pepper, stir to combine, and bring to a boil over high heat. Reduce the heat to low, cover, and simmer about 35 minutes or until the lentils are barely tender. Rinse well under cold water and drain. Discard the onion, bay leaf, clove, and garlic.

2. In a medium bowl, place the lentils, carrot, oil, vinegar, salt, pepper, onions, mashed garlic, and pimiento. Let sit at least 1 hour. Serve at room temperature or refrigerate at least 2 hours and serve cold.

Andalusian Rice Salad
Ensalada Andaluza de Arroz

MAKES 4 SERVINGS

This wonderful rice salad makes the perfect side dish to almost any meal. I have served it with meat, fish, and poultry, and it's always a big hit with my guests. Make sure the rice you choose is of the short-grain variety.

PREPARE AT LEAST 2 HOURS IN ADVANCE

Rice

1 cup short-grain rice, such as imported Spanish or Arborio

3 cups water

Olive oil

Salt

2 tablespoons finely chopped fresh cilantro or parsley

2 tablespoons canned or jarred white or light meat tuna, drained and flaked

¼ cup cooked peas

2 tablespoons finely chopped pimiento

2 tablespoons thinly sliced scallions

2 radishes, thinly sliced

2 tablespoons finely chopped pitted green olives, preferably Spanish

Dressing

3 tablespoons extra-virgin olive oil

1 tablespoon wine vinegar

Salt

Freshly ground black pepper

⅛ teaspoon sugar

½ teaspoon ground sweet paprika

1 garlic clove, finely chopped

1½ teaspoons finely chopped fresh thyme or ¼ teaspoon dried thyme

Garnishes

2 large hard-boiled eggs, cut into wedges

8 thin strips pimiento

8 cooked white or green asparagus

12 cherry tomatoes

12 pitted black olives, preferably Spanish

1. Prepare the rice: In a medium saucepan, place the rice, 3 cups water, a dash of olive oil, and salt and bring to a boil over high heat. Cover, reduce the heat to medium-low, and simmer about 15 minutes or until almost al dente, tender yet still firm to the bite. Pour into a fine-mesh strainer, rinse with cold water, and drain. Transfer to a medium bowl. Add the cilantro, tuna, peas, pimiento, scallions, radishes, and green olives and fold to combine.

2. Prepare the dressing: In a small bowl, whisk together the dressing ingredients and fold into the rice mixture. Season with salt and pepper. Let sit 30 minutes to meld flavors.

3. Transfer the salad to a serving bowl or platter. Attractively arrange the eggs, pimiento strips, asparagus, tomatoes, and black olives over the top of the salad. Serve at room temperature or refrigerate at least 2 hours and serve cold.

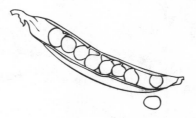

Rice Salad Ring
Ensalada de Turbante de Arroz

MAKES 4 TO 6 SERVINGS

This elegant salad makes quite a visual presentation because it is served in the form of turbante de arroz, *which translates in English to a "ring of rice."*

Rice Ring

1 cup chicken broth or vegetable broth

1 cup water

6 tablespoons unsalted butter

1 tablespoon finely chopped onion

1 cup short-grain rice, such as imported Spanish or Arborio

Salt

¼ teaspoon dried thyme

⅛ teaspoon dried tarragon

¼ sprig parsley (plus more for garnish; optional)

¼ pound mushrooms, coarsely chopped or thinly sliced

Fresh lemon juice (from ½ lemon)

Dressing

3 tablespoons extra-virgin olive oil

1 tablespoon vinegar

¼ teaspoon sugar

Salt

Freshly ground black pepper

¼ teaspoon Dijon mustard

¼ teaspoon dried thyme

1 garlic clove, mashed in a garlic press or mortar

1 fresh parsley sprig

1 anchovy fillet (canned or jarred), finely chopped

½ teaspoon anchovy oil (from the can)

1 pimiento, coarsely chopped

1. Prepare the rice ring: In a medium saucepan, bring the broth and water to a boil over medium-high heat then keep hot. Preheat the oven to 400°F.

2. Melt 3 tablespoons of the butter in a deep earthenware casserole dish or Dutch oven over medium heat. Add the onion and cook, stirring, until wilted and transparent, about 3 minutes. Stir in the rice to coat with the butter, then the hot broth and water and bring to a boil. Stir in the salt, thyme, tarragon, and parsley.

3. Transfer the dish to the oven and bake 15 minutes. Remove the dish from the oven, discard the parsley, and dab the rice with the remaining 3 tablespoons butter. Cover, and let sit on a stovetop or hot plate 10 minutes.

4. To mold the rice, grease an 8-inch ring mold with butter and fill with the rice mixture. Press down to pack well. Return to the oven and bake 2 minutes more.

5. Meanwhile, in a medium bowl, combine the mushrooms and lemon juice and let sit while preparing the dressing.

6. Prepare the dressing: In a small bowl, whisk together the remaining ingredients except the pimiento.

7. Turn the rice ring out onto a round platter. Arrange the mushrooms and pimientos around or on the rice. Pour the dressing over the rice. Garnish with parsley, if using. Serve at room temperature.

Fish Salads

Shrimp and Tomato in Sherry Vinaigrette
Salpicon de Langostino y Tomate

MAKES 6 SERVINGS

The lovely Anteojo Restaurant in Cádiz was the first place I sampled this recipe, and it quickly became one of my favorites. The salad is not meant to be mixed, so when serving, try to keep the shrimp and tomato layers intact.

PREPARE AT LEAST 2 HOURS IN ADVANCE

1 pound medium or large shrimp, unshelled

4 tablespoons sherry vinegar or red wine vinegar

8 tablespoons extra-virgin olive oil

Salt

Freshly ground black pepper

Pinch of sugar

6 tablespoons finely chopped Spanish onion

4 tablespoons finely chopped fresh flat-leaf parsley

4 medium tomatoes, coarsely chopped

1. Bring a large pot of salted water to a boil over high heat. Add the shrimp and cook until pink, 4 to 5 minutes. Let cool, then shell and devein the shrimp.

2. In a large bowl, whisk together the vinegar, oil, salt, pepper, and sugar. Add the onion, 2 tablespoons of the parsley, the shrimp, and tomatoes and stir to combine. Cover and refrigerate at least 2 hours, stirring occasionally.

3. Separate the shrimp and the tomatoes and reserve the dressing. Arrange the tomatoes over the bottom of a wide, shallow serving bowl. Arrange the shrimp in overlapping rows over the tomatoes.

Pour the dressing over the shrimp. Sprinkle with the remaining 2 tablespoons parsley and serve cold, keeping the layers intact.

Shrimp, Melon, and Apple Salad
Coctél Gran Concierto

MAKES 6 SERVINGS

This wonderful combination of tastes and textures is especially attractive when served in a melon shell.

3½ cups Cooking Liquid (page 26; partial recipe)

1 pound small shrimp, unshelled

6 tablespoons mayonnaise, (mayonesa; page 359)

2 tablespoons ketchup

¼ tablespoon Worcestershire sauce

Salt

Freshly ground black pepper

1 medium orange melon (about 2 pounds), such as Crenshaw or cantaloupe

1 apple, peeled and cut into ½-inch pieces

1. Prepare the cooking liquid as instructed. Add the shrimp and simmer over low heat until pink, 2 to 3 minutes. Drain, let cool, and shell and devein the shrimp.

2. In a small bowl, mix the mayonnaise, ketchup, Worcestershire sauce, salt, and pepper. Cut the melon crosswise in half and scoop out melon balls. Clean out any remaining loose flesh from the shells and set aside for serving.

3. In a large bowl, add the shrimp, melon balls, and apple and fold to combine. Fold in the dressing. Spoon the salad into the melon shells. Refrigerate 30 minutes to 1 hour—the salad should be served cool, not cold.

Asparagus, Shrimp, and Mushroom Salad

Ensalada de Esparrago, Gamba y Champiñón

MAKES 4 SERVINGS

There is a magnificent restaurant in Madrid, Cenador del Prado, whose talented chef, Tomás Herranz, worked for years at the Café San Martín in New York. Thomas was one of the best chefs I have ever known, but sadly, he died at a very young age. This salad is one of his delicious creations.

PREPARE AT LEAST 2 HOURS IN ADVANCE

¾ pound thin green asparagus, rinsed and trimmed

2 cups chicken broth or vegetable broth

Water, as needed

12 very small shrimp or 8 small to medium shrimp, unshelled

1 small tomato, cut into small cubes (about ½ cup)

2 medium mushrooms, rinsed, trimmed, and thinly sliced

Dressing

2 tablespoons fruity extra-virgin olive oil

2 teaspoons fresh lemon juice

Salt

Freshly ground black pepper

1 teaspoon finely chopped fresh flat-leaf parsley

⅛ teaspoon dried thyme

1. Place the asparagus in a medium skillet, add the broth plus enough water to cover, and bring to a boil over high heat. Reduce the heat to low, cover, and simmer about 5 minutes or until crisp-tender. Do not overcook. Transfer to a shallow bowl, reserving the liquid in the skillet. Bring the liquid back to a boil over high heat, add the shrimp, and cook about 2 minutes or until pink. Let cool, shell, and add to the asparagus.

2. Prepare the dressing: In a small bowl, whisk together the dressing ingredients and fold into the salad. Refrigerate at least 2 hours and serve cold.

Salad of Tiny Potatoes and Tuna

Ensalada de Cachelos y Atún

MAKES 8 SERVINGS

This recipe originated in Galicia, home to small, tender potatoes called cachelos, *a staple of Galician cooking.*

PREPARE AT LEAST 2 HOURS IN ADVANCE

1 pound tiny (about 1½ inches) red waxy or new potatoes

Kosher or sea salt

½ cup marinated light meat tuna, drained and flaked, such as Spanish

1 large hard-boiled egg

3 tablespoons extra-virgin olive oil

4 teaspoons wine vinegar, such as white

1 garlic clove, mashed in a garlic press or mortar

2 teaspoons finely chopped onion

3 tablespoons finely chopped fresh flat-leaf parsley

Ground cayenne pepper or hot pepper flakes

2 tablespoons finely chopped dill or cornichon pickle

8 small pimiento-stuffed green olives, preferably Spanish, halved crosswise

1. Place the potatoes in a medium saucepan with cold water to cover and add salt. Cover and bring to a simmer over low heat. Cook about 15 minutes or until tender when pierced with a knife. Drain and let cool slightly. Peel (or leave the skins on if you prefer), cut crosswise in half, and place in a medium bowl. Add the tuna and fold to combine.

2. Mash the egg yolk with a fork and finely chop the white. In a small bowl, whisk together the oil, vinegar, salt, and garlic. Add the onion, the egg

yolk, 2 tablespoons of the parsley, and the cayenne pepper and mix well. Fold into the potato mixture.

3. Transfer to a serving dish and sprinkle with the pickle, olives, the remaining 1 tablespoon parsley, and the egg white. Serve at room temperature or refrigerate at least 2 hours and serve cold.

Pimiento and Tuna Salad, Cazorla Style
Ensalada de Pimientos con Atún "Cazorla"

MAKES 3 TO 4 SERVINGS

Andalusians adore this salad, and it is perfect on a hot summer day. I first sampled it at the Cazorla Parador, a hotel and restaurant located in the middle of the Cazorla Mountains in the province of Jaen.

6 medium red bell peppers

Kosher or sea salt

Freshly ground black pepper

3 tablespoons canned or jarred tuna, such as light or dark meat, drained and flaked

1 large hard-boiled egg, coarsely chopped

2 tablespoons extra-virgin olive oil

1 tablespoon red wine vinegar

8 small black olives, preferably Spanish

1. Preheat the oven to 500°F. Place the peppers in a roasting pan and roast for 45 minutes, turning once. Remove from the oven, cover the pan tightly with foil, and let sit 15 minutes. Peel, core, seed, and cut into thin strips. Arrange in a single layer on a platter. Season with salt and pepper.

2. Scatter the tuna and egg over the peppers and drizzle with the oil and vinegar. Taste and adjust seasoning if necessary. Scatter the olives over the top. Let sit at least 30 minutes. Serve at room temperature.

Tuna, Egg, and Potato Salad
Ensaladilla Espartero

MAKES 4 TO 6 SERVINGS

Ensaladilla Espartero was made famous at the popular Espartero Café on Alcala Street in Madrid. Their menu features several salads—one like this one that contains potatoes and is coated in mayonnaise, and others that are made from seafood served in a spicy vinaigrette. This mixture may also be used as a filling for mini tartlet shells, in which case the potatoes and tuna should be cut into smaller pieces.

3 medium potatoes, such as red waxy

One (7-ounce) can white or light meat tuna, drained and separated into chunks

1½ teaspoons vinegar

1½ teaspoons finely chopped onion

1 tablespoon finely chopped fresh flat-leaf parsley

1 teaspoon capers in vinegar (nonpareil preferred), rinsed and drained

1 hard-boiled egg, finely chopped

Salt

Mayonnaise (mayonesa; page 359)

1 pimiento, cut into thin strips, for garnish

1. Place the potatoes in a medium saucepan with cold water to cover and add salt. Cover and bring to a simmer over low heat. Cook about 15 minutes or until tender when pierced with a knife. Drain and let cool slightly. Peel and cut into ½-inch pieces.

2. In a large bowl, combine the tuna, vinegar, onion, parsley, and capers. Fold in the potatoes, egg, and salt. Let sit at least 30 minutes.

3. Fold in the mayonnaise. It's traditional to serve this salad shaped into a dome on a flat plate and decorated with pimiento strips, but you can serve it more casually if you like—simply plated and garnished with the pimiento strips. Serve at room temperature.

Red Pepper, Tomato, and Tuna Salad, Andalusian Style

Ensalada de Pimientos Estilo Andaluz

MAKES 4 SERVINGS

This variation of Andalusian red pepper salad includes tomato, white meat tuna, and mild green olives. It is frequently served as a side dish to Andalusian fried fish.

PREPARE 8 TO 12 HOURS IN ADVANCE

6 medium to large red bell peppers

7 ounces canned or jarred white or light meat tuna, drained and separated into small chunks

½ pound medium ripe but firm tomatoes, thinly sliced, each slice cut in half

12 mild pitted green olives, preferably Spanish, such as Cerignola

2 tablespoons finely chopped fresh flat-leaf parsley

6 tablespoons fruity extra-virgin olive oil

1 tablespoon wine vinegar, such as mild white

½ teaspoon sugar

Kosher or sea salt

1. Preheat the oven to 550°F. Place the peppers in a roasting pan and bake, turning once, 30 to 40 minutes or until charred. Transfer to a deep bowl, cover tightly with foil, and let sit 15 minutes. Peel, core, and seed, reserving the juices in a medium bowl.

2. Cut the peppers into ¾-inch strips and place in the bowl with the pepper juices. Add the tuna, tomatoes, olives, and parsley and fold to combine.

3. In a small bowl, whisk together the oil, vinegar, sugar, and salt. Fold into the salad. Refrigerate overnight. Serve cold or at room temperature.

Cinta's Old-Fashioned Cod and Bean Salad

Empedrat al Estilo de Antaño de Cinta Gutierrez

MAKES 6 SERVINGS

This and the next recipe are two wonderful cod salads. My friend Cinta, whose family owns the Els Pescadors Restaurant in Girona, was kind enough to share this traditional Catalan recipe with me. Here, the cod is sliced then marinated simply with onions, tomatoes, and olives.

PREPARE 26 TO 38 HOURS IN ADVANCE

½ pound boneless skinless dried salt cod

1 cup cooked or canned white beans, drained

1 medium onion, slivered

2 plum tomatoes, coarsely chopped (about ⅔ cup)

24 small black olives, preferably Spanish

½ cup extra-virgin olive oil

¼ cup red wine vinegar

3 tablespoons finely chopped fresh flat-leaf parsley

Kosher or sea salt

1. Place the cod in a medium bowl with cold water to cover. Cover and let sit in the refrigerator 24 to 36 hours, changing the water several times, until the water no longer tastes salty. Drain and let dry on paper towels. With a thin sharp knife, cut the cod diagonally across the grain into ¼-inch slices.

2. In a flat-bottom bowl, fold together the cod, beans, onion, tomatoes, and olives.

3. In a small bowl, whisk together the oil, vinegar, parsley, and salt. Fold the dressing into the salad. Let marinate in the refrigerator 2 to 4 hours to meld flavors but no longer or some flavor will be lost. Serve cold.

Codfish Salad with Sweet Onion and Eggs
Empedrat Tarraconense

MAKES 6 SERVINGS

I was first introduced to this popular version of cod salad at the quaint Agut d'Avignon restaurant in the old quarter of Barcelona. Here the cod is shredded and the onion is baked to give it a mellow sweetness. The eggs add rich flavor.

PREPARE 26 TO 38 HOURS IN ADVANCE

1 pound boneless skinless dried salt cod

1 medium onion

1 medium tomato, thinly sliced, each slice cut in half

20 small black olives, preferably Spanish

1 cup cooked or canned white beans, drained

2 hard-boiled eggs, sliced

2 tablespoons finely chopped fresh flat-leaf parsley

8 tablespoons extra-virgin olive oil

4 tablespoons red wine vinegar

Salt

Freshly ground black pepper

1. Place the cod in a medium bowl with cold water to cover. Cover and let sit in the refrigerator 24 to 36 hours, changing the water several times, until the water no longer tastes salty. Drain. Shred the cod with your fingers.

2. Preheat the oven to 350°F. Place the onion in a shallow baking pan and bake 30 minutes or until softened. Let cool and cut into thin slivers.

3. In a large bowl, combine the cod, onion, tomato, olives, beans, eggs, and parsley. In a small bowl, whisk together the oil and vinegar and fold into the cod mixture. Season with salt and pepper. Refrigerate 2 to 4 hours but no more because some flavor will be lost. Serve cold.

Orange-Scented Salt Cod, Granada Style
Remojón Granadino

MAKES 6 SERVINGS

This is a salad typical of the olive harvest in some areas of Granada.

PREPARE 24 TO 36 HOURS IN ADVANCE

1 pound boneless skinless dried salt cod

2 tablespoons olive oil

2 oranges, peeled, cut into ½-inch slices, then each slice quartered

2 sun-dried tomatoes, coarsely chopped

2 medium onions, cut into small pieces

3 garlic cloves, finely chopped

12 black olives, sliced, preferably Spanish

Extra-virgin olive oil

Red wine vinegar

1 tablespoon ground paprika, such as Spanish smoked

2 hard-boiled eggs, cut into quarters

1. Place the cod in a medium bowl with cold water to cover. Cover and let sit in the refrigerator 24 to 36 hours, changing the water several times, until the water no longer tastes salty. Drain.

2. Heat the 2 tablespoons oil in a medium skillet over medium heat. Add the cod and cook, turning once, until tender. Transfer to paper towels with a slotted spatula and let cool slightly. Shred with your fingers.

3. Combine the oranges, tomatoes, onions, garlic, and olives in a serving bowl and place the cod on top. Drizzle with the oil and vinegar and with paprika. Decorate with the eggs. Serve at room temperature.

Avocado Salad with Pomegranate Seeds and Salmon

Ensalada de Aguacate con Granadinas y Salmon

MAKES 4 SERVINGS

The rich flavor of the smoked salmon in this recipe contrasts beautifully with the sweetness of the pomegranate seeds and the tanginess of the sherry vinegar.

¼ cup extra-virgin olive oil

2 tablespoons sherry vinegar or red wine vinegar

Kosher or sea salt

Freshly ground black pepper

1 pound avocados, cut into small cubes

1 tablespoon finely chopped scallion

¼ cup pomegranate seeds

Lettuce leaves, for presentation

¼ pound smoked salmon, thinly sliced

Mint sprigs, for garnish

In a small bowl, whisk together the oil, vinegar, salt, and pepper. Fold in the avocados, scallions, and pomegranate seeds and pour over the salad. Arrange the lettuce leaves on a platter. Spoon the salad into the center and place the salmon on top. Garnish with the mint and serve.

Escarole, Tomato, Anchovy, and Black Olive Salad with Xato Dressing

Ensalada Xato con Escarola, Tomate, Anchoa y Aceituna Negra

MAKES 4 SERVINGS

This salad combines typically Catalan ingredients, such as dried red pepper and hazelnuts, creating a taste that is both spicy and sweet.

12 hazelnuts

2 dried red chile peppers (ñoras) or 1 dried New Mexico (Anaheim) chile, stemmed and seeded

4 garlic cloves, coarsely chopped

½ teaspoon ground paprika, such as Spanish smoked

Pinch of kosher or sea salt

6 tablespoons extra-virgin olive oil

2 tablespoons wine vinegar

6 cups washed, dried, and torn escarole leaves

24 grape or cherry tomatoes

16 black olives, preferably Spanish

8 anchovy fillets

6 radishes, thinly sliced

2 tablespoons finely chopped fresh flat-leaf parsley, for garnish

1. Preheat the oven to 350°F. Arrange the hazelnuts on a cookie sheet and toast about 5 minutes or until fragrant. Meanwhile, place the bell peppers in a small bowl with warm water to cover and let soak until pliable, about 20 minutes.

2. In a food processor, place the hazelnuts and process until finely ground. Scrape the flesh from the peppers and add to the processor, along with the garlic, paprika, and salt. Process until finely chopped. With the motor running, gradually add in the oil and vinegar.

3. Arrange the escarole, tomatoes, olives, anchovies, and radishes on individual salad plates. Spoon the dressing over each portion and sprinkle with parsley. Serve.

Grilled Mackerel Topped with Tomato and Pepper Salad
Caballa a la Parrilla con Picadillo de Tomate y Pimiento

MAKES 4 SERVINGS

This recipe for mackerel smothered in a deliciously fresh tomato and pepper salad originated in Cádiz, where vegetables are at their finest. It makes for a delightful summer meal. If you can't find fresh mackerel, trout can be substituted.

5 tablespoons extra-virgin olive oil

1 tablespoon red or white wine vinegar

Salt

Freshly ground black pepper

¾ teaspoon sugar

1 small onion, slivered (about ⅓ cup)

1 medium green bell pepper, cut into ¼-inch cubes

4 (¾-pound) mackerel or 2 (1¼- to 1½-pound) mackerel, cleaned and heads on

¾ pound ripe tomatoes, cut into ½-inch cubes

1. In a small bowl, whisk together 4 tablespoons of the oil, the vinegar, salt, pepper, and sugar. Add the onion and bell pepper and stir to combine. Reserve at room temperature.

2. Brush the fish on both sides with the remaining 1 tablespoon oil. Place a barbecue grill or broiler rack about 4 inches away from the heat source and preheat the grill or broiler; or grease a stovetop griddle and heat to the smoking point (Cover the boiler pan with foil for easier cleanup, if you like.). Grill, turning once, until browned on the outside and just cooked through, about 10 minutes to each inch of thickness.

3. Add the tomatoes to the salad and fold to combine. Carefully fillet the fish and arrange on a platter or individual dishes. Spoon the salad onto the fish and serve hot or warm.

White Bean Salad with Herring
Ensalada de Judías con Arenque

MAKES 4 SERVINGS

In this winning combination, the simple, creamy white beans balance the strong flavor of the herring.

PREPARE 10 TO 14 HOURS IN ADVANCE

½ pound dried white beans, sorted and washed

1 large scallion, finely chopped

2 pickled herring, chopped with their liquid

1. Place the beans in a medium saucepan, add cold water to cover, and let soak overnight. Drain. In the same saucepan, again add cold water to cover and bring to a boil over high heat. Reduce the heat to low, cover, and simmer 1½ to 2 hours or until the beans are just tender.

2. In a medium bowl, combine the beans, scallions, and herring. Let sit 10 minutes. Serve at room temperature or refrigerate at least 2 hours and serve cold.

Lobster and Watercress Salad
Ensalada de Lubrigante con Berros

MAKES 4 SERVINGS AS A MAIN COURSE

This fabulous main-course salad is a specialty in the region of Galicia. I first tasted it at the El Nautico restaurant in the charming town of Cedeira, on the upper Galician estuaries in La Coruña province.

10 cups clam juice

4 cups water

2 (2-pound) live lobsters

1 pound red waxy potatoes

2 medium white turnips

Salt

2 bunches watercress (about ¼ pound each), rinsed and thick stems trimmed

1 garlic clove

8 black or white peppercorns

4 sprigs mint

⅛ teaspoon salt

½ teaspoon Dijon mustard

¼ cup fresh lemon juice

½ cup fruity extra-virgin olive oil

4 radishes, thinly sliced

I. Place the clam juice and water in a large pot and bring to a boil over high heat. Holding each lobster with a towel, add them to the water headfirst. Cover and boil 15 minutes or until the shells are bright red and the tails curled. Drain, transfer to a platter, and let cool. Remove the shell from the tails and claws. Cut the tail into ½-inch-thick slices and the rest into large chunks. Reserve the red coral (eggs), if desired.

2. Meanwhile, place the potatoes and turnips in a medium saucepan with cold water to cover and add salt. Cover and bring to a simmer over low heat. Cook about 20 minutes or until the potatoes and turnips are tender when pierced with a knife. Drain and let cool slightly. Peel and cut into ½-inch slices.

3. Finely chop enough watercress to make 3 tablespoons. In a mortar or mini-processor, mash the garlic, peppercorns, watercress, mint, and ⅛ teaspoon salt. Stir in the mustard and lemon juice and transfer to a small bowl. Add the oil and whisk to combine. Taste and adjust seasoning if necessary.

4. Arrange the remaining watercress on a platter. Scatter the radishes over the watercress and season with salt. Place the lobster meat in the center. Arrange the potatoes and turnips around the edge. Pour the dressing over everything and serve.

Lobster Salad, Galician Style
Salpicon de Lubrigante a la Gallega

MAKES 4 SERVINGS AS A MAIN COURSE

Like the previous recipe, this one originated at El Nautico in Cedeira. This excellent restaurant serves huge portions and is set on the colorful waterfront promenade.

10 cups bottled clam juice

4 cups water

2 (1½-pound) live lobsters

2 tablespoons finely chopped fresh flat-leaf parsley

1 large hard-boiled egg, coarsely chopped

¼ cup finely chopped onion

¼ cup finely chopped pimiento

1½ teaspoons ground paprika, such as Spanish smoked

1 large garlic clove

2 tablespoons extra-virgin olive oil

4 tablespoons wine vinegar, such as white

Salt

1. Place the clam juice and water in a large pot and bring to a boil over high heat. Holding each lobster with a towel, add them to the water headfirst. Cover and boil 15 minutes or until the shells are bright red and the tails curled. Drain, reserving 2 tablespoons of the cooking liquid. Transfer the lobsters to a platter and let cool. Remove the shell from everything but the small claws. Reserve the green tomalley, if desired. Coarsely chop the meat and place in a medium bowl. Add the unshelled claws, parsley, egg, onion, and pimiento and stir to combine.

2. Dissolve the paprika in the reserved 2 tablespoons cooking liquid. In a mortar or mini-processor, mash the garlic, then stir in the paprika mixture.

3. In a small bowl, whisk together the oil, vinegar, salt and garlic-paprika mixture. Fold it into the lobster mixture. Taste and adjust seasoning if necessary. Serve at room temperature or refrigerate at least 2 hours and serve cold.

Lobster and Endive Salad
Ensalada de Bogavante con Endivias

MAKES 4 SERVINGS

The restaurant Zalacain in Madrid is considered by many to be one of the very finest restaurants in the world. Dining there is a memorable experience, and every dish is a work of art, including this delectable lobster and endive salad.

7 cups Cooking Liquid (page 26)
One (1¾-pound) live lobster
1 head endive
1 sprig parsley, for garnish
Dressing
3 tablespoons fruity extra-virgin olive oil
1 tablespoon fresh lemon juice
Salt
Freshly ground black pepper, preferably white

1. Prepare the cooking liquid. Raise the heat to high, then holding the lobster with a towel, add it to the cooking liquid headfirst. Cover and boil 15 minutes or until the shell is bright red and the tail curled. Drain, reserving 2 tablespoons of the cooking liquid. Transfer the lobster to a platter and let cool.

2. Prepare the dressing: In a small bowl, whisk together the dressing ingredients and the reserved cooking liquid.

3. Separate the endives into individual leaves. Stack them and slice lengthwise into very thin strips.

4. Remove the lobster shell from everything but the small claws. Reserve the green tomalley, if desired. Cut the tail into ½-inch-thick slices and the rest into large chunks. Use the small claws to decorate the dish, if desired.

5. Arrange the endive on a serving platter or individual serving dishes and arrange the lobster meat attractively on top. Pour the dressing over the lobster, garnish with the parsley, and serve.

Fish and Lobster Salad
Ensalada Koshkera

MAKES 4 SERVINGS

This seafood-rich salad is a specialty of the Basque region and is usually served as a main course.

PREPARE AT LEAST 2 HOURS IN ADVANCE

Fish and Lobster

1 pound fresh cod or porgy fillets

2 tablespoons olive oil

2 tablespoons vinegar

Salt

Freshly ground black pepper

1¾ pounds live lobster

Salad

2 pimientos, cut into thin strips

One 3-ounce jar small pitted green olives (with or without pimiento), preferably Spanish

1 teaspoon vinegar

3 tablespoons extra-virgin olive oil

Salt

4 large hard-boiled eggs, cut into wedges, for garnish

1. Prepare the fish and lobster: Place the cod in a medium saucepan with water to cover. Cover and cook over medium heat 15 minutes or until tender. Drain, let cool, and pat gently with paper towels to dry. Shred with your fingers.

2. In a small bowl, whisk together the 2 tablespoons oil, 2 tablespoons vinegar, the salt, and pepper. Pour over the fish and let sit 30 minutes. Drain.

3. Meanwhile, fill a large pot with water, add salt, and bring to a boil over high heat. Add the lobster upside-down and head first, cover, and cook 12 minutes. Drain and let cool. Remove the shell and cut the lobster into thin slices.

4. Prepare the salad: Combine the fish and lobster in a serving bowl. Fold in the pimientos and olives. In a small bowl, whisk together 1 teaspoon vinegar, the 3 tablespoons oil, and the salt. Fold into the salad. Garnish with the eggs. Refrigerate at least 2 hours and serve cold.

Baby Eel Salad
Ensalada de Angulas

MAKES 2 SERVINGS

Angulas, baby eels as tiny as bean sprouts, are considered a delicacy throughout all of Spain. The eels are caught at the mouths of rivers as they complete their three-thousand-mile journey from the Sargasso Sea near Bermuda to the fresh waters of Spain's rivers. Angulas have a mild taste, which lends itself to this delicious salad recipe.

¼ pound fresh or frozen (thawed) baby eels (angulas) or mock baby eels (gulas), cleaned

2½ tablespoons extra-virgin olive oil

1½ teaspoons red wine vinegar

2 garlic cloves, mashed in a garlic press or mortar

½ dried red chile pepper, seeded and crushed

1 tablespoon finely chopped fresh flat-leaf parsley

Salt

Freshly ground black pepper

Lettuce leaves, for presentation

1. Dry the eels well and place in a salad bowl. In a small bowl, whisk together the oil, vinegar, garlic, chile pepper, parsley, salt, and black pepper. Pour over the eels and stir to combine.

2. Line a serving platter with lettuce leaves. Spoon the eels over the lettuce. Refrigerate 30 minutes to 1 hour—they should be served cool, not cold.

Fish and Vegetable Salad
Salpicon a la Valenciana

MAKES 4 SERVINGS

I first sampled this salad at the Cervecería Pema in Valencia. This colorful salad is as beautiful as it is delicious. Baby eels are a delicacy, hard to find, and very expensive but perhaps may be worth trying sometime.

PREPARE 8 TO 12 HOURS IN ADVANCE

1 dozen medium mussels

¼ pound cauliflower and/or broccoli, thick stems removed and cut into small florets

Salt

1 teaspoon fresh lemon juice

1 slice lemon

½ pound cleaned squid or 1 pound uncleaned squid (preferably very small, with tentacles)

2 ounces baby eels (angulas) or mock baby eels (gulas), cleaned (optional)

2 tablespoons finely chopped green bell pepper

3 tablespoons finely chopped tomato

1 tablespoon finely chopped scallion (about 1 small)

1 garlic clove, finely chopped

½ cup slivered onion, preferably Spanish

4 pitted black olives, preferably Spanish, sliced

1 tablespoon finely chopped dill or cornichon pickle

Dressing

2 tablespoons extra-virgin olive oil

1 tablespoon fresh lemon juice

¼ teaspoon Dijon mustard

Kosher or sea salt

1. In a large bowl, place the mussels, add cold water to cover, and let sit 30 minutes. Scrub with a stiff brush under cold running water. Cut or pull off the beards. Drain. Discard any mussels with cracked shells or that do not close tightly when touched.

2. Meanwhile, in a medium skillet, place 1 inch of water and the lemon juice and add salt. Add the cauliflower and bring to a boil over high heat. Reduce the heat to low, cover, and simmer 5 to 10 minutes or until crisp-tender. Drain and discard the liquid.

3. In the same skillet, place ½ inch water, the lemon slice, and the mussels. Bring to a boil over high heat, stirring, and remove the mussels as they open—do not overcook. Discard any unopened mussels. Remove the meat from the shells and discard the shells.

4. Make a small slit at the pointed end of each squid. Rinse thoroughly, letting the water run through the body sac. Let drain. Add them and the baby eels, if using, to the mussel liquid and cook over high heat, stirring, about 2 minutes or until just tender. Leave the squid whole if they are tiny, otherwise, cut into halves or rings. Cut the eels into small pieces.

5. In a medium bowl, combine the cauliflower, mussels, squid, baby eels (if using), bell pepper, tomato, scallion, garlic, onion, olives, and pickle.

6. Prepare the dressing: In a small bowl, whisk together the dressing ingredients and fold into the salad. Refrigerate overnight and serve cold.

Soups and Stews

GAZPACHOS

Gazpacho, Andalusian Style Ⓥ

Gazpacho, Cordoba Style Ⓥ*

Cucumber Gazpacho Ⓥ

White Gazpacho, Málaga Style Ⓥ

White Almond and Pine Nut
Gazpacho with Melon Ⓥ

Fresh Bean Gazpacho Ⓥ*

Beet Gazpacho with Melon and Goat Cheese Ⓥ

Strawberry Gazpacho Ⓥ

Fruit Gazpacho with Watermelon,
Strawberries, and Peaches Ⓥ

VEGETABLE AND BEAN SOUPS

Mint Soup Ⓥ*

Garlic Soup, Castilian Style Ⓥ*

Sherried Consommé

Onion and Almond Soup Ⓥ*

Peppers and Almond Soup Ⓥ

Tomato Soup with Goat Cheese
and Anchovy Flan

Cumin-Scented Tomato Soup with Fresh Figs Ⓥ

Potato and Mushroom Soup Ⓥ*

Thick Vegetable Soup, Mallorcan Style Ⓥ*

Watercress, Bean, and Potato Soup

Swiss Chard, Brussels Sprouts,
Lettuce, and Leek Soup

Vegetable Soup from El Bierzo

Lentil Soup

Lentils with Spinach

FISH SOUPS

Fish Broth

Fish Broth, Cádiz Style

Ⓥ = Vegetarian   Ⓥ* = Vegetarian with one change

Quick Fish Soup

Trout Soup

Fish Soup

Fish Soup with Dried Red Peppers

Basque Tuna Soup

Saffron-Scented Fish Soup

Chickpea, Spinach, and Cod Potage Lerranz

Shrimp Soup

Potato, Egg, and Shrimp Soup

Creamy Crayfish Soup

Shark Soup with Roasted Peppers

Baby Squid Soup

POULTRY AND MEAT SOUPS

Thick Chicken Broth with
Pastry Puffs

Cream of Partridge Soup

Ham Soup

Galician Meat, Potato, Greens, and Bean Soup

Meatball and Artichoke Soup

STEWS

Bean Stew

Asturian Bean Stew

Basque Red Bean Stew

Beans with Clams

Broad Beans with Sausage and Pig's Foot

Bean and Partridge Stew

Chickpea Stew, Zamora Style

Chickpea Stew with Bolos, Galician Style

Tripe and Chickpeas, Galician Style

Thick Chickpea and Chorizo Soup

Chickpea and Cuttlefish Stew

Lobster Stew, Menorca Style

Fish Stew, Catalan Style

Vinegar Fish Soup

Potted Quail

Lamb Stew, Extremadura Style

Lamb and Red Pepper Stew

Beef Stew, Catalan Style

Garlic Beef Stew

Boiled Beef and Chickpea Dinner

Tripe Stew, Madrid Style

Stew of Potatoes and Marinated Pork Ribs

*S*panish soups or *sopas* fall into two categories—soups that are light enough to be served before the main course (a more recent development in Spanish cuisine) and soups that are hearty and robust enough to be the main course. Traditionally, Spanish soups were of the hearty variety, providing inexpensive meals that were filling and delicious. But even now, the most worldly metropolitan dweller will often opt for an old fashioned, peasant-style soup that reminds him of his childhood.

Soups are a staple in Spain and much of their ingenuity was born from economic necessity. In a country whose many regions are separated by rugged, mountainous terrain, chefs and homemakers alike once relied only on the freshest local ingredients, with some of them being seasonal. On a hot summer day in Cádiz, there is nothing quite as refreshing as a crisp, cool bowl of gazpacho. On a cold day in Madrid, nothing warms your bones like a simmering stew or *cocido*, a thick soup fortified by beans, potatoes, and often meat.

Spanish soups are as varied as the regions in which they were created. Castilla is famous for their *cocidos*, Asturias for their *fabada* (thick bean stew), and Galicia for their *caldo gallego* (meat and greens stew). The Basque region is known for its *marmitako*, a fish soup usually made with tuna and potatoes and flavored with paprika and other spices from the New World. A true Basque purist will claim that the best *marmitako* can be made only upon the fishing vessels that have just caught the *bonito* needed in its preparation.

Spaniards do not like diluted flavors. Rarely will you find a soup mellowed with cream and butter, for the Spanish palate is uninterested in such refinements.

There are a limited number of soups that are appropriate for a first course. These include consommés, some garlic soups, and several of the more simple fish soups. What is most important is to pick the soup that best suits the season and best complements the other dishes that are served.

Gazpachos

Gazpacho, Andalusian Style Ⓥ
Gazpacho Andaluz

MAKES 6 SERVINGS

Everybody seems to love this classic red Andalusian gazpacho, always refreshing and delightful on a hot summer day. You won't find the usual cucumbers or onions in this version, but the recipe does call for cumin, which adds a definitive taste. Although this is a smooth, elegant soup, if you prefer gazpacho with more texture, don't strain it.

PREPARE AT LEAST 2 HOURS IN ADVANCE

2½ pounds very ripe tomatoes, quartered

2 garlic cloves, coarsely chopped

1 medium red bell pepper, coarsely chopped (about ¾ cup)

One (2-inch) chunk country (baguette) bread, crust removed

2 tablespoons sherry vinegar or red wine vinegar

2 teaspoons salt

½ teaspoon ground cumin (optional)

1 teaspoon sugar

½ cup mild extra-virgin olive oil, such as Andalusian hojiblanca

Finely chopped red and green bell peppers, for garnish (optional)

I. In a food processor, place half of the tomatoes and all of the garlic, the coarsely chopped pepper, the bread, vinegar, salt, cumin, and sugar. Process until no large pieces remain. With the motor running, add the remaining tomato and process until smooth. Drizzle in the oil until fully incorporated.

2. Pass through a fine-mesh strainer into a medium bowl, pressing with the back of a soup ladle to extract as much liquid as possible. Discard the solids. Cover and refrigerate at least 2 hours up to overnight.

3. Taste for vinegar and salt and adjust if necessary. If desired, thin the soup with ice water. Pour into individual chilled bowls. Place the finely chopped peppers, if using, in a small serving bowl. Serve the soup cold garnished with the peppers.

Gazpacho, Cordoba Style Ⓥ*
Salmorejo Cordobés

MAKES 6 SERVINGS

This recipe for gazpacho is from the Restaurant El Churrasco in Cordoba, where Andalusian cooking and traditional Arab dishes are represented at their best. The egg and ham make this a rich version of gazpacho. It is customary to also garnish this with fried eggplant, making for an extraordinary combination. Omit the ham to make this vegetarian.

PREPARE AT LEAST 2 HOURS IN ADVANCE

2 thick slices long-loaf (baguette) bread

12 medium ripe tomatoes, coarsely chopped

1 medium green bell pepper, coarsely chopped (about ⅔ cup)

½ medium red bell pepper, coarsely chopped (about ⅔ cup)

½ cup water

Kosher or sea salt

½ cup extra-virgin olive oil

2 tablespoons sherry vinegar or red wine vinegar

1 hard-boiled egg, finely chopped

Very thin 2-inch strips Serrano (Spanish cured mountain) ham or prosciutto

continues...

1. In a food processor, place all the ingredients except the egg and ham and process until smooth.

2. Pass through a fine-mesh strainer into a large bowl, pressing to extract the liquid. Discard the solids. In a small bowl, whisk together the oil and vinegar then stir it into the soup. Cover and refrigerate at least 2 hours up to overnight.

3. Taste for vinegar and salt and adjust if necessary. Pour into individual chilled bowls. Garnish with the egg and ham and serve cold.

Cucumber Gazpacho **V**
Gazpacho de Pepino

MAKES 4 SERVINGS

The simplicity of cucumber and dill blend perfectly to create a special version of green gazpacho.

PREPARE AT LEAST 2 HOURS IN ADVANCE

1 pound small cucumbers, peeled

2 teaspoons fresh dill or chives

1 small garlic clove, finely chopped

¼ cup extra-virgin olive oil

½ medium onion, coarsely chopped (about ⅓ cup)

¼ cup white wine vinegar

1 teaspoon sugar

Kosher or sea salt

Freshly ground black pepper

2 cups water

In a food processor, place all the ingredients except the water and process until smooth. With the motor running, gradually add the water. Cover and refrigerate at least 2 hours up to overnight. Taste for vinegar and salt and adjust if necessary. Pour into individual chilled bowls and serve cold.

White Gazpacho, Málaga Style **V**
Ajo Blanco Malagueño

MAKES 4 SERVINGS

Blanched almonds create the white color and creamy consistency to this gazpacho that originated in Málaga. The pungency of the garlic and vinegar is cut by the sweetness of the green grapes.

PREPARE AT LEAST 2 HOURS IN ADVANCE

One (6-inch) piece long-loaf (baguette) bread, crust removed

½ pound blanched almonds (about 1½ cups)

2 garlic cloves, coarsely chopped

2 tablespoons sherry vinegar or red wine vinegar

1 teaspoon salt

1 cup mild extra-virgin olive oil, such as Andalusian hojiblanca

4 cups ice cold water

16 peeled seedless green grapes or 16 small balls of green melon, such as honeydew or apple

12 small cooked and shelled shrimp (optional)

1. Soak the bread in water, squeeze dry, and place in a food processor. Add the almonds and garlic and process until smooth. Add the vinegar and salt and, with the motor running, drizzle in the oil until fully incorporated (the mixture will resemble mayonnaise), then gradually add the water. Transfer to a medium bowl, cover, and refrigerate at least 2 hours up to overnight.

2. Taste for vinegar and salt and adjust if necessary. Garnish each serving with 4 grapes and 3 shrimp, if using. Serve cold.

White Almond and Pine Nut Gazpacho with Melon ⓥ

Ajo Blanco de Almendras y Piñones

MAKES 6 SERVINGS

One of the many variations of white gazpacho calls for pine nuts in addition to the more commonly used almonds. The melon adds just the right amount of sweetness.

PREPARE AT LEAST 2 HOURS IN ADVANCE

⅓ cup blanched almonds (about 2 ounces)

⅓ cup pine nuts (about 2 ounces)

2 garlic cloves

1 teaspoon salt

4 (1-inch) cubes green melon, such as honeydew

4 thin slices long-loaf (baguette) bread, crust removed

6 tablespoons extra-virgin olive oil

1 tablespoon plus 1 teaspoon sherry vinegar or red wine vinegar

4 cups ice cold water

24 to 36 small cubes or balls green melon, such as honeydew

1. In a food processor, place the almonds, pine nuts, garlic, and salt and process until the nuts are as finely ground as possible (work in short bursts to prevent making a nut butter). Add the 4 cubes melon and process until smooth. Soak the bread in water and squeeze dry. With the processor motor running, add the bread, a few pieces at a time, and process until smooth. With the motor still running, drizzle in the oil until fully incorporated, then add the vinegars. Gradually pour in the water and process until incorporated. Pass through a fine-mesh strainer into a medium bowl.

2. Taste for vinegar and salt and adjust if necessary. Cover and refrigerate at least 2 hours up to overnight.

3. Taste and adjust seasoning again if necessary. Pour into individual chilled bowls. Float the melon cubes in the soup and serve cold.

GAZPACHO

Traditional bright-red gazpacho, which originated in Andalucía, is probably the most popular and well-known Spanish soup in the world. Made with only the finest vine-ripened tomatoes, extra-virgin olive oil, and vinegar with a faint sherry flavor, this refreshing chilled soup is a favorite of many.

But the word "gazpacho" does not denote one specific preparation, but rather a loose grouping of cold soups that fall within certain recognized limits. Equally delicious are other versions, among them green gazpacho, made with green vegetables and herbs, white gazpachos, *ajo blanco*, based on almonds and pine nuts, and *salmorejo*, a thick sauce-like gazpacho.

Purists insist that preparing gazpacho should be an arduous task of mashing ingredients in a mortar or passing them through a cone-shaped strainer called a chinois. But when time constraints necessitate, the use of a modern food processor or blender makes the process much easier. Bread is often used as a thickening agent, but many prefer their gazpachos without it. Always refreshing and always nutritious, gazpacho is sometimes referred to as "liquid salad."

Fresh Bean Gazpacho Ⓥ*

Gazpacho Blanco de Habas El Churrasco

MAKES 4 SERVINGS

For a new slant on the classic soup, this delicious gazpacho uses lima beans to thicken the texture. I've challenged guests to try to guess the secret ingredient, and even those with the most seasoned palates never guess lima beans. The recipe comes from the restaurant El Churrasco in the beautiful city of Cordoba. Make it vegetarian with vegetable broth.

PREPARE AT LEAST 2 HOURS IN ADVANCE

½ pound fresh or frozen lima beans

4 thin slices long-loaf (baguette) bread, crust removed

2 garlic cloves

Salt

3½ tablespoons wine vinegar

6 tablespoons extra-virgin olive oil

1 cup chicken broth or vegetable broth

16 or 24 small cubes or balls of green melon such as honeydew

1. Place the beans in a microwave-safe bowl, add water to cover, and add salt. Cover and cook on High 2 minutes (or bring to a boil in a small saucepan over high heat and cook 5 minutes). The beans will be partially cooked. Drain, reserving ¼ cup cooking liquid and adding water if necessary.

2. Soak the bread in water and squeeze dry. In a food processor, place the bread, garlic, beans, salt, and vinegar and process until smooth. With the motor running, drizzle in the oil until fully incorporated (the mixture will resemble mayonnaise). Transfer to a medium bowl and stir in the ¼ cup reserved cooking liquid and the broth. Taste for vinegar and salt and adjust if necessary. Cover and refrigerate at least 2 hours up to overnight.

3. Taste and adjust seasoning again if necessary. Pour into individual chilled bowls. Float the melon balls in the soup and serve cold.

Beet Gazpacho with Melon and Goat Cheese Ⓥ

Gazpacho de Remolacha con Queso de Cabra

MAKES 4 TO 6 SERVINGS

Beets are the star ingredient in this recipe, giving the gazpacho a much more unique flair than the familiar tomato-based gazpacho from Andalucía.

PREPARE AT LEAST 2 HOURS IN ADVANCE

3 medium beets, trimmed

3 tablespoons extra-virgin olive oil

2 tablespoons sherry vinegar or red wine vinegar

Kosher or sea salt

¼ teaspoon freshly ground black pepper

1 cup coarsely chopped onion (about 1 large)

½ teaspoon ground cumin

1 garlic clove, finely chopped

1 cup chicken broth or vegetable broth

⅓ cup chopped peeled cucumber

1 cup water

1 teaspoon fresh lemon juice

1 cup coarsely chopped green bell pepper (about 1 large)

2 large pasteurized eggs, lightly beaten

16 to 24 small cubes or balls green melon, such as honeydew

Crumbled goat cheese, for garnish

1. Place the beets in a medium saucepan with cold water to cover. Cover and bring to a simmer over low heat. Cook about 1 hour or until the beets are tender when pierced with a knife, replenishing the water if necessary. Let cool then peel them.

2. In a food processor, place the beets and all remaining ingredients except the melon and cheese and process until smooth. With the motor running, gradually add the water. Taste for vinegar and salt and adjust if necessary. If desired, add more water to thin the soup. Cover and refrigerate at least 2 hours up to overnight.

3. Taste and adjust seasoning again if necessary. Pour into individual chilled bowls. Float the melon balls in the soup and garnish with the cheese. Serve cold.

Strawberry Gazpacho Ⓥ
Gazpacho de Fresas

MAKES 4 SERVINGS

As long as gazpacho maintains its pungency with the use of tomatoes, peppers, onion, and garlic, it can be complemented with a variety of sweet fruit flavors. Strawberry gazpacho is one of my favorites. This soup is strained for a smooth finish.

PREPARE AT LEAST 2 HOURS IN ADVANCE

1 pint strawberries, hulled

8 grape tomatoes

1 medium green bell pepper, coarsely chopped (about ¾ cup)

1 medium red bell pepper, coarsely chopped (about ¾ cup)

½ medium onion, coarsely chopped (about ⅓ cup)

4 garlic cloves, coarsely chopped

½ cup extra-virgin olive oil

2 thin slices long-loaf (baguette) bread, crust removed

Kosher or sea salt

3 tablespoons sherry vinegar or red wine vinegar

1. In a food processor, place all the ingredients and process until smooth.

2. Pass through a fine-mesh strainer into a large bowl, pressing to extract the liquid. Discard the solids. Cover and refrigerate at least 2 hours up to overnight.

3. Taste for vinegar and salt and adjust if necessary. Pour into individual chilled bowls and serve cold.

Fruit Gazpacho with Watermelon, Strawberries, and Peaches Ⓥ
Gazpacho de Frutas con Sandía, Fresas y Melocotones

MAKES 4 TO 6 SERVINGS

There is nothing quite as refreshing as this light and fruity gazpacho. This recipe, which still has savory and tart elements, calls for watermelon, strawberries, and peaches, but any fresh fruit that is in season creates a delicious taste combination. This soup is wonderful for an elegant meal. It's garnished with smoked salmon and, if you like, shaved truffles.

PREPARE AT LEAST 2 HOURS IN ADVANCE

1 pound watermelon, seeded and rind removed

1 pint strawberries, hulled

½ pound peaches, peeled, pitted, and coarsely chopped

½ medium green bell pepper, coarsely chopped (about ⅓ cup)

½ medium red bell pepper, seeded and coarsely chopped (about ⅓ cup)

½ medium onion, coarsely chopped (about ⅓ cup)

1 garlic clove, coarsely chopped

2 thin slices long-loaf (baguette) bread, crust removed

continues...

Kosher or sea salt

¼ cup extra-virgin olive oil

¼ cup white wine vinegar

Smoked salmon, coarsely chopped

Truffles, finely chopped (optional)

1. In a food processor, place the watermelon, strawberries, and peaches and process until smooth. Add the peppers, onion, garlic, bread, and salt and process until smooth.

2. Pass through a fine-mesh strainer into a large bowl, pressing to extract the liquid. Discard the solids. In a small bowl, whisk together the oil and vinegar then stir into the soup. Cover and refrigerate at least 2 hours up to overnight.

3. Taste for vinegar and salt and adjust if necessary. Pour into individual chilled bowls. Garnish with the salmon and truffles, if using. Serve cold.

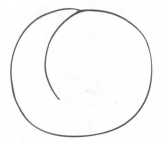

Vegetable and Bean Soups

Mint Soup ⓥ*
Sopa de Menta

MAKES 4 SERVINGS

This soup is created from a minimum of ingredients, so it is crucial to use a high-quality fruity extra-virgin olive oil. Many years ago, Spaniards considered this sopa de menta *to be a stimulant, and it was recommended for people who had delicate stomachs. It can be vegetarian with vegetable broth.*

2 cups chicken broth or vegetable broth

2 cups water

4 sprigs mint

2 thin slices long-loaf (baguette) bread, crust removed

6 tablespoons fruity extra-virgin olive oil

Kosher or sea salt

2 large eggs, lightly beaten

2 teaspoons finely chopped fresh mint, for garnish

1. In a soup pot, combine the broth, water, and mint sprigs and bring to a boil over high heat. Reduce the heat to low, cover, and simmer 20 minutes. Discard the mint.

2. Add the bread, oil, and salt and simmer uncovered 15 minutes more, whisking to break up the bread. Whisk in the eggs and simmer uncovered 10 minutes more or until blended and cooked through. Transfer to a food processor and process until smooth.

3. Pour into individual bowls and sprinkle with the mint. Serve hot or at room temperature.

Garlic Soup, Castilian Style ⓥ*

Sopa de Ajo Castellana

MAKES 4 SERVINGS

Garlic soup has been popular for centuries and was originally made by the shepherds in Castilla. It happens to be one of the easiest soups to prepare since it consists mostly of oil, garlic, bread, and egg. Traditionally, it is made with water, but broth makes for a richer version.

Instead of using whole eggs, it is also common to cover the top of the soup with beaten eggs and run the casserole dish under the broiler. In that case, reduce the number of eggs to 2. It can be vegetarian if made with water.

2 tablespoons olive oil

4 garlic cloves

4 thin slices long-loaf (baguette) bread

1 tablespoon ground paprika

4 cups beef broth, chicken broth, or water

¼ teaspoon ground cumin

Few threads of saffron

Salt

4 large eggs

1. Preheat the oven to 450°F. Heat the oil in a shallow earthenware casserole dish or Dutch oven over medium heat. Add the garlic and cook, stirring, until golden and softened, about 10 minutes (be careful not to burn them). Transfer the garlic to a small bowl, reserving the oil.

2. In the same skillet over medium heat, add the bread and cook, turning once, until golden on both sides, about 8 minutes.

3. Reduce the heat to low, then stir in the paprika. Add the broth, cumin, and saffron and simmer 5 minutes more. Return the garlic to the soup, lightly crushing them with a fork. Season with salt and simmer about 5 minutes more. Crack each egg into a bowl then slide it into the soup. Arrange the bread slices on top of the soup.

4. Transfer to the oven and bake 3 to 4 minutes or until the eggs are set—do not overcook. If using earthenware, serve hot in the dish, or transfer to individual bowls.

Sherried Consommé

Consomé al Jerez

MAKES 6 SERVINGS

There is probably no better soup to begin a three-course meal than this light and flavorful sherried consommé. If you want to make it heartier and more filling, add strips of cooked chicken breast and cured ham, which creates a delightful broth that is known as sopa real.

PREPARE AT LEAST 5 HOURS IN ADVANCE

3 pounds beef bones, such as shin, with meat on them

10 cups water

1 large carrot, peeled and halved crosswise

1 medium onion, halved

2 sprigs parsley

Salt

4 peppercorns

½ teaspoon dried thyme

2 scallions or 1 leek, trimmed and well washed

½ medium turnip, trimmed and peeled

1 medium stalk celery

1 bay leaf

2 large egg whites

2 tablespoons dry sherry, such as Fino

Chopped scallions (green part only), for garnish

continues…

1. Preheat the oven to 350°F. Place the bones in a roasting pan and roast 30 minutes, turning once, until browned. In a large pot, place the bones and all the remaining ingredients except the egg whites, sherry, and chopped scallions and add salt. Bring to a boil over high heat and skim off the foam. Reduce the heat to low and simmer uncovered until reduced by half, about 5 hours, skimming off the foam as necessary.

2. Pass the broth through a fine-mesh strainer and return to the pot. Discard the solids. In a large bowl, beat the egg whites with an electric mixer until firm but not stiff. Gradually stir the soup into the egg whites. Return to the pot and cook, stirring frequently (this clarifies the soup), over low heat about 20 minutes. Strain the broth through cheesecloth into a bowl then return it to the pot. Add the sherry and season with salt. Sprinkle with the scallions and serve hot.

Onion and Almond Soup Ⓥ*
Cebollada con Almendras

MAKES 6 SERVINGS

Ruperto de Nola, chef to King Ferdinand, wrote a sixteenth-century cookbook, the very first one in the Spanish language. In it, he provides a recipe for onion soup that is strikingly similar to what Americans refer to as "French Onion Soup," although it includes extra richness from almonds and a flavor spark from cumin. Make it vegetarian with vegetable broth.

2 tablespoons olive oil
2 large onions, thinly sliced
6 cups chicken broth or vegetable broth
1 cup dry white wine
1 bay leaf
2 sprigs parsley
Salt
Freshly ground white pepper
2 ounces blanched almonds (about 40)
¼ teaspoon ground cumin
6 thin slices long-loaf (baguette) bread, lightly toasted
½ cup grated Parmesan cheese
Sliced toasted almonds

1. Heat the oil in a soup pot over medium heat. Add the onion and cook, stirring, until wilted but not browned, about 7 minutes. Add the broth, wine, bay leaf, parsley, salt, and pepper. Reduce the heat to low, cover, and simmer 30 minutes or until blended.

2. Place the almonds in a food processor or blender and process until chopped as finely as possible (but not a paste). With the motor running, gradually add ½ cup of the broth and process until the liquid is milky white and no pieces remain. Pass through a fine-mesh strainer. (If a lot of almond remains in the strainer, return to the processor with a little broth and process again.) Discard the solids. Return to the pot and add the cumin. Cover and simmer over low heat 30 minutes more to let the flavors meld.

3. Place a broiler rack about 3 inches from the heat source and preheat the broiler. Transfer the soup to a shallow earthenware casserole dish or 6 individual shallow ovenproof bowls. Arrange the toast on top of the soup and sprinkle with the cheese. Broil until the bread and cheese are golden, 3 to 5 minutes—be careful not to let it burn. Sprinkle with the toasted almonds and serve hot.

Peppers and Almond Soup ⓥ
Sopa de Pimientos y Almendra

MAKES 6 SERVINGS

This savory recipe calls for the use of a mortar and a bit of physical exertion, but the results are well worth it because the ingredients are combined perfectly.

2 tablespoons olive oil

¼ pound blanched almonds (about ⅔ cup)

2 thin slices long-loaf (baguette) bread, crust removed

2 garlic cloves, finely chopped

½ medium red bell pepper, coarsely chopped (about ⅓ cup)

½ medium green bell pepper, coarsely chopped (about ⅓ cup)

½ medium onion (about ⅓ cup)

1 teaspoon ground paprika, such as Spanish smoked

Kosher or sea salt

1. Heat the oil in a soup pot over medium heat. Add the almonds and cook, stirring, until golden, about 3 minutes. Transfer the almonds with a slotted spoon to a mortar.

2. Add the bread and garlic to the pot and cook, turning the bread once and stirring the garlic, until golden, 2 to 3 minutes. Transfer to the mortar and mash all the ingredients.

3. Increase the heat to medium-high. Add the peppers and onion and cook, stirring, until tender, about 3 minutes. Stir in the paprika, then transfer the vegetables to the mortar. Mash until well blended.

4. Add the mortar mixture to the pot and add water to cover. Season with more paprika, if necessary, and salt. Bring to a boil over medium-high heat, then reduce the heat to low and simmer 35 minutes or until fragrant and well flavored. Serve hot.

Tomato Soup with Goat Cheese and Anchovy Flan
Sopa de Tomate con Anchoa y Queso de Cabra

MAKES 4 SERVINGS

In this modern take on a classic tomato soup, the goat cheese and anchovies give it an unusual flair and a very memorable flavor.

2 tablespoons olive oil

1 medium onion, finely chopped (about ⅔ cup)

2 garlic cloves, coarsely chopped

1 medium red bell pepper, finely chopped (about ¾ cup)

1 medium green bell pepper, finely chopped (about ¾ cup)

1 pound tomatoes, finely chopped

Kosher or sea salt

Freshly ground black pepper

¼ pound piece Serrano (Spanish cured mountain) ham or prosciutto

2 teaspoons ground bittersweet paprika, such as Spanish smoked

1 bay leaf

½ teaspoon ground cumin

1 dried sweet red pepper (ñora), stemmed and seeded

2 sprigs parsley

½ teaspoon dried oregano

4 cups vegetable broth or chicken broth

Pine nuts and basil leaves, for garnish

Flan

1 cup milk

3 tablespoons goat cheese

6 anchovy fillets

2 eggs

1 egg yolk

continues...

1. Heat the oil in a soup pot over medium heat. Add the onion, garlic, bell peppers, and ham and cook, stirring, until the peppers are slightly softened, about 3 minutes. Stir in the tomato, salt, and black pepper and cook until the tomatoes have softened and released their juice, about 3 minutes more. Stir in the paprika, bay leaf, cumin, chile pepper, parsley, and oregano. Reduce the heat to very low, cover, and cook 30 minutes or until the flavors have blended. Add the broth, simmer uncovered 30 minutes more, and remove from the heat. Remove the bay leaf.

2. Prepare the flan: Place the milk, goat cheese, and anchovies in a medium saucepan and bring to a boil over medium-high heat, stirring constantly. Cook, continuing to stir, until the cheese has melted, about 2 minutes. Pass the mixture through a fine-mesh strainer into a bowl, then stir in the eggs. Discard the solids. Transfer the milk-egg mixture to flan cups or small ramekins.

3. Place the cups in a pan of hot water, bring to a boil over medium heat, and cook 30 minutes or until just set through. Using heat pads to hold the flan cups, turn them over to release the flans into individual bowls. Divide the soup evenly over the flans. Garnish with the pine nuts and basil and serve hot.

Cumin-Scented Tomato Soup with Fresh Figs Ⓥ
Sopa de Tomate al Comino con Higos

MAKES 4 SERVINGS

When I first discovered this very unusual tomato soup, it came as a surprise that the combination of tomatoes, cumin, and figs provided such a perfect match of flavors. It is as beautiful as it is tasty.

1 tablespoon olive oil

1 garlic clove

1 small onion, finely chopped (about ⅓ cup)

4 garlic cloves, finely chopped

¼ pound green frying peppers (padróns), lightly colored red if possible, cored, seeded, and finely chopped

1 pound ripe tomatoes, peeled, seeded, and finely chopped

¼ teaspoon ground sweet paprika, such as Spanish smoked

1½ cups canned crushed tomatoes

Salt

1 bay leaf

2 sprigs parsley

¾ teaspoon ground (or mortar-crushed) cumin

1 cup ½-inch cubes crustless bread

4 fresh figs, such as purple

1. Heat the oil in a soup pot over medium heat. Add the whole garlic clove and cook, stirring, until lightly browned on all sides, 1 to 2 minutes. Transfer the garlic clove to a small bowl and reserve. Add the onion, the chopped garlic, and the peppers and cook, stirring, until softened, 2 to 3 minutes. Reduce the heat to low, cover, and cook 20 minutes more or until blended. Add the chopped tomatoes, increase the heat to medium, and cook until blended, about 5 minutes more. Stir in the paprika, the crushed tomatoes, salt, the bay leaf, parsley, ½ teaspoon of the cumin, the reserved garlic, and the water. Bring to a boil, then reduce the heat to low, cover, and simmer 1 hour more or until fragrant and flavorful.

2. Meanwhile, preheat the oven to 350°F. Arrange the bread on a cookie sheet and bake 5 to 10 minutes or until crisp and browned on all sides.

3. Remove the soup from the heat when done and add the remaining ¼ teaspoon cumin. Taste and adjust seasoning if necessary (it should be well seasoned).

4. Without slicing all the way through, cut the figs lengthwise into quarters. Divide the bread among 4 soup bowls and pour in the soup. Open each fig into the shape of a star and place in the center of each bowl. Serve hot.

Potato and Mushroom Soup Ⓥ*
Sopa de Patata y Rovellones

MAKES 4 SERVINGS

Wild mushrooms and truffles can be found in abundance in the mountain ranges and valleys of Maestrazgo and rovellones *are a prized wild mushroom in Catalunya. This is a delectable, sublime soup, created from an old family recipe and it is one of my all-time favorites. You are unlikely to find* rovellones *but use wild and cultivated mushrooms that you love. Make it vegetarian with vegetable broth.*

1 tablespoon olive oil

1 small onion, finely chopped (about ⅓ cup)

1 small tomato, peeled, seeded, and chopped (about ½ cup)

½ pound shiitake mushrooms or a mix of mushrooms, rinsed, trimmed, and finely chopped

¾ pound potatoes, peeled and coarsely grated

4 cups chicken broth or vegetable broth

Salt

Freshly ground black pepper

1 bay leaf

¾ teaspoon finely chopped fresh thyme or ⅛ teaspoon dried thyme

Heat the oil in a soup pot over high heat. Add the onion and cook, stirring, until wilted and transparent, about 5 minutes. Add the tomatoes and cook 1 minute. Add the mushrooms and potatoes and cook, stirring, until they have softened and release their juices, about 10 minutes more. Stir in the broth and season with salt, pepper, the bay leaf, and thyme. Bring to a boil, then reduce the heat to low, cover, and simmer about 1 hour or until fragrant and flavorful. Remove the bay leaf. Serve hot.

Thick Vegetable Soup, Mallorcan Style Ⓥ*
Sopa Mallorquina

MAKES 4 SERVINGS

This thick and hearty vegetable soup falls somewhere between a soup and stew. Sopas *like these are sometimes accompanied by crudités such as carrot sticks, strips of green bell pepper, radishes, and black olives. Make it vegetarian with vegetable broth.*

2 tablespoons olive oil

4 medium scallions, skins removed and finely chopped

¼ cup finely chopped onion

4 garlic cloves, finely chopped

2 medium green bell peppers, finely chopped (about 1½ cups)

2 tablespoons finely chopped fresh parsley

½ pound tomatoes, peeled, seeded, and coarsely chopped

¾ pound cabbage, coarsely chopped

3 artichoke hearts, quartered

Salt

Freshly ground black pepper

4½ cups chicken broth or vegetable broth

8 or 12 thin slices day-old country bread

Extra-virgin olive oil

continues...

1. Heat the 2 tablespoons oil in a shallow earthenware casserole dish or Dutch oven over medium heat. Add the scallions, onion, garlic, bell peppers, and parsley and cook, stirring, until softened, 1 to 2 minutes. Reduce the heat to low, stir, cover, and cook 15 minutes more or until blended. Increase the heat to medium, stir in the tomatoes, and cook, stirring, until they blend in, about 5 minutes more. Add the cabbage, artichokes, salt, and pepper. Reduce the heat to low, cover, and cook 15 minutes more. Stir in the broth, cover, and cook 20 minutes more or until blended and fragrant (the soup will be quite thick).

2. Preheat the oven to 450°F. Place half of the bread slices under the vegetable soup in the casserole dish and arrange the rest on top of the vegetables. Drizzle the bread with the oil. Bake 10 minutes or until the bread is golden. If using earthenware, serve hot in the dish, or transfer to individual bowls.

Watercress, Bean, and Potato Soup
Potaje de Berros

MAKES 6 SERVINGS

Until recently, Spaniards did little cooking with watercress, which was virtually unknown except in the Canary Islands. Its newfound popularity can be attributed in part to the influences of new wave.

PREPARE 9 TO 14 HOURS IN ADVANCE

½ pound dried white beans, sorted and washed
¼ pound salt pork
4 cups chicken broth or vegetable broth
4 garlic cloves, finely chopped
½ teaspoon salt
Freshly ground black pepper

½ teaspoon ground sweet paprika, such as Spanish smoked
½ teaspoon ground (or mortar-crushed) cumin
2 teaspoons olive oil
2 bunches (about 1 pound) watercress, rinsed, trimmed, and finely chopped
1½ pounds new potatoes, peeled and cut into 1-inch pieces

1. Place the beans in a medium bowl, add cold water to cover by 2 inches, and let soak overnight in the refrigerator. Drain. Place the beans in a soup pot, add the salt pork, 1 quart water, and the broth, and bring to a boil over high heat. Reduce the heat to low, cover, and simmer 1½ to 2 hours or until the beans are almost tender.

2. Meanwhile, in a mortar or mini-processor, mash the garlic, salt, pepper, paprika, and cumin. Stir in the oil.

3. Add the watercress and potatoes to the beans. Thin the mortar mixture by stirring in a little liquid from the pot, then stir the mortar mixture into the soup. Cover and continue cooking over low heat about 30 minutes or until the potatoes are tender. Remove from the heat, cover, and let sit 5 to 10 minutes. Pour the soup into individual soup bowls. Cut the salt pork into 6 pieces and place 1 piece in each bowl. Serve hot.

Swiss Chard, Brussels Sprouts, Lettuce, and Leek Soup
Sopa de Acederas

MAKES 6 SERVINGS

This richly flavored soup is simple to make once you have the ingredients. It usually features sorrel, which can sometimes be found in America, but you can substitute Swiss chard, which is easier to find. You can make it with or without the egg yolks, but they do add a more refined flavor.

2 tablespoons olive oil

2 cups Romaine lettuce hearts, finely sliced crosswise

2 garlic cloves, finely chopped

6 tablespoons trimmed, well washed, and finely chopped leek (white part only)

1 teaspoon dried chervil

2 tablespoons finely chopped shallots

4 cups trimmed, well washed, and finely chopped Swiss chard

6 small Brussels sprouts, trimmed and quartered

7 cups chicken broth or vegetable broth

Salt

Freshly ground black pepper

3 large egg yolks (optional)

Cooked, peeled, and cubed white or red waxy potatoes, pan-fried or boiled (optional)

6 thin slices toasted long-loaf (baguette) bread (optional)

1. Heat the oil in a soup pot over low heat. Add the lettuce, garlic, leek, chervil, shallot, chard, and Brussels sprouts and cook, stirring occasionally, until the lettuce and chard have softened and cooked down, about 8 minutes. Pour in the broth, season with salt and pepper, and bring to a boil. Cover and simmer 1 hour.

2. If using the yolks, place them into a small bowl and stir in a few tablespoons of the hot broth. Stir the mixture into the soup. Add the potatoes and bread, if using. Serve hot.

Vegetable Soup from El Bierzo
Caldo del Bierzo

MAKES 6 SERVINGS

El Bierzo is famous for the superb quality and variety of their locally grown vegetables. What is important to note about this recipe is that the beef is used only to enhance the broth. It is not part of the finished soup, as it would completely alter its essence.

7 cups water

½ pound piece beef stew meat

1 ham bone or ham hock

2 ounces (1 link) chorizo sausage, cut into ¼-inch slices

Kosher or sea salt

Freshly ground black pepper

3 cups trimmed, well washed, and coarsely chopped Swiss chard

½ pound tiny new potatoes, whole if 1½ inches or cut into ¾-inch pieces

¼ pound fresh or frozen baby fava beans or lima beans

1 tablespoon olive oil

1. In a soup pot, bring the water to a boil over high heat. Add the beef, ham bone, chorizo, salt, and pepper and return to a boil. Reduce the heat to low, cover, and simmer 1¼ hours or until the broth is flavorful and cooked through.

2. Add the chard, potatoes, beans, and oil, cover, and simmer 45 minutes more or until the potatoes and beans are tender and the flavors well blended. Taste and adjust seasoning if necessary. Discard the beef and bone (retain the chorizo). Serve hot.

Lentil Soup
Sopa de Lentejas

MAKES 4 TO 6 SERVINGS

The fine chopping of all the ingredients is what makes this lentil soup so delicious. In this version, everything is blended together, as opposed to the more traditional versions with chunks of ham and chorizo. If using Spanish lentils soak them overnight; this is not needed for American lentils. This soup can be served with a side of sardines in oil; figure about 3 to 4 sardines per person. This is actually my preferred way to enjoy lentil soup.

continues…

1 pound dried lentils, such as Spanish, picked over, rinsed, drained

6 cups water

Kosher or sea salt

Freshly ground black pepper

1 medium onion, halved

4 garlic cloves, unpeeled

2 sprigs parsley

2 bay leaves

½ cup small cubes (¼ inch) peeled red potatoes

2 medium onions, finely chopped (about 1⅓ cups)

1 large carrot, cut into ¼-inch cubes (about 2 cups)

¼ cup small cubes (¼ inch) Serrano (Spanish cured mountain) ham or prosciutto (about 2 ounces)

½ cup thin slices (¼ inch) skinned chorizo link sausage

2 teaspoons red or white wine vinegar

I. If using Spanish lentils, place them in a medium bowl, add cold water to cover by 1 inch, and let sit overnight. Drain and rinse.

2. Place the soaked Spanish lentils or other lentils in a soup pot with the water, salt, pepper, the halved onion, the garlic, parsley, and bay leaves and bring to a boil over high heat. Reduce the heat to low, cover, and simmer 1 hour until well blended. Add the potatoes, the chopped onions, the carrot, ham, chorizo, vinegar, and salt. Cover and simmer 30 minutes more or until the lentils are tender.

3. Squeeze the garlic flesh into the soup and discard the skin and the bay leaves. Serve hot.

Lentils with Spinach
Lentejas con Espinacas

MAKES 4 TO 6 SERVINGS

Spinach provides an interesting variation on traditional lentil soup. Spanish lentils must be soaked overnight while American lentils need not be.

1 pound dried lentils, such as Spanish, picked over, rinsed, drained

3 tablespoons olive oil

1 medium onion, coarsely chopped (about ⅔ cup)

5 slices bacon, coarsely chopped

5 cups water

2 cups canned crushed tomatoes

4 sprigs parsley

2 bay leaves

Salt

Freshly ground black pepper

½ teaspoon ground sweet or bittersweet paprika, such as Spanish smoked

½ teaspoon ground cumin

1 tablespoon finely chopped fresh thyme or ½ teaspoon dried thyme

1½ teaspoons finely chopped fresh rosemary or ¼ teaspoon dried rosemary

2 teaspoons wine vinegar

½ head garlic, in 1 piece, loose outer skin removed

8 tiny (1½-inch) new potatoes, peeled

½ pound fresh spinach, well washed

I. If using Spanish lentils, place in a medium bowl, add cold water to cover by 1 inch, and let soak overnight in the refrigerator. Drain.

2. Heat the oil in a soup pot over medium heat. Add the onion and cook, stirring, until wilted and transparent, about 5 minutes. Add the bacon and cook, stirring, until transparent, about 10 minutes more. Stir in the lentils and all the remaining ingredients except the potatoes and spinach and bring to a boil. Reduce the heat to low, cover, and simmer 45 minutes more or until well blended.

3. Add the potatoes, cover, and simmer 15 minutes more or until they are tender, then add the spinach, cover, and simmer 15 minutes more or until the flavors are blended. Squeeze the garlic flesh into the soup and discard the skin and the bay leaves. Serve hot.

Fish Soups

Fish Broth
Caldo de Pescado

MAKES 4 CUPS

Fish broth is an essential element of Spanish cooking; so many dishes are made richer by this flavorful base. I try to always keep some in the refrigerator. Or if you don't have it on hand, plan ahead if your recipe calls for fish broth because you will need more than an hour to prepare it.

½ dozen mussels

4 cups water

1 cup bottled clam juice

1 bay leaf

¼ teaspoon dried thyme

Kosher or sea salt

6 peppercorns

1 medium onion, halved

1 small leek, trimmed and well washed

1 small carrot, peeled

2 sprigs parsley

1 small whiting (about ¾ pound), cleaned

I. Place the mussels in a medium bowl, add cold water to cover, and let sit 30 minutes. Cut or pull off the beards. Drain. Discard any mussels with cracked shells or that do not close tightly when touched.

2. Combine all the ingredients in a large pot and bring to a boil over high heat. Reduce the heat to low, cover, and simmer 1 hour or until the broth tastes well blended.

3. Pass through a fine-mesh strainer into a medium bowl, pressing to extract as much liquid as possible. Discard the solids. Cover and store in the refrigerator up to 5 days.

Fish Broth, Cádiz Style
Caldo de Perro Gaditano

MAKES 4 SERVINGS

Fish broth known as gaditano is a soup with a very distinctive flavor that owes its subtle citrus taste to the juice of the Seville orange, which is the type commonly used to make marmalade. This orange is not easy to find in the United States, but a mixture of sweet orange juice with lemon or lime juice can produce the proper tang.

4 cups storebought or homemade Fish Broth (page 199)

1 pound whiting steaks, about ½ inch thick

Kosher or sea salt

¼ cup olive oil

2 garlic cloves

1 medium onion, finely chopped (about ⅔ cup)

Juice of 1 orange (if Seville orange is available, use 1½ oranges and eliminate the lime juice)

Juice of 1 lime or lemon

I. Prepare the broth if necessary. Season the fish with salt. Let sit 1 hour (this helps to firm the fish).

2. Heat the oil in a deep earthenware casserole dish or Dutch oven over medium heat. Add the garlic and cook, stirring it around in the oil, until golden on all sides, 2 to 3 minutes. Discard the garlic. Add the onion and cook, stirring, until wilted and transparent, about 5 minutes. Add 2 cups of the broth, reduce the heat to low, cover, and simmer 10 minutes. Add the remaining 2 cups broth and the fish, cover, and simmer 15 minutes more or until the broth is well blended.

3. Transfer the fish to a plate. Remove the skin and bones and break the fish into small pieces. Return to the broth. Stir in the orange and the lime juice, if using. If using earthenware, serve hot in the dish, or transfer to individual bowls.

Quick Fish Soup
Sopa al Cuarto de Hora

MAKES 6 SERVINGS

This soup gets its name from the 15 minute cooking time, or un cuarto de hora. *It is a familiar entry on most restaurant menus, though this soup varies from place to place depending on what ingredients the cook has in his or her kitchen that day.*

5 cups water

6 medium clams, such as Manila or littleneck

¼ cup olive oil

2 tablespoons finely chopped onion

⅓ cup finely chopped Serrano (Spanish cured mountain) ham or prosciutto (about 2 ounces)

2 medium tomatoes, peeled and finely chopped (about 1⅓ cups)

⅛ teaspoon ground paprika

1 cup storebought or homemade Fish Broth (page 199; partial recipe) or bottled clam juice

¾ pound fresh cod (skinned and boned), cut into ¾-inch pieces

½ pound medium shrimp, shelled and each cut into 3 pieces

1 cup peas

2 tablespoons cooked rice

1 tablespoon finely chopped fresh flat-leaf parsley

Salt

Freshly ground black pepper

1 large hard-boiled egg, finely chopped

I. In a medium skillet, combine ½ cup of the water and the clams. Bring to a boil over high heat, removing the clams as they open. Discard any unopened clams. Remove the clam meat from the shells, coarsely chop, and reserve. Reserve the cooking liquid.

2. In a deep earthenware casserole dish or Dutch oven, heat the oil over medium-low heat. Add the onion and ham, cover, and cook until the onion is wilted and transparent, about 3 minutes. Add the tomatoes, cover, and cook 5 minutes more or until they soften and release their juices.

3. Stir in the paprika, then gradually add the remaining 4¼ cups water, the reserved clam cooking liquid, and the fish broth. Add the cod, shrimp, peas, rice, and parsley. Season with salt and pepper. Stir in the reserved clam meat and the chopped egg. Let all cook through and blend for 2 minutes, then remove from the heat. If using earthenware, serve hot in the dish, or transfer to individual bowls.

Trout Soup
Sopa de Truchas

MAKES 4 SERVINGS

This soup could not be easier to prepare, as it requires only simple ingredients as well as a very short cooking time. The flavor is made more intense by the inclusion of onions, pepper, and paprika.

2 garlic cloves, finely chopped

⅛ teaspoon kosher or sea salt

4 teaspoons finely chopped fresh flat-leaf parsley

5 tablespoons olive oil

8 slices medium onion, finely chopped

¼ cup finely chopped green bell pepper

¼ cup finely chopped red bell pepper

2 bay leaves

Freshly ground black pepper

½ teaspoon ground bittersweet paprika, such as Spanish smoked

2 (½-pound) trout fillets (skinned), each cut crosswise into 3 pieces

4 thin slices round country loaf bread, toasted

4 cups water

I. In a mortar or mini-processor, mash the garlic, salt, and parsley. Stir in 3 tablespoons of the oil.

2. In a large skillet, heat the remaining 2 tablespoons oil over low heat. Add the onion, bell

peppers, and bay leaves and cook, stirring, until the vegetables are softened, about 10 minutes. Season with salt, black pepper, and paprika. Add the trout and stir to coat well. Add the water and the mortar mixture. Bring to a boil over medium heat, then reduce the heat and simmer until the fish is cooked through and the broth is well blended, about 10 minutes. Remove the bay leaves.

3. Break the bread into pieces and arrange in a shallow earthenware casserole dish. Arrange the trout over the bread, then pour the broth over everything. Cover and let sit 10 minutes. Serve hot.

Fish Soup

Sopa de Pescado

MAKES 4 TO 6 SERVINGS

Chef Juan Mari Arzak is truly a master of new-wave Spanish cuisine, and his restaurant was one of the few recipients of three stars in the Michelin Guide. *To my delight, he provided me with the recipe for this incredibly savory fish soup. Here, every part of the fish and shellfish is used to add flavor. If you prefer the soup to have bits of seafood, add more peeled shrimp in the last minute of cooking.*

PREPARE AT LEAST 2 HOURS IN ADVANCE

8 cups storebought or homemade Fish Broth (page 199; double recipe), vegetable broth, or bottled clam juice, or in combination

1½ pounds fish, such as scorpion fish, halibut, scrod, or monkfish

¼ cup olive oil

1 medium onion, cut into ½-inch-wide slivers

2 leeks, trimmed, well washed, and cut into 2-inch pieces then into ½-inch-wide strips

2 medium carrots, peeled and cut into 2-inch pieces then into ½-inch-wide strips

4 sprigs parsley

2 bay leaves

4 sprigs thyme or ½ teaspoon dried thyme

4 garlic cloves, unpeeled

1 large fish head, such as cod or monkfish, cut into several pieces (optional)

32 to 40 small shrimp, in their shells

3 tablespoons brandy

Salt

Freshly ground black pepper

16 to 24 shelled medium shrimp (optional)

1. Prepare the broth if necessary. Meanwhile, cut the fish into several pieces. Heat the oil in a soup pot over medium heat. Add the onion, leek, carrot, parsley, bay leaves, thyme, and garlic and cook, stirring, until the onion is wilted and transparent, about 5 minutes. Add the fish, fish head, any fish scraps, and the shrimp and cook, stirring, for 1 minute. Add the brandy. Standing well away from the pot, ignite the liquid with a match or kitchen lighter, let it burn briefly, then cover to extinguish.

2. Add the broth, bring to a boil over medium-high heat and cook until the flavors blend, about 10 minutes more. Transfer the fish and shrimp to a platter. Remove any skin and bones from the fish and shell the shrimp. Return the fish scraps and the shrimp shells to the pot. Bring to a boil over medium-high heat and cook until the liquid is reduced and the sauce thickened, about 15 minutes more. Pass through a fine-mesh strainer, pressing with the back of a soup ladle to extract as much liquid as possible, and return to the pot. Discard the solids.

3. Place the reserved shrimp in a food processor and process until as finely chopped as possible. With the motor running, add 2 tablespoons or more of the broth and process until a paste forms. Add the mixture to the pot and stir until well blended. Pass again through the strainer, pressing to extract as much liquid as possible. Return to the pot.

continues...

4. Shred the reserved fish with your fingers and stir it into the pot. Add the shelled shrimp, if using. Season with salt and pepper and bring to a boil over medium heat. Remove from the heat and let cool. Cover and let sit in the refrigerator 2 hours up to overnight. Reheat over medium-low heat, 15 to 20 minutes. Serve hot.

Fish Soup with Dried Red Peppers

Sopa de Pescado con Pimentón

MAKES 4 SERVINGS

In this simple soup made with a minimum of ingredients, the cumin and dried sweet red peppers (ñoras) give it its zing.

2½ cups storebought or homemade Fish Broth (page 199; partial recipe) or diluted bottled clam juice

1 cup water

½ pound sea bass, grouper, or snapper fillets

½ pound plum tomatoes

2 dried sweet red peppers (ñoras) or 1 dried New Mexico (Anaheim) red chile pepper, stemmed and seeded

Salt

2 garlic cloves, finely chopped

¼ teaspoon ground cumin

Freshly ground black pepper

4 teaspoons olive oil

1. Prepare the broth if necessary. In a soup pot, combine the water, broth, fish, tomatoes, chile peppers, and salt and bring to a boil over high heat. Reduce the heat to low, cover, and simmer 30 minutes or until the broth is blended.

2. Transfer the fish to a platter, and cut it into ½-inch pieces. Transfer the chile peppers to a mortar and mash. Add the garlic, cumin, and black pepper and mash, then mash in the oil. Gently mash in the tomatoes, discarding the skin.

3. Return the mortar mixture and the fish to the pot. Reheat over medium-low heat, about 15 minutes. Taste and adjust seasoning if necessary. Serve hot.

Basque Tuna Soup

Marmitako

MAKES 5 TO 6 SERVINGS

The word marmitako *is derived from the Basque word* ameiketako, *which refers to a midmorning meal. Marmitako was greatly enriched when bell peppers, potatoes, and tomatoes arrived from the New World, all of which became essential to the preparation of the soup as we know it today.*

5½ cups storebought or homemade Fish Broth (page 199; double recipe) or 4¾ cups bottled clam juice diluted with water

3 dried sweet red peppers (ñoras) or dried New Mexico (Anaheim) chile peppers, cored and seeded; or
3 medium pimientos, finely chopped

3 tablespoons extra-virgin olive oil

2 medium onions, finely chopped (about 1⅓ cups)

4 garlic cloves, finely chopped

1 pound green (Italian) frying peppers, cored, seeded, and finely chopped

2 tablespoons finely chopped fresh flat-leaf parsley

1 to 2 tablespoons ground sweet paprika, such as Spanish smoked

2 tablespoons brandy

1½ pounds potatoes, such as new or red waxy, peeled and cut into ¾-inch pieces

¾ pound tomatoes, peeled, seeded, and finely chopped

½ cup dry white wine

1 large carrot, peeled and quartered crosswise

1 medium leek, trimmed and well washed

1 dried red chile pepper, halved crosswise and seeded

Salt

Freshly ground black pepper

12 thin slices long-loaf (baguette) bread

1½ pounds tuna steaks, cut into ¾-inch chunks

1. Prepare the broth if necessary. Meanwhile, in a small bowl, place the dried sweet red chile peppers, add warm water to cover, and let soak 20 minutes. Drain.

2. In a large shallow earthenware casserole dish or Dutch oven, heat the oil over medium heat. Add the onions, garlic, frying peppers, parsley, and pimientos (if using instead of dried peppers) and cook, stirring, until the vegetables are softened, about 5 minutes. Reduce the heat to low, cover, and cook 30 minutes or until well blended.

3. Uncover and stir in the paprika (1 tablespoon if using dried peppers, 2 tablespoons if using pimientos). Increase the heat to medium and add the brandy. Standing well away from the casserole dish, ignite the liquid with a match or kitchen lighter and let it die out. Add the potatoes and cook, stirring, until coated, about 1 minute, then add the tomatoes and cook, stirring, until they soften and release their juices, about 2 minutes more. Pour in the broth and wine and add the carrot, leek, and dried red chile pepper. Scrape the flesh of the dried sweet red peppers and add it to the pot. Season with salt and black pepper. Bring to a boil, reduce the heat to low, and simmer until the potatoes are almost tender, about 30 minutes more.

4. Meanwhile, preheat the oven to 350°F. Place the bread slices on a cookie sheet and toast, turning once, about 8 minutes or until lightly golden.

5. Discard the leek, carrot, and dried red chile pepper from the pot, add the tuna, stirring, and simmer until just cooked through, about 3 minutes. Remove from the heat, cover, and let sit 5 minutes. If using earthenware, leave in the dish, or transfer to individual bowls. Serve hot, with the toasted bread placed on top of the soup or on the side.

Saffron-Scented Fish Soup
Suquet de Peix

MAKES 4 SERVINGS

This fish and shellfish soup originated in Catalunya and is made all the more delicious by the inclusion of saffron, which always adds a distinctive flavor to any type of seafood.

PREPARE AT LEAST 3 HOURS IN ADVANCE

1 dozen medium mussels

½ cup dry white wine

½ pound hake or scrod steaks

½ pound monkfish

¼ pound medium shrimp, in their shells

¼ pound bay scallops (whole) or sea scallops (halved)

Salt

Freshly ground black pepper

Pinch saffron threads

¾ teaspoon finely chopped fresh thyme or ⅛ teaspoon dried thyme

1 bay leaf

2 garlic cloves, mashed in a garlic press or mortar

Lemon juice (from ½ lemon)

Fish Broth

1 medium onion

1 small whiting (about ¾ pound)

Few sprigs parsley

1 medium carrot, peeled

½ medium stalk celery

1 small leek, trimmed and well washed, or 3 large scallions

1 bay leaf

Salt

6 peppercorns

1 cup bottled clam juice

6½ cups water

continues…

2 tablespoons olive oil

10 thin slices long-loaf (baguette) bread

1 small onion, slivered

¼ pound leeks, trimmed, well washed, and cut into
    very thin 2-inch strips

¾ pound tomatoes, peeled, seeded, and finely
    chopped

1 tablespoon finely chopped fresh flat-leaf parsley

1. In a large bowl, place the mussels, add cold water to cover, and let sit 30 minutes. Cut or pull off the beards. Drain. Discard any mussels with cracked shells or that do not close tightly when touched.

2. Place the wine and mussels in a large skillet. Bring to a boil over high heat, transferring the mussels as they open to a plate. Discard any unopened mussels. Pass the cooking liquid through a fine-mesh strainer and reserve ½ cup, adding water if necessary. Let cool. Remove the mussels from their shells.

3. Cut the hake and monkfish into ¾-inch pieces and shell the shrimp. (Save all the bones, scraps, and shells for the fish broth.) In a medium bowl, combine the mussels, shrimp, hake, scallops, and monkfish. Add the reserved cooking liquid, salt, pepper, saffron, thyme, bay leaf, 1 of the mashed garlic cloves, and the lemon juice. Cover and let marinate in the refrigerator 2 hours.

4. Meanwhile, prepare the broth: In a large soup pot, place all the ingredients, plus the reserved fish scraps, shells, and bones and bring to a boil over high heat. Reduce the heat to low and simmer uncovered until well blended, about 1 hour. Pass the broth through a fine-mesh strainer and reserve 6 cups. Discard the solids.

5. Preheat the oven to 350°F. In a cup, combine the remaining 1 tablespoon of the oil with the remaining 1 mashed garlic clove. Brush the oil on both sides of the bread and place the bread on a cookie sheet. Bake about 8 minutes, turning once, until lightly golden.

6. In a shallow earthenware casserole dish or Dutch oven, heat the remaining 1 tablespoon oil over low heat. Add the onion, the cut leeks, and the chopped garlic and cook, stirring, until the onion is wilted and transparent, about 5 minutes. Add the tomatoes and cook until they soften and release their juices, about 5 minutes more.

7. When the strained broth is ready, gradually add it to the casserole dish with the vegetables, stirring, and simmer until well blended, about 30 minutes more. Add the marinated fish with its liquid, bring to a boil, and simmer until just cooked through, about 5 minutes. Remove from the heat, cover, and let sit 10 minutes. Remove the bay leaf. If using earthenware, leave in the dish, or transfer to individual bowls. Float the bread in the soup and sprinkle with the parsley. Serve hot.

Chickpea, Spinach, and Cod Potage Lerranz
Potaje de Garbanzo Lerranz

MAKES 6 SERVINGS

This recipe came to me through my friend Tomás Herranz, a fine chef who owned both a casual tapas bar and an elegant restaurant in Madrid. Tomas is unfortunately no longer with us, but his culinary gift is very much remembered.

PREPARE 27 TO 39 HOURS IN ADVANCE

½ pound dried salt cod (boned but skin on)

1 pound dried chickpeas, sorted and washed

2 tablespoons olive oil

4 garlic cloves, finely chopped

1 medium onion, finely chopped (about ⅔ cup)

2 tablespoons finely chopped fresh flat-leaf parsley

2 teaspoons all-purpose flour

2 teaspoons ground sweet paprika, such as Spanish
    smoked

¼ teaspoon saffron threads, crumbled

10 cups water

½ head garlic, in 1 piece, loose outer skin removed

1 medium onion, halved

1 small leek, trimmed and well washed

1 bay leaf

Salt

Freshly ground black pepper

½ teaspoon ground (or mortar-crushed) cumin

½ pound new or red waxy potatoes, peeled and cut into ½-inch pieces

½ pound fresh spinach, well washed and coarsely chopped

1 large hard-boiled egg, finely chopped

1. Place the cod in a medium bowl and add cold water to cover. Cover and let sit in the refrigerator 24 to 36 hours, changing the water occasionally, until the water no longer tastes salty. Meanwhile, place the chickpeas in a medium bowl with cold water to cover. Cover and let sit in the refrigerator overnight. Drain the cod and the chickpeas.

2. Heat the oil in a large soup pot over low heat. Add the chopped garlic, chopped onion, and the parsley and cook, stirring, until the onion is wilted and transparent, about 5 minutes. Stir in the flour, paprika, and saffron. Add the water, the ½ head garlic, the halved onion, the leek, bay leaf, and cod. Bring to a boil over medium heat, removing the cod as soon as the boil is reached. Shred the cod with your fingers and reserve. Add the chickpeas to the pot, cover, and simmer 1 hour. Season with salt, pepper, and cumin, cover, and cook 1 hour more or until the chickpeas are almost tender.

3. Add the potatoes, cover, and cook about 20 minutes more or until the potatoes are almost tender. Discard the leek, the ½ head garlic, and the bay leaf.

4. Add the reserved shredded cod and the spinach, cover, and cook 5 minutes more. Remove from the heat, cover, and let sit 1 hour to thicken and meld flavors. Taste and adjust seasoning if necessary. Reheat over medium-low heat, about 15 minutes. Garnish with the egg and serve hot.

Shrimp Soup
Sopa de Langostinos

MAKES 4 SERVINGS

This simple yet sublime shrimp soup has a base of light tomato sauce combined with strong seasonings that give it a kick. I like to serve it with fried bread.

4 cups storebought or homemade Fish Broth (page 199)

3 tablespoons olive oil

¼ pound medium shrimp, in their shells

1 medium onion, thinly sliced

1 medium stalk celery, finely chopped

1 bay leaf

2 sprigs parsley

6 black peppercorns

Kosher or sea salt

3 tablespoons dry white wine

3 tablespoons tomato sauce

8 thin slices long-loaf (baguette) bread

1. Prepare the broth if necessary. Meanwhile, shell the shrimp and reserve the shells. Heat 2 tablespoons of the oil in a soup pot over medium heat. Add the shrimp shells, onion, and celery and cook, stirring, until the shrimp and vegetables are opaque, about 5 minutes. Remove and reserve the shrimp.

2. Add the broth, shrimp shells bay leaf, parsley, peppercorns, and salt, reduce the heat to low, and simmer until well blended, about 20 minutes. Pass the broth through a fine-mesh strainer and return to the pot. Discard the solids.

3. Heat the remaining 1 tablespoon oil in a medium skillet over medium heat. Add the shrimp and cook, stirring, until lightly coated with the oil, about 1 minute. Add the wine and cook about 2 minutes more. Stir in the broth and tomato sauce, reduce the heat to low, and simmer until heated through and blended, about 5 minutes more. Serve hot with the bread on the side.

Potato, Egg, and Shrimp Soup

Sopa de Patatas con Gambas y Huevo

MAKES 4 SERVINGS

This strongly seasoned broth made with diced potatoes, shrimp, and hard-boiled egg is as tasty as it is satisfying. Like most soups, the flavor is enhanced if left to sit at least 30 minutes before serving.

3 cups water

1 cup storebought or homemade Fish Broth (page 199; partial recipe) or bottled clam juice

¼ pound shrimp, in their shells

½ pound small new potatoes, peeled

1 medium tomato, halved and seeded

½ medium onion, coarsely chopped (about ⅓ cup)

¼ pound green (Italian) frying peppers, coarsely chopped

2 garlic cloves

2 sprigs parsley

1½ teaspoons finely chopped fresh thyme or ¼ teaspoon dried thyme

1½ teaspoons finely chopped fresh rosemary or ¼ teaspoon dried rosemary

⅛ teaspoon saffron threads, crumbled

1 tablespoon olive oil

2 hard-boiled eggs, coarsely chopped

Salt

1. In a soup pot, combine the water and broth, add salt, and bring to a boil over high heat. Add the shrimp and cook until just opaque, about 5 minutes. Transfer the shrimp to a bowl with a slotted spoon. Keep the liquid in the pot. Shell the shrimp, return the shells to the pot, and reserve the shrimp. Add all the remaining ingredients except the eggs and salt and bring to a boil over high heat. Reduce the heat to low, cover, and simmer 30 minutes or until the potatoes are tender.

2. Transfer the potatoes to a medium bowl. Pass the broth through a fine-mesh strainer, pressing with the back of a soup ladle to extract as much liquid as possible, and return to the pot. Discard the solids. Cut the potatoes into ½-inch pieces or, using a melon scoop, cut round pieces of a similar size. Add the potatoes to the pot along with the reserved shrimp and half of the eggs. Season with salt. Bring to a simmer over low heat and cook until blended, about 5 minutes. Remove from the heat, cover, and let sit 30 minutes.

3. Reheat over medium-low heat, about 10 minutes. Sprinkle with the remaining egg, and serve hot.

Creamy Crayfish Soup

Crema de Cangrejos

MAKES 4 SERVINGS

River crabs (crayfish) are a staple on the central plains of Castilla. If you can't find crayfish, a small lobster works just as well. This is one of the very few Spanish soup recipes that call for heavy cream.

1 cup storebought or homemade Fish Broth (page 199; partial recipe) or bottled clam juice

2 to 2½ dozen crayfish or one (1¼- to 1½-pound) freshly killed lobster

3 tablespoons unsalted butter

1 tablespoon olive oil

½ medium carrot, peeled and finely chopped (about ¼ cup)

¼ medium onion, finely chopped (about 2 tablespoons)

1 bay leaf

1 tablespoon finely chopped fresh flat-leaf parsley

1 small tomato, coarsely chopped (about ½ cup)

2 tablespoons brandy

½ cup dry white wine

⅛ teaspoon ground sweet paprika, such as Spanish smoked

3¾ cups water

⅛ teaspoon saffron threads, crumbled

1½ teaspoons finely chopped fresh thyme or
   ¼ teaspoon dried thyme

Freshly ground black pepper

Kosher or sea salt

2 large egg yolks or 2 tablespoons heavy cream

1. Prepare the broth if necessary. In a soup pot, heat 1 tablespoon of the butter and the oil over medium heat. Add the carrot, onion, and bay leaf and cook, stirring, until the onion is wilted and transparent, about 3 minutes. Add the parsley and tomato and cook, stirring, until the tomato softens and releases its juice, about 3 minutes more. Increase the heat to high, add all of the crayfish, and cook, turning once, until they turn opaque, about 5 minutes more. Remove the crayfish and remove the meat from the shells. Reserve the meat and return the shells to the broth. Add the brandy. Standing well away from the pot, ignite the liquid with a match or kitchen lighter and let die out. Stir in the broth and wine.

2. Stir in the paprika and add the water, saffron, thyme, pepper, and salt. Bring to a boil over high heat, cover, reduce the heat to low, and simmer 45 minutes or until the flavors are well blended. Pass through a fine-mesh strainer and return to the pot. Discard the solids.

3. Place the yolks in a small bowl, stir in a few tablespoons of the cooking liquid, then add to the pot. Stir in the remaining 2 tablespoons butter and the reserved crayfish meat. Simmer uncovered until the crayfish is heated through, about 3 minutes more. Serve hot.

Note: If using lobster, here's the preparation: Leaving the shell on, cut the tail from the lobster and cut into 3 rings. Cut the head into 4 pieces. Divide each large claw into 2 pieces and lightly crush the shells for easy removal of the meat. Leave the small claws whole. When cutting the lobster, reserve as much of the liquid that collects as possible.

Shark Soup with Roasted Peppers
Sopa de Cazón con Pimientos Asados

MAKES 4 SERVINGS

Cazón, *a shark found off the shores of Cádiz (which is the oldest continuously inhabited city in the western hemisphere), is a very popular staple, eaten and cooked in many different ways. You can use shark available fresh at your fishmonger or fish steak. This recipe calls for* piquillo *peppers, but if they are not available, other types of peppers may be substituted.*

6 cups storebought or homemade Fish Broth
   (page 199; double recipe)

2 dozen very small clams, such as Manila

2 tablespoons olive oil

1 large onion, finely chopped (about 1 cup)

2 garlic cloves, finely chopped

1 large tomato, finely chopped (about 1 cup)

1 pound shark or other mild fish steak, cut into
   ¾-inch chunks

6 (jarred) piquillo peppers, cut into thin strips

1 teaspoon ground cumin

⅛ teaspoon saffron threads, crumbled

2 thin slices long-loaf (baguette) bread

Kosher or sea salt

1 tablespoon mayonnaise (mayonesa; page 359)

2 teaspoons fresh lemon juice

1. Prepare the broth if necessary. Rinse the clams. Discard any with cracked shells or that do not close tightly when touched.

2. Heat the oil in a medium skillet over medium heat. Add the onion and then 2 minutes later the

continues . . .

garlic and cook until both are softened, about 3 minutes more. Add the tomato and cook, stirring, until softened and the juices release, about 5 minutes more. Add the fish and cook, stirring, until opaque on the outside, 1 to 2 minutes more.

3. Transfer the skillet contents to a large soup pot, add the fish broth, and season with salt. Add the peppers, cumin, saffron, and bread, reduce the heat to low, and simmer until blended, about 10 minutes. Place the mayonnaise in a cup, gradually stir in a few tablespoons of broth (not too hot) until blended, and stir the mixture into the pot. Stir in the clams and cook until they open. (Discard any unopened clams.) Stir in the lemon juice. Serve hot.

Baby Squid Soup
Sopa Marmitako de Chipirones

MAKES 4 SERVINGS

Marmitako *is the quintessential Basque stew, made with dried sweet red peppers, called* ñoras. *It is typically prepared with fresh tuna, as in Basque Tuna Soup, page 202, but this version calls for small squid.*

2 cups storebought or homemade Fish Broth
　　(page 199; partial recipe)

½ pound small squid

2 dried sweet red peppers (ñoras)

4 tablespoons olive oil

1 medium onion, finely chopped (about ⅔ cup)

1 garlic clove, finely chopped

2 medium green bell peppers, finely chopped
　　(about 1½ cups)

1 medium red bell pepper, finely chopped (about
　　¾ cup)

½ pound potatoes, peeled and cut into ¼-inch cubes

2 medium tomatoes, finely chopped (about 1⅓ cups)

Kosher or sea salt

Freshly ground black pepper

2 tablespoons finely chopped fresh flat-leaf parsley

1. Prepare the broth if necessary. Meanwhile, make a small slit at the pointed end of each squid. Rinse thoroughly, letting the water run through the body sac. Let drain and pat dry with paper towels. Cut into rings, if desired. Reserve. Place the chile peppers in a small bowl, add warm water to cover, and let soak 20 minutes. Drain. Scrape off the flesh from the peppers, discard the seeds, and reserve the pulp.

2. In a shallow earthenware casserole dish or Dutch oven, heat 2 tablespoons of the oil over medium heat. Add the onion and 2 minutes later the garlic and cook, stirring, until both are softened, about 3 minutes more. Add the peppers and cook, stirring, until softened, about 5 minutes. Add the broth, potatoes, the reserved pepper pulp, the tomatoes, salt, and black pepper. Reduce the heat to low and simmer until the potatoes are tender, about 20 minutes.

3. Meanwhile, heat the remaining 2 tablespoons oil in a small skillet over medium heat. Add the squid and cook, stirring, until opaque and cooked through, about 2 minutes. Add to the pot and cook 1 minute more. Sprinkle with the parsley and serve hot.

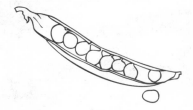

Poultry and Meat Soups

Thick Chicken Broth with Pastry Puffs
Sopas de Bunyolets Morellense

MAKES 4 SERVINGS

This is an elegant and beautifully presented soup that is garnished with unsweetened pastry puffs seasoned with ham and parsley. The recipe will probably make more puffs than you need, but they are also excellent eaten on their own. Optimally, this soup is made with the broth of a chickpea stew. If you do not have that on hand, a chicken broth thickened and flavored with cooked potatoes and chickpeas can be substituted.

Chicken Broth

½ **pound chicken parts, including the neck and gizzard**

¼-**pound piece Serrano (Spanish cured mountain) ham or prosciutto**

1 **small onion**

1 **garlic clove**

½ **cup mashed cooked chickpeas, fresh or canned**

¼ **pound potatoes, peeled and cut into ½-inch pieces**

2 **sprigs parsley**

1½ **teaspoons finely chopped fresh thyme or ¼ teaspoon dried thyme**

1 **bay leaf**

6 **peppercorns**

Salt

6½ **cups water**

Puffs (Bunyolets)

3 **tablespoons olive oil**

⅛ **teaspoon salt**

½ **cup all-purpose flour**

2 **large eggs**

Olive oil, for frying

2 **tablespoons finely chopped fresh flat-leaf parsley**

2 **tablespoons finely chopped Serrano (Spanish cured mountain) ham or prosciutto**

1. Prepare the broth: In a soup pot, combine all the broth ingredients and bring to a boil over high heat. Reduce the heat to low, cover, and simmer about 1½ hours or until blended and the liquid has concentrated. Remove the chicken pieces from the broth and discard. Pass the broth through a fine-mesh strainer, pressing with a soup ladle to push through as much solid matter as possible. Reserve ½ cup of the broth and return the rest to the pot. Discard the solids.

2. Prepare the puffs: In a medium saucepan, place the ½ cup reserved broth, the 3 tablespoons oil, and the salt and bring to a boil over high heat. Reduce the heat to medium, add the flour all at once, and stir until the mixture leaves the side of the pot and forms a ball. Continue cooking, flattening and turning the dough with a wooden spoon, about 2 minutes more. Remove from the heat and let cool 1 minute. Transfer to a food processor, add the eggs, and process until incorporated, about 15 seconds.

3. Heat at least 1 inch of oil in a medium skillet over medium-high heat (or better still, use a deep-fryer set at 375°F) until it quickly browns a cube of bread. Working in small batches, drop the dough by ½ teaspoonfuls into the oil. Reduce the heat to medium and cook, turning once, until golden and puffed. Transfer with a slotted spoon to paper towels and let drain.

4. Divide the soup among small shallow bowls and float several bunyolets in each. Serve hot.

Cream of Partridge Soup
Crema de Perdiz

MAKES 4 SERVINGS

This very rich soup is not much different than a rich chicken soup, but it is a classic recipe calling for partridge. Similar to making chicken soup, you can either make the soup using a whole bird or enjoy a meal with the cooked bird then make soup with the carcass. (If using the carcass, it is essential that the bones still have some meat on them.) This is one of the few Spanish soups that require heavy cream, and it is filling enough to be a meal on its own.

1 partridge (about 1 pound), 2 or more partridge carcasses, or 2 quail

1 small carrot, peeled and cut into pieces

1 medium onion

1 sprig parsley

¼ teaspoon dried thyme

1 whole clove

3 cups water

1 cup dry white wine

Salt

4 peppercorns

1 bay leaf

10 medium mushrooms

3 tablespoons unsalted butter

3 tablespoons all-purpose flour

½ cup milk

½ cup heavy cream

1 tablespoon dry sherry, such as Fino

1. In a soup pot, place the partridge (or carcasses), carrot, onion, parsley, thyme, clove, water, wine, salt, peppercorns, and bay leaf and bring to a boil over high heat. Reduce the heat to low, cover, and simmer 1½ hours or until well blended and the liquid is more concentrated. Discard the parsley, clove, peppercorns, and bay leaf. Transfer the partridge to a plate and skin and bone it. (If using the carcasses, discard them.) Reserve the broth in the pot.

2. In a medium skillet, heat 1 tablespoon of the butter over medium heat. Add the mushrooms and cook until softened, about 5 minutes. Transfer the mushrooms to a food processor or blender and add the partridge meat, if you used the whole bird. Add the carrot and onion from the broth and process until smooth. With the motor running, gradually add at least 6 tablespoons of the reserved broth.

3. In a medium saucepan, melt the remaining 2 tablespoons butter over medium heat. Add the flour and cook, stirring, until it absorbs the butter and starts to brown, about 1 minute. Add the remaining reserved broth (there should be about 3½ cups) and the mushroom mixture, cover, and cook 15 minutes or until blended. Pass through a fine-mesh strainer and return to the pot. Discard the solids.

4. Combine the milk and cream in a large, heatproof bowl. Gradually whisk in the hot soup until well blended. Stir in the sherry. Taste and adjust the seasoning if necessary. Serve hot (or keep warm in a double boiler, as direct heat might curdle the soup).

Ham Soup

Sopa de Jamón

MAKES 4 SERVINGS

This recipe calls for a hearty blend of cured ham and chopped hard-boiled eggs, but the ingredient that truly gives this soup its zest is the dried sweet red chile peppers.

¼ cup olive oil

4 thin slices long-loaf (baguette) bread

½ cup small cubes (¼ inch) Serrano (Spanish cured mountain) ham or prosciutto (about ¼ pound)

6 cups chicken broth or vegetable broth

4 garlic cloves

Freshly ground black pepper

4 small dried sweet red peppers (ñoras) or 2 dried red New Mexico (Anaheim) chile peppers, stemmed and seeded

Kosher or sea salt

2 large hard-boiled eggs

1 tablespoon finely chopped fresh flat-leaf parsley

1. Heat the oil in a soup pot over medium heat. Add the bread and cook, turning once, until golden on both sides, about 8 minutes. Transfer to paper towels, let drain, and reserve.

2. Add the ham to the pot and cook, stirring, 1 minute. Add the broth, garlic, black pepper, and peppers and bring to a boil over medium heat. Stir in salt. Reduce the heat to low, cover, and simmer 30 minutes.

3. Transfer the garlic and chile peppers to a mortar and mash, discarding the pepper skins. Mash in the egg yolks, adding 1 tablespoon broth to facilitate mashing. Stir the mortar mixture into the broth in the pot.

4. Finely chop the egg whites. Divide the soup among individual bowls, sprinkle with the egg white and parsley, and float the reserved bread on top. Serve hot.

Galician Meat, Potato, Greens, and Bean Soup

Caldo Gallego

MAKES 4 TO 6 SERVINGS

This common soup found throughout Spain originated in Galicia, a region with a strong Celtic heritage. Different chefs have very different—and sometimes very passionate opinions—when it comes to one of the ingredients: chorizo. *Old-fashioned recipes tend to include it, as it does make for a heartier and more filling soup.* Grelos, *the Spanish equivalent to collard greens, feature prominently here, creating an earthy flavor.*

PREPARE AT LEAST 10 TO 14 HOURS IN ADVANCE

½ pound dried white beans, sorted and washed

1 tablespoon olive oil

2 garlic cloves, finely chopped

1 teaspoon ground sweet paprika, such as Spanish smoked

7 cups water

1 pound boneless beef chuck

1 beef or ham bone

¼-pound piece Serrano (Spanish cured mountain) ham or prosciutto

2 ounces slab bacon or salt pork

1 leek, trimmed and well washed

½ pound collard greens, Swiss chard, or kale, well washed, thick stems trimmed, and coarsely chopped

¾ pound small (2-inch) new or red waxy potatoes, peeled

¼ pound sweet chorizo sausage

Salt

continues...

1. Place the beans in a medium bowl, add cold water to cover by 1 inch, and let soak overnight in the refrigerator. Drain.

2. Heat the oil in a small skillet over medium heat. Add the garlic and cook, stirring, 1 minute (the garlic should not color). Remove from the heat and stir in the paprika. Stir in 1 to 2 tablespoons of water, enough to combine the seasonings.

3. In a soup pot, stir together the water, beans, beef, bone, ham, bacon, leek, and the garlic mixture and bring to a boil over high heat. Reduce the heat to low, cover, and simmer about 2 hours or until the beans are almost tender. Add the greens, potatoes, chorizo, and salt, cover, and cook about 30 minutes more or until the potatoes are tender.

4. Transfer the beef, ham, bacon, leek, and chorizo to a bowl, cut into bite-size pieces, and return to the pot. Discard the bone. Remove from the heat, cover, and let sit 10 minutes or until slightly thickened. Reheat if necessary and serve hot.

Meatball and Artichoke Soup
Sopa de Albondiguillas y Alcachofas

MAKES 4 SERVINGS

This is an unusual soup made incredibly delicious by little pork meatballs to which I add a pinch of cinnamon and some pine nuts. Bread acts as the thickening agent, as is typical with so many Spanish soups.

3 tablespoons bread crumbs

4 cups plus 2 tablespoons chicken broth or vegetable broth

1 pound lean ground pork or a mixture of ground pork and veal

2 tablespoons finely chopped pine nuts

1 slice bacon, finely chopped

1 tablespoon finely chopped fresh flat-leaf parsley

⅛ teaspoon ground cinnamon

1 garlic clove, finely chopped

1 large egg, separated

1¼ teaspoons salt

Freshly ground black pepper

3 tablespoons olive oil

¼ cup finely chopped onion

½ teaspoon ground sweet paprika, such as Spanish smoked

4 or 6 fresh or frozen (thawed) artichoke hearts, quartered

1 slice long-loaf (baguette) bread, crust removed, cut into small cubes

1. In a medium bowl, soak the bread crumbs in 2 tablespoons of the chicken broth. Add the pork, pine nuts, bacon, parsley, cinnamon, garlic, the egg yolk, salt, and pepper and mix well with your hands. Shape into ¾-inch meatballs.

2. In a small bowl, beat the egg white with a fork until foamy. Heat 2 tablespoons of the oil in a shallow earthenware casserole dish or Dutch oven over medium-high heat. Dip the meatballs into the egg white then place them in the oil, (do not crowd them in the pan), and cook, turning each once, just until no longer pink in the middle, about 5 minutes. Transfer to a platter. Wipe out the casserole dish.

3. Heat the remaining 1 tablespoon oil in the casserole dish over medium heat. Add the onion and cook, stirring, until wilted and transparent, about 5 minutes. Stir in the paprika, then add the broth, artichokes, and meatballs. Simmer until the artichokes are tender and the broth is blended, about 15 minutes more.

4. In a medium bowl, combine the bread and 4 tablespoons of broth from the casserole dish. Whisk until smooth. Stir into the soup, taste and adjust seasoning if necessary, and serve hot in the dish, or transfer to individual bowls.

Stews

Bean Stew
Potaje de Judías

MAKES 4 TO 6 SERVINGS

This recipe for rich bean stew is definitely one of my favorites. It's a specialty in the province of Segovia, where these broad beans — with a creamy texture when cooked and similar to kidney beans — are grown. Their distinctive flavor is enhanced by the addition of dried sweet red peppers called ñoras *and saffron, which give this dish extra flair.*

PREPARE AT LEAST 10 TO
14 HOURS IN ADVANCE

1 pound large dried kidney or broad beans, such as
    Spanish judiones, sorted and washed

2 tablespoons olive oil

1 medium sweet onion, such as Vidalia, coarsely
    chopped (about ⅔ cup)

1 head garlic, loose outer skin removed

4 small or 2 medium mild dried red chile peppers
    (ñoras), such as New Mexico (Anaheim),
    stemmed and seeded

1 medium tomato, coarsely chopped (about ⅔ cup)

3 sprigs parsley

1 tablespoon finely chopped fresh thyme or
    ½ teaspoon dried thyme

8 peppercorns

Scant ¼ teaspoon saffron threads, crumbled

1 bay leaf

7 cups water

Kosher or sea salt

¼ pound sweet semi-cured chorizo sausage

¼-pound piece Serrano (Spanish cured mountain)
    ham or prosciutto

¼-pound piece slab bacon or salt pork (optional)

1. Place the beans in a large bowl, add cold water to cover by 1 inch, and let soak overnight in the refrigerator. Drain.

2. Heat the oil in a stew pot over medium heat. Add the onion, garlic, and chile peppers and cook, stirring, until the onion is softened, about 5 minutes. Add the tomato, parsley, thyme, peppercorns, saffron, and bay leaf and cook, stirring, 1 to 2 minutes. Add the water, salt, chorizo, ham, and bacon, if using, and bring to a boil. Reduce the heat to low, cover, and simmer 2 to 2½ hours or until the beans are tender and the liquid slightly thickened. Remove from the heat.

3. Transfer the peppers, garlic, chorizo, ham, and bacon to a plate. Scrape off the flesh of the peppers, add to the pot, and discard the skins. Squeeze the garlic flesh into the pot and discard the skin. Cut the chorizo into thick slices and the ham and salt pork into chunks and add them to the pot. Reheat if necessary and serve hot.

Asturian Bean Stew
Fabada Asturiana

MAKES 6 TO 8 SERVINGS

Asturias is so well known for its delectable fabada *that many of the region's other popular dishes have gone vastly unnoticed. This robust and thoroughly satisfying thick bean stew will warm your bones on a cold winter night. If you like, you can use salted pork hocks for the smoked hocks, but soak them in water for several hours and drain them before using.*

PREPARE 11 TO 15 HOURS IN ADVANCE

2 pounds very large dried white beans, sorted and
    washed

¾ pound black sausage (morcilla)

¾ pound chorizo sausage

continues...

1 pound smoked or salted pork hocks, cut into several pieces (if hocks are salted, soak several hours before using)

¾ pound slab bacon, cut into chunks

½ cup cold water

Salt

2 tablespoons olive oil

2 garlic cloves, mashed in a garlic press or mortar

1 tablespoon ground paprika

1. Place the beans in a large bowl, add cold water to cover by 1 inch, and let soak overnight in the refrigerator. Place the beans and their liquid in a stew pot. Add the black sausage, chorizo, hocks, and bacon and bring to a boil over high heat. Add the water to cut the boil, reduce the heat to low, cover, and simmer at least 2 hours or until the beans and meat are tender. Test frequently to avoid overcooking and remove from the heat immediately when done. Season with salt if necessary.

2. Heat the oil in a small saucepan over medium heat. Add the garlic and paprika and cook, stirring, until the garlic begins to sizzle. Add this to the beans, stir gently, cover, and remove from the heat. Let sit at least 1 hour or until thickened and the flavors meld.

3. Reheat the stew over medium heat and transfer to a large shallow casserole dish. Arrange the meat on top. Once you have presented the meal to your guests, cut the meat into serving pieces and serve with the beans. Guests should then proceed to cut up the meats and mix them with the beans.

Basque Red Bean Stew
Alubias Rojas del Goierri

MAKES 4 SERVINGS

Bean stews in the Basque Country are typically accompanied by long skinny hot Basque peppers called guindillas vascas. *I was fortunate to meet the world-renowned chef, Juan Mari Arzak, who credits his mother for this delicious recipe featuring these peppers. If you can't find them, use another mild chile such as New Mexico (Anaheim) or* padróns.

PREPARE AT LEAST 10 TO 14 HOURS IN ADVANCE

1 pound dried deep red beans, such as Spanish, sorted and washed

6 cups water

Kosher or sea salt

¼ cup olive oil

1 medium onion, halved

¼ pound semi-cured soft cooking sweet chorizo sausage

¼ pound black sausage with onion (morcilla)

¼ pound salt pork

2 medium green bell peppers, cored, seeded, and finely chopped

3 garlic cloves, finely chopped

Basque hot peppers (optional)

1. Place the beans in a large bowl, add cold water to cover by 1 inch, and let soak overnight in the refrigerator. Drain. Place in a stew pot with the water, salt, 2 tablespoons of the oil, and half of the onion and bring to a boil over high heat. Reduce the heat to low, cover, and simmer about 2 hours or until the beans are tender.

2. Meanwhile, prick the chorizo and black sausage with a fork and place in a medium skillet with the salt pork. Add water to cover, bring to a boil over medium-high heat, and simmer until the sausages are cooked through, about 20 minutes. Transfer the sausages and pork to a plate and cut into 1-inch pieces. Wipe out the skillet.

3. Finely chop the remaining half of the onion. Heat the remaining 2 tablespoons oil in the skillet over medium heat. Add the bell peppers, the chopped onion, and the garlic and cook, stirring, until softened, about 10 minutes. Cover and cook 15 minutes more or until the flavors meld. Stir the sausages,

pork, and the onion mixture into the beans. Taste and adjust seasoning if necessary. Serve hot with the hot peppers, if using, on top or on the side.

Beans with Clams
Fabes con Almejas

MAKES 4 TO 6 SERVINGS

I never would have guessed that beans and clams, which seem like an unlikely combination of flavors, actually blend together wonderfully and make for a unique and very unusual stew. Good crusty bread should accompany this dish.

PREPARE 10 TO 14 HOURS IN ADVANCE

1 pound dried large white beans, sorted and washed

2 medium onions, halved

4 garlic cloves

2 medium carrots, peeled and halved crosswise

2 sprigs parsley

2 bay leaves

1 cup cold water

Clams

6 tablespoons olive oil

2 tablespoons finely chopped onion

4 garlic cloves, finely chopped

2 dozen very small clams such as Manila or littleneck, at room temperature

1 tablespoon ground paprika

2 tablespoons finely chopped fresh flat-leaf parsley

½ cup white wine

½ dried red chile pepper, crushed

Salt

Freshly ground black pepper

Few threads of saffron

Salt

Fresh crusty bread

1. Place the beans in a large bowl, add cold water to cover by 1 inch, and let soak overnight in the refrigerator. Drain. Place in a stew pot with cold water to cover. Add the onions, the 4 whole garlic cloves, the carrots, parsley, and bay leaves and bring to a boil over high heat. Add the water to cut the boil, reduce the heat to low, cover, and simmer 1½ to 2 hours or until the beans are tender.

2. Meanwhile, prepare the clams: Rinse the clams. Discard any with cracked shells or that do not close tightly when touched.

3. When the beans are almost tender, heat the oil in a large skillet over medium heat. Add the onion and garlic and cook, stirring, until the onion is wilted and transparent, about 3 minutes. Increase the heat to medium-high, add the clams, and cook, stirring frequently, until they open. Remove each clam as it opens. Reserve the cooking liquid. Discard any unopened clams.

4. Stir in the paprika and parsley. Add the wine, chile pepper, salt, and black pepper and cook, stirring occasionally, until the flavors meld, about 5 minutes more.

5. Stir the saffron and salt into the beans, then add the clams and their cooking liquid. Shake the pot to mix in the clams and the liquid. Cover and cook 5 minutes more or until blended. Divide the stew among individual soup bowls and arrange the clams on top. Serve with the bread.

Broad Beans with Sausage and Pig's Foot
Judiones de la Granja

MAKES 4 TO 6 SERVINGS

Judiones are broad beans, well known for their subtle flavor and texture, and are grown almost exclusively in the province of Segovia. This is a delicious and extremely tasty bean dish, made that much heartier with the addition of pork.

PREPARE 9 TO 14 HOURS IN ADVANCE

1 pound large dried broad beans (judiones preferred) or lima beans, sorted and washed

¼ pound (2 links) chorizo sausage, cut into 1-inch pieces

¼-pound piece Serrano (Spanish cured mountain) ham or prosciutto, cut into 1-inch cubes

1 pig foot, split in half

1 pig ear (optional)

2 tablespoons olive oil

1 medium onion, finely chopped (about ⅔ cup)

2 garlic cloves, finely chopped

1 teaspoon ground paprika

1 pimiento, finely chopped

¼ pound tomatoes, finely chopped

1 tablespoon finely chopped fresh flat-leaf parsley

2 bay leaves

Salt

1. Place the beans in a large bowl, add cold water to cover by 1 inch, and let soak overnight in the refrigerator. Drain. In a stew pot, combine the beans, chorizo, ham, pig foot, and pig ear, if using, add water to cover, and bring to a boil over high heat. Reduce the heat to low, cover, and simmer 1½ to 2 hours or until the beans are almost tender.

2. Heat the oil in a medium skillet over medium heat. Add the onion and garlic and cook, stirring, until the onion is wilted and transparent, about 5 minutes. Stir in the paprika. Add the pimiento,

tomatoes, parsley, and bay leaves and cook, stirring, until the tomatoes soften and the flavors blend, about 10 minutes. Add to the beans, season with salt, and cook until the beans are tender and the flavors meld, about 30 minutes more. Take the pig foot and ear, if using, out of the pot. Remove the meat from the bone and add it to the beans. Discard the bone and the bay leaves. Serve hot.

Bean and Partridge Stew
Habichuelas con Perdiz

MAKES 4 SERVINGS

This recipe comes from a family in the tiny town of Zuheros in the province of Cordoba. A delicious stew of white beans, potatoes, and partridge (quail works just as well), it is made extra special by the flavor of the dried sweet red peppers. I first tasted this dish in the family's beautiful hotel. Partridge can dry out if overcooked, so make sure to keep it moist and stop cooking just when the flesh is no longer pink.

PREPARE 10 TO 14 HOURS IN ADVANCE

1 pound dried white beans, such as Spanish fava or navy, sorted and washed

3 tablespoons olive oil

1 medium onion, finely chopped (about ⅔ cup)

2 small green (Italian) frying peppers, finely chopped

4 garlic cloves, finely chopped

2 small dried sweet red peppers (ñoras) or 1 dried New Mexico (Anaheim) red chile pepper, stemmed and seeded

1 medium ripe tomato, finely chopped (about ⅔ cup)

6 cups water

Kosher or sea salt

Freshly ground black pepper

2 partridges or 4 quail, quartered

½ cup dry white wine

¾ cup chicken broth or vegetable broth

1 bay leaf

½ pound tiny (1½-inch) white potatoes, peeled

1. Place the beans in a large bowl, add cold water to cover by 1 inch, and let soak overnight in the refrigerator. Drain. Heat 2 tablespoons of the oil in a stew pot over medium heat. Add the onion, frying peppers, garlic, and chile peppers and cook, stirring, until the onion and peppers are softened, about 8 minutes. Stir in the tomato and cook 2 minutes. Add the beans, water, salt, and black pepper and bring to a boil over high heat. Reduce the heat to low, cover, and simmer 2 hours or until the beans are almost tender.

2. Meanwhile, season the partridges with salt. In a shallow earthenware casserole dish or Dutch oven, heat the remaining 1 tablespoon oil, add the partridges and cook, turning once, until lightly browned, about 8 minutes. Stir in the wine, broth, bay leaf, salt, and pepper and bring to a boil. Reduce the heat to low, cover, and simmer, keeping the partridge moist, 30 minutes or until the partridge is just cooked through.

3. Remove the chile peppers, scrape off the flesh, and return it to the bean pot, discarding the skin. Add the potatoes to the pot and simmer 10 minutes. Add the partridges and their cooking liquid, cover, and simmer until the potatoes and beans are tender, about 15 minutes more. Serve hot.

Chickpea Stew, Zamora Style
Garbanzos a la Zamorana

MAKES 4 TO 6 SERVINGS

This is a very simple chickpea stew that originated in Zamora in northern Spain. With its strong flavor of paprika, this hearty stew has a particular zest. It is served in small portions as a tapa at the bar in the magnificent Hotel Parador of Zamora.

PREPARE 14 TO 18 HOURS IN ADVANCE

1 pound dried chickpeas, sorted and washed

1 pound lean pork, cut into ¾-inch pieces

Marinade

1¼ teaspoons ground bittersweet paprika, such as Spanish smoked

⅛ teaspoon ground hot paprika, such as Spanish smoked, or cayenne pepper

4 garlic cloves, finely chopped

1 small onion, coarsely chopped (about ⅓ cup)

3 tablespoons finely chopped fresh flat-leaf parsley

3 tablespoons extra-virgin olive oil

¾ teaspoon ground cumin

½ teaspoon dried oregano

1 bay leaf

Kosher or sea salt

Freshly ground black pepper

¼-pound piece Serrano (Spanish cured mountain) ham or prosciutto

4 teaspoons ground bittersweet paprika, such as Spanish smoked

1 medium onion, halved

1 medium tomato, coarsely chopped (about ⅔ cup)

7 cups water

Salt

1. Place the chickpeas in a large bowl, add cold water to cover by 1 inch, and let soak overnight in the refrigerator. Drain.

2. In a medium bowl, combine marinade ingredients and mix thoroughly. Add pork and stir to coat. Cover and let marinate at least 2 hours in the refrigerator.

3. In a stew pot, combine the chickpeas, the pork and its marinade, and all the remaining ingredients and bring to a boil over high heat. Reduce the heat to low, cover, and simmer about 2 hours or until the chickpeas are almost tender. Uncover, increase the heat to medium, and cook until the chickpeas are tender, 15 to 30 minutes (there should be some liquid, but the stew should not be soupy). Season with salt. Cover and let sit 10 minutes to let the flavors meld. Serve hot.

Cocidos, stews that are sometimes known as "meals in a pot," are the ultimate comfort food in Spain and can be found in every region. Traditionally, the main ingredient was chickpeas, which came to Spain by way of the Moors, and through the centuries was dismissed as peasant food. But over time, with the addition of more expensive ingredients such as meats and sausages, the *cocido* has become to some the national dish of Spain.

The word *cocido* derives from *cocer,* which means to cook or broil. It is a direct descendent of the Sephardic stew *adafina*. Spaniards are very passionate about these long-simmering stews, first enjoyed in their youth. Ingredients can include vegetables such as potatoes, carrots, cabbage, and of course chickpeas, with each person favoring his or her regional variations. Some stews in central Spain include a kind of meatball made with chopped ingredients from the stewpot. In Catalunya, there are beans as well as chickpeas in the *cocido* called *escudella*.

The proper way to present a *cocido* is in several courses. First serve the broth, then platters with vegetables and the chickpeas, and then an array of meats. Many *cocido* lovers consider *bolos*, quenelle-like dumplings, an essential part of their time-honored stew.

Chickpea Stew with Bolos, Galician Style
Cocido Gallego con Bolos de Olla de Digna Prieto

MAKES 6 TO 8 SERVINGS

Almost every region of Spain has its own unique version of this classic chickpea stew. Whether they be Catalan, Galician, Castilian, or Andalusian, it seems that every Spaniard has fond memories of these hot, comforting stews from their childhood. Many cocido *lovers profess that* bolos, *quenelle-like dumplings, are an integral part of their favorite stew.*

PREPARE 12 TO 16 HOURS IN ADVANCE

1 pound dried chickpeas, such as Spanish, sorted and washed

18 cups water

½-pound piece meaty slab bacon

2 beef bones

Kosher or sea salt

Freshly ground black pepper

¾ pound smoked ham hock

3 chicken thighs, skin and fat removed

2 pounds beef stew meat, cut into 1½-inch pieces

4 sprigs parsley

1 small onion

1 leek, trimmed and well washed

4 whole garlic cloves

⅛ teaspoon saffron threads, crumbled

1 pound small (2½-inch) white potatoes, peeled

¾ pound semi-cured soft cooking chorizo sausage

Bolos

1 large onion, finely chopped (about 1 cup)

3 garlic cloves, finely chopped

3 teaspoons fresh mint, finely chopped

4½ tablespoons cornmeal

4½ tablespoons rye flour (can be found in health food stores)

2 tablespoons lightly beaten egg

1¾ pounds Swiss chard, well washed, thick stems trimmed, and coarsely chopped

1 cup cooked very thin pasta, such as angel hair

2 tablespoons lightly beaten egg

Kosher or sea salt

Freshly ground black pepper

1. Place the chickpeas in a medium bowl, add cold water to cover by 1 inch, and let soak overnight in the refrigerator. Drain and loosely enclose in cheesecloth or a cotton net sack.

2. In a large stew pot, combine the chickpeas, water, bacon, beef bones, salt, and pepper and bring to a boil over high heat. Reduce the heat to low, cover, and simmer 30 minutes. Add the ham hock, chicken, beef, parsley, onion, leek, and whole garlic cloves and bring to a boil. Skim off the foam, cover, and simmer 2½ hours or until the beans are tender. (If you wish, let cool and refrigerate overnight, then remove the fat that rises to the surface.) Do not remove from the heat.

3. About 40 minutes before the beans are done, transfer 4 cups broth to a smaller pot. Add the saffron, potatoes, and chorizo and bring to a boil over medium-high heat. Reduce the heat to low, cover, and simmer 40 minutes or until the potatoes are tender, while simmering the beans 40 minutes more as well.

4. Meanwhile, prepare the bolos: Heat the oil in a large skillet over medium heat. Add the onion, chopped garlic, and the mint and cook, stirring, 1 minute. Reduce the heat to low, cover, and cook about 20 minutes or until the onion is softened. Transfer to a medium bowl.

5. Add the cornmeal, rye flour, egg, and ¼ cup broth from the large pot to the bowl. Remove the bacon from the large pot, finely chop 9 tablespoons, and add to the bowl. Return the remaining piece to the pot.

6. Using your hands, mix the ingredients in the bowl. Form into sausage shapes, about 2 inches long and 1 inch wide. Add the chard and the bolos to the small pot with the potatoes and chorizo. Continue simmering both pots about 20 minutes more. Remove both pots from the heat and let sit 30 minutes.

7. Remove the meat and vegetables from both pots. Pass the broth from both pots through a fine-mesh strainer and return to the large pot. Reserve the solids.

8. Stir the salt and the cooked pasta into the pot. Discard the bones, skin, and fat from the ham hock. Cut the ham, beef, bacon, and chicken into serving pieces. Cut the chorizo into halves or thirds and the potatoes in half. Coarsely chop the leek.

9. On one large platter, place the chickpeas and chorizo. On another large platter, arrange the meat, potatoes, leek, bolos, and chard. Cover both platters with foil. Drizzle with some broth to keep moist.

10. Serve the broth hot, then serve the two platters hot as a second course. If you like, heat the platters (without the foil) briefly in a microwave before bringing them to the table.

Tripe and Chickpeas, Galician Style

Callos a la Gallega

MAKES 4 SERVINGS

The flavors of tripe and chickpeas mix splendidly in this long-cooking hearty stew from Galicia. It will have to simmer most of the day on the stove, but the taste is well worth it. Serve with fresh, crusty bread.

PREPARE 14 TO 19 HOURS IN ADVANCE

½ **pound dried chickpeas, sorted and washed**

1 **pound beef tripe**

1 **pig foot, split in half**

1 **ham or beef bone, with some meat on it**

4 **cups water**

5 **peppercorns**

Salt

2 **bay leaves**

5 **garlic cloves, unpeeled but loose outer skin removed**

1 **medium onion**

2 **tablespoons olive oil**

2 **garlic cloves, peeled**

1 **tablespoon finely chopped fresh flat-leaf parsley**

½ **cup white wine**

1 **medium onion, finely chopped (about ⅔ cup)**

2 **ounces (1 link) chorizo sausage, coarsely chopped**

1 **tablespoon all-purpose flour**

1 **tablespoon ground paprika**

Fresh crusty bread

1. Place the chickpeas in a large bowl, add cold water to cover by 1 inch, and let soak overnight in the refrigerator. Drain and reserve.

2. Rinse the tripe well. Place in a stew pot, add water to cover, and bring to a boil over high heat. Drain. Cut into 1½-inch squares and return to the pot. Add the pig foot, ham bone, water, peppercorns, salt, and 1 of the bay leaves and bring to a boil over high heat. Reduce the heat to low, cover, and simmer about 4 hours.

3. Meanwhile, when the tripe has been cooking for 2 hours, place the chickpeas in a separate large pot with water to cover. Add the unpeeled garlic cloves, the remaining 1 bay leaf, the whole onion, and salt and bring to a boil over high heat. Reduce the heat to low, cover, and simmer 1½ to 2 hours or until the chickpeas are just tender. Discard the garlic and onion. Drain the chickpeas and reserve.

4. Heat the oil in a small skillet over medium heat. Add the peeled garlic cloves and cook, stirring, until they start to brown, about 5 minutes. Transfer to a food processor, reserving the oil in the skillet. Add the parsley to the processor and blend until the garlic and parsley are finely chopped. Gradually add the wine and process until smooth. Reserve.

5. Heat the reserved oil in the skillet over medium heat. Add, the chopped onion and cook, stirring, until wilted and transparent, about 5 minutes. Add the chorizo, reduce the heat to low, and cook, stirring, until just cooked through, about 3 minutes. Stir in the flour, cook for 1 minute, and stir in the paprika. Remove from the heat.

6. Add the chickpeas to the pot with the tripe along with the processor mixture and the chorizo-onion mixture. Taste and adjust seasoning if necessary. Cover and continue cooking over low heat 2 to 3 hours more or until the tripe is very tender. Serve with the crusty bread.

Thick Chickpea and Chorizo Soup
Sopa de Garbanzos y Chorizo

MAKES 4 SERVINGS

This flavorful combination of chickpeas and chorizo falls somewhere between a soup and a stew. Some aspects of this very hearty and filling dish are reminiscent of a traditional cocido. Make it even heartier by adding potatoes.

PREPARE 10 TO 14 HOURS IN ADVANCE

¾ pound dried chickpeas, sorted and washed

3 garlic cloves

½ medium onion

2 sprigs parsley

1 bay leaf

Salt

Freshly ground black pepper

¾ pound (6 links) chorizo sausage

¼ pound slab bacon

3 potatoes, cut into 1-inch cubes (optional)

I. Place the chickpeas in a large bowl, add cold water to cover by 1 inch, and let soak overnight in the refrigerator. Drain. Place in a stew pot, add cold water to cover, and add all the remaining ingredients. Bring to a boil over high heat. Reduce the heat to low, cover, and simmer about 2 hours or until the chickpeas are tender.

2. Meanwhile, if using the potatoes, place in a medium saucepan with cold water to cover; add salt. Cover and bring to a simmer over low heat. Cook about 10 minutes to parboil. Drain and add to the pot during the last 30 minutes of simmering.

3. Skim the fat off the stew, cut the chorizo into thick slices, and cut the bacon into 4 pieces. Remove the bay leaf. Divide the soup and chorizo among 4 individual soup bowls and add 1 piece of bacon to each. Serve hot.

Chickpea and Cuttlefish Stew
Potaje de Garbanzos y Chocos

MAKES 4 SERVINGS

This delicious and easy-to-prepare stew brings together chickpeas and cuttlefish (sepia), a perfect combination and a favorite dish of many Andalusians. Although the firm texture of cuttlefish works better than finer-fleshed squid, you can substitute it if cuttlefish is not available. Cleaning and prepping cuttlefish can be quite involved, so buy it cleaned or have it cleaned by the fishmonger.

PREPARE 9 TO 14 HOURS IN ADVANCE

1 pound cleaned cuttlefish or large squid

1 pound dried chickpeas, sorted and washed

5 cups water

1 head garlic, loose outer skin removed

2 tablespoons olive oil

4 sprigs parsley

1½ teaspoons ground sweet paprika, such as Spanish smoked

1 medium tomato, finely chopped (about ⅔ cup)

1 small onion

One (1-inch) piece medium-hot dried red chile pepper, such as Basque, cored and seeded

2 bay leaves

¾ pound small (1½-inch) new potatoes, peeled

Kosher or sea salt

I. Place the chickpeas in a medium bowl, add cold water to cover by 1 inch, and let soak overnight in the refrigerator. Drain. Cut the cuttlefish tentacles into individual tentacles (if using squid, cut the tentacles in half crosswise). Cut the body lengthwise into ½-inch strips, then crosswise into 1½-inch pieces.

continues...

2. In a stew pot, combine the chickpeas, water, garlic, oil, parsley, I teaspoon of the paprika, the tomato, onion, chile pepper, and bay leaves and bring to a boil over high heat. Reduce the heat to low, cover, and simmer 1½ hours or until the chickpeas are almost tender.

3. Add the cuttlefish and potatoes, season with salt, and cook until the chickpeas, potatoes, and cuttlefish are tender, about 30 minutes more. Stir in the remaining ½ teaspoon paprika. Remove from the heat, cover, and let sit 15 minutes so the flavors meld. Remove the bay leaves. Reheat if necessary and serve hot.

Lobster Stew, Menorca Style
Calderota de Langosta Menorquina

MAKES 4 SERVINGS

This recipe comes from the Casa Burdo Restaurant on the island of Menorca. It is a bit messy to eat because guests are encouraged to use their hands to break open the lobster shells, but it is often a source of great fun at dinner parties. The lobster in this stew is tender and delicious.

6 cups storebought or homemade Fish Broth (page 199; double recipe), bottled clam juice, or water

4 (1-pound) live lobsters

1 cup olive oil

5 garlic cloves

4 medium onions, coarsely chopped (about 2⅔ cups)

2 pounds tomatoes, peeled and seeded

3 medium green bell peppers, coarsely chopped (about 2¼ cups)

2 tablespoons finely chopped fresh flat-leaf parsley

Salt

8 thin slices long-loaf (baguette) bread, lightly toasted (optional)

1. Prepare the broth if necessary. Meanwhile, place a cutting board in a rimmed cookie sheet to catch the liquid that collects. Place the lobster on its back on the cutting board. Do not remove the bands that keep the claws shut. Protect your hand with a heavy towel or pot holder and hold the lobster firmly by the head. Plunge the tip of a heavy chef's knife into the body where the tail joins the chest. Cut all the way through, separating the tail from the body. Pull out and discard the dark vein from the tail. Slice the head down the middle, discard the stomach sack, transfer the tomalley (green matter) to a mortar, and reserve the coral (red roe), if any. Cut the lobster tail into pieces at the joints and cut off the large and small claws. Partially crush the large claws for easy removal of the meat when serving. Reserve.

2. Heat the oil in a large shallow earthenware casserole dish or Dutch oven over medium heat. Add I clove of the garlic and cook, stirring, until softened, about 2 minutes. Discard the garlic clove. Add the lobster a few pieces at a time and cook only a few seconds, turning once, until the shell just turns bright red. Transfer to a platter. Repeat with the remaining lobster. Reserve 4 tablespoons of the oil in the skillet.

3. In a food processor or blender, place the onions, tomatoes, bell peppers, parsley and the 4 remaining garlic cloves and process until smooth—in several stages if necessary. Add to the casserole dish, add the broth, and cook over low heat until well blended, about 15 minutes. Add more liquid if the soup thickens too much (it is, however, a thick soup). Stir in salt. Do not remove from the heat.

4. In a processor or blender, place the reserved tomalley and coral, if any, and process until smooth. Add to the casserole dish and cook, about 15 minutes more. (Continue cooking to serve, or everything may be made in advance up to this point.) Let cool, cover, and refrigerate the lobster and the soup.

5. Add the lobster to the casserole dish, bring to a simmer over low heat, and cook 10 minutes or until heated through and the flavors meld. Take the casserole dish to the table. Place 2 slices of the bread, if using, in each soup dish and ladle the soup over the bread. Serve the lobster on a platter and let guests serve themselves, either placing in the soup or eating after the soup.

Fish Stew, Catalan Style
Suquet

MAKES 4 SERVINGS

The unusual, nutty flavor of this stew is due to the addition of toasted almonds. The tastes blend together well, creating quite an unexpectedly delightful flavor.

1½ cups storebought or homemade Fish Broth (page 199; partial recipe) or bottled clam juice

8 large clams such as Manila or littleneck

1 dozen medium mussels

¾ cups water

1 slice lemon

5 tablespoons olive oil

6 garlic cloves

4 thin slices long-loaf (baguette) bread

12 blanched almonds, lightly toasted

2 tablespoons finely chopped fresh parsley

Few threads of saffron

Salt

¾ teaspoon ground paprika

1½ tablespoons all-purpose flour

2½ pounds fish steaks, preferably of 2 types, such as halibut, striped bass, tile fish, or fresh cod (skinned and boned), cut into 1½-inch pieces

6 tablespoons dry white wine

2 tablespoons peas

Freshly ground black pepper

1. Prepare the fish broth if necessary. Meanwhile, rinse the clams and mussels well. Cut or pull off the mussel beards. Discard any clams or mussels with cracked shells or that do not close tightly when touched.

2. Place the clams and mussels in a large skillet, add the ¾ cups water and the lemon slice, and bring to a boil over high heat, removing the clams and mussels as they open. Discard any unopened shells. Remove the clam and mussel meat from the shells, cut the meat in half, and reserve. Pass the cooking liquid through a fine-mesh strainer into the pot with the broth.

3. Heat the oil in a shallow earthenware casserole dish or Dutch oven over medium heat. Add the garlic and cook, stirring, until golden on all sides. Transfer to a food processor or blender, reserving the oil in the skillet.

4. In the same skillet over medium heat, add the bread and cook, turning once, until golden, and transfer to the processor. Add to the processor the almonds, parsley, saffron, and salt and process until a paste forms. Add the paprika, flour, and ¼ cup of the broth and process until smooth. Gradually add the remaining broth.

5. Add the processor mixture to the casserole dish and bring to a boil over medium heat. Add the fish, wine, peas, salt, and pepper. Reduce the heat to low, cover, and simmer about 12 minutes or until the flavors meld. Stir in the clams and mussels. If using earthenware, serve hot in the dish, or transfer to individual bowls.

Vinegar Fish Soup
Gazpachuelo

MAKES 4 SERVINGS

Despite the misconception, this soup actually has little in common with classic gazpacho, even though its name is derived from it. I prefer to use a firm white fish such as halibut, but tilefish and fresh cod work just as well. The vinegar creates a tartness that complements the vegetables and the fish.

1 pound fish steak, such as halibut, tilefish, or fresh cod

4 cups cold water

2 tablespoons dry white wine

½ cup storebought or homemade Fish Broth or bottled clam juice

1 bay leaf

½ small onion

Salt

Freshly ground black pepper

1 pound red, waxy potatoes, peeled and cut into ¼-inch slices

1½ cups mayonnaise (mayonesa; page 359)

2 tablespoons red wine vinegar

1. In a stew pot, combine the fish, water, wine, clam juice, bay leaf, onion, salt, and pepper and bring to a boil over high heat. Reduce the heat to low and simmer until blended, about 10 minutes. Remove from the heat, cover, and let sit until cool.

2. Remove the fish from the pot, remove any skin or bone, and cut the fish into chunks. Place in a shallow medium bowl and add broth to cover. Add the potato slices to the broth in the pot, cover, and cook until the potatoes are barely tender, about 20 minutes. Transfer the potatoes to the bowl with the fish. Pass the broth through a fine-mesh strainer. Discard the solids.

3. Place the mayonnaise in a soup tureen and whisk in the vinegar. Slowly whisk in the hot broth. Fold in the potatoes and fish. Serve hot. (If the soup needs to be reheated, do so in a double boiler so the soup won't curdle.)

Potted Quail
Caldereta de Codornices

MAKES 4 SERVINGS

An extremely simple dish of quail and onion in broth, this wonderful recipe came to me by chance when I stopped into a small, nondescript restaurant in the Pyrenees.

2 tablespoons olive oil

3 medium onions, coarsely chopped (about 2 cups)

3 garlic cloves

8 quail

2 tablespoons red wine vinegar

1 bay leaf

3 sprigs parsley

6 peppercorns

4 cups water

3 cups chicken broth or vegetable broth

Salt

4 ounces thin noodles, such as angel hair (optional)

1. Heat the oil in a stew pot over medium heat. Add the onion and garlic and cook until the onion is wilted and transparent, about 5 minutes. Add all the remaining ingredients except the noodles. Reduce the heat to low, cover, and simmer 1½ hours or until the flavors meld. (Check one quail periodically to make sure they aren't overcooking; if they look cooked, remove them from the pot and cover.)

2. Remove most of the broth and pass it through a fine-mesh strainer into a small saucepan. Leave the quail in the pot and cover to keep warm. Discard the solids in the strainer.

3. If using the noodles, about 20 minutes before you're ready to serve, fill a medium saucepan with water, add salt, and bring to a boil over high heat.

Add the noodles and cook until almost al dente, tender yet still firm to the bite. Drain.

4. Add the noodles, if using, to the broth. Serve the broth hot first. Serve the quail as the main course, reheating if necessary.

Lamb Stew, Extremadura Style
Caldereta Extremeña

MAKES 4 SERVINGS

This stew comes from the Extremadura region, where lamb is traditionally raised. Tasty and robust, it is fairly easy to prepare with exceptional results. The lamb should be only of the finest quality. Serve with boiled new potatoes and a green salad. Using lard is traditional and adds a special flavor, but you can use more oil instead.

1 tablespoon olive oil

1 tablespoon lard

6 garlic cloves

1¾ pounds boneless lamb, cut into 2-inch pieces (or lamb pieces with some bone)

1 small onion, finely chopped (about ⅓ cup)

1 bay leaf

½ teaspoon dried thyme

2 teaspoons ground paprika

½ dried red chile pepper, seeded

Salt

Freshly ground black pepper

¾ cup dry red wine

¼ cup water

1 pimiento

1 tablespoon vinegar

1. Heat the oil and lard in a deep earthenware casserole dish or Dutch oven over medium heat. Add the garlic and cook, stirring, until lightly browned. Transfer to a small bowl and reserve.

2. Increase the heat to high, add the lamb, and cook, turning, until browned on all sides. Reduce the heat to low, add the onions, and cook, stirring, until wilted and transparent, about 5 minutes. Stir in the bay leaf, thyme, chile pepper, salt, and black pepper. Add the wine and simmer until slightly reduced, 1 to 2 minutes. Add the water, cover, and simmer 30 minutes or until the flavors meld.

3. Meanwhile, in a food processor or blender, place the reserved garlic and the pimiento and process until finely chopped. With the motor running, add the vinegar and 1 to 3 tablespoons of the cooking liquid from the lamb to form a smooth, thick sauce. Stir into the lamb pot and cook until the lamb is tender, at least 1 hour more, adding more water if the sauce thickens too much. Remove the bay leaf. If using earthenware, serve hot in the dish, or transfer to individual bowls.

Lamb and Red Pepper Stew
Cordero al Chilindrón

MAKES 4 SERVINGS

In Navarra, chilindrón *is the typical way to prepare lamb—with tomatoes and peppers, in this case pimientos. It is a strongly flavored stew with a bit of a kick to it. Depending on your preference, you can make it with or without the bones. Serve with boiled or roasted potatoes and a green salad.*

PREPARE AT LEAST 2 HOURS IN ADVANCE

2 tablespoons olive oil

2 to 2½ pounds lamb, cut into 2-inch pieces

Salt

Freshly ground black pepper

1 medium onion, coarsely chopped (about ⅔ cup)

1 garlic clove, finely chopped

3 pimientos, cut into thin strips

1 pound fresh or canned tomatoes, coarsely chopped

1 tablespoon finely chopped fresh flat-leaf parsley

1 bay leaf

continues...

1. Heat the oil in a deep earthenware casserole dish or Dutch oven over high heat. Add the lamb and cook, turning, until well browned on all sides. Add the onion and garlic and cook, stirring, until the onion is wilted and transparent, about 5 minutes. Stir in the pimientos, tomatoes, parsley, bay leaf, salt, and pepper.

2. Reduce the heat to low, cover, and simmer 1½ to 2 hours or until the lamb is tender. If using earthenware, serve hot in the dish, or transfer to individual bowls.

Beef Stew, Catalan Style
Estofado a la Catalana

MAKES 4 SERVINGS

The use of chocolate, nuts, or pork sausage (such as the white sausage butifarra, *which is flavored with cinnamon and nutmeg) in a dish is what is usually referred to as "Catalan style." The small amount of chocolate in this recipe adds an unpredictable tartness to the savory stew. Serve with a green bean salad.*

PREPARE AT LEAST 2 HOURS IN ADVANCE

1 tablespoon olive oil

¼ pound slab bacon, cut into 4 pieces

2 pounds beef chuck, cut into 1½-inch pieces

1 large onion, finely chopped (about 1 cup)

4 garlic cloves

1 tablespoon all-purpose flour

1 cup dry red wine

1 sprig parsley

1 bay leaf

⅛ teaspoon dried oregano

¼ teaspoon dried thyme

½ cup beef broth, chicken broth, or water

Salt

Freshly ground black pepper

½ teaspoon coarsely grated bittersweet chocolate

2 large potatoes, peeled and cubed

One (16-inch) pork sausage (butifarra) or 4 sweet Italian-style sausages

1. In a deep earthenware casserole dish or Dutch oven, place the oil and bacon and heat over low heat until the bacon turns transparent and gives off its oil. Add the beef, increase the heat to medium, and cook, turning, until well browned on all sides. Add the onion and garlic and cook, stirring, until the onion is wilted and transparent, about 5 minutes. Stir in the flour, then add the wine, parsley, bay leaf, oregano, thyme, broth, salt, and pepper. Reduce the heat to low, cover, and simmer about 2 hours or until the beef is tender.

2. Meanwhile, place the potatoes in a small saucepan, add cold water to cover, and add salt. Cover and bring to a simmer over low heat. Cook about 15 minutes or until almost tender. Drain. Add to the casserole dish, stir in the chocolate, and continue cooking until the potatoes are tender, about 10 minutes more.

3. In a medium skillet over medium heat, cook the sausage until browned and no longer pink in the center. Cut into ½-inch slices.

4. Remove the bay leaf from the casserole dish. Divide the stew among individual bowls or rimmed plates and arrange the sausage on the plate. Serve hot.

Garlic Beef Stew
Estofado de Vaca

MAKES 4 SERVINGS

Garlic adds a delicious flavor to this stew without being the least bit overpowering. Be sure to cook the garlic long enough to be certain it loses its pungency and becomes more of a subtle accent. Serve with boiled or roasted potatoes.

2 tablespoons olive oil

2 pounds beef stew meat, such as chuck, cut into
     1½-inch pieces

1 medium onion, coarsely chopped (about ⅔ cup)

1 whole head garlic, separated and peeled

1 teaspoon all-purpose flour

1 cup dry white wine

2 whole cloves

Salt

Freshly ground black pepper

1 tablespoon finely chopped fresh flat-leaf parsley

1 bay leaf

¼ teaspoon thyme

1. Heat the oil in a deep earthenware casserole dish or Dutch oven over medium heat. Add the beef and cook, turning, until well browned on all sides. Add the onion and garlic and cook, stirring, until the onion is wilted and transparent, about 5 minutes more. Stir in the flour, then add the remaining ingredients.

2. Reduce the heat to low, cover, and simmer 1½ to 2 hours or until the beef is tender. Remove the bay leaf. If using earthenware, serve in the dish, or transfer to individual bowls.

Boiled Beef and Chickpea Dinner
Cocido Madrileño

MAKES 6 TO 8 SERVINGS

Originally, cocido *became a staple meal in Spain because of its inexpensive and readily available ingredients. But because of the diversity of meats that are now commonly found in this dish, it is no longer inexpensive and is now considered more of a "special-occasion" meal. This stew from Madrid is not difficult to make, but it does take some organization to assemble and serve.*

1 pound dried chickpeas, sorted and washed

18 cups water

2 chicken thighs

2 pounds beef chuck

¼ pound slab bacon

½ pound chorizo sausage

¼ pound black sausage (morcilla; optional)

¼-pound piece Serrano (Spanish cured mountain)
     ham or prosciutto

2 ham or beef bones

Salt

Freshly ground black pepper

1 medium onion, halved

1 leek, trimmed and well washed, or 2 large scallions

2 garlic cloves

2 large carrots, peeled

4 medium new potatoes, peeled

4 ounces very thin pasta, such as angel hair
     (optional)

Meatballs (Pelotas)

1 cup shredded beef chuck (from the pot)

½ cup finely chopped bacon (from the pot)

2 large eggs

1 garlic clove, finely chopped

1 tablespoon finely chopped fresh flat-leaf parsley

2 tablespoons broth (from the pot)

Salt

Freshly ground black pepper

Bread crumbs

1 tablespoon olive oil

Sautéed Cabbage (Repollo)

2 tablespoons olive oil

2 tablespoons finely chopped onion

1 garlic clove, finely chopped

½ head cabbage, coarsely chopped

Salt

Freshly ground black pepper

continues...

1. Place the chickpeas in a large bowl, add cold water to cover, and let soak overnight in the refrigerator. Drain and reserve.

2. Meanwhile, in a large stew pot, place the water, chicken, beef, bacon, chorizo, black sausage (if using), ham, bones, salt, and pepper and bring to a boil over high heat. Skim off any foam. Reduce the heat to low and simmer until the meats are cooked through, about 1½ hours.

3. Remove the beef from the stew pot, shred 1 cup, and reserve. Return the rest to the pot. Remove the bacon, finely chop ½ cup, and reserve. Return the rest to the pot. Secure the chickpeas in a net bag or cheesecloth and add to the pot. Add the onion, leek, the 2 garlic cloves, the carrots, and potatoes. Taste and adjust seasoning if necessary. Cover and simmer 1 hour more.

4. Prepare the meatballs: In a food processor or blender, place the beef (from the beef pot), the bacon, and eggs and process until smooth. Transfer to a medium bowl and add the 1 garlic clove, the parsley, broth, salt, pepper, and enough bread crumbs to make the mixture easy to shape. Form into sausage shapes, at least 2 inches long and 1 inch wide. Heat the 1 tablespoon oil in a medium skillet over medium heat. Add the meatballs and cook, turning, until golden. Add to the pot, cover, and cook about 1½ hours more or until the chickpeas are tender. Wipe out the skillet.

5. Prepare the cabbage: Heat the 2 tablespoons oil in the same skillet over medium heat. Add the onion and garlic and cook, stirring, until the onion is wilted and transparent, about 3 minutes. Add the cabbage, salt, and pepper and cook until the cabbage is tender.

6. Meanwhile, if using the noodles, fill a medium saucepan with water, add salt, and bring to a boil over high heat. Add the noodles and cook until tender. Drain.

7. Pass the broth through a fine-mesh strainer. Ladle it into a soup tureen, but leave enough in the pot to cover the meat. Discard the bones. Add the noodles, if using, to the broth—this will be the soup. Serve hot as a first course.

8. Cut the chorizo and black sausage into thick slices. Cut the chicken, beef, bacon, ham, leek, carrots, and potatoes into pieces and leave the meatballs whole. Arrange the meat and vegetables on one or two platters and place the cabbage on one. Cover the platters with foil to retain the heat. Serve hot as the main course. (If you like, you can reheat the platters, without the foil, in the microwave.)

Tripe Stew, Madrid Style
Callos a la Madrileña

MAKES 4 TO 6 SERVINGS

This exceptionally rich Madrid stew is made with various meats, including tripe and chorizo. *Black sausage (black pudding) known as* morcilla *is also used, and often chickpeas are added as well. Lhardy, the century-old restaurant in Madrid, is famous for this down-to-earth tripe stew.*

PREPARE AT LEAST 5 HOURS IN ADVANCE

1 pound beef tripe

4 cups water

1 small onion

5 garlic cloves, coarsely chopped

4 whole cloves

5 peppercorns

1 dried hot red chile pepper, stemmed and seeded

¼-pound piece Serrano (Spanish cured mountain) ham or prosciutto

4 sprigs parsley

Kosher or sea salt

1 teaspoon ground cumin

3 tablespoons olive oil

1 medium onion, finely chopped (about ⅔ cup)

1 tablespoon ground bittersweet paprika, such as Spanish smoked

½ cup dry white wine

1 medium tomato, finely chopped (about ⅔ cup)

¼ pound (2 links) chorizo sausage, cut into thick slices

¼ pound black sausage (morcilla)

1. Rinse the tripe well. Place in a large pot, add water to cover, and bring to a boil over high heat. Drain. Cut into 1½-inch squares and return to the pot. Add the water, the whole onion, the garlic, cloves, peppercorns, hot red pepper, ham, parsley, and salt and simmer over low heat about 4 hours, until the tripe is almost tender. Discard the onion.

2. Heat the oil in a medium skillet over medium heat. Add the finely chopped onion and then 2 minutes later the finely chopped garlic. Cook, stirring, until softened, about 3 minutes more. Stir in the paprika, wine, and tomato. Add the chorizo and black sausage and cook until the sausages are just cooked through, about 1 hour more.

2. Cut the chorizo, ham, and black sausage into pieces, add them to the tripe pot, and stir the skillet contents into the pot. Continue simmering over low heat until the tripe is tender and the flavors meld, about 30 minutes. Remove the bay leaves and serve hot.

Stew of Potatoes and Marinated Pork Ribs
Patatas con Costillas de Cerdo Adobadas

MAKES 4 TO 6 SERVINGS

This flavorful stew originated in the city of Toro near Zamora. It is a delightful combination of potatoes and pork, and it is a favorite among many of my dinner guests.

PREPARE AT LEAST 4 HOURS IN ADVANCE

1 pound pork ribs

2 teaspoons ground bittersweet paprika, such as Spanish smoked

¼ teaspoon ground hot paprika, such as Spanish smoked

2 tablespoons olive oil

4 cups chicken broth or vegetable broth

2½ pounds potatoes, peeled and cut with a fork into irregular 1½-inch pieces

1 teaspoon ground cumin

1 medium onion, finely chopped (about ⅔ cup)

4 garlic cloves, finely chopped

1 teaspoon dried oregano

1 medium green bell pepper, finely chopped (about ¾ cup)

1 bay leaf

Kosher or sea salt

Freshly ground black pepper

1. Rub the ribs with the paprika and let sit in the refrigerator 2 hours. Heat the oil in a large skillet over low heat. Add the ribs and cook, turning occasionally, until browned on all sides.

2. Add the broth, cover, and simmer 1½ hours or until the meat is tender. Add the remaining ingredients, cover, and simmer about 30 minutes more or until the potatoes are tender. Remove the bay leaf. Serve hot.

Vegetables and Beans

ARTICHOKES AND ASPARAGUS

Sautéed Artichokes and Cured Ham

Sautéed Asparagus **Ⓥ**

Asparagus, Manchego Style **Ⓥ**

Asparagus with Garlic and Paprika **Ⓥ**

Asparagus in Almond Sauce **Ⓥ**

BEANS AND LEGUMES

Sautéed White Beans **Ⓥ**

Red Beans with Cabbage

Spicy Lima Beans

Sautéed Lima Beans and Ham

Limas with Artichoke and Cumin **Ⓥ**

Chickpeas with Tomatoes and Sausage

Refried Chickpeas

Chickpea Purée with Crisp Bread Bits

CABBAGE AND CRUCIFEROUS VEGETABLES

Baked Red Cabbage and Apples

Sautéed Brussels Sprouts **Ⓥ**

Cauliflower in Garlic and Paprika Sauce **Ⓥ**

EGGPLANT

Eggplant, Andalusian Style **Ⓥ**

Fried Eggplant with Honey, Mint, and Sesame Seeds **Ⓥ**

Eggplant with Cheese **Ⓥ***

Fried Eggplant

Eggplant with Shrimp and Ham

Fried Eggplant with Salmorejo Sauce

 **Ⓥ** = Vegetarian   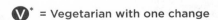 **Ⓥ*** = Vegetarian with one change

Eggplant, Peppers, and Tomatoes
with Cumin and Cilantro 🅥

MUSHROOMS

Sautéed Mushrooms 🅥

Wild Mushrooms with Garlic Bread Bits 🅥

Mushrooms in Sherry Sauce 🅥*

Mushrooms in Hazelnut Sauce 🅥

Mushrooms in Cabrales Blue Cheese Sauce 🅥

GREEN BEANS

Garlic Green Beans 🅥

Sautéed Green Beans, Cáceres Style

Garlic Green Beans with Cured Ham

Green Beans and Cured Ham

Stewed Potatoes and Green Beans,
Extremadura Style 🅥

Green Beans, Potatoes, and
Eggs, Galician Style 🅥

Green Beans with Garlic and Vinegar 🅥

ONIONS AND PEAS

Meat-Filled Baked Onions

Onions Coated with Honey and Spices 🅥

Peas with Cured Ham

Peas with Sausage

Peas, Valencia Style 🅥*

GREENS

Greens with Olive Oil 🅥

Cumin-Scented Sautéed Greens

Sautéed Greens with Croutons 🅥

Spinach Sautéed with Raisins and Pine Nuts 🅥

Sautéed Spinach with Quince and
Toasted Sesame Seeds 🅥

Sautéed Chicory with Ham and Cumin

PEPPERS

Fried Green Peppers 🅥

Sautéed Red Peppers 🅥*

Sautéed Green Peppers and Pimientos

Stuffed Peppers, Asturian Style

POTATOES

Wrinkled Potatoes Ⓥ

Widowed Potatoes Ⓥ

Castilian-Style Potatoes Ⓥ

Spicy Potatoes Ⓥ

Garlic Potatoes Ⓥ*

Poor Man's Potatoes Ⓥ

Sautéed Saffron-Scented Potatoes Ⓥ*

Potatoes with Walnuts and Cumin Ⓥ

Potatoes with Chorizo

Potatoes with Sautéed Peppers and Chorizo

Potatoes in Garlic and Almond Sauce Ⓥ*

Creamy Potato Purée with Garlic Ⓥ

Puréed Potatoes Ⓥ

Potatoes in Green Sauce Ⓥ*

Oven-Roasted Potatoes Ⓥ

Roasted Potatoes with Bell Pepper Ⓥ

Baked Stuffed Potatoes with Cured Ham

Sherry-Infused Baked Sliced Potatoes Ⓥ

Potato Fritters Ⓥ

Potatoes Vinaigrette Ⓥ

ZUCCHINI

Stewed Zucchini and Onion Ⓥ

Baked Zucchini Ⓥ

Zucchini Filled with Mushrooms Ⓥ*

Zucchini Fritters Ⓥ*

MIXED VEGETABLES

Greens and Potato Casserole Ⓥ

Mallorcan Potato and Vegetable Casserole

Vegetable Medley with Tuna,
Eggs, and Pine Nuts

Mixed Vegetables, Rioja Style

Zucchini, Green Pepper, and Tomato Medley

Vegetable Stew, Cordoba Style

The Núñez de Prado Family's
Batter-Fried Vegetables Ⓥ

Vegetable Medley, Andalusian Style

*M*any Spaniards are not especially fond of vegetables, especially when they are unadorned with other ingredients. However, when vegetables are combined with eggs, fish, or meat (particularly ham), they become much more popular. This may be somewhat rooted in history because years ago, the lack of fresh water in many parts of Spain meant that vegetables were rarely boiled. Instead, they were sautéed in oil, quick-fried, or combined in casseroles. Today, Spaniards have no lack of fresh water, but they still prefer their vegetables prepared by these traditional methods. Vegetable dishes are usually served before the main meal or as an accompaniment, although some of the recipes in this chapter are hearty enough to be a main course.

The cooking in Spain, as in all other countries, is often determined by the climate. In spring and summer, Spanish vegetables and legumes are extraordinary. The region of La Rioja produces rare white asparagus, tiny artichokes, and delicious sweet red peppers. Galicia is famous for its tiny bright green peppers, and Andalucía is best known for its lima beans (which are also used to feed the bulls to strengthen them for bullfighting).

Sweet peppers, commonly referred to as bell peppers in the United States, have been popular in Spain ever since Columbus discovered this native American vegetable in the New World. In the fall, the red peppers from La Rioja are roasted over wood-burning grills. In Extremadura, these peppers are laid out to dry and then pulverized into pimentón or paprika. It is the region of Navarra that produces the supreme kind of pepper—pimiento de piquillo. The taste of these highly desirable peppers is unlike any other.

Acelgas, with large, deep green leaves and stark white stems, are similar to chard or collard greens; the name is also used as a general term for "greens" in Spain. Greens are prepared in a variety of different ways, mainly according to region. Spaniards are also fond of green beans, especially when they are sautéed in garlic sauce. Throughout almost all of Spain they serve vegetable medleys known as *pisto*, and vegetable casseroles known as *menestras*. Dried vegetables such as beans and chickpeas are also very popular because they can keep for extended periods of time. Every region has a special way to cook them, and they are part of many traditional recipes.

Potatoes in Spain are a whole different story. Ever since they were introduced from South America in the sixteenth century, they have become a staple in Spanish cooking. To a Spaniard, a meal without potatoes is incomplete at best. Many of the potato recipes in this chapter go by their colloquial names, such as Widowed Potatoes, Poor Man's Potatoes, and Wrinkled Potatoes. Even though potatoes are usually served as a side dish, they often prove to be the highlight of the meal. There are also many recipes for potatoes that can stand on their own as the center of the meal.

Artichokes and Asparagus

Sautéed Artichokes and Cured Ham
Alcachofas Salteadas con Jamón

MAKES 4 SERVINGS

When fresh vegetables are in season, they can be simply, briefly boiled, just enough to bring out their inherent taste. But more often in Spain, vegetables are sautéed with ingredients that add more flavor, such as this dish of sautéed artichokes with cured ham.

1 pound artichoke hearts, fresh, thawed frozen (or drained canned)

2 tablespoons olive oil

¼ cup small cubes (¼ inch) Serrano (Spanish cured mountain) ham or prosciutto (about 2 ounces)

Freshly ground black pepper

2 tablespoons finely chopped fresh flat-leaf parsley

1. If using fresh or frozen artichoke hearts, place them in a medium saucepan with water to cover, add salt, and bring to a boil over high heat. Reduce the heat to medium and cook about 20 minutes or until crisp-tender. Drain.

2. Heat the oil in a medium skillet over medium heat. Add the ham, cooked or canned artichokes, and pepper and cook, stirring, about 10 minutes. Sprinkle with parsley and serve hot.

Sautéed Asparagus **V**
Espárragos Trigueros

MAKES 4 SERVINGS

*For this simple but delicious recipe for tender asparagus sautéed in olive oil and garlic, I recommend using the thinnest asparagus you can find. In Spain, wild green asparagus (*trigueros*) are typically used for this dish and are frequently found growing in wheat fields (*trigo*) in central Spain.*

¾ pound thin green asparagus, rinsed and trimmed

2 tablespoons olive oil

1 garlic clove

Kosher or sea salt

Heat the oil in a medium skillet over medium-high heat. Add the garlic and asparagus, reduce the heat to low, and cook, turning occasionally, until the asparagus is tender, about 20 minutes. Season with salt and serve hot.

Asparagus, Manchego Style **V**
Espárragos Estilo Manchego

MAKES 4 SERVINGS

The sauce for these asparagus contains egg yolk as well as cumin, a spice that reflects the influence the Moors had over Spain until they were expelled from Granada. Cumin gives this dish a very distinctive taste.

¾ pound thin asparagus, rinsed and trimmed

2 tablespoons olive oil

2 garlic cloves

2 large egg yolks

¼ teaspoon ground cumin

4 teaspoons water

Salt

Freshly ground black pepper

1. Heat the oil in a medium skillet over medium heat. Add the garlic and cook, stirring, until lightly browned. Add the asparagus, reduce the heat to low, and cook, stirring occasionally, until tender, about 20 minutes.

2. Meanwhile, in a small saucepan, mix together the egg yolks, cumin, water, salt, and pepper. Over very low heat (to avoid curdling), cook, stirring occasionally, only until warm. Pour the sauce over the asparagus. Serve hot.

Asparagus with Garlic and Paprika V
Espárragos Amargueros

MAKES 4 SERVINGS

This classic dish is beloved by many Spaniards. The asparagus is sautéed in garlic, combined with the piquant flavor of vinegar, and features the earthy accent of paprika. It is most delicious when served over fried bread.

1 pound thin asparagus, rinsed and trimmed

2 tablespoons olive oil

1 thin slice long-loaf (baguette) bread

1 garlic clove

¼ teaspoon ground paprika

½ cup water

1 tablespoon vinegar

Salt

1 tablespoon finely chopped fresh flat-leaf parsley, for garnish

1. Heat the oil in a medium skillet over medium heat. Add the bread slice and cook, turning once, until golden. Transfer to a blender or food processor. Add the garlic to the skillet and cook, stirring, until golden. Transfer to the blender. Add the asparagus to the skillet and cook, turning occasionally, about 3 minutes. Add the paprika and stir to coat. Pour in the water, cover, and cook until crisp-tender.

2. Meanwhile, in the blender, combine the bread and garlic until smooth. Gradually add the vinegar and 3 tablespoons of the cooking liquid from the asparagus. Pour this mixture over the asparagus in the skillet. Season with salt, cover, and cook 5 minutes more or until the asparagus is tender. Sprinkle with the parsley and serve hot.

Asparagus in Almond Sauce V
Trigueros Almendrados

MAKES 4 SERVINGS

This is a wonderful preparation for asparagus flavored with tomato, toasted almonds, and a generous amount of roasted garlic. The ingredients in this sauce should be beaten together to form what resembles mayonnaise, except that this recipe contains no eggs.

1 small tomato

½ small head garlic, unpeeled

¼ cup slivered blanched almonds

¼ teaspoon sherry vinegar or red wine vinegar

Salt

¼ cup plus 2 tablespoons extra-virgin olive oil

¾ pound asparagus, rinsed and trimmed

1. Preheat the oven to 350°F. Place the tomato and garlic in a cake pan and bake 15 minutes. Peel the tomato and garlic cloves. Cut the tomato in half crosswise and gently squeeze out the seeds.

2. Scatter the almonds on a cookie sheet and toast about 4 minutes or until golden.

3. In a food processor, place the tomato, garlic, almonds, vinegar, and salt and process until smooth. With the motor running, gradually drizzle in the ¼ cup oil and process until well blended and the consistency of mayonnaise. Stir in salt.

4. Heat the 2 tablespoons oil in a medium skillet over medium-high heat. Add the asparagus, reduce the heat to medium, and cook, turning occasionally, until tender, 10 to 15 minutes. Serve hot with the sauce.

Sautéed White Beans 🅥

Judías Blancas

MAKES 4 SERVINGS

This simple preparation of white beans is Catalan style. From our friend Pilar de Olmo, who uses only local ingredients in her wonderful restaurant in Scala Dei, this recipe calls for crunchy little white beans, preferably pea beans, that are boiled first and then sautéed in onion and garlic.

½ pound small dried white beans, such as pea beans

3 cups water

4 garlic cloves, unpeeled

2 sprigs fresh parsley

1 bay leaf

1 small onion

Salt

2 tablespoons extra-virgin olive oil plus more for drizzling

Freshly ground black pepper

1. Place all the ingredients except the oil and pepper in a large pot. Bring to a boil over high heat. Reduce the heat to low, cover, and simmer 1 to 2 hours, depending on the size of the beans, until the beans are tender. Remove the garlic and press with the back of a wooden spoon to extract the flesh. Discard the skin, the parsley, bay leaf, and onion. Rinse the beans in cold water and drain well.

2. Heat the 2 tablespoons oil in a medium skillet over medium-high heat. Add the beans and garlic and cook, stirring frequently, until slightly crunchy. Season with salt and pepper and drizzle with the olive oil. Serve hot.

Red Beans with Cabbage

Alubias Rojas de Tolosa con Berza

MAKES 4 SERVINGS

Tolosa, in the Basque province of Guipúzcoa along the banks of the Oria River, is an area where excellent red beans are grown. I recommend using Tolosa, Adzuki, or other dark red beans found in specialty stores, but this dish can be made with any kind of red bean. It's a delicious stew that is topped off with a spoonful or two of cabbage, which complements the flavor perfectly. I like to serve it with crusty bread.

PREPARE 8 TO 12 HOURS IN ADVANCE

Beans

1 pound small, deep-red dried beans

6 cups water

1 medium onion, halved crosswise

1 large carrot, peeled and halved crosswise

1 small leek, trimmed and well washed

¼ pound slab bacon

¼ pound sweet semi-cured chorizo

2 tablespoons olive oil

¾ cup finely chopped onion (1 medium)

6 garlic cloves, finely chopped

2 tablespoons ground sweet paprika, such as Spanish smoked

Salt

Cabbage

3 tablespoons olive oil

¼ cup finely chopped onion

2 garlic cloves, finely chopped

1 small head cabbage, coarsely chopped

Salt

Freshly ground black pepper

1. Prepare the beans: Place the beans in a medium bowl, add water to cover by 1 inch, and let soak overnight in the refrigerator. Drain. Place the beans

and the 6 cups water in a large pot and bring to a boil over high heat. Reduce the heat to low and add the onion, carrot, leek, bacon, and chorizo. Cover and simmer 1 hour.

2. Meanwhile, heat 2 tablespoons oil in a large skillet over medium heat. Reduce the heat to low, add the onion and garlic, and cook, stirring, until the onion is wilted, about 5 minutes. Stir in the paprika, then add to the beans, and season with salt. Cover and cook about 30 minutes more or until the beans are just tender. Wipe out the skillet.

3. Prepare the cabbage: Heat 3 tablespoons oil in the skillet over medium heat. Add the onion and garlic and cook, stirring, until the onion is wilted, about 5 minutes. Add the cabbage, salt, and pepper and cook, stirring, about 10 minutes. Cover and continue cooking 5 to 10 minutes more or until tender.

4. Place the beans in soup bowls and add a spoonful of cabbage off to one side—not mixed into the beans. Cut the chorizo and bacon into ½-inch slices and place a couple of slices in each bowl. Place the remaining cabbage, bacon, and chorizo in a serving bowl. Serve hot.

Spicy Lima Beans
Michirones Picanticos

MAKES 4 SERVINGS

Lima beans are commonly grown in Andalucía, and in the province of Murcia, an area famous for their fresh vegetables. Michirones picanticos is a specialty of Murcia. In Andalucía, lima beans are fed to fighting bulls to make them stronger for the bullring.

10 ounces fresh or frozen baby lima beans

1 chorizo sausage (2 ounces), cut into ½-inch slices

½ dried red chile pepper, seeded

Salt

Freshly ground black pepper

1 bay leaf

1 ham bone (optional)

½ cup water

Place all the ingredients in a medium saucepan and bring to a boil over medium-high heat. Reduce the heat to low, cover, and cook about 30 minutes or until the beans are tender and the liquid is absorbed. Remove the bay leaf and ham bone, if using. Serve hot.

Sautéed Lima Beans and Ham
Habas con Jamón

MAKES 6 SERVINGS

Beans of all types are enormously popular in Spanish cooking. The best version of habas con jamón *that I have ever eaten was served as a tapa at the Bar Lo Güeno in Málaga, near Larios Street and close to the harbor and main market. When lima beans are sautéed with ham, they make a wonderful dish and are served as a tapa in many bars.*

3 tablespoons olive oil

1¼ pounds baby lima beans

2 garlic cloves, finely chopped

2 tablespoons dry white wine

¼ pound Serrano (Spanish cured mountain) ham or prosciutto, cut into ¼-inch cubes

1 tablespoon finely chopped fresh flat-leaf parsley

Salt

Freshly ground black pepper

Heat the oil in a medium skillet over medium heat. Add the beans and garlic and cook, stirring, about 5 minutes. Stir in the wine. Reduce the heat to low, cover, and cook until the wine is absorbed and the beans are softening, about 15 minutes more. Add the ham and parsley and season with salt and pepper. Cover and cook about 15 minutes more or until the beans are tender.

Limas with Artichoke and Cumin Ⓥ

Habas a la Andaluza

MAKES 4 SERVINGS

This recipe from Andalucía is of Moorish origin, reflected by the use of characteristically Moorish ingredients such as saffron and cumin. When eggs are added, it becomes a wonderful lunch or light dinner.

1 tablespoon olive oil

2 tablespoons finely chopped onion

2 garlic cloves, finely chopped

1 small tomato, finely chopped (about ½ cup)

1 pound fresh or frozen lima beans

4 artichoke hearts, halved

¾ cup water

1 bay leaf

2 tablespoons finely chopped fresh flat-leaf parsley

Large pinch of saffron

½ teaspoon ground cumin

Salt

Freshly ground black pepper

4 large eggs (optional)

1. Heat the oil in a medium skillet over medium heat. Add the onion and garlic and cook, stirring, until the onion is wilted, about 3 minutes. Add the tomato and cook, stirring, until softened and its juices release, about 5 minutes. Stir in all the remaining ingredients except the eggs. Cover and cook 15 to 20 minutes or until the vegetables are tender, unless using the eggs.

2. If using the eggs, when the vegetables are almost tender, crack the eggs and slide them whole into the pan over the vegetables. Cover and cook about 5 minutes or until the eggs are set. Remove the bay leaf. Serve hot.

Chickpeas with Tomatoes and Sausage

Garbanzos a la Catalana

MAKES 4 SERVINGS AS A MAIN COURSE OR 6 TO 8 AS A SIDE DISH

Traditionally, chickpeas were a staple in stews and cocidos in order to provide sustenance when other more expensive ingredients were not available. They are still enormously popular today and are featured in numerous Spanish dishes. In this Catalan-style recipe, they are combined with tomatoes and sausage, creating a dish that is outstanding.

PREPARE 9 TO 13 HOURS IN ADVANCE

1 pound dried chickpeas

Salt

1 bay leaf

1 tablespoon olive oil

1 large onion, finely chopped (about 1 cup)

¼ pound sweet Italian-style or breakfast sausage, cut into ½-inch slices

2 tablespoons small cubes (¼ inch) Serrano (Spanish cured mountain) ham or prosciutto (about 1 ounce)

4 medium tomatoes, fresh or canned, finely chopped (about 4 cups)

Freshly ground black pepper

1 tablespoon finely chopped fresh flat-leaf parsley

1. Place the chickpeas in a medium bowl, add cold water to cover by 1 inch, and let soak overnight in the refrigerator. Do not drain. Place in a medium saucepan and add salt, the bay leaf, and more water to cover if necessary. Cover and bring to a boil over high heat. Reduce the heat to low and simmer 1½ to 2 hours or until the chickpeas are tender. Drain.

2. In a large skillet, heat the oil over medium heat. Add the onion, sausage, and ham and cook, stirring, until the onion is wilted, about 5 minutes. Add the tomatoes, salt, and pepper. Reduce the heat to low, cover, and cook about 15 minutes. Add the chickpeas, cover, and cook 20 minutes more or until the chickpeas are tender. Remove the bay leaf. Sprinkle with the parsley and serve hot.

Refried Chickpeas
Garbanzos Refritos

MAKES 1 SERVING

Chickpeas, or garbanzo beans, are among the most popular beans in Spain. After a cocido madrileño (chickpea stew) has been served at lunchtime, the leftover chickpeas are saved, then refried and eaten for dinner, sometimes with the company of a fried egg. Delicious!

1 tablespoon olive oil

3 tablespoons finely chopped onion

1 garlic clove, finely chopped

1 chorizo sausage (2 ounces), sliced or cut into pieces

2 cups cooked chickpeas, well drained

1 pimiento, cut into thin strips

Heat the oil in a small skillet over medium heat. Add the onion and garlic and cook, stirring, until the onion is wilted, about 3 minutes. Increase the heat to medium-high. Add the chorizo and chickpeas and cook, stirring occasionally, until the chorizo and chickpeas are lightly browned. Stir in the pimiento and serve hot.

Chickpea Purée with Crisp Bread Bits
Puré de Garbanzos con Migas

MAKES 4 SERVINGS

When cumin, cilantro, and crunchy toasted bread cubes are added to this chickpea purée, the taste is sensational. The spices reflect a Moorish influence. You can use either fresh chickpeas or canned.

PREPARE 9 TO 13 HOURS IN ADVANCE

½ pound dried chickpeas

1 ham or beef soup bone

1 cup chicken broth or vegetable broth

1 cup water

2 bay leaves

1 tablespoon plus 2 teaspoons olive oil

¼ cup finely chopped onion

2 garlic cloves, finely chopped

½ teaspoon ground sweet paprika, such as Spanish smoked

2 tablespoons finely chopped fresh cilantro

2 tablespoons finely chopped fresh flat-leaf parsley

Several threads of saffron

2 tablespoons dry white wine

¾ cup small cubes (½ inch) long-loaf (baguette) bread

1 garlic clove, mashed in a garlic press or mortar

½ plus ⅛ teaspoon ground cumin

Salt

Freshly ground black pepper

1 large hard-boiled egg, finely chopped (optional)

1. Place the chickpeas in a medium bowl, add cold water to cover by 1 inch, and let soak overnight in the refrigerator. Drain. Place the chickpeas, soup bone, broth, water, and bay leaves in a large pot. Bring to a boil over high heat. Reduce the heat to low, cover, and simmer 1 hour.

continues…

2. Meanwhile, heat 1 tablespoon of the oil in a medium skillet over medium heat. Add the onion and the chopped garlic and cook, stirring, until the onion is wilted, about 5 minutes. In a mortar or mini-processor, mash the paprika, cilantro, parsley, and saffron. Stir in the wine, and reserve.

3. Add the onion and mortar mixtures to the chickpeas, cover, and cook about 1½ hours more or until the chickpeas are tender, adding more liquid during cooking if necessary. If any liquid remains, increase the heat to medium-high and let boil until most of the liquid evaporates.

4. Preheat the oven to 350°F. In a small bowl, mix the remaining 2 tablespoons oil, the mashed garlic, and ⅛ teaspoon of the cumin. Place the bread cubes on a cookie sheet and drizzle or brush with the garlic mixture. Bake about 5 minutes or until crisp and golden.

5. Discard the bay leaves and soup bone. In a blender or food processor, blend the chickpeas until smooth. Season with the remaining ½ teaspoon cumin, the salt, and pepper. Scatter the chopped egg, if using, and toasted bread cubes over the chickpeas. Serve hot.

Cabbage and Cruciferous Vegetables

Baked Red Cabbage and Apples
Lombarda Navideña

MAKES 4 TO 6 SERVINGS

This dish is an important part of the traditional Spanish Christmas dinner in Madrid and central Spain. Red cabbage is excellent when sautéed with apples and bacon. If you want the dish to be even heartier, add cubed potatoes.

2 tablespoons lard or olive oil

1 medium onion, finely chopped (about ⅓ cup)

1 head red cabbage, tough outer leaves removed, coarsely chopped

1 large apple, peeled, cored, and cut into ½-inch pieces

¼ pound slab bacon, cut into ¼-inch cubes

2 tablespoons red wine vinegar

1 bay leaf

Salt

Freshly ground black pepper

1 tablespoon finely chopped fresh flat-leaf parsley

½ cup warm water

2 medium potatoes, cooked and cut into ½-inch cubes (optional)

1. Preheat the oven to 325°F. Melt the lard in a medium earthenware casserole dish or Dutch oven over medium heat. Add the onion and cook, stirring, until wilted, about 5 minutes. Stir in the cabbage, apple, and bacon and cook, stirring, 1 to 2 minutes more. Add the vinegar, bay leaf, salt, pepper, parsley, and warm water and bring to a boil. Remove from the heat.

2. Cover, transfer to the oven, and bake 45 minutes. Add the potatoes, if using, and bake 10 minutes more. Remove the bay leaf. If using earthenware, serve hot in the dish or transfer to individual plates.

Sautéed Brussels Sprouts V
Coles de Bruselas Salteados

MAKES 4 SERVINGS

My daughter swore she hated Brussels sprouts until she tasted this version, in which they are sautéed in olive oil, garlic, and red wine vinegar.

¾ pound Brussels sprouts

1 tablespoon olive oil

2 garlic cloves, lightly smashed

Salt

Freshly ground black pepper

2 teaspoons red wine vinegar

1. Cut off the ends of the Brussels sprouts and remove any old leaves. Place 1 inch of water in a medium saucepan, add salt, and bring to a boil over high heat. Add the sprouts, reduce the heat to low, and cook until tender, 10 to 15 minutes. Drain.

2. Heat the oil in a medium skillet over medium heat. Add the garlic and cook, stirring around the surface of the pan, until golden on all sides. Discard the garlic. Increase the heat to medium-high, add the Brussels sprouts and cook, stirring, until the sprouts are evenly coated with the oil, about 2 to 3 minutes. Add salt, pepper, and the vinegar and cook, stirring constantly, until the vinegar evaporates. Serve hot.

Cauliflower in Garlic and Paprika Sauce V
Coliflor al Ajo Arriero

MAKES 4 SERVINGS

Aragon is the region in Spain best known for their succulent red bell peppers. Once the peppers have been dried, they may be pulverized into pimentón, *or paprika. Here it lends an earthy accent to this garlic-rich preparation of cauliflower. An* arriero *is a "muleteer," originally a mule-driver but which evolved to mean a person in charge of transportation in Spain whose life is spent mostly on the road. He cooks simple food using local produce, often with exceptional results.*

1 medium cauliflower (about 1½ pounds)

2 garlic cloves

1 tablespoon finely chopped fresh flat-leaf parsley

Salt

5 tablespoons olive oil

2 tablespoons red wine vinegar

1 tablespoon ground paprika

1. Cut off the thick stems of the cauliflower and break into florets. Place 1 inch of water in a medium saucepan and add salt. Add the cauliflower and bring the water to a boil over high heat. (The cauliflower is just being steamed.) Reduce the heat to low and simmer 8 to 12 minutes or until tender. Drain, reserving the cooking liquid. Keep the cauliflower warm (covered in a turned-off oven or in a covered pot on a back burner).

2. In a food processor or blender, place 1 of the garlic cloves, the parsley, and the salt and process until finely chopped. With the motor running, gradually add 3 tablespoons of the oil and 3 tablespoons of the reserved cooking liquid and process until well blended.

continues...

3. Heat the remaining 2 tablespoons oil in a medium skillet over medium heat. Add the remaining garlic clove and cook, stirring, until browned on all sides. Discard the garlic. Turn off the heat. Stir in the vinegar, paprika, and the garlic mixture and let sit 5 minutes. Pour over the cauliflower and serve hot.

Eggplant, Andalucian Style Ⓥ
Berenjena a la Andaluza

MAKES 4 SERVINGS

This simple dish of roasted eggplant, seasoned with garlic, cumin, and paprika, is based on an old Andalusian family recipe. It is very easy to prepare and is especially suited as an accompaniment for pork dishes. This recipe comes from the Núñez de Prado family in the town of Baena.

1½ pounds baby eggplants (about 6), peeled and cut into ½-inch cubes

Kosher or sea salt

2 tablespoons finely chopped fresh parsley

2 garlic cloves, finely chopped

Freshly ground black pepper

1 teaspoon ground cumin

½ teaspoon ground sweet paprika, such as Spanish smoked

4 teaspoons olive oil

1. Preheat the oven to 400°F. Place the eggplant in a colander and sprinkle each layer with salt. Let drain at least 30 minutes, then pat dry with paper towels.

2. In a mortar or mini-processor, mash the parsley, garlic, and ¼ teaspoon salt. Mix in the pepper, cumin, paprika, and oil. Combine the eggplant and mortar mixture in a medium bowl until the eggplant is well coated. Spread the eggplant on a foil-lined cookie sheet and bake 15 to 20 minutes or until tender and browned. Serve hot.

Fried Eggplant with Honey, Mint, and Sesame Seeds Ⓥ

Berenjena con Miel

MAKES 4 SERVINGS

Our dear friend Julia who lives in the Andalucian town of Cazalla de la Sierra is an exceptional cook who specializes in recipes of Moorish origin. This fabulous dish is made from fried eggplant in Julia's special batter, with the sweetness of honey, the crunch of sesame seeds, and an unusual mint accent. Pure Moorish style.

2 cups water

Salt

One (½-pound) eggplant, peeled and cut crosswise
into ⅛-inch slices

1⅛ teaspoons kosher or sea salt

1½ tablespoons sesame seeds

⅓ cup all-purpose flour

½ teaspoon baking powder

½ cup milk

1 large egg, lightly beaten

Mild olive oil, for frying

1½ tablespoons honey

1 tablespoon finely chopped fresh mint leaves

1. Preheat the oven to 350°F. In a medium bowl, combine the water and salt. Add the eggplant and let soak 30 minutes. Meanwhile, scatter the sesame seeds in a cake pan and toast 5 to 8 minutes or until lightly golden. Reserve.

2. Drain the eggplant and pat dry with paper towels. In a small bowl, mix together the flour, the remaining ⅛ teaspoon salt, and the baking powder. Whisk in the milk and egg.

3. Heat at least ½ inch of oil in a large skillet over medium-high heat (or better still, use a deep fryer set at 375°F) until it quickly browns a cube of bread. Dip each eggplant slice in the batter, coating well, and place immediately in the hot oil. (Cook in batches if needed to avoid overcrowding.) Cook, turning once, until lightly golden, about 30 seconds per side. Transfer with a slotted spatula to paper towels and let drain.

4. Warm the honey briefly in a small saucepan over low heat or in a small microwave-safe cup in the microwave on High. Drizzle lightly over the eggplant, sprinkle with the sesame seeds and mint and serve hot.

Eggplant with Cheese Ⓥ*

Berenjena con Queso

MAKES 4 SERVINGS

This recipe for an unusual preparation of eggplant comes from a sixteenth-century cookbook by Ruperto de Nola, entitled Libro de Cozina, *and calls for a mild cheese, such as Muenster or fresh goat. Make it vegetarian with vegetable broth.*

One (1-pound) eggplant, peeled and cut crosswise
into ½-inch slices

1 cup beef broth, chicken broth, or vegetable broth

2 slices medium onion

12 blanched almonds, lightly toasted

Salt

2 slices mild cheese, such as Muenster or fresh goat

1 tablespoon grated Parmesan cheese

Freshly ground black pepper

Freshly grated nutmeg

1. Place the eggplant, broth, and onion in a medium skillet and bring to a boil over medium-high heat. Reduce the heat to low and simmer until the eggplant is just tender. Transfer to an earthenware casserole dish or Dutch oven, reserving ½ cup of the broth and adding water if necessary.

continues . . .

2. Preheat the oven to 350°F. In a food processor or blender, process the almonds until as finely chopped as possible. With the motor running, pour in the reserved broth. Stir in salt. Pour over the eggplant. Arrange the slices of cheese over the eggplant, sprinkle with the grated cheese, and season with pepper and the nutmeg. Bake 20 minutes. If using earthenware, serve hot in the dish or transfer to individual plates.

Fried Eggplant
Berenjena Frita

MAKES 4 SERVINGS

Spaniards love many of their foods fried, and vegetables are no exception. I recommend that you use extra-virgin olive oil when frying eggplant.

1 large eggplant (about 1½ pounds), peeled and cut lengthwise into ⅛-inch slices

Kosher or sea salt

All-purpose flour, for dredging

Extra-virgin olive oil, for frying

1. Place the eggplant in layers in a colander, sprinkling each layer with salt. Let drain 1 hour, then pat dry with paper towels.

2. Heat at least ½ inch of oil in a large skillet over medium-high heat (or better still, use a deep fryer set at 375°F) until it quickly browns a cube of bread. Dredge each eggplant slice in the flour and place in the oil. (Cook in batches if needed to avoid overcrowding.) Cook, turning once, until golden, about 30 seconds per side. Transfer with a slotted spatula to paper towels and let drain. Season with salt and serve hot.

Eggplant with Shrimp and Ham
Berenjenas "Rincón de Pepe"

MAKES 4 SERVINGS

The first time I tasted this dish I was at the Rincon de Pepe restaurant in Murcia, one of the best restaurants in the southeast region of Spain. This wonderful recipe combines the mild flavor of eggplant with shrimp and cured ham, creating a hearty dish that can be a meal on its own.

2 eggplants (½ pound each), peeled and cut crosswise into ¾-inch slices

Kosher or sea salt

All-purpose flour, for dredging

Olive oil, for frying

2 garlic cloves

8 medium shrimp, shelled and deveined

¼ cup very thin 1-inch strips Serrano (Spanish cured mountain) ham or prosciutto (about 2 ounces)

1 cup milk

¼ cup beef broth, chicken broth, or water

Freshly ground black pepper

2 tablespoons finely chopped onion

2 tablespoons all-purpose flour

2 tablespoons coarsely grated Swiss cheese

1. Heat at least ½ inch of oil in a large skillet over medium-high heat (or better still, use a deep fryer set at 375°F) until it quickly browns a cube of bread. Add the garlic and cook until golden. Discard. Sprinkle both sides of the eggplant with salt, dredge in the flour, and place in the oil. (Cook in batches if needed to avoid overcrowding.) Cook, turning once, until golden, about 30 seconds per side. Transfer with a slotted spatula to paper towels and let drain. Reserve 2 tablespoons of the oil.

2. Arrange the eggplant in overlapping lengthwise rows on a greased metal platter. Place the shrimp and ham on top. In a small bowl, mix the milk, broth, salt, and pepper.

3. Heat the reserved oil in the same skillet over low heat. Add the onion and cook, stirring, until tender, 2 to 3 minutes. Stir in the 2 tablespoons flour and cook about 1 minute. Gradually stir in the milk mixture and cook until smooth and thickened. Pass the sauce through a fine-mesh strainer over the eggplant.

4. Place a broiler rack about 6 inches from the heat source and preheat the broiler. (Cover the broiler pan with foil for easier cleanup, if you like.) Sprinkle the eggplant with the cheese. Place under the broiler and cook until golden. Serve hot.

Fried Eggplant with Salmorejo Sauce
Berenjena en Salmorejo

MAKES 6 TO 8 SERVINGS

Salmorejo, *a tomato sauce thickened with bread, is typical of the cooking in Córdoba and is often served as a dipping sauce. When crispy fried eggplant is sprinkled with cured ham and chopped eggs, the results are exceptional. This recipe is from the wonderful El Churrasco restaurant in Cordoba.*

Salmorejo Sauce

3 (½-inch) slices round loaf (country) bread, crust removed and cut into cubes (about 1½ cups)
1 pound medium ripe tomatoes, peeled and seeded
1 small garlic clove, finely chopped
¾ teaspoon salt
¼ cup fruity extra-virgin olive oil
1 teaspoon wine vinegar
1 hard-boiled egg, coarsely chopped
¼ cup finely chopped Serrano (Spanish cured mountain) ham or prosciutto (about 2 ounces)

One (¾-pound) eggplant, peeled and cut crosswise into ⅛-inch slices
Milk
¼ teaspoon salt
Olive oil, for frying
A mix of all-purpose flour and cornmeal, for dredging

1. Prepare the sauce: Soak the bread in water and squeeze dry. Place the tomatoes, garlic, and ¾ teaspoon salt in a food processor and process until smooth. With the motor running, gradually add the bread, then drizzle in the olive oil and finally the vinegar. Transfer to a serving bowl and sprinkle with the egg and ham.

2. With a medium bowl estimate how much milk is needed to cover the eggplant then quickly whisk in ¼ teaspoon salt. Add the eggplant. Let soak 10 minutes.

3. Heat at least 1 inch of oil in a large skillet over medium-high heat (or better still, use a deep fryer set at 375°F) until it quickly browns a cube of bread. Remove each eggplant slice from the milk—do not dry—and dredge in the flour-cornmeal mixture, patting with your fingertips so it adheres well. Immediately place in the oil and cook, turning once, until golden, about 30 seconds per side. (Cook in batches if needed to avoid overcrowding.) Transfer with a slotted spatula to paper towels and let drain. Serve hot, passing the sauce separately.

Eggplant, Peppers, and Tomatoes with Cumin and Cilantro V

Alboronia

MAKES 4 SERVINGS

Sautéed eggplant, peppers, and tomatoes are excellent when seasoned with the eastern spices of cumin and cilantro in this recipe inspired by Moorish cooking, where the flavors blend wonderfully. In Spanish, any word starting with "Al" has a Moorish Arab origin.

1 pound small eggplants, cut into ½-inch cubes

Olive oil, for brushing

1 tablespoon olive oil

2 garlic cloves

1 thin slice long-loaf (baguette) bread

1 medium onion, finely chopped (about ⅓ cup)

½ pound (about 25) green frying peppers, cored, seeded, and coarsely chopped

½ pound tomatoes, peeled, seeded, and coarsely chopped

½ teaspoon ground (or mortar-crushed) cumin

2 tablespoons finely chopped fresh cilantro

Few threads saffron, crumbled

Salt

Freshly ground black pepper

Finely chopped fresh cilantro, for garnish

1. Preheat the oven to 400°F. Place the eggplant on a cookie sheet and brush with olive oil. Bake 10 minutes, turning once. Reserve.

2. Heat the 1 tablespoon oil in a medium skillet over medium heat. Add the garlic and bread and cook, stirring the garlic and turning the bread occasionally, until the garlic is golden (do not over-brown) and the bread crisp. Transfer the garlic and bread with a slotted spoon to paper towels, reserving the oil. Let drain and cool. Transfer to a mortar or mini-processor and mash.

3. Heat the reserved oil in the skillet over medium heat. Add the onions, frying peppers, and more oil if necessary and cook, stirring, 1 to 2 minutes. Reduce the heat to low, cover, and cook 10 minutes more or until tender. Increase the heat to medium, add the tomatoes and cook until the tomatoes are softened and their juices release, about 5 minutes more. Add the eggplant and stir in the cumin, cilantro, saffron, salt, and pepper. Cover and cook 5 minutes more. Remove from the heat, stir in the mortar mixture, and let sit 5 minutes. Garnish with the cilantro and serve hot.

Garlic Green Beans Ⓥ
Judias Verdes con Ajo

MAKES 4 SERVINGS

This simple dish of green beans sautéed with garlic is as popular in my household as it is in Spain. It can be found on just about every menu in Spanish restaurants, where it is either served as a first course or a side dish. There are many variations on this recipe, but this one is the most basic. I always prepare garlic green beans the Spanish way, without any liquid.

¾ pound green beans
1 tablespoon unsalted butter
1 garlic clove, mashed in a garlic press or mortar
Kosher or sea salt

Melt the butter in a medium skillet over medium-high heat. Add the beans and cook, stirring, until they begin to brown. Reduce the heat to low, cover, and cook about 20 minutes more or until the desired tenderness, stirring occasionally. Stir in the garlic, season with salt, and serve hot.

Sautéed Green Beans, Cáceres Style
Judías Verdes Cacereñas

MAKES 4 SERVINGS

Author Luis Fausto Rodríguez wrote a book titled Recetas para Después de Una Guerra *(Post-War Recipes), which tells stories about the hardship in Spain after the Spanish Civil War. Rodríguez interweaves simple post-war recipes, always using very cheap and basic ingredients that were readily found. In*

this recipe, the green beans are made much tastier by the addition of pancetta, paprika, and vinegar.

1½ pounds broad green beans
2 tablespoons olive oil
¼ cup ¼-inch cubes pancetta or very thin 1-inch strips Serrano or prosciutto ham with some fat
¼ teaspoon ground sweet paprika, such as Spanish smoked
1 teaspoon wine vinegar
Salt

1. Fill a large pot with water, add salt, and bring to a boil over medium-high heat. Add the beans and return to a boil. Reduce the heat to medium-low and cook until done to taste, about 20 minutes. Drain.

2. Heat the oil in a large skillet over medium-high heat. Add the pancetta, reduce the heat to medium and cook, stirring, about 1 minute. Add the beans and cook, stirring, until heated through, about 2 minutes more. Reduce the heat to low, stir in the paprika and vinegar, and cook about 1 minute more. Serve hot.

Garlic Green Beans with Cured Ham
Judías Verdes Rehogadas con Jamón

MAKES 4 SERVINGS

Green beans with ham is such a beloved dish that I'm including two recipes — this one with a stronger accent of garlic and the next one, which has a balance of garlic and onion.

My husband, Luis, loves to fish for trout in the Cares River and we have frequently stayed in Niserias in Asturias, where we always ate at Casa Julián, a

continues…

restaurant known for its traditional Asturian cooking. The owners, Julián and his wife, Vicentina, are now deceased, but their memories and their recipes live on. This dish was Vicentina's favorite first course.

Salt

½ small onion

1½ pounds broad green beans

2 tablespoons olive oil

4 garlic cloves, lightly smashed and peeled

2 ounces Serrano (Spanish cured mountain) ham or prosciutto, cut into ¼-inch cubes or thin squares (about ¼ cup)

Freshly ground black pepper

1. Fill a large pot with water, add salt, and bring to a boil over high heat. Add the onion and beans and return to a boil. Reduce the heat to medium-high and cook about 20 minutes or until cooked to taste. Discard the onion and drain the beans in a colander. Rinse with cold water and let drain again. Dry on paper towels.

2. Heat the oil in a large skillet over medium heat. Add the garlic and cook, pressing the garlic with the back of a wooden spoon to release its flavor, until the garlic is golden on both sides. Add the beans and ham, season with salt and pepper, and cook, stirring, until the beans are hot. Serve hot.

Green Beans and Cured Ham
Judías Verdes "Barcena"

MAKES 4 SERVINGS

Adding cured ham to sautéed green beans makes a dish that is much richer and more flavorful. The beans should be cooked until they are tender but still slightly crunchy. I recommend adding a little vinegar to the water in which they are boiled. This recipe is from Pepe Barcena, now retired, one of the best Spanish chefs in New York.

1 tablespoon white wine vinegar

¾ pound green beans

2 tablespoons olive oil

¼ cup finely chopped onion

2 garlic cloves, finely chopped

½ cup very thin ½-inch strips Serrano (Spanish cured mountain) ham or prosciutto (about ¼ pound)

Salt

Freshly ground black pepper

1. Add the vinegar to a large pot of water and bring to a boil over high heat. Add the beans and cook 5 minutes. Drain in a colander. Rinse with cold water and let drain again. Dry with paper towels.

2. Heat the oil in a medium skillet over medium-high heat. Add the beans and cook until lightly browned, about 5 minutes. Add the onion, garlic, and ham, reduce the heat to medium, and cook 2 minutes more. Cover and cook, stirring occasionally, about 10 minutes or until the beans are tender but still slightly crunchy. Season with salt and pepper and serve hot.

Stewed Potatoes and Green Beans, Extremadura Style Ⓥ
Patatas y Judías Verdes a la Extremeña

MAKES 4 SERVINGS

Spain is credited with bringing potatoes from the New World and introducing them to the various countries of Europe. This is a stewed casserole that combines potatoes with green beans, onions, tomatoes, green peppers, and garlic. The bay leaf and parsley add the perfect accent of flavor. This recipe originated in Extremadura.

½ pound green beans

2 medium to large potatoes (about ¾ pound), peeled and cut into ¾-inch cubes

1 medium onion, finely chopped (about ⅔ cup)

1 medium tomato, finely chopped (about ⅔ cup)

1 medium green bell pepper, cut into thin strips

1 bay leaf

1 garlic clove, finely chopped

1 tablespoon finely chopped fresh flat-leaf parsley

Salt

Freshly ground black pepper

¼ cup olive oil

In a medium earthenware casserole dish or Dutch oven, combine the beans, potatoes, onion, tomato, and bell pepper. Add the bay leaf, garlic, parsley, salt, and pepper. Mix in the oil. Cover and cook over low heat, stirring occasionally, about 1 hour or until the vegetables are tender. Remove the bay leaf. If using earthenware, serve hot in the dish or transfer to individual plates.

Green Beans, Potatoes, and Eggs, Galician Style Ⓥ
Judías Verdes a la Gallega

MAKES 4 SERVINGS

Potatoes, called cachelos, *are a staple in Galicia. They are usually served as a companion to many dishes, such as meat, poultry, and other vegetables. It's a very popular side dish for octopus.*

4 small new potatoes

¾ pound broad green beans

2 tablespoons olive oil

1 medium onion, coarsely chopped (about ⅔ cup)

2 garlic cloves, coarsely chopped

Salt

Freshly ground black pepper

2 hard-boiled eggs, cut into wedges

1. Place the potatoes in a small saucepan with cold water to cover and add salt. Cover and bring to a simmer over low heat. Cook about 15 minutes or until the potatoes are tender when pierced with a knife. Drain and let cool slightly. Peel and cut in half.

2. Meanwhile, fill a large pot with water, add salt, and bring to a boil over medium-high heat. Add the beans and return to a boil. Reduce the heat to medium-low and cook until done to taste, about 20 minutes. Drain.

3. Heat the oil in a large shallow earthenware casserole dish or saucepan over medium heat. Add the onion and cook, stirring, until the onion is wilted, about 5 minutes. Add the garlic, then the beans and cook, stirring, 5 minutes. Add the potatoes, salt, and pepper and stir to combine. Place the egg wedges on top. Cover and cook 10 minutes more. If using earthenware, serve hot in the same dish, or transfer to individual plates.

Green Beans with Garlic and Vinegar Ⓥ
Judías Verdes al Ajillo con Vinagre

MAKES 6 SERVINGS

Vegetable dishes in Spain are commonly made more flavorful by the addition of ingredients such as garlic, chopped hard-boiled egg, and fried or toasted bread cubes. Here all three are featured. The tang of vinegar makes this a lovely light dish for the summertime.

1 small onion, halved

2 sprigs fresh parsley

2 whole garlic cloves

2 tablespoons plus 2 teaspoons olive oil

1 pound green beans, such as broad

2 (½-inch) slices long-loaf (baguette) bread, cut into cubes

2 garlic cloves, thinly sliced

Salt

2 teaspoons wine vinegar

1 hard-boiled egg, finely chopped

continues…

1. Fill a large pot with water, add salt, the onion, parsley, whole garlic cloves, and 1 tablespoon of the oil and bring to a boil over high heat. Add the beans, reduce the heat to low, and simmer about 20 minutes or until done to taste.

2. Meanwhile, heat 2 teaspoons of the oil in a small skillet over medium-high heat. Add the bread and cook, stirring, until browned. Transfer with a slotted spoon or spatula to paper towels and let drain. Add the remaining 1 tablespoon oil and the sliced garlic to the skillet, and cook, stirring, until golden.

3. When the green beans are done, drain them, discarding the parsley, garlic, and onion, and place on a serving platter. Pour the reserved garlic mixture over the beans, season with salt, and drizzle with the vinegar. Scatter the egg and bread over the beans and serve hot.

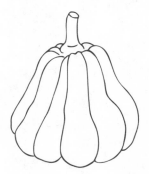

Greens with Olive Oil **V**
Acelgas Rehogadas

MAKES 3 TO 4 SERVINGS

There are very few plain vegetables my husband will eat, but this happens to be one of them. Acelgas is a general term for greens in Spain but also refers to a specific kind—its leaves are large and deep green and its stems are stark white. In the United States, the equivalents are Swiss chard and collard greens. This very simple recipe, wonderful served alongside a rich main course, calls for the greens to be boiled then drizzled with a bit of extra-virgin olive oil.

2 tablespoons extra-virgin olive oil

Salt

1 pound Swiss chard, well washed and thick stems trimmed

Add 1 tablespoon of the oil to a large pot of water, add salt, and bring to a boil over high heat. Reduce the heat to medium, add the chard and cook until just tender, about 15 minutes. Drain, pressing to extract as much liquid as possible, and chop coarsely. Drizzle with the remaining oil, season with salt, and serve hot.

Cumin-Scented Sautéed Greens
Acelgas en Rehogadillo

MAKES 6 SERVINGS

Versions of this dish are extremely popular throughout all of Spain. This recipe came from our dear belated friend Tomás Herranz who owned the excellent El Cenador del Prado restaurant in Madrid.

For many years he worked at the original San Martín restaurant and was the best Spanish chef in all of New York.

2 pounds Swiss chard, well washed and thick stems trimmed

3 tablespoons olive oil

1 thin slice long-loaf (baguette) bread, cut into small cubes

2 garlic cloves

½ teaspoon ground cumin

2 teaspoons wine vinegar

¼ cup finely chopped onion

1 medium tomato, peeled and finely chopped (about ⅔ cup)

Salt

3 hard-boiled eggs, halved (optional)

6 slices fried bread (optional)

1. Fill a large pot with water, add salt, and bring to a boil over high heat. Reduce the heat to medium, add the chard and cook until just tender, about 25 minutes. Drain, pressing to extract as much liquid as possible.

2. Heat the oil in a large skillet over medium heat. Add the bread and garlic and cook, stirring, until both are golden. Transfer to a mortar, reserving the oil, and let cool. Add the cumin and vinegar and mash.

3. Heat the reserved oil in the skillet over medium heat. Reduce the heat to low, add the onion, and cook, stirring, until wilted, about 5 minutes. Add the tomato and cook, stirring, until softened and its juices release, 2 to 3 minutes more. Stir in the mortar mixture and cook until the vinegar has evaporated. Add the chard and cook, stirring, until done to taste, a few minutes more. Season with salt. Serve hot with the eggs and bread, if using.

Sautéed Greens with Croutons Ⓥ
Acelgas Salteadas con Migas

MAKES 4 SERVINGS

This version of sautéed greens is made much more special by the addition of garlic croutons that add flavor as well as a pleasant crunch.

½ pound collard greens or Swiss chard, well washed and thick stems trimmed

Salt

5 tablespoons olive oil

1 teaspoon vinegar

2 teaspoons finely chopped onion

¾ cup small (½-inch) cubes long-loaf (baguette) bread

1 garlic clove, mashed in a garlic press or mortar

Freshly ground black pepper

1. Bring a large pot of water to a boil over high heat. Add the greens and cook 5 minutes. Drain. Return to the pot, add water to cover, salt and 1 tablespoon of the oil. Return to a boil over high heat. Reduce the heat to medium, cover, and cook about 10 minutes or until tender. Drain, pressing to extract as much liquid as possible, chop coarsely, and reserve.

2. Meanwhile, preheat the oven to 350°F. In a small bowl, mix 2 tablespoons of the remaining oil and the garlic. Place the bread cubes on a cookie sheet and drizzle or brush with the garlic mixture. Bake about 5 minutes or until crisp and golden.

3. Heat the remaining 2 tablespoons oil in a medium skillet over medium heat. Stir in the greens and cook 5 minutes. Stir in the vinegar, onions, croutons, salt, and pepper and cook until heated through, 1 to 2 minutes more. Serve hot.

Spinach Sautéed with Raisins and Pine Nuts **V**

Espinacas a la Catalana

MAKES 4 SERVINGS

Catalan style cooking is particularly creative, and it is common to combine spinach or other vegetables with raisins and pine nuts. This recipe came from Pilar de Olmo, a formidable woman despite her petite size, who runs El Robost de la Cartoixa, a restaurant in the hamlet of Scala Dei, home to the ruins of the Scala Dei Cartusian monastery. Pilar always reminds us proudly that every dish on the menu came from her grandmother's recipes.

2 tablespoons raisins

2 tablespoons pine nuts

Kosher or sea salt

1¾ pounds fresh baby spinach, well washed

2 tablespoons olive oil

2 garlic cloves, lightly smashed and peeled

Freshly ground black pepper

1. In separate small bowls, place the raisins and pine nuts, add warm water to cover, and let each soak 30 minutes. Drain and let dry on paper towels.

2. Fill a large pot with water, add salt, and bring to a boil over high heat. Add the spinach and cook until just tender, about 3 minutes. Transfer to a colander and let drain. Rinse with cold water and drain again, gently pressing to extract as much water as possible. Chop coarsely.

3. Heat the oil in a medium skillet over medium heat. Add the garlic and cook, stirring and pressing with the back of a wooden spoon to extract its flavor, until lightly browned. Sprinkle in the pine nuts and cook, stirring, until lightly golden. Stir in the spinach and raisins, season with salt and pepper, and cook 1 minute more. Reduce the heat to low, cover, and cook about 5 minutes more. Remove from the heat, cover, and let sit 10 minutes. Serve hot.

Sautéed Spinach with Quince and Toasted Sesame Seeds **V**

Espinacas con Membrillo al Sésamo

MAKES 4 TO 6 SERVINGS

Quince, a fruit somewhat similar to an apple, is very popular in Spain in preserves and is commonly served as a tapa or as a dessert with Manchego cheese. Spinach is delicious when prepared with quince, with toasted sesame seeds adding a nutty taste and texture. This excellent recipe of Moorish origin was given to me by my friend Julia who runs the restaurant Posada del Moro in Cazalla de la Sierra, near Seville.

2 teaspoons sesame seeds

2 tablespoons olive oil

1 medium sweet onion, such as Vidalia, finely chopped (about ⅔ cup)

1 quince (about ½ pound) or Golden Delicious apple, peeled and cut into ⅜-inch cubes

1½ pounds fresh spinach, well washed and coarsely chopped

Salt

Freshly ground black pepper

1. Preheat the oven to 350°F. Scatter the sesame seeds in a cake pan and bake about 5 minutes or until lightly golden.

2. Heat the oil in a large skillet over medium heat. Add the onion and quince and cook, stirring, about

2 minutes. Reduce the heat to low, cover, and cook about 10 minutes more. Stir in the spinach and season with salt and pepper. Cover and cook, stirring occasionally, until the spinach is just tender, about 5 minutes. Sprinkle with the sesame seeds and serve hot.

Sautéed Chicory with Ham and Cumin
Achicorias Salteadas

MAKES 4 SERVINGS

This recipe came from my friend Fray Juan, a monk in charge of the kitchen at the Guadalupe monastery in the region of Extremadura. Many recipes would be lost to us today had they not been preserved by convents and monasteries. Chicory, often thought of as the poor cousin of the vegetable family, is absolutely delicious when prepared with cumin, ham, paprika, and crunchy bread bits.

1 to 1½ pounds chicory, washed and trimmed

2 tablespoons olive oil

2 garlic cloves

2 (½-inch) slices long-loaf (baguette) bread, cut into cubes

¼ teaspoon salt

½ teaspoon ground cumin

¼ cup very thin 1-inch strips Serrano (Spanish cured mountain) ham or prosciutto (about 2 ounces)

½ teaspoon ground paprika, such as Spanish smoked bittersweet

1. Fill a large pot with water, add salt, and bring to a boil over high heat. Add the chicory, reduce the heat to medium, and cook until tender, 10 to 15 minutes. Drain in a colander, rinse with cold water, and let drain again, pressing to extract as much water as possible. Place between paper towels and gently squeeze out more of the water. Chop coarsely.

2. Heat the oil in a large skillet over medium-high heat. Add the garlic and bread and cook, stirring, until both are browned. Transfer with a slotted spoon to a mortar, reserving the oil, and let cool. Add the salt and cumin and mash.

3. Heat the reserved oil in the skillet over medium heat. Add the ham and cook, stirring, until lightly coated with the oil. Stir in the paprika, chicory, and the mortar mixture and cook 1 to 2 minutes more. Season with salt. Serve hot.

Sautéed Mushrooms Ⓥ
Champiñones Salteados

MAKES 4 SERVINGS

Catalunyans are mushroom connoisseurs as they have a tremendous variety of mushrooms to choose from, each with a subtly distinctive taste and texture. Here they are sautéed with butter, garlic, and bread crumbs, making an extremely tasty dish.

1 pound mushrooms, rinsed and trimmed
2 teaspoons unsalted butter
6 garlic cloves, finely chopped
2 tablespoons finely chopped fresh flat-leaf parsley
2 tablespoons bread crumbs
Salt

If the mushrooms are very large, cut them in half. Melt the butter in a large skillet over high heat. Add the mushrooms, garlic, and parsley and cook, stirring, until lightly browned. Stir in the bread crumbs and season with salt. Serve hot.

Wild Mushrooms with Garlic Bread Bits Ⓥ
Setas con Migas

MAKES 4 SERVINGS

The key to this recipe is the garlic croutons (migas), which provide a pungent contrast to the subtle flavor of the mushrooms. If you can find wild mushrooms at the store, use them, or try flavorful shiitake.

2 tablespoons fruity extra-virgin olive oil
1 garlic clove, mashed in a garlic press or mortar

1½ cups small cubes (½-inch) round loaf (country) bread, crust removed
1 pound mushrooms, such as shiitake, rinsed, trimmed, and halved or quartered
Salt
Freshly ground black pepper
1 garlic clove, finely chopped
1 tablespoon finely chopped fresh flat-leaf parsley
A squeeze of fresh lemon juice

1. Preheat the oven to 350°F. In a cup, mix 1 tablespoon of the oil with the mashed garlic. Place the bread cubes on a cookie sheet and bake, stirring occasionally, about 8 minutes or until browned. Drizzle with the oil-garlic mixture.

2. Heat the remaining 1 tablespoon oil in a large skillet over high heat. Add the mushrooms and cook, stirring, until coated with the oil and starting to soften. Add salt, pepper, the chopped garlic, the parsley, and lemon juice. Cook until the mushrooms are softened to taste. Remove from the heat and stir in the bread. Serve hot.

Mushrooms in Sherry Sauce Ⓥ*
Champiñones al Jerez

MAKES 4 SERVINGS

Sherry takes its name from its place of origin, Jerez de la Frontera in southwest Spain. It is one of the world's oldest wines, praised over the centuries for its fine quality and unique taste. Sherry greatly enhances the flavor of any dish that is cooked with it. This recipe calls for sherry of the dry or Fino variety. Make it vegetarian with vegetable broth.

1 pound mushrooms, rinsed, trimmed, whole (if small) or halved (if medium)
A squeeze of fresh lemon juice
1 tablespoon olive oil
2 tablespoons finely chopped onion
2 teaspoons all-purpose flour

¼ cup dry sherry, such as Fino

¼ cup chicken broth, beef broth, or vegetable broth

Salt

Freshly ground black pepper

1 tablespoon finely chopped fresh flat-leaf parsley

I. Place the mushrooms in a large bowl, sprinkle with the lemon juice, and fold to coat. Heat the oil in a large skillet over medium heat. Add the onion and cook, stirring, until wilted, about 3 minutes. Add the mushrooms and cook, stirring, about 3 minutes more. Transfer to a large bowl, reserving the oil.

2. Heat the reserved oil in the skillet over medium heat. Sprinkle the flour into the skillet and cook, stirring, about 1 minute. Add the sherry, broth, salt, pepper, and parsley and cook, stirring, until thickened and smooth. Return the mushrooms to the skillet and cook until the mushrooms are hot, about 2 minutes more. Serve hot.

Mushrooms in Hazelnut Sauce Ⓥ

Setas en Salsa de Avellanas

MAKES 4 SERVINGS

Here the subtle flavor of mushrooms is contrasted by a tasty mash of garlic, hazelnuts, onion, and parsley (a version of picada *sauce). I recommend shiitake mushrooms, but if they are unavailable, you can substitute a mix of mushrooms.*

2 garlic cloves, finely chopped

10 hazelnuts, shelled, skin on

2 tablespoons finely chopped fresh flat-leaf parsley

⅛ teaspoon salt

1 tablespoon olive oil

1 medium onion, slivered

1 pound mushrooms, such as shiitake or a mix, rinsed and trimmed

Salt

Freshly ground black pepper

I. In a mortar or mini-processor, mash the garlic, hazelnuts, parsley, and ⅛ teaspoon salt.

2. Heat the oil in a large skillet over medium heat. Add the onion and cook, stirring, until wilted, about 3 minutes. Reduce the heat to low, cover, and cook, stirring occasionally, 10 minutes more. Add the mushrooms and cook about 2 minutes more. Add salt, pepper, and the mortar mixture and cook until the mushrooms are done to taste. Serve hot.

Mushrooms in Cabrales Blue Cheese Sauce Ⓥ

Setas en Salsa de Cabrales

MAKES 4 SERVINGS

Although our dear friend and extraordinary cook Vicentina is now gone, her daughter-in-law Marise Zubizarreta took up where she left off. This outstanding mushroom dish uses Spain's famous Cabrales blue cheese, made in the lush mountains of Asturias, where Marise and her family live. Cabrales cheese can be found in specialty stores, but if not available, use Gorgonzola.

4 tablespoons olive oil

1½ pounds mushrooms, such as oyster, rinsed and trimmed

1 garlic clove, finely chopped

3 tablespoons finely chopped fresh flat-leaf parsley

Kosher or sea salt

3 tablespoons finely chopped onion

¼ pound Cabrales blue cheese or gorgonzola, cut into small pieces

¼ cup dry white wine

¼ cup heavy cream

continues . . .

1. Heat 3 tablespoons of the oil in a large skillet over high heat. Add the mushrooms and cook, stirring constantly, until beginning to soften, about 3 minutes. Stir in the garlic, 2 tablespoons of the parsley, and salt until the mushrooms are coated. Transfer to a large bowl. Wipe out the skillet.

2. Heat the remaining 1 tablespoon oil in the same skillet over medium heat. Reduce the heat to medium-low, add the onion, and cook, stirring, until wilted, about 3 minutes. Add the cheese, wine, and cream, and cook, stirring, until well blended. Return the mushrooms to the skillet, and cook until tender, stirring to coat with the sauce. Season with salt. Sprinkle with the remaining 1 tablespoon parsley and serve hot.

Meat-Filled Baked Onions
Cebollas Rellenas de Carne

MAKES 6 SERVINGS

These wonderful baked onions are always a big hit with my dinner guests. The onions are stuffed with a mixture of beef, veal, and pork that can be varied according to taste, as well as the flavorful addition of cured ham. I much prefer Spanish Serrano ham, but if not available, you can substitute prosciutto or capicola.

12 medium onions

3 tablespoons olive oil

3 garlic cloves, finely chopped separately

1½-pound mixture of ground beef, veal, and pork in equal parts

2 tablespoons finely chopped Serrano (Spanish cured mountain) ham or prosciutto (about 1 ounce)

3 tablespoons finely chopped fresh flat-leaf parsley

Salt

Freshly ground black pepper

1 tablespoon finely chopped fresh thyme or ½ teaspoon dried thyme

3 tablespoons seeded and finely chopped tomato

6 tablespoons finely chopped pimiento

2 large hard-boiled eggs, finely chopped

½ cup dry white wine

½ cup chicken broth or vegetable broth

1. Remove the tough outer layers of the onions and slice off the ends. Hollow out the onions, leaving a shell ¼ inch thick. Finely chop 2 cups of the removed onion and reserve.

2. Heat 2 tablespoons of the oil in a medium skillet over medium heat. Add 1 cup of the reserved chopped onions and 2 of the garlic cloves and

cook, stirring, until the onions are wilted, about 5 minutes. Add the ground meat and cook, stirring, until the meat is no longer pink. Stir in the ham, 2 tablespoons of the parsley, salt, pepper, and the thyme until incorporated, then stir in 2 tablespoons of the tomato and 4 tablespoons of the pimiento, cooking for a couple of minutes. Remove from the heat and stir in the eggs.

3. Fill the hollowed onions with the meat mixture, packing tightly. Place in a shallow baking dish.

4. Preheat the oven to 375°F. Heat the remaining 1 tablespoon oil in a medium skillet over medium heat. Add the remaining 1 cup chopped onions and 1 garlic clove and cook, stirring, until the onion is wilted, about 5 minutes. Add the remaining 2 tablespoons pimiento, 1 tablespoon tomato, and 1 tablespoon parsley. Stir in the wine and broth and season with salt and pepper. Pour over the onions. Cover and bake about 1½ hours or until tender. Spoon the sauce over the onions and serve hot.

Onions Coated with Honey and Spices **V**
Cebollas con Miel

MAKES 4 SERVINGS

There is a very interesting booklet about Moorish Andalucía that included recipes written by L. Benavides Barajas. He wrote that the Moors were prohibited from eating raw onion, both for religious reasons and the odious breath it left behind. It does include this one recipe for onions, in which their pungent flavor is tempered by honey and spices, including saffron, cloves, cumin, and nutmeg.

12 to 16 small onions (about 1½ inch in diameter)
4 teaspoons unsalted butter
2 tablespoons honey
½ teaspoon ground (or mortar-crushed) cumin
A few threads of saffron, crumbled
Pinch of ground cloves

Pinch of grated or ground nutmeg
Salt
Freshly ground black pepper

1. Trim the stem end of each onion and make an incision in the shape of a cross at the same end. Bring a large pot of water to a boil over high heat. Add the onions and cook 1 minute. Remove from the water, slip off the skins, and return to the pot. Reduce the heat to low, cover, and cook 20 minutes more.

2. Drain off all but 2 tablespoons of the water and stir in all the remaining ingredients. Bring to a simmer over medium-low heat and cook, stirring constantly (watch carefully to prevent scorching), until the liquid is absorbed and the onions are golden, about 10 minutes. Serve hot.

Peas with Cured Ham
Guisantes a la Española

MAKES 4 SERVINGS

Here the sweet flavor of peas is perfectly complemented by the savory taste of ham. This is the typical way that Spanish-style peas are prepared, and they can be found all over Spain.

2 tablespoons olive oil
¼ cup finely chopped onion
¼ cup finely chopped carrot
¼ cup finely chopped Serrano (Spanish cured mountain) ham or prosciutto (about 2 ounces)
½ pound fresh or frozen peas
Salt
Freshly ground black pepper

Heat the oil in a medium skillet over medium heat. Add the onion and carrot and cook, stirring, until the onion is wilted, about 5 minutes. Add the ham and cook, stirring, 1 minute. Stir in the peas, salt, and pepper. Cover and cook about 20 minutes or until the peas are tender. Serve hot.

Peas with Sausage
Guisantes con Salchichas

MAKES 4 SERVINGS

This recipe for peas calls for butifarra, *a very special sausage made in Catalunya. It can be found in many specialty food stores, but if it is not available, you can substitute sweet Italian or breakfast sausage. The mash of almonds and garlic completes a delicious dish.*

2 pork sausages (butifarra) or sweet Italian-style or
    breakfast sausages

1 tablespoon olive oil

1 tablespoon lard

¼ cup finely chopped onion

½ medium tomato, coarsely chopped (about ⅓ cup)

½ pound fresh or frozen peas

⅛ teaspoon finely chopped fresh mint

5 blanched almonds

1 garlic clove

1. Heat the oil and lard in a medium skillet over medium heat. Add the sausage and cook, stirring, until heated through. Transfer to a plate, reserving the oil, and thinly slice.

2. In the reserved oil over medium heat, add the onion and cook, stirring, until wilted, about 5 minutes. Add the tomato and cook, stirring occasionally, until softened and its juices release, about 15 minutes more. Transfer to a blender or food processor and blend until smooth, adding enough water to make a sauce. Return to the skillet and add the peas, sausage, and mint. Cover and cook over medium heat until the peas are almost tender.

3. In a blender or food processor, (the bowl should be clean and dry), blend the almonds and garlic until the almonds are finely ground (but not a paste). Stir into the peas and cook until the peas are tender and the nut mixture is incorporated, 3 to 4 minutes more. Serve hot.

Peas, Valencia Style Ⓥ*
Guisantes a la Valenciana

MAKES 4 SERVINGS

This is how they prepare peas in Valencia, using onions, garlic, white wine, and saffron—the perfect flavor complement to the sweetness of peas. This recipe calls for wedges of hard-boiled eggs that can be included or omitted according to preference. Make it vegetarian with vegetable broth.

1 tablespoon olive oil

1 small onion, finely chopped (about ⅓ cup)

2 garlic cloves, finely chopped

1½ cups fresh or frozen peas

2 tablespoons dry white wine

2 sprigs fresh parsley

1 bay leaf

1½ teaspoons finely chopped fresh thyme or ¼
    teaspoon dried thyme

Few threads of saffron

2 teaspoons chicken broth or vegetable broth

Salt

Freshly ground black pepper

Pimiento strips or hard-boiled egg wedges, for
    garnish (optional)

1. Heat the oil in a medium skillet over medium heat. Add the onion and half of the garlic and cook, stirring, until the onion is wilted, about 5 minutes. Stir in the peas and cook 1 minute, then stir in the wine, 2 tablespoons water, the parsley, bay leaf, and thyme. Cover, reduce the heat to low, and simmer 2 minutes.

2. Meanwhile, in a mortar or mini-processor, mash the remaining half of the garlic and the saffron, then stir in the chicken broth. Stir into the peas and season with salt and pepper. Cover and cook about 5 minutes more or until the peas are tender and the liquid has been absorbed. Remove the bay leaf. Garnish with the pimiento, if using, or hard-boiled egg, if using. Serve hot.

Fried Green Peppers ⓥ
Pimientos Fritos

MAKES 4 SERVINGS

The village of Padrón in Galicia is known for their pimientos de Padrón, tiny bright green peppers that grow mainly in summer. They are always prepared fried and sprinkled with coarse salt, and make a delicious tapa or snack. You can find imported Padrón peppers in some specialty stores or online at LaTienda.com. Or, substitute long and skinny green frying peppers, sometimes called Italian peppers. You won't need as many for a pound. Serve as is to cut at the table or stem and cut them before serving.

6 tablespoons olive oil

1 pound green frying peppers (smallest available), such as padróns or Italian peppers

Kosher or sea salt

Heat the oil in a large skillet over medium-high heat. Add the peppers, reduce the heat to medium, and cook, turning occasionally, until browned on all sides. Sprinkle with salt and serve hot.

Sautéed Red Peppers ⓥ*
Pimientos Morrones Salteados

MAKES 4 SERVINGS

This is a classic Spanish accompaniment to grilled or sautéed meat or chicken. All you need to do is stir-fry them for a minute or so in olive oil, garlic, and a bit of broth. If you don't want to work with fresh chiles, jarred prepared piquillo peppers can usually be found in well-stocked supermarkets and specialty food stores. Make this recipe vegetarian with vegetable broth.

2 tablespoons olive oil

1½ pounds fresh red chile peppers, cored and seeded, or ¾ pound (jarred) piquillo peppers, cut into thin strips

Salt

2 garlic cloves, thinly sliced

¼ cup chicken broth, vegetable broth, or water

Heat the oil in a medium skillet over medium-high heat. Add the peppers and cook, stirring, about 5 minutes (about 2 minutes for piquillos, if using). Add salt and stir in the garlic and broth. Reduce the heat to low, cover, and cook about 20 minutes more or until the peppers are softened, stirring occasionally and adding a little more broth if the pan dries out. Serve hot.

Sautéed Green Peppers and Pimientos
Pimientos del Bierzo

MAKES 4 SERVINGS

This recipe originated in El Bierzo, an area well known for their fresh vegetables, and the flavor is greatly enhanced by cured ham. It comes from the only restaurant in the tiny village of Compludo on the way to St. James.

2 tablespoons olive oil

6 green (Italian) frying peppers, cut into thin strips

3 pimientos

2 garlic cloves, finely chopped

2 tablespoons finely chopped onion

2 thin slices Serrano (Spanish cured mountain) ham or prosciutto, cut into pieces

Salt

Freshly ground black pepper

Heat the oil in a medium skillet over high heat. Add the green peppers and pimientos and cook, stirring, about 5 minutes. Stir in the garlic, onion, ham, salt, and black pepper. Reduce the heat to low, cover, and simmer about 15 minutes or until the green peppers are tender. Serve hot.

Stuffed Peppers, Asturian Style
Pimientos Rellenos a la Asturiana

MAKES 3 TO 4 SERVINGS

This Asturian specialty of peppers filled with a stuffing of meats and rice calls for a mixture of beef, veal, and pork, but you can vary it according to preference. Cured ham is added to the meat mixture, making this an especially rich dish more suited for a main course than a side dish. I like to use both red and green peppers as they make for a much more attractive and colorful presentation.

1¼-pound mixture of ground beef, veal, and pork in equal parts

2 tablespoons finely chopped Serrano (Spanish cured mountain) ham or prosciutto (about 1 ounce)

2 garlic cloves, mashed in a garlic press or mortar

1 teaspoon salt

Sauce

1 tablespoon olive oil

1 small onion, finely chopped (about ⅓ cup)

1 garlic clove, finely chopped

1 small carrot, peeled and finely chopped (about ⅓ cup)

1 small tomato, peeled, seeded, and finely chopped (about ½ cup)

1 tablespoon finely chopped fresh flat-leaf parsley

1 cup chicken broth or vegetable broth

Few threads of saffron

1 bay leaf

½ cup dry white wine

Salt

Freshly ground black pepper

1 tablespoon olive oil

1 medium onion, finely chopped (about ⅔ cup)

Freshly ground black pepper

2 tablespoons finely chopped fresh flat-leaf parsley

1 small tomato, peeled, seeded, and finely chopped (about ½ cup)

¼ cup uncooked rice, such as short grain

1 tablespoon dry white wine

8 medium red or green bell peppers, or a mix

1. In a medium bowl, mix together the ground meat, ham, garlic, and the salt and reserve.

2. Prepare the sauce: Heat the 1 tablespoon oil in a shallow earthenware casserole dish or Dutch oven over medium heat. Add the onion, garlic, and carrot and cook, stirring, until the onion is wilted, about 5 minutes. Add the tomato and parsley and cook, stirring, until the tomato is softened and its juices release, about 2 minutes. Stir in the broth, saffron, bay leaf, wine, salt, and black pepper and bring to a boil. Reduce the heat to low, cover, and simmer 15 minutes. Remove the bay leaf.

3. Meanwhile, heat the 1 tablespoon oil in a medium skillet over medium heat. Add the onion and cook, stirring, until wilted, about 5 minutes. Add the meat mixture and cook, breaking it up as it loses its color, until lightly browned. Stir in salt, black pepper, the parsley and tomato and cook 1 minute. Stir in the rice and wine and cook 5 minutes more.

4. Preheat the oven to 350°F. Cut off the tops of the bell peppers and scoop out the membranes and seeds. Fill loosely with the meat mixture and cover with the tops. Place in the casserole dish—upright or on their sides. Bake, spooning the sauce over them occasionally, about 1 hour or until the bell peppers are softened. If using earthenware, serve hot in the dish, or transfer to individual plates.

The year 1492 was a very eventful one in Spain. Queen Isabel from Castilla married King Fernando of Aragon, forming the new kingdom of Spain and for the first time achieving territorial and political unity. The Moors, who occupied Iberia for 700 years, were defeated at Granada and expelled into Africa. Christopher Columbus, representing Spain, discovered a new world, providing the Crown with a very large continent ready to be explored and colonized, and providing great riches and opportunities to anybody with a will for adventure.

The first Spaniards that arrived in America found an enormous array of products unknown in Europe that were brought back to Spain and cultivated there. This marked a huge change in Spanish and European gastronomy. Tomatoes, potatoes, peppers, corn, sugar, and chocolate (cacao) all thrived in the warm climate of Spain and were eventually popularized throughout Europe. Before long, these new ingredients became traditional staples in European dishes and dramatically changed the face of cooking in many countries. Who can imagine Italian cooking without tomato sauce, or Hungarian cuisine without paprika, or countries like Ireland and Poland without the potato?

Of all the vegetables that came from the Americas, sweet red peppers are one of the most emblematic of Spain and are commonly referred to as bell peppers in the United States. Peppers were initially used as a condiment in the Old World, first in Spain and then in other countries. In 1495, when Columbus met the Catholic Kings in the Guadalupe monastery, he showed them the vegetables he brought back from America, sweet red peppers being among them. The monks of Guadalupe cultivated them and then introduced them to other monasteries. It was in the valley of La Vera where Spanish sweet red peppers found their ideal environment.

The influence of New World products, especially vegetables, cannot be overstated. Think how different cooking would be today without beloved ingredients like peppers, tomatoes, potatoes, sugar, corn, and chocolate!

Wrinkled Potatoes ⓥ
Papas Arrugadas

MAKES 4 SERVINGS

Papas arrugadas or "wrinkled potatoes" are made with tiny potatoes, often less than an inch across, that grow in the Canary Islands and come in many varieties, including prized black potatoes. The reason they are cooked with so much salt is that the salty water draws water out of the potato by osmosis but cannot penetrate the skin. The effect is a potato dish that is very flavorful but not overly salty.

1 pound tiny (1½- to 2-inch) new potatoes
¾ cup kosher or sea salt

1. Place the potatoes in a medium saucepan with water to cover by 1 inch. Add the salt and stir until dissolved. Bring to a boil over medium-high heat, partially cover, and cook, until tender, about 20 minutes.

2. Drain off the water, leaving the potatoes in the pan. Reduce the heat to low and cook, shaking occasionally, until the potatoes are dry and the skins slightly wrinkled, about 10 minutes. Serve hot.

Widowed Potatoes ⓥ
Patatas Viudas

MAKES 4 SERVINGS

This simple dish has no major ingredients besides potatoes, and it is meant to be served alone, hence its name "Widowed Potatoes." It is enormously popular in Asturias and is also a traditional favorite of Castilian convent nuns. Many of Spain's oldest recipes have been preserved by monasteries and convents.

4 medium potatoes
Salt
2 tablespoons olive oil
¾ cup finely chopped onions
2 garlic cloves, finely chopped
2 tablespoons finely chopped fresh flat-leaf parsley
1 bay leaf
⅓ teaspoon ground sweet or hot paprika, such as Spanish smoked

1. Place the potatoes in a medium saucepan with cold water to cover and add salt. Cover and bring to a simmer over low heat. Cook about 15 minutes or until the potatoes are tender when pierced with a knife. Drain and let cool slightly. Peel and cut into ¾-inch cubes.

2. Meanwhile, heat the oil in a medium skillet over medium heat. Add the onions, garlic, parsley, and bay leaf and cook, stirring, about 2 minutes. Reduce the heat to low, cover, and cook about 10 minutes more or until the onions are softened. Stir in the paprika.

3. Drain the potatoes, reserving 4 tablespoons of the cooking liquid. Add the potatoes and reserved liquid to the skillet, turn the potatoes to coat, and cook until heated through. Remove the bay leaf. Serve hot.

Castilian-Style Potatoes ⓥ
Patatas Castellanas

MAKES 4 SERVINGS

Paprika, or pimentón, *is made from roasted red peppers and is the main product in the valley of La Vera in central Spain between Castilla and Extremadura. Pimentón from La Vera, made from sweet peppers, is considered the highest quality.*

3 tablespoons olive oil

3 tablespoons finely chopped onion

1 garlic clove, finely chopped

3 large potatoes, cut into small cubes

1 tablespoon all-purpose flour

1 teaspoon ground paprika

Salt

Freshly ground black pepper

1 bay leaf

Heat the oil in a medium skillet over medium heat. Add the onion and garlic and cook, stirring, until the onion is wilted, about 3 minutes. Add the potatoes and cook, stirring, about 5 minutes more. Sprinkle with the flour and paprika and stir to coat the potatoes. Add hot water to cover. Add salt, pepper, and the bay leaf, just cover, and cook about 20 minutes more or until the potatoes are tender and most of the liquid is absorbed. Remove the bay leaf. Serve hot.

Spicy Potatoes Ⓥ
Patatas Picantes

MAKES 4 SERVINGS

This dish, a simple version of spicy potatoes, are especially appealing to those who prefer food with a lot of heat, as this recipe calls for a generous amount of dried red chile peppers. You should always remove the seeds from the peppers before combining them with the other ingredients. Paprika adds an earthy accent.

3 medium potatoes

3 tablespoons olive oil

⅛ teaspoon ground paprika, such as Spanish smoked

⅛ teaspoon crushed seeded dried chile pepper

2 garlic cloves, finely chopped

Salt

1. Place the potatoes in a medium saucepan with cold water to cover and add salt. Cover and bring to a simmer over low heat. Cook about 15 minutes or until the potatoes are tender when pierced with a knife. Drain and let cool slightly. Peel and cut into ¼-inch slices.

2. Heat the oil in a large skillet over medium-high heat. Add the potatoes one at a time to prevent sticking. Cook, turning occasionally, until lightly browned. Sprinkle with the paprika, chile pepper, garlic, and salt. Cook, turning occasionally, about 5 minutes more. Serve hot.

onion and garlic and cook, stirring, until the onion is wilted, about 3 minutes. Stir in the tomato sauce, wine, parsley, chile pepper, hot sauce, salt, and pepper. Cook, stirring occasionally, about 20 minutes. The sauce should be thick. Pour over the potatoes and serve hot, or serve with the sauce on the side. In either case, the potatoes should be only lightly coated with the sauce.

Garlic Potatoes Ⓥ*
Patatas al Ajillo

MAKES 4 SERVINGS

Spaniards love garlic in just about everything including their potatoes. This recipe calls for them to be sliced thinly, then sautéed in a mixture of garlic, cumin, paprika, and vinegar. Make it vegetarian with vegetable broth.

3 tablespoons olive oil

4 medium potatoes, peeled and cut into ⅛-inch slices

Salt

2 garlic cloves, finely chopped

1 tablespoon finely chopped fresh flat-leaf parsley

½ teaspoon ground paprika

¼ teaspoon ground (or mortar-crushed) cumin

1 teaspoon vinegar

2 teaspoons chicken broth or vegetable broth

continues…

1. Heat the oil in a 9- to 10-inch skillet over medium heat. Add the potatoes in layers, sprinkling each layer with salt. Turn the potatoes to coat with the oil. Reduce the heat to medium-low, cover, and cook, lifting gently and turning them occasionally, about 20 minutes or until tender. (The potatoes will be separated, not in a "cake"). Increase the heat to medium-high and cook just until some of the potatoes brown.

2. Meanwhile, in a mortar or mini-processor, mash the garlic, parsley, paprika, and cumin. Stir in the vinegar and broth and drizzle over the potatoes. Serve hot.

Poor Man's Potatoes Ⓥ
Patatas Pobre

MAKES 4 SERVINGS

This is one of my family's favorite potato dishes. The colloquial term "poor man's potatoes" couldn't be further from the truth because, in fact, the love of this dish knows no economic boundaries. Years ago, whenever my husband, Luis, and I went to the Casa de España restaurant in New York, Chef Antonio Pazos would make us a batch. They were always presented beautifully, on a silver platter lined with doilies, and they were a favorite of my daughter, Elisa.

For a main dish that serves 3, break 4 eggs over the potatoes when they are done, cover, and let sit 5 minutes or until the eggs are set.

3 tablespoons olive oil
4 medium potatoes, cut into ⅛-inch slices
Salt
1 garlic clove, finely chopped, for garnish
1 tablespoon finely chopped fresh flat-leaf parsley, for garnish

Heat the oil in a 9- to 10-inch skillet over medium heat. Add the potatoes in layers, sprinkling each layer with salt. Turn the potatoes to coat with the oil. Reduce the heat to medium-low, cover, and cook, lifting gently and turning them occasionally, about 20 minutes or until tender. (The potatoes will be separated, not in a "cake"). Increase the heat to medium-high and cook just until some of the potatoes brown. Sprinkle with the garlic and parsley. Serve hot.

Sautéed Saffron-Scented Potatoes Ⓥ*
Patatas al Azafrán

MAKES 4 SERVINGS

A popular way to prepare potatoes in the Basque country, this recipe calls for sweet onions and saffron, which lends its distinctive flavor and aroma. It is an excellent side dish to accompany simple meat, poultry, or fish. Any dish prepared al azafrán includes saffron. Make it vegetarian with vegetable broth.

5 tablespoons olive oil
1 medium sweet onion, such as Vidalia, slivered
2 tablespoons chicken broth or vegetable broth
Scant ¼ teaspoon saffron threads, crumbled
4 medium potatoes, peeled and cut into ⅛-inch slices
Kosher or sea salt
2 tablespoons finely chopped fresh flat-leaf parsley

1. Heat 2 tablespoons of the oil in a 9- to 10-inch skillet over medium heat. Reduce the heat to low, add the onion and cook, stirring occasionally, about 10 minutes or until softened. Stir in the broth and saffron and cook until some of the liquid has evaporated. Transfer to a small bowl and wipe out the skillet.

2. Heat the remaining 3 tablespoons oil in the same skillet over medium heat. Add the potatoes

in layers, sprinkling each layer with salt. Turn the potatoes to coat with the oil. Reduce the heat to medium-low, cover, and cook, lifting gently and turning them occasionally, about 20 minutes or until tender. (The potatoes will be separated, not in a "cake.") Increase the heat to medium-high and cook just until some of the potatoes brown. Spoon the onions over the potatoes, sprinkle with parsley, and serve hot.

Potatoes with Walnuts and Cumin Ⓥ
Patatas Campesinas

MAKES 6 SERVINGS

A Moorish influence is reflected in this recipe for boiled potatoes covered in an exceptional sauce of walnuts, garlic, and cumin. The sauce is also excellent over other vegetables.

2 pounds new or red waxy potatoes, peeled

Salt

2 bay leaves

Few slices onion

2 garlic cloves

2 tablespoons finely chopped walnuts

½ teaspoon cumin seed or ground cumin

2 tablespoons finely chopped fresh flat-leaf parsley

2 tablespoons finely chopped pimiento

¼ cup extra-virgin olive oil

1. Place the potatoes in a medium saucepan with cold water to cover. Add salt, the bay leaves, and onions. Cover and bring to a simmer over low heat. Cook about 15 minutes or until the potatoes are tender when pierced with a knife. Drain and let cool slightly.

2. Meanwhile, in a mortar or mini-processor, mash the garlic, walnuts, ⅛ teaspoon salt, the cumin, and parsley. Mash in the pimiento. Stir in the olive oil.

3. Drain the potatoes, reserving a few tablespoons of the cooking liquid, and remove the bay leaf. Stir enough of the reserved liquid into the mortar mixture until the consistency of mayonnaise. Spoon over the potatoes and serve hot, or serve the sauce on the side.

Potatoes with Chorizo
Patatas con Chorizo

MAKES 4 SERVINGS

Chorizo is a wonderfully flavored Iberian sausage seasoned with paprika and garlic. It was adopted by Spain's former colonies in the New World and therefore is not hard to find in the United States. This delicious recipe is made richer and even more flavorful by the addition of bacon.

1 tablespoon olive oil

10 thin slices (about ⅛ inch) chorizo sausage

3 thin slices bacon, coarsely chopped

4 medium potatoes, peeled and cut into large pieces, or 12 small new potatoes, peeled and quartered

Salt

1 tablespoon finely chopped fresh flat-leaf parsley

1 garlic clove, finely chopped

Heat the oil in a large skillet over medium heat. Add the chorizo and bacon and cook, stirring, until they begin to give off their oils. Add the potatoes and season with salt. Reduce the heat to medium-low, cover, and cook until the potatoes are golden and tender. Sprinkle with the parsley and garlic. Increase the heat to medium-high, and cook, turning occasionally, until the potatoes are browned, about 5 minutes more. Serve hot.

Potatoes with Sautéed Peppers and Chorizo

Patatas Majaelrayo

MAKES 3 TO 4 SERVINGS

This mixture of potatoes, peppers, and chorizo makes a wonderful accompaniment to any simple meat or poultry dish. The recipe came from an unlikely source. My husband, Luis, and I were traveling on a dirt road in the Sierra Pobre ("Poor Mountains") in the provinces of Madrid and Guadalajara. We stopped at the village of Majaelrayo, one of the "Black Villages" named for their dark stone construction and the black slate roofs of their houses. To our surprise, we found a modern bar in this isolated town, where we were served these delicious potatoes.

2 medium potatoes, cut into ½-inch cubes

Salt

Freshly ground black pepper

2 tablespoons olive oil

2 medium green frying peppers such as Italian peppers, cored, seeded, and cut into 1-inch pieces

1 tablespoon finely chopped chorizo

I. In a greased microwave-safe small bowl, combine the potatoes, salt, black pepper, I tablespoon of the oil, and I tablespoon water. Cover and cook on High 5 minutes. Stir to coat and cook 5 minutes more or until tender. Alternatively, you can oven-roast the potatoes, omitting the water.

2. Meanwhile, heat the remaining I tablespoon oil in a small skillet over medium-high heat. Add the green peppers and salt and cook, stirring, I to 2 minutes. Reduce the heat to medium, cover, and cook until tender. Add the chorizo and cook I to 2 minutes more. Add the potatoes and cook, turning occasionally, until lightly browned. Serve hot.

Potatoes in Garlic and Almond Sauce ⓥ*

Patatas en Ajopollo

MAKES 6 SERVINGS

These potatoes in garlic sauce are made exceptional by the nutty taste and texture of the sautéed almonds. The recipe calls for saffron, which lends its distinctive flavor and aroma. It can be quite expensive, but there truly is no adequate substitute. Make it vegetarian with vegetable broth.

½ cup olive oil

1 thin slice long-loaf (baguette) bread

12 blanched almonds

2 garlic cloves

1 sprig fresh parsley

¼ teaspoon threads saffron, crumbled

Freshly ground white pepper

1 cup water

5 medium potatoes, peeled and cut into small cubes

1 cup chicken broth or vegetable broth

Salt

I. Heat the oil in a medium skillet over medium heat. Add the bread, almonds, garlic, and parsley and cook, stirring and turning the bread once, until all are lightly browned (if the almonds brown too quickly, remove them). Transfer to a food processor or blender, reserving the oil. Add the saffron and pepper to the processor and process until a paste forms. With the motor running, gradually add the water and process until smooth.

2. Place the potatoes in a medium saucepan. Add the processor mixture, the reserved oil, the broth, and salt and stir to combine. Cook over medium heat, until the potatoes are tender. Serve hot.

Creamy Potato Purée with Garlic V
Puré de Patatas a la Vasca

MAKES 4 SERVINGS

My mother in law, Clara Orozco, a Madrileño of Basque descent, taught me how to make this garlic-rich potato purée. Potatoes that are sautéed or fried are popular in many parts of Spain, but the Basques are fond of subtle, delicate flavors, and they usually prepare puréed potatoes that are thin and creamy. Clara always said that the secret to this outstanding dish was the egg yolk, which should be added to the mixture last.

2 pounds medium potatoes, peeled and halved

1 garlic clove

About 1 cup hot milk

Salt

6 tablespoons unsalted butter

1 small egg yolk

1. Place the potatoes and garlic in a medium sauce-pan with a mixture of water and ¼ cup of the milk to cover; add salt. Bring to a boil over high heat. Reduce the heat to medium, cover, and cook about 40 minutes or until the potatoes are tender.

2. Drain the potatoes (do not discard the garlic). Pass the potatoes and garlic through a ricer or strainer and back into the saucepan. Stir in the butter and enough hot milk to make the potatoes the consistency of mayonnaise. Add the egg yolk and beat with a wooden spoon until the mixture is smooth. Season with salt. Serve hot.

Puréed Potatoes V
Puré de Patata

MAKES 6 SERVINGS

This recipe comes from the quaint and unusual cookbook of two grandmothers, Isabel and Carmen García Hernández, published in its original hand-written form. These puréed potatoes are creamy and thick with a subtle accent of nutmeg. I recommend serving them with finely chopped sautéed mushrooms.

2 pounds small new potatoes, peeled and quartered

2 garlic cloves

¾ cup warm milk

2 tablespoons unsalted butter

3 to 4 tablespoons extra-virgin olive oil

½ teaspoon freshly ground nutmeg

Salt

Freshly ground black pepper

8 mushrooms, such as brown or shiitake, finely chopped (optional)

1. Place the potatoes and garlic in a medium sauce-pan with cold water to cover and add salt. Cover and bring to a simmer over low heat. Cook until the potatoes are tender. Drain.

2. Pass the potatoes and garlic through a ricer or strainer into a medium bowl. Add the milk, butter, 3 tablespoons of the oil, the nutmeg, salt, and pep-per and mix until well blended.

3. If using the mushrooms, heat the remaining 1 tablespoon oil in a small skillet over medium heat. Add the mushrooms and cook, stirring, until soft-ened. Fold into the potatoes. Serve hot.

Potatoes in Green Sauce ⓥ*
Patatas en Salsa Verde

MAKES 4 SERVINGS

Traditionally, this green sauce is called for in seafood recipes, but it also makes an excellent sauce for these potatoes sautéed with onion, garlic, and olive oil. This is a classic Spanish dish most likely Basque in origin. Make it vegetarian with vegetable broth.

3 tablespoons olive oil

1 garlic clove

1 tablespoon finely chopped onion

4 medium potatoes, peeled and cut into ⅛-inch slices

¾ cup hot chicken broth, vegetable broth, or water

Salt

Freshly ground black pepper

3 tablespoons finely chopped fresh flat-leaf parsley

1. Heat the oil in a 9- to 10-inch skillet over medium heat. Add the garlic clove and cook, stirring, until lightly browned. Transfer the garlic to a mortar or mini-processor, reserving the oil. Mash and reserve.

2. Heat the reserved oil in the skillet over medium heat. Add the onion and cook, stirring, until wilted, about 3 minutes.

3. Add the potatoes one at a time to prevent sticking. Turn the potatoes to coat with the oil. Increase the heat to medium-high and cook until lightly browned, lifting and turning occasionally. Stir in the broth, salt, pepper, the reserved garlic, and the parsley. Reduce the heat to low and cook until the potatoes are tender, about 10 minutes more. Serve hot.

Oven-Roasted Potatoes ⓥ
Papas Panaderas

MAKES 4 SERVINGS

A popular and extremely simple recipe for sliced roasted potatoes, perfectly seasoned with onion, garlic, paprika, and thyme sautéed in olive oil. I recommend putting bay leaves between the layers of potatoes and garnishing the dish with parsley.

2 to 2½ pounds potatoes, peeled and cut into ¼-inch slices

1 medium onion, cut into ¼-inch slices

8 garlic cloves, thinly sliced

Freshly ground black pepper

½ teaspoon ground sweet paprika, such as Spanish smoked

1½ teaspoons finely chopped fresh thyme or ¼ teaspoon dried thyme

2 tablespoons olive oil

2 bay leaves

1 tablespoon finely chopped fresh flat-leaf parsley

3 tablespoons water

Preheat the oven to 400°F. Grease a square baking pan. In two layers using half of each ingredient, add the potatoes, scatter the onion and garlic over the potatoes, season with salt, pepper, paprika, and thyme, drizzle with olive oil, and add 1 bay leaf. Drizzle with 3 tablespoons water over the top layer. Bake about 45 minutes. Remove the bay leaves. Garnish with the parsley and serve hot.

Roasted Potatoes with Bell Pepper ⓥ

Patatas al Horno con Pimiento

MAKES 4 SERVINGS

This simple recipe of roasted potatoes with pimientos has minimal ingredients and takes hardly any time to make.

4 large scallions, trimmed

3 tablespoons olive oil

4 medium potatoes, peeled, cut into ¼-inch slices, each slice cut in half

1 medium green bell pepper, cut into very thin 2-inch strips

2 garlic cloves, finely chopped

1 small onion, thinly sliced

1 tablespoon finely chopped fresh flat-leaf parsley

Salt

1. Cut both the green and white parts into 1½-inch pieces, then cut each piece lengthwise in half.

2. Preheat the oven to 350°F. Heat the oil in a shallow earthenware casserole dish or Dutch oven over medium-high heat. Add the potatoes, bell pepper, garlic, and onion and cook, turning occasionally, about 10 minutes. Sprinkle with the parsley and season with salt. Cover with foil and bake 15 to 20 minutes or until the potatoes are tender. If using earthenware, serve hot in the dish, or transfer to individual plates.

Baked Stuffed Potatoes with Cured Ham

Patatas Asadas Rellenas

MAKES 4 SERVINGS

In the United States, I have seen versions of this potato preparation referred to as "twice baked." This recipe calls for the potatoes to be scooped out and then the contents puréed with butter, milk, salt, and pepper and returned to the potato skins. In typical Spanish style, this recipe includes cured ham, making this potato dish even more rich and flavorful.

4 large baking potatoes

3 tablespoons unsalted butter

Salt

¼ to ½ cup milk, or as needed, heated

Freshly ground black pepper

¼ pound Serrano (Spanish cured mountain) ham or prosciutto, cut into ¼-inch cubes

4 teaspoons bread crumbs

Unsalted butter

1. Preheat the oven to 400°F. Gently scrub the potatoes but do not peel. Pierce the potatoes several times with a fork to allow steam to escape. Bake 1 hour to 1 hour 15 minutes or until the potatoes are tender when pierced with a fork. Leave the oven on.

2. Cut off a thin slice from the top of each potato. Scoop out the potato, leaving the skin intact, and place in a medium bowl. Add the butter, salt, and pepper and beat with an electric mixer until smooth. Beat in enough milk for the desired consistency. Stir in the ham. Fill the potato shells with the potato mixture, sprinkle with bread crumbs, and dot with butter. Return to the oven and bake 10 minutes more. Serve hot.

Sherry-Infused Baked Sliced Potatoes Ⓥ
Patatas al Jerez

MAKES 4 SERVINGS

This recipe came from our friend Fernando Hermoso who owns the restaurant Casa Bigote in Sanlucar de Barrameda. Everything on the menu is delicious, but the real crowd pleaser is always Fernando's baked, sliced potatoes. The secret to the flavor of this dish is the Manzanilla, *the bone-dry sherry produced in this town.*

3½ tablespoons olive oil

1½ pounds potatoes, peeled and cut into ⅛-inch slices

Kosher or sea salt

Freshly ground black pepper

2 bay leaves, halved

¼ medium onion, slivered

3 tablespoons dry sherry, such as Manzanilla or Fino

2 tablespoons finely chopped fresh flat-leaf parsley

1. Preheat the oven to 300°F. Grease a 9 x 13-inch roasting pan with ½ tablespoon of the oil. Add half of the potatoes in a slightly overlapping layer and season with salt and pepper. Scatter the bay leaves and onion over the potatoes. Add the remaining potatoes and season with salt and pepper. Drizzle the remaining 3 tablespoons oil over the potatoes. Bake 30 minutes. Turn the potatoes, cover lightly with foil, and cook about 20 minutes more or until the potatoes are almost tender.

2. Increase the oven temperature to 450°F. Sprinkle the sherry over the potatoes, cover with foil, and bake about 10 minutes more or until the sherry is absorbed and the potatoes are tender. Sprinkle with parsley and serve hot.

Potato Fritters Ⓥ
Patatas Huecas

MAKES 4 SERVINGS (ABOUT 16 FRITTERS)

A truly elegant potato dish, this recipe came to me from Pilar Monteoliva, mother of our friend Pilar Vico. These potato fritters are soft with a delicious thin, crispy coating. Cinnamon adds an unusual flavor, and lemon gives it a wonderful zest.

1 pound small potatoes

1 tablespoon olive oil

1⅛ teaspoons ground cinnamon

¼ teaspoon lemon zest

1 tablespoon all-purpose flour

½ teaspoon baking powder

2 tablespoons milk

1 large egg, lightly beaten

1 garlic clove, mashed in a garlic press or mortar

1 tablespoon finely chopped fresh flat-leaf parsley

Salt

Olive oil, for frying

1. Place the potatoes in a medium saucepan with cold water to cover and add salt. Cover and bring to a simmer over low heat. Cook about 15 minutes or until the potatoes are tender when pierced with a knife. Drain and let cool slightly and peel. Pass through a ricer or strainer into a medium bowl. Add all the remaining ingredients except the oil and mix until well blended.

2. Heat at least ½ inch of oil in a large skillet over medium-high heat (or better still, use a deep fryer set at 375°F) until it quickly browns a cube of bread. Drop the potato mixture by rounded teaspoons into the oil and cook until golden, turning once. Transfer with a slotted spoon to paper towels and let drain. Serve hot.

Potatoes Vinaigrette Ⓥ
Patatas Fritas a la Vinagreta

MAKES 4 SERVINGS

A perfect light and refreshing side dish to a summer meal, these potatoes can also be served as a tapa.

4 medium red waxy potatoes, peeled and cut into
    ½-inch slices

½ cup plus 3 tablespoons olive oil

Salt

¼ cup vinegar

2 garlic cloves, thinly sliced

¼ teaspoon freshly ground black pepper

1. Heat 3 tablespoons oil in a 9- to 10-inch skillet over medium heat. Add the potatoes one at a time to prevent sticking. Season with salt. Cook until tender but not browned, lifting and turning occasionally. Transfer to a shallow earthenware casserole dish or Dutch oven and arrange in layers.

2. In a medium saucepan, place the vinegar, garlic, and pepper and bring to a boil over medium heat. Reduce the heat to low and simmer 2 minutes. Remove from the heat. Whisk in the remaining ½ cup oil and pour over the potatoes. Let sit in a warm place 10 minutes. Pour off the liquid. Serve warm or at room temperature. If using earthenware, serve hot in the dish, or transfer to individual plates.

Zucchini

Stewed Zucchini and Onion Ⓥ
Zarangollo Rincón de Pepe

MAKES 4 SERVINGS

Murcia is a region in Spain famed for their wide variety of fresh vegetables. This simple, traditional dish was popular with field workers in Murcia, who could literally find all the ingredients within their reach. This recipe comes from one of the region's finest restaurants, Rincón de Pepe, where Raimundo Frutos and his son and daughter take great pride in their restaurant and its regional dishes.

2 tablespoons olive oil

2 garlic cloves, finely chopped

1 medium onion, slivered

½ teaspoon ground sweet paprika, such as Spanish
    smoked

1½ pounds zucchini, cut into ¼-inch slices

Salt

Freshly ground black pepper

1 tablespoon finely chopped fresh oregano or
    ½ teaspoon dried oregano

Heat the oil in a medium skillet over medium heat. Add the garlic and onion and cook, stirring, until softened, 3 to 5 minutes. Reduce the heat to low, cover, and cook 10 minutes more. Stir in the paprika and zucchini. Season with salt, pepper, and the oregano, cover, and cook 10 minutes more or until the zucchini is done to taste. Serve hot.

Baked Zucchini ⓥ

Calabacín al Horno

MAKES 4 SERVINGS

One of the most popular preparations of vegetables in Spain is to bake them in a casserole dish. The zucchini should be baked, then sprinkled with bread crumbs, garlic, and parsley, and run under the broiler until the top is golden.

2 medium zucchini (about 1 pound total)

4 tablespoons olive oil

Salt

Freshly ground black pepper

1 tablespoon bread crumbs

1 garlic clove, finely chopped

1 tablespoon finely chopped fresh flat-leaf parsley

1. Preheat the oven to 350°F. Using a vegetable peeler, peel the zucchini in thin, alternating strips of green to create a decorative stripe effect. Cut off the ends, cut in half lengthwise, then cut crosswise in half. Grease a baking dish with 1 tablespoon of the oil. Arrange the zucchini in the dish and drizzle with the remaining 3 tablespoons oil. Season with salt and pepper. Bake, brushing occasionally with the pan juices, about 20 minutes or until tender.

2. Place a broiler rack about 6 inches from the heat source and preheat the broiler. (Cover the broiler pan with foil for easier cleanup, if you like.) Sprinkle the zucchini with the bread crumbs, garlic, and parsley and spoon the pan juices over the top. Place under the broiler until the top is golden. Serve hot.

Zucchini Filled with Mushrooms ⓥ*

Calabacín Relleno de Setas

MAKES 4 TO 6 SERVINGS

I obtained this unique recipe from our friends Reme Domínguez and Ximo Boix, owners and chefs at the magnificent Tasca del Puerto in Castellón de la Plana, a restaurant famous for their extraordinary arroz negro *(black rice). It is magnificent with the small addition of fragrant truffles (*trufas*) but still excellent if you leave them out. Make it vegetarian with vegetable broth.*

Leek Sauce

1 pound leeks, trimmed and well washed

1 tablespoon olive oil

1 medium onion, coarsely chopped (⅔ cup)

1 teaspoon unsalted butter

1 tablespoon all-purpose flour

2 cups milk

Salt

2 pounds small thin zucchini, each about ¼ pound or less

1 tablespoon olive oil

¾ cup finely chopped onion

2 garlic cloves, finely chopped

½ pound mushrooms, such as shiitake, rinsed, trimmed, and finely chopped

Salt

Freshly ground black pepper

2 teaspoons finely chopped black truffles (optional)

¼ cup chicken broth or vegetable broth

1. Prepare the sauce: Place enough water to cover the leeks in a large pot and add salt. Bring to a boil over high heat. Add the leeks, reduce the heat to low, cover, and cook about 15 to 20 minutes or until tender. Drain and coarsely chop.

2. Heat the oil in a medium skillet over medium heat. Add the onion and cook, stirring, 1 to 2 minutes. Reduce the heat to low, cover, and cook 10 minutes more. Stir in the butter, then add the leeks. Sprinkle with the flour and gradually stir in the milk. Season with salt. Bring to a boil and cook, stirring occasionally, until thickened. Let cool slightly. Transfer to a food processor, and process until smooth. The sauce should have a medium thickness; if too thin, return to the skillet and boil over medium-high heat, stirring occasionally, until the desired consistency. Reserve.

3. Cut the zucchini in half crosswise and with a small spoon hollow out each half, leaving a ¼-inch shell. Finely chop the pulp. Heat the oil in a medium skillet over medium heat. Add the onions and garlic and cook, stirring, 1 to 2 minutes. Reduce the heat to low, cover, and cook about 10 minutes more or until the onions are softened. Add the mushrooms and cook 1 minute more, then stir in the zucchini pulp and cook until the zucchini is softened, about 2 minutes more. Season with salt and pepper and stir in the truffles, if using. Fill the zucchini halves with the pulp mixture.

4. Preheat the oven to 350°F. Arrange the zucchini in a baking dish and pour the broth into the dish. Bake 15 minutes or until the liquid is absorbed and the zucchini are tender.

5. Warm the sauce in a small saucepan over medium heat. Spoon onto 4 individual plates and place the zucchini on top. Serve hot.

Zucchini Fritters Ⓥ*
Buñuelos de Buangos

MAKES 14 FRITTERS

An excellent recipe that can be served as a side dish or a tapa, these zucchini fritters are seasoned with onion, parsley, and thyme and made richer by milk, cheese, and an egg white. Make it vegetarian with vegetable broth.

1 tablespoon olive oil

1 medium onion, finely chopped

1 garlic clove, finely chopped

¼ pound zucchini, coarsely grated

2 tablespoons finely chopped fresh flat-leaf parsley

1½ teaspoons finely chopped fresh thyme or
    ¼ teaspoon dried thyme

Salt

Freshly ground black pepper

1 tablespoon chicken broth, vegetable broth, or water

6 tablespoons all-purpose flour

1 teaspoon baking powder

¼ cup milk

1 teaspoon grated aged Manchego or Parmesan
    cheese

1 large egg white

Olive oil, for frying

1. Heat 1 tablespoon oil in a medium skillet over medium heat. Reduce the heat to low, add the onion and garlic, and cook, stirring, until the onion is wilted, about 5 minutes. Stir in the zucchini, parsley, thyme, salt, and pepper. Cover and cook 5 minutes. Add the broth, cover, and cook 10 minutes more.

2. In a small bowl, combine together the flour and baking powder. Add the milk and mix until smooth. Add the zucchini mixture, cheese, and salt and mix until well blended. In another small bowl, beat the egg white with an electric mixer until stiff but not dry (a peak will just hold its shape when the beater is lifted) and fold it into the batter.

3. Heat at least 1 inch of oil in a large skillet over medium-high heat (or better still, use a deep fryer set at 375°F) until it quickly browns a cube of bread. Drop the zucchini mixture by rounded tablespoons into the oil and cook until golden, turning once. Transfer with a slotted spoon to paper towels and let drain. Serve hot.

Greens and Potato Casserole Ⓥ
Menestra a la Extremeña

MAKES 4 SERVINGS

This version of greens, potatoes, and eggs makes an excellent light supper, especially in the summer. It came from Charito de Pablos, an old family friend, who was originally from Córdoba but lived in Madrid for most of her adult life. She spent many of her weekends and vacations at her family's country house in Extremadura, hence the Spanish name of this recipe.

1 pound Swiss chard, well washed and thick stems trimmed

6 romaine lettuce leaves

¼ cup olive oil

1 large potato, peeled and cut into ⅛-inch slices

1 medium sweet onion, such as Vidalia, thinly sliced

Salt

1 garlic clove, finely chopped

1 tablespoon finely chopped fresh flat-leaf parsley

¼ teaspoon ground sweet paprika, such as Spanish smoked

⅛ teaspoon salt

1 large egg, lightly beaten

1. Fill a large pot with water, add salt, and bring to a boil over high heat. Add the chard and lettuce, reduce the heat to medium, and cook until almost tender, about 15 minutes. Reserve ⅓ cup of the cooking liquid, then drain the chard, pressing to extract as much liquid as possible. Chop coarsely and return to the pot.

2. Meanwhile, heat the oil in a medium skillet over medium-high heat. Add the potatoes one at a time to prevent sticking, alternating them with the onion. Season each layer with salt. Reduce the

heat to medium-low and cook, lifting and turning occasionally, until the potatoes are almost tender, about 20 minutes (the potatoes should not brown). Transfer with a slotted spoon or spatula to paper towels and let drain.

3. In a mortar or mini-processor, mash the garlic, parsley, paprika, and ⅛ teaspoon salt. Add a few drops of the reserved liquid and continue mashing. Stir in the remaining reserved liquid.

4. With a rubber spatula, gently fold the potatoes and the mortar mixture into the greens. Bring to a simmer over low heat and cook until the potatoes are tender and the liquid is absorbed, about 8 minutes. Transfer to a shallow casserole dish.

5. Preheat the broiler. Pour the egg evenly over the casserole and place under the broiler until the top is lightly browned, about 3 minutes. Serve hot.

Mallorcan Potato and Vegetable Casserole
Tumbet Mallorquín

MAKES 4 TO 5 SERVINGS

Tumbet is a very popular vegetable dish in Mallorca and a perfect meatless meal. It includes red and green peppers, potatoes, zucchini, eggplant, and tomato. The original preparation calls for these vegetables to be fried, but the results can be somewhat greasy, so I usually choose to boil them instead. This dish can be prepared in advance, then baked right before serving.

1¼ eggplants, cut crosswise into ¼-inch slices

Kosher or sea salt

2 tablespoons olive oil, plus oil for brushing

Freshly ground black pepper

2 medium green bell peppers

1 medium red bell pepper

½ pound zucchini, cut crosswise into ¼-inch slices

4 garlic cloves, finely chopped separately

½ teaspoon ground sweet paprika, such as Spanish smoked

1 cup canned stewed tomatoes, finely chopped

2 tablespoons finely chopped fresh flat-leaf parsley

2 medium potatoes, peeled and cut into ⅛-inch slices

2 tablespoons water

1. Sprinkle the eggplant on both sides with salt, place in a colander, and let drain 1 hour. Pat dry with paper towels.

2. Preheat the oven to 400°F. Arrange the eggplant on a cookie sheet, brush both sides with olive oil, and season with salt and pepper. Bake 10 minutes, turning once. Reserve.

3. Increase the oven to 500°F. Place the green and red peppers in a roasting pan and bake 20 minutes, turning once. Let cool, then core, seed, and cut into ½-inch strips. Reserve.

4. Heat 1 tablespoon of the oil in a medium skillet over medium heat. Add the zucchini and cook, stirring, 1 minute. Add the peppers, salt, pepper, and 1 chopped garlic clove and cook, stirring, 1 minute. Reserve. Wipe out the skillet.

5. Heat the remaining 1 tablespoon oil in the same skillet over medium heat. Add the remaining chopped garlic and cook, stirring, a few seconds, then add the paprika, tomatoes, and 1 tablespoon of the parsley. Reduce the heat to low and simmer 5 minutes. Reserve.

6. Grease a microwave-safe dish and arrange the potatoes in layers, drizzling each layer with olive oil and seasoning with salt. Sprinkle the water over the potatoes, cover, and microwave on High 8 minutes. Turn the potatoes, cover, and cook on High in 8 minutes more or until the potatoes are tender. (Alternatively, the potatoes can be drizzled with oil [eliminate the water], salted, and baked in a greased roasting pan, tightly covered with foil, in a 350°F oven about 1 hour or until tender.)

7. Preheat the oven to 400°F. In a shallow 13 x 7-inch earthenware casserole dish or baking dish, arrange the potatoes, spoon the zucchini-pepper mixture over the potatoes, and arrange the eggplant slices over the top. Pour the tomato sauce over the casserole and bake 15 minutes. Sprinkle with the remaining parsley and serve hot.

Vegetable Medley with Tuna, Eggs, and Pine Nuts
Pisto Albarracín

MAKES 3 SERVINGS AS A MAIN COURSE OR 6 AS A SIDE DISH

Our dear friend Maria Pilar is an excellent cook whom we have known for many years. She lives in the beautiful town of Albarracín, preserved as a national monument, in the region of Aragon. This recipe comes from her friend María Teresa, a retired cook with a sterling reputation in the village, who carefully wrote it out for me by hand. This is an exceptional recipe for Spain's traditional vegetable medley commonly known as pisto. María Teresa's version calls for the unusual additions of tuna, pine nuts, and hard-boiled egg. A perfect summer meal.

2 tablespoons olive oil

½ pound green frying peppers, cut into ½-inch pieces

¼ pound red frying peppers, cut into ½-inch pieces

¾ pound zucchini, cut into ½-inch cubes

1 medium sweet onion, such as Vidalia, finely chopped (about 1 cup)

2 garlic cloves, finely chopped

One (16-ounce) can crushed tomatoes

Salt

Freshly ground black pepper

¼ teaspoon sugar

One (5½-ounce) jar or can tuna in olive oil, preferably Spanish, broken into small chunks

2 hard-boiled eggs, finely chopped

3 tablespoons pine nuts

4 (jarred) piquillo peppers or 2 pimientos, cut into thin strips

continues...

One (8-ounce) can tomate frito or 8 ounces stewed
 diced tomatoes

1. Heat the oil in a large skillet over medium heat. Reduce the heat to low, add the green and red peppers, and cook, stirring occasionally, until softened, about 8 minutes. Transfer to a medium bowl. Add the zucchini and cook, stirring occasionally, about 5 minutes. Transfer to the bowl. Add the onion and cook, stirring, until wilted, about 5 minutes, then add the garlic and cook 2 minutes more. Transfer the onion and garlic to a deep earthenware casserole dish or Dutch oven.

2. Add the crushed tomato, salt, pepper, and sugar to the onion-garlic mixture in the casserole dish and mix well. Bring to a boil over high heat. Reduce the heat to medium-low and cook, stirring occasionally, 15 minutes. Add the reserved peppers and zucchini, the tuna, egg, pine nuts, piquillos, and stewed tomato. Simmer, stirring occasionally, about 10 minutes. If using earthenware, serve hot in the dish, or transfer to individual plates.

Mixed Vegetables, Rioja Style
Menestra a la Riojana

MAKES 4 SERVINGS

La Rioja, located in the Ebro River valley, is an area known for its peppers and other vegetables, including artichokes, peas, beans, leeks, and cauliflowers. These vegetables are harvested in the spring, and the resulting mixture or menestra *is the specialty in all the local restaurants. This recipe contrasts the taste and texture of boiled and fried vegetables with cured ham and hard-boiled eggs, creating a dish that is hearty and delicious. Much more than a simple vegetable medley, this is a complete meal. It can also be baked and served in four individual casserole dishes if you like.*

2 medium carrots, peeled
½ pound green beans

½ head cauliflower, thick stems removed and cut into
 small florets
2 leeks, trimmed and well washed (white part only)
4 small artichoke hearts
¼ pound peas
2 tablespoons olive oil
4 thin slices Serrano (Spanish cured mountain) ham
 or prosciutto, cut into small pieces
1 small onion, finely chopped (about ⅓ cup)
1 garlic clove, finely chopped
Olive oil, for frying
All-purpose flour, for dusting
1 large egg, lightly beaten
2 large hard-boiled eggs, cut into wedges, for garnish
1 pimiento, cut into thin strips, for garnish
Salt

1. Place the peas in a small saucepan, add water to cover and salt, and bring to a boil over high heat. Reduce the heat to low and cook until tender, 5 to 10 minutes. Drain and reserve.

2. Meanwhile, in a large skillet (cook in batches if needed to avoid overcrowding), add ½ inch of water, add salt, and bring to a boil over high heat. Add the carrots, beans, cauliflower, leeks, and artichokes. Cover and cook the vegetables until tender. If some vegetables are done before others, transfer them with a slotted spoon to a colander and let drain while the others continue cooking. Do not overcook. Drain. Cut the carrots and leeks into 1½-inch pieces. Reserve.

3. Heat the 2 tablespoons oil in a medium skillet over medium heat. Add the ham and cook, stirring, about 1 minute. Add the onion and garlic and cook, stirring, until the onion is wilted, about 5 minutes. Add the carrots, beans, and peas and cook, stirring, about 2 minutes. Transfer to an earthenware casserole dish.

4. Heat at least 1 inch of oil in a large skillet over medium-high heat (or better still, use a deep fryer set at 375°F) until it quickly browns a cube of bread. Dredge the cauliflower, leeks, and artichokes

in the flour, dip in the beaten egg, and place in the hot oil. Cook, turning occasionally, until lightly browned. Transfer with a slotted spoon or spatula to paper towels and let drain. Place over the other vegetables in the casserole dish. Decorate with the egg wedges and pimiento strips. Season with salt. Serve hot.

Zucchini, Green Pepper, and Tomato Medley

Pisto Manchego

MAKES 4 TO 6 SERVINGS

This recipe originated in La Mancha in central Spain (the land of Don Quixote) and is a staple of that region's cuisine. The addition of bacon and potatoes makes this traditional vegetable dish heartier and tastier. Many people like to also add fried egg.

1 tablespoon olive oil

¼ cup small cubes (¼ inch) slab bacon

1 large onion, coarsely chopped (about 1 cup)

1 garlic clove, finely chopped

1 medium potato, peeled and cut into ½-inch cubes

2 medium green bell peppers, cut into thin strips

2 large tomatoes, coarsely chopped (about 2 cups)

2 medium zucchini, cut into ¼-inch slices

1 tablespoon finely chopped fresh flat-leaf parsley

¼ cup chicken broth or vegetable broth

Salt

Freshly ground black pepper

In a medium skillet over medium heat, heat the oil and cook the bacon, stirring occasionally, until the bacon is transparent. Add the onion and garlic and cook, stirring, until the onion is wilted, about 5 minutes. Add the potato and bell peppers and cook, stirring occasionally, about 10 minutes. Mix in the tomatoes, zucchini, parsley, broth, salt, and pepper. Cover and cook until the vegetables are tender, about 20 minutes. Serve hot.

LA TOMATINA

Spaniards love to have a good time and use any excuse to organize and celebrate with festivals. The most famous festival is San Fermín, the "running of the bulls." There are even a multitude of festivals involving the harvest of vegetables: The Pepper festival in La Rioja, the Vendimia (grape crop and wine festivities) in La Mancha, and the Calçots (celebrating scallions) in Tarragona. Many of these festivals attract international spectators, but there is nothing in the world like *La Tomatina*, the annual Spanish tomato festival.

La Tomatina takes place in Buñol, a small town near Valencia, where they celebrate the tomato harvest with song and dance, a huge paella (free for everybody), and wine from the area of Utiel-Requena. But this tame celebration of the harvest didn't attract crowds until one year when someone threw a tomato at someone else, and others joined in. This became a tradition, and now on the last Wednesday of August, Spaniards and tourists alike gather for the "world's largest food fight."

Over the years, *La Tomatina* has become a rowdy and raucous celebration with a party-like atmosphere. Sometimes as many as 40,000 people participate in throwing over 100 tons of ripe tomatoes in the street. With crowds of people hurling tomatoes at each other, it was decided that some rules needed to be put into place: *La Tomatina* starts at 11 am with the sound of a rocket being fired and ends exactly one hour later. Participants need to squash the tomatoes before they are thrown so they have less impact when they hit someone. The moment the second shot is heard, everybody must stop throwing tomatoes. It is quite a sight to see thousands of people covered in tomato from head to toe. Only in Spain!

Vegetable Stew, Córdoba Style
Pisto Cordobés

MAKES 4 TO 6 SERVINGS

When I was in Córdoba, I found this recipe from a charming hand-written booklet issued by the producers of olive oil from the Baena appellation of origin. Most vegetable stews in Spain are based on a mixture of tomatoes, peppers, and zucchini. This version is made with eggs and served with crisp garlic bread rounds.

2 garlic cloves, mashed in a mortar or garlic press

5 tablespoons extra-virgin olive oil

8 to 12 thin slices long-loaf (baguette) bread

1 medium onion, coarsely grated

2 garlic cloves, finely chopped

1½ pounds zucchini, cut into ¾-inch cubes

2 pounds potatoes, peeled and cut into 1-inch cubes

2 large green bell peppers, cut into ½-inch strips

2 tablespoons finely chopped fresh flat-leaf parsley

1½ pounds tomatoes, halved crosswise, seeded, and coarsely grated down to the peel

¼ teaspoon sugar

¾ cup water

Salt

Freshly ground black pepper

4 large eggs

1. Preheat the oven to 350°F. Mix the mashed garlic and 2 tablespoons of the oil in a cup. Place the bread on a cookie sheet and bake about 8 minutes, turning once, or until lightly toasted. Brush with the oil-garlic mixture and reserve.

2. Heat the remaining 3 tablespoons oil in a large skillet over medium heat. Add the onion and chopped garlic and cook, stirring, until the onion is wilted, about 5 minutes. Stir in the zucchini, potatoes, peppers, parsley, tomatoes, and sugar, then add the water. Season with salt and pepper. Reduce the heat to low, cover, and simmer 25 minutes.

3. In a small bowl, lightly beat the eggs and season with salt. Pour over the stew and stir until the egg is set. Serve hot with the garlic toast.

The Núñez de Prado Family's Batter-Fried Vegetables Ⓥ
Verduras de la Huerta de la Familia Núñez de Prado

MAKES 4 SERVINGS

The famed olive oil of the Núñez de Prado estate, owned by our friend Paco Núñez de Prado, adds a subtle but delectable flavor to every dish prepared in the family's home. The estate, located in the Cordoban city of Baena, has been making olive oil for seven centuries, and Paco takes great pride in his groves of olive trees that stretch as far as the eye can see. Paco told us that any olives that fall to the ground and bruise are unworthy of his family name. This is his delicious recipe for vegetables, cut into thin strips and fried, of course, in his family's famous olive oil, easily found in the United States.

1 cup water

½ teaspoon salt

¼ pound small or baby eggplant, peeled, cut into ¼-inch crosswise slices, each slice cut into ¼-inch strips, then the strips into 1½-inch lengths

Kosher or sea salt

¼ cup milk

1 large egg

All-purpose flour, for dredging

½ medium red bell pepper, cut into 1½ x ¼-inch strips

½ medium-large green bell pepper, cut into 1½ x ¼-inch strips

¼ medium onion, slivered

¼ pound zucchini, cut into ¼-inch crosswise slices, each slice cut into ¼-inch strips

Olive oil, for frying

1. Combine the water and ½ teaspoon salt in a medium bowl. Add the eggplant and let soak 20 minutes. Drain and let dry on paper towels.

2. In a shallow bowl, beat the milk and egg together with a fork. Place the flour on a piece of wax paper. Heat at least ½ inch of oil in a large skillet over medium-high heat (or better still, use a deep fryer set at 375°F) until it reaches the smoking point.

3. Preheat the oven to 200°F. Place the vegetables in the milk-egg mixture. Remove with a slotted spoon, draining off the excess liquid. Toss the vegetables in the flour, coating very lightly, and place in the oil, shaking the skillet carefully to spread them out rapidly in the oil. Do not crowd. (Cook in batches if necessary to avoid overcrowding.) Cook until lightly golden, about 2 minutes. Transfer with a slotted spoon to paper towels and let drain. Transfer to an ovenproof dish and place in the oven to keep warm while preparing the remaining batches. Season with coarse salt and serve hot.

Vegetable Medley, Andalucian Style
Pisto Andaluz

MAKES 4 SERVINGS

Although La Mancha is the region typically associated with this type of vegetable medley called pisto *(usually containing onion, peppers, tomato, and zucchini), it is found all over Spain. My favorite version comes from La Bobadilla in Andalucía, an exquisite hotel and restaurant in the hills of the province of Granada. This recipe includes dried sweet red peppers (* ñoras *) which give this vegetable dish an extra kick. I recommend that you cut all the vegetables into very small pieces.*

2 tablespoons olive oil

1 medium sweet onion, such as Vidalia, finely chopped (about ⅔ cup)

1 garlic clove, finely chopped

2 tablespoons finely chopped Serrano (Spanish cured mountain) ham or prosciutto

2 medium red bell peppers, cut into ¼-inch pieces

2 medium green bell peppers, cut into ¼-inch pieces

1 small dried sweet red pepper (ñora) or 1 New Mexico (Anaheim) chile pepper, stemmed and seeded

¾ pound tomatoes, finely chopped

1 small zucchini, cut into ¼-inch cubes

1 tablespoon dry sherry, such as Fino, or white wine

1 tablespoon finely chopped fresh flat-leaf parsley

Salt

Freshly ground black pepper

¼ teaspoon ground cumin

Heat the oil in a medium skillet over medium heat. Reduce the heat to low, add the onion, garlic, and ham and cook, stirring, until the onion is wilted, about 8 minutes. Add the bell peppers and the dried pepper and cook, stirring, until the peppers begin to soften. Stir in the remaining ingredients. Reduce the heat to low, cover, and simmer about 30 minutes, or until done to taste.

2. Press the dried pepper with the back of a wooden spoon to extract its flavor, then discard the skin. Serve hot or store in a covered container in the refrigerator, where it will keep very well for several days.

Paella and Rice Dishes

THE PERFECT ACCOMPANIMENT

Garlic Sauce Ⓥ

VEGETABLE AND BEAN PAELLA

Saffron Rice with Pine Nuts Ⓥ

Mushroom Paella Ⓥ

Vegetable Paella with Spicy Garlic Sauce Ⓥ*

Spinach and Pine Nut Paella Ⓥ*

Rice with Zucchini Ⓥ*

Squash Paella with Basil Ⓥ*

Brown Rice–Vegetable Paella with Pine Nuts Ⓥ*

Chickpea Stew Paella

Crusted Paella

Bean-Pebbled Paella Ⓥ*

Rice with Black Beans

Rice with Fried Eggs and Bananas Ⓥ

SHELLFISH AND SEAFOOD PAELLA

Soupy Rice with Seafood

Three-Color Paella with Cheese and Almonds Ⓥ

Eggplant, Olive, and Caper Paella Ⓥ*

Seafood-Flavored Rice, Alicante Style

Rosemary-Scented Shellfish and Egg Paella

Rice with Shrimp and Fresh Tuna

Scallop and Mushroom Paella

Scallop, Shrimp, and Seaweed Paella

Shrimp Paella with Red Pepper Sauce

Rice with Squid and Shrimp

 = Vegetarian   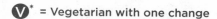 = Vegetarian with one change

Garlic Clam Paella

Mussel Paella

Lobster Paella Casa Roberto

Crab Meat Paella with Peas and Carrots

Seafood Rice, Murcia Style

Fresh Tuna and Rabbit Paella

Cod Paella, Catalan Style

Cod, Bean, and Hot Green Pepper Paella

Salt Cod, Cauliflower, and Artichoke Paella

Salmon and Asparagus Paella
with Capers and Dill

Rice with Monkfish and Roasted Tomatoes

Monkfish and Almond Paella, Alicante Style

Monkfish, Swiss Chard, and Sesame Seed Paella

Black Rice

Squid Paella "El Faro"

Squid and Scallion Paella

Mixed Seafood Paella

Pesto Seafood Paella

Seafood Pasta Paella

POULTRY AND GAME PAELLA

Rice with Chicken

Valencia's Traditional Paella

Mixed Chicken and Seafood Paella

Chicken with Rice, Andalusian Style

Chicken Paella Pepitoria

Ruperto's Marinated Chicken Paella

Chicken, Peppers, and Eggplant Paella

Sweet-and-Sour Paella with Caramelized Walnuts

Catalan Sea and Mountain Paella

Rice with Duck, Sausage, and Chickpeas

Duck, Bean, Grape, and Nut Paella

Rabbit Paella with Red Peppers and Almonds

Quail and Mushroom Paella

Rabbit, Spinach, and Artichoke Paella

Paella, Sevilla Style

Stewed Rabbit Paella

Rabbit Paella with Sausage,
Pork Ribs, and Pea Pods

MEAT PAELLA

Pork and Pomegranate Paella

Rice with Garlic-Paprika-
Marinated Rib Pork Chops

Pork, Chickpea, and Red Pepper Paella

Rice with Pork, Potato, and
Egg, Galician Style

Cumin-Scented Pork and Watercress Paella

Pork Paella, Catalan Style

Mushroom and Meatball Paella,
Dársena Style

Rice with Lamb and Chickpeas

Lamb, Lentil, and Eggplant Paella

Lamb and Red Pepper Paella

Monastic Paella with Chorizo and Olives

Baked Rice with Black Sausage and Garlic

Cabbage and Chopped Meat Paella

Paella is not just one dish but rather a technique for preparing many Spanish rice dishes that are categorized by the use of a paella pan and the method in which they cook. Paella comes in endless varieties, depending on the region and the availability of ingredients. The only indispensable ingredients are rice, water, and olive oil. No matter what kind of paella it is, to a Spaniard, the most important part is the flavor of the rice, which must be of the short-grain variety.

Valencia, with rice paddies that stretch as far as the eye can see, is the region in Spain where paella originated. Born from economic necessity, these rice dishes were traditionally made over an open fire for laborers in the fields when other more expensive ingredients were not accessible. As Spain grew richer as a nation, paellas transformed from simple rice dishes to culinary masterpieces and works of art. There are now innumerable versions of paella, but they all owe their origin to the recipe for Valencia's traditional paella.

Rice production in Valencia would not have been possible without the Moors, who arrived from North Africa thirteen hundred years ago. They created elaborate irrigation systems to channel river water from the mountains that otherwise would be lost to the sea. The water in Valencia is not the best for drinking, but it is by far the best for preparing rice. The Moors are also credited with bringing saffron to Spain, a spice that is integral to most paellas because it creates a distinctive flavor, a yellow color, and a wonderful aroma.

A Valencian paella purist would insist that a true paella should consist of only the original ingredients of rice, snails, and green beans. Some other paella lovers believe that a paella should contain either seafood or meat, but the two should never be combined. However, when it comes to Spanish restaurants in the United States, the most popular paella by far is the mixed variety. The essence of an excellent paella is its *socarrat*, the dark crust of rice that forms on the bottom of the pan. It is usually scraped off and served after the paella so that everybody can have a taste.

Paellas are not difficult to make at home, and since most of the ingredients are cooked in one pan, cleanup is minimal. The other advantage is that most paellas can be prepared in advance and then baked once guests arrive. A paella should always be served in the paella pan and garnished with ingredients that make for a beautiful presentation.

Garlic Sauce Ⓥ
Alioli

MAKES 1¼ CUPS

This delectable alioli *is a garlic-rich sauce that is the perfect accompaniment for many paellas. The eggs are not cooked; use only the freshest, highest-quality eggs.*

10 garlic cloves, mashed in a garlic press or mortar

1 teaspoon salt

1 large egg

3 teaspoons fresh lemon juice

1 cup olive oil

In a food processor or blender, place the garlic and salt and process until finely chopped. Add the egg and lemon juice and process until smooth and a uniform pale yellow. With the motor running, gradually drizzle in the oil and process until well emulsified.

Transfer to a serving bowl and leave at room temperature. If made more than 1 hour up to 48 hours in advance, cover and refrigerate, then bring to room temperature and serve.

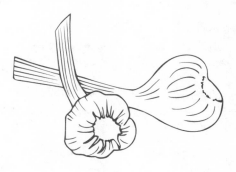

Saffron Rice with Pine Nuts Ⓥ
Arroz al Azafrán con Piñones

MAKES 4 SERVINGS

This basic rice dish can be used to accompany seafood, meat, or poultry. The saffron gives the rice a wonderful flavor that is delicious on its own but is also perfectly complemented by a variety of different sauces.

2 tablespoons unsalted butter

2 tablespoons finely chopped onion

2 tablespoon pine nuts

1 cup short-grain rice, such as imported Spanish or Arborio

1 cup vegetable broth or chicken broth

1 cup water

2 tablespoons finely chopped fresh flat-leaf parsley

1½ teaspoon finely chopped fresh thyme or ¼ teaspoon dried thyme

Few threads of saffron, crumbled

Salt

1. Preheat the oven to 400°F. Melt the butter in a deep earthenware casserole dish or Dutch oven over medium heat. Add the onion and pine nuts and cook until the onion is wilted and transparent, about 3 minutes. Stir in the rice, coating it with the butter. Add the broth and water, stir in the parsley, thyme, saffron, and salt, and bring to a boil. Remove from the heat, cover, and transfer to the oven.

2. Bake 15 minutes or until the liquid is absorbed and the rice almost al dente, tender yet still firm to the bite. Cover and let sit on top of the stove 5 to 10 minutes or until the rice is cooked to taste. If using earthenware, serve hot in the dish, or transfer to individual plates.

1. Use only short-grain rice. It may be imported from Valencia or you can use Italian Arborio rice or short-grain pearl rice grown in California (Spanish or Japanese style). Do not rinse it before using unless indicated in the recipe. Long-grain rice produces rice dishes entirely different in character, flavor, and texture from those made with short-grain rice. I discourage such a substitute, but in the case that short-grain rice is absolutely unavailable, use the long-grain rice in the proportion of 1 cup rice to 2½ cups liquid.

2. For most rice recipes, it is important that the dish is wide and shallow and that the rice cooks uncovered—this prevents it from steaming, which is undesirable in a paella. Recipes in this chapter call for two basic types of pans:

   • Paella pans: The inexpensive thin metal types imported from Spain with handles on either side are the best. Recipes in this chapter are geared for pans that are about a 15- to 15½-inch diameter at the base and about a 17-to-18-inch diameter at the top, excluding handles (be sure to measure your oven width and depth before purchasing a pan of this size).

   • Earthenware casserole dishes: Ones that are 12 inches in diameter and about 2 inches deep are perfect for other rice dishes.

3. The broth in which the rice is cooked is extremely important to the flavor of the finished dish. Therefore, when cooking other kinds of meals, always be thinking of the leftovers that might make great broth for rice—such things as chicken carcasses, lobster and shrimp shells, or fish heads. When boiling shellfish, always save the cooking liquid.

4. Home stove burners are not large enough to accommodate a paella pan, so it will need to be placed over 2 burners and turned frequently to equalize the heat. Stirring the rice, frowned upon by purists, becomes necessary when the heat is uneven.

5. Never wait until the rice tastes "done" before removing it from the stove or oven. The rice must finish cooking away from the heat; otherwise the rice grains will burst and turn mushy.

6. Most rice dishes can be partially prepared in advance. However, the final cooking must be done at the last minute. The dish never quite tastes the same when re-heated, although I must admit I enjoy leftover paella. When cooking for company, it is advisable to do some of the cooking in advance—recipes will indicate up to what point this may be done. (The component or ingredients that are cooked in advance should not be refrigerated—they will keep with no problem for several hours). Since paella pans are shallow, there is a quite a bit of splattering at the beginning, which can be cleaned up earlier in the day. The final stages are easy and no problem to handle after the guests have arrived.

7. Saffron is not included in all rice dishes, but when it is called for, it should be the real thing—imported from Spain and in threads, not powdered. It is fantastically expensive. Fortunately, only small amounts are needed, and a tiny container goes a long way. Many people are under the misconception that saffron is merely a colorant, when actually it imparts a very definite flavor and aroma to the rice.

Mushroom Paella Ⓥ

Paella de Setas

MAKES 6 TO 8 SERVINGS

This excellent mushroom paella can be served vegetarian style or, if preferred, with the addition of cured ham. The more different kinds of mushrooms you use, the better this paella will be. If you are using portobello mushrooms, I recommend that you remove the dark spongy underside or else the rice will get discolored. As with most paellas, it is the distinctive taste of saffron that flavors the rice.

¼ teaspoon saffron threads, crumbled

¼ cup finely chopped shallots

¼ teaspoon salt

¼ cup finely chopped fresh flat-leaf parsley

4 garlic cloves, finely chopped

6 cups vegetable broth or chicken broth

7 tablespoons olive oil

4 medium leeks, trimmed, well washed, and finely chopped (white part only)

2 medium onions, finely chopped (about 1⅓ cups)

½ pound Serrano (Spanish cured mountain) ham or prosciutto, cut into ¼-inch cubes (optional)

2 medium tomatoes, peeled, seeded, and finely chopped (about 1⅓ cups)

¾ cup dry white wine

1½ pounds mushrooms, such as shiitake, oyster, or cepes, rinsed, trimmed, and coarsely chopped

3 cups short-grain rice, such as imported Spanish or Arborio

1. In a mortar or mini-processor, mash the saffron, shallots, salt, parsley, and garlic and reserve. Place the broth and saffron in a large pot and heat over the lowest heat on a back burner to keep hot until needed.

2. Preheat the oven to 400°F. In a 17- to 18-inch paella pan or a similar-size shallow earthenware casserole dish, heat the oil over medium heat, placing over two burners if necessary. Add the leeks and onions and cook, stirring, until softened, about 8 minutes. Add the ham, if using, stir 1 minute, then add the tomato and cook, stirring, 1 to 2 minutes more. Add the wine and cook until evaporated.

3. Add the mushrooms to the paella pan and cook until softened, 1 to 2 minutes more. Stir in the rice and coat well with the pan mixture. Add the broth and bring to a boil. Taste and adjust seasoning if necessary. Add the mortar mixture and cook, stirring occasionally and rotating the pan if over two burners, until the bubbles rising from the pan look slightly thick and the rice begins to be visible at the surface, about 15 minutes more.

4. Transfer to the oven and bake until the liquid is absorbed and the rice almost al dente, tender yet still firm to the bite, about 10 minutes. Remove from the oven, cover with foil, and let sit 5 to 10 minutes or until the rice is cooked to taste. Serve hot.

Vegetable Paella with Spicy Garlic Sauce Ⓥ*

Paella de Verduras con Salsa Picante de Ajo

MAKES 6 TO 8 SERVINGS

Out of all the vegetarian paellas I have ever sampled or prepared, this one is my all-time favorite. The recipe calls for twelve different kinds of vegetables, but obviously any of them can be omitted if not desired or accessible. To most Spaniards, the spicy garlic sauce is the very essence of this vegetable paella, but it can also be prepared without it. Make it vegetarian with vegetable broth.

Spicy Garlic Sauce

¼ cup finely chopped red bell pepper

1 teaspoon finely chopped fresh red or green chile
    pepper

½ teaspoon ground cumin

½ teaspoon salt

4 garlic cloves, finely chopped

1½ teaspoons finely chopped fresh thyme or
    ¼ teaspoon dried thyme

¼ teaspoon dried oregano

4 tablespoons finely chopped fresh flat-leaf parsley

½ cup olive oil

1 medium zucchini, cut into ½-inch slices, each slice
    quartered

2 cups coarsely chopped, trimmed, and rinsed fresh
    spinach

2 medium red bell peppers, finely chopped (about
    1½ cups)

4 teaspoons finely chopped fresh hot red or green
    chile peppers

6 artichoke hearts, quartered

⅔ cup fresh or frozen lima beans

6 large shiitake or other mushrooms, rinsed, trimmed,
    and coarsely chopped (about ½ pound)

½ cup fresh or frozen peas

8 medium scallions, coarsely chopped (about ½ cup)

1 medium tomato

6 cups chicken broth or vegetable broth

¼ teaspoon saffron threads, crumbled

7 tablespoons olive oil

4 garlic cloves, finely chopped

1 teaspoon ground sweet paprika, such as Spanish
    smoked

1 teaspoon ground cumin

2 tablespoons finely chopped fresh flat-leaf parsley

3 cups short-grain rice, such as imported Spanish or
    Arborio

Salt

½ pound snow peas

1. Prepare the sauce: In a mortar or mini-processor, mash the bell and chile peppers, cumin, salt, garlic, thyme, oregano, and 2 tablespoons of the parsley. Stir in the oil and remaining 2 tablespoons parsley. Transfer to a small serving bowl and reserve.

2. In a large bowl, combine the zucchini, spinach, bell and chile peppers, artichokes, beans, mushrooms, peas, and scallions. Cut the tomato in half crosswise and gently squeeze each half to extract the seeds. With a coarse grater held over a small bowl, grate down to the skin, draining off any excess juices. Reserve the pulp and discard the skin. Place the broth and saffron in a medium saucepan and heat over the lowest heat on a back burner to keep hot until needed.

3. Preheat the oven to 400°F. In a 17- to 18-inch paella pan or similar-size shallow earthenware casserole dish, heat the oil over high heat, placing over two burners if necessary. Add the vegetable mixture and cook, stirring, until the vegetables are slightly softened, about 3 minutes. Stir in the tomato, garlic, paprika, cumin, and parsley and cook 2 minutes more, then add the rice and coat well with the pan mixture.

4. Add the broth and salt and bring to a boil. Cook, stirring occasionally and rotating the pan if over two burners, until the bubbles rising from the pan look slightly thick and the rice begins to be visible at the surface, about 5 minutes more. Stir in the snow peas.

5. Transfer to the oven and bake 10 to 12 minutes or until the liquid is absorbed and the rice almost al dente, tender yet still firm to the bite. Remove from the oven, cover with foil, and let sit 5 to 10 minutes or until the rice is cooked to taste. Serve hot with the sauce on the side.

Spinach and Pine Nut Paella ⓥ*

Paella de Espinacas, Piñones y Garbanzos

MAKES 6 TO 8 SERVINGS

This delicious vegetable paella features spinach, chick-peas, the distinctive taste of cumin, and the crunch of pine nuts. Make it vegetarian with vegetable broth.

¾ cup canned chickpeas

About 5 cups vegetable broth or chicken broth

½ cup dry white wine

7 tablespoons olive oil

¼ cup pine nuts

1 large red bell pepper, finely chopped (about 1 cup)

16 garlic cloves, finely chopped

2 medium tomatoes, finely chopped (about 1⅓ cups)

2 tablespoons finely chopped fresh flat-leaf parsley

½ pound fresh spinach, rinsed, trimmed, well dried, and coarsely chopped

4 teaspoons ground sweet paprika, such as Spanish smoked

1 tablespoon finely chopped fresh thyme or ½ teaspoon dried thyme

½ teaspoon ground cumin

½ teaspoon dried oregano

Salt

1. Drain the chickpeas and combine the liquid with the chicken broth to make 5½ cups. Place in a large saucepan, add the wine and saffron, and heat over the lowest heat on a back burner to keep hot until needed.

2. Preheat the oven to 400°F. In a 17- to 18-inch paella pan or similar-size shallow earthenware cas-serole dish, heat the oil over medium heat, placing over two burners if necessary. Add the pine nuts and cook, stirring, until lightly browned, then add the bell pepper and garlic and cook, stirring, 1 to 2 minutes more. Add the tomato, parsley, and spin-ach and cook, stirring, until the spinach is wilted,

2 to 3 minutes more. Stir in the paprika, thyme, cumin, and oregano, and add the rice and coat well with the pan mixture.

3. Add the broth and bring to a boil. Stir in salt, add the chickpeas, and cook, stirring occasionally and rotating the pan if over two burners, until the bubbles rising from the pan look slightly thick and the rice begins to be visible at the surface.

4. Transfer to the oven and bake about 10 minutes or until the liquid is absorbed and the rice almost al dente, tender yet still firm to the bite. Remove from the oven, cover with foil, and let sit 5 to 10 minutes or until the rice is cooked to taste. Serve hot.

Rice with Zucchini ⓥ*

Arroz con Calabacín

MAKES 4 TO 6 SERVINGS

Zucchini is featured in this paella, which can be served as either the main course or a side dish.

½ cup olive oil

½ dried sweet red pepper (ñora), or New Mexico (Anaheim) pepper, stemmed and seeded

1 small tomato, cut into large pieces

1 garlic clove

1 small onion, coarsely chopped (⅓ cup)

½ medium zucchini, cut into ½-inch cubes (about ¼ pound)

¼ pound green beans

1 cup short-grain rice, such as imported Spanish or Arborio

2 cups chicken broth or vegetable broth

Salt

1. Heat the oil in an 8- to 9-inch earthenware cas-serole dish or Dutch oven over medium heat. Add the chile pepper and cook, turning once, until soft-ened (be careful not to let it burn). Cut the pep-per into pieces and place in a food processor or blender. In the same oil, add the tomato and garlic

and cook, stirring, until the garlic is golden. Transfer the tomato and garlic to the processor. In the same oil, add the onion and cook, stirring, until wilted and transparent, about 5 minutes. Add the zucchini and beans and cook, stirring, about 10 minutes. Add the rice and stir to coat well with the pan mixture.

2. Preheat the oven to 325°F. Blend the processor ingredients until a paste forms. Slowly add the broth and blend until smooth. Add to the casserole dish, season with salt, and bring to a boil, Reduce the heat to low and simmer, stirring occasionally, until the bubbles rising from the pan look slightly thick and the rice begins to be visible at the surface, about 5 minutes more.

3. Transfer to the oven and bake 15 minutes or until the liquid is absorbed and the rice almost al dente, tender yet still firm to the bite. Remove from the oven, cover with foil, and let sit 5 to 10 minutes or until the rice is cooked to taste. Serve hot.

Squash Paella with Basil Ⓥ*
Paella de Basílico y Calabacín

MAKES 4 SERVINGS

The strong taste of pesto in this recipe lends a delicious flavor to the rice. Make it vegetarian with vegetable broth.

3 cups chicken broth or vegetable broth

⅛ teaspoon saffron threads, crumbled

¼ cup olive oil

2 tablespoons pine nuts

½ small onion, finely chopped

1 long thin green chile pepper, finely chopped (about 3 tablespoons)

½ medium green bell pepper, finely chopped (about ⅓ cup)

3 ounces mushrooms, such as oyster, rinsed, trimmed, and coarsely chopped (about 1 cup)

1 cup coarsely chopped, trimmed, and rinsed spinach

½ pound medium zucchini, cut into ½-inch cubes

½ pound medium yellow squash, cut into ½-inch cubes

3 tablespoons finely chopped tomato

¼ teaspoon ground sweet paprika, such as Spanish smoked

1½ cups short-grain rice, such as imported Spanish or Arborio

3 tablespoons pesto sauce

Kosher or sea salt

1. Preheat the oven to 400°F. In a medium saucepan, combine the broth and saffron and place over the lowest heat on a back burner to keep hot until needed. Heat the oil in a 13-inch paella pan or a similar-size shallow earthenware casserole dish over medium heat. Add the pine nuts and cook, stirring, until browned. Add the onion and the chile and bell peppers and cook, stirring, until the vegetables are softened, about 5 minutes more. Stir in the mushrooms, spinach, zucchini, and squash and cook, stirring, until the vegetables are softened, 2 to 3 minutes. Stir in the tomato and paprika. Add the rice and coat well with the pan mixture.

2. Add the broth and bring to a boil. Season with salt. Add the pesto and cook until the bubbles rising from the pan look slightly thick and the rice begins to be visible at the surface.

3. Transfer to the oven and bake 10 minutes or until the liquid is absorbed and the rice almost al dente, tender yet still firm to the bite. Remove from the oven, cover with foil, and let sit 5 to 10 minutes or until the rice is cooked to taste. Serve hot.

Brown Rice–Vegetable Paella with Pine Nuts Ⓥ*

Arroz Integral Hortelano

MAKES 6 SERVINGS

Preparing brown rice paella takes longer than other paellas because the rice must first be boiled in a pot to partially cook it before transferring to the paella pan, where it continues to cook with the vegetables. I really enjoy this delicious paella, and I find the extra effort to be well worth it. Make it vegetarian with vegetable broth.

2½ cups brown short-grain rice, such as imported Spanish or Arborio

8 cups chicken broth or vegetable broth

¼ teaspoon saffron threads, crumbled

2 medium tomatoes

7 tablespoons olive oil

½ cup pine nuts

2 medium red bell peppers, finely chopped (about 1½ cups)

2 bunches scallions (about ½ pound)

6 garlic cloves, finely chopped

½ cup fresh or frozen peas

1 cup cooked fresh or canned lima beans, drained if canned

6 artichoke hearts, quartered

¼ cup finely chopped fresh flat-leaf parsley

1 teaspoon ground sweet paprika, such as Spanish smoked

⅛ teaspoon ground cayenne pepper

¼ pound snow peas

1. Wash the rice, place in a large saucepan with 6 cups of the broth and the saffron, and bring to a boil over high heat. Reduce the heat to low, cover, and simmer 30 minutes.

2. Cut the tomatoes in half crosswise and gently squeeze to extract the seeds. With a coarse grater over a small bowl, grate each half down to the skin, draining off any excess juices. Reserve the pulp and discard the skin.

3. Preheat the oven to 350°F. In a 17- to 18-inch paella pan or similar-size shallow earthenware casserole dish, heat the oil over medium heat, placing over two burners if necessary. Add the pine nuts, cook, stirring, until browned, and transfer to a small bowl. In the same oil, add the peppers and cook, stirring, until softened. Add the scallions and garlic and cook, stirring, about 1 minute more. Stir in the tomato and parsley, increase the heat to medium-high, and cook until the liquid from the tomato has cooked away. Reduce the heat to medium and stir in the peas, beans, and artichokes.

4. Add the rice to the paella pan and mix well with the vegetables. Stir in the remaining 2 cups broth and bring to a boil. Reduce the heat to low and simmer until the bubbles rising from the pan look slightly thick and the rice begins to be visible at the surface, about 15 minutes more (there should be less liquid remaining than for other paellas since brown rice absorbs liquids more slowly). Stir in the snow peas.

5. Transfer to the oven and bake about 25 minutes or until the liquid is absorbed and the rice almost al dente, tender yet still firm to the bite. Remove from the oven, cover with foil, and let sit 5 to 10 minutes or until the rice is cooked to taste. Serve hot.

Chickpea Stew Paella

Arroz al Horno

MAKES 4 TO 6 SERVINGS

This dish is basically Spain's famous beloved chickpea stew with the addition of rice, so the preparation takes a bit longer than most other paellas. Hearty and filling, this is a classic recipe that was given to me by Tino Salcedo, a native Valencian. It is a very traditional preparation based on chickpeas, which were once relied upon for sustenance when other more expensive ingredients such as meats and fishes were not available. Noteworthy about this recipe is that while most paellas can be finished in the oven, this one calls for the rice to bake solely in the oven.

PREPARE 10 TO 14 HOURS IN ADVANCE

⅓ cup dried chickpeas

6 cups water

1 pound beef bones

One (½-pound) piece lean beef stew meat

½ pound lean meaty pork ribs, cut into 1½-inch pieces

1 medium onion

1 leek, trimmed and well washed

2 (1-inch) cubes fresh or salt pork, or 1 piece slab bacon (about 2 ounces)

Salt

1 head garlic, loose skin removed

¼ teaspoon saffron threads, crumbled

¼ cup olive oil

¼ pound black sausage (morcilla), such as Spanish style with onion

1 medium potato, peeled and cut into ¼-inch slices

2 small tomatoes, peeled, seeded, and finely chopped

3 garlic cloves, finely chopped

½ teaspoon ground sweet paprika, such as Spanish smoked

2 cups short-grain rice, such as imported Spanish or Arborio

1. Place the chickpeas in a medium bowl, add cold water to cover by 1 inch, add salt, and let soak overnight. Drain. In a large saucepan, combine the water, bones, beef, pork ribs, onion, leek, salt pork, chickpeas, and salt and bring to a boil over high heat. Reduce the heat to low, cover, and simmer 2 to 2½ hours or until the chickpeas are tender. Add the whole head of garlic and simmer 10 minutes more. Pass through a fine-mesh strainer, discard the bones and leek and reserve the beef garlic, ribs, and chickpeas. Cut the beef into 1-inch cubes. In the same saucepan, combine 4 cups of the broth, salt, and the saffron and heat over the lowest heat on a back burner to keep hot until needed.

2. Preheat the oven to 375°F. Heat the oil in a 13-inch earthenware casserole dish or Dutch oven over medium heat. Add the black sausage and cook until browned. Transfer to a platter. In the same oil, add the potatoes and cook, turning occasionally, until tender. Transfer to the platter. Add the tomatoes to the casserole dish and cook, turning once, until softened. Transfer to the platter. Add the beef, ribs, and chopped garlic and cook until the meat is browned. Transfer to the platter. Stir in the paprika. Add the rice and stir to coat well with the pan mixture. Return the head of garlic to the casserole dish and place in the center of the rice. Place the meat mixture over the rice and arrange the tomatoes, potatoes, and black sausage over the top.

3. Pour in the broth all at once, bring to a boil, then transfer the dish to the oven. Bake 30 to 35 minutes or until the liquid is absorbed and the rice almost al dente, tender yet still firm to the bite. Remove from the oven, cover with foil, and let sit 5 to 10 minutes until the rice is done to taste. If using earthenware, serve hot in the dish, or transfer to individual plates.

Crusted Paella
Arroz con Costra

MAKES 4 SERVINGS

This classic recipe comes from a sixteenth-century cookbook written by Ruperto de Nola, Catalan chef to the Spanish King of Naples. This outstanding paella has a tasty egg crust that allows the rice to be cut like a deep-dish pizza.

⅔ cup canned chickpeas

About 2½ cups chicken broth or vegetable broth

⅛ teaspoon saffron threads, crumbled

¼ pound boneless chicken, such as thigh meat, cut into ½-inch pieces

¼ pound lean pork loin, cut into ½-inch pieces

¼ pound sausage, such as bratwurst, cut diagonally into ½-inch slices

¼ cup olive oil

1 small onion, finely chopped (about ⅓ cup)

1 garlic clove, finely chopped

½ medium red bell pepper

1 medium tomato, finely chopped (about ⅔ cup)

1 tablespoon finely chopped fresh flat-leaf parsley

¼ teaspoon ground sweet paprika, such as Spanish smoked

1¾ cups short-grain rice, such as imported Spanish or Arborio

Salt

Freshly ground black pepper

4 large eggs

1. Drain the chickpeas and combine the liquid with the broth and saffron to make 3½ cups. Place the broth mixture in a medium saucepan. Pass ⅓ cup of the chickpeas through a fine-mesh strainer or a ricer into the broth mixture and mix well. Reserve another ⅓ cup for the rice. Heat the broth over the lowest heat on a back burner to keep hot until needed.

2. Preheat the oven to 400°F. Heat the oil in a 13-inch paella pan or similar-size shallow earthenware casserole dish over medium heat. Add the chicken, pork, and sausage and cook, stirring, until lightly browned (they need not be cooked through). Transfer to a platter. In the same oil, add the onion, garlic, and bell pepper and cook, stirring, until softened, about 5 minutes more. Add the tomato and parsley and cook, stirring, about 3 minutes more. Stir in the paprika, add the rice, and stir to coat well with the pan mixture.

3. Add the broth, the remaining ⅓ cup chickpeas, the reserved chicken and pork (the sausage will be added later), salt, and pepper. Bring to a boil and cook until the bubbles rising from the pan look slightly thick and the rice begins to be visible at the surface. Transfer to the oven and bake about 10 minutes or until the liquid is absorbed and the rice almost al dente, tender yet still firm to the bite.

4. Increase the oven to 550°F. In a small bowl, beat the eggs well with a fork and add a little salt. Pour over the rice and arrange the sausage over the rice. Bake about 10 minutes more or until the egg coating is golden brown. Remove from the oven and let sit, uncovered, 5 minutes. Cut into wedges, transfer to dinner plates, and serve hot.

Bean-Pebbled Paella Ⓥ*
Arroz Empedrat

MAKES 6 TO 8 SERVINGS

Made predominantly with beans, this paella has a pebble-like appearance, which accounts for its name. The recipe calls for chickpeas, pinto beans, red beans, and black beans, which makes quite a colorful presentation. If you like, the addition of cured ham makes it a heartier dish. Or, leave it out and make it vegetarian with vegetable broth.

⅔ cup each canned chickpeas, pinto beans, red beans, and black beans

4 cups chicken broth or vegetable broth

¼ teaspoon saffron threads, crumbled

7 tablespoons olive oil

2 bunches scallions (about ½ pound)

12 garlic cloves, finely chopped

2 medium red bell peppers, finely chopped (about 1½ cups)

3 cups coarsely chopped, trimmed, and well washed Swiss chard

6 tablespoons small cubes (¼ inch) Serrano (Spanish cured mountain) ham or prosciutto (about 6 ounces; optional)

1 medium tomato, finely chopped (about ⅔ cup)

2 tablespoons finely chopped fresh flat-leaf parsley

2 teaspoons ground sweet paprika, such as Spanish smoked

1 teaspoon ground cumin

3 cups short-grain rice, such as imported Spanish or Arborio

Salt

1. Drain the beans and reserve the liquid from all the cans except the black beans. Rinse the beans and reserve. In a medium saucepan, combine the broth with 2 cups of the bean liquid and the saffron and heat over the lowest heat on a back burner to keep hot until needed.

2. Preheat the oven to 400°F. In a 17- to 18-inch paella pan or similar-size shallow earthenware casserole dish, heat the oil over medium heat, placing over two burners if necessary. Add the scallions, garlic, bell peppers, chard, and ham, if using, and cook until the peppers are softened. Add the tomato and parsley and cook 1 to 2 minutes more, then stir in the paprika and cumin.

3. Add the rice and stir to coat well with the pan mixture. Add the broth, the reserved beans, and salt and bring to a boil. Cook, stirring and rotating the pan occasionally if over two burners, until the bubbles rising from the pan look slightly thick and the rice begins to be visible at the surface, about 5 minutes more.

4. Transfer to the oven and bake about 10 minutes or until the liquid is absorbed and the rice almost al dente, tender yet still firm to the bite. Remove from the oven, cover with foil, and let sit 5 to 10 minutes or until the rice is cooked to taste. Serve hot.

Rice with Black Beans
Moros y Cristianos

MAKES 4 TO 6 SERVINGS

For more than seven hundred years, Moorish invaders from North Africa controlled Spain, and the name of this recipe is rooted in Spanish history. Moros y Cristianos, *black beans contrasted with white rice, alludes to the racial and religious strife that permeated that period of Spain's history. This dish, cooked decoratively in a ring, can be served as a main course or a side dish. You can also serve this more casually —after the rice sits in step 3, serve the beans under or alongside the rice.*

½ pound dried black beans (frijoles negros), sorted and washed

4 cups cold water

½ pound onions

Freshly ground black pepper

2 garlic cloves

2 tablespoons olive oil

1 medium onion, chopped

2 garlic cloves, finely chopped

¼ cup small cubes (¼ inch) slab bacon

½ teaspoon ground paprika

1 teaspoon all-purpose flour

Salt

1 sprig parsley, for garnish

continues . . .

Rice Ring (Turbante De Arroz)

1 cup chicken broth or vegetable broth

1 cup water

6 tablespoons unsalted butter

1 tablespoon finely chopped onion

1 cup short-grain rice, such as imported Spanish or Arborio

Salt

1 sprig parsley

¼ teaspoon dried thyme

⅛ teaspoon dried tarragon

1. Place the beans in a large saucepan, add 2 cups of the cold water, and let soak 1 hour. Drain. Add the remaining 2 cups cold water to the beans in the saucepan, add the ½ pound onion, the pepper, and the whole garlic cloves, and bring to a boil over high heat. Reduce the heat to low, cover, and simmer 1 hour.

2. Meanwhile, heat the oil in a small skillet over medium heat. Add the chopped onion, chopped garlic, and bacon and cook, stirring, until the bacon is lightly browned. Stir in the paprika and flour. Add to the saucepan, stir in salt, and cook until the beans are done, about 1 hour more, adding some water if necessary (the beans should have very little liquid when done). Discard the ½ pound onion. Preheat the oven to 400°F.

3. Prepare the rice: In a small saucepan, combine the broth and water and bring to a boil over high heat. Meanwhile, melt 3 tablespoons of the butter in a deep earthenware casserole dish or Dutch oven over medium heat. Add the chopped onion and cook, stirring, until wilted and transparent, about 3 minutes. Add the rice, stir to coat with the butter, then stir in the broth, salt, parsley, thyme, and tarragon. Cover and bake 15 minutes or until the liquid is absorbed and the rice almost al dente, tender yet still firm to the bite. Remove from the oven, discard the parsley, and dot the rice with the remaining 4 tablespoons butter. Cover and let sit 5 to 10 minutes or until the rice is cooked to taste.

4. To mold the rice, generously grease an 8-inch ring mold with butter. Fill with the rice and press down so the rice is well packed. Return to the oven and bake 2 minutes more. Place the beans on a slightly concave serving platter. Turn the rice out over the beans to form a crown. Decorate with the parsley. Serve hot.

Rice with Fried Eggs and Bananas V
Arroz a la Cubana

MAKES 4 SERVINGS

In the sixteenth century, Spain introduced bananas, which grow in abundance in the Canary Islands, to the New World. However, cooking with bananas originated in South America, which is why Spaniards refer to this delicious dish of bananas, rice, eggs, and tomato sauce as "Cuban-Style Rice."

Tomato Sauce

3 tablespoons olive oil

1 medium onion, finely chopped (about ⅔ cup)

2 garlic cloves, finely chopped

1⅓ cups puréed fresh or canned tomatoes

Salt

Freshly ground black pepper

5 tablespoons unsalted butter

2 tablespoons ¼-inch cubes slab bacon

2 garlic cloves, finely chopped

1½ cups short-grain rice, such as imported Spanish or Arborio

1½ cups chicken broth or vegetable broth

1½ cups water

Salt

Freshly ground black pepper

Olive oil, for frying

3 unripe bananas, peeled and halved lengthwise then crosswise

All-purpose flour, for dredging

1 large egg, lightly beaten

8 whole eggs

1 tablespoon finely chopped fresh flat-leaf parsley, for garnish

1. Prepare the tomato sauce: Heat the oil in a medium saucepan over low heat. Add the onion and garlic, cover, and cook until the onion is softened but not browned, about 10 minutes. Add the tomatoes, salt, pepper, and enough water to make a tomato-sauce consistency. Cover and cook 30 minutes more. Transfer to a small serving bowl and reserve.

2. Preheat the oven to 350°F. In a small saucepan, combine the broth and water and bring to a boil over high heat. Meanwhile, in a shallow 12-inch earthenware casserole dish or Dutch oven, heat the butter over medium heat. Add the bacon and garlic and cook, stirring until the bacon begins to brown. Add the rice, stir to coat with the butter, then stir in the broth, salt, and pepper. Cover and bake 15 minutes or until the liquid is absorbed and the rice almost al dente, tender yet still firm to the bite. Remove from the oven and let sit, covered, 10 minutes or until the rice is cooked to taste.

3. Meanwhile, place the flour and the beaten egg in separate shallow bowls. Heat ¼ inch of oil in a small skillet over medium heat. Dredge the bananas in the flour, dip in the egg, and place in the oil. Cook, turning once, until just golden. Transfer with a slotted spoon to paper towels and let drain.

4. Fry the whole eggs as instructed in Fried Eggs, Spanish style (page 107). If using a Dutch oven, transfer the rice to a serving dish. Arrange the bananas and eggs decoratively over the rice. Sprinkle with the parsley. Serve hot with the sauce on the side.

SAFFRON

Saffron is the world's most expensive spice, literally worth its weight in gold. The word "saffron" is derived from the Arab word *asafran*, which translates in English to "yellow." Saffron comes from the stigmas of the purple crocus flower. Once a year in October, a dense carpet of purple crocus sprouts up from the dry earth. The flowers must be picked before dawn, and the stigmas must be removed and roasted immediately to conserve the flavor and aroma. Each crocus flower produces just three stigmas, and ten thousand flowers will only yield one ounce of dried saffron. This, and the laborious process of harvesting them, is why saffron is so very expensive. In some places, it can sell for upwards of $6,000 an ounce. Luckily, a tiny bit of saffron goes a long way.

The very best saffron in the world comes from Spain and, more specifically, from a small area centering around the town of Membrilla in La Mancha, where the perfect climate for the crocus flower exists. The Moors rescued saffron and introduced it to Europe by way of the Iberian Peninsula. They planted the crocus flowers in Andalucía, Valencia, and southern Castilla.

Despite its high cost, saffron is an indispensable spice in many Spanish recipes, especially those for paella. I recommend that you buy saffron threads instead of powder so you know what you are getting—the threads should have a uniformly deep red color. When a recipe calls for saffron, it is essential that you use the real thing. Substitutes such as Mexican marigold petals, turmeric, or artificial coloring simply will not do. Once you become acquainted with saffron at its best, you will learn that all substitutes pale in comparison.

Soupy Rice with Seafood
Arroz Caldoso de Marisco

MAKES 4 SERVINGS

Arroz Caldoso or "soupy rice" is not exactly a paella, but rather another kind of rice dish that also originated in the Valencia region. It is not as dry as a paella and is more like a thick, hearty soup. The most traditional soupy rice dishes contain ingredients such as dried beans and fresh vegetables. This version is filled with seafood and flavored with saffron.

2 tablespoons Garlic Sauce (alioli; page 284)

4 cups bottled clam juice or storebought or homemade Fish Broth (page 199)

5 cups water

¼ pound medium shrimp, in their shells

¼ pound bay scallops, whole, or sea scallops, halved

1 pound monkfish or grouper, cut into ¾-inch pieces

Kosher or sea salt

2 tablespoons finely chopped fresh flat-leaf parsley

2 garlic cloves, mashed in a garlic press or mortar

¼ cup dry white wine

1 tablespoon fresh lemon juice

1½ teaspoons finely chopped fresh thyme or ¼ teaspoon dried thyme

1 leek, trimmed and well washed

¼ teaspoon saffron threads, crumbled

1 bay leaf

2 sprigs parsley

6 peppercorns

12 thin slices long-loaf (baguette) bread

2 tablespoons olive oil, plus more for brushing

1 small onion, slivered

2 garlic cloves, finely chopped

1 medium tomato, peeled, seeded, and finely chopped (about ⅔ cup)

1⅓ cups short-grain rice, such as imported Spanish or Arborio

2 dozen medium mussels, thoroughly cleaned

1. Prepare the sauce if necessary. In a soup pot, combine the clam juice and water. Shell the shrimp and add the shells to the broth. In a large bowl, combine the shrimp, scallops, and monkfish. Add salt, the minced parsley and mashed garlic, the wine, lemon juice, and thyme and refrigerate until needed.

2. Preheat the oven to 350°F. Cut off the green part of the leek and add to the broth (finely chop the white part and reserve), along with the saffron, bay leaf, parsley sprigs, peppercorns, and salt. Bring to a boil over high heat. Reduce the heat to low, cover, and simmer 20 minutes. Pass through a fine-mesh strainer and reserve 8 cups. Discard the solids.

3. Brush the bread on both sides with the oil, place on a cookie sheet, and toast, turning once, until crusty but not browned.

4. In a shallow earthenware casserole dish or Dutch oven, heat the 2 tablespoons oil over medium heat. Add the onion, the chopped garlic, and the reserved leek and cook, stirring, until the onion is wilted and transparent, about 5 minutes. Add the tomato and cook, stirring, until softened and its juices release, 2 to 3 minutes more, then add the broth and bring to a boil. Reduce the heat to low, cover, and simmer about 10 minutes. Add the rice, return to a boil, and simmer uncovered until the rice is almost al dente, tender yet still firm to the bite, about 12 to 15 minutes. Add more liquid if desired (it should have the consistency of a thick soup).

5. Stir in the fish (with any liquid) and the mussels in their shells. Cook 4 minutes, stirring occasionally, until the mussels open. Remove from the

heat, cover, and let sit 5 minutes. Transfer to wide shallow soup bowls. Discard any unopened mussels. Divide the toast among individual plates and place a dollop of garlic sauce on each piece. Serve hot. Each person should float the toast in the soup when they begin to eat (otherwise the bread will turn soggy).

Three-Color Paella with Cheese and Almonds Ⓥ
Paella Tres Colores con Queso y Almendra

MAKES 6 SERVINGS

This is a wonderful vegetarian paella in which the rice is flavored by cheese and almonds. For a non-vegetarian dish with a little more flavor, add the anchovy fillets. The recipe calls for red, yellow, and green bell peppers, which creates a delicious and exceptionally colorful paella.

¼ cup slivered almonds

2 medium red bell peppers

2 medium yellow bell peppers

2 medium green bell peppers

¼ cup finely chopped fresh flat-leaf parsley

4 garlic cloves, coarsely chopped

Salt

6 jarred anchovy fillets, chopped (optional)

¼ cup grated aged Spanish Manchego or Parmesan cheese

7 tablespoons olive oil

2 medium onions, finely chopped (about 1⅓ cup)

1 medium tomato, finely chopped (about ⅔ cup)

¼ cup fresh or frozen peas

3 cups short-grain rice, such as imported Spanish or Arborio

6 cups vegetable or chicken broth

1. Preheat the oven to 350°F. Scatter the almonds on a cookie sheet and toast about 8 minutes or until golden. Transfer to a mortar or mini-processor. Increase the oven to 555°F, arrange the bell peppers in a roasting pan, and roast, turning once, about 20 minutes or until the skins are browned and separated from the flesh.

2. Meanwhile, add the parsley, garlic, and salt to the mortar and mash. Mash in the anchovies, if using, then the almonds, adding 1 teaspoon water to facilitate the process. Add the cheese and 1 more teaspoon water and mash.

3. Remove the peppers from the oven, cover with a towel, and let cool. Peel, core, seed, and cut half of each pepper into ½-inch strips. Coarsely chop the remaining halves.

4. Reduce the oven to 400°F. In a 17- to 18-inch paella pan or similar-size shallow earthenware casserole dish, heat the oil over medium heat, placing over two burners if necessary. Add the onion and cook, stirring, until wilted and transparent, about 5 minutes. Increase the heat to high and add the tomato, the chopped peppers and the peas and cook, stirring, about 3 minutes more.

5. Add the rice and stir to coat with the pan mixture. Add the broth and bring to a boil. Stir in the mortar mixture and salt and cook, stirring and rotating the pan occasionally if over two burners, until the bubbles rising from the pan look slightly thick and the rice begins to be visible at the surface.

6. Arrange the pepper strips in a starburst pattern over the rice, transfer to the oven, and bake about 10 minutes or until the liquid is absorbed and the rice almost al dente, tender yet still firm to the bite. Remove from the oven, cover with foil, and let sit about 5 minutes or until the rice is cooked to taste. Serve hot.

Eggplant, Olive, and Caper Paella ⓥ*

Paella de Berenjena con Aceituna y Alcaparras

MAKES 6 SERVINGS

According to preference, this all-vegetable paella can be prepared with or without anchovies. This is a boldly flavored paella, and the chile peppers add an extra zest. Make it vegetarian with vegetable broth.

9 tablespoons olive oil

4 garlic cloves, mashed in a garlic press or mortar

2½ pounds small to medium eggplants, cut crosswise into ⅛-inch slices

¼ teaspoon kosher or sea salt

¼ cup finely chopped fresh flat-leaf parsley

8 garlic cloves, finely chopped

6 cups chicken broth or vegetable broth

¼ teaspoon saffron threads, crumbled

1 medium red bell pepper, finely chopped (about ¾ cup)

1 medium green bell pepper, finely chopped (about ¾ cup)

2 fresh red medium-hot chile peppers, finely chopped

1 small onion, finely chopped (about ⅓ cup)

2 medium scallions, finely chopped (about ¼ cup)

1 medium tomato, finely chopped (about ⅔ cup)

1 teaspoon ground sweet paprika, such as Spanish smoked

10 medium black olives, preferably Spanish, such as kalamata, coarsely chopped

8 anchovy fillets, coarsely chopped (optional)

½ teaspoon nonpareil capers, whole, or larger capers, finely chopped

3 cups short-grain rice, such as imported Spanish or Arborio

1. Preheat the oven to 425°F. In a small bowl, combine 4 tablespoons of the oil and the mashed garlic. Season the eggplant well with salt, place in a colander, and let drain at least 20 to 30 minutes. Dry well between paper towels. Grease a cookie sheet and arrange the eggplant in a single layer. Brush with the garlic-oil mixture and bake 10 minutes, turning once. Reserve about one quarter of the eggplant for garnish and coarsely chop the remainder.

2. In a mortar or mini-processor, mash the parsley, ¼ teaspoon salt, and the chopped garlic. In a soup pot, combine the broth and saffron and heat over the lowest heat on a back burner to keep hot until needed.

3. In a 17- to 18-inch paella pan or similar-size shallow earthenware casserole dish, heat the oil over medium-high heat, placing over two burners if necessary. Add the bell pepper, chile peppers, and onion and cook, stirring, until the peppers are slightly softened. Add the scallions and tomato and cook, stirring, about 2 minutes more. Stir in the paprika, olives, anchovies, if using, capers, and the reserved chopped eggplant.

4. Reduce the oven to 400°F. Add the rice and stir to coat well with the pan mixture. Add the broth, bring to a boil, and taste and adjust seasoning if necessary. Cook, stirring and rotating the pan occasionally if over two burners, until the bubbles rising from the pan look slightly thick and the rice begins to be visible at the surface.

5. Arrange the eggplant slices over the rice and transfer to the oven. Bake about 10 minutes or until the liquid is absorbed and the rice almost al dente, tender yet still firm to the bite. Remove from the oven, cover with foil, and let sit 5 to 10 minutes or until the rice is cooked to taste. Serve hot.

Seafood-Flavored Rice, Alicante Style
Arroz a Banda

MAKES 6 TO 8 SERVINGS

Arroz a Banda or "rice on its own" is the ultimate rice as it must stand without the pieces of clam, shrimp, lobster, or other seafood usually found in rice dishes. The key to this dish is a well-seasoned broth and it is best served with a garlic-rich sauce. This recipe is from El Pegoli restaurant in Dénia, a region known for its delicious red bell peppers.

1 recipe Garlic Sauce (alioli; page 284)

¾ pound medium shrimp, in their shells

Fish Broth

1 pound whiting or similar fish, cleaned, boned, and head on

1 cup bottled clam juice

1 bay leaf

½ cup white wine

2 sprigs parsley

1 slice medium onion

1 slice lemon

Salt

6 peppercorns

¾ cup olive oil

2 garlic cloves

1 dried sweet red pepper (ñora), or New Mexico (Anaheim), stemmed and seeded, or 1 pimiento

Salt and freshly ground black pepper

2 tablespoons finely chopped fresh flat-leaf parsley

2 teaspoons ground paprika

⅛ teaspoon saffron threads, crumbled

2 garlic cloves, finely chopped

1 large tomato, finely chopped (about 1 cup)

3 cups short-grain rice, such as imported Spanish or Arborio

1. Prepare the sauce. Place only enough water to cover the shrimp in a large saucepan, add salt, and bring to a boil over high heat. Add the shrimp and cook 1 to 2 minutes or until pink. Drain and reserve the cooking liquid, adding enough water to make 6 cups. Shell the shrimp, reserve the shells, and finely chop the meat. Reserve.

2. Prepare the broth: In the same large saucepan, add the reserved cooking liquid, the reserved shells, and all the remaining broth ingredients and bring to a boil over high heat. Reduce the heat to low, cover, and simmer at least 1½ hours—the broth must have a strong seafood flavor but at the same time not be overly salty. Pass through a fine-mesh strainer and reserve 6 cups. Discard the solids. Shred the whiting with your fingers and reserve.

3. In a 15-inch paella pan or similar-size shallow earthenware casserole dish, heat the oil over medium heat. Add the whole garlic cloves and cook, stirring, until golden on all sides. Transfer to a food processor or blender, reserving the oil in the pan. Add the chile pepper and cook, turning once, until softened (do not burn). Cut into pieces and add to the processor along with the salt, black pepper, parsley, paprika, and saffron. Process until finely chopped. Gradually add 1 cup of the broth. (May be made in advance up to this point.)

4. Preheat the oven to 350°F. In a medium saucepan, heat the remaining 5 cups broth to a boil over high heat. Meanwhile, heat the reserved oil in the paella pan over medium heat. Add the chopped garlic and tomato and cook, stirring, until the tomato is softened and its juices release, 2 to 3 minutes.

5. Add the rice, stir to coat well with the pan mixture, and cook, stirring, about 3 minutes more. Add the processor mixture, the remaining 5 cups broth, the shrimp and whiting. Increase the heat to medium-high, bring to a boil, and cook until the bubbles rising from the pan look slightly thick and the rice begins to be visible at the surface, about 7 minutes more.

continues...

6. Transfer to the oven and bake 15 minutes or until the liquid is absorbed and the rice almost al dente, tender yet still firm to the bite. Do not stir. Remove from the oven, cover with foil, and let sit 10 minutes or until the rice is cooked to taste. Serve hot with the sauce on the side.

Rosemary-Scented Shellfish and Egg Paella

Arroz con Marisco y Huevo Duro al Romero

MAKES 4 SERVINGS

The warm climate of Spain is ideal for rosemary to grow wild, and this distinctively flavored herb has made its way into numerous recipes. This is a wonderful shellfish paella of shrimp, clams, mussels, and squid, made richer by hard-boiled eggs.

¼ pound tiny Manila or cockle clams or ½ dozen very small littleneck clams

½ dozen very small mussels

½ pound cleaned squid

2 hard-boiled eggs

3 cups bottled clam juice or storebought or homemade Fish Broth (page 199)

⅛ teaspoon saffron threads, crumbled

½ pound small to medium shrimp, in their shells

2 garlic cloves, finely chopped

1 small onion, finely chopped (about ⅓ cup)

1 medium green bell pepper, finely chopped (about ¾ cup)

1 tablespoon finely chopped fresh rosemary or ½ teaspoon dried rosemary

1 small tomato, finely chopped (about ⅓ cup)

1 tablespoon finely chopped fresh flat-leaf parsley

¼ teaspoon ground sweet paprika, such as Spanish smoked

1½ cups short-grain rice, such as imported Spanish or Arborio

2 medium scallions, finely chopped (about ¼ cup)

12 snow peas

1 pimiento, cut into ½-inch strips

Few sprigs rosemary, for garnish

1. Rinse the clams and mussels well. Cut or pull off the mussel beards. Discard any clams or mussels with cracked shells or that do not close tightly when touched. If using littleneck clams, place ¼ cup water in a medium saucepan and bring to a boil over high heat. Add the clams and cook until they open. Drain and reserve any pan liquid for the broth. Discard any unopened clams.

2. Cut the squid body into ½-inch rings and the tentacles in half, reserving any scraps for the broth. Reserve.

3. Coarsely chop half of 1 hard-boiled egg and cut the remainder into slices. Combine the broth and saffron in a soup pot. Shell the shrimp and reserve. Add the shells and any squid scraps to the broth and bring to a boil over high heat. Reduce the heat to low, cover, and simmer 20 minutes. Pass through a fine-mesh strainer and return 3 cups to the pot. Discard the solids. Heat over the lowest heat on a back burner to keep hot until needed.

4. Preheat the oven to 400°F. Generously salt the shrimp and squid. Heat the oil in a 13-inch paella pan or shallow similar-size earthenware casserole dish over medium-high heat. Add the shrimp and squid, turning once, and cook about 1 minute (they should not be fully cooked because they will continue to cook in the oven). Transfer the shrimp to a platter. Add the garlic, onion, bell pepper, and 1½ teaspoons of the chopped rosemary (or ¼ teaspoon of the dried), reduce the heat to medium, and cook until the peppers are slightly softened, about 3 minutes. Add the tomato and parsley and cook 2 to 3 minutes more or until the tomato is softened and its juices release.

5. Stir in the paprika, add the rice, and stir to coat with the pan mixture. Add the broth, bring to a boil, and cook, stirring, about 2 minutes more. Taste and

adjust seasoning if necessary. Add the shrimp, the chopped egg, scallions, and snow peas and cook until the bubbles rising from the pan look slightly thick and the rice begins to be visible at the surface. Arrange the pimiento, clams, and mussels attractively over the rice.

6. Transfer to the oven and bake about 10 minutes or until the liquid is absorbed and the rice almost al dente, tender yet still firm to the bite. Remove from the oven, arrange the sliced egg over the rice, cover with foil, and let sit 5 to 10 minutes or until the rice is cooked to taste. Sprinkle with the remaining 1½ teaspoons minced rosemary and garnish with the rosemary sprigs. Serve hot.

Rice with Shrimp and Fresh Tuna

Arroz con Langostinos y Atún

MAKES 4 SERVINGS

From the province of Alicante, this dish relies on the garlic and dried red peppers for flavor. If the peppers are not available, more paprika can be substituted. Garlic sauce (alioli) is the perfect complement.

3½ cups storebought or homemade Fish Broth (page 199) or 2½ cups bottled clam juice diluted with 1 cup water

1 recipe Garlic Sauce (alioli; page 284)

½ pound small to medium shrimp, in their shells

8 jumbo shrimp, in their shells

Kosher salt

2 medium tomatoes

1 teaspoon ground paprika (increase to 2 tablespoons if not using dried sweet red peppers)

7 tablespoons olive oil

17 garlic cloves

2 teaspoons finely chopped fresh flat-leaf parsley

¾ pound fresh tuna, cut into 1-inch chunks

2 dried sweet red peppers (ñoras) or mild New Mexico (Anaheim) chile peppers, stemmed, seeded, and broken into several pieces

¼ teaspoon saffron threads, crumbled

1¾ cups short-grain rice, such as imported Spanish or Arborio

1 pimiento, cut into ½-inch strips

1. Prepare the broth and sauce if necessary. Place the sauce in a serving bowl and reserve. Meanwhile, shell the small shrimp, add the shells to the broth for added flavor, coarsely chop the shrimp, and reserve. Pass the broth through a fine-mesh strainer and return 3½ cups to the pot. Discard the solids.

2. In a medium bowl, season the chopped shrimp and the jumbo shrimp in their shells with salt and let sit until needed. Cut the tomatoes in half crosswise and gently squeeze to extract the seeds. With a coarse grater over a small bowl, grate each half down to the skin, draining off any excess juices. Reserve the pulp and discard the skin. Stir in the 1 teaspoon paprika (2 tablespoons if not using dried red bell peppers). Season the tuna on all sides with salt. In a mortar or mini-processor, mash 1 clove of the garlic. Add 1 tablespoon of the oil and the parsley and mash. Brush over the tuna and let marinate until needed. Peel 8 of the remaining garlic cloves and coarsely chop the other 8.

3. Heat 1 tablespoon of the oil in a small skillet over medium-low heat. Add the bell pepper and the whole garlic cloves and cook, stirring, 1 to 2 minutes, until the peppers are softened and the garlic very lightly browned. Finely chop the peppers and transfer to a mortar or mini-processor, add the cooked garlic cloves and the saffron, and mash. Add to the tomato mixture and mix well.

4. Preheat the oven to 375°F. Heat the remaining 5 tablespoons oil in a 13-inch paella pan or similar-size shallow earthenware casserole dish over medium-high heat. Add the tuna and jumbo shrimp in their shells and cook until the shells just

continues . . .

turn pink (they will continue to cook later). Transfer to a platter. Reduce the heat to medium, add the chopped shrimp and chopped garlic and cook only a few seconds. Add the rice and cook, stirring frequently, about 5 minutes more.

5. Stir in the tomato mixture and cook 1 minute more, then add the broth. Increase the heat to high, bring to a boil, and cook, stirring constantly, until the bubbles rising from the pan look slightly thick and the rice begins to be visible at the surface. Taste and adjust seasoning if necessary (it should be well seasoned). Stir in the tuna and attractively arrange the whole shrimp and the pimientos over the rice.

6. Transfer to the oven and bake 10 minutes or until the liquid is absorbed and the rice almost al dente, tender yet still firm to the bite. Remove from the oven, cover with foil, and let sit 10 minutes. Serve hot, passing the sauce separately. Everyone should place a small amount on the side of their dish, taking a little with each forkful of paella.

Scallop and Mushroom Paella
Arroz con Vieiras y Setas

MAKES 6 SERVINGS

The region of Galicia is famous for its delectable scallops, which when mixed with mushrooms, give this paella a more subtle flavor than most. I first sampled this superb dish in the restaurant of Toñi Vicente in the historic city of Santiago de Compostela.

4½ cups storebought or homemade Fish Broth (page 199; double recipe) or 3½ cups bottled clam juice diluted with 1 cup water

1 pound bay scallops, whole, or sea scallops, halved

Kosher salt

½ cup dry white wine

2 tablespoons fresh lemon juice

¼ teaspoon saffron threads, crumbled

2 teaspoons finely chopped fresh thyme or ¼ teaspoon dried thyme

2 teaspoons finely chopped fresh rosemary or ¼ teaspoon dried rosemary

5 tablespoons olive oil

6 tablespoons finely chopped shallots

½ pound oyster mushrooms, rinsed. trimmed, and coarsely chopped

4 tablespoons finely chopped fresh flat-leaf parsley

¼ cup small cubes (¼ inch) Serrano (Spanish cured mountain) ham or prosciutto (about 2 ounces)

2½ cups short-grain rice, such as imported Spanish or Arborio

Lemon wedges, for garnish

1. Prepare the broth if necessary. Meanwhile, in a medium bowl, season the scallops on all sides with salt and let sit until needed. Add the wine, lemon juice, saffron, thyme, and rosemary to the broth and place on a back burner over the lowest heat to keep hot until needed.

2. Preheat the oven to 375°F. In a 16- to 17-inch paella pan or similar-size shallow earthenware casserole dish, heat the oil over high heat, placing over two burners if necessary. Add the scallops and cook, stirring, about 2 minutes. Transfer to a platter. Reduce the heat to low, add the shallots, and cook, stirring, about 1 minute more. Stir in the mushrooms, 2 tablespoons of the parsley, and the ham and cook about 2 minutes more.

3. Add the rice and stir 1 minute more. Add the broth, bring to a boil, and cook, stirring and rotating the pan occasionally if over two burners, until the bubbles rising from the pan look slightly thick and the rice begins to be visible at the surface. Taste and adjust seasoning if necessary (it should be well seasoned). Stir in the scallops and any juices from their platter. Transfer to the oven and bake 10 minutes or until the liquid is absorbed and the rice almost al dente, tender yet still firm to the bite. Remove from the oven, cover with foil, and let sit 10 minutes or until the rice is cooked to taste. Sprinkle with the remaining 2 tablespoons parsley and garnish with the lemon wedges. Serve hot.

Scallop, Shrimp, and Seaweed Paella
Paella de Vieiras, Gambas y Algas

MAKES 6 TO 8 SERVINGS

I was surprised to find seaweed as an ingredient in paella and equally surprised at how delicious it was. Here the delicate taste of shrimp and scallops is perfectly contrasted by the strong flavor of the seaweed.

5½ cups storebought or homemade Fish Broth (page 199; double recipe) or bottled clam juice

1 pound bay scallops, whole, or sea scallops, halved

1 pound shrimp, shelled and cut crosswise into ½-inch pieces

Kosher or sea salt

1 cup dried seaweed pieces or strips, such as wakame

¼ teaspoon saffron threads, crumbled

½ cup dry white wine

2 tablespoons fresh lemon juice

5 tablespoons olive oil

2 medium green bell peppers, finely chopped (about 1½ cups)

¼ cup finely chopped shallots

1⅓ cups trimmed, well-washed, finely chopped leeks (white part only)

2 tablespoons finely chopped fresh flat-leaf parsley

3 cups short-grain rice, such as imported Spanish or Arborio

1. Prepare the broth if necessary. Meanwhile, in a medium bowl, season the scallops and shrimp with salt and let sit 15 minutes. In a small bowl, place the seaweed, add warm water to cover, and let soak until softened. Drain. Add the saffron, wine, and lemon juice to the broth and place on a back burner over the lowest heat to keep hot until needed.

2. Preheat the oven to 400°F. In a 17- to 18-inch paella pan or similar-size shallow earthenware casserole dish, heat the oil over medium heat, placing over two burners if necessary. Add the scallops and shrimp and cook, turning once, until the seafood just turns opaque on the surface, about 1 minute. Transfer to a platter and reserve. Add the bell pepper and cook, stirring, until slightly softened. Stir in the shallots and leeks and cook 1 minute, then stir in the seaweed and parsley.

3. Add the rice and stir to coat well with the pan mixture. Add the broth, bring to a boil, and cook, stirring and rotating the pan occasionally if over two burners, until the bubbles rising from the pan look slightly thick and the rice begins to be visible at the surface. Taste and adjust seasoning if necessary. Add the reserved scallops and shrimp (and any liquid from their platter).

4. Transfer to the oven and bake 10 minutes or until the liquid is absorbed and the rice almost al dente, tender yet still firm to the bite. Remove from the oven, cover with foil, and let sit 5 to 10 minutes or until the rice is cooked to taste. Serve hot.

Shrimp Paella with Red Pepper Sauce
Arroz con Gambas y Salsa Salmorreta

MAKES 6 TO 8 SERVINGS

Dried sweet red peppers once again lend their distinctive flavor to this delicious paella prepared Alicante style. The broth has a more concentrated flavor if made with fresh clams, but clam juice may be substituted. This paella is perfectly complemented by the garlic-rich salmorreta sauce on the side. If the dried red peppers are not available, use paprika and a fresh red bell pepper may be substituted.

1 dozen large clams such as Manila or littleneck

8 cups water or bottled clam juice

¼ teaspoon saffron threads, crumbled

Salt

continues…

2 sprigs parsley

2 dried sweet red peppers (ñoras) or mild New Mexico (Anaheim) chile peppers, stemmed and seeded (or 2 tablespoons ground sweet paprika, and 1 fresh red bell pepper)

4 whole small tomatoes

1 pound small to medium shrimp, in their shells

½ pound jumbo shrimp, in their shells, preferably with heads

Salmorreta Sauce

3 dried sweet red peppers (ñoras) or mild New Mexico (Anaheim) chile peppers, stemmed and seeded

2 tablespoons finely chopped fresh flat-leaf parsley

2 teaspoons ground sweet paprika, such as Spanish smoked

6 garlic cloves, finely chopped

¼ teaspoon salt

6 tablespoons extra-virgin olive oil

1 teaspoon fresh lemon juice

Reserved tomatoes from paella recipe

2 large cleaned squid (about ½ pound), with or without tentacles, finely chopped

7 tablespoons olive oil

12 garlic cloves, finely chopped

2 tablespoons finely chopped fresh flat-leaf parsley

1 teaspoon ground sweet paprika, such as imported Spanish smoked

3 cups short-grain rice, such as imported Spanish or Arborio

1. Prepare the broth: Rinse the clams. Discard any with cracked shells or that do not close tightly when touched.

2. In a soup pot, combine the clams, water, saffron, salt, parsley sprigs, chile peppers, and tomatoes. Shell the small shrimp, add the shells to the broth, and reserve the shrimp. Bring to a boil over high heat, reduce the heat to low, and simmer about 30 minutes. Transfer the chile peppers and

2 of the tomatoes to a platter and reserve. Pass the remaining broth through a fine-mesh strainer, pressing with the back of a soup ladle to extract as much liquid as possible, and return 6 cups to the pot. Discard the solids. Scrape the flesh from the chile peppers and add to the broth. Place on a back burner over the lowest heat to keep hot until needed.

3. Prepare the sauce: Peel and seed the 2 reserved tomatoes. In a mortar or mini-processor, mash the bell peppers, 2 tablespoons parsley, 6 chopped garlic cloves, and salt. Mash in the tomatoes, then stir in the oil and lemon juice. Let sit 30 minutes. (May be made up to 24 hours ahead and stored covered in the refrigerator.)

4. Cut the small shrimp crosswise into halves or thirds. Season the cut small shrimp, the unshelled jumbo shrimp, and the squid with salt. In a 17- to 18-inch paella pan or similar-size shallow earthenware casserole dish, heat the oil over medium heat, placing over two burners if necessary. Add the jumbo shrimp and cook, stirring, until just pink. Transfer to a platter, reserving the oil in the skillet.

5. Preheat the oven to 400°F. In the same oil over medium heat, add the 12 chopped garlic cloves, the small shrimp, squid, and 2 tablespoons parsley to the pan and cook, stirring, until the shrimp turn pink. Stir in the paprika and 4 tablespoons of the sauce, then add the rice and stir to coat well with the pan mixture. Add the broth, bring to a boil, and cook, stirring and rotating the pan occasionally if over two burners, until the bubbles rising from the pan look slightly thick and the rice begins to be visible at the surface.

6. Transfer to the oven and bake about 10 minutes or until the rice is almost al dente, tender yet still firm to the bite and the shrimp is cooked through. Remove from the oven, arrange the jumbo shrimp over the rice, cover with foil, and let sit 5 to 10 minutes or until the rice is done to taste. Serve hot with the sauce on the side, to use with the rice and as a dip for the jumbo shrimp.

Rice with Squid and Shrimp

Arrosetxat

MAKES 4 TO 6 SERVINGS

Arrosetxat *refers to the golden color of the rice that results from sautéing it before stirring in the liquid in which it will cook. This is a typical dish of Castellón de la Plana, but other versions of it can be found in Catalunya.*

1 recipe Garlic Sauce (alioli; page 284)

1 pound cleaned squid with tentacles, coarsely chopped

¼ pound medium shrimp

Fish Broth

1 small whiting, cleaned, head on

1 small onion

6 peppercorns

2 sprigs thyme or ¼ teaspoon dried thyme

1 bay leaf

1 slice lemon

Salt

2 sprigs parsley

1 cup bottled clam juice

3 cups water

1 medium green (Italian) frying pepper, cored and seeded

1 small tomato, halved

⅛ teaspoon saffron threads, crumbled

3 garlic cloves

5 tablespoons olive oil

2 cups short-grain rice, such as imported Spanish or Arborio

5 garlic cloves, finely chopped

1 small tomato, peeled, seeded, and finely chopped (about ⅓ cup)

2 teaspoons ground sweet paprika, such as Spanish smoked

½ cup dry white wine

Salt

1. Prepare the sauce. Shell the shrimp, reserve the shells, and cut each shrimp into 3 pieces. In a soup pot, combine all the broth ingredients, add the shrimp shells and any squid scraps, and bring to a boil over high heat. Reduce the heat to low and simmer about 40 minutes. Pass through a fine-mesh strainer and reserve 3½ cups (boil down if there is more). Discard the solids.

2. In a mortar or mini-processor, mash the saffron and the 3 whole cloves garlic. Stir in ¼ cup of the broth and reserve.

3. Preheat the oven to 375°F. In a 17- to 18-inch paella pan or similar-size shallow earthenware casserole dish, heat the oil over low heat, placing over two burners if necessary. Add the squid and shrimp and cook, stirring, about 10 minutes. Increase the heat to medium, add the rice, the chopped garlic, the tomato, and paprika, and cook, stirring constantly, until the rice is lightly golden. (May be made in advance up to this point.) Add the remaining 3¼ cups broth, the wine, and the mortar mixture and bring to a boil.

4. Add the rice and cook, stirring and rotating the pan occasionally if over two burners, until the bubbles rising from the pan look slightly thick and the rice begins to be visible at the surface.

5. Taste and adjust seasoning if necessary. Transfer to the oven and bake 10 minutes or until most of the liquid is absorbed and the rice almost al dente, tender yet still firm to the bite. Remove from the oven, cover with foil, and let sit 5 to 10 minutes or until the rice is cooked to taste. Serve hot with the sauce on the side.

Garlic Clam Paella
Arroz de Almejas a la Marinera

MAKES 4 SERVINGS

Clams are the star attraction in this wonderful paella. The recipe calls for large clams for chopping, and small clams to leave whole, with a rice perfectly seasoned with garlic, onion, and parsley.

1 dozen large littleneck clams

1 to 1½ dozen very small littleneck clams

3 cups water

8 garlic cloves, finely chopped

⅛ teaspoon saffron threads, crumbled

7 tablespoons finely chopped fresh flat-leaf parsley

⅛ teaspoon kosher or sea salt

¼ cup dry white wine

2 teaspoons fresh lemon juice

¼ cup olive oil

½ cup finely chopped onion

¼ cup trimmed, well washed, and finely chopped leek (white part only)

1 small green bell pepper, finely chopped (about ⅓ cup)

1 bay leaf

One (½-inch) piece dried red chile pepper or ¼ teaspoon crushed red pepper

¼ teaspoon ground paprika, such as Spanish smoked

1½ cups short-grain rice, such as imported Spanish or Arborio

I. Rinse the clams. Discard any clams with cracked shells or that do not close tightly when touched. Reserve the small clams. In a large skillet, place the large clams and the water and bring to a boil over high heat. Cover and cook until the clams have opened. Discard any unopened clams, reserving 2¾ cups of the cooking liquid. Finely chop the clams. Return the cooking liquid to the saucepan and place on a back burner over the lowest heat to keep hot until needed.

2. Preheat the oven to 400°F. In a mortar or mini-processor, mash the garlic, saffron, 6 tablespoons of the parsley, and the salt. Mash in the wine and lemon juice. Heat the oil in a 13-inch paella pan or similar-size shallow earthenware casserole dish over low heat. Add the onion, leek, bell pepper, bay leaf, and chile pepper and cook, stirring, until the vegetables are softened, about 8 minutes. Add the chopped clams and cook, stirring, about 5 minutes more. Remove the bay leaf and chile pepper and stir in the paprika.

3. Add the rice and stir to coat well with the pan mixture. Add the broth and bring to a boil. Taste and adjust seasoning if necessary. Add the mortar mixture and cook until the bubbles rising from the pan look slightly thick and the rice begins to be visible at the surface.

4. Transfer to the oven and bake about 10 minutes or until the rice is almost al dente, tender yet still firm to the bite. Remove from the oven. Arrange the large clams over the rice, cover with foil, and let sit 5 to 10 or minutes until the rice is cooked to taste. Sprinkle with the remaining 1 tablespoon parsley and serve hot.

Mussel Paella
Paella de Mejillones

MAKES 6 TO 8 SERVINGS

Mussels are most commonly used in paella to impart their flavor to the rice and other seafood and as a decorative garnish. Here they are featured prominently.

About 5¼ cups storebought or homemade Fish Broth (page 199; double recipe) or bottled clam juice

6 pounds small mussels

⅔ cup white wine

1 tablespoon finely chopped fresh thyme or ½ teaspoon dried thyme

1 tablespoon finely chopped fresh rosemary or ½ teaspoon dried rosemary

¼ cup fresh lemon juice

7 tablespoons olive oil

1 medium onion, finely chopped (about ⅓ cup)

8 garlic cloves, finely chopped

2 tablespoons finely chopped shallots

¼ cup finely chopped fresh flat-leaf parsley

¼ teaspoon saffron threads, crumbled

2 pimientos, finely chopped

3 cups short-grain rice, such as imported Spanish or
    Arborio

Salt

A generous amount freshly ground black pepper

2 pimientos, cut into ½-inch strips

1. Prepare the broth if necessary. Rinse the mussels well. Cut or pull off the mussel beards. Drain. Discard any mussels with cracked shells or that do not close tightly when touched. Reserve 6 to 10 mussels per portion depending on their size.

2. In a large skillet, add the wine into a skillet, add the mussels, cover, and bring to a boil over high heat. Cook, transferring the mussels to a platter as they open. Discard any unopened mussels. Reserve the cooking liquid, combine it with enough fish broth to make 6 cups and return to the soup pot. Add the thyme, rosemary, and lemon juice and place on a back burner over the lowest heat to keep hot until needed. Remove the mussel meat from the shells, chop coarsely, and reserve.

3. Preheat the oven to 400°F. Heat the oil in a 17- to 18-inch paella pan or similar-size shallow earthenware casserole dish over medium heat. Add the onion, garlic, shallots, parsley, and saffron and cook, stirring, until the onion has softened. Add the chopped mussel meat and the chopped pimientos and cook, stirring, 1 minute, then add the rice and stir to coat well with the pan mixture. Increase the heat to high, add the broth, salt, and pepper and bring to a boil. Cook until the bubbles rising from the pan look slightly thick and the rice begins to be visible at the surface, about 5 minutes more.

4. Arrange the pimiento strips and the reserved mussels attractively over the rice with the edge of the mussel that will open facing up. Bake 10 to 15 minutes or until the rice is almost al dente, tender yet still firm to the bite. Remove from the oven, cover with foil, and let sit 5 to 10 minutes. Serve hot.

Lobster Paella Casa Roberto
Paella de Langosta Casa Roberto

MAKES 6 SERVINGS

In Spain as in America, lobster is quite expensive and often considered a luxury item. Therefore, I was quite surprised to find lobster paella on the menu at the Valencian restaurant Casa Roberto, a casual, laid-back establishment lacking any pretentiousness. The lobster paella is their specialty, and it was as good if not better than those I've had in more elegant restaurants. Thanks to master chef Juana for sharing this recipe.

6 cups storebought or homemade Fish Broth (page
    199; double recipe) or bottled clam juice

3 (1¼-pound) live lobsters or 6 frozen (thawed)
    lobster tails

¼ teaspoon saffron threads, crumbled

1½ teaspoons finely chopped fresh thyme or
    ¼ teaspoon dried thyme

1 pound monkfish, cut into ½-inch chunks

Kosher or sea salt

7 tablespoons olive oil

1 medium onion, finely chopped (about ⅓ cup)

4 garlic cloves, finely chopped

2 tablespoons finely chopped cooked carrot

2 tablespoons finely chopped fresh flat-leaf parsley

1 bay leaf

1 medium tomato, peeled, seeded, and finely
    chopped (about ⅔ cup)

1 teaspoon ground sweet paprika, such as Spanish
    smoked

3 cups short-grain rice, such as imported Spanish or
    Arborio

continues...

1. Prepare the broth if necessary. Place a cutting board in a rimmed cookie sheet to catch the liquid that collects. Place the lobster on its back on the cutting board. Do not remove the bands that keep the claws shut. Protect your hand with a heavy towel or pot holder and hold the lobster firmly by the head. Plunge the tip of a heavy chef's knife into the body where the tail joins the chest. Cut all the way through, separating the tail from the body. Pull out and discard the dark vein from the tail. Slice the head down the middle, discard the stomach sack, and transfer the tomalley (green matter) to a mortar, and reserve the coral (red roe), if desired. Mash the tomalley.

2. Add the clam juice, tomalley, and saffron to the broth and place the pot on a back burner over the lowest heat to keep hot until needed. Season the monkfish all over with salt.

3. Preheat the oven to 400°F. In a 17- to 18-inch paella pan or similar-size shallow earthenware casserole dish, heat the oil over high heat, placing over two burners if necessary. Add the lobster halves meat side down on both sides of the pan and cook about 2 minutes (it will barely be cooked). Transfer to a platter. Add the monkfish, cook until lightly browned on both sides, turning once (not cooked through), and transfer to the platter, reserving the oil in the pan.

4. Reduce the heat to medium, add the onion, garlic, carrot, parsley, and bay leaf and cook, stirring, until the onion is slightly softened, about 5 minutes. Add the tomato and cook, stirring, until softened and its juices release, 2 to 3 minutes more. Stir in the paprika, then add the rice and stir to coat well with the pan mixture. Add the broth and bring to a boil. Taste and adjust seasoning if necessary. Return the lobster to the pan and cook about 3 minutes. Transfer the lobster to the platter, add the monkfish, and cook, stirring and rotating the pan occasionally if over two burners, until the bubbles rising from the pan look slightly thick and the rice begins to be visible at the surface.

5. Arrange the lobster halves over the rice, transfer to the oven, and bake about 10 minutes or until the rice is almost al dente, tender yet still firm to the bite. Return the paella to the stovetop over high heat and cook, without stirring, until a crust of rice forms at the bottom of the pan (be careful not to let it burn), about 2 minutes. Remove from the heat, cover with foil, and let sit 5 to 10 minutes or until the rice is cooked to taste. Remove the bay leaf and serve hot.

Crab Meat Paella with Peas and Carrots
Paella de Centolla con Guisantes y Zanahorias

MAKES 6 TO 8 SERVINGS

In Spain, this paella is made with centolla, *the large spider crabs found off the coast, but other types of crab will do nicely. You can use cooked lump crabmeat that is fresh or frozen, but be certain it is 100% crab and not the fish mixture that often passes for crab. For an attractive presentation, garnish this dish with crab claws or legs.*

6 cups storebought or homemade Fish Broth (page 199; double recipe) or bottled clam juice

1 live crab or 3 ounces fresh or frozen lump crab meat (optional)

8 garlic cloves, finely chopped

¼ teaspoon kosher or sea salt

¼ cup finely chopped fresh flat-leaf parsley

1 tablespoon finely chopped fresh thyme or ½ teaspoon dried thyme

⅛ teaspoon ground cayenne pepper

1 bay leaf, crumbled

¼ teaspoon saffron threads, crumbled

2 medium tomatoes

7 tablespoons olive oil

1 medium onion, finely chopped (about ⅓ cup)

6 tablespoons trimmed, well-washed, and finely chopped leek (white part only)

½ cup finely chopped carrot (1 medium)

¼ teaspoon ground sweet paprika, such as Spanish smoked

¼ cup brandy

3 cups short-grain rice, such as imported Spanish or Arborio

1 cup fresh or frozen peas

½ pound fresh or frozen (thawed) cooked lump crab meat

1. Prepare the broth if necessary. If using the live crab, fill a large pot with water and heat to a boil over high heat. Add the crabs, cover, and return to a boil. Reduce the heat to low and simmer 10 minutes. Drain. Place the crab on its back on a cutting board. Using your thumb, pry up the tail flap, twist off, and discard. Turn the crab over, pry up the top shell and discard. Cut off the gills on both sides and discard. Discard the internal organs and transfer the tomalley (green matter) and the coral (red roe), if any, to a mortar or mini-processor. Twist off the claws and legs and crack their shells at the joints. Using a nutpick, remove the meat and place in a small bowl. Break the body in half, remove the meat, and place in the bowl. Discard the shell and reserve the meat.

2. In a mortar or mini-processor, mash 4 of the garlic cloves, the salt, parsley, thyme, cayenne pepper, bay leaf, and the reserved tomalley or coral (if using whole crabs in their shells). Reserve. In a large saucepan, combine the broth and saffron and place on a back burner over the lowest heat to keep hot until needed.

3. Preheat the oven to 400°F. In a 17- to 18-inch paella pan or similar-size shallow earthenware casserole dish, heat the oil over medium heat, placing over two burners if necessary. Reduce the heat to low, add the onion, the remaining 4 cloves garlic, the leek, and carrot, and cook, stirring, until the vegetables are softened, about 8 minutes. Add the

tomato and brandy, increase the heat to high, and cook until no liquid remains. Stir in the paprika, then add the rice and stir to coat well with the pan mixture. Add the broth, taste and adjust seasoning if necessary, and bring to a boil. Add the mortar mixture and the peas and cook, stirring and rotating the pan occasionally if over two burners, until the bubbles rising from the pan look slightly thick and the rice begins to be visible at the surface.

4. Stir in the crabmeat, transfer to the oven and bake about 10 minutes or until the rice is almost al dente, tender yet still firm to the bite. Remove from the oven, cover with foil, and let sit 5 to 10 minutes or until the rice is cooked to taste. Remove the bay leaf and serve hot.

Seafood Rice, Murcia Style
Arroz de Caldera Murciano

MAKES 6 SERVINGS

Spaniards adore garlic, and this recipe for paella calls for a generous amount of it, both in the recipe and in the garlic sauce that accompanies it. Murcia, famous for its fresh vegetables, is also a rice-producing region, where rice was traditionally cooked in an iron kettle hung by chains over a fire. Besides the abundance of garlic, the flavor of this paella relies heavily on the dried red bell pepper.

2 cups storebought or homemade Fish Broth (page 199; partial recipe)

1 recipe Garlic Sauce (alioli; page 284)

4 tablespoons olive oil

1 head garlic (about 20 medium cloves), separated and peeled

10 dried sweet red peppers (ñoras), 6 mild dried New Mexico (Anaheim) chile peppers, stemmed and seeded, or 5 tablespoons ground sweet paprika, such as Spanish smoked

½ cup coarsely chopped onion

continues...

2 large tomatoes, coarsely chopped (about 1 pound)

11 cups bottled clam juice or water

1 pound whiting, cleaned

¼ teaspoon saffron threads, crumbled

Salt

1-pound boneless piece 1½-inch-thick striped bass or other blue fish, with skin

1½ pounds monkfish

3 cups short-grain rice, such as imported Spanish or Arborio

1. Prepare the broth if necessary. Meanwhile, prepare the alioli if necessary. In a heavy pot, heat 3 tablespoons of the oil over low heat. Add the garlic and peppers and cook, turning occasionally, until the garlic is golden and the peppers slightly softened (be careful not to burn them). Transfer the garlic and peppers with a slotted spoon to a food processor, reserving the oil in the pot. Process until finely chopped. With the motor running, gradually add the broth and process until smooth.

2. In the reserved oil over medium heat, add the onion and cook, stirring, until wilted and transparent, about 5 minutes. Add the tomatoes and cook 1 minute, then add 8 cups of the clam juice, the whiting, saffron, salt, and the processor mixture. Bring to a boil over high heat, reduce the heat to low, and simmer 30 minutes.

3. Pass the broth through a fine-mesh strainer, pushing through as much of the solid material as possible, and discard the remaining solids. Return the broth to the pot, add the bass and monkfish, and simmer about 15 minutes, or 10 minutes for each inch of thickness. Transfer the fish to another pot, add broth to cover, cover, and keep in a warm spot until ready to serve.

4. Measure the remaining broth to 9 cups, adding liquid or boiling down if necessary. Bring the broth to a boil over high heat, and add the rice. Reduce the heat to low and simmer until the rice is almost al dente, tender yet still firm to the bite, about 15 minutes. Remove from the heat, cover, and let rest

until the rice is cooked to taste, about 5 minutes. Serve hot with the sauce on the side.

Fresh Tuna and Rabbit Paella
Paella de Atún y Conejo

MAKES 6 SERVINGS

Tuna and rabbit may seem to be an unusual combination, but their tastes and textures blend together perfectly, especially with the added zest of paprika.

16 garlic cloves, finely chopped

2 tablespoons finely chopped fresh flat-leaf parsley

1½ teaspoons finely chopped fresh thyme or ¼ teaspoon dried thyme

¼ teaspoon dried oregano

A generous amount of freshly ground black pepper

¼ teaspoon kosher or sea salt

2 pimientos, finely chopped

4 teaspoons ground paprika, such as Spanish smoked

½ teaspoon ground cumin

½ cup white wine

2 medium tomatoes

1 pound boneless rabbit, cut into ½-inch pieces, or boneless, skinless chicken, such as thigh meat, cut into ½-inch pieces

1 pound fresh tuna, cut into ½-inch chunks

5½ cups chicken broth or vegetable broth

¼ teaspoon saffron threads, crumbled

7 tablespoons olive oil

1 medium onion, finely chopped (about ⅔ cup)

3 cups short-grain rice, such as imported Spanish or Arborio

1. In a mortar or mini-processor, mash the garlic, parsley, thyme, oregano, pepper, and the salt. Mash in the pimientos, paprika, and cumin. Stir in the wine.

2. Cut the tomatoes in half crosswise and gently squeeze to extract the seeds. With a coarse grater over a small bowl, grate each half down to the skin, draining off any excess juices. Reserve the pulp and

discard the skin. Season the chicken and tuna well with salt and let sit 10 minutes.

3. Preheat the oven to 400°F. In a medium pot, combine the broth and saffron and place a back burner over the lowest heat to keep hot until needed. Heat the oil in a 17- to-18-inch paella pan or similar-size shallow earthenware casserole dish over high heat. Add the rabbit and tuna and cook, turning once, until lightly browned. Transfer to a platter. Reduce the heat to low, add the onion, and cook, stirring, until softened but not browned. Add the tomatoes and cook, stirring, about 5 minutes more.

4. Add the rice and stir to coat well with the pan mixture, then add the mortar mixture and the broth. Taste and adjust seasoning if necessary. Bring to a boil and cook about 3 minutes. Add the tuna and chicken and cook until the bubbles rising from the pan look slightly thick and the rice begins to be visible at the surface.

5. Transfer to the oven and bake about 10 minutes or until the rice is almost al dente, tender yet still firm to the bite. Return to the stovetop and cook over high heat until a crust of rice forms at the bottom of the pan (be careful not to let it burn), about 2 minutes. Remove from the heat, cover with foil, and let sit 5 to 10 minutes or until the rice is cooked to taste. Serve hot.

Cod Paella, Catalan Style
Paella de Bacalao a la Catalana

MAKES 6 SERVINGS

Catalan-style dishes tend to be especially creative and often combine sweet and savory flavors. This version of paella dates back to medieval times when cod was naturally preserved with salt and was more readily available than other types of fish. Here the cod is combined with spinach sautéed with raisins and pine nuts, creating a paella with a flavor that is unique and delicious.

PREPARE 24 TO 36 HOURS IN ADVANCE

½ **pound dried boneless skinless salt cod, about ¾ inch thick (if thicker, slice to this thickness)**

6 **cups storebought or homemade Fish Broth (page 199; double recipe) or bottled clam juice**

¼ **cup raisins**

¼ **teaspoon saffron threads, crumbled**

7 **tablespoons olive oil**

¼ **cup pine nuts**

2 **medium onions, finely chopped (about 1⅓ cups)**

½ **medium green bell pepper, finely chopped (¾ cup)**

1 **small tomato, finely chopped (about ⅓ cup)**

10 **garlic cloves, finely chopped**

¼ **cup finely chopped fresh flat-leaf parsley**

¾ **pound spinach leaves, rinsed, trimmed, well dried, and coarsely chopped**

¾ **cup dry white wine**

3 **cups short-grain rice, such as imported Spanish or Arborio**

1. Place the cod in a medium bowl and add cold water to cover. Cover and let sit in the refrigerator 24 to 36 hours, changing the water occasionally, until the water no longer tastes salty. Drain.

2. Prepare the broth if necessary. Meanwhile, place the raisins in a small bowl, add warm water to cover, and let sit 15 minutes or until rehydrated. Drain.

3. Preheat the oven to 400°F. Add the saffron to the broth and place on a back burner over the lowest heat to keep hot until needed. In a 16- to 17-inch paella pan or similar-size shallow earthenware casserole dish, heat the oil over medium heat, placing over two burners if necessary. Add the cod and cook, turning once, about 1 minute per side. Transfer to a platter, shred with your fingers or finely chop, and reserve.

4. In the same oil over medium heat, add the pine nuts and cook, stirring, until lightly browned. Add the onion and peppers and cook, stirring, until softened, about 8 minutes more. Stir in the tomato,

continues...

garlic, and parsley and cook 1 to 2 minutes more, then add the spinach and cook, stirring, until wilted. Add the wine and cook until no liquid remains.

5. Add the rice and stir to coat well with the pan mixture. Add the broth, raisins, and cod and cook, stirring and rotating the pan occasionally if over two burners, until the bubbles rising from the pan look slightly thick and the rice begins to be visible at the surface.

6. Transfer to the oven and bake until the liquid is absorbed and the rice almost al dente, tender yet still firm to the bite, about 10 minutes. Remove from the oven, cover with foil, and let sit about 5 minutes or until the rice is cooked to taste. Serve hot.

Cod, Bean, and Hot Green Pepper Paella

Paella de Bacalao, Habichuelas y Pimientos Picantes

MAKES 6 TO 8 SERVINGS

When the cod is of good quality and properly desalted, it is enormously popular in Spanish cooking, and there are many paella recipes that depend on it. If you can't find cod, you can substitute monkfish, but in my opinion the result is not quite as good. This dish is best served with garlic oil.

PREPARE 24 TO 36 HOURS IN ADVANCE

¼ pound dried boneless skinless salt cod or fresh monkfish, about 1 inch thick (if the cod is thicker, slice in half lengthwise)

⅓ cup dried kidney beans, sorted and washed (for 2 cups cooked)

3½ cups bottled clam juice diluted with ½ cup water or 4 cups storebought or homemade Fish Broth (page 199)

¼ teaspoon saffron threads, crumbled

Salt

Garlic Oil (Ajo Aceite)

3 tablespoons finely chopped mildly hot green chile peppers

5 garlic cloves, finely chopped

¾ cup extra-virgin olive oil

5 tablespoons olive oil

4 long thin mildly hot green chile peppers

1 medium green bell pepper, finely chopped (about ¾ cup)

6 garlic cloves, finely chopped

2 medium ripe tomatoes, peeled, seeded, and finely chopped (about 1⅓ cups)

½ teaspoon ground sweet paprika, such as Spanish smoked

Salt

3 cups short-grain rice, such as imported Spanish or Arborio

1. Place the cod in a medium bowl and add cold water to cover. Cover and let sit in the refrigerator 24 to 36 hours, changing the water occasionally, until the water no longer tastes salty. Drain and dry between paper towels.

2. Meanwhile, place the beans in a small bowl, add cold water to cover by 1 inch, and let soak overnight in the refrigerator. Drain. Place in a medium saucepan with water to cover by 2 inches and bring to a boil over high heat. Reduce the heat to low, cover, and simmer 1 hour. Drain, reserving 2 cups of the liquid. Transfer the beans to a medium bowl. Add the diluted clam juice, the saffron, and salt to the pan and place on a back burner on the lowest heat to keep hot until needed.

3. In a mortar or mini-processor, mash the chile peppers and garlic. Mash in 1 tablespoon of the oil. Gradually stir in the remaining oil. Reserve.

4. Preheat the oven to 375°F. In a 17- to 18-inch paella pan or similar-size shallow earthenware casserole dish, heat the oil over medium heat, placing over two burners if necessary. Add the cod and cook, turning once, about 1 minute per side. Transfer to

a platter. Add the whole hot and chopped bell peppers and cook, stirring occasionally, until the peppers are softened. Meanwhile, coarsely chop the cod. Add the garlic and cook 1 minute more, then add the tomato and cod and cook about 2 minutes more. Stir in the paprika, beans, and salt then add the rice and stir to coat well with the pan mixture. Cook 1 to 2 minutes more.

5. Add the broth and bring to a boil. Reduce the heat to low, and cook, stirring and rotating the pan occasionally if over two burners, until the bubbles rising from the pan look slightly thick and the rice begins to be visible at the surface.

6. Transfer to the oven and bake 10 minutes or until the liquid is absorbed and the rice almost al dente, tender yet still firm to the bite. Remove from the oven, cover with foil, and let sit 10 minutes more or until the rice is cooked to taste. Serve hot with the oil on the side to drizzle over each portion.

Salt Cod, Cauliflower, and Artichoke Paella

Arroz con Bacalao, Coliflor y Alcachofas

MAKES 4 TO 6 SERVINGS

While most Spanish preparations of cod demand that it be soaked for days in order to lose its saltiness, this unique recipe does not. Instead, use mostly water for the cooking liquid and do not add any additional salt to the recipe. That, combined with the milder flavors of cauliflower and artichokes, compensates for the saltiness of the cod.

½ pound dried boneless skinless salt cod

6 garlic cloves, finely chopped

¼ teaspoon saffron threads, crumbled

2 whole cloves

2 tablespoons finely chopped fresh flat-leaf parsley

1 teaspoon water

1 cup storebought or homemade Fish Broth or bottled clam juice

4 cups water

7 tablespoons olive oil

2 medium onions, finely chopped (about 1⅓ cups)

4 medium green (Italian) frying peppers or 2 medium green bell peppers, finely chopped (about 1½ cups)

1 medium tomato, finely chopped (about ⅔ cup)

4 artichoke hearts, quartered

¾ pound cauliflower (6 flowers), cut into ½- to 1-inch florets and stems removed

½ teaspoon ground paprika

Freshly ground black pepper

¼ cup fresh or frozen peas

2½ cups short-grain rice, such as imported Spanish or Arborio

1 pimiento, cut into ½-inch strips, for garnish

1. Rinse the cod well to remove all the salt and let dry on paper towels. In a mortar or mini-processor, mash the garlic, saffron, cloves, and parsley. Add the 1 teaspoon water and mash to incorporate.

2. In a medium saucepan, combine the broth and the 4 cups water and place on a back burner over the lowest heat to keep hot until needed.

3. In a 17- to 18-inch paella pan or similar-size shallow earthenware casserole dish, heat the oil over medium heat, placing over two burners if necessary. Add the cod and cook, turning once, until lightly softened, about 1 minute. Transfer to a platter, reserving the oil in the pan.

4. Cut the cod into ½-inch strips and place in a medium bowl with warm water to cover. Let sit about 30 minutes, changing the water occasionally. Drain and let dry on paper towels, pressing to extract the salt and moisture. Shred with your fingers and reserve.

continues...

5. Preheat the oven to 400°F. In the reserved oil over medium heat, add the onions and frying peppers and cook, stirring, until softened, about 8 minutes. Add the tomato, artichokes, and cauliflower and cook, stirring, about 5 minutes more. Stir in the paprika, pepper, and peas. Add the rice and cod, stirring to coat the rice well with the pan mixture. Add the broth and the mortar mixture, bring to a boil, and cook, stirring and rotating the pan occasionally if over two burners, until the bubbles rising from the pan look slightly thick and the rice begins to be visible at the surface.

6. Arrange the pimiento over the rice. Transfer to the oven and bake about 10 minutes or until the liquid is absorbed and the rice almost al dente, tender yet still firm to the bite. Remove from the oven, cover with foil, and let sit 5 to 10 minutes or until the rice is cooked to taste. Serve hot.

Salmon and Asparagus Paella with Capers and Dill

Paella de Salmón y Espárragos con Alcaparras y Eneldo

MAKES 6 SERVINGS

Smoked salmon has a very strong flavor and when enhanced with the equally strong flavors of onions, capers, and dill, it gives the rice in this paella an added pungency and zest.

6 cups storebought or homemade Fish Broth (page 199; double recipe) or bottled clam juice

Topping

3 tablespoons finely chopped onion

3 tablespoons capers, rinsed, drained, and whole (if nonpareil) or finely chopped

1½ tablespoons finely chopped fresh dill

2 large hard-boiled eggs, finely chopped

6 ounces chopped smoked salmon or lox

½ cup dry white wine

¼ teaspoon saffron threads, crumbled

1 pound boneless salmon, cut into ½-inch chunks

Kosher or sea salt

7 tablespoons olive oil

1 medium onion, finely chopped (about ⅓ cup)

1 medium green bell pepper, finely chopped (about ¾ cup)

4 garlic cloves, finely chopped

1 large scallion, finely chopped

¼ cup finely chopped fresh chives or 2 teaspoons dried chives

2 tablespoons finely chopped fresh dill or 1 teaspoon dried dill

1 medium tomato, finely chopped (about ⅔ cup)

½ teaspoon ground paprika, such as Spanish smoked

2 teaspoons capers, rinsed, drained, and whole (if nonpareil) or finely chopped

3 cups short-grain rice, such as imported Spanish or Arborio

12 cooked green asparagus, rinsed and trimmed

1. Prepare the broth if necessary.

2. Prepare the topping: Place each topping ingredient in a small serving bowl (or mix them all together in one serving bowl).

3. In a medium saucepan, combine the wine, broth, and saffron and place on a back burner over the lowest heat to keep hot until needed. Season the salmon with salt and let sit 10 minutes.

4. In a 16- to 17-inch paella pan or similar-size shallow earthenware casserole dish, heat the oil over high heat, placing over two burners if necessary. Add the salmon and cook, stirring gently, until lightly browned. Transfer to a platter, reserving the oil in the skillet.

5. Preheat the oven to 400°F. In the same oil over medium heat, add the onion, bell pepper, garlic, scallion, chives, and dill and cook, stirring, until the onions and peppers are softened, about 8 minutes. Add the tomato, and cook, stirring, 2 minutes,

then stir in the paprika and the capers. Add the rice and stir to coat well with the pan mixture. Add the broth and cook until the liquid is reduced slightly. Add the reserved salmon and cook, stirring and rotating the pan occasionally if over two burners, until the bubbles rising from the pan look slightly thick and the rice begins to be visible at the surface.

6. Arrange the asparagus attractively over the rice. Transfer to the oven and bake 10 to 15 minutes or until the liquid is absorbed and the rice almost al dente, tender yet still firm to the bite. Remove from the oven, cover with foil, and let sit about 5 minutes or until the rice is cooked to taste. Serve hot with the toppings on the side.

Rice with Monkfish and Roasted Tomatoes
Arroz a Banda con Rape y Tomate Asado

MAKES 6 SERVINGS

This version of Arroz a Banda, "rice on its own," calls for monkfish to be cooked independently from the rice, and then served as a separate course. The monkfish is prepared by coating it with garlic and parsley and simmering it with roasted tomatoes. Since the rice is "plain," it is essential that this fish broth be strongly flavored. The rice is best served with garlic sauce.

6 cups storebought or homemade Fish Broth (page 199; double recipe) or bottled clam juice

1 recipe Garlic Sauce (alioli; page 284)

Tomatoes

3 medium tomatoes, halved crosswise

Salt

Freshly ground black pepper

1 tablespoon finely chopped fresh thyme or
    ½ teaspoon dried thyme

1 small onion, slivered

2 garlic cloves, finely chopped

2 tablespoons finely chopped fresh flat-leaf parsley

1 tablespoon dried bread crumbs

1 tablespoon olive oil

Fish

1½ pounds monkfish, cut lengthwise into ½ inch slices
    then crosswise in half if the slices are long

Kosher or sea salt

Fresh lemon juice

2 garlic cloves, finely chopped

2 tablespoons finely chopped fresh flat-leaf parsley

1½ teaspoons finely chopped fresh thyme or
    ¼ teaspoon dried thyme

⅛ teaspoon salt

9 tablespoons olive oil

All-purpose flour, for dusting

Rice

2 dried sweet red peppers (ñoras), stemmed and
    seeded (optional)

¼ teaspoon saffron threads, crumbled

2 medium onions, finely chopped (about 1½ cups)

4 garlic cloves, finely chopped

1 medium tomato, chopped (about ⅔ cup)

1 teaspoon ground paprika (add 4 more teaspoons if
    not using dried sweet peppers)

2 tablespoons finely chopped fresh flat-leaf parsley

3 cups short-grain rice, such as imported Spanish or
    Arborio

1. Prepare the broth if necessary. Meanwhile, preheat the oven to 375°F. Prepare the sauce if necessary.

2. Prepare the tomatoes: Arrange the tomatoes in a baking dish. Season with salt, black pepper, and thyme. Scatter the onion over the tomatoes and sprinkle with the garlic, parsley, and bread crumbs. Drizzle with the oil. Roast 30 minutes.

3. Prepare the fish: Season the fish with salt, sprinkle with the lemon juice, and let sit 10 minutes.

continues...

Meanwhile, in a mortar or mini-processor, mash the garlic, parsley, thyme, and salt. Stir in 4 tablespoons of the oil.

4. Place the flour in a shallow bowl. In a 17- to 18-inch paella pan or similar-size shallow earthenware casserole dish, heat the oil over medium-high heat, placing over two burners if necessary. Dredge the fish in the flour, place in the oil, and cook, turning once, just until browned (it should not be completely cooked because it will continue cooking in the oven). Transfer to a shallow earthenware casserole dish or Dutch oven, reserving the oil in the pan.

5. Prepare the rice: In a small bowl, place the chile peppers, add warm water to cover, and let sit until softened. Drain and finely chop.

6. Preheat the oven to 400°F. Add the saffron to the broth and place on a back burner over the lowest heat to keep hot until needed. In the reserved oil over medium heat, add the onion and garlic and cook, stirring, until the onion is wilted and transparent, about 5 minutes. Stir in the tomato, dried pepper, if using, the paprika, and parsley and cook about 2 minutes more. Add the rice and stir to coat well with the pan mixture. Add the broth and cook, stirring and rotating the pan occasionally if over two burners, until the bubbles rising from the pan look slightly thick and the rice begins to be visible at the surface.

7. Transfer to the oven and bake 10 minutes or until the liquid is absorbed and the rice almost al dente, tender yet still firm to the bite. Remove from the oven (leave the oven on), cover with foil, and let sit 5 to 10 minutes or until the rice is cooked to taste.

8. Meanwhile, place the fish in the oven and bake about 7 minutes or until just cooked through and flakes easily with a fork. Place the fish on a serving platter, pouring any pan juices over the fish. Reheat the tomatoes if necessary and place on the platter with the fish. Serve hot with the rice.

Monkfish and Almond Paella, Alicante Style

Arroz con Rape y Almendras a la Alicantina

MAKES 6 TO 8 SERVINGS

This outstanding paella prepared Alicante style — with lots of dried red bell pepper and garlic — features monkfish, which has a solid consistency and does not fall apart when cooking. The almonds add a nutty taste and texture.

8 cups bottled clam juice or storebought or homemade Fish Broth (page 199; double recipe)

1 medium onion

7 tablespoons olive oil

2 medium red bell peppers, coarsely chopped (about ½ pound)

2 heads garlic, separated into cloves, loose skin removed

1 medium tomato, coarsely chopped (about ⅔ cup)

4 tablespoons finely chopped fresh flat-leaf parsley

¼ teaspoon saffron threads, crumbled

2 tablespoons ground sweet paprika, such as Spanish smoked

1 pound monkfish, grouper, or other firm-fleshed fish steaks, cut into ¾-inch chunks

Kosher or sea salt

3 cups short-grain rice, such as imported Spanish or Arborio

1 cup ground blanched almonds (about 5 ounces)

1. In a large pot, combine the clam juice and onion and place on a back burner over the lowest heat to keep hot until needed. In a 17- to 18-inch paella pan or similar-size shallow earthenware casserole dish, heat 3 tablespoons of the oil over medium heat, placing over two burners if necessary. Add the garlic and cook, stirring, until lightly browned. Add the peppers and cook, stirring, 1 minute more. Add

the tomato and 2 tablespoons of the parsley and cook, stirring, 2 minutes more. Stir in the saffron and paprika and transfer to the pot. Deglaze the paella pan, adding a few tablespoons of the liquid from the pot, stirring, and scraping up any bits of flavor. Add to the pot and bring to a boil over high heat. Reduce the heat to low and simmer about 20 minutes. Wipe out the pan.

2. Season the fish well with salt. Heat the remaining 4 tablespoons oil in the paella pan over medium-high heat. Add the monkfish and cook, turning, until lightly browned (it should not be fully cooked because it will continue cooking in the oven). Transfer to a platter. Add the rice and all but 2 tablespoons of the almonds. Cook, stirring until the rice is well coated with the pan mixture, about 1 to 2 minutes. Remove from the heat.

3. Preheat the oven to 425°F. Pass the broth through a fine-mesh strainer, pushing through as much of the solid matter as possible. Discard the solids. Return 6½ cups to the pot and bring to a boil over high heat.

4. Add the broth to the paella pan and bring to a boil over medium-high heat. Cook, stirring and rotating the pan occasionally if over two burners, until the bubbles rising from the pan look slightly thick and the rice begins to be visible at the surface, about 5 minutes more. Stir in the monkfish, sprinkle with the remaining 2 tablespoons parsley and the remaining almonds and transfer to the oven.

5. Bake 10 to 12 minutes or until the rice is almost al dente, tender yet still firm to the bite. Remove from the oven, cover with foil, and let sit 5 to 10 minutes or until the rice is cooked to taste. Serve hot.

Monkfish, Swiss Chard, and Sesame Seed Paella
Paella de Rape, Acelgas y Sésamo

MAKES 4 SERVINGS

Here the relatively mild taste of monkfish is complemented by the slightly pungent Swiss chard and the nutty flavor of sesame seeds. I recommend sprinkling more sesame seeds on this finished rice as it creates a wonderful, crunchy texture.

½ pound monkfish, grouper, or other firm-fleshed fish steaks, cut into ½-inch chunks

Kosher or sea salt

¾ pound Swiss chard, well washed and thick stems trimmed

¼ cup sesame seeds

6 garlic cloves, finely chopped

3 tablespoons finely chopped fresh flat-leaf parsley

⅛ teaspoon kosher or sea salt

3 cups bottled clam juice or vegetable broth

⅛ teaspoon saffron threads, crumbled

¼ cup olive oil

1 small onion, finely chopped

2 tablespoons finely chopped shallots

1 small tomato, finely chopped (about ½ cup)

¼ teaspoon ground sweet paprika, such as imported Spanish smoked

1½ cups short-grain rice, such as imported Spanish or Arborio

1. Preheat the oven to 425°F. Season the fish well with salt. Cut the chard to separate the stems from the leaves, and coarsely chop each. Place the sesame seeds on a cookie sheet and toast about 3 minutes or until lightly browned. In a mortar or mini-processor, mash half of the garlic, 2 tablespoons of the parsley, and the ⅛ teaspoon salt.

2. Preheat the oven to 400°F. In a medium saucepan, combine the broth and saffron and place on

continues...

a back burner over the lowest heat to keep hot until needed. Heat the oil in a 13-inch paella pan or similar-size shallow earthenware casserole dish over medium-high heat. Add the monkfish and cook, stirring, about 1 minute (it should not be fully cooked because it will continue to cook in the oven). Transfer to a platter.

3. Reduce the heat to medium, add the remaining half of the garlic, the onion, shallots, and chard stems, and cook, stirring, until the vegetables are softened. Add the tomato and cook, stirring, 2 to 3 minutes, then stir in the paprika. Add the rice and stir to coat it well with the pan mixture. Add the broth and bring to a boil. Stir in the mortar mixture and cook until the bubbles rising from the pan look slightly thick and the rice begins to be visible at the surface. Stir in 2 tablespoons of the sesame seeds and the chard leaves.

4. Transfer to the oven and bake about 10 minutes or until the rice is almost al dente, tender yet still firm to the bite. Remove from the oven, cover with foil, and let sit 5 to 10 minutes or until the rice is cooked to taste. Sprinkle with the remaining 2 tablespoons sesame seeds and the remaining 1 tablespoon parsley. Serve hot.

Black Rice
Arroz Negro

MAKES 6 TO 8 SERVINGS

Arroz Negro is in a class by itself, and if you haven't ever tried black rice, I strongly recommend you do. It is almost jet black, colored by the squid ink, and filled with pieces of squid, shrimp, and monkfish. This paella is absolutely extraordinary and ranks amongst my favorites. Vacuum packs of squid ink are now available by mail order or at specialty fishmongers, which makes the preparation process much easier. Black rice, best served with garlic sauce, is an extraordinary paella not to be missed.

1 recipe Garlic Sauce (alioli; page 284)

2 pounds cleaned small squid (with tentacles) cut into ½-inch rings

½ pound medium shrimp, in their shells

½ pound monkfish or other firm-fleshed fish, skinned and cut into ½-inch pieces

Kosher or sea salt

8 garlic cloves, finely chopped

2 tablespoons finely chopped fresh flat-leaf parsley

⅛ teaspoon kosher or sea salt

6 (4-gram) packets squid ink

6 cups bottled clam juice or storebought or homemade Fish Broth (page 199; double recipe)

2 tablespoons fresh lemon juice

¼ teaspoon saffron threads, crumbled

4 tablespoons olive oil

2 medium red bell peppers, finely chopped (about 1½ cups)

1 medium onion, finely chopped (about ⅔ cup)

2 medium tomatoes, finely chopped (about 1⅓ cups)

2 teaspoons ground sweet paprika, such as Spanish smoked

3 cups short-grain rice, such as imported Spanish or Arborio

4 frozen or canned artichoke hearts, cut into quarters

1 large pimiento, cut into ½-inch strips

Lemon wedges, for garnish

1. Prepare the sauce if necessary. Season the squid, shrimp, and monkfish with salt and let sit 10 minutes at room temperature.

2. Meanwhile, in a mortar or mini-processor, mash half of the garlic, all of the parsley, and the ⅛ teaspoon salt, then stir in the squid ink and reserve. Combine the clam juice, lemon juice, and saffron in a soup pot and place on a back burner over the lowest heat to keep hot until needed.

3. Preheat the oven to 350°F. In a 17- to 18-inch paella pan or similar-size shallow earthenware casserole dish, heat 2 tablespoons of the oil over high heat, placing over two burners if necessary. Add the

squid, shrimp, and monkfish and cook, stirring, 2 minutes. Do not cook them completely. Transfer to a platter.

4. Reduce the heat to medium-high. Add 2 more tablespoons of the oil, the bell peppers, and onion to the paella pan and cook, stirring, until the onion is wilted and transparent, about 5 minutes. Stir in the tomatoes and the remaining half of the garlic. Stir in the paprika. Add the rice and stir to coat well with the pan mixture. Add the broth and bring to a boil. While stirring, add the mortar mixture and the artichokes. Cook, stirring and rotating the pan occasionally if over two burners, about 2 minutes more. Add the squid, shrimp, and monkfish and the juices from the platter. Continue to boil until most of the liquid is absorbed, about 5 minutes more.

5. Arrange the pimiento strips over the rice, transfer to the oven, and bake 10 to 15 minutes or until the rice is almost al dente, tender yet still firm to the bite. Remove from the oven, cover with foil, and let sit 5 to 10 minutes or until the rice is cooked to taste. Remove the foil and arrange the lemon wedges around the pan. Serve hot with the sauce on the side.

Squid Paella "El Faro"
Arroz con Chocos "El Faro"

MAKES 6 SERVINGS

This creative recipe came to me from my friend Gonzalo Córdoba, owner of the excellent El Faro restaurant in Cádiz. In typical Andalucian style, the pungency of the squid and onions is contrasted by the sweetness of the sherry, creating a rice with an incredible flavor.

6 cups storebought or homemade Fish Broth (page 199; double recipe) or bottled clam juice

2 pounds small squid

7 tablespoons olive oil

2 thin slices long-loaf (baguette) bread

3 medium onions, finely chopped (about 2 cups)

2 bay leaves

2 tablespoons white wine

Salt

10 garlic cloves, finely chopped

¼ teaspoon saffron threads, crumbled

2 tablespoons finely chopped fresh flat-leaf parsley

¼ teaspoon salt

2 tablespoons medium-sweet sherry, such as Oloroso, or more white wine

½ large red bell pepper

1 large green bell pepper

3 cups short-grain rice, such as imported Spanish or Arborio

1. Prepare the broth if necessary. Meanwhile, make a small slit at the pointed end of each squid. Rinse thoroughly, letting the water run through the body sac. Cut the body into 1-inch rings and tentacles lengthwise in half at the base.

2. Heat 2 tablespoons of the oil in a large shallow earthenware casserole dish or Dutch oven over medium heat. Add the bread and cook, turning once, until golden on both sides. Transfer to paper towels and let drain. Increase the heat to medium-high, add about 1½ cups of the chopped onions and the bay leaves, and cook, stirring, about 2 minutes. Increase the heat to high, add the squid, and cook, stirring, 1 minute. Add the wine and salt and reduce the heat to low. Cover and simmer about 30 minutes or until the squid is tender.

3. Meanwhile, wet the bread, squeeze dry, and place in a mortar or mini-processor. Add the garlic, saffron, parsley, and the ¼ teaspoon salt. Stir in the sherry.

4. When the squid is done, add the mortar mix to the casserole dish (clean out the mortar or processor container with some of the squid juices, adding to the casserole dish), cover, and simmer 10 minutes more.

continues...

5. Preheat the oven to 400°F. In a 16- to 17-inch paella pan or similar-size shallow earthenware casserole dish, heat the remaining 5 tablespoons oil over medium heat, placing over two burners if necessary. Add the remaining ½ cup onion and the bell pepper and cook, stirring, until softened. Add the rice and stir to coat well with the pan mixture. Add the squid with its cooking liquid and the broth and cook, stirring and rotating the pan occasionally if over two burners, until the bubbles rising from the pan look slightly thick and the rice begins to be visible at the surface.

6. Transfer to the oven and bake about 10 minutes or until the rice is almost al dente, tender yet still firm to the bite. Remove from the oven, cover with foil, and let sit 10 minutes or until the rice is cooked to taste. Remove the bay leaf. Serve hot.

Squid and Scallion Paella
Arroz de Chipirones y Ajos Tiernos

MAKES 6 SERVINGS

Squid can often be found in many of Spain's paellas, but in this recipe it is the star ingredient. The rice is prepared Alicante style with dried sweet red peppers (ñoras) or paprika and enhanced by a generous amount of scallions. As with many paellas, I recommend serving this one with garlic sauce (alioli).

1 recipe Garlic sauce (alioli; page 284) (optional)

1½ pounds squid

6½ cups bottled clam juice or storebought or homemade Fish Broth (page 199; double recipe)

¼ teaspoon saffron threads, crumbled

7 tablespoons olive oil

8 garlic cloves, coarsely chopped

3 sweet or mild dried red peppers (ñoras), stemmed and seeded, or 1 fresh red bell pepper, finely chopped, plus 3 heaping teaspoons ground sweet paprika, such as Spanish smoked

3 medium tomatoes, coarsely chopped (about 2 cups)

Salt

1 pound (about 4 bunches) scallions, trimmed and coarsely chopped

3 cups short-grain rice, such as imported Spanish or Arborio

1. Prepare the sauce, if using. Place in a small serving bowl and reserve. Make a small slit at the pointed end of each squid. Rinse thoroughly, letting the water run through the body sac. Cut the body into ½ inch rings and the tentacles lengthwise in half at the base.

2. In a large pot, combine the clam juice and saffron. In a 17- to 18-inch paella pan or similar-size shallow earthenware casserole dish, heat 2 tablespoons of the oil over medium heat, placing over two burners if necessary. Add the garlic and dried pepper and cook, stirring, about 2 minutes (be careful not to let it burn). Or, if using the fresh pepper, add to the garlic in the casserole dish and cook, stirring, until softened. Transfer the pepper to the broth, reserving the garlic and oil in the casserole dish.

3. In the casserole dish over medium heat, add the tomato and paprika, if using, and cook, stirring, about 2 minutes more. Add the pan mixture to the broth and bring to a boil over high heat. Reduce the heat to low and simmer about 20 minutes. Pass through a fine-mesh strainer, pressing with the back of a wooden spoon to extract as much liquid as possible. Discard the solids. Return 6 cups to the pot and place on a back burner over the lowest heat to keep hot until needed. Wipe out the paella pan.

4. Preheat the oven to 400°F. Heat the remaining 5 tablespoons oil in the paella pan over high heat. Add the squid and cook, stirring, about 5 minutes. Reduce the heat to medium, add the scallions and cook 1 to 2 minutes more. Add the rice and stir to coat well with the pan mixture. Add the broth and taste and adjust seasoning if necessary. Return to a

boil and cook, stirring and rotating the pan occasionally if over two burners, until the bubbles rising from the pan look slightly thick and the rice begins to be visible at the surface, about 5 minutes more.

5. Transfer to the oven and bake about 10 minutes or until the rice is almost al dente, tender yet still firm to the bite. Remove from the oven, cover with foil, and let sit 5 to 10 minutes or until the rice is cooked to taste. Serve hot with the sauce on the side.

Mixed Seafood Paella
Arroz a la Marinera de Pescado

MAKES 6 SERVINGS

Mixed seafood paella is one of the most popular and well known of all of Spain's paellas. Over the years, I have sampled innumerable versions, but I think this recipe is my very favorite. It emphasizes fish over shellfish, and it is best prepared with grouper, monkfish, or another firm-fleshed fish that will hold together when cooking. Like all paella recipes, it is the saffron that gives the rice its distinctive flavor and aroma.

7 cups storebought or homemade Fish Broth (page 199; double recipe) or bottled clam juice

1 pound small squid with tentacles

2 dozen small mussels

¾ cup water

¾ pound monkfish

¾ pound grouper

12 to 18 large shrimp, in their shells

⅛ teaspoon kosher salt

2 tablespoons finely chopped fresh flat-leaf parsley

8 garlic cloves, coarsely chopped

1 tablespoon finely chopped fresh thyme or ½ teaspoon dried thyme

⅛ teaspoon kosher or sea salt

2 teaspoons ground sweet paprika, such as Spanish smoked

¼ teaspoon saffron threads, crumbled

7 tablespoons olive oil

1 medium onion, finely chopped (about ⅔ cup)

6 small scallions (white part only), finely chopped

2 medium red bell peppers, finely chopped (about 1½ cups)

1 medium tomato, finely chopped (about ⅔ cup)

3 cups short-grain rice, such as imported Spanish or Arborio

1. Prepare the broth if necessary. Meanwhile, make a small slit at the pointed end of each squid. Rinse thoroughly, letting the water run through the body sac. Cut the body into ½-inch rings and cut the tentacles lengthwise in half at the base. Reserve.

2. In a medium skillet, place 1 dozen of the mussels and the water. Cover and bring to a boil over high heat, removing the mussels as they open. Discard any unopened mussels, and transfer the cooking liquid to a large pot. Remove the mussels from their shells, discard the shells, and reserve the meat.

3. Cut the monkfish and grouper into ½-inch chunks, reserving the scraps. Place the fish scraps and the broth in the pot with the mussel liquid and bring to a boil over high heat. Reduce the heat to low, cover, and simmer 30 minutes. Season the squid, fish, and shrimp well with salt and let sit 10 minutes. In a mortar or mini-processor, mash the parsley, garlic, thyme, and the ⅛ teaspoon salt. Stir in the paprika and a little water, if necessary, until a paste forms. Pass the broth through a fine-mesh strainer. Return 6 cups to the pot and add the saffron. Place on a back burner over the lowest heat to keep hot until needed.

4. Preheat the oven to 400°F. In a 17- to 18-inch paella pan or similar-size shallow earthenware casserole dish, heat the oil over medium heat, placing over two burners if necessary. Add the squid, fish, and shrimp and cook, stirring, until lightly browned but not fully cooked. Transfer the fish and shrimp to a platter. Reduce the heat to low, add the onion,

continues . . .

scallions, and bell peppers and cook, stirring, until the vegetables are softened, about 8 minutes. Raise the heat to medium-low, add the tomato, and cook, stirring, until softened and its juices release, 2 to 3 minutes more.

5. Add the rice to the paella pan and stir to coat well with the pan mixture. Add the broth, bring to a boil, and cook about 3 minutes. Stir in the reserved monkfish and grouper, the reserved mussels, and the mortar mixture and cook, stirring and rotating the pan occasionally if over two burners, until the bubbles rising from the pan look slightly thick and the rice begins to be visible at the surface.

6. Arrange the shrimp and the uncooked 1 dozen mussels over the rice with the side that will open facing up. Transfer to the oven and bake until the rice is almost al dente, tender yet still firm to the bite, about 10 minutes. Remove from the oven, cover with foil, and let sit 5 minutes or until the rice is cooked to taste. Serve hot.

Pesto Seafood Paella

Paella de Marisco con Puré de Basílico

MAKES 4 SERVINGS

This paella features pesto sauce, which gives the rice a very strong flavor that is tempered by the mild taste of shellfish. I recommend using fresh basil and the smallest clams you can find.

½ pound cockles or other very small clams

1 dozen jumbo shrimp, in their shells

½ pound bay scallops, whole, or sea scallops, cut into ¾-inch chunks

Kosher or sea salt

3 cups bottled clam juice or storebought or homemade Fish Broth (page 199)

⅛ teaspoon saffron threads, crumbled

Pesto Sauce

2 cups packed fresh basil leaves

3 tablespoons pine nuts

4 garlic cloves, finely chopped

½ cup finely chopped fresh flat-leaf parsley

2 tablespoons grated aged Manchego or Parmesan cheese

1 tablespoon olive oil

½ teaspoon salt

Generous amount of freshly ground black pepper

3 tablespoons olive oil

2 tablespoons pine nuts

½ small onion, finely chopped (about ¼ cup)

3 ounces oyster or other mushrooms, rinsed, trimmed, and coarsely chopped (about 1 cup)

1 long thin hot green chile pepper, finely chopped (about 2 tablespoons)

3 tablespoons finely chopped tomato

1½ cups short-grain rice, such as imported Spanish or Arborio

2 tablespoons finely chopped fresh flat-leaf parsley, for garnish

1. Rinse the cockles. Discard any cockles with cracked shells or that do not close tightly when touched. Meanwhile, season the shrimp and scallops well with salt. Let sit 10 minutes. In a medium saucepan, combine the broth and saffron.

2. Prepare the sauce: In a food processor, place the sauce ingredients and process until as finely chopped as possible. With the motor running, gradually add 4 tablespoons of the broth from the pot. Reserve.

3. Preheat the oven to 400°F. Place the broth on a back burner over the lowest heat to keep hot until needed. Heat the oil in a 13-inch paella pan or similar-size shallow earthenware casserole dish. Add the shrimp and scallops and cook, stirring, until the shrimp is just pink and the scallops are lightly browned (they should not be fully cooked

because they will continue to cook in the oven). Transfer to a platter. Add the 2 tablespoons pine nuts and cook, stirring, until lightly browned. Add the onion, mushrooms, and chile pepper and cook, stirring, until the onion is slightly softened, about 5 minutes more. Add the tomato and cook, stirring, until softened and its juices release, about 2 to 3 minutes more.

4. Add the rice to the paella pan and stir to coat well with the pan mixture. Add the broth, taste and adjust seasoning if necessary, and bring to a boil. Stir in 4 tablespoons of the pesto sauce. Stir in the scallops and clams and cook until the bubbles rising from the pan look slightly thick and the rice begins to be visible at the surface, about 5 minutes more.

5. Arrange the shrimp over the rice and transfer to the oven. Bake about 10 minutes or until the rice is almost al dente, tender yet still firm to the bite. Remove from the oven, cover with foil, and let sit 5 to 10 minutes or until the rice is cooked to taste. Sprinkle with the parsley and serve hot.

Seafood Pasta Paella

Fideuà

MAKES 6 SERVINGS

This is a highly unusual paella because instead of being made with rice, it is made with pasta. It is prepared in a paella pan just like a paella, and it contains similar ingredients. This recipe originated in Valencia where fideos, pasta similar to thin spaghetti, is popular. The thin, narrow shape allows all the flavors of the broth to permeate the pasta. When it is done, run it under the broiler for a few minutes to give it a crisp finish and serve it with garlic sauce. Seafood pasta prepared paella style is an extraordinary and truly memorable creation.

1 recipe Garlic Sauce (alioli; page 284)

½ pound squid

2 dozen tiny clams, such as cockles or Manila or 1 dozen very small littlenecks

2 dozen very small mussels

½ pound shrimp, whole if small or halved crosswise if medium, shelled

½ pound monkfish, grouper, or other firm-fleshed fish, cut into ½-inch chunks

Kosher or sea salt

7 cups bottled clam juice or storebought or homemade Fish Broth (page 199; double recipe)

¼ teaspoon saffron threads, crumbled

7 tablespoons olive oil

1 medium green bell pepper, finely chopped (about ¾ cup)

16 garlic cloves, finely chopped

2 medium tomatoes, finely chopped (about 1⅓ cups)

2 tablespoons finely chopped fresh flat-leaf parsley

½ cup dry white wine

1 pound perciatelli pasta, broken into 1½-inch pieces

2 teaspoons ground sweet paprika, such as Spanish smoked

½ teaspoon ground cayenne pepper or 1 teaspoon ground hot paprika, such as Spanish smoked

1. Prepare the sauce if necessary. Place in a small serving bowl and reserve. Rinse the clams and mussels well. Cut or pull off the mussel beards. Discard any clams or mussels with cracked shells or that do not close tightly when touched. Reserve.

2. Meanwhile, make a small slit at the pointed end of each squid. Rinse thoroughly, letting the water run through the body sac. Let drain and pat dry with paper towels. Cut the body into 1-inch rings and the tentacles lengthwise in half at the base.

continues…

3. Season the squid, shrimp, and monkfish well with salt. In a large saucepan, combine the broth and saffron and place on a back burner over the lowest heat to keep hot until needed.

4. Preheat the oven to 400°F. In a 17- to 18-inch paella pan or similar-size shallow earthenware casserole dish, heat the oil over high heat, placing over two burners if necessary. Add the shrimp and monkfish and cook, stirring, just until the shrimp is pink and the surface of the monkfish opaque, less than 1 minute. Transfer to a platter. Reduce the heat to medium-high, add the pepper and squid and cook, stirring, until the pepper is slightly softened. Add the garlic, tomatoes, parsley, and wine, bring to a boil, and cook until the liquid is evaporated.

5. Add the pasta to the paella pan and stir to coat well with the pan mixture. Cook, stirring constantly, about 2 minutes, then add the sweet paprika, cayenne pepper, and broth. Bring to a boil and taste and adjust seasoning if necessary. Cook, stirring and rotating the pan occasionally if over two burners, until the bubbles rising from the pan look slightly thick and the pasta begins to be visible at the surface.

6. Return the shrimp and fish to the paella pan and mix in the clams and mussels. Transfer to the oven and bake about 7 minutes or until the pasta is almost al dente, tender yet still firm to the bite and most of the liquid is absorbed. Remove from the oven, cover with foil, and let sit 5 to 10 minutes or until the pasta is cooked to taste. Place a broiler rack about 6 inches from the heat source and preheat the broiler. Uncover the pasta and place under the broiler, about 1½ minutes or until the pasta is browned and crisp. Serve hot with the sauce on the side.

Rice with Chicken
Arroz con Pollo

MAKES 4 TO 6 SERVINGS

This popular Spanish dish is basically a simplified version of paella that can be prepared in almost no time at all with ingredients commonly found in the supermarket.

One (3-pound) chicken

Salt

6 tablespoons olive oil

2 medium green bell peppers, coarsely chopped (about 1½ cups)

1 medium onion, coarsely chopped (about ⅓ cup)

2 garlic cloves, finely chopped

2 medium tomatoes, peeled and coarsely chopped (about 1⅓ cups)

2 pimientos, coarsely chopped

3½ cups chicken broth

3 tablespoons ground paprika

¼ teaspoon saffron threads, crumbled

2 cups short-grain rice, such as imported Spanish or Arborio

½ cup dry white wine

Freshly ground black pepper

1 tablespoon finely chopped fresh flat-leaf parsley, for garnish

1. Hack or cut the chicken with kitchen shears into 1½-inch pieces, hacking off the bony ends of the leg and dividing the wings into two pieces, discarding the tips. Sprinkle the chicken all over with salt. Heat the oil in a 15-inch paella pan or similar-sized shallow earthenware casserole dish over medium heat. Add the chicken and cook, turning

occasionally, until golden on all sides. Transfer to a platter. Add the bell peppers, onion, and garlic and cook, stirring, until the bell pepper is tender, about 8 minutes more. Add the tomato and pimientos and cook, stirring occasionally, 10 minutes more.

2. Preheat the oven to 325°F. Place the broth in a small saucepan and bring to a boil over high heat. Add the paprika and saffron to the paella pan, then add the rice, and stir to coat well with the pan mixture. Add the broth, wine, salt, and black pepper and bring to a boil, stirring occasionally, until the bubbles rising from the pan look slightly thick and the rice begins to be visible at the surface, about 7 minutes more.

3. Arrange the chicken over the rice, transfer to the oven, and bake until the liquid is absorbed and the rice almost al dente, tender yet still firm to the bite. Cover with foil, and let sit 5 to 10 minutes or until the rice is cooked to taste. Garnish with the parsley and serve hot.

Valencia's Traditional Paella
Paella Tradicional de Valencia

MAKES 6 TO 8 SERVINGS

Valencia, with its abundance of rice paddies, is indisputably the region of Spain where paella originated. Once an economic necessity, these rice dishes were traditionally prepared over an open fire for laborers in the fields. There are now innumerable versions of paella but they all owe their origin to this recipe for Valencia's traditional paella. Land snails are typical to this dish, but since they are not easy to find, I have omitted them here. Authentic paella must have the quintessential socarrat—*a thin layer of rice at the bottom of the pan that becomes browned and crusty and is considered the very essence of the paella. It is scraped off after the rice is served and passed around so everyone can have a piece of it.*

2 cups chicken broth

4 cups water

6 sprigs rosemary or ½ teaspoon dried rosemary

Half of a 2½-pound chicken

Half of a 2-pound rabbit

Kosher or sea salt

½ pound snap or snow peas

¼ teaspoon saffron threads, crumbled

7 tablespoons olive oil

2 green (Italian) frying peppers or 1 medium green bell pepper, finely chopped (about ¾ cup)

1 medium onion, finely chopped (about ⅓ cup)

8 garlic cloves, finely chopped

2 medium tomatoes, finely chopped (about 1⅓ cups)

2 tablespoons finely chopped fresh flat-leaf parsley

½ pound green beans, such as broad, halved crosswise

4 artichoke hearts, quartered

1 teaspoon ground paprika, such as Spanish smoked

3 cups short-grain rice, such as imported Spanish or Arborio

1. In a large saucepan, combine the broth, water, rosemary, salt, and saffron and simmer over low heat, about 20 minutes. Discard the rosemary. Place the broth on a back burner over the lowest heat to keep hot until needed.

2. Meanwhile, hack or cut the chicken with kitchen shears into 2-inch pieces, hacking off the bony ends of the leg and dividing the wings into two pieces, discarding the tips. Hack or cut with kitchen shears the rabbit into 2-inch pieces. Sprinkle the chicken and rabbit all over with salt. Reserve a few snap peas for garnish.

3. Preheat the oven to 400°F. In a 17- to 18-inch paella pan or similar-sized shallow earthenware casserole dish, heat the oil over high heat, placing over two burners if necessary. Add the chicken and rabbit and cook, turning occasionally, until golden but not fully cooked. Add the frying peppers, onion,

continues...

and garlic and cook, stirring, until softened, keeping the heat high. Add the green beans, snap peas, and artichokes and cook, stirring, about 3 minutes more. Add the tomato and parsley, cook 1 minute more, then stir in the paprika.

4. Add the rice and stir to coat well with the pan mixture. Add the broth, bring to a boil, and cook, stirring and rotating the pan occasionally if over two burners, until the bubbles rising from the pan look slightly thick and the rice begins to be visible at the surface, about 5 minutes more.

5. Arrange the reserved snap peas over the rice and transfer to the oven. Bake 10 to 12 minutes or until the liquid is absorbed and the rice almost al dente, tender yet still firm to the bite. Return to the stovetop over high heat and cook, without stirring, until a crust of rice forms at the bottom of the pan (be careful not to let it burn), about 2 minutes. Remove from the heat, cover with foil, and let sit 5 to 10 minutes or until the rice is cooked to taste. Serve hot.

Mixed Chicken and Seafood Paella
Paella Mixta Valenciana

MAKES 6 TO 8 SERVINGS

Although a Valencian paella purist would frown upon combining seafood and chicken, this mixed paella has become one of the most popular versions, especially in Spanish restaurants in the United States. This is a recipe for a typical mixed paella which can be varied according to preference. For a truly exceptional paella, I suggest you add lobsters and mussels, which lend great flavor to the rice and creates a spectacular presentation.

½ pound cleaned squid, cut into ½ inch rings, the tentacles in half lengthwise

6 garlic cloves, finely chopped

2 tablespoons finely chopped fresh flat-leaf parsley

¼ teaspoon saffron threads, crumbled

⅛ teaspoon kosher or sea salt

Half of a 2½-pound chicken or rabbit

¼ pound pork loin, cut into ½-inch pieces

½ pound monkfish, grouper, or other firm-fleshed fish, cut into ½-inch chunks

6½ cups chicken broth or vegetable broth

7 tablespoons olive oil

½ pound large shrimp, in their shells

¼ pound (2 links) mild chorizo sausage, cut into ¼-inch slices

1 medium onion, finely chopped (about ⅔ cup)

1 medium red bell pepper, finely chopped (about ¾ cup)

1 medium tomato, finely chopped (about ⅔ cup)

½ teaspoon ground paprika, such as Spanish smoked

½ cup fresh or frozen peas

3 cups short-grain rice, such as imported Spanish or Arborio

2 lemons, cut into quarters, for garnish

1. In a mortar or mini-processor, mash the garlic, parsley, saffron, and salt. Cut the chicken wing into 2 parts, discarding the tip. Hack off the bony end of the leg. Hack or cut with kitchen shears the rest of the chicken into 1½-inch pieces. Sprinkle the squid, chicken, pork, and monkfish all over with salt.

2. Preheat the oven to 400°F. Prepare the broth, if necessary, and place on a back burner over the lowest heat to keep hot until needed. In a 17- to 18-inch paella pan or similar-sized shallow earthenware casserole dish, heat the oil over medium heat, placing over two burners if necessary. Add the shrimp and cook, stirring, until pink, then transfer to a platter. Add the chicken and cook, turning occasionally, until browned but not fully cooked. Transfer to the platter. Add the pork, monkfish, and chorizo and cook, stirring, until browned. Transfer to the platter.

3. Add the squid and cook, stirring, I minute and leave in the pan. Add the onion and bell pepper and cook, stirring, until softened, about 8 minutes more. Stir in the tomato, cook I minute more, then add the paprika. Add the rice and stir to coat well with the pan mixture. Add the broth and the mortar mixture and cook, stirring and rotating the pan occasionally if over two burners, until the bubbles rising from the pan look slightly thick and the rice begins to be visible at the surface, about 3 minutes more. Add the reserved monkfish and pork and the peas and cook until the rice is no longer soupy but enough liquid remains to continue cooking the rice, about 2 minutes more.

4. Arrange the chicken and shrimp over the rice, transfer to the oven and bake 10 to 12 minutes or until the liquid is absorbed and the rice almost al dente, tender yet still firm to the bite. Remove from the oven, cover with foil, and let sit about 5 minutes or until the rice is done to taste. Garnish with the lemon wedges and serve hot.

Chicken with Rice, Andalucian Style
Arroz con Pollo Estilo Andaluz

MAKES 6 SERVINGS

Picada, *a mash of fresh herbs and garlic, lends a wonderful taste to this paella of chicken, ham, and vegetables. The cumin adds a distinctive flavor, and the toasted almonds adds a delightful texture.*

5 cups chicken broth

16 asparagus

Picada

1 tablespoon olive oil

2 tablespoons slivered blanched almonds

4 garlic cloves

2 tablespoons finely chopped fresh flat-leaf parsley

¼ cup dry sherry, such as Fino, or dry white wine

¼ teaspoon saffron threads, crumbled

One (3-pound) chicken

Kosher or sea salt

6 tablespoons olive oil

1 medium onion, finely chopped (about ⅓ cup)

1 cup finely chopped green bell pepper (from about 1 large)

1 bay leaf

¼ cup small cubes Serrano (Spanish cured mountain) ham or prosciutto, cut from a ⅛-inch thick slice (about 2 ounces)

2 medium tomatoes

1½ cups coarsely chopped oyster mushrooms, rinsed and trimmed

¼ pound cooked green beans, cut into 1-inch pieces

2½ cups short-grain rice, such as imported Spanish or Arborio

1 pimiento, cut into ½-inch strips

1. Prepare the broth, if necessary. Place the asparagus in a medium skillet with water to cover, add salt, and bring to a boil over high heat. Reduce the heat to low, cover, and simmer 5 to 10 minutes or until crisp-tender.

2. Meanwhile, prepare the picada: Heat the oil in a small skillet over medium heat. Add the almonds and garlic and cook, stirring, until golden. Transfer to a mortar or mini-processor, add the parsley, and mash. Stir in the sherry and saffron. Reserve.

3. Hack or cut the chicken with kitchen shears into 2-inch pieces, hacking off the bony ends of the legs and dividing the wings into two pieces, discarding the tips. Sprinkle all over with salt.

4. In a 16- to 17-inch paella pan or similar-size shallow earthenware casserole dish, heat the oil over medium-high heat, placing over two burners if necessary. Add the chicken and cook, turning occasionally, about 10 minutes. Transfer to a platter. Add the onion, bell pepper, bay leaf, and ham and cook, stirring, until the onion and pepper are softened, about 5 minutes.

continues…

5. Meanwhile, place the broth on a back burner over the lowest heat to keep hot until needed. Cut the tomatoes in half crosswise and gently squeeze to extract the seeds. With a coarse grater held over a small bowl, grate each half down to the skin, draining off any excess juices. Reserve the pulp and discard the skin. Add to the paella pan along with the mushrooms and green beans and cook, stirring, about 5 minutes more.

6. Preheat the oven to 375°F. Stir the rice into the paella pan and cook 2 minutes more. Add the broth, taste and adjust seasoning if necessary, and bring to a boil. Reduce the heat to low and simmer about 5 minutes. Remove the bay leaf and stir in the picada. Add the chicken and cook, stirring and rotating the pan occasionally if over two burners, until the bubbles rising from the pan look slightly thick and the rice begins to be visible at the surface.

7. Arrange the asparagus and pimiento attractively over the rice and transfer to the oven. Bake 10 minutes or until the liquid is absorbed and the rice almost al dente, tender yet still firm to the bite. Remove from the oven, cover with foil, and let sit 10 minutes or until the rice is cooked to taste. Serve hot.

Chicken Paella Pepitoria
Paella de Pepitoria

MAKES 6 SERVINGS

This chicken paella is made extraordinary by the distinctive tastes of Spanish sherry and nutmeg, complemented by the picada *sauce of almonds, garlic, and parsley. The garnish of chopped egg makes it richer and more visually appealing.*

6 cups chicken broth or vegetable broth
One (3-pound) chicken
Kosher or sea salt
2 tablespoons blanched slivered almonds
6 garlic cloves, finely chopped
10 tablespoons finely chopped fresh flat-leaf parsley
¼ teaspoon saffron threads, crumbled
7 tablespoons olive oil
1 medium onion, finely chopped
¼ cup small cubes (¼ inch) Serrano (Spanish cured mountain) ham or prosciutto (about 2 ounces)
1 medium red bell pepper, finely chopped (about ¾ cup)
1 bay leaf
1 medium tomato, finely chopped (about ⅔ cup)
A generous grating of nutmeg
1 teaspoon ground sweet paprika, such as Spanish smoked
¼ cup dry sherry, such as Fino
1½ cups short-grain rice, such as imported Spanish or Arborio
2 hard-boiled eggs, coarsely chopped

1. Prepare the broth if necessary. Hack or cut the chicken with kitchen shears into 1½-inch pieces, hacking off the bony ends of the legs and dividing the wings into two pieces, discarding the tips. Sprinkle all over with salt. In a mortar or mini-processor, mash the almonds, garlic, 6 tablespoons of the parsley, and the saffron. Add 1 tablespoon of the broth, mash to incorporate, then mash in another 1 tablespoon broth. Reserve.

2. Place the broth on a back burner over the lowest heat to keep hot until needed. Heat the oil in a 13-inch paella pan or similar-size shallow earthenware casserole dish over high heat. Add the chicken and cook, turning once, about 5 minutes (do not remove from the pan). Reduce the heat to medium-high, add the onion, ham, bell pepper, and bay leaf and cook, stirring, until the vegetables are softened, about 5 minutes. Add the tomato, cook 1 minute more, then stir in the nutmeg, paprika, and sherry. Increase the heat to high and cook, stirring constantly, until the sherry has evaporated.

3. Preheat the oven to 400°F. Add the rice to the paella pan and stir to coat well with the pan mixture. Add the broth and bring to a boil. Stir in the

mortar mixture, taste and adjust seasoning if necessary, and cook until the bubbles rising from the pan look slightly thick and the rice begins to be visible at the surface.

4. Discard the bay leaf and transfer the rice to the oven. Bake about 10 minutes or until the rice is almost al dente, tender yet still firm to the bite. Remove from the oven, cover with foil, and let sit 5 to 10 minutes or until the rice is cooked to taste. Sprinkle with 2 tablespoons of the parsley and with half of the eggs. Serve hot, sprinkling the remaining half of the eggs and 2 tablespoons parsley over each portion.

Ruperto's Marinated Chicken Paella

Paella de Pollo Marinado Ruperto

MAKES 6 SERVINGS

Chef Ruperto of Sevilla was kind enough to share this recipe with me which features chicken in his famous marinade sauce. The rice is flavored with sherry, cumin, thyme, and nutmeg, which creates a truly extraordinary paella with a Moorish influence.

Marinade

8 teaspoons dry sherry, such as Fino, or dry white wine

7 tablespoons extra-virgin olive oil

1 teaspoon ground cumin

Freshly ground black pepper

6 teaspoons finely chopped fresh thyme or 1 teaspoon dried thyme

4 whole cloves, mashed in a garlic press or mortar

½ teaspoon ground nutmeg

4 bay leaves, crumbled

1 teaspoon crushed red pepper

¼ cup finely chopped fresh flat-leaf parsley

4 teaspoons fresh lemon juice

12 garlic cloves, peeled and lightly smashed

2 teaspoons ground sweet paprika, such as Spanish smoked

Salt

One (3- to 3½-pound) chicken

Kosher or sea salt

3 tablespoons olive oil

6 cups chicken broth or vegetable broth

¼ teaspoon saffron threads, crumbled

6 garlic cloves, finely chopped

1 medium onion, finely chopped (about ⅓ cup)

2 medium green bell peppers, finely chopped (about 1½ cups)

1 bay leaf

1 medium tomato, finely chopped (about ⅔ cup)

3 tablespoons finely chopped fresh flat-leaf parsley

3 cups short-grain rice, such as imported Spanish or Arborio

1. Prepare the marinade: Combine all the marinade ingredients in a large shallow bowl.

2. Hack or cut the chicken with kitchen shears into 1½-inch pieces, hacking off the bony ends of the legs and dividing the wings into two pieces, discarding the tips. Add the chicken to the marinade, turning to coat well. Cover and let marinate in the refrigerator at least 1 hour.

3. Remove the chicken from the marinade, reserving the marinade. Place the chicken on paper towels and let dry, then season with salt. In a large saucepan, combine the reserved marinade (discard the garlic and swirl a little of the chicken broth in the bowl to remove all the marinade), the broth, and saffron. Place on a back burner over the lowest heat to keep hot until needed.

4. Preheat the oven to 400°F. In a 17- to 18-inch paella pan or similar-size shallow earthenware casserole dish, heat the oil over medium-high heat, placing over two burners if necessary. Add the chicken and cook, turning once, about 5 minutes (it should not be fully cooked). Transfer to a platter.

continues…

5. Add the garlic, onion, bell peppers, and bay leaf and cook, stirring, until the vegetables are softened, about 8 minutes. Stir in the tomato and parsley and cook 2 to 3 minutes more. Add the rice and stir to coat with the pan mixture. Add the broth and bring to a boil. Add the peas, taste and adjust seasoning if necessary, and cook, stirring and rotating the pan occasionally if over two burners, until the bubbles rising from the pan look slightly thick and the rice begins to be visible at the surface.

6. Discard the bay leaves and arrange the chicken pieces over the rice. Transfer to the oven and bake about 10 minutes or until the rice is almost al dente, tender yet still firm to the bite. Remove from the oven, cover with foil, and let sit 5 to 10 minutes or until the rice is cooked to taste. Serve hot.

Chicken, Peppers, and Eggplant Paella
Arroz de Pollo y Chanfaina

MAKES 4 SERVINGS

Eggplant is the perfect contrast to this paella that features chicken with a generous amount of bell peppers and onion. If the chicken is cut into smaller pieces, it adds more flavor to the rice.

One (1-pound) eggplant
Kosher or sea salt
4 garlic cloves, finely chopped
1 tablespoon finely chopped fresh flat-leaf parsley
⅛ teaspoon salt
Half of a 3-pound chicken
Olive oil, for drizzling
Freshly ground black pepper
3 cups chicken broth or vegetable broth
⅛ teaspoon saffron threads, crumbled
¼ cup olive oil
2 tablespoons small cubes (¼ inch) Serrano (Spanish cured mountain) ham or prosciutto
1 large onion, such as yellow (Spanish) or Vidalia, slivered
1 medium green bell pepper, cut into ½-inch strips
1 medium red bell pepper, cut into ½-inch strips
1½ teaspoons finely chopped fresh thyme or ¼ teaspoon dried thyme
1 bay leaf
1 large tomato, finely chopped (about 1 cup)
½ cup dry white wine
1½ cups short-grain rice, such as imported Spanish or Arborio

1. Preheat the oven to 425°F. Cut 5 inches of the eggplant crosswise into 20 (¼-inch) rounds. Using a vegetable peeler, peel the remaining piece in alternating strips for decorative effect and cut into ½-inch cubes. Arrange the eggplant slices and cubes in layers in a colander, sprinkling each well with salt, and let drain 20 minutes. Meanwhile, in a mortar or mini-processor, mash the garlic, parsley, and the ⅛ teaspoon salt. Hack or cut the chicken thigh into 1½- to 2-inch pieces. Hack off the bony end of the leg and divide the wing into two pieces, discarding the tip. Cut the breast into ½-inch boneless cubes. Sprinkle the chicken all over with salt.

2. Pat the eggplant dry with paper towels and place on a greased cookie sheet. Drizzle with oil, season with black pepper, and bake about 10 minutes or until tender.

3. In a small saucepan, combine the broth and saffron and place on a back burner over the lowest heat to keep hot until needed. Heat the oil in a 13-inch paella pan or similar-size shallow earthenware casserole dish over high heat. Add all the chicken except the breast cubes and cook, turning once, about 5 minutes (they should not be fully cooked). Transfer to a platter. Add the chicken breast cubes, cook, stirring, 1 minute, and transfer to the platter.

4. Add the ham, onion, bell peppers, thyme, and bay leaf to the paella pan, reduce the heat to medium-low, cover, and cook 20 minutes. Add the tomato, increase the heat to medium high and cook,

uncovered, until any liquid has evaporated. Add ¼ cup of the wine and cook until evaporated, then stir in the remaining ¼ cup wine and cook again until evaporated. Stir in the eggplant cubes, reduce the heat to medium and cook 2 minutes more. Discard the bay leaf.

5. Preheat the oven again to 425°F. Add the rice to the paella pan and stir to coat well with the pan mixture. Add the broth, stir in the mortar mixture, and bring to a boil. Taste and adjust seasoning if necessary. Cook until the bubbles rising from the pan look slightly thick and the rice begins to be visible at the surface.

6. Stir in the cubed chicken and arrange the remaining chicken pieces and the eggplant slices over the rice. Transfer to the oven and bake 10 to 15 minutes or until the rice is almost al dente, tender yet still firm to the bite. Remove from the oven (if the rice still has liquid, place the pan over high heat until it has evaporated), cover with foil, and let sit 5 to 10 minutes until the rice is cooked to taste. Serve hot.

Sweet-and-Sour Paella with Caramelized Walnuts
Paella de Pollo Agridulce con Nueces Garrapiñadas

MAKES 6 TO 8 SERVINGS

This delicious chicken paella has a Catalan influence as is evidenced by the combination of sweet and sour ingredients. The sugar-coated walnuts are the very essence of this recipe. Spain's finest orange groves are in Valencia, so it is typical of their paellas and other dishes to use oranges in their recipes. The result here is a highly unusual paella with an extraordinary mix of tastes and textures.

One (3- to 3½-pound) chicken
Kosher or sea salt
2 tablespoons sugar

2 tablespoons water
5⅓ cups plus 1 tablespoon chicken broth or vegetable broth
⅔ cup plus 1 tablespoon fresh orange juice
2 tablespoons medium-sweet sherry, such as Oloroso, or medium-sweet wine
2 teaspoons wine vinegar
5 tablespoons honey
¾ cup pieces (½ inch) walnuts
7 tablespoons olive oil
¼ teaspoon saffron threads, crumbled
1 medium onion, finely chopped (about ⅔ cup)
6 garlic cloves, finely chopped
2 medium red bell peppers, finely chopped (about 1½ cups)
2 medium tomatoes, finely chopped (about 1⅓ cups)
¼ cup finely chopped fresh flat-leaf parsley
3 cups short-grain rice, such as imported Spanish or Arborio
¼ pound snow peas
6 to 8 orange slices, halved, for garnish

1. Hack or cut the chicken with kitchen shears into 1½-inch pieces, hacking off the bony ends of the legs and dividing the wings in two pieces, discarding the tips. Sprinkle all over with salt.

2. In a small saucepan, heat the sugar and water over medium heat, stirring frequently, until the sugar is lightly caramelized. Remove from the heat. Slowly and carefully drizzle and stir in 1 tablespoon broth, 1 tablespoon of the orange juice, the sherry, vinegar, and 1 tablespoon of the honey. Reserve.

3. In a small skillet, combine the remaining 4 tablespoons honey and the walnuts. Cook over low heat until the honey clings to the walnuts and forms a crackling coating. Reserve.

4. In a medium saucepan, combine the remaining 5⅓ cups broth and ⅔ cup orange juice and the saffron and place on a back burner over the lowest heat to keep hot until needed. In a 17- to 18-inch paella pan

continues...

or similar-size shallow earthenware casserole dish, heat the oil over high heat, placing over two burners if necessary. Add the chicken and cook, turning once, until browned, about 5 minutes. Transfer to a platter, reserving the oil in the pan. Spoon a little of the reserved sugar mixture over the chicken pieces. Stir the remaining mixture into the broth.

5. Preheat the oven to 400°F. In the same oil over medium-high heat, add the onion, garlic, and peppers and cook, stirring, until the peppers are slightly softened. Add the tomato and parsley and cook, stirring, 2 minutes more, then add the rice and stir to coat well with the pan mixture. Add the broth and bring to a boil, stirring and rotating the pan occasionally if over 2 burners, until the bubbles rising from the pan look slightly thick and the rice begins to be visible at the surface.

6. Stir in the snow peas and transfer to the oven. Bake about 10 minutes or until the rice is almost al dente, tender yet still firm to the bite. Remove from the oven, cover with foil, and let sit 5 to 10 minutes or until the rice is cooked to taste. Sprinkle each portion with the caramelized walnuts, garnish with the oranges, and serve hot.

Catalan Sea and Mountain Paella

Paella Mar y Montaña

MAKES 6 SERVINGS

This hearty paella originated in Catalunya as reflected by the typical Catalan-style mash of nuts, garlic, and parsley used for flavor. It features chicken and seafood, a combination that is discouraged in the traditional paellas of Valencia, but extremely delicious nonetheless.

4 cups chicken broth or vegetable broth

2 tablespoons ground sweet paprika, such as Spanish smoked

¼ teaspoon saffron threads, crumbled

1½ teaspoons finely chopped fresh thyme or ¼ teaspoon dried thyme

¼ teaspoon dried oregano

1 bay leaf

2 cups water

8 leeks, trimmed and well washed

½ pound small-medium shrimp, in their shells

One (3-pound) chicken (breast and thigh only)

1 cup dry white wine

7 tablespoons olive oil

¼ cup blanched slivered almonds

8 garlic cloves, finely chopped

¼ teaspoon kosher or sea salt

Finely chopped fresh flat-leaf parsley

2 tablespoons brandy

1 medium onion, finely chopped (about ⅔ cup)

1 medium tomato, finely chopped (about ⅔ cup)

3 cups short grain rice, such as imported Spanish or Arborio

1. In a soup pot, combine the broth, paprika, saffron, thyme, oregano, bay leaf, and water. Cut off the green portion of the leeks and add to the broth. Finely chop the white portion and reserve. Shell the shrimp and add the shells to the broth. Bring the broth to a boil over high heat, then reduce the heat to low and simmer about 30 minutes.

2. Cut the shrimp crosswise in half. Hack or cut the chicken with kitchen shears into 2-inch pieces. Sprinkle the shrimp and chicken all over with salt.

3. Pass the broth through a fine-mesh strainer. Discard the solids. Return 5 cups to the pot, add the wine, and place on a back burner over the lowest heat to keep hot until needed. In a 17- to 18-inch paella pan or similar-size shallow earthenware casserole dish, heat the oil over medium heat, placing over two burners if necessary. Add the almonds and cook, stirring, until golden. Transfer to a mortar or mini-processor, reserving the oil in the pan. Mash the almonds, half of the garlic, the salt, and parsley. Gradually mash in the brandy. Reserve.

4. In the same oil over high heat, add the chicken and cook, turning once, until browned, about 7 minutes (it should not be fully cooked). Transfer to a platter. Reduce the heat to medium. Add the reserved leek, the onion, and the remaining half of the garlic and cook, stirring, until the onion is slightly softened, about 4 minutes. Add the tomato and cook until softened and its juices release, 2 to 3 minutes more, then stir in half of the mortar mixture.

5. Preheat the oven to 400°F. Add the rice to the paella pan and stir to coat well with the pan mixture. Add the broth and bring to a boil. Taste and adjust seasoning if necessary. Cook, stirring and rotating the pan occasionally if over two burners, until the bubbles rising from the pan look slightly thick and the rice begins to be visible at the surface.

6. Arrange the chicken pieces over the rice and transfer to the oven. Bake about 10 minutes or until the rice is almost al dente, tender yet still firm to the bite. Remove from the oven, cover with foil, and let sit 5 to 10 minutes or until the rice is cooked to taste. Remove the bay leaf and serve hot.

Rice with Duck, Sausage, and Chickpeas
Arroz con Pato

MAKES 4 TO 6 SERVINGS

In Spain, this rice dish of duck, sausage, chickpeas, and pine nuts is usually made during duck hunting season. The La Albufera lagoon, just outside of Valencia, used to be a fertile breeding ground for ducks, but due to changes in ecology, ducks cannot be found in the abundance they once were. I pre-roast the duck before combining it with the rice in order to eliminate most of the fat.

PREPARE 8 TO 10 HOURS IN ADVANCE

One (4 to 4½-pound) duck, trussed (with the neck if available)

4 cups chicken broth or vegetable broth

Several threads of saffron

¼ pound fresh sweet sausage, such as Italian style

3 tablespoons olive oil

1 small onion, slivered

2 garlic cloves, finely chopped

1 cup finely chopped red bell peppers (from 1 large)

1 teaspoon ground sweet paprika, such as Spanish smoked

1¼ cups peeled, seeded, and finely chopped tomatoes (from 2 medium)

2 tablespoons finely chopped fresh flat-leaf parsley

2 cups short-grain rice, such as imported Spanish or Arborio

3 cups freshly cooked or canned chickpeas, rinsed and drained

½ cup fresh or frozen peas

2 tablespoons pine nuts

Salt

1 pimiento, cut into thin strips

1. Place the duck and the neck, if using, in a roasting pan and roast 1½ hours, pouring off the fat occasionally. Transfer to a platter and cut into serving pieces. Deglaze the pan, adding ¼ cup chicken broth, stirring, and scraping up any bits of flavor. Transfer to a large saucepan.

2. Add the remaining broth and the saffron to the saucepan and place on a back burner over the lowest heat to keep hot until needed. In a greased shallow earthenware casserole dish or Dutch oven, add the sausage and cook until lightly browned. Cut into ¾-inch slices and reserve. Wipe out the casserole dish.

3. Preheat the oven to 350°F. Heat the oil in the casserole dish over medium heat. Add the onion, garlic, and bell peppers and cook, stirring, until

continues...

the onion and peppers are softened, about 5 minutes. Stir in the paprika, then add the tomatoes and parsley and cook until the tomatoes have softened and their juices release, 2 to 3 minutes more. Add the rice and stir to coat well with the casserole dish mixture. Add the broth, sausage, chickpeas, peas, and pine nuts and cook until the bubbles rising from the pan look slightly thick and the rice begins to be visible at the surface. Taste and adjust seasoning if necessary.

4. Arrange the pimiento and duck over the rice and transfer to the oven. Bake 15 to 18 minutes or until the rice is almost al dente, tender yet still firm to the bite. Remove from the oven, cover with foil, and let sit 5 to 10 minutes or until the rice is cooked to taste. Serve hot.

Duck, Bean, Grape, and Nut Paella
Arroz Tropical Tasca del Puerto

MAKES 6 TO 8 SERVINGS

Some of the most wildly innovative paella dishes I have tasted were at the Tasca del Puerto restaurant in the Valencian region's city of Castellón de la Plana. Reme Domínguez and Ximo Boix—owners, chefs, and paella aficionados—are certainly not afraid to take chances. This recipe of paella made with duck, grapes, raisins, walnuts, and sesame oil is typical of their exceptionally creative flair.

One (4- to 4½-pound) duck, trussed (with the neck if available)

Kosher or sea salt

5½ cups chicken broth or vegetable broth

½ cup dry white wine

¼ teaspoon saffron threads, crumbled

7 tablespoons olive oil

2 tablespoons pine nuts

2 tablespoons chopped walnuts

1 medium red bell pepper, finely chopped (about ¾ cup)

1 medium green bell pepper, finely chopped (about ¾ cup)

¼ cup raisins

¼ pound spinach, rinsed, trimmed, well dried, and finely chopped

2 tablespoons finely chopped fresh flat-leaf parsley

1¼ cups small cauliflower florets (about ½ pound)

¼ pound green beans, such as broad, cut into 1-inch pieces

4 garlic cloves, finely chopped

2 medium tomatoes, finely chopped (about 1⅓ cups)

2 teaspoons ground sweet paprika, such as Spanish smoked

3 cups short-grain rice, such as imported Spanish or Arborio

4 teaspoons sesame oil

½ cup cooked white beans, drained

24 red seedless grapes

24 green seedless grapes

Thin pimiento strips, for garnish

1. Preheat the oven to 375°F. Prick the duck all over with a fork. Sprinkle inside and out with salt. Place the duck and the neck, if using, in a roasting pan and bake 1¾ hours. Discard the neck and wings, split the duck in half, and remove the backbone. Separate the legs and cut the rest into 2-inch pieces. Deglaze the pan, adding ½ cup of the broth, stirring, and scraping up any bits of flavor. Transfer to a large saucepan and add enough broth to make 5½ cups. Add the wine and saffron and place on a back burner over the lowest heat to keep hot until needed.

2. Preheat the oven to 400°F. In a 17- to 18-inch paella pan or similar-size shallow earthenware casserole dish, heat the oil over medium-high heat, placing over two burners if necessary. Add the pine nuts and walnuts and cook, stirring, until the pine nuts just begin to color. Reduce the heat to medium, add the peppers, raisins, spinach, parsley, cauliflower, and green beans, and cook, stirring,

until the spinach has wilted, about 5 minutes. Add salt, the garlic, and tomato and cook 2 minutes more, then stir in the paprika. Add the rice and sesame oil and stir to coat the rice well with the pan mixture. Add the broth, taste and adjust seasoning if necessary, and bring to a boil. Stir in the white beans and grapes and continue to cook until bubbles rising from the pan look slightly thick and the rice begins to be visible at the surface.

3. Arrange the duck and pimiento over the rice, transfer to the oven and bake about 10 minutes or until the rice is almost al dente, tender yet still firm to the bite. Remove from the oven, cover with foil, and let sit 5 to 10 minutes or until the rice is cooked to taste. Serve hot.

Rabbit Paella with Red Peppers and Almonds
Paella de Conejo con Pimientos y Almendras

MAKES 6 SERVINGS

Hispania, *the Roman name for Spain, means "land of rabbits." Rabbit meat, which is tasty and lean, is often used in Spanish recipes. If you prefer, chicken may be substituted here, but I recommend you first remove the skin. Noteworthy about this paella is that it is typically made in a* cazuela, *an earthenware casserole dish, instead of a paella pan.*

2 tablespoons slivered blanched almonds
One (15-ounce) can chickpeas
About 5½ cups chicken broth or vegetable broth
4 garlic cloves, finely chopped
2 tablespoons finely chopped fresh flat-leaf parsley
¼ teaspoon saffron threads, crumbled
¼ teaspoon kosher or sea salt
One (2½-pound) rabbit or skinless chicken
7 tablespoons olive oil
1 medium onion, finely chopped (about ⅔ cup)

1 medium red bell pepper, finely chopped (about ¾ cup)
2 medium tomatoes, finely chopped (about 1⅓ cups)
3 cups short-grain rice, such as imported Spanish or Arborio

1. Preheat the oven to 350°F. Scatter the almonds on a cookie sheet and toast about 4 minutes or until lightly browned. Drain the chickpeas, combine the liquid from the can with the broth to make 6 cups, and place in a large saucepan. Pass ½ cup of the chickpeas through a fine-mesh strainer or a ricer into the broth. Reserve ¾ cup (if there is more, reserve for another use).

2. In a mortar or mini-processor, mash the garlic, parsley, saffron, almonds, and salt. Mash in 1 tablespoon of the broth. Hack or cut with kitchen shears the rabbit into 2-inch pieces and discard the rib portion. Sprinkle all over with salt.

3. Place the broth on a back burner over the lowest heat to keep hot until needed. Heat the oil in a shallow 15-inch earthenware casserole dish or Dutch oven over medium-high heat. Add the rabbit and cook about 5 minutes (it should not be fully cooked). Transfer to a platter. Reduce the heat to low, add the onion and pepper and cook, stirring occasionally, until softened, about 10 minutes. Increase the heat to medium, add the tomato, and cook, stirring, until softened and its juices release, 2 to 3 minutes more.

4. Preheat the oven to 400°F. Add the rice to the casserole dish and stir to coat well with the pan mixture. Add the broth and bring to a boil. Add the reserved ¾ cup chickpeas, the rabbit, and the mortar mixture and taste and adjust seasoning if necessary. Cook until the bubbles rising from the pan look slightly thick and the rice begins to be visible at the surface, about 5 minutes more.

5. Transfer to the oven and bake about 10 minutes or until the rice is almost al dente, tender yet still firm to the bite. Remove from the oven, cover with foil, and let sit 5 to 10 minutes or until the rice is cooked to taste. Serve hot.

Quail and Mushroom Paella
Paella de Codornices y Setas

MAKES 6 TO 8 SERVINGS

Spaniards adore eating quail, and it is featured in Spanish dishes much more often than chicken. This recipe calls for a small amount of slab bacon, which makes this paella that much more savory. The subtle flavor of mushrooms provides the perfect contrast.

8 quail, butterflied (split in half)

Kosher or sea salt

6 cups chicken broth or vegetable broth

6 tablespoons olive oil

¼ cup small cubes (¼ inch) slab bacon (about 2 ounces)

2 medium red bell peppers, cut into ½-inch pieces

2 medium green bell peppers, cut into ½-inch pieces

1 medium onion, finely chopped (about ⅔ cup)

½ pound mushrooms, such as shiitake, rinsed, trimmed, and coarsely chopped

One (2-inch) piece dried red chile pepper or ¼ teaspoon crushed red pepper

1 medium tomato, finely chopped (about ⅔ cup)

8 garlic cloves, finely chopped

1½ teaspoons finely chopped fresh thyme, or ¼ teaspoon dried thyme

2 tablespoons finely chopped fresh flat-leaf parsley

¼ teaspoon saffron threads, crumbled

1 cup dry white wine

3 cups short-grain rice, such as imported Spanish or Arborio

1. Sprinkle the quail all over with salt. In a large saucepan, heat the broth on a back burner over the lowest heat to keep hot until needed.

2. In a 17- to 18-inch paella pan or similar-size shallow earthenware casserole dish, heat the oil over high heat, placing over two burners if necessary. Add the quail and cook, turning once, until lightly browned (it should not be fully cooked). Transfer to a platter.

3. Reduce the heat to medium, add the bacon and cook, stirring, until its fat is rendered. Add the bell peppers, onion, and mushrooms and cook, stirring, until softened, about 8 minutes more. Add the tomato and chile pepper and cook, stirring, until the vegetables are tender.

4. Meanwhile, in a mortar or mini-processor, mash the garlic, thyme, parsley, and saffron. Gradually mash in a few tablespoons of the broth and brush the quail lightly with a small amount, reserving the rest.

5. Preheat the oven to 400°F. Add the wine to the paella pan and cook until the liquid has evaporated. Discard the chile pepper. Add the rice and stir to coat well with the pan mixture. Add the broth, taste and adjust seasoning if necessary, and bring to a boil. Cook, stirring and rotating the pan occasionally if over two burners, until the bubbles rising from the pan look slightly thick and the rice begins to be visible at the surface.

6. Stir in the mortar mixture and arrange the quail over the rice. Transfer to the oven and bake about 10 minutes or until the rice is almost al dente, tender yet still firm to the bite. Remove from the oven, cover with foil, and let sit 5 to 10 minutes or until the rice is cooked to taste. Serve hot.

Rabbit, Spinach, and Artichoke Paella
Paella de Conejo, Espinacas y Alcachofas

MAKES 4 TO 5 SERVINGS

In Spain it is common to eat rabbit meat, which is tasty, lean, and nutritious. When combined with spinach and artichokes, the results are excellent.

One (2½-pound) rabbit, skin and fat removed

Kosher or sea salt

5 cups chicken broth or vegetable broth

¼ teaspoon saffron threads, crumbled

5 tablespoons olive oil

4 garlic cloves, coarsely chopped

½ pound tomatoes, peeled, seeded and coarsely
    chopped

½ pound fresh spinach, rinsed, trimmed, well dried,
    and coarsely chopped

2½ cups short-grain rice, such as imported Spanish
    or Arborio

8 artichoke hearts, halved

1. Cut or hack the rabbit into 2-inch pieces, discarding the bony tips of the legs. Sprinkle all over with salt. In a large saucepan, combine the broth and saffron and place on a back burner over the lowest heat to keep hot until needed.

2. Preheat the oven to 375°F. In a 17- to 18-inch paella pan or similar-size shallow earthenware casserole dish, heat the oil over medium-high heat. Add the rabbit and cook, turning once, until lightly browned, about 5 minutes (it should not be fully cooked). Transfer to a platter. Reduce the heat to medium, add the garlic, tomatoes, and spinach, and cook, stirring, until the spinach is wilted.

3. Add the rice and stir to coat well with the pan mixture. Increase the heat to high, add the broth and artichokes, and cook, stirring constantly, until the bubbles rising from the pan look slightly thick and the rice begins to be visible at the surface. Stir in the rabbit and any juices from the platter. Taste and adjust seasoning if necessary.

4. Transfer to the oven and bake 10 minutes or until the liquid is absorbed and the rice almost al dente, tender yet still firm to the bite. Remove from the oven, cover with foil, and let sit 10 minutes or until the rice is cooked to taste. Serve hot.

Paella, Sevilla Style
Paella a la Sevillana

MAKES 4 TO 6 SERVINGS

This wonderful version of paella is a signature dish of Seville and consists of duck simmered in a sauce of green olives and sherry.

One (4½- to 5-pound) duck

Kosher or sea salt

½ cup coarsely chopped pitted green olives,
    preferably Spanish

¾ cup plus 2 tablespoons dry white wine

About 4¾ cups chicken broth or vegetable broth

¼ teaspoon saffron threads, crumbled

½ cup dry sherry, such as Fino

5 tablespoons olive oil

¼ cup finely chopped onion

2 garlic cloves, finely chopped

1 cup finely chopped red bell pepper (from 1 large)

¼ cup finely chopped carrot

2 tablespoons finely chopped fresh flat-leaf parsley

1 tablespoon finely chopped fresh thyme or
    ½ teaspoon dried thyme

½ cup finely chopped tomato

3 cups short-grain rice, such as imported Spanish or
    Arborio

1. Preheat the oven to 375°F. Prick the duck all over with a fork. Sprinkle inside and out with salt. Place in a roasting pan and bake 1 hour, pour off the fat, and continue baking 30 minutes more. Meanwhile, in a small saucepan, combine the olives and 6 tablespoons of the white wine, bring to a boil over high heat, and cook 5 minutes. Drain.

2. Remove the duck from the roasting pan. Separate the legs, cut the breast into 8 serving pieces and the thighs into 8 serving pieces, and discard the wings. Deglaze the roasting pan, using ½ cup of the white wine, the broth, and sherry, stirring, and

continues...

scraping up any bits of flavor. Transfer 6 cups of the liquid to a large saucepan and stir in the saffron. Place on a back burner over the lowest heat to keep hot until needed.

3. Preheat the oven to 400°F. In a 17- to 18-inch paella pan or similar-size shallow earthenware casserole dish, heat the oil over medium heat, placing over two burners if necessary. Add the onion, garlic, pepper, carrot, parsley, and thyme and cook, stirring, until the vegetables are softened, about 10 minutes. Add the tomato and cook, stirring, until softened and its juices release, 2 to 3 minutes more.

4. Add the rice and stir to coat well with the pan mixture. Add the broth and cook, stirring and rotating the pan occasionally if over two burners, until the bubbles rising from the pan look slightly thick and the rice begins to be visible at the surface.

5. Arrange the duck over the rice and bake 10 minutes or until the liquid is absorbed and the rice is almost al dente, tender yet still firm to the bite. Remove from the oven, cover with foil, and let sit 5 to 10 minutes or until the rice is cooked to taste. Serve hot.

Stewed Rabbit Paella

Paella de Conejo Estofado

MAKES 6 TO 8 SERVINGS

This paella takes a bit longer to prepare than most because it is essential that the rabbit meat be stewed to make it more tender and flavorful, but the rich taste is memorable.

PREPARE AT LEAST 4 HOURS IN ADVANCE

One (2½-pound) rabbit or chicken

Kosher or sea salt

7 tablespoons olive oil

2 medium onions, finely chopped (about 1⅓ cup)

2 medium red bell peppers, finely chopped (about 1½ cups)

20 garlic cloves, finely chopped

2 tablespoons finely chopped fresh flat-leaf parsley

6¼ cups chicken broth or vegetable broth

¼ cup dry white wine

2 (1-inch) pieces dried hot red chile pepper

1 tablespoon finely chopped fresh rosemary or ½ teaspoon dried rosemary

1 tablespoon finely chopped fresh thyme or ½ teaspoon dried thyme

½ teaspoon ground sweet paprika, such as Spanish smoked

2 bay leaves

¼ teaspoon saffron threads, crumbled

2½ cups short-grain rice, such as imported Spanish or Arborio

1. Cut or hack the rabbit into 1½-inch pieces. Sprinkle all over with salt. Heat 2 tablespoons of the oil in a shallow casserole dish or Dutch oven over medium-high heat. Add the rabbit and cook, turning once, until browned on all sides, about 5 minutes. Add 1 of the onions, 1 of the bell peppers, the garlic, and parsley and cook until the vegetables are softened, about 8 minutes. Stir in ¼ cup of the broth, the wine, chile pepper, rosemary, thyme, paprika, and bay leaves. Reduce the heat to low, cover, and simmer 40 minutes.

2. Discard the bay leaves and chile peppers. If there is still liquid in the casserole dish, boil down until thickened. In a large saucepan, combine the remaining 6 cups broth and the saffron and place on a back burner over the lowest heat to keep hot until needed.

3. Preheat the oven to 400°F. In a 17- to 18-inch paella pan or similar-size shallow earthenware casserole dish, heat the remaining 5 tablespoons oil over medium heat, placing over two burners if necessary. Add the remaining 1 onion and 1 pepper and cook, stirring, until softened, about 8 minutes.

4. Add the rice and stir to coat well with the pan mixture. Add the broth and cook, stirring and rotating the pan occasionally if over two burners,

about 3 minutes. Stir in the rabbit. Deglaze the casserole dish, adding a few tablespoons of the broth, stirring, and scraping up any bits of flavor. Add to the paella pan. Cook, stirring and rotating the pan occasionally if over two burners, until the bubbles rising from the pan look slightly thick and the rice begins to be visible at the surface.

5. Transfer to the oven and bake about 10 minutes or until the rice is almost al dente, tender yet still firm to the bite. Remove from the oven, cover with foil, and let sit 5 to 10 minutes or until the rice is cooked to taste. Serve hot.

Rabbit Paella with Sausage, Pork Ribs, and Pea Pods
Arroz a la Catalana

MAKES 6 SERVINGS

This Catalan-style paella calls for butifarra, *a sausage native to Catalunya. If you can't find it, sweet Italian sausage may be substituted. Pork ribs and pea pods are typical in Catalan-style cooking.*

One (3-pound) rabbit or chicken

Salt

8 tablespoons olive oil

½ pound pork ribs, cut into individual ribs

1 medium onion, chopped (about ⅔ cup)

One (12-inch) piece sausage (butifarra) or 3 sweet
    Italian-style sausages, cut into ¾-inch pieces

¼ pound Serrano (Spanish cured mountain) ham or
    prosciutto, cut into ¼-inch cubes

1 medium tomato, chopped (about ⅔ cup)

2½ cups short-grain rice, such as imported Spanish
    or Arborio

5 cups chicken broth or vegetable broth

2 garlic cloves, finely chopped

2 tablespoons finely chopped fresh flat-leaf parsley

¼ pound snow pea pods

2 pimientos, cut into thin strips

1. Preheat the oven to 350°F. Cut or hack the rabbit into 1½-inch pieces. Sprinkle all over with salt. Cut the pork into individual serving-size ribs. Heat the oil in a 17- to 18-inch paella pan or similar-size shallow earthenware casserole dish over medium-high heat. Add the rabbit and pork ribs and cook, turning once, until browned. Transfer both to a roasting pan, reserving the oil in the paella pan. Bake 15 minutes.

2. Meanwhile, in the same oil over medium heat, add the onion, sausage, and ham and cook, stirring, until the onion is wilted and transparent, about 5 minutes. Add the tomato and cook, stirring, until softened and its juices release, 2 to 3 minutes more. (May be made in advance up to this point).

3. Add the rice to the paella pan and stir to coat well with the pan mixture. Add the broth, garlic, parsley, and salt and bring to a boil. Cook, stirring frequently, until the bubbles rising from the pan look slightly thick and the rice begins to be visible at the surface. Add the pea pods.

4. Reduce the oven to 325°F. Arrange the rabbit, ribs, and pimientos over the rice and bake 20 minutes or until the liquid is absorbed and the rice is almost al dente, tender yet still firm to the bite. Remove from the oven, cover with foil, and let sit 5 to 10 minutes or until the rice is cooked to taste. Serve hot.

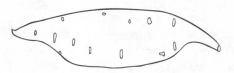

Meat Paella

Pork and Pomegranate Paella
Paella de Magro y Granadinas

MAKES 4 TO 6 SERVINGS

The city of Granada is named after the pomegranate, and Spaniards have a long history with this unusual fruit. The pomegranate is part of the Spanish national coat of arms, dating back to the conquest of Granada. Here the flavor adds a unique sweetness to the savory taste of the marinated pork.

2 pomegranates

1 bay leaf, crumbled

1 tablespoon finely chopped fresh rosemary or
   ½ teaspoon dried rosemary

4 tablespoons finely chopped fresh flat-leaf parsley

1½ teaspoons ground cumin

8 garlic cloves, finely chopped

Kosher or sea salt

Freshly ground black pepper

¼ cup dry white wine

1 pound pork loin, cut into ½-inch pieces

5¾ cups chicken broth or vegetable broth

¼ teaspoon saffron threads, crumbled

7 tablespoons olive oil

1 medium onion, finely chopped (about ⅔ cup)

1½ cups finely chopped watercress (mostly leaves)

3 cups short-grain rice, such as imported Spanish or
   Arborio

1. Cut the pomegranates into quarters and remove the seeds in the sink over a bowl of cold water. (Be careful not to splash the juice; it can stain.) Place the seeds in a food processor and with quick pulses, process a few seconds, just long enough to release the juice. Pass through a fine-mesh strainer. Discard the solids and transfer the juice to a small saucepan. Bring to a boil over high heat and cook until reduced by half and slightly syrupy. Let cool.

2. In a large bowl, combine the pomegranate syrup, bay leaf, half of the rosemary, 2 tablespoons of the parsley, ¾ teaspoon of the cumin, half of the garlic, the salt, pepper, and wine. Stir in the pork, cover, and let marinate in the refrigerator 1 hour.

3. Transfer the meat to paper towels and pat dry. In a large saucepan, combine the marinade, broth, and saffron and place on a back burner over the lowest heat to keep hot until needed.

4. Preheat the oven to 400°F. Season the pork with salt. In a 17- to 18-inch paella pan or similar-size shallow earthenware casserole dish, heat the oil over medium-high heat, placing over two burners if necessary. Add the pork and cook, stirring, until lightly browned but not fully cooked. Transfer to a platter.

5. Add the onion and the remaining half of the garlic and cook, stirring, until the onion is wilted and transparent, about 5 minutes. Stir in the watercress, the remaining halves of the rosemary and parsley, and the remaining ¾ teaspoon cumin and cook 1 minute more. Add the rice and stir to coat well with the pan mixture. Add the broth, bring to a boil, and cook 3 minutes more. Stir in the pork and cook until the bubbles rising from the pan look slightly thick and the rice begins to be visible at the surface, about 2 minutes more.

6. Transfer to the oven and bake about 10 minutes or until the rice is almost al dente, tender yet still firm to the bite. Remove from the oven, cover with foil, and let sit 5 to 10 minutes. Remove the bay leaf and serve hot.

Rice with Garlic-Paprika-Marinated Rib Pork Chops
Arroz con Costillas Adobadas

MAKES 5 TO 6 SERVINGS

This is an especially flavorful paella made with pork marinated in olive oil, garlic, paprika, and herbs. The well-seasoned pork loin adds a rich flavor to the rice.

PREPARE 8 TO 12 HOURS IN ADVANCE

Marinade

2 tablespoons olive oil

1 tablespoon dry white wine

1½ teaspoons ground paprika

2 garlic cloves, mashed in a garlic press or mortar

1 bay leaf

1 teaspoon finely chopped fresh thyme or
⅛ teaspoon dried thyme

¼ teaspoon dried oregano

Salt

Freshly ground black pepper

1 pound rib pork chops, 1 inch thick, trimmed of fat, and hacked into 1½-inch pieces

4¾ cups chicken broth or vegetable broth

2 medium tomatoes (about ½ pound)

5 tablespoons olive oil

6 garlic cloves

¼ teaspoon saffron threads, crumbled

2 tablespoons finely chopped fresh flat-leaf parsley

Salt

¼ cup dry white wine

2 large red bell peppers, finely chopped (about 1½ cups)

2 teaspoons ground sweet paprika, such as Spanish smoked

2½ cups short-grain rice, such as imported Spanish or Arborio

⅔ cup fresh or frozen peas

1. Combine all marinade ingredients in a large bowl. Add the pork and stir to coat well. Cover and refrigerate overnight.

2. Place the broth in a medium saucepan on a back burner over the lowest heat to keep hot until needed. Cut the tomatoes in half crosswise and gently squeeze to extract the seeds. With a coarse grater held over a small bowl, grate each half down to the skin, draining off any excess juices. Reserve the pulp and discard the skin. Remove the pork from the marinade and pat dry with paper towels.

3. Preheat the oven to 375°F. In a 16- to 17-inch paella pan or similar-size shallow earthenware casserole dish, heat the oil over medium-high heat, placing over two burners if necessary. Add the pork and cook, stirring, until lightly browned but not fully cooked. Transfer to a platter. Add the garlic and cook, stirring, until browned, then transfer to a mortar or mini-processor. Reduce the heat to medium, add the red pepper and cook, stirring, until softened, about 5 minutes. Meanwhile, add the saffron, parsley, and salt to the mortar and mash. Stir in the wine.

4. Add the tomato to the paella pan, cook 1 minute, then stir in the paprika and the mortar mixture. Add the rice and stir to coat well with the pan mixture. Add the broth and peas and bring to a boil. Cook, stirring and rotating the pan occasionally if over two burners, until the bubbles rising from the pan look slightly thick and the rice begins to be visible at the surface, about 5 minutes more.

5. Stir in the pork and transfer to the oven. Bake about 10 minutes or until the liquid is absorbed and the rice almost al dente, tender yet still firm to the bite. Remove from the oven, cover with foil, and let sit 10 minutes or until the rice is cooked to taste. Return to the stovetop over high heat and cook, without stirring, until a crust of rice forms at the bottom of the pan (be careful not to let it burn), about 2 minutes. Serve hot.

Pork, Chickpea, and Red Pepper Paella

Paella con Magro, Garbanzos y Pimientos Rojos

MAKES 4 TO 6 SERVINGS

The excellent La Dársena restaurant in Alicante has over fifty different and delicious paellas on their menu. This one, which features pork and a generous amount of red bell peppers, is very popular with their customers.

PREPARE 10 TO 14 HOURS IN ADVANCE

¾ pound boneless pork loin, cut into ½-inch pieces

2 garlic cloves, mashed in a garlic press or mortar

3 tablespoons finely chopped fresh flat-leaf parsley

6 tablespoons olive oil

Kosher or sea salt

Freshly ground black pepper

4 cups chicken broth or vegetable broth

¼ teaspoon saffron threads, crumbled

2½ cups cooked or canned chickpeas, drained

2 teaspoons ground paprika, such as Spanish smoked

2 large red bell peppers, cut into ¾-inch pieces

10 garlic cloves, finely chopped

2 tablespoons small cubes (¼ inch) Serrano (Spanish cured mountain) ham or prosciutto (about 1 ounce)

1 medium tomato, finely chopped (about ⅔ cup)

2 cups short-grain rice, such as imported Spanish or Arborio

1. In a large bowl, combine the meat, the mashed garlic, 1 tablespoon of the parsley, 1 tablespoon of the oil, salt, and black pepper. Let sit 20 minutes. Place the broth in a medium saucepan. Pass ½ cup of the chickpeas through a fine-mesh strainer or a ricer into the broth, and add the saffron. Place on a back burner over the lowest heat to keep warm until needed.

2. Preheat the oven to 400°F. Heat the remaining 5 tablespoons oil in a 13-inch paella pan or similar-size shallow earthenware casserole dish over medium-high heat. Add the pork and cook, stirring, until lightly browned but not fully cooked. Transfer to a platter. Reduce the heat to medium, add the bell peppers and cook 1 minute. Add the chopped garlic, the ham, tomato, and the remaining 2 tablespoons parsley and cook, stirring, 2 minutes more. Stir in the paprika and pork. Add the rice and stir to coat well with the pan mixture. Add the broth, the remaining 2 cups chickpeas, taste and adjust seasoning if necessary, and bring to a boil. Cook until the bubbles rising from the pan look slightly thick and the rice begins to be visible at the surface.

3. Transfer to the oven and bake 10 to 12 minutes or until the rice is almost al dente, tender yet still firm to the bite. Remove from the oven, cover with foil, and let sit 5 to 10 minutes or until the rice is cooked to taste. Serve hot.

Rice with Pork, Potato, and Egg, Galician Style

Arroz a la Gallega

MAKES 4 SERVINGS

The marinated pork in this traditional Galician recipe creates a strongly flavored rice that is contrasted perfectly by the subtle taste and texture of baked eggs and new potatoes.

PREPARE 8 TO 12 HOURS IN ADVANCE

¾ pound boneless pork loin, cut into ½-inch pieces

¼ teaspoon kosher or sea salt

4 teaspoons ground sweet paprika, such as Spanish smoked

6 garlic cloves, finely chopped

1 small bay leaf, crumbled

8 tiny (1½-inch) new potatoes

3 cups chicken broth or vegetable broth

⅛ teaspoon saffron threads, crumbled

¼ cup olive oil

½ medium red bell pepper, finely chopped (about
⅓ cup)

½ medium green bell pepper, finely chopped (about
⅓ cup)

1 medium tomato, finely chopped (about ⅔ cup)

1 tablespoon finely chopped fresh flat-leaf parsley

¼ teaspoon ground hot paprika, such as Spanish
smoked, or ground cayenne pepper

1½ cups short-grain rice, such as imported Spanish or
Arborio

4 large eggs

12 to 16 small green asparagus spears, cooked

Thin pimiento strips

1. In a large bowl, combine the meat, salt, 2 teaspoons of the sweet paprika, the garlic, and bay leaf. Cover and let marinate in the refrigerator overnight.

2. Meanwhile, place the potatoes in a small saucepan and add cold water to cover and salt. Cover and bring to a simmer over low heat. Cook until tender when pierced with a knife. Drain and let cool slightly. Peel. In a medium saucepan, combine the broth and saffron and place on a back burner over the lowest heat to keep hot until needed.

3. Preheat the oven to 400°F. Heat the oil in a 13-inch paella pan or similar-size shallow earthenware casserole dish over medium-high heat. Add the peppers and cook, stirring, until softened, about 5 minutes. Add the pork and cook, stirring, until it loses its color (it should not be fully cooked). Transfer to a platter.

4. Add the tomato and parsley, cook 2 to 3 minutes more, then stir in the remaining 2 teaspoons sweet paprika and the hot paprika. Add the rice and stir to coat well with the pan mixture. Add the broth and bring to a boil. Cook 3 minutes more, then add the pork and taste and adjust seasoning if necessary. Cook until the bubbles rising from the pan look slightly thick and the rice begins to be visible at the surface.

5. Stir in the potatoes, then crack the eggs over the rice and arrange the asparagus and pimientos over the rice. Transfer to the oven and bake about 10 minutes or until the rice is almost al dente, tender yet still firm to the bite, and the eggs are set. Remove from the oven, cover with foil, and let sit 5 to 10 minutes or until the rice is cooked to taste. Serve hot.

Cumin-Scented Pork and Watercress Paella

Arroz de Magro y Berros al Comino

MAKES 4 SERVINGS

Delicious and simple to prepare, this paella features pork complemented by watercress and cumin.

¼ to ½ pound small red waxy potatoes

3 cups chicken broth or vegetable broth

⅛ teaspoon saffron threads, crumbled

¾ pound boneless pork loin, cut into ½-inch pieces

Kosher or sea salt

5 tablespoons olive oil

¾ cup finely chopped onion

4 garlic cloves, finely chopped

½ medium green bell pepper, finely chopped (about
⅓ cup)

1 bunch (about ½ pound) watercress, rinsed, thick
stems trimmed, and coarsely chopped (about
3 cups)

1 tablespoon finely chopped fresh flat-leaf parsley

½ teaspoon ground cumin

½ teaspoon ground sweet paprika, such as Spanish
smoked

1½ cups short-grain rice, such as imported Spanish or
Arborio

½ cup cooked white beans, drained, or canned white
beans, drained and rinsed

continues…

1. Place the potatoes in a small saucepan and add cold water to cover and salt. Cover and bring to a simmer over low heat. Cook until tender when pierced with a knife. Drain and let cool slightly. Peel. In a medium saucepan, combine the broth and saffron and place on a back burner over the lowest heat to keep hot until needed. Season the pork with salt.

2. Preheat the oven to 400°F. In a 13-inch paella pan or similar-size shallow earthenware casserole dish, heat the oil over medium-high heat. Add the pork and cook, stirring, until it loses its color (it should not be fully cooked). Transfer to a platter. Reduce the heat to medium, add the onion, garlic, and peppers, and cook, stirring, until the vegetables are slightly softened. about 5 minutes. Add the watercress and parsley and cook, stirring, until the watercress is wilted, then stir in the cumin and paprika.

3. Add the rice and stir to coat well with the pan mixture. Add the broth and bring to a boil. Stir in the beans and pork, taste and adjust seasoning if necessary, and cook until the bubbles rising from the pan look slightly thick and the rice begins to be visible at the surface.

4. Stir in the potatoes and transfer to the oven. Bake about 10 minutes or until the rice is almost al dente, tender yet still firm to the bite. Remove from the oven, cover with foil, and let sit 5 to 10 minutes or until the rice is cooked to taste. Serve hot.

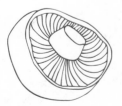

Pork Paella, Catalan Style
Arroz a la Catalana

MAKES 6 TO 8 SERVINGS

Catalan-style paella is as innovative and exciting as one would expect from the cuisine of that region. Many of the paellas that originated there typically combine the savory with the sweet. This version, featuring pork, artichokes, and almonds, is one of my very favorites.

12 blanched slivered almonds

2 tablespoons pine nuts

4 garlic cloves, coarsely chopped

¼ cup finely chopped fresh flat-leaf parsley

¼ teaspoon saffron threads, crumbled

¼ teaspoon kosher or sea salt

5 tablespoons water

6 cups chicken broth or vegetable broth

7 tablespoons olive oil

½ pound pork loin, cut into ½-inch pieces

¼ pound Serrano (Spanish cured mountain) ham or prosciutto, cut into ¼-inch cubes

½ pound lean, mildly spiced sausage, such as Spanish (butifarra) or bratwurst

4 medium red bell peppers, finely chopped

2 medium onions, finely chopped (about 1⅓ cups)

2 teaspoons ground sweet paprika, such as Spanish smoked

1 pound tomatoes, finely chopped

3 cups short-grain rice, such as imported Spanish or Arborio

6 tablespoons fresh or frozen peas

12 artichoke hearts, quartered

Thin pimiento strips, for garnish (optional)

1. Preheat the oven to 350°F. Arrange the almonds and pine nuts on a cookie sheet and toast until golden. In a mortar or mini-processor, mash the almonds, pine nuts, garlic, parsley, saffron, and salt. Mash in 1 tablespoon of the water. Stir in another

3 tablespoons water. Place the broth in a large saucepan on a back burner over the lowest heat to keep hot until needed.

2. Increase the oven to 400°F. In a 17- to 18-inch paella pan or similar-size shallow earthenware casserole dish, heat 2 tablespoons of the oil over medium-high heat, placing over two burners if necessary. Add the pork, ham, and sausage and cook, stirring, until lightly browned (the pork should not be fully cooked). Drain off most of the fat and oil. Reduce the heat to medium. Add the remaining 5 tablespoons oil, the bell peppers and onions, and cook, stirring, until the vegetables are softened, about 8 minutes. Stir in the paprika and tomatoes and cook until the tomatoes are softened and their juices release, 2 to 3 minutes more. Reduce the heat to low and cook about 15 minutes more.

3. Add the rice and stir to coat well with the pan mixture. Add the broth, the mortar mixture, the peas, and artichokes, taste and adjust seasoning if necessary, and bring to a boil. Cook, stirring and rotating the pan occasionally if over two burners, until the bubbles rising from the pan look slightly thick and the rice begins to be visible at the surface.

4. Arrange the pimientos, if using, over the rice and transfer to the oven. Bake about 10 minutes or until the rice is almost al dente, tender yet still firm to the bite. Remove from the oven, cover with foil, and let sit 5 to 10 minutes or until the rice is cooked to taste. Serve hot.

Mushroom and Meatball Paella, Dársena Style

Arroz con Setas y Albondigas la Darsena

MAKES 4 TO 5 SERVINGS

This unusual paella recipe is from La Dársena restaurant in the province's capital city of Alicante. It features mushrooms and dried red bell peppers

Alicante style, with the unexpected addition of pork and pine nut mini meatballs.

4 cups canned chicken broth or vegetable broth

2 sprigs parsley

1 dried sweet or mild red pepper (ñora), stemmed and seeded or 1 fresh red bell pepper, halved

10 garlic cloves

⅛ teaspoon saffron threads, crumbled

1 large tomato, chopped (about 1 cup)

2 tablespoons ground paprika (3 if using the fresh red bell pepper)

Meatballs

¾ cup lean ground pork

1 large egg

2 tablespoons finely chopped fresh flat-leaf parsley

1 teaspoon salt

3 tablespoons finely chopped pine nuts

¼ cup dried bread crumbs

1 garlic clove, finely chopped

2 tablespoons chicken broth or vegetable broth

Generous amount of freshly ground black pepper

¼ cup olive oil

1 medium red bell pepper, cut into ½-inch pieces (2 if not using the dried sweet red pepper)

¾ pound boneless pork loin, cut into ½-inch pieces

8 garlic cloves, finely chopped

1 ounce mushrooms, such as oyster, rinsed, trimmed, and coarsely chopped

1½ cups short-grain rice, such as imported Spanish or Arborio

2 large egg whites, lightly beaten with a fork

1. In a medium saucepan, combine the broth, parsley, dried bell pepper, the whole garlic cloves, saffron, half of the chopped tomato, and the paprika and bring to a boil over high heat. Reduce the heat to low and cook uncovered about 30 minutes. Pass through a fine-mesh strainer into a bowl, pushing

continues...

through as much of the solids as possible. Discard the remaining solids. Return 3 cups to the pan and place on a back burner over the lowest heat to keep hot until needed.

2. Meanwhile, prepare the meatballs: In a medium bowl, combine all the meatball ingredients. Shape into 1-inch meatballs and reserve.

3. Preheat the oven to 400°F. In a 13-inch paella pan or similar-size shallow earthenware casserole dish, heat the oil over medium-high heat. Add the chopped red pepper and cook, stirring, until softened. Add the pork, breaking it up as it cooks, until it loses its color. Add the remaining half of the tomato, the chopped garlic, and the mushrooms and cook 2 to 3 minutes more.

4. Add the rice and stir to coat well with the pan mixture. Add the broth. Coat the meatballs with the egg white and stir into the rice. Taste and adjust seasoning if necessary and bring to a boil. Cook until the bubbles rising from the pan look slightly thick and the rice begins to be visible at the surface.

5. Transfer to the oven and bake 10 to 12 minutes or until the rice is almost al dente, tender yet still firm to the bite. Remove from the oven, cover with foil, and let sit 5 to 10 minutes or until the rice is cooked to taste. Serve hot.

Rice with Lamb and Chickpeas
Arroz con Cordero

MAKES 4 TO 6 SERVINGS

This Valencian recipe calls for lamb, which is not typically found in Spanish rice dishes. When chickpeas, pig foot, and sausage are added, it creates a rich and robust meal.

PREPARE 8 TO 12 HOURS IN ADVANCE

½ **pound dried chickpeas**

9 **tablespoons olive oil**

½ **boneless lamb, such as shoulder, cut into ½-inch pieces (about 8 pieces)**

Kosher or sea salt

1 **medium tomato, finely chopped**

6 **cups water**

2 **pork bones**

1 **pig foot, split in half**

2 **ounces slab bacon, cut into ½-inch cubes**

1 **small onion, halved**

Few threads of saffron

2 **whole cloves**

Freshly ground black pepper

1 **head garlic, separated and peeled**

2 **cups short-grain rice, such as imported Spanish or Arborio**

2 **tablespoons finely chopped parsley**

1 **medium tomato, cut into ⅛-inch slices**

¼ **pound black sausage (morcilla), cut into ¼-inch slices**

1 **pimiento, cut into strips**

1. Place the chickpeas in a medium bowl, add salt, add cold water to cover by 1 inch, and let soak overnight. Drain and reserve.

2. Heat 6 tablespoons of the oil in a medium skillet over medium-high heat. Season the lamb with salt and cook, stirring, until lightly browned (it should not be fully cooked). Transfer to a platter. Reduce the heat to medium. Add the chopped tomato and cook, stirring, until softened and its juices release, 2 to 3 minutes.

3. In a soup pot, place the chickpeas, water, the bones, pig foot, bacon, lamb, and the onion. Bring to a boil over high heat. Reduce the heat to low, cover, and simmer 1 hour. Add the saffron, cloves, pepper, garlic, and salt and cook until the chickpeas are tender, about 1 hour more. Pass through a fine-mesh strainer and return 4 cups to the pot. Discard the bones. Bone and finely chop the pig foot and return to the pot. Reserve.

4. Preheat the oven to 325°F. In a 12-inch shallow earthenware casserole dish or Dutch oven, heat the remaining 3 tablespoons oil over medium heat. Add the rice and parsley, stir to coat the rice well with the pan mixture, and cook 2 minutes. Add the reserved contents from the soup pot and bring to a boil. Cook, uncovered and stirring occasionally, until the bubbles rising from the pan look slightly thick and the rice begins to be visible at the surface, about 4 to 5 minutes more.

5. Arrange the sliced tomato, sausage, and pimiento over the rice. Bake about 20 minutes or until the liquid is absorbed but the rice is almost al dente, tender yet still firm to the bite. Remove from the oven, cover, and let sit 5 minutes or until the rice is cooked to taste. Serve hot.

Lamb, Lentil, and Eggplant Paella

Arroz de Cordero, Lentejas y Berenjena

MAKES 6 TO 8 SERVINGS

This is an especially hearty paella in which the flavors of lamb, eggplant, and lentils blend together perfectly. The recipe calls for cumin and cilantro, reflecting a Moorish influence.

1 pound eggplant, cut into ½-inch pieces

Kosher or sea salt

6 cups chicken broth or a mixture of chicken broth and beef broth

¼ teaspoon saffron threads, crumbled

1½ pounds boneless leg of lamb, cut into ½-inch pieces

1 small onion (about ⅓ cup)

8 garlic cloves, finely chopped

1 medium green bell pepper, finely chopped (about ¾ cup)

1 medium tomato, finely chopped (about ⅔ cup)

2 tablespoons finely chopped fresh flat-leaf parsley

1 cup freshly cooked or canned lentils, drained and rinsed

1 tablespoon finely chopped fresh oregano or ½ teaspoon dried oregano

½ teaspoon ground cumin

3 cups short-grain rice, such as imported Spanish or Arborio

2 tablespoons finely chopped fresh cilantro, for garnish

1. Place the eggplant in a colander and sprinkle well with salt. Let sit 30 minutes. Pat dry with paper towels. In a large saucepan, combine the broth and saffron and place on a back burner over the lowest heat to keep hot until needed.

2. Preheat the oven to 400°F. In a 17- to 18-inch paella pan or similar-size shallow earthenware casserole dish, heat the oil over medium-high heat, placing over two burners if necessary. Add the lamb and cook, stirring and sprinkling with salt, until lightly browned (it should not be fully cooked). Transfer to a platter.

3. In the same oil over medium heat, add the onion, garlic, and peppers and cook until the vegetables are softened, about 8 minutes. Add the eggplant and cook, stirring, 1 minute, then stir in the tomato, parsley, lentils, oregano, and cumin. Add the rice and stir to coat well with the pan mixture. Add the broth and bring to a boil. Taste and adjust seasoning if necessary. Cook, stirring and rotating the pan occasionally if over two burners, until the bubbles rising from the pan look slightly thick and the rice begins to be visible at the surface.

4. Transfer to the oven and bake 10 to 12 minutes or until the rice is almost al dente, tender yet still firm to the bite. Remove from the oven, cover with foil, and let sit 5 to 10 minutes or until the rice is cooked to taste. Sprinkle with the cilantro and serve hot.

Lamb and Red Pepper Paella
Paella de Cordero Chilindrón

MAKES 6 SERVINGS

This paella is a regional specialty of Aragon, an area of mountains and valleys that is perfect for lambs to graze. The region is also well known for its bell peppers, which make a perfect combination with the lamb. Because here the lamb is not stewed first, use a tender cut like the leg for this recipe.

1⅓ cups canned chickpeas

6½ cups chicken broth or vegetable broth

12 garlic cloves, coarsely chopped

4 sprigs parsley

2 sprigs rosemary or ¼ teaspoon dried rosemary

2 sprigs thyme or ¼ teaspoon dried thyme

2 sprigs oregano or ¼ teaspoon dried oregano

1 bay leaf

1 medium onion

½ teaspoon ground cumin

¼ teaspoon saffron threads, crumbled

½ cup dry white wine

7 tablespoons olive oil

1½ pounds boneless leg of lamb, cut into ¾-inch pieces

Kosher or sea salt

2 medium red bell peppers, cut into ½-inch pieces

1 small onion, finely chopped (about ⅓ cup)

1 medium tomato, finely chopped (about ⅔ cup)

2 tablespoons brandy

3 cups short-grain rice, such as imported Spanish or Arborio

1 pimiento, cut into ½-inch strips

12 (¼-inch) slices medium tomato

2 tablespoons finely chopped fresh flat-leaf parsley, for garnish

1. Drain the chickpeas and reserve the liquid. In a mortar or mini-processor, mash ⅔ cup of the chickpeas. In the saucepan, combine the broth, chickpeas, the reserved liquid, the garlic, parsley sprigs, the rosemary, thyme, oregano, bay leaf, the whole onion, the cumin, and saffron and bring to a boil over high heat. Reduce the heat to low, cover, and simmer 30 minutes. Pass through a fine-mesh strainer and return 5½ cups to the pot along with the wine. Discard the solids. Place on a back burner over the lowest heat to keep hot until needed.

2. Preheat the oven to 400°F. In a 17- to 18-inch paella pan or similar-size shallow earthenware casserole dish, heat the oil over medium-high heat, placing over two burners if necessary. Add the lamb, season with salt, and cook, stirring, until lightly browned (it should not be fully cooked). Transfer to a platter.

3. In the same oil over medium-high heat, add the bell pepper and the chopped onion and cook, stirring, until the vegetables are softened, about 5 minutes. Stir in the chopped tomato and the brandy and cook until the brandy has evaporated. Add the rice and stir to coat well with the pan mixture. Add the broth and the reserved ⅔ cup chickpeas. Taste and adjust seasoning if necessary and bring to a boil. Cook 2 minutes, then stir in the lamb and cook, stirring and rotating the pan occasionally if over two burners, until the bubbles rising from the pan look slightly thick and the rice begins to be visible at the surface.

4. Arrange the pimiento and the sliced tomato over the rice. Transfer to the oven and bake about 10 to 12 minutes or until the rice is almost al dente, tender yet still firm to the bite. Remove from the oven, cover with foil, and let sit 5 to 10 minutes or until the rice is cooked to taste. Sprinkle with the chopped parsley and serve hot.

Monastic Paella with Chorizo and Olives
Paella Monacal Santa Clara

MAKES 6 TO 8 SERVINGS

I was very fortunate to obtain this recipe handed down from the Clarisa nuns of the Santa Clara convent in Briviesca, in the Castilian province of Burgos. Chorizo is frequently found in many different paellas, but here it is the main ingredient. Spaniards adore their chorizo, a sausage seasoned with garlic and paprika. When combined with capers, cured ham, and green and black olives, the results are outstanding.

¼ cup coarsely chopped pitted green olives, preferably Spanish

¼ cup coarsely chopped pitted black olives, preferably Spanish

½ cup dry white wine

6 cups chicken broth or a mixture of chicken broth and beef broth

¼ teaspoon saffron threads, crumbled

7 tablespoons olive oil

½ pound (4 links) chorizo, skinned and cut into ½-inch slices

1 medium onion, finely chopped (about ⅔ cup)

4 garlic cloves, finely chopped

1 medium red bell pepper, finely chopped (about ¾ cup)

¼ pound Serrano (Spanish cured mountain) ham or prosciutto, cut into ¼-inch cubes

¼ cup finely chopped fresh flat-leaf parsley

3 cups short-grain rice, such as imported Spanish or Arborio

Salt

24 snow pea pods

1. Combine the olives and wine in a small saucepan and bring to a boil over high heat. Reduce the heat to low and simmer 5 minutes. Drain. In a large saucepan, combine the broth and saffron and place on a back burner over the lowest heat to keep hot until needed.

2. Preheat the oven to 400°F. In a 17- to 18-inch paella pan or similar-size shallow earthenware casserole dish, heat the oil over medium heat, placing over two burners if necessary. Add the chorizo and cook, stirring, 1 minute, then add the onion, garlic, pepper, ham, and parsley and cook, stirring, until the peppers are slightly softened, about 5 minutes more.

3. Add the olives and rice and stir to coat the rice well with the pan mixture. Add the broth, taste and adjust seasoning if necessary, and bring to a boil. Cook, stirring and rotating the pan occasionally if over two burners, until the bubbles rising from the pan look slightly thick and the rice begins to be visible at the surface.

4. Stir in the snow peas and transfer to the oven. Bake about 10 minutes or until the rice is almost al dente, tender yet still firm to the bite. Remove from the oven, cover with foil, and let sit 5 to 10 minutes or until the rice is cooked to taste. Serve hot.

Baked Rice with Black Sausage and Garlic
Arroz al Horno con Morcilla y "Perdiu"

MAKES 6 SERVINGS

If you omit the sausage, this is a traditional Lenten dish consisting of baked rice, potatoes, sliced tomato, and chickpeas. But morcilla (black sausage) is extremely delicious and makes a much more flavorful rice. The "perdiu" (partridge) refers to the whole head of garlic that is placed symbolically in the center of the rice. In times of old, when ovens were not

continues...

common in home kitchens, villagers often took their casseroles to the local baker for cooking.

PREPARE 10 TO 14 HOURS IN ADVANCE

⅔ cup dried chickpeas or 2 cups canned chickpeas, liquid reserved

1 head garlic, loose skin removed

About 5½ cups broth, such as a mixture of chicken broth and beef broth

¼ teaspoon saffron threads, crumbled

1 medium tomato

½ pound black sausage (such as morcilla), chorizo, or any other sausage, cut diagonally into ½-inch slices

7 tablespoons olive oil

1 medium potato, peeled and cut into ¼-inch slices

2 medium tomatoes, cut into ½-inch slices

Kosher or sea salt

1 medium onion, finely chopped (about ⅔ cup)

1 medium green bell pepper, finely chopped (about ¾ cup)

2 garlic cloves, finely chopped

2 tablespoons finely chopped fresh flat-leaf parsley

½ teaspoon ground sweet paprika, such as Spanish smoked

3 cups short-grain rice, such as imported Spanish or Arborio

1. Place the chickpeas in a medium bowl, add salt, add cold water to cover by 1 inch, and let soak overnight. Drain, place in a medium saucepan, add cold water to cover, and bring to a boil over high heat. Reduce the heat to low, cover, and simmer, stirring occasionally, 2 to 2½ hours or until tender. Drain and reserve the liquid.

2. Place the head of garlic in a baking dish and bake until needed. Meanwhile, pass ⅔ cup of the chickpeas through a fine-mesh strainer or a ricer into a medium saucepan. Combine the broth and about ½ cup of reserved chickpea liquid to make

6 cups and transfer to the saucepan. Stir in the saffron. Place the saucepan on a back burner over the lowest heat to keep hot until needed.

3. Cut the whole tomato in half crosswise and gently squeeze to extract the seeds. With a coarse grater held over a small bowl, grate each half down to the skin, draining off any excess juices. Reserve the pulp and discard the skin. In a 17- to 18-inch paella pan or similar-size shallow earthenware casserole dish, heat the oil over medium heat, placing over two burners if necessary. Add the sausage and cook, turning once, until lightly browned on both sides. Transfer to paper towels to drain, then place on a platter.

4. Drain off any fat in the pan, then add the oil and heat over medium heat. Add the potatoes and cook, turning once, until browned and tender, about 5 minutes. Transfer to paper towels to drain, then place on the platter. Add the sliced tomatoes to the pan, and cook, turning once, until softened and their juices release, 2 to 3 minutes. Transfer to the platter. Season the tomatoes and potatoes with salt.

5. Preheat the oven to 400°F. In the same oil over low heat, add the onion, pepper, and garlic and cook, stirring, until softened, about 8 minutes. Stir in the grated tomato and the parsley and cook 5 minutes. Add the paprika, then add the rice and stir to coat well with the pan mixture. Add the broth and about 1 cup chickpeas (reserve the remaining chickpeas for another use) and bring to a boil. Cook just until enough liquid has cooked away so that the garnishes will sit on top, about 3 minutes.

6. Remove the garlic from the oven and place in the center of the paella pan. Arrange the potatoes, tomatoes, and sausages attractively over the rice. Transfer to the oven and bake about 15 minutes or until the rice is almost al dente, tender yet still firm to the bite. Remove from the oven, cover with foil, and let sit 5 minutes or until the rice is cooked to taste. Serve hot.

Cabbage and Chopped Meat Paella
Arroz con Repollo y Carne Picada

MAKES 4 SERVINGS

This paella could not be more unconventional, but it is delicious nonetheless. It's an extremely rich dish featuring ground beef, cured ham, and bacon, and made spicy by the addition of jalapeño peppers. The cabbage adds a pleasing contrast.

3 cups chicken broth or vegetable broth

⅛ teaspoon saffron threads, crumbled

3 thin slices lean bacon

¼ cup olive oil

¾ pound lean ground beef

Salt

1 large onion, finely chopped (about 1 cup)

1 jalapeño pepper, cored, seeded, and finely chopped (about 2 teaspoons)

2 tablespoons small cubes (¼ inch) Serrano (Spanish cured mountain) ham or prosciutto (about 1 ounce)

¼ head (about ½ pound) cabbage, finely chopped (about 3¼ cups)

1½ cups short-grain rice, such as imported Spanish or Arborio

1 bunch scallions, finely chopped

10 snow peas, cut into very thin strips

1. In a medium saucepan, combine the broth and saffron and place on a back burner over the lowest heat to keep hot until needed. In a 13-inch paella pan or similar-size shallow earthenware casserole dish, heat the oil over medium heat. Arrange the bacon strips and cook, turning occasionally, until crisp. Transfer to paper towels and let drain. Crumble and reserve. Pour off the fat from the pan or leave some in the pan for added flavor.

2. Preheat the oven to 400°F. Add 2 tablespoons of the oil to the pan and heat over medium heat. Add the beef, sprinkling with salt and stirring and separating into small pieces, until no longer pink. Transfer to a platter. Add the remaining 2 tablespoons oil, the onion, pepper, and ham and cook, stirring, until the vegetables are softened, about 8 minutes. Add the cabbage and cook, stirring, until slightly wilted, then add in the rice and stir to coat well with the pan mixture. Add the broth, scallions, beef, and half of the bacon, taste and adjust seasoning if necessary, and bring to a boil. Cook until the bubbles rising from the pan look slightly thick and the rice begins to be visible at the surface.

3. Transfer to the oven and bake 10 to 12 minutes or until the rice is almost al dente, tender yet still firm to the bite. Remove from the oven, cover with foil, and let sit 5 to 10 minutes or until the rice is cooked to taste. Scatter the snow peas and the remaining bacon over the rice. Serve hot.

Fish

SOLE AND FLOUNDER

Marinated Fillet of Sole Stuffed
with Pimientos

Fillet of Sole with Pine Nuts

Fillet of Sole with Green Mayonnaise

Fillet of Sole in Mushroom Sauce

Fillet of Sole in Wine and Mushroom Sauce

Fillet of Sole Stuffed with
Shrimp in Almond Sauce

Fillet of Sole Stuffed with Shrimp and
Asparagus in Txakoli Wine Sauce

Crunchy Fillet of Sole Stuffed
with Shrimp and Vegetables

Fillet of Sole Stuffed with
Red and Green Peppers

Flounder in Almond Sauce

Flounder in Lemon Sauce

Fried Flounder with Ham

Flounder with Mushrooms, Shrimp, and Sherry

TROUT

Pickled Trout

Trout with Almonds Stuffed
with Piquillo Peppers

Baked Trout with Onion and Wine

Trout, Segovia Style

STRIPED BASS

Striped Bass Stuffed with Mushrooms

Striped Bass in Fennel Sauce

Striped Bass with Lemon and Orange

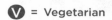 

Striped Bass in a Pine Nut Crust

Striped Bass with Garlic and Bay Leaves

Striped Bass with White Wine and Garlic

Striped Bass in Almond Sauce

Striped Bass in Orange Cream Sauce

PORGY

Porgy with Garlic and Vinegar Sauce

Baked Porgy and Peppers with Brandy

Stuffed Porgy

Butterflied Porgy, Bilbao Style

Porgy Baked in Salt

Porgy in Wine and Pine Nut Sauce

Baked Porgy, Madrid Style

Marinated Fried Red Bream

TUNA

Fresh Tuna Smothered in Onions

Fresh Tuna in Spicy Tomato Sauce

Marinated Tuna Steak

Honey-Coated Fried Tuna

Tuna in Balsamic Vinegar

Tuna in Piquillo Sauce

Tuna Medallions with Leeks
and Pine Nuts

Tuna with Pine Nuts and Capers

Tuna in Sherry Sauce with
Peppercorns

SNAPPER AND TURBOT

Red Snapper in Beer Sauce

Sautéed Turbot with Mushrooms
from Juan Mari's Mother

Turbot in Garlic, Vinegar, and
Toasted Flour Sauce

Baked Turbot with Bell Peppers and Potatoes

Turbot in Romesco Sauce

Stewed Turbot with Potatoes
and Peppers

Turbot with Tomatoes, Vinegar, and
Ham over Roasted Potatoes

Turbot with Greens and Clams

Stuffed Red Mullet

GROUPER

Grilled Grouper with Tomatoes
and Olive Sauce

Grouper with Scallops

Grouper with Swiss Chard

Roasted Grouper with Wine,
Potatoes, and Pine Nuts

HAKE

Hake in Hard Cider Sauce

Hake, Galician Style

Hake with Capers

Hake with Peas in Saffron Sauce

Hake in Saffron Sauce

Hake Filled with Tomato and Ham

Hake Filled with Shrimp in Sweet Sherry

Hake in Garlic Sauce with Fried Garlic

Carmen's Stuffed Hake with Two Sauces

Hake Stuffed with Shrimp,
Mushrooms, and Capers

Hake in Green Sauce with Peas

Hake, Andalusian Style, with
Shellfish and Pine Nuts

Hake and Shellfish in Green Sauce

Hake with Garlic Sauce and Parsley

Hake with Ham and Cheese

Coated Hake Filled with
Ham and Olives

Hake, Pine Nut, and Piquillo Pepper Pie

Hake Loaf

Hake Roll with Green Sauce

MONKFISH AND SHARK

Old-Style Marinated Monkfish

Monkfish Marinera

Monkfish with Rosemary

Monkfish in Black Olive Sauce

Monkfish with Sherry and Fried Bread

Monkfish and Shrimp Brochette

Monkfish Filled with Large Shrimp

Casserole of Monkfish with
Shrimp and Nuts

Shark with Shrimp and Peas

FRESH COD AND SALT COD

Baked Fresh Cod with Eggplant
and Onion

Codfish Fritters with Garlic Sauce

Salt Cod, Basque Style

Salt Cod with Eggplant and Peppers

Salt Cod with Tomatoes and Peppers

Salt Cod in Onion Sauce

Salt Cod in Creamy Garlic
Sauce with Mushrooms

Salt Cod in Honey-Garlic Sauce

Salt Cod with Honey

Salt Cod with Cream, Honey, and Mustard

FISH FRYS AND STEWS

Andalucian Fish Fry

Fish Baked with Potatoes, Onions,
Saffron, and Paprika

Grilled Fish with Ruperto's
Anchovy Caper Sauce

Rockfish with Vegetables, Sun-
Dried Tomatoes, and Potatoes

Mediterranean Fish Stew

Catalan Fish and Potatoes
with Garlic Sauce

SARDINES AND ANCHOVIES

Sardines, Santander Style

Sardines, Meson Style

Luisa Osborne's Stuffed Sardines

Marinated Sardines with Sweet
Tomato Marmalade

Marinated Anchovies
with Asparagus

Anchovies Layered with Tomato,
Capers, Bread Crumbs, and Cheese

Mackerel Vinaigrette

SHELLFISH

Prawns Smothered in Onion

Crayfish with Paprika, Onion, and Brandy

Crabmeat with Brandy and Wine

Crab in Wine, Brandy, and Tomato Sauce

Lobster Casserole with Garlic,
Nuts, and Chocolate

Lobster Stew

Shellfish Casserole with Saffron
and White Wine

Marinated Shellfish with Pickles
and Capers

Mixed Shellfish in
Brandy and Tomato Sauce

OCTOPUS AND SQUID

Octopus with Paprika in
Simmered Onions

Octopus with Paprika, Galician Style

Octopus in Red Wine Sauce

Baby Squid in Ink Sauce

Stewed Squid with Peppers

Stewed Squid with Peppers and Sherry

Baked Stuffed Squid in Almond Sauce

Squid Filled with Shrimp

Marinated Frog Legs

*S*pain has the highest fish consumption in all of Europe and also a very high life expectancy—perhaps, in part, because of the numerous health benefits of fish. Spain is blessed with the longest coastline in Europe, so fishermen have access to the Mediterranean Sea, the Bay of Biscay, and the Atlantic Ocean. This provides an overwhelming variety of seafood choices, and Spaniards will accept only the very best and the very freshest. At a typical Spanish fish market, you will find hake, bass, tuna, turbot, squid, cuttlefish, langoustine, red mullet, and many others. Spaniards frown upon over-seasoning fish dishes as it tends to mask the sublime and delectable flavor of the fish itself. Many chefs consider even a tiny squirt of lemon to be unnecessary and even insulting.

A typical three-course Spanish lunch tends to be heavier and more elaborate than a Spanish dinner. Traditionally, meat is served at lunch, and fish, because it is lighter, is served for supper. Fish is also commonly used in tapas such as Shrimp in Garlic Sauce and Fried Squid (see the Tapas chapter).

Some varieties of fish that are caught in Spain are the very same family as those that are found here, such as porgy, flounder, bass, cod, and mackerel. In general, Spaniards like their fish small, the most famous being their *angulas*, baby eels, which are as tiny as bean sprouts. When eels are caught by fisher-

men, they are plunged briefly into hot water where a piece of cigar is added for flavor. They are almost always prepared *a la bilbaína*, in a light oil and garlic sauce. Spain is also known for tuna. It may be called *atún* or *bonito*. If *ventresca* is called for, it is for the "choice" tender tuna belly.

In Spain's interior regions, saltwater fish is less commonly eaten, while freshwater fish such as trout reigns supreme. Flounder caught in the salt flats of Cádiz are considered far more desirable than open-water flounder. One of Spain's most beloved fish, hake or *merluza*, is at its best when it comes from the Bay of Biscay. Fish are hooked instead of netted since that way the fish fights and preserves the flavor. When netted, the fish is entangled and drowns. Fish markets mark the fish "hooked" and price them higher.

While the freshness of the fish is of utmost importance to every Spaniard, recipes vary greatly according to region. In Asturias, they prepare fish using cider, in Galicia they use wine, and in Andalucía they use sherry. Despite the abundance of delicious fish recipes, the most popular mode of preparation is the traditional fish fry, which originated in Cádiz. Spaniards have perfected the art of frying fish and they only use the purest and finest fresh olive oil. The result is crunchy on the outside, moist on the inside, and never ever greasy.

Sole and Flounder

Marinated Fillet of Sole Stuffed with Pimientos
Lenguado Empanado a la Sevillana

MAKES 4 SERVINGS

One of my very favorite dishes, this recipe requires first marinating the fillet of sole in lemon and milk, then breading and frying it. The addition of piquillo *peppers adds a particular zest. This can be served on its own or with tartar sauce.*

4 thin sole or similar fish fillets (about 6 ounces each)

Kosher or sea salt

Freshly ground black pepper

½ cup fresh lemon juice

¼ cup milk

2 tablespoons finely chopped fresh flat-leaf parsley

2 garlic cloves, finely chopped

2 large eggs, lightly beaten

1 cup bread crumbs, such as regular mixed with panko, for dredging

One (6- to 7-ounce) jar pimientos, such as (jarred) piquillo peppers, cut into 2-inch strips

Olive oil, for frying

1. In a flat bottomed bowl or deep plate, arrange the fish in a single layer. Season both sides with salt and pepper. In a small bowl, combine the lemon juice, milk, parsley, and garlic and pour over the fish. Let marinate 30 to 40 minutes at room temperature. Drain and let dry on paper towels.

2. Place the eggs and bread crumbs in separate wide shallow bowls. Place the pimiento strips along half of the length of each fish. Fold the fish in half crosswise and secure with a toothpick. Dip in the eggs, dredge in the bread crumbs, coating well, place on a wire rack, and let dry about 20 minutes

3. Heat at least ½ inch of oil in a medium skillet over medium-high heat (or better still, use a deep fryer set at 375°F) until it quickly browns a cube of bread. Place the fish in the oil and cook, turning once, until the crumbs are golden, about 3½ minutes. Transfer with a slotted offset spatula to paper towels and let drain. Remove the toothpicks and serve hot.

Fillet of Sole with Pine Nuts
Lenguado con Piñones "Tres Carabelas"

MAKES 4 SERVINGS

Spaniards are famous for dishes combining fish with meat, the most well known of which is paella. This fish dish features fillet of sole covered in a beef sauce, with pine nuts added for texture and flavor. The recipe originated in the Casa de España restaurant in New York City quite a few years ago. The restaurant has been gone for a long time.

All-purpose flour, for dredging

4 sole or flounder fillets (about 4 to 6 ounces each)

3 tablespoons olive oil

1 tablespoon all-purpose flour

1 cup beef or veal broth (such as flavored with wine)

1 tablespoon fresh lemon juice

Salt

Freshly ground black pepper

1 ounce pine nuts (about 3 tablespoons)

1. Place the flour in a shallow bowl. Heat the oil in a medium skillet over medium-high heat. Dredge the fish in the flour and place in the oil. Cook, turning once, until golden and just barely opaque when cut in the thickest part. Transfer to a warm platter.

2. Reduce the heat to medium, and stir the 1 tablespoon of flour into the remaining oil until well blended. Gradually stir in the broth and lemon juice and cook, stirring constantly, until thickened and smooth. Season with salt and pepper. Stir in the pine nuts and pour over the fish. Serve hot.

Fillet of Sole with Green Mayonnaise

Filete de Lenguado con Mayonesa Verde

MAKES 4 SERVINGS

Homemade mayonnaise is vastly superior to its storebought counterpart. Since it is an ingredient that features prominently in so many Spanish recipes, I highly encourage that you make your own. This mayonnaise recipe owes its green color to the addition of parsley, capers, and pickled cucumber.

Green Mayonnaise

1 recipe Mayonnaise (or 1½ cups prepared mayonnaise)

3 tablespoons finely chopped fresh flat-leaf parsley

2 tablespoons capers, rinsed, drained, and whole (if nonpareil) or finely chopped

½ dill pickle, drained and finely chopped

½ cup milk

4 sole or flounder fillets (about 4 to 6 ounces each)

Salt

All-purpose flour, for dredging

2 large eggs, lightly beaten

Bread crumbs, for dredging

¼ cup olive oil

8 rolled anchovies with capers, for garnish

8 lemon slices, for garnish

MAYONNAISE (MAYONESA)

MAKES 1½ CUPS

Mayonnaise is used for much more than a sandwich condiment; it's used to moisten foods during cooking and serves as the base of a sauce. I like to make it from scratch when possible and keep it on hand. It will keep stored in a closed jar or container for about a week.

1 whole egg

1 egg yolk

¼ teaspoon Dijon mustard

1 teaspoon salt

2 tablespoons fresh lemon juice

1 cup extra-virgin olive oil

Place the whole egg, egg yolk, mustard, salt, and lemon juice in a food processor and process until combined. With the motor running, gradually drizzle in the oil and process until emulsified. When done, it should be thick and silky.

1. Prepare the green mayonnaise: Combine the mayonnaise ingredients in a small bowl. Cover and let marinate in the refrigerator at least 1 hour.

2. Place the milk in a shallow medium bowl. Add the fish, turn to coat, and let soak 30 minutes, turning occasionally. Drain and let dry on paper towels. Place the flour, eggs, and bread crumbs in separate shallow bowls. Season both sides of the fish with salt. Dredge each fish in the flour, dip in the eggs, and dredge in the bread crumbs. Let sit 15 minutes.

3. Heat the oil in a large skillet over medium-high heat. Add the fish and cook, turning once, until the crumbs are golden and the fish is just barely opaque when cut in the thickest part. Decorate with the anchovies and lemons. Serve hot with the green mayonnaise on the side.

Fillet of Sole in Mushroom Sauce
Lenguado en Salsa de Setas

MAKES 4 SERVINGS

This creamy mushroom sauce is delicious with fish. It's best to cook thick fillets separately from the sauce so they cook more quickly, then serve the sauce on the side.

3 tablespoons olive oil

1 pound mushrooms, rinsed, trimmed, and thinly sliced

2 tablespoons unsalted butter

1 tablespoon shallots, finely chopped

2 tablespoons leeks, trimmed, well washed, and finely chopped

2 tablespoons storebought or homemade Fish Broth or bottled clam juice

Kosher or sea salt

2 tablespoons heavy cream

4 sole or other thick fillets (about 6 ounces each)

2 tablespoons finely chopped fresh flat-leaf parsley, for garnish

1. Heat the oil in a medium skillet over medium heat. Add the mushrooms, shallots, and leeks and cook, stirring, until they release their juices, about 4 minutes. Add the broth and salt and cook, stirring, until the mushrooms are softened, about 2 minutes more. Stir in the cream and butter and cook 1 minute more.

2. Grease a stovetop griddle and heat over high heat. Place the fish on the griddle and cook, turning once, until just barely opaque when cut in the thickest part. Transfer the fillets to plates, spoon the sauce over the fish, sprinkle with the parsley, and serve hot.

Fillet of Sole in Wine and Mushroom Sauce
Lenguado al Albariño

MAKES 4 SERVINGS

Galicia is well known for its white Albariño wine, which is fruity and dry, making it excellent for cooking. Fortunately, it is not very hard to find in the United States, but any dry wine can be substituted. The sauce, made with eggs and heavy cream, is richer than most.

4 tablespoons olive oil

¼ cup finely chopped onion

2 garlic cloves, finely chopped

2 tablespoons all-purpose flour

¾ cup medium-dry white wine

¾ cup storebought or homemade Fish Broth or bottled clam juice

½ cup milk

3 tablespoons fresh lemon juice

Salt

Freshly ground black pepper

2 cups thinly sliced mushrooms

4 sole or flounder fillets (about 4 to 6 ounces each)

All-purpose flour, for dredging

4 large egg yolks

2 tablespoons heavy cream

1 tablespoon finely chopped fresh flat-leaf parsley

1. Heat 2 tablespoons of the oil in a medium skillet over medium heat. Add the onion and garlic and cook, stirring, until the onion is wilted, about 5 minutes. Sprinkle in the 2 tablespoons of flour and cook, stirring, 1 minute more. Gradually stir in the wine, broth, milk, lemon juice, salt, and pepper and cook, stirring, until thickened and smooth. Reduce the heat to low, add the mushrooms, and simmer while preparing the fish.

2. Place the flour in a wide shallow bowl. Heat the remaining 2 tablespoons of oil in a large skillet over medium-high heat. Dredge each fish in the flour and place in the oil. Cook until the crumbs are golden and the fish is just barely opaque when cut in the thickest part. Transfer to a warm platter.

3. In a small bowl, lightly beat the egg yolks and heavy cream with a fork. Stir in a few tablespoons of the sauce, then return this mixture to the skillet with the sauce and stir, about 1 to 2 minutes. Pour over the fish, sprinkle with the parsley and serve hot.

Fillet of Sole Stuffed with Shrimp in Almond Sauce
Filetes de Lenguado Rellenos en Salsa de Almendra

MAKES 4 SERVINGS

In order to properly prepare this dish, each individual fish fillet should be stuffed with four shrimp and then rolled. The sauce is made with cream, so therefore is quite rich with the almonds adding a subtle, nutty flavor.

4 sole fillets (about 4 to 6 ounces each)

16 small shrimp, shelled and deveined

All-purpose flour, for dredging

2 tablespoons unsalted butter

¼ pound ground blanched almonds

½ cup storebought or homemade Fish Broth or bottled clam juice

¼ cup dry white wine

½ cup heavy cream

1. Place four shrimp in each fillet, roll up, and secure with a toothpick. Place the flour in a wide shallow bowl.

2. Heat the butter in a medium skillet over medium-high heat. Dredge each fish roll in the flour and place in the butter. Cook, turning once,

until browned. Transfer to a warm platter. Wipe out the skillet.

3. Reduce the heat to medium, add the almonds, broth, and wine and cook, stirring occasionally, until the liquid is reduced and the sauce is thickened, about 10 minutes. Add the cream and cook, stirring, until the sauce is blended.

4. Return the fish rolls to the skillet, pour the sauce over the fish, and turn gently to coat. Cook over medium heat until heated through. Serve hot.

Fillet of Sole Stuffed with Shrimp and Asparagus in Txakoli Wine Sauce
Lenguado Relleno de Gambas y Txakoli

MAKES 4 SERVINGS

The wine commonly used for cooking in the Basque Country is a young green wine called txakoli. *It adds a mild fruity flavor to this excellent preparation of sole. Because it can be hard to find in the United States, you can substitute Spanish* Albariño *wine or Portuguese* vinho verde.

4 thin asparagus

8 medium shrimp, shelled and deveined

4 sole fillets (about 4 to 6 ounces each)

2 garlic cloves, finely chopped

¼ cup very dry white wine

½ cup storebought or homemade Fish Broth or bottled clam juice

1 teaspoon cornstarch

1 tablespoon olive oil

All-purpose flour, for dredging

1. Place the asparagus in a small skillet with water to cover, add salt, and bring to a boil over high heat.

continues...

Reduce the heat to low, cover, and simmer 5 minutes or until crisp-tender. Drain. Cut to the size of the fillets and use the tip part only.

2. Place 2 shrimp and 1 asparagus on each fillet, roll up, secure with a toothpick, and reserve. In a small saucepan, combine the garlic, wine, and broth and bring to a boil over high heat. Cook, stirring occasionally, about 15 minutes. Stir in a little bit of cornstarch and cook until blended and thickened.

3. Heat the oil in a large skillet over medium heat. Place the flour in a small shallow bowl. Dredge each fish roll in the flour and place in the oil. Cook, turning gently, until golden and cooked through. Pour the sauce over the rolls and cook 1 minute more. Serve hot.

Crunchy Fillet of Sole Stuffed with Shrimp and Vegetables
Crujiente de Lenguado con Langostinos

MAKES 4 SERVINGS

Phyllo dough of Greek origin is called for in more than a few Spanish recipes, especially in the region of Galicia, which is famous for its delectable meat and fish pies. Thin fillets of sole work better for this recipe as they must be stuffed with the shrimp before covered with the phyllo and fried until crisp.

2 tablespoons olive oil

1 garlic clove, finely chopped

1 small zucchini, finely chopped (about 1 cup)

1 small red bell pepper, finely chopped (about ¾ cup)

1 small carrot, finely chopped (about ⅓ cup)

1 small leek, trimmed, well washed, and finely chopped

12 large shrimp, shelled, deveined, and coarsely chopped

12 very thin sole fillets (about 2 to 3 ounces each)

Kosher or sea salt

Olive oil, for frying

4 sheets phyllo pastry dough, thawed in the refrigerator

Freshly ground black pepper

1. Heat the 2 tablespoons oil in a medium skillet over medium heat. Add the garlic, zucchini, bell pepper, carrot, and leek and cook, stirring, until the vegetables are softened, about 8 minutes. Add the shrimp and cook 1 minute more. Remove from the heat.

2. Season the fillets with salt. Top each with the vegetable-shrimp mixture. Lay each fillet on a phyllo sheet. Roll up to enclose the fillets and filling.

3. Heat the frying oil in a large skillet over medium heat. Place the phyllo rolls in the skillet seam side down. Cook, turning gently with a spatula, until crisp. Serve hot.

Fillet of Sole Stuffed with Red and Green Peppers
Lenguado Rías Baixas

MAKES 4 SERVINGS

Peppers are commonly used in the northwestern area of Spain. Any dish designated chilindrón *style or* a la riojana *has bell peppers as a principal ingredient. This dish is in the chilindrón style, but the Spanish title refers to region it's from, Rías Baixas, in Galicia, which is also known for its Albariño white wine.*

2 tablespoons olive oil

1 medium onion, finely chopped (about ⅔ cup)

½ medium red bell pepper, finely chopped (about ⅓ cup)

½ medium green bell pepper, finely chopped (about ⅓ cup)

2 garlic cloves, finely chopped

Kosher or sea salt

4 thick sole fillets (about 6 ounces each)

¼ cup brandy

¾ cup dry white wine

1. Preheat the oven to 375°F. Heat 2 tablespoons of the oil in a shallow earthenware casserole dish or Dutch oven over medium heat. Add the onion, bell peppers, garlic, and salt and cook, stirring, until softened, about 8 minutes. Heat the remaining 1 tablespoon oil in another medium skillet over medium-high heat. Add the sole and cook, turning once, until golden, about 2 minutes per side. Add the brandy and, standing well away from the skillet, ignite the brandy with a match or kitchen lighter and let die out.

2. Cook until the liquid is reduced and the sauce is thickened slightly. Stir in the wine, then the onion mixture. Transfer to the oven and bake 10 minutes. If using earthenware, serve hot in the dish, or transfer to individual plates.

Flounder in Almond Sauce
Lenguado con Almendra

MAKES 4 SERVINGS

Hearty and filling, this recipe combines flounder fillets with bread and potatoes, creating a satisfying meal that requires nothing else on the table. What's nice about this dish is that it can be made in advance then reheated in the oven. The subtle flavor of almonds greatly enhances the taste.

4 tablespoons olive oil

3 thin slices long-loaf (baguette) bread

2 medium potatoes, cut into ⅛-inch slices

Salt

Freshly ground black pepper

All-purpose flour, for dredging

4 flounder or sole fillets (about 6 ounces each)

1 medium onion, finely chopped (about ⅔ cup)

8 blanched almonds

3 garlic cloves, coarsely chopped

3 tablespoons finely chopped fresh flat-leaf parsley

1 cup dry white wine

¼ cup water

1. Heat 2 tablespoons of the oil in a large skillet over medium heat. Add the bread slices and cook, turning once, until golden. Transfer to a plate and reserve. Reduce the heat to low, add the potatoes, and cook, turning occasionally, until tender but not browned. Season with salt and pepper. Transfer to and arrange in a large shallow earthenware casserole dish or Dutch oven, reserving the oil in the skillet.

2. Place the flour in a wide shallow bowl. Heat the reserved oil over medium-high heat. Dredge the fish in the flour and place in the oil, adding more oil if necessary. Cook, turning once, until golden and just barely opaque when cut in the thickest part. Transfer to the casserole dish, arranging over the potatoes.

3. Heat the remaining 2 tablespoons oil in the same skillet over medium heat. Add the onion and cook, stirring, until wilted, about 5 minutes. In a blender or food processor, place the almonds, garlic, 2 tablespoons of the parsley, and the bread and blend until finely chopped. With the motor running, add the onion, and gradually pour in the wine and water until well blended. Return to the skillet and cook about 15 minutes. Taste and adjust seasoning if necessary.

4. Preheat the oven to 350°F. Pass the sauce through a fine-mesh strainer over the fish and potatoes, pushing through as much of the mixture as possible. Bake 15 minutes. Sprinkle with the remaining 1 tablespoon parsley. If using earthenware, serve hot in the dish, or transfer to individual plates.

Flounder in Lemon Sauce
Lenguado al Limón

MAKES 4 SERVINGS

This tart, citrus-based sauce has accents of ginger and mustard. While it is particularly well suited for flounder, it can be just as delicious when served with other types of fish.

All-purpose flour, for dredging

4 flounder or sole fillets (about 4 to 6 ounces each)

Salt

2 tablespoons unsalted butter

¾ cup dry white wine

Freshly ground white pepper

½ teaspoon Dijon mustard

½ teaspoon ground ginger

Juice of 1 lemon

¾ cup heavy cream

1 tablespoon finely chopped fresh flat-leaf parsley, for garnish

1. Place the flour in a wide shallow bowl. Melt 1 tablespoon of the butter in a large skillet over medium-high heat. Season the fillets with salt, dredge in the flour, and place in the oil. Cook, turning once, until golden and just barely opaque when cut in the thickest part, 2 to 3 minutes per side. Transfer to a warm platter. Wipe out the skillet.

2. Melt the remaining 1 tablespoon butter in the same skillet over medium heat. Add the wine, pepper, mustard, salt, ginger, and lemon juice and bring to a boil. Cook, stirring, until the liquid is reduced by half and the sauce has thickened slightly. Reduce the heat to low, stir in the cream, and simmer, stirring occasionally, until the sauce is thickened and smooth. Pour over the fish, sprinkle with the parsley, and serve hot.

Fried Flounder with Ham
Lenguado "El Anteojo"

MAKES 4 SERVINGS

Spaniards are experts at frying, which when done well yields a fish that is moist on the inside and crunchy on the outside. This recipe, which includes cured ham, came to me from the quaint El Anteojo restaurant in Cádiz.

Flour, for dredging, such as semolina

Salt

Freshly ground black pepper

Oil, for frying, such as a mix of olive and soybean

4 flounder fillets (about 4 to 6 ounces each)

¼ pound Serrano (Spanish cured mountain) ham or prosciutto, cut into ¼-inch cubes

12 tablespoons unsalted butter

2 tablespoons fresh lemon juice

2 tablespoons finely chopped fresh flat-leaf parsley

1 garlic clove, finely chopped

1. In a wide shallow bowl, mix together the flour, salt, and pepper. Heat at least ¼ inch of oil in a large skillet over medium-high heat (or better still, use a deep fryer set at 375°F) until it quickly browns a cube of bread. Dredge each fish in the flour mixture and place in the oil. Cook, turning once, until golden and the fish is just barely opaque when cut in the thickest part. Transfer to an ovenproof serving platter and scatter the ham over the fish.

2. Preheat the oven to 500°F. Melt the butter in a small skillet over medium heat and let it brown lightly. Remove from the heat and stir in the lemon juice, parsley, garlic, salt, and pepper. Pour only across the middle of the fish—do not cover completely. Bake 3 minutes. Spoon the sauce over the fish and serve hot.

Flounder with Mushrooms, Shrimp, and Sherry

Lomito de Gallo con Champiñones, Gambas y Oloroso

MAKES 4 SERVINGS

While this recipe calls for flounder, fillet of sole works just as well. Both are delicious when prepared with an onion and garlic sauce made with shrimp and mushrooms. While most recipes call for cooking with dry sherry, in this case, I recommend you use one that is medium-sweet.

All-purpose flour, for dredging

4 flounder fillets (about ¼ pound each)

2 tablespoons olive oil

¼ pound onions, finely chopped

2 garlic cloves, finely chopped

¼ pound mushrooms, rinsed, trimmed, and thinly sliced

¼ cup medium-sweet sherry, such as Oloroso

¼ cup storebought or homemade Fish Broth or bottled clam juice

¼ pound shrimp, shelled and deveined

Kosher or sea salt

Place the flour in a wide shallow bowl. Heat the oil in a medium skillet over medium-high heat. Dredge the fish in the flour and place in the oil. Cook, turning once, until golden and the fish is just barely opaque when cut in the thickest part. Transfer to a warm platter. Add the onion and garlic and cook, stirring, until the onion is wilted, about 5 minutes. Add the mushrooms and cook 10 minutes. Add the sherry, broth, shrimp, and salt and cook about 5 to 6 minutes. Add the fish and serve hot.

MADRID: "THE BEST SEAPORT IN SPAIN"

Although geographically located in the center of Spain with the nearest port in Alicante, about 185 miles (300 kilometers) east, Madrid is called "The Best Seaport in Spain" by Spaniards. The reason is that Madrileños love their fresh fish so much that they will pay high prices for the freshest catch. All along the seashores of the Mediterranean and Atlantic, the fishing boats arrive around 5 pm. The fish is immediately sent to auction, where representatives from restaurants and fish markets bid on the day's catch.

The fish is then placed on large trucks or high-speed trains, or even planes that start toward the interior cities of Spain, including Madrid. They arrive in Madrid in the early morning, where the fish are auctioned again to restaurants and fish markets. At many restaurants, waiters may present the fish at the table before it's cooked so that the customer can appreciate the freshness.

The tradition of rapid transportation of fish has been present for many years, even before the era of mechanized transport. Charles I, Emperor of the Holy Roman Empire, abdicated the throne in the sixteenth century in favor of his son, Philip II, and retired to a monastery in Yuste, in the mountains of central Spain. He was a well-known gourmand and insisted on the freshest fish available, including his favorite oysters, which were brought to him by means of caravans of mules. One of the most popular fish in Madrid is *besugo matamulos* (literally "Porgy Mule Killer") which "proves" how fresh the porgy were because the mules could die transporting it quickly.

Trout

Pickled Trout
Truchas en Escabeche "Valle de Arán"

MAKES 4 SERVINGS

Trout is very popular in the inland regions of Spain as they are plentiful in the rivers of the mountainous terrain. This classic dish with its very simple marinade is very refreshing in the summertime. Serve either a whole trout per person as a main course or a fillet as a first course, leaving the skin on.

PREPARE AT LEAST 2 HOURS IN ADVANCE

2 medium trout (about ¾ pound each; cleaned and heads on or off)

Kosher or sea salt

Freshly ground black pepper

¾ cup olive oil

4 (2-inch) pieces leeks, trimmed and well washed (white part only)

2 medium carrots, peeled and cut into very thin 2-inch strips

4 garlic cloves, cut into very thin strips

4 (2-inch) pieces celery, cut into very thin strips

½ medium onion, slivered

½ teaspoon ground bittersweet paprika, such as Spanish smoked

2 bay leaves

1 tablespoon finely chopped fresh thyme or ½ teaspoon dried thyme

½ teaspoon dried oregano

¾ cup dry white wine

¾ cup wine vinegar, such as white

1. Season the fish with salt and pepper and let sit 10 minutes. In a shallow earthenware casserole dish or Dutch oven, heat the oil over low heat. Add the leeks, carrots, garlic, celery, and onion and cook, stirring, until the vegetables are softened, about 8 minutes.

2. Stir in the paprika, bay leaves, thyme, oregano, salt, and pepper. Reduce the heat to medium-low, arrange the fish over the vegetables and cook, turning once, 7 to 10 minutes. Add the wine and vinegar, bring to a full boil over high heat, and boil for 1 minute. Remove from the heat and let cool completely. Cover and refrigerate at least 2 hours up to 2 days, turning occasionally. Cut each trout in half and transfer to 4 individual plates. Spoon the vegetables and marinade over each. Remove the bay leaves. Serve cold.

Trout with Almonds Stuffed with Piquillo Peppers
Truchas con Almendras

MAKES 4 SERVINGS

Trout is easily accessible to most Spaniards as the rivers are filled with them. Here the piquillo *peppers and the dried red chile peppers give it an extra flair, while the almonds add a more subtle, nutty flavor.*

1 tablespoon bread crumbs

1 tablespoon wine vinegar

All-purpose flour, for dredging

4 (jarred) piquillo peppers, stemmed and seeded

4 medium trout (about ¾ pound each; cleaned and heads on or off)

2 tablespoons olive oil

2 tablespoons blanched almonds

2 garlic cloves, finely chopped

2 dried sweet red peppers (ñoras), stemmed, seeded, and finely chopped

Kosher or sea salt

Freshly ground black pepper

½ cup dry white wine

½ cup dry sherry, such as Fino

1 tablespoon finely chopped fresh flat-leaf parsley

1. In a small bowl, combine the bread crumbs and vinegar and reserve. Place the flour in a wide shallow bowl. Place 1 piquillo pepper inside each fish. Heat the oil in a shallow earthenware casserole dish or Dutch oven over medium-high heat. Dredge each fish in the flour and place in the oil. Cook, turning once, until browned on each side. Transfer the fish to a platter.

2. Add the almonds, garlic, and chile peppers and cook, stirring, until the almonds are golden and peppers are softened, about 3 minutes. Transfer to a mortar, add the soaked bread crumbs, salt, and black pepper, and mash. Add to the casserole dish and stir in the wine and sherry. Arrange the trout over the vegetables and cook, stirring gently, 3 to 4 minutes. Sprinkle with the parsley and cook until the fish is opaque when cut with a small sharp knife near the bone. If using earthenware, serve hot in the dish, or transfer to individual plates.

Baked Trout with Onion and Wine
Trucha al Horno

MAKES 4 SERVINGS

Due to Spain's mountainous terrain, there are many streams where trout are plentiful. Fishing for trout is very common, and this preparation, which I discovered in the town of Albarracín, is a favorite of many.

4 medium trout (about ¾ pound each; cleaned and heads on or off)

Kosher or sea salt

2 tablespoons olive oil

1 medium onion, coarsely grated (about ⅔ cup)

2 garlic cloves, finely chopped

1 tablespoon finely chopped fresh flat-leaf parsley

½ cup dry white wine

Freshly ground black pepper

1. Preheat the oven to 350°F. Season the fish with salt and place in a greased roasting pan.

2. Heat the oil in a medium skillet over medium heat. Add the onion, garlic, and parsley and cook, stirring, until the onion is wilted, about 4 minutes. Add the wine and pepper, increase the heat to high, bring to a boil, and cook about 2 minutes more. Pour the sauce over the fish and bake 12 to 15 minutes or until the flesh is just opaque when cut with a small sharp knife near the bone. Serve hot.

Trout, Segovia Style
Trucha a la Segoviana

MAKES 4 SERVINGS

This style of cooking originated in the town of Segovia in the region of Castile, where their lush green lands are perfect for animals to graze, and many mountain rivers are rich with trout. Pairing fish with meat is a common preparation. This particular dish is made richer and more flavorful with the addition of bacon.

All-purpose flour, for dredging

4 trout (about ¾ pound each; cleaned)

4 tablespoons olive oil

1 medium onion, slivered

2 garlic cloves, finely sliced

continues…

3 slices bacon, finely chopped

2 tablespoons finely chopped fresh flat-leaf parsley

1 teaspoon dried thyme

¼ cup storebought or homemade Fish Broth

½ cup dry white wine

Juice of 1 lemon

Salt

1. Place the flour in a wide shallow bowl. Heat 3 tablespoons of the oil in a medium skillet over medium heat. Dredge the fish in the flour and place in the oil. Cook, turning once, until browned. Reserve. Wipe out the skillet.

2. Heat the remaining 1 tablespoon oil over medium heat. Add the onion, garlic, and bacon and cook, stirring, until the onions are softened and the bacon is browned, 4 to 5 minutes. Add the parsley, thyme, broth, wine, and lemon juice and cook about 10 minutes. Stir in salt if necessary. Serve hot.

Striped Bass Stuffed with Mushrooms
Lubina Rellena

MAKES 4 SERVINGS

This excellent preparation of striped bass is one in which you sew the fish around the filling. In this case, the stuffing consists of mushrooms, bread crumbs, parsley, salt, pepper, lemon juice, and paprika.

5 tablespoons olive oil

6 tablespoons finely chopped onion

2 garlic cloves, finely chopped

½ pound mushrooms, rinsed, trimmed, and finely chopped

6 tablespoons bread crumbs

2 tablespoons finely chopped fresh flat-leaf parsley

Salt

Freshly ground black pepper

3 teaspoons fresh lemon juice

2 tablespoons dry sherry, such as Fino

¼ teaspoon ground paprika

4 striped bass or similar fish (¾ pound each; cleaned, boned, and head on)

1. Heat 2 tablespoons of the oil in a small skillet over medium heat. Add the onion and garlic and cook, stirring, until the onion is wilted, about 5 minutes. Add the mushrooms and cook about 5 minutes more. Add the bread crumbs, parsley, salt, pepper, 1 teaspoon of the lemon juice, the sherry, and paprika. Remove from the heat.

2. Preheat the oven to 350°F. Fill the cavity of each fish with the mushroom mixture. Sew up the fish with a thick, sterilized needle and heavy thread. Spread the remaining 3 tablespoons oil in a

roasting pan. Add the fish and turn to coat with the oil. Sprinkle with the remaining 2 teaspoons lemon juice and season with salt. Bake about 45 minutes or until the fish flesh is flaky. Remove the thread. Serve hot.

Striped Bass in Fennel Sauce
Lubina al Hinojo

MAKES 4 SERVINGS

The flavor of fennel adds a delightful accent to almost any fish you prepare. This sauce is particularly suited for fresh bass, but other types of fish can be substituted.

All-purpose flour, for dredging

4 striped bass fillets (about 6 ounces each)

6 tablespoons unsalted butter

2 tablespoons all-purpose flour

¾ cup storebought or homemade Fish Broth or bottled clam juice

¾ cup dry white wine

½ cup milk

Salt

Freshly ground white pepper

½ teaspoon crushed fennel seed

1 tablespoon finely chopped fresh flat-leaf parsley, for garnish

I. Place the flour in a wide shallow bowl. Heat 4 tablespoons of the butter in a medium skillet over medium heat. Dredge the fish in the flour and place in the oil. Cook, turning once, until golden and just opaque inside when tested with a small sharp knife. Transfer to a warm platter. Wipe out the skillet.

2. Melt the remaining 2 tablespoons of butter in the skillet over medium heat. Add the 2 tablespoons of flour and cook, stirring, I minute. Stir in the broth, wine, milk, salt, pepper, and fennel and cook, stirring, until the sauce is smooth and thickened. Pour over the fish and sprinkle with the parsley. Serve hot.

Striped Bass with Lemon and Orange
Lubina al Horno al Estilo de Cudillero

MAKES 4 SERVINGS

The Seville orange, the type used to make marmalade, is far superior to all others but not readily available in the United States. But as long as the sweet juice of an orange is mixed with the bitter juice of a lemon, it can provide the proper acidity.

2 tablespoons olive oil

3 medium potatoes, peeled and thinly sliced

2 medium onions, slivered

2 garlic cloves, coarsely chopped

3 medium tomatoes, peeled and cut into small cubes

1 bay leaf

½ cup dry white wine

Juice of ½ lemon

Juice of ½ orange

2 tablespoons unsalted butter

3 pounds striped bass (cleaned, boned, and head on)

Kosher or sea salt

Freshly ground black pepper

1 tablespoon finely chopped fresh flat-leaf parsley, for garnish

I. Preheat oven to 350°F. Heat the oil in a medium skillet over medium heat. Add the potatoes, onions, and garlic and cook, turning the potatoes once, until the potatoes are softened and the onion is wilted, about 8 minutes. Transfer the potatoes to a platter. Reduce the heat to low, add the tomatoes and bay leaf and cook, stirring, about 10 minutes more. Add the wine, salt, lemon and orange juices, and butter and cook, stirring, about 5 minutes more. Reserve.

2. Season the fish with salt. Place the potatoes in the bottom of a shallow earthenware casserole dish or Dutch oven. Arrange the fish over the potatoes.

continues...

Pour the sauce over the fish and transfer to the oven. Bake 20 minutes or until the sauce is cooked and the fish is just opaque inside when tested with a small knife. Remove the bay leaf. Sprinkle with the parsley. If using earthenware, serve hot in the dish, or divide into individual portions on plates.

Striped Bass in a Pine Nut Crust
Lubina en Costra de Piñones

MAKES 4 SERVINGS

Prunes are the surprising addition to this delicious baked fish that is enhanced by the delicate flavor of pine nuts. Dishes that include fruit are typical of Catalan-style cooking, which often has an innovative and highly creative flair.

1 medium onion, thinly sliced

¼ teaspoon dried thyme

4 striped bass fillets (about 6 ounces each)

Kosher or sea salt

12 pitted prunes

2 tablespoons olive oil

1 garlic clove, finely chopped

4 tablespoons pine nuts

Freshly ground black pepper

1 tablespoon fresh lemon juice

¼ cup storebought or homemade Fish Broth or bottled clam juice

1. Preheat the oven to 350°F. Arrange the onion in a shallow earthenware casserole dish or Dutch oven and sprinkle with the thyme. Season the fish with salt and arrange over the onion. Arrange the prunes over the fish. Drizzle with the oil and reserve.

2. In a mortar or mini-processor, mash the garlic, 2 tablespoons of the pine nuts, salt, and pepper. Add the lemon juice and gradually stir in the broth. Transfer to a small saucepan and cook, stirring

occasionally, until thickened and creamy. Pour over the fish and sprinkle with the remaining 2 tablespoons whole pine nuts.

3. Transfer the casserole dish to the oven and bake 10 to 15 minutes or until the fish is browned and just barely opaque when cut in the thickest part. If using earthenware, serve hot in the dish, or transfer to individual plates.

Striped Bass with Garlic and Bay Leaves
Lubina al Ajo Pescador

MAKES 4 SERVINGS

Garlic is enormously popular in Spanish cooking and is featured prominently in innumerable recipes. This version calls for the garlic cloves to be sautéed with lemon zest and bay leaves before it is poured over the striped bass.

2 tablespoons olive oil

4 striped bass fillets (about ½ pound each)

10 garlic cloves

5 bay leaves

Zest of ½ lemon

Few drops of vinegar

Kosher or sea salt

Freshly ground black pepper

1. Preheat the oven to 350°F. Heat the oil in a shallow earthenware casserole dish or Dutch oven over medium heat. Add the fish, skin side up, and cook, turning once, until browned on each side, about 2 minutes. Transfer to a greased baking pan. Add the garlic, bay leaves, and lemon zest to the pan and cook, stirring, about 2 minutes. Stir in the vinegar, salt, and pepper then pour over the fish.

2. Transfer to the oven and bake 10 to 15 minutes, or until the fish is just barely opaque when cut in the thickest part. If using earthenware, serve hot in the dish, or transfer to individual plates.

Striped Bass with White Wine and Garlic
Lubina a la Marinera

MAKES 4 SERVINGS

A la marinera, in its simplest form, is a sauce of white wine and garlic. In this version, Manila clams are added as well as chopped, blanched almonds.

2 dozen Manila clams

2 tablespoons olive oil

1¾ pounds striped bass (cleaned and boned), cut into 4 pieces

½ medium onion, finely chopped

6 garlic cloves, finely chopped

¼ cup dry white wine

¼ teaspoon saffron threads, crumbled

½ cup storebought or homemade Fish Broth or bottled clam juice

2 tablespoons finely chopped fresh flat-leaf parsley

2 tablespoons finely chopped blanched almonds

Kosher or sea salt

Freshly ground black pepper

I. In a large bowl, place the clams, add cold water to cover, and let sit 30 minutes. Drain. Discard any clams with cracked shells or that do not close tightly when touched.

2. Heat the oil in a medium skillet over medium heat. Add the fish and cook, turning once, until browned, about 3 minutes per side. Transfer to a platter.

3. Add the onion and garlic and cook, stirring, until the onion is softened and translucent, about 4 minutes. Add the white wine and saffron and bring to a boil. Cook, stirring occasionally, until the liquid is absorbed. Add the broth, parsley, clams, almonds, salt, and pepper and cook, stirring occasionally, until the liquid is reduced and the sauce is thickened slightly. Add the fish, spooning some of the sauce over them, and cook until the flesh is just opaque when cut with a small sharp knife. Discard any clams that do not open. Serve hot.

Striped Bass in Almond Sauce
Lubina "Albufera"

MAKES 4 SERVINGS

In the middle of the rice lands of Valencia, there is a vast lagoon called Albufera, for which this recipe is named. Some say that this style of cooking was originated by the French, who occupied much of Spain during the early nineteenth century. This version, with a sauce rich with garlic and almonds, definitely has a Spanish flavor.

6 garlic cloves

¼ cup finely chopped fresh flat-leaf parsley

¼ teaspoon dried oregano

¼ teaspoon dried mint

3 tablespoons ground blanched almonds

2 tablespoons all-purpose flour

1 tablespoon olive oil

¼ teaspoon ground paprika

4 striped bass fillets (about ½ pound each)

Thin strips pimiento, for garnish

I. In a food processor or blender, place the garlic, parsley, oregano, mint, and I tablespoon of the almonds and process until a paste forms.

2. Preheat the oven to 350°F. In a medium skillet, place the flour and the remaining 2 tablespoons almonds. Stir in the oil and cook over low heat until the flour and almonds turn golden. Add the processor mixture and the paprika and cook, stirring constantly, until blended. Add the broth and cook, stirring constantly, until the sauce is thickened and smooth.

3. Place the fish in a greased shallow earthenware casserole dish or Dutch oven. Pour the sauce over the fish. Transfer to the oven and bake about 20 minutes,

continues...

or until the fish is just barely opaque when cut in the thickest part. Decorate the fish with the pimiento. If using earthenware, serve hot in the dish, or transfer to individual plates.

Striped Bass in Orange Cream Sauce
Lubina a la Naranja

MAKES 4 SERVINGS

This is an unusual but interesting recipe for striped bass with an orange cream sauce flavored with orange juice and peel.

About 3 cups storebought or homemade Fish Broth (page 199) or bottled clam juice

1 cup water

Peel of ½ orange (orange part only)

½ cup fresh orange juice

½ cup heavy cream

Salt

Freshly ground black pepper

1½ tablespoons unsalted butter

4 skin-on striped bass fillets (about ½ pound each)

1. Prepare the broth if necessary. Heat the water in a small saucepan over medium-high heat, add the orange peel, and cook about 5 minutes. Drain and cut into very thin strips.

2. In the same saucepan, combine the orange juice, ½ cup of the broth, the cream, salt, and pepper and cook until the liquid is reduced by half. Stir in the butter and the orange strips. Reserve.

3. In a large skillet, place the remaining 2½ cups broth and bring to a boil over high heat. Reduce the heat to low, add the fish skin side down, cover, and simmer about 4 minutes for every ½ inch of thickness or until the fish is just barely opaque when cut in the thickest part. Transfer the fish to individual plates. Reheat the sauce if necessary, spoon it over the fish, and serve hot.

Porgy with Garlic and Vinegar Sauce
Besugo a la Espalda Artiés

MAKES 4 SERVINGS

This recipe is from my friend Irene who lives in the beautiful village Artiés high up in the Pyrenees. Since the freshness of the fish is the most important factor to Spaniards, many tend to reject recipes featuring sauces or heavy seasoning. Here just a little garlic, vinegar, and dried chile pepper create a taste that is simple yet delicious.

5 tablespoons olive oil

2 porgies or red snapper (about 2 pounds each; cleaned and heads on)

Kosher or sea salt

Freshly ground black pepper

4 garlic cloves, thinly sliced

2 (1-inch) pieces medium-hot dried red chile pepper, such as Spanish guindilla

2 tablespoons red wine vinegar

2 tablespoons finely chopped fresh flat-leaf parsley, for garnish

1. Preheat the oven to 450°F. In a shallow earthenware casserole dish or Dutch oven in which the fish just fits, place 1 tablespoon of the oil, add the fish, and turn to coat with oil. Season with salt and black pepper, and let sit 10 minutes.

2. Meanwhile, in a small skillet, heat the remaining 4 tablespoons oil over low heat. Add the garlic and chile pepper and cook, stirring, until the garlic begins to sizzle but is not yet browned. Add the vinegar and cook, stirring, until the liquid has evaporated. Reserve.

3. Transfer the fish to the oven and bake 15 to 20 minutes or until the flesh is just opaque inside when cut with a small sharp knife. Remove from the oven and fillet, leaving the skin on or removing it, as desired. Reheat the sauce and spoon over each fish. Sprinkle with the parsley. If using earthenware, serve hot in the dish, or divide into four portions and serve on individual plates.

Baked Porgy and Peppers with Brandy
Urta a la Roteña

MAKES 4 SERVINGS

The city of Cádiz, well known for its seafood, lies directly across the bay from the small but beautiful village of Rota, where seafood is equally plentiful. This delicious recipe for baked porgy is named after the town where it originated.

2 porgies (about 2 pounds each; cleaned and heads on)

6 thin lemon wedges

8 tablespoons olive oil

4 medium green bell peppers, cut into thin strips

4 medium onions, thinly sliced

5 garlic cloves, finely chopped

4 medium tomatoes, peeled and finely chopped (4 cups)

1 bay leaf

Salt

Freshly ground black pepper

½ teaspoon dried thyme

1 cup dry white wine

½ cup brandy, such as Spanish brandy, or Cognac

1. Preheat the oven to 350°F. Make 3 incisions in one side of each fish. Insert the lemon wedges so that only the rind is exposed. Reserve. In a large shallow earthenware casserole dish or Dutch oven, heat 4 tablespoons of the oil over medium heat. Add the bell peppers, onions, and garlic and cook,

stirring, until the onion is wilted, about 5 minutes. Add the tomatoes, bay leaf, salt, and pepper, cover, and simmer 10 minutes.

2. Place the fish on top of the mixture, sprinkle with the remaining 4 tablespoons olive oil, the thyme, salt, and pepper. Transfer to the oven and bake 15 minutes. Pour in the wine and brandy and bake 25 minutes more or until the fish is just opaque inside when cut with a small sharp knife near the bone. Remove the bay leaf. If using earthenware, serve hot in the dish, or divide into four portions and serve on individual plates.

Stuffed Porgy
Besugo Relleno

MAKES 4 SERVINGS

In order to prepare this dish, the porgy needs to be stuffed with a mixture of egg, ham, pimiento, olives, and onion, then sewn up with a needle and thick thread. This method may take a little practice, but the results are well worth it.

1½ cups storebought or homemade Fish Broth (page 199; partial recipe) or bottled clam juice

1 large hard-boiled egg, finely chopped

½ cup small cubes (¼ inch) Serrano (Spanish cured mountain) ham or prosciutto (about ¼ pound)

1 pimiento, finely chopped

10 green olives (with or without pimiento), preferably Spanish, finely chopped

1 tablespoon finely chopped onion

3 to 3½ pounds porgy or other mild fish (boned—except backbone left in, butterflied, and head and tail on)

¼ cup olive oil

1 garlic clove, finely chopped

1 tablespoon all-purpose flour

1 tablespoon finely chopped fresh flat-leaf parsley

continues…

1. Prepare the broth if necessary. In a medium bowl, combine the egg, ham, pimiento, olives, and onion and stuff into the fish. Sew up with a needle and heavy thread.

2. Preheat the oven to 350°F. In a large, shallow earthenware casserole dish or Dutch oven, heat the oil in a medium skillet over medium heat. Add the garlic and cook, stirring, until softened—do not let it brown—about 2 minutes. Stir in the flour and parsley, then add the broth. Cook, stirring occasionally, until thickened and smooth.

3. Transfer the fish to the casserole dish and bake 30 minutes, basting occasionally, or until the fish is opaque when cut with a small sharp knife near the bone. Remove the string. If using earthenware, serve hot in the dish, or divide into four portions and serve on individual plates.

Butterflied Porgy, Bilbao Style
Besugo a la Bilbaína

MAKES 4 SERVINGS

This simple recipe for porgy in a light oil and garlic sauce gets its name from the Basque city of Bilbao. This method of preparation has become immensely popular throughout all the regions of Spain.

4 porgies (about ¾ pound each; boned—except backbone left in, butterflied, and head and tail on or off)

6 tablespoons olive oil

4 large garlic cloves, thinly sliced

½ dried red chile pepper, seeded and cut into several pieces

Fresh lemon juice

2 tablespoons finely chopped fresh flat-leaf parsley

8 lemon wedges, for garnish

1. Preheat the oven to 300°F and place an oven-proof platter on the middle rack. Pat dry with paper towels.

2. Heat 2 tablespoons of the oil in a large skillet over high heat. Open the butterflied fish and place flesh side down in the oil. Cook, turning once, until browned, about 1 to 2 minutes per side. Transfer to the heated platter, skin side down, and place in the oven.

3. Heat the remaining 4 tablespoons of oil in a small skillet over medium heat. Add the garlic and chile pepper and cook, stirring, until the garlic begins to sizzle—do not let it brown. Remove from the heat. Remove the fish from the oven and sprinkle with the lemon juice. Spoon the garlic sauce over the fish. Sprinkle with the parsley and decorate with lemon wedges. Serve hot.

Porgy Baked in Salt
Urta a la Sal

MAKES 2 SERVINGS

Spaniards adore porgy a la sal, a method of preparing fish that is very popular in Cádiz. While this recipe calls for an unusually large amount of salt, it does not create a salty fish. Rather, the salt acts as an insulating layer protecting the sweet, tender meat of the fish. The porgy should be presented on a platter surrounded by salt, decorated with parsley sprigs, and accompanied by one or more sauces (serving all three is common). Any fish can be prepared by following this method. Round out the meal, perhaps, with boiled new potatoes and a green vegetable such as Green Beans and Serrano Ham.

Green Mayonnaise (page 359; omit the capers and add 2 garlic cloves, mashed in a garlic press or mortar), to taste

Salpicón Marinade sauce (page 424; omit the hard-boiled egg), to taste

Romesco Sauce (page 156), to taste

2 porgy or other fish (about ¾ pound each; skin and head on)

About 2 cups kosher or sea salt

Parsley sprigs, for garnish

1. Depending on the sauce or sauces you're using: Prepare the mayonnaise as instructed in step 1 of the recipe. Prepare the salpicón marinade sauce as instructed in step 3 of the recipe. Prepare the romesco sauce as instructed in step 1 of the recipe. Place each sauce in a small serving bowl and reserve.

2. Preheat the oven to 350°F. Grease an oval oven-proof serving platter or baking dish in which the fish fits fairly snugly. Place the fish on the platter and pour the salt over it, covering it completely—you may need more or less salt, depending on the pan and fish size. Bake about 40 minutes (the flesh should be opaque inside).

3. Brush the salt off the top of the fish and decorate the platter with the parsley sprigs. Bring to the table for the diners' viewing. To serve, brush off all the salt. Remove the skin and discard. Carefully bone the fish and arrange the filets attractively on individual plates. Serve warm (the fish will be warm, not hot) with the sauces at room temperature.

Porgy in Wine and Pine Nut Sauce
Besugo con Piñones

MAKES 4 SERVINGS

This is a delightful combination of tastes and textures. The porgy is lightly fried, creating a crunchy effect, and the delicious white wine sauce is perfectly complemented by the pine nuts.

4 porgy fillets (½ pound each; skinned)

Salt

All-purpose flour, for dredging

4 tablespoons olive oil

1 large onion, finely chopped

3 garlic cloves, finely chopped

3 tablespoons pine nuts

2 tablespoons finely chopped fresh flat-leaf parsley

¾ cup medium-dry white wine

¾ cup storebought or homemade Fish Broth or bottled clam juice

1½ tablespoons fresh lemon juice

Freshly ground black pepper

1. Place the flour in a shallow bowl. Sprinkle the fish with salt and dredge in the flour. Heat 2 tablespoons of the oil in a large skillet over high heat. Add the fish and cook, turning once, about 1 minute per side. Transfer to a platter. Wipe out the skillet.

2. In the same skillet, heat 1 of the remaining tablespoons oil over medium heat. Add the onion, garlic, and pine nuts and cook, stirring, until the onion is wilted, about 5 minutes. Transfer to a food processor or blender. Add 1 tablespoon of the parsley and the remaining 1 tablespoon oil and process until smooth. With the motor running, gradually add the wine, ½ cup of the broth, the lemon juice, salt, and pepper. Pass through a fine-mesh strainer into the skillet and stir in the remaining ¼ cup broth.

3. Add the fish and spoon some sauce over the tops. Reduce the heat to low, cover, and simmer 15 minutes or until the fish is just opaque inside when cut with a small sharp knife. Sprinkle with the remaining tablespoon of parsley and serve hot.

Baked Porgy, Madrid Style
Besugo a la Madrileña

MAKES 4 SERVINGS

Porgy baked in white wine and tomato sauce can of course be served any time, but it is an essential part of the traditional Spanish Christmas Eve dinner in Madrid.

4 small porgies (about ¾ pound each) or 1 large
    porgy (about 4 pounds) (skinned and heads on)
1 lemon, cut into thin wedges
Juice of 1 lemon
½ cup olive oil
3 tablespoons finely chopped onion
½ cup tomato sauce
Salt
Freshly ground black pepper
1 bay leaf
1 cup dry white wine
3 garlic cloves, finely chopped
¼ cup finely chopped fresh flat-leaf parsley
6 tablespoons bread crumbs
2 large potatoes, peeled, cubed, and parboiled
    (optional)

I. Make 2 incisions in each side of each porgy for 4 total per fish (or 4 incisions in each side if using a large porgy for 8 total). Insert the lemon wedges so that only the rind is exposed. Sprinkle with lemon juice and let sit 30 minutes.

2. Meanwhile, heat 2 tablespoons of the oil in a small skillet over medium heat. Add the onion and cook, stirring, until wilted, about 3 minutes. Add the tomato sauce, salt, pepper, and bay leaf. Reduce the heat to low, cover, and simmer 15 minutes.

3. Preheat the oven to 350°F. Grease the bottom of a roasting pan with 2 tablespoons of the remaining oil. Place the fish in the pan and season with salt and pepper. Brush with the remaining ¼ cup oil.

Bake 5 minutes. Add ½ cup of the wine and cook 10 minutes more.

4. In a small bowl, mix the garlic, parsley, and bread crumbs. Spoon tomato sauce over each fish, then sprinkle with the garlic mixture. Pour the remaining ½ cup wine around the sides of the pan (not over the fish). Bake about 45 minutes more, adding the potatoes, if using, for the last 20 minutes. Serve hot.

Marinated Fried Red Bream
Palometas Adobadas

MAKES 4 SERVINGS

This dish from Cádiz in the South of Spain is commonly known as bien me sabe, *which translates in English to "tastes good."*

PREPARE 24 HOURS IN ADVANCE

¾ pound red bream, cleaned, boned, and cut into
    1-inch chunks
1 tablespoon vinegar
¼ teaspoon ground sweet paprika, such as Spanish
    smoked
¼ teaspoon dried oregano
2 garlic cloves, mashed in a garlic press or mortar
Olive oil, for frying
All-purpose flour, for dredging

I. In a medium bowl, combine the vinegar, paprika, oregano, and garlic. Add the fish, stir to coat, cover, and let marinate in the refrigerator at least 24 hours.

2. Drain then pat the fish dry with paper towels. Place the flour in a shallow bowl. Heat at least I inch of oil in a medium skillet over medium-high heat (or better still, use a deep fryer set at 375°F) until it quickly browns a cube of bread. Dredge the fish in the flour and place in the oil. Cook, turning occasionally, until golden brown and just cooked through. Let drain on paper towels. Serve hot.

Fresh Tuna Smothered in Onions
Bonito Encebollado

MAKES 4 SERVINGS

Tuna are plentiful in Cádiz, as they migrate from the colder water of the Atlantic to the Mediterranean in search of spawning grounds. This simple recipe for tuna with onions is especially easy to prepare.

2 tablespoons olive oil

4 medium onions, finely chopped (about 2⅔ cups)

2 medium green bell peppers, finely chopped (about 1½ cups)

½ pound tuna steak, about 1 inch thick, cut into 1-inch chunks

Kosher or sea salt

Freshly ground black pepper

Heat the oil in a large skillet over low heat. Add the onions and bell peppers and cook, stirring, until softened, about 10 minutes. Increase the heat to medium. Add the tuna and cook, stirring until browned, about 5 minutes. (Cook longer if you prefer tuna cooked through, but not too long or it will get dry.) Season with salt and black pepper. Serve hot.

Fresh Tuna in Spicy Tomato Sauce
Bonito con Tomate

MAKES 4 SERVINGS

This flavorful tomato sauce with its dried red bell peppers and pimientos really brings out the best in a fresh tuna steak. The recipe is from my late mother-in-law's cookbook.

All-purpose flour, for dredging

2 tablespoons olive oil

4 tuna steaks (about ½ pound each), about 1 inch thick

3 medium red onions, slivered

4 garlic cloves, thinly sliced

1 dried hot red chile pepper, stemmed and seeded

8 medium tomatoes, finely chopped (about 6 cups)

2 pimientos, finely chopped

1 tablespoon finely chopped fresh flat-leaf parsley

Kosher or sea salt

Freshly ground black pepper

1. Place the flour in a wide shallow bowl. Heat the oil in a shallow earthenware casserole dish or Dutch oven over medium-high heat. Dredge the tuna in the flour and place in the oil. Cook, turning once, until browned, 2 to 4 minutes per side, and transfer to a platter.

2. In the same oil over medium heat, add the onion, garlic, and chile pepper and cook, stirring, until the onion is wilted, about 10 minutes. Reduce the heat to medium low. Stir in the tomatoes, pimientos, and parsley and cook, stirring occasionally, about 15 minutes more. Pass through a fine-mesh strainer and return to the casserole dish. Season with salt and black pepper.

3. Return the tuna to the casserole dish. Simmer until just heated through. If using earthenware, serve hot in the dish, or transfer to individual plates.

Marinated Tuna Steak

Atún en Escabeche

MAKES 4 SERVINGS

Escabeche, used for centuries as a way to preserve food before refrigeration, is a blend of water or broth, wine, vinegar, herbs, and spices. This simple marinated tuna is not at all saucy, very tender, and unusually flavorful. If cut into smaller chunks, this tuna can also be served as a tapa.

PREPARE AT LEAST 24 HOURS IN ADVANCE

6 tablespoons olive oil

4 tuna steaks (about ½ pound each), about 1 inch thick

2 medium onions, thinly sliced

6 garlic cloves, thinly sliced

2 bay leaves

1 teaspoon dried oregano

½ teaspoon ground bittersweet paprika, such as Spanish smoked

¼ cup sherry wine vinegar

Kosher or sea salt

Freshly ground black pepper

I. Heat the oil in a medium skillet over medium-high heat. Add the tuna, and cook, turning once, until lightly browned, 2 to 4 minutes per side. Transfer to a platter.

2. Reduce the heat to medium, add the onion, garlic, and bay leaves and cook, stirring, until the onion is wilted, about 8 minutes. Stir in the oregano and paprika, then add the vinegar, salt, and pepper. Reduce the heat to low, cover, and simmer about 5 minutes more. Let cool.

3. Cut the tuna into chunks and place in a wide shallow bowl. Pour the sauce over the tuna and stir to coat. Cover and let marinate in the refrigerator at least 24 hours. Remove the bay leaves and serve cold.

Honey-Coated Fried Tuna

Atún Frito con Miel

MAKES 4 SERVINGS

A Moorish influence is reflected in this sweet and savory recipe. The combination of tuna with honey makes for a very unusual taste.

All-purpose flour, for dredging

2 pounds tuna steaks (about ½ pound each), about 1 inch thick

Kosher or sea salt

2 large eggs

½ teaspoon dried parsley flakes

Olive oil, for frying

Honey, for coating

I. Season the tuna on both sides with salt and let sit 10 minutes. In a wide shallow bowl, lightly beat the eggs and parsley with a fork. Place the flour in another wide shallow bowl.

2. Heat at least ⅛ inch of oil in a medium skillet over medium-high heat. Spread a light coating of honey on each side of the tuna steaks, dredge the tuna in the flour, dip in the egg mixture, and place in the oil. Cook, turning once, until the coating is golden and the tuna cooked to taste, about 2 minutes per side for rare or more until done to taste. Serve hot.

Tuna in Balsamic Vinegar
Lomo de Atún al Vinagre Balsamico

MAKES 4 TO 6 SERVINGS

When the tuna is fresh, and of course Spaniards will accept nothing less, its flavor is perfectly complemented by a quick, tangy splash of balsamic vinegar.

1½ pounds tuna steaks, about 1 inch thick

Kosher or sea salt

All-purpose flour, for dredging

2 tablespoons olive oil

1 medium onion, slivered

2 bay leaves

½ cup balsamic vinegar

1 cup storebought or homemade Fish Broth (page 199; partial recipe) or bottled clam juice

1 teaspoon sugar

1. Place the flour in a wide shallow bowl. Season the tuna with salt and dredge in the flour.

2. Heat the oil in a large skillet over medium-high heat. Add the tuna and cook, turning once, until golden, 2 to 4 minutes per side. Transfer to a platter. Reduce the heat to low, add the onion, and cook, stirring, until softened, about 5 minutes. Add the peppercorns, bay leaves, and vinegar and cook until the liquid is reduced and the sauce is thickened slightly, about 3 minutes more. Increase the heat to medium, add the broth, and cook, stirring occasionally, about 10 minutes more. Add the tuna and cook, stirring, about 2 minutes more. Stir in the sugar. Divide among plates. Serve hot.

Tuna in Piquillo Sauce
Taco de Atún en Salsa de Piquillo

MAKES 4 SERVINGS

Imported piquillo *peppers can be found in gourmet stores, jarred. This version of a* piquillo *sauce for tuna is especially rich as it calls for both butter and cream.*

3 tablespoons olive oil

½ medium onion, slivered

1 medium red bell pepper, cored, seeded, and chopped (about ¾ cup)

2 garlic cloves, finely chopped

2 tablespoons unsalted butter, softened

6 (jarred) piquillo peppers

2 tablespoons heavy cream

½ pound tuna steaks, about 1 inch thick, cut into chunks

2-3 tablespoons storebought or homemade Fish Broth or bottled clam juice

1. Heat 2 tablespoons of the oil in a medium skillet over medium heat. Add the onion and cook, stirring, until wilted, about 3 minutes. Transfer to a small bowl. Add the bell pepper, garlic, and butter and cook, stirring, until softened, about 3 minutes. Stir the onion back into the skillet.

2. In a food processor or blender, place the piquillo peppers and cream and process until smooth. With the motor running, gradually add as much broth as needed to make a smooth sauce. Add to the onion and bell pepper mixture.

3. Brush the tuna on both sides with the remaining 1 tablespoon oil. Place a barbecue grill or broiler rack about 4 inches away from the heat source and preheat the grill or broiler, or grease a stovetop griddle and heat over high heat. (Cover the broiler pan with foil for easier cleanup, if you like.) Grill, turning once, about 3 minutes per side for rare or more until done to taste. Pour the sauce over the bottom of a serving platter and place the fish on the sauce. Serve hot.

Tuna Medallions with Leeks and Pine Nuts

Medallones de Atún con Puerros Confitados

MAKES 4 SERVINGS

This is a simple tuna dish, with leeks and other ingredients first sautéed, then baked.

4 tablespoons olive oil

2 pounds tuna steaks (about ½ pound each), about 1 inch thick

3 medium leeks, trimmed, well washed, and finely chopped

1 medium carrot, coarsely grated

2 garlic cloves, finely chopped

2 tablespoons pine nuts

Kosher or sea salt

Freshly ground black pepper

1 teaspoon Dijon mustard

2 tablespoons finely chopped fresh flat-leaf parsley

¼ cup dry white wine

1. Heat 2 tablespoons of the oil in a medium skillet over medium-high heat. Add the tuna and cook, turning once, until seared on both sides, 2 to 4 minutes per side. Transfer to a platter.

2. Preheat the oven to 350°F. In a shallow earthenware casserole dish or Dutch oven, heat the remaining 2 tablespoons oil over low heat. Add the leeks, carrots, garlic, and pine nuts and cook, stirring, until softened, about 8 minutes. Add salt, pepper, the mustard, and parsley and cook, stirring, until incorporated, about 2 minutes more. Stir in the wine.

3. Add the tuna to the casserole dish, transfer to the oven, and bake about 10 minutes. If using earthenware, serve hot in the dish, or transfer to individual plates.

Tuna with Pine Nuts and Capers

Atún con Piñones

MAKES 4 SERVINGS

Capers are the flowers of the caper bush that proliferate in warm, Mediterranean climates. They have an extremely strong and distinct flavor and are to be used quite sparingly.

2 tablespoons olive oil

4 garlic cloves, finely chopped

2 bay leaves

3 tablespoons pine nuts

2 pounds tuna steak, cut into 4 pieces

½ cup dry white wine

¼ cup storebought or homemade Fish Broth or bottled clam juice

2 tablespoons capers (nonpareil preferred), rinsed and drained

1. Heat the oil in a medium skillet over medium-high heat. Add the tuna and cook, turning once, until seared on both sides, about 2 minutes. Transfer to a platter.

2. Reduce the heat to medium, add the garlic, bay leaves, and pine nuts and cook, stirring, until golden, about 2 minutes. Stir in the wine, capers, and broth and cook, stirring occasionally, until the liquid is reduced and the sauce has thickened. Add the tuna and cook about 2 minutes for rare or more until done to taste. Remove the bay leaves and serve hot.

Tuna in Sherry Sauce with Peppercorns
Bonito al Jerez

MAKES 4 SERVINGS

This version of sherry sauce is predominantly flavored by the distinctive taste of peppercorns. I prefer this dish with tuna, but it can also be made with mackerel steaks as long as they are fresh.

½ cup olive oil

1 large onion, thinly sliced

3 garlic cloves, lightly smashed and peeled

4 tuna steaks (about ½ pound each), about 1 inch thick

1 tablespoon peppercorns, crushed

2 bay leaves

Kosher or sea salt

Freshly ground black pepper

1 tablespoon ground bittersweet paprika, such as Spanish smoked

1 cup Manzanilla or other dry sherry

1. Preheat the oven to 350°F. Heat the oil in a shallow earthenware casserole dish or Dutch oven over medium-high heat. Add the onion, garlic, and tuna and cook, turning the tuna once, until the tuna is golden, 2 to 4 minutes per side.

2. Reduce the heat to medium, add the sherry, peppercorns, bay leaves, and paprika. Season with salt and pepper, then transfer the dish to the oven. Bake 10 minutes for rare or until done to taste. Transfer the tuna to a warm serving platter.

3. Transfer the sauce to a medium saucepan and cook, stirring occasionally, until the liquid is reduced and the sauce has thickened slightly. Remove the bay leaves. Spoon the sauce over the tuna and serve hot.

Snapper and Turbot

Red Snapper in Beer Sauce
Cherne con Salsa de Cerveza

MAKES 4 SERVINGS

Spaniards love their fish cooked over a thin layer of potatoes, creating a hearty all-in-one meal. If fresh red snapper is not available, grouper or bass work just as well.

2 tablespoons olive oil

1 medium onion, chopped (about ⅔ cup)

1 garlic clove, finely chopped

1 medium potato, thinly sliced

3 tablespoons canned crushed tomatoes

4 (jarred) piquillo peppers, cut into thin strips

1 tablespoon ground sweet paprika, such as Spanish smoked

¾ cup beer

¼ cup storebought or homemade Fish Broth or bottled clam juice

2 tablespoons finely chopped fresh flat-leaf parsley

2 skin-on red snapper, grouper, or bass fillets (1½ pounds each)

Kosher or sea salt

Freshly ground black pepper

Heat the oil in a medium skillet over low heat. Add the onion and garlic and cook, stirring, until golden and slightly tender, about 5 minutes. Add the potato, onion, tomato sauce, and piquillo peppers. Stir in the paprika, add the beer and broth, and sprinkle in the parsley and simmer 2 to 3 minutes more. Add the fish, spooning the sauce over the top, and cook until the fish is just opaque inside when cut with a small sharp knife. Serve hot.

Sautéed Turbot with Mushrooms from Juan Mari's Mother
Rodaballo con Hongos de la Madre de Juan Mari Arzak

MAKES 4 SERVINGS

This recipe comes from the mother of celebrated chef Juan Mari Arzak, and it uses mushrooms to complement the fish. I recommend using shiitake mushrooms, but brown mushrooms or oyster mushrooms will suffice. This dish can be prepared in minutes.

4 turbot or halibut steaks (about ½ pound each), about 1 inch thick

Kosher or sea salt

6 tablespoons olive oil

5 tablespoons unsalted butter

4 garlic cloves, finely chopped

2 tablespoons trimmed, well washed, and finely chopped leek or scallion (white part only)

1 pound mushrooms, such as brown, shiitake, or oyster, rinsed trimmed, and thinly sliced lengthwise

2 tablespoons finely chopped fresh flat-leaf parsley, for garnish

1. Season the fish with salt and let sit 10 minutes. In a medium skillet over low heat, add the oil, butter, garlic, and leek and cook, stirring, until the garlic just begins to sizzle. Increase the heat to medium, add the mushrooms and salt and cook, stirring and adding more oil if necessary, until the mushrooms are softened.

2. Grease a stovetop griddle and heat over high heat. Place the fish on the griddle and cook, turning once, until rare, about 4 minutes per side, or until done to taste. Spoon the mushrooms over the fish and sprinkle with the parsley. Serve hot.

Turbot in Garlic, Vinegar, and Toasted Flour Sauce
Rodaballo en Salsa de Sobrehueso "Casa Bigote"

MAKES 4 SERVINGS

Prepared with dry sherry called Manzanilla, this tasty and filling recipe is best with a mild white fish. Much of its flavor comes from the sauce, which is made with toasted flour. Sobrehueso is the term used by fishermen in Cádiz when referring to the part of the catch of the day that is not good enough to sell. It is sometimes eaten on the boats by the fishermen.

1¼ cups storebought or homemade Fish Broth (page 199; partial recipe) or bottled clam juice

4 fish steaks (about 8 ounces each), such as turbot or fresh cod, monkfish, or swordfish, about 1 inch thick

Kosher or sea salt

2 tablespoons all-purpose flour

2 tablespoons olive oil

3 garlic cloves, coarsely chopped

1 bay leaf

2 tablespoons wine vinegar, such as white

1. Prepare the broth if necessary. Season the fish on both sides with salt and let sit at room temperature and set aside. Place the flour in a small heavy skillet over medium heat and toast, stirring constantly, until lightly browned.

2. Heat the oil in a large skillet over low heat. Add the garlic and bay leaf and cook, stirring, until the garlic turns lightly golden. Stir in the flour. Add the broth, vinegar, and salt and simmer, stirring constantly, until slightly thickened.

3. Add the fish, cover, and cook about 10 minutes or until just opaque when cut in the thickest part. Remove the fish to a platter. If the sauce has thinned, cook again over low heat until thickened. Remove the bay leaf. Spoon the sauce over the fish and serve hot.

Baked Turbot with Bell Peppers and Potatoes
Rodaballo al Horno

MAKES 4 SERVINGS

Bell peppers are at their best in the fertile grounds of the Rioja region in the northeastern interior of Spain. This tasty baked dish with potatoes calls for both red and green peppers and makes an unusually colorful presentation.

2 tablespoons olive oil plus more, for drizzling

1 medium onion, thinly sliced

2 garlic cloves, finely chopped

½ medium red bell pepper, chopped (about ⅓ cup)

½ medium green bell pepper, chopped (about ⅓ cup)

2 medium tomatoes, coarsely chopped (about 1⅓ cups)

4 turbot steaks (about ½ pound each), about 1 inch thick

4 medium potatoes, peeled and cut into ⅛-inch slices

Kosher or sea salt

Freshly ground black pepper

¼ cup dry white wine

¼ cup storebought or homemade Fish Broth or bottled clam juice

2 tablespoons finely chopped fresh flat-leaf parsley, for garnish

1. Preheat the oven to 350°F. Heat the oil in a shallow earthenware casserole dish or Dutch oven over medium heat. Add the onion, garlic, and bell peppers and cook, stirring, until the vegetables are softened, about 8 minutes. Add the tomatoes and cook until softened and their juices release, about 5 minutes more.

2. Arrange the fish over the vegetables, cut several slits in each fish, and drizzle with olive oil. Arrange the potatoes around the fish. Season the fish and potatoes with salt and pepper, then add the wine and broth. Bake 15 to 20 minutes or until the fish is just opaque inside when cut with a small, sharp knife. Sprinkle with the parsley. If using earthenware, serve hot in the dish, or transfer to individual plates.

Turbot in Romesco Sauce
Rodaballo al Romesco

MAKES 4 SERVINGS

Romesco, or spicy red pepper sauce, originated in the province of Tarragona in Catalunya. Its more elaborate version, Romesco de Peix, *is an excellent casserole dish. Both versions use bread as a thickening agent.*

1 pound shrimp, shelled and deveined

1 pound turbot steak, cut into 8 pieces

6 garlic cloves, coarsely chopped

3 dried sweet red peppers (ñoras), stemmed and seeded

10 shelled hazelnuts

3 slices long loaf (baguette) bread, crust removed and toasted

3 medium tomatoes

¾ cup dry white wine

2 tablespoons olive oil

Kosher or sea salt

1. Heat the oil in a shallow earthenware casserole dish or Dutch oven over medium heat. Add the shrimp and turbot and cook, turning once, until the shrimp is pink and the fish is golden, about 2 minutes per side. Transfer to a platter and reserve.

2. In a mortar or mini-processor, mash the garlic, red peppers, hazelnuts, and bread as fine as possible. Transfer to a food processor, add the tomatoes, and process until smooth. Add the wine and process until well blended.

3. Transfer the processor mixture to the casserole dish. Arrange the fish and shrimp in the dish and cook over medium heat until heated through. Serve hot.

Stewed Turbot with Potatoes and Peppers

Rodaballo Guisado

MAKES 4 SERVINGS

On a cold winter night, Spaniards love nothing more than an old-fashioned stew, made that much heartier by the addition of potatoes. If you can't find turbot, another firm fish will do.

Seasoning Mash

4 garlic cloves

2 tablespoons finely chopped fresh flat-leaf parsley

1 tablespoon olive oil

2 tablespoons dry white wine

Kosher or sea salt

4 turbot or other firm-fleshed fish steaks (about ½ pound each)

2 medium potatoes, peeled and thinly sliced

½ medium onion, slivered

1 medium green bell pepper, cut into thin strips

1 medium red bell pepper, cut into thin strips

½ medium tomato, coarsely chopped (about ⅓ cup)

2 tablespoons olive oil

½ cup wine

Kosher or sea salt

1. Prepare the seasoning: In a mortar or mini-processor, mash the garlic and parsley, then stir in the oil, wine, and salt and reserve.

2. Preheat the oven to 350°F. In a shallow earthenware casserole dish or Dutch oven, add the potatoes in layers with the onion, peppers, and tomato and drizzle with the olive oil and wine. Add salt, then add the fish, Spread the mortar mixture over the fish.

3. Transfer to the oven and bake about 15 minutes or until the fish is just opaque inside when cut with a small sharp knife. If using earthenware, serve hot in the dish, or transfer to individual plates.

Turbot with Tomatoes, Vinegar, and Ham over Roasted Potatoes

Rodaballo con Tomate, Vinagre y Jamón con Patatas Panaderas

MAKES 4 SERVINGS

Although a true fish purist might frown upon it, combining seafood with meat is immensely popular in Spanish cuisine, especially in areas that have access to both. This tasty preparation with Spanish ham or its substitute, prosciutto, is extraordinary when served over sautéed potatoes.

1 thin slice Serrano (Spanish cured mountain) ham or prosciutto

4 turbot steaks (about ½ pound each)

Kosher or sea salt

Freshly ground black pepper

4 medium tomatoes, cut into ¼-inch cubes

2 tablespoons olive oil

¼ cup balsamic vinegar

2 tablespoons finely chopped fresh flat-leaf parsley

Roasted Potatoes

2 tablespoons olive oil

2 medium potatoes, peeled and coarsely grated

Kosher or sea salt

Freshly ground black pepper

1. Preheat the oven to 350°F. Place the ham in a roasting pan and bake 10 minutes. Let cool and chop very finely. Reserve the oil in the pan.

2. Increase the oven temp to 400°F. Season the fish with salt and pepper, place in the roasting pan, and bake 7 minutes or until the fish is just barely opaque when cut in the thickest part. Meanwhile, in a medium bowl, place the tomatoes and sprinkle with the 2 tablespoons oil. Add the vinegar and parsley, mix well, and reserve.

3. Prepare the potatoes: Heat the 2 tablespoons oil in a medium skillet over medium-high heat. Add the potatoes and flatten with an offset spatula. Cook until browned on the bottom, season with salt and pepper, and flip over. Reduce the heat to medium and cook until browned on the bottom and tender throughout. Season again with salt and pepper. Transfer to a serving platter. Arrange the fish over the potatoes, spoon the tomato salad over the fish, and sprinkle with the ham. Serve hot.

Turbot with Greens and Clams
Rodaballo con Grelos y Almejas

MAKES 4 SERVINGS

Many Spaniards prefer their fish unadorned with vegetables, but here the addition of collard greens and small clams makes for a winning combination.

½ pound collard greens or Swiss Chard, well washed
    and thick stems removed

Salt

6 tablespoons olive oil

4 fish steaks (about 8 ounces each), such as turbot,
    about 1 inch thick

All-purpose flour, for dredging

Fresh lemon juice

¼ cup finely chopped onion

2 garlic cloves, finely chopped

Freshly ground black pepper

2 teaspoons vinegar

1 bay leaf

2 tablespoons finely chopped fresh flat-leaf parsley

1 dozen small clams, such as Manila or littleneck,
    cleaned

1. In a large saucepan, place the greens and add cold water to cover, salt, and 1 tablespoon of the oil. Bring to a boil over high heat and cook 5 minutes. Drain and chop coarsely. Reserve.

2. Place the flour in a wide shallow bowl. Heat 3 more tablespoons of the oil in a shallow earthenware casserole dish or Dutch oven over medium-high heat. Dredge the fish in the flour and place in the oil. Cook, turning once, until lightly browned, 2 to 3 minute per side. Transfer to a warm platter and sprinkle with lemon juice. Wipe out the dish.

3. Heat the remaining 2 tablespoons of oil in the casserole dish over medium heat. Add the onion and garlic and cook, stirring, until the onion is wilted, about 3 minutes. Stir in the greens, salt, pepper, vinegar, bay leaf, and parsley. Return the fish to the dish and arrange the greens around the fish. Reduce the heat to low, cover, and cook 15 minutes more.

4. Meanwhile, rinse the clams. Discard any with cracked shells or that do not close tightly when touched. Place the clams in a medium saucepan with ½ cup water. Bring to a boil over high heat, and cook until the clams open, removing each clam as it opens. Discard any unopened clams. Reserve the cooking liquid, remove the clams, and chop the clam meat. Add the clam meat and the reserved liquid to the fish, cover, and cook 5 minutes more. Remove the bay leaf. If using earthenware, serve hot in the dish, or transfer to individual plates.

Stuffed Red Mullet
Salmonetes Rellenos a la Plancha

MAKES 4 SERVINGS

This dish is much easier to prepare than you might think. It is a delectable recipe of red mullet, stuffed with bread crumbs, garlic, onion, parsley, and Serrano ham.

4 skin-on red mullet or red snapper fillets (about
    ½ pound)

Kosher or sea salt

4 tablespoons olive oil

continues...

¼ cup finely chopped onion

2 garlic cloves, finely chopped

¼ cup finely chopped fresh flat-leaf parsley

¼ cup finely chopped Serrano (Spanish cured mountain) ham or prosciutto (about 2 ounces)

½ teaspoon ground sweet paprika, such as Spanish smoked

¼ cup dry white wine

¼ cup bread crumbs

Freshly ground black pepper

8 lemon wedges, for garnish

1. Make several shallow slits in the skin side of the fish. Season all over with salt.

2. Heat 2 tablespoons of the oil in a medium skillet over medium heat. Add the onion, garlic, parsley, and ham and cook, stirring, until the onion is wilted, about 3 minutes. Stir in the paprika, add the wine, and cook until the liquid is reduced by half. Remove from the heat. Stir in the bread crumbs and add salt and pepper.

3. Spread the bread crumb mixture over each of 2 fillets. Place the remaining 2 fillets on top and secure each pair with kitchen string. Wipe out the skillet and heat the remaining 2 tablespoons oil over medium heat. Add the fish and cook, turning once, until browned and just barely opaque when cut in the thickest part, 8 to 10 minutes per inch of thickness.

4. Remove the string. Cut each fish crosswise into 2 portions. Garnish with the lemon wedges and serve hot.

Grouper

Grilled Grouper with Tomatoes and Olive Sauce
Mero Sobre Tomates Confitados y Salsa de Aceitunas

MAKES 4 SERVINGS

This is a relatively simple dish of grilled fish with two sauces that work beautifully together. In order to maintain its full flavor, the tomato compote in this dish must simmer slowly before the fish is added. The olive sauce is a simple mixture of olive oil and mashed black olives.

Tomato Compote

2 tablespoons olive oil, plus more for brushing

2 garlic cloves, finely chopped

2 tablespoons finely chopped onion

1 bay leaf

1 pound tomatoes, finely chopped

¼ teaspoon sugar

Kosher or sea salt

Freshly ground black pepper

½ teaspoon dried thyme

½ teaspoon dried oregano

Black Olive Sauce

20 pitted black olives, preferably Spanish

4 tablespoons olive oil

4 grouper or other fish fillets (about 6 ounces each)

1. Brush a grill or broiler rack with olive oil and place about 4 inches away from the heat source. Preheat the grill or broiler. (Cover the broiler pan with foil for easier cleanup, if you like.)

2. Prepare the compote: Heat the 2 tablespoons oil in a medium skillet over medium heat. Add the garlic, onion, and bay leaf and cook, stirring, until the onion is wilted, about 3 minutes. Reduce the heat to low, add the tomatoes, sugar, salt, thyme, and oregano, and cook until the tomatoes are softened and release their juices, about 3 minutes. Reserve, discarding the bay leaf.

3. Prepare the sauce: In a food processor, place the olives and oil and process until smooth. Transfer to a small serving bowl.

4. Season the fish with salt and pepper. Grill over direct heat, turning once, until browned on each side and just barely opaque when cut in the thickest part, 2 to 3 minutes per side. On each of 4 individual plates, spread the compote in the center. Place the fish over the compote and the sauce to one side.

Grouper with Scallops
Mero con Salsa de Vieiras

MAKES 4 SERVINGS

The very best scallops in the world can be found in the region of Galicia, and this popular shellfish has made its way into innumerable Spanish recipes featuring fillets of fish. This version is particularly tasty as the scallops are only lightly grilled to maintain their tender texture.

4 grouper fillets (about ½ pound each)

2 tablespoons olive oil

4 garlic cloves

¼ cup finely chopped onion

Kosher or sea salt

¼ cup dry white wine

¼ cup storebought or homemade Fish Broth or bottled clam juice

Preheat the oven to 350°F. Preheat a grill or grill pan. In a shallow earthenware casserole dish or Dutch oven, add the fish, oil, garlic, onion, salt, and wine. Place in the oven while making the scallops.

Grill the scallops, turning once, until browned, about 2 minutes per side. Add to the casserole dish and add the broth. Bake 15 to 20 minutes or until the fish is just barely opaque when cut in the thickest part. Serve hot.

Grouper with Swiss Chard
Mero con Grelos

MAKES 4 SERVINGS

Delicious and very easy to prepare, this is a typical Spanish recipe for fish with greens or grelos, a vegetable that is almost identical to our Swiss chard. This version also calls for potatoes, which make the dish that much more filling and substantial.

2 garlic cloves, coarsely chopped

2 teaspoons ground bittersweet paprika, such as Spanish smoked

2 tablespoons olive oil plus more, for drizzling

4 grouper or other fish steaks (about ½ pound each), about 1 inch thick

2 medium potatoes, peeled and cut into ¼-inch slices

Kosher or sea salt

½ pound Swiss chard, well washed, thick stems trimmed, and coarsely chopped

¼ cup finely chopped onion

1 tablespoon vinegar

1. Preheat the oven to 350°F. In a mortar or mini-processor, mash the garlic, paprika, and the 2 tablespoons oil and reserve. Season the fish with salt.

2. In a greased baking dish, arrange the potatoes in layers, season with salt, and spread with the mortar mixture. Arrange the Swiss chard over the potatoes, and sprinkle with the onion and vinegar. Cover and bake about 15 minutes or until the potatoes are tender. Arrange the fish over the casserole, drizzle with oil, and bake about 5 minutes more or until the fish is just barely opaque inside when cut with a small sharp knife. Serve hot.

Roasted Grouper with Wine, Potatoes, and Pine Nuts

Mero con Patatas, Vino Blanco y Piñones

MAKES 4 SERVINGS

Wine sauce heavily flavored with onion and garlic is what gives this popular dish its essence. When baked with potatoes and pine nuts, the results are excellent.

2 medium potatoes, peeled and thinly sliced

2 large onions, thinly sliced

¼ cup olive oil plus more, for drizzling

4 grouper steaks (about ½ pound each), cut into 4 pieces

2 medium tomatoes, chopped (about 1⅓ cup)

8 garlic cloves, coarsely chopped

3 tablespoons pine nuts

2 tablespoons finely chopped fresh flat-leaf parsley

¼ cup dry white wine

Kosher or sea salt

Freshly ground black pepper

Preheat the oven to 350°F. In a greased baking dish, place the potatoes and onions and bake, stirring once or twice, about 20 minutes or until the potatoes are tender. Add the fish, tomatoes, garlic, pine nuts, and parsley. Drizzle with oil and add the wine. Bake about 10 minutes more or until the fish is just barely opaque inside when cut with a small sharp knife. Serve hot.

Hake in Hard Cider Sauce

Merluza a la Sidra

MAKES 4 SERVINGS

Asturias in the northern region of Spain is famous for its hard ciders, which is both the most popular drink and the ingredient of choice for cooking. Most recipes call for hard cider, drier than common cider and with a higher alcohol content.

1 dozen small clams

4 tablespoons olive oil

2 large new potatoes, peeled and thinly sliced

Salt

1 cup water

1 bay leaf

½ teaspoon dried thyme

4 peppercorns

1 slice medium onion

1 sprig parsley

4 fish steaks, such as hake or fresh cod (about ½ pound each), about 1 inch thick, cut into 4 pieces

2 medium onions, finely chopped (about 1⅓ cups)

2 garlic cloves, finely chopped

2 tablespoons all-purpose flour

1 tablespoon ground paprika

1 cup hard cider

1 tablespoon finely chopped fresh flat-leaf parsley

1. In a large bowl, place the clams, add cold water to cover, and let sit 30 minutes. Drain. Discard any clams with cracked shells or that do not close tightly when touched.

2. Heat 2 tablespoons of the oil in a medium skillet over medium heat. Add the potatoes in layers, season with salt, cover, and cook, turning occasionally, until the potatoes are tender but not browned, about 15 minutes. Arrange the potatoes in the bottom of 4 individual earthenware casserole dishes.

3. In a medium skillet, arrange the clams and add the water. Bring to a boil over high heat, removing the clams as they open. Discard any unopened clams, reserving the liquid in the skillet. Arrange 3 clams around the side of each casserole dish.

4. In the skillet, add the bay leaf, thyme, peppercorns, onion slice, and parsley sprig. Arrange the fish in the skillet, cover, and cook about 10 minutes. Transfer the fish to the casserole dishes. Pass the cooking liquid through a fine-mesh strainer and reserve 1½ cups, adding water or clam juice if necessary. Discard the solids. Wipe out the skillet.

5. Preheat the oven to 350°F. In the skillet, heat the remaining 2 tablespoons oil over medium heat. Add the onion and garlic and cook, stirring, until the onion is wilted, about 5 minutes. Reduce the heat to low, add the flour and paprika, and cook, stirring, 2 to 3 minutes. Gradually add the reserved cooking liquid and the cider. Sprinkle in the parsley and simmer about 10 minutes. Pour the sauce over the fish. Transfer to the oven and bake 15 minutes. Serve hot in the casserole dishes.

Hake, Galician Style
Merluza a la Gallega

MAKES 4 SERVINGS

Paprika is the predominant spice used in most dishes that originated in Galicia. It adds a delightful zest to this flavorful baked fish recipe.

½ cup plus 4 teaspoons olive oil

1 medium onion, chopped (about ⅔ cup)

2 garlic cloves, mashed in a garlic press or mortar

2 tablespoons finely chopped fresh flat-leaf parsley

2 teaspoons ground paprika

1½ pounds new potatoes, peeled and cut into ⅛-inch slices

1 tablespoon all-purpose flour

Salt

Freshly ground black pepper

Dash of ground cloves

½ teaspoon dried thyme

1 bay leaf

4 fish steaks, such as hake or fresh cod (about ½ pound each), about 1 inch thick

1. Preheat the oven to 350°F. Heat the ½ cup oil in a medium skillet over medium heat. Add the onion and cook, stirring, until wilted, about 5 minutes. Stir in the garlic, 1 tablespoon of the parsley, and the paprika. Add the potatoes and turn to coat well with the oil. Sprinkle in the flour, then add water to cover. Sprinkle with salt, pepper, cloves, and thyme and add the bay leaf. Cover and cook 25 minutes more or until the potatoes are just tender.

2. Divide the potatoes among 4 individual earthenware casserole dishes and arrange a fish steak on top. Season with salt and pepper. Drizzle the remaining 4 teaspoons oil over the fish, 1 teaspoon per fish. Bake 15 minutes or just until the fish flakes when tested with a fork.

Hake with Capers
Merluza con Alcaparras

MAKES 4 SERVINGS

Capers are the flower buds of the caper bush that thrive in the warmer climates of southern Spain. Capers are typically available either bottled in brine or dried in sea salt. Here, they enhance a lemon sauce served over fried hake.

4 fish steaks, such as hake or fresh cod (about ½ pound each), about 1 inch thick

Salt

All-purpose flour, for dredging

Olive oil, for frying

2 large eggs, lightly beaten

6 tablespoons unsalted butter

2 tablespoons capers (nonpareil preferred), rinsed and drained

8 lemon wedges, for garnish

1. Place the flour and eggs into separate wide shallow bowls. Season the fish with salt. Heat at least ½ inch of oil in a medium skillet over medium-high heat (or better still, use a deep fryer set at 375°F) until it quickly browns a cube of bread. Dredge the fish in the flour, dip into the egg, and place in the oil. Cook, turning once, until golden and cooked through. Transfer with a slotted spatula to paper towels and let drain. Transfer to individual plates.

2. Meanwhile, melt the butter in a small saucepan over low heat. Add the capers and cook 3 to 4 minutes. Pour over the fish. Garnish with the lemon wedges and serve hot.

Hake with Peas in Saffron Sauce
Merluza en Amarillo a la Gaditana

MAKES 4 SERVINGS

Amarillo (yellow) is the color of the sauce in this very popular Andalucian dish. The sauce combines the distinctive flavor of saffron, which also lends its color, with the sweetness of the pea.

1½ cups storebought or homemade Fish Broth (page 199; partial recipe) or bottled clam juice

4 hake or scrod steaks (about ½ pound each), about 1 inch thick

Kosher or sea salt

3 tablespoons olive oil

6 garlic cloves, finely chopped

1 medium onion, finely chopped (about ⅔ cup)

2 bay leaves

½ cup dry white wine

1 tablespoon all-purpose flour

⅔ cup fresh or frozen peas

Scant ¼ teaspoon saffron threads, crumbled

1. Prepare the broth if necessary. Season the fish on both sides with salt and let sit at room temperature 15 minutes. Heat the oil in a medium skillet over medium heat. Add the fish and cook, turning once, until the flesh just turns opaque inside, 8 to 9 minutes. Transfer the fish to a shallow earthenware casserole dish, reserving the oil in the skillet.

2. In the skillet over medium heat, add the garlic, onion, and bay leaf and cook, stirring, until the onion is wilted, about 5 minutes. Add the wine and cook until the wine has evaporated. Stir in the flour and cook 1 minute, then add the peas, broth, and saffron. Reduce the heat to low and simmer, stirring frequently, about 5 minutes. Remove from the heat and let sit 15 minutes. Remove the bay leaf and pour over the fish. Return the casserole dish to the stovetop over medium heat to reheat and serve hot.

Hake in Saffron Sauce
Merluza al Azafrán

MAKES 4 SERVINGS

Saffron adds a distinctive taste, yellow color, and wonderful aroma to this dish. It has a very strong flavor and should be used only in small quantities. Try to use saffron from the La Mancha region of Spain—I consider it the best.

All-purpose flour, for dredging

2 tablespoons olive oil

1½ pounds hake steak, about 1 inch thick, cut into
    4 pieces

1 medium onion

2 garlic cloves

2 medium green bell peppers

3 medium tomatoes, finely chopped (about 2 cups)

½ cup white wine or ¼ cup brandy

¼ cup storebought or homemade Fish Broth or
    bottled clam juice

¼ teaspoon saffron threads, crumbled

2 tablespoons finely chopped fresh flat-leaf parsley

Kosher or sea salt

1. Place the flour in a wide shallow bowl. Heat the oil in a medium skillet over medium heat. Dredge the fish in the flour and place in the oil. Cook, turning once, until golden, 2 to 4 minutes per side. Transfer to a platter.

2. Add the onion, garlic, bell peppers, tomatoes, wine, broth, saffron, and parsley to the pan and cook, stirring, until the vegetables soften. Arrange the fish over the vegetables, and cook, turning the fish once, until just barely opaque inside when cut with a small sharp knife. Serve hot.

Hake Filled with Tomato and Ham
Merluza Rellena

MAKES 4 SERVINGS

Spaniards adore their hake and enjoy it prepared in a seemingly endless array of ways. This delicious and popular version of merluza *calls for tomato, ham, egg, bread crumbs, and wine.*

1 medium tomato, finely chopped (about ⅔ cup)

¼ cup finely chopped Serrano (Spanish cured
    mountain) ham or prosciutto (about 2 ounces)

1 tablespoon finely chopped fresh flat-leaf parsley

2 tablespoons bread crumbs

1 garlic clove, finely chopped

Juice of 1 lemon

1 hard-boiled egg, sliced

1½ to 2 pounds hake (skinned, boned, and
    butterflied)

¼ cup dry white wine

2 tablespoons olive oil

Kosher or sea salt

1 tablespoon capers (nonpareil preferred), rinsed and
    drained, for garnish

Preheat the oven to 400°F. In a medium bowl, combine the tomato, ham, parsley, bread crumbs, garlic, lemon juice, and egg. Stuff the fish cavity with this mixture and secure with kitchen string. Place in a shallow earthenware casserole dish or Dutch oven. Pour the wine over the fish, drizzle with the olive oil, and season with salt. Bake, basting occasionally with the sauce, about 15 minutes or until the fish is just opaque inside when cut with a small sharp knife. Scatter the capers over the fish. If using earthenware, serve hot in the dish, or divide into portions and transfer to individual plates.

Hake Filled with Shrimp in Sweet Sherry

Merluza Rellena al Pedro Ximénez

MAKES 4 SERVINGS

In the region of Andalucía, it is common to cook fish using sherry. Most dishes call for a dry sherry, but this recipe uses sweet Pedro Ximénez sherry. You'll need to gently pound the fish into thin fillets before stuffing them with the shrimp.

¼ cup finely chopped onion

2 tablespoons olive oil

1 pound hake steak, about 1 inch thick, cut into 4 pieces

12 small shrimp, shelled and deveined

Kosher or sea salt

Freshly ground black pepper

¼ cup sweet sherry, such as Spanish cream

¼ cup storebought or homemade Fish Broth or bottled clam juice

1. Preheat the oven to 350°F. Heat the oil in a medium skillet over medium heat. Add the onion and cook, stirring, until wilted, about 5 minutes. To stuff the fish, pound each fish to ½ inch thick. With a sharp knife split each pounded fish steak in half. On each steak, place 3 shrimp and ¼ of the onion, and season with salt and pepper. Cover with the remaining 4 steak pieces and close with toothpicks.

2. Place the stuffed fish pieces in a shallow earthenware casserole dish or Dutch oven. Pour in the broth. Bake about 10 minutes or until the fish is almost done. Add the sherry and bake about 5 minutes more, or until the sauce is reduced and thickened slightly and the fish is just barely opaque inside when cut with a small sharp knife. If using earthenware, serve hot in the dish, or transfer to individual plates.

Hake in Garlic Sauce with Fried Garlic

Merluza a la Vasca con Ajo Frito

MAKES 4 SERVINGS

One of the easiest and most popular ways to prepare hake or fresh cod is a la vasca, which means in garlic sauce. In this version, the fish is made with the addition of fried garlic and parsley.

½ pound cockles or 12 Manila or littleneck clams

4 hake or scrod steaks (about ½ pound each), about 1 inch thick

Kosher or sea salt

8 tablespoons extra-virgin olive oil

8 garlic cloves, finely chopped

1 tablespoon all-purpose flour

¼ cup storebought or homemade Fish Broth or bottled clam juice

4 tablespoons finely chopped fresh flat-leaf parsley

1. In a large bowl, place the cockles, add cold water to cover, and let sit 30 minutes. Drain. Discard any cockles with cracked shells or that do not close tightly when touched.

2. Season the fish with salt and let sit a few minutes. In a shallow earthenware casserole dish or Dutch oven, heat 4 tablespoons of the oil over medium heat. Add half of the garlic and cook, stirring, until lightly colored. Add the fish and clams and sprinkle the flour over the fish. Gently shake the casserole dish, adding the broth and continuing to shake the pan so that the sauce becomes smooth and slightly thickened. Reduce the heat to medium low, cover, and cook 3 minutes more.

3. Turn the fish and continue gently shaking the casserole dish. Sprinkle the parsley over the fish, shake again, cover, and cook about 3 minutes more or until the fish is just barely opaque when cut with a small sharp knife. Discard any unopened clams.

4. Heat the remaining 4 tablespoons oil in a small skillet over medium heat. Add the remaining half of the garlic and cook, stirring, until it begins to color. Spoon the garlic and hot oil over the fish and parsley (the oil will fry the parsley). Shake again. If using earthenware, serve hot in the dish, or transfer to individual plates.

Carmen's Stuffed Hake with Two Sauces

Merluza Rellena Dos Salsas de Mi Amiga Carmen

MAKES 4 SERVINGS

This dish is served cold stuffed with egg slices and pimientos and accompanied by both mayonnaise, preferably fresh, and vinaigrette.

PREPARE AT LEAST 2 HOURS IN ADVANCE

Vinaigrette

½ cup extra-virgin olive oil

2 tablespoons wine vinegar, such as white

2 tablespoons chopped cornichon or dill pickle

2 teaspoons capers in vinegar (nonpareil preferred), drained

2 tablespoons finely chopped onion

2 tablespoons finely chopped (jarred) piquillo peppers or pimiento

1 tablespoon finely chopped fresh flat-leaf parsley

Salt

Freshly ground black pepper

4 hake steaks (about 6 ounces each), about ¾ inch thick

2 hard-boiled eggs, sliced

4 (jarred) piquillo peppers or 2 pimientos, cut into ½-inch strips

Kosher or sea salt

2 tablespoons bottled clam juice or water

2 tablespoons fresh lemon juice

2 tablespoons extra-virgin olive oil

Mayonnaise (mayonesa, page 359)

1. Prepare the vinaigrette: In a small bowl, whisk together the oil and vinegar, then stir in the remaining ingredients. Reserve.

2. To stuff the fish, with a sharp knife split the steaks in half. Arrange the egg and pimiento over half of the steaks. Sprinkle with salt and cover with the remaining steaks. Season the top of the fish with salt.

3. Preheat the oven to 400°F. In a shallow earthenware casserole dish or Dutch oven, combine the clam juice, lemon juice, and oil. Arrange the fish in the dish. Bake, basting with the juices occasionally, about 15 minutes or until the fish is just opaque inside when cut with a small sharp knife. Let cool.

4. Cover the fish and let marinate in the refrigerator at least 2 hours. Slice the fish crosswise into pieces about 1 inch wide. Serve hot with the mayonnaise and vinaigrette on the side.

Hake Stuffed with Shrimp, Mushrooms, and Capers
Cola de Merluza "Monte Igueldo"

MAKES 4 SERVINGS

My friend Pedro Subijana has a restaurant high up on Monte Igueldo, a mountain in the city of San Sebastián with a beautiful view of the sea. He was kind enough to share this recipe with me, which came from his father. You can also serve this with cooked sliced potatoes and eggs. If you do, spoon the juices and parsley over them as well before serving.

2 pounds hake, about ¾ inch thick

Salt

Freshly ground black pepper

8 teaspoons fresh lemon juice

2 tablespoon olive oil

1 medium onion, finely chopped (about ⅔ cup)

1 small garlic clove, finely chopped

6 medium white or brown mushrooms, rinsed, stems removed, and thinly sliced lengthwise

12 small shrimp, shelled, deveined, and halved lengthwise

2 hard-boiled eggs, finely chopped

7 tablespoons dry white wine

1 slice good-quality sandwich bread, crust removed, grated or cut into very small pieces

2 teaspoons capers in vinegar (nonpareil preferred), drained

1 large egg, separated

Olive oil, for brushing

2 tablespoons unsalted butter, cut into small pieces

3 tablespoons chicken broth or vegetable broth

2 tablespoons finely chopped fresh flat-leaf parsley

1. Butterfly the fish and season inside with salt, pepper, and 4 teaspoons of the lemon juice. Heat the oil in a medium skillet over medium heat. Add the onion and garlic, and cook, stirring, until the onion is wilted, about 5 minutes. Add the mushrooms and shrimp and cook, stirring, until the shrimp are pink, about 2 minutes more. Stir in the chopped eggs and 4 tablespoons of the wine. Sprinkle with the bread and capers.

2. Preheat the oven to 450°F. In a small bowl, beat the egg white with an electric hand-held beater until stiff, then beat in the yolk. Stir into the onion mixture and season well with salt. Spread on one side of the butterflied fish and cover with the top portion. Tie with kitchen string and wrap the cut edge with foil.

3. Place the fish in a greased baking dish and brush the top with oil. Scatter the butter in the baking dish and add the remaining 3 tablespoons wine and the broth.

4. Bake 15 to 20 minutes until just opaque inside. Sprinkle with the remaining 4 teaspoons lemon juice. Cut the fish into 4 pieces and spoon the pan juices over the fish. Sprinkle with the parsley and serve hot.

Hake in Green Sauce with Peas
Merluza en Salsa Verde con Guisantes

MAKES 4 SERVINGS

This delicious recipe for hake prepared in green sauce gets its color from parsley and peas. This is a very popular sauce based on a traditional recipe often used by fishermen.

All-purpose flour, for dredging

4 hake or scrod steaks (about ½ pound each), about 1 inch thick

¼ cup olive oil

¼ cup finely chopped onion

6 garlic cloves, finely chopped

6 tablespoons finely chopped fresh flat-leaf parsley

½ cup dry white wine

¼ cup storebought or homemade Fish Broth or
    bottled clam juice

Kosher or sea salt

Freshly ground black pepper

⅔ cup peas

1-inch piece dried red chile pepper, seeded

Place the flour for dredging in a wide shallow bowl and dredge the fish in the flour. Heat the oil in a medium skillet over medium-high heat. Add the onion, garlic, and 4 tablespoons of the parsley and cook, stirring, until wilted, about 4 minutes. Add the wine, broth, salt, black pepper, peas, chile pepper, and fish and bring to a boil. Cook about 5 minutes more. Sprinkle with the remaining 2 tablespoons parsley and serve hot.

Hake, Andalucian Style, with Shellfish and Pine Nuts
Merluza a la Andaluza

MAKES 4 SERVINGS

Even though Andalucía has access to an abundance of different seafood, the region's beloved hake with its delicate flavor is always a favorite. This recipe is enhanced by the addition of small clams with an added accent created by the pine nuts.

2 dozen small clams, such as Manila

2 squid, cleaned

2 tablespoons olive oil

4 garlic cloves, finely chopped

2 tablespoons pine nuts

4 hake steaks (about ½ pound each), about 1 inch
    thick

Kosher or sea salt

Freshly ground black pepper

⅓ cup dry white wine

¾ cup storebought or homemade Fish Broth or
    bottled clam juice

2 tablespoons finely chopped fresh flat-leaf parsley

8 large shrimp, shelled and deveined

1. Rinse the clams. Discard any clams with cracked shells or that do not close tightly when touched. Meanwhile, cut the squid body into rings and the tentacles into bite-size pieces.

2. Heat the oil in a shallow earthenware casserole dish or Dutch oven over medium heat. Add the garlic and pine nuts and cook, stirring, until golden, about 4 minutes. Add the squid and hake, sprinkle with salt and pepper, stir in the wine, and cook 1 minute. Add the broth, parsley, clams, and shrimp and cook until the clams open. Discard any unopened clams. If using earthenware, serve hot in the dish, or transfer to individual plates.

Hake and Shellfish in Green Sauce
Merluza a la Vasca

MAKES 4 SERVINGS

Hake is found in abundance and prepared with great variations in all the many regions of Spain. This recipe is as delicious as it is beautiful, as each individual casserole dish (cazuela) is served with clams, mussels, parsley, and chopped egg. The clams and mussels are not merely decorative; their juices add flavor to the sauce. Boiled potatoes may also be added to this dish if you like.

1 dozen small clams, such as Manila or littleneck

1 dozen small mussels

All-purpose flour, for dredging

4 fish steaks, such as hake (about ½ pound each),
    about 1 inch thick

Salt

Freshly ground black pepper

continues . . .

4 tablespoons olive oil

1 tablespoon fresh lemon juice

4 garlic cloves, finely chopped

3 tablespoons finely chopped onion

2 tablespoons all-purpose flour

¾ cup white wine

¾ cup storebought or homemade Fish Broth or bottled clam juice

6 tablespoons finely chopped fresh flat-leaf parsley

¾ cup fresh or frozen peas

1 hard-boiled egg, finely chopped

1. Rinse the clams and mussels well. Cut or pull off the mussel beards. Discard any clams or mussels with cracked shells or that do not close tightly when touched. Place the flour in a wide shallow bowl.

2. Meanwhile, season the fish with salt and pepper. Heat 2 tablespoons of the oil in a large skillet over medium-high heat. Dredge the fish in the flour and place in the oil. Cook, turning once, about 1 minute per side. Transfer to individual earthenware casserole dishes and sprinkle with lemon juice. Wipe out the skillet.

3. Preheat the oven to 350°F. Heat the remaining 2 tablespoons oil in the skillet over medium heat. Add the garlic and onion and cook, stirring, until the onion is wilted, about 3 minutes. Stir in the 2 tablespoons flour and gradually add the wine and broth. Cook, stirring, until the liquid is reduced and the sauce is thickened and smooth. Stir in 5 tablespoons of the parsley, the peas, salt, and pepper.

4. Spoon sauce over each fish and garnish each with 3 clams and 3 mussels. Bake about 20 minutes or until the fish is just opaque inside and the shellfish have opened. Discard any unopened shellfish. Spoon the sauce over the fish and divide the clams and mussels to each plate. Sprinkle each dish with the remaining 1 tablespoon parsley and the egg. Serve hot.

Hake with Garlic Sauce and Parsley
Colitas de Merluza con Alioli y Perejil

MAKES 4 SERVINGS

*This recipe, as well as so many others, derives its flavor from garlic sauce (*alioli*), a sauce made from olive oil and garlic, sometimes with a touch of egg.*

¼ cup Garlic Sauce (alioli; partial recipe; page 284)

3 tablespoons olive oil

2 tablespoons finely chopped fresh flat-leaf parsley

1 medium red bell pepper, cut into very thin strips

1 medium onion, cut into very thin strips

2 leeks, trimmed, well washed, and cut into very thin strips

1 medium tomato, coarsely chopped (about ⅔ cup)

4 fresh hake steaks or scrod fillets (about ½ pound each), 1 inch thick

1 tablespoon vinegar

2 tablespoons finely chopped fresh flat-leaf parsley

Bread crumbs

1. Prepare the sauce if necessary. Preheat the oven to 400°F. Heat 2 tablespoons of the oil in a medium skillet over medium heat. Add the bell pepper, onion, leeks, and tomato and cook, stirring, until softened, about 8 minutes.

2. Transfer to a roasting pan, and arrange the fish over the vegetables. Drizzle with the vinegar and the remaining 1 tablespoon oil. Spread the garlic sauce over the fish and sprinkle with the parsley and bread crumbs. Roast 15 to 20 minutes or until the fish is just barely opaque inside when cut with a small sharp knife. Serve hot.

Hake with Ham and Cheese
Merluza a la Madrileña

MAKES 4 SERVINGS

This simple recipe is one of my very favorites. The fish steaks are stuffed with a delicious filling of cured ham and cheese, rolled in bread crumbs, then topped with fresh tomato sauce.

4 hake steaks (about ½ pound each), about 1¼ inches thick

4 thin slices Serrano (Spanish cured mountain) ham or prosciutto

4 thin slices mild cheese, such as Jarlsberg or Fontina

All-purpose flour, for dredging

2 large eggs, lightly beaten

Bread crumbs

3 tablespoons olive oil

Fresh Tomato Sauce

1 tablespoon olive oil

1 medium onion, finely chopped (about ⅔ cup)

2 medium ripe tomatoes, finely chopped (about 1⅓ cups)

1 tablespoon finely chopped fresh flat-leaf parsley

Salt

Freshly ground black pepper

1. Divide each steak lengthwise into 2 medallions. To stuff the fish, with a sharp knife split each medallion horizontally in half. Place 1 slice of ham and 1 slice of cheese on 4 of the medallions. Cover with the remaining 4 medallions.

2. Place the flour, eggs, and bread crumbs in separate wide shallow bowls. Dredge each medallion in the flour, coating the sides well, dip in the egg, and dredge in the bread crumbs. Let sit on a platter about 20 minutes or until dry.

3. Meanwhile, prepare the sauce: Heat the 1 tablespoon oil in a medium skillet over low heat. Add the onion, cover, and cook until wilted, about 5 minutes. Add the tomatoes, parsley, salt, and pepper and cook uncovered until the tomatoes are tender, 10 to 15 minutes.

4. In a large skillet, heat the 3 tablespoons oil over medium-high heat until it reaches the smoking point. Add the fish, reduce the heat to medium, and cook until browned and just opaque inside, 2 to 4 minutes per side. Spoon the tomatoes over the fish and serve hot, or serve with the tomatoes on the side.

Coated Hake Filled with Ham and Olives
Merluza Rellena de Jamón y Aceitunas "Bodegas Osborne"

MAKES 4 SERVINGS

I first tasted this delicious and beautifully presented dish at the Bodegas Osborne in Puerto de Santa María. You can prepare the fish ahead of time, but its gratin of mayonnaise and egg white should be broiled right before serving.

2 pounds hake or scrod steaks, ¾ to 1 inch thick

Kosher or sea salt

12 pitted green olives, preferably Spanish

¼ cup finely chopped Serrano (Spanish cured mountain) ham or prosciutto (about 2 ounces)

3 tablespoons olive oil

All-purpose flour, for dredging

2 large eggs, lightly beaten

1 small egg white

¾ cup mayonnaise (mayonesa; page 359)

1. To stuff the fish, with a sharp knife split the steaks in half. Season the fish on all sides. Arrange the olives and sprinkle the ham on half of the steaks. Cover with the remaining pieces of fish. Place the flour and beaten eggs in separate wide shallow bowls.

2. Heat the oil in a medium saucepan over medium heat. Dredge the fish in the flour, dip in the egg, and place in the oil. Cook, turning once, until the fish is just barely opaque inside when cut with a small sharp knife, about 8 minutes. Transfer to an ovenproof baking dish.

3. Place a broiler rack about 4 inches from the heat source and preheat the broiler. (Cover the broiler pan with foil for easier cleanup, if you like.) In a small bowl, beat the egg white with an electric hand-held beater until stiff but not dry (peaks hold their shape). Fold in the mayonnaise. With a rubber spatula, spread the mixture over the top of each fish. Broil about 1 minute or until browned—watch carefully. Serve hot.

Hake, Pine Nut, and Piquillo Pepper Pie
Pastel de Merluza

MAKES ONE 9-INCH PIE

This is a classic dish from Albacete where my friend Pilar grew up. The key ingredients in this sensational fish pie are pine nuts and piquillo peppers. The crust is surprisingly light because it is made with olive oil and not butter.

Pastry Crust

About 1½ cups all-purpose flour

½ teaspoon salt

½ cup mild olive oil

½ cup dry white wine

1 tablespoon plus 2 teaspoons cold water

¾ pound scrod steak, 1 to 1½ inches thick

About ½ cup storebought or homemade Fish Broth or bottled clam juice

¼ cup olive oil

3 tablespoons pine nuts

2 tablespoons finely chopped onion

¼ cup all-purpose flour

¼ cup milk

2 tablespoons dry white wine

Salt

Freshly ground black pepper

A generous amount of grated or ground nutmeg

1 tablespoon finely chopped fresh flat-leaf parsley

4 (jarred) piquillo peppers or 2 pimientos, cut into ½-inch strips

2 hard-boiled eggs, sliced

1 large egg, lightly beaten

1. Prepare the crust: Combine the flour and salt in a medium bowl. Add the oil and wine and enough water to make a dough. Shape into a ball, cover with plastic wrap, and reserve.

2. Place the fish in a large saucepan, add broth to cover, and bring to a boil over high heat. Reduce the heat to low, cover, and simmer about 10 minutes. Transfer the fish to a platter and chop finely. Reserve ½ cup plus 2 tablespoons of the cooking liquid. Wipe out the saucepan.

3. In the same saucepan, heat the oil over medium heat. Add the pine nuts and cook, stirring, until golden. Transfer with a slotted spoon to paper towels and let drain. Add the onion and cook, stirring, until wilted, about 3 minutes. Add the flour and cook, stirring, until the mixture is smooth and bubbly. Gradually add the milk, the reserved cooking liquid, and the wine and cook, stirring constantly, until thickened and smooth. Season with salt, pepper, and nutmeg, then stir in the fish and parsley.

4. Preheat the oven to 375°F. Divide the dough in half. Roll 1 piece into an 11-inch round and place on a cookie sheet. Spread the fish mixture over the dough to within 1 inch of the edge and arrange the piquillos and eggs over the fish mixture. Scatter the pine nuts over the top.

5. Roll the remaining 1 piece dough into an 11-inch round and place over the pie. Roll up the edges and pinch to seal. Cut decorative slits in the top crust with a sharp thin knife and brush with the beaten egg. Bake about 40 minutes or until the crust is browned. Let cool 15 minutes, then cut into wedges and serve hot.

Hake Loaf

Pastel de Merluza de la Mamá de Luis

MAKES 6 TO 8 SERVINGS

This recipe comes from Clara Orozco, my mother-in-law and one of the greatest cooks I have known. Born in the Basque city of San Sebastián, she lived in Madrid all her life and taught me a lot about Spanish cooking. This version of fish loaf was one of her favorite dishes.

PREPARE AT LEAST 3 HOURS IN ADVANCE

2 tablespoons butter

1 medium onion, finely chopped (about ⅔ cup)

1 medium carrot, peeled and cut into several pieces

1 leek, trimmed and well washed

1 cup dry white wine

1 pound hake steaks, about 1 inch thick (skinned and boned)

1 bay leaf

2 sprigs parsley

Kosher or sea salt

1½ thin slices sandwich bread, crust removed

2 tablespoons tomato sauce

1 pimiento, finely chopped

5 large eggs

3 tablespoons heavy cream

Freshly ground black pepper

⅛ teaspoon nutmeg

Mayonnaise (mayonesa, page 359)

1. Grease a 9¼ x 5¼-inch loaf pan. Heat the butter in a shallow earthenware casserole dish or Dutch oven over medium heat. Add the onion, carrot, and leek and cook, stirring, until all are softened, about 8 minutes. Increase the heat to high, add the wine, and cook until the liquid is reduced by half. Add the fish, add water to cover, then add the bay leaf, parsley, and salt, and bring to a boil. Reduce the heat to low, cover, and simmer 15 minutes. Transfer the fish to a plate and shred with your fingers. Pass the cooking liquid through a fine-mesh strainer into a medium shallow bowl and reserve ¾ cup (add water if there is not enough cooking liquid).

2. Add the bread to the reserved liquid. Add the shredded fish, tomato sauce, pimiento, and raisins. In a small bowl, beat the eggs and cream with a fork and add to the fish mixture. Season with salt, pepper, and nutmeg. Pour into the loaf pan and cover tightly with foil.

3. In a skillet large enough to hold the loaf pan, place enough water to reach halfway up the loaf pan and bring to a boil over high heat. Reduce the heat to medium, place the loaf pan in the water, and cook about 1½ hours, replenishing the water as necessary. Remove the pan from the water, loosen the foil, and let cool. Refrigerate at least 2 hours.

4. Place the mayonnaise in a small serving bowl. Loosen the sides of the loaf with a knife and unmold onto a serving platter. Cut into slices and serve cold with the mayonnaise.

Hake Roll with Green Sauce

Rollo de Merluza

MAKES 4 TO 6 SERVINGS

This delicious recipe calls for the fish to be mixed in a bowl with bread crumbs, ham, eggs, and salt—and then shaped into a roll. The flavors blend perfectly, and it makes for a beautiful presentation.

2½ pounds hake steak, about 1 inch thick

1 cup bread crumbs

½ pound Serrano (Spanish cured mountain) ham or prosciutto, cut into ¼-inch cubes

3 large eggs

Salt

All-purpose flour, for dredging

3 tablespoons olive oil

continues...

Green Sauce

¾ cup finely chopped fresh flat-leaf parsley

3 garlic cloves, coarsely chopped

¼ teaspoon salt

2 tablespoons olive oil

2 teaspoons all-purpose flour

I. Place the fish in a medium pot and add water to cover (at least 3 cups). Bring to a boil over medium-high heat and cook until opaque inside. Transfer the fish to a plate, reserving 2 cups of the cooking liquid (add more water if there is not enough). Shred the fish with your fingers. In a small bowl, mix the bread crumbs and ½ cup of the reserved liquid. In a large bowl, mix the fish, bread crumbs, ham, eggs, and salt. Shape the mixture into a 10 x 3-inch roll. Place the flour in a large plate.

2. Heat the 3 tablespoons oil in a deep earthenware casserole dish or Dutch oven over medium heat. Dredge the fish roll in the flour and place in the oil. Cook, turning occasionally, until browned on all sides. Transfer to a platter. Wipe out the casserole dish.

3. Prepare the green sauce: In a food processor or blender, place the parsley, garlic, and salt and process until as finely chopped as possible. Gradually add the remaining 1½ cups reserved cooking liquid.

4. Heat 2 tablespoons of the oil in a deep earthenware casserole dish or Dutch oven over medium heat. Stir in the flour, then add the processor mixture. Cook, stirring, until slightly thickened. Add the fish roll, cover, and cook 20 minutes. Cut the roll into thick slices, and spoon the sauce over the slices. If using earthenware, serve hot in the dish, or transfer to individual plates.

Monkfish and Shark

Old-Style Marinated Monkfish
Escabeche de Rape a la Antigua

MAKES 4 SERVINGS

Escabeche *in Spanish cooking generally refers to a spiced vinegar and wine combination in which the fish first cooks then marinates. A la antigua indicates that the recipe is old and traditional. Monkfish, once known as "the poor man's lobster" is perfect for this recipe, but other firm fish such as tuna or halibut work just as well.*

PREPARE AT LEAST 8 HOURS IN ADVANCE

4 monkfish, tuna, or halibut steaks (about ½ pound each), about 1 inch thick

Kosher or sea salt

Freshly ground black pepper

2 tablespoons olive oil

2 medium onions, slivered

1 medium carrot, peeled and cut crosswise into ¼-inch slices

½ cup wine vinegar

1 cup dry white wine

One coin-size slice fresh ginger, peeled and crushed with the back of a wooden spoon

8 peppercorns

6 coriander seeds

½ teaspoon ground cumin

Scant ⅛ teaspoon saffron threads, crumbled

1 garlic clove

1 bay leaf

I. Season the fish with salt and pepper. Heat the oil in a shallow earthenware casserole dish or Dutch oven over medium heat. Add the fish and cook, turning once, until golden, 2 to 5 minutes per side. Transfer to a platter.

2. In the same oil, add the onion and carrots and cook, stirring, 1 minute. Reduce the heat to low, cover, and cook until the carrots are softened, about 10 minutes more. Add the remaining ingredients and bring to a boil over medium-high heat. Reduce the heat to medium and cook about 15 minutes more to reduce the liquid. Let cool.

3. Return the fish to the casserole dish, cover, and let marinate in the refrigerator at least 8 hours up to 48 hours, turning the fish and spooning the marinade over them occasionally. Arrange the vegetables over and around the fish and spoon the marinade over the top. Remove the bay leaf. Serve cold or at room temperature.

Monkfish Marinera

Rape Marinera

MAKES 4 SERVINGS

Serving this in individual cazuelas (earthenware casserole dishes) keeps this dish hot, makes it a charming presentation, and gives it an authentic Spanish flair.

2 tablespoons olive oil

4 monkfish steaks (about ½ pound each), about 1 inch thick

2 garlic cloves, thinly sliced

⅛ teaspoon saffron threads, crumbled

½ cup dry white wine

1 medium tomato, chopped (about ⅔ cup)

1. Heat the oil in a medium skillet over medium-high heat. Add the fish and cook, turning once, until browned, 2 to 5 minutes per side. Lower the heat to medium and cook until the fish is just barely opaque inside when cut with a small sharp knife. Transfer each fish to an individual earthenware casserole dish.

2. Add the garlic, saffron, wine, and tomato to the skillet and cook over medium heat, stirring until the sauce is well blended. Spoon the sauce over each fish and serve hot.

Monkfish with Rosemary

Rape al Romero

MAKES 4 SERVINGS

Al romero or "with rosemary" is a popular way to prepare fish in the northeastern region of Spain, well known for its fine spices. Rosemary is found in the wild all over Spain. It adds a distinctive Spanish flavor to this monkfish dish, but to ensure it's not overpowering, don't add more than a half teaspoon.

2 tablespoons olive oil

4 monkfish steaks (about ½ pound each), about 1 inch thick

All-purpose flour, for dredging

1 medium onion, cut into very thin strips

5 garlic cloves, thinly sliced

2 bay leaves

½ teaspoon dried rosemary

1 tablespoon finely chopped fresh flat-leaf parsley

Kosher or sea salt

¾ cup dry white wine

1 pimiento, cut into thin strips, for garnish

1. Place the flour in a wide shallow bowl. Heat the oil in a medium skillet over medium-high heat. Dredge the fish in the flour and place in the oil. Cook, turning once, until golden, 2 to 5 minutes. Transfer to a platter.

2. Add the onion and garlic and cook, stirring, until the onion is wilted, about 5 minutes. Reduce the heat to low, return the fish to the skillet, add the bay leaves, rosemary, ½ tablespoon of the parsley, the salt, and wine and simmer until the fish is just barely opaque when cut with a small sharp knife. Remove the bay leaves. Garnish with the remaining parsley and the pimiento strips. Serve hot.

Monkfish in Black Olive Sauce

Medallones con Salsa de Aceitunas Negras

MAKES 4 TO 6 SERVINGS

The sweetness and firm texture of monkfish make it an excellent fish to serve grilled. The black olive sauce is the perfect complement.

2 tablespoons olive oil

2 medium onions, finely chopped (about 1⅓ cup)

3 shallots, finely chopped

3 garlic cloves, thinly sliced

1 pound tomato, peeled and finely chopped

½ teaspoon dried thyme

Kosher or sea salt

Freshly ground black pepper

Pinch of sugar

Black Olive Sauce

2 tablespoons olive oil

1 medium onion, finely chopped (about ⅔ cup)

¼ pound pitted black olives, preferably Spanish, coarsely chopped

2 tablespoons storebought or homemade Fish Broth or bottled clam juice

Kosher or sea salt

Freshly ground black pepper

4 monkfish steaks (about ½ pound each), about 1 inch thick

1. Heat the 2 tablespoons oil in a medium skillet over low heat. Add the 2 chopped onions, the shallots, and garlic and cook, stirring, until the onions are wilted, about 5 minutes. Add the tomato and thyme and cook until the liquid has evaporated, then add the sugar.

2. Prepare the sauce: Heat the 2 tablespoons oil in another medium skillet over medium heat. Add the 1 chopped onion and the olives and cook, stirring, until the onion is wilted, about 5 minutes. Add the broth and cook, stirring, until the liquid is evaporated. Pass the sauce through a fine-mesh strainer and return to the skillet. Discard the solids. Stir in a little olive oil.

3. Grease a stovetop griddle and heat over high heat. Season the fish on both sides with salt and pepper. Cook the fish, turning once, until browned on both sides, 2 to 5 minutes per side. Place the tomato mixture on a warm platter and arrange the fish on top. Pour the sauce over the fish. Let sit 10 minutes. Serve warm.

Monkfish with Sherry and Fried Bread

Rape al Pan Frito

MAKES 4 SERVINGS

In Andalucía, fish is often prepared using sherry. This simple recipe calls for dry Manzanilla sherry, but any dry sherry will do nicely.

4 monkfish steaks (about ½ pound each), about 1 inch thick

3 tablespoons olive oil

2 slices country bread

6 garlic cloves, finely chopped

1 small onion, finely chopped (about ⅓ cup)

2 tablespoons finely chopped fresh flat-leaf parsley

1 dried sweet red pepper (ñora), stemmed and seeded, or ½ dried New Mexico (Anaheim) chile, stemmed and seeded

2 teaspoons ground sweet paprika, such as Spanish smoked

¼ cup dry sherry, such as Manzanilla or Fino

½ cup dry white wine

2 bay leaves

1. Season the fish with salt. Heat the oil in a medium skillet over medium heat. Add the bread and cook, turning once, until crisp. Transfer to a mortar or mini-processor. In the same oil, add the

garlic and onion and cook, stirring, until the onion is wilted, about 5 minutes. Add the parsley, chile pepper, and paprika and cook until the pepper softens. Transfer to the mortar and mash.

2. In the same skillet over medium heat, add the mortar mixture, 2 tablespoons of the sherry, and the wine and cook, stirring, 1 minute. Reduce the heat to low, add the fish, and simmer 10 minutes or until just barely opaque inside when cut when cut with a small sharp knife. Transfer the fish to a warm platter.

3. Add the remaining 2 tablespoons sherry and the bay leaves and cook, stirring constantly, until the liquid is reduced and thickens slightly. Remove the bay leaves. Pour the sauce over the fish and serve hot.

Monkfish and Shrimp Brochette
Brocheta de Rape y Langostinos

MAKES 4 SERVINGS

These simple skewers of cubed monkfish and shrimp are easy to prepare. For a light meal, they can be eaten alone, seasoned with salt and pepper. For a heavier meal, they can be covered in this cream-based sauce, rich with garlic and tomatoes.

1 pound monkfish steak, about 1 inch thick, cut into 16 chunks

16 large shrimp, shelled and deveined

Kosher or sea salt

Freshly ground black pepper

2 tablespoons olive oil

1 garlic clove, finely chopped

2 bay leaves

2 tablespoons brandy

½ pound tomatoes

2 tablespoons heavy cream

1 large scallion, finely chopped

1. Place a barbecue grill or broiler rack about 4 inches away from the heat source. Preheat the grill

or broiler. (Cover the broiler pan with foil for easier cleanup, if you like.) Onto each of 8 skewers, thread 2 pieces monkfish and 2 shrimp. Grill the fish and shrimp until the fish is browned and the shrimp is pink. Transfer to a platter and season with salt and pepper.

2. Heat the oil in a medium skillet over medium heat. Add the garlic and bay leaves and cook, stirring, until browned, about 2 minutes. Add the brandy and tomatoes and cook, stirring, 2 to 3 minutes more. Add the cream and cook, stirring constantly, until the liquid is reduced and the sauce is thickened slightly. Remove the bay leaves.

3. Onto each of 4 small individual plates, spoon the sauce and arrange 2 skewers on the sauce. Sprinkle with the scallion and serve hot.

Monkfish Filled with Large Shrimp
Rape Relleno de Cigalas

MAKES 4 SERVINGS

Monkfish, sometimes called "poor man's lobster," has a firm consistency that is perfect for stuffing, but bake works as well. In this recipe, you should pound the fish until thin, and then enclose the shrimp.

8 asparagus, rinsed and trimmed

2 monkfish steaks (about ½ pound each), about 1 inch thick

8 large raw shrimp, shelled, deveined, and halved lengthwise

Kosher or sea salt

All-purpose flour, for dredging

2 tablespoons olive oil

3 garlic cloves, finely chopped

½ cup storebought or homemade Fish Broth or bottled clam juice

continues . . .

1. Place the asparagus in a medium skillet with water to cover, add salt, and bring to a boil over high heat. Reduce the heat to low, cover, and simmer 5 to 10 minutes or until crisp-tender. Drain and reserve. Cut each steak lengthwise into medallions. Pound each medallion to an even thickness. Place 2 shrimp on each fish, roll up, and secure with a toothpick. Season with salt. Place the flour in a wide shallow bowl.

2. Heat the oil in a medium skillet over medium-high heat. Dredge the fish rolls in the flour and place in the oil seam side down. Cook, turning once, until seared. Add the asparagus, garlic, and broth. Season with salt and cook until the shrimp are pink and the fish is just opaque inside. Serve hot.

Casserole of Monkfish with Shrimp and Nuts
Cazuela de Rape con Gambas

MAKES 4 TO 6 SERVINGS

This recipe pairs a firm fish steak with shellfish, in this case, shrimp. The picada *sauce made with almonds and hazelnuts makes this dish extraordinary.*

2 tablespoons olive oil

4 monkfish steaks (about ½ pound each), about
      1 inch thick

Kosher or sea salt

Freshly ground black pepper

12 large shrimp, shelled and deveined

2 garlic cloves, finely chopped

1 medium onion, finely chopped (about ⅔ cup)

1 small tomato, chopped (about ⅓ cup)

1 cup storebought or homemade Fish Broth (page
      199; partial recipe) or bottled clam juice

1 teaspoon ground sweet paprika, such as Spanish
      smoked

2 tablespoons finely chopped fresh flat-leaf parsley,
      for garnish

Picada

2 garlic cloves, finely chopped

2 tablespoons ground blanched almonds

2 tablespoons ground hazelnuts

1. Heat the oil in a medium skillet over medium heat. Add the monkfish, season with salt and pepper, and cook, turning once, until browned, about 2 to 5 minutes per side. Add the shrimp and cook 1 minute until pink. Transfer the fish and shrimp to a platter and reserve.

2. Add the garlic and onion, and cook, stirring, until the onion is wilted, about 5 minutes. Add the tomato and paprika and cook 5 minutes more. Add the broth and cook 5 minutes more.

3. While the sauce is thickening slightly, prepare the picada: Place the garlic, almonds, and hazelnuts in a mortar and mash.

4. Transfer the sauce and the picada to a blender and purée. Return the sauce to the pan over medium heat. Add the monkfish and shellfish and cook 5 minutes, spooning the sauce over the fish, until the fish is just opaque inside when cut with a small sharp knife. Sprinkle with the parsley and serve hot.

Shark with Shrimp and Peas

Cazón al Azafrán con Langostinos y Guisantes

MAKES 4 SERVINGS

Most important to this recipe is the addition of saffron, which admittedly is quite expensive. But once you become acquainted with saffron at its best, nothing less will do. If you prefer not to use shark, try other firm steaks.

2 tablespoons olive oil

1 medium onion, finely chopped (about ⅔ cup)

1 garlic clove, finely chopped

Kosher or sea salt

Freshly ground black pepper

¼ teaspoon saffron threads, crumbled

1 cup dry sherry, such as Fino

1 cup storebought or homemade Fish Broth (page 199; partial recipe) or bottled clam juice

1 medium potato, peeled and thinly sliced

¼ cup cooked peas

4 firm-fleshed fish steaks, such as shark or monkfish (about ½ pound each), about 1 inch thick

12 shrimp, shelled and deveined

Heat the oil in a large skillet over medium-high heat. Add the onion and garlic, and cook, until the onion is wilted, about 5 minutes. Stir in salt, pepper, and saffron, then add the sherry and broth. Add the potatoes and peas, and cook, turning the potatoes occasionally, until the potatoes are crisp-tender. Add the fish and shrimp and cook, turning the fish once, until the shrimp are pink and the fish is just opaque inside when cut with a small sharp knife. Serve hot.

Fresh Cod and Salt Cod

Baked Fresh Cod with Eggplant and Onion

Bacalao Gratinado sobre Berenjenas y Cebolla

MAKES 4 SERVINGS

The thick texture of fresh cod makes it perfect for baking, and the sautéed eggplants and onions make it especially flavorful. This dish is very rich, as it is one of the few Spanish fish recipes that call for cream.

2 tablespoons olive oil

4 baby eggplants, cut into thin sticks

4 medium onions, thinly sliced

4 fresh cod or scrod steaks (about ½ pound each), about 1 inch thick

¼ cup heavy cream

4 large egg yolks

Salt

Freshly ground black pepper

½ cup dry white wine

1. Preheat the oven to 400°F. Lightly coat the bottom of a roasting pan with olive oil. Heat the 2 tablespoons oil in a medium skillet over medium heat. Add the onions and eggplants and cook, stirring, until softened, about 10 minutes. Transfer to the roasting pan in a single layer.

2. In a small bowl, gently whisk together the cream and egg yolks. Season the cod with salt and pepper. Place the cod on the vegetables. Drizzle the wine evenly over the cod. Roast about 8 minutes. Pour the cream mixture over the cod. Bake about 10 minutes more or until browned and the flesh is just opaque inside when tested with a small sharp knife. Serve hot.

Codfish Fritters with Garlic Sauce

Tortillas de Bacalao al Alioli

MAKES 4 SERVINGS

*Codfish fritters, like all fried Spanish seafood, are moist inside and crunchy outside. The desired effect is accomplished by frying in very hot oil for a minimum amount of time. Garlic sauce (*alioli*) is now available in specialty stores, but I recommend that you make your own, as it is a simple sauce consisting of olive oil, garlic, and sometimes eggs. Either dried salt cod or fresh cod can be used in this recipe. If you can't find fresh cod, there are a variety of other fishes that will work nicely.*

1 cup Garlic Sauce (alioli; page 284)

2 large egg whites, lightly beaten

3 tablespoons olive oil

2 pounds fresh cod steaks, cut into 8 pieces

1 pound tomatoes, peeled and finely chopped

1. Prepare the sauce as instructed. Combine the sauce and egg whites in a small saucepan. Over low heat, cook, stirring, until the eggs are well blended and the sauce is hot, 1 to 2 minutes. Do not boil.

2. Heat the oil in a large skillet over medium-high heat. Add the cod and cook, turning once, until golden, 1 to 2 minutes per side. Transfer to a platter. Add the tomatoes and cook, stirring, until softened and their juices release, 2 to 3 minutes.

3. Place a broiler rack about 4 inches from the heat source and preheat the broiler. (Cover the broiler pan with foil for easier cleanup, if you like.) Arrange a layer of tomatoes in the pan, place the cod on top, and spoon some sauce over each piece of cod. Broil 2 to 3 minutes or until the tops are browned and the fish is opaque inside when cut with a small sharp knife. Serve hot.

Salt Cod, Basque Style

Bacalao a la Vizcaína

MAKES 4 SERVINGS

The Basque Country is home to the Bay of Biscay, one of the finest fishing areas in the world. But even though fresh fish is readily abundant there, people in the Basque region have a penchant for salt cod, as evidenced in so many of their recipes. Bacalao a la Vizcaína — one of their most popular dishes — derives much of its flavor from the dried red peppers. This dish is considered better when served the day after it is made.

PREPARE 24 TO 36 HOURS IN ADVANCE

1 pound dried boneless skinless salt cod

4 dried sweet red peppers (ñoras), or 2 dried New Mexico (Anaheim) chiles, stemmed and seeded

3 tablespoons olive oil

3 large onions, finely chopped (about 3 cups)

2 garlic cloves, lightly smashed

2 sprigs parsley

¼ cup small cubes (¼ inch) slab bacon (about 2 ounces)

½ cup small cubes (¼ inch) Serrano (Spanish cured mountain) ham or prosciutto (about ¼ pound)

1 large hard-boiled egg yolk

1½ cups hot water

1 bay leaf

Salt

Freshly ground black pepper

½ dried red chile pepper, seeded and crumbled

1. Place the cod in a medium bowl and add cold water to cover. Cover and let sit in the refrigerator 24 to 36 hours, changing the water occasionally, until the water no longer tastes salty. Place the dried sweet chile peppers in a small bowl, add warm water to cover, and soak 1 hour. Drain. Cut the peppers into small pieces.

2. Heat the oil in a large skillet over medium heat. Add the onion, garlic, and parsley and cook, stirring, until the onion is wilted, about 10 minutes. Reduce the heat to low, cover, and cook about 30 minutes more but not until browned. Meanwhile, in a small skillet, add the bacon and ham and cook, stirring, until browned. Reserve.

3. Preheat the oven to 300°F. Transfer the onion mixture to a food processor or blender. Add the drained sweet peppers and egg yolk and process until smooth. With the motor running, gradually add the hot water. Pass through a fine-mesh strainer and return to the skillet. Add the bay leaf, salt, black pepper, the reserved ham-bacon mixture, and the chile pepper. Cover and cook over low heat 20 minutes.

4. Drain the cod and place in a large saucepan with water to cover. Bring to a boil over high heat and remove immediately from the heat. Drain. Cut into 1½-inch pieces.

5. In a shallow earthenware ovenproof casserole dish or Dutch oven, spread a few tablespoons of the onion-peppers mixture. Add the cod and cover with the remaining onion-pepper mixture. Bake about 1½ hours or until the cod is tender, adding a little water if the sauce dries out too much. Remove the bay leaf. If using earthenware, serve hot in the dish, or transfer to individual plates. Or, let cool, cover, and store in the refrigerator, then reheat at 300°F.

Salt Cod with Eggplant and Peppers
Bacalao en Chanfaina

MAKES 4 SERVINGS

Salt cod has a strong taste that admittedly is not for everybody, so you can substitute fresh cod or other fish if you prefer. This recipe pairs it with an onion-flavored white wine sauce that is quite delicious when sautéed with eggplant and bell peppers. If using salt cod, start at least 24 hours in advance.

PREPARE 24 TO 36 HOURS IN ADVANCE

1 pound dried boneless skinless salt cod or fresh cod, tuna, or other fish steaks, about 1 inch thick

All-purpose flour, for dredging

¼ cup olive oil

2 medium onions, finely chopped (about 1⅓ cups)

1 eggplant (about 1 pound), peeled and cut into ½-inch cubes

2 medium green bell peppers, cut into thin strips

4 medium tomatoes, peeled and chopped

½ cup dry white wine

Salt

Freshly ground black pepper

1. Place the salt cod in a large bowl with cold water to cover. Cover and let sit in the refrigerator 24 to 36 hours, changing the water occasionally, until the water no longer tastes salty. Drain and place in a soup pot with water to cover. Bring to a boil over high heat and remove immediately from the heat. Drain and let dry on paper towels.

2. Place the flour in a large shallow bowl. Cut the fish into 1½-inch chunks. Heat the oil in a large skillet over medium heat. Lightly dredge the fish in the flour and place in the oil. Cook, turning once, until golden on both sides. Transfer to a platter lined with paper towels.

3. In the remaining oil over low heat, add the onions, eggplant, and bell peppers and cook, stirring, until softened, about 10 minutes. Add the tomatoes, wine, salt, and black pepper. Cover and cook about 20 minutes or until the vegetables are tender. Add the fish and cook 10 minutes more or until the fish is just opaque inside. Serve hot.

Two of the three provinces of the Basque Country are located on the Bay of Biscay, a rich fishing area with a great variety of fish and shellfish. A lot of the great Basque cuisine is based on fish dishes, but it's interesting to note that some of the signature specialty dishes of this area are based on salted, dried codfish (bacalao), not fresh.

Since the sixteenth century, the Basques were known to travel as far as the grand banks of Newfoundland for whale and cod. They built small villages in Newfoundland as a base for their fishing expeditions. Obviously, cod became a staple in Basque cooking, and there are two codfish dishes considered the greatest of Basque cuisine: Codfish "a la bilbaína," in a very basic oil and garlic sauce, and the even more popular "al pil pil," in a garlic sauce that is prepared in a special way to make it appear "creamy" even though it has no cream (see page 410). Salted codfish remains beloved in Spanish cuisine, and traditionally, no one in Spain eats fresh codfish.

If you don't get to the Basque region, when in Madrid, look for Soldaditos de Pavía, small cubes of cod dredged in flour and egg and deep fried. Go to Casa Labra on Tetuán Street just across from the main entrance of El Corte Inglés, Madrid's most prestigious department store. Or, see Fried Cod Sticks, page 44, to make them at home.

Salt Cod with Tomatoes and Peppers
Bacalao al Ajo Arriero

MAKES 4 SERVINGS

Spain is credited with bringing native American foods, such as tomatoes, bell peppers, and potatoes to the Old World, and they soon became some of the most important ingredients in Spanish cooking. Two are showcased here. For a pretty presentation, garnish this dish with piquillo peppers.

PREPARE 24 TO 36 HOURS IN ADVANCE

1½ pounds dried boneless skinless salt cod, cut into 4 pieces

All-purpose flour, for dredging

3 tablespoons olive oil

8 garlic cloves, thinly sliced

1 medium onion, slivered

2 bay leaves

4 medium tomatoes, finely chopped

2 tablespoons finely chopped fresh flat-leaf parsley

2 teaspoons ground bittersweet paprika, such as Spanish smoked

3 (jarred) piquillo peppers, cut into strips, for garnish

1. Place the cod in a medium bowl and add cold water to cover. Cover and let sit in the refrigerator 24 to 36 hours, changing the water occasionally, until the water no longer tastes salty. Drain.

2. Preheat the oven to 375°F. Place the flour in a large shallow bowl. Heat 2 tablespoons of the oil in a shallow earthenware casserole dish or Dutch oven over low heat. Lightly dredge the fish on all sides in the flour and place in the oil. Cook, turning once, until lightly browned, about 5 minutes per side. Transfer to a platter.

3. In the same skillet, heat the remaining 1 tablespoon oil over medium heat. Add the onion and

garlic and cook, stirring, until the onion is wilted, about 5 minutes. Stir in the tomatoes, parsley, and paprika and simmer until the tomatoes are softened and their juices release, about 5 minutes more.

4. Transfer to the oven and bake 10 minutes or until the fish is just opaque inside. Remove the bay leaves. Garnish with the pepper strips. If using earthenware, serve hot in the dish, or transfer to individual plates.

Salt Cod in Onion Sauce

Lomos de Bacalao Encebollados y Brandy

MAKES 4 SERVINGS

This recipe calls for cooking the salt cod in brandy. The onion sauce, also featuring tomatoes and garlic, is pungent and extremely flavorful.

PREPARE 24 TO 36 HOURS IN ADVANCE

1 pound dried boneless skinless salt cod, cut into 4 pieces

½ pound asparagus, rinsed and trimmed

2 tablespoons olive oil

2 medium onions, slivered

3 garlic cloves, finely chopped

6 medium tomatoes, crushed

½ teaspoon sugar

¼ cup brandy

2 bay leaves

1 teaspoon dried oregano

1 medium carrot, peeled and cut into very thin strips

½ cup storebought or homemade Fish Broth

Kosher or sea salt

Freshly ground black pepper

2 medium potatoes, peeled and cut into ¼-inch slices

1. Place the cod in a medium bowl and add cold water to cover. Cover and let sit in the refrigerator 24 to 36 hours, changing the water occasionally, until the water no longer tastes salty. Drain.

2. Place the asparagus in a medium skillet with water to cover, add salt, and bring to a boil over high heat. Reduce the heat to low, cover, and simmer 5 to 10 minutes or until crisp-tender. Reserve.

3. Heat the oil in a shallow earthenware casserole dish or Dutch oven over low heat. Add the onions and garlic and cook, stirring, until the onions are wilted, about 5 minutes. Stir in the tomatoes, and sugar. Add the brandy and, standing well away from the pot, ignite the liquid with a match or kitchen lighter and let it die out. Stir in the bay leaves, oregano, potatoes, carrots and cod. Cook about 10 minutes. Add the asparagus and broth and cook, stirring occasionally, about 5 minutes more, until the vegetables are tender and the fish is just opaque inside. Remove the bay leaves. If using earthenware, serve hot in the dish, or transfer to individual plates.

Salt Cod in Creamy Garlic Sauce with Mushrooms
Bacalao Confitado al Pil Pil

MAKES 4 SERVINGS

This creamy garlic sauce actually contains no cream. Instead olive oil is shaken in the pan until it emulsifies to a white creamy texture. The subtle flavor of mushrooms makes this dish all the more delicious.

PREPARE 24 TO 36 HOURS IN ADVANCE

1 pound dried boneless skinless salt cod

½ cup olive oil

4 garlic cloves, thinly sliced

1-inch piece dried red chile pepper, seeded and broken into several pieces

All-purpose flour, for dredging

Small mushrooms, rinsed, trimmed, and thinly sliced

1. Place the cod in a medium bowl and add cold water to cover. Cover and let sit in the refrigerator 24 to 36 hours, changing the water occasionally, until the water no longer tastes salty. Drain.

2. Heat the oil in a large skillet over low heat. Add the garlic and chile and cook, stirring, until the garlic turns lightly golden. Transfer the garlic and chile to a small plate and reserve. Transfer all but 2 tablespoons of the oil to a small bowl.

3. Place the flour in a large shallow bowl. Lightly dredge the fish on all sides in the flour. In the same oil over medium-low heat, add the fish and cook, turning once, until golden on both sides and just opaque inside, about 5 minutes per side. Transfer to a platter (preferably an ovenproof platter warmed in the oven) and cover.

4. Add 1 tablespoon of the reserved garlic oil to the skillet, constantly shaking the skillet until the oil emulsifies to a white creamy consistency. Repeat, adding the remaining oil 1 tablespoon at a time, until all the oil has been incorporated.

5. Add the mushrooms and cook, stirring, until soft, browned, and their juices have been incorporated into the sauce. Garnish the fish with the reserved garlic and chile and serve hot with the sauce on the side.

Salt Cod in Honey-Garlic Sauce
Bacalao al Alioli de Miel

MAKES 4 SERVINGS

This delicious recipe pairs the saltiness of cod with a special garlic sauce that is sweetened with honey, creating a delicious taste sensation. Dishes that are sweet and savory are characteristic of Catalan-style cooking, which reflects a Mediterranean influence.

PREPARE 24 TO 36 HOURS IN ADVANCE

2 pounds dried boneless skinless salt cod

½ cup Garlic Sauce (alioli; page 284)

1 tablespoon honey

All-purpose flour, for dredging

2 tablespoons olive oil

1. Place the cod in a medium bowl and add cold water to cover. Cover and let sit in the refrigerator 24 to 36 hours, changing the water occasionally, until the water no longer tastes salty. Drain.

2. Meanwhile, prepare the sauce and combine with the honey in a small serving bowl. Reserve, covered, in the refrigerator.

3. When ready to cook, place a broiler rack about 4 inches from the heat source and preheat the broiler. (Cover the broiler pan with foil for easier cleanup, if you like.) Place the flour in a large shallow bowl. Heat the oil in a shallow earthenware casserole dish or Dutch oven over medium heat. Dredge the fish in the flour and place in the oil. Cook, turning once, until browned. Spoon the reserved sauce over the cod. Transfer to the broiler and cook until the sauce is browned. If using earthenware, serve hot in the dish, or transfer to individual plates.

Salt Cod with Honey

Bacalao a la Miel

MAKES 4 SERVINGS

Here the saltiness of the cod is contrasted with the sweetness of the honey. Raisins are added for extra sweetness and texture.

PREPARE 24 TO 36 HOURS IN ADVANCE

½ pound dried boneless skinless salt cod

1 cup all-purpose flour

2 teaspoons baking powder

1 teaspoon salt

½ cup water

½ cup milk

1 tablespoon olive oil

Olive oil, for frying

½ cup storebought or homemade Fish Broth or bottled clam juice

1 tablespoon honey

Kosher or sea salt

1 tablespoon heavy cream

2 tablespoons raisins

1. Place the cod in a medium bowl and add cold water to cover. Cover and let sit in the refrigerator 24 to 36 hours, changing the water occasionally, until the water no longer tastes salty. Drain.

2. Cut the cod into sticks the size of a finger. In a shallow bowl, combine the flour, baking powder, and the salt. Stir in the water, milk, and oil and mix until smooth. Line a plate with paper towels.

3. Heat at least 1 inch of oil in a medium skillet over medium-high heat (or better still, use a deep fryer set at 375°F) until it quickly browns a cube of bread. Dip each cod stick in the batter and place in the oil. Cook, turning once, until golden. (Cook in batches if needed to avoid overcrowding.) Transfer to paper towels to drain.

4. In a medium saucepan over medium-high heat, combine the broth, honey, and salt and bring to a boil, stirring occasionally, and cook until thickened. Reduce the heat to medium, add the cream and raisins, and cook, stirring, until the sauce is blended. Season with salt. Drizzle over and around the cod and serve hot.

Salt Cod with Cream, Honey, and Mustard

Bacalao a la Crema de Miel con Mostaza

MAKES 4 SERVINGS

Cream, honey, and mustard may seem to be an unlikely combination of flavors, but in this simple recipe they complement each other beautifully.

PREPARE 24 TO 36 HOURS IN ADVANCE

¾ pound dried boneless skinless salt cod

2 tablespoon olive oil

All-purpose flour, for dredging

1 tablespoon unsalted butter

2 tablespoons honey

1 tablespoon coarse mustard

¼ cup heavy cream

1. Place the cod in a medium bowl and add cold water to cover. Cover and let sit in the refrigerator 24 to 36 hours, changing the water occasionally, until the water no longer tastes salty. Drain.

2. Place the flour in a large shallow bowl. Heat the oil in a medium skillet over medium-low heat. Dredge the fish in the flour and place in the oil. Cook, turning once, until golden, about 5 minutes per side. Reserve. Wipe out the skillet.

3. In the same skillet over medium heat, add the butter, honey, and mustard and cook, stirring occasionally, until blended. Stir in the cream and cook, stirring, until the liquid is reduced and the sauce is thickened. Pour over the cod and serve hot.

Andalucian Fish Fry
Pescado Frito a la Andaluza

MAKES 4 SERVINGS

This famous dish, sometimes referred to as Pescadito Frito a la Gaditana, *originated in Cádiz and is probably one of the most popular fish preparations found throughout all of Spain. The chefs of Cádiz seem to have a special knack for frying the fish to just the right point, making it moist, crisp, and greaseless. The region of Andalucía, with its access to some of the finest fish in Spain, is credited with the creation of the fish fry, as popular today as it was back then.*

1½ pounds whiting (smallest available) or other small fish (skinned and heads on or off)

4 very small whole flounders (about ¼ pound each; skinned and heads off)

4 very small snappers (about ¼ pound each; skinned and heads on or off)

Fresh lemon juice

Kosher or sea salt

¾ cup all-purpose flour

¾ cup cornmeal

Olive oil, for frying

Lemon wedges, for garnish

Wet both sides of the fish with water and sprinkle with the lemon juice and salt. Combine the flour and cornmeal in a small bowl. Heat at least 1 inch of oil in a medium skillet over medium-high heat (or better still, use a deep fryer set at 365°F) until it turns a cube of bread light brown in 60 seconds. Dredge the fish in the flour mixture and place in the oil. (Cook in batches if needed to avoid overcrowding.) Cook, turning once, until lightly golden and very crisp. Transfer with a slotted spatula to paper towels and let drain. Garnish with the lemon wedges and serve hot.

Fish Baked with Potatoes, Onions, Saffron, and Paprika
Pescado al Horno "Crisol"

MAKES 4 SERVINGS

This hearty dish of fish and potatoes has a Galician-style influence in which saffron and paprika figure prominently. The recipe calls for a rather large amount of onion as this is what gives this dish such a wonderful flavor.

1½ to 2 pounds firm fish fillets, such as striped bass, turbot, or grouper (skin on)

Kosher or sea salt

½ cup fresh lemon juice

5 tablespoons olive oil

1 pound baking potatoes, peeled and cut into ⅛-inch slices

2 cups very finely chopped sweet onions, such as Vidalia

Scant ¼ teaspoon saffron threads, crumbled

½ teaspoon ground sweet paprika, such as Spanish smoked

2 tablespoons finely chopped fresh flat-leaf parsley

1. Season the fish with salt and arrange in a flat-bottom bowl or pie plate. Pour the lemon juice over the fish and let sit until needed.

2. In a shallow earthenware casserole dish or Dutch oven, heat 3 tablespoons of the oil over medium heat. Add the potatoes in layers and sprinkle each layer with salt. Turn the potatoes to coat with the oil and cook 2 minutes. Stir in the onion, ⅛ teaspoon of the saffron, and ¼ teaspoon of the paprika, and cook 2 minutes more. Cover and cook, lifting and turning the potatoes occasionally, 15 to 20 minutes or until the potatoes are almost tender.

3. Preheat the oven to 375°F. Drain the fish and arrange over the potatoes. Drizzle the remaining 2 tablespoons oil over the fish and season with salt and the remaining ⅛ teaspoon saffron and ¼ teaspoon paprika. Bake about 15 minutes or until the fish is just barely opaque when cut in the thickest part. If using earthenware, sprinkle with the parsley and serve hot in the dish. Or transfer to individual plates, arrange the potatoes around and over the fish, and sprinkle with the parsley.

Grilled Fish with Ruperto's Anchovy Caper Sauce

Pescado a la Parrilla con Salsa de Anchoa de Ruperto Blanco

MAKES 4 SERVINGS

My friend Ruperto Blanco first introduced me to this recipe in his bar Las Codornices in the Triana neighborhood in Seville. The strongly flavored anchovy and caper sauce enhances just about any grilled fish it is served with.

4 fish steaks (about ½ pound each), such as
    monkfish, turbot, or swordfish, about 1 inch thick

Kosher or sea salt

Anchovy Caper Sauce

2 tablespoons finely chopped fresh flat-leaf parsley

4 teaspoons finely chopped scallions (white part
    only)

2 tablespoons finely chopped celery

2 garlic cloves, finely chopped

2 tablespoons capers (nonpareil preferred), rinsed
    and drained

4 large anchovies, finely chopped

¼ teaspoon dried oregano

1½ teaspoons finely chopped fresh thyme or
    ¼ teaspoon dried thyme

2 tablespoons extra-virgin olive oil

1½ tablespoons red wine vinegar

Salt

Freshly ground black pepper

1. Season the fish with salt and reserve.

2. Prepare the sauce: In a mortar or mini-processor, mash the parsley, scallions, celery, garlic, capers, anchovies, oregano, and thyme. Stir in the oil, vinegar, salt, and pepper.

3. Grease a stovetop grill and heat over medium-high heat until very hot. Grill the fish, turning once, until just barely opaque when cut in the thickest part, 8 to 10 minutes. Spoon the sauce over the fish and serve hot.

Rockfish with Vegetables, Sun-Dried Tomatoes, and Potatoes

Pescado de Roca con su Jugo Confitado, Tomates y Verduras

MAKES 4 SERVINGS

This is another meal-in-one, with layers of fish, potatoes, and vegetables. The sun-dried tomatoes add an extra flair, and I recommend serving this dish with alioli.

Garlic Sauce (alioli; page 284), to taste

2 tablespoons olive oil

4 rockfish steaks (about ½ pound each), about 1 inch
    thick

1 medium green bell pepper, finely chopped (about
    ¾ cup)

1 head garlic, chopped

1 bay leaf

¼ teaspoon dried thyme

1 sun-dried tomato, finely chopped

2 medium tomatoes, chopped (about 1⅓ cups)

2 medium potatoes, peeled and thinly sliced

½ cup dry white wine

continues...

1. Prepare the sauce. Heat the oil in a medium skillet over medium-high heat. Add the fish and cook, turning once, until golden, 2 to 5 minutes per side. Transfer to a platter.

2. Reduce the heat to medium. Add the bell pepper, garlic, bay leaf, thyme, and sun-dried tomato and cook, stirring, until the vegetables are softened. Transfer to a shallow earthenware casserole dish or Dutch oven.

3. In the same oil, add the chopped tomatoes and cook, stirring, until softened and their juices release, 2 to 3 minutes. Transfer to the casserole dish.

4. Arrange the potatoes over the vegetables and the fish over the potatoes. Pour the wine over everything, reduce the heat to low, and simmer 10 minutes more. If using earthenware, serve hot in the dish, or transfer to individual plates. Serve the sauce on the side.

Mediterranean Fish Stew
Suquet de Pescado Mediterráneo

MAKES 4 SERVINGS

Suquet, *which originates in Catalunya, is a typical way of preparing fish in the coastal villages.*

Garlic Sauce (alioli; page 284), to taste

1 dozen littleneck clams

1 tablespoon olive oil

3 thin slices long-loaf (baguette) bread

6 garlic cloves

2 tablespoons finely chopped fresh flat-leaf parsley

12 blanched almonds, finely chopped

¼ teaspoon saffron threads, crumbled

1 dried sweet red pepper (ñora), stemmed, seeded, and finely chopped

1 pound monkfish, cut into stew-size pieces

½ pound scrod, cut into 1- to 2-inch pieces

1 dozen large shrimp, shelled and deveined

1. Prepare the sauce. Rinse the clams. Discard any clams with cracked shells or that do not close tightly when touched. Reserve.

2. Heat the oil in a small skillet over medium heat. Add the bread and cook, turning once, until golden on both sides. Transfer to paper towels and let drain.

3. In a mortar or mini-processor, mash the garlic, bread, parsley, almonds, saffron, and red pepper. Transfer to a shallow earthenware casserole dish or Dutch oven over low heat. Cook, stirring, just until fragrant. Stir in the broth and cook about 15 minutes more. Arrange the fish and shrimp in the casserole dish. Season with salt and pepper and cook, stirring, about 2 minutes more. Add the clams and cook until they open and the fish is still tender but just cooked through. Discard any unopened clams. Serve hot with the alioli on the side.

Catalan Fish and Potatoes with Garlic Sauce
Suquet de Pescado "La Escala"

MAKES 4 SERVINGS

Hearty and simple to prepare, this Catalan-style fish stew has been warming the bellies of Spaniards for centuries. Different versions are served throughout the various regions of Spain, but this recipe made with garlic sauce is a particular favorite of mine. I first tasted this dish in the town of La Escala.

3 cups storebought or homemade Fish Broth (page 199)

Garlic Sauce (alioli)

5 garlic cloves, finely chopped

½ teaspoon kosher or sea salt

1 teaspoon fresh lemon juice

1½ tablespoons lightly beaten egg

1 cup mild olive oil

1 pound monkfish steak, about 1 inch thick

4 (¼ pound) turbot or other firm-fleshed fish steaks, such as halibut, about 1 inch thick

Kosher or sea salt

3 tablespoons olive oil

4 garlic cloves, thinly sliced

1 pound plum tomatoes, peeled and coarsely chopped

1¼ pound potatoes, peeled and cut into ½-inch cubes

2 tablespoons finely chopped fresh flat-leaf parsley, for garnish

1. Prepare the broth if necessary.

2. Prepare the sauce: Mash the garlic and salt in a mortar. Mash in the lemon juice, then stir in the egg. Using a rubber spatula, transfer the mortar mixture to a food processor. With the motor running, add the oil in a thin steady stream, pausing to scrape down the sides with a rubber spatula if necessary. Transfer to a serving bowl and reserve.

3. Season the fish with salt. Heat the oil in a shallow earthenware casserole dish or Dutch oven over medium heat. Add the garlic and cook, stirring, until it turns lightly golden. Add the tomatoes and potatoes and cook, stirring, until the tomatoes soften and their juices release, 2 to 3 minutes more. Add the broth, bring to a boil, and cook about 10 minutes more. Add the fish, and cook about 10 minutes more, adding some water and seasoning with salt if the liquid evaporates.

4. Transfer the fish to a platter. Transfer the potatoes with a slotted spoon to a medium bowl, reserving the sauce in the casserole dish, and coarsely mash the potatoes with a fork. Arrange the fish and potatoes on dinner plates. Add a little water if necessary to the remaining sauce to ensure there is enough for each fish portion and pour over the fish. Sprinkle the fish and potatoes with the parsley. Serve hot with the alioli on the side.

Sardines, Santander Style
Sardinas a la Montañesa

MAKES 4 SERVINGS

The small sardines in this recipe are wrapped in grape leaves to help hold them together during cooking. Sardines have an unusually strong taste, which is perfectly complemented by the subtle flavor of the grape leaves.

12 grape leaves packed in brine

12 small sardines (about 1½ pounds)

Salt

Freshly ground black pepper

¼ teaspoon mint

1 medium onion, finely chopped (about ⅔ cup)

1 medium leek or 3 scallions, trimmed, well washed, and finely chopped

3 medium tomatoes, finely chopped (about 2 cups)

2 garlic cloves, finely chopped

¼ cup olive oil

½ cup dry white wine

½ teaspoon ground paprika

1. Fill with water a pot large enough to fit the grape leaves and bring to a boil over high heat. Working in batches if necessary, separate the grape leaves and place them in the water. Cook about 3 minutes. Transfer to paper towels and let drain.

2. Season the sardines with salt and pepper. Wrap each in a grape leaf, leaving the heads exposed. In a deep earthenware casserole dish or Dutch oven, arrange the sardines seam side down in crisscrossing layers. Sprinkle each layer lightly with the mint.

continues...

3. In a medium bowl, mix the onion, leek, tomatoes, garlic, oil, wine, paprika, salt, and pepper. Pour over the sardines and shake the pot to distribute the sauce. Bring to a boil over medium-high heat. Reduce the heat to low, cover, and simmer 25 minutes or until the sardines are cooked through.

4. Turn the contents of the casserole dish out onto a large platter (the sardines may break if you try to serve them directly from the dish). Carefully remove the grape leaves and place 3 sardines on each of 4 individual plates. Spoon the sauce around, not over, the sardines and add a piece of grape leaf as garnish. Serve hot.

Sardines, Mesón Style
Sardinas Mesoneras

MAKES 6 SERVINGS

A mesón is a down-to-earth inn, inexpensive and serving mostly the working class. By extension here, it refers to simple, flavorful, peasant-style food, which is always filling.

PREPARE 24 HOURS IN ADVANCE

2 pounds small sardines (cleaned, boned, and heads removed)

2 cups white wine vinegar

1 teaspoon ground cumin

4 garlic cloves, coarsely chopped

3 tablespoons olive oil

1 medium onion, thinly sliced

½ pound (8 ounces) canned whole tomato, finely chopped

Kosher or sea salt

Freshly ground black pepper

1. Wash the sardines well and place in a large bowl. Add the vinegar, cover, and let marinate in the refrigerator 24 hours.

2. In a mortar or mini-processor, mash the cumin and garlic. Mash in the oil, onion, tomato, salt, and pepper. Remove the sardines from the vinegar and let drain on paper towels. Place in a serving bowl and pour the mortar mixture over them and serve.

Luisa Osborne's Stuffed Sardines
Sardinas del Puerto de Santa María

MAKES 4 SERVINGS

Since these tasty sardines, stuffed with cured ham and pimiento, are bite-size, they can also be served as a tapa. They are prepared by dusting them in flour, dipping them in egg, and frying them at the last possible minute.

1 pound small sardines, no more than 4 to 5 inches long

¼ cup finely chopped Serrano (Spanish cured mountain) ham or prosciutto

¾ cup finely chopped pimientos, such as (jarred) piquillo peppers

All-purpose flour, for dredging

2 large eggs, lightly beaten

Kosher or sea salt

1. Butterfly the sardines. Wash the sardines, remove the bones and heads, and leave the tail fins on. In a small bowl, combine the ham and pimiento and fill each sardine with about 1 teaspoon of the mixture. Close and press to seal. Place the flour and eggs in separate wide shallow bowls.

2. Heat at least ½ inch of oil in a medium skillet over medium-high heat (or better still, use a deep fryer set at 375°F) until it quickly browns a cube of bread. Dredge the sardines in the flour, dip into the egg, and place in the oil. Cook, turning once, until lightly golden, about 5 minutes. Transfer with a slotted spoon to paper towels and let drain. Season with salt and serve hot.

Marinated Sardines with Sweet Tomato Marmalade

Sardinas Marinadas con Mermelada de Tomate

MAKES 4 SERVINGS

Sardines are so adored in Spain that were they not so inexpensive, they might very well be considered a delicacy. In this recipe, the saltiness of the sardines is contrasted by the sweetness of the tomato marmalade. I like to serve this dish topped with chopped sun-dried tomato and croutons.

START PREPARATION AT LEAST
8 HOURS IN ADVANCE

2 pounds medium sardines, cleaned

¼ cup sherry vinegar or red wine vinegar

¼ cup dry white wine

Kosher or sea salt

Tomato Marmalade

2 tablespoons olive oil

1 pound tomatoes, finely chopped

½ teaspoon dried thyme

1 teaspoon sugar

Kosher or sea salt

Freshly ground black pepper

2 tablespoons olive oil

1½ teaspoons finely chopped fresh thyme or
 ¼ teaspoon dried thyme

1 bunch watercress

Sun-dried tomatoes, cut into thin strips, for garnish

Croutons, for garnish

1. In a medium bowl, combine the sardines, vinegar, wine, and salt. Cover and let marinate in the refrigerator at least 8 hours.

2. Prepare the marmalade: In a medium pot over medium heat, combine 1 tablespoon of the oil, the tomatoes, thyme, sugar, salt, and pepper and cook, stirring occasionally, until thickened and gelatinous. Stir in the remaining 1 tablespoon oil. Reserve.

3. Remove the sardines from the marinade and butterfly them, discarding the bones and the marinade. Drizzle with the oil and sprinkle with the thyme. Arrange the watercress and sardines on a platter. Arrange the sun-dried tomato over them and scatter the croutons over the top. Drizzle a thin strip of marmalade across the middle. Serve at room temperature.

Marinated Anchovies with Asparagus

Escabeche de Espárragos con Boquerones

MAKES 4 SERVINGS

Spaniards tend to prefer small fish to large fish whenever they are available. Here the unusually strong flavor and firm texture of anchovies are perfectly combined with the subtle taste of asparagus. White asparagus is recommended, but if it can't be found, green asparagus is an adequate substitute.

½ pound asparagus, rinsed and trimmed

¾ pound fresh anchovies, cleaned

Kosher or sea salt

All-purpose flour, for dredging

4 tablespoons olive oil

¼ teaspoon saffron threads, crumbled

1 tablespoon water

⅓ cup wine vinegar

10 garlic cloves, sliced

10 peppercorns

Peel of ½ orange (orange part only), cut into several
 pieces

1 bay leaf

continues...

1. Place the asparagus in a medium skillet with water to cover, add salt, and bring to a boil over high heat. Reduce the heat to low, cover, and simmer 5 to 10 minutes or until crisp-tender. Drain. Reserve.

2. Season the anchovies with salt. Place the flour in a shallow bowl. Heat 2 tablespoons of the oil in a medium skillet over medium heat. Dredge the anchovies in the flour and place in the oil. Cook, turning once, until golden. Reserve.

3. In a mortar or mini-processor, mash the saffron, salt, water, vinegar, and the remaining 2 tablespoons oil. Pour into a shallow earthenware casserole dish or Dutch oven. Add the garlic, peppercorns, orange peel, bay leaf, and asparagus and bring to a boil. Reduce the heat to low and simmer until reduced by half. Add the anchovies, and spoon the sauce over the anchovies. Remove from the heat, cover, and let sit 15 to 30 minutes. Remove the bay leaf. If using earthenware, serve at room temperature in the dish, or transfer to individual plates.

Anchovies Layered with Tomato, Capers, Bread Crumbs, and Cheese

Cazuela de Boquerones Alpujarreña

MAKES 6 SERVINGS

This baked fish is easy to prepare and cooks in almost no time at all. If you can't find fresh anchovies, then bass, trout, or another strong-tasting fish can be substituted.

½ cup grated aged Manchego or Parmesan cheese

¾ cup bread crumbs

2 teaspoons finely chopped fresh oregano or 1 teaspoon dried oregano

Kosher or sea salt

Freshly ground black pepper

2 tablespoons finely chopped capers (nonpareil preferred), rinsed and drained

2 tablespoons finely chopped fresh flat-leaf parsley

4 garlic cloves, finely chopped

1½ pounds fresh anchovies (butterflied and boned), or 6 bass or trout fillets (skin on)

1½ pounds large cherry tomatoes, cut into ¼-inch slices

6 tablespoons dry white wine

¼ cup olive oil plus more, for greasing

1. Preheat the oven to 450°F. In a small bowl, combine the cheese, bread crumbs, oregano, salt, pepper, capers, parsley, and garlic. Generously grease with olive oil a shallow earthenware casserole dish or Dutch oven.

2. If using fresh anchovies, arrange the ingredients in layers: First, arrange a layer of the anchovies, skin side down, in the dish. Season with salt, scatter some of the tomatoes over the fish, and season again with salt. Sprinkle some of the crumb mixture over the tomatoes. Repeat the layers until all the fish and crumbs have been used. (If using bass or trout, arrange half of the fish, skin side down, in the casserole dish. Season with salt, scatter half of the tomatoes over the fish, and season again with salt. Sprinkle with half of the crumbs. Arrange the remaining fish, skin side up, over the top, then scatter the remaining tomato over the fish and sprinkle with the crumb mixture.)

3. Drizzle the wine and the ¼ cup oil over the fish. Bake 20 minutes or until the fish is just barely opaque when cut in the thickest part. If using earthenware, serve hot in the dish, or transfer to individual plates.

Mackerel Vinaigrette
Caballa en Vinagreta

MAKES 4 SERVINGS

Cádiz, world renowned for its seafood, has an abundance of mackerel, a fish considered highly desirable in all parts of Spain. It is often served in the summer with a light and tangy vinaigrette.

PREPARE AT LEAST 2 HOURS IN ADVANCE

8 tablespoons olive oil

3 tablespoons red wine vinegar

Salt

Freshly ground black pepper

1 teaspoon capers (nonpareil preferred), rinsed and drained

1 tablespoon finely chopped fresh flat-leaf parsley

2 tablespoons finely chopped onion

2 garlic cloves, mashed in a garlic press or mortar

Pinch of sugar

4 skinned mackerel fillets (about ½ pound each)

I. Place a broiler rack about 4 inches away from the heat source and preheat the broiler. (Cover the broiler pan with foil for easier cleanup, if you like.) In a small bowl, mix 6 tablespoons of the oil and all the remaining ingredients except the fish. Grease a broiler pan and brush the fish lightly on both sides with the remaining 2 tablespoons oil.

2. Broil the fish, turning once, until just barely opaque when cut in the thickest part, about 2 minutes per side—be careful not to overcook. Let cool to room temperature. Place in a deep dish, pour the vinaigrette over the fish, and let marinate in the refrigerator at least 2 hours, spooning the sauce over the fish occasionally. Serve cold.

Shellfish

Prawns Smothered in Onion
Langostinos Encebollado

MAKES 4 SERVINGS

This recipe is very simple and can be prepared in almost no time at all. Prawns are preferred over smaller shrimp since they tend to have a firmer consistency. In order for this dish to have the intended pungency, make sure you use enough onions.

2 tablespoons olive oil

30 large shrimp, shelled and deveined

¾ pound onion, finely chopped

3 garlic cloves, finely chopped

2 medium tomatoes, chopped (about 1⅓ cups)

Kosher or sea salt

Freshly ground black pepper

I. Heat the oil in a large skillet over medium heat. Add the shrimp and cook, stirring occasionally, until pink. Transfer to a plate.

2. Add the onion and garlic and cook, stirring, until the onion is wilted, about 5 minutes. Add the tomatoes and cook, stirring, until softened and their juices release, about 2 to 3 minutes more. Add the shrimp and stir in salt and pepper. Cook until the shrimp are just heated through and the sauce is blended, 2 to 3 minutes more. Serve hot.

Crayfish with Paprika, Onion, and Brandy

Cangrejos de Río Guisados con Pimentón, Cebolla y Brandy

MAKES 4 SERVINGS

While the inland areas of Spain don't always have access to the kinds of seafood found in the ocean, the rivers that run through the mountainous regions have an abundance of river crabs, or crayfish, called cangrejos. *Here they are prepared simply but with great flavor.*

2 tablespoons olive oil

32 river crab tails or large shrimp (in their shells)

2 tablespoons brandy

3 tablespoons finely chopped onions

¼ teaspoon red chile pepper

1 tablespoon ground bittersweet paprika, such as Spanish smoked

2 tablespoons finely chopped tomato

1 bay leaf

1 garlic clove, finely chopped

Heat the oil in a large skillet over medium heat. Add the crabs and cook, stirring occasionally, until the shells turn red. Add the brandy. Standing well away from the skillet, ignite the liquid with a match or kitchen lighter and let die out. Transfer to a plate. Add the onions, chile pepper, paprika, tomato, and bay leaf and cook until the onions are wilted, about 5 minutes. Add the crabs and cook about 5 minutes more. Remove the bay leaf. Serve hot.

Crabmeat with Brandy and Wine

Txangurro a la Vasca

MAKES 4 SERVINGS

Txangurro *is the name of a very popular Basque dish made from flaked and well-seasoned* centollo, *the spider crab found off Spain's northern coast. Alaskan king crab can also be used. This and the next recipe are similar but with slightly different approaches from different cooks. Both are delicious.*

This richer version features brandy, sherry, whole tomatoes, and fish broth and gets a little heat from a chile, but it is lighter on aromatics such as shallot and leek. The next recipe is lighter with more of the flavor from aromatics such as onion, leeks, and garlic. It uses white wine and brandy and tomato sauce, but no fish broth. Try them both!

2 tablespoons olive oil

¼ cup peeled and finely chopped carrot

1 medium onion, finely chopped (about ⅔ cup)

1 leek, trimmed, well washed, and finely chopped

1 shallot, finely chopped

2 medium tomatoes, finely chopped (about 1⅓ cups)

¼ cup storebought or homemade Fish Broth or bottled clam juice

3 tablespoons brandy

4 tablespoons dry sherry, such as Fino

3 tablespoons finely chopped fresh flat-leaf parsley

¼ teaspoon dried tarragon

½ medium dried chile pepper, stemmed and seeded

Kosher or sea salt

Freshly ground black pepper

1 pound cooked crabmeat, coarsely chopped

Unsalted butter

Bread crumbs

1. Preheat the oven to 400°F. Heat the oil in a medium skillet over medium heat. Add the carrot, onion, leek, and shallot and cook, stirring, until the vegetables are softened, about 8 minutes. Lower the heat to low and stir in the tomatoes, broth, brandy, sherry, parsley, tarragon, chile pepper, salt, and pepper. Let simmer several minutes. Stir in the crabmeat and cook until the crabmeat is heated through and the sauce well blended.

2. Fill the 4 individual ovenproof ramekins with the crab mixture, dot with the butter, and sprinkle with the bread crumbs. Bake 10 minutes or until the bread crumbs are browned. Serve hot.

Crab in Wine, Brandy, and Tomato Sauce
Centollo a la Donostiarra

MAKES 4 SERVINGS

Centollo is the Spanish word for spider crabs, which are immensely popular in the region of Asturia. It is found exclusively in the Bay of Biscay. Called txangurro *in Basque, it is usually served in its shell. If you have scallop shells or can get them from the fishmonger, serving this in the shells makes a lovely presentation.*

2 tablespoons olive oil

¼ cup finely chopped carrot

1 medium onion, finely chopped (about ⅔ cup)

2 medium scallions, finely chopped (about ¼ cup)

3 medium leeks, trimmed, well washed, and finely chopped

2 garlic cloves, finely chopped

½ teaspoon ground bittersweet paprika, such as Spanish smoked

Kosher or sea salt

Freshly ground black pepper

1 pound cooked crabmeat, coarsely chopped

¼ cup dry white wine

¼ cup brandy

½ cup tomato sauce

Unsalted butter

Bread crumbs

1. Preheat the oven to 400°F. Heat the oil in a medium skillet over medium heat. Add the carrot, onion, scallions, leeks, and garlic, and season with paprika, salt, and pepper. Reduce the heat to low, and cook, stirring, until the vegetables are softened, about 10 minutes. Add the crabmeat, wine, brandy, and tomato sauce and cook, stirring, a few minutes to combine.

2. Transfer to 4 cleaned scallop shells, 4 individual ramekins, or a roasting pan. Dot with the butter and sprinkle with the bread crumbs. Bake about 10 minutes or until the bread crumbs are golden. Serve hot.

Lobster Casserole with Garlic, Nuts, and Chocolate
Cazuela de Langosta a la Catalana

MAKES 2 SERVINGS

Inventiveness and creativity are typical in Catalan-style cooking. Recipes like this one that call for bittersweet chocolate are definitely a reflection of the influence of the new products and ingredients brought from America by Spain in the sixteenth century.

One (2-pound) live lobster

2 tablespoons olive oil

1 medium onion, coarsely chopped (about ⅔ cup)

1 medium tomato, chopped (about ⅔ cup)

⅓ cup white wine

⅓ cup storebought or homemade Fish Broth or bottled clam juice

Picada

4 garlic cloves

2 tablespoons finely chopped fresh flat-leaf parsley

10 hazelnuts

16 blanched almonds

1½ teaspoons grated bittersweet chocolate

I. Place a cutting board in a rimmed cookie sheet to catch the liquid that collects. Place the lobster on its back on the cutting board. Do not remove the bands that keep the claws shut. Protect your hand with a heavy towel or pot holder and hold the lobster firmly by the head. Plunge the tip of a heavy chef's knife into the body where the tail joins the chest. Cut all the way through, separating the tail from the body. Pull out and discard the dark vein from the tail. Slice the head down the middle and discard the stomach sack. Reserve the liquid, the tomalley (green matter), and the coral (red roe), if any, for another use. With sturdy kitchen scissors, cut off the large and small claws

and reserve. Remove the tail meat from the shell and cut crosswise into pieces.

2. Heat the oil in an earthenware casserole dish or Dutch oven. Add the lobster meat and cook, stirring occasionally until just tender. Transfer to a platter. Add the onion and cook, stirring, until wilted, about 5 minutes. Add the tomato and cook, stirring, 5 minutes more. Stir in the wine and broth.

3. Meanwhile, in a mortar or mini-processor, mash the picada ingredients and add it and the reserved lobster claws to the casserole dish. Cook until the lobster is just heated through and has absorbed some of the sauce, about 10 minutes more. If using earthenware, serve hot in the dish, or transfer to individual plates.

Lobster Stew
Caldereta de Langosta

MAKES 4 SERVINGS

The most famous dish to originate on the island of Menorca is this wonderful lobster stew flavored with almonds, garlic, peppers, and tomatoes. I learned this recipe from my friend Pepe Sanz.

6 cups storebought or homemade Fish Broth (page 199; double recipe) or bottled clam juice

2 (2-pound) live lobsters

¼ cup olive oil

3 medium onions, finely chopped (about 2 cups)

6 cloves garlic, finely chopped

2 medium green bell peppers, finely chopped (about 1½ cups)

3 medium tomatoes, finely chopped (about 2 cups)

2 (jarred) piquillo peppers

¼ pound ground blanched almonds

I. Prepare the broth if necessary. Place a cutting board in a rimmed cookie sheet to catch the liquid that collects. Place the lobster on its back on the cutting board. Do not remove the bands that keep the claws shut. Protect your hand with a heavy towel or pot holder and hold the lobster firmly by the head. Plunge the tip of a heavy chef's knife into the body where the tail joins the chest. Cut all the way through, separating the tail from the body. Pull out and discard the dark vein from the tail. Slice the head down the middle, discard the stomach sack, and reserve the tomalley (green matter) and the coral (red roe), if any. Cut off the large and small claws and reserve. Remove the tail meat from the shell and cut crosswise into pieces.

2. Heat the oil in a large earthenware casserole dish or Dutch oven over medium heat. Add the lobster meat and stir briefly. Transfer to a platter.

3. Add the onions, garlic, and bell peppers and cook, stirring, until softened, about 10 minutes. Add the reserved tomalley and coral, the tomatoes, piquillo peppers, and almonds. Stir in the broth and cook, stirring occasionally, about 15 minutes more. Add the lobster meat and the reserved claws and cook until the lobster is cooked but still tender, the claws are red, and the sauce has been absorbed, 10 minutes more. If using earthenware, serve hot in the dish, or transfer to individual plates.

Once you work with lobsters at home a few times, it really isn't that difficult. For the freshest taste, killing them right before cooking is best; you can do so with a knife or put them into a pot of boiling water.

Killing: Place a cutting board in a rimmed cookie sheet to catch the liquid that collects and reserve it. Place the lobster on its back on the cutting board. Do not remove the bands that keep the claws shut. Protect your hand with a heavy towel or pot holder and hold the lobster firmly by the head. Plunge the tip of a heavy chef's knife into the body where the tail joins the chest. Cut all the way through, separating the tail from the body.

Cleaning: Pull out and discard the dark vein from the tail. Slice the head down the middle, discard the stomach sack, and transfer the tomalley (green matter) to a mortar, and reserve the coral (red roe), if any.

Cooking live: Holding each lobster with a towel, add them to the water headfirst. Cover and boil 15 minutes or until the shells are bright red and the tails curled.

Shellfish Casserole with Saffron and White Wine
Cazuela de Marisco al Albariño

MAKES 4 SERVINGS

Catalunya and the Balearic Islands are sometimes referred to as "the region of the casseroles." This version is a delicious mix of lobster, shrimp, and clams in a wine sauce with a saffron accent. Albariño's acidic flavor lends a pleasant flavor to this dish. It is a young white wine produced exclusively in Galicia, which has become quite popular, and can easily be found in the United States.

2 dozen small Manila clams

2 (1½-pound) live lobsters

2 tablespoons olive oil

¼ cup finely chopped onion

1 garlic clove, finely chopped

Few threads of saffron, crumbled

1 bay leaf

12 large shrimp, shelled

½ cup dry white wine

½ cup storebought or homemade Fish Broth or bottled clam juice

2 tablespoons tomato paste

1. Rinse the clams. Discard any with cracked shells or that do not close tightly when touched.

2. Meanwhile, place a cutting board in a rimmed cookie sheet to catch the liquid that collects. Place each lobster on its back on the cutting board. Do not remove the bands that keep the claws shut. Protect your hand with a heavy towel or pot holder and hold the lobster firmly by the head. Plunge the tip of a heavy chef's knife into the body where the tail joins the chest. Cut all the way through, separating the tail from the body. Pull out and discard the dark vein from the tail. Slice the head down the middle and discard the stomach sack. Reserve the liquid, the tomalley (green matter), and the coral (red roe), if any, for another use. With sturdy kitchen scissors, cut off the large and small claws and reserve. Remove the tail meat from the shell, cut in half lengthwise, then cut into pieces and reserve. Do not discard the lobster carcasses.

3. Preheat the oven to 400°F. Heat the oil in a shallow earthenware casserole dish or Dutch oven over medium heat. Add the lobster meat, claws, and carcasses and cook, stirring, until the lobster is cooked but still tender and the claws are red. Transfer to a platter and discard the carcasses.

4. In the casserole dish, add the onion, garlic, saffron, and bay leaf and cook, stirring, until softened. Add the shrimp and cook, stirring, until pink. Add the wine, broth, tomato paste, clams, and the reserved lobster meat and claws. Transfer to the oven and bake until the clams open. Discard any unopened clams and the bay leaf. If using earthenware, serve hot in the dish, or transfer to individual plates.

Marinated Shellfish with Pickles and Capers
Salpicón de Marisco

MAKES 4 SERVINGS

Lobster, shrimp, and crabmeat are delicious in this simple marinade flavored with pickles and capers. Salpicón is very often served as a first course or as a tapa, most frequently in summer months.

One 1½-pound live lobster

¾ pound large shrimp, in their shells

½ pound cooked lump crabmeat

Marinade

½ cup olive oil

3 tablespoons white wine vinegar

5 cornichon or dill pickles, finely chopped

2 tablespoons capers (nonpareil preferred), rinsed
and drained

2 tablespoons finely chopped onion

2 tablespoons finely chopped pimiento

1 tablespoon finely chopped fresh flat-leaf parsley

2 teaspoons Dijon mustard

1 hard-boiled egg, finely chopped

Kosher or sea salt

Freshly ground black pepper

1. Bring a large pot of water to a boil. Holding the lobster with a towel, add it to the water head-first. Cover and boil 15 minutes or until the shell is bright red and the tail curled. Transfer to a platter and let cool. Keep the water at a boil and add the shrimp. Cook just until the shrimp turn pink.

2. Remove the shells from the lobster and shrimp and cut the lobster into chunks.

3. Prepare the marinade: In a large bowl, whisk together the oil and vinegar. Mix in the pickles, capers, onion, pimientos, parsley, and mustard. Fold in the egg, salt, and pepper.

4. Fold in the lobster and shrimp until well coated. Cover and refrigerate at least 1 hour and serve cold.

Mixed Shellfish in Brandy and Tomato Sauce
Zarzuela de Marisco

MAKES 4 SERVINGS

The Spanish word zarzuela *is a term for a musical performance originally produced at the Zarzuela Palace. The varied music of the zarzuela is considered a form of opera. This dish is*

a dazzling array of shellfish, including lobster, shrimp, Manila clams, and mussels, composing a symphony of flavors.

1 dozen small Manila clams

1 dozen mussels

2 (1½-pound) live lobsters

10 tablespoons olive oil

12 large shrimp, in their shells

2 tablespoons finely chopped onion

2 garlic cloves, finely chopped

2 tablespoons brandy

2 medium tomatoes, finely chopped (about 1⅓ cups)

1 teaspoon ground bittersweet paprika, such as
Spanish smoked

1 bay leaf

Freshly ground black pepper

⅛ teaspoon saffron threads, crumbled

½ cup dry white wine

1 small dried red chile pepper, stemmed and seeded

1 tablespoon Worcestershire sauce

Few drops hot sauce, such as Tabasco

Kosher or sea salt

2 tablespoons finely chopped fresh flat-leaf parsley

Lemon wedges, for garnish

1. Rinse the clams and mussels well. Cut or pull off the mussel beards. Discard any clams or mussels with cracked shells or that do not close tightly when touched.

2. Meanwhile, place a cutting board in a rimmed cookie sheet to catch the lobster liquid that collects. Place the lobster on its back on the cutting board. Do not remove the bands that keep the claws shut. Protect your hand with a heavy towel or pot holder and hold the lobster firmly by the head. Plunge the tip of a heavy chef's knife into the body where the tail joins the chest. Cut all the way through, separating the tail from the body. Pull

continues...

out and discard the dark vein from the tail. Slice the head down the middle and discard the stomach sack. Reserve the liquid, the tomalley (green matter), and the coral (red roe), if any, for another use. With sturdy kitchen scissors, cut off the large and small claws. Remove the tail meat from the shell, cut in half lengthwise, then cut into pieces.

3. Preheat the oven to 400°F. Heat the oil in a very large shallow earthenware casserole dish or Dutch oven. Add the lobster claws and meat and the shrimp and cook, stirring, until they just turn pink. Transfer to a platter.

4. Add the onion and garlic and cook, stirring, until the onion is wilted, about 3 minutes. Add the brandy and, standing well away from the casserole dish, ignite the liquid with a match or kitchen lighter and let die out.

5. Add the tomatoes, paprika, bay leaf, pepper, and saffron and cook, stirring, until the tomatoes are softened and their juices release, 2 to 3 minutes more. Add the wine and cook, stirring occasionally, 5 minutes more. Add the lobster, shrimp, clams, mussels, and chile pepper and stir in the Worcestershire and hot sauces. Cover and cook 10 minutes. Remove any unopened clams or mussels. Taste and adjust seasoning if necessary. Sprinkle with the parsley and garnish with the lemon wedges. If using earthenware, serve hot in the dish, or transfer to individual plates.

Octopus with Paprika in Simmered Onions
Pulpo Encebollado a la Gallega

MAKES 4 SERVINGS

Octopus is extremely popular in the region of Galicia, where it is boiled in steaming metal drums and often presented on a wooden dish drizzled with oil and sprinkled with paprika. Preparing octopus is easier than you might think, although it does involve a rather unusual ritual of dunking it several times in boiling water. This gives shape to the octopus and makes it tender.

2 pounds small octopus, cleaned

2 tablespoons olive oil

4 garlic cloves, thinly sliced

2 medium sweet onions, such as Vidalia, finely chopped

2 teaspoons ground sweet paprika, such as Spanish smoked

Salt

Ground hot paprika, such as Spanish smoked

1. Before cooking the octopus, tenderize it by throwing it with force into the kitchen sink. Repeat at least 10 times.

2. Bring a large pot of water to a boil over high heat. Dunk the octopus in the boiling water for a few seconds, remove, and repeat 2 more times, leaving the octopus out of the water a minute between dunkings. Reduce the heat to low, put the octopus in the water, and simmer until tender, about 1 hour. Drain and let cool. Scrape away any loose skin. Cut off the ends of the tentacles with kitchen shears, discard the sac-like mouth, then cut the octopus into 1-inch pieces. Wipe out the pot.

3. In the same pot, heat the oil over medium heat, add the garlic and onions and cook, stirring, about 1 minute. Reduce the heat to low, cover, and simmer about 20 minutes more or until the onion is softened but not browned. Stir in the sweet paprika, octopus, and salt. Increase the heat to medium-low, cover, and cook 10 minutes more or until the flavors are incorporated. Sprinkle with the hot paprika and serve hot.

Octopus with Paprika, Galician Style
Pulpo a la Gallega

MAKES 4 SERVINGS

Octopus is most popular in Spain's northern provinces. In Galicia, it always appears during fiestas, where it is boiled in metal drums. Any dish described as a la gallega *denotes the presence of paprika and oil.*

1½ pounds octopus (2 preferred; about ¾ pound each), cleaned

12 cups water

1 bay leaf

½ medium onion

4 peppercorns

2 sprigs parsley

Kosher or sea salt

Freshly ground black pepper

4 garlic cloves, finely chopped

¼ cup olive oil

2 teaspoons ground bittersweet paprika, such as Spanish smoked

¼ teaspoon crushed hot red pepper flakes

1. Before cooking the octopus, tenderize it by throwing it with force into the kitchen sink. Repeat at least 10 times.

2. In a large pot, bring the water to a boil over high heat. For each octopus, submerge in the water and remove immediately; repeat two more times. Return the water to a boil and add the bay leaf, onion, peppercorns, parsley, and salt. Return the octopus to the pot, reduce the heat to low, cover, and simmer until tender, 45 to 60 minutes. Drain and let cool. Scrape away any loose skin. Cut the bodies and tentacles into bite-size pieces with kitchen shears.

3. In a medium bowl, mix the garlic, oil, paprika, pepper flakes, salt, and pepper and stir in the octopus. Serve.

Octopus in Red Wine Sauce
Pulpo al Vino Tinto

MAKES 4 SERVINGS

This dish is very easy to prepare as it is composed of octopus in a simple red wine sauce. I recommend using a small octopus because the meat is more tender.

2 pounds small octopus, cleaned

2 tablespoons olive oil

3 medium red onions, slivered

8 garlic cloves, finely chopped

6 bay leaves

Kosher or sea salt

Freshly ground black pepper

1½ cups dry red wine

1. Before cooking the octopus, tenderize it by throwing it with force into the kitchen sink. Repeat at least 10 times. Cut the tentacles with kitchen shears into 1-inch pieces and remove any loose skin.

2. Heat the oil in a medium skillet over medium heat. Add the onions, garlic, bay leaves, salt, and pepper, and cook, stirring, until softened. Add the wine and cook until the liquid is reduced by half, about 15 minutes. Reduce the heat to low, add the octopus, and cook until tender, about 1 hour. Serve hot.

Baby Squid in Ink Sauce
Chipirones en su Tinta

MAKES 4 SERVINGS

While the Spanish word calamar *generally refers to large squid,* chipirón *in the Basque Country means baby squid. For any squid dish requiring slow cooking, they are far superior because of their more delicate flesh. I recommend serving this dish surrounded by white rice and fried bread.*

1¾ pounds very small squid, cleaned

2 tablespoons olive oil

2 large onion, chopped

6 garlic cloves, finely chopped

1 medium green bell pepper, finely chopped (about ¾ cup)

Kosher or sea salt

Freshly ground black pepper

2 tablespoons finely chopped fresh flat-leaf parsley

2 teaspoons ground bittersweet paprika, such as Spanish smoked

2 cups storebought or homemade Fish Broth (page 199; partial recipe) or bottled clam juice

1 medium tomato, chopped (about ⅔ cup)

¼ cup dry white wine

¼ cup squid ink

Finely chop the squid tentacles and fill the bodies with them. Heat the oil in a medium skillet over medium heat. Add the squid, onion, garlic, bell pepper, salt, pepper, parsley, and paprika and cook, stirring to incorporate. Reduce the heat to low. Add the broth, tomato, wine, and squid ink, cover, and cook 2 hours. Serve hot.

Stewed Squid with Peppers
Chipirones Estofados

MAKES 4 SERVINGS

This simple recipe of squid stew is quite easy to prepare, although it does require slow cooking 2 hours after the squid and other ingredients are added.

2 tablespoons olive oil

4 medium onions, sliced

4 green frying peppers, finely chopped

4 garlic cloves, finely chopped

24 small squid, cleaned and thinly sliced

¾ cup dry white wine

Heat the oil in a medium skillet over medium heat. Add the onions and cook, stirring, until wilted, 10 to 12 minutes. Add the frying peppers, garlic, and squid, and cook, turning occasionally, until the peppers are softened. Add the wine and cook, stirring, until the squid is tender and the sauce is blended, about 2 hours. Serve hot.

Stewed Squid with Peppers and Sherry
Guiso de Calamares

MAKES 4 SERVINGS

Rings of squid are best for this stew as it requires them to be fried before they are submerged in a sherry sauce that works well to soften the squid.

2 pounds squid, cleaned

All-purpose flour

Olive oil, for frying

2 tablespoons olive oil

2 medium onions, chopped (about 1⅓ cups)

1 medium green bell pepper, cut into very thin strips

1 medium red bell pepper, cut into very thin strips

2 tablespoons finely chopped fresh flat-leaf parsley

2 medium tomatoes, finely chopped (about 1⅓ cups)

Kosher salt

Freshly ground black pepper

¼ cup dry sherry

1. Cut the squid bodies into rings. Place the flour in a wide shallow bowl.

2. Heat at least ½ inch of oil in a medium skillet over medium-high heat (or better still, use a deep fryer set at 365°F) until it turns a cube of bread light brown in 60 seconds. Dredge the squid in the flour, place in the oil, and cook until golden. Transfer with a slotted spoon to paper towels and let drain.

3. Heat the 2 tablespoons oil in a large skillet over medium heat. Add the onion, bell peppers, and parsley and cook, stirring, until softened, about 8 minutes. Add the tomatoes, salt, and black pepper and cook, stirring, until the tomatoes are softened and their juices release, 2 to 3 minutes more. Reduce the heat to low, add the squid and sherry, and simmer until the squid is softened, about 45 minutes. Serve hot.

Baked Stuffed Squid in Almond Sauce

Calamares al Horno "Triana"

MAKES 4 SERVINGS

This squid is stuffed with a mixture of its tentacles, garlic, and parsley, then baked in a wine sauce and covered with toasted almonds. The results are outstanding.

1½ pounds squid with tentacles, bodies no more than 3 inches long

4 tablespoons finely chopped fresh flat-leaf parsley

2 garlic cloves, finely chopped

½ plus ⅛ teaspoon kosher or sea salt

2 tablespoons olive oil

12 blanched almonds

2 thin slices long-loaf (baguette) bread, crust removed

¾ cup plus 2 tablespoons dry white wine

1 medium onion, slivered

½ cup storebought or homemade Fish Broth or bottled clam juice

Freshly ground black pepper

1½ teaspoons finely chopped fresh thyme or ¼ teaspoon dried thyme

1 bay leaf

1. Make a small slit at the pointed end of each squid. Rinse thoroughly, letting the water run through the body sac. Let drain on paper towels. Finely chop the tentacles and combine in a small bowl with 2 tablespoons of the parsley, half of the garlic, and the ½ teaspoon salt. Stuff the squid bodies with this mixture and reserve.

2. Heat the oil in a shallow earthenware casserole dish or Dutch oven over medium heat. Add the almonds and bread and cook, stirring the almonds and turning the bread once, until the almonds are browned and the bread golden. Transfer to a mortar, reserving the oil in the casserole dish, add the remaining 2 tablespoons parsley and the ⅛ teaspoon salt, and mash as finely as possible. Add 2 tablespoons of the wine and mash until a paste forms.

3. Preheat the oven to 350°F. In the casserole dish over medium heat, add the onion, the remaining half of the garlic, and a little more oil if necessary. Reduce the heat to low and cook, stirring, until the onion is wilted, about 5 minutes.

4. Add the mortar mixture and stir in the remaining ¾ cup wine, the broth, salt, pepper, thyme, and bay leaf. Cook, stirring, 1 minute, then add the squid. Transfer to the oven and bake 45 minutes, basting the squid occasionally. Remove the bay leaf. If using earthenware, serve hot in the dish, or transfer to individual plates.

Squid Filled with Shrimp
Calamares Rellenos de Cigalas

MAKES 4 TO 6 SERVINGS

In this popular recipe, the squid is stuffed with a mixture of ham, egg, shrimp, and tentacles, then rolled in bread crumbs and fried until golden.

1¾ pounds medium squid

24 medium shrimp, shelled, deveined, and coarsely chopped

1 hard-boiled egg, finely chopped

½ pound mushrooms

3 garlic cloves, finely chopped

1 teaspoon kosher or sea salt

2 tablespoons finely chopped fresh flat-leaf parsley

Sauce

2 tablespoons olive oil

1 medium onion, finely chopped (about ⅔ cup)

1 teaspoon all-purpose flour

1 cup dry white wine

Freshly ground black pepper

Kosher or sea salt

1. Make a small slit at the pointed end of each squid. Rinse thoroughly, letting the water run through the body sac. Cut the tentacles lengthwise in half at the base.

2. Preheat the oven to 350°F. In a mortar or mini-processor, mash the garlic, salt, and parsley. Mash in the egg, then stir in the tentacles. Stuff into the squid bodies and close with a toothpick. Place in a shallow earthenware casserole dish or Dutch oven and reserve.

3. Prepare the sauce: Heat the oil in a medium skillet over medium heat. Add the onion and cook, stirring, until wilted, about 5 minutes. Add the flour and cook, stirring, until golden brown. Stir in the wine, salt, and pepper. Pour over the squid.

4. Transfer the casserole dish to the oven and bake about 25 minutes. If using earthenware, serve hot in the dish, or transfer to individual plates.

Marinated Frog Legs
Ancas de Rana a la Valenciana

MAKES 4 SERVINGS

The region of Valencia is filled with rice paddies in a swampy terrain in which frogs thrive. Since frogs are small in Spain, their legs make perfect tapas or serve with rice for a main dish.

PREPARE AT LEAST 3 HOURS IN ADVANCE

Marinade

½ cup dry white wine

½ teaspoon thyme

1 tablespoon olive oil

1 tablespoon finely chopped fresh flat-leaf parsley

1½ pounds medium frog legs (about 10 to 12 pairs)

Salt

Freshly ground black pepper

All-purpose flour, for dredging

2 large eggs, lightly beaten

Bread crumbs

Oil, such as a mix of olive and salad, for frying

1 garlic clove, mashed in a garlic press or mortar

Juice of 1 lemon

4 peppercorns

Salt

1. Prepare the marinade: Mix the marinade ingredients in a small bowl.

2. Separate the frog legs, if the pairs are joined, and place in a shallow earthenware casserole dish or Dutch oven. Pour the marinade over the legs. Cover and refrigerate at least 3 hours. Place the flour, eggs, and bread crumbs in separate small shallow bowls. Transfer the legs to paper towels and let drain. Season both sides with salt and pepper.

3. Heat at least ½ inch of oil in a large skillet over medium-high heat (or better still, use a deep fryer set at 375°F) until it browns a cube of bread quickly. Dredge the legs in the flour, dip in the egg, roll in the bread crumbs, and place in the oil. Cook, turning once, until golden. Transfer with a slotted spoon to paper towels and let drain. Serve hot. Alternatively, they may be kept warm in a 200°F oven up to 30 minutes if you like and served warm.

Poultry and Game

ROASTED CHICKEN

Roast Chicken in Lemon Sauce

Rosemary and Lemon-Scented
Chicken with Potatoes

Chicken with Crispy Bits and Lemon

Roast Chicken with Orange Sauce

Roast Chicken with Sherry

Roast Chicken in Wine Sauce

Roast Chicken with Figs

Chicken with Peaches in Syrup

Chicken in Pomegranate Sauce

Spit-Roasted Chicken Brushed with
Honey-Cumin Marinade

Broiled Marinated Chicken
with Garlic and Lemon

Broiled Marinated Chicken with Garlic Sauce

Baked Stuffed Chicken Breast

SAUTÉED AND FRIED CHICKEN

Garlic Chicken

Chalo's Breaded Chicken Cutlets with Alioli

Béchamel-Coated Fried Chicken

Chicken in Garlic Sauce

Yesterday's Chicken

Chicken Livers in Sherry and Onion Sauce

Garlic Chicken Livers with Hazelnuts

BRAISED AND STEWED CHICKEN

Braised Chicken in Brandy Sauce

Chicken in Garlic with Brandy and Parsley

Chicken in Brandy Sauce with Shrimp

 = Vegetarian    = Vegetarian with one change

Garlic Chicken with Wine and Peppers

Braised Chicken and Onion

Chicken Braised with Onions, Garlic, and Saffron

Chicken with Ham, Olives, and Sherry

Chicken with Pine Nuts

Chicken with Red Peppers

Chicken with Vegetables

Chicken with Apples and Raisins

Lemon Chicken with Ginger and Pine Nuts

Chicken and Sparerib Stew

Chicken in Egg and Almond Sauce

Pepita's Stewed Chicken with Almonds and Egg

Stewed Chicken with Cream and Truffles

Chicken with White Wine,
Grape Juice, and Cilantro

Chicken with Green Olives

"The Good Woman's" Chicken

Chicken and Chorizo in Red Wine Sauce

Cándida's Stewed Chicken with Potatoes

Chicken with Stewed Vegetables
in Caramelized Sugar Sauce

Grandma's Stewed Chicken

Chicken in Black Currant and Sherry Sauce

Chicken in Fino Sherry Sauce

Chicken in Puréed Onion and Wine Sauce

Chicken with Almonds and Honey

Lobster with Chicken

Chicken with Shrimp in Almond
and Hazelnut Sauce

Turkey "Fricassee" Faín

PHEASANT, PARTRIDGE, AND QUAIL

Roasted Pheasants with Port

Partridges in White Wine Sauce, Toledo Style

Partridges in Escabeche

Partridges with Stuffed Cabbage Leaves

Stewed Partridges

Fermín's Saffron-Marinated Partridge

Partridges in Chocolate-Flavored Sauce

Braised Quail

Braised Marinated Quail

Quail with Beans

Braised Quail in Grape Leaves

Grilled Quail with Garlic and Parsley

Quail in Green Peppers

Sautéed Small Birds with Crumb Topping

Quail in a Nest

DUCK AND GOOSE

Duck with Sherry and Green Olives, Sevilla Style

Duck in Orange Sauce

Duck with Prunes and Pine Nuts

Roasted Duck with Quince Sauce

Baby Goose with Pears

RABBIT

Broiled Rabbit with Garlic Sauce

Rabbit Coated with Honey-Garlic Mayonnaise

Rabbit in Tomato Sauce

Marinated Rabbit in Sherry Sauce

Rabbit Stew, Zamora Style

Sautéed Rabbit, Batter-Fried with Sesame Seeds

Rabbit with Almonds and Pine Nuts

Rabbit in Garlic and Dried Red Pepper Sauce

Rabbit with Red Peppers and Zucchini

Rabbit with Crisp Bread Bits

Rabbit in Egg and Lemon Sauce

Rabbit in Garlic Sauce

Rabbit in Tomato and White Wine

Rabbit, Hunter Style

Potted Rabbit

Rabbit in Almond and Olive Sauce

Rabbit with Blackberries and Brown Sugar

$\mathcal{T}$he reasons why Spain is known around the world as a hunter's paradise are twofold. The first is Spain's topography and climate. Much of Spain is mountainous terrain, which creates many acres of low mountain brushlands that are ideal for pheasants, partridge, quail, and rabbits to breed. The second reason is its geographic location. Spain is on the migratory path of millions of European birds that travel to Africa for the winter. In spring, when they return to their homeland, most of them pass through Spain, where they tend to bear their offspring before continuing their journey.

Because Spain has such an abundance of game, restaurant menus tend to feature partridge, quail, and rabbit almost as frequently as chicken, and these other birds are also cooked at home. Chickens in Spain wander around freely on small farms, eating whatever they choose—they are free-range in the truest sense of the word.

It's very important to use only high-quality poultry. If you can use free-range, please do to ensure the best taste and texture. The most popular way to prepare chicken is *al ajillo* or in garlic sauce, and there are innumerable versions of this classic recipe. Garlic chicken in Catalunya often includes fruit or other sweet ingredients which create a flavor that is both savory and sweet. Garlic chicken in Aragon tends to be spicier as it includes the fresh, succulent red bell peppers found in that region. Out of the many garlic chicken dishes that I have tasted, my favorite one is served at Casa Lucio, the extraordinary restaurant in the old quarter of Madrid.

Pheasant and partridge have a more muscular meat, and cooks usually prepare them by stewing for hours in order to tenderize them. Quail, a small bird with lots of flavor, is especially beloved by Spaniards. Its tiny size is perfect for elaborate dishes such as quail wrapped in grape leaves, quail stuffed in green peppers, and quail surrounded by a "nest" of fried potatoes.

In addition to game birds, rabbits also have a long history in Spain. In the third century B.C., when the ancient Romans reached the Iberian Peninsula, they found so many rabbits in the untamed lush green lands that they named it "Hispania," which means "land of the rabbit." Spaniards are inordinately fond of rabbit, and it is eaten with more frequency than even chicken. Unfortunately, its popularity has yet to spread to the United States, which is a shame because rabbit meat is tasty, lean, and nutritious. In fact, it is much healthier than chicken because the skin is never eaten, and the meat, which is all white, is virtually fat free. This chapter contains several rabbit recipes, but if you truly have an aversion to it, chicken can always be substituted. Still, I urge you to at least try rabbit, which can now be commonly found frozen in many American supermarkets.

Roasted Chicken

Roast Chicken in Lemon Sauce
Pollo al Limón

MAKES 4 SERVINGS

Chicken roasted with lemons and rosemary is always a favorite with my dinner guests. The paprika, wine, and pine nuts complete a great dish.

2 tablespoons olive oil

One (3- to 3½-pound) chicken

12 garlic cloves, lightly smashed

2 lemons, cut into wedges

Kosher or sea salt

Freshly ground black pepper

½ teaspoon dried rosemary

½ teaspoon ground bittersweet paprika, such as Spanish smoked

¼ cup dry white wine

¼ cup chicken broth or vegetable broth

¼ cup pine nuts

1. Detach the chicken wings and legs. Hack off the bony ends of the legs and the tips of the wings and discard. Hack or cut with kitchen shears the breast into 4 pieces and each thigh crosswise in half.

2. Preheat the oven to 350°F. Arrange the chicken in a greased roasting pan. Scatter the garlic cloves and lemon wedges around the pan, season with salt, pepper, the rosemary, and paprika, and add the wine, broth, and pine nuts. Roast about 40 minutes or until the dark meat inside just turns opaque. Serve hot.

Rosemary and Lemon-Scented Chicken with Potatoes
Pollo al Romero y Limón con Patatas

MAKES 4 SERVINGS

Rosemary grows wild in Spain, and it is the perfect complement to this dish of lemon-scented chicken, made heartier by the addition of potatoes.

One (3- to 3½-pound) chicken, preferably free-range

2 tablespoons olive oil

12 garlic cloves, loose skin removed and lightly smashed

Salt

Freshly ground black pepper

¾ pound baking potatoes, peeled and cut into ¾-inch pieces

4 lemon slices, halved

3 sprigs rosemary or ½ teaspoon dried rosemary

¼ cup dry white wine

¼ cup chicken broth or vegetable broth

1. Preheat the oven to 450°F. Detach the chicken wings and legs. Hack off the bony ends of the legs and the tips of the wings and discard. Hack or cut with kitchen shears the breast into 4 pieces and each thigh crosswise in half.

2. Grease a roasting pan with 1 tablespoon of the oil. Arrange the chicken, skin side up, and scatter the garlic cloves around the chicken. Brush the chicken with the remaining 1 tablespoon oil and season with salt and pepper. Roast 10 minutes, reduce the heat to 350°F, scatter the potatoes around the chicken, and season them with salt.

3. Scatter the lemon and rosemary sprigs around the pan (or sprinkle the chicken and potatoes with the dried rosemary) and bake 5 minutes more. Add the wine and bake 10 minutes more, then add the broth and bake 30 minutes more or until the dark meat just turns opaque inside (remove the white

meat sooner if needed), adding more broth or water if necessary to keep some liquid in the pan. Serve hot.

Chicken with Crispy Bread Bits and Lemon
Pollo con Migas y Limón

MAKES 4 SERVINGS

The key to this variation on lemon chicken is the croutons, which soak up the flavor of the sauce and make this delicious recipe all the more hearty.

1 cup crustless ½-inch torn pieces bread

2 tablespoons plus 1 to 2 teaspoons olive oil

One (3- to 3½-pound) chicken

Salt

All-purpose flour, for dredging

1 medium onion, finely chopped (about ⅔ cup)

2 ounces Serrano (Spanish cured mountain) ham or prosciutto, cut into ¼-inch cubes (about ¼ cup)

¾ cup dry white wine

¼ cup chicken broth or vegetable broth

½ lemon, thinly sliced

Finely chopped fresh flat-leaf parsley, for garnish

I. Preheat the oven to 350°F. Grease a cookie sheet with the 1 to 2 teaspoons oil and arrange the bread on the sheet. Bake about 5 minutes, stirring occasionally, until golden on all sides. Reserve.

2. Detach the chicken wings and legs. Hack off the bony ends of the legs and the tips of the wings and discard. Hack or cut with kitchen shears the breast into 4 pieces and each thigh crosswise in half. Season the chicken with salt. Place the flour in a wide shallow bowl and dredge the chicken in the flour.

3. Heat the remaining 2 tablespoons oil in a shallow earthenware casserole dish or Dutch oven over medium-high heat. Add the chicken and cook, turning once, until browned on all sides. Add the

onion and ham and cook, stirring, until the onion is wilted and transparent, about 5 minutes. Add the wine and broth, scatter the lemon slices around the chicken, and bring to a boil.

4. Transfer the oven and bake 45 minutes or until the dark meat just turns opaque inside, adding more broth if necessary to ensure there is always some liquid in the pan. Scatter the bread over the chicken and sprinkle with the parsley. If using earthenware, serve hot in the dish, or transfer to a platter.

Roast Chicken with Orange Sauce
Pollo Asado con Salsa de Naranja

MAKES 4 SERVINGS

The sweetness of the orange is tempered by the vinegar in this delicious sweet-sour recipe of Catalan origin.

3- to 3½-pound chicken, trussed

Salt and freshly ground black pepper

¾ cup chicken broth or vegetable broth

5 teaspoons powdered (confectioners) sugar

3½ teaspoons vinegar

Juice of 2 oranges (about ¾ cup)

2 teaspoons cornstarch

1 tablespoon water

I. Preheat the oven to 375°F. Place the chicken in an oval earthenware casserole dish or a roasting pan. Season with salt and pepper. Bake, basting occasionally, about 1 hour or until the skin is golden, the internal temperature of the dark meat reaches 165°F, and the legs move easily when gently lifted or twisted. Transfer to a warmed platter and cover loosely with foil. Being careful to retain the juices, pour off the fat from the casserole dish. Deglaze the dish, adding ¼ cup of the broth, stirring, and scraping up any bits of flavor. Reserve.

continues…

2. In a medium skillet, place 4½ teaspoons of the sugar and heat over low heat, stirring constantly, until the sugar turns golden and caramelizes. Remove from the heat and add 3 teaspoons of the vinegar, the orange juice, the remaining ½ cup broth, and the reserved liquid. Add the remaining ½ teaspoon sugar and ½ teaspoon vinegar. Return to the stove on low heat, cover, and simmer until blended and reduced, about 10 minutes.

3. In a cup, dissolve the cornstarch in the water. Add to the sauce and cook, stirring constantly, until thickened and smooth. Remove the string from the chicken and cut into serving pieces. Spoon the sauce over the chicken and serve.

Roast Chicken with Sherry
Pollo al Horno

MAKES 4 SERVINGS

Cádiz is famous for a succulent roast chicken dish that uses sherry produced in Jerez. I've sampled many different versions of pollo al horno *throughout the various regions of Spain, but this original recipe remains the best that I have found.*

One (3- to 3½-pound) chicken

2 tablespoons olive oil

Salt

Freshly ground black pepper

1 tablespoon finely chopped fresh flat-leaf parsley

2 garlic cloves, cut into several pieces

¼ cup medium-sweet sherry, such as Oloroso

2 tablespoons lard or unsalted butter

1. Detach the chicken wings and legs. Hack off the bony ends of the legs and the tips of the wings and discard. Hack or cut with kitchen shears the breast into 4 pieces and each thigh crosswise in half.

2. Preheat the oven to 375°F. Grease the bottom of a roasting pan with the oil. Arrange the chicken pieces skin side up, in the pan and season with salt, pepper, and parsley. Scatter the garlic around the chicken and pour in the sherry. Dot the chicken with the lard or butter.

3. Roast about 50 minutes, basting the chicken frequently and adding water to ensure there is always some liquid in the pan, until the dark meat is opaque inside (remove the white meat sooner if needed). Serve hot.

Roast Chicken in Wine Sauce
Pollo al Vino

MAKES 4 SERVINGS

Even though this recipe has similar ingredients to other roast chicken recipes, this dish has a taste all its own. The Paúles monks of the village of Tardajos in Burgos province are credited for keeping this recipe alive through the years.

One (3- to 3½-pound) chicken

Fresh lemon juice

Kosher or sea salt

Freshly ground black pepper

1 medium onion, slivered

2 garlic cloves, finely chopped

2 tablespoons finely chopped fresh flat-leaf parsley

2 tablespoons olive oil

¼ cup dry white wine

Chicken broth or vegetable broth

1. Detach the chicken wings and legs. Hack off the bony ends of the legs and the tips of the wings and discard. Hack or cut with kitchen shears the breast into 4 pieces and each thigh crosswise in half.

2. Preheat the oven to 375°F. Arrange the chicken in a large roasting pan. Sprinkle with the lemon

juice, salt, and pepper and scatter the onion around the chicken.

3. In a mortar or mini-processor, mash the garlic, parsley, a little salt, and pepper. Stir in the oil and wine. Pour over the chicken.

4. Transfer to the oven and bake about 40 minutes until the flavors are blended and the dark meat is opaque inside (remove the white meat sooner if needed), adding broth if necessary to ensure there is always some liquid in the pan. Spoon the sauce over the chicken and serve hot.

Roast Chicken with Figs
Pollo con Higos

MAKES 4 SERVINGS

It is typical of Catalan-style cooking to combine the savory flavor of meat with the sweet flavor of fruit. Fig trees grow in abundance all over the Mediterranean, and this recipe for chicken with figs creates a dish that is unusual but outstanding.

PREPARE AT LEAST 4 HOURS IN ADVANCE

Figs

¾ cup sugar

¾ cup water

½ cup vinegar

1 slice lemon

1 cinnamon stick

1 pound fresh figs or jarred figs, drained

½ cup medium sweet white wine

Peel of ½ lemon (yellow part only)

One (3- to 3½-pound) chicken

Kosher or sea salt

Freshly ground black pepper

½ cup small cubes (¼ inch) slab bacon

1 tablespoon olive oil

3 tablespoons beef broth, chicken broth, or water

1. Prepare the figs: In a medium saucepan, mix the sugar, water, vinegar, lemon, and cinnamon and bring to a boil over medium heat. Cook, stirring occasionally, about 5 minutes. Add the figs, return to a boil, and simmer about 10 minutes more (only 5 minutes for jarred figs). Cover and let sit at room temperature at least 4 hours.

2. Drain the figs, discarding the lemon and cinnamon, and place in a medium bowl. Add the wine and lemon peel. Let sit while preparing the chicken.

3. Detach the chicken wings and legs. Hack off the bony ends of the legs and the tips of the wings and discard. Hack or cut with kitchen shears the breast into 4 pieces and each thigh crosswise in half. Season with salt and pepper.

4. Place the bacon in a large shallow earthenware casserole dish or Dutch oven over low heat. Cook, stirring, until its fat is rendered and it turns golden. Transfer the bacon with a slotted spoon to paper towels and let drain, reserving its oil.

5. Preheat the oven to 375°F. In the same oil over medium-high heat, stir in the olive oil, add the chicken, and cook, turning occasionally, until golden on all sides. Very gradually add the wine in which the figs have been soaking (discard the lemon peel), then increase the heat to high and cook until the wine is reduced and syrupy.

6. Transfer to the oven and bake 20 minutes, adding water if necessary to ensure there is always some liquid in the casserole dish. Return the casserole dish to the stovetop over medium heat. Add the broth and figs, cover, and cook 10 minutes more until the flavors are blended and the dark meat is opaque inside (remove the white meat sooner if needed). If using earthenware, serve hot in the dish, or transfer to a platter.

Chicken with Peaches in Syrup

Pollo al Vino con Melocotones en Jarabe

Catalunya is unrivalled when it comes to innovative recipes that pair fruits with meat, seafood, and poultry. This delightful dish combines chicken with peaches that have been cooked in sugar syrup.

Peaches

1 cup water

⅓ cup sugar

½ cinnamon stick

1 slice lemon

3 medium peaches, peeled, halved, and pitted

One (3- to 3½-pound) chicken

Kosher or sea salt

1 tablespoon olive oil

1 garlic clove, finely chopped

¼ cup dry white wine

¼ cup chicken broth or vegetable broth

1. In a medium saucepan, combine the water, sugar, cinnamon, and lemon, bring to a boil over low medium heat, then lower the heat and simmer about 5 minutes. Add the peaches, simmer 1 minute, remove from the heat, cover, and let steep while the chicken cooks.

2. Detach the chicken wings and legs. Hack off the bony ends of the legs and the tips of the wings and discard. Hack or cut with kitchen shears the breast into 4 pieces and each thigh crosswise in half. Season all over with salt.

3. Preheat the oven to 400°F. In a shallow earthenware casserole dish or Dutch oven, heat the oil over medium-high heat. Add the chicken and cook, turning once, until browned on all sides. Add the garlic and cook, stirring, 1 minute. Reduce the heat to low, add the wine, and bring to a boil. Cook until the wine is reduced by half. Add the broth, cover, and simmer 20 minutes. Add the peaches and 2 tablespoons of the peach syrup.

4. Transfer to the oven and bake 15 minutes or until the dark meat just turns opaque inside. If using earthenware, serve hot in the dish, or transfer to a platter.

Chicken in Pomegranate Sauce

Pollo en Salsa de Granadas

Spain has a long history and association with the pomegranate that dates back to the conquest of Granada in 1492 when the pomegranate was incorporated by the Catholic Kings to the coat of arms of Spain. But the idea of combining this unusual fruit with main courses was inspired by the creative flair typical of the dishes of Catalunya.

PREPARE 2 HOURS IN ADVANCE

One (3- to 3½-pound) chicken

Kosher or sea salt

2 large pomegranates

4 teaspoons cumin seeds or ground cumin

2 whole cloves

2 teaspoons peppercorns

¼ teaspoon grated or ground nutmeg

Dash of ground cinnamon

4 garlic cloves

2 tablespoons extra-virgin olive oil

¼ cup chicken broth or vegetable broth

1. Detach the chicken wings and legs. Hack off the bony ends of the legs and the tips of the wings and discard. Hack or cut with kitchen shears the breast into 4 pieces and each thigh crosswise in half. Season all over with salt.

2. Quarter the pomegranates and place the seeds in a food processor. Beat only a few seconds, just until the seeds are crushed and the juice extracted. Pass through a fine-mesh strainer into a small saucepan (there should be about 1½ cups juice). Discard the solids. Bring to a boil over medium heat and cook, stirring occasionally, until the liquid is reduced and the consistency of syrup—you should have about ½ cup. Let cool.

3. In a mortar or mini-processor, mash the cumin, whole cloves, peppercorns, nutmeg, cinnamon, salt, and garlic cloves. Stir in the pomegranate juice and oil.

4. Arrange the chicken pieces in a shallow bowl, skin side up, and spread the marinade over the chicken with a rubber spatula. Cover and let marinate in the refrigerator at least 2 hours.

5. Preheat the oven to 375°F. Transfer the chicken with its marinade to a roasting pan and pour the broth around the chicken. Bake about 40 minutes until the flavors are blended and the dark meat is opaque inside (remove the white meat sooner if needed), adding more broth to ensure there is always some liquid in the pan. Serve hot.

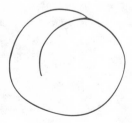

Spit-Roasted Chicken Brushed with Honey-Cumin Marinade
Pollo al Ast Glaseado

MAKES 4 SERVINGS

Although this recipe calls for the chicken to be spit-roasted, it can also be prepared in the oven. This dish is multicultural—it combines the sweet and sour flavors of Catalan-style cooking with the Moorish influence of cumin.

¼ **cup olive oil**
1½ **tablespoons vinegar**
2 **teaspoons ground cumin**
2 **garlic cloves, mashed in a garlic press or mortar**
2 **tablespoons honey**
1 **tablespoon salt**
One (3- to 3½-pound) chicken, trussed

1. In a small bowl, mix all the ingredients except the chicken. Place the chicken in a shallow bowl and pour the marinade evenly over the chicken. Cover and let marinate in the refrigerator at least 1 hour, turning and brushing the chicken with the marinade frequently. Transfer the remaining marinade to a small saucepan and reserve.

2. Preheat the oven to 375°F. Place the chicken on a spit or in a shallow earthenware casserole dish or Dutch oven and bake 1 hour or until the internal temperature of the dark meat reaches 165°F, and the legs move easily when gently lifted or twisted.

3. Meanwhile, bring the marinade to a boil over high heat and cook until reduced by half into a sauce, about 5 minutes. Brush the chicken frequently with the sauce as it roasts. Remove the string and serve hot.

Broiled Marinated Chicken with Garlic and Lemon
Pollo al Ajillo con Limón

MAKES 4 SERVINGS

The nuns of the Santa Clara monastery in Briviesca, in Northern Castilla preserved this recipe. The lemon lends a wonderful zest to the pungency of this broiled garlic chicken. The marinated chicken can also be grilled.

PREPARE AT LEAST 2 HOURS IN ADVANCE

One (3- to 3½-pound) chicken

5 garlic cloves

1 tablespoon finely chopped fresh flat-leaf parsley

1½ teaspoons finely chopped fresh thyme or ¼ teaspoon dried thyme

¼ teaspoon salt

2 tablespoons fresh lemon juice

¼ cup extra-virgin olive oil

¼ cup dry white wine

Freshly ground black pepper

1. Detach the chicken wings and legs. Hack off the bony ends of the legs, then hack or cut with kitchen shears the wings into two parts, discarding the tips, the breast into 4 pieces, and each thigh crosswise in half. Hack or cut the remaining chicken into 2-inch pieces.

2. In a mortar or mini-processor, mash the garlic, parsley, thyme, and ¼ teaspoon salt. Stir in the lemon juice, oil, and wine. Arrange the pieces in a shallow earthenware casserole dish or Dutch oven. Pour the mortar mixture over the chicken, cover, and let marinate in the refrigerator at least 2 hours.

3. Place a broiler rack about 5 inches from the heat source and preheat the broiler. (Cover the broiler pan with foil for easier cleanup, if you like.) Remove the chicken from the marinade (leave the marinade in the casserole dish) and place the chicken skin down on a broiler pan. Broil 5 minutes or until browned. Turn, baste with the marinade, and broil 5 minutes more. Return the chicken, skin side up, to the marinade in the casserole and season with salt and pepper.

4. Preheat the oven to 400°F. Transfer the chicken to the oven and bake 15 minutes, basting occasionally, or until the dark meat just turns opaque inside (remove the white meat sooner if needed). If using earthenware, serve hot in the dish, or transfer to a platter.

Broiled Marinated Chicken with Garlic Sauce
Pollo la Parrilla con Alioli

MAKES 4 SERVINGS

Garlic sauce is the perfect complement to so many Spanish dishes, including vegetables, meat, seafood, and poultry. Here it is delicious when served with broiled—or grilled—chicken.

PREPARE AT LEAST 2 HOURS IN ADVANCE

1 recipe Garlic Sauce (alioli; page 284)

One (3- to 3½-pound) chicken, butterflied (split in half)

Marinade

¾ cup dry white wine

¾ cup extra-virgin olive oil

2 bay leaves, crumbled

4½ teaspoons finely chopped fresh thyme or ¾ teaspoon dried thyme

3 cloves garlic, mashed in a garlic press or mortar

½ teaspoon ground (or mortar-crushed) cumin

Salt

Freshly ground pepper

1. Prepare the sauce. Gently pound each half of the chicken with a meat mallet or small heavy pan until flat.

2. Prepare the marinade: In a large shallow bowl, mix the marinade ingredients. Add the chicken to the marinade, turn to coat well, and place skin side down. Cover and let marinate in the refrigerator at least 2 hours, basting occasionally.

3. Place a broiler rack about 5 inches from the heat source and preheat the broiler. (Cover the broiler pan with foil for easier cleanup, if you like.) Remove the chicken from the marinade and place skin side down on a broiler tray. Broil, turning once and basting occasionally with the marinade, about 7 minutes per side or until browned.

4. Preheat the oven to 400°F. Turn the chicken skin side up and transfer to the oven. Bake, basting occasionally, about 15 minutes more or until the meat just turns opaque inside. Serve hot with the sauce on the side.

Baked Stuffed Chicken Breast
Pechuga de Pollo Rellena

MAKES 4 SERVINGS

This popular dish is prepared by covering each chicken cutlet with a slice of ham and olives, rolling it, and then holding it in place with toothpicks while it cooks. The bold flavors complement each other wonderfully, and the results are outstanding.

4 tablespoons chopped pitted olives, preferably Spanish

¼ cup water

4 thin (or pounded) chicken cutlets

4 thin slices Serrano (Spanish cured mountain) ham or prosciutto

4 tablespoons olive oil

All-purpose flour, for dredging plus 2 tablespoons all-purpose flour

6 tablespoons finely chopped onion

2 garlic cloves, finely chopped

1 cup chicken broth or vegetable broth

1 cup dry white wine

1 tablespoon finely chopped fresh flat-leaf parsley

Salt

Freshly ground black pepper

¼ pound mushrooms, sliced

1. In a small saucepan, place the chopped olives and the water, bring to a boil over medium heat, and cook, 3 minutes. Drain. Season the cutlets with salt and pepper. On a long end of each cutlet, place 1 slice of the ham and 1 tablespoon of the chopped olives and roll up. Secure with toothpicks. Place the flour in a wide shallow bowl. Dredge the cutlets in the flour.

2. Heat the oil in a medium skillet over medium heat. Add the cutlets seam side down and cook, turning occasionally, until golden on all sides, 4 to 6 minutes. Transfer to a shallow earthenware casserole dish or Dutch oven. Reserve 2 tablespoons of the oil in the skillet.

3. Preheat the oven to 350°F. In the skillet oil over medium heat, add the onion and garlic and cook, stirring, until the onion is wilted and transparent, about 5 minutes. Stir in the 2 tablespoons flour, add the broth, wine, parsley, salt, and pepper, and cook, stirring, about 10 minutes more. Add the mushrooms. Pour the sauce over the chicken. Cover and bake 25 minutes until all the flavors blend. If using earthenware, serve hot in the dish, or transfer to a platter.

Garlic Chicken
Pollo al Ajillo Casa Lucio

MAKES 4 SERVINGS

Casa Lucio is a famous restaurant in Old Madrid that has been around for centuries. It has a stellar reputation for down-to-earth cooking and is frequented by movie stars, foreign dignitaries, and even Spain's king. Everything on their menu is sensational, but their garlic chicken is by far the best I have ever tasted. Contrary to most garlic chicken recipes that tend to be saucy, Lucio's version has no sauce. Instead the chicken is garlic flavored, then complemented by a little saffron, vinegar, and wine.

One (3-pound) chicken, preferably free-range

Kosher or sea salt

Olive oil, for frying

1 head garlic, divided into cloves, loose skin removed, unpeeled, and lightly smashed

2 garlic cloves, finely chopped

1 tablespoon wine vinegar

1 tablespoon dry white wine

1 tablespoon chicken broth or vegetable broth

Several threads of saffron, crumbled

I. Detach the chicken wings and legs. Hack off the bony ends of the legs, then hack or cut with kitchen shears the wings into 2 parts, discarding the tips. Divide the remainder of the chicken into quarters, then hack or cut into 2-inch pieces. Season all over with salt and let sit 10 minutes at room temperature.

2. Heat ½ inch of oil in a large skillet over medium-high heat (or better still, use a deep fryer set at 375°F) until it quickly browns a cube of bread. Add the chicken and the smashed garlic and cook, shaking the skillet carefully and turning the pieces frequently, until well browned and the meat inside is opaque, about 12 minutes. Drain the chicken in a fine-mesh strainer, discarding the oil, and leave in the strainer. Wipe out the skillet.

3. In the same skillet, combine the chopped garlic, the vinegar, wine, broth, saffron, and a pinch of salt and bring to a boil over medium heat. Add the chicken and cook, turning frequently, until the liquid is absorbed. Serve hot.

Chalo's Breaded Chicken Cutlets with Alioli
Filetes de Pollo al Alioli de Chalo Peláez

MAKES 4 SERVINGS

This dish is one of my granddaughter's favorites, which is fitting as this recipe came from Chalo Peláez, one of our dearest friends in Spain, who has a child-like enthusiasm for fine food and wine. The secret to Chalo's recipe is that under the crisp bread-crumb coating, he adds a thin layer of alioli sauce.

3 tablespoons Garlic Sauce (alioli; partial recipe; page 284)

2 large eggs

½ teaspoon dried parsley

1 tablespoon grated aged cheese, such as Manchego or Parmesan

1 cup bread crumbs, such as a mix of regular and Japanese-style panko, for dredging

8 very thin chicken cutlets (about ¾ to 1 pound)

Olive oil, for frying

Kosher or sea salt

1. Prepare the alioli. In a small shallow bowl, beat together the eggs, parsley, and cheese with a fork. Place the bread crumbs in another small shallow bowl.

2. Brush each cutlet with about 1 teaspoon alioli per side. Dip the cutlets in the egg mixture and dredge in the crumbs, patting lightly so they adhere well. Let dry on a wire rack.

3. Heat ⅛ inch of oil in a large skillet over medium-high heat to the smoking point. Add as many cutlets as will comfortably fit and cook, turning once, until lightly golden and the meat is just opaque inside when tested with a fork. Transfer with a slotted spatula to paper towels and let drain. Season with salt. Serve immediately, or keep warm briefly in a 200°F oven.

Béchamel-Coated Fried Chicken
Pechuga de Pollo Villeroy

MAKES 4 SERVINGS

This recipe for fried chicken coated with a rich béchamel sauce is actually much easier to prepare than it may seem. The trick is to chill the béchamel sauce first so that it clings to the chicken during cooking. I have eaten the best "Chicken Villeroy" several times at LHardy in Madrid.

PREPARE AT LEAST 3 HOURS IN ADVANCE

4 chicken breast halves
Kosher or sea salt
Freshly ground black pepper
¼ teaspoon dried thyme
1 bay leaf
½ medium onion
1 sprig parsley

Béchamel Sauce

5 tablespoons unsalted butter
6 tablespoons all-purpose flour
¾ cup milk
Salt
Freshly ground black pepper
⅛ teaspoon ground nutmeg

1 large egg, lightly beaten
Bread crumbs, for dredging
Olive oil, for frying

1. Remove the small rib bones from the chicken, leaving the breast bone intact and reserving the rib bones. Place the chicken in a large saucepan, add water to cover, and add the salt, pepper, thyme, bay leaf, onion, parsley, and the reserved rib bones. Bring to a boil over medium-high heat, then lower the heat to medium, and cook until the white meat is just opaque inside, about 15 minutes (the juices should run clear). Transfer the chicken to a platter and let cool. Cook the broth 30 minutes more. Pass the broth through a fine-mesh strainer into a bowl and reserve ¾ cup for the sauce. After the chicken is cooled, cover and refrigerate at least 2 hours.

2. Meanwhile, prepare the sauce: Melt the butter in a small saucepan over low heat. Add the flour, stirring constantly to incorporate, 1 to 2 minutes. Stir in the reserved broth, the milk, salt, pepper, and nutmeg. Cook, stirring constantly, until the sauce is thickened and smooth. Let cool completely, stirring occasionally. Cover and refrigerate at least 2 hours.

3. Dip the chicken into the sauce, coating completely. Arrange on a plate and refrigerate until the sauce hardens, at least 1 hour. Place the egg and bread crumbs in separate shallow bowls.

4. Heat at least 1 inch of oil in a medium skillet over medium-high heat (or better still, use a deep fryer set at 365°F) until it browns a cube of bread in 60 seconds. Dip the chicken in the egg, dredge in the bread crumbs, and place in the oil. Cook, turning once, until the coating is golden. Transfer to paper towels with a slotted spatula and let drain. Serve hot.

My friend Lucio Blazquez owns a very special restaurant in Madrid, Casa Lucio. The place used to be called El Mesón del Segoviano, and Lucio started his career there as a waiter at a young age. Eventually, through hard work and perseverance, he was able to own the place and converted it into the most iconic restaurant in Madrid. Today the who's who of Spanish society, including even the king, go to Casa Lucio to splurge on his simple home cooking. Besides his great shellfish, hams, and veal chops, one of his signature dishes is *pollo al ajillo* (chicken in garlic sauce).

I once asked him what was the secret for the high quality of his chickens, and very seriously he said to me, "Chickens have to exercise. They have to move; otherwise, they are a ball of fat. I have a small farm where I breed my chickens near Burgos (about 150 miles away from Madrid). When I need to be supplied, I call by phone and tell them how many I need, and right away they put them on the road and they come walking all the way to the restaurant!" We all laughed at Lucio's humor, had a glass of wine with him, and devoured our *ajillo* chicken. Sure enough, it tasted like they had just arrived from the farm.

Chicken in Garlic Sauce
Pollo al Ajillo

MAKES 4 SERVINGS

In Spain, pollo al ajillo *is the most popular way to prepare chicken and can be found on just about every menu. This recipe comes from the El Mesón del Duque restaurant in Osuna, a small town in southern Spain.*

One (3- to 3½-pound) chicken
Kosher or sea salt
¼ cup olive oil
15 garlic cloves, lightly smashed
½ dried red chile pepper, stemmed and seeded
¼ cup dry white wine
3 tablespoons chicken broth or vegetable broth
2 bay leaves
2 tablespoons finely chopped fresh flat-leaf parsley,
    for garnish

1. Detach the chicken wings and legs. Hack off the bony ends of the legs, then hack or cut with kitchen shears the wings into two parts, discarding the tips. Divide the remainder of the chicken into quarters, then hack or cut into 2-inch pieces. Season with salt.

2. Heat the oil in a shallow earthenware casserole dish or Dutch oven over medium-high heat. Add the chicken and garlic and cook, turning occasionally, until the garlic is lightly colored. Transfer the garlic to a small bowl. Continue cooking the chicken, turning occasionally, until browned. Return the garlic to the casserole dish, add the chile pepper, wine, broth, and bay leaves and cook until the dark meat just turns opaque (remove the white meat sooner if needed). Sprinkle with the parsley. If using earthenware, serve hot in the dish, or transfer to a platter.

Yesterday's Chicken
Pollo del Día Anterior

MAKES 4 SERVINGS

The reason this is called "yesterday's" chicken is that this dish is just as delicious when served several days after it is prepared. Escabeche sauce, a marinade of oil, garlic, and vinegar, once served as a natural preservative for fish, meat, and poultry before the advent of refrigeration. This is the perfect dish to keep on hand for days when you do not feel like cooking. It should be kept in the refrigerator, but I recommend serving it at room temperature.

PREPARE AT LEAST 4 HOURS IN ADVANCE

One (3- to 3½-pound) chicken

2 medium onions, halved crosswise

3 bay leaves

Salt

3 large eggs, lightly beaten

All-purpose flour, for dredging

¼ cup olive oil

5 garlic cloves, lightly smashed

3 tablespoons wine vinegar

1. Detach the chicken wings and legs. Hack off the bony ends of the legs, then hack or cut with kitchen shears the wings into two parts, discarding the tips. Hack or cut with kitchen shears the breast into 6 pieces and each thigh crosswise in half.

2. In a stew pot, place the chicken, onions, I of the bay leaves, and salt, add water to cover, and bring to a boil. Reduce the heat to low, cover, and simmer 45 minutes. Transfer the chicken to a platter and the broth to a medium saucepan. Cover the broth and place in the refrigerator at least 2 hours, then skim off the fat and reserve.

3. Place the eggs and flour in separate wide shallow bowls. Heat the oil in a shallow earthenware casserole dish or Dutch oven over medium-high heat. Dredge the chicken in the flour, dip in the egg, and place in the oil. Cook, turning occasionally, until browned on all sides and the dark meat just turns opaque inside (remove the white meat sooner if needed). Add the garlic, the remaining 2 bay leaves, and the vinegar and cook, stirring, until the garlic is golden.

4. In the saucepan, reheat the broth to the boiling point over medium heat and pass through a fine-mesh strainer over the chicken. Discard the solids. Bring to a boil over medium heat and cook about 2 minutes. Let cool. Refrigerate at least 4 hours up to 3 days. Remove the bay leaves. Bring to room temperature and serve or reheat and serve hot. If using earthenware, serve in the dish, or transfer to a platter.

Chicken Livers in Sherry and Onion Sauce
Higadillos de Pollo al Jerez

MAKES 4 SERVINGS

Chicken livers (higadillos) are popular in an area of southwestern Spain referred to as "Spain's Sherry Triangle." They are typically sautéed over low heat with lots of onion and dry sherry, then served over fried bread. This is also very good when served with a simple white rice.

¼ cup olive oil

4 slices sandwich bread, quartered in triangles

2 medium sweet onions, such as Vidalia, slivered

2 pounds chicken livers, gristle removed

Salt

Freshly ground black pepper

6 tablespoons dry sherry, such as Fino

2 tablespoons finely chopped fresh flat-leaf parsley

1½ teaspoons finely chopped fresh thyme or
    ¼ teaspoon dried thyme

1 bay leaf, crumbled

continues…

1. Heat 2 tablespoons of the oil in a medium skillet over medium heat. Add the bread and cook, turning once, until golden. Transfer to paper towels and let drain.

2. Add the onion and cook, stirring, 2 minutes, adding a little more oil if necessary. Reduce the heat to low, cover, and cook about 20 minutes more or until very tender but not browned. Transfer the onion to a small bowl. Wipe out the skillet.

3. Heat the remaining 2 tablespoons oil in the skillet over high heat to the smoking point. Add the livers and cook, turning once, sprinkling with salt and pepper, until browned (the livers should not be cooked through). Reduce the heat to medium and deglaze the skillet, adding the sherry, stirring in and around the livers, and scraping up any bits of flavor. Cook until the liquid is reduced by half. Stir in the onions, parsley, thyme, and bay leaf, and cook 1 minute to blend flavors. Remove the bay leaf. Arrange 4 bread triangles on each of 4 individual plates. Spoon the livers over the bread and serve hot.

Garlic Chicken Livers with Hazelnuts

Higadillos de Pollo al Ajillo con Avellana

MAKES 4 SERVINGS

This Andalusian recipe comes from a cookbook written by Juan Martinez titled La Cocina de Doñana el Rocio; Recipes from Grandparents, Fishermen, Hunters, and Men of the Marshlands. *The sherry, vinegar, and hazelnuts add a wonderful flavor to the chicken liver. Doñana is an expansive and beautiful marshland south of Seville. It is a breeding area for many species of birds that stop there on their migrations between Africa and Europe.*

16 hazelnuts, shelled and finely chopped
2 teaspoons sherry vinegar or red wine vinegar
½ cup dry white wine
3 tablespoons olive oil
2 pounds chicken livers, gristle removed, each cut into 2 pieces
Salt
Freshly ground black pepper
6 garlic cloves, finely chopped
½ cup slivered sweet onion, such as Vidalia
2 tablespoons finely chopped fresh flat-leaf parsley, for garnish

1. In a mortar or mini-processor, mash the hazelnuts. Gradually mash in the vinegar and a little of the wine, then stir in the remaining wine.

2. Heat the oil in a large skillet over medium-high heat to the smoking point. Season the livers with salt and pepper, add to the skillet, and cook, turning occasionally, until browned on all sides. Reduce the heat to medium, add the garlic and onion, and cook 2 to 3 minutes. Stir in the mortar mixture and cook until the liquid is reduced and the sauce slightly thickened. Sprinkle with the parsley and serve hot.

Braised and Stewed Chicken

Braised Chicken in Brandy Sauce
Pollo Asado al Coñac

MAKES 4 SERVINGS

A trick I learned from several recipes of Andalucian origin is that if you cover the stew pot with an inverted cover, it helps to retain the liquid, in this case the brandy. When combined with a generous amount of garlic, this creates a tender and flavorful chicken dish.

One (3- to 3½-pound) chicken, preferably free-range

Kosher or sea salt

6 garlic cloves, finely chopped

½ teaspoon dried oregano

2 tablespoons finely chopped fresh flat-leaf parsley

⅛ teaspoon kosher or sea salt

2 tablespoons olive oil

1 small onion, thinly sliced

2 bay leaves

¼ cup brandy

1. Detach the chicken wings and legs. Hack off the bony ends of the legs and the tips of the wings and discard. Hack or cut with kitchen shears the breast into 4 pieces and each thigh crosswise in half. Season all over with salt.

2. In a mortar or mini-processor, mash two-thirds of the garlic, the oregano, parsley, and the ⅛ teaspoon salt and reserve. In a deep earthenware casserole dish or Dutch oven, heat the oil over medium-high heat. Add the chicken and cook, turning, until browned on all sides. Add the onion, the remaining one-third of the garlic, and the bay leaves and cook, stirring, 1 to 2 minutes. Add the brandy and, standing well away from the casserole dish, ignite the liquid with a match or kitchen lighter, and let die out.

3. Stir in the mortar mixture and cover with an inverted lid or a shallow soup bowl (it should fit snugly). Reduce the heat to low. Fill the lid with a few tablespoons water and simmer the chicken about 30 minutes more, turning occasionally, until the dark meat is opaque inside (remove the white meat sooner if needed); add a little water from the lid if necessary to keep the chicken moist. When done, remove the bay leaf. If using earthenware, serve hot in the dish, or transfer to a platter.

Chicken in Garlic with Brandy and Parsley
Pollo al Ajillo con Brandy y Perejil

MAKES 4 SERVINGS

As I have traveled through Spain over the years, the multitude of garlic chicken recipes I have come across never ceases to amaze me. What makes this version slightly different from the others is that it is cooked in brandy, and the garlic and parsley are mashed into a picada.

One (3- to 3½-pound) chicken

Kosher or sea salt

3 tablespoons olive oil

16 garlic cloves, coarsely chopped

2 bay leaves

2 tablespoons brandy

½ cup dry white wine

Scant ¼ teaspoon saffron threads, crumbled

⅛ teaspoon kosher or sea salt

4 peppercorns

¼ cup finely chopped fresh flat-leaf parsley

continues…

1. Detach the chicken wings and legs. Hack off the bony ends of the legs and the tips of the wings and discard. Hack or cut with kitchen shears the breast into 4 pieces and each thigh crosswise in half. Season all over with salt and let sit 10 minutes at room temperature.

2. Heat the oil in a shallow earthenware casserole dish or Dutch oven over medium-high heat. Add the chicken and cook, turning once, until browned. Remove from the heat. Add half of the garlic and the bay leaves and let the garlic sizzle in the casserole dish. Return to the heat and cook over medium heat until hot; add the brandy. Standing well away from the casserole dish, ignite the liquid with a match or kitchen lighter and let die out. Add the wine and bring to a boil. Reduce the heat to low, cover, and cook about 35 minutes.

3. Meanwhile, in a mortar or mini-processor, mash the remaining half of the garlic, the saffron, the ⅛ teaspoon salt, the peppercorns, and 2 tablespoons of the parsley. Stir into the casserole dish, cover, and cook 15 minutes more, stirring occasionally. (Check that the dark meat inside is opaque). Sprinkle with the remaining parsley. If using earthenware, serve hot in the dish, or transfer to a platter.

Chicken in Brandy Sauce with Shrimp
Pollastre Amb Gambes al Coñac

MAKES 4 SERVINGS

The taste of chicken and shrimp blend perfectly together, especially when sautéed in this wonderful brandy sauce. This is yet another creative recipe that originated in Catalunya, also home to langosta con pollo *(Lobster with Chicken, page 466), another famous dish that pairs chicken with shellfish.*

One (3- to 3½-pound) chicken
Kosher or sea salt
Freshly ground black pepper
3 tablespoons olive oil
¼ pound medium to large shrimp, in their shells
1 medium onion, finely chopped (about ⅔ cup)
1 garlic clove, finely chopped
1 medium carrot, peeled and finely chopped
¼ cup brandy, such as Cognac
1½ teaspoons all-purpose flour
½ cup dry white wine
¼ cup beef broth, chicken broth, or water
2 tablespoons finely chopped fresh flat-leaf parsley

1. Detach the chicken wings and legs. Hack off the bony ends of the legs and the tips of the wings and discard. Hack or cut with kitchen shears the breast into 4 pieces and each thigh crosswise in half. Season all over with salt and pepper.

2. Heat the oil in a large shallow earthenware casserole dish or Dutch oven over medium-high heat. Add the chicken and shrimp. Cook the shrimp, turning once, until pink, about 1 minute, transfer to a medium bowl, and reserve. Continue cooking the chicken until golden on all sides. Add the onion, garlic, and carrot and cook, stirring, until the onion is wilted and transparent, about 5 minutes. Add the brandy and, standing well away from the casserole dish, ignite the liquid with a match or kitchen lighter, and stir until the flames die out.

3. Stir in the flour, cook 1 minute, then add the wine, broth, 1 tablespoon of the parsley, salt, and pepper. Reduce the heat to low, cover, and cook 20 minutes. Add the reserved shrimp and cook 10 minutes more or until the chicken meat inside just turns opaque.

4. Transfer the chicken and shrimp to a platter. Pass the sauce through a fine-mesh strainer over the chicken and shrimp. Discard the solids. Sprinkle with the remaining 1 tablespoon parsley. If using earthenware, serve hot in the dish, or transfer to a platter.

Garlic Chicken with Wine and Peppers
Pollo al Ajillo con Vino y Ñoras

MAKES 4 SERVINGS

Here's yet another preparation of garlic chicken, this time sautéed in white wine. The addition of dried sweet red peppers (ñoras) makes this version a bit spicier than the rest. If you can't find them try mild New Mexico (Anaheim) chiles. This recipe comes from the town of Alcalá de Henares in the province of Madrid, the location of the old University and the birthplace of Cervantes.

One (3- to 3½-pound) chicken

Kosher or sea salt

2 tablespoons olive oil

4 garlic cloves, sliced

1 tablespoon wine vinegar

1 bay leaf

¼ cup dry white wine

1-inch piece dried red pepper (ñora), stemmed and
    seeded, or ¼ teaspoon crushed red pepper

¼ teaspoon ground paprika

Freshly ground black pepper

Pinch of sugar

1 tablespoon finely chopped fresh flat-leaf parsley

1. Detach the chicken wings and legs. Hack off the bony ends of the legs and the tips of the wings and discard. Hack or cut with kitchen shears the breast into 4 pieces and each thigh crosswise in half. Season all over with salt.

2. Heat the oil in a large shallow earthenware casserole dish or Dutch oven over medium-high heat. Add the chicken and cook, turning, until browned on all sides. Add the garlic and cook, stirring, until it just begins to color. Add the vinegar and cook until it evaporates. Stir in the bay leaf, wine, chile pepper, paprika, black pepper, sugar, and parsley.

Reduce the heat to low, cover, and simmer 45 minutes more, stirring occasionally, or until the dark meat just turns opaque inside. Remove the bay leaf. If using earthenware, serve hot in the dish, or transfer to a platter.

Braised Chicken and Onion
Pollo Encebollado

MAKES 4 SERVINGS

This is a traditional and very down-to-earth Spanish dish in which the chicken is braised with a generous amount of onion and garlic.

One (3- to 3½-pound) chicken

Kosher or sea salt

Freshly ground black pepper

5 garlic cloves, finely chopped

2 tablespoons finely chopped fresh flat-leaf parsley

⅛ teaspoon kosher or sea salt

½ cup dry white wine

3 tablespoons olive oil

2 medium onions, chopped (about ⅔ cup)

1. Detach the chicken wings and legs. Hack off the bony ends of the legs and the tips of the wings and discard. Hack or cut with kitchen shears the breast into 4 pieces and each thigh crosswise in half. Cut the chicken into small serving pieces, detaching the wings and legs and dividing the breast into 4 pieces and each thigh in half crosswise. Season all over with salt and pepper.

2. In a mortar or mini-processor, mash the garlic, parsley, and the ⅛ teaspoon salt. Stir in the wine and reserve.

3. Heat the oil in a shallow earthenware casserole dish or Dutch oven over medium-high heat. Add the chicken and cook, turning, until browned on all sides. Add the onions and cook, stirring

continues...

occasionally, until they have softened, about 5 minutes more. Stir in the mortar mixture, cover, and simmer 45 minutes more, stirring occasionally, until the flavors are blended and the dark meat is opaque inside (remove the white meat sooner if needed). If using earthenware, serve hot in the dish, or transfer to a platter.

Chicken Braised with Onions, Garlic, and Saffron
Pollo en Salsa de Cebolla

MAKES 4 SERVINGS

With simple ingredients and minimal preparation, this dish of chicken rich with the pungency of onions and garlic has a wonderful flavor and is very popular amongst Spaniards. What makes this recipe different than the traditional pollo encebollado *is that it features the whole head of garlic and is enhanced by saffron.*

One (3- to 3½-pound) chicken
Salt
Freshly ground black pepper
All-purpose flour, for dredging
2 tablespoons olive oil
2 medium onions, finely chopped (about 1⅓ cups)
⅔ cup dry white wine
6 tablespoons chicken broth or vegetable broth
1 head garlic, loose skin removed
1 bay leaf
Several threads of saffron, crumbled

I. Cut the chicken into small serving pieces, detaching the wings and legs and dividing the breast in 4 pieces and each thigh crosswise in half. Season all over with salt and pepper. Place the flour in a wide shallow bowl and dredge the chicken in the flour.

2. Heat the oil in a shallow earthenware casserole dish or Dutch oven over medium-high heat. Add the chicken and cook, turning, until browned on all sides. Add the onions and cook, stirring, until transparent, about 5 minutes more. Stir in the wine and broth.

3. Cut the garlic head vertically halfway through and add to the casserole dish along with the bay leaf, saffron, salt, and pepper. Reduce the heat to low, cover, and simmer about 40 minutes or until until the flavors are blended and the dark meat is opaque inside (remove the white meat sooner if needed), adding more broth if necessary (the sauce should be fairly thick). Squeeze the garlic flesh into the sauce and discard the skin and the bay leaf. If using earthenware, serve hot in the dish, or transfer to a platter.

Chicken with Ham, Olives, and Sherry
Pollo a la Sevillana

MAKES 4 SERVINGS

A la Sevillana refers to a dish made with ham, olives, and Spanish (dry) Fino sherry. In southwestern Spain, where sherry is produced, it is a popular way to prepare chicken, duck, and a variety of other poultry. I much prefer this dish when it is made with imported Serrano ham, but if you can't find it you can substitute prosciutto.

One (3- to 3½-pound) chicken
Kosher or sea salt
½ cup sliced pitted green olives, preferably Spanish
½ cup dry white wine
3 tablespoons olive oil
½ medium sweet onion, such as Vidalia, finely chopped
2 garlic cloves, finely chopped

¼ cup small cubes (¼ inch) Serrano (Spanish cured mountain) ham or prosciutto

1 teaspoon all-purpose flour

6 tablespoons dry sherry, such as Fino

½ cup chicken broth or vegetable broth

Freshly ground black pepper

1 tablespoon finely chopped fresh thyme or ½ teaspoon dried thyme

1. Detach the chicken wings and legs. Hack off the bony ends of the legs and the tips of the wings and discard. Hack or cut with kitchen shears the breast into 4 pieces and each thigh crosswise in half. Season all over with salt and let sit 10 minutes at room temperature.

2. In a small saucepan, combine the olives and wine, and bring to a boil over low heat. Simmer about 5 minutes. Drain and reserve the olives.

3. In a shallow earthenware casserole dish or Dutch oven, heat the oil over medium-high heat. Add the chicken and cook, turning, until browned on all sides. Reduce the heat to low, add the onion and garlic, and cook, stirring, about 5 minutes more. Add the ham and cook 1 minute, then stir in the flour. Add the sherry, broth, salt, pepper, and thyme. Cover and cook 40 minutes more, stirring occasionally, until the flavors are blended and the dark meat is opaque inside (remove the white meat sooner if needed).

4. Add the reserved olives and simmer uncovered until the olives are heated through, about 2 minutes more. Taste and adjust seasoning if necessary. If using earthenware, serve hot in the dish, or transfer to a platter.

Chicken with Pine Nuts
Pollo con Piñones

MAKES 4 SERVINGS

Pine nuts add a nice nutty taste and a crunchy texture when combined with this chicken in white wine sauce.

One (3- to 3½-pound) chicken

Kosher or sea salt

Freshly ground black pepper

3 tablespoons olive oil

1 teaspoon all-purpose flour

2 tablespoons finely chopped shallots

½ teaspoon dried thyme

2 tablespoons finely chopped fresh flat-leaf parsley

1 bay leaf

½ cup dry white wine

2 ounces pine nuts (about ⅓ cup)

1. Detach the chicken wings and legs. Hack off the bony ends of the legs and the tips of the wings and discard. Hack or cut with kitchen shears the breast into 4 pieces and each thigh crosswise in half. Season all over with salt and pepper.

2. Heat the oil in a large shallow earthenware casserole dish or Dutch oven over medium-high heat. Add the chicken and cook, turning, until golden on all sides. Stir in the flour and add the remaining ingredients. Reduce the heat to low, cover, and cook 30 minutes more, turning occasionally, or until the flavors are blended and the dark meat is opaque inside (remove the white meat sooner if needed). Taste and adjust seasoning if necessary. Remove the bay leaf. If using earthenware, serve hot in the dish, or transfer to a platter.

Chicken with Red Peppers
Pollo Chilindrón

MAKES 4 SERVINGS

A hearty and delicious chicken dish, originally from the region of Aragon where red peppers are abundant and used every day in cooking, this is one of my very favorite chicken recipes.

One (3- to 3½-pound) chicken

Kosher or sea salt

2 tablespoons olive oil

1 medium onion, finely chopped (about ⅔ cup)

2 garlic cloves, finely chopped

2 tablespoons small cubes (¼ inch) Serrano (Spanish cured mountain) ham or prosciutto

1 medium tomato, finely chopped (about ⅔ cup)

1-inch piece dried red chile pepper, stemmed and seeded

4 pimientos, such as (jarred) piquillo peppers, cut into thin strips

Freshly ground black pepper

1. Detach the chicken wings and legs. Hack off the bony ends of the legs and the tips of the wings and discard. Hack or cut with kitchen shears the breast into 4 pieces and each thigh crosswise in half. Season all over with salt.

2. Heat the oil in a large shallow earthenware casserole dish or Dutch oven over medium-high heat. Add the chicken and cook, turning, until browned on all sides. Add the onion, garlic, and ham and cook, stirring, until the onion softens and garlic starts to brown, 2 to 3 minutes. Reduce the heat to low, stir in the tomato, chile pepper, pimientos, salt, and pepper, and simmer 45 minutes, turning occasionally, until the flavors are blended and the dark meat is opaque inside (remove the white meat sooner if needed). If using earthenware, serve hot in the dish, or transfer to a platter.

Chicken with Vegetables
Pollo en Chanfaina

MAKES 4 SERVINGS

A Catalan specialty, this is a light and very healthy way to prepare chicken that includes eggplant, bell peppers, and tomatoes. The colorful medley of ingredients is why this recipe is called chanfaina, *a word that has the same root as the English word "symphony."*

One (3- to 3½-pound) chicken

Kosher or sea salt

2 tablespoons olive oil

1¼ pounds Serrano (Spanish cured mountain) ham or prosciutto, cut into ¼-inch cubes

1 medium onion, coarsely chopped (about ⅔ cup)

1 garlic clove, finely chopped

1 medium eggplant, peeled or unpeeled, cut into 1-inch cubes

1 medium green bell pepper, cut into 1-inch strips

1 pound tomatoes, peeled and coarsely chopped

1 bay leaf

½ teaspoon dried thyme

1 tablespoon finely chopped fresh flat-leaf parsley

Freshly ground black pepper

½ cup dry white wine

1. Detach the chicken wings and legs. Hack off the bony ends of the legs and the tips of the wings and discard. Hack or cut with kitchen shears the breast into 4 pieces and each thigh crosswise in half. Season all over with salt.

2. Heat the oil in a large shallow earthenware casserole dish or Dutch oven over medium-high heat. Add the chicken and cook, turning, until golden on all sides. Transfer to a platter, reserving the oil.

3. Reduce the heat to medium. Add the ham and cook, stirring, 1 minute, then add the onion and garlic and cook, stirring, until the onion is wilted

and transparent, about 5 minutes more. Add the eggplant and bell pepper and cook, stirring, about 5 minutes more. Add the tomatoes, bay leaf, thyme, parsley, salt, and pepper and cook 1 minute, then stir in the wine. Add the chicken and spoon some sauce over it. Reduce the heat to low, cover, and simmer 1 hour, turning occasionally, until the flavors are blended and the dark meat is opaque inside (remove the white meat sooner if needed). Remove the bay leaf. If using earthenware, serve hot in the dish, or transfer to a platter.

Chicken with Apple and Raisins
Pollo con Manzanas y Pasas

MAKES 4 SERVINGS

Here's an unusual dish that is extremely easy to prepare. The chicken sautéed with the pungency of onions is perfectly contrasted by the sweetness of the apples and raisins. This recipe originally appeared in a Granada newspaper, contributed by a local housewife.

One (3- to 3½-pound) chicken
Kosher or sea salt
2 tablespoons olive oil
2 medium onions, finely chopped (about 1⅓ cup)
2 medium apples, peeled, cored, and cut into ⅛-inch wedges
¼ cup raisins
¾ cup dry white wine

1. Detach the chicken wings and legs. Hack off the bony ends of the legs and the tips of the wings and discard. Hack or cut with kitchen shears the breast into 4 pieces and each thigh crosswise in half. Season all over with salt.

2. Heat the oil in a large shallow earthenware casserole dish or Dutch oven over medium heat. Add the chicken and cook, turning, until browned on all sides. Transfer to a platter.

3. Add the onions and cook, stirring, until softened, about 5 minutes. Stir in the apples, raisins, wine, and salt. Reduce the heat to low, cover, and simmer about 45 minutes more, turning occasionally, until the dark meat is opaque inside (remove the white meat sooner if needed) and the onion and apples are softened. If using earthenware, serve hot in the dish, or transfer to a platter.

Lemon Chicken with Ginger and Pine Nuts
Pollo al Agraz con Piñones

MAKES 4 SERVINGS

Several Spanish cookbooks from the seventeenth and eighteenth centuries feature different versions of this classic recipe. The addition of ginger is the perfect complement to the lemon flavor of the sauce, and the pine nuts lend a wonderful accent.

2 tablespoons pine nuts
1 garlic clove, finely chopped
2 tablespoons finely chopped fresh flat-leaf parsley
⅛ teaspoon saffron threads, crumbled
⅛ teaspoon kosher or sea salt
One (3- to 3½-pound) chicken
2 tablespoons olive oil
1 medium onion, finely chopped (about ⅔ cup)
½ cup chicken broth or vegetable broth
2 tablespoons fresh lemon juice
1 bay leaf
½ teaspoon grated fresh ginger
Freshly ground black pepper

1. In a mortar or mini-processor, mash the pine nuts, garlic, parsley, saffron, and the salt. Reserve.

2. Detach the chicken wings and legs. Hack off the bony ends of the legs and the tips of the wings and

continues...

discard. Hack or cut with kitchen shears the breast into 4 pieces and each thigh crosswise in half. Season all over with salt.

3. Heat the oil in a shallow earthenware casserole dish or Dutch oven over medium-high heat. Add the chicken and cook, turning, until browned on all sides. Reduce the heat to medium. Add the onion and cook, stirring, until the onion is wilted and transparent, about 5 minutes more. Add the broth, lemon juice, bay leaf, ginger, and pepper and bring to a boil. Reduce the heat to low, cover, and simmer 30 minutes, turning occasionally. Stir in the reserved mortar mixture and cook 15 minutes more, turning occasionally, until the flavors are blended and the dark meat is opaque inside (remove the white meat sooner if needed). Remove the bay leaf. If using earthenware, serve hot in the dish, or transfer to a platter.

Chicken and Sparerib Stew
Guiso Caldoso de Aldea Antigua

MAKES 4 TO 6 SERVINGS

I found this traditional dish that combines chicken with pork in an old village in the region of Galicia. Cumin and saffron are both spices characteristic of Moorish-style cooking. This rich, hearty stew is a very popular dish in Spain, especially in the winter.

2 tablespoons olive oil

1 pound pork spare ribs or baby back ribs, fat trimmed and cut into 2-inch pieces

Kosher or sea salt

Freshly ground black pepper

One (3- to 3½-pound) chicken

¾ cup chicken broth or vegetable broth

⅓ cup water

¼ pound pancetta, cut into ¾-inch cubes

1 medium carrot, peeled and finely chopped (about ½ cup)

4 garlic cloves, finely chopped

1 medium onion, finely chopped (about ⅔ cup)

¼ cup finely chopped fresh flat-leaf parsley

½ pound small (2-inch) new potatoes, peeled and halved

½ cup fresh or frozen peas

¼ teaspoon ground cumin

⅛ teaspoon saffron threads, crumbled

1. In a shallow earthenware casserole dish or Dutch oven, heat 1 tablespoon of the olive oil over medium heat. Add the pork ribs and cook, turning occasionally and sprinkling with salt and pepper once or twice as they cook, until browned. Add the broth and water and bring to a boil over high heat. Reduce the heat to low, cover, and simmer 1 hour (may be made in advance).

2. Meanwhile, detach the chicken wings and legs. Hack off the bony ends of the legs and the tips of the wings and discard. Hack or cut with kitchen shears the breast into 4 pieces and each thigh crosswise in half. Season with salt and let sit 10 minutes at room temperature.

3. Transfer the ribs to a warm platter, and reserve 1½ cups of the broth, adding water if there is less and reserve. Skim off the fat that rises to the surface. Wipe out the casserole dish.

4. In the casserole dish, heat the remaining 1 tablespoon oil over medium-high heat. Add the chicken and pancetta and cook, turning the chicken once and stirring the pancetta, until both are browned. Reduce the heat to medium, add the carrot, garlic, onion, and parsley and cook, stirring, until the vegetables are softened, 8 to 10 minutes.

5. Add the reserved ribs, the reserved broth, and the potatoes and bring to a boil. Reduce the heat to low, cover, and simmer 25 minutes, stirring occasionally. Stir in the peas, cumin, saffron, salt, and pepper, cover, and cook 15 minutes more or until the flavors are blended and the dark meat just turns opaque inside (remove the white meat sooner than needed). If using earthenware, serve hot in the dish, or transfer to a platter.

Chicken in Egg and Almond Sauce
Pollo en Pepitoria

MAKES 4 SERVINGS

Chicken cooked with hard-boiled egg, saffron, and almonds is among the most traditional chicken dishes in Spain. The word pepitoria, *a little obscure in origin, implies that many ingredients are mixed together to cook and always include eggs.*

One (3- to 3½-pound) chicken

Kosher or sea salt

2 tablespoons olive oil

1 medium onion, chopped (about ⅔ cup)

2 garlic cloves, finely chopped

3 tablespoons finely chopped fresh flat-leaf parsley

¼ cup dry sherry, such as Fino

¾ cup chicken broth or vegetable broth

¼ teaspoon saffron threads, crumbled

1 bay leaf

1 medium tomato, chopped (about ⅔ cup)

Freshly ground black pepper

10 toasted blanched almonds, finely chopped

1 hard-boiled egg, finely chopped

1. Detach the chicken wings and legs. Hack off the bony ends of the legs and the tips of the wings and discard. Hack or cut with kitchen shears the breast into 4 pieces and each thigh crosswise in half. Season all over with salt.

2. Heat the oil in a large shallow earthenware casserole dish or Dutch oven over medium-high heat. Add the chicken and cook, turning once, until browned. Transfer to a platter. Reduce the heat to medium, add the onion, garlic, and parsley and cook, stirring, until the vegetables soften. Reduce the heat to low, add the tomato, sherry, saffron, and broth, and simmer about 10 minutes more. Add the chicken and the almonds, cover, and cook 40 minutes more, stirring occasionally, or until the flavors are blended and the dark meat just turns opaque inside. Sprinkle with the hard-boiled egg and serve hot.

Pepita's Stewed Chicken with Almonds and Egg
Pepitoria de Pepita Alía

MAKES 4 SERVINGS

In this delicious variation of Spain's classic pollo pepitoria, *the eggs are placed whole in the casserole dish where they hard-boil as the chicken is stewed. The saffron adds a wonderful flavor and aroma, and the almonds add a subtle taste and a crunchy texture. My friend Pepita Alía from the village of Lagartera in central Spain created this dish. Lagartera is known for the quality of their embroidery, and Pepita owns the most important* atelier, *providing her craft to many institutions, including the Royal house of the Netherlands and Spain.*

One (3- to 3½-pound) chicken

Kosher or sea salt

Freshly ground black pepper

All-purpose flour, for dredging

3 tablespoons olive oil

¼ medium onion, cut into ⅛-inch slices

1 garlic clove, loose skin removed

Scant ¼ teaspoon saffron threads, crumbled

2-ounce piece Serrano (cured mountain) ham or prosciutto

1 bay leaf

20 blanched almonds

3 sprigs parsley

2 cups chicken broth or vegetable broth

¼ cup dry white wine

continues . . .

2 large eggs, in their shells, well washed

1 tablespoon finely chopped fresh flat-leaf parsley, for garnish

1. Detach the chicken wings and legs. Hack off the bony ends of the legs and the tips of the wings and discard. Hack or cut with kitchen shears the breast into 4 pieces and each thigh crosswise in half. Season all over with salt and pepper. Place the flour in a wide shallow bowl and dredge the chicken in the flour.

2. Heat the oil in a shallow earthenware casserole dish or Dutch oven over medium-high heat. Add the chicken and cook, turning once, until golden. Add the onion, garlic, saffron, ham, bay leaf, almonds, and parsley sprigs and cook, stirring, until the onion is softened, about 5 minutes. Reduce the heat to medium, add the broth, wine, and the whole eggs, and bring to a boil. Cover and simmer about 45 minutes, stirring occasionally, until the flavors are blended and the dark meat just turns opaque inside. Transfer the chicken to a warm platter.

3. With a fork or slotted spoon, transfer the ham, parsley, almonds, onion, and garlic to a medium bowl. Finely chop the almonds and reserve. Press the garlic with the back of a wooden spoon to extract its flesh, discarding the skin, and reserve. Finely chop the ham and return it to the casserole dish. Remove the eggs and shell them.

4. Finely chop the egg whites and reserve. Mash the egg yolks in a mortar. Add the reserved almonds and the reserved garlic to the mortar and mash as finely as possible. Mash in the parsley sprigs, onion, and ham.

5. Stir the mortar mixture into the casserole dish, and cook over medium heat until blended. Reduce the heat to low, add the chicken, cover, and simmer 10 minutes or until the mixture is incorporated. Sprinkle with the chopped parsley and the reserved egg white. If using earthenware, serve hot in the dish, or transfer to a platter.

Stewed Chicken with Cream and Truffles
Pularda a la Suprema de Trufas

MAKES 4 TO 6 SERVINGS

Here a simple preparation of boiled chicken is made extravagant by the addition of cream and truffles. This recipe comes from our friend Irene España who runs a charming restaurant, Casa Irene, set high up in the Pyrenees Mountains in the Aran Valley where the French Garonne River originates.

One (4½ to 5-pound) chicken, with neck if possible, preferably free-range

6 cups chicken broth, vegetable broth, or water

Salt

10 peppercorns

2 medium carrots, peeled

1 leek, trimmed and well washed

4 sprigs parsley

4 sprigs thyme or ½ teaspoon dried thyme

2 bay leaves

2 tablespoons unsalted butter

2 tablespoons all-purpose flour

2 tablespoons heavy cream

4 jarred truffles, finely chopped, plus 2 teaspoons truffle juice

1. Place the chicken in a stew pot, add the broth, salt, peppercorns, carrots, leek, parsley, thyme, and bay leaves, and bring to a boil over high heat. Skim off the foam. Reduce the heat to low, cover, and simmer, partially covered for 1½ hours or until the dark meat inside just turns opaque. Transfer the chicken to a warm platter and cut into quarters, discarding the wing tips and the skin. Remove the ribs and the wing bones.

2. Pass the broth through a fine-mesh strainer into a medium bowl and reserve 2¼ cups (if there is more, boil down in a small saucepan). Discard the

solids. Return the chicken to the pot and add ¼ cup of the reserved broth. Cover and keep warm.

3. Melt the butter in a medium saucepan. Add the flour and cook, stirring constantly, 1 minute. Stir in the cream, then gradually add the remaining 2 cups broth, the truffles, and truffle juice. Cook, stirring constantly, until smooth and thickened. Spoon the sauce over the chicken and serve hot.

Chicken with White Wine, Grape Juice, and Cilantro
Pollo a la Uva Blanca con Cilantro

MAKES 4 SERVINGS

The cilantro reflects a Moorish influence on this delicious chicken recipe from Andalucía, where Palomino white grapes are grown to make sherry. The onion-flavored wine sauce blends perfectly with the sweetness of the grape juice.

One (3- to 3½-pound) chicken
Kosher or sea salt
Freshly ground black pepper
3 tablespoons olive oil
1 small to medium onion, slivered
¾ cup dry white wine
¼ cup plus 2 tablespoons white grape juice
6 tablespoons finely chopped fresh cilantro

1. Detach the chicken wings and legs. Hack off the bony ends of the legs and the tips of the wings and discard. Hack or cut with kitchen shears the breast into 4 pieces and each thigh crosswise in half. Season all over with salt and pepper.

2. Heat the oil in a shallow earthenware casserole dish or Dutch oven over medium-high heat. Add the chicken and cook, turning once, until golden on both sides. Reduce the heat to medium, add the onion, and cook, stirring, until wilted and transparent, about 5 minutes. Add the wine, grape juice,

and 3 tablespoons of the cilantro and bring to a boil. Reduce the heat to low, cover, and simmer 45 minutes or until the juice of the chicken is clear when the thickest piece is cut to the bone (at least 165°F). Transfer the chicken to a warm platter.

3. Increase the heat to medium-high and cook until the liquid is reduced and the sauce slightly thickened. Pour over the chicken. Sprinkle with the remaining 3 tablespoons cilantro and serve hot.

Chicken with Green Olives
Pollo con Aceitunas

MAKES 4 SERVINGS

Olives are plentiful in Spain and therefore a common ingredient in Spanish cooking. Here they add their distinctive flavor to a chicken recipe that is made richer with the addition of bacon.

One (3- to 3½-pound) chicken

3 ounces pitted green olives, preferably Spanish, halved crosswise

Kosher or sea salt

3 tablespoons olive oil

3 garlic cloves, finely chopped

1 medium onion, slivered

¼ pound slab bacon, cut into ¼-inch cubes

¾ cup dry white wine

½ cup chicken broth or vegetable broth

Freshly ground black pepper

1. Detach the chicken wings and legs. Hack off the bony ends of the legs and the tips of the wings and discard. Hack or cut with kitchen shears the breast into 4 pieces and each thigh crosswise in half. Season all over with salt.

2. In a small saucepan, place the olives, add water to cover, and bring to a boil over medium heat. Cook 5 minutes, drain, and reserve.

3. Heat the oil in a shallow earthenware casserole dish or Dutch oven over medium-high heat. Add the chicken and cook, turning once, until golden. Add the bacon and cook for a minute, stirring, then add the onion and garlic and cook until the onion softens and the bacon browns. Add the wine and broth, season with pepper, and bring to a boil. Reduce the heat to low, add the olives, cover, and simmer 45 minutes or until the flavors blend and the dark meat just turns opaque inside. If using earthenware, serve hot in the dish, or transfer to a platter.

"The Good Woman's" Chicken
Pollo Buena Mujer

MAKES 4 SERVINGS

Not only have I seen this oddly titled recipe in more than a few Spanish cookbooks, but the French derived their own version which they call Bonne Femme. *This is an extraordinary chicken dish from Andalucía in which the sweetness of orange juice and orange segments is perfectly complemented by mushrooms, brandy, and a dash of saffron.*

One (3- to 3½-pound) chicken

Kosher or sea salt

Freshly ground black pepper

2 tablespoons olive oil

3 garlic cloves, finely chopped

1 small onion, finely chopped

⅓ pound mushrooms, rinsed, trimmed, and cut into ¼-inch slices

3 tablespoons brandy

5 tablespoons fresh orange juice

1 small orange, peeled and divided into segments

⅓ cup chicken broth or vegetable broth

⅛ teaspoon saffron threads, crumbled

1. Detach the chicken wings and legs. Hack off the bony ends of the legs and the tips of the wings and discard. Hack or cut with kitchen shears the breast into 4 pieces and each thigh crosswise in half. Season all over with salt and pepper.

2. Heat the oil in a shallow earthenware casserole dish or Dutch oven over medium-high heat. Add the chicken and cook, turning once, until golden on all sides. Add the garlic, onion, and mushrooms and cook, stirring, until the onion is wilted and transparent, about 5 minutes. Stir in the brandy and orange juice, add the orange segments, broth, and saffron, and bring to a boil. Reduce the heat to

low, cover, and simmer 45 minutes, stirring occasionally, or until the flavors blend and the dark meat just turns opaque inside. Taste and adjust seasoning if necessary. If using earthenware, serve hot in the dish, or transfer to a platter.

Chicken and Chorizo in Red Wine Sauce
Pollo al Vino Tinto y Chorizo

MAKES 4 SERVINGS

This recipe for chicken simmered in a sauce of red wine and brandy is an outstanding chicken dish that is especially rich and hearty. If you can't find Spanish brandy, I suggest that you use Cognac instead. And remember that, for cooking, you do not need to buy an expensive bottle of wine.

One (3- to 3½-pound) chicken

Salt

Freshly ground black pepper

All-purpose flour, for dredging

¼ cup olive oil

1 large onion, finely chopped (about 1 cup)

1 garlic clove, finely chopped

1 medium carrot, peeled and finely chopped (about ½ cup)

2 ounces (1 link) chorizo sausage, chopped

2 tablespoons brandy, such as Spanish brandy or Cognac

1 pimiento, finely chopped

2 tablespoons finely chopped fresh flat-leaf parsley

1 bay leaf

1 tablespoon finely chopped fresh thyme or ½ teaspoon dried thyme

½ cup chicken broth or vegetable broth

1 cup dry red wine

1. Detach the chicken wings and legs. Hack off the bony ends of the legs and the tips of the wings and discard. Hack or cut with kitchen shears the breast into 4 pieces and each thigh crosswise in half. Season all over with salt and pepper. Place the flour in a wide shallow bowl and dredge the chicken in the flour.

2. Heat the oil in a large shallow earthenware casserole dish or Dutch oven over medium-high heat. Add the chicken and cook, turning once, until browned on all sides. Add the onion, garlic, carrot, and chorizo and cook, stirring, until the onion is wilted and transparent and the chorizon browns, about 5 minutes more. Add the brandy and, standing well away from the casserole dish, ignite the liquid with a match or kitchen lighter, and let die out.

3. Stir in the pimiento, parsley, salt, pepper, bay leaf, thyme, broth, and wine. Reduce the heat to low, cover, and simmer about 1½ hours, stirring occasionally until the flavors blend. (Check that the dark meat is just opaque inside; add water if the dish gets dry.) If using earthenware, serve hot in the dish, or transfer to a platter.

Cándida's Stewed Chicken with Potatoes
Pollo de Corral de Cándida

MAKES 4 SERVINGS

El Bierzo is a region famous for its vegetables, which are the freshest that can be found in all of Spain. This is a wonderful dish in which chicken is sautéed with locally grown onions, carrots, peppers, and potatoes. Cándida Acebo, a woman from the beautiful, quaint, and old village of Compludo in the mountains of León on the way to St. James, runs a simple restaurant with great traditional home cooking. This is her recipe.

continues...

One (3- to 3½-pound) chicken

Kosher or sea salt

Freshly ground black pepper

2 garlic cloves, coarsely chopped

2 tablespoons finely chopped fresh flat-leaf parsley

⅛ teaspoon salt

½ teaspoon ground sweet paprika, such as Spanish smoked

1¼ cups dry red wine

6 tablespoons olive oil

1 medium sweet onion, such as Vidalia, finely chopped

1 medium carrot, finely chopped (about ½ cup)

1 medium red bell pepper, finely chopped (about ¾ cup)

1 large baking potato, peeled and cut into ½-inch pieces

1. Detach the chicken wings and legs. Hack off the bony ends of the legs and the tips of the wings and discard. Hack or cut with kitchen shears the breast into 4 pieces and each thigh crosswise in half. Season all over with salt and black pepper.

2. In a large mortar, mash the garlic, parsley, and the ⅛ teaspoon salt. Mash in the paprika, then stir in the wine and reserve.

3. Heat 3 tablespoons of the oil in a shallow earthenware casserole dish or Dutch oven over medium-high heat. Add the chicken and cook, turning once, until browned on both sides. Add the onion, carrot, and bell pepper and cook, stirring, until the vegetables are softened, about 8 minutes. Reduce the heat to low, stir in the mortar mixture, and cook, stirring occasionally, about 30 minutes.

4. Meanwhile, in a large skillet, heat the remaining 3 tablespoons oil over medium heat. Add the potatoes one at a time in a single layer, season with salt, and cook, turning with a slotted offset spatula, about 2 minutes. Reduce the heat to medium-low, cover, and cook, turning occasionally with the spatula, about 10 minutes or until tender.

5. Drain off the oil from the potatoes. After the chicken has cooked 30 minutes, add the potatoes to the casserole dish and cook 5 minutes more. If using earthenware, serve hot in the dish, or transfer to a platter.

Chicken with Stewed Vegetables in Caramelized Sugar Sauce
Pollo en Salsa Caramelizada con Chanfaina

MAKES 4 SERVINGS

Chanfaina ("symphony" in English) refers to the traditional vegetable medley of eggplant, peppers, and tomatoes that can be found in many classic Spanish recipes. This dish, with its obvious Catalan inspiration, contrasts the stewed vegetables with a caramelized sugar that coats the chicken, creating a dish that is unique and memorable.

1 eggplant

Kosher or sea salt

3 tablespoons olive oil plus more, for brushing

Freshly ground black pepper

1 medium onion, slivered

1 garlic clove, finely chopped

1 medium red bell pepper, cut into ½-inch pieces

2 medium tomatoes, peeled, seeded, and coarsely chopped (about 1⅓ cups)

1 tablespoon finely chopped fresh flat-leaf parsley

¼ cup chicken broth or vegetable broth

One (3- to 3½-pound) chicken

3 tablespoons sugar

¼ cup water

1. Preheat the oven to 400°F. With a vegetable peeler, partially peel the eggplant, leaving alternating strips of skin. Cut into ¾-inch pieces and place in a colander in layers, sprinkling each layer with salt. Let drain 30 minutes and pat dry with paper

towels. Place on a greased baking sheet. Brush with oil, season with salt and black pepper, and bake about 15 minutes or until tender.

2. Heat 1 tablespoon of the oil in a shallow earthenware casserole dish or Dutch oven over low heat. Add the onion, garlic, and bell pepper and cook, stirring, until the vegetables have softened, about 8 minutes. Increase the heat to medium, add the tomatoes, parsley, salt, and broth, and cook about 15 minutes more. Add the eggplant, cook 5 minutes to meld flavors, and reserve.

3. Detach the chicken wings and legs. Hack off the bony ends of the legs and the tips of the wings and discard. Hack or cut with kitchen shears the breast into 4 pieces and each thigh crosswise in half. Season all over with salt.

4. Heat 2 tablespoons of the oil in a large skillet over medium-high heat. Add the chicken and cook, turning occasionally, until the chicken is browned and the dark meat just turns opaque inside, about 20 minutes. Drain off the oil.

5. Sprinkle the sugar in the skillet and add the water. Cook over low heat, spooning the liquid over the chicken, until the liquid is lightly golden, thickened, and caramelized. Transfer the chicken to a warm platter; pour about half of the remaining liquid into a small pot. Add the reserved vegetable mixture to the skillet and stir to coat well with the caramelized sugar in the pan. Cook over medium heat until the vegetables are heated through and transfer to another platter. Arrange the chicken over the vegetables and spoon the remaining half of the caramelized sugar over the chicken. Serve hot.

Grandma's Stewed Chicken
Pollo de la Abuela

MAKES 4 SERVINGS

Reme Domínguez and Ximo Boix, the remarkable chefs and owners of restaurant Tasca del Puerto in Castellón de la Plana, developed this innovative creation. They told me that the secret to the recipe is that you do not stir the stew while cooking because the broth will blend the onion and tomato into the sauce by itself.

One (3½- to 4-pound) chicken
Kosher or sea salt
2½ pounds ripe tomatoes
3 tablespoons olive oil
3 tablespoons brandy
5 garlic cloves
2 bay leaves
4 large onions, cut into fine slivers
2½ cups chicken broth or vegetable broth

1. Detach the chicken wings and legs. Hack off the bony ends of the legs and the tips of the wings and discard. Hack or cut with kitchen shears the breast into 4 pieces and each thigh crosswise in half. Season all over with salt and let sit at room temperature until needed.

2. Cut the tomatoes in half crosswise and gently squeeze to extract the seeds. With a coarse grater held over a small bowl, grate each half down to the skin, draining off any excess juices. Reserve the pulp and discard the skin.

3. Heat the oil in a shallow earthenware casserole dish or Dutch oven over medium-high heat. Add the chicken and cook, turning once, until well browned on all sides. Add the brandy and, standing well away from the casserole dish, ignite the liquid

continues . . .

with a match or kitchen lighter and let it die out. Scatter the garlic and bay leaves around the chicken. Scatter the onions over the chicken and tomato over the onions. Season with salt. Add the broth and bring to a boil.

4. Reduce the heat to low and cook until the liquid is reduced by half, about 1½ hours—do not stir. Taste and adjust seasoning if necessary. If using earthenware, serve hot in the dish, or transfer to a platter.

Chicken in Black Currant and Sherry Sauce
Pollo en Salsa de Jerez y Grosella

MAKES 4 SERVINGS

Sherry takes its name from its place of origin, Jerez de la Frontera in Spain. This is an unusual recipe of Catalan origin that combines sweet and savory flavors with the distinctive taste of saffron. This dish has a Moorish influence seen in the use of cumin and the sweet-sour flavor of the black currant sauce. The orange rind adds a subtle tartness.

One (3- to 3½-pound) chicken

Kosher or sea salt

2 tablespoons olive oil plus more, for brushing

2 garlic cloves, mashed in a garlic press or mortar

Freshly ground black pepper

1 tablespoon finely chopped fresh thyme or
    ½ teaspoon dried thyme

1 tablespoon finely chopped fresh rosemary or
    ½ teaspoon dried rosemary

½ cup medium-sweet sherry, such as Oloroso

Chicken broth, vegetable broth, or water

¼ cup black currant jelly

½ teaspoon orange zest

2 tablespoons dry white wine

½ teaspoon ground cumin

2 garlic cloves, finely chopped

2 tablespoons finely chopped fresh flat-leaf parsley

1. Preheat the oven to 400°F. Detach the chicken wings and legs. Hack off the bony ends of the legs and the tips of the wings and discard. Hack or cut with kitchen shears the breast into 4 pieces and each thigh crosswise in half. Season all over with salt.

2. Brush a roasting pan with oil and arrange the chicken in the pan. In a small bowl, combine the mashed garlic and 2 tablespoons of the oil and brush over the chicken. Season with salt, pepper, thyme, and rosemary and pour the sherry into the pan. Bake 30 minutes, basting occasionally and adding a little broth if necessary to ensure there is always some liquid in the pan.

3. Meanwhile, in a small saucepan, combine the jelly, orange zest, wine, cumin, the chopped garlic, and the parsley and heat over low heat until blended. Brush over the chicken and continue baking and basting with the pan juices 15 minutes more or until the dark meat just turns opaque inside.

4. Transfer the chicken to a platter. Drain the fat from the pan and deglaze, adding some broth, stirring, and scraping up any bits of flavor. Spoon the sauce over the chicken and serve hot.

Chicken in Fino Sherry Sauce
Pollo al Jerez

MAKES 4 SERVINGS

The history of Jerez and its sherry goes back thousands of years, when Phoenician settlers introduced grape vines to this area of southern Spain. Sherry takes many forms from bone dry to syrupy sweet, and all the ranges in between. This simple chicken dish calls for sherry of the dry variety called Fino.

One (3- to 3½-pound) chicken

⅛ teaspoon kosher or sea salt

2 tablespoons olive oil

3 garlic cloves, peeled and lightly smashed

Scant ⅛ teaspoon saffron threads, crumbled

¼ cup chicken broth or vegetable broth

⅓ cup dry sherry, such as Fino

1. Detach the chicken wings and legs. Hack off the bony ends of the legs and the tips of the wings and discard. Hack or cut with kitchen shears the breast into 4 pieces and each thigh crosswise in half. Season all over with salt.

2. Heat the oil in a shallow earthenware casserole dish or Dutch oven over medium heat. Add the garlic and cook, turning once and pressing with the back of a wooden spoon to extract its flavor, until lightly browned. Transfer to a mortar, reserving the oil in the casserole dish. Add the ⅛ teaspoon salt and the saffron and mash. Mash in a little of the broth, then stir in the rest.

3. Heat the reserved oil in the casserole dish over medium-high heat, add the chicken, and cook, turning once, until browned on all sides. Stir in the sherry and the mortar mixture and bring to a boil. Reduce the heat to medium-low, cover, and cook about 35 minutes more or until the dark meat just turns opaque inside. If using earthenware, serve hot in the dish, or transfer to a platter.

Chicken in Puréed Onion and Wine Sauce
Pollo a la Castellana

MAKES 4 SERVINGS

Delicious and simple to prepare, this recipe from Castilla calls for the chicken to be sautéed in a pungent wine sauce flavored with onion, garlic, and parsley.

2 tablespoons olive oil

1 medium onion, finely chopped (about ⅔ cup)

1 garlic clove

Kosher or sea salt

Freshly ground black pepper

One (3- to 3½-pound) chicken

3 tablespoons finely chopped fresh flat-leaf parsley

Pinch of saffron

½ cup dry white wine

½ cup chicken broth or vegetable broth

¼ teaspoon thyme

1 bay leaf

1. Heat the oil in a shallow earthenware casserole dish or Dutch oven over medium heat. Add the onion and garlic and cook, stirring, until the onion is wilted and transparent, about 5 minutes. Transfer the onion and garlic to a food processor or blender, reserving the oil in the casserole dish. Reserve.

2. Detach the chicken wings and legs. Hack off the bony ends of the legs and the tips of the wings and discard. Hack or cut with kitchen shears the breast into 4 pieces and each thigh crosswise in half. Season all over with salt and pepper.

3. Heat the reserved oil in the casserole dish over medium-high heat. Add the chicken and cook, turning once, until browned, adding more oil if necessary.

4. Meanwhile, in the food processor, place 2 tablespoons of the parsley, the saffron, salt, and pepper with the onion and garlic and process until blended. Gradually add the wine and broth and process until smooth. Pass through a fine-mesh strainer over the chicken. Discard the solids. Sprinkle with the thyme and add the bay leaf.

5. Reduce the heat to low, cover, and cook, adding more broth if the sauce becomes too thick, 30 minutes or until the dark meat just turns opaque inside. Remove the bay leaf. Sprinkle with the remaining 1 tablespoon parsley. If using earthenware, serve hot in the dish, or transfer to a platter.

Chicken with Almonds and Honey

Pollo al Andalus

MAKES 4 SERVINGS

Here the Moorish influence on Andalucian cooking is reflected by the use of honey and spices such as cilantro, saffron, and cumin. The almonds should be lightly browned in a small skillet before they are added because this greatly enhances their flavor.

One (3- to 3½-pound) chicken

Kosher or sea salt

Freshly ground black pepper

2 tablespoons plus 1 teaspoon olive oil

1 medium onion, finely chopped (about ⅔ cup)

1 tablespoon cilantro

1 tablespoon finely chopped fresh flat-leaf parsley

¼ teaspoon peeled and grated fresh ginger

Few threads saffron, crumbled

¼ teaspoon ground (or mortar-crushed) cumin

⅛ teaspoon ground nutmeg

½ cup chicken broth or vegetable broth

¼ cup dry white wine

2 tablespoons finely chopped blanched almonds

1 tablespoon honey

2 tablespoons water

1. Detach the chicken wings and legs. Hack off the bony ends of the legs and the tips of the wings and discard. Hack or cut with kitchen shears the breast into 4 pieces and each thigh crosswise in half. Season all over with salt and pepper.

2. Heat the 2 tablespoons oil in a shallow earthenware casserole dish or Dutch oven over medium-high heat. Add the chicken and cook, turning occasionally, until lightly browned on all sides. Add the onion and cook, stirring, until wilted and transparent, about 5 minutes. Sprinkle in the cilantro,

parsley, ginger, saffron, cumin, and nutmeg and stir in the broth and wine. Reduce the heat to low, cover, and cook 40 minutes or until the dark meat just turns opaque inside.

3. In a very small skillet, heat the 1 teaspoon oil over medium heat. Add the almonds and cook, stirring, until lightly browned. Add the honey and water and cook until most of the liquid has evaporated. Spoon over the chicken, cover, and cook 5 minutes more. If using earthenware, serve hot in the dish, or transfer to a platter.

Lobster with Chicken

Langosta con Pollo

MAKES 4 SERVINGS

The combination of shellfish and poultry that originated in Catalunya has become enormously popular in Spain, as well as many other countries. This dish is usually served with a typical lobster sauce. But here I include the original Catalan recipe, which calls for chocolate, almonds, and hazelnuts, making this dish much more unusual. You can find the aguardiente or grappa in most liquor stores.

2 whole chicken breasts, split in half

Salt

Freshly ground black pepper

2 (1- to 1½-pound) live lobsters

¼ cup olive oil

1 medium onion, finely chopped (about ⅔ cup)

2 tablespoons finely chopped fresh flat-leaf parsley

1 bay leaf

½ teaspoon dried thyme

½ pound fresh or canned tomatoes, peeled and finely chopped

1 cup dry white wine

2 tablespoons aguardiente or grappa

Few threads saffron, crumbled

4 garlic cloves

16 blanched almonds

10 hazelnuts, shelled

1½ teaspoons grated bittersweet chocolate

⅛ teaspoon sugar

1. Season the chicken with salt and pepper. Set aside. Place a cutting board in a rimmed cookie sheet to catch the lobster liquid that collects. Place each lobster on its back on the cutting board. Do not remove the bands that keep the claws shut. Protect your hand with a heavy towel or pot holder and hold the lobster firmly by the head. Plunge the tip of a heavy chef's knife into the body where the tail joins the chest. Cut all the way through, separating the tail from the body. Pull out and discard the dark vein from the tail. Slice the head down the middle, discard the stomach sack, and transfer the tomalley (green matter) to a small bowl and reserve.

2. In a large saucepan, place the bodies and small claws, add water to cover and salt, and bring to a boil over high heat. Reduce the heat to low, cover, and simmer 30 minutes or until the shells are red and the liquid is seasoned. Discard the body and reserve the small claws for future use. Reserve 1 cup of the cooking liquid.

3. Heat the oil in a medium skillet over medium heat. Add the chicken and cook, turning once, until golden on both sides. Transfer to another platter. Increase the heat to medium-high, add the lobster tails and large claws, and cook just a few minutes until they turn pink. Transfer to the platter with the chicken.

4. Reduce the heat to medium, add the onion, and cook, stirring, until wilted and transparent, about 5 minutes. Add 1 tablespoon of the parsley, the bay leaf, thyme, tomatoes, wine, aguardiente, salt, and pepper, cover, and cook 15 minutes. Add the chicken and lobster, reduce the heat to low, cover, and cook about 10 minutes more or until they absorb the sauce. Remove the bay leaf.

5. Meanwhile, in a food processor or blender, combine the reserved tomalley, the saffron, garlic, almonds, hazelnuts, the remaining 1 tablespoon parsley, the chocolate, and sugar and process until as smooth as possible. Gradually add the reserved 1 cup cooking liquid. Pour over the chicken and lobster, stir to coat well, cover, and cook 15 minutes more or until the chicken just turns opaque.

6. Remove the shell from the lobster tails and large claws. Cut the lobster meat into ¼-inch slices. On each of 4 individual plates, place 1 chicken breast half and arrange lobster slices on the chicken. Pour the sauce over the top (it may be passed through a fine-mesh strainer if you prefer). Serve hot.

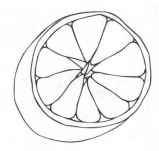

Chicken with Shrimp in Almond and Hazelnut Sauce

Pollastre con Gambas Almendras y Avellanas

MAKES 4 SERVINGS

This delicious dish combining poultry, shellfish, and nuts is a regional specialty of Catalunya. The flavors blend perfectly, and the subtle almond and hazelnut wine sauce is excellent.

One (3- to 3½-pound) chicken

Salt

Freshly ground black pepper

All-purpose flour, for dredging

20 medium shrimp, in their shells

3 tablespoons olive oil

1 medium onion, finely chopped (about ⅔ cup)

2 garlic cloves, finely chopped

1 medium tomato, peeled, seeded, and finely chopped (about ⅔ cup)

2 tablespoons finely chopped fresh flat-leaf parsley

1½ teaspoons finely chopped fresh oregano or ¼ teaspoon dried oregano

1½ teaspoons finely chopped fresh thyme or ¼ teaspoon dried thyme

1 bay leaf

3-inch piece leek, trimmed, well washed, and quartered lengthwise (white part only)

½ cup chicken broth or vegetable broth

¼ cup dry white wine

5 blanched almonds

5 hazelnuts

⅛ teaspoon salt

1 tablespoon brandy

1. Detach the chicken wings and legs. Hack off the bony ends of the legs and the tips of the wings and discard. Hack or cut with kitchen shears the breast into 4 pieces and each thigh crosswise in half. Season all over with salt and pepper. Place the flour in a wide shallow bowl and dredge the chicken in the flour. Shell the shrimp, reserving the shells. Season the shrimp with salt and dredge in the flour.

2. Heat the oil in a shallow earthenware casserole dish or Dutch oven over medium-high heat. Add the chicken and cook, turning occasionally, until browned on all sides. Transfer to a platter. Add the shrimp and cook, turning once, until pink. Transfer to the platter.

3. Reduce the heat to medium, add the onion and garlic, and cook, stirring, until the onion has softened, about 5 minutes. Stir in the tomato, parsley, oregano, thyme, bay leaf, and leek, then add the broth, wine, and the reserved shrimp shells. Add the chicken, cover, and cook 30 minutes or until the meat inside just turns opaque.

4. In a mortar or mini-processor, mash the almonds, hazelnuts, and the ⅛ teaspoon salt. Stir in the brandy. Add to the casserole dish and cook 5 minutes more until the flavors blend. Remove the bay leaf. If using earthenware, serve hot in the dish, or transfer to a platter.

Turkey "Fricassee" Faín
Pavo Guisado al Estilo de Faín

MAKES 4 SERVINGS

Our friend Soledad Gil runs a small hotel in the peaceful country estate of Faín near the beautiful town of Arcos de la Frontera in the Cádiz province. His turkey fricassee is one of the best versions I have ever tasted.

3 to 3½ pounds turkey parts, such as wings, drumsticks, and/or thighs

Kosher or sea salt

2 tablespoons olive oil

1 medium sweet onion, such as Vidalia, slivered

2 garlic cloves, finely chopped

1 small dried sweet red pepper (ñora); or ½ dried red New Mexico (Anaheim) chile pepper, stemmed and seeded

1 medium tomato, finely chopped (about ⅔ cup)

1 tablespoon finely chopped fresh flat-leaf parsley

¾ cup chicken broth or vegetable broth

½ cup dry white wine

Scant ⅛ teaspoon saffron threads, crumbled

Generous amount freshly grated black pepper

¼ teaspoon ground cumin

1. Season the turkey parts all over with salt.

2. Heat the oil in a large shallow casserole dish or Dutch oven over medium-high heat. Add the turkey and cook, turning occasionally, until browned on all sides. Reduce the heat to medium, add the onion, garlic, and chile pepper, and cook, stirring, until the onion is wilted and transparent, about 5 minutes. Stir in the tomato and parsley and cook, stirring, about 2 minutes. Reduce the heat to low and add the broth, wine, saffron, black pepper, and cumin.

3. Cover and simmer 1¼ hours until the dark meat is just opaque inside (add water if the pan gets dry). If using earthenware, serve hot in the dish, or transfer to a platter.

Roasted Pheasants with Port
Faisán al Modo de Alcántara

MAKES 4 SERVINGS

Monasteries might seem to be an unlikely source of recipes, when in fact the opposite is true. There are many centuries-old recipes that were it not for monasteries would be lost to us today. This recipe from the old Benedictine Monastery at Alcántara on the River Tajo in Extremadura has a great story behind it (see sidebar, page 471).

PREPARE 2 TO 3 DAYS IN ADVANCE

2 dozen small truffles; 3 ounces dried morel mushrooms; or 3 ounces chanterelle mushrooms (1 pound if fresh, 6 ounces if canned)

1 bottle port wine, such as tawny

2 (2 to 2½-pound) pheasants, with necks

Salt

Freshly ground black pepper

10 duck or chicken livers, gristle removed, each cut into 4 pieces

¼ pound unsalted butter

Lard

1. Place half of the truffles in a medium saucepan and add ¾ cup of the wine. Bring to a boil over low heat and simmer 10 minutes. Drain and thinly slice. Season the pheasant inside and out and the livers on both sides with salt and pepper.

2. Melt the butter in a medium skillet over low heat. Add the livers, cover, turn once, and cook about 15 minutes. Transfer the livers to a food processor or

continues...

blender and process until smooth, adding a little of the butter if the purée is too thick (it should hold together but not be pasty). Add the truffles and process until smooth. Fill the pheasant cavities with this mixture and truss.

3. Place the pheasants in a deep bowl in which they fit fairly snugly. Pour the remaining port over the pheasants, cover with foil, and let marinate 2 to 3 days in the refrigerator. (If the port doesn't quite cover, either add more port, or turn the birds occasionally as they marinate.)

4. Preheat the oven to 350°F. Drain and dry the pheasants, reserving the port for marinade. Rub well with the lard and season with salt and pepper. Place in a shallow earthenware casserole dish or Dutch oven (along with the necks, if available).

5. Bake, turning occasionally and basting regularly, about 55 minutes (24 minutes per pound) or until the internal temperature reaches at 165°F to 170°F, and the legs move easily when gently lifted or twisted. Do not overcook.

6. Meanwhile, place the reserved marinade and the remaining half of the truffles in a small saucepan. Bring to a simmer over low heat and cook, stirring occasionally, until the liquid is reduced by half and the marinade is slightly thickened. During the last 10 minutes of roasting, pour the cooked marinade over the pheasants and cover the pheasant breasts with foil. Let rest 10 minutes.

7. Cut the birds in half and place each half on an individual plate. Serve hot.

Partridges in White Wine Sauce, Toledo Style
Perdiz a la Toledana

MAKES 4 SERVINGS

The province of Toledo in the La Mancha region is famous for its partridges. They are very common in the fields, making this area a Mecca for hunters from all over the world during hunting season. This recipe is slightly more elaborate than other preparations, but it creates a rich sauce that is absolutely out of this world. (You may need to preorder game birds like partridge and quail, or try substituting Cornish hens.)

2 partridges or pheasants (2 to 3 pounds each)
Salt
Freshly ground black pepper
2 tablespoons olive oil
1 large onion, finely chopped (about 1 cup)
12 garlic cloves, lightly smashed and peeled
2 tablespoons trimmed, well washed, and finely chopped leek or scallion (white part only)
2 tablespoons brandy
1 tablespoon wine vinegar
1 cup dry white wine
1 medium carrot, peeled, and cut into 4 pieces
Few threads of saffron
1 bay leaf
4 peppercorns
1 tablespoon finely chopped fresh flat-leaf parsley
1½ tablespoons finely chopped fresh thyme or ¼ teaspoon dried thyme

1. Season the partridges inside and out with salt and pepper and truss.

2. In a stew pot in which the birds will fit closely, heat 1 tablespoon of the oil over medium heat.

Several years ago, I went to Montréal with my husband, Luis, to promote one of my cookbooks. One evening we went to a highly recommended French restaurant called Chez la Mère Michel for dinner. The restaurant was elegant and comfortable, and we felt very much at ease. We ordered a couple of drinks and asked to see the menu. I was deciding what to order when my husband became very excited after reading that one of their specialties was "Pheasant Alcántara Style." He immediately called over the maître d', and speaking to him in French, ordered the pheasant. I was very surprised when a few minutes later the maître d' came back and said to Luis, "Sir, I told the chef to cook the pheasant the best he can because I realized that you are Spanish."

I was quite intrigued and tried to find more information about the recipe. I found the answer in a famous French cookbook, *Le Guide Culinaire*, written by A. Escoffier in 1903, and I was fascinated by the story behind the recipe. In 1812, during the so-called Wars of Independence by the Spaniards (or Peninsular Wars by the British), a group of Spanish guerrillas took refuge in the Monastery of Alcántara near the Tajo River in Extremadura. A fierce battle ensued in which the Spaniards were killed and the Monastery was left in ruins. (It still is today.)

After the battle, a soldier walking through the ruins found a manuscript containing several recipes from the kitchen of the monks that he gave to his superior, Jean-Andoche Junot. Junot took the manuscript back to Paris with him and eventually gave it to the Duchess of Abrantes. Her memoirs included some of the recipes, and the pheasant dish became a signature dish of French cuisine. The ingredients include pheasant, foie gras, and truffles cooked in Port wine. Escoffier was surprised to learn that truffles and foie gras were not exclusive to Languedoc and Gascony in France, but were also common in Extremadura where today pheasants are still found in the wild. Even truffles are not difficult to find in Spain under the encinas trees. In his book, Escoffier makes it clear that the only good thing the French obtained from their unfortunate campaign in Spain was the discovery of this recipe. We loved the dinner in Montréal, and in homage to France for saving the recipe, we drank a delicious Armagnac.

Add the partridges and cook, turning occasionally, until browned on all sides. Stir in the remaining 1 tablespoon oil, the onion, garlic, and leek and cook, stirring, until the onion is wilted and transparent, about 5 minutes. Add the brandy. Standing well away from the pot, ignite the liquid with a match or kitchen lighter and let die out. Stir in all the remaining ingredients and salt. Reduce the heat to low, cover, and simmer about 1 hour (15 to 20 minutes per pound), adding a little water or chicken broth if necessary and turning the partridges occasionally. They are done when the internal temperature reaches 165°F to 170°F and the legs move easily when lifted or twisted.

3. Transfer the partridges to a warm platter. Pass the sauce through a fine-mesh strainer into a bowl, pressing with the back of a wooden spoon to extract as much liquid as possible. Discard the solids. Split the partridges in half and place each on an individual plate. Spoon the sauce over each partridge and serve hot.

Partridges in Escabeche
Perdiz Escabechada

MAKES 4 SERVINGS

Escabeche, *a form of marinade, has been used for centuries as a way to preserve food long before refrigeration. It has a tangy taste and does a wonderful job of bringing out the flavors of the food with which it is prepared. You can keep Partridges in* escabeche *in the refrigerator for several days, but I recommend serving it at room temperature. (You may need to pre-order game birds like partridge and quail, or try substituting Cornish hens.)*

PREPARE AT LEAST 2 HOURS IN ADVANCE

7 tablespoons olive oil

4 partridges (about 2 pounds each) or 8 European quail or Cornish hens (1 pound each)

¾ cup white wine vinegar

2 cups dry white wine

1 large onion, slivered

12 garlic cloves, coarsely chopped

3 bay leaves

15 peppercorns

¼ teaspoon dried thyme

¼ teaspoon saffron threads, crumbled

2 sprigs parsley

½ teaspoon kosher or sea salt

Jarred pickles and caperberries, for garnish

1. Heat the oil in a shallow earthenware casserole dish or Dutch oven over medium heat. Add the partridges and cook, turning occasionally, until browned. Add the vinegar, wine, onion, garlic, bay leaves, peppercorns, thyme, saffron, parsley, and salt and bring to a boil. Reduce the heat to low, cover, and simmer, basting the birds periodically. Cook about 45 minutes (15 to 20 minutes per pound)

or until the internal temperature reaches 165°F to 170°F and the legs move easily when gently lifted or twisted. Let cool, lightly covered with foil, at least 2 hours.

2. Place the pickles and caperberries in a small serving bowl. Serve the partridges at room temperature with the pickles and caperberries.

Partridges with Stuffed Cabbage Leaves
Perdiz con Col y Cerdo

MAKES 4 SERVINGS

This is a variation of a classic Catalan dish consisting of partridge stuffed in cabbage and tied into small packets. It includes ground pork, which makes the dish much richer. I have prepared this recipe without the pork, but I much prefer this version from my friend Irene España, who runs Casa Irene, a marvelous restaurant high in the Pyrenees in the small village of Artíes. (You may need to preorder game birds like partridge and quail, or try substituting Cornish hens.)

12 cabbage leaves

4 partridges (about 2 pounds each) or 8 European quail or Cornish hens (about 1 pound each), butterflied (split in half)

Salt

Freshly ground black pepper

Stuffing

2 tablespoons bread crumbs

2 teaspoons milk

1 pound ground pork

1 teaspoon salt

Freshly ground black pepper

¼ cup finely chopped Serrano (Spanish cured mountain) ham or prosciutto

1 large egg, lightly beaten

2 tablespoons finely chopped fresh flat-leaf parsley

2 garlic cloves, finely chopped

1½ teaspoons finely chopped fresh thyme or
¼ teaspoon dried thyme

¼ teaspoon dried oregano

Vegetables

¼ cup olive oil

All-purpose flour, for dusting

1 small onion, finely chopped (about ⅓ cup)

½ cup trimmed, well washed, and finely chopped leek
(white part only)

1 medium carrot, peeled and finely chopped (about
½ cup)

¼ cup finely chopped celery

2 garlic cloves, finely chopped

1 medium tomato, finely chopped (about ⅔ cup)

2 tablespoons finely chopped fresh flat-leaf parsley

2 bay leaves

½ teaspoon dried oregano

2 teaspoons all-purpose flour

1¼ cups dry white wine

Picada

2 garlic cloves, coarsely chopped

2 tablespoons finely chopped fresh flat-leaf parsley

Scant ¼ teaspoon saffron threads, crumbled

¼ teaspoon salt

1. Bring a large pot of water to a boil over high heat. Add 2 cabbage leaves and cook about 2 minutes. Drain and transfer to a platter. Repeat for the remaining leaves.

2. Season the partridges inside and out with salt and pepper and let sit while stuffing the cabbage leaves. In a large bowl, combine the stuffing ingredients, lightly mixing with your hands. Place 2 tablespoons of the stuffing in the center of each cabbage leaf. Fold in the two sides of the leaves, then fold over the top and bottom, forming 2- to 2½-inch rectangles. Tie with kitchen string like a ribbon on a gift.

3. Heat 2 tablespoons of the oil in a large shallow earthenware casserole dish or Dutch oven over medium heat. Add the partridge and cook, turning once, until browned. Transfer to a platter. Place the flour in a small shallow bowl, dredge the cabbages in the flour, and add to the casserole dish. Over medium heat, cook, turning once, until browned on both sides. Transfer to the platter.

4. Prepare the vegetables: Add the remaining 2 tablespoons oil to the casserole dish. Add the onion, leek, carrot, celery, and garlic and cook, stirring, until the vegetables are softened. Add the tomato, parsley, bay leaves, oregano, salt, and pepper and cook, stirring, about 2 minutes more. Sprinkle in the flour, then stir in the wine. Reduce the heat to low, cover, and simmer 15 minutes.

5. Add the cabbage rolls and partridges to the casserole dish, cover, and simmer 30 minutes more, turning once, or until the internal temperature of the partridge reaches 165°F.

6. Meanwhile, prepare the picada: Mash all the ingredients in a mortar or mini-processor.

7. Transfer the partridges and cabbage rolls to a platter. Pass the vegetables through a food mill or a fine-mesh strainer, pressing with the back of a soup ladle to extract as much liquid as possible. Discard the solids. Return the strained liquid to the casserole dish and stir in the picada. Add the partridges and cabbage rolls and reheat over medium-low heat. Remove the string from the cabbage rolls and serve hot.

Stewed Partridges
Perdiz Estofada "Casa Paco"

MAKES 4 SERVINGS

This is my husband's favorite recipe for partridges, which we were fortunate to obtain from Casa Paco, a quaint tavern in Madrid in the middle of the old and historic neighborhood known as the "Madrid of the Austrias," which is the name of the old royal family in the sixteenth century. To make the dish more substantial, parboiled cubed or whole new potatoes may be added for the last 15 minutes of cooking. You can substitute Cornish hens, which don't need to rest for several days.

PREPARE 2 TO 3 DAYS IN ADVANCE

4 partridges (about 2 pounds each), butterflied (split in half)

¼ cup olive oil

1 large onion, finely chopped (about 1 cup)

6 garlic cloves, lightly smashed

2 bay leaves

6 peppercorns

1 cup dry white wine

1 medium carrot, sliced

8 small pearl onions

Salt

1. Place the partridges in a large pot or bowl, cover, and let sit in the refrigerator 2 to 3 days—this helps tenderize the meat.

2. Heat the oil in a deep earthenware casserole dish or Dutch oven over medium heat. Add the partridges and cook, turning occasionally, until browned on all sides. Add the chopped onion, the garlic, and bay leaves and cook until the onion is wilted and transparent, about 5 minutes more. Stir in the peppercorns, wine, carrot, pearl onions, and salt. Reduce the heat to low, cover tightly, and simmer about 1 hour or until the internal temperature reaches at least 165°F to 170°F. Serve hot.

Fermín's Saffron-Marinated Partridge
Perdiz en Escabeche de Fermín

MAKES 4 SERVINGS

Chef Fermín Merino Sánchez from the region of La Mancha has created a unique Escabeche marinade that is light on vinegar and heavy on saffron. I first tasted this unusual version of Escabeche at the magnificent Parador of Albacete, where Fermín has worked for much of his life. Because the recipe calls for so little vinegar, this Escabeche marinade is less tangy and more subtle than most others.

PREPARE AT LEAST 4 DAYS IN ADVANCE

4 partridges (about 2 pounds each), butterflied (split in half); or 8 quail (about 1 pound each), whole and trussed; or 2 Cornish game hens, butterflied

2 cups water

1 cup chicken broth or vegetable broth

1 head garlic, separated and peeled

½ teaspoon salt

3 bay leaves

10 peppercorns

2 sprigs rosemary or ¼ teaspoon dried rosemary

4 sprigs thyme or ¼ teaspoon dried thyme

1 cup white or amber wine vinegar

½ teaspoon saffron threads, crumbled

1. Place the partridges breast down in a shallow earthenware casserole dish or Dutch oven. Add all the remaining ingredients except the saffron and bring to a boil over medium-high heat. Reduce the heat to low, cover, and simmer about 40 minutes (15 to 20 minutes per pound) or until the internal

temperature reaches 165°F to 170°F. Transfer the partridges to a deep bowl or other container in which they fit snugly. Transfer the garlic to a food processor. Reserve the bay leaves and cooking liquid in the casserole dish.

2. Add the saffron and 3 tablespoons of the cooking liquid to the processor and blend until smooth. Stir into the casserole dish and taste and adjust seasoning if necessary.

3. Pour the marinade over the partridges (it should cover them). Cover and let marinate in the refrigerator at least 4 days up to several weeks. Remove the bay leaf. Bring to room temperature and serve.

Partridges in Chocolate-Flavored Sauce
Perdiz con Chocolate

MAKES 4 SERVINGS

Chocolate came to Spain after the discovery of the New World, and it spread from Spain throughout Europe. Still, it took many years for this ingredient to make its way into recipes other than desserts. This dish is not at all sweet, as the chocolate the recipe calls for is of the bitter variety. It adds an unusual flavor that enhances rather than overwhelms the other ingredients.

PREPARE AT LEAST 2 TO 3 DAYS IN ADVANCE

2 or 4 partridges (about 2 pounds each); or other
    game bird, butterflied (split in half)

Kosher or sea salt

Freshly ground black pepper

3 tablespoons olive oil

2 garlic cloves, finely chopped

1 medium onion, finely chopped (about ⅔ cup)

1 tablespoon all-purpose flour

2 tablespoons vinegar

½ cup dry white wine

½ cup chicken broth or vegetable broth

2 bay leaves

2 whole cloves

1 teaspoon grated bittersweet chocolate

1. Place the partridges in a large pot or bowl, cover, and let sit in the refrigerator 2 to 3 days—this helps tenderize the meat.

2. Season the partridges on both sides with salt and pepper. Heat the oil in a deep earthenware casserole dish or Dutch oven over medium heat. Add the partridges and cook, turning once, until browned. Add the garlic and onion and cook, stirring, until the onion is wilted and transparent, about 5 minutes more. Stir in the flour. Add the vinegar, wine, broth, salt, pepper, bay leaves, and cloves. Turn the partridges skin side down if necessary. Reduce the heat to low, cover, and simmer about 40 minutes more (15 to 20 minutes per pound) or until the internal temperature reaches 165°F to 170°F. Transfer the partridges to a warm platter.

3. Add the chocolate to the sauce in the casserole dish and stir until dissolved. Return the partridges to the dish and cook, covered, 10 minutes more. Remove the bay leaf. If using earthenware, serve hot in the dish, or transfer to a platter.

Braised Quail
Codornices Estofadas

MAKES 4 SERVINGS

The first time I was introduced to this odd cooking method, in which the stew pot is covered with a dish filled with water and onion slices, I admit that I was a bit perplexed. My close friend Carmen Serrano explained the logic behind it: The dish on top simulates a pressure cooker by holding in the steam.

continues…

If the stew needs extra liquid, the water and onion in the plate can be used. This method, and Carmen's wonderful recipe, creates an especially tender and flavorful braised quail that is not to be missed.

8 quail or Cornish hens (about 1 pound each), butterflied (split in half)

Kosher or sea salt

2 tablespoons olive oil

2 medium sweet onions, such as Vidalia, each cut into 8 pieces

3 garlic cloves, halved crosswise

3 sprigs parsley

1 bay leaf

Freshly ground black pepper

¼ cup water

4 slices medium onion

1. Season the quail on both sides with salt. Coat a large stew pot with 1 tablespoon of the oil and arrange the quail in the pot, skin side down. Scatter the 8 onion pieces and the garlic around the quail, then drizzle with the remaining 1 tablespoon oil.

2. Heat over medium-high heat and cook, leaving the quail skin side down, until it begins to brown. Add the parsley, bay leaf, and pepper. Cover the pot with a deep plate or shallow soup bowl that fits tightly over the pot. Add the water and sliced onion to the plate.

3. Reduce the heat to low and cook 30 to 40 minutes or until the onion is tender and the quail is cooked through, removing the plate occasionally to stir and adding water from the plate if necessary. Serve hot.

Braised Marinated Quail
Codorniz en Escabeche Casa Irene

MAKES 4 SERVINGS

Quail marinated in escabeche *is a common preparation that can be found in all parts of Spain. It is particularly delicious when Irene España gives it her special flair by gently flattening the quail first and adding nutmeg and rosemary to the marinade.*

PREPARE 8 TO 12 HOURS IN ADVANCE

8 quail (about 1 pound each)

7 tablespoons extra-virgin olive oil

6 garlic cloves, lightly smashed

2 bay leaves

¼ teaspoon freshly ground nutmeg

2 sprigs rosemary or ½ teaspoon dried rosemary

10 peppercorns

¼ cup wine vinegar

Salt

2 tablespoons chicken broth or vegetable broth

1. Leave the quail whole, but gently pound the breast bone to flatten the birds slightly. In a shallow earthenware casserole dish or Dutch oven in which the quail fit closely, heat 1 tablespoon of the oil over medium-high heat. Add the quail and cook, turning occasionally, until browned on all sides. Transfer to a platter and wipe out the casserole dish.

2. Heat the remaining 6 tablespoons oil in the casserole dish over medium heat. Add the garlic, bay leaves, nutmeg, rosemary, peppercorns, vinegar, and a little salt and cook, stirring, until the mixture comes to a sizzle. Reduce the heat to low, add the quail breast side down, cover, and simmer about 45 minutes (15 to 20 minutes per pound), turning once, until the internal temperature reaches 165°F to 170°F and the legs move easily when gently lifted or twisted.

3. Remove the quail and cut into quarters. Add the broth to the casserole dish, bring to a boil, and remove from the heat. Return the quail to the casserole dish and spoon some of the sauce over them. Let cool. Cover and let marinate overnight in the refrigerator, turning occasionally. Bring to room temperature and serve.

Quail with Beans
Cordornices con Pochas "Santo Domingo de la Calzada"

MAKES 4 SERVINGS

This recipe originated in the heart of Rioja wine country, in a magnificent parador which was a hospital for pilgrims on their way to St. James in the twelfth century. Santo Domingo not only established the hospital, but he also paved the roads that led to it. Santo Domingo de la Calzada translates in English to "Santo Domingo of the Road." The parador is visually breathtaking, and every item on their menu is delicious, including this traditional dish of quail with large lima beans.

PREPARE 1 DAY IN ADVANCE

1 pound dried lima beans, sorted and washed

8 cups water

5 tablespoons olive oil

Kosher or sea salt

8 quail (about 1 pound each) trussed

1 medium onion, finely chopped (about ⅔ cup)

2 garlic cloves, finely chopped

1 medium tomato, finely chopped (about ⅔ cup)

Freshly ground black pepper

1 bay leaf

4 (1-inch) cubes slab bacon

¼ pound (2 links) chorizo sausage, each cut into 4 pieces

1. Place the beans in a large bowl, add cold water to cover by 1 inch, and let soak overnight in the refrigerator. Drain. In a large saucepan, place the beans and the 8 cups water and bring to a boil over high heat. Reduce the heat to low, cover, and simmer 1½ to 2 hours.

2. Meanwhile, season the quail with salt. Heat the oil in a large skillet over medium-high heat. Add the quail and cook, turning occasionally, until golden on all sides. Transfer to a platter.

3. Add the onion and garlic and cook, stirring, until the onion is wilted and transparent, about 5 minutes. Add the tomato and cook, stirring, 3 minutes more. Add this mixture to the beans along with the salt, pepper, bay leaf, bacon, chorizo, and the quail. Cover and cook 30 minutes or until the beans are tender, and the internal temperature of the quail reaches 165°F to 170°F and the legs move easily when gently lifted or twisted. (The quail should not be cooked longer than 30 minutes). Remove the bay leaf and serve hot.

Braised Quail in Grape Leaves
Codornices en Hoja de Parra

MAKES 4 SERVINGS

Grape leaves are common in all Mediterranean countries, and they are featured in more than a few Spanish dishes. Here, is the quail wrapped in grape leaves and covered with pancetta (bacon), creating a dish that is succulent and flavorful. This recipe comes from Jerez de la Frontera—sherry and brandy country. I found it at Bodegas Osborne.

8 grape leaves, packed in brine

8 quail (about 1 pound each) necks trimmed

8 thin slices pancetta or bacon

2 tablespoons olive oil

6 tablespoons finely chopped onion

continues...

2 tablespoons brandy, such as Spanish brandy or
   Cognac

1¼ cups chicken broth or vegetable broth

Salt

1. Fill with water a pot large enough to fit the grape leaves and bring to a boil over high heat. Separate the grape leaves and place them in the water. (Cook in batches if necessary to avoid overcrowding.) Cook about 3 minutes. Transfer to paper towels and let drain.

2. Fold the wing tip of the quail under the breast and push the legs up towards the breast. Fit a grape leaf over and around each quail, pressing lightly so that the leaf adheres. Place a slice of pancetta over each breast and tie the quail lengthwise and crosswise with kitchen string as you would a package.

3. Heat the oil in a shallow earthenware casserole dish or Dutch oven over medium heat. Add the onion and cook, stirring, until wilted and transparent, about 5 minutes. Stir in the brandy and cook until evaporated. Add the quail, breast side down, and cook 5 minutes. Turn the breasts over and add the broth and salt. Increase the heat to medium-high, cover, and cook about 25 minutes, checking occasionally and adding more broth if necessary. The quail are done when the internal temperature reaches 165°F to 170°F and the legs move easily when gently lifted or twisted.

4. Transfer the quail to a platter and remove the string, leaving the leaf and pancetta over the quail. If using earthenware, serve hot in the dish, or transfer to a platter. Serve the sauce on the side.

Grilled Quail with Garlic and Parsley

Codornices a la Parrilla con Ajo y Perejil

MAKES 4 SERVINGS

In this extremely simple way to prepare quail, it is grilled quickly and covered with a pungent mixture of olive oil, garlic, and parsley.

4 garlic cloves, finely chopped

¼ cup finely chopped fresh flat-leaf parsley

⅛ teaspoon salt

3 tablespoons extra-virgin olive oil, plus more for
   brushing

8 quail (about 1 pound each)

Freshly ground black pepper

1. In a mortar or mini-processor, mash the garlic, parsley, and the salt. Stir in the oil.

2. Butterfly the quail by splitting the breasts down the center to open. Pound the quail lightly with a wide, flat knife, metal pan, or wooden spoon to flatten. Brush both sides with the mortar mixture and season with salt and pepper.

3. Place a broiler rack about 6 inches from the heat source and preheat the broiler. (Cover the broiler pan with foil for easier cleanup, if you like.) Broil the quail about 5 minutes per side or until browned and cooked through. (Watch them; they will cook quickly.) Spoon the sauce over the quail and serve hot.

Quail in Green Peppers
Codornices en Zurrón

MAKES 4 SERVINGS

The Spanish word zurrón *refers to the shoulder bags carried by shepherds in the field to hold their food and belongings. This recipe calls for the quail to be wrapped in cured ham and placed inside green peppers, which is why this dish is sometimes called "Quail in a Knapsack."*

8 tiny quail (less than a pound), trussed

¼ cup brandy, such as Spanish brandy or Cognac

Kosher or sea salt

Freshly ground black pepper

6 tablespoons olive oil

8 pearl onions

8 thin slices Serrano (Spanish cured mountain) ham or prosciutto

8 green frying peppers, each large enough to hold a quail

2 medium carrots, peeled and cut into ¼-inch slices

2 garlic cloves, finely chopped

8 large cherry tomatoes

1½ teaspoons all-purpose flour

½ cup chicken broth or vegetable broth

¼ cup white wine

1. Fill the cavity of each quail with about 1½ teaspoons brandy. Season outside with salt and pepper. Heat the oil in a large skillet over medium-high heat. Add the quail and cook, turning occasionally, until browned on all sides. Transfer the quail to a platter and reserve the oil in the skillet.

2. Fill a small saucepan with water and bring to a boil over high heat. Add the pearl onions and cook 3 minutes. Rinse under cold water and slip off the skins.

3. Preheat the oven to 350°F. Wrap each quail in a slice of ham. For each bell pepper, remove the stem, make a lengthwise slit in the side, and remove the seeds. Place a quail in each pepper. Arrange, slit side down, in a shallow earthenware casserole dish or Dutch oven. Scatter the onions, carrots, garlic, and tomatoes around the quail and drizzle the reserved oil over everything.

4. Bake 30 minutes. Remove from the oven. Sprinkle the flour in the casserole dish and stir to combine, then stir in the broth and the wine. Season with salt and black pepper. Transfer to the stovetop over low heat and cook 20 minutes more.

5. Place a broiler rack about 6 inches from the heat source and preheat the broiler. (Cover the broiler pan with foil for easier cleanup, if you like.) Place the casserole dish under the broiler and broil until the frying peppers are browned. If using earthenware, serve hot in the dish, or transfer to a platter.

Sautéed Small Birds with Crumb Topping
Chimbos a la Bilbaína

MAKES 4 SERVINGS

Small birds, or chimbos, *are a delicacy in Spain and there are numerous ways to prepare them. This outstanding recipe in which the quail or Cornish hen is coated in crunchy fried bread crumbs originated in Bilbao. If quail or hen is not available, chicken may be substituted.*

2 quail or Cornish hens (about 1 pound each), quartered

Salt

Freshly ground black pepper

2 tablespoons olive oil

2 tablespoons bread crumbs

2 garlic cloves, finely chopped

2 tablespoons parsley

continues...

1. Sprinkle the hens all over with salt and pepper. Heat the oil in a shallow earthenware casserole dish or Dutch oven over high heat. Add the quail or hens and cook, turning once, until golden on both sides. Reduce the heat to medium high, cover, and cook about 20 minutes until the internal temperature reaches 165°F to 170°F and the legs move easily when gently lifted or twisted.

2. Meanwhile, in a small bowl, combine the bread crumbs, garlic, and parsley.

3. When the hens are done, transfer to a warm platter. Add the bread crumb mixture to the casserole dish and cook, stirring, until crisp. Spoon the crumbs over the hens. Serve hot.

Quail in a Nest
Codornices al Nido

MAKES 4 SERVINGS

This exceptional recipe is always a crowd pleaser, but it requires the use of a potato nest basket for a deep fryer. It is worth the extra effort because this dish of tiny quail in a nest of fried potatoes is truly sensational. Because the quail are tiny, two per person would be needed for a meal or this could be a small course for 8.

1 recipe Braised Quail (page 475)
6 cups shredded peeled potatoes
Olive oil, for frying
Watercress, for garnish

1. Prepare the quail. Preheat the oven to 200°F, cover the quail, and keep warm. Meanwhile, place the potatoes in a medium bowl with cold water to cover and let soak 30 minutes. Drain and let dry on paper towels.

2. Heat enough oil to cover a potato nest basket in a large skillet over medium-high heat (or better still, use a deep fryer set at 365°F) until it turns a cube of bread light brown in 60 seconds. Dip the potato nest basket into the oil to coat, then line with the potatoes, about ¾ cup per nest. Secure with the smaller nest basket that fits inside.

3. Dip each nest into the oil and cook until lightly browned. Let drain on paper towels, then place on a cookie sheet and transfer to the oven to keep warm. Repeat for the remaining 7 nests,

4. Place 1 quail in each nest, spoon the sauce over the quail, and decorate with the watercress. Serve hot.

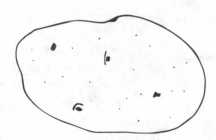

Duck with Sherry and Green Olives, Seville Style

Pato a la Sevillana

MAKES 4 SERVINGS

This is a typical recipe from Seville where both green olives and ducks can be found in abundance. Seville is situated close to the mouth of the Guadalquivir River and not far away from the Coto Doñana, a breeding ground where birds stop during their migration to and from Africa. Ducks in the United States tend to have more fat than ducks native to Spain, so I recommend always pre-roasting your duck before combining it with the other ingredients.

One (4½-pound) duck, with neck

2 medium onions, thinly sliced

2 garlic cloves

½ cup dry white wine

½ cup thinly sliced pitted green olives, preferably Spanish

2 tablespoons olive oil

1 medium onion, finely chopped (about ⅔ cup)

2 garlic cloves, finely chopped

½ cup dry sherry, such as Fino

½ cup chicken broth or vegetable broth

2 medium carrots, peeled and thinly sliced

1 sprig parsley

¼ teaspoon dried thyme

1 bay leaf

4 peppercorns

Kosher or sea salt

1. Preheat the oven to 400°F. Place the onions and the whole garlic cloves in the duck cavity and truss. Prick the duck deeply with a fork. Place in a roasting pan with the neck and roast 1 hour or until lightly browned. Transfer to a platter and cut into quarters. Drain all fat from the pan and deglaze, adding ¼ cup of the wine, stirring, and scraping up any bits of flavor. Reserve the pan juices and discard the neck.

2. In a small saucepan, place the olives and the remaining ¼ cup wine, bring to a boil over high heat, and cook 5 minutes. Drain. Heat the oil in a shallow earthenware casserole dish or Dutch oven over medium heat. Add the chopped onion and the chopped garlic and cook, stirring, until the onion is wilted and transparent, about 5 minutes. Add the sherry, broth, carrots, parsley, thyme, bay leaf, peppercorns, salt, and the reserved pan juices. Reduce the heat to low and simmer 5 minutes. Add the duck, spooning some sauce over it, cover, transfer to the oven, and roast 45 minutes or until the internal temperature of the thigh reaches 175°F.

3. Pass the sauce through a fine-mesh strainer into a small saucepan, pressing with the back of a wooden spoon to extract as much liquid as possible. Discard the solids. Deglaze the casserole dish, adding some broth, stirring, and scraping up any bits of flavor. Add to the sauce. Stir in the olives and pour over the duck. Serve hot.

Duck in Orange Sauce

Pato a la Naranja

MAKES 4 SERVINGS

Orange groves stretch as far as the eye can see in Valencia, and the nearby Albufera Lagoon is an area where many ducks thrive. Therefore it's natural to assume that Spain is the country in which pato a la naranja *originated, although the French might beg to differ.*

One (4½-pound) duck, with neck and giblets

Salt

Freshly ground black pepper

1 medium onion

3 garlic cloves

1 medium carrot, peeled and cut into thick slices

Duck Broth

1 tablespoon olive oil

1 medium onion, coarsely chopped (about ⅔ cup)

1 garlic clove, finely chopped

1 medium carrot, peeled and thickly sliced

1½ cups chicken broth or vegetable broth

1 sprig parsley

Salt

Freshly ground black pepper

3 oranges

½ cup medium-sweet sherry, such as Oloroso

Peel of ½ lemon (yellow part only)

1. Preheat the oven to 400°F. Prick the duck deeply all over with a fork. Season inside and out with salt and pepper. Cut 2 slices from the onion and place in the duck cavity with 1 clove of the garlic. Truss. Place the duck in a roasting pan and scatter the remainder of the onion in 1 piece, the remaining 2 cloves garlic, and the carrot slices around the pan. Bake 1 hour, pour off the fat, and roast about 45 minutes more or until the internal temperature of the thigh reaches 175°F and the legs move easily when gently lifted or twisted.

2. Meanwhile, prepare the duck broth: Heat the oil in a medium saucepan, add the neck and giblets, and cook, stirring, until well browned. Add the onion, garlic, and carrot and cook, stirring, until the onion is wilted and transparent, about 5 minutes. Reduce the heat to low, add the chicken broth, parsley, salt, and pepper, cover, and simmer 1 hour. Pass through a fine-mesh strainer and reserve.

3. Prepare the oranges: Peel 2 of the oranges and cut the rind (orange part only) into very thin strips. Place in a small saucepan with water to cover, bring to a boil over medium heat, and cook 5 minutes. Rinse under cold water, drain, and reserve. Remove and discard the pith (white part only) from the 2 peeled oranges and separate them into sections. Reserve. Squeeze the remaining 1 orange and reserve the juice (save the orange for another use).

4. When the duck is done, transfer it to a platter. Discard the onion, garlic, and carrot. Skim off as much fat from the pan liquid as possible. Deglaze the pan, adding the sherry, stirring, and scraping up any bits of flavor. Bring to a boil over medium heat and cook until the liquid is reduced by half and the sauce thickens slightly. Add the lemon peel, orange strips, duck broth, and the reserved orange juice and cook 2 minutes. Discard the lemon peel, add the reserved orange sections, and cook until heated through. Cut the duck into serving pieces. Pour the sauce over the duck. Serve hot.

Duck with Prunes and Pine Nuts

Pato a la Catalana

MAKES 4 SERVINGS

This is a Catalan-style recipe that contrasts the savory flavor of duck with the sweetness of prunes and subtle crunch of pine nuts.

2 4½-pound ducks, trussed and with necks

Salt

Freshly ground black pepper

1½ cups chicken broth or vegetable broth

1 tablespoon olive oil

1 medium onion, finely chopped (about ⅔ cup)

4 garlic cloves, finely chopped

1 medium carrot, peeled and thinly sliced

2 tablespoons pine nuts

1 bay leaf

1½ teaspoons finely chopped fresh thyme or ¼ teaspoon dried thyme

¾ cup dry white wine

1 tablespoon brandy

12 pitted prunes

½ cup orange or other fruit juice

1. Preheat the oven to 350°F. Prick the ducks all over with a fork. Season inside and out with salt and pepper. Place the ducks and necks in a shallow earthenware casserole dish or Dutch oven. Roast 1½ hours, spooning off the fat occasionally, until the internal temperature reaches 165°F to 170°F and the legs move easily when lifted or twisted. The ducks should be only lightly browned. Transfer to a platter and let cool. Cut the ducks into quarters, remove the small rib bones from the breasts, remove the backbones, and reserve the bones and necks. Transfer the duck to a roasting pan.

2. Pour off any remaining fat from the casserole dish and deglaze, adding the chicken broth, stirring, and scraping up any bits of flavor. Add the necks and bones and bring to a boil over high heat. Reduce the heat to low, cover, and simmer 30 minutes. Pass the liquid through a fine-mesh strainer into a bowl then return it to the casserole dish. Cook over low heat until the liquid is reduced to ½ cup, then transfer to a small bowl and reserve. Wipe out the casserole dish.

3. In the casserole dish, heat the oil over medium heat. Add the onion, garlic, carrot, pine nuts, bay leaf, and thyme and cook, stirring, 2 to 3 minutes. Reduce the heat to low, cover, and cook 15 minutes more or until the onion is tender but not browned. Add the wine, brandy, and the reserved broth, cover, and simmer 10 minutes more. Add the prunes, cover, and simmer about 15 minutes more or until the prunes are tender. (Can be made in advance up to this point.)

4. Preheat the oven to 550°F. Turn the duck skin side up in the roasting pan if necessary. Pour the orange juice over the duck and roast 10 minutes or until the skin is richly browned and crispy. Spoon the sauce over the duck, remove the bay leaf, and garnish with the prunes. Serve hot.

Roasted Duck with Quince Sauce

Pato con Membrillo a la Aragonesa

MAKES 4 SERVINGS

Catalunya is credited with most recipes for preparing duck, but this one comes from the nearby region of Aragon. Quince is a fruit found in the Mediterranean that resembles an apple, but it holds up much better than an apple during cooking. When combined with the savory juice of duck, it creates a sweet-sour flavor that is out of this world. If quince is unavailable, I recommend using Golden Delicious apples.

continues…

Two (4½-pound) ducks, trussed

2 duck necks (if available)

Salt

Freshly ground black pepper

1½ cups chicken broth or vegetable broth

2 tablespoons olive oil

1 medium onion, finely chopped (about ⅔ cup)

2 cloves garlic, finely chopped

1 medium carrot, peeled and finely chopped (about ½ cup)

1 bay leaf

1½ teaspoon finely chopped fresh thyme or ¼ teaspoon dried thyme

Dash of ground cinnamon

Freshly grated or ground nutmeg

1 whole clove

¾ pound quince or firm Golden Delicious apples, peeled, cored, and cut into ½-inch wedges

1 tablespoon honey

¾ cup dry white wine

½ cup fresh orange juice or other fruit juice

1. Preheat the oven to 350°F. Prick the ducks all over with a fork. Place with the necks, if using, in a shallow earthenware casserole dish or Dutch oven. Season with salt and pepper. Roast 1½ hours, spooning off the fat occasionally, or until the internal temperature reaches 165°F to 170°F and the legs move easily when lifted or twisted. The ducks should be only lightly browned. Transfer to a platter and let cool.

2. Cut the ducks into quarters, remove the small rib bones from the breasts, remove the backbones, and reserve the bones and necks. Transfer the ducks to a roasting pan.

3. Pour off any remaining fat from the casserole dish and deglaze, adding the chicken broth, stirring, and scraping up any bits of flavor. Add the necks and bones and bring to a boil over high heat. Reduce the heat to low, cover, and simmer

30 minutes. Pass through a fine-mesh strainer into a small bowl (there should be about 1 cup) and reserve. Wipe out the casserole dish.

4. In the casserole dish, heat the oil over medium heat. Add the onion, garlic, and carrot and cook, stirring, 2 to 3 minutes. Add the bay leaf, thyme, cinnamon, nutmeg, and clove. Reduce the heat to low, cover, and cook about 15 minutes more or until the onion is tender but not browned. Add the quince, honey, wine, salt, and pepper, cover, and simmer 45 minutes more.

5. Meanwhile, about midway through the simmering, preheat the oven to 500°F. Turn the duck skin side up in the roasting pan if necessary. Pour the orange juice over the duck and roast 10 minutes or until the skin is browned and crispy. Spoon the sauce over the duck, remove the bay leaf, and serve hot.

Baby Goose with Pears
Oca con Peras

MAKES 4 SERVINGS

In typical Catalan style, this signature dish combines savory goose meat with the sweetness of raisins and pears. It makes a beautiful presentation as the pears are coated with caramelized sugar and arranged in a circle around the goose. If you can't find goose, duck may be substituted. Look for the aguardiente or grappa in stores.

One (4-pound) baby goose or duck, quartered

2 slices medium onion

2 garlic cloves

1 bay leaf

7 tablespoons chicken broth or vegetable broth

1 tablespoon olive oil

1 medium onion, finely chopped (about ⅔ cup)

1 garlic clove, finely chopped

1 tablespoon finely chopped fresh flat-leaf parsley

2 tablespoons pine nuts

¼ cup raisins

4 very small pears, peeled and stems on

2 teaspoons aguardiente or grappa (available in liquor stores)

½ cup sugar

¼ cup water

1. Preheat the oven to 350°F. Place the goose, skin side up, in a roasting pan and scatter the onion slices, 2 of the garlic cloves, and the bay leaf around the goose. Prick the goose deeply all over with a fork. Roast 1 hour or until lightly browned. Transfer to a platter. Pour off the fat and deglaze the roasting pan, adding 4 tablespoons of the chicken broth, stirring, and scraping up any bits of flavor. Reserve the pan juices.

2. Meanwhile, in a large shallow casserole dish, heat the oil over medium heat. Add the chopped onion and the chopped garlic and cook, stirring, until the onion is wilted and transparent, about 5 minutes. Add the parsley, pine nuts, raisins, and pears and cook 5 minutes. Stir in the remaining 3 tablespoons chicken broth and the aguardiente, cover, and simmer 15 minutes. Add the goose and the reserved deglazed pan juices to the casserole dish. Cover and cook 45 minutes more or until the internal temperature reaches 165°F to 170°F and the legs move easily when lifted or twisted. Transfer the pears to a warm platter and stand them upright.

3. In a small saucepan, combine the sugar and water and heat over low heat, stirring constantly, until syrupy and light golden. Quickly pour some over each pear (it will harden right away).

4. Transfer the goose and its sauce to a serving platter. Arrange the pears around the sides. Spoon the sauce over the goose. Serve hot.

Broiled Rabbit with Garlic Sauce
Conejo Alioli

MAKES 4 SERVINGS

Rabbit meat is tasty, nutritious, and readily available in Spain. The two most popular ways to prepare it are either in tomato sauce (see 486) or with this recipe that calls for the rabbit to be broiled in seasoned oil, baked in white wine, and sautéed in a pungent garlic sauce (alioli).

PREPARE AT LEAST 2 HOURS IN ADVANCE

1 recipe Garlic Sauce (alioli; page 284), reducing the amount of garlic if desired

½ cup olive oil

1 bay leaf, crumbled

½ teaspoon thyme

One (2½- to 3-pound) rabbit, cut into serving pieces

Fresh lemon juice

Salt

Freshly ground black pepper

½ cup white wine

1. In a small bowl, combine the oil, the bay leaf, and thyme and let sit at least 2 hours to meld flavors. Prepare the garlic sauce and place in a small serving bowl.

2. Place a broiler rack about 6 inches from the heat source and preheat the broiler. (Cover the broiler pan with foil for easier cleanup, if you like.) Grease a broiler pan. Sprinkle the rabbit with the lemon juice and brush with the oil mixture. Season with salt and pepper. Broil 8 minutes per side, basting with the oil mixture, or until browned.

continues...

3. Preheat the oven to 450°F. Transfer the rabbit to a roasting pan. Add the broiler pan juices and the wine and roast 15 minutes, basting regularly, until the meat is tender and opaque inside. Serve hot with the sauce on the side.

Rabbit Coated with Honey-Garlic Mayonnaise
Conill Amb Alioli Gratinat

MAKES 4 SERVINGS

Here's a different version of rabbit with a garlic sauce: the rabbit is cooked first over lower heat then broiled to brown. The first time I tasted this dish was at the charming Masia del Cadet in the province of Tarragona in Catalunya. It is a simple yet delicious preparation of sautéed rabbit coated with a honey-garlic mayonnaise, with accents of thyme and bay leaf. I am grateful to Merce Vidal, who enthusiastically shared this recipe with me.

Honey-Garlic Mayonnaise

2 garlic cloves, mashed in a garlic press or mortar

Salt

1 large egg or ¼ cup egg substitute made with egg white

1 teaspoon fresh lemon juice

¼ teaspoon Dijon mustard

1 tablespoon honey

⅔ cup extra-virgin olive oil

2 tablespoons finely chopped fresh thyme or 1 teaspoon dried thyme

1 bay leaf, finely crumbled

½ teaspoon freshly ground black pepper

One (2½- to 3-pound) rabbit or 4 skinless chicken breast halves

Kosher or sea salt

1 tablespoon olive oil

1 tablespoon unsalted butter

1. Prepare the mayonnaise: In a food processor, place the garlic, salt, egg, lemon juice, mustard, and honey and process a few seconds until combined. With the motor running, drizzle in the oil until emulsified. Add the thyme, bay leaf, and pepper and blend. Transfer to a small bowl and stir in enough hot water to give the mayonnaise the consistency of a sauce.

2. Cut the rabbit into 1½-inch pieces and remove any fat and as many of the bones as possible. Season with salt. Heat the oil and butter in a shallow earthenware casserole dish or Dutch oven over medium-high heat. Add the rabbit and cook, turning once, until lightly browned, about 15 minutes.

3. Place a broiler rack about 6 inches from the heat source and preheat the broiler. (Cover the broiler pan with foil for easier cleanup, if you like.) Spoon the mayonnaise over the rabbit and place under the broiler until the rabbit is richly browned, tender, and just opaque inside. Serve hot.

Rabbit in Tomato Sauce
Conejo con Tomate

MAKES 4 SERVINGS

The two most popular ways to prepare rabbit in Spain are either broiled with garlic sauce (alioli; see the previous recipe) or served in a robust tomato sauce. This traditional recipe for conejo con tomate *comes from Malacatín, one of the oldest taverns in Madrid, which is also renowned for their great* Cocido Madrileño *(Boiled Beef and Chickpea Dinner), page 227.*

One (2½- to 3-pound) rabbit, cut into serving pieces

1 garlic clove, halved

1 cup dry white wine

3 garlic cloves, finely chopped

Kosher or sea salt

Freshly ground black pepper

2 tablespoons olive oil

1 large onion, finely chopped (about 1 cup)

1 medium green bell pepper, finely chopped (about ⅔ cup)

2 cups crushed tomato, fresh or canned

¼ teaspoon thyme

2 tablespoons finely chopped fresh flat-leaf parsley

1 bay leaf

½ dried red chile pepper, seeded, crumbled

3 teaspoons red wine vinegar

1. Rub the rabbit with the garlic halves. Place in a large bowl, add the wine and the chopped garlic, cover, and let marinate in the refrigerator at least 1 hour. Drain well, reserving the liquid and the garlic. Season with salt and pepper.

2. Heat the oil in a large shallow earthenware casserole dish or Dutch oven over medium-high heat. Add the rabbit and cook, turning occasionally, until browned on all sides. Transfer to a platter. Add the onion and bell pepper and cook, stirring, until the onion is wilted and transparent, about 5 minutes. Add the tomato, thyme, parsley, bay leaf, chile pepper, vinegar, and the reserved wine and garlic. Return the rabbit to the dish, reduce the heat to low, cover, and cook 2 hours or until the meat is very tender and opaque inside. Remove the bay leaf. If using earthenware, serve hot in the dish, or transfer to a platter.

Marinated Rabbit in Sherry Sauce
Conejo Mirabel

MAKES 3 TO 4 SERVINGS

In order to prepare this dish properly, the rabbit must be first marinated for several days in sherry, garlic, and herbs. This recipe comes from the monastery of Guadalupe, where the monks supposedly led a life of luxury. Fine food was not only prepared for the monastic table, but also for the monastery's hotels, where kings, conquistadores, and famous writers such as Cervantes came to worship the Virgin of Guadalupe. Some of my most treasured recipes came from Fray Juan Barrera González, the monk who at one time was in charge of the kitchen.

PREPARE 3 DAYS IN ADVANCE

One (2½- to 3-pound) rabbit, cut into serving pieces

Marinade

2 garlic cloves, finely chopped

1 bay leaf

1½ teaspoons finely chopped fresh thyme or ¼ teaspoon dried thyme

1½ teaspoons finely chopped fresh marjoram or ¼ teaspoon dried marjoram

1½ teaspoons finely chopped fresh rosemary or ¼ teaspoon dried rosemary

Freshly ground black pepper

½ cup dry sherry, such as Fino

Salt

Freshly ground black pepper

2 tablespoons olive oil

1 small onion, slivered

2 garlic cloves, finely chopped

1 teaspoon all-purpose flour

1-inch piece dried red chile pepper

continues...

1. Arrange the rabbit in a shallow bowl. Combine all the marinade ingredients in a medium bowl. Pour over the rabbit. Cover and let marinate 3 days in the refrigerator, turning the rabbit occasionally. Transfer the rabbit to paper towels, reserving the marinade in the bowl, and let dry. Season with salt and pepper.

2. Heat 1 tablespoon of the oil in a shallow earthenware casserole dish or Dutch oven over low heat. Add the onion and garlic and cook, stirring, until the onion is wilted and transparent, about 5 minutes. Stir in the flour, then add this mixture to the marinade. Wipe out the casserole dish.

3. Heat the remaining 1 tablespoon oil in the casserole dish over medium-high heat. Add the rabbit and cook, turning occasionally, until well browned, about 10 to 15 minutes. Reduce the heat to low, add the marinade and the chile pepper, cover, and simmer about 30 minutes or until the rabbit is very tender and the meat is opaque inside. If using earthenware, serve hot in the dish, or transfer to a platter.

Rabbit Stew, Zamora Style
Conejo a la Zamorana

MAKES 4 SERVINGS

This fabulous recipe comes from the parador in Zamora that was once the fifteenth century palace of the counts of Alba and Aliste. This is a delicious rabbit stew with carrot and herb-scented sauce, flavored with smoked paprika, an ingredient characteristic of this part of Castile.

One (2½- to 3-pound) rabbit, cut into serving pieces
Kosher or sea salt
3 tablespoons olive oil
1 medium sweet onion, such as Vidalia, finely chopped (about ⅔ cup)
3 garlic cloves, finely chopped

2 medium carrots, peeled and finely chopped (about 1 cup)
½ teaspoon ground sweet paprika, such as Spanish smoked
¾ cup dry white wine
¼ cup plus 2 tablespoons chicken broth or vegetable broth
2 tablespoons finely chopped fresh flat-leaf parsley
4 sprigs thyme
4 sprigs rosemary
½ teaspoon dried oregano
1 bay leaf
Freshly ground black pepper

1. Season the rabbit well with salt. Heat the oil in a shallow earthenware casserole dish or Dutch oven over medium-high heat. Add the rabbit and cook, turning once, until well browned. Reduce the heat to medium, add the onion, garlic, and carrots and cook, stirring, about 5 minutes more. Stir in the paprika, then add the wine, broth, parsley, thyme, rosemary, oregano, bay leaf, salt, and pepper and bring to a boil.

2. Reduce the heat to low, cover, and simmer 45 minutes or until the rabbit is very tender and the meat is opaque inside. Remove the bay leaf. If using earthenware, serve hot in the dish, or transfer to a platter.

Sautéed Rabbit, Batter-Fried with Sesame Seeds
Conejo con Ajonjolí

MAKES 4 SERVINGS

This recipe is from the province of Córdoba, where hunting is a longtime tradition in the mountains of the Sierra Morena. It calls for sautéing the rabbit, dipping it in a batter, coating it with sesame seeds, and frying it. The outside gets crunchy while the inside stays moist and tender.

2 tablespoons olive oil

One (2¾- to 3-pound) rabbit, cut into 8 pieces

2 garlic cloves, lightly smashed

1 small onion, cut into rings

Salt

Freshly ground black pepper

1½ cups chicken broth or vegetable broth

1 cup sesame seeds, for dredging

About ½ cup all-purpose flour, for dredging

2 large eggs, separated

Olive oil, for frying

1. Heat the oil in a shallow earthenware casserole dish or Dutch oven over medium-high heat. Add the rabbit and cook, turning once, until lightly browned. Add the garlic, onion, salt, and pepper and cook, stirring, until the onion is wilted and transparent, about 5 minutes. Add the broth and bring to a boil. Reduce the heat to low, cover, and simmer 30 minutes or until tender. Transfer the rabbit to paper towels and let dry, reserving the broth for another use if you like. (The broth will not be used, but it makes a delicious soup.) Wipe out the casserole dish.

2. Spread the sesame seeds on wax paper. Place the flour in a small shallow bowl. In another small bowl, beat the egg whites with an electric mixer until soft peaks form. Fold in the yolks and season with salt and pepper.

3. Heat at least ½ inch of oil in a large skillet over medium-high heat (or better still, use a deep fryer set at 375°F) until it quickly browns a cube of bread. Dredge each rabbit piece in the flour, dip in the egg, dredge in the sesame seeds, and place in the oil. Cook, turning once, until just golden. Season with salt and serve hot.

Rabbit with Almonds and Pine Nuts
Conejo con Almendras y Piñones

MAKES 4 SERVINGS

Rabbit is excellent when accompanied by almonds and pine nuts that lend a nutty taste and texture. This recipe comes from the charming La Posada de Javier restaurant in Torrecaballeros, a small town near Segovia with a beautiful Romanesque church. Pine trees are abundant around the town, providing the pine nuts.

All-purpose flour, for dredging

3 tablespoons olive oil

One (2½- to 3-pound) rabbit, cut into serving pieces

1 large onion, finely chopped (about 1 cup)

1 cup dry white wine

1 tablespoon finely chopped fresh flat-leaf parsley

½ tablespoon dried thyme

1 bay leaf

Salt

Freshly ground black pepper

2 garlic cloves, finely chopped

2 tablespoons pine nuts

¼ cup slivered blanched almonds (1½ ounces)

1. Place the flour in a small shallow bowl. Heat the oil in a shallow earthenware casserole dish or Dutch oven over medium-high heat. Dredge each rabbit piece in the flour, place in the oil, and cook, turning occasionally, until browned on all sides.

2. Reduce the heat to medium, add the onion and cook, stirring, until wilted and transparent, about 5 minutes. Stir in the wine, parsley, thyme, bay leaf, salt, pepper, garlic, pine nuts, and almonds. Reduce the heat to low, cover, and simmer until the rabbit is tender, 1 to 1½ hours. Remove the bay leaf. If using earthenware, serve hot in the dish, or transfer to a platter.

Rabbit in Garlic and Dried Red Pepper Sauce
Conejo en Salmorejo

MAKES 4 SERVINGS

Chef Carlos Gamonal of the wonderful Mesón el Drago restaurant in the Canary Islands has won many awards for his unique rendition of traditional island dishes, including this recipe, in which the piquant marinade becomes the sauce. The dried sweet red peppers add a distinctive zest.

3 tablespoons olive oil

One (2½- to 3-pound) rabbit, cut into serving pieces

¼ cup blanched almonds

10 garlic cloves

1 thin slice long-loaf (baguette) bread

2 dried sweet red chile peppers (ñoras), such as New Mexico (Anaheim), stemmed and seeded

1 teaspoon dried oregano

⅛ teaspoon saffron threads, crumbled

¾ cup dry white wine

Kosher or sea salt

Freshly ground black pepper

I. Heat the oil in a shallow earthenware casserole dish or Dutch oven over medium-high heat. Add the rabbit and cook, turning occasionally, until browned on all sides. Transfer to a platter. Add the almonds, garlic, bread, chile peppers, oregano, and saffron and cook, stirring, until lightly browned. Transfer to a mortar and mash. Stir in the wine, salt, and black pepper and return to the casserole dish.

2. Reduce the heat to low, add the rabbit, and simmer until the rabbit is tender, I to I½ hours. If using earthenware, serve hot in the dish, or transfer to a platter.

Rabbit with Red Peppers and Zucchini
Conejo con Pisto

MAKES 4 SERVINGS

When rabbit is sautéed with fresh vegetables, it creates a hearty and flavorful stew. The Spanish word pisto *refers to a vegetable medley that originated in Castile.*

One (2½- to 3-pound) rabbit, cut into serving pieces

Kosher or sea salt

2 tablespoons olive oil

1 medium onion, thinly sliced

2 garlic cloves, finely chopped

2 pimientos, cut into ½-inch strips

1 medium zucchini, cut into ½-inch slices

3 bay leaves

Freshly ground black pepper

½ teaspoon dried thyme

3 tablespoons dry white wine

I. Season the rabbit with salt. Heat the oil in a deep earthenware casserole dish or Dutch oven over medium-high heat. Add the rabbit and cook, turning occasionally, until browned on all sides. Transfer to a platter. Reduce the heat to medium, add the onion, garlic, pimientos, and zucchini and cook, stirring, until the onion is wilted and transparent, about 5 minutes.

2. Reduce the heat to low, add the rabbit, bay leaves, salt, pepper, thyme, and wine, cover, and cook I to I½ hours or until the rabbit is very tender. Remove the bay leaves. If using earthenware, serve hot in the dish, or transfer to a platter.

Rabbit with Crisp Bread Bits
Conejo con Migas

MAKES 4 SERVINGS

Once considered peasant food, this dish was traditionally prepared by shepherds in the field. Rabbits thrive in Las Bardenas, a dry and desolate region east of the city of Zaragoza. When bread was added for substance, this became a hearty meal that is still popular today.

One (2½- to 3-pound) rabbit, cut into serving pieces; or skinless chicken, all fat removed, cut into serving pieces

Salt

2 tablespoons olive oil

1 garlic clove, finely chopped

1 small onion, finely chopped (about ⅓ cup)

1-inch piece dried red chile pepper, seeded and crumbled

¼ cup chicken broth or vegetable broth

¼ cup water

2 cups day-old baguette bread, torn into ½-inch pieces

1. Season the rabbit with salt. Heat the oil in a large skillet over medium-high heat. Add the rabbit and cook, turning occasionally, until browned on all sides.

2. Reduce the heat to low, add the garlic, onion, and chile pepper, and cook, stirring occasionally, about 25 minutes more. Increase the heat to medium, add the broth and water and bring to a boil. Add the bread and cook, stirring occasionally, until the liquid is absorbed, the meat is tender, and the bread crisp, about 10 to 15 minutes more. Serve hot.

Rabbit and Egg and Lemon Sauce
Conejo en Pepitoria

MAKES 4 SERVINGS

This traditional egg and lemon sauce goes back hundreds of years, where it originated in the Canary Islands. The mild taste of artichokes and mushrooms perfectly complements the rich sauce.

2 tablespoons lard or olive oil

One (2½- to 3-pound) rabbit, cut into serving pieces

1 medium onion, coarsely chopped (about ⅔ cup)

¾ cup chicken broth or vegetable broth

6 artichoke hearts, halved

Salt

Freshly ground black pepper

½ teaspoon dried thyme

2 tablespoons finely chopped fresh flat-leaf parsley

¼ pound mushrooms, halved or quartered

2 large egg yolks

2 tablespoons fresh lemon juice

1. Heat the lard in a deep earthenware casserole dish or Dutch oven over medium-high heat. Add the rabbit and cook, turning occasionally, until browned on all sides. Add the onion and cook, stirring, until the onion is wilted and transparent, about 5 minutes more. Stir in the broth, artichokes, salt, pepper, thyme, and 1 tablespoon of the parsley. Reduce the heat to low, cover, and cook 45 minutes more. Stir in the mushrooms, cover, and cook 15 minutes more or until the rabbit is tender and the meat opaque. Transfer the rabbit to a serving platter.

2. In a small bowl, beat the egg yolks with a fork. Beat in the lemon juice, then 2 tablespoons of the sauce from the casserole dish. Stir the egg mixture into the casserole dish and cook 1 minute more. Pour over the rabbit and sprinkle with the remaining 1 tablespoon parsley. If using earthenware, serve hot in the dish, or transfer to a platter.

Rabbit in Garlic Sauce
Conejo al Ajillo

MAKES 4 SERVINGS

This is a quick and easy way to prepare rabbit, and many Spaniards prefer conejo al ajillo *to its chicken equivalent. Rabbits and other game thrive in the expansive areas of Spain's wilderness and have always been a staple in Spanish cooking.*

One (2½- to 3-pound) rabbit, cut into serving pieces

Kosher or sea salt

2 tablespoons olive oil

10 garlic cloves, coarsely chopped

2 dried sweet red peppers (ñoras)

1 tablespoon finely chopped fresh flat-leaf parsley

2 teaspoons peppercorns, smashed

½ teaspoon dried oregano

½ teaspoon dried rosemary

2 dried bay leaves

¼ teaspoon saffron threads, crumbled

½ cup dry white wine

¼ cup chicken broth or vegetable broth

1. Season the rabbit with salt and let sit 10 minutes. Heat the oil in a shallow earthenware casserole dish or Dutch oven over medium-high heat. Add the rabbit and cook, turning occasionally, until browned on all sides.

2. Reduce the heat to low, add the garlic, chile peppers, parsley, peppercorns, oregano, rosemary, and bay leaves. Stir in the saffron, wine, and broth, cover, and simmer about 35 minutes more or until the rabbit is tender and the meat opaque inside. Remove the bay leaves. If using earthenware, serve hot in the dish, or transfer to a platter.

Rabbit in Tomato and White Wine
Conejo con Tomate y Vino Blanco

MAKES 4 SERVINGS

This classic country recipe is favored by hunters in the field at the end of the day using their catch. It's a great way to prepare rabbit—a healthy meal that is tasty, nutritious, and low in fat.

One (2½- to 3-pound) rabbit, cut into serving pieces

Kosher or sea salt

2 tablespoons olive oil

10 garlic cloves, finely chopped

1 medium green bell pepper (about ¾ cup), finely chopped

2 bay leaves

6 black peppercorns, smashed

¼ teaspoon dried rosemary

¼ teaspoon dried thyme

¼ teaspoon dried oregano

2 large scallions, finely chopped

¾ cup dry white wine

2 medium tomatoes, finely chopped (about 1⅓ cups)

1. Season the rabbit with salt and let sit 10 minutes. Heat the oil in a shallow earthenware casserole dish or Dutch oven over medium-high heat. Add the rabbit and cook, turning occasionally, until browned on all sides. Stir in the garlic, bell pepper, bay leaves, peppercorns, rosemary, thyme, oregano, and scallions. Add the wine and cook, stirring occasionally, until reduced by half.

2. Reduce the heat to low, add the tomato and salt, cover, and simmer 45 minutes more or until the rabbit is tender and the meat opaque inside. Remove the bay leaves. If using earthenware, serve hot in the dish, or transfer to a platter.

Rabbit, Hunter Style
Conejo a la Cazadora

MAKES 4 SERVINGS

Hunting is a very popular activity in Spain due to the abundance of large and small game. This recipe calls for the rabbit to be simmered in brandy with the savory addition of diced ham.

3 tablespoons olive oil

One (2½- to 3-pound) rabbit, cut into serving pieces

1 medium onion, finely chopped (about ⅔ cup)

¼ pound Serrano (Spanish cured mountain) ham or prosciutto, cut into ¼-inch cubes

1 garlic clove, finely chopped

2 tablespoons brandy, such as Spanish brandy or Cognac

1 cup dry white wine

1½ cups chopped tomato or tomato sauce

½ teaspoon dried thyme

1 tablespoon finely chopped fresh flat-leaf parsley

Salt

Freshly ground black pepper

¾ cup sliced mushrooms

1. Heat the oil in a large shallow earthenware casserole dish or Dutch oven over medium-high heat. Add the rabbit and cook, turning occasionally, until browned on all sides. Add the onion, ham, and garlic and cook until the onion is wilted and transparent, about 5 minutes. Add the brandy. Standing well away from the pot, ignite the liquid with a match or kitchen lighter and let die out.

2. Add the wine, tomato, thyme, parsley, salt, and pepper, cover, and simmer 1 to 1½ hours or until the meat is tender. Stir in the mushrooms and cook uncovered 15 minutes more until the mushrooms release their juices and are absorbed into the sauce. If using earthenware, serve hot in the dish, or transfer to a platter.

Potted Rabbit
Conejo Salmantino

MAKES 4 SERVINGS

Conejo Salmantino is a dish that originated in the mountains of Las Hurdes in the province of Salamanca. The rabbit is prepared in a deep cazuela, or earthenware casserole dish, using a generous amount of garlic and vinegar.

2 tablespoons olive oil

One (2½- to 3-pound) rabbit, cut into serving pieces

¼ cup vinegar

1 medium onion, finely chopped (about ⅔ cup)

Salt

Freshly ground black pepper

1 bay leaf

½ head garlic, separated and unpeeled

1. Heat the oil in a deep earthenware casserole dish or Dutch oven over medium-high heat. Add the rabbit and cook, turning occasionally, until browned on all sides.

2. Reduce the heat to low, add the vinegar, onion, salt, pepper, bay leaf, and garlic, cover tightly, and cook about 2 hours or until the rabbit is tender and most of the liquid has evaporated. If it evaporates too quickly, add a little water. Remove the bay leaf. If using earthenware, serve hot in the dish, or transfer to a platter.

Rabbit in Almond and Olive Sauce

Conejo Aurora

MAKES 4 SERVINGS

I got this wonderful recipe from our dear friend Pepe Sanz, whose wife, Aurora, grew up in Jaén, an Andalucian province that is covered with olive trees. Spaniards tend to be inordinately fond of olives, and they have made their way into more than a few recipes. Here they are the perfect accent for this rabbit dish sautéed in a garlicky almond sauce.

3 ounces pitted green olives, preferably Spanish, halved crosswise

1½ ounces blanched almonds (about ¼ cup)

All-purpose flour, for dredging

One (2½- to 3-pound) rabbit, cut into serving pieces

Kosher or sea salt

3 tablespoons olive oil

3 garlic cloves, lightly smashed and peeled

1 large onion, finely chopped (about 1 cup)

¾ cup dry white wine

½ cup chicken broth or vegetable broth

Freshly ground black pepper

1. Preheat the oven to 350°F. Place the olives in a small saucepan, add water to cover, and bring to a boil over high heat. Cook 5 minutes, drain, and reserve. Scatter the almonds on a cookie sheet and toast about 5 minutes or until fragrant and lightly browned. Let cool, transfer to a mortar or mini-processor, and reserve. Place the flour in a small shallow bowl.

2. Season the rabbit with salt and dredge in the flour. Heat the oil in a shallow earthenware casserole dish or Dutch oven over medium-high heat. Add the rabbit and cook, turning occasionally, until browned on all sides. Transfer to a platter.

3. Add the garlic and cook, stirring, until lightly browned. Transfer to a mortar, add the almonds, and mash. Add the onion to the casserole dish and cook, stirring, about 2 minutes. Add the rabbit, wine, broth, salt, pepper, the reserved olives, and the reserved mortar mixture, and bring to a boil.

4. Reduce the heat to low, cover, and simmer about 1 to 1½ hours or until the rabbit is tender. If using earthenware, serve hot in the dish, or transfer to a platter.

Rabbit with Blackberries and Brown Sugar

Conejo con Moras y Azúcar Moreno

MAKES 4 SERVINGS

From Andalucía, this recipe contains ingredients that are characteristic of Moorish cooking. The savory taste of rabbit combined with the sweetness of the brown sugar coating creates a dish that is as unique as it is delicious.

½ cup dry white wine

One (3-pound) rabbit or chicken, cut into serving pieces

Kosher or sea salt

Freshly ground black pepper

½ teaspoon sweet ground paprika, such as Spanish smoked

3 tablespoons finely chopped fresh thyme or 1½ teaspoons dried thyme

½ cup chicken broth or vegetable broth

Sauce

2 tablespoons packed light brown sugar

2 tablespoons mashed blackberries or blackberry preserves

2 tablespoons wine vinegar, such as white

2 garlic cloves, finely chopped

1 teaspoon olive oil

¼ teaspoon sweet ground paprika, such as Spanish smoked

¼ teaspoon ground (or mortar-crushed) cumin

½ cup blackberries (optional)

1. Preheat the oven to 375°F. Pour ¼ cup of the wine into a roasting pan. Arrange the rabbit pieces in the pan (do not crowd) and season with salt, pepper, paprika, and thyme. Roast, basting occasionally, 35 minutes, adding the remaining wine as the liquid evaporates and then adding the broth to ensure there is always some liquid in the pan.

2. Meanwhile, in a small bowl, mix the sauce ingredients and spoon them over the rabbit. Continue cooking and basting with the pan juices for 10 minutes more or until tender. Spoon the sauce over the rabbit, garnish with the blackberries, if using, and serve hot.

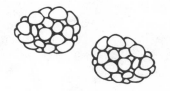

Meat

BEEF STEAKS AND ROASTS

Filet Mignon with Toasted Garlic Sauce

Breaded Beef Steaks

Steak with Blue Cheese Sauce

Sliced Beef, Castilian Style

Beef Roast in Garlic Sauce

BEEF STEWS

Garlic Beef Stew

Beef Stew with Mushrooms and
Piquillo Peppers

Beef Stew with Pearl Onions

Beef Stew with Cumin and Coriander

Beef Stew, Catalan Style

Beef Stew Larded with Ham,
Olives, and Scallions

Oxtail Stew

Pedro's Oxtail Stew with Juniper Berries

Tripe, Madrid Style

GROUND BEEF

Beef Patties

Three-Meat Loaf

Meat-Filled Red Peppers in Red Pepper Sauce

Stuffed Green Peppers and Zucchini

Stuffed Red Cabbage

Meat-Filled Potatoes

Hash Casserole, Spanish Style

 = Vegetarian   = Vegetarian with one change

LAMB CHOPS

Grilled Baby Lamb Chops

Grilled Lamb Chops with
Garlic and Parsley

Lamb Chops and Sliced Potatoes
with Garlic and Vinegar

Marinated Lamb Chops and Mushrooms

Béchamel-Coated Breaded Lamb Chops

LAMB STEWS

Sautéed Marinated Lamb Stew

Lamb Stew with Honey

Potted Lamb with Lemon

Lamb with Lemon

Lamb with Garlic and
Dried Red Peppers

Lamb Stew in Garlic Sauce

Lamb Stew with New Potatoes

Lamb Stew, Extremadura Style

Lamb Stew with Raisins and Honey

Moorish Lamb Stew with Fruits

Smothered Lamb Stew

Lamb and Red Pepper Stew

Lamb Meatballs in Brandy Sauce

Lamb Meatballs, Moorish Style

LAMB ROASTS

Roast Lamb and Potatoes

Rosemary-Scented Lamb Roast
with Olives

Roast Lamb, Castilian Style

Roast Lamb, Aragon Style

Roast Lamb, Sepulveda Style

Rack of Lamb Stuffed with
Mushrooms and Scallions

PORK CHOPS

Seasoned Broiled Pork Chops

Baked Pork Chops with Garlic and Lemon

Pork Chops with Apples in Cider Sauce

Pork Chops with Sherry

Marinated Breaded Pork Chops

Pork Chops, Rioja Style

Pork Chops, Green Pepper, and Ham

Pork Chops with Prunes

Pork Chops in Clove-Spiced
Lemon and Honey Sauce

Pork and Sausage Casserole

Pimiento- and Cheese-Filled Pork Cutlets

Breaded Pork Cutlets Filled with Sobrasada

PORK LOIN AND ROASTS

Lemon- and Garlic-Marinated
Grilled Pork Loin

Marinated Pork Tenderloin
with Garlic and Parsley

Pork Tenderloin in Sweet Sherry Sauce

Pork Tenderloin in Orange Sauce

Pork Tenderloin with Stewed Onions

Pork Tenderloin with Sun-Dried
Tomatoes, Pine Nuts, and Raisins

Roast Pork Tenderloin with
Sherry, Garlic, and Parsley

Breaded Pork Tenderloin with Béchamel

Sausage Rolled in Pork Fillet

Stuffed Pork Loin

Pork Loin Stuffed with Spinach,
Prunes, and Pine Nuts

Pork Loin Marinated in Pomegranate Syrup

Sliced Pork Loin with Pearl Onions
and Olives, Murcia Style

Pork Loin with Prunes and Pears

Roasted Pork Loin with Onions and Leeks

Seasoned Pork Loin Roast

Marinated Pork and Potatoes

Pork Roast Simmered in Milk

Pork Roast with Peppers and Eggplant

Pork in Almond Sauce

Pepita's Pork Stew

Sweet-and-Sour Pork with Prunes

Meatballs Salvador

OTHER PORK DISHES

Baked Sausage and Mushrooms

Sausages with Sweet-and-Sour Figs

Roast Suckling Pig

Pork-Stuffed Baked Apples

Stuffed Pig's Feet

VEAL CUTLETS AND CHOPS

Veal Medallions with Fresh Tomato Sauce

Breaded Veal Cutlets, Spanish Style

Veal with Chorizo and Green Peppers

Veal Chops, Shepherd Style

Veal Chops with Beans

Veal Chops with Ham,
Mushrooms, and Pimiento

Veal Shanks with Apples and Pine Nuts

VEAL ROASTS, STEWS, AND GROUND MEAT

Roast Veal

Potted Veal Roast

Veal Stew, Catalan Style

Veal Stew in Sherry Sauce

Old-Fashioned Veal Stew with Almonds,
Hazelnuts, and Mushrooms

Meatballs with Green Pepper and Tomato

Meatballs in Lemon Sauce

Meatballs with Pine Nuts in Tomato Sauce

ORGAN MEATS

Calves' Liver with Garlic and Vinegar

Calves' Liver and Green Peppers

Liver in Sorrel Sauce

Kidneys in Sherry Sauce

*P*ork is by far the most popular meat in Spain, followed by lamb and veal, with beef being eaten less frequently, although still quite wonderful. Spaniards often travel hundreds of miles on the weekends to their favorite village inns for the sole purpose of eating roasted delectable tiny lambs and succulent baby pigs. These dishes originated in Castilla y Leon, where the standards are set quite high: The pigs must not have run in the field, and for nourishment, they must have had only their mother's milk, which transmits the flavors of the wild herbs from the field. Purists insist they should be roasted in a traditional clay *cazuela* in a wood-burning baker's oven scented with thyme, rosemary, or oak. The only seasoning needed for tiny lambs and baby pigs is a dash of salt and pepper. The meat is so tender that you can cut it without a knife.

In other parts of Spain, where tiny lambs and pigs are not available, recipes tend to call for heavier seasoning and sauces. Each region has its specialties—sometimes stews, sometimes meat in combination with peppers, sometimes sausage and chopped meat dishes. Catalunya is famous for its *fricandó*, veal made with ground almonds, and their *estofado a la catalana*, beef with bitter chocolate. Extremadura has a stew rich in paprika and garlic, and another piquant version called *cochifrito*. In Asturias, pork is baked in Asturian hard apple cider. The Rioja region prepares pork with their local red peppers. No matter what the preparation, the traditional Spanish accompaniment is potatoes.

Sausages are also very popular in Spain, either eaten on their own, or combined with other meats. *Chorizo*, the quintessential Iberian sausage, has become popular all over the world. It is a wonderfully flavorful cured sausage seasoned with paprika and garlic and sometimes with nutmeg, oregano, and pepper. The other type of sausage that Spain is best known for is their delicious *butifarra*, which comes from Catalunya, as well as black sausages made with rice or onion.

One of the most traditional and beloved preparations is *filetes de ternera empanados*, Spanish-style breaded veal cutlet. Although this simple dish is sometimes not even featured on the menu, there is not a restaurant in Spain that won't serve it to you if you ask. Also popular are *albóndigas*, meatballs made of a breaded mixture of pork, veal, and sometimes beef.

Almost all of the recipes in this chapter call for cuts of meat that are readily available here—such as beef steaks, pork loin, veal chops, and leg of lamb. I recommend using the freshest meat you can find, which should always be purchased from a reputable butcher. One note: Veal in Spain, usually older than American or Italian veal, is preferred when it is *añojo*, meaning it is at least one year old. The meat of this veal is a little more mature and has more flavor. This is why some of the veal recipes that follow in the chapter can also be made with beef.

Filet Mignon with Toasted Garlic Sauce
Solomillo al Ajo Tostado

MAKES 4 SERVINGS

Our beloved friend Tomás Herranz was one of Madrid's star chefs, dividing his time between the elegant restaurant El Cenador del Prado and his upscale tapas bar, Lerranz, around the corner. This was his recipe for filet mignon coated with a garlic sauce and then run under the broiler.

4 filet mignons, about 1 inch thick
Salt, to taste
½ cup Garlic Sauce (alioli; partial recipe; page 284)
Fresh parsley sprigs, for garnish

1. Place a broiler rack about 6 inches from the heat source and preheat the broiler. Line a broiler pan with foil and arrange the filets on the pan. Season with salt on both sides. Broil, turning once, until browned on both sides and cooked to taste, about 3 minutes per side for rare up to about 6 minutes per side for well. (You can also pan-fry the filets if preferred.)

2. Prepare the garlic sauce. Spread about 1½ tablespoons of the sauce over the top of each filet. (If you pan-fried the steaks, transfer them to a foil-lined broiler pan.) Broil until the sauce is lightly browned, about 2 minutes. Garnish with the parsley sprigs and serve hot.

Breaded Beef Steaks
Filetes Empanados

MAKES 4 SERVINGS

My daughter is crazy about this simple beef dish that requires few ingredients and minimal time to prepare. I recommend using the heel of your hand to press the bread crumb mixture into the meat so that it adheres well. In Spain, when traveling, everybody carries filetes empanados *for lunch.*

1 garlic clove, finely chopped
2 tablespoons finely chopped fresh flat-leaf parsley
½ teaspoon salt
¼ pound beef steak, such as round, very thinly sliced
2 eggs, lightly beaten
Bread crumbs, for dredging
5 tablespoons olive oil

1. In a blender or a food processor, blend the garlic, parsley, and salt until the garlic and parsley are as finely chopped as possible. Spread on the beef with a rubber spatula (it needs not be evenly distributed), pressing with the heel of your hand so that it adheres.

2. Place the eggs and bread crumbs in separate wide shallow bowls. Dip both sides of the beef into the egg, dredge both sides in the crumbs, and let sit at least 20 minutes or until the coating is dried.

3. Preheat the oven to 200°F. Heat the oil in a large skillet over medium-high heat. Place the beef in the oil and cook, turning once, just until the coating is browned. (Cook in batches if necessary to avoid overcrowding.) Let drain on paper towels. Transfer to a platter and keep warm in the oven while cooking the remaining batches. Serve hot, or let cool, wrap in foil, and store in the refrigerator.

Steak with Blue Cheese Sauce
Entrecot al Queso Cabrales

MAKES 4 SERVINGS

Queso Cabrales, *a strong blue cheese aged in caves and wrapped in leaves, is produced in Asturias, where this recipe originated. It can now be found in specialty stores or by mail order, but if it is not available, Roquefort cheese may be substituted. This is a very popular way of preparing steak in Spain.*

¼ pound blue cheese, such as Cabrales or Roquefort

4 teaspoons white wine

1 teaspoon fresh lemon juice

1 tablespoon finely chopped fresh flat-leaf parsley

1 garlic clove, mashed in a garlic press or mortar

Dash of ground paprika

Dash of freshly ground black pepper

1 tablespoon unsalted butter

4 beef steaks, such as rib-eye or club, 1 inch thick

3 tablespoons beef broth or water

Salt

1. Preheat the oven to 200°F. Fill the bottom of a double boiler or pot with one inch of water. In the top of the double boiler or a medium bowl that will sit firmly on the pot, combine the cheese, wine, lemon juice, parsley, garlic, paprika, and pepper. Lower the heat to low and cook, stirring occasionally, until the cheese mixture is smooth. Place the sauce in the oven to keep warm while the steak is cooking.

2. Heat the butter in a large skillet over high heat until it starts to brown. Add the steaks and cook, turning once, until browned on both sides and cooked to taste, about 4 minutes per side for rare up to 6 minutes per side for well. Transfer to a platter and cover lightly with foil.

3. Add the broth to the skillet and season with salt. Deglaze the pan, stirring with a rubber spatula and scraping up any bits of flavor. Stir 2 tablespoons

into the reserved sauce. Pour the sauce over the steaks and serve hot.

Sliced Beef, Castilian Style
Carne a la Castellana

MAKES 4 SERVINGS

In this rich and hearty dish made with steak and cured ham, the beef should be thinly sliced and then fried very quickly, just to the point where it is browned. The onions and garlic are sautéed in red wine, completing a highly flavorful dish.

5 tablespoons olive oil

2 medium onions, sliced (about 1⅓ cup)

2 garlic cloves, finely chopped

4 long, thin slices Serrano (Spanish cured mountain) ham or prosciutto, each cut into 4 pieces

1½ pounds beef steak, such as sirloin, cut into ¼-inch slices

2 tablespoons all-purpose flour

1½ cups beef broth, chicken broth, or water

½ cup dry red wine

1. Heat 2 tablespoons of the oil in a large skillet over low heat. Add the onion and garlic, cover, and cook about 20 minutes or until the onion is tender. Stir in the ham and remove from the heat and reserve.

2. In a separate large skillet, heat another 1 tablespoon of the oil over high heat. Add the beef and cook, turning once, just until browned on both sides, about 4 minutes per side for rare up to 6 minutes per side for well. Transfer to a warm platter with slotted spatula and cover lightly with foil.

3. Reduce the heat to medium and add the remaining 2 tablespoons oil to the skillet. Stir in the flour and cook 1 minute. Add the broth and wine and stir gently and continuously until smooth and thickened. Add the onion mixture and cook, stirring occasionally, about 5 minutes. Add the beef

and cook just until the beef is heated through, 1 to 2 minutes. Serve hot.

Beef Roast in Garlic Sauce
Solomillo All-i-Pebre

MAKES 4 SERVINGS

All-i-pebre *is a Valencian expression that refers to anything in a garlic and pepper or paprika sauce. This dish is at its best when prepared with beef tenderloin (the Châteaubriand section), but other cuts will do. Because it simmers in a well-seasoned red wine vinegar sauce, the beef that results is somewhere between a pot roast and a roast beef.*

All-purpose flour, for dredging

1½ to 1¾ pounds beef tenderloin; or a roast beef cut, such as sirloin tip or round

Kosher or sea salt

2 tablespoons lard or olive oil

8 small pearl onions, halved lengthwise

1½ tablespoons red wine vinegar

3 garlic cloves, mashed in a garlic press or mortar

1 tablespoon finely chopped fresh flat-leaf parsley

¼ teaspoon freshly ground black pepper

½ cup beef broth, chicken broth, or water

1. Place the flour on wax paper. Season the beef with salt and dredge in the flour. Melt the lard or oil in a deep earthenware casserole dish or Dutch oven over medium-high heat. Add the beef and cook over high heat, turning once, until browned on both sides. Reduce the heat to low, add the onions and vinegar, cover, and cook, turning occasionally, about 15 minutes.

2. Meanwhile, in a blender or food processor, process the garlic, parsley, and pepper until combined. With the motor running, gradually add the broth. After the beef has cooked 15 minutes, pour over the beef, cover, and cook 10 to 15 minutes more or until cooked to taste. Let sit for 5 minutes, then slice and serve hot.

Beef Stews

Garlic Beef Stew
Estofado de Vaca

MAKES 4 SERVINGS

Because this dish simmers for a while, the garlic loses some of its pungency so the flavor is subtle and not at all overpowering.

PREPARE AT LEAST 2 HOURS IN ADVANCE

2 tablespoons olive oil

2 pounds beef for stew, such as chuck, cut into 1½-inch pieces

1 medium onion, chopped (about ⅔ cup)

1 whole head garlic, separated and peeled

1 teaspoon all-purpose flour

1 cup dry white wine

2 whole cloves

Salt

Freshly ground black pepper

1 tablespoon finely chopped fresh flat-leaf parsley

1 bay leaf

¼ teaspoon thyme

1. Heat the oil in a deep earthenware casserole dish or Dutch oven over medium heat. Add the beef and cook, stirring, until well browned on all sides. Add the onion and garlic and cook, stirring, until the onion is wilted and transparent, about 5 minutes more. Stir in the flour, then add the wine, cloves, salt, pepper, parsley, bay leaf, and thyme.

2. Reduce the heat to low, cover, and simmer 1½ to 2 hours or until the meat is tender and well flavored. Remove the bay leaf and serve hot.

Beef Stew with Mushrooms and Piquillo Peppers

Estofado de Ternera con Setas y Piquillo

MAKES 4 TO 6 SERVINGS

Here the mortar mash of sautéed onion and garlic gives extra flavor and texture to the stew, and the piquillo peppers add a wonderful zest. I got this recipe from Antonia Rollón at the Bodegas Fariña in Toro, a city next to the Duero River. The Bodegas produce great wines, including dry and robust reds and very good sweet dessert whites. Antonia loved to cook for guests, and I always had great meals with her.

PREPARE AT LEAST 2 HOURS IN ADVANCE

3 tablespoons olive oil

1 medium sweet onion, such as Vidalia, slivered

6 garlic cloves, finely chopped

1¼ cups dry white wine

2 pounds beef stew meat, cut into 1-inch pieces

Kosher or sea salt

Freshly ground black pepper

2 medium carrots, peeled and thinly sliced

1 teaspoon dried oregano

2 tablespoons finely chopped fresh flat-leaf parsley

¼ pound small mushrooms, such as cremini, rinsed, trimmed, and quartered

1 cup thin strips (jarred) piquillo peppers or pimientos

2 teaspoons tomato paste

1. Heat 2 tablespoons of the oil in a stew pot over medium-high heat. Reduce the heat to low, add the onion and garlic, and cook, stirring, until the onion is wilted and transparent, about 5 minutes. Transfer the onion and garlic with a slotted spoon to a large mortar, reserving the oil in the pot, and mash the onion mix. Stir in the wine.

2. In the stew pot, heat the remaining 1 tablespoon of oil over medium heat. Add the beef and cook, stirring and seasoning with salt and black pepper, until well browned on all sides. Stir in the mortar mixture, the carrots, oregano, and parsley.

3. Reduce the heat to low, cover, and simmer 1 hour. Add the mushrooms, piquillo peppers, and tomato paste and simmer until the meat is tender and the sauce flavors have been absorbed, ¾ to 1 hour more. Serve hot.

Beef Stew with Pearl Onions

Ternera con Cebollitas

MAKES 4 SERVINGS

This recipe comes from my friend Cinta's grandmother, who was from the village of Cassa de la Selva in the Catalan province of Girona. The cinnamon adds a wonderful accent to this dish rich with savory pearl onions. If you can't find pearl onions, you can substitute another kind of sweet onion.

PREPARE AT LEAST 2 HOURS IN ADVANCE

28 or 32 medium pearl onions (about ¾ pound)

2 pounds beef stew meat, cut into 1-inch pieces

3 tablespoons olive oil

8 or 12 tiny (1½-inch) new potatoes, peeled

3 tablespoons brandy

A 1½-inch piece cinnamon stick

2 bay leaves

Salt

12 peppercorns

Beef broth, chicken broth, or water

1. Bring a medium pot of water to a boil over high heat, add the onions, and cook 3 minutes. Drain, rinse under cold water, and slip off the skins. (Parboiling makes the onions easier to peel.)

2. In a large stew pot, combine all the remaining ingredients except the broth. Cover tightly and simmer over low heat about 2 hours or until the beef is tender and the sauce well blended, adding a little broth to keep the pot from getting dry and to have enough sauce when serving. Remove the bay leaves. Serve hot.

Beef Stew with Cumin and Coriander
Ternera Estilo Coto Doñana

MAKES 4 SERVINGS

This wonderful dish was served to me at the palace of Las Marismillas in Coto Doñana when I spent four days there in the 1970s with my husband and daughter. The cook was kind enough to share the recipe with me.

PREPARE AT LEAST 2 HOURS IN ADVANCE

2 tablespoons olive oil

1½ to 2 pounds beef stew meat, cut into 1-inch pieces

2 medium sweet onions, such as Vidalia, thinly sliced

4 garlic cloves, finely chopped

1 pound tomatoes, finely chopped

1½ teaspoons ground cumin

1½ teaspoons ground coriander seeds

3 tablespoons finely chopped fresh cilantro

½ teaspoon crushed hot red pepper, or to taste

¼ cup water

½ cup beef broth or chicken broth, low sodium if canned, or water

1. Heat the oil in a stew pot over medium-high heat. Add the beef and cook, stirring and seasoning with salt, until well browned.

2. Reduce the heat to low, add the onion and garlic, and cook until the onion is wilted and transparent, about 5 minutes. Stir in the tomatoes, 1 teaspoon of the cumin, the coriander, 2 tablespoons of the cilantro, and the hot pepper and cook, stirring, 2 minutes more. Add the water and broth, bring to a boil, cover, and simmer 1½ hours.

3. Stir in the remaining ½ teaspoon cumin and simmer 30 minutes more or until the beef is tender and well flavored. Sprinkle with the remaining 1 tablespoon cilantro and serve hot.

Beef Stew, Catalan Style
Estofado a la Catalana

MAKES 4 SERVINGS

My dinner guests are always surprised when I tell them this beef stew has chocolate in it. It has just a touch of it, which lends an unexpected tartness but also richness to the sauce. Chocolate is frequently called for in Catalan-style cooking, as are nuts and sausage. Butifarra is the typical sausage of that region and can often be found in the United States in specialty stores. If it's not available, you may substitute sweet Italian-style sausages.

PREPARE AT LEAST 2 HOURS IN ADVANCE

2 large potatoes, peeled and cut into 1-inch pieces

1 tablespoon olive oil

¼ pound slab bacon, cut into 4 pieces

2 pounds beef chuck, cut into 1-inch pieces

1 large onion, finely chopped (about 1 cup)

4 garlic cloves

1 tablespoon all-purpose flour

1 cup dry white wine

1 sprig parsley

1 bay leaf

⅛ teaspoon dried oregano

¼ teaspoon dried thyme

½ cup beef broth, chicken broth, or water

Salt

continues...

Freshly ground black pepper

½ teaspoon coarsely grated bittersweet chocolate

One (16-inch) pork sausage (butifarra) or 4 sweet
   Italian-style sausages

1. Place the potatoes in a medium saucepan with cold water to cover and add salt. Cover and bring to a simmer over low heat. Cook about 20 minutes or until tender when pierced with a knife. Drain and reserve.

2. Place the oil and bacon in a deep stew pot over low heat and cook until the bacon begins to sizzle. Add the beef, increase the heat to medium-high, and cook, stirring, until well browned on all sides. Reduce the heat to medium, add the onion and garlic, and cook until the onion is wilted and transparent, about 5 minutes more. Stir in the flour, then add the wine, parsley, bay leaf, oregano, thyme, and broth. Season with salt and pepper. Reduce the heat to low, cover, and cook about 2 hours or until the beef is tender.

3. Stir in the chocolate, add the reserved potatoes, and cook until the potatoes are tender, about 10 minutes more.

4. Meanwhile, place the sausage in a small skillet over medium heat and cook, stirring, until browned and cooked through. Cut the sausage into ½-inch slices. Spoon the stew into individual shallow bowls and arrange the sausage around the edge. Remove the bay leaf. Serve hot.

Beef Stew Larded with Ham, Olives, and Scallions
Carne Mechada

MAKES 4 SERVINGS

Carne mechada is one of the most popular ways in Spain of preparing beef. It is a robust and hearty meal, made even richer if you add potatoes. The meat is also very good chilled or at room temperature as a sandwich meat when cut into thin slices.

PREPARE AT LEAST 3 HOURS IN ADVANCE

1½ pounds beef stew meat

2 "sticks" Serrano (Spanish cured mountain) ham or
   prosciutto, about 5 inches long and ¼ inch thick,
   for larding

10 to 12 small pimiento-stuffed green olives,
   preferably Spanish

2 large scallions

2 tablespoons olive oil

Kosher or sea salt

2 medium sweet onions, such as Vidalia, cut into
   thin rings

2 garlic cloves

2 tablespoons finely chopped fresh flat-leaf parsley

1 tablespoon finely chopped fresh thyme or
   ½ teaspoon dried thyme

5 peppercorns

1 bay leaf

¼ cup dry white wine

1¼ cups chicken broth or vegetable broth

⅛ teaspoon saffron threads, crumbled

1. Using the handle of a thick wooden spoon, make 6 holes through the length of the meat, twisting to enlarge the hole. Push the ham sticks into 2 of the holes, the olives into 2 more holes, and the scallions into the remaining 2 holes.

2. In a stew pot in which the meat fits closely, heat the oil over medium-high heat. Add the beef and cook, stirring and seasoning with salt as it cooks, until well browned on all sides. Transfer to a platter. Reduce the heat to low, add the onions, garlic, parsley, thyme, peppercorns, and bay leaf and cook, stirring, until the onion is wilted and transparent, about 8 minutes. Add to the pot, stir in the wine, broth, and saffron, and bring to a boil. Cover and simmer about 3 hours (or ¾ to 1 hour in a pressure cooker) until the meat is tender.

3. Transfer the meat to a warm platter. Pass the sauce through a fine-mesh strainer into a bowl, pressing with the back of a soup ladle to extract as much liquid as possible, and return sauce to the pot. Discard the solids. Bring the sauce to a boil over low heat and cook until slightly thickened. Cut the meat into ½-inch slices, add to the sauce, and simmer until the meat is heated through, 2 to 3 minutes. Remove the bay leaf. Serve hot.

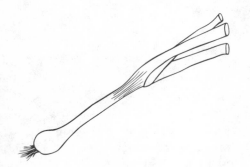

Oxtail Stew
Rabo de Toro

MAKES 4 SERVINGS

Oxtail stew or rabo de toro *is popular in Andalucía. This dish originated in the city of Cordoba. It makes sense that this dish comes from Andalucía, traditionally breeding grounds for fighting bulls.*

PREPARE AT LEAST 2 HOURS IN ADVANCE

2 tablespoons olive oil

3 to 4 pounds oxtail, cut into 2-inch pieces

2 medium onions, coarsely chopped (about 1⅓ cup)

1 head garlic, finely chopped

1 dried red chile pepper, stemmed and seeded

3 bay leaves

Kosher or sea salt

10 black peppercorns

1 medium carrot, peeled and cut into thick slices

3 sprigs parsley

2 sprigs rosemary

2 sprigs thyme

1 cup dry white wine

Beef broth or water

Heat the oil in a large skillet over medium-high heat. Add the oxtail and cook, stirring, until browned. Add the onion, garlic, chile pepper, bay leaves, salt, and peppercorns and cook until the onion is wilted and starts to brown. Add the carrot, parsley, rosemary, thyme, and wine. Reduce the heat to low, cover, and simmer about 2 hours, adding some beef broth as needed if the sauce evaporates too soon. Remove the bay leaves. Serve hot.

Pedro's Oxtail Stew with Juniper Berries
Rabo de Toro Pedro

MAKES 4 SERVINGS

This recipe comes from our good friend Pedro Narro, who runs the El Chorro restaurant in the breathtaking mountain village of Albarracín. Traditionally, Andalucía is the region where oxtail stew is most popular, but I prefer Pedro's Aragon version, partly because he adds juniper berries from the forestlands in the region. Pedro is not only a great cook, but also in the Aragonese tradition, a magnificent singer.

2 tablespoons olive oil

3½ to 4 oxtail, cut into 1½- to 2-inch rounds and fat trimmed

1 medium onion, finely chopped (about ⅔ cup)

1 medium carrot, peeled and cut into ¼-inch slices

Salt

¼ teaspoon ground paprika

1½ teaspoons finely chopped fresh thyme or ¼ teaspoon dried thyme

1½ teaspoons finely chopped fresh oregano or ¼ teaspoon dried oregano

5 dried juniper berries

6 peppercorns

1 small tomato, peeled, seeded, and finely chopped (about ½ cup)

2 cups dry white wine

Heat the oil in a deep pot over medium-high heat. Add all the ingredients except the tomato and wine and cook, stirring frequently, until the oxtail is lightly browned and the onion is wilted. Add the tomato and cook about 3 minutes more, then add the wine and bring to a boil. Reduce the heat to low and simmer about 3 hours or until most of the liquid is evaporated (leaving a thick gravy) and the oxtail is tender. If the liquid is absorbed sooner than this, cover the pot and continue cooking. Serve hot.

Tripe, Madrid Style
Callos a la Madrileña

MAKES 4 TO 6 SERVINGS

My husband Luis has always adored tripe, but I never shared his enthusiasm until I tasted this spicy version from Madrid that includes chorizo. *Tripe is best when prepared the day before and then reheated. Cooking times vary, but it is important that the tripe be very tender before eating. This dish requires a lot of cooking time but is mostly unattended. It is enormously popular with Spaniards and can be served as either a first course or the main meal.*

PREPARE AT LEAST 6 TO
9 HOURS IN ADVANCE

1 pound beef tripe

3 cups water

½ cup dry white wine

1 fresh or canned small tomato, finely chopped (about ½ cup)

2 sprigs parsley

10 peppercorns, lightly smashed

2 whole cloves, mashed in a garlic press or mortar

Dash of grated or ground nutmeg

2 bay leaves

½ teaspoon dried thyme

Salt

1 small onion, coarsely chopped (about ⅓ cup)

6 garlic cloves

1 pig foot, split in half

2 tablespoons olive oil

1 small onion, finely chopped (about ⅓ cup)

¼ pound (2 links) chorizo, cut into ¼-inch slices

¼ cup small cubes (¼ inch) Serrano (Spanish cured mountain) ham or prosciutto

1 tablespoon all-purpose flour

1 tablespoon ground paprika

½ dried red chile pepper, seeded and crumbled

1. Rinse the tripe well. Place in a large pot, add water to cover, and bring to a boil over high heat. Drain immediately. Cut the tripe into 1½-inch squares and return to the pot. Add the 3 cups water, the wine, tomato, parsley, peppercorns, cloves, nutmeg, bay leaves, thyme, salt, coarsely chopped onion, garlic, and pig foot. Reduce the heat to low, cover, and simmer 4 to 5 hours or until the tripe is almost tender.

2. Heat the oil in a medium skillet over medium heat. Add the finely chopped onion and cook, stirring, until wilted and transparent, about 5 minutes. Add the chorizo and ham and cook, stirring, about 5 minutes more. Stir in the flour and paprika and cook 1 minute more. Add ½ cup of the cooking liquid from the tripe pot and cook, stirring, until the liquid is reduced and the sauce thickens slightly. Stir into the tripe pot, add the chile pepper, cover, and cook 1 to 2 hours more. Uncover and cook 1 to 2 hours more or until extremely tender.

3. Remove the bone from the pig foot and discard. Cut the meat into pieces and stir into the tripe pot. Remove the bay leaves. Divide the tripe among individual soup bowls or shallow individual earthenware casserole dishes. Serve hot.

Beef Patties
Fricadelas

MAKES 4 TO 6 BEEF PATTIES

Here is Spain's version of the hamburger, a recipe that comes from Cartageña in Murcia. The ground beef is made richer by the addition of chopped bacon, so you can use lean beef if you like. The escarole adds a little tartness for balance. I like it best when served on French-style bread.

2 slices bacon

1 pound ground beef

1 cup finely chopped escarole

Salt

Freshly ground black pepper

1 tablespoon dry sherry, such as Fino

4 tablespoons olive oil

4 to 6 thin slices long-loaf (baguette) bread

1. In a small skillet over medium heat, cook the bacon until browned but not crisp. In a large bowl, combine the beef, bacon, escarole, salt, pepper, and sherry.

2. Shape into 4 to 6 equal patties. Heat 1 tablespoon of the oil in a large skillet over medium-high heat. Add the patties and cook, turning once, until browned on both sides and cooked to taste, about 3 minutes per side for rare up to about 7 minutes per side for well. Reserve in the skillet.

3. Heat the remaining 3 tablespoons oil in a medium skillet over medium-high heat. Add the bread, and cook, turning once, until lightly golden. Arrange the bread on individual plates, place 1 patty on each slice and spoon the pan juices over the patties. Serve hot.

Three-Meat Loaf
Pastel de Tres Carnes

MAKES 4 SERVINGS

This is somewhere between a meatloaf and pâté — the chopped meats are sandwiched between chicken cutlets and enclosed in bacon. The Spanish word pastel *may refer to either a dessert pastry or to a pâté. This dish has a much more elegant flavor than a standard meatloaf.*

¼ pound thinly sliced bacon

1¼ pound thin (¼ inch) chicken cutlets

Kosher or sea salt

2 tablespoons bread crumbs

2 tablespoons milk

1½-pound mixture of ground veal and ground pork

1 large egg

2 garlic cloves, finely chopped

1½ teaspoons kosher or sea salt

¼ teaspoon freshly ground black pepper

2 tablespoons dry sherry, such as Fino

3 tablespoons finely chopped fresh flat-leaf parsley

1. Preheat the oven to 450°F. Arrange half of the bacon in the bottom of a 9 x 5-inch loaf pan, overlapping if necessary. Arrange half of the chicken in the bottom of the pan, cutting the pieces to fit if necessary. Season with salt and pepper.

2. In a cup, combine the bread crumbs and milk until the crumbs are soaked. In a medium bowl, place the ground meat, the egg, garlic, the 1½ teaspoons salt, the pepper, sherry, parsley, and the soaked crumbs and mix well to combine. Spread evenly in the loaf pan and arrange the remaining half of the cutlets over the meat mixture (cutting to fit if necessary). Season with salt and pepper and arrange the remaining half of the bacon (overlapping if necessary).

3. Fill a larger baking pan with 1 inch of hot water. Place the loaf pan into the larger pan and bake about 1 hour or until crisp on top but still moist in the center. Loosen the loaf around the edges with a knife, then drain off and reserve the juices. Turn the loaf out onto a serving platter and cut into 8 slices. Spoon the juices over the loaf and serve hot.

Meat-Filled Red Peppers in Red Pepper Sauce
Pimientos del Piquillo Rellenos de Carne en Salsa de Pimientos

MAKES 4 SERVINGS

Pimientos del piquillo, *the sweet red peppers that thrive in Navarra, are immensely popular in local dishes. They are sometimes served stuffed, with meat being the traditional filling, in a puréed red pepper sauce. It is hard to find fresh* piquillos *here; you can use jarred.*

8 (jarred) piquillo peppers or 16 jarred pimentos, drained

½ pound mixture ground veal, beef, and pork, in equal parts

1 garlic clove, finely chopped

2 tablespoons finely chopped fresh flat-leaf parsley

Red Pepper Sauce

2 tablespoons olive oil

1 small onion, finely chopped (about ⅓ cup)

1 garlic clove, finely chopped

½ pound red (jarred) piquillo peppers or one (7-ounce) jar pimientos, drained and finely chopped

2 teaspoons brandy

½ cup plus 2 tablespoons chicken broth or vegetable broth

Salt

1 garlic clove, mashed in a garlic press or mortar

2 tablespoons liverwurst or other liver pâté

Generous amount of freshly grated or ground nutmeg

1. In a medium bowl, mix the ground meats, the chopped garlic, and the parsley. Let sit 10 minutes.

2. Prepare the sauce: Heat 1 tablespoon of the oil in a medium skillet over medium heat. Add the onion and cook, stirring, until wilted and transparent, about 5 minutes. Add the garlic and cook, stirring, until softened, about 2 minutes more. Add the reserved chopped peppers and pour the brandy around the pan. Standing well away from the pan, ignite the liquid with a match or kitchen lighter and let die out. Stir in ½ cup of the broth and salt. Reduce the heat to low, simmer about 10 minutes, and let cool.

3. Preheat the oven to 400°F. Transfer the sauce to a food processor and blend until smooth. The sauce should be of a medium thickness; if too thick, add 2 tablespoons broth.

4. Heat the remaining 1 tablespoon oil in a large skillet over medium-high heat. Add the garlic and cook briefly. Add the meat mixture, the liverwurst, and the nutmeg, and cook, breaking it up and stirring as it cooks, until the meat is no longer pink.

5. Season each piquillo pepper with salt and stuff with 1 tablespoon of the meat mixture. Arrange the stuffed peppers in a shallow earthenware casserole dish or Dutch oven and pour the sauce over the peppers. Roast about 15 minutes or until the meat is cooked through. If using earthenware, serve hot in the dish, or transfer to a platter.

Stuffed Green Peppers and Zucchini
Pimientos y Calabacines Rellenos

MAKES 6 SERVINGS

This dish makes a beautiful presentation but might take a little practice to prepare.

3 medium zucchini

6 medium green bell peppers

2 tablespoons olive oil

2 large onions, finely chopped (about 2 cups)

3 garlic cloves

2 pounds ground beef or a mixture of beef, veal, and pork

Salt

Freshly ground black pepper

2 tablespoons finely chopped fresh flat-leaf parsley

2 tablespoons dry red wine

2 tablespoons finely chopped Serrano (Spanish cured mountain) ham or prosciutto

2 medium tomatoes, peeled and finely chopped (about 1⅓ cups)

½ cup uncooked short- or long-grain rice

¾ cup tomato sauce

¾ cup water

1. Cut the zucchini crosswise in half. Scoop out the flesh and place in a medium bowl. Reserve the shells. Cut off the caps of the green peppers and reserve. Scoop out and discard the seeds and membrane and reserve the shells.

2. Heat the oil in a large skillet over medium heat. Add the onion and garlic and cook, stirring, until the onion is wilted and transparent, about 5 minutes. Add the beef and cook, breaking it up and stirring as it cooks, until the beef is lightly browned. Season with salt and pepper. Add the parsley, wine,

continues...

ham, tomatoes, and zucchini flesh and cook about 5 minutes more. Stir in the rice and cook about 5 minutes more. Reserve.

3. Preheat the oven to 350°F. In a small bowl, combine the tomato sauce and water and season with salt and pepper. Pour into a 13 x 9-inch baking dish.

4. Stuff the zucchini and peppers about three-quarters full with the meat mixture. Place the caps on the peppers. Arrange the zucchini and peppers in the baking dish. Bake, basting occasionally with the sauce, about 1 hour or until the vegetables are tender and the meat has browned more, adding more water if the sauce thickens too much. Serve hot.

Stuffed Red Cabbage
Lombarda Rellena

MAKES 4 SERVINGS

In Spain, this is a traditional yuletide dish. The delicious sausage and apple filling is the perfect complement to the sweetness of the red cabbage. Serve this dish with a bit of grated Manchego cheese on top.

1 medium head red cabbage

2 tablespoons olive oil

1 medium onion, finely chopped (about ⅔ cup)

1 pound sweet Italian-style sausage

1 garlic clove, finely chopped

1 tablespoon finely chopped fresh flat-leaf parsley

¼ cup dry red wine

½ apple, peeled, cored, and cut into ¼-inch pieces

½ cup cooked rice

Salt

Freshly ground black pepper

2 large eggs, lightly beaten

½ cup beef broth, chicken broth, or water, plus more if needed

1 tablespoon melted unsalted butter

2 tablespoons coarsely grated cheese, such as aged Manchego

1. Select and separate 8 of the outer leaves of the cabbage (if the leaves are hard to separate, boil the cabbage head briefly). Finely chop the rest of the cabbage to make about 2 cups. Fill a large pot with water and bring to a boil over high heat. Add the cabbage leaves and cook until tender enough to fold for stuffing—do not overcook because the leaves will lose their color. Drain.

2. Heat the oil in a large skillet over medium-high heat. Add the onion and cook, stirring, until wilted and transparent, about 5 minutes. Add the sausage and cook, breaking it up and stirring as it cooks, until the sausage is browned.

3. Pour off and discard any excess fat from the skillet. Reduce the heat to medium. Stir in the garlic, parsley, chopped cabbage, wine, and apple and cook, stirring occasionally, about 15 minutes. Remove from the heat and stir in the cooked rice, salt, and pepper. Mix in the eggs.

4. Preheat the oven to 350°F. Fill each cabbage leaf with several tablespoons of the filling. Fold up the 2 sides of the cabbage, then roll to enclose the filling.

5. Combine the broth and melted butter in a roasting pan and coat the bottom. Arrange the cabbage in the pan, seam side down, and sprinkle with the cheese. Bake about 30 minutes, adding more broth as necessary. Serve hot.

Meat-Filled Potatoes
Patatas Rellenas Casa Julián

MAKES 3 TO 4 SERVINGS

Casa Julián, a small restaurant and hotel on the banks of the Cares River in Asturias, was run by Julián, his wife Vicentina, and their sons. The restaurant has a spectacular view of the mountainous scenery of the Picos de Europa, and many of their dishes are superb. Vicentina, an extraordinary cook, shared this recipe for patatas rellenas, *one of her specialties. Julián and Vicentina are no longer with us, but their memory and restaurant is maintained by their children, now in charge of the place.*

2 tablespoons olive oil

1 medium onion, finely chopped (about ⅔ cup)

1 garlic clove, finely chopped

1 pound mixture of beef, veal, and pork, in equal parts

Salt

Freshly ground black pepper

½ pound tomatoes, peeled, seeded, and finely chopped

2 tablespoons finely chopped pimiento

2 tablespoons finely chopped fresh flat-leaf parsley

16 small (2-inch) potatoes

2 tablespoons finely chopped Serrano (Spanish cured mountain) ham or prosciutto

1 teaspoon all-purpose flour

1¼ cups chicken broth or vegetable broth

¼ cup dry white wine

1. Heat 1 tablespoon of the oil in a shallow earthenware casserole dish or Dutch oven over medium heat. Add the onion and garlic and cook, stirring, until the onion is wilted and transparent, about 5 minutes. Transfer to a small bowl and reserve 2 tablespoons for the sauce. Add the meat and cook, breaking it up and stirring as it cooks, until the meat is no longer pink. Season with salt and pepper. Reduce the heat to low, add the tomatoes, pimiento, and parsley and cook, stirring, about 10 minutes. Reserve. Wipe out the casserole dish.

2. Peel the potatoes and hollow out with a small spoon or melon scoop, leaving a shell about ⅜ inch thick. Fill each potato with about 1 tablespoon of the meat mixture and cover with a scrap of potato.

3. Heat the remaining 1 tablespoon oil in the casserole dish over medium heat. Add the reserved onion mixture, the ham, and flour and stir in the broth and wine. Arrange the potatoes in the casserole dish and spoon some of the sauce over them. Reduce the heat to low, cover, and simmer until the potatoes are tender, about 1 hour, basting occasionally with the sauce. If using earthenware, serve hot in the dish, or transfer to individual plates.

Hash Casserole, Spanish Style
Pastel de Carne y Patata

MAKES 4 SERVINGS

Here is the Spanish version of hash, in which a touch of brandy and nutmeg give the meat and potatoes a delicious flavor that is complemented by the addition of the egg, cheese, and bread crumb topping.

4 tablespoons olive oil, plus oil for greasing

2 medium onions, finely chopped (about 1⅓ cup)

1½ pounds ground beef

Kosher or sea salt

Generous amount of freshly ground black pepper

1 medium tomato, finely chopped (about ⅔ cup)

3 tablespoons finely chopped fresh flat-leaf parsley

1 teaspoon freshly grated or ground nutmeg

¼ cup brandy

2 pounds medium Idaho potatoes, peeled and halved crosswise

2 garlic cloves

About 1 cup warm milk

1 cup bread crumbs

2 large eggs

1 tablespoon unsalted butter, cut into small cubes

Grated aged Manchego or Parmesan cheese

1. Heat 2 tablespoons of the oil in a large skillet over medium-high heat. Add the onion and cook about 2 minutes. Reduce the heat to low, cover, and cook, stirring occasionally, until wilted and transparent, about 10 minutes more. Increase the heat to high. Add the beef and cook, breaking it up and

continues . . .

stirring—as well as seasoning with salt and pepper—as it cooks, until no longer pink. Add the tomato, parsley, nutmeg, and brandy, and cook, stirring, about 5 minutes more.

2. Place the potatoes in a large saucepan with cold water to cover, add the garlic, and add salt. Cover and bring to a simmer over low heat. Cook about 20 minutes or until tender when pierced with a knife. Drain.

3. Transfer the potatoes and garlic to a medium bowl. Add the remaining 2 tablespoons oil and beat with an electric mixer until smooth, adding as much of the warm milk as necessary for the potatoes to be spreadable but not liquid. Season with salt and pepper.

4. Preheat the oven to 350°F. Grease a 12 x 8-inch glass baking dish with oil and sprinkle with half of the bread crumbs. Arrange a layer of potatoes over the bread crumbs, and cover with a layer of the meat mixture. Repeat the layers several times, ending with potatoes.

5. Place the eggs in a small bowl and beat with a electric hand-held beater until thick, creamy, and lemon colored. Pour over the potatoes. Dot with the butter and sprinkle with the remaining half of the bread crumbs and the cheese. Bake about 30 minutes or until browned. Loosen the edges with a knife and cut into portions, removing with an offset spatula. Serve hot.

Grilled Baby Lamb Chops
Chuletillas de Cordero a la Parrilla

MAKES 4 SERVINGS

Spaniards have become accustomed to delectable milk-fed baby lamb, usually no more than several weeks old. They are so tender that they can be cut without a knife and so flavorful that the only seasoning they require is a dash of salt and pepper. In the United States, the smallest lamb I have been able to find are sold as a rack of lamb and need to be sliced into chops. I recommend either using a stovetop griddle or cooking them on a charcoal grill.

12 baby rib lamb chops, ¾- to 1- inch thick
Olive oil
A bunch of rosemary and/or thyme sprigs, dampened (optional)
Salt
1 garlic clove, finely chopped
1 tablespoon finely chopped fresh flat-leaf parsley

1. Place a barbecue grill rack about 4 inches away from the heat source. Preheat the grill.

2. Brush the chops on both sides with the oil. Scatter the rosemary and/or thyme sprigs, if using, over the hot coals. Place the chops on the grill and cook, turning once, until done to taste, about 3 minutes per side for rare and about 7 minutes per side for well. Transfer to a warm platter. Season with salt and sprinkle with the garlic and parsley. Serve hot.

Grilled Lamb Chops with Garlic and Parsley

Chuletas de Cordero con Ajo y Perejil

MAKES 4 SERVINGS

The central plains of Spain is an area where baby lambs are raised, and Spaniards have become accustomed to this delicacy. Droves of Madrileños don't hesitate to drive long distances into the countryside just to eat baby lamb at centuries-old inns in beautiful Castilian villages. This recipe came to me from my friend Cándida Acebo, who lives in the charming village of Compludo on the way to St. James where she runs the only bar and restaurant.

4 garlic cloves, finely chopped

¼ cup finely chopped fresh flat-leaf parsley

¼ teaspoon kosher or sea salt

2 tablespoons extra-virgin olive oil, plus more for brushing

2 tablespoons dry red wine

2 pounds loin lamb chops, 1 to 1¼ inch thick

1. Place a barbecue grill rack about 4 inches away from the heat source. Preheat the grill. In a mortar or mini-processor, mash the garlic, parsley, and the salt. Stir in the oil and wine.

2. Brush the chops on both sides with oil and season with salt. Place the chops on the grill and cook, turning once, until done to taste. Transfer to a warm platter. Spoon the mortar mixture over the chops and season with salt. Serve hot.

Lamb Chops and Sliced Potatoes with Garlic and Vinegar

Chuletas de Cordero al Ajo Cabañil Rincón de Pepe

MAKES 4 SERVINGS

Ajo cabañil refers to the garlic and vinegar sauce that seasons the meat as well as the potatoes. This recipe came from Raimundo Frutos, who owns Rincón de Pepe, the finest restaurant in the city of Murcia in southeastern Spain.

12 garlic cloves, mashed in a garlic press or mortar

¼ cup white wine vinegar

½ cup chicken broth or vegetable broth

½ teaspoon sugar

1 pound potatoes, peeled and cut into very thin slices

3 tablespoons olive oil

Salt

Freshly ground black pepper

2 tablespoons water

2½ pounds rib lamb chops, ¾ to 1 inch thick

1. In a small bowl, combine the garlic, vinegar, broth, and sugar. In a greased microwave-safe dish, arrange the potatoes in layers, sprinkling each layer with oil (a total of about 1 tablespoon), salt, and pepper. Drizzle 2 tablespoons of water over the potatoes, cover, and cook on High 7 minutes.

2. Fold in half of the garlic mixture, cover, and microwave about 8 minutes more or until the potatoes are tender. (Alternatively, the potatoes can be roasted: omit the water, cover with foil, and bake in a 350°F oven about 1 hour, adding the garlic mixture after 30 minutes.)

3. Meanwhile, heat the remaining 1 tablespoon oil in a large skillet over high heat. Add the chops and

continues...

cook, turning once, until browned on both sides. Season with salt and pepper and stir in the remaining half of the garlic mixture. Reduce the heat to low and simmer 10 minutes more or until cooked to taste.

4. Place the potatoes in the center of individual dinner plates or a serving platter and arrange the chops around the potatoes. Serve hot.

Marinated Lamb Chops and Mushrooms

Chuletas de Cordero y Chámpiñones Aliñados

MAKES 4 SERVINGS

The subtle taste of mushrooms is the perfect accent for these marinated and well-seasoned lamb chops. The paprika, parsley, and celery seed make this an especially good marinade.

PREPARE AT LEAST 2 HOURS IN ADVANCE

¼ cup wine vinegar

¾ cup extra-virgin olive oil

¼ teaspoon celery seed

2 tablespoons finely chopped fresh flat-leaf parsley

½ teaspoon ground paprika, such as Spanish smoked

½ teaspoon salt

Freshly ground black pepper

1 small onion, slivered

2 pounds lamb chops, about 1 inch thick

½ pound mushrooms, rinsed and trimmed

1. In a shallow bowl, whisk together the vinegar, oil, celery seed, parsley, paprika, salt, and pepper. Stir in the onion, then add the chops and mushrooms and turn to coat well with the marinade. Let marinate at least 2 hours at room temperature in the refrigerator, turning occasionally. Drain.

2. If the chops were in the refrigerator, let them sit at room temperature for a few minutes. Place a broiler rack about 6 inches from the heat source and preheat the broiler or preheat a stovetop griddle over high heat. (Cover the broiler pan with foil for easier cleanup, if you like.) Arrange the chops and mushrooms on a broiler pan or the griddle and cook, turning once, until the chops are browned on each side and done to taste, about 3 minutes per side for rare up to 7 minutes per side for well. The mushrooms will cook more quickly than the chops, so remove them once they're done. Serve hot.

Béchamel-Coated Breaded Lamb Chops

Chuletas de Cordero Empanadas

MAKES 4 SERVINGS

This recipe calls for several steps — the chops need to be marinated, fried, dipped in a creamy white (béchamel) sauce, and then browned again. This creates an exceptional lamb chop that is tender on the inside and crunchy on the outside, a wonderful dish that is well worth the extra effort.

PREPARE AT LEAST 2 HOURS IN ADVANCE

½ cup olive oil

3 garlic cloves, mashed in a garlic press or mortar

1 tablespoon finely chopped fresh flat-leaf parsley

Salt

Freshly ground black pepper

12 small rib lamb chops, about ½ inch thick

2 large eggs, lightly beaten

Bread crumbs, for dredging

Olive oil, for frying

White Sauce (Béchamel)

7½ tablespoons unsalted butter

9 tablespoons all-purpose flour

1 cup chicken broth or vegetable broth

1¼ cups milk

Salt

Freshly ground black pepper

1. In a shallow bowl, combine the ½ cup olive oil, garlic, parsley, salt, and pepper. Add the chops, turn to coat, and let marinate at least 2 hours at room temperature or in the refrigerator, turning occasionally. Drain. Discard the marinade.

2. If the chops were in the refrigerator, let them sit at room temperature for a few minutes. Lightly grease a large skillet and heat over medium-high heat. Add the chops and cook, turning once, until browned on both sides and done to taste. Transfer to paper towels with a slotted spatula and let drain, patting both sides to absorb the grease. Reserve.

3. Prepare the white sauce: Melt the butter in a medium saucepan over medium heat. Add the flour and cook 1 minute. Gradually add the broth, milk, salt, and pepper and cook, stirring constantly, until very thick and smooth. Let cool and spread out on a dinner plate. Coat the chops lightly with the sauce, on both sides and along the rib bone. Place on a greased platter and refrigerate 30 minutes or until the sauce solidifies.

4. Place the eggs and bread crumbs in separate shallow bowls. Dip the chops in the egg and dredge in the bread crumbs. Heat ⅛ inch of oil in a large skillet over medium-high heat. Add the chops and cook, turning once, until browned on both sides. Transfer with a slotted spatula to paper towels and let drain. Serve hot.

Sautéed Marinated Lamb Stew
Frite Cacereño

MAKES 4 SERVINGS

This dish is a specialty of the Restaurant Pizarro located in historic Trujillo, the birthplace of Pizarro. Isabel Carrasco runs this beautiful restaurant, which has been in her family for over sixty years. This is Isabel's delicious version of sautéed marinated leg of lamb.

PREPARE AT LEAST 2 HOURS IN ADVANCE

1¾ to 2 pounds boneless leg of lamb, cut into 1½-inch pieces

1 bay leaf, crumbled

4 garlic cloves, peeled

⅛ teaspoon salt

Freshly ground black pepper

1 tablespoon ground paprika, such as Spanish smoked

1 tablespoon finely chopped fresh oregano or ½ teaspoon dried oregano

½ cup olive oil, plus 2 tablespoons

2 garlic cloves, unpeeled and lightly smashed

1. Place the lamb in a medium bowl. In a mortar or mini-processor, mash the bay leaf, peeled garlic, salt, pepper, paprika, and oregano and gradually stir in the ½ cup oil. Pour over the lamb and stir to coat well. Cover and let marinate 2 hours. Drain and discard the marinade.

2. Heat the remaining 2 tablespoons oil in a medium skillet over medium heat. Add the unpeeled garlic and cook, turning once and pressing with the back of a wooden spoon to extract its flavor, until golden. Discard the garlic.

3. Add the meat and cook, turning once, until browned on the outside but still lightly pink within. Season with salt and serve hot.

When you travel in Spain, you cannot avoid the sight of large flocks of lambs grazing in the fields under the attentive care of a lonely shepherd (and often accompanied by one or two dogs). Lamb has the best flavor if it has never grazed and has only been fed its mother's milk. Traditionally, lamb has been a staple in Spain, cooked in many different ways, but the quintessential preparation is baby lamb roasted in a clay pot in a brick oven with nothing added but a touch of salt and a little water. The wood used in the oven is ideally vine branches or wood from *encinas*, which are similar to oak trees.

This way of cooking is typical of Castilla, north of Madrid. On weekends, many families leave Madrid on their way to several little villages and restaurants to indulge in a great *corderada* which translates as "lamb debauchery." Villages such as Sepulveda, Pedraza, and Penafiel have great *mesones* (country taverns) and great lamb roasts. For many years, my favorite restaurant has been Meson Zute, owned by my friend Martin Antoranz in the beautiful village of Sepulveda. It is recognized as the best roaster of lamb, even by many of its competitors.

There are two breeds of lambs in Spain: merinos, bred for their wool, and churras, bred for their meat. The lambs migrate from north to south and back, looking for the proper climate to thrive. These migrations are made through trails called *Real Cañadas* that were established hundreds of years ago by Royal Decree and are still in use today. Alcala, the main street in Madrid, is still a *Cañada* where every year a few thousand lambs with their shepherds and dogs are brought to cross Madrid, in order to maintain its rights to the trail. Traffic comes to a standstill, and it is a great spectacle.

If you are ever in Madrid, I would suggest that you go to Posada de la Villa on Cava Baja Street and order a quarter of roasted lamb. Just remember that the purists always ask for the front quarters and, whenever possible, they prefer the right side because the lambs tend to sleep lying on their left, and that makes the meat on the left side somewhat tougher!

Lamb Stew with Honey
Cordero a la Miel

MAKES 4 SERVINGS

Here the savory taste of lamb is contrasted by the sweetness of honey in this dish of Moorish origin. Córdoba was the capital of Moorish Spain. This recipe came to me by way of José García Marín, owner of Córdoba's excellent El Caballo Rojo restaurant specializing in Moorish recipes.

1 tablespoon olive oil

3 to 3½ pounds lamb stew meat with bone, cut into 1½- to 2-inch pieces

Salt

1 medium onion, finely chopped (about ⅔ cup)

1 small green bell pepper, finely chopped (about ⅓ cup)

1 teaspoon ground paprika, such as Spanish smoked

1 tablespoon brandy

⅓ cup dry white wine

Few threads of saffron

½ cup chicken broth or vegetable broth

2 tablespoons wine vinegar

1½ tablespoons honey

1. Heat the oil in a stew pot over medium-high heat. Add the lamb and cook, stirring, until well browned on all sides. Season with salt. Add the

onion and bell pepper and cook, stirring, until the vegetables are softened, about 5 minutes. Reduce the heat to low, stir in the paprika, then the brandy, wine, and saffron, and simmer 5 minutes more.

2. Add the broth and bring to a boil. Simmer 1 to 1½ hours more or until the lamb is tender. Stir in the vinegar and honey, taste and adjust seasoning if necessary, and simmer 10 minutes more. Serve hot.

Potted Lamb with Lemon
Cochifrito

MAKES 4 SERVINGS

Lemon adds the perfect zest to this classic Spanish dish of potted lamb. I recommend that you sauté the lamb, then simmer it for about 2 hours so that the meat will be tender. This recipe calls for butter, which makes a wonderfully rich sauce.

PREPARE AT LEAST 2 HOURS IN ADVANCE

1 tablespoon olive oil

1 tablespoon unsalted butter

2 pounds boneless lamb, cut into 2-inch pieces (or use lamb pieces with bones and increase the weight)

Salt

Freshly ground black pepper

2 garlic cloves, finely chopped

¼ cup fresh lemon juice

¼ cup chicken broth or water

1 teaspoon dry sherry, such as Fino

1. In a deep earthenware casserole dish or Dutch oven, heat the oil and butter over medium-high heat until the butter begins to brown. Add the lamb and cook, stirring, until well browned on all sides. Reduce the heat to medium. Season with salt and pepper, add the garlic, and cook 5 minutes more. Stir in the lemon juice, broth, and sherry.

2. Reduce the heat to low and cook 1½ to 2 hours or until the lamb is very tender, adding some water if necessary to prevent it from getting dry—but this dish shouldn't have a lot of sauce. If using earthenware, serve hot in the dish, or transfer to individual plates.

Lamb with Lemon
Cordero con Limón

MAKES 4 SERVINGS

This version of lamb-with-lemon stew omits the butter and broth but features tomato and brandy. The recipe came to me by way of my dear friend Carmen Serrano who learned it from her friend Maria, whose family is from the central plains of La Mancha where lambs roam in huge flocks.

2 tablespoons olive oil

2 pounds boneless lamb, cut into 1½-inch pieces

Salt

Freshly ground black pepper

2 garlic cloves, finely chopped

1 medium tomato, peeled, seeded, and finely chopped (about ⅔ cup)

1 bay leaf

¼ cup fresh lemon juice

2 tablespoons brandy

1. Heat the oil in a deep earthenware casserole dish or Dutch oven over medium-high heat. Add the lamb and cook, stirring and seasoning with salt and pepper as it cooks, until browned on all sides. Add the garlic and cook, stirring, 1 minute, then stir in the tomato and bay leaf and cook 2 minutes more. Add the lemon juice and brandy, bring to a boil, and taste and adjust seasoning if necessary.

2. Reduce the heat to low, cover, and simmer 1½ hours or until the lamb is tender. Remove the bay leaf. Serve hot. If using earthenware, serve hot in the dish, or transfer to individual plates.

Lamb with Garlic and Dried Red Peppers
Cordero al Ajillo

MAKES 4 SERVINGS

Lambs in Spain belong to either one of these two types, merino, bred for its wool, or churra, bred for its meat and its milk for cheese. This recipe calls for a generous amount of garlic (which mellows as it cooks) and dried red chile peppers — it's an outstanding lamb dish.

PREPARE AT LEAST 2 HOURS IN ADVANCE

2 tablespoons plus 1 teaspoon olive oil

3 pounds boneless lamb, cut into 2-inch pieces

25 garlic cloves, peeled

1 tablespoon ground sweet paprika, such as Spanish smoked

3 bay leaves

¼ teaspoon dried oregano

Kosher or sea salt

Freshly ground black pepper

1 cup dry white wine

½ cup tomato sauce

1 thin slice long-loaf (baguette) bread

2 dried red chile peppers, stemmed and seeded

1. Heat the 2 tablespoons oil in a shallow earthenware casserole dish or Dutch oven over medium-high heat. Add the lamb and 20 of the garlic cloves and cook, stirring, until the lamb is well browned on all sides. Stir in the paprika, then the bay leaves, oregano, salt, black pepper, wine, and tomato sauce.

2. Meanwhile, heat the 1 teaspoon oil in a small skillet over medium heat. Add the bread and cook, turning once, until crisp. Transfer to a mortar. Add the remaining 5 garlic cloves and the chile peppers and mash. Add to the lamb.

3. Cover and simmer 2 hours or until the lamb is tender and the sauce thickens slightly. Remove the bay leaves. If using earthenware, serve hot in the dish, or transfer to individual plates.

Lamb Stew in Garlic Sauce
Cordero al Ajillo

MAKES 4 SERVINGS

Spaniards love their lamb in garlic sauce and here it is paired with even more garlic and fried bread. The sweet red peppers enhance the flavor of the sauce and the paprika adds an earthy accent. This is wonderful served with sautéed, thickly sliced potatoes.

PREPARE AT LEAST 2 HOURS IN ADVANCE

4 tablespoons olive oil

2 thin slices long-loaf (baguette) bread

3 heads garlic, finely chopped separately

3 dried sweet red peppers (ñoras), stemmed and seeded

3 pounds boneless lamb, cut into 1½-inch pieces

1 tablespoon ground sweet paprika, such as Spanish smoked

3 bay leaves

1 teaspoon dried oregano

Kosher or sea salt

Freshly ground black pepper

¼ cup dry white wine

1 pound tomatoes, finely chopped

1. Heat 2 tablespoons of the oil in a small skillet over medium-high heat. Add the bread and cook, turning once, until golden on both sides. Transfer to a mortar or mini-processor, add 1 head of the garlic and the peppers, and mash.

2. In a shallow earthenware casserole dish or Dutch oven, heat the remaining 2 tablespoons of the oil over medium heat. Add the remaining 2 heads of

the garlic and cook, stirring, until fragrant and lightly browned. Add the lamb and cook, turning occasionally, until browned on all sides. Stir in the paprika, bay leaves, oregano, salt, black pepper, wine, and tomatoes. Stir in the mortar mixture, cover, and let cook 2 hours more. If using earthenware, serve hot in the dish, or transfer to individual plates.

Lamb Stew with New Potatoes
Caldereta de Cordero

MAKES 4 SERVINGS

My friend Carmen Serrano gave me this wonderful recipe. There are few ingredients, but the taste is exceptional—it's the dried red peppers (ñoras) that makes the difference.

3 tablespoons olive oil

6 garlic cloves

2 small dried sweet red peppers (ñoras) or 1 dried New Mexico (Anaheim) chile pepper, stemmed and seeded

2 to 2½ pounds boneless leg of lamb, cut into 1½-inch pieces

Kosher or sea salt

Freshly ground black pepper

¾ pound tiny (1½ inch) new potatoes, peeled

⅓ cup dry white wine

¾ cup chicken broth or vegetable broth

1. Heat the oil in a stew pot over medium-low heat. Add the garlic and chile peppers and cook 1 to 2 minutes. Add the meat, season with salt and pepper, and cook, stirring, until the meat is lightly browned. Cover and simmer 30 minutes.

2. Transfer the garlic and dried peppers to a mortar, mash, and return to the pot. Add the potatoes, wine, and broth, cover, and cook, about 8 minutes more or until the potatoes are tender. Serve hot.

Lamb Stew, Extremadura Style
Caldereta Extremeña

MAKES 4 SERVINGS

Extremadura, land of the conquistadores and home to some of Spain's most beautiful villages, has a cuisine that is similar to that of Castile, where Spain's most popular dish, cocido *(a mixture of meats, sausage and chickpeas) originated. Stewing makes the lamb meat more tender and flavorful.*

1 tablespoon olive oil

1 tablespoon lard

6 garlic cloves

1¾ pounds boneless lamb, cut into 1½-inch pieces (or use lamb pieces with bone and increase weight)

1 small onion, finely chopped (about ⅓ cup)

1 bay leaf

½ teaspoon thyme

2 teaspoons ground paprika

½ dried red chile pepper, seeded

Salt

Freshly ground black pepper

¾ cup dry red wine

¼ cup water

1 pimiento

1 tablespoon vinegar

1. Heat the oil and lard in a deep earthenware casserole dish or Dutch oven over low heat. Add the garlic and cook, stirring, until lightly browned. Transfer to a food processor or blender and reserve, and reserve the oil in the casserole dish.

2. Increase the heat to high, add the lamb, and cook, stirring, until browned on all sides. Reduce the heat to medium, add the onion, and cook, stirring, until wilted, about 5 minutes. Stir in the bay leaf, thyme, paprika, chile pepper, salt, and black pepper. Add

continues...

the wine, bring to a boil, and cook until the liquid is reduced and the sauce thickened slightly. Stir in the water, cover, and cook 30 minutes.

3. Meanwhile, add the pimiento to the food processor or blender and process until finely chopped. With the motor running, add the vinegar and enough liquid from the meat (a few tablespoons) to form a smooth, thick sauce. Stir into the lamb, cover, and cook at least 1 hour more or until the meat is tender, adding more water if the sauce thickens too much. Remove the bay leaf. If using earthenware, serve hot in the dish, or transfer to individual plates.

Lamb Stew with Raisins and Honey
Cordero a la Mediterránea

MAKES 4 SERVINGS

The cumin, ginger, cilantro, cinnamon, and honey in this dish are all ingredients characteristic of Moorish cooking. Spain is home to some of the most tender lamb in the world, and most Spaniards prefer lamb to beef. These all join forces in this fabulous recipe where once again the savory is contrasted with the sweet.

2 tablespoons olive oil

3 pounds boneless leg of lamb, cut into 1½-inch pieces

3 medium onions, chopped (about 2 cups)

Kosher or sea salt

Freshly ground black pepper

½ cup chicken broth or vegetable broth

¼ cup raisins

1 teaspoon ground cumin

1 teaspoon ground ginger

1 tablespoon finely chopped fresh cilantro

⅛ teaspoon ground cinnamon

¼ cup honey

1. Heat the oil in a shallow earthenware casserole dish or Dutch oven over medium-high heat. Add the lamb and cook, stirring and seasoning with salt and pepper as it cooks, until browned. Add the onion and cook, stirring, until softened, about 10 minutes. Reduce the heat to low, cover, and simmer 1¼ hours.

2. Stir in the raisins, cumin, ginger, cilantro, and cinnamon, cover, and cook 15 minutes more. Stir in the honey, cover, and cook until the meat is tender. If using earthenware, serve hot in the dish, or transfer to individual plates.

Moorish Lamb Stew with Fruits
Cordero Mozárabe

MAKES 4 SERVINGS

In the province of Seville, there is a wonderful restaurant in Cazalla de la Sierra that specializes in dishes of Moorish influence. It is owned and run by two sisters, Julia and Lucia, who gave me this recipe for pork simmered with cinnamon, nutmeg, and ginger with the addition of prunes, figs, and raisins. The restaurant serves many dishes that combine meat with fruit, but Julia says this one is her favorite.

PREPARE AT LEAST 2 HOURS IN ADVANCE

1½ pounds leg of lamb (boned, reserving the bone)

2 cups dry red wine

1 teaspoon sugar

¼ teaspoon ground cinnamon

1 small onion, finely chopped (about ⅓ cup)

1 bay leaf

6 peppercorns

½ teaspoon finely chopped fresh ginger

⅛ teaspoon grated or ground nutmeg

2 tablespoons brandy

2 cups water

Kosher or sea salt

8 pitted prunes

6 dried figs, cut crosswise into ¼-inch slices

1 tablespoon raisins

Freshly ground black pepper

I. In a stew pot, combine the lamb bone, wine, ⅛ teaspoon of the cinnamon, the onion, bay leaf, peppercorns, ginger, nutmeg, brandy, water, and salt and bring to a boil over high heat. Reduce the heat to low, cover, and simmer 1 hour.

2. Uncover the pot and cook until the liquid is considerably reduced and the sauce slightly thickened. Pass through a fine-mesh strainer, pressing with the back of a soup ladle to extract as much liquid as possible, and return to the pot. Discard the solids. Add the prunes, figs, and raisins and bring to a boil. Reduce the heat to low, cover, and simmer 10 minutes more. Reserve.

3. Preheat the oven to 450°F. Place the meat (tied with string if necessary) in a greased shallow earthenware casserole dish or Dutch oven. Season with salt, pepper, and the remaining ⅛ teaspoon cinnamon. Brush with a little of the sauce. Transfer to the oven and reduce the temperature to 325°F. Roast about 1 hour or until the meat is still slightly pink inside, about 160°F on a meat thermometer.

4. Reheat the sauce. Slice the lamb and spoon the sauce over the lamb. Serve hot. If using earthenware, serve hot in the dish, or transfer to individual plates.

Smothered Lamb Stew
Cordero Estofado

MAKES 6 SERVINGS

I was surprised to find that this recipe calls for a whole head of garlic, but that and the vinegar give this stewed lamb dish its delicious flavor, with paprika adding an earthy accent.

3 tablespoons olive oil

3 pounds boneless lamb, cut into 2-inch pieces

1 large onion, coarsely chopped (about 1 cup)

1 head garlic, separated but unpeeled

1 bay leaf

1 teaspoon ground paprika

½ cup red wine vinegar

Salt

Freshly ground black pepper

I. Heat the oil in a deep earthenware casserole dish or Dutch oven over medium-high heat. Add the lamb and cook, stirring, until well browned on all sides. Add the onions and cook, stirring, until wilted and transparent, about 5 minutes. Stir in the garlic, bay leaf, paprika, vinegar, salt, and pepper.

2. Reduce the heat to low, cover, and cook about 2 hours or until the meat is tender, adding some water if necessary to keep the casserole dish from getting dry. Remove the bay leaf. If using earthenware, serve hot in the dish, or transfer to individual plates.

Lamb and Red Pepper Stew

Cordero al Chilindrón

MAKES 4 SERVINGS

Las Pocholas is a restaurant in Pamplona made famous in the 1930s when travelers from all over the world, including Ernest Hemingway, would gather for the "running of the bulls" in early July. Las Pocholas, run by the six daughters of the original owner, was one of the most famous and elegant restaurants in all of Pamplona. Their cordero al chilindrón, made with a generous amount of red peppers, is the best version I have ever tasted.

PREPARE AT LEAST 2 HOURS IN ADVANCE

2 tablespoons olive oil

2 to 2½ pounds lamb (the amount depends on whether you prefer your stew with or without bones), cut into 1½-inch pieces

Salt

Freshly ground black pepper

1 medium onion, coarsely chopped (about ⅔ cup)

1 garlic clove, finely chopped

3 pimientos, cut into thin strips

1 pound fresh or canned tomatoes, coarsely chopped

1 tablespoon finely chopped fresh flat-leaf parsley

1 bay leaf

I. Heat the oil in a deep earthenware casserole dish or Dutch oven. Add the lamb and cook, stirring, until well browned. Season with salt and pepper. Add the onion and garlic and cook, stirring, until the onion is wilted and transparent, about 5 minutes more. Add the pimientos, tomatoes, parsley, bay leaf, salt, and pepper (if necessary).

2. Reduce the heat to low, cover, and simmer 1½ to 2 hours or until the lamb is tender. Remove the bay leaf. If using earthenware, serve hot in the dish, or transfer to individual plates.

Lamb Meatballs in Brandy Sauce

Albóndigas "Sant Climent"

MAKES 6 SERVINGS AS A MAIN COURSE OR ABOUT 60 APPETIZER-SIZE MEATBALLS

In a valley of the Pyrenees Mountains is a small village, San Clemente de Tahull (Sant Climent in the Catalan language), which is famous for its meticulously preserved church, one of the finest works of Romanesque architecture in all of Spain. This charming village was at one time abandoned, but now it is flourishing, as is the restaurant Sant Climent. Their delicious lamb meatballs in brandy sauce are the best I have ever eaten. To make this more substantial, parboiled potatoes may be added for the last few minutes of cooking.

2 pounds ground lamb

2 large eggs

4 garlic cloves, mashed in a garlic press or mortar

¼ cup finely chopped fresh flat-leaf parsley

Salt

2 tablespoons coarsely ground black pepper

1 cup bread crumbs

¼ cup dry red wine

2 tablespoons olive oil

1 medium onion, finely chopped (about ⅔ cup)

¼ cup brandy, such as Spanish brandy or Cognac

3 tablespoons tomato sauce

1 cup beef broth or lamb broth

I. In a large bowl, combine the lamb, eggs, garlic, parsley, salt, and pepper. In a small bowl, combine the bread crumbs and wine until softened, then add to the lamb mixture and mix well. Shape into about 25 meatballs (or about 60 bite-size meatballs if they are to be served as appetizers).

2. Heat the oil in a large earthenware casserole dish or Dutch oven over medium-high heat. Add the meatballs and cook, turning, until browned on all sides. Add the onion and cook, stirring, until wilted and transparent, about 5 minutes more.

3. Add the brandy. Standing well away from the pot, ignite the liquid with a match or kitchen lighter, then stir until the flames die out. Add the tomato sauce and broth. Taste and adjust seasoning if necessary. Reduce the heat to low, cover, and simmer 45 minutes or until the meatballs are no longer pink and the sauce thickens slightly. If using earthenware, serve hot in the dish, or transfer to individual plates.

Lamb Meatballs, Moorish Style
Albóndigas Al-Andalus

MAKES 4 SERVINGS

What makes these meatballs different from the others in this chapter is that they include a picada of almonds, garlic, and saffron, creating a much richer taste. This recipe originated in Andalucía and calls for ginger and cilantro, again reflecting a Moorish influence.

2 tablespoons olive oil

1 large onion, finely chopped (about 1 cup)

2 pounds ground lamb

1 large egg, lightly beaten

1 teaspoon finely chopped fresh ginger

3 tablespoons finely chopped fresh cilantro

½ teaspoon ground (or mortar-crushed) cumin

2 tablespoons finely chopped fresh flat-leaf parsley

1½ teaspoons salt

Freshly ground black pepper

1½ teaspoons finely chopped fresh thyme or
   ¼ teaspoon dried thyme

1½ teaspoon finely chopped fresh marjoram or
   ¼ teaspoon dried marjoram

2 small sprigs basil

All-purpose flour, for dredging

3 tablespoons finely chopped onion

¾ cup beef broth

½ cup water

Picada

2 garlic cloves, finely chopped

⅛ teaspoon salt

1 tablespoon finely chopped fresh cilantro

Few threads of saffron

8 blanched almonds, finely chopped

1. Heat 1 tablespoon of the oil in a large shallow earthenware casserole dish or Dutch oven over low heat. Add the large chopped onion and cook, stirring, about 5 minutes. Cover and cook until tender but not browned, about 10 minutes more.

2. Meanwhile, in a large bowl, combine the lamb, egg, ginger, 2 tablespoons of the cilantro, the cumin, parsley, salt, pepper, thyme, marjoram, and basil. Add the onions and mix until well combined. Shape into 1½- to 2-inch meatballs. Place the flour in a small shallow bowl and lightly dredge the meatballs in the flour.

3. Heat the remaining 1 tablespoon oil in the casserole dish over medium-high heat. Add the meatballs and cook, turning, until browned on all sides. Add the 3 tablespoons chopped onion and cook, stirring, until the onion is wilted, about 3 minutes more. Stir in the broth and water, cover, and cook 40 minutes.

4. Meanwhile, prepare the sauce: Place all the sauce ingredients in a mortar or mini-processor and mash. When the meatballs are done, stir in the mortar mixture and cook 5 minutes more. Sprinkle with the remaining 1 tablespoon cilantro. If using earthenware, serve hot in the dish, or transfer to individual plates.

Lamb Roasts

Roast Lamb and Potatoes
Cordero Estilo San Vicente

MAKES 4 SERVINGS

In Galicia, long before kitchens had their own ovens, roast lamb prepared in traditional cazuelas were brought to village wood-burning bakery ovens on festive occasions. This delicious recipe for marinated lamb roasted with potatoes came to me from my friend Digna Prieto. In the beautiful fishing village of Cambados, Digna cooked at and managed her restaurant, Crisol, from when she was 17 years old until she was in her eighties.

PREPARE 8 TO 12 HOURS IN ADVANCE

14 garlic cloves, finely chopped

2 bay leaves, crumbled

2 tablespoons finely chopped fresh flat-leaf parsley

¼ teaspoon kosher or sea salt

8 tablespoons olive oil

6 tablespoons dry white wine

1½ to 2 pounds boneless leg of lamb, cut into 2-inch pieces

¼ cup chicken broth or vegetable broth

2 whole cloves

Freshly ground black pepper

1 pound baking potatoes, peeled and cut into ½-inch pieces

⅛ teaspoon saffron threads, crumbled

1. In a mortar or mini-processor, mash one-quarter of the garlic, the bay leaves, parsley, and salt. Stir in 4 tablespoons of the oil and 2 tablespoons of the wine. Transfer to a large bowl, add the lamb and stir to coat well. Cover and let marinate overnight in the refrigerator.

2. Preheat the oven to 375°F. Heat another 2 tablespoons of the oil in a large shallow earthenware casserole dish or Dutch oven over high heat. Add the lamb with its marinade and cook, stirring, until browned. Remove from the heat and add the remaining 2 tablespoons oil, the remaining 4 tablespoons wine, the broth, the remaining three-quarters of the garlic, the cloves, salt, and pepper.

3. Bake 30 minutes. Add the potatoes, season with salt and the saffron, and bake about 30 minutes more or until the potatoes are tender. Serve hot. If using earthenware, serve hot in the dish, or transfer to a platter.

Rosemary-Scented Lamb Roast with Olives
Cordero al Romero con Aceitunas

MAKES 4 SERVINGS

This delightful dish of lamb is flavored by rosemary, olives, and lemon, which add a pleasant zest. In order to prepare it properly, you must sauté the olives with the meat, as they are an integral part of the recipe and not merely a garnish. Rosemary (romero) grows profusely all over Spain and is one of the most popular herbs for cooking with lamb.

PREPARE 8 TO 12 HOURS IN ADVANCE

2 pounds boneless lamb

1 tablespoon ground cinnamon

1 teaspoon ground ginger

1 tablespoon ground hot paprika, such as Spanish smoked

2 lemons, sliced

2 tablespoons olive oil

1 pound onions, sliced

½ pound pitted black olives, preferably Spanish, coarsely chopped

¾ cup dry white wine

½ cup chicken broth or vegetable broth

1 sprig rosemary

1 sprig thyme

Kosher or sea salt

Freshly ground black pepper

1. Rub the meat with the cinnamon, ginger, and paprika. Scatter the lemon over the meat, cover, and refrigerate overnight to meld flavors.

2. Heat the oil in a shallow earthenware casserole dish or Dutch oven over medium-high heat. Add the lamb and cook, stirring, until browned on all sides. Add the onions and olives and cook, stirring, until softened, about 5 minutes. Reduce the heat to low, add the wine, broth, rosemary, and thyme, cover, and cook 45 minutes or until the meat is tender. If using earthenware, serve hot in the dish, or transfer to individual plates.

Roast Lamb, Castilian Style
Cordero Asado, Estilo Castellano

MAKES 6 SERVINGS

Two hundred and fifty years ago, Casa Botín was an inn or posada *in the heart of Madrid's old commercial center. Because travelers who stopped to rent a room and rest their horses also needed something to eat,* posadas *often became restaurants as well. This recipe comes from Casa Botín, which is now a landmark in Old Madrid, famous for the roast baby lamb and roast suckling pig. Popularized by Ernest Hemingway, Casa Botín is next to another popular eatery, near a large sign that proclaims, "Hemingway never ate here."*

3- to 4-pound leg of baby lamb or a 3- to 4-pound shank portion of a leg of lamb

2 tablespoons lard

Salt

Freshly ground black pepper

¼ teaspoon ground paprika

1 garlic clove, mashed in a garlic press or mortar

2 cups water

2 garlic cloves

3 slices medium onion

1 bay leaf

2 sprigs parsley

2 tablespoons vinegar

¼ teaspoon dried rosemary

¼ teaspoon dried oregano

¼ teaspoon ground cumin

Juice of 1 lemon

1. Preheat the oven to 450°F. Rub the lamb with the lard and season with salt, pepper, and the paprika. Rub in the mashed garlic. Place the lamb in a roasting pan and roast 15 minutes.

2. Meanwhile, in a medium saucepan, combine the remaining ingredients and bring to a boil over high heat. Reduce the heat to low and simmer, uncovered, while roasting the lamb, replenishing the sauce with more water if necessary.

3. Reduce the oven to 350°F. Pour about ½ cup of the sauce over the lamb and roast 12 to 20 minutes to the pound (which ranges from medium-rare to well done), depending on the desired doneness. Baste every 10 minutes with more sauce. Slice the lamb. Spoon the sauce onto individual plates and arrange the lamb over the sauce. Serve hot.

Roast Lamb, Aragon Style
Ternasco a la Aragonesa

MAKES 4 SERVINGS

The baby lambs in Castilla are considered the most desirable as they are only a few weeks old. They are usually prepared by simply roasting them in a wood-burning oven. But the lambs eaten in Aragon tend to be older, and they are typically prepared with heavy seasoning, in this case herbs, garlic, and dry white wine. The word ternasco *refers to young lamb. This flavorful dish is even more delicious when served over a bed of potatoes.*

2 pounds new potatoes, peeled and cut into
　　¼-inch slices

Salt

3 tablespoons olive oil, plus more for drizzling

2 (1½-pound) racks of lamb, well trimmed of fat
　　(reserve any meaty scraps)

2 garlic cloves, mashed in a garlic press or mortar

Freshly ground black pepper

1 tablespoon finely chopped fresh thyme or
　　½ teaspoon dried thyme

1 tablespoon finely chopped fresh rosemary or
　　½ teaspoon dried rosemary

¼ cup chicken broth or vegetable broth

4 garlic cloves

¼ cup finely chopped fresh flat-leaf parsley

¼ teaspoon salt

6 tablespoons dry white wine

2 tablespoons brandy

1 teaspoon finely chopped black truffle (optional)

1. Preheat the oven to 400°F. Arrange the potatoes in layers in a well-greased roasting pan, sprinkling each layer with salt and drizzling with a little oil. Sprinkle 2 teaspoons water over the potatoes. Roast 25 minutes.

2. Meanwhile, arrange the racks of lamb, meaty side up, and the lamb scraps, if using, in another roasting pan. Rub with the mashed garlic, brush with 1 tablespoon of the oil, and season with salt, pepper, thyme, and rosemary. Pour the broth around the lamb.

3. When the potatoes have roasted 25 minutes, place the lamb in the same oven, turn the potatoes, and roast 15 minutes more.

4. Meanwhile, in a mortar or mini-processor, mash the 4 whole garlic cloves, the parsley, and the ¼ teaspoon salt. Stir in the remaining 2 tablespoons oil, the wine, brandy, and truffle, if using. Pour over the lamb and continue roasting, adding more broth or water if necessary to keep the pan from drying out, about 10 to 15 minutes more or until the meat registers 145°F on a meat thermometer for medium-rare, or to taste.

5. Transfer the lamb to the stovetop and let sit 10 minutes (you can leave the potatoes in the oven—with the oven off—if they are not overly browned). Cut the lamb into chops and arrange on individual plates with the potatoes. Spoon the pan juices over the chops and potatoes and serve hot.

Roast Lamb, Sepulveda Style
Cordero Asado a la Sepulvedana

MAKES 6 SERVINGS

The village of Sepulveda is located in the province of Segovia where baby lambs are at their finest. This is their version of roast lamb, made more flavorful with garlic and sherry.

3- to 4-pound leg of baby lamb or a 3- to 4-pound shank portion of a leg of lamb

Salt

Freshly ground black pepper

½ teaspoon dried thyme

4 garlic cloves, mashed in a garlic press or mortar

3 tablespoons pure lard

2 tablespoons medium-sweet sherry, such as Oloroso

Preheat the oven to 350°F. Rub the lamb with salt, pepper, the thyme, garlic, and lard. Place in a roasting pan and bake 30 minutes. Pour the sherry around the lamb and roast 12 to 20 minutes to the pound (which ranges from medium-rare to well done), depending on the desired doneness. Baste every 10 minutes, adding water if necessary to prevent the juices from burning. Serve hot.

Rack of Lamb Stuffed with Mushrooms and Scallions
Lomito de Cordero Relleno de Hongos

MAKES 4 TO 6 SERVINGS

In the United States, it is nearly impossible to find lambs as tiny as they are in Spain, so instead I substitute small New Zealand lamb, which are similar in size. The first time I tasted this wonderful rack of lamb dish stuffed with mushrooms and scallions was at the Parador in Plasencia, run by chef Félix Durán in a beautiful historic hotel. Plasencia's most important product is paprika (pimentón). It is interesting to note, though, that pimentón is not included in this recipe.

2 racks baby lamb, about ¾ to 1 pound each

2 tablespoons olive oil, plus more for drizzling

½ cup finely chopped scallions

1½ cups finely chopped mushrooms, such as brown or shiitake, rinsed and trimmed

Salt

Freshly ground black pepper

¼ cup medium-sweet sherry, such as Oloroso

About 2 tablespoons finely chopped fresh thyme or 1 teaspoon dried thyme

3 tablespoons dry white wine

1½ tablespoons fresh lemon juice

1. With a very sharp knife, slit the meatiest part between the chops to create pockets, following the center of each bone and cutting about halfway through. Heat the oil in a medium skillet over low heat. Add the scallions and mushrooms, season with salt and pepper, and cook, stirring, until the mushrooms are softened. Add the sherry and cook until it evaporates. Fill each slit in the racks of lamb with about 1½ teaspoons of the scallion-mushroom mixture. Tie up the racks with kitchen string.

2. Preheat the oven to 400°F. Arrange the racks in a greased roasting pan, drizzle with oil, and season with salt, pepper, and thyme. Roast 15 minutes. Add the wine and lemon juice and roast about 10 minutes more or until the lamb reaches an internal temperature of about 145°F for medium-rare, (or to taste), adding a little water or broth if necessary to keep the pan from drying out. Cut the lamb into individual chops by slicing between the bones. Spoon any pan juices over the lamb and serve hot.

Seasoned Broiled Pork Chops
Chuletas de Cerdo a la Madrileña

MAKES 4 SERVINGS

This popular Spanish dish could not be any easier to prepare. Just broil the pork chops, then top them with garlic, parsley, onion and paprika. An extremely simple dish that is always a favorite with my guests.

Salt
Freshly ground black pepper
4 pork loin chops, about 1 inch thick
2 garlic cloves, finely chopped
2 tablespoons finely chopped fresh flat-leaf parsley
3 tablespoons finely chopped onion
1½ teaspoon ground paprika
3 tablespoons olive oil

1. Season the chops with salt and pepper. In a small bowl, mix the garlic, parsley, onion, paprika, and oil.

2. Place a broiler rack about 6 inches from the heat source and preheat the broiler. Arrange the pork on a greased broiler pan. Spread half of the garlic mixture over the chops. Broil about 5 minutes, turn, spread with the remaining garlic mixture, and broil 5 minutes more or until the internal temperature of the chops reaches 145°F for medium-rare (or to taste). Serve hot.

Baked Pork Chops with Garlic and Lemon
Chuletas de Cerdo al Horno con Ajo y Limón

MAKES 4 SERVINGS

The perfect pork chop recipe for garlic lovers, this recipe is enhanced with the tangy zest of lemons. When served over seasoned roast potatoes, this is a fabulous meal.

8 garlic cloves
¼ cup finely chopped fresh flat-leaf parsley
¼ teaspoon salt
4 tablespoons olive oil
¼ cup fresh lemon juice
3 medium baking potatoes, cut into ⅛-inch slices
Freshly ground black pepper
4 pork chops, 1¼ to 1½ inches thick
¼ cup chicken broth or vegetable broth

1. In a mortar or mini-processor, mash the garlic, parsley, and salt. Stir in 3 tablespoons of the oil and the lemon juice. Spread 2 teaspoons of this mixture over the bottom of a shallow earthenware casserole dish or Dutch oven and arrange half of the potatoes in the dish. Season with salt and pepper. Brush with a little of the garlic mixture.

2. Preheat the oven to 350°F. Heat the remaining 1 tablespoon oil in a medium skillet over medium-high heat. Add the chops and cook until browned on both sides. Season with salt and pepper, brush with some of the garlic mixture, and arrange the chops over the potatoes. Arrange the remaining half of the potatoes over the chops, season with salt and pepper, and spoon the remaining garlic mixture over the potatoes. Add the broth.

3. Cover and bake 45 to 60 minutes or until the potatoes are tender and the internal temperature of the chops reaches 145°F. If using earthenware, serve hot in the dish, or transfer to individual plates.

Pork Chops with Apples in Cider Sauce
Chuletas de Cerdo a la Asturiana

MAKES 4 SERVINGS

Asturias is the region in Spain that produces hard cider. It is a popular drink as well as a common cooking ingredient. In this dish, it is accompanied by apples, which creates a special pork chop dish. Hard cider can be found here in most liquor stores.

All-purpose flour, for dredging

4 pork loin chops, ¾ to 1 inch thick

Salt

1 tablespoon olive oil

2 tablespoons unsalted butter

½ pound apples, peeled, cored, and cut into ½-inch slices

2 tablespoons chicken broth or vegetable broth

½ cup hard cider

Freshly ground black pepper

1. Place the flour on a plate. Season the chops with salt and dredge in the flour. Heat the oil and butter in a large skillet over medium-high heat. Add the chops and cook, turning once, until lightly browned on both sides. Transfer to a platter. Add the apples to the skillet and cook, turning once, about 1 minute.

2. In a shallow earthenware casserole dish or Dutch oven, arrange half of the apples, arrange the chops over the apples, then arrange the remaining apples over the chops.

3. Preheat the oven to 350°F. Deglaze the skillet, adding the broth, cider, salt, and pepper, stirring, and scraping up any bits of flavor. Bring to a boil over medium heat and cook until blended, about 3 minutes, then pour over the chops. Lower the heat to low, cover tightly, and roast 35 minutes, until the pork is tender and cooked through. If using earthenware, serve hot in the dish, or transfer to individual plates.

SPANISH PORK

Pork is more popular than any other meat in Spain. It is rich in flavor, inexpensive, and nutritious. Many people are surprised to learn that pork is actually very low in cholesterol, which led to it being called "the other white meat" in an ad campaign. Spaniards love their pork, whether it is eaten alone or in combination with other meat.

The supreme breed of pigs in Spain is the Iberian pig, which produces the best-quality pork in the world. Iberian pigs are not kept in pens but allowed to roam freely in the *dehesas* of southwestern Spain. The term *dehesa* refers to large expanses of land where pigs and cattle graze and thrive. The predominant trees on the *dehesas* are *encinas*, part of the oak tree family that produces acorns, which are the main diet of the Iberian pigs. The pigs are given a scanty diet until the acorns (*bellotas*) appear in September. Then the pigs roam the fields, free to eat as much as they want until February. By then, they have doubled or tripled their weight. The *bellotas* give a very unique, nutty flavor to the meat. Hams specified "of only *bellota*" are the Rolls Royce of the world's hams. Today, several companies in the United States import these Serrano hams. They are not cheap, but they are a true delicacy.

In February, all throughout Spain, the *matanza* (the killing of the pigs) occurs amid all kinds of celebrations. Then hams, *chorizos*, and sausages are made, usually as a community affair. They are used all year long for cooking because, as they say in Spain, if you want to improve your food, "Add to it some pork!"

Pork Chops with Sherry
Chuletas de Cerdo al Jerez

MAKES 6 SERVINGS

In this recipe, medium-sweet sherry or Oloroso produced in Jerez adds a delightful sweetness to the pork chops. (Cream sherry will make this dish far too sweet.) The slivered blanched almonds lend a nutty taste and texture.

3 tablespoons olive oil

6 pork loin chops, about 1 inch thick

3 ounces slivered blanched almonds

½ cup medium-sweet sherry, such as Oloroso

Salt

1. Heat the oil in a large skillet over high heat. Add the chops and cook, turning once, until browned on both sides. Reduce the heat to medium and cook, turning once, until the internal temperature of the chops reaches 145°F for medium-rare. Transfer to a warm platter.

2. In the same oil over medium heat, add the almonds and cook until lightly golden. Transfer to the platter. Deglaze the skillet, adding the sherry, stirring, and scraping up any bits of flavor. Season with salt. Reduce the heat to low and simmer until the liquid is reduced and the sauce slightly thickened, about 5 minutes more. Pour over the chops. Serve hot.

Marinated Breaded Pork Chops
Chuletas de Cerdo Aliñadas y Empanadas

MAKES 4 SERVINGS

Here the chops are marinated with herbs, garlic, and olive oil, then breaded and sautéed. This results in a tender and especially flavorful meat.

PREPARE 8 TO 12 HOURS IN ADVANCE

Marinade

¼ cup extra-virgin olive oil

1½ tablespoons fresh lemon juice

1 garlic clove, mashed in a garlic press or mortar

1 bay leaf, crumbled

1½ teaspoons finely chopped fresh thyme or
    ¼ teaspoon dried thyme

¾ teaspoon finely chopped fresh oregano or
    ⅛ teaspoon dried oregano

¾ teaspoon finely chopped fresh marjoram or
    ⅛ teaspoon dried marjoram

1½ teaspoons finely chopped fresh rosemary or
    ¼ teaspoon dried rosemary

Salt

Freshly ground black pepper

1½ pounds boneless lean pork loin chops, ½ to ¾ inch
    thick

1 large egg, lightly beaten with 1 teaspoon water

Bread crumbs, seasoned with salt and pepper

2 tablespoons olive oil

1. Prepare the marinade: In a large wide shallow bowl in which the chops will fit in one layer, combine all the marinade ingredients. Add the chops and turn to coat well. Cover and let marinate overnight in the refrigerator.

2. Remove the chops from the marinade and pat dry with paper towels (to make them easier to coat). Discard the marinade. Place the egg wash

and bread crumbs in separate wide shallow bowls. Dip each chop in the egg and dredge in the bread crumbs, coating well.

3. Heat the 2 tablespoons oil in a large skillet over medium heat. Add the chops and cook, turning once, until golden and the internal temperature of the chops reaches 145°F, about 4 minutes per side. Serve hot.

Pork Chops, Rioja Style
Chuletas de Cerdo a la Riojana

MAKES 4 SERVINGS

Any dish that is prepared with the delicious red peppers from the Rioja region is referred to as either a la riojana *or* chilindrón. *This delicious recipe of pork chops with red peppers (here, pimientos) is very popular with Spaniards.*

2 tablespoons olive oil

4 pork chops, ¾ to 1 inch thick

1 medium onion, finely chopped (about ⅔ cup)

1 garlic clove, finely chopped

3 pimientos, cut into thin strips

2 fresh or canned tomatoes, finely chopped

Salt

Freshly ground black pepper

Heat the oil in a large skillet over medium-high heat. Add the chops and cook, turning once, until browned on both sides. Add the onion and garlic and cook, stirring, until the onion is wilted and transparent, about 5 minutes more. Stir in the pimientos, tomatoes, salt, and pepper. Reduce the heat to low, cover, and simmer about 20 minutes more; the pork should be tender. Transfer the chops to individual plates and spoon the vegetables over the top. Serve hot.

Pork Chops, Green Pepper, and Ham
Chuletas de Cerdo con Pimiento y Jamón

MAKES 4 SERVINGS

Another great recipe for pork chops with red peppers, this one adds cured ham and green pepper and omits the tomatoes, creating a meal that is hearty and rich. I like to serve this dish with the pepper mixture on the side instead of on top.

4 tablespoons olive oil

2 medium onions, thinly sliced

1 medium green bell pepper, cut into strips

1 pimiento

1 garlic clove, finely chopped

4 pork loin chops, ¾ to 1 inch thick

¼ pound Serrano (Spanish cured mountain) ham or prosciutto, cut into ¼-inch cubes

Salt

Freshly ground black pepper

1. Heat 2 tablespoons of the oil in a large skillet over low heat. Add the onion, bell pepper, pimiento, and garlic and cook, stirring, about 5 minutes. Cover and cook until the bell pepper is tender.

2. Meanwhile, heat the remaining 2 tablespoons of oil in a large shallow earthenware casserole dish or Dutch oven over high heat. Add the chops and cook, turning once, until browned on both sides. Add the ham and cook, stirring, until lightly browned.

3. Spoon the onion-pepper mixture over the chops and season with salt and pepper. Reduce the heat to low, cover, and cook 20 minutes more; the pork should be tender. If using earthenware, serve hot in the dish, or transfer to individual plates.

Pork Chops with Prunes
Chuletas de Cerdo con Ciruela Pasa

MAKES 4 SERVINGS

Prunes are typical of Catalan-style recipes, where meat is commonly combined with fruit for a sweet and savory flavor. In this dish, the pork chops simmer in prune juice, which tenderizes the meat and gives it an excellent taste.

PREPARE AT LEAST 2 HOURS IN ADVANCE

½ pound pitted prunes

Salt

Freshly ground black pepper

4 pork loin chops, ¾ to 1 inch thick

½ cup red wine

½ cup water

1 cinnamon stick

2½ teaspoons sugar

2 tablespoons olive oil

½ teaspoon cornstarch

½ teaspoon water

1. Place the prunes in a small bowl and add warm water to cover. Let sit at least 2 hours.

2. Season the chops with salt and pepper and let sit while preparing the prunes. Drain the prunes and place in a medium saucepan. Add the wine, water, cinnamon, and sugar and bring to a boil over low heat. Cover and simmer about 20 minutes. Transfer the prunes to a small bowl, reserving the liquid in the saucepan.

3. Heat the oil in a large skillet over high heat. Add the chops and cook, turning once, until browned on both sides. Meanwhile, heat the reserved prune liquid over medium-high heat. In a small cup, dissolve the cornstarch in the water, stir into the prune liquid, and cook 2 minutes until thickened. Spoon the prunes and the sauce over the chops. Serve hot.

Pork Chops in Clove-Spiced Lemon and Honey Sauce
Chuletas de Cerdo en Limón y Miel

MAKES 4 SERVINGS

Here are pork chops Catalan style with Moorish influence reflected by the combination of the sweet-sour flavors of honey and lemon. The cloves and hint of cinnamon complete this tasty, unusual dish.

PREPARE 8 TO 12 HOURS IN ADVANCE

Juice of 1 lemon

Salt

Freshly ground black pepper

4 tablespoons olive oil

3 garlic cloves, finely chopped

4 center-cut rib pork chops, about ¾ inch thick

1½ tablespoons honey

½ cup chicken broth

3 tablespoons dry white wine

3 bay leaves

4 whole cloves

1 cinnamon stick

1. In a deep earthenware casserole dish or Dutch oven, combine the lemon, salt, pepper, 2 tablespoons of the oil, and the garlic. Add the chops, cover, and let marinate overnight in the refrigerator, turning occasionally. Transfer the chops to a platter, reserving the marinade and removing the bay leaves. Season the chops with salt and pepper.

2. Heat the oil in a large skillet over medium-high heat. Add the chops and cook, turning once, until browned on both sides, about 5 minutes. Add the honey, broth, wine, bay leaves, cloves, and cinnamon. Reduce the heat to low, cover, and simmer until the the pork is no longer pink inside, about 5 minutes more.

3. Transfer the chops to a platter and cover lightly with foil. Deglaze the skillet, adding the reserved marinade, stirring, and scraping up any bits of flavor. Cook, stirring constantly, until the liquid is reduced and the sauce syrupy. Add the chops to the sauce and cook, turning to coat, just until heated through. Serve hot.

Pork and Sausage Casserole
Cazuela de Lomo y Butifarra

MAKES 4 SERVINGS

Most recipes that include butifarra *sausage originated in Catalunya. This pork and sausage casserole is a classic Catalan specialty.* Butifarra *can be found in specialty stores.*

1 tablespoon olive oil

4 boneless pork loin chops, ¾ inch thick

½ pound pork sausage (butifarra) links or sweet Italian-style sausage

1 medium onion, chopped (about ⅔ cup)

2 garlic cloves, finely chopped

½ cup dry white wine

4 fresh or canned plum tomatoes, finely chopped (about 1⅓ cups)

1 bay leaf

Salt

Freshly ground black pepper

1 tablespoon finely chopped fresh flat-leaf parsley

I. Heat the oil in a shallow earthenware casserole dish or Dutch oven over medium-high heat. Add the chops and sausage and cook, turning the chops once and the sausage occasionally, until browned. Add the onion and garlic and cook, stirring, until the onion is wilted and transparent, about 5 minutes more. Stir in the wine, tomatoes, bay leaf, salt, pepper, and parsley.

2. Preheat the oven to 350°F. Cover and roast 30 minutes. Transfer the chops to a platter. When done, slice the sausage and add to the chops. Spoon the sauce over the meat. Remove the bay leaf. If using earthenware, serve hot in the dish, or transfer to a platter.

Pimiento- and Cheese-Filled Pork Cutlets
Filetes de Cerdo "Cantamañanas"

MAKES 4 SERVINGS

Cantamañanas *is an expression often used by children in Spain to refer to breaded pork cutlets, a favorite. In this recipe, a mixture of cheese and pimiento is sandwiched between two cutlets.*

1 pound pork cutlets (8 thin cutlets)

4 slices mild cheese, such as Fontina or Jarlsberg

2 pimientos, cut into thin strips

All-purpose flour, for dredging

2 large eggs, lightly beaten

Bread crumbs, for dredging

3 tablespoons olive oil

I. Match up the cutlets by size and shape so that 2 will fit together. Arrange I slice of cheese and several strips of pimiento over 4 of the cutlets. Top with the other 4 cutlets. Pound the edges lightly with a meat pounder (mallet) to seal. Place the flour, eggs, and bread crumbs in separate wide shallow bowls. Dredge each "sandwich" in the flour, dip in the egg, and dredge in the bread crumbs. Let sit about 20 minutes.

2. Heat the oil in a large skillet over medium-high heat. Add the cutlets and cook, turning once, until lightly browned and cooked through, about 2 minutes per side. Transfer to paper towels and let drain. Repeat with any remaining cutlets if needed. Serve hot.

Breaded Pork Cutlets Filled with Sobrasada
Lomo Relleno a la Mallorquina

MAKES 4 SERVINGS

Sobrasada is a soft, spreadable chorizo *from the Balearic Islands that also makes a terrific tapa. It can be found in specialty food stores in the United States and is also available through mail order. This simple recipe calls for a layer of* sobrasada *to be sandwiched between two thin, breaded pork cutlets.*

1½ pounds pork cutlets, (8 thin cutlets)

¼ pound sobrasada, cut into ⅛-inch slices

2 large eggs, lightly beaten

About 1 cup bread crumbs, such as a mix of bread crumbs and Japanese-style panko, for dredging

¼ teaspoon dried thyme

¼ teaspoon dried oregano

¼ teaspoon dried parsley flakes

3 tablespoons olive oil

1. Arrange the slices of sobrasada over 4 of the cutlets. Cover with the remaining 4 cutlets and pound the edges lightly with a meat pounder (mallet) to seal. Place the eggs in a wide shallow bowl. In another wide shallow bowl, combine the bread crumbs, thyme, oregano, and parsley. Dip each cutlet "sandwich" in the egg and dredge in the crumb mixture.

2. Heat the oil in a large skillet over medium-high heat. Add as many cutlets as will comfortably fit and cook, turning once, until lightly browned and cooked through, about 2 minutes per side. Transfer to paper towels and let drain. Repeat with any remaining cutlets if needed. Serve hot.

Lemon- and Garlic-Marinated Grilled Pork Loin
Lomo de Cerdo a la Plancha Bar Bahía

MAKES 4 SERVINGS

Here's a simple dish with few ingredients that appeals to almost everybody. This recipe came from our friend Salvador Lucero who runs Bar Bahía in Cádiz, one of my favorite cities in Spain. Salvador is a real genius at cooking.

4 boneless pork loin medallions, ¼-inch thick

½ lemon

4 garlic cloves, finely chopped

¼ teaspoon dried oregano

Salt

Freshly ground black pepper

1. Arrange the meat in one layer on a platter and sprinkle with the lemon juice and garlic. Cover with foil or plastic wrap and let sit 1 hour at room temperature. (If longer, refrigerate.)

2. Grease a stovetop griddle and heat over medium-high heat to the smoking point. Add the pork and cook, turning once, until browned on both sides and cooked through, about 1 minute per side. Season with the oregano, salt, and pepper. Serve hot.

Marinated Pork Tenderloin with Garlic and Parsley
Medallones de Solomillo Ibérico con Una Majada de Ajo y Perejil

MAKES 4 SERVINGS

I have tasted versions of this dish at some of Spain's most famous restaurants, but never has it been so delicious as when served at the famed olive oil estate of Paco Núñez de Prado, known for their traditional home cooking and their fantastic olive oil, found easily in the United States. They prepare their pork tenderloin using native Iberian pigs, which are the source of the finest ham. This dish can be replicated using the pork tenderloin more commonly found in the United States, but be sure to marinate the meat overnight, as this greatly enhances the flavor.

PREPARE 8 TO 12 HOURS IN ADVANCE

8 garlic cloves, finely chopped
½ cup finely chopped fresh flat-leaf parsley
½ teaspoon salt
6 tablespoons olive oil
1½ pounds pork tenderloin, cut into ½-inch slices

1. In a mortar or mini-processor, mash the garlic, parsley, and salt, then stir in the oil. Place the pork slices in a shallow flat-bottom bowl. Pour the mortar mixture over the pork and turn to coat well. Cover and let marinate overnight in the refrigerator. Drain the pork, letting some marinade cling to it, and reserve the marinade.

2. Grease a stovetop griddle or large skillet with oil and heat over medium-high heat. Add the pork and cook, turning once and brushing with the marinade occasionally, until very lightly browned and just cooked through—do not overcook; the meat should be slightly pink inside. (Cook in batches if necessary to avoid overcrowding.) Season with salt and serve hot.

Pork Tenderloin in Sweet Sherry Sauce
Lomo en Dulce

MAKES 4 SERVINGS

This recipe from the mother of our friend Pilar Vico shows the influence of Andalucía's Moorish heritage in its sweet and savory combination of flavors. It relies on sherry, the quintessential Andalucian wine, to give the pork its distinctive flavor.

All-purpose flour, for dredging
1½ pounds pork tenderloin
Kosher or sea salt
Freshly ground black pepper
2 tablespoons olive oil
½ medium onion, slivered
2 bay leaves
2 tablespoons finely chopped fresh flat-leaf parsley
⅓ cup chicken broth or water
½ cup sweet sherry, such as Spanish cream sherry
¼ teaspoon ground cumin

1. Preheat the oven to 400°F. Place the flour on a dinner plate. Season the pork on all sides with salt and pepper, and dredge in the flour. Heat the oil in a shallow earthenware casserole dish or Dutch oven over medium-high heat. Add the pork and cook, turning occasionally, until browned on all sides. Add the onion and cook, stirring, until wilted and transparent, about 5 minutes more. Stir in the bay leaves and parsley and cook 1 minute more, then stir in the broth, sherry, and cumin and bring to a boil.

2. Cover the casserole dish, transfer to the oven, and roast 35 minutes or until the internal temperature of the pork reaches 150°F. Check occasionally and add a little more broth if necessary to prevent the pan from drying out. Remove the bay leaves. Cut the pork at an angle into ½-inch slices and place on a platter. Spoon the sauce over the pork. Serve hot.

Pork Tenderloin in Orange Sauce
Lomo de Cerdo Asado a la Naranja

MAKES 4 SERVINGS

In this Catalan-inspired dish, the savory flavor of pork is combined with the sweetness of orange juice. I have seen many different versions of this recipe, some dating back to the sixteenth century.

2 tablespoons olive oil

2 (¾-pound) pork tenderloins

Kosher or sea salt

Freshly ground black pepper

½ medium onion, slivered

6 garlic cloves, finely chopped

1 tablespoon finely chopped fresh flat-leaf parsley

1½ teaspoons finely chopped fresh thyme or
    ¼ teaspoon dried thyme

Scant ⅛ teaspoon saffron threads, crumbled

½ cup plus 2 tablespoons fresh orange juice

½ cup plus 2 tablespoons chicken broth or vegetable broth

I. Preheat the oven to 350°F. In a shallow earthenware casserole dish or Dutch oven, heat the oil over medium-high heat. Add the tenderloins and cook, turning and seasoning with salt and pepper occasionally, until browned on all sides. Transfer to a platter. Add the onion and garlic and cook, stirring, until the onion is wilted and transparent, about 5 minutes more. Return the tenderloins to the pan, add the parsley, thyme, saffron, orange juice, and broth, and bring to a boil.

2. Cover the casserole dish, transfer to the oven, and bake about I hour or until the internal temperature of the tenderloins reaches 150°F. Transfer to a platter and cut into ½-inch slices. Spoon the sauce over the pork and serve hot.

Pork Tenderloin with Stewed Onions
Solomillo de Cerdo "Chalo"

MAKES 6 SERVINGS

This pork dish is prepared with a hint of mustard and a generous amount of sweet onions. It is meant to simmer for at least a few hours, which makes the meat tasty and tender. This recipe comes from Chalo Pelaez, a native Madrileño, and one of our dearest friends in the world.

2 (¾-pound) pork tenderloins

Kosher or sea salt

Freshly ground black pepper

2 tablespoons coarse Dijon mustard

2 tablespoons olive oil

4 medium sweet onions, such as Vidalia, coarsely chopped

8 peppercorns

1 tablespoon sugar

Chicken broth or vegetable broth

4 tablespoons ground mustard, mixed with
    3 tablespoons water (optional)

I. Season the tenderloins with salt and pepper, patting the meat so that the salt and pepper adhere. Brush on all sides with the mustard.

2. Heat the oil in a large shallow earthenware casserole dish or Dutch oven over medium-high heat. Add the tenderloins and cook, turning occasionally, until well browned on all sides (it should not be cooked through). Transfer to a platter.

3. Add the onions and cook, stirring, until slightly softened. Reduce the heat to low and cook uncovered, stirring occasionally, about I hour. Stir in the peppercorns and sugar, cover, and cook, stirring occasionally, I hour more, adding some broth if necessary to prevent the casserole dish from drying out.

4. Return the tenderloins to the casserole dish. Cover and cook about 35 minutes or until the internal temperature reaches 145°F. Cut the meat at an angle into ¼-inch slices. Spoon the onions and sauce over the pork, adding more broth if necessary to ensure is enough sauce. Place the mustard dipping sauce, if using, in a small serving bowl. Serve hot with the mustard sauce.

Pork Tenderloin with Sun-Dried Tomatoes, Pine Nuts, and Raisins

Solomillo con Tomates Secos, Piñones y Uvas Pasas

MAKES 4 SERVINGS

This Catalan-style recipe combines the sweetness of raisins, which are produced in the sun-drenched province of Málaga, with the savory taste of pork and sun-dried tomatoes. Pine nuts, which are abundant throughout Castilla, add a perfect nutty taste and texture.

1 (1½-pound) pork tenderloin

Kosher or sea salt

Freshly ground black pepper

2 tablespoons olive oil

2 tablespoons pine nuts

12 garlic cloves, finely chopped

2 sun-dried tomatoes, chopped

1 dried sweet red pepper (ñora), stemmed, seeded, and finely chopped

¼ teaspoon dried oregano

¼ teaspoon dried thyme

10 peppercorns, smashed

2 tablespoons golden raisins

½ cup dry white wine

1 medium tomato, finely chopped (about ⅔ cup)

2 pimientos, cut into thin strips

1. Season the tenderloin with salt and pepper. Heat the oil in a shallow earthenware casserole dish or Dutch oven over medium-high heat. Add the pine nuts, garlic, sun-dried tomatoes, and red pepper, and cook, stirring, until the garlic and nuts begin to color. Add the tenderloin, season with the oregano, thyme, peppercorns, and raisins, and cook, turning occasionally, until browned all around. Add the wine and bring to a boil, then add the chopped tomato.

2. Cover and cook about 15 minutes or until the internal temperature of the tenderloin reaches 150°F. Let sit 5 minutes. Garnish with the pimientos. If using earthenware, serve hot in the dish, or transfer to a platter.

Roast Pork Tenderloin with Sherry, Garlic, and Parsley

Lomo "Huerta de Arriba"

MAKES 6 SERVINGS

Sherry adds its distinctive flavor to this delicious recipe that calls for a minimum of ingredients and is very easy to prepare. Huerta de Arriba *indicates that the pork used in the recipe is bred and fed in the* dehesa *where there are many oak trees on the hilltops and acorns are plentiful (see page 531).*

PREPARE AT 8 TO 12 HOURS IN ADVANCE

6 garlic cloves, finely chopped

½ cup finely chopped fresh flat-leaf parsley

¼ teaspoon Kosher or sea salt

2 (1-pound) pork tenderloins

6 tablespoons dry sherry such as Fino

Chicken broth or vegetable broth

1. In a small bowl, combine the garlic, parsley, and salt. Pat the mixture all over the tenderloins so that it adheres. Let sit overnight in the refrigerator.

continues . . .

2. Preheat the oven to 400°F. Place the tenderloins in a roasting pan and add the sherry. Roast 35 minutes or until the internal temperature of the tenderloins reaches 150°F, stirring in a little broth occasionally to prevent the pan from drying out. Let sit 5 minutes. Cut into thick slices and pour the juice over them. Serve hot.

Breaded Pork Tenderloin with Béchamel
Lomo Empanado de Clara Orozco

MAKES 4 SERVINGS

I owe much of what I know about Spanish cooking to my mother-in-law, Clara Orozco, who lived in Madrid for 88 years. The secret to these breaded pork tenderloins is that they are coated with Clara's "White Sauce," also known as béchamel. She was an excellent cook.

White Sauce (Béchamel)

2 tablespoons unsalted butter

3 tablespoons olive oil

6 tablespoons all-purpose flour

¾ cup chicken broth or vegetable broth

¾ cup milk

Kosher or sea salt

Freshly ground black pepper

⅛ teaspoon grated or ground nutmeg

2 tablespoons olive oil

1 pound pork tenderloin, cut into ⅜-inch slices

Kosher or sea salt

2 large eggs

1 tablespoon grated cheese, such as aged Manchego or Parmesan

½ teaspoon dried parsley flakes

1 cup bread crumbs, such as a mix of bread crumbs and Japanese panko, for dredging

Olive oil, for frying

1. Prepare the sauce: Melt the butter with the oil in a medium saucepan over low heat. Add the flour and cook, stirring, 1 to 2 minutes. Gradually stir in the broth, milk, salt, pepper, and nutmeg and cook, stirring constantly, until thickened and smooth. Let cool, stirring occasionally and reserve.

2. Heat the oil in a large skillet over medium-high heat. Add the pork and cook, turning once and seasoning with salt, until lightly browned and cooked through. (Cook in batches if necessary to avoid overcrowding.) Transfer to a warm platter and repeat for the remaining pork.

3. Dip each pork slice in the sauce, coating completely on both sides. Place on a platter and let sit at least 1 hour in the refrigerator until the sauce solidifies.

4. In a wide shallow bowl, beat the eggs, cheese, and parsley with a fork. Dip the pork in the egg, then dredge in the crumbs. Heat at least ⅛ inch of oil in a large skillet over high heat to the smoking point. Reduce the heat to medium-high. Add the pork and cook, turning once, until lightly golden. (Cook in batches if necessary to avoid overcrowding.) Transfer to paper towels and let drain. Repeat with the remaining pork. Serve hot, or keep warm briefly in a 200°F oven.

Sausage Rolled in Pork Fillet
Lomo Relleno de Salchicha

MAKES 4 SERVINGS

Pork fillets stuffed with sausage are an extremely rich and flavorful combination, especially when sautéed in an onion-and-garlic red wine sauce, and with the addition of sweet diced carrots.

1 pound thin pork sausage links

One (¾-pound) pork loin, cut into 8 very thin slices

All-purpose flour, for dredging

2 tablespoons olive oil

1 medium onion, chopped (about ⅔ cup)

1 garlic clove, finely chopped

1 medium carrot, finely chopped (about ½ cup)

1 tablespoon finely chopped fresh flat-leaf parsley

¾ cup dry red wine

Salt

Freshly ground black pepper

1. Wrap each sausage link in 1 slice of pork loin. Secure with a toothpick. Place the flour in a wide shallow bowl and dredge each link in the flour.

2. Heat the oil in a shallow earthenware casserole dish or Dutch oven over medium-high heat. Add the sausage rolls and cook, turning occasionally, until browned on all sides. Add the onion, garlic, and carrot and cook, stirring, until the onion is wilted and transparent, about 5 minutes more. Add the parsley, wine, salt, and pepper. Reduce the heat to low, cover, and cook 30 minutes. If using earthenware, serve hot in the dish, or transfer to individual plates.

Stuffed Pork Loin

Lomo Relleno

MAKES 4 SERVINGS

One of my favorite tapas bars in Sevilla is Casa Ruperto, which is run by my good friend José Manuel who serves many exceptional dishes created by his uncle Ruperto. This is one of their special dishes—pork loin stuffed with egg, Serrano ham, and pimiento. Ruperto, a charismatic man and a great cook, is now in his eighties but still going strong. Whenever my husband Luis sees Ruperto, they take great joy in singing flamenco songs together.

One (1½- to 1¾-pound) boneless pork loin

Kosher or sea salt

Freshly ground black pepper

1 garlic clove, finely chopped

1 tablespoon finely chopped fresh flat-leaf parsley

2 (jarred) piquillo peppers or 1 small pimiento, cut into thin strips

1 large hard-boiled egg, thinly sliced crosswise

1 ounce Serrano (Spanish cured mountain) ham or prosciutto, cut into very thin strips

2 tablespoons olive oil

All-purpose flour, for dredging

1 small onion, finely chopped (about ⅓ cup)

2 tablespoons finely chopped tomato

2 garlic cloves

4 peppercorns

½ cup dry white wine

1. Butterfly the pork and season with salt, pepper, the chopped garlic, and the parsley. Stuff the pork, arranging the piquillo peppers, egg, and ham over one cut side of the pork. Close the pork and tie securely lengthwise and crosswise with kitchen string as you would a package.

2. Place the flour on a dinner plate. Heat the oil in a stew pot over medium-high heat. Dredge the pork in the flour and place in the oil. Cook, turning occasionally, until browned on all sides. Add the onion and cook, stirring, until translucent. Add the tomato, the whole garlic cloves, and the peppercorns and cook, stirring, 2 minutes more. Reduce the heat to low. Stir in the wine and salt, cover, and simmer 50 minutes to 1 hour more (about 35 minutes per pound) or until the internal temperature of the pork reaches 150°F.

3. Transfer the pork to a warm platter. Continue cooking the sauce, stirring occasionally, until the liquid is reduced and the sauce thickened slightly. Press the garlic cloves with the back of a wooden spoon to extract the flesh, stir into the sauce, and discard the skin. Remove the string from the pork. Cut into ¾-inch slices. Spoon the sauce over the pork and serve hot.

Pork Loin Stuffed with Spinach, Prunes, and Pine Nuts
Lomo de Cerdo Relleno de Espinacas, Ciruelas, y Piñones

MAKES 4 SERVINGS

This wonderful recipe, characteristic of Mallorcan cooking, comes from the Es Menjador restaurant in Manacor. The dish consists of pork loin stuffed with spinach, prunes, and pine nuts and is complemented by a light honey-mustard sauce.

8 prunes

¾ cup cranberry or apple juice

2 cups coarsely chopped spinach leaves, well washed and left slightly damp

Salt

4 teaspoons Dijon mustard

2 teaspoons honey

One (1½-pound) boneless pork loin

Freshly ground black pepper

¼ cup dry white wine

4 teaspoons finely chopped pine nuts

All-purpose flour, for dredging

2 tablespoons olive oil

1 small onion, finely chopped (about ⅓ cup)

½ cup chicken broth or vegetable broth

1. In a small saucepan, combine the prunes and cranberry juice and bring to a boil over low heat. Cover and simmer about 15 minutes or until tender. Meanwhile, place the spinach in a microwave-safe medium bowl, season with salt, cover, and microwave 4 minutes on Low or until softened (or place in a medium saucepan with water to cover and simmer on the stovetop over low heat about 10 minutes). Drain and squeeze dry between paper towels.

2. In a small cup, combine the mustard and honey. Butterfly the pork by cutting horizontally and splitting lengthwise just far enough so that the meat opens up into one flat piece. Brush the cut sides lightly with the mustard-honey mixture and season with salt and pepper. Add the wine to the remaining honey mustard, mix well, and reserve.

3. Drain, pit, and coarsely chop the prunes, discarding the cooking liquid. Arrange the spinach and prunes over one side of the pork and sprinkle with the pine nuts. Close the pork and tie securely lengthwise and crosswise with kitchen string as you would a package. Place the flour on a dinner plate. Season the pork with salt and pepper and dredge in the flour.

4. Heat the oil in a deep stew pot over medium-high heat. Add the pork and cook, turning occasionally, until browned on all sides. Add the onion and cook, stirring, until wilted and transparent, about 5 minutes. Stir in the mustard-honey mixture, the broth, salt, and pepper, cover, and simmer about 45 minutes or until the internal temperature of the pork (not the stuffing) reaches 150°F. Cut the pork diagonally into ¾-inch slices, and spoon the sauce over the pork. Serve hot.

Pork Loin Marinated in Pomegranate Syrup
Lomo de Cerdo en Jarabe de Granada

MAKES 4 TO 6 SERVINGS

The Balearic Islands, where this recipe originated, was home to the Moors for over five hundred years, and many of their local dishes reflect that influence. Meat is often combined with fruit, and pork marinated in pomegranate syrup is a classic dish. Spain has a long history with the pomegranate dating back to 1492 when the Moors were finally expelled from Granada. Pomegranates were incorporated into the Spanish coat of arms to signal the end of Moorish rule in Spain.

PREPARE AT LEAST 2 HOURS IN ADVANCE

2 large pomegranates

½ medium onion, slivered

1 tablespoon finely chopped fresh thyme or
⠀⠀½ teaspoon dried thyme

2 bay leaves, crumbled

1 tablespoon finely chopped fresh rosemary or
⠀⠀½ teaspoon dried rosemary

2 tablespoons finely chopped fresh flat-leaf parsley

¼ cup dry white wine

3 tablespoons extra-virgin olive oil

Salt

Freshly ground black pepper

One (2-pound) boneless pork loin

1. Cut the pomegranate into quarters, remove the seeds, and place them in a food processor. Blend 2 to 3 seconds, just long enough to break the seeds and release the juice. Pass through a fine-mesh strainer—there should be about 1½ cups juice. Place in a small saucepan over medium-high heat and cook until reduced by half. Let cool completely.

2. In a deep medium bowl, combine the pomegranate syrup and all remaining ingredients except the pork. Add the meat and turn to coat. Let marinate in the refrigerator at least 2 hours, turning occasionally.

3. Preheat the oven to 375°F. Transfer the pork to a roasting pan, scatter the onion from the marinade around the pork, and add just enough of the marinade to moisten the pan. Roast about 1 hour 10 minutes (about 35 minutes per pound), adding more marinade occasionally to keep the pan juices from burning, until a meat thermometer inserted into the center of the pork reads 145°F. Remove

from the heat, cover with foil, and let stand 10 minutes until the thermometer reads 150°F. By the time the meat is done, you should have added all the marinade (if more liquid is necessary, add chicken broth or water). Remove the bay leaves.

4. Cut the pork into ¾-inch slices and spoon the sauce over the pork. Serve hot.

Sliced Pork Loin with Pearl Onions and Olives, Murcia Style
Filetes de Lomo con Cebollitas y Aceitunas al Estilo de Murcia

MAKES 4 SERVINGS

Pork loin slices with a sauce of onions, olives, saffron, and hard-boiled egg yolk, is a traditional preparation in the southeastern region of Murcia, an area known for its fresh produce.

20 pearl onions

3 tablespoons olive oil

2 garlic cloves

1 medium carrot, peeled and cut into ⅛-inch slices

¼ cup dry white wine

About ¾ cup chicken broth or vegetable broth

1 bay leaf

Scant ⅛ teaspoon saffron threads, crumbled

⅛ teaspoon kosher or sea salt

Freshly ground black pepper

¼ teaspoon grated or ground nutmeg

1 hard-boiled egg yolk

4 teaspoons fresh lemon juice

16 small green pitted olives, preferably Spanish,
⠀⠀rinsed of their brine

1½ pounds boneless pork loin, cut into ½-inch slices

continues...

1. Bring a large saucepan of water to a boil over high heat, add the onions, and cook 3 minutes. Drain, rinse under cold water, and slip off the skins. (Parboiling makes the onions easier to peel.)

2. Heat 1 tablespoon of the oil in a shallow earthenware casserole dish or Dutch oven over medium heat. Add the garlic and cook, stirring, until browned on all sides. Transfer to a mortar. Add the onions and carrot to the casserole dish and cook, stirring, 1 to 2 minutes. Cover and cook 10 minutes more. Add the wine, ¼ cup of the broth, and the bay leaf, cover, and simmer about 20 minutes or until the carrots are tender.

3. Meanwhile, add to the mortar the saffron, salt, pepper, and nutmeg and mash. Mash in the egg yolk, then stir in the lemon juice and another ¼ cup of the broth. Add the mortar mixture and the olives to the casserole dish, cook 1 minute more, and remove from the heat. Reserve.

4. Heat the remaining 2 tablespoons oil in a large skillet over high heat until very hot. Add the pork and cook, turning once, until browned on both sides and just cooked through. Transfer to a warm platter.

5. Deglaze the skillet, adding a little broth, stirring, and scraping up any bits of flavor, and add to the casserole dish. Heat the sauce over medium heat and cook, stirring constantly and adding more broth as needed to make a medium-thick sauce. Remove the bay leaf. Pour over the meat and serve hot.

Pork Loin with Prunes and Pears

Lomo de Cerdo con Ciruelas y Peras

MAKES 4 SERVINGS

Pork and fruit combine in traditional Catalan style in this recipe, which comes from the island of Mallorca. It calls for the addition of ground almonds and garlic, completing an excellent dish.

½ pound ripe but firm pears, such as small Seckel

Fresh lemon juice

About 1 cup plus 5 tablespoons dry red wine

1 cinnamon stick, broken into 3 pieces

One (1½-pound) boneless pork loin

Salt

Freshly ground black pepper

2 tablespoons olive oil

2 tablespoons brandy

1 small onion, finely chopped (about ⅓ cup)

1 bay leaf

¾ cup chicken broth or vegetable broth

2 ounces blanched almonds (about ⅓ cup)

2 garlic cloves, finely chopped

1½ teaspoons finely chopped fresh thyme or
    ¼ teaspoon dried thyme

1½ teaspoons finely chopped fresh oregano or
    ¼ teaspoon dried oregano

¼ pound mushrooms, rinsed, trimmed, and quartered

12 prunes

1. Peel the pears with a vegetable peeler, rub with the lemon juice, and place in a small saucepan. Add about 1 cup red wine to cover and the cinnamon stick and bring to a boil over high heat. Reduce the heat to low and simmer until the pears are tender when pierced with a knife, about 20 minutes. Remove from the heat, cover, and let the pears steep until needed.

2. Season the pork with salt and pepper. Heat the oil in a deep earthenware casserole dish or Dutch oven over medium-high heat. Add the pork and cook, turning occasionally, until browned on all sides. Add the brandy and, standing well away from the casserole dish, ignite the liquid with a match or kitchen lighter, and let die out. Reduce the heat to medium, add the onion, and cook, stirring, until wilted and transparent, about 3 minutes more. Stir in the 5 tablespoons wine and cook until the liquid is reduced to less than half and the sauce has thickened slightly. Reduce the heat to low, add the bay leaf and ½ cup of the broth, cover, and cook 20 minutes more.

3. Meanwhile, preheat the oven to 350°F. Scatter the almonds on a cookie sheet and toast about 5 minutes or until lightly golden. Let cool. Transfer to a food processor with the garlic, thyme, and oregano and blend until as smooth as possible. With the motor running, gradually add the remaining ¼ cup broth.

4. Add the mushrooms, the almond mixture, and the prunes to the casserole dish. Cover and cook 30 minutes more or until the internal temperature of the pork reaches 145°F.

5. Cut the pears into quarters, core, and cut into ½-inch wedges. Fold into the casserole dish and remove from the heat. Transfer the pork to a platter and cut into ½-inch slices. Arrange the pears in overlapping rows around the pork and arrange the prunes around the pork. Spoon the sauce over the pork and serve hot.

Roasted Pork Loin with Onions and Leeks

Lomo de Cerdo al Horno con Cebolla y Puerros

MAKES 4 SERVINGS

This is a delicious all-in-one meal where pork, vegetables, and potatoes are all roasted together. The recipe calls for leeks, but you should only use the white part and the light-green inner shoots. If you cut them into very thin strips, they will impart more flavor to the rest of the ingredients, as well as making an attractive presentation.

½ pound leeks, trimmed and well washed

2 medium potatoes, peeled

One (1½-pound) boneless pork loin

2 medium onions, slivered

2 medium carrots, peeled and cut into very thin
    2-inch strips

2 garlic cloves

Salt

Freshly ground black pepper

Olive oil

½ cup dry white wine

Chicken broth or vegetable broth

1. Trim and wash the leeks well. Using the white and light-green inner shoots only, cut into very thin 2-inch strips. With a melon scoop or a small spoon, scoop out 1-inch balls of potato.

2. Preheat the oven to 400°F. Place the pork in the center of a roasting pan. Arrange the leeks, potatoes, onions, carrots, and garlic around the pork. Season the pork and vegetables with salt and pepper and drizzle with oil. Roast 15 minutes, then stir in the wine. Bake 45 minutes more, stirring the vegetables occasionally and adding more broth to prevent the pan from drying out, until a meat thermometer inserted into the center of the pork reads 145°F. Remove from the heat, cover with foil, and let stand 10 minutes until the thermometer reads 150°F.

3. Transfer the pork to a platter and cut into ½-inch slices. Spoon the vegetables over the pork and arrange the potatoes around the pork. Deglaze the pan over medium heat, adding a little broth, stirring and scraping up any bits of flavor. Pour over the pork and serve hot.

Seasoned Pork Loin Roast

Lomo de Cerdo Adobado

MAKES 4 SERVINGS

Lomo adobado, when served on a slice of bread, is popular in many tapas bars throughout Spain. This recipe requires that you marinate the pork roast in an olive oil and garlic mixture at least overnight or up to several days. It will keep in your refrigerator for up to a week, and when you are ready to serve it, simply slice the meat and sauté it in oil or butter.

continues...

1 tablespoon ground paprika

2 garlic cloves, mashed in a garlic press or mortar

6 tablespoons olive oil

¼ teaspoon dried thyme

1 bay leaf, crushed

Salt

One (1½-pound) boneless pork loin

Chicken broth or vegetable broth

I. In a small bowl, mix the paprika, garlic, 3 tablespoons of the oil, the thyme, bay leaf, and salt. Rub the pork on all sides with this mixture. Place in a shallow bowl and cover with foil. Let marinate in the refrigerator at least overnight up to several days. Drain and discard the marinade. Remove the bay leaf.

2. Cut the pork into ½-inch slices. Heat the remaining 3 tablespoons oil in a large skillet over medium-high heat. Add the pork and cook, turning once, until browned, about I minute per side. Transfer to a platter. Deglaze the skillet over medium heat, adding a little broth, stirring and scraping up any bits of flavor. Pour over the pork. Serve hot.

Marinated Pork and Potatoes

Picadillo

MAKES 4 SERVINGS

This delicious version of Spanish-style pork hash featuring pork originated in Rioja.

PREPARE 8 TO 12 HOURS IN ADVANCE

3 large potatoes

⅓ cup olive oil

1 bay leaf, crumbled

Salt

Freshly ground black pepper

1 tablespoon finely chopped onion

1 garlic clove, mashed in a garlic press or mortar

1 tablespoon finely chopped fresh flat-leaf parsley

2 teaspoons ground paprika

1¼ pounds pork loin, cut into ½-inch pieces

I. Place the potatoes in a medium saucepan with cold water to cover and add salt. Cover and bring to a simmer over low heat. Cook about 20 minutes or until tender when pierced with a knife. Drain and let cool slightly. Peel and cut into ½-inch pieces.

2. In a large bowl, mix the oil, bay leaf, salt, pepper, onion, garlic, parsley, and paprika. Add the pork and stir to coat well. Cover and let marinate in the refrigerator overnight. Drain and discard the marinade, reserving I tablespoon.

3. Heat the reserved I tablespoon marinade in a large skillet over high heat. Add the pork and cook, stirring, until the slices are lightly browned. Add the potatoes and cook, stirring, until the meat is no longer pink inside and the potatoes are browned. Serve hot.

Pork Roast Simmered in Milk

Lomo de Cerdo con Leche

MAKES 4 TO 5 SERVINGS

This is one of my all-time favorite recipes. Pork is never as tender as when it is simmered in milk, which adds subtle, creamy flavor to a sauce rich in onion, garlic, and peppercorns. This recipe comes from my mother-in-law, an exceptional cook with a Basque background. The milk makes this dish quite special.

PREPARE AT LEAST 2 HOURS IN ADVANCE

1 tablespoon lard or olive oil

One 2-pound boneless pork loin

1 medium onion, coarsely chopped (about ⅔ cup)

1 medium carrot, peeled and coarsely chopped (about ½ cup)

2 cups warm milk

2 garlic cloves, unpeeled

3 peppercorns

Salt

1 tablespoon finely chopped fresh flat-leaf parsley, for garnish

I. Heat the lard in a deep earthenware casserole dish or Dutch oven over medium-high heat. Add the pork and cook, turning occasionally, until browned on all sides. Add the onion and carrot and cook, stirring, until the onion is wilted and transparent, about 5 minutes more. Stir in the milk, garlic, peppercorns, and salt and bring to a boil. Reduce the heat to low, cover, and simmer about 2 hours.

2. Transfer the pork to a platter and the sauce to a food processor or blender. Blend the sauce until smooth, then pass through a fine-mesh strainer into the casserole dish, pressing with the back of a soup ladle to extract as much liquid as possible. Add the pork and cook over medium heat until the pork is heated through. Cut the pork into ½-inch slices. Pour the sauce over the pork and sprinkle with the parsley. Serve hot.

Pork Roast with Peppers and Eggplant
Lomo de Cerdo con Escalibada

MAKES 4 SERVINGS

Roast pork is excellent when served with escalibada, a Catalan mixture of eggplant and peppers. This dish is quite tasty on its own, though I particularly enjoy it with this picante sauce, a spicy cucumber and caper sauce.

Picante Sauce

¼ cup finely chopped onion

1 tablespoon tarragon vinegar

1½ teaspoons white wine

1 pickled cucumber, finely chopped

¼ teaspoon capers, small (nonpareil; whole) or large (finely chopped)

1 tablespoon tomato sauce

Salt

1 tablespoon unsalted butter

2 teaspoons finely chopped fresh flat-leaf parsley

One (2-pound) boneless pork loin

1 garlic clove, mashed in a garlic press or mortar

Dried thyme

Salt

Freshly ground black pepper

2 medium red bell peppers

1 medium green eggplant

One (½-pound) eggplant

1 tablespoon olive oil

1 tablespoon finely chopped fresh flat-leaf parsley, for garnish

¼ cup beef broth or water

I. Prepare the sauce: In a small saucepan, place the onion, vinegar, and wine and bring to a boil over low heat and simmer until the liquid is absorbed, about 5 minutes. Add the cucumbers, capers, tomato sauce, and salt and cook, stirring occasionally, about 10 minutes more. Stir in the butter and parsley. Place on a back burner over the lowest heat to keep hot until needed.

2. Preheat the oven to 450°F. Place the roast in a roasting pan. Rub with the garlic and season with the thyme, salt, and pepper. Place in the oven, reduce the heat to 350°F, and roast 15 minutes. Add the bell peppers and eggplants and roast, turning the vegetables occasionally, 30 minutes more. Transfer the vegetables to a platter. Continue roasting the pork 60 to 70 minutes (about 30 to 35 minutes per pound) or until a meat thermometer inserted into the center of the pork reads 145°F. Remove from the heat, cover with foil, and let stand 10 minutes until the thermometer reads 150°F. Transfer to a separate platter.

continues...

3. Meanwhile, peel the peppers and eggplants and core and seed the peppers. Cut both into strips. Combine the peppers and eggplant in rows (not tossed together) on the platter and season with salt and pepper. Drizzle with the oil and garnish with the parsley. Keep warm (this should not be hot).

4. Deglaze the skillet over medium heat, adding a few tablespoons of broth, stirring and scraping up any bits of flavor. Cut the pork into ½-inch slices and arrange on its platter. Pour the pan juices over the pork. Serve hot with the vegetables on the side.

Pork in Almond Sauce

Carne en Salsa Mesón Poqueira

MAKES 4 SERVINGS

This is a delicious pork dish, enriched with almonds and spiced with plenty of peppercorns. I got the recipe from Mesón Poqueira, a wonderful family-run restaurant in the quaint village of Capileira, which is set high up in the majestic snow-capped Alpujarra mountains of Granada. The almonds reflect an influence by the Moors, who were not expelled from Granada until 1492.

1 teaspoon black peppercorns

2 pounds boneless pork loin, cut into 1-inch pieces

Kosher or sea salt

2 to 3 tablespoons olive oil

1 thin slice long-loaf (baguette) bread

20 blanched almonds

1 dried sweet red pepper (ñora) or ½ New Mexico (Anaheim) chile pepper, cored and seeded

2 garlic cloves

⅛ teaspoon kosher or sea salt

2 tablespoons dry white wine

2 tablespoons finely chopped tomato

1 bay leaf

½ cup chicken broth or vegetable broth

1. In a mortar or mini-processor, crack the peppercorns, transfer to a small bowl, and reserve. Season the pork with salt and let sit at room temperature until needed.

2. Heat the oil in a shallow earthenware casserole dish or Dutch oven over medium heat. Add the bread, almonds, chile pepper, and garlic and cook, turning the bread once and stirring, then transferring each ingredient to the mortar when it turns golden and the pepper when it is slightly softened. Reserve the oil in the pan and remove from the heat. Add the ⅛ teaspoon salt to the mortar and mash, adding the wine a little at a time to aid the mashing.

3. Heat the reserved the oil over medium-high heat. Add the pork and cook, stirring, until browned. Reduce the heat to low, add the tomato and bay leaf, and cook 1 minute more. Stir in the broth, cover, and simmer 15 minutes more. Add the mortar mixture and the reserved peppercorns and simmer 15 minutes more, adding more broth or water if necessary. Remove the bay leaf. If using earthenware, serve hot in the dish, or transfer to individual plates.

Pepita's Pork Stew

Landrilla de Lagartera de Pepita Alía

MAKES 4 SERVINGS

When I was first introduced to this simple recipe, I was surprised at how just a few ingredients could create such a delicious dish. Our friend Pepita, who lives in the village of Lagartera, which is famed for its intricate needlework, is as talented at cooking as she is at embroidering. This is one of the many recipes she has shared with me over the years.

2 tablespoons olive oil

2 pounds boneless pork loin, cut into 1-inch pieces

Kosher or sea salt

1 medium onion, slivered

1 medium tomato, finely chopped (about ⅔ cup)

2 garlic cloves

½ cup dry white wine

1. Heat the oil in a deep earthenware casserole dish or Dutch oven over medium-high heat. Add the pork and cook, stirring and seasoning with salt, until browned on all sides. Add the onion and cook, stirring, until wilted and transparent, about 5 minutes more, then stir in the tomato and cook 1 minute. Reduce the heat to low, cover, and simmer 45 minutes, adding a little water if necessary to prevent the casserole dish from drying out.

2. Meanwhile, mash the garlic in a mortar, then stir in the wine. Stir the mixture into the casserole dish and simmer 15 minutes more. If using earthenware, serve hot in the dish, or transfer to individual plates.

Sweet-and-Sour Pork with Prunes

Estofado de Cerdo Agridulce con Ciruelas Pasas

MAKES 4 SERVINGS

I had my doubts about using 2 tablespoons of sugar in this sauce, but it proved to be an extraordinary dish. The sweetness of the sauce is contrasted by the acidity of the vinegar. This recipe comes from Seville.

12 pearl onions

2 tablespoons olive oil

2 tablespoons wine vinegar

2 tablespoons sugar

2 pounds boneless pork, such as tenderloin, cut into 1-inch pieces

3 garlic cloves, finely chopped

1 medium sweet onion, such as Vidalia, slivered

Kosher or sea salt

Freshly ground black pepper

½ cup chicken broth or vegetable broth

8 pitted prunes

1. Bring a medium saucepan of water to a boil over high heat, add the pearl onions, and cook 3 minutes. Drain, rinse under cold water, and slip off the skins. (Parboiling makes the onions easier to peel.)

2. In a small bowl, combine 1 tablespoon of the oil, the vinegar, and sugar and stir until the sugar is dissolved.

3. Heat the remaining 1 tablespoon oil in a stew pot over medium-high heat. Add the pork, garlic, and the slivered onion and cook, stirring and seasoning with salt and pepper, until the onion is wilted and transparent, about 5 minutes. Stir in the broth, the vinegar mixture, and the prunes. Reduce the heat to low, cover, and simmer 1 hour. Add the pearl onions, cover, and simmer 15 minutes more. Serve hot.

Meatballs Salvador

Albóndigas Salvador

MAKES 4 SERVINGS

This recipe is as simple as it is delicious and is from our friend Salvador Lucero, who owns the Bar Bahía in Cádiz.

continues…

¾ cup bread crumbs

¾ cup chicken broth or vegetable broth

½ pound ground pork

½ pound ground veal

4 garlic cloves, finely chopped

2 tablespoons finely chopped fresh flat-leaf parsley

7 tablespoons finely chopped onion

Generous amount of freshly ground black pepper

⅛ teaspoon grated or ground nutmeg

½ teaspoon salt

1 small egg, lightly beaten

2 tablespoons olive oil

All-purpose flour, for dredging

1 bay leaf

1 small tomato, peeled, seeded, and finely chopped
    (about ½ cup)

¼ cup dry white wine

1. In a large bowl, combine the bread crumbs and ½ cup of the broth until the crumbs are soaked. Lightly mix in the meat, half of the garlic, 1 tablespoon of the parsley, 3 tablespoons of the onion, the pepper, nutmeg, salt, egg, and 1 tablespoon of the oil. Shape into 1½-inch balls. Place the flour in a small shallow bowl and dredge the meatballs in the flour.

2. Heat the remaining 1 tablespoon oil in a shallow earthenware casserole dish or Dutch oven over medium-high heat. Add the meatballs and cook, turning occasionally, until browned on all sides. Add the remaining half of the garlic, 4 tablespoons onion, 1 tablespoon parsley and the bay leaf and cook, stirring, until the onion is wilted and transparent. Stir in the tomato, the remaining ¼ cup broth, and the wine, and season with salt and pepper.

3. Reduce the heat to low, cover, and simmer 45 minutes, adding more broth or water if necessary to prevent the casserole dish from drying out. Remove the bay leaf. If using earthenware, serve hot in the dish, or transfer to individual plates.

Baked Sausage and Mushrooms
Butifarra con Setas

MAKES 4 SERVINGS

Butifarra con setas, *one of Catalunya's most famous dishes, is made with the local sausage combined with wild mushrooms. Catalunyans are mushroom connoisseurs as they have a tremendous variety of mushrooms to choose from, each with a subtly distinctive taste and texture. The flavor of this dish will be slightly different according to which type of mushroom you use. It may also be made in individual casserole dishes.*

1 tablespoon olive oil

1½ pounds pork sausage (butifarra) or sweet Italian-style sausage

¼ cup dry white wine

1 pound mushrooms, small (whole) or medium (halved)

1 garlic clove, finely chopped

1 tablespoon finely chopped fresh flat-leaf parsley

Salt

Freshly ground black pepper

1. Preheat the oven to 400°F. Heat the oil in a large ovenproof casserole dish or Dutch oven over medium-high heat. Add the sausage and cook, stirring, until browned on all sides. Pour off and discard the excess fat.

2. Deglaze the casserole dish, adding the wine, stirring, and scraping up any bits of flavor. Stir in the mushrooms, garlic, parsley, salt, and pepper.

3. Transfer to the oven and roast about 20 minutes or until the mushrooms have softened and the sausages are no longer pink inside. Serve hot.

Sausages with Sweet-and-Sour Figs

Salchichas con Higos Agri-Dulces

MAKES 4 SERVINGS

This Catalan-style recipe pairs sausages with figs in a sweet-and-sour sauce. In the sixteenth century, it was common to prepare flavorful sweet-and-sour sauces, possibly as a means to disguise poor-quality food. But for many years, this type of sauce fell out of favor in Spanish cooking. This dish, which originated in Extremadura, is a rare example of this type of sauce.

PREPARE 8 TO 12 HOURS IN ADVANCE

Figs

1 cup sugar

1 cup red wine vinegar

1 cinnamon stick

4 whole cloves

1 slice lemon

1 pound fresh small green figs

1 tablespoon olive oil

4 tablespoons white wine

1½ pounds sausage, such as sweet Italian-style

¼ cup water

2 teaspoons tomato sauce

Salt

Freshly ground black pepper

1. Prepare the figs: In a medium saucepan, combine the sugar, vinegar, cinnamon, cloves, and lemon and bring to a boil over high heat. Reduce the heat to low and simmer about 5 minutes. Add the figs, cover, and simmer 20 minutes more. Let cool, then cover and let sit overnight at room temperature.

2. Heat the oil and 2 tablespoons of the wine in a medium skillet over medium heat. Add the sausages and cook, turning occasionally, until the sausages are browned. Add the wine and stir the sausages until the wine has been absorbed and the sausages are no longer pink inside. Transfer to a platter.

3. Pour off and discard most of the excess fat. Deglaze the pan, adding the water and the remaining 2 tablespoons wine, stirring, and scraping up any bits of flavor. Reduce the heat to low, add the tomato sauce, salt, and pepper, and simmer about 2 minutes.

4. Drain the figs (the syrup will not be used). Add to the skillet, cover, and cook until the figs are heated through. Serve hot.

Roast Suckling Pig

Cochinillo Asado

MAKES 4 SERVINGS

On weekends, it is not out of the ordinary for Spaniards to travel for miles to small villages that specialize in roast suckling pig, a Castilian specialty. Cochinillo is considered a delicacy, and great care is given to its preparation. An authentic cochinillo should be roasted in a wood-burning baker's oven, using woods such as pine, thyme, or ash to give added aroma to the roast. This can also be done in a home oven, providing you can find pigs that are small enough. The village of Arevalo and the city of Segovia where Meson de Candido, one of the oldest inns in Spain, was located next to the magnificent Roman Aqueduct, are the capitals of roast suckling pig. Have the butcher butterfly the pig if you like.

continues…

5 tablespoons lard

3 garlic cloves, lightly smashed

One (7-pound) baby pig, head on

1 tablespoon water

Salt

1 tablespoon dry white wine

Thyme

1. In a small saucepan, melt the lard with 2 of the garlic cloves over the lowest heat and keep warm until needed. Butterfly the pig by splitting the underside and leaving the backbone and the head intact. Pound on the skin side to flatten slightly. Season both sides with salt.

2. Preheat the oven to 450°F. Put the pig skin side down in a shallow earthenware casserole dish or Dutch oven and add the water and wine. Roast 10 minutes, then reduce the heat to 350°F and roast until the side facing down begins to brown (be careful not to let it stick in the pan). Turn the pig skin side up and pierce the skin several times with a fork. Cover the ears with foil to prevent burning. Continue roasting, basting frequently with the lard, until the skin is deeply golden, shiny, and crunchy. Figure cooking time at somewhere around 3 hours.

3. Remove from the oven and brush once more with the lard. Season with salt. Add to the pan juices a sprinkling of thyme, the remaining 1 garlic clove, well smashed, and a little more wine if desired. Remove the foil from the ears. Present the pig at the table in the casserole dish, if using, or transfer to a platter and pour the juices over the pig and present. Then cut the pig into quarters, remove the head, and serve hot, with its juices.

Pork-Stuffed Baked Apples
Manzanas Rellenas de Cerdo

MAKES 4 SERVINGS

This centuries-old Catalan recipe is still popular today. Baked apples are usually thought of as dessert, but here they are stuffed with a delectable mixture of ground pork, carrots, and raisins, which creates a delicious and unusual main course.

2 tablespoons raisins

8 medium Golden Delicious apples, peeled

Fresh lemon juice

1 tablespoon olive oil

1 large onion, finely chopped (about 1 cup)

2 medium carrots, peeled and finely chopped (about ½ cup)

1½ pounds lean ground pork

Salt

Dash of ground cinnamon

½ teaspoon lemon zest

¾ cup dry white wine

2 tablespoons coarsely chopped pine nuts

½ cup chicken broth or vegetable broth

1 large egg, lightly beaten

½ teaspoon sugar

1. Place the raisins in a small bowl with warm water to cover and let soak 10 minutes. Drain. Hollow out the apples, leaving a shell ¼ inch thick, and reserve the shells. Sprinkle inside and out with the lemon juice. Save several scraps of apple to cover the pork filling as it bakes.

2. Heat the oil in a medium skillet over medium heat. Add the onion and carrots and cook, stirring, 1 to 2 minutes. Reduce the heat to low, cover, and cook 15 minutes more. Increase the heat to medium-high, add the pork, and cook, breaking it up and stirring, until no longer pink. Stir in the salt, cinnamon, and lemon zest, add ¼ cup of the wine, and cook, stirring occasionally, until the

liquid has evaporated. Reduce the heat to low, add the pine nuts, raisins, and ¼ cup of the broth, and simmer about 10 minutes more. Remove from the heat, let cool slightly, then stir in the egg.

3. Preheat the oven to 350°F. In a shallow earthenware casserole dish or Dutch oven, combine the remaining ¼ cup broth, the remaining ½ cup wine, and the sugar. Fill each apple with about 5 tablespoons of the pork mixture, cover with a scrap of apple, and arrange in the dish. Bake about 15 minutes or until the apples have softened. If using earthenware, serve hot in the dish, or transfer to individual plates.

Stuffed Pig's Feet
Manos de Cerdo Rellenas

MAKES 2 SERVINGS

My husband, Luis, is a big fan of this dish— although I will admit that it is not for everyone. You have to like the gelatinous consistency of pig's feet to appreciate it or be an adventurous eater. This version stuffed with mushrooms is quite tasty. Pig's feet are popular in the region of La Mancha, where they are typically served with mashed potatoes. This recipe is easy to double or triple to serve more people.

PREPARE AT LEAST 7 HOURS IN ADVANCE

2 pig's feet, split in half

2 (1-inch) cubes slab bacon

½ carrot, peeled and cut into thick slices

1 small onion, studded with 4 cloves

1 sprig parsley

¼ teaspoon thyme

1 bay leaf

1 cup dry red wine

3 cups chicken broth or vegetable broth

4 peppercorns

Salt

Stuffing

5 tablespoons unsalted butter

¼ cup finely chopped onion

2 garlic cloves, finely chopped

1⅓ cups finely chopped mushrooms (about ½ pound)

1½ tablespoons finely chopped fresh flat-leaf parsley

3 tablespoons bread crumbs

4 teaspoons dry white wine

Salt

Freshly ground black pepper

4 tablespoons olive oil

Bread crumbs, for dredging

1. Tie each pig's foot with kitchen string at 1-inch intervals so it does not fall apart during cooking. Place in a deep pot and add the bacon, carrot, the studded onion, the parsley sprig, the thyme, bay leaf, red wine, broth, peppercorns, and salt. Bring to a boil over high heat. Reduce the heat to low, cover, and simmer at least 7 hours or until the pig's feet are extremely tender. Carefully transfer the pig's feet to a platter, let cool, and remove the string. Gently remove the bones, being careful to keep the feet whole.

2. Prepare the stuffing: Melt the butter in a medium skillet over medium heat. Add the chopped onion and cook, stirring, until wilted and transparent, about 5 minutes. Add the garlic, mushrooms, and the chopped parsley and cook, stirring, about 3 minutes more. Remove from the heat and stir in the 3 tablespoons bread crumbs, white wine, salt, and pepper. Stuff the pig's feet with this mixture.

3. Place a broiler rack about 6 inches from the heat source and preheat the broiler. (Cover the broiler pan with foil for easier cleanup, if you like.) Place the oil and bread crumbs in separate wide shallow bowls. Turn each foot in the oil to coat, then carefully roll in the bread crumbs. Place skin side up in a baking dish and broil 3 to 4 minutes or until golden. Serve hot.

Veal Medallions with Fresh Tomato Sauce
Escalopines Madrileños

MAKES 4 SERVINGS

This is an immensely popular dish in Spain. I have tasted many versions but none as superb as the one served in the beautiful restaurant of the Hostal de San Marcos in León, one of the most magnificent hotels I have ever been in. Their tomato sauce is outstanding.

Tomato Sauce

1 tablespoon olive oil
1 medium onion, finely chopped (about ⅔ cup)
2 medium tomatoes, finely chopped (about 1½ cups)
1 tablespoon finely chopped fresh flat-leaf parsley
Salt
Freshly ground black pepper

Veal

2 large eggs, lightly beaten
1 tablespoon finely chopped fresh flat-leaf parsley
1 garlic clove, mashed in a garlic press or mortar
¼ cup all-purpose flour
1½ pounds veal medallions, cut into very thin slices
¼ cup olive oil

1. Prepare the sauce: Heat the 1 tablespoon oil in a medium skillet over medium heat. Add the onion and cook, stirring, until wilted and transparent, about 5 minutes. Reduce the heat to low, add the tomatoes, the 1 tablespoon parsley, salt, and

pepper, and cook until the tomato is just tender, about 10 to 15 minutes more. (The sauce should have a fresh, rather than cooked, taste.) Place in a serving bowl and reserve.

2. Prepare the veal: Place the eggs in a wide shallow bowl. In another wide shallow bowl, combine the parsley, garlic, and flour. Dredge the veal in this mixture, pressing with the palm of your hand so that it adheres well.

3. Heat the ¼ cup oil in a large skillet over high heat to the smoking point. Dip the veal in the eggs and place in the oil. Cook, turning once, until lightly browned, removing each slice as it browns to a warm platter. Serve hot with the tomato sauce on the side.

Breaded Veal Cutlets, Spanish Style
Filetes de Ternera Empanados

MAKES 4 SERVINGS

This simple dish is a staple at almost every restaurant in Spain and is beloved by children as well as adults — and a favorite of my husband, Luis. A hint of parsley, a splash of lemon juice, and a few tablespoons of olive oil for frying are what make these veal cutlets Spanish style. When you coat the cutlets with the egg mixture and bread crumbs, make sure to press the crumbs into the meat so they adhere well.

1 large egg
1 teaspoon fresh lemon juice
Bread crumbs, for dredging
1 tablespoon finely chopped fresh flat-leaf parsley
1 pound veal cutlets, very thinly sliced
Salt
Freshly ground black pepper
3 tablespoons olive oil

1. In a wide shallow bowl, beat together the egg and lemon juice with a fork. In another wide shallow bowl, combine the bread crumbs and parsley. Season the cutlets on both sides with salt and pepper. Dip in the egg mixture and dredge in the bread crumbs, pressing so that they adhere well. Let sit 20 minutes or until dry.

2. Heat the oil in a medium skillet over high heat to the smoking point. Reduce the heat to medium, add the cutlets, and cook, turning once, until golden on both sides. Serve hot.

Veal with Chorizo and Green Peppers
Ternera a la Extremeña

MAKES 4 SERVINGS

Not only are Spaniards inordinately fond of this veal dish, but it appears on the menu of just about every traditional Spanish restaurant in New York City. I recommend that the veal be of top quality and sliced very thinly. The chorizo makes this an especially rich meal.

1½ pounds veal cutlets, thinly sliced

Kosher or sea salt

1 tablespoon olive oil

1 medium onion, chopped (about ⅔ cup)

1 garlic clove, finely chopped

1 medium green bell pepper, finely chopped (about ⅔ cup)

2 ounces (1 link) chorizo, thinly sliced

6 tablespoons dry sherry, such as Fino

6 tablespoons chicken broth or vegetable broth

2 tablespoons tomato sauce

½ teaspoon dried thyme

1 bay leaf

Freshly ground black pepper

1. Season the cutlets on both sides with salt. Heat the oil in a large shallow earthenware casserole dish or Dutch oven over high heat. Add the cutlets and cook, turning once, until browned on both sides. Transfer to a platter.

2. Reduce the heat to medium, add the onion, garlic, and bell pepper, and cook, stirring, about 5 minutes. Add the chorizo and cook, stirring, about 2 minutes more. Stir in the sherry, broth, tomato sauce, thyme, bay leaf, salt, and pepper. Reduce the heat to low, add the cutlets, and spoon some sauce over them. Cover and cook 15 minutes. Remove the bay leaf. Serve hot.

Veal Chops, Shepherd Style
Chuleta de Ternera al Ajo Cabañil

MAKES 4 SERVINGS

This is a recipe typical of the region of Murcia, famed for their fresh vegetables. Ajo cabañil refers to any sautéed meat prepared with garlic, vinegar, and paprika.

2 tablespoons olive oil

4 veal rib chops, about ¾ inch thick

2 garlic cloves, finely chopped

Salt

Freshly ground black pepper

½ teaspoon ground paprika

1 tablespoon vinegar

1 tablespoon chicken broth, vegetable broth, or water

Heat the oil in a large skillet over high heat. Add the chops and cook, turning once, until well browned. Stir in the garlic, salt, pepper, paprika, vinegar, and broth. Reduce the heat to low, cover and cook about 15 minutes more or until the chops are cooked to taste. Serve hot.

Veal Chops with Beans
Chuleta de Ternera con Habas

MAKES 4 SERVINGS

The most important thing to remember about this dish is that it is not supposed to be a stew. Instead, the veal and beans remain separate but complementary. Galicia is famous for its tender veal, and I first tasted this dish at the Duna 2.0 in La Coruña, a restaurant well known for its Galician specialties.

PREPARE 10 TO 14 HOURS IN ADVANCE

½ pound dried beans, such as white, kidney, or small limas, sorted and washed

1 veal bone

2-ounce piece slab bacon

1 small leek, trimmed and well washed

2 tablespoons olive oil

1 small onion, finely chopped (about ⅓ cup)

2 garlic cloves, finely chopped

3 tablespoons tomato sauce

½ dried red chile pepper, seeded and crumbled

1 bay leaf

Kosher or sea salt

Freshly ground black pepper

4 veal loin chops, about 1 inch thick

1 tablespoon finely chopped fresh flat-leaf parsley, for garnish

1. Place the beans in a large bowl, add cold water to cover by 1 inch, and let soak overnight in the refrigerator. Drain. Place in a stew pot with water to cover. Add the bone, bacon, and leek and bring to a boil over high heat. Reduce the heat to low, cover, and simmer 1 hour.

2. Heat 1 tablespoon of the oil in a medium skillet over medium heat. Add the onion and garlic and cook, stirring, until the onion is wilted and transparent, about 5 minutes. Add to the beans, then stir in the tomato sauce, chile pepper, bay leaf, salt, and

black pepper. Cover and cook about 1 to 1½ hours more or until the beans are tender. Remove the bay leaf. Remove from the heat and let sit covered while preparing the chops.

3. Season the chops with salt. Heat the remaining 1 tablespoon oil in a large skillet over medium-high heat. Add the chops and cook, turning once, until browned. Reduce the heat to medium and continue cooking, turning once, until the chops are still slightly pink in the center, about 15 minutes more. Place on individual plates and place the beans next to the chops. Sprinkle with the parsley and serve hot.

Veal Chops with Ham, Mushrooms, and Pimiento
Chuleta de Ternera Hortelana

MAKES 4 SERVINGS

This delicious dish makes a beautiful presentation due to the colorful, finely chopped vegetables that cover the veal chops. I recommend using the best veal that your butcher has available.

3 tablespoons olive oil

½ cup finely chopped onion

1 garlic clove, finely chopped

2 tablespoons finely chopped Serrano (Spanish cured mountain) ham or prosciutto

1 cup finely chopped mushrooms

2 pimientos, finely chopped

Kosher or sea salt

Freshly ground black pepper

¼ teaspoon dried thyme

4 veal rib chops, about 1 inch thick

¼ cup dry white wine

1 bay leaf

Chicken broth, vegetable broth, or water

1 tablespoon finely chopped fresh flat-leaf parsley, for garnish

1. Heat 2 tablespoons of the oil in a medium skillet over medium heat. Add the onion and garlic and cook, stirring, until the onion is wilted and transparent, about 5 minutes. Add the ham, mushrooms, pimiento, salt, pepper, and thyme and cook, stirring, about 5 minutes more.

2. Meanwhile, season the chops with salt and pepper. Heat the remaining I tablespoon oil in a large skillet over low heat. Add the chops and cook, turning once, until slightly pink in the center, about 15 minutes. Arrange on a warm platter.

3. Deglaze the skillet over low heat, adding the wine, stirring and scraping up any bits of flavor. Stir in salt and pepper, add the bay leaf, and cook 2 or 3 minutes, adding broth if it gets too dry. Arrange the vegetable mixture on top of the chops. Pour the sauce over the chops and sprinkle with the parsley. Serve hot.

Veal Shanks with Apples and Pine Nuts

Jarrete de Ternera con Manzana y Piñones

MAKES 4 SERVINGS

This meal has always been a favorite with my dinner guests. The recipe was given to me by Mercè Vidal who owns Maísa del Cadet restaurant, which is a stone's throw away from the magnificent Poblet monastery in Tarragona. Mercè runs both the restaurant and the hotel like a one-woman show, doing everything from answering phones to helping with luggage. But her true talents come out when she is in the kitchen, and I am very grateful for all the wonderful recipes she has shared with me.

2½ pounds veal shanks, about 1½ inches thick
Salt
Freshly ground black pepper

3 tablespoons olive oil
1 medium onion, chopped (about ⅔ cup)
¼ pound green (Italian) frying peppers, cored, seeded, and finely chopped
16 garlic cloves, finely chopped
2 medium tomatoes, skinned, seeded, and finely chopped (about 1⅓ cups)
2 bay leaves
1 tablespoon finely chopped fresh thyme or ½ teaspoon dried thyme
¼ cup dry white wine
1¼ cups chicken broth or vegetable broth
2 Golden Delicious apples, peeled, cored, and cut into ¼-inch wedges
2 tablespoons pine nuts
2 tablespoons sugar
¼ cup brandy

1. Preheat the oven to 350°F. Season the shanks with salt and pepper. Heat 2 tablespoons of the oil in a shallow earthenware casserole dish or Dutch oven over medium-high heat. Add the shanks and cook, turning once, until browned on both sides. Transfer to a platter. Add the onion, peppers, and garlic and cook, stirring, until the onion is wilted and transparent, about 5 minutes. Add the tomatoes, bay leaves, thyme, salt, and pepper and cook 2 minutes, then stir in the wine.

2. Return the shanks to the casserole dish. Cover and roast 30 minutes. Add the broth and roast I hour more.

3. Heat the remaining I tablespoon oil in a medium skillet over medium heat. Add the apples and pine nuts and cook, stirring, until the nuts are golden. Sprinkle with the sugar and add the brandy. Standing well away from the skillet, ignite the liquid with or match or kitchen lighter and let it die out. Cover and simmer until the apples are softened.

4. Transfer the shanks to a serving platter. Pass the sauce through a fine-mesh strainer and pour over the shanks. Discard the solids. Arrange the apples in overlapping rows around the shanks. Serve hot.

Veal Roasts, Stews, and Ground Meat

Roast Veal
Ternera Asada

MAKES 6 SERVINGS

Here's a preparation for roast veal that could not be easier. Since veal in the United States is not as tender as veal in Spain, I suggest you use a boneless veal roast, cut from either the leg or loin.

2 tablespoons olive oil

One (3-pound) boneless veal roast, cut from the leg or loin

1 medium onion, quartered

¼ teaspoon dried thyme

Salt

Freshly ground black pepper

About 1 cup dry white wine

1. Heat the oil in a large earthenware casserole dish or Dutch oven over medium-high heat. Add the veal and cook, turning occasionally, until browned on all sides. Add the onion and cook until transparent, about 6 minutes.

2. Preheat the oven to 350°F. Transfer the veal to a roasting pan. Season with the thyme, salt, and pepper. Deglaze the casserole dish over medium heat, adding ¼ cup of the wine, stirring and scraping up any bits of flavor. Add to the roasting pan and add another ¼ cup of the wine.

3. Roast about 1¼ hours (about 25 minutes per pound) or until a meat thermometer registers 145°F or to desired doneness, adding more wine as the liquid evaporates. Let sit 10 minutes. Cut the roast into ½-inch slices, pour the pan juices over the slices, and serve hot.

Potted Veal Roast
Caldereta de Ternera

MAKES 6 SERVINGS

This hearty potted veal roast requires that the veal simmer close to two hours in order to properly absorb the flavors of the different ingredients, especially the dry sherry. For this recipe, I recommend a boneless veal roast, cut from the leg or loin. This is a very traditional dish.

2 tablespoons olive oil

One (3-pound) boneless veal roast, cut from the leg or loin

2 large onions, coarsely chopped (about 2 cups)

2 garlic cloves, lightly smashed

½ cup dry sherry, such as Fino

½ cup chicken broth, vegetable broth, or water

2 whole cloves

Salt

Freshly ground black pepper

¼ pound mushrooms, quartered

1. Heat the oil in a deep earthenware casserole dish or Dutch oven over medium-high heat. Add the veal and cook, turning occasionally, until browned on all sides. Add the onion and garlic and cook, stirring, until the onion is wilted and transparent, about 10 minutes.

2. Reduce the heat to low. Add the sherry, broth, cloves, salt, and pepper, cover, and cook about 1 hour (about 20 minutes per pound). Stir in the mushrooms, cover, and cook 15 minutes more, until the mushrooms soften and release their juice and a meat thermometer inserted into the veal registers 145°F or to desired doneness.

3. Let sit 10 minutes. Cut the veal into ½-inch slices, spoon the sauce over the slices, and serve hot.

Veal Stew, Catalan Style
Fricandó de Ternera a la Catalana

MAKES 4 SERVINGS

The stewed veal in this signature Catalan recipe is complemented by a paste of almonds, garlic, parsley, and saffron that is similar to a picada *mash but with a taste all its own.*

All-purpose flour, for dredging

1½ pounds boneless veal, such as shoulder, cut into
     1½-inch pieces

Salt

4 tablespoons olive oil

1 medium onion, chopped (about ⅔ cup)

2 medium tomatoes, peeled and chopped
     (about 1⅓ cups)

1 cup dry white wine

1 cup veal broth, chicken broth, or vegetable broth

1 bay leaf

1 sprig parsley

¼ teaspoon dried thyme

Freshly ground black pepper

6 medium mushrooms, quartered

6 blanched almonds

2 garlic cloves, coarsely chopped

Few threads of saffron

1 tablespoon finely chopped fresh flat-leaf parsley

1. Place the flour in a wide shallow bowl. Season the veal with salt, then dredge in the flour. Heat 2 tablespoons of the oil in a deep earthenware casserole dish or Dutch oven over medium-high heat. Add the veal and cook, stirring, until browned on all sides. Transfer to a platter.

2. Add the onion to the casserole dish, adding more oil if necessary, and cook, stirring, until wilted and transparent, about 5 minutes Add the tomatoes and wine, bring to a boil, and cook until the liquid is reduced by half. Return the veal to the casserole dish, then add the broth, bay leaf, parsley sprig, thyme, salt, pepper, and mushrooms. Reduce the heat to low, cover, and simmer 1 hour.

3. In a food processor, process the almonds until a paste forms. Beat in the garlic, saffron, chopped parsley and the remaining 2 tablespoons oil. Add to the veal, cover, and cook 30 minutes more. Remove the bay leaf. If using earthenware, serve hot in the dish, or transfer to individual plates.

Veal Stew in Sherry Sauce
Ternera en Salsa de Jerez

MAKES 4 SERVINGS

*Jerez is famous for its sherry production, partly because of the sunny weather and partly because of the chalky (*albariza*) soil, which creates the perfect condition for grape vines to thrive. A small amount of dry sherry makes a big difference in the flavor of the sauce.*

2 tablespoons olive oil

1 medium carrot, peeled and thinly sliced

1 small onion, slivered

2 garlic cloves, finely chopped

1 bay leaf

2 pounds boneless veal, such as shoulder, cut into
     ½-inch pieces

Kosher or sea salt

Freshly ground black pepper

¼ cup dry sherry, such as Fino

¾ cup chicken broth or vegetable broth

¼ cup fresh or frozen peas

2 tablespoons finely chopped fresh flat-leaf parsley,
     for garnish

continues...

1. Heat the oil in a stew pot over medium heat. Add the carrot, onion, garlic, and bay leaf and cook, stirring, until the onion is wilted and transparent, about 5 minutes. Add the veal and cook, stirring occasionally and seasoning with salt and pepper as it cooks, until the veal begins to brown.

2. Add the sherry and cook until the liquid is reduced by half. Add the broth, bring to a boil over high heat, cover, lower the heat to low and simmer 1 hour. Add the peas, cover, and cook 10 minutes more.

3. Uncover and cook, if necessary, until the sauce is thickened slightly. Remove the bay leaf. Sprinkle with the parsley and serve hot.

Old-Fashioned Veal Stew with Almonds, Hazelnuts, and Mushrooms
Fricandó al Estilo Antiguo

MAKES 4 TO 6 SERVINGS

This very old recipe was handed down through generations to my friend Cinta Rodríguez of El Pescador restaurant in the town of La Scala. In Cinta's region of Catalunya, the addition of nuts to sauces enhances a great many dishes. The secret to this recipe is the picada *mash, typical in Catalan cooking.*

1½ ounces dried mushrooms, such as porcini

2 tablespoons olive oil

1 thin slice long-loaf (baguette) bread

All-purpose flour, for dredging

2 pounds veal stew meat, cut into ½-inch steaks

Kosher or sea salt

2 medium sweet onions, such as Vidalia, finely
    chopped (about 1⅓ cups)

⅔ cup tomato sauce

Freshly ground black pepper

1¼ cups vegetable broth

½ cup chicken broth

Picada

8 blanched almonds

6 hazelnuts, shelled

¼ teaspoon kosher or sea salt

Freshly ground black pepper

1 teaspoon olive oil

1 teaspoon all-purpose flour

6 tablespoons dry white wine

1. Place the mushrooms in a small bowl, add hot water to cover by 2 inches, and let soak until softened, about 30 minutes. Heat the oil in a shallow earthenware casserole dish or Dutch oven over medium-high heat. Add the bread and cook, turning once, until golden. Transfer to a mortar or food processor and reserve, reserving the oil in the casserole dish.

2. Place the flour on a plate. Sprinkle the veal with salt, then dredge in the flour. In the casserole dish over medium-high heat, add the veal and cook, turning once, until lightly browned on both sides. Transfer to a warm platter and reserve.

3. Drain the mushrooms and let dry on paper towels. In the casserole dish over medium heat, add the mushrooms and cook, stirring, until browned, and transfer to the platter. Add the onions and cook, stirring, 1 to 2 minutes. Reduce the heat to low, cover, and cook 20 minutes more.

4. Stir in the tomato sauce, salt, and pepper, cover, and cook 10 minutes more. Add the reserved meat and mushrooms and the broths, cover, and simmer 45 minutes.

5. Meanwhile, prepare the picada: Preheat the oven to 400°F. Spread the almonds and hazelnuts on a cookie sheet and toast about 5 minutes or until golden. Let cool, transfer to the mortar with the reserved bread, and add salt and pepper. Mash until as fine as possible. Mash in the oil and then the flour. Stir in the wine. Add to the veal, cover, and cook 15 minutes more. If using earthenware, serve hot in the dish, or transfer to individual plates.

Meatballs with Green Pepper and Tomato
Albóndigas en Salsa

MAKES 3 TO 4 SERVINGS

The recipe for albóndigas en salsa *calls for onion, green pepper, and tomato to be added to both the meatballs and the sauce. When the meatballs are coated with egg and cooked briefly, the results are outstanding. This recipe came from our friend Marisé Zubizarreta at Casa Julián in Asturias.*

Meatballs

3 tablespoons olive oil

1 garlic clove, finely chopped

¼ medium onion, finely chopped

½ medium green bell pepper, finely chopped (about ⅓ cup)

One (¼-pound) tomato

1 pound mixture ground veal and ground pork

About 1½ teaspoons salt

Generous amount of freshly ground black pepper

3 large eggs

3 tablespoons bread crumbs

All-purpose flour, for dredging

Sauce

¼ medium onion, finely chopped

1 garlic clove, finely chopped

½ medium green bell pepper, finely chopped (about ⅓ cup)

1 teaspoon all-purpose flour

1 tablespoon tomato sauce

¼ cup dry white wine

1 cup chicken broth or vegetable broth

Kosher or sea salt

Freshly ground black pepper

1. Prepare the meatballs: Heat 1 tablespoon of the oil in a shallow earthenware casserole dish or Dutch oven over low heat. Add the garlic, onions, and bell pepper and cook, stirring, until softened, about 5 minutes. Transfer to a mixing bowl and wipe out the casserole dish.

2. Cut the tomato in half crosswise and gently squeeze to extract the seeds. With a coarse grater held over the mixing bowl, grate each half down to the skin. Discard the skin. Add the meat, salt, pepper, 1 of the eggs, and the bread crumbs. Blend with your hands until well mixed, then shape into 1½-inch meatballs. Place the flour in another small shallow bowl. In a small shallow bowl, lightly beat the remaining 2 eggs.

3. Heat the remaining 2 tablespoons oil in the casserole dish over medium heat. Dredge the meatballs in the flour, dip in the eggs, then place in the oil. Cook, turning occasionally, until browned on all sides and cooked through. Transfer to a platter, reserving the oil in the casserole dish.

4. Prepare the sauce: In the same oil (add a little more if necessary) over medium heat, add the onion, garlic, and bell pepper and cook, stirring, until the vegetables are softened, about 5 minutes. Stir in the flour, then the tomato sauce, wine, broth, salt, and pepper. Reduce the heat to low, cover, and simmer 20 minutes. Return the meatballs to the skillet and cook until heated through. If using earthenware, serve hot in the dish, or transfer to individual plates.

Meatballs in Lemon Sauce
Albóndigas en Salsa de Limón

MAKES 4 SERVINGS

This delicious recipe for pork and veal meatballs has an unusual sauce consisting of lemon, egg yolk, and the distinctive flavor of saffron. It came to me from the mother of our friend Pilar Vico. These meatballs are out of this world and have a taste that is very different than other meatballs I have come across in Spanish restaurants.

6 tablespoons bread crumbs

¼ cup milk

1½ pounds mixture ground veal and ground pork

2 tablespoons finely chopped Serrano (Spanish cured mountain) ham or prosciutto

5 tablespoons finely chopped fresh flat-leaf parsley

3 garlic cloves, finely chopped

1½ plus ⅛ teaspoons salt

½ teaspoon freshly ground black pepper

3 tablespoons plus 1 teaspoon fresh lemon juice

2 large eggs

2 tablespoons olive oil

¼ cup finely chopped onion

¾ cup chicken broth or vegetable broth

3 tablespoons dry white wine

2 large egg yolks

⅛ teaspoon salt

Scant ⅛ teaspoon saffron threads, crumbled

1. In a small bowl, combine the bread crumbs and milk. In a large bowl, mix the ground meat, ham, 2 tablespoons of the parsley, two-thirds of the garlic, the 1½ teaspoons salt, the pepper, 2 tablespoons plus 2 teaspoons of the lemon juice, the softened bread crumbs, and the 2 whole eggs. Shape into 1½-inch balls and dredge in the flour.

2. Heat the oil in a shallow earthenware casserole dish or Dutch oven over medium-high heat. Add the meatballs and cook, turning, until browned on all sides. Add the onion and cook, stirring, until softened, about 5 minutes more. Stir in the broth and wine, bring to a boil, cover, and simmer 40 minutes.

3. In a mortar or mini-processor, mash 2 more tablespoons of the parsley, the remaining one-third of the garlic, the ⅛ teaspoon salt, and the saffron.

4. Transfer the meatballs to a platter. Pass the sauce through a fine-mesh strainer, pressing with the back of a soup ladle to extract as much liquid as possible. Discard the solids. Return the sauce to the casserole dish and stir in remaining 2 teaspoons lemon juice and the mortar mixture.

5. In a small bowl, beat the egg yolks lightly with a fork and stir in a little hot broth. Stir into the casserole dish. Reduce the heat to low and cook, stirring constantly, until thickened (if too thick, add a little more broth or water). Return the meatballs to the sauce and cook until heated through, 2 to 3 minutes. Sprinkle with the remaining 1 tablespoon parsley. If using earthenware, serve hot in the dish, or transfer to individual plates.

Meatballs with Pine Nuts in Tomato Sauce
Albóndigas con Salsa y Piñones

MAKES 6 SERVINGS

What makes these meatballs unusual is that they have no egg or bread fillers. They are comprised of veal and pork seasoned with garlic and parsley. They are not meant to be slowly simmered. Instead, they should be cooked only briefly. The pine nuts add a wonderful taste and texture.

2 pounds mixture ground veal and ground pork

2 garlic cloves, finely chopped

¼ cup finely chopped fresh flat-leaf parsley

¼ cup coarsely chopped pine nuts

1 tablespoon kosher or sea salt

Coarsely ground black pepper

All-purpose flour, for dredging

3 tablespoons olive oil

4 medium carrots, peeled and very finely chopped (about 2 cups)

1 large onion, very finely chopped (about 1 cup)

1 large leek, trimmed, well washed, and very finely chopped

3 cups chicken broth or vegetable broth

¾ cup tomate frito or a mixture of strained tomatoes, 1½ teaspoons sugar, salt, and 1 tablespoon olive oil

12 to 18 tiny (1½-inch) new potatoes

1. In a medium bowl, combine the ground meat, garlic, parsley, pine nuts, salt, and pepper. Place the flour in a small shallow bowl. Shape into 1½-inch meatballs and dredge in the flour.

2. Heat the oil in a large shallow earthenware casserole dish or Dutch oven over medium-high heat. Add the meatballs and cook, turning occasionally, until well browned (they should not be cooked through). Transfer to a platter. Add the carrots, onion, and leek and cook, stirring, 1 minute. Reduce the heat to low, add ¼ cup of the broth, cover, and cook about 35 minutes or until the vegetables are tender.

3. Meanwhile, place the potatoes in a medium saucepan with cold water to cover and add salt. Cover and bring to a simmer over low heat. Cook about 10 minutes or until tender when pierced with a knife. Drain and let cool slightly. Peel.

4. Stir the tomato and the remaining 2¾ cups broth into the casserole dish and simmer 10 minutes. Add the meatballs and simmer 3 to 4 minutes more or until the meatballs are heated through. Stir in the potatoes and cook about 1 minute more. If using earthenware, serve hot in the dish, or transfer to individual plates.

Organ Meats

Calves' Liver with Garlic and Vinegar
Higado en Ajo Cabañil

MAKES 2 SERVINGS

In this recipe, the strong taste of liver is tempered by a zesty vinegar and paprika combination. The liver should be fried very quickly over high heat.

2 tablespoons olive oil

½ to ¾ pound calves' liver, thinly sliced

6 tablespoons water

2 garlic cloves, finely chopped

2 tablespoons red wine vinegar

½ teaspoon ground paprika

Salt

Freshly ground black pepper

1. Heat the oil in a medium skillet over high heat. Add the liver and cook, turning once, until browned but not yet cooked. Transfer the liver to a platter.

2. Reduce the heat to medium. Deglaze the skillet, adding the water, stirring and scraping up any bits of flavor. Add the garlic, vinegar, paprika, salt, and pepper, then the liver slices and cook, turning once, until the liver is cooked to taste, adding more water if necessary to prevent the skillet from drying out. Serve hot.

Calves' Liver and Green Peppers

Higado con Pimientos Verdes

Here is a simple recipe for thinly sliced liver sautéed with peppers and onions in a dry white wine sauce.

2 tablespoons olive oil

2 medium onions, thinly sliced

3 medium green bell peppers, cut into strips

Kosher or sea salt

1 pound calves' liver, thinly sliced

¼ cup dry white wine

Freshly ground black pepper

1. Heat the oil in a medium skillet over medium heat. Add the onions and cook, turning occasionally, until wilted and transparent, about 8 minutes. Transfer to a medium bowl and reserve. In the same oil (add more if necessary) over medium heat, add the bell peppers and cook, stirring, 2 minutes. Reduce the heat to low, cover, and cook 10 to 15 minutes more or until tender. Transfer to the bowl with the onions, reserving the oil in the skillet.

2. Season the liver with salt. In the reserved oil (add more if necessary) over high heat, add the liver and cook, turning once, until cooked to taste. Transfer to a warm platter.

3. Deglaze the pan over medium heat, adding the wine, stirring, and scraping up any bits of flavor. Pour over the liver. Return the onions and peppers to the skillet, season with salt and pepper, and cook until the vegetables are heated through. Spoon the vegetables over the liver and serve hot.

Liver in Sorrel Sauce

Figado con Ruibarbo

MAKES 4 SERVINGS

The quaint Mesón de Cándido in the historic city of Segovia is one of the oldest inns in Spain. Located at the foot of the city's two-thousand-year-old Roman aqueduct, its longtime owners, Cándido and his family, have an impressive display of memorabilia—from gastronomic awards they have won to photographs of famous guests, and even a special display cabinet reserved for royal signatures only. Mesón de Cándido is best known for its Castilian specialties such as baby lamb and suckling pig roasted in a wood-burning oven. Figado con ruibarbo, liver cooked in a sauce of lettuce, sorrel, vinegar, and wine, is one of Cándido's lesser known dishes. In Spain, this is prepared with rhubarb leaves, but here I have substituted sorrel leaves.

3 tablespoons olive oil

1 medium onion, slivered

1¼ pounds calves' liver, cut into 1¼-inch pieces

1½ teaspoons all-purpose flour

1 teaspoon ground paprika

⅛ teaspoon ground cayenne pepper

1 Romaine lettuce heart (about 2 ounces), coarsely chopped

¼ pound sorrel leaves, stems trimmed (if unavailable use 2 teaspoons sorrel purée)

¼ cup red wine vinegar

¼ cup dry red wine

2 garlic cloves, coarsely chopped

½ teaspoon dried thyme

1 bay leaf

Salt

Freshly ground black pepper

1 tablespoon finely chopped fresh flat-leaf parsley, for garnish

1. Assemble all the ingredients and do all the cutting and chopping before beginning; otherwise, the liver will overcook. Heat the oil in a medium skillet over high heat. Add the onion and liver and cook, stirring, until both are browned.

2. Reduce the heat to low and stir in the flour, paprika, and cayenne pepper. Add the lettuce and the sorrel and cook, stirring, until the sorrel is wilted (or the puree is heated through). Stir in the vinegar, wine, garlic, thyme, bay leaf, salt, and pepper and simmer until the liver is lightly pink within. Remove the bay leaf. Sprinkle with the parsley and serve hot.

Kidneys in Sherry Sauce
Riñones al Jerez

MAKES 4 SERVINGS

The most popular way of preparing kidneys in Spain is in sherry sauce, or al Jerez. I was not a fan of kidneys until I tasted this recipe, in which the sherry provides the perfect contrast. Use only the freshest kidneys from a reputable butcher.

3 pounds very fresh veal kidneys

Juice of 3 lemons

Kosher or sea salt

Freshly ground black pepper

2 tablespoons olive oil

2 medium onions, finely chopped (about 1⅓ cups)

2 garlic cloves, finely chopped

2 tablespoons finely chopped fresh flat-leaf parsley

2 tablespoons all-purpose flour

1½ cups dry sherry, such as Fino

1½ cups beef broth, chicken broth, or water

1. Place the kidneys in a medium bowl, add the lemon juice, and let sit 10 minutes. Cut into ¾-inch pieces, removing all fat and membrane. Rinse under hot water and let drain on paper towels. Season with salt and pepper.

2. Heat the oil in a medium skillet over high heat. Add the kidneys and cook, turning once, about 1 minute. Transfer to a platter. Add the onions, garlic, and parsley and cook, stirring, until the onion is wilted and transparent, about 5 minutes, adding more oil if necessary. Stir in the flour and cook 1 minute. Add the sherry and broth and cook, stirring, until thickened and smooth. Reduce the heat to low, cover, and simmer 10 minutes more.

3. Pass through a fine-mesh strainer and return to the skillet. Discard the solids. Add the kidneys to the skillet and simmer until the kidneys are just slightly pink within, 5 to 10 minutes more—do not overcook because the kidneys will become tough. Serve hot.

Desserts and Drinks

COOKIES

Crisp Butter Cookies Ⓥ

Old-Fashioned Olive Oil Wafers Ⓥ

Crisp Almond Wafers Ⓥ

Almond Crisps Ⓥ

Raspberry Almond-Crisp Sandwiches Ⓥ

Crispy Almond Tile Cookies Ⓥ

Meringue Wafers with Almond Butter Ⓥ

Cream Cookies Ⓥ

"Cat's Tongue" Cookies Ⓥ

Almond–Pine Nut Cookies Ⓥ

Sugar Cookies "Uncastillo" Ⓥ*

Saint Clara's Cookie Rings of Aunt Javiera Ⓥ

Almond Cookies, Granada Style Ⓥ*

Almond Cookie "Sandwiches" Ⓥ

Cinnamon and Lemon-Scented Cookies Ⓥ

Flan-Filled Fried Cookies Ⓥ

Albarracín Almond Cookies Ⓥ*

Chewy Almond Cookies Ⓥ

Powdered Sugar Cookies, Seville Style Ⓥ

Powdered Sugar Flower Cookies Ⓥ

Powdered Sugar Cookies with Lemon Zest

Powdered Sugar Cookies with Wine Ⓥ*

Flaky Sugar Cookies Ⓥ*

CAKES AND TARTS

Almond Cupcakes Ⓥ

Spanish-Style Cupcakes Ⓥ*

Galician Almond Cake Ⓥ

Almond and Potato Cake Ⓥ

Orange Cake Ⓥ

Orange-Almond Cake Ⓥ

Ⓥ = Vegetarian   Ⓥ* = Vegetarian with one change

Orange Yogurt Cake Ⓥ

Orange Ice Cream Cake Ⓥ

Chocolate Custard Cake Ⓥ

Custard-Filled, Liqueur-Flavored Cake Ⓥ

Segovia's Custard and Marzipan Cake Ⓥ

Custard-Filled Cake Roll Ⓥ

Chocolate Charlotte Ⓥ

Peach Yogurt Torte Ⓥ

Apple Tart from Madrid Ⓥ

Basque Apple Custard Tart Ⓥ

Almond and Egg Yolk Tart Ⓥ*

Cheese Tart, Extremadura Style Ⓥ

Puff Pastry Tart Ⓥ

Sixteenth-Century Cheesecake Ⓥ

Apple Flan Loaf with Caramelized
Sugar Syrup Ⓥ

~~~~~~

PASTRIES AND TURNOVERS

Breakfast Fritters Ⓥ

Apple Fritters Ⓥ

Basic Fritters Ⓥ

Cream-Filled Fritters Ⓥ

Sweetened Chickpea Fritters Ⓥ

Fritters from Xàtiva Ⓥ

Fresh Goat Cheese Fritters Ⓥ

Anise-Flavored Fried Pastries Ⓥ

Fried Pastries with Anise and Sesame Seeds Ⓥ

Sugar-Dusted Pastry Puffs Ⓥ

Sugared Puff Pastry Strips with Almonds Ⓥ

Sweet Potato Dessert Turnovers Ⓥ*

Goat's Milk Cheese Tartlets Ⓥ

Spiced Stewed Apples in Puff Pastry Ⓥ

Frosted Puff Pastries Ⓥ

Spanish "French Toast" Ⓥ

Fried Bread and Honey Ⓥ

Crisply Sautéed Bread in Honey Syrup Ⓥ

Pastries with Squash Marmalade and Honey Ⓥ

Spiced Doughnuts Ⓥ

Miniature Anise-Flavored Doughnuts Ⓥ

Custard-Filled Mini Doughnuts Ⓥ

Baked Doughnuts Bathed in Honey Ⓥ

Custard-Filled Fried Pastries Ⓥ

Spaghetti Squash Turnovers Ⓥ*

Almond and Marmalade
Puff Pastry Strips Ⓥ

Custard Horns Ⓥ

Sweet Spinach Custard in
Puff Pastry Horns Ⓥ

Pastries Filled with Marmalade
and Almonds Ⓥ*

Walnut-Filled Turnovers Ⓥ

Fig and Candied Squash Pastries Ⓥ

Sweetened Potato Puffs Ⓥ

Candied Egg Yolk Pastries Ⓥ

Walnut-Filled Fried Pastries with Honey Ⓥ

Mallorcan Orange-Flavored
Turnover Dough Ⓥ*

Cheese Turnovers Ⓥ

Córdoba's Sugar-Coated Fried Pastries Ⓥ*

Flowers Coated with Honey Ⓥ

Puff Pastry Pie with Spaghetti
Squash Marmalade Ⓥ

Strawberries Fried in Sherry Batter Ⓥ

Custard-Filled Dessert Crepes Ⓥ

Crepes Filled with
Cinnamon Apple Sauce Ⓥ

FLAN, CUSTARDS, AND PUDDINGS

Caramel Custard (Flan) Ⓥ

Flan, Canary Style Ⓥ

Apple Flan Ⓥ

Orange Flan Ⓥ

Coconut Flan Ⓥ

Chocolate Flan with Almond-
Flavored Chocolate Sauce Ⓥ

Walnut and Egg White Flan in
Caramelized Custard Sauce Ⓥ

Sugar-Crusted Custard Ⓥ

Rich Caramel Mini Custards Ⓥ

Almond Milk Custard

Gossamer Lemon Custard Ⓥ

Soft Custard with Walnuts Ⓥ

Grandma's Soft Custard with Walnuts
and Cornmeal Fritters Ⓥ

Fried Custard Ⓥ

Rice Pudding, Asturian Style Ⓥ

Rice Pudding Flan with Rum

Apple Pudding with Custard Sauce Ⓥ

Warm Anise-Scented Pudding
with Fried Bread Bits Ⓥ

Chocolate-Sherry Chiffon Pudding Ⓥ

Rennet Pudding with Honey Ⓥ*

Cottage Cheese Bread Pudding Ⓥ

Pastries in Soft Custard Ⓥ

Almond "Soup" Ⓥ

Banana and Almond Cream Ⓥ

Sweetened Condensed Milk Ⓥ

Caramelized Condensed Milk Ⓥ

Strawberry Meringues Ⓥ

Vanilla Ice Cream with Hot Banana Sauce Ⓥ

Frozen Almond Cream Ⓥ

Prune Ice Cream with
Orange Liqueur Sauce Ⓥ

Frozen Walnut "Cake" with Candied
Walnuts and Chocolate Sauce Ⓥ

Coffee-Flavored Refrigerator Log Ⓥ

Cream Cheese Ice Cream
with Raspberry Purée Ⓥ

Crackling Caramelized Pine Nuts with
Ice Cream Bathed in Honey Sauce Ⓥ

FROZEN DESSERTS

Frozen Lemon Cream in Lemon Shells Ⓥ

Red Wine Sangria Sorbet Ⓥ

White Sangria Sorbet with
Melon and Kiwi Fruit Ⓥ

Cava Sorbet Ⓥ

Strawberry and Wine Vinegar Sorbet Ⓥ

Frozen Orange Custard with
Blackberry Sauce Ⓥ

Turrón Ice Cream Ⓥ

Almond Crisps with Yogurt Ice
Cream and Honey Ⓥ

FRUIT DESSERTS

Almond- and Raisin-Filled Baked Apples Ⓥ

Baked Apples with Raisins in
Custard Sauce Ⓥ

Baked Apples Filled with
Catalan Custard Ⓥ

Caramelized Oranges Ⓥ

Bananas with Honey and Pine Nuts Ⓥ

Melon Balls in Sweet Sherry Ⓥ

Summer Berries with Yogurt Cream Ⓥ

Apples in Spiced Wine Syrup Ⓥ

Stewed Prunes and Apricots Ⓥ

Autumn Fruit in Grape Syrup Ⓥ

Pears Steeped in Red Wine and
Sherry Syrup Ⓥ

Dried Apricots in Red Wine Syrup Ⓥ

Oranges in Honey and Olive
Oil "Núñez de Prado" Ⓥ

Peaches Steeped in Red Wine Ⓥ

Baked Peaches in Sherry Syrup Ⓥ

Pears in Wine Sauce Ⓥ

Strawberries with Sugar and Vinegar Ⓥ

SAUCES AND MARMALADES

Rich Almond Sauce Ⓥ

Raspberry Purée Ⓥ

Strawberry and Kiwi Fruit Purée Ⓥ

Peach or Apricot Marmalade Ⓥ

Quince Marmalade Ⓥ

Candied Spaghetti Squash Marmalade Ⓥ

CANDY

Candied Almonds Ⓥ

Candied Egg Yolks Ⓥ

Almond and Egg Yolk Candies Ⓥ

Candied Egg Yolk in Almond Roll Ⓥ

Marzipan Candies Ⓥ

Coconut Candies Ⓥ

DRINKS

Sangria Ⓥ

Tiger Nut Milk Ⓥ

Flaming Liquor with Apples Ⓥ

Cinnamon-Flavored Ice Milk Ⓥ

Hot Chocolate, Spanish Style Ⓥ

Dessert courses are not nearly as popular in Spain as they are in the United States, and many Spanish restaurants feature only very simple desserts on their menu. At the end of a meal, typical offerings include cheese and fruit, flan, or ice cream. Extraordinary pastries are always sold in great variety at local *pastelerías*, but more often than not, they are eaten as snacks between meals, with afternoon tea, or as Sunday treats.

Many Spanish desserts are often linked to religious events and are traditionally eaten on holidays. On All Saints Day, *Huesos De Santo* ("Saint's Bones") and *Buñuelos de Viento* (light and airy fritters) are popular. On Christmas, turrón and marzipan candies are served. Two kinds of *turrón* are available commercially in specialty stores and supermarkets that have Latin and Spanish products: soft (*jijona*) and hard (*alicante*). *Jijona* is a sweet almond paste and is the one that is referred to in the recipes. On Easter, *torrijas* (sugar-coated fried bread or what Americans call "French Toast") are found all over. During the festival of Madrid's patron Saint, San Isidro, all the pastry shops sell *Buñuelos de San Isidro* (Crème Filled Fritters), and on Saint Clara's Day *rosquillas de Santa Clara* (iced doughnuts) are the pastries to buy.

The link between Spain's desserts and religion is much more encompassing than just the tradition of eating certain desserts on specific holidays. Candy making was once the domain of nuns. There are many wine companies in Rioja and Jerez de la Frontera that used egg whites as a method for removing any particles that could make the wine cloudy. When the wine makers found themselves with a surplus of egg yolks, they donated them to convents. Subsequently, the nuns built thriving businesses selling *yemas* (egg yolk candies), and to this day these convent recipes are closely guarded

secrets. The heavy use of egg yolks has become characteristic in Spanish dessert recipes. Egg whites are mainly used for meringues, for iced milk desserts, and as the leavening agent for cakes.

Dessert making in Spain owes much to the influence of the Moors, who were not expelled from Granada until the fifteenth century. Ingredients such as almonds, egg yolks, and honey have been staples in Spain ever since. Ground almonds often replace flour in cake baking. Milk desserts are often spiced with cinnamon and lemon, sometimes with anisette liqueur added. The most popular dessert in Spain is fried pastries, which are often coated with honey and flavored with anise seeds. No matter how many I buy or make, they disappear in no time. Surprisingly, even though Spain brought chocolate from the New World and introduced it to the rest of Europe, there are only a handful of Spanish dessert recipes that call for chocolate.

Marmalades and purées are often included in other dessert recipes. They are the perfect accompaniment to simple custards and ice creams and are also delicious fillings for pastries and turnovers. Some of the desserts you will find here are traditional and classic, while some are more innovative and exotic. All of them can be prepared with ingredients easily found in the United States.

Spain is known throughout the world for its wines, even more so in recent years, and Spaniards love wine with their meals. Other drinks are enjoyed as well, and I finish this chapter with several classic drinks, such as Sangria and Cinnamon-Flavored Ice Milk (*leche merengada*). Several, such as Iced Tiger-Nut Milk (*horchata*) are enjoyed in summer months almost like slushy frozen desserts.

Cookies

Crisp Butter Cookies ⓥ
Galletas María de Reinosa

MAKES ABOUT 35 COOKIES

Called galletas María, *these are the most common cookies in Spain. They are not too sweet and are very crisp, as opposed to* pastas, *which are sweeter and richer; see Almond Pine Nut Cookies, page 577, and Powdered Sugar Cookies, page 582, for example. They are based on the traditional butter cookies from the town of Reinosa in the mountains of Santander, an area known for its fine-quality butter. To this day, Reinosa continues to be one of the principal cookie-producing centers of Spain, and every household there has a large box of these* galletas.

1¾ cups all-purpose flour

⅛ teaspoon salt

2 tablespoons cornstarch

½ teaspoon baking soda

½ teaspoon cream of tartar

1 teaspoon powdered malted milk

½ cup plus 2 tablespoons sugar

¼ pound (1 stick) unsalted butter, cut into small cubes

1 large egg

1 tablespoon honey

1 teaspoon grated coconut

¼ teaspoon pure vanilla extract

1. In a large bowl with a fork or in the bowl of a food processor or mixer, combine the flour, salt, cornstarch, baking soda, cream of tartar, malted milk, and sugar. Cut the butter into the flour mixture using two knives or forks pulled in opposite directions, or blend in the processor or mixer, until the mixture resembles fine crumbs.

2. In a small bowl, whisk together the egg, honey, coconut, and vanilla. Stir into the flour mixture with a rubber spatula or add to the processor or mixer. Work the mixture with your hands, or process or mix, until a dough forms.

3. On a floured surface, roll the dough out into a wide rectangle ¼ inch thick.

4. Preheat the oven to 300°F. Line a cookie sheet with foil and grease the foil. To imprint the cookies, you can gently cut a design partway through the dough with the dull side of a knife (or better still, press an imprinted rolling pin, the kind used to make sprinkle cookies, over the dough, then cut with a knife to separate into individual cookies, following the imprinted lines). Otherwise, cut the dough into 1¾ x 2-inch rectangles.

5. Place on the cookie sheet 1 inch apart and bake, turning the tray frequently from back to front and side to side to brown evenly, 15 to 18 minutes or until a very deep golden color. Remove from the oven, transfer to a cooling rack, and let cool. Serve at room temperature. Store in a covered container.

Old-Fashioned Olive Oil Wafers ⓥ
Antiguas Tortas de Aceite

MAKES 6 LARGE WAFERS

This recipe originated centuries ago, in the town of Castilleja de la Cuesta, just outside of Seville. These large, flaky wafers are not overly sweet, and they are usually eaten for breakfast or as an afternoon snack. They are also the perfect accompaniment to custards and frozen desserts. Tortas de aceite *are derived from Moorish* alcorzas, *little wafers that were baked or fried. It is not unusual to find them in American supermarkets, but they are better homemade.*

1 tablespoon sesame seeds

2 teaspoons ground anise seeds

¼ cup mild olive oil

Peel of ¼ lemon (yellow part only)

¼ pound uncooked pizza dough

1½ teaspoons sweet anise liqueur

About ½ cup all-purpose flour

About 2 tablespoons sugar

I. Preheat the oven to 350°F. Spread the sesame and anise seeds in a cake pan and toast, stirring occasionally, about 8 minutes or until lightly browned. Transfer to a mortar or mini-processor and mash until as finely ground as possible.

2. In a small skillet, heat the oil and lemon peel over high heat until the peel is blackened. Discard the peel, let the oil cool, and reserve.

3. In a large bowl, combine the seeds, dough, the reserved oil, and the liqueur. Gradually work in the flour until the dough holds together. Turn out onto a work surface and knead lightly, incorporating more flour if necessary. Roll the dough out with a rolling pin until it has the thickness of a nickel. Cut into 4¼-inch rounds, using an inverted bowl of that size as a guide or a biscuit cutter.

4. Place a broiler rack about 5 inches from the heat source. Increase the oven temperature to 375°F. Grease a cookie sheet. Roll the rounds lightly with the rolling pin to return them to their 4¼-inch size (the rounds tend to shrink once cut). Transfer with an offset spatula to the cookie sheet then sprinkle I teaspoon of the sugar over each wafer.

5. Bake on the middle oven rack about 12 minutes or until the bottoms of the wafers are lightly browned.

6. Meanwhile, preheat the broiler. Place the cookie sheet under the broiler and broil until the tops are golden and the sugar melted. Serve at room temperature. Store individually wrapped in wax paper in a covered container.

Crisp Almond Wafers ⓥ
Almendrados Carmen

MAKES 20 LARGE COOKIES

Almond cookies are very popular in Spain and there are countless recipes for their preparation. This version of large, airy almond wafers comes from our dear friend Carmen Martín, who got the recipe from the handwritten cookbook of her mother.

1 cup sugar

½ pound blanched almonds (about 1⅓ cups)

2 large eggs, separated

1 teaspoon lemon zest

Ground cinnamon

I. Preheat the oven to 350°F. Place the sugar and almonds in a food processor and blend until the almonds are finely chopped (but not a paste).

2. In a medium bowl, beat the egg whites with an electric mixer until thick and stiff (and hold their shape when you lift the beater) but not dry. Gently fold in the egg yolks and the lemon zest, then fold in the sugar-almond mixture.

3. Line a cookie sheet with foil and grease the foil. Drop the dough, 2 tablespoons at a time, onto the cookie sheet 3 inches apart—the cookies will more than double in size during baking.

4. Sprinkle with the cinnamon and bake about 10 minutes or until golden. Let cool on the cookie sheet and peel off the foil. Serve at room temperature.

Almond Crisps Ⓥ
Crujientes de Almendra

MAKES TWELVE 3½-INCH COOKIES

These delectably crisp, almond-flavored cookies are among my very favorites. They are extremely easy to prepare and can be served alone or with other desserts, such as ice cream or custard.

⅔ cup (about 4 ounces) slivered blanched almonds
⅔ cup sugar
2 tablespoons all-purpose flour
½ teaspoon lemon zest
⅛ teaspoon salt
6 tablespoons sweet unsalted butter

1. Preheat the oven to 350°F. Line a cookie sheet with foil and grease the foil. In the bowl of a food process or, place the almonds, sugar, flour, lemon zest, and salt and beat until the almonds are as finely chopped as possible. Add the butter and pulse until the butter is fully incorporated and the mixture holds together.

2. Shape the dough into 12 (1½-inch) balls and place on the cookie sheet 2 inches apart. Flatten gently with your fingers into 2½-inch rounds. Bake about 10 minutes or until golden all over. Let cool slightly, then carefully transfer with an offset spatula to a cooling rack and let cool. Serve at room temperature. Store in a covered container.

Raspberry Almond-Crisp Sandwiches Ⓥ
Pastelillos de Frambuesa

MAKES 6 SANDWICH COOKIES

Cookie sandwiches (two cookies with a filling in between them) are very popular in Spain. In this recipe, raspberries and whipped cream are sandwiched between two almond wafers and covered with raspberry purée. The tastes and textures blend beautifully, creating an excellent dessert.

1 recipe (12) Almond Crisps (at left)
1½ recipes (12 tablespoons) Raspberry Purée (page 596)
12 tablespoons thick whipped cream, sweetened to taste
¾ pound fresh raspberries or other berries
Powdered (confectioners) sugar, for dusting
Raspberries or other berries, for garnish

1. Prepare the cookies and purée. Spread 1 tablespoon of the whipped cream on each of 6 cookies. Divide about 24 raspberries among the cookies, arranging them on the whipped cream. Spread each of the remaining 6 cookies with 1 tablespoon whipped cream and place cream side down over the raspberries to make 6 cookie sandwiches.

2. Spoon 2 tablespoons of the raspberry purée onto each of 6 dessert plates. Place 1 cookie sandwich on top of the sauce, then dust with powdered sugar and garnish with 1 or more raspberries on top of the cookie. If not serving all the cookies immediately, fill as many as you are serving. Reserve the remaining cookies and filling, separated, to fill at a later date.

Crispy Almond Tile Cookies Ⓥ
Tejas de Almendra

MAKES ABOUT 16 COOKIES

The name of these crispy almond cookies comes from the Spanish word teja, meaning a curved roof tile, which is the shape they resemble. These delectable cookies are on the menu of many of Spain's most elegant restaurants, and at the end of the meal, they are often served complimentary with coffee and after-dinner drinks. They can be eaten on their own or as accompaniments to ice cream, custard, or fruit desserts.

6 tablespoons unsalted butter, softened

1¼ cups sifted powdered (confectioners) sugar

3 large unbeaten egg whites

½ cup all-purpose flour

Sliced almonds

1. Preheat the oven to 325°F. Line a cookie sheet with foil and grease the foil well with butter (you will have to make the cookies in several batches). In a large bowl with a wooden spoon or in the bowl of a mixer, beat the butter and powdered sugar until combined. Add the egg whites one at a time and mix well after each addition. Stir in the flour and continue to mix until the batter is smooth and thin, about the consistency of a pancake batter.

2. Drop the batter by level tablespoons onto the cookie sheet 2 inches apart. With a rubber spatula, spread with a swirling motion into thin rounds about 3 inches across. Sprinkle well with the almonds. Bake about 12 minutes or until the edges are lightly browned and the center is cooked.

3. Remove from the oven and let cool a few seconds on the cookie sheet, then carefully lift one cookie at a time with a metal offset spatula and place the underside of the cookie over a rolling pin. Press the cookie edges down to give it a good shape. Transfer to cooling rack and let cool. Repeat for the remaining cookies (if the cookies become too crisp to shape, return them to the oven for a minute to soften). Serve at room temperature. Store in a covered container.

Meringue Wafers with Almond Butter Ⓥ

Láminas de Merengue con Mantequilla de Almendra

MAKES 8 SERVINGS

When my husband Luis was a child in Madrid, every Sunday his grandfather would take him to El Riojano pastry shop, still open today on Mayor Street, to buy meringues for the afternoon meal. Meringues are made with egg whites and have always been popular in Spain as they are airy, light, and delicious. This recipe is for meringue wafers coated with rich almond butter and constructed like Napoleons.

4 large egg whites, at room temperature

½ teaspoon cream of tartar

½ cup superfine sugar

1 cup sifted powdered (confectioners) sugar

5 ounces blanched almonds, whole or slivered (about 1 cup)

¾ cup plus 2 tablespoons unsalted butter

Sliced almonds, skin on, for garnish

1. Preheat the oven to 200°F. Line two lightly greased cookie sheets with parchment paper. Cut a piece of heavy cardboard to 5½ x 4 inches. With a razor blade or similarly sharp tool, cut out a 3½ x 2-inch rectangle from the center of the cardboard, leaving a 1-inch frame.

2. In a small bowl, beat the egg whites with an electric mixer until foamy, add the cream of tartar, and gradually beat in the superfine sugar. Continue beating until thick and stiff (and hold their shape when you lift the beater) but not dry. Fold in the powdered sugar. Place the cardboard frame on the parchment paper and, with a rubber spatula, fill the frame with a ¼-inch layer of meringue. Carefully remove the frame and repeat to make 16 rectangles, using 2 cookie sheets. If there is extra meringue, make a few more to allow for breakage.

3. Bake 2 hours or until crisp and dry all the way through (they should not brown). Turn off the oven, leave the door slightly ajar, and let sit in the oven 15 minutes more. Remove from the oven and let cool on the cookie sheets. Carefully lift the meringues from the parchment and replace.

continues…

4. Turn the oven on and set to 400°F. Scatter the almonds on a cookie sheet and toast about 5 minutes or until well browned. Let cool, then transfer to a food processor and blend until very finely chopped. Add the butter, blend until well mixed (may be made ahead and refrigerated until ready to use).

5. With a narrow rubber spatula, spread about 2 tablespoons of the almond butter (slightly softened if refrigerated), over 8 meringues. Cover each with a second meringue and spread a very thin coating of the almond butter on top. Place in paper or foil cupcake liners. Sprinkle with the sliced almonds and serve at room temperature.

Cream Cookies V
Galletas de Nata

MAKES ABOUT 18 COOKIES

The recipe for these coconut cookies from the Canary Islands calls for butter, a touch of cream, a lot of lemon peel, and a little coconut. These rich and buttery short cookies are best when sprinkled with sugar.

6 tablespoons unsalted butter

1 large egg yolk

5 tablespoons sugar

½ teaspoon lemon zest

2 tablespoons heavy cream

¼ teaspoon ground cinnamon

1 tablespoon flaked or shredded coconut

⅛ teaspoon ground anise seeds

1 cup plus 3 tablespoons all-purpose flour

¼ teaspoon baking soda

1 large egg, lightly beaten with 1 teaspoon water, for brushing

Granulated sugar, for sprinkling

1. Preheat the oven to 350°F. In a medium bowl, beat the butter with an electric mixer until light colored and fluffy. Beat in the egg yolk and sugar, then beat in the lemon zest, cream, cinnamon, coconut, and anise. In a small bowl, combine the flour and baking soda and stir into the butter mixture until a smooth dough forms.

2. Roll out on a floured surface to ¼ inch thick and cut with a cookie cutter (about 2½-inch size) into desired shapes. Brush with the egg and sprinkle with sugar.

3. Bake 10 to 12 minutes or until well browned. Serve at room temperature.

"Cat's Tongue" Cookies V
Lenguas de Gato

MAKES ABOUT 70 COOKIES

Lenguas de gato are crisp, wafer-thin cookies that are the perfect accompaniment to custard desserts or ice cream. These traditional cookies can be found in pastry shops all over Madrid. Because they are so thin, you have to be careful not to burn them.

¼ pound (1 stick) unsalted butter

¾ cup powdered (confectioners) sugar

¼ teaspoon pure vanilla extract

⅛ teaspoon lemon peel (optional)

2 large egg whites

¾ cup all-purpose flour

Pinch of salt

1. In a medium bowl, beat the butter with an electric mixer until light colored and fluffy. Add the powdered sugar, vanilla, and lemon zest and beat another minute. Add the egg whites and beat until the mixture is smooth and very light textured. Gradually stir in the flour and add the salt.

2. Put the dough in a pastry bag or cake decorator fitted with a ¼-inch round opening (#11 or #12). Squeeze the dough in 2½-inch lengths onto a greased cookie sheet 2 inches apart (the dough will spread when baked).

3. Preheat the oven to 350°F. Bake 5 minutes or until the cookies are very lightly browned around the edges—watch carefully because they burn easily. Transfer with an offset spatula to a cooling rack and let cool. Serve at room temperature.

Almond–Pine Nut Cookies Ⓥ
Pastas de Piñones

MAKES 12 COOKIES

Whenever I am in Madrid, I go to the El Riojano bakery off the Puerta del Sol to buy a box of these sensational cookies. Most Spanish almond cookies are crisp, but these, made with ground almonds instead of flour, are soft and chewy with the delightful crunch of pine nuts.

¼ cup pine nuts
¼ pound slivered blanched almonds (about 1 cup)
½ cup sugar
1 large egg white
1 teaspoon anisette or other sweet liqueur
¼ teaspoon ground cinnamon
½ teaspoon lemon zest

1. Preheat the oven to 350°F. Spread the pine nuts on a cookie sheet and bake about 5 minutes—watch carefully because they burn easily. Remove from the oven, let cool on the cookie sheet, and reduce the oven temperature to 325°F. Line a cookie sheet with foil and grease the foil.

2. In a food processor, place the almonds and sugar and process until as finely ground as possible. Pulse in the egg white, anisette, cinnamon, and lemon zest until a dough forms. Shape into 12 (1-inch)

balls and place on the cookie sheet 2 inches apart. Press with your fingers into 2-inch rounds, then lightly press some pine nuts into the cookies. Bake about 10 minutes or until lightly colored. Serve at room temperature.

Sugar Cookies "Uncastillo" Ⓥ*
Mantecados Uncastillo

MAKES ABOUT 14 COOKIES

This recipe for sugar cookies comes from Uncastillo, a charming town named after its castle on top of a hilltop in Navarra, and home to the magnificent Romanesque Santa Maria church. My husband Luis and I stopped in to a very crowded local bakery to buy a bag of sugar cookies, cut into a variety of shapes. They were so sensational that I immediately went back to the bakery to acquire the recipe from the chief baker. Make it vegetarian with vegetable shortening or butter.

1½ cups all-purpose flour
⅓ cup sugar
1½ tablespoons lightly beaten egg
¼ pound lard, preferably pure lard, vegetable shortening, or unsalted butter, softened

1. Preheat the oven to 350°F. Line a cookie sheet with foil and grease the foil. Place all the ingredients in a medium bowl and work the mixture with your hands until a dough forms.

2. Roll out on a floured surface to ½ inch thick. Cut into shapes about 2½ inches in size.

3. Place on the cookie sheet 1 inch apart and bake 15 minutes or until well browned. Serve at room temperature.

Saint Clara's Cookie Rings of Aunt Javiera ⓥ
Rosquillas Listas de Santa Clara de la Tía Javiera

MAKES ABOUT 20 COOKIES

Pastelería del Pozo, located in Callejón del Pozo, a small street in Madrid, has been one of the most famous pastry shops in Madrid for over two hundred years. These cookies are typically eaten on the day of San Isidro (patron saint of Madrid) and come in three varieties: listas (literally the "clever" cookies, bathed in sugar syrup and dipped in a lemon and sugar glaze), tontas (the "stupid" ones, with no glaze), and those of Santa Clara, covered in an egg white and sugar wash. My favorites have always been the Santa Clara version with its white coating. Many years ago, pastry makers from surrounding villages set up stands in Madrid on the day of San Isidro. The most popular stand was run by a woman referred to as Aunt Javiera. Ever since that time, these delicious but not too sweet cookie rings (rosquillas) have been linked to her name.

Cookies

2 large eggs
2 large egg yolks
1 large egg white
2 tablespoons granulated sugar
5 tablespoons mild olive oil
1 teaspoon ground anise seeds
2 tablespoons sweet anisette liqueur
2¼ cups all-purpose flour

Glaze

1 large egg white
1 cup powdered (confectioners) sugar

1. Preheat the oven to 400°F. Line a cookie sheet with foil and grease lightly. In a medium bowl, whisk together the whole eggs and egg yolks until foamy. Whisk in the granulated sugar, the oil, anise seeds, and anisette. Stir in the flour, then work the mixture with your hands to form a smooth ball. Cover with plastic wrap and let sit in a cool spot 1 hour.

2. Divide the dough into 20 equal pieces. Shape each piece into a 5 x ½-inch rope. Join the ends to make a circle, sealing the ends well. Place on the cookie sheet about 2 inches apart and bake about 15 minutes or until lightly golden. Let cool on the cookie sheet.

3. Meanwhile, prepare the glaze: In a small bowl, whisk the egg white until foamy. Add the powdered sugar and beat until smooth and thickened.

4. Dip the tops of the cookies in the sugar glaze and return to the cookie sheet, glazed side up. Place for a few minutes in a warm oven (with the heat off) to dry. Serve at room temperature.

Almond Cookies, Granada Style ⓥ*
Granadinas

MAKES 20 COOKIES

When the Moors controlled Granada, they planted almond tree groves that flourished in that climate. These almond-rich cookies called Granadinas are native to Granada. These cookies will stay crisp several weeks in a metal tin. In Spain, however, they are eaten soft. To soften, wrap the cookies lightly in wax paper and let sit at room temperature about 6 days. Make it vegetarian with vegetable shortening.

1 cup all-purpose flour

¾ cup finely ground blanched almonds

½ cup granulated sugar

Pinch of salt

¼ teaspoon ground cinnamon

¼ pound (½ cup) lard or vegetable shortening

1 large egg, lightly beaten

Powdered (confectioners) sugar, for dusting

1. Preheat the oven to 300°F. Place the flour in a heavy skillet over low heat and cook, stirring occasionally with a wooden spoon, until golden but not browned, about 7 minutes. (This process gives the flour a "nutty" flavor.) Let cool and transfer to a medium bowl. Add the almonds, sugar, salt, and cinnamon and mix to combine. Add the lard and egg and work the mixture with your hands until a dough forms. Shape the dough into 20 (1-inch) balls and place on an ungreased cookie sheet 2 inches apart. Flatten the centers of the cookies with your index finger.

2. Bake about 30 minutes or until golden. Let cool. Dust with powdered sugar. Serve at room temperature. Store in a metal tin or wrapped in wax paper depending on your cookie texture preference.

Almond Cookie "Sandwiches" Ⓥ
Rusos de Alfaro

MAKES ABOUT 24 SANDWICH COOKIES

These are the cookies that made the town of Alfaro famous. They are made with only almonds, sugar and egg white, with a filling of almonds and egg cream. "Cookie sandwiches" are very popular in Spain, and there are many different versions. Rusos de Alfaro cookies are commonly found at roadside stops along the main routes in La Rioja. They are wafer thin and extraordinary.

½ pound blanched almonds (about ⅔ cup)

1½ cups powdered (confectioners) sugar, plus more for dusting

4 large eggs, separated

2 tablespoons granulated sugar

2 tablespoons water

2 tablespoons unsalted butter

1. Preheat the oven to 350°F. Line a 15 x 10-inch rimmed cookie sheet with foil, grease the foil with butter, and dust with flour. In a food processor, place the blanched almonds and the 1½ cups powdered sugar and process until the almonds are ground as finely as possible. Reserve 2 tablespoons. In a small bowl, beat the egg whites with an electric mixer until thick and stiff (and hold their shape when you lift the beater) but not dry. Fold in the remaining almond mixture.

2. Spread the egg-almond mixture evenly with a rubber spatula over the cookie sheet and bake about 12 minutes or until lightly browned. Let cool. Trim off any edges that are irregular or too brown and cut into 2½ x 1½-inch rectangles.

3. In a very small saucepan, combine the granulated sugar and the water and bring to a boil over low heat. Simmer, stirring constantly, until the liquid is reduced and the sauce thickens slightly, about 5 minutes. In another small saucepan, whisk the egg yolks and then gradually whisk in the syrup. Heat over low heat and cook, stirring constantly, about 5 minutes, then increase the heat to medium and cook, stirring constantly, until thickened. Stir in the reserved 2 tablespoons almond mixture, let cool briefly, then stir in the butter.

4. Spread the egg and almond mixture over the bottoms of half of the cookies. Place a second cookie bottom side down on the filling. Sprinkle with powdered sugar and serve at room temperature.

Cinnamon and Lemon-Scented Cookies
Perrunillas

MAKES ABOUT 30 COOKIES

Spaniards almost always use lard for baking. It has less saturated fat than butter, it makes excellent biscuits and pie crust, and it lends a distinctively Spanish flavor. It is important that you use pure fresh lard, not the cheap, hydrogenated kind sold in supermarkets. These cinnamon- and lemon-scented cookies are deliciously light and flaky. They are slightly thicker than most cookies, and you can make them into whatever shape you wish. I like them best when cut with a round scalloped-edge cookie cutter.

½ pound lard, preferably pure lard
½ cup sugar, plus more for sprinkling
½ teaspoon ground cinnamon
½ teaspoon lemon zest
1 large egg, separated
1½ tablespoons beaten egg
2 cups all-purpose flour

1. Preheat the oven to 425°F. Line a cookie sheet with foil. In a medium bowl, place the lard and sugar and beat with an electric mixer until light and fluffy. Stir in the cinnamon, lemon zest, the egg yolk, and the beaten egg. Add the flour and work the mixture with your hands until the flour is fully incorporated, adding more flour if the dough is sticky.

2. Roll out on a floured surface to ½ inch thick. Cut with a 1¾-inch scalloped-edge cookie cutter. Place on the cookie sheet about 2 inches apart.

3. In a small bowl, lightly beat the egg white with a fork. Brush the cookies with the egg white, sprinkle well with sugar, and bake 13 to 15 minutes or until well browned. Serve at room temperature.

Flan-Filled Fried Cookies ⓥ
Galletas Fritas

MAKES 8 SANDWICH COOKIES

This dessert is best when you use Spanish María biscuits or other lightly sweetened butter biscuits found in supermarkets. It is important that they be thin and not too sweet. This is a simple preparation of fried cookies filled with flan, another delicious recipe that came from our friend Ruperto.

2 homemade flans (partial recipe; page 627) or storebought flans, about 2½-inches wide
16 thin crisp cookies, such as María biscuits or butter biscuits, about 2½-inches wide
Mild olive oil, for frying
2 large eggs, lightly beaten
A mixture of sugar and ground cinnamon, for dusting

1. Turn out the flans onto a plate, drain the liquid, and cut each crosswise into 4 (⅜-inch) slices. Place each slice on the bottom of 1 cookie and cover with a second cookie, bottom side down.

2. Heat at least 1 inch of oil in a medium skillet over medium-high heat (or better still, use a deep fryer set at 365°F) until it browns a cube of bread quickly. Dip each sandwich cookie in the egg, coating all sides, then using tongs, place it in the oil. Fry, turning once, until the egg coating is golden. Transfer with an offset spatula to paper towels and let drain. Sprinkle with the sugar-cinnamon mixture and serve hot.

Albarracín Almond Cookies Ⓥ*

Mantecados de Almendra de Albarracín

MAKES 8 TO 10 LARGE COOKIES

This version of almond cookie from Albarracín, a region known for its fresh bread, is one of my very favorites. I much prefer these cookies when made with lard, but you may substitute vegetable shortening instead and make them vegetarian.

2 ounces blanched almonds (about ⅓ cup)

1 cup all-purpose flour

¼ cup lard or vegetable shortening

¼ cup sugar

1 large egg yolk

⅛ teaspoon lemon zest

8 to 10 whole almonds, skin on

1 large egg, lightly beaten

1. Preheat the oven to 350°F. Place the blanched almonds in a food processor, add 2 tablespoons of the flour, and process until the almonds are as finely chopped as possible.

2. In a medium bowl, beat the lard with an electric mixer until light and fluffy, then beat in the sugar, egg yolk, lemon zest, and the chopped almonds until well blended. Stir in the remaining flour. Work the mixture with your hands until a dough forms. Roll out the dough on a floured work surface to ⅜ inch thick. Cut with a 2-inch heart shaped cookie cutter and place on a lightly greased cookie sheet 1 inch apart.

3. Press a whole almond into the center of each cookie and brush with the beaten egg. Bake about 15 to 17 minutes or until well browned. Serve at room temperature.

Chewy Almond Cookies Ⓥ

Amargos

MAKES ABOUT 24 COOKIES

In this version of almond cookies from the Balearic Islands, no egg yolks or shortening are used. These are chewy instead of crisp, similar in consistency to macaroons.

1½ cups sugar

10 ounces blanched almonds (about 1⅔ cup)

2 large egg whites

2 teaspoons honey

½ teaspoon lemon zest

¼ teaspoon ground cinnamon

¼ teaspoon pure vanilla extract

1. Preheat the oven to 350°F. Place the sugar and almonds in a food processor and blend until the almonds are finely ground (but not a paste).

2. In a medium bowl, beat the egg whites with an electric mixer until the whites are thick and stiff (and hold their shape when you lift the beater) but not dry. Fold in the almond-sugar mixture, the honey, lemon zest, cinnamon, and vanilla.

3. With wet hands, shape the mixture into 1¼-inch balls and place on a greased cookie sheet 2 inches apart. Bake about 8 minutes or until golden. Serve at room temperature.

Powdered Sugar Cookies, Seville Style V

Polvorones Sevillanos

MAKES ABOUT 20 COOKIES

Seville is famous for these cookies of Arab origin but they can also be found all throughout Spain, served, typically, at Christmas.

½ pound (2 sticks) unsalted butter, at room temperature

1 large egg yolk

1 tablespoon powdered (confectioners) sugar

1 tablespoon brandy, such as Spanish brandy or Cognac

2 cups all-purpose flour

½ teaspoon ground cinnamon

About 2 cups powdered (confectioners) sugar, sifted, for coating

1. Preheat the oven to 300°F. Place the butter in a large bowl and beat with an electric mixer until light colored and fluffy. In a small cup, lightly beat the egg yolk and the 1 tablespoon powdered sugar with a fork. Stir in the brandy. Add to the creamed butter and beat until well blended.

2. Into a large bowl, sift the flour with the cinnamon. Gradually incorporate the flour with a rubber spatula or wooden spoon into the butter mixture. The dough should be slightly sticky. With floured hands, shape the dough into ovals, about 2 inches long, 1 inch wide, and ½ inch thick. Place on an ungreased cookie sheet about 2 inches apart. Bake about 30 minutes or until the cookies are lightly golden and the center is cooked. The cookies should not brown. Remove from the oven and let cool slightly on the cookie sheet 2 to 3 minutes.

3. Sift the powdered sugar onto a sheet of wax paper. Roll the warm cookies carefully in the sugar, coating them lightly on all sides. Let cool completely, then coat heavily with more powdered sugar.

4. Serve as they are at room temperature, or place in miniature paper cupcake liners. Store in a covered container.

Powdered Sugar Flower Cookies

Pasta Flora

MAKES 30 COOKIES

This version of powdered sugar cookies comes from Madrid's oldest bakery, Pastelería del Pozo, founded in 1830. It is a tiny bakery that specializes in traditional cakes and pastries. I always go there to buy these deliciously crumbly cookies that are sold by the box. As with most pastries that come from Spain, pasta floras are much better when made with lard.

2½ cups all-purpose flour

1 tablespoon ground cinnamon

¼ cup granulated sugar

½ pound lard, preferably pure lard, softened

¼ cup dry white wine

Powdered (confectioners) sugar, for dusting

1. Place an oven rack in the upper position. Preheat the oven to 400°F. In a large bowl, combine 2 cups of the flour, the cinnamon, and the granulated sugar. Add the lard and work in with your hands until well combined, then mix in the wine. Add enough of the remaining ½ cup flour to make a dough that can be rolled.

2. Roll out the dough on a floured work surface to ¼ inch thick. Cut with a 2½-inch scalloped-edge cookie cutter.

3. Place on a lightly greased cookie sheet 1 inch apart and bake 8 to 10 minutes or until well browned. Let cool slightly, then coat both sides heavily with powdered sugar. Serve at room temperature.

Powdered Sugar Cookies with Lemon Zest

Pastissets

MAKES ABOUT 30 COOKIES

These wonderful scalloped cookies are flavored with cinnamon and lemon zest, then sprinkled with powdered sugar. This is a cookie recipe for which I urge you to use lard because they just won't taste the same without it.

⅔ cup lard, vegetable shortening, or unsalted butter, softened

⅓ cup unsalted butter, softened

½ cup granulated sugar

1 large egg yolk

½ teaspoon lemon zest

¼ teaspoon ground cinnamon

2 cups all-purpose flour

Sifted powdered (confectioners) sugar, for dredging

1. Preheat the oven to 350°F. In a medium large bowl, add the lard and butter and beat with a wooden spoon until blended. Add the sugar, egg yolk, and lemon zest and beat until still thick but more pliable. In a small bowl, combine the cinnamon and flour, then stir into the lard-sugar mixture. Work the mixture with your hands to form a smooth dough.

2. Roll the dough out on a floured work surface to a scant ¼ inch thick. Cut with a 3-inch scalloped-edge cookie cutter (or other shape if you wish).

3. Place the cookies on a greased cookie sheet and bake about 10 minutes or until golden. Let cool, then dredge both sides in the powdered sugar.

Powdered Sugar Cookies with Wine Ⓥ*

Mantecados de Vino Castellanos

MAKES ABOUT 16 COOKIES

The recipe for these sugar cookies from Castilla calls for dry white wine. They are coated with powdered sugar after baking, but there is no sugar at all in the dough. The result is a cookie that is unusually light and delicate. Make it vegetarian with vegetable shortening.

½ pound lard, preferably pure lard, vegetable shortening, or unsalted butter

½ cup dry white wine

2 cups all-purpose flour

Sifted powdered (confectioners) sugar, for dusting

1. Preheat the oven to 350°F. In a medium bowl, beat the lard with an electric mixer until light and fluffy. Beat in the wine, then gradually stir in the flour until the dough holds together. Remove the dough from the bowl and pat between your hands to make a smooth shape.

2. On a lightly floured work surface, roll out the dough to ⅜ inch thick. Cut into 2½-inch rounds with a fluted-edge cookie-cutter (or other shape if you wish). Place on a greased cookie sheet and let sit uncovered at room temperature at least 1 hour.

3. Bake 15 to 20 minutes or until lightly golden. Let cool, then coat both sides heavily with powdered sugar. Serve at room temperature.

Flaky Sugar Cookies Ⓥ*
Mantecados Ossa de Montiel

MAKES ABOUT 14 COOKIES

This variation on sugar cookies, which are particularly flaky and light, includes anisette liqueur and comes from the town of Ossa de Montiel in the province of Albacete. These short cookies are made with lard, which adds a distinctive flavor and an especially flaky texture. Make it vegetarian with vegetable shortening.

¼ pound lard, preferably pure lard or vegetable shortening

¼ cup sugar

1 teaspoon anisette liqueur

1 tablespoon dry white wine

1¼ cups all-purpose flour

1 large egg, lightly beaten

About ¼ cup granulated sugar, for sprinkling

1. Preheat the oven to 350°F. In a medium bowl, beat the lard and sugar with an electric mixer until the mixture is light and fluffy, then beat in the anisette and wine. Stir in the flour and work the mixture with your hands until a dough forms.

2. Roll out the dough on a floured surface to ¾ inch thick. Cut with a 1½-inch fluted-edge cookie cutter. Place on a lightly greased cookie sheet 1 inch apart.

3. Brush each cookie with the egg and sprinkle with ¼ teaspoon sugar. Bake about 30 minutes or until golden. Serve at room temperature.

Almond Cupcakes Ⓥ
Almendrados

MAKES 12 CUPCAKES

What is most surprising about these sensational moist almond cupcakes is that they are cholesterol free, as the recipe calls for neither egg yolk nor shortening. They are always a big hit at my dinner parties.

¾ pound blanched almonds (about 2 cups)

1 cup powdered (confectioners) sugar

¼ teaspoon ground cinnamon

½ teaspoon lemon zest

3 large egg whites

1. Preheat the oven to 350°F. Grease 6 jumbo or 12 regular-size muffin cups. Scatter the almonds on a cookie sheet and toast about 5 minutes or until lightly browned. Let cool. Transfer to a food processor, add ½ cup of the powdered sugar and the cinnamon, and pulse in short bursts until a fine consistency but not a paste.

2. In a medium bowl, mix the remaining ½ cup sugar and the egg whites with an electric mixer on low speed until just combined, then increase the speed to medium and beat until soft peaks form. Gently fold in the almond mixture until combined.

4. Divide the batter evenly among the muffin cups. Bake 15 to 20 minutes or until the cupcakes gently spring back when pressed lightly in the center. Serve at room temperature.

Spanish-Style Cupcakes Ⓥ*
Mantecadas de Astorga

MAKES 20 CUPCAKES

Light and airy cupcakes, mantecadas, *are usually made with lard and are sometimes more like cookies than cake. Many variations of these cupcakes can be found all over Spain. This is the most well-known recipe, which comes from Astorga, a town in the butter-producing province of León. Astorga is a train stop on the main line to Galicia and Asturias, and passengers always stock up on* mantecadas *for the rest of the trip.*

¼ pound (1 stick) unsalted butter or pure lard

1 cup sifted all-purpose flour

⅛ teaspoon salt

¼ teaspoon ground cinnamon

3 large eggs

½ cup granulated sugar

Powdered (confectioners) sugar, for dusting

1. Preheat the oven to 350°F. Place paper baking cups in each of 20 regular-size muffin cups. Melt the butter in a small saucepan over low heat and let cool. Meanwhile, in a medium bowl, combine the flour, salt, and cinnamon.

2. In a small bowl, beat the eggs with an electric beater until foamy. Gradually add the granulated sugar and beat until very light and fluffy, about 4 minutes. Lightly fold in the cooled butter. Divide the batter evenly among the muffin cups, filling each about two-thirds full.

3. Bake 15 minutes or until just lightly golden. Let cool slightly and dust with powdered sugar. Serve warm.

Galician Almond Cake Ⓥ
Tarta de Santiago

MAKES ONE 8-INCH CAKE

Tarta de almendra *is a simple and moist, single layer almond cake that originated in the region of Galicia. It is sometimes called* Tarta de Santiago *because the cross of Spain's patron saint Santiago is emblazoned with caramelized sugar in the center of the cake. This version, which is the best I have ever tasted, comes from Alfonso Merlo, owner of O Merlo in the capital city of Pontevedra.*

6 ounces blanched almonds (about 1 cup)

6 tablespoons all-purpose flour

¾ cup granulated sugar

3 large eggs

Powdered (confectioners) sugar

1. Place 2 ounces (about ⅓ cup) of the almonds and the flour in a food processor and pulse until the almonds are coarsely chopped. Remove from the processor and reserve. Place the remaining 4 ounces almonds and ¼ cup of the granulated sugar in the processor, and blend until the almonds are chopped as finely as possible.

2. Preheat the oven to 350°F. In a medium bowl, beat the eggs with an electric mixer until foamy. Add the remaining ½ cup granulated sugar and beat until the mixture is light colored and thick. Beat in the almond-flour and almond-sugar mixtures until well blended. Pour into a greased and floured 8-inch springform pan.

3. Bake 35 to 40 minutes or until the cake springs back slightly when touched in the center. Let cool. Remove the rim of the pan and sprinkle heavily with the powdered sugar. To burn the traditional cross in the sugar, use a pot holder to hold a thin metal skewer over a flame until the lower portion is red hot.

continues...

Press the skewer over the center of the cake to caramelize the sugar. Wipe off the skewer, reheat, and repeat to form a cross. Serve at room temperature.

Almond and Potato Cake 🅥
Tarta de Almendra y Patata

MAKES ONE 8½- OR 9-INCH CAKE

The unusual addition of potatoes makes this cake extremely moist and also lends a subtle flavor. It tastes very similar to a pound cake but is made without any butter. It relies on ground almonds instead of flour to create the cake consistency. This is an old family recipe that came to me from Reme Domínguez at the excellent Tasca del Puerto in Castellón de la Plana, a restaurant well known for its unique and innovative recipes.

½ pound blanched almonds (about 1⅓ cups)

2½ cups granulated sugar

1 pound potatoes, such as Idaho, peeled

6 large eggs

¾ cup all-purpose flour

Powdered (confectioners) sugar, for dusting

1. Place the almonds and 1 cup of the granulated sugar in a food processor and blend until the almonds are as finely ground as possible (but not a paste).

2. Place the potatoes in a medium saucepan with cold water to cover and add salt. Cover and bring to a simmer over low heat. Cook about 20 minutes or until tender when pierced with a knife. Drain and let cool slightly. Pass through a ricer or fine-mesh strainer into a medium bowl and stir in the almond-sugar mixture.

3. Preheat the oven to 350°F and grease a 9-inch springform cake pan. In a large bowl, beat the eggs with an electric mixer on high speed until the yolks and whites are blended, about 1 minute. Gradually add the remaining 1½ cups granulated sugar and beat until the mixture is thick and pale lemon colored. Gradually beat in the flour until thoroughly incorporated, then the potato-almond mixture. Pour into the cake pan.

4. Bake 1 to 1¼ hours or until a toothpick inserted in the center comes out almost clean (there can still be a couple of crumbs attached, but it shouldn't be wet). Let cool. Turn out upside down onto a serving dish. Dust heavily with the powdered sugar. Serve at room temperature. Wrap and store at room temperature—it will stay fresh and moist several days.

Orange Cake 🅥
Bizcocho de Naranja

MAKES AN 8-INCH BUNDT CAKE

A delightfully moist orange-flavored cake, perfect when served with coffee or tea. This cake can either be served plain, or brushed with apricot jam and orange liqueur. It's also delicious with ice cream.

3 large eggs

1 cup granulated sugar

1 cup fresh orange juice

1 tablespoon orange zest

½ cup mild olive oil

2 cups all-purpose flour

1 tablespoon baking powder

Powdered (confectioners) sugar, for dusting

1. Preheat the oven to 350°F. Grease and flour an 8-inch fluted tube cake pan. In a large bowl, beat the eggs with an electric mixer until thickened and light colored. Gradually beat in the granulated sugar, then—in this order—the orange juice, orange zest, and oil. Beat in the flour and, finally, the baking powder.

2. Pour the batter into the pan and bake about 45 minutes or until a toothpick inserted in the center comes out clean and the cake springs back when pressed lightly in the center. Let cool slightly,

then turn out onto a serving dish. Dust with confectioners sugar. Serve at room temperature.

Orange-Almond Cake Ⓥ
Tarta de Naranja

MAKES ONE 8-INCH CAKE

The sweetness of the cake is tempered by the addition of orange zest in this classic Spanish dessert flavored with ground almonds and cinnamon.

4 large eggs, separated

½ cup sugar

Zest of 2 oranges

¼ pound blanched almonds, finely ground

Syrup

Juice of 2 oranges

⅓ cup sugar

1 cinnamon stick

1 teaspoon orange liqueur, such as Gran Torres or Grand Marnier

I. Preheat the oven to 350°F. In a medium bowl, beat the egg yolks, the ½ cup sugar, and the orange zest with an electric mixer until fluffy and lemon colored. Gradually beat in the almonds. In a small bowl, beat the egg whites with the electric mixer until thick and stiff (and hold their shape when you lift the beater) but not dry, then fold into the yolk mixture. Turn out into a greased and floured 8-inch square or round cake pan. Bake about 45 minutes or until well browned. Let cool slightly, then remove the cake from the pan and place top side up on a serving dish.

2. Prepare the syrup: In a small saucepan, combine the orange juice, ⅓ cup sugar, and the cinnamon stick and bring to a boil over medium heat. Reduce the heat to low and simmer about 5 minutes. Remove from the heat and stir in the liqueur. Let cool, then pour evenly over the cake. Serve at room temperature.

Orange Yogurt Cake Ⓥ
Bizcocho de Naranja

MAKES ONE 8- OR 9-INCH CAKE

La Gomera, a tiny volcanic island, is famous all over the Canaries for its superb desserts. This recipe is for an orange, almond, and yogurt cake that is wonderfully moist. According to history books, the island of La Gomera is where Columbus stayed with his mistress before his journey to the new world.

3 cups all-purpose flour

½ teaspoon salt

2¼ teaspoons baking powder

5 large eggs, separated

1½ cups sugar

Zest of ¼ lemon

Zest of 1 orange

½ cup fresh orange juice

¼ pound (1 stick) unsalted butter, melted

¾ cup whole milk yogurt

¼ cup ground blanched almonds

I. Preheat the oven to 350°F. Grease a deep 8- or 9-inch springform cake pan with butter and dust with flour. Sift together the flour, salt, and baking powder into a medium bowl. In a large bowl, beat the egg yolks with an electric mixer until light colored, then beat in the sugar, lemon zest and orange zest, orange juice, butter, and yogurt. Gradually stir in the flour mixture until thoroughly incorporated.

2. In a small bowl, beat the egg whites with the electric mixer until thick and stiff (and hold their shape when you lift the beater) but not dry, then fold into the batter. Pour into the cake pan and sprinkle with the almonds. Bake at about 55 minutes or until a toothpick inserted in the center comes out clean. Let cool briefly, remove the side of the pan, and let cool completely. Serve at room temperature.

Orange Ice Cream Cake Ⓥ
Tarta "Huerto de Cura"

MAKES 8 SERVINGS

An elegant variation on ice cream cake, this one comes from Elche, the city with the largest date palm forest in Europe. This dessert is a combination of two dessert recipes found in this chapter—frozen orange custard and "drunken" cake.

PREPARE 16 TO 24 HOURS IN ADVANCE

½ recipe Frozen Orange Custard with Blackberry Sauce (page 647), using 2 teaspoons orange peel and omitting the blackberry sauce

1 recipe Custard-Filled, Liqueur-Flavored Cake (page 589), omitting the filling and syrup

1 pint vanilla ice cream, softened

½ pint heavy cream

8-ounce jar English orange marmalade

½ cup orange liqueur, such as Gran Torres or Grand Marnier

Instant coffee powder, for dusting

1. Prepare the custard as instructed in steps 1 through 3 of the recipe, except pour into an 8-inch round cake pan. Prepare the cake as instructed in step 1 of the recipe, except pour into 8-inch round cake pan.

2. When the custard is frozen and the cake cool, quickly assemble the ice cream cake. Cut the cake horizontally into 3 layers. Spread the vanilla ice cream over the first layer and cover with the second layer of cake. Spread the custard over the second layer, and cover with the remaining layer of cake. Spread the orange marmalade over the top layer. Lightly cover with foil and place in the freezer overnight to harden.

3. In a small bowl, beat the cream with an electric mixer until soft peaks form. In a small microwave-safe bowl, heat the orange marmalade in the microwave on High a few seconds to soften slightly.

4. Remove the cake from the freezer and let soften slightly. Cut into wedges and place on their sides on individual dishes. Pour about 1 tablespoon of the orange liqueur onto each wedge so that it penetrates the cake. Top with the whipped cream and dust lightly with the coffee. Serve cold.

Chocolate Custard Cake Ⓥ
Pan de Munición

MAKES ONE 9¼ X 5¼-INCH LOAF
(6 SERVINGS)

This is very different from the sweet chocolate cakes found in the United States. Even though Spain was responsible for introducing chocolate from the New World to the rest of Europe, it took quite a while for this ingredient to make its way into dessert recipes. Pan de munición produces a dense, bittersweet chocolate taste in a cake that is somewhat more of a custard. This traditional recipe is over a hundred years old. The orange flower water is available in specialty food stores.

1⅓ cups unsweetened cocoa powder

½ cup orange flower water

½ cup water

¼ cup (½ stick) unsalted butter, softened

¾ cup plus 1 tablespoon sugar

4 large eggs

½ cup ground almonds

½ teaspoon orange zest

2 large egg whites

¼ cup chopped almonds

Chocolate Sauce

1⅓ cups milk

3 squares unsweetened chocolate

Pinch of salt

⅓ cup sugar

2 teaspoons cornstarch

1 teaspoon pure vanilla extract

⅓ cup heavy cream

1. Preheat the oven to 350°F. In a small bowl, combine the cocoa, orange flower water, and water and mix until smooth. In a medium bowl, beat the butter and sugar with an electric mixer until light and fluffy. Beat in the whole eggs, then stir in ¼ cup of the ground almonds, the cocoa mixture, and the orange rind until well blended.

2. In a small bowl, beat the egg whites with the electric mixer until thick and stiff (and hold their shape when you lift the beater) but not dry. Fold into the chocolate mixture along with the chopped almonds. Pour the batter into a greased 9¼ x 5¼-inch loaf pan. Bake 40 minutes. Let cool, then turn out onto a serving dish, top side up.

3. Prepare the sauce: In the top of a double boiler or a bowl over a pot, combine the milk, chocolate, and salt and cook, stirring occasionally, until the chocolate is melted. Add the sugar and cook, stirring occasionally, until dissolved. In a small bowl, mix the cornstarch with enough cold water to form a paste. Add to the chocolate mixture and stir until smooth, thickened, and no cornstarch taste remains. Let cool, then stir in the vanilla. Stir in enough of the heavy cream to make the sauce the consistency of heavy cream.

4. Cut the cake into slices and pour the chocolate sauce over each. Sprinkle with the remaining ¼ cup ground almonds. Serve at room temperature.

Custard-Filled, Liqueur-Flavored Cake Ⓥ
Bizcocho Borracho a la Crema

MAKES 36 SMALL CAKE SQUARES

Because this cake is soaked in liquor, in Spain they call this "drunken" cake. The rum and the orange liqueur add a different and unusual flavor to this moist, custard-filled cake. In Spain, it is traditional to cut cake into squares rather than wedges.

Cake

4 large eggs

½ cup sugar

1 cup all-purpose flour

2 tablespoons unsalted butter, melted and cooled

Powdered (confectioners) sugar, for dusting

Syrup

6 tablespoons granulated sugar

6 tablespoons water

1 cinnamon stick

5 tablespoons rum

4 tablespoons orange liqueur, such as Gran Torres or Grand Marnier

Custard Filling

1 cup milk

Peel of ½ lemon (yellow part only)

3 large egg yolks

¼ cup granulated sugar

¼ cup all-purpose flour

2 teaspoons unsalted butter

1. Preheat the oven to 350°F. In a medium bowl, add the 4 whole eggs and the ½ cup granulated sugar and beat with an electric mixer until the mixture is light and fluffy, about 3 minutes. Gradually beat in the 1 cup flour, then the melted butter. Pour

continues...

the batter into a greased and floured 8-inch square baking pan. Bake about 25 minutes or until the cake springs back when pressed lightly in the center. Let cool slightly.

2. Meanwhile, prepare the syrup: In a small saucepan, combine the 6 tablespoons granulated sugar, the water, and cinnamon stick and bring to a boil over low heat. Simmer about 5 minutes, remove from the heat, and discard the cinnamon. Stir in the rum and liqueur. While the cake is still warm in the pan, pour half of the syrup evenly over the cake. It will take only a moment for the syrup to soak in. Carefully turn the cake out upside down onto a plate and pour the remaining syrup over the cake.

3. Prepare the custard: In another small saucepan, combine the milk and lemon peel and bring to a boil over medium heat. Reduce the heat to low and simmer 10 minutes. Discard the lemon peel. Place the 3 egg yolks in a medium saucepan and gradually stir in the ¼ cup sugar, then gradually stir in the flour and the hot milk. Cook over medium heat, stirring constantly, until thickened and smooth and no flour taste remains. Remove from the heat and stir in the butter. Let cool, stirring occasionally.

4. Cut the cake horizontally in half. Spread the custard on the cut side of the bottom half and cover with the top half. Cut into 6 rows by 6 rows (36 squares). Dust each square heavily with powdered sugar. Use a pot holder to hold a thin metal skewer over a flame until the lower portion is red hot. Press the skewer on the tops of the cakes, making a gridiron design by caramelizing the sugar. Wipe off the skewer and reheat as necessary. Serve the cakes in miniature paper baking cups.

Segovia's Custard and Marzipan Cake Ⓥ
Ponche Segoviano

MAKES 6 SERVINGS

Ponche segoviano, *a cake moistened with rum-flavored syrup, filled with custard, and covered with a thin coating of almond paste, can be found in just about every restaurant and pastry shop in the ancient city of Segovia. The best version I have ever tasted came from Casa Cándido, also famous for their traditional roast suckling pig. Typically,* ponche segoviano *is served with an attractive design burned into the sugar coating of the cake.*

Cake

4 large eggs, separated

½ cup granulated sugar

¼ teaspoon salt

2 tablespoons unsalted butter, melted and cooled

¼ teaspoon lemon zest

1 cup all-purpose flour

4 ounces pure almond paste

Powdered (confectioners) sugar, for dusting

Syrup

6 tablespoons granulated sugar

6 tablespoons water

1 small cinnamon stick

1 tablespoon rum

Custard

1 cup milk

Peel of ½ lemon (yellow part only)

3 large egg yolks

¼ cup granulated sugar

2 tablespoons cornstarch

2 teaspoons unsalted butter

1. Prepare the cake: Preheat the oven to 350°F. Grease and flour an 8-inch square baking pan. In a medium bowl, beat the 4 egg yolks, ½ cup granulated sugar, the salt, the 2 tablespoons butter, and the lemon zest with an electric mixer until pale yellow and spongy. Gradually beat in the flour until thoroughly incorporated.

2. In a small bowl, beat the 4 egg whites with the electric mixer until soft peaks form. Gently fold into the batter. Pour into the baking pan and bake about 20 minutes or until a toothpick inserted in the center comes out clean and the cake springs back when pressed lightly in the center.

3. Meanwhile, prepare the syrup: In a very small saucepan, combine the 6 tablespoons granulated sugar, the water, and cinnamon and bring to a boil over low heat. Simmer, stirring occasionally, 10 minutes. Remove from the heat and stir in the rum. Let cool.

4. When the cake is done, remove from the oven and shake to loosen it in the pan. Pour half of the syrup evenly over the cake. Carefully turn the cake out upside down onto a plate and pour the remaining syrup over the cake. Let cool.

5. Meanwhile, prepare the custard: In a small saucepan, combine the milk and lemon peel and bring to a boil over low heat. Cover and simmer 10 minutes. Discard the lemon peel. In a small bowl, whisk together the 3 egg yolks, then whisk in the ¼ cup granulated sugar and the cornstarch. Gradually pour in the hot milk, return to the saucepan over medium heat, and cook, stirring constantly, until thickened and smooth. Remove from the heat and stir in the 2 teaspoons butter. Let cool, stirring occasionally.

6. Cut the cake horizontally in half. Place the top half upside down on a serving plate and spread the custard over the cake. Cover with the other half of the cake, cut side down. On a work surface, roll the almond paste to ⅛ inch (it should be slightly larger than the cake). Place the almond paste over the cake and trim to size with a sharp knife. Gently press so that the almond paste adheres to the cake. Sprinkle generously with the powdered sugar.

7. Use a pot holder to hold a thin metal skewer over a flame until the lower portion is red hot. Create a rhombus (slanted square) design by holding the skewer over the cake and burning 2 horizontal parallel lines. Wipe off the skewer, reheat, and burn 2 diagonal lines connecting the first 2. Or create the design of your choice. Serve warm.

Custard-Filled Cake Roll ⓥ
Brazo de Gitano

MAKES 1 ROLLED CAKE
(AT LEAST 8 SERVINGS)

The elongated shape of this Spanish rolled cake is probably the reason for this oddly named recipe. In English, Brazo de Gitano *literally means "Gypsy's Arm." It is quite popular and found in pastry shops all over Spain.*

¼ pound (1 stick) unsalted butter

3 large eggs

½ cup granulated sugar

½ teaspoon lemon zest

1 cup sifted all-purpose flour

⅛ teaspoon salt

Filling

2¾ cups milk

1 cinnamon stick

Peel of ½ lemon

8 large egg yolks

¾ cup granulated sugar

¾ cup all-purpose flour

3 tablespoons sweet sherry, such as cream

1 tablespoon unsalted butter

2 ounces pine nuts (about ⅓ cup)

Powdered (confectioners) sugar, for dusting

Ground cinnamon, for dusting

continues...

1. Place an oven rack in the upper-middle position. Preheat the oven to 375°F. Melt the ¼ pound butter in small saucepan over low heat and let cool. In a medium bowl, beat the eggs with an electric mixer until foamy. Gradually add the ½ cup granulated sugar and the lemon zest. Beat until very light and fluffy, about 4 minutes. In another small bowl, combine the flour and salt, then stir into the batter. Lightly fold in the cooled butter. Grease well a 15 x 10-inch rimmed cookie sheet. Pour the batter into the pan and distribute evenly.

2. Bake 9 to 10 minutes or until the cake is done (prick it with a toothpick to test that no batter clings) but only lightly golden on the bottom (otherwise, the cake will be difficult to roll).

3. Sprinkle a piece of thin cloth, at least the length of the cake and a few inches wider, heavily with the powdered sugar. Invert the cake while still warm onto the cloth. Trim any browned edges. Starting with a long side, roll the cake in the cloth, being sure the ends are well covered. Let cool and leave wrapped until needed.

4. Prepare the filling: In a small saucepan, add the milk, cinnamon, and lemon peel and bring to a boil over medium heat. Reduce the heat to low and simmer, stirring occasionally, about 15 minutes. Discard the cinnamon stick and the lemon peel. Whisk together the egg yolks in a heavy saucepan. Whisk in the ¾ cup granulated sugar until the eggs are a pale yellow color. Stir in the flour. Gradually stir in the hot milk and 2 tablespoons of the sherry. Increase the heat to medium and cook, stirring constantly, until thickened and smooth and beginning to bubble. (The custard may seem lumpy for a while, but it will smooth out when done.) Remove from the heat and stir in the 1 tablespoon butter and the remaining 1 tablespoon sherry. Let cool, stirring occasionally.

5. When the custard is at room temperature, unroll the cake, leaving it on the cloth. Spread the custard over the cake and sprinkle with the pine nuts. Reroll, using the cloth to aid in rolling. Transfer to a serving dish. Sift the powdered sugar over the cake and dust with the cinnamon. Serve at room temperature.

Chocolate Charlotte Ⓥ
Charlote de Xocolate

MAKES 8 SERVINGS

This simple yet elegant dessert with just a few ingredients is similar to French charlotte desserts, because the recipe originated in the region of the Pyrenées that borders France. The ladyfingers that line the cake mold should be arranged close together but with enough space to create chocolate swirls. Ladyfingers can be found in almost any supermarket.

PREPARE 8 TO 12 HOURS IN ADVANCE

About 9 ladyfingers, each cut horizontally in half
¼ pound (1 stick) unsalted butter
5 ounces good quality bittersweet chocolate
½ cup sugar
3 large eggs, separated

1. Line the bottom and sides of a 1½-quart charlotte mold with the ladyfingers. If you don't have one, you may use a bowl of a similar capacity, about 6½ inches across the top, 4 to 5 inches tall, and 4 to 6 inches across the bottom. In a large saucepan, combine the butter and chocolate and melt over medium heat, stirring constantly. Add the sugar and cook, stirring constantly, until the mixture is smooth and the sugar dissolved. Remove from the heat and let cool slightly.

2. Place the egg yolks in a small bowl and stir in a few tablespoons of the chocolate mixture. Add to the saucepan and stir vigorously until well combined.

3. In a small bowl, beat the egg whites with an electric mixer until soft peaks form. Fold into the chocolate mixture. Let cool slightly. Pour into the mold, cover with plastic wrap, and refrigerate overnight.

Loosen the side with a knife and turn out upside down onto a serving dish. Serve cold.

Peach Yogurt Torte Ⓥ
Tarta de Yogur y Melocotón

MAKES ONE 8½-INCH TORTE

The recipe for this superb peach torte glazed with apricot marmalade uses yogurt instead of milk and olive oil instead of butter. It's flavored with almond extract and hints of cinnamon and nutmeg.

1 cup all-purpose flour

2 teaspoons baking powder

⅛ teaspoon salt

1 large egg

½ cup plus 2 tablespoons sugar

¼ cup lemon or vanilla yogurt

3 tablespoons olive oil

¼ teaspoon almond extract

2 ripe peaches, peeled, pitted, and cut into
 ½-inch wedges

1 teaspoon fresh lemon juice

¼ teaspoon ground cinnamon

¼ teaspoon ground nutmeg

2 tablespoons apricot preserves

2 tablespoons sliced almonds

Whipped cream

1. Preheat the oven to 350°F. Sift together the flour, baking powder, and salt into a small bowl. In a large bowl, beat the egg with an electric mixer until frothy, then gradually beat in the ½ cup sugar and continue beating until light and lemon colored. Beat in the yogurt, oil, and almond extract, then gradually beat in the flour mixture until thoroughly mixed.

2. Pour into a well-greased and floured 8½-inch springform pan. Arrange the peaches in slightly overlapping rows over the batter. Sprinkle with the remaining 2 tablespoons sugar, the lemon juice, cinnamon, and nutmeg. Bake about 1 hour or until a toothpick inserted in the center comes out clean. Let cool and remove the side of the pan. In a small microwave-safe bowl, heat the apricot preserves in the microwave on Medium until warm and liquefied and brush over the torte. Sprinkle with the almonds and top each serving with a dollop of whipped cream. Serve at room temperature.

Apple Tart from Madrid Ⓥ
Tarta Madrileña de Manzana

MAKES ONE 9-INCH TART

Spain has many versions of apple tarts. This is the classic recipe favored by Madrileños.

Crust

¼ pound (1 stick) unsalted butter

½ cup sugar

1 large egg yolk

1½ cups sifted all-purpose flour

Pinch of salt

⅛ teaspoon baking powder

Custard

1 cup milk

Peel of ½ lemon (yellow part only)

3 large egg yolks

¼ cup sugar

¼ cup all-purpose flour

1½ teaspoons unsalted butter

Filling

¼ cup sugar

1 teaspoon fresh lemon juice

½ teaspoon ground cinnamon

4 apples, peeled, cored, and cut into ¼-inch slices

½ cup apple jelly

continues…

1. Prepare the crust: In a medium bowl, beat the ¼ pound butter with an electric mixer until light colored and fluffy. Gradually beat in the ½ cup sugar, then the 1 egg yolk until well blended. In a small bowl, combine the 1½ cups flour, salt, and baking powder and stir into the butter mixture. Work the dough with your hands to form a ball. Press into and up the side of a loose-bottom, 9-inch tart pan and trim any excess by pressing and cutting off at the rim. Refrigerate while preparing the custard.

2. Prepare the custard: In a small saucepan, combine the milk and lemon peel and bring to a boil over medium heat, stirring occasionally. Reduce the heat to low and simmer, stirring occasionally, about 10 minutes. Discard the lemon peel. Place the 3 egg yolks in another small saucepan, gradually stir in the ¼ cup sugar, and beat with a whisk until pale yellow. Whisk in the flour and gradually add the hot milk. Cook over medium heat, stirring constantly, until thickened and smooth and no flour taste remains. Remove from the heat and stir in the 1½ teaspoons butter. Let cool, stirring occasionally.

3. Meanwhile, preheat the oven to 350°F. Prepare the filling: In a small bowl, combine the ¼ cup sugar, the lemon juice, and cinnamon. Fold in the apples.

4. Spread the custard over the dough and arrange the apples on top in overlapping circles. Bake about 1 hour or until the crust is well browned. Let cool.

5. In a small saucepan, melt the jelly over low heat. Spoon over the apples to glaze the tart. Remove the side of the quiche pan, leaving the tart on the bottom circle. Serve at room temperature or refrigerate at least 2 hours and serve cold.

Basque Apple Custard Tart Ⓥ
Tarta Vasca de Manzana

MAKES 8 SERVINGS

This sensational tart, filled with creamy custard and topped with sliced apples marinated in spiced apple syrup, is typical of the Basque Country. This recipe comes from the pastry chef at Baserri Maitea, a magnificent eighteenth-century country house on an isolated hilltop just north of Guernica near Bilbao. Guernica was the subject of Picasso's famous painting depicting the bombing of that village in the Spanish Civil War.

PREPARE AT LEAST 2 HOURS IN ADVANCE

2 Golden Delicious apples, peeled, cored, quartered, and cut into ⅛-inch slices

1½ cups apple juice

3 tablespoons sugar

2 whole cloves

¼ teaspoon ground nutmeg

Crust

1 cup all-purpose flour

2 tablespoons sugar

½ teaspoon baking powder

6 tablespoons chilled unsalted butter

1 tablespoon egg yolk

2 tablespoons heavy cream

Custard

1 cup milk

½ cinnamon stick

Peel of ½ lemon (yellow part only)

2 large egg yolks

¼ cup sugar

2 tablespoons cornstarch

2 teaspoons unsalted butter

2 tablespoons apricot preserves

1. Arrange the apples in a flat-bottom bowl. In a small saucepan, combine the apple juice, 3 tablespoons sugar, the cloves, and nutmeg and bring to a boil over medium heat. Reduce the heat to low and simmer, stirring occasionally, until the liquid is reduced by half and the sauce syrup thickened. Pour over the apples and let sit at room temperature at least 2 hours.

2. Prepare the crust: Preheat the oven to 350°F. In a medium bowl, combine the flour, sugar, and baking powder. Work in the butter with your fingers, then stir in the 1 egg yolk and beat with a fork until combined. Turn out onto a work surface and work lightly with your hands to form a ball. Sprinkle lightly with flour and roll out between sheets of wax paper to an 11-inch round (chill briefly if the dough becomes too soft). Press into the bottom and up the side of a 9-inch loose-bottom tart pan and trim any excess by pressing and cutting off at the rim. Prick all over with a fork and bake about 15 minutes or until lightly browned.

3. Prepare the custard: In a small saucepan, combine the milk, cinnamon stick, and lemon peel and bring to a boil over medium heat, stirring occasionally. Reduce the heat to low, cover, and simmer, stirring occasionally, about 20 minutes. Let cool briefly, then discard the cinnamon and lemon.

4. In a medium bowl, whisk together the 2 egg yolks and the ¼ cup sugar, then whisk in the cornstarch and gradually stir in the warm milk. Return to the saucepan over medium heat, stirring constantly, until thickened and smooth. Remove from the heat and stir in the butter. Let cool, stirring occasionally.

5. Preheat the oven to 450°F. Pour the custard into the crust. Remove the apples from the syrup and arrange in tightly overlapping rows over the custard. Bake 10 minutes.

6. Place the preserves in a microwave-safe bowl, heat in the microwave on Medium until warm and liquefied, and brush over the tart. Let cool, remove the side of the tart pan, and serve warm.

Almond and Egg Yolk Tart ⓥ*
Técula Mécula

MAKES 8 TO 10 SERVINGS

This fine recipe was given to me by Félix Durán, chef at the magnificent Parador de Plasencia, which specializes in traditional dishes from the region of Extremadura. Félix told me that the secret to this tart is to add the ingredients one at a time and in the specified order. These rich candy-like tarts made with almond and egg yolk are always a favorite at my dinner parties. As for the name of the recipe, técula mécula, I have no idea where it came from; it was not shared with me, and neither word appears in the dictionary. Make it vegetarian with butter.

½ pound puff pastry dough, homemade (page 135; partial recipe) or storebought
¼ pound blanched almonds (about ⅔ cup)
3 tablespoons all-purpose flour
1¼ cups granulated sugar
½ cup water
1 tablespoon unsalted butter, softened
2 tablespoons lard or an additional 2 tablespoons unsalted butter, softened
5 large egg yolks
1½ tablespoons lightly beaten egg

Sugar Glaze
½ egg white
½ cup powdered (confectioners) sugar

1. Preheat the oven to 400°F. Roll out the pastry to an 11-inch square, then trim the corners to make a circle. Press into and up the sides of an 8-inch fluted loose-bottom tart pan and trim any excess by pressing and cutting off at the rim. Be sure the pastry adheres to the sides—if necessary, dampen

continues...

the underside and press lightly. Prick all over with a fork and bake about 15 minutes or until lightly browned.

2. Meanwhile, place the almonds and flour in a food processor and blend until the almonds are as finely ground as possible. In a large saucepan, stir together the 1¼ cups granulated sugar and the water and bring to a boil over high heat. Lower the heat to simmer and cook until syrupy, about 2 minutes. Let cool slightly.

3. Add to the saucepan—one at a time and in the following order—the almond mixture, the butter, stirring until melted, then the lard, stirring again until melted, the egg yolks, and finally the whole egg. Cook over medium-low heat until the mixture begins to bubble, stirring occasionally, about 15 minutes. Pour into the tart pan and bake 13 to 15 minutes or until lightly browned on top. Let cool briefly, then remove the side of the tart pan.

4. In a small bowl, whisk the egg white until foamy, add the powdered sugar, and whisk until smooth and thickened. While the tart is still warm, paint the top with the glaze (there will be extra glaze that you can use, if you wish, for some other confection). Cut into small pieces and serve at room temperature.

Cheese Tart, Extremadura Style Ⓥ
Tarta de la Serena

MAKES 8 SERVINGS

This recipe for a heavenly cheese tart comes from Félix Durán at the Parador de Plasencia in Extremadura, a region that produces two excellent cheeses—Torta de La Serena and Torta del Casar. Both of these cheeses, which are considered highly desirable by cheese aficionados in the United States, are soft and runny (and available in American specialty stores). They lend an exotic flavor, but you may substitute another soft cheese such as Brie or Camembert. I always serve this with raspberry purée.

PREPARE AT 8 TO 12 HOURS IN ADVANCE

1 cup (10 ounces) small curd cottage cheese

6 ounces cream cheese

2 ounces Serena Torta del Casar, Camembert, or Brie, rind removed

1 cup sugar

4 large eggs

2 large egg yolks

¾ cup heavy cream

Fresh raspberries (optional)

Raspberry Purée (optional)

1⅓ cups fresh or frozen raspberries

¼ cup sugar

1½ teaspoons dry orujo (a Spanish liqueur similar to grappa), aquavit, Kirshwasser, or water

1. Preheat the oven to 350°F. In a medium bowl, beat the cottage, cream, the Serena cheeses, and the 1 cup sugar with an electric mixer until well blended. Beat in the whole eggs and yolks, one at a time, until the mixture is smooth and creamy. Gradually stir in the cream.

2. Lightly grease a 9-inch square or round cake pan, then line the bottom and sides with parchment paper or foil. Place about 1 inch of hot water in a roasting pan large enough to hold the cake pan. Pour in the cheese mixture and place the cake pan inside the roasting pan. Bake 1 hour 20 minutes to 1 hour 30 minutes or until fairly firm to the touch. Remove from the pan of water and let cool completely. Invert onto a plate, remove the parchment paper, and invert again onto the plate. Cover and refrigerate overnight.

3. Prepare the purée, if using: Combine the 1⅓ cups raspberries, the ¼ cup sugar and the liqueur in a food processor and blend until smooth. Pass through a fine-mesh strainer into a small bowl. Discard the solids.

4. Spoon the purée onto individual dessert dishes. Place 1 slice of the tart on top and scatter the fresh raspberries, if using, around the dish. Serve at room temperature.

Puff Pastry Tart Ⓥ
Tarta del Convento

MAKES ONE 12 X 7-INCH TART
(6 TO 8 SERVINGS)

This recipe comes from the beautiful parador Via de la Plata at Mérida, a building that was once an ancient convent. The restaurant of this parador has received several gastronomic awards for its excellent regional cooking. These delectable pastry tarts are filled with cream and coated with a chocolate glaze.

PREPARE AT LEAST 2 HOURS IN ADVANCE

8¼ pounds puff pastry dough, homemade (page 135; triple recipe) or storebought

Filling

½ cup water

⅓ cup granulated sugar

3 large egg whites

Few drops fresh lemon juice

1 teaspoon powdered (confectioners) sugar

¼ teaspoon pure vanilla extract

1 cup heavy cream

Chocolate Glaze

3 ounces unsweetened chocolate

10 tablespoons granulated sugar

6 tablespoons water

1. Prepare the pastry dough if necessary. Preheat the oven to 450°F. Place an oven rack in the upper position. Divide the dough into 3 equal parts. Wrap 2 parts in plastic wrap and reserve in the refrigerator. Roll 1 part on a floured work surface into a 15 x 10-inch rectangle. Transfer to a lightly greased cookie sheet of the same size and refrigerate until needed. Prepare the 2 remaining parts of dough in the same manner (if 3 cookie sheets are not available, you will have to bake the dough in 2 or more stages).

2. Prick the dough all over with a fork. It is best to bake 1 cookie sheet at a time, or as many as will fit on the upper oven rack. Bake 10 minutes, opening the oven every 2 minutes or so to prick the dough some more so that it does not puff too much, or until well browned all over (don't worry if the edges overcook). Let cool, then trim the edges to make one 12 x 7-inch rectangle. Repeat with the remaining rectangles if necessary.

3. Prepare the filling: Place the ½ cup water and ⅓ cup granulated sugar in a small saucepan and bring to a boil over high heat. Reduce the heat to low and simmer until the syrup reaches the soft-ball stage, about 15 to 20 minutes. (It will reach 234-240°F on a candy thermometer and when a small amount is dropped into very cold water, forms a soft ball that flattens when pressed.)

4. Meanwhile, place the egg whites and lemon juice in a small bowl and beat with an electric mixer until foamy. Add the powdered sugar and vanilla and beat until they are thick and stiff (and hold their shape when you lift the beater) but not dry. Gradually beat in the hot syrup and continue beating 10 minutes more. Cover and refrigerate at least 2 hours to chill.

5. Place the cream in a deep bowl and beat with the electric mixer until soft peaks form; fold the cream into the egg white mixture.

6. Place 1 sheet of pastry on a serving dish. Spread half of the filling over the pastry, top with a second sheet, and spread the remaining filling over the top. Cover with the third sheet.

7. Prepare the glaze: Melt the chocolate, either in a double boiler or by letting it sit in a saucepan on top of a warm stove. In a small saucepan, combine

continues...

the 10 tablespoons sugar and 6 tablespoons water and bring to a boil over high heat. Reduce the heat to low and simmer until it reaches the thread stage. (It will reach 220-233°F on a candy thermometer and a drop of syrup lengthens to a thread when placed in a glass of cold water.) Gradually pour the syrup into the chocolate, stirring vigorously. Spread over the top layer of the tart. Cut into rectangular or square serving pieces. Serve at room temperature.

Sixteenth-Century Cheesecake Ⓥ

Flaón

MAKES ONE 8-INCH TART

This recipe is from the 1525 cookbook of Ruperto de Nola, the oldest cookbook in Spain and one of the oldest in Europe. It produces a cheesecake that is flat and uniquely flavored and is a specialty of Ibiza.

Dough

1 cup all-purpose flour
¼ teaspoon salt
2½ tablespoons water
3 tablespoons vegetable oil

2 large eggs
½ pound cottage cheese
½ cup sugar
⅛ teaspoon dried mint
⅛ teaspoon anisette liqueur
3 tablespoons honey
1 teaspoon rose water
Ground cinnamon, for dusting

1. Prepare the dough: Preheat the oven to 350°F. In a small bowl, combine the flour and salt, add in the water and oil, and mix well until a dough forms. Roll out on a work surface and fold lengthwise in thirds, business-letter fashion. Roll again to the previous size and fold, then roll and fold 2 more times (for a total of four times). Press into and up the side of an 8-inch loose-bottom tart pan and trim any excess by pressing and cutting off at the rim.

2. In a small bowl, beat the eggs, cottage cheese, sugar, mint, and anisette with an electric mixer until smooth. Spread onto the dough and bake 40 minutes or until the filling is set.

3. In another small bowl, combine the honey and rose water. Drizzle over the cheesecake, then dust with the cinnamon. Serve warm.

Apple Flan Loaf with Caramelized Sugar Syrup Ⓥ

Flan de Manzana con Azúcar Acaramelado

MAKES 5 TO 6 SERVINGS

Milk is a characteristic ingredient of flan, but in this recipe puréed apples and egg provide the body to set the custard. I first tasted this unusual apple flan loaf in the picturesque seaside city of San Sebastián in northern Spain at the exquisite Panier Fleuri restaurant. María Jesús Fombellida, the talented chef who ran the restaurant, was known for her incredible desserts.

PREPARE AT LEAST 2 HOURS IN ADVANCE

1 pound Golden Delicious apples, peeled, cored, and cut into eighths
¼ cup (½ stick) unsalted butter, cut into several pieces
1 tablespoon fresh lemon juice

2 tablespoons dry white wine

⅛ teaspoon ground cinnamon

⅛ teaspoon ground nutmeg

5 large eggs

½ cup sugar

Fresh berries, for garnish (optional)

Caramelized Sugar Syrup

½ cup sugar

½ cup hot water

1. In a medium saucepan, combine the apples, butter, lemon juice, wine, cinnamon, and nutmeg. Cover, bring to a boil over low heat, and simmer about 20 minutes or until the apples are tender.

2. Meanwhile, prepare the syrup: In a small saucepan, combine the ½ cup sugar and 3 tablespoons of the water and cook over high heat, stirring constantly. until syrupy and light golden. Remove from the heat. Gradually and very carefully stir in the remaining 5 tablespoons water. Pour into a 7½ x 3½-inch loaf pan.

3. Preheat the oven to 350°F. When the apples are done, uncover, increase the heat to medium and cook, stirring occasionally, until the liquid has evaporated. Pass through a fine-mesh strainer. Discard the solids. In a medium bowl, whisk together the eggs and the ½ cup sugar, then whisk in the apples. Pour into the loaf pan.

4. Place about 1 inch of hot water in a 13 x 9-inch baking pan and place the loaf pan inside it. Bake about 1 hour and 10 minutes or until the custard is fairly firm when touched at the center.

5. Let cool, then refrigerate at least 2 hours up to 24 hours to chill. Turn out onto a serving dish, top side up. Cut into ½-inch slices and place two slices on each dessert dish. Spoon the caramelized sugar over the top and garnish with berries, if using. Serve warm or at room temperature.

Pastries and Turnovers

Breakfast Fritters Ⓥ
Churros

MAKES 30 FRITTERS

Churros, or wand-shaped donuts, which are made from nothing but a fried batter of flour and water, are eaten in Spain mostly for breakfast, but really, anytime the urge strikes. Churros should be eaten right after they are made, or they will lose their delightful crunch. You will need a churro maker or pastry bag to pipe the fluted shape of the churros. The fluted shape is essential because the pastries will turn out hard and doughy otherwise. Churro makers are available in specialty shops and online (see box, page 602).

2 cups water

1 tablespoon vegetable oil

¼ teaspoon salt

2 cups all-purpose flour

Olive oil, for frying

Sugar, for dipping

1. In a medium saucepan, combine the water, oil, and salt and bring to a boil over high heat. Add the flour all at once, reduce the heat to low, and stir vigorously with a wooden spoon until a ball forms. Let cool slightly. Transfer to a churro maker or to a pastry bag or cake decorator fitted with a ⅜-inch fluted tube (#105 is good).

2. Heat at least ½ inch of oil in a medium skillet over medium-high heat (or better still, use a deep fryer set at 375°F) until it browns a cube of bread

continues . . .

quickly. Reduce the heat to medium and press out 3 or 4 strips of dough 4 inches long into the oil (the strips may also be shaped into loops). Fry, turning once, until they barely begin to color. Transfer to paper towels with an offset spatula and let drain.

3. Repeat with the remaining batter, cooking in small batches so you can keep a watchful eye to prevent overcooking. Place the sugar in a small serving bowl. Serve warm with the sugar, for dipping.

Apple Fritters Ⓥ
Buñuelos de Manzana

MAKES 4 SERVINGS

Buñuelos de Manzana *are enormously popular in Catalunya. They are commonly served with different sauces, which should be spooned in a pool on the plate rather than poured over the fritters because that would detract from their crunchiness. This recipe includes two different sauces: an apricot sauce and a light creamy custard. Both of them are delicious.*

Batter

¾ cup all-purpose flour

1½ teaspoons baking powder

⅛ teaspoon salt

¼ cup plus 1 tablespoon water

¼ cup milk

2 tablespoons mild olive oil

1 large egg white

Apricot Sauce

½ cup apricot preserves

1 teaspoon medium-sweet sherry, such as Oloroso

4 teaspoons fruit juice, such as apple

Light Custard Sauce

2 large egg yolks

3 tablespoons sugar

1 tablespoon all-purpose flour

⅛ teaspoon salt

2 cups milk

¼ cup sugar

¼ teaspoon ground cinnamon

¼ teaspoon fresh lemon juice

Generous amount of freshly grated nutmeg

1 apple, such as McIntosh or Golden Delicious, peeled, cored, and cut into 12 (¼-inch) rings or wedges

Olive oil, for frying

1. Prepare the batter: In a medium bowl, combine the flour, baking powder, and salt. Gradually stir in the water, milk, and oil and mix until smooth. In a small bowl, whisk the egg white until soft peaks form and fold into the batter.

2. Prepare the apricot sauce, if using: Combine all the ingredients in a small serving bowl and reserve.

3. Prepare the custard sauce, if using: In the top of a double boiler or bowl over a pot (not yet over the heat), whisk together the egg yolk, sugar, flour, and salt until pale yellow, and gradually stir in the 2 cups milk. Place over boiling water and cook, stirring constantly, until thickened to a soft custard consistency. Let cool, stirring frequently. Reserve.

4. In a small shallow bowl, combine the sugar, cinnamon, lemon juice, and nutmeg. Dredge each apple slice in this mixture.

5. Heat at least 1 inch of oil in a medium skillet over medium-high heat (or better still, use a deep fryer set at 375°F) until it quickly browns a cube of bread. Dip each apple slice in the batter and place in the oil. Fry, turning once, until lightly golden. Transfer with a slotted spoon to paper towels and let drain.

6. Spoon the sauce of your choice onto 4 dessert dishes and arrange 3 apple fritters over the sauce on each dish. Serve warm.

Basic Fritters V

Buñuelos de Viento

MAKES ABOUT 50 FRITTERS

Fritters of all kinds are very popular in Spain. These heavenly light and tiny doughnuts are typically eaten on All Saints Day, celebrated on November 1. Buñuelos de viento translates in English to "puffs of wind," a name that could not be more fitting.

1 cup water

6 tablespoons unsalted butter, cut into pieces

¼ teaspoon salt

2 tablespoons granulated sugar

1 cup all-purpose flour

¼ teaspoon lemon zest (optional)

4 large eggs

Olive oil, for frying

Powdered (confectioners) sugar, for dusting

1. In a small saucepan, combine the water, butter, salt, and granulated sugar and bring to a boil over medium heat. Add the flour all at once and stir until well blended. Reduce the heat to low, add the lemon zest, if using, and stir with a wooden spoon until a ball forms. Cook, flattening and turning the dough with a wooden spoon, about 2 minutes. Remove from the heat and let cool 1 to 2 minutes. Transfer to a food processor and process 15 seconds. Add the eggs and process 30 seconds more.

2. Heat at least 1 inch of oil in a medium skillet over medium-high heat (or better still, use a deep fryer set at 365°F) until it turns a cube of bread light brown in 60 seconds. Working in small batches because the fritters will double in size, drop the dough by the teaspoon into the oil. Fry, turning occasionally, until completely puffed and hollow within. Transfer with a slotted spoon to paper towels and let drain and cool. Repeat with the remaining dough. Dust with the powdered sugar. Serve at room temperature.

Cream-Filled Fritters V

Buñuelos de San Isidro

MAKES 40 FRITTERS

On May 16, Spaniards celebrate San Isidro, the patron saint of Madrid, in a festival that is followed by a month of daily bullfighting. These cream-filled puffs can be found in all the local bakeries and are traditionally eaten during this time of year.

1 cup milk

Peel of ½ lemon

3 egg yolks

¼ cup sugar

¼ cup flour

2 teaspoons butter

1 recipe Basic Fritters (at left)

Powdered (confectioners) sugar, for dusting

1. In a small saucepan, heat the milk and lemon peel over high heat to the boiling point. Reduce the heat to low and simmer about 10 minutes. Discard the lemon peel. Place the egg yolks in a separate small saucepan and stir in the sugar. Beat the yolk mixture with a whisk until pale yellow. Beat in the flour and gradually add the hot milk. Cook over medium heat, stirring constantly, until thickened. Remove from the heat and stir in the butter. Let cool.

2. Prepare the fritters as instructed in the recipe, but do not sprinkle with the powdered sugar.

3. Cut open a flap in the top of each fritter. Fill with custard and close the flap. (The custard may also be injected if you have a device for that purpose known as a Bismarck filler.) Dust with the powdered sugar. Serve at room temperature.

It is amazing that, with all the different pastries, cookies, tarts, and fritters that are so plentiful in Spanish cuisine, whenever anybody asks me what the quintessential Spanish dessert is, I answer without any doubt "*Churros!*" There are many other desserts more sophisticated, involving many more ingredients and dependent sometimes upon specialized cooking techniques. But to me, *churros*, or wand-shaped donuts often coated with sugar crystals, are the premier delicacy (yes, delicacy) and the most cherished snack throughout all of Spain. Commonly served with coffee, tea, or hot chocolate, *churros* (page 599) are eaten for breakfast, as mid-afternoon snacks, and sometimes for dessert. They are also enormously popular at three or four in the morning, when Spaniards are winding down after a late night of partying.

Churros, such a simple staple and one of the greatest accomplishments of Spanish gastronomy, consist of very simple ingredients—water, flour, a touch of salt, and olive oil for frying. They are found all over Spain—in Castilla, Andalucía, Catalunya, Gali-cia, the Balearic Islands, and the Basque Country. *Churros* are beloved by Spaniards in every region.

In Spain, *churros* are sold in *churrerías*, not bakeries or pastry shops, and they are usually the only product the vendors make and sell. *Churrerías* have their "unique" hours to cater to their clients—they open around 4 am and close around 10 am, then reopen at 5 pm and close at 9 pm. These hours are well known all over the country, and during business hours, the churrerias are mobbed. If you are ever in Madrid, I recommend that you go at about 3 or 4 in the morning to Churreria San Gines, near Madrid's main square, the Puerta del Sol. This is the place where people gather to end the night's festivities with hot chocolate and *churros*. It is an experience not to be missed.

Churros should be eaten right after they are fried, and the only addition should be a dish with granulated sugar for dipping. As the Spaniards say, "*Churros* keep Spain going!"

Sweetened Chickpea Fritters

Buñuelos de Garbanzos

MAKES ABOUT 20 FRITTERS

While chickpeas are enormously popular in Spain, they don't usually make their way into dessert recipes. These sweet chickpea fritters from the island of Lanzarote have an interesting texture, much like a cake. It's a very unusual combination of ingredients, as is typical of the Canary Islands.

½ pound cooked chickpeas, drained, or canned chickpeas, rinsed and drained

2 large eggs, separated

⅛ teaspoon salt

1 tablespoon anisette liqueur

1 tablespoon mild olive oil or vegetable oil

¼ cup granulated sugar

¼ teaspoon ground cinnamon

¼ teaspoon lemon zest

7 tablespoons all-purpose flour

Olive oil, for frying

Powdered (confectioners) sugar, for dusting

1. Place the chickpeas in a food processor and blend until smooth. Add the egg yolks, salt, anisette, and oil and blend until smooth. Add the granulated sugar, the cinnamon, lemon zest, and flour and pulse to blend.

2. In a medium bowl, beat the egg whites with an electric mixer until soft peaks form. Fold in the chickpea mixture.

3. Heat at least 1 inch of oil in a large skillet over medium-high heat (or better still, use a deep fryer set at 375°F) until it quickly browns a cube of bread. Drop the chickpea mixture by the tablespoon into the oil and fry, turning once, until golden on both sides. Transfer with a slotted spoon to paper towels and let dry.

4. Arrange on a platter and dust with the powdered sugar. Serve at room temperature.

Fritters from Xátiva Ⓥ
Toronjas de Xátiva Que Son Almojábanas

**MAKES 12 TO 14 FRITTERS
(SERVES ABOUT 4)**

The Spanish word almojábana *in Moorish times meant "cheese torte," although today the word refers to a fritter that does not necessarily include cheese. The word* toronja *refers to the size and shape of these fritters. This oddly titled recipe comes from the sixteenth-century cookbook* El Llibre del Cuiner *by Ruperto de Nola, who was chef to Spanish King Fernando of Naples when Naples was a Spanish possession.*

⅓ cup all-purpose flour

⅛ teaspoon salt

½ teaspoon baking powder

½ pound farmer's cheese, crumbled

5 tablespoons sugar

1 large egg

4 teaspoons finely chopped fresh mint

Mild olive oil, for frying

½ cup honey, thinned with 1 tablespoon water

Ground cinnamon, for dusting

1. In a medium bowl, combine the flour, salt, and baking powder. Stir in the cheese, sugar, egg, and mint and mix until well blended.

2. Heat at least ½ inch of oil in a large skillet over medium heat (or better still, use a deep fryer set at 375°F) until it quickly browns a cube of bread. Drop the cheese mixture by heaping teaspoons into the oil and fry until the fritters are, in the words of Ruperto de Nola, "the color of gold." Transfer with a slotted spoon to paper towels and let drain.

3. Arrange the fritters on individual dessert plates. In a microwave-safe bowl, combine the honey and water and heat in the microwave on High until warm. Spoon over the fritters. Dust with the cinnamon and serve warm.

Fresh Goat Cheese Fritters

Bollos de Cuajada

MAKES 24 FRITTERS (SERVES 6 TO 8)

These fritters are served on holidays in the Canary Islands. They are heavenly puffs of cheese bathed in honey, with accents of lemon and cinnamon. They should be served right after they are prepared so that they do not lose their crunchiness.

1 pound fresh goat cheese or farmer's cheese

½ teaspoon lemon zest

½ teaspoon ground cinnamon

3 tablespoons sugar

1 tablespoon melted unsalted butter

½ teaspoon brandy

⅛ teaspoon salt

⅛ teaspoon baking powder

4 large eggs

¼ cup all-purpose flour

Olive oil, for frying

½ cup honey

2 tablespoons water

1 teaspoon fresh lemon juice

Ground cinnamon, for dusting

1. In a medium bowl, mash the cheese with a fork. Stir in the lemon zest, cinnamon, sugar, butter, brandy, salt, and baking powder, then beat in the eggs with an electric mixer until combined. Stir in the flour until well blended.

2. Preheat the oven to 200°F. Heat at least 1 inch of oil in a large skillet over medium-high heat (or better still, use a deep fryer set at 375°F) until it quickly browns a cube of bread. Drop the batter by tablespoons into the oil and fry, turning frequently, until golden and crisp (do not crowd them in the pan). Transfer with a slotted spoon to paper towels and let drain. Arrange on a heatproof plate and place in the oven to keep warm while preparing the honey mixture.

3. In a small saucepan, combine the honey, water, and lemon juice and heat over low heat until thinned and smooth. Place a cooling rack over wax paper to catch any drips. Dip each fritter in the honey, place on the cooling rack, and let drain. Arrange on a platter and dust with the cinnamon. Serve warm.

Anise-Flavored Fried Pastries

Pestiños al Anís

MAKES 70 TO 80 PASTRIES

These are one of the most popular Spanish pastries. Today the word pestiño *refers to delicious, anise-flavored pastries that puff when fried and are then dipped in honey and covered with powdered sugar. Originally, it referred to a room where bread or pastries were baked. These pastries should be prepared several hours before serving so that the honey has a chance to penetrate the crisp pastry. They stay crisp for many days and, in my opinion, are better the following day.*

PREPARE AT LEAST 2 HOURS IN ADVANCE

½ cup vegetable oil

Peel of ½ lemon (yellow part only)

2 tablespoons ground anise seeds

½ cup dry white wine

2 cups all-purpose flour

1 cup honey

¼ cup water

Olive oil, for frying

Powdered (confectioners) sugar, for dusting

1. In a small skillet, combine the oil and lemon peel, heat over high heat, and cook until the peel turns black. Remove from the heat and discard the peel. Let cool slightly, then stir in the anise and let cool completely.

2. Pass the oil through a fine-mesh strainer into a medium bowl and discard the anise seeds. Stir in the wine and gradually mix in the flour until fully incorporated. Turn the dough out onto a work surface and knead lightly into a smooth ball. Wrap in plastic wrap and let sit 30 minutes.

3. Roll out the dough on a lightly floured work surface to the thickness of a nickel. Cut into 2 x 1-inch rectangles and let sit 30 minutes.

4. In a small saucepan, combine the honey and water and bring to a boil over high heat. Reduce the heat to low and simmer 15 minutes. Reserve.

5. Meanwhile, heat at least ½ inch of oil in a medium skillet over medium-high heat (or better still, use a deep fryer set at 375°F) until it quickly browns a cube of bread. Reduce the heat to medium (340°F). Place as many dough rectangles as will comfortably fit in the oil (they will puff) and fry, turning once, until lightly browned. (Cook in batches if necessary to avoid overcrowding.) Transfer with an offset spatula to paper towels and let drain. Repeat with the remaining rectangles.

6. Place a cooling rack over a sheet of foil or wax paper to catch the excess honey. Dip each pastry into the honey, place on the cooling rack, and let drain. On a round serving tray, arrange the pastries attractively in an overlapping "starburst" design and dust with the powdered sugar. Let sit 2 to 3 hours to allow the honey to penetrate the pastry. Serve at room temperature. Store on a platter covered with foil.

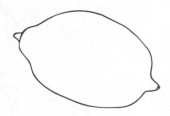

Fried Pastries with Anise and Sesame Seeds Ⓥ
Borrachuelos

MAKES 60 PASTRIES

Very similar to pestiños (Anise-Flavored Fried Pastries) these borrachuelos are larger, more moist, and seasoned with sesame seeds. This is the recipe for them in their simplest form—there are also a variety of more elaborate desserts that are based on borrachuelos. They will keep for several days.

⅔ cup vegetable oil

Peel of ¼ orange (orange part only)

2 teaspoons sesame seeds

1 teaspoon ground anise seeds

⅓ cup sweet white wine

⅓ cup dry white wine

3 tablespoons fresh orange juice

2¾ cups all-purpose flour

Olive oil, for frying

1 cup honey (one 12-ounce jar)

¼ cup water

Powdered (confectioners) sugar, for dusting

1. In a small skillet, combine the ⅔ cup oil and the orange peel, heat over high heat, and cook until the peel turns black. Remove from the heat, discard the peel, and let the oil cool. Pour the oil into a medium bowl and stir in the sesame seeds, anise seeds, sweet and dry wines, and the orange juice. Gradually mix in the flour until thoroughly incorporated. Turn the dough out onto a work surface and knead lightly, adding flour if necessary. Wrap in plastic wrap and let sit 30 minutes.

2. Divide the dough into 60 equal pieces and shape into ¾-inch balls. On a lightly floured work surface, roll each ball out with a rolling pin into a 4 x 2-inch oval.

continues...

3. Heat at least ½ inch of oil in a medium skillet over medium-high heat (or better still, use a deep fryer set at 375°F) until it quickly browns a cube of bread. Reduce the heat to medium. Place as many pastries as will comfortably fit in the oil (they will puff) and fry, turning once, until lightly browned. (Cook in batches if necessary to avoid overcrowding.) Transfer with a slotted spoon to paper towels and let drain. Repeat with the remaining pastries.

4. In a small saucepan, combine the honey and water and bring to a boil over high heat. Reduce the heat to low and simmer 5 minutes.

5. Place the powdered sugar in a wide shallow bowl. Place a cooling rack over a sheet of foil or wax paper to catch the excess honey. Dip each pastry into the honey, place on the cooling rack, and let drain. Roll in the powdered sugar and arrange on a platter. Serve at room temperature. Store on a platter covered with foil.

Sugar-Dusted Pastry Puffs Ⓥ
Soplillos de Sery Bermeo

MAKES ABOUT 30 PASTRIES

As is typical of Castilian cooking, the ingredients are simple and the results are delicious. These wonderful pastries that puff up as they fry are flavored with a hint of orange and anise. This recipe comes from Sery Bermeo and her husband Eugenio who run Mesón de la Villa, a wonderful restaurant in Aranda de Duero, in the heart of northern Castile. Soplillos will keep for several days at room temperature wrapped in foil.

2 tablespoons mild olive oil

2 tablespoons dry white wine

2 tablespoons anisette liqueur

2 tablespoons fresh orange juice

1 teaspoon orange zest

¼ teaspoon pure vanilla extract

About 1 cup all-purpose flour

Mild olive oil, for frying

Sugar, for dredging

1. In a medium bowl, combine the oil, wine, liquor, orange juice, orange zest, and vanilla. Gradually add the flour until thoroughly incorporated and a soft dough forms. Turn out on a work surface and knead briefly, adding more flour as necessary, so the dough is not sticky. Wrap in plastic wrap and let sit about 20 minutes.

2. Roll out the dough on a floured work surface to less than ⅛ inch thick in a rectangle. Cut the dough diagonally at 1-inch intervals with a thin sharp knife, then cut diagonally in the opposite direction at 3-inch intervals, crisscrossing to form rhombus shapes (slanted rectangles).

3. Heat at least ½ inch of oil in a medium skillet over medium-high heat (or better still, use a deep fryer set at 375°F) until it quickly browns a cube of bread. Place as many pastries as will comfortably fit in the oil (they will puff) and fry, turning once, until well browned. (Cook in small batches if necessary to avoid overcrowding.) Transfer with an offset spatula to paper towels and let drain. Repeat with the remaining rectangles. Place the sugar in a wide shallow bowl. While the pastries are still warm, dredge each in the sugar and arrange on a platter. Serve at room temperature.

Sugared Puff Pastry Strips with Almonds ⓥ

Almendrados de Villalcázar de Sirga

MAKES ABOUT 20 PASTRIES

Whenever I prepare these pastries, I smile at the memory of the exuberant man who gave me this recipe. Pablo El Mesonero, already in his nineties when we met him, was the proud owner of the centuries-old restaurant Los Templarios in the town of Villalcázar de Sirga, an important stop on the pilgrimage route known as El Camino de Santiago (the Way to St. James). Pablo used to dress as a pilgrim, donning a brown cape, a wide brimmed hat, and a red striped wool scarf over one shoulder. What was significant about the brown cape was the scallop shells on the shoulder, a symbol of St. James. Scallop shells, quite common in Galicia, were used by pilgrims as a way to prove they had completed their pilgrimage. Pablo has passed on, but in his memory, his staff and cape adorn a corner of the restaurant that his children now run.

½ pound puff pastry dough, homemade (page 135; partial recipe) or storebought

1 large egg white, lightly beaten

4 to 5 tablespoons finely chopped sliced almonds, skin on

4 to 5 tablespoons sugar

1. Preheat the oven to 450°F. Roll the puff pastry to ⅛ inch thick and cut into 2¾ x 1½-inch rectangles. Arrange on a greased cookie sheet. Brush each pastry with the egg and sprinkle with about ½ teaspoon of the sugar and about ½ teaspoon of the almonds.

2. Bake 8 minutes or until golden brown. Turn off the oven, leave the door slightly ajar, and let cool in the oven about 5 minutes or until thoroughly crisped. Serve at room temperature.

Sweet Potato Dessert Turnovers ⓥ*

Truchas Canarias

MAKES ABOUT 25 MINI TURNOVERS

Nobody seems to know why these turnovers are called truchas *(trout) since they come from the Canary Islands where there are no rivers, let alone trout. They are made with a flaky pastry filled with* batata *(sweet potato), almonds, and a touch of anise—and are typical Canary Island Christmas treats.* Truchas canarias *can be baked or fried, but I most definitely prefer them fried. Make it vegetarian with vegetable shortening.*

PREPARE AT LEAST 3 HOURS IN ADVANCE

Pastry Dough

¼ cup mild olive oil or vegetable oil

¼ cup dry white wine

⅛ teaspoon salt

3 tablespoons lard or vegetable shortening, softened

2 cups all-purpose flour

Sweet Potato

1 pound sweet potatoes, unpeeled

2 large egg yolks

¼ pound ground almonds

¼ cup sugar

1 teaspoon ground cinnamon

¼ teaspoon lemon zest

2 teaspoons anisette liqueur

¼ teaspoon ground anise seeds

Olive oil, for frying

A mixture of sugar and ground cinnamon, for sprinkling

1 egg, lightly beaten, for brushing

continues...

1. Prepare the dough: In a medium bowl, mix with a fork the oil, wine, salt, and lard. Gradually mix in the flour until thoroughly incorporated. Turn out onto a floured work surface and knead lightly until smooth. Wrap in plastic wrap and let sit 2 hours.

2. Meanwhile, prepare the filling: Place the potatoes in a large saucepan with cold water to cover. Cover and bring to a simmer over low heat. Cook about 30 minutes or until tender when pierced with a knife. Drain and let cool slightly. Peel and transfer to a medium bowl. Mash with a fork, then stir in the egg yolks, almonds, sugar, cinnamon, lemon zest, anisette, and anise seeds. Cover and let sit 1 hour.

3. Roll out the dough to ⅛ inch and cut into 3½-inch rounds with an empanadilla or biscuit cutter. Place 2 teaspoons filling in the center of each round. Fold in half and press the edges with a fork to seal.

4. Fry or bake the turnovers as desired:

To fry: Heat at least 1 inch of oil in a medium skillet over medium-high heat (or better still, use a deep fryer set at 365°F) until it turns a cube of bread of bread light brown in 60 seconds. Place the turnovers in the oil and cook, turning once, and fry until golden. (Cook in small batches if necessary to avoid overcrowding.) Transfer with a slotted spoon to paper towels and let drain. Repeat with the remaining turnovers.

To bake: Preheat the oven to 350°F. Brush each turnover with the egg. Arrange on a lightly greased cookie sheet and bake about 15 minutes. Let cool.

5. Sprinkle with the sugar-cinnamon mixture and arrange on a platter. Serve at room temperature.

Goat's Milk Cheese Tartlets Ⓥ
Quesadillas Canarias

MAKES 12 TARTLETS

Because of the Canary Islands' terrain, most of their best cheeses are made from goat's milk, which has more flavor than cow's milk. These pastry tartlets filled with sweetened goats milk flavored with the distinctive accent of anise originated there, and so are called quesadillas canarias. *They are best when served cold.*

PREPARE AT LEAST 2 HOURS IN ADVANCE

Pastry Dough

⅔ cup all-purpose flour

2 tablespoons unsalted butter, softened

2 tablespoons sugar

2 tablespoons beaten egg

⅛ teaspoon lemon zest

Filling

¼ pound fresh goat cheese or farmer's cheese, crumbled

2 tablespoons sugar

1 tablespoon honey

1 large egg, lightly beaten

¼ teaspoon ground anise seeds

⅛ teaspoon ground cinnamon

¼ teaspoon lemon zest

Pinch of salt

1. Prepare the dough: Place all the dough ingredients in a small bowl and work with your fingers until a dough forms.

2. Prepare the filling: In another small bowl, mix the cheese and sugar until well blended. Add the honey, whole beaten egg, the anise, cinnamon, lemon zest, and salt and stir until well blended.

3. Preheat the oven to 350°F. Roll out the dough to less than ⅛ inch thick and cut into 2½-inch rounds.

Fit 1 round in the bottom and up the side of each of 12 (1¾-inch) lightly buttered mini tartlet pans. Fill each with 1 tablespoon of the filling. Bake 25 to 30 minutes or until the filling is set. Refrigerate at least 2 hours and serve cold.

Spiced Stewed Apples in Puff Pastry Ⓥ

Hojaldre de Manzana

MAKES 4 TO 5 SERVINGS

Puff pastries have been popular in Spain for centuries and are traditionally prepared with lard rather than butter. This is a delicious dessert of spiced stewed apples in a puff pastry covered with either whipped cream or ice cream. This recipe comes from Asturias, a region that has the ideal climate for growing apples.

6 ounces puff pastry dough, homemade (page 135; partial recipe) or storebought

½ cup plus 2 tablespoons sugar

½ cup apple juice

½ cup white wine

1 cinnamon stick

Peel of ½ lemon (yellow part only)

¼ teaspoon ground nutmeg

5 whole cloves

2 large Golden Delicious apples, peeled, cored, and cut into ¾-inch pieces

Melted vanilla ice cream or sweetened heavy cream

Powdered (confectioners) sugar, for dusting

1. Prepare the pastry dough if necessary. Preheat the oven to 450°F.

2. Roll out the pastry dough to ⅛ inch thick and cut into 4 x 3-inch rectangles. Place on a greased cookie sheet and bake about 8 minutes until puffed and golden brown. Turn off the oven, leave the door slightly ajar, and let sit in the oven about 5 minutes more to further crisp.

3. In a small saucepan, combine the sugar and 3 tablespoons of the apple juice and cook over high heat, stirring constantly, until syrupy and lightly golden. Remove from the heat. Gradually and very carefully stir in the remaining 5 tablespoons apple juice. Stir in the wine, cinnamon stick, lemon peel, nutmeg, and cloves and bring to a boil over medium heat. Reduce the heat to low and simmer about 10 minutes more. Add the apples, bring again to a boil, and simmer uncovered about 30 minutes more. Increase the heat to medium and cook, stirring constantly, until the liquid is reduced and the mixture syrupy, about 2 minutes more. Let cool. Discard the lemon peel, cinnamon stick, and cloves.

4. Split open each pastry and fill with about 2 tablespoons of the apples. Spoon a pool of melted ice cream or sweetened heavy cream onto individual dessert plates and place a pastry in the center. Dust with the powdered sugar and serve warm.

Frosted Puff Pastries Ⓥ

Corbatas de Unquera

MAKES 10 TO 12 PASTRIES

In Spanish, the word corbata *means "necktie" or "bow tie," which is how these puff pastries, twisted in the center like the knot of a tie, got their name. Wonderfully light and airy, frosted, and absolutely delicious, these pastries are very popular in all the pastry shops in the town of Unquera, in the northern coast of Cantabria. They are often served with coffee and are very popular as snacks in the mid-afternoon.*

½ pound puff pastry dough, homemade (page 135; partial recipe) or storebought

1 large egg white

¼ cup honey

¼ cup sugar

continues...

1. Place an oven rack in the upper position and preheat the oven to 425°F. Roll the puff pastry to ⅛ inch thick and cut into 5 x 1½-inch rectangles, being sure the dough stays chilled (refrigerate briefly if necessary). Twist one short side 180 degrees so that it looks like a bowtie. Place on a cookie sheet lined with foil.

2. Bake about 10 minutes or until the pastries are golden. Turn off the oven and leave the pastries in the oven with the door ajar about 5 minutes to dry the inner layers of dough. Let cool.

3. In a small bowl, beat the egg white with an electric mixer until soft peaks form. In a small saucepan, combine the honey and sugar, and stir over medium-high heat until it comes to a boil. Reduce the heat to low and simmer 5 minutes. Add the egg white and stir until smooth. Spread about 2 teaspoons over each pastry. Serve warm.

Spanish "French Toast" Ⓥ
Torrijas

MAKES 8 SERVINGS

Torrijas are Spain's version of what Americans call French toast. The recipe calls for day-old bread slices to be soaked in a custard-like milk mixture, coated with beaten eggs, and fried. It should be crisp on the outside and creamy within. I recommend using crusty bread. Torrijas are served always at Easter and mostly in popular taverns. In days of old, caballeros would arrive at a tavern, tie their horse at the door, and say to the bartender, "A glass of wine for me and a torrija for the horse!"

2 cups milk

6 tablespoons sugar

1 cinnamon stick

Peel of 1 lemon (yellow part only), cut into pieces

2 large eggs, lightly beaten

Mild olive oil, for frying

16 (¾-inch) slices day-old long-loaf (baguette) bread

Sugar, for sprinkling

Ground cinnamon, for sprinkling

1. In a medium saucepan, whisk the milk, sugar, cinnamon stick, and lemon peel together and bring to a boil over high heat. Reduce the heat to low and cook 1 minute. Return to a full boil over high heat, continuing to whisk, then reduce to low again and cook 1 minute more. Repeat 4 to 5 times until the milk is slightly thickened, then simmer about 5 minutes more. Let cool until barely warm and pour into a large deep plate.

2. Preheat the oven to 200°F. Place the eggs in a wide shallow bowl. Place the bread slices in the warm milk and let soak about 1 minute on each side. Meanwhile, heat at least 1 inch of oil in a large skillet over medium-high heat (or better still, use a deep fryer set at 365°F) until it turns a cube of bread light brown in 60 seconds. Dip each bread slice in the egg and place in the oil. (Cook in batches if necessary to avoid overcrowding.) Fry, turning once, until golden. Transfer with an offset spatula to paper towels and let drain. Place on a cookie sheet and keep warm in the oven while preparing the remaining bread.

3. Arrange the bread on a serving platter and sprinkle generously with the sugar and cinnamon. Serve warm or at room temperature.

Fried Bread and Honey **V**
Tostadas

MAKES 4 SERVINGS

This is a more elaborate version of torrijas *(Spanish "French Toast," page 610) in which the delicious fried bread is bathed in a honey and white wine syrup.*

½ cup milk

⅓ cup honey

8 (¾-inch) slices day-old long-loaf (baguette) bread (the bread should not be "airy")

Mild olive oil, for frying

1 large egg, beaten

Syrup

½ cup sugar

½ cup water

¼ cup white wine

Peel of ½ lemon (yellow part only)

1. Place the milk in a microwave-safe wide shallow bowl and heat in the microwave on Medium until lukewarm. Stir in the honey. Dip each bread slice in this mixture, turning several times to coat well, and place on a platter. Let sit 1 hour.

2. Prepare the syrup: In a small saucepan, combine all the syrup ingredients and bring to a boil over medium heat. Reduce the heat to low and simmer, stirring occasionally, about 10 minutes. Keep warm over the lowest heat until needed.

3. Heat at least ½ inch of oil in a large skillet over medium-high heat (or better still, use a deep fryer set at 375°F) until it quickly browns a cube of bread. Reduce the heat to medium. Place the egg in a small shallow bowl. Dip the bread in the egg and place in the oil. Fry, turning once, until golden on both sides. Transfer with an offset spatula to paper towels and let drain. Place 2 slices of bread on each of 4 deep plates and pour the syrup over the bread. Serve warm.

4. Tostadas are still good 1 or 2 days later. To reheat, place the bread and its syrup in a 350°F oven until heated and the bread is crisp.

Crisply Sautéed Bread in Honey Syrup **V**
Torrijas Taberna de Antonio Sánchez

MAKES 4 SERVINGS

This outstanding version of torrijas *(Spanish "French Toast," page 610) comes from La Taberna de Antonio Sanchez, a historic and very famous tavern in Madrid. It was owned by a retired bullfighter who became an artist, and the walls of this wonderfully rustic tavern are filled with his paintings and bullfighting memorabilia. At one time, this was a popular gathering place for Madrid's literati and today remains a quaint, old-fashioned tavern that serves excellent tapas and still has* torrijas *on the menu.*

1 large egg

1 tablespoon sugar

⅛ teaspoon ground cinnamon

1 cup milk

Peel of ½ lemon, cut into several strips (yellow part only)

4 (1-inch) slices dense but fine-textured day-old country bread, 4 x 3 inches

Mild olive oil, for frying

Honey Syrup

¼ cup water

2 tablespoon sugar

⅛ teaspoon ground cinnamon

2 tablespoons honey

Peel of ¼ lemon, cut into several strips (yellow part only)

continues...

1. In a small saucepan, whisk together the egg, the 1 tablespoon sugar, and the ⅛ teaspoon cinnamon, then stir in the milk and the ½ lemon peel. Heat over medium-low heat, stirring constantly, until the mixture begins to bubble and becomes the thickness of a soft custard. Let cool, remove the lemon peel, and pour into a large deep plate (the custard should not be too thick—thin with some milk if necessary). Add the bread and let sit, turning occasionally, until all the custard is absorbed, about 30 minutes.

2. Meanwhile, prepare the syrup: In a small saucepan, combine all the syrup ingredients and bring to a boil over medium heat. Reduce the heat to low and simmer about 5 minutes. Let cool and discard the lemon peel.

3. Transfer the bread to a cooling rack and let dry 10 minutes. Heat ⅛ inch of oil in a medium skillet over medium heat. Add the bread and cook, turning once, until golden. Transfer with an offset spatula to paper towels and let drain. Place 1 slice of bread on each of 4 individual plates, and pour the syrup over the bread. Serve warm.

Pastries with Squash Marmalade and Honey Ⓥ
Torrijas con Mermelada de Calabaza y Miel

MAKES ABOUT 15 PASTRIES

This is one of my favorite desserts that comes from the Canary Islands. I got the recipe from La Era, a rustic restaurant on the island of Lanzarote that serves only local specialties. Fried pastries filled with squash marmalade are even better when coated with honey.

PREPARE 8 TO 12 HOURS IN ADVANCE

2¾ cups all-purpose flour

¼ teaspoon ground cinnamon

¼ teaspoon ground anise seeds

1 teaspoon baking powder

⅛ teaspoon salt

6 large eggs, lightly beaten

2 tablespoons milk

¼ teaspoon lemon zest

1 recipe Candied Spaghetti Squash Marmalade (page 664)

Olive oil, for frying

Honey

1. In a medium bowl, combine the flour, cinnamon, anise, baking powder, and salt. Stir in the eggs, milk, and lemon zest until a soft dough forms.

2. Turn out onto a work surface and knead briefly until smooth, adding a little more flour if the dough is too sticky. Wrap loosely in oiled plastic wrap and let sit at room temperature overnight. Meanwhile, prepare the marmalade as instructed in the recipe.

3. Divide the dough into about 15 equal pieces and shape into 1½-inch balls. With a rolling pin, roll each out on a floured work surface into a 6 x 3-inch oval.

4. Heat at least 1 inch of oil in a large skillet over medium-high heat (or better still, use a deep fryer set at 365°F) until it turns a cube of bread light brown in 60 seconds. Place the pastries in the oil and fry, turning once, until slightly puffed but not browned. Transfer with a slotted spoon to paper towels and let drain.

5. Drizzle with the honey and spoon a dollop of marmalade over the top. Serve warm.

Spiced Doughnuts Ⓥ

Rosquillas

MAKES ABOUT 15 DOUGHNUTS

These fragrant spiced doughnuts, flavored with anise, nutmeg, and cloves, reflect a Moorish influence. They should be fried quickly in hot oil so they are crispy on the outside but still doughy within.

1½ cups all-purpose flour

⅛ teaspoon salt

1 tablespoon baking powder

½ teaspoon freshly grated or ground nutmeg

6 whole cloves, finely crushed

½ teaspoon ground or finely crushed anise seeds

1 large egg

¼ cup granulated sugar

1½ tablespoons cold milk

2 tablespoons melted unsalted butter, cooled

Mild olive oil, for frying

Powdered (confectioners) sugar for dusting

1. Sift together the flour, salt, and baking powder into a small bowl. Stir in the nutmeg, cloves, and anise.

2. In a medium bowl, beat the egg and granulated sugar with an electric mixer, about 20 minutes. (Beating for this long helps develop the dough.) Beat in the milk and butter, then add the flour mixture and stir until incorporated. Turn out onto a floured work surface and knead about 5 minutes, adding more flour as necessary, until the dough no longer sticks to your hands (do not add more flour than necessary).

3. Roll out the dough on a floured surface to ¼ inch thick. Cut with a doughnut cutter and let sit 10 minutes.

4. Heat at least 1 inch of oil in a medium skillet over medium heat (or better still, use a deep fryer set at 350°F) until it slowly browns a cube of bread (in about a minute). Place as many doughnuts as will comfortably fit in the oil and fry, turning once, until golden. (Cook in small batches if necessary to avoid overcrowding.) Transfer with an offset spatula to paper towels and let drain and cool. Dust with the powdered sugar. Serve at room temperature.

Miniature Anise-Flavored Doughnuts Ⓥ

Rosquillas Riojanas

MAKES ABOUT 40 MINI DOUGHNUTS

This is an old family recipe that I got from my mother-in-law, Clara Orozco, a Madrileña of Basque descent. Before the advent of measuring cups and spoons, any recipe calling for eggs used the egg half shells to measure the other ingredients. These doughnuts are a favorite of my husband because of the unusual flavor and texture.

PREPARE AT LEAST 2 HOURS IN ADVANCE

¾ cup (6 half egg shells) salad oil

1½ teaspoons ground anise seeds

1 large egg

¼ cup granulated sugar

¾ cup (6 half egg shells) dry white wine

2½ cups all-purpose flour

Olive oil, for frying

Powdered (confectioners) sugar, for dredging and dusting

Ground cinnamon, for dusting (optional)

continues...

1. In a small skillet, combine the oil and anise seeds, heat over medium heat, and cook, stirring, until the seeds are browned. Let cool. Pass through a fine-mesh strainer into a small bowl. Discard the anise.

2. In a medium bowl, whisk the egg until light and frothy. Gradually add the sugar, then the oil and wine. Gradually stir in the flour until incorporated to make a dough that can be worked with the hands but is slightly sticky. Cover the bowl with foil and let rest 2 hours.

3. Divide the dough into about 40 equal pieces. With floured hands, roll each piece into a 4 x ½-inch rope. Shape into a ring, pressing the ends together so they are firmly joined.

4. Heat at least 1 inch of oil in a large skillet over high heat to the smoking point (or better still, use a deep fryer set at 375°F) until it quickly browns a cube of bread. Reduce the heat to medium-high (about 365°F). Place as many doughnuts as will comfortably fit in the skillet (they will puff) and fry, turning 2 or 3 times, until golden—they should brown slowly. Transfer with an offset spatula to paper towels and let drain.

5. Sift the powdered sugar into a wide shallow bowl. Roll each doughnut in the powdered sugar. Arrange on a platter and sift additional powdered sugar over the doughnuts. Sprinkle with the cinnamon, if using. Serve at room temperature.

Custard-Filled Mini Doughnuts Ⓥ
Brevas de Soria

MAKES ABOUT 30 MINI DOUGHNUTS

This version of miniature doughnuts filled with custard comes from a small corner cafeteria in Soria, a beautiful town where the famous poet Antonio Machado lived and taught. The beauty of Soria is always present in his magnificent poetry. People line up down the block to buy these great doughnuts.

PREPARE AT LEAST 2 HOURS IN ADVANCE

1 package (2½ teaspoons) active dry yeast

¼ cup warm water (100° to 110°F)

3½ cups all-purpose flour

½ teaspoon salt

½ cup sugar

1 large egg, lightly beaten

1 cup warm milk

2 tablespoons unsalted butter, melted

½ recipe Custard Filling (page 615)

Olive oil, for frying

Sugar, for dredging

1. In a small cup, sprinkle the yeast over ¼ cup of the warm water. Let sit until the yeast is creamy, about 2 minutes. Stir until the yeast dissolves. In a medium bowl, combine the flour, salt, and the ½ cup sugar. Stir in the egg until well blended, then stir in the milk, butter, and the yeast mixture. Turn out onto a work surface and knead a minute or so, just until the dough is smooth and no longer sticky, adding more flour as necessary. Grease a large bowl with oil, place the dough in the bowl, and turn to coat. Cover with a towel and let rise in a warm draft-free spot 1½ hours or until double in size.

2. Meanwhile, prepare the custard as instructed in steps 2 and 3, omitting the lemon peel and adding ¼ teaspoon vanilla with the butter after the custard has cooked. Let cool, stirring occasionally.

3. Punch down the dough, divide into about 30 equal pieces and shape into 2 x 1-inch ovals. Arrange on a cookie sheet and let sit in a warm draft-free spot 1 hour more.

4. Heat at least ½ inch of oil in a large skillet over medium-high heat (or better still, use a deep fryer set at 375°F) until it quickly browns a cube of bread. In a skillet, heat the oil, at least ½ inch deep, until very hot. Reduce the heat to medium (about 340°F). Place as many doughnuts as will comfortably fit in the skillet (they will puff) and fry, turning frequently, until golden and well puffed. Transfer with a slotted spoon to paper towels and let drain.

5. Place the sugar in a shallow bowl and roll each doughnut in the sugar. Slit lengthwise with a sharp knife, as for a baked potato, and fill doughnut with about 1 teaspoon of custard. Serve immediately.

Baked Doughnuts Bathed in Honey
Almojábanas

MAKES ABOUT 40 DOUGHNUTS

Any Spanish word that begins with the prefix "al" means it is of Arab origin. Almojábanas are baked doughnuts coated with honey and are the typical pastries of Albarracín, a village that to this day reflects the culinary influence the Moors have had on Spain.

1 recipe dough puffs (Bunyolets; page 309), substituting water for the chicken broth, omitting the ham and parsley, and adding 1 teaspoon sugar

Olive oil

½ cup honey

Powdered (confectioners) sugar

1. Prepare the puffs dough as instructed in step 2 of the recipe. Preheat the oven to 350°F. Drop the dough by the teaspoon onto a greased cookie sheet. Dip a finger in oil and press a hole into the center of each pastry, then bake about 25 minutes or until puffed and lightly browned.

2. Place the honey in a small saucepan and heat over low heat until thinned. Place a cooling rack over a cookie sheet to catch any drips. Dip each doughnut in the honey, place on the cooling rack, and let drain. Sprinkle with the powdered sugar. Serve at room temperature.

Custard-Filled Fried Pastries
Bartolillos

MAKES 15 TO 20 PASTRIES

Custard-filled fried pastries are popular all throughout Spain but this version, called Bartolillos, *is a specialty of Madrid.*

½ cup vegetable oil

Peel of ½ lemon (yellow part only)

½ cup white wine

2 cups all-purpose flour

Pinch of salt

Custard Filling

2 cups milk

Peel of ½ lemon (yellow part only)

5 large egg yolks

½ cup granulated sugar

½ cup all-purpose flour

1 tablespoon unsalted butter

Olive oil, for frying

Powdered (confectioners) sugar, for dusting

Ground cinnamon, for dusting

continues...

1. In a small skillet, combine the ½ cup oil and the ½ lemon peel, heat over high heat, and cook until the peel turns black. Discard the peel and let the oil cool. Transfer to a medium bowl and add the wine, flour, and salt. Work into a ball with your hands, kneading lightly. Wrap in plastic wrap and let sit 30 minutes.

2. Meanwhile, prepare the filling: In a small saucepan, combine the milk and the ½ lemon peel and bring to a boil over medium heat. Reduce the heat to low and simmer, stirring occasionally, about 10 minutes. Discard the lemon peel.

3. Place the egg yolks in another small saucepan and gradually stir in the sugar, then beat with a whisk until the yolks are pale yellow. Beat in the flour and gradually add the milk. Cook over medium heat, stirring constantly, until thickened and smooth and no flour taste remains. Remove from the heat and stir in the butter. Let cool, stirring occasionally.

4. While the custard is cooling, roll out the dough on a floured work surface to the thickness of a nickel. Cut into triangles that are 3 x 3 x 2 inches and let sit 30 minutes more.

5. Place about 1 teaspoon of the custard down the middle of each of half the triangles. Cover with the remaining triangles and press the edges with a fork to seal.

6. Heat at least ½ inch of oil in a large skillet over medium heat (or better still, use a deep fryer set at 350°F) until it slowly browns a cube of bread (in about a minute). Place as many pastries as will comfortably fit in the oil and fry, turning once, until golden. (Cook in batches if necessary to avoid overcrowding.) Transfer with an offset spatula to paper towels and let drain and cool.

7. Arrange on a platter and dust with the powdered sugar and cinnamon. Serve at room temperature.

Spaghetti Squash Turnovers Ⓥ*
Farinosos

MAKES 12 MINI TURNOVERS

These turnovers are always a big hit with my guests, but they can never guess the secret ingredient. Spaghetti squash has been a staple in Spanish dessert making for centuries, but it is relatively new in the United States. In Spain, it is called cabello de angel *which translates to "angel's hair." This recipe calls for candied spaghetti squash (marmalade), a wonderfully sweet and unusual filling, but you can also substitute other kinds of marmalade. Make it vegetarian with vegetable shortening.*

1 recipe Candied Spaghetti Squash Marmalade (page 664)
1¼ cups all-purpose flour
2 tablespoons mild olive oil
1 tablespoon sugar
⅛ teaspoon salt
4 tablespoons (¼ cup) lard or vegetable shortening
1 tablespoon beaten egg
1 tablespoon honey
Olive oil, for brushing
Sugar, for sprinkling

1. Prepare the marmalade as instructed in the recipe. In a medium bowl, combine the flour, oil, 1 tablespoon sugar, the salt, lard, egg, and honey and work with your hands to form a dough. Wrap in plastic wrap and let sit 30 minutes.

2. Roll the dough on a floured surface to a scant ⅛ inch thick and cut into 3½-inch rounds with an empanadilla or biscuit cutter. Place about 2 teaspoons of candied spaghetti squash in the center of each round. Fold in half and press the edges with a fork to seal. Arrange on a greased cookie sheet and let sit 1 hour.

3. Preheat the oven to 350°F. Brush the turnovers with the oil and sprinkle with the sugar. Bake about 10 minutes or until golden. Serve warm.

Almond and Marmalade Puff Pastry Strips **V**
Banda de Almendra

MAKES 12 PASTRIES

I like this classic and elegant Spanish pastry best when prepared with quince marmalade or candied squash marmalade, but any other fruit marmalade can be substituted.

½ pound puff pastry dough, homemade (page 135; partial recipe) or storebought

¾ cup Quince Marmalade (page 663), Candied Spaghetti Squash Marmalade (page 664), or other fruit marmalade or preserves, such as apricot

⅓ cup sliced almonds

Powdered (confectioners) sugar, for dusting

1. Prepare the pastry dough and marmalade as instructed in the recipes.

2. Place an oven rack in the upper position and preheat the oven to 425°F. Roll the dough out to ⅛ inch thick and cut into 4 x 1½-inch strips. Arrange on a cookie sheet. Bake 7 minutes, remove from the oven, and leave the oven on.

3. Spread about 1 tablespoon of the marmalade on each strip. Return to the oven and bake about 5 minutes more or until golden. Let cool slightly.

4. Arrange the almonds in overlapping rows along the length of the pastry. When completely cool, dust with the powdered sugar. Serve at room temperature.

Custard Horns **V**
Canutillos

MAKES ABOUT 15 PASTRIES

Canutillos are specialties of Navarra. These custard-filled horns are served warm and sprinkled with powdered sugar and cinnamon. You will need horn-shaped molds to get the traditional look.

10 ounces puff pastry dough, homemade (page 135; partial recipe) or storebought

1 recipe Custard Filling (page 615), at room temperature

Egg yolk, for sealing

Powdered (confectioners) sugar, for dusting

Ground cinnamon, for dusting

1. Prepare the pastry dough as instructed in the recipe, if necessary. Prepare the custard as instructed in steps 2 and 3 of the recipe.

2. Place an oven rack in the upper position. Preheat the oven to 425°F. Roll out the pastry dough to the thickness of a dime. Cut into ½-inch-wide strips and wrap, in slightly overlapping circles, around 4-inch-long baking horn molds. If more than 1 strip is needed for each horn, seal the seams well with egg yolk. Place on a cookie sheet, seam side down and bake about 5 minutes or until the horns are golden. Let cool slightly. Carefully remove the molds from the horns. Reduce the oven to 350°F.

3. Fill each horn with the custard and place on the cookie sheet. Bake about 5 minutes or until the custard is heated through. Turn off the oven and leave the horns in the oven for a few minutes to dry the inner layers of dough. Place on a platter, dust with the powdered sugar and cinnamon, and serve warm.

Sweet Spinach Custard in Puff Pastry Horns Ⓥ

Crema de Espinacas en Canutillos

MAKES ABOUT 30 PASTRIES

This very unusual dessert of spinach and custard was popular in Bilbao at the beginning of the century, and it is still popular throughout Spain today. The sweet spinach custard is served either as a filling for pastry horns or in a tart shell. This recipe for stuffed puff pastry horns came from Genaro Pildain, the talented chef at Bilbao's outstanding Guria restaurant. I have also included the directions for making the tart.

1 pound storebought or homemade puff pastry
(page 135; partial recipe), chilled

2 ounces fresh spinach leaves, well washed
(about 1 cup)

3 tablespoons cornstarch

2 cups plus 2 tablespoons milk

Peel of ¼ lemon (yellow part only)

2 large eggs

⅛ teaspoon salt

½ cup granulated sugar

Powdered (confectioners) sugar

1 large egg yolk, for sealing

1. If preparing your own pastry dough, make it at least 1 hour in advance and refrigerate until ready to use.

2. Place the spinach in a microwave-safe dish (if the spinach is damp, no water is necessary; otherwise, sprinkle lightly with water). Cover and microwave on High 4 minutes or until tender. (Or place in a small saucepan, add water to cover, and bring to a boil over high heat. Reduce the heat to low, cover, and simmer until tender, about 10 minutes.) Drain well, then wrap in paper towels and squeeze out any liquid. Chop finely and reserve. Wipe out the saucepan.

3. In a small bowl, dissolve the cornstarch in 2 tablespoons of the milk and reserve. In the small saucepan, combine the remaining 2 cups milk and the lemon peel and bring to a boil over medium heat. Reduce the heat to low and simmer, stirring occasionally, about 10 minutes.

4. In a medium saucepan, whisk together the eggs, salt, granulated sugar, and the cornstarch mixture. Discard the lemon peel and stir in the milk. Cook over medium heat, stirring constantly, until the mixture begins to thicken. Add the spinach and cook, stirring occasionally, until the custard begins to bubble. Remove immediately from the heat and let cool without stirring (stirring will thin the custard). Reserve at room temperature.

The Puff Pastry Horns:

5. Prepare the pastry horns: Place an oven rack in the upper position and preheat the oven to 425°F. Line a cookie sheet with foil. Roll out the pastry dough into a rectangle that is a scant ⅛ inch thick. Cut into ½-inch-wide strips and wrap each strip, in slightly overlapping circles, around a 4-inch-long baking horn-shaped mold. If more than 1 strip is needed for each horn, seal the seams well with egg yolk.

6. Arrange the horns, seam side down, on a cookie sheet and bake about 5 minutes or until the horns are golden. Turn off the oven and leave the horns in the oven for a few minutes to dry the inner layers of dough. Carefully remove the molds from the horns and let the horns cool.

7. Fill each horn with about 4 tablespoons of the custard and sprinkle with the powdered sugar. Serve warm or at room temperature.

The Puff Pastry Tart:

5. Place an oven rack in the upper position and preheat the oven to 425°F. Divide the dough into 2 equal parts. Roll out 1 dough part into a round that is a scant ⅛ inch thick. Cut into a round large enough to cover the bottom and side of a 9-inch tart pan. Prick all over with a fork and bake about

10 minutes or until golden, pricking occasionally to deflate the pastry. Leave the oven on.

6. Meanwhile, roll the remaining dough part into a rectangle that is a scant ⅛ inch thick and cut into 6 (9 x ½-inch) strips. Refrigerate at least 1 hour to chill.

7. Spoon the custard into the tart shell and lay 3 parallel strips of dough across the top. Interweave the remaining 3 strips through the others to create a lattice top. Brush with the egg yolk and bake 10 minutes more or until the pastry strips are golden. Let cool. Serve at room temperature.

Pastries Filled with Marmalade and Almonds *

Formetjades Rellenos de Mermelada y Almendra

MAKES 12 SMALL PASTRIES

These delicate marmalade- and almond-filled pastries are typical of the many filled pastries (both sweet and savory) from the Balearic Islands. I strongly recommend using lard as it creates a light and flaky pastry. I like these best with either peach or apricot marmalade. Make it vegetarian with vegetable shortening.

2⅔ cups all-purpose flour

1 large egg yolk

1 tablespoon sugar

¼ pound lard, preferably pure lard or vegetable shortening

¼ cup water

¼ cup mild olive oil

1 ounce blanched almonds (about 18)

¾ cup peach or apricot marmalade, or other fruit marmalades or preserves

1 large egg, lightly beaten with 1 teaspoon water

1. In a large bowl, mix the flour, egg yolk, sugar, lard, water, and oil. Work the mixture lightly with your hands to form a smooth dough. Wrap in plastic wrap and let sit 1 hour.

2. Meanwhile, preheat the oven to 350°F. Scatter the almonds on a cookie sheet and toast 3 to 4 minutes or until lightly golden and fragrant. Let cool. Transfer to a food processor and blend until as finely chopped as possible (but not a paste). Transfer to a small bowl and stir in the marmalade until well blended.

3. Preheat the oven to 325°F. Roll out the dough on a floured surface to a scant ⅛ inch thick and cut into 3½-inch rounds with an empanadilla or biscuit cutter. Place about 1 tablespoon of the marmalade mixture in the center of half of the rounds and cover each with another round. Press the edges together with your fingers, then curl up the edges and press to seal.

4. Brush the top of each pastry with the egg wash, arrange on a greased cookie sheet, and bake 25 to 30 minutes or until golden. Serve at room temperature.

Walnut-Filled Turnovers Ⓥ

Casadielles

MAKES 20 MINI TURNOVERS

Asturia's variation on walnut-filled turnovers, casadielles, are extremely popular in the northern part of that region. This recipe differs from the Moorish version in that it does not contain any honey.

1 pound storebought or homemade puff pastry (page 135; partial recipe), chilled

1 cup coarsely ground walnuts

½ cup sugar

¼ teaspoon ground cinnamon

1 tablespoon anisette liqueur

continues...

1 tablespoon unsalted butter, melted and cooled

1 large egg, lightly beaten, for sealing

Sugar, for dusting

I. Prepare the pastry dough, if necessary. Place an oven rack in the upper position and preheat the oven to 425°F. In a small bowl, combine the nuts, sugar, and cinnamon. Stir in the anisette and butter.

2. Roll out the pastry dough to ⅛ inch thick and cut into 4-inch rounds with an empanadilla or biscuit cutter. Spoon 3 teaspoons of the walnut mixture into the center of each round. Brush the edge with the beaten egg, fold the round in half, and press the edges with a fork to seal.

3. Arrange the turnovers on a cookie sheet and bake about 10 minutes or until golden. Let cool slightly, then dust with the sugar. Serve warm or at room temperature.

Fig and Candied Squash Pastries Ⓥ

Pasteles de Higo

MAKES 12 PASTRIES

This recipe for pastries with its unusual filling of dried figs and candied squash came from Simón Tomás of the great Sol-Ric restaurant in the ancient city of Tarragona, home to many monuments of its Roman past.

1 pound storebought or homemade puff pastry (page 135; partial recipe), chilled

12 tablespoons Candied Spaghetti Squash Marmalade (page 664; partial recipe)

12 dried figs, hard stems removed, lightly mashed

1 egg yolk, for sealing

Powdered (confectioners) sugar, for dusting

Ground cinnamon, for dusting

I. Prepare the pastry dough if necessary and the marmalade. Place an oven rack in the upper position and preheat the oven to 425°F.

2. Roll out the pastry dough to ⅛ inch thick and cut into 6 x 4 x 4-inch triangles. Place I tablespoon of the marmalade in the center of each triangle and place I fig in the center of the marmalade. Brush the edges with the beaten egg, cover with another triangle, and press the edges with a fork to seal.

3. Arrange on a cookie sheet and bake 10 to 15 minutes or until golden. Let cool slightly. Dust with the powdered sugar and cinnamon and serve warm.

Sweetened Potato Puffs Ⓥ

Boladillas de Patatas Dulces

MAKES ABOUT 20 PUFFS

An elegant dessert perfect for parties, these sweetened potato puffs have a crunchy sugar coating and are filled with custard.

½ pound potatoes

3 large egg yolks

¼ cup sugar

6 tablespoons all-purpose flour

1 teaspoon baking powder

Mild olive oil, for frying

A mixture of ground cinnamon and granulated sugar, for dusting

I. Place the potatoes in a medium saucepan with cold water to cover and add salt. Cover and bring to a simmer over low heat. Cook about 20 minutes or until tender when pierced with a knife. Drain and let cool slightly. Peel and pass through a ricer or strainer into a medium bowl. Stir in the egg yolks, sugar, flour, and baking powder until well blended.

2. Heat at least I inch of oil in a large skillet over medium-high heat (or better still, use a deep fryer

set at 365°F) until it turns a cube of bread light brown in 60 seconds. Drop the potato mixture by heaping teaspoons into the oil and fry, turning frequently, until golden on all sides. Transfer with a slotted spoon to paper towels and let drain.

3. Sprinkle with the cinnamon-sugar mixture and serve warm.

Candied Egg Yolk Pastries Ⓥ
Tecla de Yema

MAKES 9 TO 10 PASTRIES

Traditionally, candied egg yolks (yemas) were prepared by nuns in convents who created quite a thriving business selling these highly sought-after treats. The egg yolks were often donated by wine makers who used egg whites to clarify their wines, leaving them with a surplus of egg yolks. These delectable, candy-like pastries are delicious and easy to prepare. All this recipe requires is filling puff pastries with a candied egg yolk mixture.

¾ pound puff pastry dough, homemade (page 135) or storebought

1 recipe Candied Egg Yolks (page 665)

1. Prepare the pastry dough if necessary and the egg yolks. Place an oven rack in the upper position and preheat the oven to 450°F.

2. Roll out the pastry dough to a rectangle ⅛ inch thick and cut into 3½ x 1½-inch rectangles. Spread 1 heaping teaspoon of filling over each rectangle to within ¼ inch of the edges. Cover with a second rectangle and press the edges with a fork to seal.

3. Arrange on a cookie sheet and bake 10 to 15 minutes or until golden. Serve at room temperature.

Walnut-Filled Fried Pastries with Honey Ⓥ
Hidromiel de Nuez

MAKES 40 PASTRIES

A recipe clearly of Moorish origin, this dessert features honey, nuts, cloves, anise, oranges, and sesame seeds. The best version that I ever tasted of these honey-coated walnut pastries was served by Juan Durillo, chef at the magnificent parador at the top of a precipice in the city of Ronda in Andalucía.

4 ounces shelled walnuts

1 cup plus 6 tablespoons honey

4 whole cloves, ground or smashed

¼ teaspoon ground cinnamon

¼ cup olive oil

Peel of ¼ orange (orange part only)

1 tablespoon ground anise seeds

¼ cup white wine

1 tablespoon fresh orange juice

1 teaspoon sesame seeds

1 cup all-purpose flour

Mild olive oil, for frying

3 tablespoons rose water (available in specialty stores or Italian delis) or water

1. Mash the nuts in a large mortar until as finely ground as possible. In a small saucepan, combine 6 tablespoons of the honey, the cloves, cinnamon, and the nuts. Heat over medium-low heat, stirring constantly until the mixture holds together, about 3 minutes. Let cool.

2. Heat the oil in a small skillet over medium heat. Add the orange peel and cook until blackened. Remove from the heat and immediately stir in the anise. Let the oil cool, then pass through a fine-mesh strainer into a medium bowl. Discard

continues...

the solids. Stir in the wine, orange juice, and sesame seeds. Gradually incorporate the flour until a dough forms. Turn out onto a floured surface and knead lightly until smooth and elastic, adding more flour as necessary. Wrap in plastic wrap and let sit 30 minutes.

3. Divide the dough into 2 equal parts. Roll each part into a long, narrow, paper-thin strip about 1¾ inches wide and cut into 3-inch lengths. Let sit 30 minutes more. Take ¼ teaspoon of the nut mixture and roll between your palms into 2½-inch-long "sticks," then place along the length of a pastry strip, leaving ¼ inch free at each end. Roll up and press the seams and ends to seal. Repeat for the remaining mixture and strips.

4. Heat at least ½ inch of oil in a large skillet over medium-high heat (or better still, use a deep fryer set at 375°F) until it quickly browns a cube of bread. Place as many pastries as will comfortably fit in the oil and fry, turning frequently, until golden brown on all sides. (Cook in small batches if necessary to avoid overcrowding.) Transfer with a slotted spoon to paper towels and let drain.

5. In a medium saucepan, combine the remaining 1 cup honey and the rose water and bring to a boil over medium heat. Cook, stirring constantly, about 2 minutes, then remove from the heat. Place a cooling rack over a rimmed cookie sheet to catch any drips. Working in batches, place the pastry rolls in the honey and let sit a minute, then transfer to the cooling rack and let drain.

6. Serve at room temperature, or warm briefly in a microwave. The pastries are best if left several hours or overnight at room temperature before serving.

Mallorcan Orange-Flavored Turnover Dough Ⓥ*
Masa de Empanadilla a la Mallorquina

MAKES DOUGH FOR 1 LARGE OR 8 SMALL TARTS

This is the dough that is typically used for most Mallorcan desserts. You can fill it with cottage cheese, marmalade, or any other kind of sweetened filling. This dough is easy to make and good to keep on hand. It is used in the next recipe, Cheese Turnovers (below). Make it vegetarian with vegetable shortening.

2 tablespoons fresh orange juice

3 tablespoons mild olive oil or vegetable oil

1 large egg yolk

1 cup all-purpose flour

2 teaspoons sugar

Pinch of salt

2 tablespoons lard or vegetable shortening

In a small bowl, whisk together the juice, oil, and egg yolk. In a food processor, combine the flour, sugar, and salt, then add the lard and pulse to incorporate evenly into the flour mixture. Pulse in the juice mixture. Wrap in plastic wrap and refrigerate 1 hour. The dough is ready to use or to store for future use in the refrigerator or freezer.

Cheese Turnovers
Rubiols de Requesón

MAKES 12 TURNOVERS

These sweetened cheese turnovers from Mallorca are excellent on their own, and better with preserves.

1 recipe Mallorcan Orange-Flavored Turnover Dough (see above)

1 pound farmer's cheese, crumbled, or cottage cheese

½ teaspoon lemon zest

½ cup plus 2 tablespoons sugar

½ teaspoon ground cinnamon

⅛ teaspoon salt

1 large egg, lightly beaten with 1 teaspoon water

Sugar, for dusting

1. Prepare the turnover dough. In a small bowl, combine the cheese, lemon zest, sugar, cinnamon, and salt.

2. Preheat the oven to 350°F. Roll out the dough on a floured work surface to less than ⅛ inch thick and cut into 5- to 6-inch rounds. Place 2 tablespoons of the cheese mixture in the center of each round. Fold in half and press the edges together with a fork to seal.

3. Brush with the egg wash and dust well with the sugar. Bake about 20 minutes or until lightly browned. Serve warm or at room temperature.

Córdoba's Sugar-Coated Fried Pastries ⓥ*

Pestiños Cordobeses

MAKES ABOUT 36 TO 40 PASTRIES

Pestiños can be found all over Spain, but this version from Córdoba is scented with spices and heavily coated with sugar and cinnamon. They are wonderfully light and flaky. Make it vegetarian with vegetable shortening.

PREPARE AT LEAST 2 HOURS IN ADVANCE

2 cups all-purpose flour

Pinch of salt

1½ teaspoons ground anise seeds

1½ teaspoons sesame seeds

1 whole clove, crushed to a powder

½ teaspoon lemon zest

3 tablespoons lard or vegetable shortening, softened

¼ cup mild olive oil

¼ cup dry white wine

Olive oil, for frying

½ cup sugar

¼ teaspoon ground cinnamon

1. In a large bowl, combine the flour, salt, anise, sesame seeds, clove, and lemon zest. Add the lard and, working with your fingers, incorporate it into the flour mixture. Stir in the olive oil and white wine. Turn out onto a work surface and knead lightly until smooth. Shape into a ball, wrap in plastic wrap, and let sit at room temperature 2 hours.

2. On a floured work surface, briefly knead the dough, then roll out to the thickness of a nickel. With a sharp knife or pizza cutter, cut into 4 x 2-inch strips. Fold each strip lengthwise in half, moisten the edges with water, and press with your fingers to seal.

3. Heat at least 1 inch of oil in a medium skillet over medium-high heat (or better still, use a deep fryer set at 365°F) until it turns a cube of bread light brown in 60 seconds. Place the strips in the oil and fry, turning once, until golden brown. (Cook in batches if necessary to avoid overcrowding.) Transfer with a slotted spoon to paper towels and let drain.

4. Combine the sugar and cinnamon in a small shallow bowl and dredge each pastry in the mixture. Arrange on a platter and sprinkle heavily with more of the sugar-cinnamon mixture. Serve warm or at room temperature.

Flowers Coated with Honey **V**
Flores de Miel

MAKES ABOUT 60 PASTRIES

A rosette iron—a flower-shaped iron device with a long handle—is necessary to make this dessert. You can find them in specialty shops and online. The rosette iron is used to dip the "flowers" into the batter and then into the hot oil, creating a crispy, light fried pastry.

3 large eggs

1 cup milk

¼ teaspoon lemon zest

¼ teaspoon ground cinnamon

Pinch of salt

1 cup flour, such as bread flour

Oil, such as mild olive oil, for frying

Peel of ½ lemon, cut into thin strips (yellow part only)

½ cup honey

2 tablespoons water

Powdered (confectioners) sugar

1. In a medium bowl, beat the eggs with an electric mixer until foamy. Add the milk, lemon zest, cinnamon, and salt and beat 1 minute, then add the flour and beat at a low speed until smooth—the batter should be quite thin.

2. Heat at least 1 inch of oil in a large skillet over medium heat (or better still, use a deep fryer set at 365°F) until browns a cube of bread in 60 seconds. Add the strips of lemon peel and fry until they blacken. Discard.

3. Place the rosette iron in the oil until the metal becomes very hot, then dip in the batter. Be careful to coat the mold only to the top of the rim—if the batter covers more, it will be more difficult to separate the pastries when done. Transfer immediately to the oil. Hold the mold in the oil until the batter

becomes golden. Remove from the oil; the pastry should slip off easily from the mold; otherwise, use the point of a knife to gently loosen. Let drain on paper towels. Repeat, immersing the mold in the oil briefly each time before dipping in the batter.

4. In a small saucepan, combine the honey and water and heat over low heat until thinned and smooth. Drizzle over the flowers and dust with the powdered sugar. Serve at room temperature.

Puff Pastry Pie with Spaghetti Squash Marmalade **V**
Pastel Cordobés

MAKES 8 SERVINGS

Puff pastry filled with marmalade is a common dessert in Spain, and spaghetti squash makes for a particularly delicious marmalade. This recipe comes from the quaint Taberna San Miguel in Córdoba, a famous tavern with walls filled with bullfighting memorabilia and a meeting place for cordobeses (bullfighters).

¾ pound storebought or homemade puff pastry (page 135; partial recipe)

½ cup Candied Spaghetti Squash Marmalade (page 664; partial recipe)

1 large egg, lightly beaten with 1 teaspoon water

Sugar, for sprinkling

1. Prepare the pastry dough if necessary as instructed in the recipe. Prepare the marmalade as instructed in the recipe. Place an oven rack in the upper position and preheat the oven to 425°F.

2. Roll out the pastry dough to an 18 x 10-inch rectangle. Cut into 2 (8½-inch) squares, then trim each square into an 8½-inch round. Place one round on a cookie sheet that has been dampened with water.

3. Spread the marmalade on 1 pastry round with a rubber spatula to within 1½ inches of the edges. Cover with the other pastry round and press the edges to seal. Cut several slits in the top and brush with the egg wash and bake about 25 minutes or until golden.

4. Turn off the oven and leave the pastry in the oven 20 minutes more to dry the inner pastry layers. Let cool and sprinkle heavily with the sugar. Serve at room temperature.

Strawberries Fried in Sherry Batter ⓥ

Buñuelos de Fresones en Pasta de Jerez

MAKES 4 SERVINGS

This batter with its distinctive taste of sherry is best when used to coat strawberries or whole fresh figs, but it also works well for any small whole fruits or fruit wedges. For a more attractive presentation, I recommend serving these fruit puffs over a raspberry purée.

¼ cup sweet sherry, such as Spanish cream

¼ cup milk

½ cup all-purpose flour

2 tablespoons plus 1 teaspoon sugar

1½ teaspoons oil

Pinch of salt

1 large egg white

Mild olive oil, for frying

All-purpose flour, for dredging

16 medium strawberries, with stems and leaves if possible, or 4 fresh figs (whole) or other fruits (cut into ½-inch wedges)

¼ teaspoon ground cinnamon

Mint leaves, for garnish

1. In a small bowl, mix the sherry, milk, flour, 1 teaspoon of the sugar, the oil, and salt until well blended. In another small bowl, beat the egg white with an electric mixer until soft peaks form, then fold into the batter.

2. Heat at least 1 inch of oil in a medium skillet over medium heat (or better still, use a deep fryer set at 375°F) until it quickly browns a cube of bread. Place the flour in a small shallow bowl. Dredge the strawberries in the flour, dip in the batter, and place in the oil. Fry, turning occasionally, until golden on all sides. Transfer with a slotted spoon to paper towels and let drain. If using figs, cut each lengthwise into quarters, without cutting all the way through, and open out (it will look like a flower).

3. In a small shallow bowl, combine the remaining 2 tablespoons sugar and the cinnamon. Dredge each strawberry in this mixture and place on a platter. Garnish with mint leaves and serve hot.

Custard-Filled Dessert Crepes ⓥ

Filloas a la Crema

MAKES ABOUT 12 CREPES

Filloas a la crema is a typical Galician dessert. When these custard-filled dessert crepes are flamed with anisette, they make for a more elaborate presentation and taste even better.

PREPARE AT LEAST 2 HOURS IN ADVANCE

Crepes

1 large egg

½ cup milk

½ cup water

1 cup all-purpose flour

1 teaspoon sugar

Pinch of salt

continues . . .

Filling

9 large egg yolks

9 tablespoons sugar

¾ cup milk

3 tablespoons unsalted butter

1 tablespoon anisette liqueur (optional)

Sugar, for dusting (optional)

Powdered (confectioners) sugar, for dusting (optional)

Ground cinnamon, for dusting (optional)

1. Prepare the crepes: In a food processor or blender, combine the egg, the ½ cup milk, the water, flour, 1 teaspoon sugar, and the salt and process until smooth. Let the batter rest 2 to 3 hours at room temperature.

2. Prepare the filling: In the bottom of a double boiler or a medium pot, bring 1 inch of water to a simmer over low heat. In the top of the double boiler or a bowl fitted securely over the pot, whisk the egg yolks. Add the sugar and whisk until smooth and lemon colored.

3. In a separate small saucepan, heat the ¾ cup milk over medium heat until heated through and slightly thickened. Gradually stir the milk into the yolk mixture. Make sure there is simmering water in the pot (or add more if needed) and cook, stirring constantly, until the mixture is thickened. If any lumps appear, pass the mixture through a fine-mesh strainer and discard the solids. Let cool.

4. Grease a small skillet or crepe pan and heat over medium-high heat. Swirl in just enough batter to coat the pan, about 1 tablespoon. Cook the crepe on one side until the edges look crisp and the crepe underneath is golden, about 1 minute; turn with a spatula and cook the other side briefly, about 30 seconds—do not brown. (The crepes may be cooked in advance and stored between pieces of wax paper at room temperature until ready to use.)

5. Spread 1 tablespoon of the filling on each crepe. Fold in half, then in half again.

If using anisette: Melt the 3 tablespoons butter in a large skillet over low heat. Add the crepes and cook, turning once, until heated through. Turn, dust with the sugar, and pour in the anisette. Standing well away from the skillet, ignite the liquid with a match or kitchen lighter then let die out. Serve hot.

If not using anisette: Preheat the oven to 350°F. Melt the 3 tablespoons butter in a baking pan. Arrange the custard-filled crepes in the pan and bake, turning once, until heated through. Dust with the powdered sugar and cinnamon. Serve hot.

Crepes Filled with Cinnamon Apple Sauce ⓥ
Frixuelos Rellenos de Salsa de Manzana

MAKES ABOUT 14 CREPES

In Asturias, these dessert crepes are called frixuelos, *while in Galicia, they are called* filloas. *They can be served with a sprinkle of sugar or filled with pastry cream. Because Asturias is a region where apple trees thrive, this version calls for applesauce. I got this recipe from the country inn La Tahona, set in the majestic Picos de Europa mountains.*

1 recipe Crepes (page 625), adding 1 teaspoon sugar to the batter

1¾ cups applesauce

1 teaspoon ground cinnamon

¼ teaspoon ground nutmeg

½ teaspoon lemon zest

1 tablespoon melted unsalted butter

About 2½ tablespoons sugar, or to taste

1 tablespoon vegetable oil or butter

Sugar, for sprinkling

Ground cinnamon, for sprinkling

1. Prepare the crepes as instructed in step 1 of the recipe.

2. In a small bowl, mix the applesauce, cinnamon, nutmeg, lemon zest, and butter until well blended. Stir in the sugar—the amount will depend on whether the applesauce is sweetened or not. However, since only a small amount fills each pancake and it is being used as a dessert filling, the applesauce should be sweeter than customary so I recommend adding about 2½ tablespoons of sugar.

3. Spoon about 2 tablespoons of the applesauce down the middle of each crepe. Fold over one side, then the other. Heat the oil in a medium skillet over medium heat. Add as many crepes as will fit comfortably, seam side down. Cook until lightly golden, turn, and lightly brown the other side. Sprinkle with the sugar and cinnamon and serve hot.

Caramel Custard (Flan) Ⓥ

Flan del Gran Flanero

MAKES 6 SERVINGS

This is Spain's classic flan, which has become the most popular Spanish dessert served around the world. Legend has it that there was once a man who was known in Madrid as "El Gran Flanero"—the Great Flan Maker. Supposedly, the society elite in Madrid would not dream of making any important decisions without first eating one of these "good luck" flans. James Michener's book Iberia *includes a comprehensive chapter about El Gran Flanero. This recipe produces a custard that is smooth and rich.*

PREPARE AT LEAST 2 HOURS IN ADVANCE

Caramelized Sugar

10 tablespoons sugar

5 teaspoons water

Custard (Flan)

3 whole eggs

3 large egg yolks

¼ teaspoon lemon zest

6 tablespoons sugar

2½ cups milk

1. Prepare the caramelized sugar: Combine the 10 tablespoons sugar and water in a small skillet and heat over medium-high heat, stirring constantly, until golden. Immediately remove from the heat and pour into 6 ovenproof custard cups.

continues...

2. Prepare the custard: In a medium bowl, whisk together lightly the whole eggs and the egg yolks. Whisk in the lemon zest, 6 tablespoons sugar, and the milk. Pour into the custard cups. Place about 1 inch of hot water in a shallow earthenware casserole dish or Dutch oven and arrange the cups in the dish. Cook over medium heat about 1 hour, adding more water if necessary.

3. Meanwhile, preheat the oven to 350°F. Transfer the skillet to the oven and bake 25 minutes or until a knife inserted in the center comes out clean.

4. Remove the cups from the water and let cool. Refrigerate least 2 hours, Loosen the sides of the custards with a knife and turn out upside down onto individual dessert dishes. Serve cold.

Flan, Canary Style Ⓥ

Quesillo

MAKES 5 SERVINGS

Canary-style flan is richer than most other flans because it is made from condensed milk, with ground almonds adding a special taste and texture. This recipe comes from the Restaurante Los Abrigos, a local fish restaurant overlooking the port of Los Abrigos in the south of Tenerife.

PREPARE 8 TO 12 HOURS IN ADVANCE

1 recipe Caramelized Sugar Syrup (page 627)

3 large eggs

½ cup condensed milk, homemade or canned

2 cups whole milk

⅓ cup ground blanched almonds

1. Preheat the oven to 350°F. Prepare the caramelized sugar and divide evenly among 5 ovenproof custard cups. In a large bowl, whisk the eggs, then add the condensed milk and fresh milk. Stir in the almonds. Divide evenly among the custard cups.

2. Place 1 inch of warm water in a 13 x 9-inch baking pan and place the custard cups in the pan. Bake 20 minutes. Remove from the water and let cool. Refrigerate overnight. Loosen the side of each custard with a knife and turn out upside down onto individual dessert dishes. Serve room temperature.

Apple Flan Ⓥ

Flan de Manzana

MAKES 4 TO 5 SERVINGS

This is a delicious apple custard flavored with cinnamon and vanilla bean. The custard should be served over slices of baked apple.

¼ cup light brown sugar, packed

½ cup water

¼ teaspoon ground cinnamon

1 apple, peeled, cored, and cut into ⅛-inch slices

Caramelized Sugar

5 tablespoons granulated sugar

2½ teaspoons water

Custard

¼ cup granulated sugar

2 cups milk

⅛ teaspoon salt

1-inch piece vanilla bean pod

2 whole eggs

2 large egg yolks

1. In a medium saucepan, combine the brown sugar, water, and cinnamon and heat over low heat, stirring occasionally, until the sugar is dissolved. Add the apple and simmer, stirring occasionally, until tender. Drain and arrange in the bottoms of 4 or 5 greased ovenproof custard cups.

2. Prepare the caramelized sugar: In a small saucepan, heat the 5 tablespoons sugar and the water over medium heat, stirring constantly, until syrupy and light golden. Immediately pour over the apple slices.

3. Prepare the custard: In another small saucepan, combine the ¼ cup sugar, milk, salt, and vanilla and bring to a boil over medium heat, stirring occasionally. Reduce the heat to low and simmer, stirring occasionally, about 10 minutes. Discard the vanilla bean.

4. Preheat the oven to 350°F. In a medium bowl, lightly whisk together the whole eggs and egg yolks. Gradually pour in the hot milk and whisk until well blended. Divide among the custard cups.

5. Place about 1 inch of hot water in a 13 x 9-inch baking pan and place the custard cups in the pan. Bake 45 to 60 minutes or until a knife inserted in the custard comes out clean. Let cool, then refrigerate at least 2 hours to chill.

6. Loosen the side of each custard with a knife and turn out upside down onto individual dessert dishes. Serve cold.

Orange Flan 🅥
Flan de Naranja

MAKES 6 SERVINGS

In this simple but delicious orange custard, the orange zest provides the perfect contrast to the sweetness of the caramelized sugar.

Caramelized Sugar

½ cup sugar

4 teaspoons water

6 large eggs

5 tablespoons granulated sugar

Juice of 4 oranges (about 1⅓ cups)

1 teaspoon orange zest

1. Prepare the caramelized sugar: In a small saucepan, combine the 8 tablespoons sugar and the water and heat over medium heat, stirring constantly, until the sugar is golden. Immediately pour into 6 ovenproof custard cups.

2. Preheat the oven to 350°F. In a small bowl, lightly whisk the eggs until light colored. Whisk in the sugar, then gradually whisk in the orange juice and the orange rind until well blended. Pour the egg mixture into the custard cups.

3. Place 1 inch of hot water in a 13 x 9-inch baking pan and place the custard cups in the pan. Bake 45 minutes or until a knife inserted in the custard comes out clean. Remove from the water and let cool.

4. Loosen the side of each custard with a knife and turn out upside down onto 4 dessert dishes. Spoon the caramelized sugar syrup over the custards and serve.

Coconut Flan 🅥
Flan de Coco

MAKES 5 SERVINGS

This coconut custard is very rich because it is made with condensed milk and covered with caramelized sugar, so serve it in small portions.

PREPARE AT LEAST 2 HOURS IN ADVANCE

⅜ cup finely grated fresh coconut

1⅞ cups whole milk

½ cup plus 2 tablespoons condensed milk (sweetened)

3 large eggs

1½ tablespoons sugar

Caramelized Sugar

5 tablespoons sugar

2½ teaspoons water

continues...

1. Place the coconut and ½ cup of the milk in a small bowl and let soak 2 hours.

2. Prepare the caramelized sugar: In a small saucepan, combine the sugar and the water and cook over high heat, stirring constantly, until syrupy and light golden. Divide among 5 ovenproof custard cups. Let cool.

3. In a small saucepan, heat the remaining 1⅜ cups milk and the condensed milk over medium heat, stirring constantly, until it reaches a boil. Remove from the heat.

4. Preheat the oven to 350°F. In a small bowl, lightly whisk the eggs, then whisk in the sugar. Drain the coconut, discarding the milk. Stir the coconut into the eggs, then gradually stir in the hot milk.

5. Pour the custard into the caramelized cups. Place 1 inch of hot water in a 13 x 9-inch baking pan and place the custard cups in the pan. Bake about 45 minutes or until a knife inserted in the custard comes out clean.

6. Loosen the side of each custard with a knife and turn out upside down onto 5 dessert dishes. Serve warm or at room temperature, or refrigerate at least 2 hours to chill and serve cold.

Chocolate Flan with Almond-Flavored Chocolate Sauce Ⓥ
Flan de Chocolate con Salsa de Chocolate al Sabor de Almendra

MAKES 6 SERVINGS

Spain is responsible for introducing the rest of Europe to a variety of products they brought from the New World—chocolate being one of them. But surprisingly, although chocolate is well loved in Spain as a candy, it has never been a popular dessert ingredient. One of the exceptions is this recipe for rich chocolate flan flavored with almond liqueur and topped with almond-flavored chocolate sauce. It's absolutely out of this world.

Flan

4 ounces dark unsweetened chocolate, cut into pieces

2 cups warm milk

⅛ teaspoon salt

2 whole eggs plus 2 egg yolks

½ cup sugar

¼ cup almond liqueur, such as Amaretto

Whipped cream (optional)

Sliced almonds

Chocolate Sauce

2 ounces unsweetened dark chocolate, cut into pieces

1 tablespoon unsalted butter

½ cup sugar

Pinch of salt

½ cup water

2 tablespoons almond liqueur, such as Amaretto

¼ teaspoon almond extract

1. Prepare the flan: Place the 4 ounces chocolate in a small microwave-safe bowl and melt in the microwave on low. In a medium saucepan, combine the milk and the ⅛ teaspoon salt, then stir in the melted chocolate. Cook over medium heat, stirring frequently, until the chocolate is fully incorporated. Remove from the heat.

2. Preheat the oven to 350°F. In a small bowl, whisk together the whole eggs, the egg yolks, and the ½ cup sugar. Gradually stir in the milk-chocolate mixture and the ¼ cup almond liqueur. Grease 6 custard cups and pour in the flan. Place 1 inch of hot water in a 13 x 9-inch baking pan and place the custard cups in the pan. Bake 1 hour or until set. Let cool.

3. Meanwhile, prepare the sauce. Place the 2 ounces chocolate and the butter in a microwave-safe cup or small bowl and melt in the microwave on Low. In a small saucepan, combine the sugar, salt, and water. Whisk in the chocolate mixture and cook over medium heat, stirring constantly, until thickened (do not boil). Let cool slightly, then stir in the 2 tablespoons almond liqueur and almond extract.

4. Spoon about 2 tablespoons chocolate sauce onto 6 dessert plates. Unmold the flan upside down over the sauce and spoon a dollop of whipped cream, if using, on top. Sprinkle with the almonds. Serve at room temperature or refrigerate at least 2 hours to chill and serve cold.

Walnut and Egg White Flan in Caramelized Custard Sauce ⓥ

Dulce de Nuez

MAKES 6 SERVINGS

The flan in this recipe is made only with egg whites, walnuts, and a splash of sherry. The egg yolks are used to make the custard sauce, which has no sugar but is sweetened when mixed with part of the caramelized sugar. This recipe comes from our dear friend Mari Carmen Martín.

Caramelized Sugar

½ cup sugar

7 tablespoons hot water

Flan

5 large egg whites

5 tablespoons sugar

¼ cup finely chopped walnuts

1 tablespoon semisweet sherry, such as Oloroso, or port

Custard Sauce

5 large egg yolks

1 cup milk

¾ teaspoon pure vanilla extract

12 walnuts, halved

1. Prepare the caramelized sugar: Preheat the oven to 325°F. In a small saucepan, combine the ½ cup sugar and 3 tablespoons of the water and cook over high heat, stirring constantly, until syrupy and light golden. Remove from the heat. Gradually and very carefully stir in the remaining 4 tablespoons water. Pour into a greased 8-inch bundt pan or savarin mold.

2. Prepare the flan: In a large bowl, beat the egg whites with an electric mixer until soft peaks form. Beat in the sugar, the chopped nuts, and the sherry. Spoon into the bundt pan. Place 1 inch of hot water in a 13 x 9-inch baking pan and place the bundt pan in the pan. Bake about 25 minutes or until set. Remove from the water and let cool.

3. Meanwhile, prepare the sauce: In the top of a double boiler or a bowl over a pot, whisk the egg yolks until pale yellow. Gradually stir in the milk. Place over boiling water and cook, stirring constantly, until thickened to a soft custard consistency. Remove from the heat and stir in the vanilla.

4. Unmold the flan onto a plate, returning to the mold any caramelized sugar that is still liquid. Pour the sauce into the mold and mix with a spoon to loosen and blend any remaining sugar.

5. Spoon the sauce onto 6 dessert plates. Cut the flan into 6 portions and place over the custard. Garnish with the walnut halves. Serve warm.

Sugar-Crusted Custard Ⓥ
Crema Catalana

MAKES 6 SERVINGS

This heavenly, soft Catalan custard with a crackling caramelized sugar coating is beloved by Spaniards and is featured on the menus of most Spanish restaurants. Traditionally, in Catalunya restaurants, the sugar is caramelized with a salamander—an iron disk with a long handle—but the sugar can also be caramelized with a small kitchen torch made for that purpose. Both are available in kitchenware shops, but if you don't have either, you can use the bottom of a small hot saucepan. This classic Spanish dessert is very popular in Madrid and also the favorite of my granddaughter Ruby.

2 tablespoons plus ½ teaspoon cornstarch

2⅔ cups plus 2 tablespoons milk

6 large egg yolks

¾ cup plus 2 tablespoons sugar

Peel of ½ lemon, cut into several pieces
    (yellow part only)

1 cinnamon stick

1. In a small bowl, dissolve the cornstarch in 2 tablespoons of the milk. Stir in the egg yolks until well blended.

2. In a small saucepan, combine the remaining 2⅔ cups milk, ½ cup of the sugar, the lemon peel, and cinnamon stick and bring to a boil over medium heat, stirring occasionally. Reduce the heat to low and simmer, stirring occasionally, 15 minutes. Gradually stir into the cornstarch mixture. Return to the saucepan, increase the heat to medium, and cook, stirring constantly, until the custard starts to bubble. Discard the lemon peel and cinnamon stick and divide the mixture among 6 shallow dessert bowls, such as earthenware. Let cool without stirring.

3. Sprinkle each custard with 1 tablespoon of the remaining sugar. Using a kitchen torch, melt the sugar until it is shiny and crispy. Serve at room temperature.

Rich Caramel Mini Custards Ⓥ
Tocinillos del Cielo

MAKES ABOUT 15 MINI CUSTARDS

My husband Luis is not a big fan of desserts, but this one is his very favorite. This caramelized custard is so rich that it is almost like a candy, so it should be served in small portions. Many centuries ago, it was customary for winemakers to donate egg yolks to convents since only egg whites were used to clarify their wines. Tocinillos and other Spanish candy desserts rely on egg yolks for their rich consistency.

1⅓ cups sugar

1 cup water

1 recipe Caramelized Sugar Syrup (page 627)

6 large egg yolks

¼ teaspoon pure vanilla extract

¼ teaspoon lemon zest

1. In a small saucepan, combine the sugar and water and bring to a boil over high heat. Reduce the heat to low and simmer until a drop of syrup lengthens to a thread when placed in a glass of cold water, about 15 minutes. Let cool. Lightly coat the sides of about 15 (1¼-inch) mini muffin cups or individual mini custard molds with slightly less than 1 tablespoon syrup.

2. Prepare the caramelized sugar as instructed in step 2 of the recipe, but do not pour into the loaf pan. Set aside to cool. In a small bowl, whisk together the egg yolks, vanilla, and lemon zest. Gradually whisk in the cooled syrup. Fill each muffin cup to the rim with this mixture, about 2 tablespoons.

3. Fill a saucepan halfway with water and bring to a boil over high heat. Place a cooling rack atop the rim of the saucepan. Place the muffin pan on the rack, cover, and cook about 13 minutes, adding more water to the pan if it evaporates, or until the custard is just set—do not overcook. Let cool.

4. Loosen the side of each custard and turn out upside down onto a serving plate. Serve at room temperature.

Almond Milk Custard
Mató Catalan

MAKES 4 SERVINGS

This pure white custard, a Catalan specialty, has no eggs. The recipe calls for gelatin and almonds, with the almonds being used to flavor the milk. The result is a delectably light custard with a subtle nutty flavor. Best served with fresh fruit.

PREPARE AT LEAST 6 HOURS IN ADVANCE

¼ pound slivered blanched almonds (about 1 cup)

⅓ cup sugar

⅔ cup water

1 envelope (¼ ounce) gelatin

1⅓ cups milk

1 cinnamon stick

Peel of ½ lemon (yellow part only)

Sliced or chopped fresh fruit

1. In a food processor, blend the almonds and sugar until the almonds are as finely ground as possible. With the motor running, gradually add the water. Transfer to a small bowl, cover, and let rest in the refrigerator about 4 hours. Pass through a fine-mesh strainer, pressing with the back of a wooden spoon to extract as much liquid as possible. Discard the solids.

2. In a small saucepan, combine 1 cup of the milk, the cinnamon stick, and lemon peel, bring to a simmer over low heat, and simmer, stirring occasionally,

about 15 minutes. In a cup or small bowl, combine the gelatin and the remaining ⅓ cup milk and stir until the gelatin is softened. Stir into the saucepan and simmer, stirring occasionally, about 2 minutes more or until the gelatin is dissolved. Let cool.

3. Discard the cinnamon stick and lemon peel. Pour the almond milk into 4 custard cups. Refrigerate at least 2 hours or until the gelatin has set, then bring to room temperature.

4. Loosen the side of each custard with a knife and turn out upside down onto 4 dessert dishes. Garnish with the fresh fruit. Serve at room temperature.

Gossamer Lemon Custard
Delicia de Limón

MAKES 6 SERVINGS

This recipe is adapted from the elegant Urepel restaurant in the beautiful seaside city of San Sebastián in northern Spain. It is a supremely light lemon custard, thickened only with a small amount of egg. I recommend serving it over a strawberry or kiwi fruit purée and garnishing it with fruit and whipped cream.

Unsalted butter, for greasing

15 tablespoons (1 cup minus 1 tablespoon) fresh strained lemon juice

1 cup sugar

¾ teaspoon lemon zest

3 large eggs

12 tablespoons strawberry or kiwi fruit purée

6 strawberries (whole) or kiwi fruit (cut into thin slices), for garnish

1. Grease 6 ovenproof custard cups well with the butter. In a small bowl, beat the lemon juice, sugar, and lemon zest with an electric mixer until well blended. Add the eggs, one at a time, and beat about 1 minute after each addition. Divide evenly among the custard cups.

continues...

2. Place 1 inch of hot water in a 13 x 9-inch baking pan and place the custard cups in the pan. Bake about 15 to 20 minutes or until just set. Remove from the water and let cool.

3. Spoon 2 tablespoons of the fruit purée onto 6 dessert dishes. Unmold the custard upside down over the purée. Top with a dollop of whipped cream and garnish with whole or cut up strawberries or kiwi fruit. Serve at room temperature or refrigerate at least 2 hours and serve cold.

Soft Custard with Walnuts Ⓥ
Natillas con Nueces

MAKES 4 SERVINGS

Here walnuts lend an interesting taste and texture when mixed with a simple soft custard. These are best when served cold.

PREPARE AT LEAST 2 HOURS IN ADVANCE

2 cups milk

Peel of ½ lemon (yellow part only)

4 large egg yolks

3 tablespoons sugar

⅛ teaspoon salt

2 ounces walnut pieces

1. In a small saucepan, combine the milk and lemon peel and bring to a boil over medium heat, stirring occasionally. Reduce the heat to low and simmer, stirring occasionally, about 10 minutes. Discard the lemon peel.

2. In the top of a double boiler or a bowl over a pot, whisk together the egg yolks, sugar, and salt until the yolks turn pale yellow. Gradually stir in the milk. Place over hot water and cook, stirring constantly, until the custard is thickened. Divide among 4 wide shallow dessert dishes, such as earthenware. Let cool, then refrigerate at least 2 hours to chill. Sprinkle with the walnut pieces and serve cold.

Grandma's Soft Custard with Walnuts and Cornmeal Fritters Ⓥ
Natillas de la Abuela con Nueces y Tortas de Maíz

MAKES 4 SERVINGS

Corn was one of the products that Spain introduced to Europe after the discovery of America. It never became a common cooking ingredient, but it does appear in some very old recipes, especially those from the northern regions of Spain. Galicia, Asturias, Cantabria, and the Basque Country all have ideal climates for growing corn. This recipe is from Javier González Martínez, who comes from Torrelavega in the mountains of Cantabria.

These crunchy cornmeal puffs perfectly complemented by creamy custard are absolutely delicious. I recommend sprinkling walnuts on top and adding a splash of orujo (Spain's version of grappa).

Custard

2 cups plus 2 teaspoons milk

½ cup sugar

Peel of ¼ lemon (yellow part only)

A 1-inch piece cinnamon stick

2½ teaspoons cornstarch

3 large egg yolks

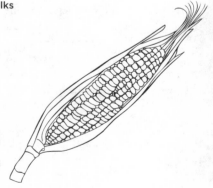

Fritters

¾ cup stone-ground yellow cornmeal

¼ cup all-purpose flour

¾ cup sparkling water

¼ teaspoon salt

1 tablespoon olive oil

Mild olive oil, for frying

6 walnuts, quartered

Ground cinnamon

1 teaspoon Spanish orujo or grappa (optional)

I. In a medium saucepan, combine 2 cups of the milk, the sugar, lemon peel, and cinnamon stick and bring to a boil, stirring occasionally, over medium heat. Reduce the heat to low and simmer, stirring occasionally, about 10 minutes. In a small bowl, combine the cornstarch and the remaining 2 teaspoons milk. Whisk in the egg yolks, add a few tablespoons of the hot milk, and stir this mixture into the saucepan. Simmer without boiling, stirring constantly until thickened and smooth, about 2 minutes more. Let cool, stirring occasionally. Discard the cinnamon stick and lemon peel.

2. Prepare the fritters: In a medium bowl, combine the cornmeal, flour, sparkling water, salt, and the 1 tablespoon oil and stir until smooth. Heat at least 1 inch of oil in a large skillet over medium heat (or better still, use a deep fryer set at 365°F) until it turns a cube of bread light brown in 60 seconds. Drop the batter by heaping teaspoons into the oil and fry, turning frequently, until golden on all sides. Transfer to paper towels and let drain.

3. Divide the custard among 4 flat-bottom dessert bowls, such as earthenware. Arrange the fritters and 4 walnut pieces over each custard. Sprinkle with the cinnamon and a splash of the liqueur, if using. Serve warm.

Fried Custard Ⓥ
Leche Frita

MAKES 6 TO 8 SERVINGS

This dessert is a custard made without eggs, but thickened by cornstarch and flour. It solidifies when refrigerated and then can be deep-fried or sautéed. This version of this popular recipe came from our friend Soledad Gil, who owns an estate surrounded by olive groves near Arcos de la Frontera. In English, leche frita *translates to "fried milk," which does not sound nearly as appetizing as this dessert actually is. Although the recipe comes from Soledad in Andalucía,* leche frita *is a quintessential Basque dessert. My husband's mouth still waters at the very thought of the* leche frita *from his grandmother, a native Basque.*

PREPARE AT LEAST 2 HOURS IN ADVANCE

3 cups milk

1 cinnamon stick

Peel of 1 lemon (yellow part only)

¼ cup cornstarch

¼ cup all-purpose flour

10 tablespoons sugar

2 teaspoons ground cinnamon

All-purpose flour, for dredging

2 large eggs, lightly beaten with 1 teaspoon water

Mild olive oil, for frying

I. In a medium saucepan, combine 2½ cups of the milk, the cinnamon stick, and lemon peel and bring to a boil over medium heat. Reduce the heat to low and simmer, stirring occasionally, about 30 minutes. Discard the cinnamon stick and lemon peel.

2. Grease an 8-inch-square baking pan. In a large bowl, combine the cornstarch, flour, and 6 tablespoons of the sugar. Gradually stir in the remaining

continues...

½ cup cold milk, then stir in the hot milk. Return this mixture to the saucepan and cook, stirring constantly, until the custard is thickened and just begins to bubble, about 15 minutes more. Pour the custard into the baking pan and let cool 5 minutes—do not stir. Refrigerate at least 2 hours up to overnight or until the custard is firm.

3. In a cup or small bowl, combine the remaining 4 tablespoons sugar and the cinnamon and reserve. Cut the custard diagonally at 1½-inch intervals, then repeat in the opposite direction, crisscrossing to form rhombus shapes (slanted squares).

4. Place the flour and egg wash in separate small shallow bowls. Heat at least ¼ inch of oil in a large skillet over medium-high heat (or better still, use a deep fryer set at 375°F) until it quickly browns a cube of bread. Dredge the custard pieces in the flour, dip in the eggs, and place in the oil. Fry, turning frequently, until browned on all sides. Transfer with a slotted spoon to paper towels and let drain.

5. Dredge the custards in the reserved sugar-cinnamon mixture and serve warm.

Rice Pudding, Asturian Style Ⓥ
Arroz con Leche Casa Lucio

MAKES 8 SERVINGS

The region of Asturias is famous for its rice pudding. Although this recipe has no eggs, no cream, and is not particularly sweet, it is some of the purest rice pudding I have ever had. The recipe comes from Casa Lucio, one of the finest restaurants in Madrid. Whenever making rice pudding, be sure to use only short-grain rice.

PREPARE AT LEAST 3 HOURS IN ADVANCE

¾ cup short-grain rice, such as imported Spanish or Arborio

8 cups whole milk

⅛ teaspoon salt

1 cinnamon stick

1 cup plus 2 tablespoons sugar

1. Rinse the rice in a fine-mesh strainer and drain well. Place in a deep pot, add the milk, salt, and cinnamon, and bring to a boil over medium-high heat, watching carefully. Reduce the heat to the lowest possible simmer, and simmer, stirring frequently, until the mixture has the consistency of a soft custard, about 3 hours. Stir in ½ cup plus 2 tablespoons of the sugar and simmer, stirring frequently, about 15 minutes more. Let cool, stirring occasionally.

2. Divide the pudding among 8 dessert bowls, such as flat-bottom earthenware. Refrigerate at least 2 hours to chill or keep at room temperature.

3. Sprinkle 1 tablespoon of the sugar across the surface of each pudding. Standing well away from the bowls and using a match or kitchen lighter, light the sugar to melt it until it is shiny and crispy. Serve immediately (the sugar will soften if left more than a few minutes).

Rice Pudding Flan with Rum
Pastel de Arroz con Leche al Ron

MAKES 4 SERVINGS

Pedro Subijana of the Akelarre restaurant in San Sebastián credits his father, a baker, with inventing this recipe. This is an unusual combination of Spanish-style rice pudding and Spanish flan, flavored with rum and caramelized sugar. Make sure you use short-grain rice.

5 tablespoons golden raisins

2 tablespoons rum

4 cups milk

½ cup short-grain rice, such as imported Spanish or Arborio

½ cup sugar

1 cinnamon stick

Peel of ½ lemon (yellow part only)

2 large eggs

4 large egg yolks

Caramelized Sugar

½ cup sugar

7 tablespoons hot water

1. In a small bowl, combine the raisins and rum and let soak 20 to 30 minutes. In a large saucepan, combine the milk, rice, sugar, cinnamon stick, and lemon peel and bring to a boil over medium heat. Reduce the heat to low and simmer, stirring frequently, about 30 minutes. Let cool 10 minutes. Discard the lemon peel and cinnamon stick.

2. Prepare the caramelized sugar: Preheat the oven to 350°F. In a small saucepan, combine the sugar and 3 tablespoons of the water and bring to a boil over medium heat. Cook, stirring constantly, until syrupy and light golden. Remove from the heat. Gradually and very carefully stir in the remaining 4 tablespoons water. Pour into the bottom of an 8-inch bundt pan or savarin mold.

3. In a large bowl, lightly whisk together the whole eggs and the egg yolks. Stir in the milk mixture, the raisins, and rum. Pour into the bundt pan.

4. Place about 1 inch of hot water in a 13 x 9-inch baking pan and place the bundt pan in the baking pan. Bake 45 to 60 minutes or until the custard is set. Loosen the sides of the custard with a knife and turn out upside down onto a serving dish. Serve warm or at room temperature, or refrigerate at least 2 hours and serve cold.

Apple Pudding with Custard Sauce ⓥ
Pudín de Manzana con Natillas

MAKES 6 SERVINGS

This wonderful dessert takes a little extra time to prepare since the apples cook for three hours and must be stirred occasionally. This is a specialty at Casa Cámara in Pasajes de San Juan, a charming seaside village with a busy port near San Sebástian. It was also home for a time to famed writer Victor Hugo during his exile from France.

PREPARE AT LEAST 4 HOURS IN ADVANCE

2½ pounds apples, peeled and cored

5 tablespoons sugar

¼ cup (½ stick) unsalted butter

1 teaspoon fresh lemon juice

¼ teaspoon lemon zest

¼ teaspoon ground cinnamon

Pinch of salt

2 large eggs, lightly beaten

Caramelized Sugar

½ cup sugar

4 teaspoons water

Custard

2 large eggs, lightly beaten

¼ cup sugar

⅛ teaspoon salt

2 cups hot milk

½ teaspoon pure vanilla extract

1. Coarsely grate the apples, place in a heavy medium saucepan, and add the 5 tablespoons sugar, the butter, lemon juice, lemon zest, cinnamon, and salt. Bring to a simmer over low heat,

continues...

cover, and cook, stirring occasionally, about 3 hours. If any liquid remains, uncover, increase the heat to medium, and cook, stirring constantly, until the liquid is evaporated, 2 to 3 minutes. Let cool slightly, then mix in the eggs until well blended.

2. Prepare the caramelized sugar: Grease 6 oven-proof custard cups. In a small saucepan, combine the ½ cup sugar and the water and cook over medium-high heat, stirring constantly, until syrupy and light golden. Divide evenly among the custard cups.

3. Preheat the oven to 350°F. Spoon the apple mixture over the custard. Place 1 inch of hot water in a 13 x 9-inch baking pan and place the custard cups in the pan. Bake 1½ hours. Remove from the water and let cool.

4. Prepare the custard: In the bottom of a double boiler or a medium, heavy saucepan bring 1 inch of water to a simmer over low heat. In the top of the double boiler or a bowl that fits snugly on top of the saucepan, whisk together the eggs, the ¼ cup sugar, and the salt. Gradually stir in the milk. Cook the mixture, stirring constantly until the custard coats a spoon. Stir in the vanilla and let cool, stirring occasionally.

5. Loosen the side of each custard with a knife and turn out upside down onto 6 dessert plates. Serve at room temperature.

Warm Anise-Scented Pudding with Fried Bread Bits Ⓥ

Puches Dulces

MAKES 6 SERVINGS

Puches dulces *is a warm pudding consisting of little more than flour, water, and sugar. The secret to this recipe is not the pudding, but the crunchy bread cubes with the added flavor of anise seeds. This recipe came from our dear friend Tomás Herranz, one of Madrid's finest chefs, who owned the Cenador del Prado restaurant for many years. This anise-scented pudding can be made with either water or milk (Tomas preferred water), but it must be served warm.*

3 tablespoons mild olive oil

Peel of ½ lemon (yellow part only)

2 cups (½-inch) bread cubes, cut from long-loaf (baguette) bread (do not remove the crust)

½ teaspoon ground anise seeds

¼ cup all-purpose flour

2 cups hot water or milk

½ cup sugar

1. In a small skillet, heat the oil and lemon peel over high heat until the peel is blackened. Discard the peel. Add the bread and fry, stirring, until golden. Transfer with a slotted spoon to paper towels and let drain, reserving the oil. Pass the oil through a fine-mesh strainer and return to the skillet. Discard the solids. Let cool slightly and reduce the heat to medium. Add the anise seeds and cook, stirring, until browned, being careful not to burn them. Reduce the heat to low, add the flour, and cook, stirring, 1 to 2 minutes.

2. Gradually stir in the water, then the sugar, and simmer, stirring occasionally, until the thickness of custard, 3 to 4 minutes. Divide among 6 flat-bottom dessert bowls, such as earthenware.

3. Sprinkle the puddings with the bread bits and serve warm.

Chocolate-Sherry Chiffon Pudding
Crema de Jerez

MAKES 6 SERVINGS

A rare Spanish dessert with chocolate, this ultra-light pudding is made with sherry and gelatin, and topped with whipped cream.

PREPARE AT LEAST 2 HOURS IN ADVANCE

1½ packages gelatin

1 cup sweet sherry, such as cream

1 cup milk

3 ounces unsweetened chocolate, cut into pieces

¼ cup finely ground hazelnuts

2 large eggs, separated

1 cup plus 2 tablespoons sugar

1 teaspoon pure vanilla extract

½ cup heavy cream

Whipped cream, for garnish (optional)

1. In a cup, combine the gelatin and ¼ cup of the sherry and stir until the gelatin is softened. In a small saucepan, combine the milk, chocolate, and gelatin mixture and cook over medium heat, stirring occasionally, until the chocolate is completely melted and the gelatin dissolved. Stir in the hazelnuts and let cool, stirring occasionally.

2. In a small bowl, beat the egg yolks, ¾ cup of the sugar, and the vanilla with an electric mixer until well blended. Add the remaining ¾ cup sherry. Stir into the cooled chocolate mixture.

3. In a medium bowl, beat the egg whites and the remaining 6 tablespoons of sugar with the electric mixer until stiff and glossy. In another medium bowl, beat the heavy cream until stiff peaks form. Stir the chocolate mixture into the whipped cream. Gradually fold this into the egg whites, mixing gently but thoroughly so that there are no lumps. Divide among individual dessert dishes and refrigerate at least 2 hours or until set.

4. Spoon a dollop of whipped cream, if using, onto each pudding. Serve cold.

Rennet Pudding with Honey Ⓥ*
Cuajada con Miel

MAKES 4 SERVINGS

Homemade rennet pudding has a completely different taste than the artificially flavored storebought kind. This has become a very popular dessert in many Spanish restaurants. In Spain, it is usually prepared unsweetened with honey poured over it. You can buy rennet in many specialty food stores; make it vegetarian with vegetarian rennet. If you prefer to have the custard sweeter, omit the honey and add 4½ tablespoons sugar to the milk before heating.

PREPARE AT LEAST 3 HOURS IN ADVANCE

3 cups milk

1 cinnamon stick

3 rennet tablets, crushed

Honey, for drizzling

Chopped walnuts (optional)

1. In a medium saucepan, combine the milk and cinnamon and heat over medium heat until very warm but not hot. Add the rennet and stir gently until it is completely dissolved but the milk has not yet begun to set. Discard the cinnamon.

2. Pour into individual dessert dishes (in Spain narrow earthenware mugs without handles are used). Let sit 1 hour, undisturbed, then refrigerate at least 2 hours to chill.

3. Drizzle with honey, sprinkle with the chopped walnuts, if using, and serve cold.

Cottage Cheese Bread Pudding ⓥ

Pastel de Greixonera

MAKES 8 SERVINGS

This dessert of Mallorcan origin is a bread pudding with a consistency somewhere between a cake and a custard. Cottage cheese, while not a traditional ingredient, makes this dessert even richer and more delicious. The recipe gets its name from the word greixonera, which refers to the earthenware casserole dish in which many Mallorcan dishes and desserts are prepared. I use a shallow oval earthenware casserole dish, similar to what is typically used for this dessert. It is excellent when served with peach marmalade or fresh berries.

PREPARE AT LEAST 2 HOURS IN ADVANCE

1 pound small-curd cottage cheese

¼ cup heavy cream

¼ cup sugar

4 large eggs

⅛ teaspoon salt

¼ teaspoon lemon zest

¼ teaspoon ground cinnamon, plus more for sprinkling

1¼ cups milk

3 ounces ladyfingers or light sponge cake, crumbled

2 tablespoons unsalted butter, melted

Granulated sugar, for dusting

Powdered (confectioners) sugar, for dusting

1. In a medium bowl, beat the cottage cheese with an electric mixer until smooth, then beat in the cream and sugar. Add the eggs, salt, lemon zest, and cinnamon and beat until smooth. Stir in the milk and ladyfingers and let sit 10 minutes. Beat again until smooth.

2. Preheat the oven to 350°F. Brush an oval-shaped mold or shallow oval earthenware casserole dish with the butter and dust well with the granulated sugar. Pour the batter into the pan and bake about 50 minutes or until the mixture is set. Let cool, then refrigerate at least 2 hours to chill.

3. Divide among dessert plates or bowls and dust with the cinnamon and powdered sugar. Serve cold.

Pastries in Soft Custard ⓥ

Natillas con Borrachuelos

MAKES 30 PASTRIES

This dessert is not custard in pastries, but rather pastries in custard. In this recipe, the pastries are crunchier than most similar ones, so soaking in the custard will not make them soggy. Even though the pastries and custard combine into one sensational dessert, they are often eaten separately. This recipe comes from the restaurant of Ubeda's beautiful parador, a sixteenth-century palace in a town filled with Renaissance architecture. We frequently go to Ubeda to visit our friend Natalio Rivas, owner of the beautiful sixteenth-century palace near the parador that he likes to show to visitors.

PREPARE AT LEAST 2 HOURS IN ADVANCE

Pastries

1 large egg yolk

1 tablespoon sugar

¼ teaspoon ground anise seeds

⅛ teaspoon ground cinnamon

⅛ teaspoon pure vanilla extract

1 tablespoon fresh orange juice

1 tablespoon grappa (aguardiente) or brandy

¼ cup white wine

¼ cup mild olive oil

1 strip lemon peel (yellow part only)

1¼ cups all-purpose flour

Soft Custard

2 cups milk

4 large egg yolks

¼ cup powdered (confectioners) sugar, plus more for dusting

½ teaspoon pure vanilla extract

Mild olive oil, for frying

1. Prepare the pastries: In a medium bowl, mix together with a wooden spoon the 1 egg yolk and the 1 tablespoon sugar. Stir in the anise, cinnamon, vanilla, orange juice, grappa, and white wine until blended.

2. In a small skillet, combine the oil and the lemon peel and heat over medium heat until the peel turns black. Discard the peel and let the oil cool. Stir into the egg mixture. Gradually stir in the flour until fully incorporated to make a smooth dough. Cover with plastic wrap and let rest at least 2 hours.

3. Meanwhile, prepare the custard: In a medium saucepan, bring the milk to a boil over medium heat, then let cool slightly. In the top of a double boiler or a bowl over a pot (not yet over the heat), whisk the egg yolks until lemon colored. Whisk in the sugar and gradually stir in the milk. Place over hot water and cook, stirring constantly, until thickened to a soft custard consistency. Remove from the heat and add the vanilla. Let cool, stirring frequently.

4. Roll out the dough on a floured surface to ⅛ inch thick and cut into 1½- to 1¾-inch-wide strips. Then cut across at a 45-degree angle to form rhombuses (slanted squares).

5. Heat at least ½ inch of oil in a large skillet over medium-high heat (or better still, use a deep fryer set at 375°F) until it quickly browns a cube of bread. Add as many pastries as will comfortably fit in the oil (they will puff) and fry, turning once, until browned on both sides. (Cook in batches if necessary to avoid overcrowding.) Transfer with a slotted spoon to paper towels and let drain. Repeat

with the remaining pastries. Let cool slightly, then dust with the sugar.

6. Divide the custard evenly among wide shallow bowls, such as earthenware, and float several pastries on top of each. Serve at room temperature.

Almond "Soup" Ⓥ

Sopa de Almendra

MAKES 4 TO 6 SERVINGS

Although this dessert is called almond "soup," it is actually an almond custard topped with sugar-coated fried bread. In this version, the almonds are toasted, and a dash of anisette is added. This recipe came from our dear friend Pepita Alias, who grew up in Lagartera, a town near Toledo that is famous for its intricate needlework. Pepita is as talented at cooking as she is at embroidering, being the supplier of lace for the royal houses of Spain and The Netherlands.

½ pound blanched almonds (about 1⅓ cups)

½ cup sugar

4 cups milk

Peel of 1 lemon (yellow part only), cut into strips

2 cinnamon sticks

Mild olive oil, for frying

8 thin slices long-loaf (baguette) bread

Powdered (confectioners) sugar, for sprinkling

1. In a food processor, process the almonds and sugar until the almonds are as finely ground as possible.

2. In a medium saucepan, combine the milk, lemon peel, and cinnamon sticks and bring to a boil over medium heat. Reduce the heat to low and simmer, stirring occasionally, about 10 minutes. Add the processor mixture, return to a boil, and simmer, stirring constantly, until the consistency of a soft custard, about 3 minutes. Let cool.

continues...

3. Remove the lemon peel and cinnamon stick. Pass the custard through a fine-mesh strainer, pressing with the back of a soup ladle to extract as much liquid as possible. Discard the solids. Divide the custard among individual flat-bottom bowls, such as small earthenware bowls and reserve at room temperature or refrigerate at least 2 hours to chill.

4. Heat at least ¼ inch of oil in a medium skillet over medium-high heat (or better still, use a deep fryer set at 375°F) until it quickly browns a cube of bread. Add the bread and fry, turning once, until golden. Transfer with an offset spatula to paper towels and let drain. (Alternatively, brush the bread with oil, place on a cookie sheet, and bake until golden in a 350°F oven—but the bread is far better when fried.)

5. Sprinkle the custards with the sugar. Garnish with the fried bread and serve at room temperature or refrigerate at least 2 hours and serve cold.

Banana and Almond Cream
Crema de Plátano con Almendra

MAKES 4 SERVINGS

Crema de plátano con almendra is a popular dessert in the Canary Islands, where bananas thrive in the subtropical climate. This needs to be served the same day it is prepared, or else the bananas will discolor.

¼ cup blanched almonds (about 1¾ ounces)

3 tablespoons cornstarch

2 cups plus 2 tablespoons milk

Pinch of salt

Peel of ½ lemon (yellow part only)

1 cinnamon stick

2 large eggs

⅓ cup sugar

2 medium bananas, peeled, mashed, and sprinkled with fresh lemon juice

Strawberry wedges, for garnish

1. Preheat the oven to 350°F. Scatter the almonds on a cookie sheet and toast about 5 minutes or until lightly golden. Let cool. Transfer to a food processor and blend until ground as finely as possible. In a cup, combine the cornstarch and 2 tablespoons of the milk until the cornstarch is dissolved. In a medium saucepan, combine the remaining 2 cups milk, the salt, lemon peel, and cinnamon and bring to a boil over medium heat, stirring frequently. Reduce the heat to low and simmer, stirring constantly, about 20 minutes. Discard the lemon peel and cinnamon stick.

2. In another medium saucepan, whisk together the eggs, sugar, bananas, the cornstarch mixture, and the almonds. Stir in the milk and bring to a boil over medium heat, stirring constantly. Remove from the heat and immediately divide among individual dessert bowls—do not stir. Garnish with the strawberries and serve at room temperature.

Sweetened Condensed Milk ⓥ
Dulce de Leche

MAKES 1½ CUPS

What is known here as the candy or caramel sauce dulce de leche *literally translates to sweetened condensed cream. Traditionally, though, first you would condense and sweeten milk before cooking and reducing it to the caramel stage. Here is how to make the cream. The next recipe is for the caramel sauce using homemade or canned condensed milk.*

MAKES ABOUT 1½ CUPS

1 quart whole milk

1 cup sugar

In a medium saucepan, combine the milk and sugar and bring to a boil over medium heat, stirring frequently. Reduce the heat to medium-low and cook, stirring constantly, until thickened to the consistency of condensed milk and slightly darkened in color, about 1 hour. Serve warm or at room temperature.

Caramelized Condensed Milk ⓥ
Leche Condensada al Caramelo

MAKES 1½ CUPS

My husband Luis, a native Madrileño, craves this so often that we always keep some on hand in the refrigerator. The preparation is simple—you only need put an unopened can of condensed milk into boiling water—and the result is a mouthwatering chewy candy or sauce. Dulce de leche tastes fresher if you make the sweet milk yourself, but canned condensed milk has been popular in Spain for decades. You can pour this over ice cream, serve it with cookies or churros for dipping, or use it as a filling for pastries.

One (14-ounce) can sweetened condensed milk or 1 recipe Sweetened Condensed Milk (Dulce de Leche) (at left)

1. Remove the label from the unopened can of condensed milk, place on its side in a medium saucepan, and add water to cover. If using Sweet Cream of Milk (Dulce de Leche), prepare and pour into a jar. Cover tightly with foil, place in a medium saucepan, and add water that comes three-quarters of the way up the jar.

2. Bring the water to a boil over high heat. Reduce the heat to low and simmer about 2½ hours, adding more water as necessary (make sure the closed can is always covered by water). Remove from the water and let cool. If made in a closed can, do not open until cool; if the milk is not caramelized enough, return the open can, standing upright, to the water and simmer until caramelized. Serve at room temperature.

Strawberry Meringues ⓥ
Merengues de Fresa

MAKES 20 SMALL MERINGUES

This version of strawberry meringue is meant to be eaten with a spoon as it is slightly crunchy on the outside and soft and creamy within. It is made with egg whites, which create a light and airy consistency. This fruity dessert is particularly beloved by children in Spain. For flavor variation, you can use an equal amount of other berries. Note that humidity can interfere with making the meringues; you may need to bake them longer on humid days.

¼ pound strawberries (about 8 medium), washed and stemmed

½ cup hot water

1 cup granulated sugar

4 large egg whites

14 drops fresh lemon juice

2 tablespoons powdered (confectioners) sugar, plus more for dusting

Strawberries, or other berries, for garnish

1. In a food processor or blender, process the strawberries until smooth, then add the hot water and process until smooth. Pass through a fine-mesh strainer into a medium saucepan. Discard the solids. Stir in the granulated sugar and bring to a boil over medium heat, stirring occasionally. Reduce the heat to low and simmer, stirring occasionally, until the syrup reaches the soft-crack stage (when a small amount is dropped into ice water, hard threads will form that can be bent but not broken), about 25 to 30 minutes.

continues...

2. When the syrup is almost done, combine the egg whites and lemon juice in a small bowl with an electric mixer until the whites start to stiffen. Add the 2 tablespoons powdered sugar and continue beating until stiff (but not dry) and glossy peaks form. With the electric mixer still on, very gradually pour the hot syrup into the egg white and beat about 10 minutes more.

3. Preheat the oven to 500°F. Place 20 miniature paper baking cups on a cookie sheet and drop the meringue by 3 tablespoons full into each cup (the meringue may be made larger or smaller). Dust heavily with the powdered sugar. Bake 1 minute. Transfer the meringue cups from the pan to a cooling rack and let cool. Decorate with wedges of strawberry—about 1 strawberry for each meringue. Serve at room temperature.

Frozen Lemon Cream in Lemon Shells Ⓥ

Crema de Limón con Miel

MAKES 4 TO 5 SERVINGS

Frozen sorbets served in fresh fruit shells are very popular all over Spain. This recipe from Mesón La Ráfaga in Andalucía offers a unique slant on this dessert—the filling is more of a soft cream than an ice cream or sorbet. The delicious lemon filling is served inside of a lemon shell. You should use the largest lemons you can find, making sure that the outsides are not bruised. For an even more attractive presentation, you can garnish it with a few berries.

PREPARE 8 TO 12 HOURS IN ADVANCE

4 to 5 large unblemished lemons

2 cups milk

Peel of ½ lemon (yellow part only), cut into several strips

1 cinnamon stick

2 large egg yolks

½ teaspoon lemon zest

¼ cup honey

1½ tablespoons granulated sugar

2 teaspoons fresh lemon juice

⅓ cup all-purpose flour

Small raspberries or blueberries

Powdered (confectioners) sugar, sifted, for dusting

1. Slice off the tops of the lemons and, with the aid of a grapefruit knife or a very small spoon, scrape the pith and membrane from the tops into a small bowl. Scrape out the rest of the lemon in

the same way and transfer to the bowl, trimming with kitchen shears any remaining membrane so that only the shells (yellow part only) remain. Pass the juice through a fine-mesh strainer and reserve 2 teaspoons (reserve the rest for another use). Slice off a small piece from the bottoms of the lemons, if necessary, so they stand upright.

2. In a small saucepan, combine the milk, lemon peel, and cinnamon stick and heat over medium heat, stirring occasionally, until the milk barely comes to a boil. Reduce the heat to low and simmer, stirring occasionally, about 10 minutes. Discard the lemon peel and cinnamon stick.

3. In a medium saucepan, whisk together the egg yolks, lemon zest, honey, granulated sugar, and the lemon juice. Stir in the flour until fully incorporated, then gradually stir in the hot milk. Cook over medium heat, stirring constantly, until the custard is thickened and smooth, begins to bubble, and no flour taste remains. Let cool, stirring occasionally. Fill the lemon shells with the custard, cover with the caps, and refrigerate overnight.

4. Dust 4 or 5 dessert dishes with the powdered sugar and place a lemon in the center of each dish. Remove the caps and arrange some berries over the custard, then partially cover with the caps. Scatter more berries around each plate. Serve at room temperature.

Red Wine Sangria Sorbet Ⓥ
Sorbete de Sangria

MAKES 4 SERVINGS

In this quintessentially Spanish sorbet made from sangria, sugar, citrus juices, and peach pulp, the sweetness is tempered by the tartness of the citric juices, creating a light and refreshing sorbet that is a delightful ending to any meal. It is especially good in the summertime.

PREPARE AT LEAST 8 TO
12 HOURS IN ADVANCE

½ cup sugar

¾ cup water

Peel of 1 lemon (yellow part only), cut into several strips

Peel of 1 orange (orange part only), cut into several strips

1 cinnamon stick

¼ cup fresh lemon juice

½ cup fresh orange juice

¾ cup dry red wine

2 tablespoons orange liqueur, such as Gran Torres or Grand Marnier

1 ripe peach, peeled, pitted, and coarsely chopped

1. Freeze the ice cream machine bowl at least 8 hours in advance. In a small saucepan, combine the sugar, water, lemon and orange peels, and cinnamon stick and bring to a boil over high heat. Reduce the heat to low and simmer, stirring occasionally, about 20 minutes. Let cool. Transfer to a medium bowl, cover, and refrigerate at least 2 hours to chill. Discard the lemon and orange peels. Stir in the lemon and orange juice, wine, and liqueur.

2. Place the peach in a food processor and chop as finely as possible. With the motor running, gradually add as much of the wine mixture as needed to make a smooth thick sauce, then mix in the rest. Transfer to an ice cream machine, churn, then freeze at least 30 minutes; it will be somewhat soft. Transfer to a container and freeze several hours until solid but scoopable. (As an alternative to an ice cream machine, you can make and freeze this in a bowl until set.) Serve immediately, or store, covered, in the freezer until serving.

White Sangria Sorbet with Melon and Kiwi Fruit **V**

Sorbete de Sangria Blanca con Melon y Kiwi

MAKES 6 SERVINGS

This version of sangria sorbet is made with white wine Sangria instead of red. The sorbet has an unusual appearance—it is pure white but speckled with black kiwi fruit seeds. I often serve white sangria sorbet alongside another fruit sorbet, usually raspberry, to provide a contrast of flavors and colors.

PREPARE AT LEAST 8 TO 12 HOURS IN ADVANCE

1 cup sugar

1½ cups water

Peel of 1 lemon (yellow part only), cut into several strips

2 kiwi fruits, peeled and coarsely chopped

2 (1½-inch) wedges honeydew melon or other light-fleshed melon

½ cup fresh lemon juice

¼ cup orange liqueur, such as Gran Torres or Grand Marnier

1½ cups dry white wine

Sliced kiwi fruit, for garnish

1. Freeze the ice cream machine bowl up at least 8 hours in advance. In a medium saucepan, combine the sugar, water, and lemon peel and bring to a boil over medium heat, stirring occasionally. Reduce the heat to low and simmer about 20 minutes. Let cool. Transfer to a medium bowl, cover, and refrigerate at least 2 hours to chill. Discard the lemon peel.

2. Meanwhile, in a food processor, add the kiwi and melon and process until as finely chopped as possible. Gradually add the lemon juice and the liqueur and process until smooth. Add the wine and process until blended. Transfer to an ice cream machine, churn, then freeze at least 30 minutes; it will be somewhat soft. Transfer to a container and freeze several hours until solid but scoopable. (As an alternative to an ice cream machine, you can make and freeze this in a bowl until set.) Garnish with the kiwi slices and serve cold.

Cava Sorbet **V**

Sorbete de Cava

MAKES 6 SERVINGS

In the summertime, I can't think of a dessert more refreshing than this splendid sparkling wine sorbet. It's made with orange peel and lemon peel, so it is not particularly sweet. Spanish cavas are sparkling wines produced by the same method as champagne. They are crisp, fresh, and fruity and perfect for sorbet.

PREPARE AT LEAST 8 TO 12 HOURS IN ADVANCE

½ cup sugar

¾ cup water

Peel of 1 orange (orange part only)

Peel of 1 lemon (yellow part only)

1¼ cups fresh orange juice

¼ cup fresh lemon juice

¾ cup cava (Spanish sparkling wine)

1. Freeze the ice cream machine bowl at least 8 hours in advance. In a medium saucepan, combine the sugar, water, and orange and lemon peels and bring to a boil over medium heat, stirring occasionally. Reduce the heat to low and simmer, stirring occasionally, about 30 minutes. Discard the orange and lemon peels. Stir in the orange juice, lemon juice, and champagne.

2. Transfer to an ice cream machine, churn, then freeze at least 30 minutes; it will be somewhat soft. Transfer to a container and freeze several hours until solid but scoopable. (As an alternative to an ice cream machine, you can make and freeze this in

a bowl until set.) Let sit briefly at room temperature to soften slightly and serve cold.

Strawberry and Wine Vinegar Sorbet Ⓥ
Sorbete de Fresa y Vinagre

MAKES 4 SERVINGS

Vinegar adds a subtle tang to this otherwise sweet and fruity strawberry sorbet. This recipe is based on a simple Spanish dessert of strawberries prepared with sugar and vinegar. The fruit liqueur can either be added or omitted, according to preference.

PREPARE AT LEAST 2 HOURS IN ADVANCE

3 cups water

¾ cup sugar

Peel of 1 lemon (yellow part only), cut into several pieces

2¼ pounds strawberries, washed and stemmed

3 tablespoons fresh lemon juice

3 tablespoons red wine vinegar

6 tablespoons fruit-flavored aquavit, Kirschwasser, or other fruit liqueur

Strawberries, for garnish

I. In a medium saucepan, combine the water, sugar, and lemon peel and bring to a boil over medium heat, stirring occasionally. Reduce the heat to low and simmer, stirring occasionally, about 20 minutes. Let cool and discard the lemon peel. Transfer to a medium bowl, cover, and refrigerate at least 2 hours to chill.

2. In a food processor, place with the strawberries, lemon juice, vinegar, and liqueur and process until smooth. Pass through a fine-mesh strainer into the chilled sugar mixture, discarding the solids, and mix until well blended.

3. Transfer to an ice cream machine, churn, then freeze at least 30 minutes; it will be somewhat soft.

Transfer to a container and freeze several hours until solid but scoopable. (As an alternative to an ice cream machine, you can make and freeze this in a bowl until set.) Garnish with the strawberries and serve cold.

Frozen Orange Custard with Blackberry Sauce Ⓥ
Babarrua de Naranja con Salsa de Mora

MAKES 6 SERVINGS

An unusual dessert with a consistency somewhere between a sorbet and a custard, this is excellent when topped with a mixture of orange liqueur and blackberry preserves.

Custard

1½ teaspoons gelatin

¼ cup cold water

¼ cup heavy cream

1¾ cups fresh orange juice

1 cup plus ½ teaspoon sugar

4 large eggs, separated

½ teaspoon orange zest

3 teaspoons orange liqueur, such as Gran Torres or Grand Marnier

Topping

1 cup blackberry preserves

3 teaspoons orange liqueur, such as Gran Torres or Grand Marnier

I. Prepare the custard: In a cup, combine the gelatin and water and let sit until the gelatin is softened. In a small saucepan, combine the cream and ¼ cup of the orange juice. Stir in the gelatin and cook over medium heat, stirring occasionally, until the gelatin is dissolved. Let cool.

continues...

2. In a medium bowl, beat together 1 cup of the sugar, the egg yolks, and orange zest until well blended, then gradually beat in the gelatin mixture, the remaining 1½ cups of orange juice, and the orange liqueur until well blended. In another medium bowl, beat the egg whites and the remaining ½ teaspoon of sugar with an electric mixer until stiff (but not dry) peaks form. Fold the egg yolk mixture into the egg whites.

3. Transfer to an ice cream machine, churn, then freeze at least 30 minutes; it will be somewhat soft. Transfer to a container and freeze several hours until solid but scoopable. (As an alternative to an ice cream machine, you can make and freeze this in a bowl until set.)

4. Prepare the topping: In a small bowl, mix the preserves and liqueur. Let the custard sit briefly at room temperature until slightly softened, then scoop into dessert bowls. Spoon the sauce over the custard and serve cold.

Turrón Ice Cream
Sorbete de Turrón

MAKES 4 TO 6 SERVINGS

Turrón, an almond and honey candy of Arab origin, is wildly popular in Spain. Therefore it is no surprise that turrón *ice cream is the favorite flavor of many Spaniards. This recipe calls for the crackling-hard type of* turrón *(Alicante style) as well as soft* turrón *(Jijona style). Both are excellent and available in specialty stores in the United States.*

One simple dessert featuring the candy is to crumble soft turrón *over ice cream. In this recipe, the* turrón *is blended into the ice cream (similar to the popular mix-ins in ice cream shops). This is excellent served with chocolate syrup.*

PREPARE AT LEAST 2 HOURS IN ADVANCE

5 ounces (½ package) Jijona (soft) turrón, crumbled

1½ cups powdered milk

½ cup sugar

½ cup heavy cream

½ cup water

12 ice cubes, crushed

5 ounces (½ package) Alicante (hard) turrón, broken into pieces

1. In a small saucepan, combine the Jijona turron, powdered milk, sugar, cream, and water and heat over medium heat, stirring occasionally, until the sugar dissolves. Let cool. Transfer to a food processor or blender and process until smooth.

2. Add the crushed ice and blend with an on/off motion until no large pieces remain. Add the Alicante turrón and blend with the on/off motion until no large pieces remain. Transfer to a bowl and refrigerate at least 2 hours or until hardened. Serve cold.

Almond Crisps with Yogurt Ice Cream and Honey
Crujiente de Almendra con Helado de Yogurt y Miel

MAKES 6 SERVINGS

This is a classic and popular finish to any Spanish meal; the ingredients complement each other beautifully.

½ recipe Almond Crisps (page 574)

1 pint vanilla ice cream or frozen yogurt

6 tablespoons honey

Fresh mint leaves (optional)

Prepare the almond crisps as instructed in the recipe. Place one on each of 6 dessert plates. Top each crisp with a large scoop of ice cream or frozen yogurt and drizzle with the honey. Garnish with the mint leaves, if using, and serve cold.

Vanilla Ice Cream with Hot Banana Sauce Ⓥ

Helado de Vainilla con Salsa Caliente de Plátano

MAKES 6 SERVINGS

This recipe comes from the Canary Islands, the only part of Spain that has a subtropical climate hot enough to grow bananas. This quick-cooking banana topping is sautéed with a brown sugar sauce that is flavored with cinnamon, nutmeg, and lemon zest. Then it is flamed with orujo, *a Spanish liquor made from grape skins. If* orujo *is not available, you may substitute Italian grappa or aquavit.*

¼ cup (½ stick) unsalted butter

3 bananas, cut into ½-inch slices

2 tablespoons brown sugar

¼ teaspoon ground cinnamon

¼ teaspoon lemon zest

¼ teaspoon ground nutmeg

2 tablespoons orujo, grappa, or other liqueur

1 pint vanilla ice cream

¼ cup sliced almonds

1. Melt the butter in a medium skillet over low heat. Add the bananas and sprinkle with the sugar, cinnamon, lemon zest, and nutmeg. Simmer, turning the bananas occasionally with a rubber spatula, about 2 minutes.

2. Pour the liqueur over the bananas. Standing well away from the skillet, ignite the liquid with a match or kitchen lighter and let the flame die out.

3. Scoop the ice cream into 6 dessert bowls. Spoon the sauce over the ice cream, sprinkle with the almonds, and serve immediately.

Frozen Almond Cream Ⓥ

Biscuit de Almendras

MAKES 8 SERVINGS

This wonderful frozen dessert has no egg yolks and only a little bit of cream, yet richer than it actually is. It's best when accompanied by bienmesabe *almond sauce (page 662).*

PREPARE AT LEAST 4 HOURS IN ADVANCE

¼ pound blanched almonds (about ⅔ cups)

½ cup sugar

8 large egg whites or 1 cup egg substitute made with egg whites

⅔ cup heavy cream

Pinch of salt

½ teaspoon pure vanilla extract

1. Preheat the oven to 350°F. Scatter the almonds on a cookie sheet and toast 3 to 4 minutes or until golden. Let cool. Transfer to a food processor, add ¼ cup of the sugar, and process until as finely ground as possible.

2. In a small bowl, beat the egg whites with an electric mixer until frothy, then beat in the remaining ¼ cup sugar and beat until the egg whites are stiff but not dry (a peak will just hold its shape when you lift the beater; if using egg substitute, the mixture will be very thick, but not stiff). In a medium bowl, beat the cream, salt, and vanilla with the electric mixer until soft peaks form. Stir in all but 2 tablespoons of the almond mixture, then gently fold in the egg whites in batches.

3. Grease a loaf pan (or line it with plastic wrap with long overhang) and dust with the remaining 2 tablespoons of the almond mixture. Pour the egg white mixture into the pan, cover with plastic on top (or the plastic overhang) and freeze at least 4 hours or until firm. Remove the loaf from the pan. Cut into slices and serve cold.

Prune Ice Cream with Orange Liqueur Sauce ⓥ

Helado de Ciruela "Casa Irene"

MAKES 6 SERVINGS

This outstanding recipe comes from Casa Irene, one of the finest restaurants in all of Spain, located in Arties, a tiny village high in the Pyrenees Mountains. When our friend Irene served me this wonderful ice cream with orange liqueur, I never would have guessed her "secret" ingredient was prunes. Delicious and very unusual.

¼ pound prunes

2 pints vanilla ice cream

½ cup orange liqueur, such as Gran Torres or Grand Marnier

1. Stew the prunes according to package directions. Reserve the liquid. Coarsely chop the prunes, removing the pits. Return the pits to the reserved liquid to give it added flavor.

2. Place the ice cream in a large bowl and let sit at room temperature until softened. Fold in the prunes with a rubber spatula and return the ice cream to the freezer to harden. Pass the prune juice through a fine-mesh strainer into a small bowl and discard the solids. (If there is more than ½ cup juice, you may wish to boil it down for stronger flavor.) Stir in the orange liqueur.

3. Scoop the ice cream into individual dessert dishes and spoon a few tablespoons of the sauce over the ice cream. Serve cold.

Frozen Walnut "Cake" with Candied Walnuts and Chocolate Sauce ⓥ

Biscuit de Nueces Garrapiñadas y Salsa de Chocolate

MAKES 8 TO 10 SERVINGS

This ice cream dish has the appearance of a cake because it is prepared in a loaf pan, but really it is not a cake at all. The ground walnuts and beaten egg whites give the mixture a texture that can best be described as cake-like. I always serve it with chocolate sauce and candied walnuts.

PREPARE AT LEAST 4 HOURS IN ADVANCE

Unsalted butter, for greasing

1 cup walnuts

5 tablespoons sugar

Pinch of salt

6 large egg whites or 1 cup egg substitute made with egg whites

¾ cup heavy cream

¼ teaspoon pure vanilla extract

1 recipe Chocolate Sauce (page 589)

¼ cup powdered (confectioners) sugar

⅛ teaspoon cinnamon

⅛ teaspoon salt

4 ounces walnuts (about ¾ cup)

1. Grease a 9¼ x 5¼-inch loaf pan (or cover the bottom with plastic wrap with long overhang). In a food processor, place the walnuts and 2 tablespoons of the granulated sugar and process until the walnuts are finely ground. Reserve. In a small bowl, beat the egg white with an electric mixer until foamy, then add the remaining 3 tablespoons granulated sugar and the pinch of salt and beat until

stiff but not dry (a peak will just hold its shape when you lift the beater; or until very thick, if using egg substitute).

2. In a medium bowl, beat the cream and vanilla with the electric mixer until stiff (but not dry) peaks form, then fold in the egg white mixture and the 1 cup walnuts. Pour into the loaf pan. Cover with foil and freeze overnight.

3. Prepare the sauce as directed in step 3 of the recipe. Preheat the oven to 375°F. In a small bowl, combine the powdered sugar, the ⅛ teaspoon salt, and cinnamon.

4. Place the ¾ cup walnuts in a small saucepan with water to cover and bring to a boil over high heat; lower and simmer 3 minutes. Drain well, then immediately roll the walnuts in the sugar mixture. Transfer to a cookie sheet. Bake 20 to 25 minutes or until browned, turning the nuts so they do not burn. Let cool.

5. Briefly place the bottom of the loaf pan in hot water to loosen the cake. Turn out the loaf upside down (removing the plastic wrap if necessary) onto a serving plate and present at the table. Cut into slices and place each on an individual dessert plate. Pour the sauce over the ice cream and sprinkle with the candied walnuts. Serve cold.

Coffee-Flavored Refrigerator Log Ⓥ
Brazo de Fabiola

MAKES 6 TO 8 SERVINGS

Elegant but simple, this dessert is made with María biscuit cookies (a biscuit-type cookie that isn't overly sweet), layered in coffee frosting and covered in meringue. This is a very rich dessert that should be served in small portions. The recipe comes from our friend Reme Domínguez, a talented and innovative chef at Tasca del Puerto in Castellón de la Plana. You can usually find María cookies in the international or Goya-brand section of the supermarket.

PREPARE 8 TO 12 HOURS IN ADVANCE

½ **pound (2 sticks) unsalted butter, at room temperature**

½ **cup sugar**

2 **teaspoons instant espresso coffee**

½ **cup fresh espresso, regular coffee, or liquid instant espresso, cooled**

½ **package María biscuits (about 14 cookies)**

1 **large egg white**

1. In a small bowl, beat the butter and 6 tablespoons of the sugar with an electric mixer until light and fluffy. Add the instant coffee and 2 teaspoons of the liquid coffee and beat until smooth.

2. Pour the remaining liquid coffee into a shallow bowl and dip each cookie quickly in the coffee (don't leave the cookies in the coffee any longer or they will break up). Spread about 2 teaspoons of the butter mixture on each cookie and form a "log" by gently pressing the cookies together.

3. In a small bowl, beat the egg white and the remaining 2 tablespoons sugar with the electric mixer until stiff (but not dry) peaks form. Using a rubber spatula, cover the log with the meringue, forming swirls and soft peaks. Refrigerate overnight. Cut diagonally into thin slices and serve cold.

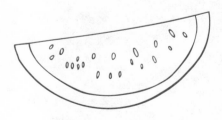

Cream Cheese Ice Cream with Raspberry Purée ⓥ

Helado de Queso con Salsa de Frambuesa

MAKES 4 SERVINGS

For this creamy and delicious dessert, you may either make your own cream cheese ice cream or use a fine-quality storebought vanilla ice cream.

PREPARE AT LEAST 2 HOURS IN ADVANCE

3 ounces cream cheese, softened

1 pint vanilla ice cream, softened

Fresh raspberries or small strawberries

1 recipe Raspberry Purée (page 662)

Mint leaves, for garnish (optional)

1. In a medium bowl, beat the cream cheese with an electric mixer until smooth. Add the ice cream and beat again until smooth. Freeze at least 2 hours, stirring occasionally.

2. Meanwhile, prepare the purée. Spoon 2 tablespoons of the purée onto individual dessert plates. Place a scoop of ice cream in the center, scatter the raspberries over the ice cream, and garnish with the mint, if using. Serve cold.

Crackling Caramelized Pine Nuts with Ice Cream Bathed in Honey Sauce ⓥ

Helado de Piñones Garrapiñados en Salsa de Miel

MAKES 4 SERVINGS

Of Moorish origin, this dessert contains ingredients such as nuts, honey, and sugar. Sugar- or honey-coated nuts are enormously popular in Spain and are sold on the street by vendors with pushcarts. Although candied almonds are the most popular, candied pine nuts are equally delicious.

Unsalted butter

½ cup pine nuts

½ cup sugar

½ cup water

¼ teaspoon ground cinnamon

1 pint vanilla ice cream

Honey Sauce

½ cup honey

2 teaspoons warm water

½ teaspoon ground cinnamon

1. Line a cookie sheet with foil and grease the foil well with butter. In a small skillet, combine the pine nuts, sugar, water, and ¼ teaspoon cinnamon and bring to a boil over high heat, stirring constantly, and cook, continuing to stir, until the sugar turns dark golden, about 5 minutes. Pour onto the cookie sheet and spread with a rubber spatula into a thin layer. Let cool. Peel off the foil and break or lightly pound the nut candy into small pieces.

2. Prepare the sauce: In a small bowl, combine the honey, water, and cinnamon and spoon onto individual dessert plates. Place a scoop of ice cream in the center and sprinkle with the nuts. Serve cold.

Almond- and Raisin-Filled Baked Apples ❤️
Manzanas Asadas

MAKES 4 SERVINGS

These delicious baked apples filled with almonds and raisins are a classic dessert in Spain. Egg yolks are used to make the filling richer, and rum adds a wonderful accent of flavor. The apples are coated with lemon juice in order to prevent discoloration.

2 ounces blanched almonds (about ⅓ cup)

2 tablespoons light rum

½ cup plus 1 tablespoon water

2 tablespoons raisins

4 large apples suitable for baking, such as McIntosh

Fresh lemon juice

2 egg yolks

6 tablespoons sugar

3 tablespoons unsalted butter, melted and cooled

1. Preheat the oven to 350°F. Scatter the almonds on a cookie sheet and toast about 5 minutes or until lightly golden. Let cool. Transfer to a food processor, and blend until as finely ground as possible (but not a paste). Leave the oven on.

2. In a small saucepan, combine the rum, the 1 tablespoon water, and the raisins and heat over medium heat, stirring occasionally, until warm. Remove from the heat and reserve.

3. Peel and core each apple, leaving a base of ½ inch at the bottom so they will stand upright. Scoop out the inside, leaving a hollow "cylinder" about 1½ inches in diameter. Rub the apples with the lemon juice to prevent discoloration.

4. In a small bowl, mix the egg yolks, 5 tablespoons of the sugar, the almonds, and butter until well blended. Drain the raisins, reserving the liquid. Stir the raisins into the egg mixture. Fill each apple with about 2 tablespoons of the mixture.

5. Place the apples in an 8-inch square baking pan and pour in the reserved liquid, the ½ cup water, and the remaining 1 tablespoon sugar. Bake 30 minutes, basting occasionally and adding more water if the liquid evaporates. Cover with foil and bake 15 to 20 minutes more or until the apples are tender. Serve warm.

Baked Apples with Raisins in Custard Sauce ❤️
Manzanas Asadas con Uvas Pasas a la Crema

MAKES 6 SERVINGS

Spanish sherry adds its distinct flavor to this traditional dessert of baked apples, made more unique and delicious by the addition of rich custard. The apples are baked in the sherry with raisins and cinnamon, with the custard providing the perfect creamy complement. Each apple is stuffed with a strawberry. I suggest using strawberries with their leaves on, but if the leaves are not available, you can garnish with mint leaves.

3 large apples suitable for baking, such as McIntosh or Golden Delicious, peeled, halved lengthwise, and cored

Fresh lemon juice

2 cinnamon sticks, each cut into 3 pieces

2 tablespoons sugar

2 tablespoons honey

2 tablespoons sweet sherry or other sweet wine

3 tablespoons raisins

continues . . .

Peel of ½ lemon (yellow part only), cut into several
  pieces

¼ cup water

Custard Sauce

2 large eggs, lightly beaten

¼ cup sugar

⅛ teaspoon salt

2 cups hot milk

½ teaspoon pure vanilla extract

6 large strawberries, preferably with their leaves
  (otherwise, use mint leaves)

Sliced almonds, for garnish

1. Preheat the oven to 350°F. Rub the apples all over with the lemon juice. In a shallow baking dish in which the apples will comfortably fit, combine the cinnamon sticks, sugar, honey, sherry, raisins, lemon peel, and water.

2. Arrange the apples in the baking dish, cored side up, cover, and bake, basting occasionally, about 40 minutes or until the apples are just tender—do not overcook. Let cool.

3. Meanwhile, prepare the sauce: In the top of a double boiler or a medium bowl, lightly beat the eggs, sugar, and salt with a fork. Gradually stir in the milk. Over medium heat (the water should not boil), cook in the double boiler or the bowl over a pot of water, stirring constantly, until the custard coats a spoon. Stir in the vanilla and let cool.

4. Transfer the apples, cinnamon sticks, and raisins to a platter, reserving the liquid. Discard the lemon peel. Stir the liquid into the custard.

5. Spoon about 3 tablespoons of the custard onto each of 6 dessert plates and place 1 apple half, cored side up, over the custard. Fill the hollow of the apple with a strawberry. Scatter the raisins around the custard and garnish each plate with 1 piece of cinnamon stick. Sprinkle with the almonds and serve warm or at room temperature.

Baked Apples Filled with Catalan Custard Ⓥ

Manzanas Rellenas de Crema Catalana Quatre Barres

MAKES 8 SERVINGS

This Catalan-style recipe comes from Chef Josep Lladonosa i Giró, the founder of the Quatre Barres restaurant in Barcelona. Baked apples are very popular in Spain, and I have tasted many versions. This one, filled with Catalan custard and bathed in caramelized sugar, is truly exceptional.

Custard

1 tablespoon plus ¼ teaspoon cornstarch

1⅓ cups plus 1 tablespoon milk

3 large egg yolks

¼ cup sugar

Peel of ¼ lemon, cut into several pieces (yellow part
  only)

½ cinnamon stick

Apples

8 apples suitable for baking, such as Golden Delicious

Fresh lemon juice

½ cup water

½ cup white wine

½ cinnamon stick

Peel of ½ lemon (yellow part only), cut into several
  pieces

¼ cup sugar

Caramelized Sugar Syrup

½ cup sugar

½ cup hot water

1. Prepare the custard: In a small bowl, dissolve the cornstarch in 1 tablespoon of the milk. Stir in the egg yolks until well blended.

2. In a small saucepan, combine the remaining 1⅓ cups milk, the ¼ cup sugar, ¼ lemon peel, and ½ cinnamon stick and bring to a boil over medium heat, stirring occasionally. Reduce the heat to low and simmer, stirring occasionally, 15 minutes. Gradually stir into the cornstarch mixture. Return to the saucepan, increase the heat to medium, and cook, stirring constantly, until the custard starts to bubble. Discard the lemon peel and cinnamon stick. Reserve.

3. Prepare the apples: Preheat the oven to 350°F. Peel the apples and rub with the lemon juice to prevent discoloration. Hollow out enough of each apple, removing the core and seeds, so there is room for 2 tablespoons of the custard. In a shallow baking dish in which the apples will comfortably fit, combine the water, wine, the ½ cinnamon stick, and ½ lemon peel. Arrange the apples in the baking dish and sprinkle with the ¼ cup sugar. Bake 30 to 40 minutes or until softened, basting occasionally and adding more water if the liquid evaporates. Cover with foil and bake 10 minutes more. Let cool.

4. Prepare the syrup: In a very small saucepan, combine the sugar and 3 tablespoons of the water and bring to a boil over high heat, stirring constantly, and cook, continuing to stir, until the syrup is light golden. Gradually and very carefully stir in the remaining 5 tablespoons water.

5. Spoon some of the liquid from the baking pan onto each of 8 dessert dishes. Fill each apple with about 2 tablespoons of the custard and place 1 on each dish. Spoon the caramelized sugar over the apples. Serve warm or at room temperature.

Caramelized Oranges ⓥ
Naranjas en Azúcar Acaramelado

MAKES 4 SERVINGS

When sweet, juicy oranges are coated with a caramelized sugar glaze, the results are outstanding. These sugar-coated oranges are delicious on their own, but I recommend serving them over a raspberry purée. The oranges can be prepared earlier in the day because the coating will stay hard for several hours.

2 large oranges, peeled

1 cup sugar

2 tablespoons water

2 teaspoons vinegar

3 tablespoons orange liqueur, such as Gran Torres or Grand Marnier

1 recipe Raspberry Purée (page 662; optional)

Mint sprigs and fresh raspberries, for garnish (optional)

1. Clean the pith from the oranges, removing as much as possible. Divide into segments, keeping the membrane intact. Place on paper towels and let dry. Set out a cooling rack over a tray or foil.

2. In a small saucepan, combine the sugar, water, and vinegar and bring to a boil over high heat, stirring constantly, and cook, continuing to stir, until light golden, about 4 minutes. Lower the heat to low, and gradually and very carefully stir in the orange liqueur.

3. For this step, keep your fingers away from the sugar because it is very hot. Working quickly before the syrup hardens (it can be liquefied by reheating), use a fork or a slotted spoon to dip the orange segments in the syrup. Place upright on the cooling rack to dry.

4. Prepare the purée. Spoon 2 tablespoons of the purée onto individual dessert plates. Place a few orange segments in the center of each, and garnish with the mint, if using. Serve at room temperature.

Bananas with Honey and Pine Nuts
Plátanos con Miel y Piñones

MAKES 4 SERVINGS

The climate of the Canary Islands is ideal for grow-ing bananas, and most desserts based on bananas originated there. This recipe is so simple that you can prepare it in less than 10 minutes. It is very good over vanilla ice cream.

¼ cup (½ stick) unsalted butter

4 bananas, peeled and halved lengthwise then crosswise

½ cup honey

3 tablespoons warm water

1 teaspoon fresh lemon juice

3 tablespoons anisette liqueur

¼ cup pine nuts

Melt the butter in a skillet or chafing dish over medium heat. Add the bananas and cook, turning once, about 1 minute. In a small bowl, stir together the honey, water, and lemon juice. Add to the bananas, reduce the heat to low, and cook about 1 minute more. Add the anisette and cook about 2 minutes more. Sprinkle with the pine nuts and serve hot.

Melon Balls in Sweet Sherry
Melón al Jerez Dulce

MAKES 4 SERVINGS

The sweet sherry in this recipe gives these melon balls their distinctively Spanish flavor. You can try it using other fruits, but I've always found that melon works best for this very simple and refreshing dessert.

½ cup sherry, such as Spanish cream, or sweet red wine

½ cup cranberry or fresh orange juice

½ teaspoon fresh lemon juice

1 tablespoon sugar

¼ teaspoon lemon zest

1 tablespoon chopped fresh mint or ½ teaspoon dried mint

¼ teaspoon ground mace

1 ripe orange melon, such as cantaloupe or Crenshaw

Combine all ingredients except the melon in a medium bowl. With a melon scoop or a small spoon, scoop out 1-inch balls of melon. Fold the melon into the juice mixture, cover, and refrigerate about 30 minutes, stirring occasionally. Serve cool.

Summer Berries with Yogurt Cream
Bayas con Crema de Yogur

MAKES 6 SERVINGS

This rich, creamy dessert is so simple that it can be prepared in under 5 minutes and then frozen. You can use blueberries, raspberries, blackberries, or a combination depending on your preference. This recipe came from the Claretian monks from Aranda de Duero in Castilla. I garnish it with fresh mint.

PREPARE AT LEAST 2 HOURS IN ADVANCE

¾ cup plain yogurt

¾ cup storebought or homemade Dulce de Leche (page 642; partial recipe) or sweetened condensed milk

¼ cup fresh lemon juice

3 cups berries, such as blueberries, raspberries, and/or blackberries

12 mint sprigs, for garnish (optional)

In a medium bowl, lightly whisk together the yogurt, Dulce de Leche, and lemon juice. Cover and refrigerate at least 2 hours to chill. Spoon the yogurt mixture onto each of 6 dessert dishes and arrange the berries around the yogurt. Garnish with the mint, if using, and serve cold.

Apples in Spiced Wine Syrup Ⓥ
Manzanas en Jarabe

MAKES 4 SERVINGS

This recipe happens to be the very last one in the sixteenth-century Spanish cookbook written by Robert Nola. After this recipe, Nola writes, "And here this book comes to an end." Fortunately, all the recipes this famous cookbook has inspired have not come to an end and instead continue to flourish in all parts of Spain. This dessert of apples in spiced wine has a Moorish influence reflected by the use of nutmeg, cloves, cinnamon, and cardamom.

¼ cup slivered blanched almonds

1 cup dry white wine

¼ cup sugar

¼ teaspoon ground nutmeg

4 whole cloves

1 cinnamon stick

¼ teaspoon ground cardamom

Peel of ½ small orange (orange part only), cut into very thin strips, then finely chopped

2 large Golden Delicious apples, peeled, cored, and quartered

Whipped cream or ice cream, for garnish (optional)

1. Preheat the oven to 350°F. Scatter the almonds on a cookie sheet and toast about 5 minutes or until lightly golden.

2. In a medium saucepan, combine the wine, sugar, almonds, nutmeg, cloves, cinnamon stick, cardamom, and orange peel and bring to a boil over high heat, stirring occasionally. Reduce the heat to low and simmer, stirring occasionally, about 10 minutes. Add the apples and continue cooking until the apples are tender, about 30 minutes. Turn off the heat, transfer the apples to a medium bowl, and continue to cook the syrup at a high simmer until it has thickened to a heavy syrup consistency and is slightly caramelized. Return the apples to the syrup and let steep until ready to serve.

3. Slice the apples into thin wedges and arrange attractively on 4 dessert plates. Spoon the syrup over the apples. Serve hot with a little cream or a scoop of ice cream, if using.

Stewed Prunes and Apricots Ⓥ
Zurracapote

MAKES 4 TO 6 SERVINGS

This typical Christmas Eve dessert is from the Basque country. Prunes and dried apricots are stewed in red wine, brown sugar, and cinnamon, creating a wonderfully spicy fruit dessert. It will keep for weeks in a jar, either refrigerated or at room temperature, but it is best when served warm.

PREPARE AT LEAST 3 HOURS IN ADVANCE

1 cup full-bodied red wine

1 cup water

1 cup firmly packed brown sugar

1 cinnamon stick

Peel of ½ lemon (yellow part only)

½ pound prunes

½ pound dried apricots

In a medium saucepan, combine the wine, water, brown sugar, cinnamon, and lemon peel and bring to a boil over high heat. Reduce the heat to low and simmer about 5 minutes. Add the prunes and apricots, cover, and simmer 15 minutes more. Remove from the heat and let sit covered at least 3 hours in the syrup. Reheat over medium heat and serve warm.

Autumn Fruit in Grape Syrup Ⓥ
Mostillo

MAKES 6 SERVINGS

This seasonal dessert is only served in the fall for two reasons. The first is that the fruits this recipe calls for—pears, figs, melon, and spaghetti squash—are freshest in the fall. The second is that fall is the time when the grapes of La Rioja and Aragon are pressed to make the region's incredible wines. Grape juice in Spain is sometimes referred to as grape "must," which is why this dessert is called mostillo.

PREPARE AT LEAST 2 HOURS IN ADVANCE

5 cups white grape juice

½ pound ripe but firm green or orange melon, cut into 1-inch cubes

½ pound spaghetti squash, peeled and cut into 1-inch cubes

½ pound ripe but firm sweet pears, such as seckel, peeled, cored, and cut into 1½-inch pieces

12 very small fresh or dried figs

Peel of ½ orange (orange part only)

1 cinnamon stick

2 tablespoons walnut pieces

2 tablespoons raisins

1. In a large saucepan, bring the grape juice to a boil over high heat. Reduce the heat to low and simmer uncovered about 1 hour. It should be reduced but not thick.

2. Add all the remaining ingredients, increase the heat to medium, and cook, stirring occasionally, until the grape juice becomes a thick syrup, about 1 hour more. Let cool. Serve at room temperature. Store in a covered container in the refrigerator, but bring to room temperature before serving.

Pears Steeped in Red Wine and Sherry Syrup Ⓥ
Peras en Jarabe de Vino y Jerez

MAKES 4 SERVINGS

This is a very simple recipe, but it does need to be prepared one day in advance. The pears are steeped overnight in a sauce of red wine, sweet cream sherry, and spices that is boiled down to a syrup. The pears absorb the delicious flavor of the syrup, and the results are sensational.

PREPARE AT LEAST 8 TO 12 HOURS IN ADVANCE

4 medium to large ripe but firm pears

Juice of ½ lemon

3 cups dry red wine

2 cups water

½ cup sugar

2 cinnamon sticks, halved

2 (¼-inch) lemon slices, halved

¼ cup sherry, such as Spanish cream, or sweet red wine

¼ teaspoon ground mace

1 tablespoon honey

Whipped cream (optional)

1. Peel the pears and dip in the lemon juice to prevent discoloration. In a deep saucepan in which the pears will fit fairly closely, combine the wine, water, sugar, cinnamon, and lemon and bring to a boil over high heat, stirring occasionally. Reduce the heat to low. Add the pears, cover, and simmer about 20 minutes or until the pears are tender. Transfer the pears to a plate, reserving the liquid.

2. Add the sherry and mace to the wine mixture and cook over high heat, stirring occasionally, until the liquid is reduced and the mixture is syrupy (you should have about 1½ cups). Remove from the

heat, stir in the honey, and return the pears to the syrup. Let sit covered at room temperature overnight, turning the pears occasionally in the syrup.

3. Cut the pears into quarters, removing the core. Cut into ¼- to ½-inch wedges and arrange in overlapping rows on 4 dessert plates. Spoon the syrup over the pears and garnish with the cinnamon and lemon. Spoon a dollop of whipped cream, if using, in the center. Serve at room temperature.

Dried Apricots in Red Wine Syrup Ⓥ
Orejones al Vino Tinto

MAKES 4 SERVINGS

Because of the shape of dried apricots, in Spain they are called orejones, *which translates to "big ears." The first time I tasted this delicious dessert was at the Meseguer restaurant in Alcaniz, a restaurant that is well known for its simple Aragonese dishes.*

PREPARE AT LEAST 8 TO 12 HOURS IN ADVANCE

1 cup water

¼ cup sugar

1 slice lemon

1 cinnamon stick

½ pound dried apricots or a mix of dried apricots and dried prunes

½ cup dry red wine

1. In a medium saucepan, bring the water and sugar to a boil over high heat. Reduce the heat to low, add the lemon, cinnamon, and apricots, cover, and simmer, stirring occasionally, about 10 minutes. Stir in the wine, cover, and simmer, stirring occasionally, 10 minutes more or until the apricots are tender.

2. Transfer the apricots to a heatproof glass jar. Cook the remaining liquid over medium-high heat, stirring occasionally, until reduced and syrupy. Let

cool and pour over the apricots. Cover and let sit at room temperature overnight, then serve. Store covered in the refrigerator.

Oranges in Honey and Olive Oil "Núñez de Prado" Ⓥ
Naranjas con Miel Aceite de Oliva "Núñez de Prado"

MAKES 6 SERVINGS

Our dear friend Paco Núñez de Prado of the famous Núñez de Prado olive oil estate in the Córdoban city of Baena, has introduced me to innumerable recipes featuring his family's sublime and distinguished extra-virgin olive oil. I guess I shouldn't have been surprised when, for dessert, we were served sliced oranges bathed in a blend of honey and the finest extra-virgin olive oil. It turned out to be extremely delicious and quite possibly the highlight of the meal.

6 navel oranges

½ cup water

2 tablespoons honey

1½ cups sugar

2 tablespoons fresh orange juice

2 tablespoons finest extra-virgin olive oil

2 tablespoons orange liqueur, such as Gran Torres or Grand Marnier

1. Remove a thin peel (orange part only) from 2 oranges and cut into very thin strips. Clean the pith, removing as much as possible. Place the strips in a small saucepan, add 1 inch of water, bring to a boil over low heat, and simmer about 10 minutes. Drain and rinse under cold water.

2. In another small saucepan, combine the water, honey, sugar, and orange juice and bring to a boil over high heat, stirring occasionally, until the liquid

continues...

is reduced and the mixture syrupy, about 10 minutes (230°F on a candy thermometer). Add the orange peel and remove from the heat. Let cool. Stir in the olive oil and orange liqueur.

3. Slice the remaining 4 oranges and arrange in a large shallow bowl. Pour the syrup over the oranges and let sit at room temperature at least 1 hour. Divide the orange slices among 6 dessert plates and spoon the sauce over the top. Serve at room temperature.

Peaches Steeped in Red Wine Ⓥ
Melocotón con Vino

MAKES 4 SERVINGS

Aragon is the region in Spain that is famous for its extraordinary quality of peaches. They are sold everywhere in huge jars, peeled and preserved whole in sugar syrup. This popular recipe from Aragon calls for the peaches to be steeped in a mixture of syrup and wine. The peaches traditionally come from Calanda, the birthplace of Luis Buñuel, the famous Spanish-born movie director.

In Aragon, the peaches are served whole in small bowls with some of the wine syrup, but for a more elegant presentation, cut the peaches into wedges.

PREPARE AT LEAST 3 TO 4 DAYS IN ADVANCE

4 cups sugar

4 cups water

1 cinnamon stick

2 slices lemon

⅛ teaspoon salt

About 4 large, firm but ripe peaches, skinned

2 cups full-bodied dry red wine

I. In a medium saucepan, combine the sugar, water, cinnamon, lemon, and salt and bring to a boil over medium heat. Reduce the heat to low and simmer, stirring occasionally, about 15 minutes. Let cool. Place the peaches in a deep bowl or jar in which they fit fairly closely, then pour the syrup over the peaches (it should cover them). Cover and refrigerate at least 2 days.

2. Pour off 2 cups of the syrup (you can reserve it for making more peaches or other preserved fruits) and replace it with the wine. Mix well.

3. Refrigerate at least 24 up to 48 hours. Leave the peaches whole or cut into wedges and place 1 on each of 4 dessert plates. Either drizzle with the syrup or bathe in a small pool of the syrup. Serve at room temperature.

Baked Peaches in Sherry Syrup Ⓥ
Melocotón al Horno en Jarabe de Vino

MAKES 4 SERVINGS

Here is another version of Aragon's famous peaches steeped in wine, except that this preparation is a bit more elaborate. The peaches are baked and served warm in a syrup made with vino rancio, *which translates to "rancid" wine. The wine is exposed to light, giving it a sherry-like flavor. I recommend using* amontillado, *a Spanish semi-dry sherry that can be purchased at many specialty stores. The first time I tasted this dessert was at La Cocina Aragonesa in the city of Jaca.*

4 ripe but still firm peaches

¼ cup water

1 cup sugar

1 cup vino rancio or semi-dry sherry, such as Spanish amontillado

1. Preheat the oven to 350°F. Place the peaches in an 8-inch square or round cake pan, add the water, and bake about 45 minutes or until the peaches are tender (the skin will be firm), adding more water if it evaporates. Let cool slightly and peel.

2. Meanwhile, in a small saucepan, combine the sugar and wine and bring to a boil over high heat, stirring occasionally. Reduce the heat to low and simmer, stirring, until the liquid is reduced and the mixture syrupy, 10 to 15 minutes. Place 1 peach on each of 4 dessert plates, spoon the syrup over the peaches, and serve warm.

Pears in Wine Sauce Ⓥ
Peras con Vino

MAKES 4 SERVINGS

This dessert is most attractive when the pears are cut into slices and arranged in overlapping rows on dessert plates.

PREPARE 8 TO 12 HOURS IN ADVANCE

2 cups water

½ cup sugar

2 slices lemon

2 cinnamon sticks

4 pears, peeled but not cored, stems on

¾ cup red wine

Lemon slices, for garnish

Cinnamon sticks, for garnish

1. In a medium saucepan, combine the water and sugar and bring to a boil over high heat, stirring occasionally. Reduce the heat to low, add the lemon slices, cinnamon sticks, and pears, cover, and simmer, stirring, about 10 minutes. Add the wine and simmer 10 minutes more or until the pears are tender. Transfer the pears to a plate and reduce (boil down) the sauce until slightly thickened and syrupy. Return the pears to the syrup and let sit at room temperature overnight.

2. Core the pears, cut into slices and arrange in overlapping rows on dessert plates. Garnish each plate with a cinnamon stick or a slice of lemon. Spoon the syrup over each pear. Serve at room temperature.

Strawberries with Sugar and Vinegar Ⓥ
Fresones al Vinagre

MAKES 4 SERVINGS

Here strawberries and sugar are given an unusual tang by adding a splash of vinegar. This simple fruit preparation comes from an Augustine monastery in Burgos and is one of the many recipes that would be lost to us today had they not been preserved by a monastery or convent. Serve them, if you wish, drizzled with heavy cream or topped with a dollop of whipped cream.

PREPARE AT LEAST 2 HOURS IN ADVANCE

1½ pounds medium strawberries, hulled and quartered, or small whole strawberries

6 tablespoons sugar

1 tablespoon red wine vinegar

In a medium bowl, combine the strawberries and sugar. Cover and let sit at room temperature 30 minutes. Fold in the vinegar and refrigerate at least 2 hours to chill. Serve cold.

Sauces and Marmalades

Rich Almond Sauce Ⓥ
Bienmesabe

MAKES 8 SERVINGS

In English, the word bienmesabe translates literally to "it tastes good to me." This is an incredibly rich candy-like sauce that is often served by itself as a dessert in the Canary Islands. I like it best with vanilla ice cream or Frozen Almond Cream, page 649. To serve this with vanilla or any ice cream, spoon about 3 tablespoons onto each dessert plate or bowl and put a scoop of ice cream over the sauce.

½ pound blanched almonds (about 1⅓ cups)

1 cup sugar

1 cup water

½ cup honey

1 teaspoon lemon zest

½ teaspoon ground cinnamon

4 large egg yolks

1. In a food processor, combine the almonds and sugar and process until the nuts are ground as finely as possible (but not a paste). Transfer to a large saucepan, add the water, honey, lemon zest, and cinnamon, and bring to a boil over high heat. Reduce the heat to low and simmer, stirring frequently, until the liquid is reduced and the mixture thickened, about 15 minutes. Let cool slightly.

2. In a small bowl, whisk the egg yolks, then gradually whisk in a few tablespoons of the almond mixture and add to the saucepan. Increase the heat to medium-high and cook, stirring constantly, until the mixture begins to bubble. Let cool, stirring occasionally. The almond sauce should have the consistency of a thick custard; thin with water if necessary.

3. Serve at room temperature or store in a sealable crock or covered container in the refrigerator.

Raspberry Purée Ⓥ
Puré de Frambuesa

MAKES ABOUT ½ CUP

Many Spanish desserts, including pastries, ice creams, and simple custards, are even more delicious when accompanied by homemade marmalade or purées. Vary the amount of liqueur to taste, or substitute water if you prefer.

1⅓ cups fresh or frozen raspberries

1¼ cups sugar

1½ to 2 teaspoons fruit-flavored aquavit, Kirshwasser, orange liqueur, or water

1. Combine the raspberries and sugar in a food processor and blend until smooth. With the motor running gradually add enough liqueur until puréed.

2. Pass the purée through a fine-mesh strainer into a small bowl. Discard the solids. Store in a covered container in the refrigerator. Serve as desired.

Strawberry or Kiwi Fruit Purée Ⓥ
Puré de Fresas o Kiwi

MAKES ABOUT ¾ CUP

A delicious purée that is the perfect complement to many simple desserts, this one is made from strawberries or kiwi fruit.

1½ cups cut-up strawberries or 4 to 5 peeled kiwi fruit

3 tablespoons sugar

1½ to 2 teaspoons fruit-flavored aquavit,
Kirschwasser, orange liqueur, and/or water

1. Combine the strawberries or the kiwi fruit and sugar in a food processor and blend until finely chopped. With the motor running, gradually add enough liqueur until puréed.

2. Pass the purée through a fine-mesh strainer into a small bowl. Discard the solids. Store in a covered container in the refrigerator. Serve as desired.

Peach or Apricot Marmalade Ⓥ
Mermelada de Melocotón o Albaricoque

MAKES ABOUT ½ CUP

The recipe for this delicious marmalade is a variation on the dessert Apples in Spiced Wine Syrup (Manzanas en Jarabe, page 657). The apples and almonds are eliminated and, instead, the main ingredient is peaches, apricots, or pears. Accents of nutmeg, cinnamon, and cardamom complete the wonderfully complex flavor of this marmalade, which is excellent served with simple custards.

½ cup dry white wine
½ cup fresh orange juice
½ cup sugar
¼ teaspoon ground nutmeg
4 whole cloves
1 cinnamon stick
¼ teaspoon ground cardamom
Peel of ¼ small orange (orange part only), cut into very thin strips, then finely chopped
½ pound fresh peaches, apricots, or pears, peeled, pitted or cored, and cut into ¾-inch pieces

1. In a small saucepan, combine the wine, orange juice, sugar, nutmeg, cloves, cinnamon stick, cardamom, and orange peel and bring to a boil over high heat. Reduce the heat to low and simmer, stirring occasionally, until the liquid is reduced and the mixture slightly thickened, about 10 minutes. Add the peaches and simmer, stirring occasionally, until the peaches are tender and the syrup thick, about 30 minutes more.

2. To serve as a sauce rather than a marmalade, thin with a little water. Let cool. Store in a sealable crock or jar in the refrigerator. Serve as desired.

Quince Marmalade Ⓥ
Dulce de Membrillo

MAKES ABOUT 1 CUP

Quince, a fruit similar in taste and consistency to an apple, has been popular since ancient times. Sometimes you can find it fresh, but if not, it is readily available canned or as a paste in specialty food stores. In Spain, quince paste is often eaten with Manchego cheese or simply spread on a piece of toast. It is also used to accompany a variety of desserts, most notably Almond and Marmalade Puff Pastry Strips (page 617).

2 quince (about 1½ pounds), peeled, cored, and cut into ½-inch slices
10 tablespoons sugar

1. Place the quince in a small saucepan, add water to cover, and bring to a boil over high heat. Reduce the heat to low, cover, and simmer about 15 minutes or until the quince is tender. Drain.

2. Place the quince in a food processor or blender and process until smooth. With the motor running, gradually add the sugar. Return to the saucepan and cook over low heat, stirring frequently, until thickened to marmalade consistency, about 20 minutes. Let cool. Store in a sealable crock or jar in the refrigerator. Serve as desired.

Candied Spaghetti Squash Marmalade **V**

Cabello de Ángel

MAKES ABOUT 1 CUP

Sweetened spaghetti squash (called "angel hair" in Spanish), an unusual alternative to other fruit marmalades, is a typical Spanish topping or filling. The reason it is called angel hair is its golden color. This is frequently used as a filling for fritters and puff pastries.

1-pound piece of spaghetti squash, seeded and quartered

½ cup plus 2 tablespoons honey

2 tablespoons warm water

1 cinnamon stick

Peel of ½ lemon (yellow part only)

1. Place the spaghetti squash in a large saucepan, add water to cover and bring to a boil over high heat. Reduce the heat to low, cover, and simmer 15 to 25 minutes or until the flesh is tender. Drain and let cool slightly. Using a fork, scrape the flesh down to the rind to form thread-like strands.

2. Return the squash to the saucepan. Mix in the honey, water, cinnamon stick, and lemon peel and bring to a boil over medium heat. Reduce the heat to low and simmer uncovered until thickened to a marmalade consistency, about 35 minutes. Let cool. Store in a sealable crock or jar in the refrigerator. Serve as desired.

Candied Almonds **V**

Almendras Garrapiñadas

MAKES ¼ POUND

Candied almonds, a popular Spanish snack, are often sold by vendors with pushcarts on the street. Many vendors carry other items as well, but these delectable candied almonds sell faster than they can make them.

¼ pound almonds with skins

½ cup sugar

2 tablespoons honey

2 teaspoons water

1. Preheat the oven to 350°F. Scatter the almonds on a cookie sheet and toast about 5 minutes or until lightly golden.

2. In a heavy small skillet, combine the sugar, honey, and water, heat over medium heat, stirring constantly, and cook, continuing to stir, until the sugar is melted and well caramelized. Add the almonds and cook, stirring with a wooden spoon, until they are completely coated with the sugar.

3. Turn the candy out onto a greased marble slab or cookie sheet (on a heatproof surface). While the sugar is hardening, continuously move the nuts with a wooden spoon, so that the sugar adheres to them.

4. When cool enough to handle but not yet completely hard, separate the nuts, each one with its sugar coating, and let harden completely. Serve at room temperature.

Candied Egg Yolks ⓥ
Yemas de Santa Teresa

MAKES 12 CANDIES

Centuries ago, Spanish egg yolk candies originated in convents. The convent of Saint Teresa, best known as the founder of the Descalza reform movement of Carmelite nuns in the city of Ávila, christened these candies with her name. Yemas are still made in the convents today, and they are also available in pastry shops.

PREPARE 8 TO 12 HOURS IN ADVANCE

½ cup sugar

¼ cup water

1 cinnamon stick

5 large egg yolks

⅛ teaspoon fresh lemon juice

Zest of ½ lemon

Sugar, for dredging

1. In a small saucepan, combine the ½ cup sugar, the water, and cinnamon stick and bring to a boil over high heat. Reduce the heat to low and simmer, stirring occasionally, until the syrup reaches the soft-ball stage (234-240°F on a candy thermometer; when dropped in cold water, a soft ball will form that flattens when pressed). Remove from the heat and discard the cinnamon stick.

2. Fill a medium bowl with ice. In a small bowl, whisk together the egg yolks, lemon juice, and lemon zest until pale yellow. Gradually add to the syrup in a slow stream, whisking constantly. Increase the heat to medium and cook, whisking constantly, until thickened, about 4 minutes. Remove from the heat and continue whisking until the candy stiffens, then place the saucepan in the ice and beat with a wooden spoon until very stiff.

3. Line a cookie sheet with wax paper and lightly butter the paper. Transfer the candy mixture to

the wax paper and, with a buttered rubber spatula, shape into a 12 x 1-inch "log." Refrigerate until stiff enough to handle—do not let harden.

4. Cut the roll into 1-inch slices. Using buttered hands, shape each slice into a round "yolk." Roll in the sugar. Arrange the candies on a plate or cookie sheet and cover with foil. Let sit at room temperature overnight until slightly crystallized on the outside. Place each candy in a paper or candy cup. Serve at room temperature.

Almond and Egg Yolk Candies ⓥ
Bocaditos de Monja

MAKES 12 TO 15 CANDIES

These candies are called "Nun's Morsels" in Spanish because like many egg yolk candies, the recipes originated in the convents of Spain.

PREPARE 2 DAYS IN ADVANCE

5 ounces blanched almonds (about 1 cup)

¼ teaspoon lemon zest

1 cup water

2 large egg yolks

¾ cup granulated sugar

Powdered (confectioners) sugar, for dusting

1. Place the almonds in a food processor or blender and process until as finely ground as possible (but not a paste). Add the lemon zest and pulse once to combine. Transfer to a small saucepan, add the water, and bring to a boil over medium heat, then cook about 5 minutes. Pass through a fine-mesh strainer over a bowl, reserving the liquid (there will be a few tablespoons). Let cool. Transfer the almonds to another small bowl, add the egg yolks, and mix well.

continues...

2. Fill a medium bowl with ice. Place the reserved liquid and the granulated sugar in a small saucepan and bring to a boil over high heat. Cook, stirring occasionally, until it reaches the thread stage (230-233°F on a candy thermometer; thin thread will form when dropped off a spoon into a glass of cold water). Gradually pour the syrup over the nut mixture, mixing constantly with a wooden spoon. Return to the saucepan and cook, stirring constantly, until thickened, about 5 minutes more. Place the saucepan in the ice and mix with the wooden spoon until stiff. Refrigerate until firm enough to handle.

3. Dust your hands with the powdered sugar. Shape the candy into 1-inch balls and roll each in the powdered sugar. If the sugar is absorbed, roll the candies in it again. Arrange on a plate or cookie sheet and let dry, uncovered, at room temperature 48 hours. Place each candy in a paper or foil candy cup. Serve at room temperature.

Candied Egg Yolk in Almond Roll ⓥ

Huesos de Santo

MAKES 10 CANDIES

Huesos de santo *are eaten on All Saints Day (November 1) when it is traditional for the living to pay their respects to the dead. In English,* huesos de santo *translates into "bones of the saint," a fitting and humorous description for these hollowed white candy rolls filled with candied egg yolk.*

PREPARE 10 TO 14 HOURS IN ADVANCE

2 ounces potato (about ¼ of a large potato), peeled

½ cup sugar

¼ cup water

⅛ teaspoon lemon zest

3½ ounces finely ground almonds (about ⅞ cup)

Filling

6 large egg yolks

6 tablespoons sugar

¼ cup water

Coating

1 cup sugar

½ cup water

2 teaspoons fresh lemon juice

1. Place the potato in a small saucepan, add cold water to cover and add a pinch of salt. Cover and bring to a simmer over low heat. Cook until tender when pierced with a knife. Drain and let cool slightly. Peel. Pass through a fine-mesh strainer into a small bowl. Discard the solids. Wipe out the saucepan.

2. In the saucepan, combine the ½ cup sugar, the ¼ cup water, and the lemon zest and bring to a boil over high heat. Cook until the mixture reaches hard-ball stage—when dropped into very cold water, a hard ball forms that holds its shape when squeezed between the fingers but is still pliable (the sugar will have thickened and darkened slightly). Add the ground almonds and stir with a wooden spoon. Add the potato and cook, stirring constantly, until the mixture leaves the side of the pan. Remove from the heat and let cool until firm enough to handle. Turn out onto a floured work surface and flatten to about ½ inch thick. Let sit 1 to 2 hours, turning occasionally with the aid of a knife, until dry.

3. Roll out the candy on a floured work surface to ¼-to ⅜-inch thickness. Cut into 10 (3 x 2-inch) rectangles and roll each lengthwise around a ½-inch-diameter cylindrical object to form a "bone"—the handle of a wooden spoon works well. Remove the cylinder and place the candy, seam side down, on a cookie sheet. Repeat with the remaining rectangles. Let sit uncovered at room temperature overnight until dry and hardened.

In my youth, when I was a junior at Vassar, I spent my summer vacation in Spain studying at Madrid University. I met a lot of friends as well as my future husband, Luis. I have to say that I had never thought of making a career of writing about gastronomy, but one of the things that impressed me the most was the distinctive relationship Spaniards have with food. Luis and I used to travel long distances on weekends to see beautiful small villages and the sights around Madrid, Toledo, Escorial, and Aranjuez. One time, while in Ávila, my friends took me to a convent of cloistered nuns. We walked inside, and in a small hallway in front of a turnstile, we rang a bell. From inside a voice greeted us, and someone in the group asked for cookies and *yemas*. We put the money in the turnstile, and in exchange we got a box of delicious cookies and a box of *Yemas de Santa Teresa*, Candied Egg Yolks, page 665—one of the most delicious sweets I ever had.

For the 50 years since then, I have patronized convents all over Spain. I have bought *Yemas de San Leandro* in Sevilla, egg yolk empanadas in the Santa Clara Convent in Tordesillas, cookies and doughnuts at the Santa Clara convent in Trujillo, cupcakes and sponge cakes at the Dominicas in Jerez, and many other sweets at convents throughout Spain. After a while, I became addicted to discovering new convent specialties—always of great quality and very often at a better price than similar products in pastry shops. I always advise travelers to ask the concierge at their hotel for the addresses of local convents, in order to visit them and buy their specialties. Nobody has ever been disappointed.

We owe a great debt to these convents and their nuns for keeping many traditional recipes alive through the years that otherwise would have disappeared. The nuns are not only responsible for preserving candy and dessert recipes, but there are also complicated cooking techniques that would be lost to us without them. Spanish cuisine would not be what it is today without the invaluable contribution of the nuns.

4. Prepare the filling: In a small bowl, whisk the egg yolks until light yellow. In a small saucepan, combine the 6 tablespoons sugar and the ¼ cup water and cook over high heat until the mixture reaches hard-ball stage. Gradually add the egg yolks in a thin stream, beating constantly with a whisk. Cook, stirring constantly, with a wooden spoon until the mixture stiffens. Let cool. With the aid of a pastry tube (or use a small spoon if a tube is not available), fill the cylinders with the yolk mixture.

5. Prepare the coating: In another small saucepan, combine the 1 cup sugar and the ½ cup water and heat over high heat until the mixture reaches the hard-ball stage. Remove from the heat and add the lemon juice. Whisk until the syrup turns white, thickens, and forms a ball. Transfer to a bowl and let cool.

6. Place the sugar syrup ball in the top of a double boiler or a medium bowl and add 1 teaspoon hot water. Over low heat, cook in the double boiler or the bowl over a pot of water until the sugar is completely liquefied. Dip each candy in the liquid and place on wax paper. Let sit at least 1 hour or until dry. Serve at room temperature.

Marzipan Candies Ⓥ

Melindres de Yepes

MAKES ABOUT 50 CANDIES

The Moors introduced Spain to marzipan candies hundreds of years ago, and they are just as popular now as they were back then. The sweetened lemon glaze makes them even better.

PREPARE 8 TO 12 HOURS IN ADVANCE

½ pound blanched almonds (about 1⅓ cups)

1 cup granulated sugar

¼ cup water

Powdered (confectioners) sugar, for dusting

Glaze

½ cup powdered (confectioners) sugar

1 large egg white

1 teaspoon fresh lemon juice

1. In a food processor or blender, process the almonds until a paste forms. Add the sugar and process until blended. With the motor running, add the water and process until a malleable dough forms.

2. Dust a work surface with powdered sugar. Shape the dough into about 50 rings the thickness of a pencil and about 1½ inches in diameter. Arrange on cookie sheets and let sit uncovered overnight to dry.

3. Prepare the glaze: In a small bowl, beat the powdered sugar and egg white with an electric mixer until white, creamy, and thickened. Add the lemon juice and beat about 5 minutes more.

4. Dip the top of each candy into the glaze. Place on the cookie sheet and let sit until the glaze hardens. Serve at room temperature.

Coconut Candies Ⓥ

Yemas de Coco

MAKES ABOUT 10 CANDIES

Yemas de coco are sweet rich coconut candies that are even more delicious when flamed with Spanish brandy or cognac.

PREPARE 8 TO 12 HOURS IN ADVANCE

3 ounces finely grated fresh coconut (about ¾ cup)

¾ cup milk

6 tablespoons sugar

1 teaspoon brandy, such as Spanish brandy, or cognac

Sugar, for dredging

1. Combine the coconut and milk in a small bowl and let soak overnight in the refrigerator. Drain well. (Reserve the coconut milk for another use.)

2. In a small saucepan, combine the coconut and the 6 tablespoons sugar and heat over low heat, stirring occasionally, until the sugar is dissolved. Increase the heat to medium and cook, stirring constantly, about 5 minutes more. The mixture should be very stiff; if there is too much liquid, increase the heat and cook, stirring constantly, until it evaporates. Stir in the brandy. Remove from the heat. Standing well away from the skillet, ignite the liquid and let die out. Let cool.

3. When the candy is still slightly warm, shape into 10 (¾-inch) balls. Roll in the sugar and place in paper or foil candy cups. Cover with foil and let sit at room temperature overnight to dry. Serve at room temperature.

Drinks

Sangria Ⓥ

MAKES 4 SERVINGS

Sangria is probably the most famous and popular Spanish drink. It is found in bars, restaurants, chiringuitos (seasonal cheap restaurants for beachgoers), as well as in the homes of Spaniards all over the country. The main ingredients are a robust, not-too-expensive red wine, fruit, sugar, and gaseosa (a mildly sweet seltzer). To these, each person adds something to his or her taste—some people add Cointreau (as I do), cognac, a little rum, or other spirits, although classic sangria makers try to avoid strong alcoholic complements.

To make white sangria, use a dry white wine instead of the red, such as a Rueda, Jumilla, or Valdepeñas.

PREPARE AT LEAST 2 HOURS IN ADVANCE

1 bottle (750 ml) red wine, full bodied and dry, such as Mancha, Toro, or Valencia

Juice from 2 oranges

1 to 3 tablespoons sugar, to taste

2 to 3 tablespoons Cointreau or Triple Sec

Fruit, such as slices of orange, lemon, apple, or peach

1 cup club soda or sparkling water

1. In a large jar or pitcher, such as ceramic, mix together all the ingredients except the club soda. Taste and adjust sweetness if necessary. Refrigerate at least 2 hours to chill and meld flavors.

2. Stir in the club soda and add a few ice cubes. Pour into large wine glasses, adding some fruit into each glass. Serve cold.

Tiger Nut Milk Ⓥ
Horchata

MAKES 6 SERVINGS

This is a refreshing summer drink native to Valencia but now found all over Spain from May to October. The main ingredient is a small dried root called chufa or tiger nut, similar to a tiny potato, grown in a small area just north of Valencia in the town of Alboraya. The chufa was brought to Spain from Africa by the Arab invaders that held.

The drink is served very chilled or really "slushy" and closer to frozen but still drinkable through a straw. Look for chufas in specialty stores. Plan ahead because they need to soak for many hours.

PREPARE AT LEAST 10 HOURS IN ADVANCE

2 pounds tiger nuts (chufas)

14 cups water

3 cups sugar

One 2-inch-long piece lemon peel (yellow part only)

1 cinnamon stick

1. Sort through the tiger nuts and discard any that are discolored or blemished. Place in a large bowl and add the water. Wash in the same water (do not discard or rinse) and let sit at room temperature until softened, about 10 hours.

2. Drain the tiger nuts, reserving all the water. Add the nuts to a food processor. Working with 2 cups of the reserved water, add a small amount to the processor and blend until the mixture is a creamy consistency. Working in batches, add the remainder of the 2 cups reserved water a small amount at a time to maintain the creamy consistency and process until fully incorporated and creamy.

continues...

3. Transfer the tiger nut cream to a jar or pitcher, such as earthenware. Add the remaining reserved water, the sugar, lemon peel, and cinnamon stick. Stir thoroughly until the sugar is dissolved. Discard the cinnamon stick and lemon peel. Freeze until close to frozen but still drinkable (it might be called slushy). (You can also use an ice cream machine to achieve a near-frozen texture.) Serve chilled in glasses with straws.

Flaming Liquor with Apples Ⓥ
Queimada

MAKES 6 SERVINGS

Queimada comes from the region of Galicia in northwestern Spain, an area with a large Celtic heritage, observed in the local music, architecture, and cuisine. The land of Galicia is green and misty, rain is common, and forests cover much of the land. The tradition of witches and magic is very strong here, and it is believed that queimada, loosely translated as "burned," is the drink that witches brew when they get together. The base of this drink usually served in winter, is orujo, a liquor distilled from the skins and pits of grapes, similar to Italian grappa. If you can't find orujo, use grappa instead. The other ingredients are sugar, apples, and sometimes a few coffee beans. The flaming preparation of the drink is very important and dramatic (but take safety precautions). There is a custom of singing Celtic or Galician songs when the brew is set aflame.

1 bottle (750 ml) orujo, such as from Galicia, or Italian grappa

6 tablespoons sugar

2 apples, cored and cut into wedges

7 or 8 whole coffee beans

1. In a large saucepan or Dutch oven, combine the orujo, 3 tablespoons of the sugar, and the cut apples.

2. In a large, heat-resistant serving spoon, such as earthenware, add 1 tablespoon of the sugar, then fill the spoon with orujo. Do not add to the pan. With a match or kitchen lighter, set the liquor aflame in the spoon. (For safety, if you prefer, hold the spoon with an oven mitt.)

3. Let the flame continue briefly until the sugar is amber colored, then lower the spoon slowly to the pan and gently light all of the orujo aflame. (The flame will be low.) Stir the flaming mixture with a long heat-resistant spoon. You can let it burn as long as you wish—the longer it burns, the lower the alcohol content. Extinguish the flame by covering the pan with a lid. Serve hot or warm, with slices of apple.

Cinnamon-Flavored Ice Milk Ⓥ
Leche Merengada

MAKES 6 SERVINGS

My husband Luis often reminisces about summer nights in Madrid spent with his grandfather after dinner at Sakuskilla, a seasonal aguaducho (drink stand) that had a few tables al fresco (outdoors). People would meet there to talk and find respite from the heat, and Luis's grandfather would often order leche merengada. The famous Café Gijón on Paseo de Recoletos, the "scene" for literati, actors, and bullfighters, still lures customers with its leche merengada, as they have done for almost a hundred years. You can serve this as a drink or a frozen dessert. For dessert, use an ice cream machine, or freeze the mixture in small ramekins. For a blanco y negro ("black and white"), stir chilled black coffee into the milk mixture when slightly frozen.

3 cups milk

1 cup sugar

1 cup heavy cream

3 cinnamon sticks

4 large egg whites

Zest of 1 lemon

Juice of ½ lemon

Ground cinnamon, for dusting

1. In a medium saucepan, combine the milk, cream, ¾ cup of the sugar, the cinnamon sticks, and the lemon zest and bring to a boil over medium-high heat. Reduce the heat to low and simmer, stirring occasionally, about 30 minutes. Remove from the heat and let cool. Refrigerate at least 2 hours to chill. Discard the cinnamon sticks and lemon peel.

2. In a large bowl using an electric mixer on medium-high speed, briefly beat the egg whites and lemon juice, then gradually add 2 to 3 tablespoons of the sugar. Continue beating until the mixture becomes fairly thick but not dry. Gently fold in the milk mixture.

3. Refrigerate at least 1 hour to chill and serve as a drink, or freeze at least 2 hours or until firm and serve as a dessert. Either way, dust with the cinnamon and serve cold.

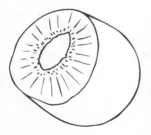

Hot Chocolate, Spanish Style Ⓥ
Chocolate a la Española

MAKES 1 SERVING

Chocolate was brought to Europe by Spain after the discovery of America. It became popular and a staple of Spanish gastronomy during the 1600s, before it was known in the rest of Europe. To this day, hot chocolate, enjoyed by Spain's Princess María (who brought it to France when she married Louis XIV), is beloved by children, and it is part of many Spaniards' daily breakfast. For some, that means capping off a long night of partying by going to a churrería *at dawn to enjoy hot chocolate and* churros *before heading home.*

1 cup milk

1 ounce good-quality unsweetened chocolate, broken into small pieces

2 tablespoons sugar, or to taste

In a small saucepan, combine all the ingredients and heat over low heat, stirring constantly, until the chocolate is melted. Increase the heat to medium and bring to a boil, stirring constantly. When the liquid starts bubbling up and reaches the top of the saucepan, remove the pan from the heat and whisk gently until the bubbles subside a bit. Repeat the process, boiling then whisking, two or three times more, until the chocolate appears thick and frothy. Serve hot.

Index

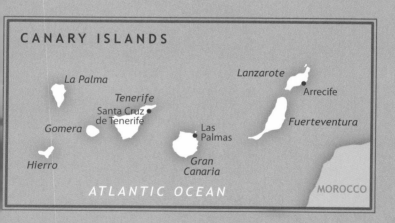

CANARY ISLANDS

La Palma

Tenerife

Santa Cruz
de Tenerife

Gomera

Hierro

Las
Palmas

Gran
Canaria

Lanzarote

Arrecife

Fuerteventura

MOROCCO

ATLANTIC OCEAN